The Developing Child

Helen Bee

The Developing Child

NINTH EDITION

Allyn and Bacon

Boston • London • Toronto • Sydney • Tokyo • Singapore

Editor-in-Chief: Priscilla McGeehon
Executive Editor: Rebecca Dudley Pascal
Supplements Editor: Cyndy Taylor
Marketing Manager: Anne Wise
Project Manager: Bob Ginsberg
Design Manager and Text and Cover Designer: Rubina Yeh
Cover Photograph: © Michael Goldman/FPG International LLC
Art Studio: ElectraGraphics, Inc.
Photo Researcher: Photosearch, Inc.
Electronic Page Makeup: York Production Services

Copyright © 2000 by Allyn & Bacon
A Pearson Education Company
160 Gould Street
Needham Heights, MA 02194

www.abacon.com

Library of Congress Cataloging-in-Publication Data

Bee, Helen L., (date)
　　　　The developing child / Helen Bee. — 9th ed.
　　　　　　p.　　cm.
　　　　Includes bibliographical references and indexes.
　　　　ISBN 0-321-04709-5
　　　　1. Child psychology. 2. Child development. I. Title.
　　BF721.B336 1999　　　　　　　　　　　　98-31711

　　155.4—dc21　　　　　　　　　　　　　　　CIP

Printed in the United States of America
10 9 8 7 6 5 4 3 2 1　VHP　03 02 01 00

Credits appear on pages 547–548, which constitute a continuation of the
copyright page.

To my grandchildren: Sam, Maggie, and Will
and to their parents, Rex and Jenny

Brief Contents

Contents

Part 4 The Thinking Child 162

Chapter 6 Cognitive Development I: Structure and Process 162

Part 5   The Social Child   258

Part 6   The Whole Child   376

Chapter 13   The Ecology of Development: The Child Within the Family System   376

Boxes in the Text

To the Student

Hello and welcome. Let me invite you into the study of a fascinating subject—children and their development. This is a bit like inviting you into my own home, since I have lived in the world of the study of children for a great many years. Unfortunately, I cannot know each of you individually, but by writing this book as if it were a conversation between you and me, I hope I can make your reading and studying as personal a process as possible.

Because such personal involvement is one of my goals, you will find that I often write in the first person and that I have included a number of anecdotes about my own life. It is for this same reason that I give you the full name of many of the researchers and theorists I quote—so that you will have some sense that these are real people doing the research and proposing the theories. By giving the first names, I can also make it clear that at least half of them are women!

Welcome, too, to the adventure of science. From the very first edition of this book, one of my goals has been to try to convey a sense of excitement about scientific inquiry. I want each of you to gain some feeling for the way psychologists think, the kinds of questions we ask, and the ways we go about trying to answer those questions. I also want you to take away with you some sense of the theoretical and intellectual ferment that is part of any science. Think of psychology as a kind of detective story. We discover clues after hard, often painstaking work; we make new guesses or hypotheses; and then we search for new clues to check on those hypotheses.

Of course, I also want you to come away from reading this book with a firm grounding of knowledge in the field. Although there is much that we do not yet know or understand, a great many facts and observations have accumulated. These facts and observations will be of help to you professionally if you are planning (or are already in) a career with children—such as teaching, nursing, social work, medicine, or psychology; the information will also be useful to you as parents, now or in the future. I hope you enjoy the reading as much as I have enjoyed the writing.

HELEN BEE

To the Instructor

It is amazing to find myself writing the preface for a ninth edition of this topically organized text. When I began working on the first edition 25 years ago, I certainly did not imagine that I would still be engaged in this process so many years later. What is perhaps most surprising is that the process has continued to be a challenge and an adventure over all nine editions.

The greatest challenge is to stay open to new theories and concepts and be willing to rethink and reorganize whole chapters, rather than sticking reflexively (or defensively) to old rubrics. One must also give up favorite examples that are now out of date, and search for new metaphors that will speak to current students. Perhaps hardest of all, one must cut as well as add. Over many editions, the changes accumulate, so that when I compare this edition to the first edition, published in 1975, I find that there are almost no common sentences, let alone common paragraphs. Still, I can see the common threads running from the first to this ninth edition. In particular, the same central goals have guided my writing in every edition:

- To **actively engage the student** in as many ways as possible;
- To find that difficult but **essential balance between theory, research, and practical application;**
- To **present the most current thinking and research.**

In addition, this edition, like the seventh and eighth editions, reflects a further goal:

- To **maintain a strong emphasis on culture.**

Actively Engaging the Student

If a text is scientifically sound but does not engage the student, you've lost half the battle. I have made every effort to catch and maintain the student's interest, through a variety of means:

- *An informal, personal narrative style.* This edition, like all my texts, is written in the first person, as if it were a conversation with the student. I have also used personal examples where they help to make a point. Students report that they enjoy reading the text—surely the first hurdle.
- *Critical thinking questions.* As in the past several editions, I have included **critical thinking questions** in every chapter, designed to encourage the students to ponder, analyze, and think more creatively. These questions, which appear in the margins, ask the student to pause and consider a particular point before going on. Often they ask the reader to consider how the material may apply to his

or her own life. In other cases, they ask the student to think about how to design a study to answer a particular question. Sometimes they ask theoretical questions or ask the student to analyze her or his own point of view or feelings on the subject at issue. These questions may be useful for provoking class discussion; it is also my hope that they will make the reading process more active and thus make learning deeper. They may also help the student to gain greater skill in the important process of critical thinking—learning how to think about and evaluate his or her own feelings, thoughts, and behavior so as to clarify and improve them.

• *Real World boxes.* Almost every chapter includes at least one boxed discussion of a practical, applied question. My intent with these boxes is not only to show students that it is possible to study such applied questions with scientific methods, but also to show that all the theory and research they are reading about has some relevance to their own lives.

Balancing Research, Theory, and Application

My goal has always been to write a scientifically rigorous book, strongly based on both theory and research. Texts that are primarily compendia of research facts with relatively little theory are hard for students to absorb; those that are heavy on theory can provide a useful framework but may leave the student without enough information to evaluate the theories or a sufficient understanding of our current body of knowledge. I have tried throughout to balance the two:

• *Classic theories and newer models are used as the basis for the organizational structure of most chapters,* supplemented by extensive discussion of current research findings.

• *Research Report* boxes amplify the research emphasis, each exploring a specific study or a body of research on a particular topic, such as Ann Streissguth's work on fetal alcohol syndrome (Chapter 2), or Judith Langlois' research on babies' preference for attractive faces (Chapter 5).

• *Real World* boxes provide the balancing perspective, pointing students toward potential applications. Examples include a box on sports for children in Chapter 4, and one on the pros and cons of spanking in Chapter 13.

Current Thinking and Research

Any revision involves an enormous amount of updating. I have sometimes chosen to continue to include a discussion of an older study when it has become a classic, or when it is still the best example to be found, but in most cases I have searched for the most current examples I can find, not only in the text but in the tables and figures. Some examples:

• A number of *new theories or models have been added* to the discussion, including Siegler's new model for the development of strategies (Chapter 6) and Sroufe's branching-tree conceptualization of developmental psychopathology (Chapter 15). I have also considerably expanded the coverage of Vygotsky's theory—surely not new, but of increased importance to the thinking of many developmentalists.

• *Twenty-three new figures or tables* are included in this edition, most based on very recent research. Some examples include a new figure showing stages in the prenatal development of the brain (Figure 2.6), one showing the risk of death in the first year of life for children in industrialized versus developing countries (Figure 4.9), and one showing Siegler's new "overlapping wave" model of strategy development (Figure 6.5).

- *17 boxes are new or substantially updated.* Examples include a new Research Report box describing Claude Steele's work on stereotype threat (Chapter 7), a Research Report on bullies and victims (Chapter 11), and a Real World box on latchkey children (Chapter 14).

Emphasis on Culture

Finally, in this edition, I have built on the emphasis on cultural variations introduced in the seventh and eighth editions:

- The distinction between *collectivist* and *individualist* cultural systems has been used as a basis for contrast throughout the text;
- *Cultures and Contexts* boxes have been expanded and updated. For example, the new discussion of "Sleeping Arrangements for Infants" in Chapter 3 compares the typical individualist cultural practice of separate sleeping with the common collectivist cultural system of cosleeping with parents.
- The growing body of excellent research comparing developmental patterns among children in major U.S. ethnic groups has also made it possible to expand the discussions of ethnic variations throughout this edition.

What Else Is New in This Edition?

Those of you who have taught from earlier editions of this book will find the structure largely the same, except for one major change:

Intelligence Chapter Moved

At the suggestion of a number of reviewers, I have shifted the chapter on intelligence so that it now comes *after* the chapter on cognitive structure. Reviewers of earlier editions had sometimes suggested this same change, but I resisted it—perhaps out of sheer laziness, since this is a major shift. This time around I mulled it over at some length and finally decided that the reviewers were right: It simply makes more sense to talk about the developmental changes first, followed by the discussion of individual differences. Those of you who are wedded to the old sequence are of course free to assign these two chapters in reverse order!

New or Expanded Topics and Themes

Beyond this one major change, most of the changes in this edition involve additions or expansions of topics and themes. Some I have mentioned earlier. Here are other illustrations from each chapter:

- Chapter 2: Significant expansion and updating of the impact of **diet during pregnancy,** including very new information on folic acid.
- Chapters 2 and 4: Expanded discussion of **prenatal and postnatal brain development,** using the most recent research and thinking.
- Chapter 3: A new section on the **infant's expression of emotion,** including a summary table.
- Chapter 4: New data on **hormone changes during puberty,** including a new figure, as well as a major discussion of **child abuse,** a greatly expanded discussion of **sexually transmitted diseases,** and new material on **poverty and health.**

- Chapter 5: Expanded discussion of the infant and child's **ability to read social signals.**
- Chapter 6: Expanded discussion of **emotional regulation.**
- Chapter 7: A new box on the **impact of schooling on IQ,** based on the recent work of Ceci and Williams.
- Chapter 8: Expanded discussion of the effect of **variations in richness of the child's early language environment,** including a new table showing vocabulary differences among children living in various degrees of poverty.
- Chapter 9: New data on the **heritability of temperament,** based on the most recent research.
- Chapter 10: A shift to the use of **William James's distinction between the I and Me selves** as the basic organizational rubric for the discussion of the development of the self-concept.
- Chapter 11: A new box on **intergenerational transmission of secure/insecure attachments;** expanded and updated discussion of **adolescent peer groups and peer pressure.**
- Chapter 12: A new box describing the **PATHS and Fast Track programs** devised by Greenberg, Coie, Dodge, and others; the addition of **Rest's four factors affecting moral development** as a basis for the discussion of moral reasoning and moral behavior; the addition of a discussion of **Turiel's distinction between conventional and moral rules.**
- Chapter 13: A brief discussion of Sulloway's ideas about **birth order;** a new section on the **impact of the marital relationship on the parent-child relationship.**
- Chapter 14: A new box on **latchkey children;** expanded coverage of **poverty effects.**
- Chapter 15: An updated discussion of **ADHD** with the newest research; an entirely new section on **inclusive education.**
- Chapter 16: The addition of Rutter's **five principles of person/environment interaction** as the organizational basis for part of the chapter.

Same Old Good Features

In addition to all these expansions and changes, I have naturally tried to keep all the qualities and features that you have appreciated in earlier editions: the engaging and clear writing style; the critical thinking questions in the margins; the annotated lists of suggested readings; the "Real World," "Research Report," and "Cultures and Contexts" boxes that allow exploration of some of the byways of research and application; and boldfaced key terms defined at the end of each chapter as well as in the glossary.

Supplements

Naturally, there are also a variety of supplements available to the instructor and the student.

Instructor's Manual. Written by Helen Bee, the IM for this edition is an expansion and updating of the extensive manual prepared for the eighth edition. This IM, like the earlier versions, lays out a whole course using *The Developing Child,* including pre-planning, a sample syllabus, suggested organization of the lectures, and lecture material for each chapter. I have added new material for each chapter, including good new sources. The IM also includes, as before, a set of transparency masters as well as an updated film/video guide.

Test Bank. Written by Carolyn Meyer, Lake Sumter Community College, the test bank contains approximately 2000 questions, 50 percent of which are new for this edition. Each of these multiple-choice and essay questions is referenced to page number, topic, and skill. Some questions also appear in the student study guide or SuperShell II software tutorial and are referenced as such.

Study Guide. (ISBN 0-321-05992-1). Written by Betty Sunerton, each chapter of the comprehensive study guide contains a brief chapter outline, learning objectives, a definition of key terms, lists of key concepts and important individuals, and three practice tests containing multiple-choice, matching, and fill-in-the-blank questions with their answers.

Computerized Test Bank. ESA-Test is a flexible, easy-to-master computerized test bank that includes all the test items in the printed test bank. ESA-Test is available in Macintosh, Windows, and DOS formats from your Allyn and Bacon sales representative, or by calling 1-800-852-8024.

Video. (ISBN 0-321-02059-6). We have created a custom video to accompany this edition of *The Developing Child*. It consists of a wide variety of brief segments to illustrate developmental concepts. These "lecture launchers" (each two to eight minutes long) cover topics such as the Apgar test, the Kohlberg dilemma, language development, and fetal alcohol syndrome. This video is also available from your sales representative.

Website. A website has been developed to accompany this edition. Information for both students and instructors can be found at: www.abacon.com/bee. An icon 🖥 in the text links material with related activities on the Bee website.

Transparency Set. (ISBN 0-321-04043-0). A set of 100 full-color transparencies includes images from the text and beyond. These transparencies are appropriate for use in both small and large classrooms.

Bouquets

My work on this edition, as with every edition, has been greatly aided by the criticism and commentary provided by colleagues, who take the time to look at earlier editions or early drafts. I am enormously appreciative of the thoughtful comments and suggestions made by Janette B. Benson, University of Denver; Marvin W. Berkowitz, Marquette University; Joan Cook, County College of Morris; Rita M. Curl, Minot State University; Wallace E. Dixon, Jr., Heidelberg College; Donna Frick-Horbury, Appalachian State University; Betty K. Hathaway, University of Arkansas at Little Rock; Patricia A. Jarvis, Illinois State University; and Ric Wynn, County College of Morris.

My work is also made enormously easier because of the fine team of people at Addison Wesley Longman—the same team I have worked with on several books. By now, we know each other's strengths and weaknesses, and the process has become remarkably smooth. Becky Dudley Pascal, the acquisitions editor, is extremely energetic, full of new ideas, always willing to listen, and blessed with that most delightful of traits: She answers her mail immediately! Becky Kohn is certainly the best development editor on the face of the earth. She has been less involved in this edition than in many of my other books, but I do not want to miss an opportunity to say thank you once more for her steady and intelligent assistance. Bob Ginsberg, the project manager for this book, also deserves special thanks. Bob and I have worked together several times before, always with humor and goodwill. For this edition, I asked specially if I could work with him again. He keeps the system working efficiently and clearly, all the while providing wonderful support, both personal and professional. I have not yet persuaded him that the forests and mountains of Washington State are to be preferred over the canyons of Manhattan, but other than that we are compatible spirits. He has even convinced me that e-mail is worth the effort.

Last but never least, there is my personal "convoy," who truck along with me through each book. My husband, Carl de Boor, solves computer puzzles and sometimes keeps me from tearing out my hair in clumps when deadlines become too tight or chapter structures defy solution. My women friends—Sarah Brooks, Diane Edie,

To the Instructor

Miriam Schneider, and Deb Harville—are willing to listen to me rant and rave over some unfindable journal article or other frustrations; their good sense and humor keep me on an even keel. Quite literally, I could not live without these very special people. Thank you.

HELEN BEE

Basic Questions

In traditional Kenyan culture, still seen in some rural areas, babies are carried in slings all day and allowed to nurse on demand at night. This cultural pattern, quite different from what we see in most Western societies, seems to have an effect on the baby's sleep/wake cycle.

Each summer, I spend several months at an unusual camp in the state of Washington, where adults of all ages as well as families with young children come each year to live for a short time in a kind of temporary community. Because many of the same people come back year after year, bringing their children (and often later their grandchildren), I see these growing children in once-a-year snapshots. When a family arrives, I am quite naturally struck by how much the children have changed, and I find myself saying to the kids, "Good grief, you've grown a foot" or "Last time I saw you, you were only this big." (I say these things, even remembering full well how much I hated it when people said these things to me at the same age. Of *course* I had grown. And because I was always taller than anyone else my age, I didn't like to be reminded of this peculiarity.)

At the same time, I am also struck by the consistency in these kids from year to year. Sweet-tempered young Malcolm and ebullient Crystal always give me many hugs; Malcolm's older brother Elliot, far shyer, still gazes at me silently from some measured distance. He warms up as the days go by, but his behavior is quite different from his brother's and remains noticeably constant from year to year. Even 18-year-old Stacey, now fully grown, still has the same dreamy and slow-moving pattern he showed throughout his childhood. Each of these children has a particular style, a particular set of skills, a particular personality, and these qualities appear to be at least somewhat consistent from year to year, perhaps even into adult life.

These simple examples illustrate one of the key points about human development: It involves both change and continuity. To understand development, we will need to look at both. Equally important, we need to understand which developmental changes, and which types of consistency or continuity, are shared by individuals in all cultures and which are unique to a given culture, to a group within a culture, or to a particular individual. For example, you probably know that in the first weeks after they are born, babies do not sleep through the night; they wake every two hours or so to be fed. It is only at about 6 to 8 weeks of age that most babies are able to string several two-hour stretches together and begin to show something approximating a day/night sleeping pattern (Bamford et al., 1990). That certainly sounds like a basic biological change, one that would occur pretty much regardless of the child's environment. Yet according to one study (Super & Harkness, 1982), babies in rural Kenya who are carried about by their mothers in a sling all day and fed on demand at night do not show any shift toward a nighttime sleep pattern over the first 8 months of life. Instead, they continue to wake intermittently throughout the 24-hour period. So what seems like a universal, biological process turns out not to be universal at all. It is affected by culture—by attitudes and values expressed through variations in care and handling. This issue of what is universal and what is not will be a persistent theme.

This example also makes it clear that to understand development, we will need to explore both *nature* and *nurture,* both biology and environment, and how they interact to explain both consistency and change. Throughout these chapters, I will be trying to sort out the relative impact of nature and nurture in each domain of development and at each age. That task will be a great deal easier if you have at least a grounding in some of the basic concepts and theories that form the framework for such an analysis. So let me take you on a quick tour of current ideas about nature and nurture, and an equally brief look at the major theoretical approaches to explaining both consistency and individuality in development.

Nature and Nurture: An Ancient Debate

The argument about nature versus nurture, also referred to as *heredity versus environment* or *nativism versus empiricism,* is one of the oldest and most central theoretical issues within philosophy as well as psychology. When asked by developmental psychologists, the question is basically whether a child's development is governed by a pattern built in at birth or whether it is shaped by experiences after birth. Historically, the nativist/nature side of the controversy was represented principally by Plato and (in the more modern era) René Descartes, both of whom believed that at least some ideas were innate. On the other side of the philosophical argument were a group of British philosophers called *empiricists,* such as John Locke, who insisted that at birth the mind is a blank slate—in Latin, a *tabula rasa.* All knowledge, they argued, is created by experience.

No developmental psychologist today would cast this issue in such black-and-white terms. We agree that essentially every facet of a child's development is a product of some pattern of interaction of nature and nurture. Even clearly physical developments have some environmental component. For example, in every culture, puberty occurs sometime between approximately age 9 and age 16, but the timing is affected by environmental factors such as diet. Similarly, some temperamental patterns may be inherited, but they can be and are modified by the parents' style of caregiving. *No* aspect of development is entirely one or the other. Nonetheless, psychologists have always had lively disagreements about the relative importance of these two factors.

Until fairly recently, the theoretical pendulum was well over toward the environmental end of the continuum. Most developmental research, and the majority of the theorizing by developmental psychologists, focused on environmental effects of one type or another. In the last decade or so, though, we have seen a strong and growing emphasis on the biological roots of behavior and development. In part, this shift has grown out of new technology that allows physiologists and psychologists to study the functioning of the brain in much greater detail; it also rests on the development of new statistical techniques that have made it possible to study genetic influences in new ways. The shift may also have occurred because it became clear that we needed more balance in our explanations of development. Whatever the reasons, a significant resurgence of interest in the biological roots of behavior has occurred, evident in a number of important themes.

Critical Thinking

See if you can identify one of your own characteristics or behavior patterns that has been strongly affected by "nature" and one pattern that you think is strongly a result of your upbringing.

Inborn Biases and Constraints

One example of this resurgence is an increasing popularity of the concepts of "inborn biases" or "constraints" on development. The argument, which is in some ways a modern descendent of Descartes' notion of inborn ideas, is that children are born with tendencies to respond in certain ways. In computer language, we could say that infants are born with certain "default options"; the system is *already* programmed or "biased."

For instance, from the earliest days of life, babies seem to listen more to the beginnings and ends of sentences than to the middle parts (Slobin, 1985a), and they respond visually to motion and to shifts from dark to light (Haith, 1980). Similarly, in the study of infants' cognitive development, researchers such as Elizabeth Spelke (1991) have concluded that babies come into the world with certain "preexisting conceptions" or constraints in their understanding of the behavior of objects. Very young babies already seem to understand that unsupported objects will move downward and that a moving object will continue to move in the same direction unless it encounters an obstacle. Unlike Descartes, current theorists do not propose that these built-in response patterns are the end of the story; rather, they see them as the starting point. What then develops is a result of experience filtered through these initial biases, but those biases *constrain* the number of developmental pathways that are possible (Campbell & Bickhard, 1992).

Maturation

Nature can shape processes after birth in other ways as well, most clearly through genetic programming that may determine whole sequences of later development. This is not a new idea; Arnold Gesell (1925; Thelen & Adolph, 1992) proposed such an idea seventy years ago. He used the term **maturation** to describe such genetically programmed sequential patterns of change, and this term is still uniformly used today. Changes in body size and shape, changes in hormones at puberty, changes in muscles and bones, and changes in the nervous system all may be programmed in this way. You can probably remember your own physical changes during adolescence. The timing of these pubertal changes differs from one teenager to the next, but the basic sequence is essentially the same for all children. Such sequences, which begin at conception and continue until death, are shared by all members of our species. The instructions for these sequences are part of the specific hereditary information that is passed on at the moment of conception.

Any maturational pattern is marked by three qualities: It is *universal,* appearing in all children, across cultural boundaries; it is *sequential,* involving some pattern of unfolding skill or characteristics; and it is *relatively impervious to environmental influence.* In its purest form, a maturationally determined developmental sequence occurs regardless of practice or training. You don't have to practice growing pubic hair; you don't have to be taught how to walk. In fact, it would take almost herculean efforts to *prevent* such sequences from unfolding. Yet even confirmed maturational theorists agree that experience plays a role. These powerful, apparently automatic maturational patterns require at least some minimal environmental support, such as adequate diet and opportunity for movement and experimentation.

Modern research also tells us that specific experience interacts with maturational patterns in intricate ways. For example, Greenough (1991) notes that one of the proteins required for the development of the visual system is controlled by a gene whose action is triggered only by visual experience. So *some* visual experience is needed for the genetic program to operate. In normal development, of course, every (nonblind) child will have some such experience. Still, examples like this one tell us that maturational sequences do not simply "unfold" automatically. The system appears to be "ready" to develop along particular pathways, but it requires experience to trigger the movement.

I should point out that the term *maturation* does not mean quite the same thing as *growth,* although the two terms are sometimes used as if they were synonyms. *Growth* refers to some kind of step-by-step change in quantity, as in size, and it can occur either with or without an underlying maturational process. A child's body could grow because her diet has significantly improved, or it could grow because she is getting older. The first of these has no maturational component while the second does. To put it another way, the term *growth* is a *description* of change, while the concept of maturation is one *explanation* of change.

The shift from crawling to walking is a classic example of a maturationally based universal developmental change: It follows the same basic pattern in boys and girls, in Asians, blacks, Latinos, and Caucasians.

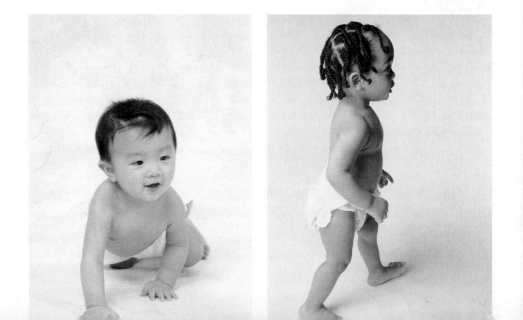

Behavior Genetics

The idea of inborn biases and the concept of maturation are both designed to account for patterns and sequences of development that are the *same* for all children. At the same time, nature contributes to *variations* from one individual to the next, since genetic inheritance is individual as well as collective. The study of genetic contributions to individual behavior, called **behavior genetics,** has become a particularly vibrant and influential research area in recent years and has contributed greatly to the renewed interest in the biological roots of behavior.

Using two primary research techniques—the study of identical and fraternal twins and the study of adopted children (described more fully in the Research Report on p. 6)—behavior geneticists have shown that specific heredity affects a remarkably broad range of behaviors. Included in the list are not only obvious physical differences such as height, body shape, or a tendency to skinniness or obesity, but also cognitive abilities such as general intelligence (about which I will have a great deal more to say in Chapter 7), more specific cognitive skills such as spatial visualization ability, or problems like reading disability (Rose, 1995). Newer research is also showing that many aspects of pathological behavior are genetically influenced, including alcoholism, schizophrenia, excessive aggressiveness or antisocial behavior, depression or anxiety, even anorexia (Goldsmith et al., 1997b; Gottesman & Goldsmith, 1994; McGue, 1994). Finally, and importantly, behavior geneticists have found a significant genetic influence on children's temperament, including such dimensions as emotionality (the tendency to get distressed or upset easily), activity (the tendency toward vigorous, rapid behavior), and sociability (the tendency to prefer the presence of others to being alone) (Saudino, 1998).

Paradoxically, a child's genetic heritage may also affect her environment (Plomin, 1995), a phenomenon that could occur via either or both of two routes. First, the child inherits her genes from her parents, who *also* create the environment in which she is growing up. So knowing something about the child's genetic heritage may allow us to predict something about her environment as well. For example, parents who themselves have higher IQ scores are not only likely to pass their "good IQ" genes on to their children; they are also likely to create a richer, more stimulating environment for their child. Similarly, children who inherit a tendency toward aggression and hostility from their parents are likely to live in a family environment that is higher in criticism and negativity—because those are expressions of the parents' own genetic tendencies toward aggressiveness or hostility (Reiss, 1998).

Second, each child's unique pattern of inherited qualities affects the way she behaves with other people, which in turn affects the way adults and other children respond to her. A cranky or temperamentally difficult baby may receive fewer smiles and more scolding than an easy, sunny-dispositioned one; a genetically brighter child may demand more personal attention, ask more questions, or seek out more complex toys than would a less bright child (Saudino & Plomin, 1997). Furthermore, children's interpretations of their experiences are affected by all their inherited tendencies, including not only intelligence but temperament or pathologies. For example, in one study of twins and step-siblings, Robert Plomin and his colleagues (1994) found that identical twin adolescents described their parents in more similar terms than did fraternal twins.

The study of identical twins, like these two girls, is one of the classic methods of behavior genetics. Whenever pairs of identical twins are more like one another in some behavior or quality than are pairs of fraternal twins, it indicates the presence of a genetic influence.

Research Report

How Do Behavior Geneticists Identify Genetic Effects?

Investigators can search for a genetic influence on a trait in either of two primary ways: They can study identical and fraternal twins, or they can study adopted children. Identical twins share exactly the same genetic patterning, because they develop from the same fertilized ovum. Fraternal twins each develop from a separate ovum, separately fertilized. They are therefore no more alike than are any other pair of siblings, except that they have shared the same prenatal environment and grow up in the same sequential niche within the family. If identical twins turned out to be more like one another on any given trait than fraternal twins, that would be evidence for the influence of heredity on that trait.

A powerful variant of the twin strategy is to study twins who have been reared apart. If identical twins are still more like one another on some dimension, despite having grown up in different environments, we have even clearer evidence of a genetic contribution for that trait.

In the case of adopted children, the strategy is to compare the degree of similarity between the adopted child and his birth parents (with whom he shares genes but not environment) with the degree of similarity between the adopted child and his adoptive parents (with whom he shares environment but not genes). If the child should turn out to be more similar to his birth parents than to his adoptive parents, or if his behavior or skill is better predicted by the characteristics of his birth parents than by characteristics of his adoptive parents, that would again demonstrate the influence of heredity.

In very recent years, behavior geneticists have devised a method that combines some of the elements of the twin and adoption strategies by studying twins along with children growing up in stepfamilies. Stepfamilies can include full siblings, half siblings, and step-siblings. Studying these families allows us to see whether the degree of similarity on some trait matches the degree of genetic similarity in any pair of children.

Let me give you two examples, both from studies of intelligence, measured with standard IQ tests. Bouchard and McGue (1981, p. 1056, Fig. 1) have combined the results of dozens of twin studies on the heritability of IQ scores, with the following results:

Identical twins reared together	.85
Identical twins reared apart	.67
Fraternal twins reared together	.58
Siblings (including fraternal twins) reared apart	.24

The numbers here are correlations—a statistic I'll explain more fully later in this chapter. For now you need to know only that a correlation can range from 0 to +1.00 or –1.00. The closer it is to 1.00, the stronger the relationship it describes. In this case, the number reflects how similar the IQs are in the two members of a twin pair. You can see that identical twins reared together have IQs that are highly similar, much more similar than what occurs for fraternal twins reared together. You can also see, though, that environment plays a role, since identical twins reared apart are less similar than are those reared together.

The same conclusion comes from two well-known studies of adopted children, the Texas Adoption Project (Loehlin et al., 1994) and the Minnesota Transracial Adoption Study (Scarr et al., 1993). In both studies, the adopted children were recently given IQ tests at approximately age 18. Their scores on this test were then correlated with the earlier-measured IQ scores of their natural mothers and of their adoptive mothers and fathers. Here are the results:

	Texas	Minnesota
Correlation with the biological mother's IQ score	.44	.29
Correlation with the adoptive mother's IQ score	.03	.14
Correlation with the adoptive father's IQ score	.06	.08

In both cases, the children's IQs were at least somewhat predicted by their natural mothers' IQs, but *not* by the IQs of their adoptive parents, with whom they had spent their entire childhood. Thus, the adoption studies, like the twin studies of IQ, tell us that there is indeed a substantial genetic component in what we measure with an IQ test.

In this same study, full siblings described their parents more similarly than did genetically unrelated step-siblings. It appears that identical twins are *experiencing* their parents, and their family environment, in more similar ways. This does *not* mean that there is somehow an "experiencing the environment" gene. Rather, the full genetic pattern of each child or adult affects the way he or she experiences and interprets. Because identical twins have the same genetic makeup, they experience and interpret more similarly.

Research of this kind has forced developmental psychologists to rethink some long-held assumptions about the effects of environment. At the same time, I want to emphasize that no behavior geneticist is saying that heredity is the *only* cause of behavior, or even the most central one in many cases. Indeed, as Robert Plomin points out, behavior genetic research has been as important in showing the significant effect of environment as in proving the centrality of heredity (1995). For some characteristics, such as inherited diseases, genetic influences are clearly dominant. For most aspects of development, however, such as variations in personality or intellectual abilities, the effect of a particular genetic pattern is more a matter of probability than certainty. We know there is *some* genetic effect because identical twins are a lot more alike in personality, IQ, or many specific behavior patterns than are fraternal twins. Yet even identical twins are not identical in these characteristics. For example, studies of adult criminals, done in the United States, Germany, Japan, Norway, and Denmark, show that if one of a pair of identical twins has been jailed for some criminal act, the probability that the other twin has also been jailed is about 50 percent. Among fraternal twins, this "concordance rate" is only 23 percent (Gottesman & Goldsmith, 1994). This shows a clear genetic effect, but the role of environment is also obvious. In virtually every case, specific outcomes for a given child depend on the interaction of that child's genetic patterning with the particular environment the child encounters and creates.

Models of Environmental Influence

Everything I've said so far should underline the fact that theories and models of the role of nature in development have become more subtle and complex in recent years, with much more attention paid to the ways in which nurture interacts with nature. On the nurture side of the theoretical issue we see the same increased subtlety and complexity. One particularly good example is a set of models of environmental influence summarized by Richard Aslin (1981a), based on earlier work by Gottlieb (1976a; 1976b), shown schematically in Figure 1.1 (see p. 8). In each drawing the dashed line represents the path of development of some skill or behavior that would occur without a particular experience; the solid line represents the path of development if the experience were added.

For comparison purposes, the first of the five models actually shows a maturational pattern with *no* environmental effect. The second model, which Aslin calls *maintenance,* describes a pattern in which some environmental input is necessary to sustain a skill or behavior that has already developed maturationally. For example, kittens are born with full binocular vision, but if you cover one of their eyes for a period of time, their binocular skill declines. Similarly, muscles will atrophy if not used.

The third model shows a *facilitation* effect of the environment in which a skill or behavior develops earlier than it normally would because of some experience. For example, children whose parents talk to them more often in the first 18 to 24 months of life, using more complex sentences, appear to develop two-word sentences and other early grammatical forms somewhat earlier than do children talked to less. Yet less talked-to children do eventually learn to create complex sentences and use most grammatical forms correctly, so there is no permanent gain.

When a particular experience does lead to a permanent gain or to an enduringly higher level of performance, Aslin calls it *attunement.* For example, children born to poverty-level families who attend special enriched day care in infancy and early childhood have consistently higher IQ scores throughout childhood than do children from the same kinds of families who do not have such enriched experience (Campbell & Ramey, 1994; Ramey, 1993; Ramey & Campbell, 1987). Similarly, children whose parents talk to them a lot, using a wide-ranging vocabulary, appear to have a permanent advantage in total vocabulary size over children whose parents talk to them less (Hart & Risley, 1995). Thus, a rich early language environment seems to have a facilitation effect on basic grammatical development, but an attunement effect on vocabulary.

Critical Thinking

Another example: Behavior genetic evidence (McGue & Lykken, 1992) shows that the concordance rate for divorce is about .45 among adult identical twins (that is, if one identical twin is divorced, the probability that the co-twin will also be divorced is .45). The equivalent "concordance rate" among adult fraternal twins is only .30. How can you explain such a difference?

Critical Thinking

Several decades ago, educators devised the preschool program called Head Start to improve the school preparation of children growing up in poor families. Which of Aslin's models do you think best describes what the designers of Head Start thought (or hoped) would be the result of the program?

Figure 1.1

Aslin's five models of possible relationships between maturation and environment. The top model shows a purely maturational effect; the bottom model (*induction*) shows a purely environmental effect. The other three show interactive combinations: *maintenance*, in which experience prevents the deterioration of a maturationally developed skill; *facilitation*, in which experience speeds up the development of some maturational process; and *attunement*, in which experience increases the ultimate level of some skill or behavior above the "normal" maturational level.

(*Source:* Aslin, Richard N., "Experimental Influences and Sensitive Periods in Perceptual Development," *Psychobiological Perspectives*, Vol. 2, *The Visual System* (1981), p. 50. Reprinted by permission of Academic Press and the author.)

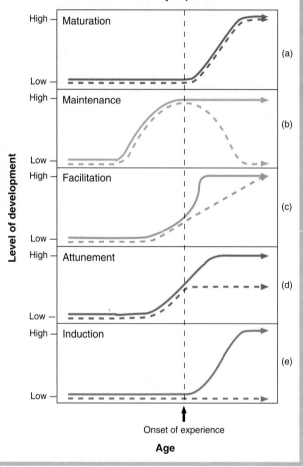

Aslin's final model, *induction,* describes a pure environmental effect: In the absence of some experience, a particular behavior would not develop at all. Giving a child tennis lessons or exposing him to a second language would fall into this category.

Helpful as they are, Aslin's models still don't take us far enough. At least three other aspects of the environmental side of the equation are also significant in current thinking about development: the timing of experience, the child's own interpretation of experience, and the total ecological/cultural system in which experiences occur.

The Timing of Experience

Just as the importance of nature may vary from one time in development to another, so the timing of specific experiences may matter as well. The impact of day care on an infant may be quite different when he is 6 months old than when he is 16 months old; moving from one school to another may have a different effect when it coincides with puberty than when it does not; and so forth.

Our thinking about the importance of timing was stimulated, in part, by research on other species that showed that specific experiences had different or stronger effects at some points in development than at others. The most famous example is that baby ducks will become *imprinted* on (become attached to and follow) any duck or any other quacking, moving object that happens to be around them 15 hours after they hatch. If nothing is moving or quacking at that critical point, they don't become imprinted at all (Hess, 1972). So the period just around 15 hours after hatching is a **critical period** for the duck's development of a proper following response.

We can see similar critical periods in the action of various **teratogens** in prenatal development. (A teratogen is any outside agent or chemical that causes a birth defect.) While some teratogens can have negative consequences at any time in gestation, most have effects only during some critical period. For example, if a mother contracts the disease rubella (commonly called German measles) during a narrow range of days in the first three months of pregnancy, some damage or deformity occurs in the fetus. Infection with the same virus after the third month of pregnancy rarely has such an effect.

We can also see critical periods in some aspects of brain development after birth—specific weeks or months during which the child needs to encounter certain types of stimulation or experience for the nervous system to develop normally and fully (Hirsch & Tieman, 1987).

The broader and somewhat looser concept of a **sensitive period** has also been widely used. A sensitive period is a span of months or years during which a child may be particularly responsive to specific forms of experience, or particularly influenced by their absence. For example, the period from 6 to 12 months of age may be a sensitive period for the formation of a core attachment to the parents. Other periods may be particularly significant for intellectual development or language (Tamis-LeMonda & Bornstein, 1987).

Internal Models of Experience

Another concept that offers us a more subtle and complex way of thinking about environmental effects is that of an **internal model of experience.** The key idea is that the effect of some experience lies in an individual's *interpretation* or *representation* of it, the *meaning* the individual attaches to it, rather than in the objective properties of the experience. You can easily come up with everyday examples from your own life. For instance, suppose a friend says to you, "Your new haircut looks great. I think it's a lot

If the first year of life is a sensitive period for the establishment of a secure attachment (as some contend), then are these infants in day care, separated from their parents every day, less likely to establish such a secure attachment? There has been hot debate among psychologists on this point.

more becoming when it's short like that." Your friend intends it as a compliment, but what determines your reaction is how you *hear* the comment, not what is intended. If your internal model of your self includes the basic idea "I usually look okay," you will likely hear your friend's comment as a compliment; but if your internal model of self or relationships includes some more negative elements, such as "I usually do things wrong, so other people criticize me," then you may hear an implied criticism in your friend's comment ("Your hair used to look awful").

Theorists who emphasize the importance of such meaning systems argue that each child creates a set of internal models—a set of assumptions or conclusions about the world, about himself, and about relationships with others—through which all subsequent experience is filtered (Epstein, 1991; Reiss, 1998). John Bowlby expressed this idea when he talked about the child's "internal working model" of attachment (1969; 1980). A child with a secure model of attachment may assume that someone will come when he cries and that affection and attention are reliably available. A child with a less secure model may assume that if a grown-up frowns, it probably means she will be yelled at. Such expectations are certainly based in part on actual experiences, but once formed into an internal model, they generalize beyond the original experience and affect the way the child interprets future experiences. A child who expects adults to be reliable and affectionate will be more likely to interpret the behavior of new adults in this way and will re-create friendly and affectionate relationships with others outside the family; a child who expects hostility will read hostility into otherwise fairly neutral encounters.

A child's self-concept seems to operate in much the same way, as an internal working model of "who I am" (Bretherton, 1991). This self-model is based on experience, but it also shapes future experience.

To be sure, these internal models of experience may well have some "nature" component to them. In particular, children with different inborn temperaments may have an initial bias toward one or another type of internal model. For example, an extraverted baby with a generally positive mood may be more likely to create a secure working model of attachment than will a crankier, more difficult infant. But whatever factors contribute to the creation of such an internal model, be they nature or nurture or some combination of the two, once formed, the internal model affects the way the child interprets future experience.

The Ecological Perspective

A third facet of current thinking about environmental effects is a growing emphasis on casting a wider environmental net. Until quite recently, most research on environmental influences focused on a child's family (frequently only the child's mother) and on the stimulation available in the child's home, such as the kinds of toys or books available to the child. If we looked at a larger family context at all, it was usually in terms of the general wealth or poverty of the family.

In the past ten or fifteen years, however, there has been a strong push to widen our scope, to consider the *ecology* or *context* in which each child develops. Urie Bronfenbrenner, one of the key figures in this area (1979; 1989), emphasizes that each child grows up in a complex social environment (a social ecology) with a distinct cast of characters: brothers, sisters, one or both parents, grandparents, baby-sitters, pets, schoolteachers, friends. And this cast is itself embedded within a larger social system: The parents have jobs that they may like or dislike; they may or may not have close and supportive friends; they may be living in a safe neighborhood or one full of dangers; the local school may be excellent or poor, and the parents may have good or poor relationships with the school. Bronfenbrenner's argument is that we must not only include descriptions of these more extended aspects of the environment in our research, we must also understand the ways in which all the components of this complex system interact with one another to affect the development of an individual child.

Critical Thinking

How would you describe the "ecology" of your own childhood? What sort of family did you grow up in? What sort of neighborhood and school? What other significant people were in your life? What significant events affected your parents' lives and in turn affected you?

A particularly impressive example of research that examines such a larger system of influences is Gerald Patterson's work on the origins of antisocial (highly aggressive) behavior in children (1996; Patterson et al., 1989). His studies show that parents who use poor discipline techniques and poor monitoring of their child are more likely to have noncompliant or antisocial children. Once established, however, the child's antisocial behavior pattern has repercussions in other areas of his life, leading both to rejection by peers and to academic difficulty. These problems, in turn, are likely to push the young person toward a deviant peer group and still further delinquency (Dishion et al., 1991; Vuchinich et al., 1992). So a pattern that began in the family is maintained and exacerbated by interactions with peers and with the school system.

These relationships are of interest in themselves, but Patterson does not stop there. He adds important ecological elements, arguing that the family's good or poor disciplinary techniques are not random events but are themselves shaped by the larger context in which the family exists. He finds that those parents who were raised using poor disciplinary practices are more likely to use those same poor strategies with their children. He also finds that even parents who possess good basic child-management skills may fall into poor patterns when the stresses in their own lives are increased. A recent divorce or a period of unemployment increases the likelihood that parents will use poor disciplinary practices and thus increases the likelihood that the child will develop a pattern of antisocial behavior. Figure 1.2 shows Patterson's conception of how these various components fit together. Clearly, by taking into account the larger social ecological system in which the family is embedded, we greatly enhance our understanding of the process.

Figure 1.2

Patterson's model describes the many factors that influence the development of antisocial behavior. The core of the process, in this model, is the interaction between the child and the parent (the orange box). One might argue that the origin of antisocial behavior lies in that relationship. But Patterson argues that there are larger ecological or contextual forces that are also "causes" of the child's delinquency, some of which are listed in the two blue boxes on the left.

(*Source:* Patterson, G. R.; DeBaryshe, B. D.; and Ramsey, E., 1989. "A Developmental Perspective on Antisocial Behavior," *American Psychologist,* 44, pp. 331 and 332. Copyright © 1989 by the American Psychological Association. Adapted with permission of the American Psychological Association and B. D. DeBaryshe.)

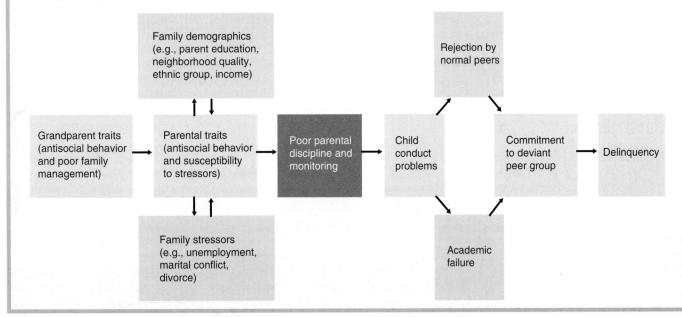

Cultural Influences

One aspect of such a larger ecology, not emphasized in Patterson's model but clearly part of Bronfenbrenner's thinking, is the still broader concept of **culture.** There is no commonly agreed-on definition for this term, but in essence it describes *a system of meanings and customs,* including values, attitudes, goals, laws, beliefs, morals, and physical artifacts of various kinds, such as tools and forms of dwellings. The majority U.S. culture, for example, is strongly shaped by the values expressed in the Constitution and the Bill of Rights; it also includes a strong emphasis on "can-do" attitudes and on competition. At a more specific level, the cultural beliefs include the assumption that the ideal form of living is for each family to have a separate house—a belief that contributes to a more spread-out pattern of housing in the United States than what exists in Europe.

For such a system of meanings to be called a culture, it must be *shared by some identifiable group,* whether that group is a subsection of some population or a larger unit; it must then be *transmitted from one generation of that group to the next* (Betancourt & Lopez, 1993; Cole, 1992). Families and children are clearly embedded in culture, just as they are located within an ecological niche within the culture.

Most of us are aware of the powerful impact of culture or subculture only when we find ourselves outside our own cultural milieu, or when we are in a situation in which we must interact consistently with others of another subculture. My own awareness was greatly enhanced recently by a year spent living in Germany. I found that small cultural differences often left me feeling dislocated and uncertain. One fairly trivial example: As an American, I quite naturally smiled at strangers I might pass while out walking on one of the many special paths crisscrossing the country. Yet those I met rarely made eye contact and never smiled at me. Indeed, they often seemed quite put off by my friendliness. I experienced their behavior as coldness and felt quite isolated, even when my logical mind told me that I was merely encountering a different cultural pattern. Experiences like this convinced me that Edward Sapir was right when he said, "The worlds in which different societies live are distinct worlds, not merely the same world with different words attached" (1929, p. 209).

Individualism and Collectivism. Anthropologists point out that a key dimension on which cultural worlds differ from one another is that of **individualism** versus **collectivism** (e.g., Kim et al., 1994). Cultures with an individualistic emphasis assume that the world is made up of independent persons whose achievement and responsibility is individual rather than collective. Most European cultures are based on such individualistic assumptions, as is the Euro-American culture (the dominant U.S. culture created primarily by whites who came to the United States from Europe). In contrast, most of the remainder of the world's cultures operate with a collectivist belief system in which the emphasis is on collective rather than individual identity, on group solidarity, sharing, duties and obligations, and group decision making (Greenfield, 1994). A person living in a collectivist system is integrated into a strong, cohesive group that protects and nourishes that individual throughout his life. Collectivism is the dominant theme in most Asian countries, as well as in many African and South American cultures. Strong elements of collectivism are also part of the African-American, Latino, Native American, and Asian-American subcultures.

Greenfield (1995) gives a wonderful example of how the difference between collectivist and individualist cultures can affect actual child-rearing practices as well as our judgments of others' child rearing. She notes that mothers from the Zinacanteco Maya culture maintain almost constant bodily contact with their young babies and do not feel comfortable when they are separated from their infants. They believe that their babies *require* this contact to be happy. When these mothers saw a visiting anthropologist put her own baby down, they were shocked and blamed the foreign baby's regular crying on the fact that he was separated from his mother so often. Greenfield argues that the constant bodily contact of the Mayan mothers is a logical outgrowth of their collectivist approach because their basic goal is *inter*dependence rather than independence. The

U.S. anthropologist, in contrast, operates with a basic goal of independence for her child and so emphasizes more separation. Each group judges the other's form of child rearing to be less optimal or even inadequate.

This example makes it clear that the distinction between individualism and collectivism provides a useful conceptual hook on which we may be able to hang some of our analyses of cultural differences and cultural effects. Greenfield's analysis, and her example, also remind us that developmental psychology, as a scientific endeavor, has been almost entirely embedded in an individualistic cultural system. We have assumed that children naturally develop as individuals. Even when we acknowledge that development may be influenced by context and culture, our unit of study and analysis is almost always the individual, not the family or the village or some other collective. Now we must begin to try to look at development through collectivist eyes as well.

Two Basic Reasons for Studying Cultural Variations. As I see it, there are two fundamental reasons why we need to study cultural variations. First, if we are to understand "nurture," surely we must understand culture as part of the environment in which the child is growing up. How are developmental patterns changed by cultural variations, as in the example of sleeping through the night I already mentioned? How do different cultural values affect the way children experience their childhood and adolescence? For instance, might it be, as some have argued, that one consequence of the individualist U.S. culture is a much higher level of tolerance of aggression and violence than is true in many collectivist societies (Lore & Schultz, 1993)? Such tolerance, in turn, might manifest in a variety of ways, including the astonishingly high percentage of teenagers who carry weapons in the United States.

A second basic reason for studying cultural variations is, paradoxically, to uncover those developmental patterns or processes that are truly universal. If research with white middle-class U.S. children points to the existence of some basic developmental sequence or process, we need to observe or test children from a variety of subcultural or cultural groups, from as wide an array of cultures as possible, to check on the universality of the developmental pattern.

Fortunately, our store of cross-cultural research is growing steadily. In a few areas, such as the study of language, moral development, and attachment, we already have a fair amount of information about developmental patterns in myriad cultures. In many other areas, our research is still highly Eurocentric, but I will bring in cross-cultural or subcultural research wherever I can find it.

Interactions of Nature and Nurture

Nature and nurture do not act independently in shaping each child's development; they interact in complex and fascinating ways. I've suggested several such interactions as I've gone along, such as the need for certain specific types of environmental experience to trigger some maturational development. It is also possible that the interactions between nature and nurture *vary* from one child to another. In particular, the *same* environment may have quite different effects on children who are born with different characteristics. One influential research approach exploring such an interaction is the study of *vulnerable* and *resilient* children.

In the Latino subculture, families like the Limons, shown here at their annual reunion, are tightly knit, with frequent contact and support. Their interactions are based on a *collectivist* belief system. Such a cultural pattern may have wide repercussions.

American researchers have concluded that this kind of physical aggression is normal among 2-year-olds like Laura and Megan. But perhaps it is more likely in "individualist" cultures than in "collectivist" cultures. How could you find out?

Research Report
Resilience Among Children Growing Up in Poverty

On average, children who grow up in chronic poverty turn out less well than do children reared in more stable and economically well-off families. At the same time, some children reared in poverty nonetheless do very well as adults. How are these *resilient* children different from equally disadvantaged peers? Several fascinating studies begin to give us some answers.

Emmy Werner and Ruth Smith (1992), in their famous study of a group of 505 children born on the Hawaiian island of Kauai in 1955, found that certain specific risk factors predicted serious problems for children later in development: chronic poverty, a low level of education in the mother, family instability (particularly the absence of one parent), and significant physical problems in the infant, prenatally or at birth. Yet among the children in their sample who had experienced high levels of these kinds of risks, about a third managed to avoid the various problems of adolescence and young adulthood, including delinquency, learning problems, teenage pregnancy, or mental health problems. Werner found that these resilient young people had certain protective factors in common:

- As infants and toddlers, they had been affectionate, good-natured, and easy to deal with.
- As infants, they had had an opportunity to form a positive bond with at least one loving caregiver.
- In elementary school and high school, they got along well with classmates and had better language and reasoning skills than the children with poorer outcomes. They had many interests and hobbies, often participating in organized groups such as 4-H or the YMCA or YWCA.

A study by Janis Long and George Vaillant (1984) of 456 boys who grew up in inner-city neighborhoods in Boston in the 1930s and 1940s points to similar protective factors. The researchers found that the majority of men who had spent their youth in poverty nonetheless became effective adults. These men earned adequate incomes, married, and reared their children. Still, some had been much more successful than others, and these more resilient men shared two protective factors: higher IQ scores, and good "coping skills" as children. They had had good relationships with parents, teachers, and peers.

Thus, an engaging, easy temperament; an ability to get along with others; adequate or good intellectual skills, and access to supportive adults all seem to be protective factors for children growing up in poverty. These results have obvious practical relevance as we think about designing programs for inner-city children. They also have theoretical importance because they underline the fact that the same or similar environments (poverty and chaotic family life, in this case) have different effects on different children, depending on the qualities and skills the children bring to the interaction. Environments don't just "happen" to children, willy-nilly. Children interact with their environment.

Vulnerability and Resilience

In her long-term study of a group of children born on the island of Kauai, Hawaii, in 1955 (a study described more fully in the Research Report above), Emmy Werner and Ruth Smith (Werner, 1993; 1995; Werner & Smith, 1992) found that only about two-thirds of the children who grew up in poverty-level, chaotic families turned out to have serious problems themselves as adults. The other third, despite their poor environmental support, turned out to be "competent, confident, and caring adults" (Werner, 1995, p. 82). Thus, similar environments were linked to quite different outcomes.

Theorists such as Norman Garmezy, Michael Rutter, Ann Masten, and others (Garmezy, 1993; Garmezy & Rutter, 1983; Masten & Coatsworth, 1995; Rutter, 1987) argue that the best way to make sense out of results like Werner's is to think of each child as born with certain *vulnerabilities,* such as a difficult temperament, a physical abnormality, allergies, or a genetic tendency toward alcoholism. Each child is also born with some *protective factors,* such as high intelligence, good coordination, an easy temperament, or a lovely smile, that tend to make her more resilient in the face of stress. These vulnerabilities and protective factors then interact with the child's environment so that the *same* environment can have quite different effects, depending on the qualities the child brings to the interaction.

A more general model describing an interaction between the qualities of the child and the environment comes from Fran Horowitz, who proposes that the key ingredients are each child's vulnerability or resilience and the "facilitativeness" of the environment (1987; 1990). A highly facilitative environment is one in which the child has loving and responsive parents and is provided with a rich array of stimulation. If the relationship between vulnerability and facilitativeness were merely additive, we would find that the best outcomes occurred for resilient infants reared in optimum environments, the worst outcomes for vulnerable infants in poor environments, with the two mixed combinations falling halfway between. But that is not what Horowitz proposes, as you can see schematically in Figure 1.3. Instead she is suggesting that a resilient child in a poor environment may do quite well, since such a child can take advantage of all the stimulation and opportunities available. Similarly, she suggests that a vulnerable child may do quite well in a highly facilitative environment. According to this model, it is only the double whammy—the vulnerable child in a poor environment—that leads to really poor outcomes.

In fact, as you will see throughout the book, a growing body of research shows precisely this pattern. For example, very low IQ scores are most common among children who were low-birth-weight *and* reared in poverty-level families, while low-birth-weight children reared in middle-class families have essentially normal IQs, as do normal-weight infants reared in poverty-level families (Werner, 1986). Further, among low-birth-weight children who are reared in poverty-level families, those whose families show "protective" factors (such as greater residential stability, less crowded living

Figure 1.3

Horowitz's model describes one possible type of interaction between the vulnerability of the child and the quality of the environment. The height of the surface shows the "goodness" of the developmental outcome (such as IQ or skill in social relationships). In this model, only the combination of a vulnerable infant and a nonfacilitative environment will result in really poor outcomes.

(*Source:* Horowitz, F. D., *Exploring Developmental Theories: Toward a Structural/Behavioral Model of Development*, Fig. 1.1, p. 23. © 1987 by Lawrence Erlbaum Associates, Inc. By permission of the publisher and author.)

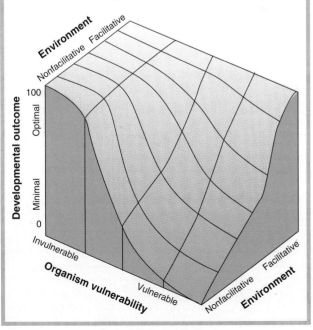

Critical Thinking

Another possible variation of this same idea: Do you think it is possible that girls and boys, beginning in infancy, respond differently to the *same* environments? If this is true, what would be the ramifications of such a pattern?

conditions, and more acceptance, more stimulation, and more learning materials) turn out better than do equivalently low-birth-weight children reared in the least optimum poverty conditions (Bradley et al., 1994). The key point here is that the same environment can have quite different effects, depending on the qualities or capacities the child brings to the equation.

The Nature of Developmental Change

The nature/nurture controversy is not the only "big question" in developmental psychology. An equally central dispute concerns the nature of developmental change itself: Is a child's expanding ability just "more of the same," or does it reflect a new kind of activity? For example, a 2-year-old is likely to have no individual friends among her playmates, while an 8-year-old is likely to have several. We could think of this as a *quantitative* change (a change in amount) from zero friends to some friends. Or we could think of it as a *qualitative* change (a change in kind or type) from disinterest in peers to interest, or from one sort of peer relationship to another. Where a given researcher or theorist stands on this question has a profound effect on the way he or she perceives children and their behavior. Does a child simply get better and better at things, such as walking or running or reading? That is, are the *processes* the same and only the efficiency or the speed different, or are there different processes at different ages? Do older children use different strategies, develop different understandings, organize their behavior differently? These issues are particularly central in discussions of cognitive development, which I'll be talking about in Chapters 6 and 12.

Stages and Sequences

An important related question, also especially relevant to discussions of cognitive development, concerns the existence of *stages* in the course of development. If development consists only of additions (quantitative change), then the concept of stages is not needed. However, if development involves reorganization or the emergence of wholly new strategies, qualities, or skills (qualitative change), then the concept of stages may become attractive. Certainly we hear a lot of "stagelike" language in everyday conversation about children: "He's just in the terrible twos" or "It's only a stage she's going through." Although there is not always agreement on just what would constitute evidence for the existence of discrete stages, the usual description is that a stage shift involves not only a change in skills but some discontinuous change in underlying *structure* (McHale & Lerner, 1990). The child in a new stage approaches tasks differently, sees the world differently, is preoccupied with different issues.

As we move through the following chapters, you will see that stage theories are common in studies of development, although the concept has come under considerable recent attack. John Flavell (1985; 1992), a major thinker in the area of cognitive development, points out that research on children's thinking in the past several decades has yielded only limited evidence of stages. What one does see are *sequences* of development in each of a large number of content areas—sequences in the development of concepts of gender, sequences in the development of memory strategies, sequences in the acquisition of language skills. Each of these sequences appears to be common across children and to reflect qualitative as well as quantitative changes, but the many sequences do not seem to be organized into cohesive wholes that we might think of as broad stages. A child might be very advanced in one sequence and only average in several others, for example, rather than being equally fast or slow in all areas.

Thus, the idea of stages of development, which seems at first blush to be a tidy way of organizing information, a simple way of describing changes with age, has turned out to be slippery and difficult to sustain. You should keep that in mind as you encounter the various stage theories that are still part of our theoretical language. You should also

Many people would explain this boy's behavior by saying he is in a "stage"—the so-called terrible twos—in which tantrums are common. Most psychologists, however, use the term *stage* to imply more than simply a behavior that is particularly visible at a particular age. A stage, in this usage, requires some change in internal structure, some reorganization of ways of thinking or feeling.

note, however, that it is not necessary to assume stages in order to argue that the nature of developmental change is qualitative as well as (or instead of) quantitative. Qualitative change may be gradual as well as abrupt, sequential rather than stagelike.

Theories of Development

In talking about the several key questions addressed by developmental psychologists—nature versus nurture, developmental universals versus unique developmental patterns, continuity and change, or the nature of developmental change—I have discussed each one as if it could be dealt with separately. In fact, though, scientists (and nonscientists) have a strong urge to organize information and ideas into larger structures we call **theories.** By laying out basic assumptions and giving answers to the key questions, a theory provides a kind of road map. Without such a road map, you can get lost in the minutiae of observation, just as you can get lost if you are trying to make your way in a strange city without a map. To use another analogy, theories help us to see the size and shape of the forest instead of the individual trees.

In developmental psychology, we have many types or layers of theories. At the broadest level, we have three **grand schemes**—psychoanalytic theory, learning theory, and cognitive-developmental theory—each designed to describe and explain the great sweep of human development and human behavior. These grand schemes have been and continue to be influential, shaping the language we use, the assumptions we make, the kinds of questions we ask.

Despite their residual impact, however, these grand schemes are less potent than they once were. Most psychologists today, although still influenced by these major theoretical proposals, work primarily with smaller-scale theories that we might call **models.** Behavior genetics offers one such model; Bronfenbrenner's ecological approach is another. Neither model is designed to account for all behavior or to explain all development. Yet each model points us toward important sources of information, toward key questions or hypotheses.

Finally, we have **minitheories,** each designed to explain a narrow range of behavior. For example, Susan Harter proposes a minitheory about the origins of variations in self-esteem, which I'll talk about in Chapter 10; Laurence Steinberg suggests a minitheory to explain the rise in parent-child conflict at the beginning of adolescence (see Chapter 11). Information processing theorists have brought concepts from computer simulations of adult intelligence to the problem of explaining children's cognitive development (see Chapter 6), and so on. Many such minitheories have their roots in the grand schemes, but the newer theorists' goals are much more modest. They aren't trying for a theory to explain everything, merely a theory that will handle the data in a narrow area. Ultimately, of course, we hope to be able to add up these minitheories and models into new grand schemes.

My primary goal in this brief introduction to theories is to introduce you to the three grand schemes. A second goal is to make clear just how real and potentially important the differences among these various theories and models can be, affecting not only the way researchers interpret data, but also the way parents and teachers interact with the children they deal with every day.

Let me give you an example. Imagine you hear two teachers arguing. The first one says:

> I want my kids to have time to *explore,* to figure things out for themselves. If I have everything scheduled down to a gnat's eyelash, they don't have any time to play with objects or ideas.

The second teacher replies:

> I don't want my kids to "explore" on their own. I want them to stay focused on the tasks I think are important. I want to have control over the classroom so that I can

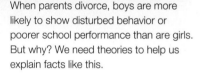

When parents divorce, boys are more likely to show disturbed behavior or poorer school performance than are girls. But why? We need theories to help us explain facts like this.

emphasize the important things, reward the kids for good behavior, and restrain their wildness.

These two teachers are probably both very good at their jobs, yet because they have different theories about children and their development, they go about their task very differently. The first teacher is basing her argument on the assumption that children are necessarily active participants in their own development, that they reach understanding by their own explorations and experiments—an argument central to cognitive-developmental theory. The second teacher is basing her argument on the assumption that children are *shaped* by their environment, so for learning to occur she must control that environment—an argument central to learning theories of development.

Like teachers, scientists are profoundly affected by their explicit and implicit theories. We make every attempt to be objective in our observations and collection of facts, but both the collection of the facts and the interpretation of them is guided by theory. For example, here's a fact: Virtually all children show some negative effects when their parents divorce, such as increases in aggression or a deterioration in school performance. Further, on average, these negative effects are slightly larger for boys than for girls (e.g., Hetherington, 1989; Kline et al., 1989).

This fact is extremely interesting in and of itself, but the fact alone doesn't provide an explanation. Do mothers treat their sons and daughters differently after a divorce? Do boys suffer more from the absence of the father? Or perhaps boys are somehow inherently less able to handle stress of any kind. Each of these alternative explanations is derived from a different theory or model; each suggests different types of additional research we might do to check on the validity of the explanation. If differential treatment of sons and daughters is the answer, then we ought to study family interactions in recently divorced families in some detail. If the absence of the father in the son's life is the crucial factor, then we ought to study boys and girls living with their fathers after divorce. If response to stress is involved, we should look at other stressful occurrences in family life, such as unexpected parental unemployment, the death of a family member, or a major move, and see whether in these cases, too, boys show more extreme responses.

The key point is that no fact stands alone without any explanation or framework; instead, we all interpret and create theories about each fact that comes our way, whether in our personal experience or in scientific endeavor. I'll be examining each of the major theories in much greater detail in later chapters, but to give you some feeling for the kinds of road maps developmental psychologists have used to guide their work, let me briefly introduce you to the three grand schemes here.

Psychoanalytic Theories

Theorists in the psychoanalytic tradition have been interested in explaining human behavior by understanding the underlying processes of the *psyche,* a Greek term referring to the soul, spirit, or mind. Sigmund Freud (1856–1939) is usually credited with originating the psychoanalytic approach (1905; 1920), and his terminology and many of his concepts have become part of our intellectual culture, even while his explicit influence on developmental psychology has waned. Two other theorists in this tradition, however, remain directly influential: Erik Erikson and John Bowlby.

The most distinctive and central assumption of the psychoanalytic approach is that behavior is governed by *unconscious* as well as conscious processes. Some of these unconscious processes are present at birth; others develop over time. For example, Freud proposed the existence of a basic unconscious, instinctual sexual drive he called the **libido.** He argued that this energy is the motive force behind virtually all our behavior. Freud also proposed that unconscious material is created over time through the functioning of the various defense mechanisms—those automatic, normal, unconscious strategies for reducing anxiety that we all use daily, such as repression, denial, or projection.

A second basic assumption is that personality has a structure and that this structure develops over time. Freud proposed three parts: the **id,** which is the center of the libido; the **ego,** a much more conscious element, the executive of the personality; and the **superego,** which is the center of conscience and morality, since it incorporates the norms and moral strictures of the family and society. In Freud's theory, these three parts are not all present at birth. The infant and toddler is all id, all instinct, all desire, without the restraining influence of the ego or the superego. The ego begins to develop in the years from age 2 to about 4 or 5 as the child learns to adapt his instant-gratification strategies. Finally, the superego begins to develop just before school age, as the child incorporates the parents' values and cultural mores.

Psychoanalytic theorists also see development as fundamentally stagelike, with each stage centered on a particular form of tension or a particular task. The child moves through these stages, resolving each task, reducing each tension as best he can. There is direction to this development, an ideal sequence.

The stages themselves are conceived somewhat differently in the various theories in this tradition. Freud thought they were strongly influenced by maturation. In each of Freud's five **psychosexual stages,** the libido is invested in that part of the body that is most sensitive at that age. In a newborn, the mouth is the most sensitive part of the body, so libidinal energy is focused there. The stage is therefore called the *oral* stage. As neurological development progresses, the infant has more sensation in the anus (hence the *anal* stage) and later the genitalia (the *phallic* and eventually the *genital* stages).

The stages Erikson proposes, called **psychosocial stages,** are influenced much less by maturation and much more by common cultural demands for children of a particular age, such as the demand that the child become toilet trained at about age 2 or that the child learn school skills at age 6 or 7. In Erikson's view, each child moves through a fixed sequence of tasks or dilemmas, each centered on the development of a particular facet of identity. For example, the first task, central to the first 12 to 18 months of life, is to develop a sense of basic trust. If the child's caregivers are not responsive and loving, however, the child may develop a sense of mistrust, which will affect her responses at all the later stages.

In both theories, however, the critical point is that the degree of success a child experiences in meeting the demands of these various stages will depend very heavily on the interactions he has with the people and objects in his world. This *interactive* element in Freud's and all subsequent psychoanalytic theories is absolutely central. Basic trust cannot be developed unless the parents or other caregivers respond to the infant in a loving, consistent manner. The oral stage cannot be fully completed unless the infant is given sufficient gratification of the desire for oral stimulation. And when a stage is not fully resolved, the old patterns or the unmet need is carried forward, affecting the individual's ability to handle later tasks or stages. So, for example, a young adult who developed a sense of mistrust in the first years of life may have a more difficult time establishing a secure intimate relationship with a partner or with friends—a pattern that has been found in a growing number of studies (e.g., Hazan & Shaver, 1990; Senchak & Leonard, 1992; Simpson, 1990).

This emphasis on the formative role of early experience, particularly early family experience, is a hallmark of psychoanalytic theories. In this view, the first five or six years of life are a kind of sensitive period for the creation of the individual personality.

Cognitive-Developmental Theories

In psychoanalytic theories, the quality and character of a child's relationships with a few key people are seen as central to the child's whole development. The child's encounters with the inanimate world—with toys and objects, with sights and sounds—are rarely discussed. Most cognitive-developmental theorists, whose interest has been primarily in cognitive development rather than personality, reverse this order of importance, emphasizing the centrality of the child's explorations of objects.

Critical Thinking

Does this make sense to you—this idea that one carries unresolved issues forward into adulthood? Can you think of any examples in your own experience?

The central figure in cognitive-developmental theory has been Jean Piaget (1896–1980), a Swiss psychologist whose theories shaped the thinking of several generations of developmental psychologists (1952; 1970; 1977; Piaget & Inhelder, 1969). Piaget, along with other early cognitive theorists such as Lev Vygotsky (1962) and Heinz Werner (1948), was struck by the great regularities in the development of children's thinking. He noticed that all children seemed to go through the same kinds of sequential discoveries about their world, making the same sorts of mistakes and arriving at the same solutions. For example, 3- and 4-year-olds all seem to think that if you pour water from a short, fat glass into a tall, thin one, there is more water in the thin glass since the water level is higher there than it was in the fat glass. In contrast, most 7-year-olds realize that the amount of water is the same in either case.

Piaget's detailed observations of such systematic shifts in children's thinking led him to several assumptions, the most central of which is that it is the nature of the human organism to *adapt* to its environment. This is an active process. In contrast to many learning theorists, Piaget does not think that the environment *shapes* the child. Rather, the child (like the adult) actively seeks to understand his environment. In the process, he explores, manipulates, and examines the objects and people in his world.

The process of adaptation, in Piaget's view, is made up of several important subprocesses—*assimilation, accommodation,* and *equilibration*—all of which I will define fully in Chapter 6. What you need to understand at this preliminary point is that Piaget thought that the child develops a series of fairly distinct "understandings" or "theories" about the way the world works, based on her active exploration of the environment. Each of these "theories" comprises a specific stage. Since Piaget thought that virtually all infants begin with the same skills and built-in strategies, and since the environments children encounter are highly similar in important respects, he believed that the stages through which their thinking moves are also similar. Piaget proposed a fixed sequence of four major stages, each growing out of the one that preceded it, and each consisting of a more or less complete system or organization of concepts, strategies, and assumptions.

Vygotsky's Theory. Russian psychologist Lev Vygotsky (1896–1934) is normally thought of as belonging to the cognitive-developmental camp because he, too, was primarily concerned with understanding the origins of the child's knowledge (1978). Vygotsky differs from Piaget, however, in one key respect: He was convinced that complex forms of thinking have their origins in *social* interactions rather than primarily in the child's private explorations as Piaget proposed (Duncan, 1995). According to Vygotsky, children's learning of new cognitive skills is guided by an adult (or a more skilled child, such as an older sibling), who models and structures the child's learning experience, a process Jerome Bruner later called **scaffolding** (Wood et al., 1976). Such new learning, Vygotsky suggested, is best achieved in what he called the **zone of proximal development**—that range of tasks that are too hard for the child to do alone but that she can manage with guidance. As the child becomes more skilled, the zone of proximal development steadily shifts upward, including ever harder tasks. Vygotsky thought the key to this interactive process lay in the language the adult used to describe or frame the task. Later, the child could use this same language to guide her independent attempts to do the same kinds of tasks.

Learning Theories

Learning theories represent a very different theoretical tradition, one in which the emphasis is much more on the way the environment *shapes* the child than on how the child understands his experiences. No learning theorist is arguing that genetics or built-in biases are unimportant, but theorists of this group see human behavior as enormously plastic, shaped by predictable processes of learning. The most central of these processes are classical conditioning and operant conditioning. If you have encountered these concepts in earlier courses, you may be able to skim the next section. For those of you who lack such a background, a brief description is needed.

Classical Conditioning. This type of learning, made famous by Pavlov's experiments with his salivating dog, involves the acquisition of new signals for existing responses. If you touch a baby on the cheek, he will turn toward the touch and begin to suck. In the technical terminology of **classical conditioning,** the touch on the cheek is the **unconditional stimulus;** the turning and sucking are **unconditioned responses.** The baby is already programmed to do all that; these are automatic reflexes. Learning occurs when some *new* stimulus is hooked into the system. The general model is that other stimuli that are present just before or at the same time as the unconditional stimulus will eventually trigger the same responses. In the typical home situation, for example, a number of stimuli occur at about the same time as the touch on the baby's cheek before feeding: the sound of the mother's footsteps approaching, the kinesthetic cues of being picked up, and the tactile cues of being held in the mother's arms. All these stimuli may eventually become **conditional stimuli** and may trigger the infant's response of turning and sucking, even without any touch on the cheek.

Classical conditioning is of special interest in our study of child development because of the role it plays in the development of emotional responses. For example, things or people present when you feel good will become conditional stimuli for that same sense of well-being, while those previously associated with some uncomfortable feeling may become conditional stimuli for a sense of unease or anxiety. This is especially important in infancy, since a child's mother or father is present so often when nice things happen—when the child feels warm, comfortable, and cuddled. In this way mother and father usually come to be a conditional stimulus for pleasant feelings, a fact that makes it possible for the parents' mere presence to reinforce other behaviors as well. A tormenting older sibling might come to be a conditional stimulus for angry feelings, even after the sibling has long since stopped the tormenting. These classically conditional emotional responses are remarkably powerful. They begin to be formed very early in life, continue to be created throughout childhood and adulthood, and profoundly affect each individual's emotional experiences.

Operant Conditioning. The second major type of learning is most often called **operant conditioning,** although you will also see it referred to as *instrumental conditioning.* Unlike classical conditioning, which involves attaching an old response to a new stimulus, operant conditioning involves attaching a new response to an old stimulus, achieved by the application of appropriate principles of reinforcement. Any behavior that is reinforced will be more likely to occur again in the same or in a similar situation. There are two types of reinforcements. A **positive reinforcement** is any event that, following some behavior, increases the chances that the behavior will occur again in that situation. Certain classes of pleasant consequences, such as praise, a smile, food, a hug, or attention, serve as reinforcers for most people most of the time. But strictly speaking, a reinforcement is defined by its effect; we don't know something is reinforcing unless we see that its presence increases the probability of some behavior.

The second major type is a **negative reinforcement,** which occurs when something an individual finds *unpleasant* is *stopped.* Suppose your little boy is whining and begging you to pick him up. At first you ignore him, but finally you do pick him up. What happens? He stops whining. So your picking-up behavior has been *negatively reinforced* by the cessation of his whining, and you will be *more* likely to pick him up

A daily achievement chart, like this one for 5-year-old Aaron, can be highly reinforcing for many children.

the next time he whines. At the same time, his whining has probably been *positively reinforced* by your attention, so he will be more likely to whine on similar occasions.

Both positive and negative reinforcements strengthen behavior. **Punishment,** in contrast, is intended to weaken some undesired behavior. Sometimes punishments involve eliminating nice things (like "grounding" a child, taking away TV privileges, or sending her to her room). Often they involve administering unpleasant things such as a scolding or a spanking. What is confusing about the idea of punishment is that it doesn't always do what it is intended to do: It does not always suppress the undesired behavior. If your child has thrown his milk glass at you to get your attention, spanking him may be a positive reinforcement instead of the punishment you intended.

In laboratory situations, experimenters can be sure to reinforce some behavior every time it occurs, or to stop reinforcements completely so as to produce *extinction* of the response. In the real world, however, consistency of reinforcement is the exception rather than the rule. Much more common is a pattern of **partial reinforcement,** in which a behavior is reinforced on some occasions but not others. Studies of partial reinforcement show that children and adults take longer to learn some behavior under partial reinforcement conditions, but once established, such behaviors are much more resistant to extinction. If you smile at your daughter only every fifth or sixth time she brings a picture to show you (and if she finds your smile reinforcing), she'll keep on bringing pictures for a very long stretch, even if you quit smiling altogether.

Bandura's Social Cognitive Theory. Albert Bandura, whose variation of learning theory is by far the most influential among developmental psychologists today, has built upon the base of these traditional learning concepts but has added several other key ideas (1977; 1982; 1989). First, he argues that learning does not always require direct reinforcement. Learning may also occur merely as a result of watching someone else perform some action. Learning of this type, called **observational learning** or **modeling,** is involved in a wide range of behaviors. Children learn ways of hitting from watching other people in real life and on TV. They learn how to be generous by watching others donate money or goods.

Bandura also calls attention to another class of reinforcements called **intrinsic reinforcements** or *intrinsic rewards,* such as pride or discovery. These are reinforcements internal to the individual, such as the pleasure a child feels when she figures out how to draw a star, or the sense of satisfaction you may experience after strenuous exercise.

Finally, and perhaps most important, Bandura has gone far toward bridging the gap between learning theory and cognitive-developmental theory by emphasizing important *cognitive* (mental) elements in observational learning. Indeed, he now calls his theory "social cognitive theory" rather than "social learning theory," as it was originally labeled (Bandura, 1986; 1989). For example, Bandura now stresses the fact that modeling can be the vehicle for learning abstract as well as concrete skills or information. In this *abstract modeling,* the observer extracts a rule that may be the basis of the model's behavior, then learns the rule as well as the specific behavior. A child who sees his parents volunteering one day a month at a food bank may extract a rule about the importance of "helping others," even if the parents never articulate this rule specifically. In this way a child or adult can acquire attitudes, values, ways of solving problems, even standards of self-evaluation through modeling.

Critical Thinking

Think again about your own upbringing. What values or attitudes do you think you learned through modeling? How were those values and attitudes displayed (modeled) by your parents or others?

Learning to use chopsticks through modeling is only one of the myriad skills, attitudes, beliefs, and values that are learned in this way.

Table 1.1

Comparison of Developmental Theories on Some Key Questions About Development

Issue	Learning Theory	Psychoanalytic Theory	Cognitive-Developmental Theory
What is the major influence on development: nature or nurture?	Primarily nurture	Both	The child's own internal processing of experience
Is developmental change qualitative or quantitative?	Quantitative (both in Bandura's version)	Qualitative	Qualitative
Are there stages or sequences?	No stages; some sequences	Stages	Piaget said stages
Examples of research questions emerging from that theoretical tradition	Impact of TV on behavior; origins of social behaviors such as aggression	Attachment; fantasies	Development of logic; gender concepts; moral development

Collectively, these additions to traditional learning theory make the system far more flexible and powerful, although it is still not a strongly *developmental* theory. That is, Bandura has little to say about changes with age in what or how a child may learn from modeling. In contrast, both psychoanalytic and cognitive-developmental theories are strongly developmental, emphasizing sequential, often stagelike qualitative change over age.

Contrasting the Theories

No doubt by now your head is swimming with theories. I can help you make some order out of the array by returning to some of the central issues I discussed earlier in the chapter and looking at how the various theories differ along these dimensions—an analysis you can see in Table 1.1. In this table, as in my descriptions of the theories, I have intentionally oversimplified the contrasts to help you keep the alternatives clearly separate. However, as we go along through the book, you will find that many current theories involve very interesting mixtures of these approaches. You've already seen this in the cognitive elements now contained in Bandura's theories and in the ecological concepts added to a basic learning theory approach in Patterson's work. Other examples are easy to find, such as newer theories of the child's attachment to her parents that combine basic psychoanalytic concepts with clearly cognitive themes such as the notion of an internal working model. And in virtually every area of study we see a return to an emphasis on biological roots—an emphasis not strongly present in any of these three grand schemes. Having distinctly separate theories may be tidy, but I find the new blends, the new syntheses, far more intriguing.

Finding the Answers: Research on Development

I've asked an enormous number of questions already in this chapter. But before you can understand the answers—before I can get to the really interesting stuff you are probably most curious about—you need one more tool, namely, at least a modicum of familiarity with the methods researchers use when they explore questions about development. You'll need such a familiarity to make sense out of the research I'll be talking about throughout this book, and you'll need it in the future if you are going to be an intelligent consumer of research information provided through newspapers and magazines.

Let me walk you through the various alternative methods by using a concrete example with clear practical ramifications. Imagine that you are a social scientist. One day you get a call from your local state representative. She has become seriously concerned about the apparently rising levels of crime and lawlessness among teenagers and wants to propose new legislation to respond to this problem. First, though, she wants to have some answers to a series of basic questions:

1. Does the same problem exist everywhere in the world, or only in the United States? If the latter, then what is it about our culture that promotes or supports such behavior?

2. At what age does the problem begin to be visible?

3. Which kids are most at risk for such delinquent behavior, and why?

How would you, could you, go about designing one or more studies that might answer such questions? You would face a number of decisions:

- To answer the question about the age at which delinquent acts begin, should you compare groups of children and teenagers of different ages, or should you select a group of younger children and follow them over time, as they move into adolescence? And should you study young people in many settings or cultures, or in only one setting, such as inner-city youth in the United States? These are questions of *research design*.

- How will you measure delinquent behavior? Can you observe it? Can you ask about it? Can you rely on official records? What other things about each young person might you want to know to begin to answer the "why" question? Family history and relationships? Relationships with peers? Self-esteem? These are questions of *research methodology*.

- How will you analyze the data you collect, and how will you interpret your findings? Suppose you find that young people whose families live in poverty are considerably more likely to be delinquent. Would you be satisfied to stop there, or would you want to analyze the results separately for each of several ethnic groups, for children growing up with single mothers, or in other ways that might clarify the meaning of your results? These are questions of *research analysis*.

Research Design

Choosing a research design is crucial for any research, but especially so when the subject matter you are trying to study is change (or continuity) with age. You have basically three choices: (1) You can study different groups of people of different ages, called a **cross-sectional design.** (2) You can study the same people over a period of time, called a **longitudinal design.** (3) Or you can combine the two in some fashion, using what is called a **sequential design** (Schaie, 1983; 1994). Finally, if you want to know whether the same patterns hold across different cultures or contexts, you will need to do some kind of **cross-cultural research,** in which equivalent or parallel methods are used in more than one context.

Cross-Sectional Designs

The key feature of a cross-sectional design is that the researcher assesses separate age groups, with each subject tested only once. To study delinquency cross-sectionally, you might select groups of subjects at each of a series of ages, such as 8, 10, 12, 14, and 16. You would then measure each child or teen's delinquent behavior, along with whatever other characteristics you had decided were important. To get some feeling for what the results from such a study might look like, take a look at Figure 1.4, which shows the rate of "conduct disorders" in a large random sample of all children between the ages of 4 and 16 in the province of Ontario, Canada (Offord et al., 1991). (A conduct disorder is akin to what is called delinquency in everyday language.) It is clear that conduct disorders in this sample were far more common in adolescents and in boys. Such a pattern of results is typical of cross-sectional studies in a number of Western countries in which equivalent studies have been done (e.g., Martin & Hoffman, 1990).

Cross-sectional research is often enormously useful. It is relatively quick to do, and when age differences are indeed found, they may suggest new hypotheses about developmental processes. When the investigators collect a rich array of additional information about each subject, such studies can yield highly interesting results. In the Ontario study shown in Figure 1.4, for example, Offord and his colleagues found that the probability of a conduct disorder was four times as high in low-income families, nearly three times as high in "dysfunctional" families (those in which the parents reported serious difficulty in communicating, planning, or organizing normal family activities), three times as high in families with domestic violence, and so forth. Thus, a research design of this type can begin to tell us *which* children are at risk and give us some hints about whys.

At the same time, cross-sectional designs have several major problems or limitations. The first of these is the "cohort problem."

The Cohort Problem. Social scientists use the word **cohort** to describe groups of individuals born within some fairly narrow band of years who share the same cultural/

Figure 1.4

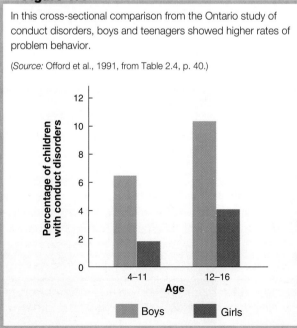

In this cross-sectional comparison from the Ontario study of conduct disorders, boys and teenagers showed higher rates of problem behavior.

(*Source:* Offord et al., 1991, from Table 2.4, p. 40.)

historical experiences at the same times in their lives. Within any given culture, successive cohorts may have quite different life experiences. For example, the 4-year-olds in the Offord study were born in 1979; the 16-year-olds were born in 1967. In that span of 12 years in the United States, the percentage of children whose mothers were working rose about 14 points; the proportion of children living in single-parent families increased from about 11 percent to about 19 percent (Hernandez, 1994). Assuming that similar trends (albeit probably less extreme) have also been true of Canada, then the two age groups in Figure 1.4 differ not just in age, but also in family experiences. Is the higher level of delinquency in the older group linked to age per se or to changes in culture?

When we compare different age groups in a single study, as we do in any cross-sectional design, we are also inevitably comparing cohorts to some degree. Thus, *cohort* and *age* are totally confounded, and we cannot tell whether some apparent age difference is really attributable to age or only to cohort differences. When the age groups we are comparing are close in age, as is true in most studies of children, this is not usually a major problem, since we can assume similar life circumstances. Over age ranges of as much as 10 years, however, the cohort differences may be significant.

Origins, Sequences, and Consistency. A second and perhaps more important limitation is that cross-sectional research cannot tell us much about *sequences* of development or about the cumulative development of some pattern over time. The Ontario study doesn't tell us what happens—in children or in families—to lead to increased rates of conduct disorders in adolescence. It also doesn't tell us if there is some typical sequence through which a child passes, such as from minor misbehavior to more serious lawlessness.

Similarly, cross-sectional studies will not tell us anything about the consistency of individual behavior over time. In this case, it won't tell us if the children who show conduct disorders at 6 or 7 or 8 are likely to show the same kind of problem in adolescence.

Longitudinal Designs

Both of these problems can be addressed with longitudinal designs, in which the *same* individuals are studied over a period of time. They allow us to look at sequences of change and individual consistency or inconsistency over time. And because they compare performances by the same people at different ages, they get around the cohort problem.

Only by studying the same children over time (that is, longitudinally), such as this boy at three ages, can we identify consistencies (or changes) in behavior across age.

Because of these advantages, longitudinal research has become increasingly common. As just one example, research on the origins of aggression and delinquency includes a number of well-known longitudinal studies. Leonard Eron (Eron et al., 1991) followed a group of 632 children from third grade to age 30, looking specifically at the links between childhood aggression and adult antisocial or criminal behavior; Gerald Patterson and his colleagues (1991; Vuchinich et al., 1992), as part of their research testing the model you've seen in Figure 1.2 (see p. 11), have followed groups of boys thought to be at high risk for later delinquency from fourth grade through junior high school; Terrie Moffitt (Caspi et al., 1993; Moffitt, 1990) has looked at the origins of delinquency in a group of more than 1000 children born in the town of Dunedin, New Zealand, in 1972 and 1973. Collectively, such longitudinal research adds greatly to our understanding of the origins of delinquency or aggression.

Longitudinal designs obviously have enormous advantages, but they are not a panacea. In particular, they are time-consuming and expensive. For this reason, longitudinal researchers often study quite small samples, making it hard to generalize the findings to broader groups. It is also very hard to keep track of all the subjects over many years, so you end up with smaller and smaller subgroups as the study progresses—a problem made more serious by the fact that the least stable or most troubled families or children are most likely to drop out of the study.

Sequential Designs

Sequential designs offer at least partial solutions to a number of these problems. All sequential designs involve either combinations of cross-sectional designs, combinations of longitudinal designs, or both. A repeated longitudinal study is called a *cohort-sequential design*. Gerald Patterson's major study, for example, involved two groups of children, with each group followed from fourth grade to seventh grade. This makes it possible to check results found on the first group and increases our confidence that a given pattern is not unique to some special set of children.

If you do two parallel cross-sectional studies in different years, you create a **time-lag design,** a procedure used primarily to try to look specifically at historical or cohort changes. For example, if you want to know whether rates of teenage drug use are rising or falling, you could collect data on the same age groups—perhaps 12- and 16-year-olds—every few years. This is exactly what the Centers for Disease Control do in their repeated studies of this question.

The most complex sequential design is called a **cross-sequential design.** It involves selecting a set of cross-sectional groups and then following *each* group longitudinally. For example, Rolf Loeber and his colleagues, in their Pittsburgh Youth Study (1991; Lynam et al., 1993; Maguin et al., 1993), have been studying three groups of boys longitudinally, aged 7, 10, and 13 at the beginning of the study. Each group will be followed for five years, which gives the research design shown schematically in Figure 1.5 (see p. 28). Such a design gives you an approximation of a longitudinal study covering the ages of 7 to 18, but it only takes five years to complete. And by overlapping the age groups, Loeber now has multiple sets of information on some ages.

Complex sequential designs like these are becoming much more prevalent as researchers struggle to find ways to uncover basic developmental patterns.

Cross-Cultural or Cross-Context Designs

Also increasingly common are studies specifically designed to compare cultures or contexts, a task that researchers have approached in several ways.

One strategy involves what anthropologists call an **ethnography**—a detailed description of a single culture or context, based on extensive observation. Often the observer lives within the culture for a period of time, perhaps as long as several years.

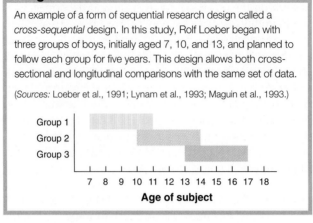

Figure 1.5

An example of a form of sequential research design called a *cross-sequential* design. In this study, Rolf Loeber began with three groups of boys, initially aged 7, 10, and 13, and planned to follow each group for five years. This design allows both cross-sectional and longitudinal comparisons with the same set of data.

(*Sources:* Loeber et al., 1991; Lynam et al., 1993; Maguin et al., 1993.)

Alternatively, investigators may attempt to compare two or more cultures directly, by studying or testing samples of children in each of several cultures or contexts, using the same or comparable instruments or measures. Sometimes this involves comparing across different countries, as in the research described in the Cultures and Contexts box on mothers' speech patterns (opposite). Sometimes the comparisons are between subcultures within the same country, such as the increasingly common research in the United States involving comparisons of children living in different ethnic groups or communities, such as African Americans, Latinos, Asian Americans, and Euro-Americans. You'll see many examples of this kind of work as we go along.

Such cross-cultural or cross-context comparisons are immensely difficult to do well. One of the troublesome difficulties is the problem of equivalence of measurement. Is it enough just to translate some test into another language? Will the same measure or assessment technique be equally valid in all cultures? Do behaviors have the same *meaning* in other contexts, other cultures? For example, Anne-Marie Ambert (1994) makes the point that when Western researchers study parent behavior, they begin with the assumption that the mother is the most central figure in a child's upbringing. Yet in many cultures in the world, multiple mothering is the rule and the biological mother may do relatively little nurturing. If we then try to measure the "quality" of the mother's caregiving behavior by counting the number of her nurturing acts or the frequency of her smiles or verbal interactions, we may come to quite erroneous conclusions.

Despite these difficulties, cross-cultural research is vitally important if we are to uncover universal patterns of development and if we are to understand the ways in which environmental and cultural variation affects children's development.

Experimental Designs

Most of the research designs I have described so far are alternative ways to look at changes with age. If we are interested in examining a basic process—such as learning or memory—or in *explaining* any observed phenomena, we need to do an **experiment.**

An experiment is normally designed to test a specific hypothesis, a particular causal explanation. For example, Patterson hypothesized that the beginning of the chain of causal events implicated in aggressive and delinquent behavior lies in family discipline patterns. To test this, he could devise an intervention experiment in which some families of aggressive children are given training in better discipline techniques and other families, with similar children, are given no training. He could then check at the end of the training, and perhaps some months or years later, to see if the children whose families had had the training were less likely to show aggression or delinquency.

A key feature of an experiment is that subjects are assigned *randomly* to participate in one of several groups. Subjects in the **experimental group** receive the treatment the experimenter thinks will produce an identified effect, while those in the **control group** receive either no special treatment or a neutral treatment. The presumed causal element in the experiment is called the **independent variable.** In the mythical Patterson experiment, the training is the independent variable. Any behavior that the independent variable is expected to influence is called a **dependent variable.** In the example I'm using, later levels of aggression or delinquency would be dependent variables.

Problems with Experiments in Studying Development. Experiments like this, which are essential for our understanding of many aspects of development, have created an important core of knowledge. At the same time, you should be aware that two special problems in studying child or adult development limit the use of experimental designs in some cases.

First, many of the questions we want to answer have to do with the effects of particular unpleasant or stressful experiences on individuals—abuse, prenatal influences such as the mother's drinking, family poverty, or parental unemployment. For obvious ethical reasons, we cannot manipulate these variables. We cannot ask one set of pregnant women to have two alcoholic drinks a day and others to have none; we cannot randomly assign adults to become unemployed. So to study the effects of such experiences, we must rely on nonexperimental designs, including longitudinal and sequential studies.

Cultures and Contexts
An Example of a Cross-Cultural Comparison Study

Ann Fernald and Hiromi Morikawa's research on Japanese and U.S. mothers' speech to their infants shows both strong cross-cultural similarities and interesting cultural variations (1993). The investigators took video and audio recordings of 30 Japanese and 30 U.S. mothers with their infants, in the family's own home, playing with the infant's own toys. Ten of the infants in each cultural group were 6 months old, ten were 12 months old, and ten were 19 months old. So in each culture, Fernald and Morikawa have a cross-sectional study.

There are striking similarities in the ways these two groups of mothers speak to their infants—patterns that have been found in studies of mothers in many cultures (e.g., Fernald et al., 1989). Both groups simplify their speech, repeat themselves frequently, use intriguing sounds to attract the child's attention, and speak in a higher-pitched voice than usual. Collectively this pattern is often labeled *motherese* or *infant-directed speech.*

Yet the mothers from these two cultural groups also differed, particularly in the kinds of things they said. One such difference was in the mothers' tendency to label toys or parts of toys for their infants. U.S. mothers did this more often than did Japanese mothers, as you can see in the accompanying figure. The Japanese mothers, in contrast, used many more social routines—greetings such as *hello* and *bye-bye* (*konnichiwa* or *o'genki desu ka* in Japanese), or exchange routines involving of-

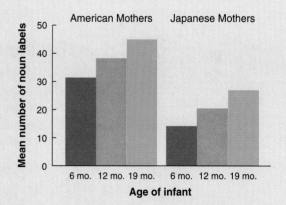

fering and accepting things politely, such as "here you are" or "thank you" (in Japanese, *dozo*), "please help yourself" (*choodai*), and "thank you" (*arigato*). One consequence of these differences in the content of mothers' speech appears to be that U.S. children learn more object words sooner. The U.S. 19-month-olds in this study knew significantly more such words than did their Japanese counterparts.

Thus, this cross-cultural study not only tells us something about how these two cultures differ, it also gives us important new insights about the whole process of language development during infancy and toddlerhood.

Second, the independent variable in which we are very often interested is age it-self, and *we cannot assign subjects randomly to age groups*. We can compare 4-year-olds and 6-year-olds in their approach to a particular task, such as searching for a lost object, but the children differ in a host of ways in addition to their ages. Older children have had more and different experiences. Thus, unlike psychologists studying other aspects of behavior, developmental psychologists *cannot* systematically manipulate some of the variables we are most interested in.

To get around this problem, we can use any one of a series of strategies that are sometimes called *quasi experiments,* in which we compare groups but do not assign the subjects randomly. Cross-sectional comparisons are a form of quasi experiment; so are studies in which we select naturally occurring groups that differ in some dimension of interest, such as children whose parents choose to place them in day-care programs compared to children whose parents rear them at home, or children in single-parent families versus those in two-parent families.

Such comparisons have built-in problems, because groups that differ in one way are likely to be different in other ways as well. Families who place their children in day care, compared to those who rear them at home, are also likely to be poorer, may more often be single-parent families, and may have different values or religious back-grounds. If we find that the two groups of children differ in some fashion, is it because they have spent their daytime hours in different places or because of these other differences in their families? We can make such comparisons a bit cleaner if we select our comparison groups initially so that they are matched on those variables we think might matter, such as income or marital status or religion. Even with such careful matching, however, quasi experiments, by their very nature, will always yield more ambiguous results than will a fully controlled experiment.

Happily, fully controlled experiments are possible in a great many areas within developmental psychology, allowing us to explore causes more directly and to test alternative theories.

Research Methods

Choosing a research design is only the first crucial decision an investigator must make. Equally important is to decide what subjects to study and how to study them.

Choosing the Subjects. Because we would like to uncover basic developmental patterns that are true for all children, all adolescents, or all adults, the ideal strategy would be to choose and study a random sample of all people in the world. This is clearly impractical, so some kind of compromise is necessary. One compromise, becoming more and more common in today's research, is to select large samples that are representative of some subgroup or population—such as the Ontario study I've already described. This strategy is widely used in sociology and epidemiology, and it can be very fruitful in psychology as well. But because it is difficult to collect highly detailed information from or about large numbers of subjects, we frequently trade off depth for breadth.

The other alternative, very common in psychological research on children, is to focus on studying a smaller group of subjects in greater depth and detail, in an attempt to uncover very basic processes. For instance, Alan Sroufe and his colleagues (Sroufe, 1989; Sroufe et al., 1990; Weinfield et al., 1997) have studied a group of 267 children and families, beginning before the birth of the child. Families were deliberately chosen from among those thought to be at high risk for later caregiving problems, such as low-education single mothers with unplanned pregnancies. The children have now been repeatedly studied, each time in considerable detail. The sample is not representative of the population as a whole, but the results are enormously informative nonetheless and may tell us more about the process of emotional and social development than we could possibly glean from larger samples studied more broadly. Neither strategy is better than the other; both are useful. In either case, we need to remember that the conclusions we can draw will be limited by the sample we studied and by the type of information we could obtain.

The two time-honored ways of gathering information about individuals are observation and asking questions. Because infants and young children are not particularly good at answering questions, observation has been an especially prominent research strategy among developmental psychologists.

Observation. Any researcher planning to use observation to collect information about children or their environments will have to make at least three further decisions: What shall I observe? Where shall I observe? How shall I record the observations?

The decision about *what* to observe can be divided still further: Should you try to observe everything a child does or focus only on selected behaviors? Should you observe only the child or also the immediate environment—such as the responses of the people around the child—or the quality of the home? Which you choose will depend largely on the basic question you are trying to address. If you are interested in the child's first words, you do not need to pay much attention to how close the child is sitting to an adult or to whether the child exchanges mutual gazes with the adults in his vicinity. But you might want to make note of what the child is playing with, whether other people are present, and what they say to the child. On the other hand, if you are interested in the development of attachment, you will want to make note of mutual gazes as well as how close or far away from the parent the child is standing or sitting.

It is also no simple matter to decide *where* to observe. You can observe in a natural setting, such as a child's home or school, in which case you are introducing an enormous amount of variability into the system and increasing the complexity of the observation immensely. Or you can choose a controlled setting, keeping it the same for each child observed. For example, the most commonly used measure of the security of a child's attachment to an adult is obtained in what is called the *Strange Situation:* The child is observed in a series of episodes in a laboratory setting, including periods with the mother, with the mother and a stranger, alone with a stranger, and reunited with the mother. By standardizing the situation, researchers gain the enormous advantage of having comparable information for each child, but they may lose some ecological validity. Investigators cannot be sure that what they observe in this strange laboratory is representative of the child's behavior in more accustomed settings.

Questionnaires and Interviews. Questionnaires and interviews can often provide an excellent alternative to observation. Many widely used measures of infant and toddler behavior are based on standardized interviews with or questionnaires completed by a mother or father. Examples are measures of problem behavior such as the Child Behavior Checklist (Achenbach, 1991) or the Communicative Development Inventories that ask parents detailed questions about their child's language comprehension and production (Fenson et al., 1994). School-age children and adolescents may also be interviewed directly or asked to complete questionnaires. Such strategies have been widely used in studies of children's moral development (which you'll read about in Chapter 12), as well as in studies of peer relationships among children of elementary school and high school age.

Each of these alternatives has costs and benefits. Structured laboratory tests give the experimenter excellent control over the situation so that each subject is confronted with the same task, the same stimuli. Yet because they are artificial, such tests may not give us an accurate portrayal of how individuals behave in the more complex natural environment. Interviews, especially very open-ended ones in which the subject is only guided toward general topics, may give a rich picture of an individual's thoughts and feelings, but how do you reduce the answers to a set of scores that will allow you to compare groups or individuals with one another? Questionnaires solve some of this problem, but the trade-off may be the richness and individuality of replies. Often the

Careful observation of children's behavior, such as activities recorded by this psychology student in a day-care center, have provided one essential source of information about early development.

Research Report

Ethical Issues in Research on Development

Anytime we try to understand human behavior by observing, testing, and asking questions, we are probing into personal lives. If we go into a home to observe the way the parents interact with their children, we are invading their privacy. We may even inadvertently give the impression that there must be something wrong with the way the parents are raising their family. If we give adults or children laboratory tests, some subjects will do very well, and others will not. How will the less successful subjects interpret this experience? What is the risk that some subject will become depressed over what he perceives as a poor performance?

Any research on human behavior involves some risks and raises some ethical questions. Because of this, psychologists and other social and biological scientists have established clear procedures and guidelines that must be followed before any observation can be undertaken or any test given. In every university or college—the setting in which most such research is done—a committee of peers must approve any research plan involving human subjects. The most basic guideline is that subjects must always be protected from any potential mental or physical harm. More specific principles include:

Informed Consent

Each adult subject must give written consent to participate. When research involves children, informed consent must be obtained from the parent or guardian. In every case, the procedure and its possible consequences must be explained in detail. If there are potential risks, these must be described. For example, if you were studying patterns of communication between teenagers and their parents, you might want to observe each

family while they talked about some unresolved issue between them. As part of your informed consent request, you would have to explain to each family that while such discussions often lead to greater clarity, they also occasionally increase tension. And you would need to provide support and debriefing at the end of the procedure, to assist any family who found the task stressful or destabilizing.

Right of Privacy

Subjects must be assured that highly personal information they may provide will be kept entirely private—including information about income, or attitudes, or illegal behavior like drug taking. Researchers can use the information *collectively,* but they cannot report it individually in any way that will associate a subject's name with some piece of data—unless the subject has specifically given permission for such use, or unless the information given reveals some real risk to the subject, such as evidence of child abuse, potential suicide, or homicide, in which cases the researcher has certain legal obligations to act.

In virtually all cases, it is also considered unethical to observe through a one-way mirror without the subject's knowledge or to secretly record behavior.

Testing Children

These principles are important for any research but particularly so for research on children. Any child who balks at being tested or observed must *not* be tested or observed; any child who becomes distressed must be comforted; any risk to the child's self-esteem must be avoided.

best strategy—although one not always possible because of cost in time or money—is to collect many different kinds of information from or about each subject.

Research Analysis

Finally, you need to analyze the results of your research. In studies of development, researchers use two broad forms of analysis.

First, they can compare different age groups by simply calculating the average score of each group on some measure, just as the Ontario researchers did in comparing rates of conduct disorders for each age or gender group in the results shown in Figure 1.4 (see p. 25).

A second strategy allows us to look at relationships between two separate variables, most often using a statistic called a correlation. A **correlation** is simply a number ranging from −1.00 to +1.00 that describes the strength of a relationship between two variables. A zero correlation shows no linear relationship between those variables. For instance, you might expect to find a zero or near-zero correlation between the length of big toes and IQ. People with toes of all sizes have high IQs, and those with toes of all sizes have low IQs. The closer a correlation comes to −1.00 or +1.00, the stronger the relationship being described. If the correlation is positive, it indicates that high scores on the two dimensions tend to go together and that low scores tend to go together, such as length of big toes and shoe size. Height and weight are also strongly positively correlated, as are age and memory span.

If the correlation is negative, it describes a relationship in which high scores on one variable are associated with low scores on the other. For example, there is a negative correlation between the amount of disorder and chaos in a family and the child's later IQ: High chaos is associated with lower IQ, and low chaos with higher IQ.

Perfect correlations (−1.00 or +1.00) do not happen in the real world, but correlations of .60 to .80 clearly do occur and are interpreted as reflecting strong relationships. As one further example, the correlation between grades in the first year of college and grades in the second year of college are usually about .75. Correlations between .30 and .60 are more common in psychological research, describing relationships that may suggest important hypotheses or allow helpful predictions. For instance, in the Patterson study I have mentioned several times, the correlation between fourth-grade ratings of antisocial behavior and eighth-grade delinquency was .46—a moderate relationship, well above chance but still with a fair amount of variation.

Correlations are an enormously useful descriptive tool. They can tell us about consistency over time, or about links between two environmental variables, or between the child's behavior and some experience he may have had. Useful as they are, though, correlations have a major limitation: They do not tell us about *causal* relationships. For example, several researchers have found a moderate positive correlation between the "difficultness" of a child's temperament and the amount of punishment the child receives from his parents: The more difficult the temperament, the more punishment the child experiences. The problem is to figure out which way the causality runs. Do difficult children *elicit* more punishment? Or does a greater rate of punishment lead to a more difficult temperament? Or is there some third factor that may cause both, such as perhaps some genetic contribution both to the child's difficultness and to the parent's tendency to be punitive? The correlation alone does not allow us to choose among these alternatives. Stating the point more generally: No correlation, standing alone, can prove causality. A correlation may point in a particular direction or suggest possible causal links, but to discover the causes, we must then explore such possibilities with other techniques, including experiments.

A Final Word

It may seem to you that these details about research design are of interest and value only to professional researchers. But that is not true. You will find that knowledge of this kind has many practical, daily applications, even if you never take another course in psychology.

An example: An issue of *Time* magazine several years ago included an article about a system for providing stimulation for the unborn baby. The pregnant woman was supposed to wear a belt full of audio equipment, on which tapes of various complex patterns of heartbeat sounds were played. The article reported that the maker of this gadget had done some "research" to demonstrate that this procedure produced smarter, faster-developing babies. To quote *Time:* "Last year 50 of the youngsters [whose mothers had worn the belt], ranging in age from 6 months to 34 months, were given standardized language, social and motor-skills tests. Their overall score was 25% above the national norm" (September 30, 1991, p. 76).

Table 1.2

Guidelines for Critical Thinking About Popular Presentation of Research Findings

- If an experiment is reported, does it include appropriate control or comparison groups—such as a group that did *not* receive the particular treatment?

- If an experiment is described, were the subjects assigned randomly to the treatment and control groups?

- If a survey is reported, were the subjects chosen randomly (or through some systematic process), or were they entirely self-selected (as you often see with surveys reported in magazines in which readers have been invited to respond to a questionnaire)? Information collected in the latter way is essentially useless.

- If a quasi experiment is described, have the various groups been matched as closely as possible on the qualities or traits that might be important?

- Are the subjects being studied representative of the total group of interest? For example, studies of health habits and disease among adults have frequently been done with only male subjects. This is not inherently wrong, but it poses a problem when the researchers or writers generalize the conclusions to "adults." Another example might be studies of "poor children" that include only white poor or only African-American poor. Without direct study, we can't be sure that the same processes are at work on all subgroups.

I hope you would not go out and buy this apparatus on the basis of that finding! After reading what I've said about research design, you should be able to see immediately that self-selection is a major problem here. What kind of mothers will buy such a gadget? How are they likely to differ from mothers who would not buy it? In fact, this reported "research" tells us nothing. It isn't even a quasi experiment because there is no comparison group. Equivalent reports of research on children and adolescents appear in the newspapers and popular magazines every day. Obviously, I want you to be critical analysts of the research I'll talk about in this book. Even more basically, I want you to become very critical consumers of popularly presented research information, asking yourself questions such as the ones listed in Table 1.2. Some of the research described in such popular sources is very good. Some of it is bunk, or at the very least inconclusive. I hope you are now in a better position to tell the difference.

Summary

1. To understand children's development, we must understand both change and consistency, both universality and individuality.

2. Both nature and nurture, biology and culture, are involved in all aspects of development, although there has been long-standing disagreement on the relative importance of these factors.

3. Current thinking about the nature side of the equation not only emphasizes the role of maturation, but also points to potential inborn strategies of perceiving or responding to the environment.

4. Genetic differences, yet another aspect of the influence of nature, also clearly play a significant role in a great many patterns of behavior.

5. Current thinking about the nurture side of the equation emphasizes not only the potential importance of the timing of some experience and

the significance of a child's interpretation of some experience, but also the importance of examining the entire ecological system in which development occurs, including culture.

6. One important dimension along which cultures vary widely is individualism versus collectivism. Most Western cultures emphasize individualism, while Asian, Latin, and African cultures are more likely to emphasize collectivism.

7. Nature and nurture may not interact in precisely the same way for each child. Children with different inborn qualities (vulnerability or resilience) may be affected differently by the same environment.

8. Another key question concerns the nature of developmental change itself, whether it is qualitative or quantitative, continuous or stagelike.

9. Theories designed to answer the many questions about development can be divided into three rough groupings, depending on their scope: grand schemes, models, and minitheories.

10. Three grand schemes have been influential within developmental psychology: psychoanalytic, cognitive-developmental, and learning theories.

11. Psychoanalytic theorists such as Freud and Erikson have primarily studied the development of personality, emphasizing the interaction of internal instincts and environmental influences in producing shared stages of development as well as individual differences in personality.

12. Cognitive-developmental theorists such as Piaget and Vygotsky emphasize the child's own active exploration of the environment as a critical ingredient leading to shared stages of development. They strongly emphasize qualitative change.

13. Learning theorists generally place strongest emphasis on environmental influences, thought to produce largely quantitative change. Bandura's influential version of learning theory includes more cognitive elements and the crucial concept of modeling.

14. A first major question in planning research is the basic research design. Cross-sectional studies compare different children of different ages; longitudinal studies observe the same children as they develop over time; sequential studies combine some of these features; and cross-cultural studies compare children, their rearing, or nature/nurture relationships in differing cultures or subcultures.

15. Each of these designs has particular strengths and drawbacks.

16. To study causal connections, researchers normally use experimental designs. In an experiment, the researcher controls (manipulates) one or more relevant variables and assigns subjects randomly to different treatment and control groups.

17. In a quasi experiment, subjects are not randomly assigned to separate groups; rather, existing groups are compared. Quasi experiments are needed in developmental research because subjects cannot be randomly assigned either to age groups or to experience such negative treatments as poverty or abuse or poor attachment.

18. Decisions about research methods include the choice of subjects to be studied and the methods to be used to observe or assess them.

19. When research results are analyzed, the two most common methods are comparing average scores between groups and describing relationships among variables with the statistic called a correlation. It can range from +1.00 to −1.00 and describes the strength of a relationship.

Key Terms

behavior genetics The study of the genetic basis of behavior, such as intelligence or personality. **p. 5**

classical conditioning One of three major types of learning. An automatic unconditioned response such as an emotion or a reflex comes to be triggered by a new cue, called the conditional stimulus (CS), after the CS has been paired several times with the original unconditional stimulus. **p. 21**

cohort A group of persons of approximately the same age who have shared similar major life experiences, such as cultural training, historical events, or general economic conditions. **p. 25**

collectivism A cultural perspective or belief system, contrasted with individualism, in which the emphasis is on collective rather than individual identity, and on group solidarity, decision making, duties and obligations. Characteristic of most Asian, Latino, and African cultures. **p. 12**

conditional stimulus In classical conditioning, the stimulus that, after being paired a number of times with an unconditional stimulus, comes to trigger the unconditioned response. (E.g., the sound of the mother's footsteps may become a conditional stimulus for the baby's turning his head as if to suck.) **p. 21**

control group The group of subjects in an experiment that receives either no special treatment or some neutral treatment. **p. 29**

correlation A statistic used to describe the degree or strength of a relationship between two variables. It can range from +1.00 to −1.00. The closer it is to 1.00, the stronger the relationship being described. **p. 32**

critical period Any time period during development when the organism is especially responsive to and learns from a specific type of stimulation. The same stimulation at other points in development has little or no effect. **p. 9**

cross-cultural research Research involving in-depth study of another culture, or research involving comparisons of several cultures or subcultures. **p. 24**

cross-sectional design A form of research in which samples of subjects from several different age groups are studied at the same time. **p. 24**

cross-sequential design A complex combination of cross-sectional and longitudinal research designs in which groups of subjects of several different ages are initially selected and compared, and then all groups are followed longitudinally. **p. 27**

culture A system of meanings and customs shared by some identifiable group or subgroup, and transmitted from one generation of that group to the next. **p. 12**

dependent variable The variable in an experiment that is expected to show the impact of manipulations of the independent variable; also called the outcome variable. **p. 29**

ego In Freudian theory, that portion of the personality that organizes, plans, and keeps the person in touch with reality. Language and thought are both ego functions. **p. 19**

ethnography A detailed description of a single culture or context, based on extensive observation by a resident observer. **p. 27**

experiment A research strategy in which subjects are assigned randomly to experimental and control groups. The experimental group is then provided with some designated experience that is expected to alter behavior in some fashion. **p. 28**

experimental group The group (or groups) of subjects in an experiment that is given a special treatment intended to produce some specific consequence. **p. 29**

grand schemes Phrase used in this book to describe the three most comprehensive theories of development: psychoanalytic, cognitive-developmental, and learning theories. **p. 17**

id In Freudian theory, the first, primitive portion of the personality; the storehouse of basic energy, continually pushing for immediate gratification. **p. 19**

independent variable A condition or event an experimenter varies in some systematic way in order to observe the impact of that variation on the subjects' behavior. **p. 29**

individualism A cultural perspective or belief system, contrasted with collectivism, in which the emphasis is placed on the separateness and independence of individual development and behavior. Characteristic of most Western cultures. **p. 12**

internal model of experience Currently popular theoretical concept emphasizing that each child creates a set of core ideas or beliefs about the nature of relationships, the self, and the world. The most commonly discussed example is the child's "inner working model" of attachment. **p. 9**

intrinsic reinforcements Those inner sources of pleasure, pride, or satisfaction that serve to increase the likelihood that an individual will repeat the behavior that led to the feeling. **p. 22**

libido The term used by Freud to describe the pool of sexual energy in each individual. **p. 18**

longitudinal design A research design in which the same subjects are observed or assessed repeatedly over a period of months or years. **p. 24**

maturation The sequential unfolding of physical characteristics, governed by instructions contained in the genetic code and shared by all members of a species. **p. 4**

minitheories Term used in this text to describe the narrower, more limited types of theories designed to explain only a particular, somewhat specific phenomenon. **p. 17**

modeling A term used by Bandura and others to describe observational learning. **p. 22**

models Term used in this book to describe the middle level of theories, less comprehensive than a grand scheme, but broader than a minitheory; examples are biological and ecological models. **p. 17**

negative reinforcement The strengthening of a behavior because of the removal or cessation of an unpleasant stimulus. **p. 21**

observational learning Learning of motor skills, attitudes, or other behaviors through watching someone else perform them. **p. 22**

operant conditioning That type of learning in which the probability of a person performing some behavior is strengthened by positive or negative reinforcements. **p. 21**

partial reinforcement Reinforcement of behavior on some schedule less frequent than every occasion. **p. 22**

positive reinforcement Strengthening of a behavior by the presentation of some pleasurable or positive stimulus. **p. 21**

psychosexual stages The stages of personality development suggested by Freud, including the oral, anal, phallic, latency, and genital stages. **p. 19**

psychosocial stages The stages of personality development suggested by Erikson, including trust, autonomy, initiative, industry, identity, intimacy, generativity, and ego integrity. **p. 19**

punishment Unpleasant consequences, administered after some undesired behavior by a child or adult, with the intent of extinguishing the behavior. **p. 22**

scaffolding Term used by Bruner to describe the process by which a teacher (parent, older child, or person in the official role of teacher) structures a learning encounter with a child, so as to lead the child from step to step—a process consistent with Vygotsky's theory of cognitive development. **p. 20**

sensitive period Similar to a critical period except broader and less specific. A time in development when a particular type of stimulation is particularly important or effective. **p. 9**

sequential design A family of research designs involving multiple cross-sectional, or multiple longitudinal, studies, or a combination of the two. **p. 24**

superego In Freudian theory, the "conscience" part of personality that develops as a result of the identification process. The superego contains the parental and societal values and attitudes incorporated by the child. **p. 19**

teratogen Any outside agent, such as a disease or a chemical, that causes a birth defect. **p. 9**

theory A relatively broad explanatory system, with specific assumptions and propositions, designed to explain some set of observations. **p. 17**

time-lag design A comparison of groups of subjects of the *same* age in different cohorts, such as studying drug use in a separate sample of 15-year-olds each year for 20 years; allows a direct examination of cohort changes in some behavior. **p. 27**

unconditioned response In classical conditioning, the basic unlearned response that is triggered by the unconditional stimulus. A baby's turning of his head when touched on the cheek is an unconditioned response. **p. 21**

unconditional stimulus In classical conditioning, the cue or signal that automatically triggers the unconditioned response. A touch on a baby's cheek, triggering head turning, is an unconditional stimulus. **p. 21**

zone of proximal development In Vygotsky's theory, the zone is that range of tasks or skills that is slightly too difficult for a child to do alone but that she can do successfully with guidance or "scaffolding" by an adult or more experienced child. **p. 20**

Suggested Readings

Bornstein, M. H. (Ed.). (1987). *Sensitive periods in development. Interdisciplinary perspectives.* Hillsdale, NJ: Erlbaum. Bornstein's own paper in this collection of reports is an excellent introduction to the concept of sensitive periods, but the book also contains a number of reports of research exploring potential sensitive periods both in humans and in other animals.

Cole, M. (1992). Culture in development. In M. H. Bornstein & M. E. Lamb (Eds.), *Developmental psychology: An advanced textbook* (3rd ed., pp. 731–789). Hillsdale, NJ: Erlbaum. Not at all easy reading, but one of the best analyses I have yet seen on this very complicated subject.

Greenfield, P. M., & Cocking, R. R. (Eds.). (1994). *Cross-cultural roots of minority child development.* Hillsdale, NJ: Erlbaum. One of the central themes in this excellent collection of papers is the impact of

individualism and collectivism on the lives of children in different cultural contexts.

Plomin, R., & McClearn, G. E. (Eds.). (1993). *Nature, nurture, & psychology.* Washington, DC: American Psychological Association. If you think the "great debate" about nature and nurture is an old issue, this book will quickly persuade you otherwise. The controversy is alive and well, although the papers in this book reflect the efforts of many people to recast it in more useful terms.

Rowe, D. C. (1994). *The limits of family influence: Genes, experience, and behavior.* New York: Guilford Press. A clear, well-reasoned book arguing that developmental psychologists have greatly exaggerated the effects of "nurture" on personality, intelligence, and other characteristics and greatly underestimated the effects of heredity.

This is another good introduction to some current thinking on the nature/nurture controversy.

Seitz, V. (1988). Methodology. In M. H. Bornstein & M. E. Lamb (Eds.), *Developmental psychology: An advanced textbook* (2nd ed., pp. 51–84). Hillsdale, NJ: Erlbaum. This paper is no longer brand-new, but it is still one of the clearest descriptions I have found of the various methods of research.

Thomas, R. M. (Ed.). (1990). *The encyclopedia of human development and education. Theory, research, and studies.* Oxford: Pergamon Press. This is a very useful volume. It includes brief descriptions of virtually all the theories I have described in this chapter as well as a helpful chapter on the concept of stages. Each chapter is quite brief but covers many of the critical issues.

2

Prenatal Development

When my daughter-in-law, Jenny, was pregnant with their first child (my grandson Sam, now aged 6), I had dinner one night at a restaurant with her and my son Rex. She ordered a glass of wine. After a long pause, during which I tried to calculate whether I thought the research evidence was clear and strong enough for me to risk sounding like a bossy, intrusive mother-in-law, I decided I really needed to say something. I began by asking her what her doctor had advised her about alcohol. His advice, it turned out, was that the occasional glass was okay. More pause for thought on my part. Finally, I said that I thought that perhaps her doctor hadn't seen the most recent information; the occasional glass *might* be okay, but all the evidence suggested that there was no level of alcohol that could be guaranteed completely safe.

This brief encounter gives you a glimpse of some of the complexities—personal as well as scientific—involved in making good decisions during pregnancy. The list of "do's" and "don'ts" for pregnant women has become very long indeed, so that it is hard for a conscientious woman (and her partner) to be sure of what is okay and what is not. One of my goals in this chapter is to give you the very best information we now have about all those do's and don'ts. To do that, I need to explore what we know about the basic processes of development from conception to birth, as well as what we have learned about the things that can interfere with those basic processes.

Beyond this practical question, it is also essential for any complete understanding of child development that we begin our search at the beginning—at conception and pregnancy. The heredity passed on to the new individual at the moment of conception, and the neurological and other physical developments in these first months, set the stage for all that is to follow.

Conception

The first step in the development of a single human being is that moment of conception when a single sperm cell from the male pierces the gelatinous coating surrounding the ovum of the female, as shown in Figure 2.1 (see p. 40). Ordinarily, a woman produces one **ovum** (egg cell) per month from one of her two ovaries. This occurs roughly midway between two menstrual periods. If it is not fertilized, the ovum travels from the ovary down the **fallopian tube** toward the **uterus,** where it gradually disintegrates and is expelled as part of the next menstruation.

If a couple has intercourse during the crucial few days when the ovum is in the fallopian tube, one of the millions of sperm ejaculated as part of each male orgasm may travel the full distance through the woman's vagina, cervix, uterus, and fallopian tube and penetrate the ovum. A child is conceived. The now fertilized ovum then continues on its journey down the fallopian tube, where instead of disintegrating, it implants itself in the wall of the uterus. Interestingly, only about half of conceptuses are likely to survive to birth. About a quarter are lost in the first few days after conception, well before implantation, often because of a flaw in the genetic material. Another quarter are aborted spontaneously ("miscarried") at a later point in the pregnancy (Wilcox et al., 1988).

The Basic Genetics of Conception

It is hard to overstate the importance of the genetic events accompanying conception. The combination of genes from the father in the sperm and from the mother in the ovum creates a unique genetic blueprint—the **genotype**—that characterizes that specific individual. To explain how that occurs, I need to back up a few steps.

Except in individuals with particular types of genetic abnormality, the nucleus of each cell in the body contains a set of 46 **chromosomes,** arranged in 23 pairs. These

Figure 2.1

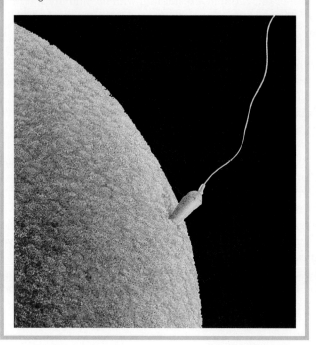

The moment of conception when a single sperm has pierced the coating around the ovum.

chromosomes include all the genetic information for that individual, governing not only individual characteristics like hair color, height, body shape, temperament, and aspects of intelligence, but also all those characteristics shared by all members of our species, such as patterns of physical development and "built-in biases" of various kinds.

The only cells that do *not* contain 46 chromosomes are the sperm and the ovum, collectively called **gametes** or germ cells. In the early stages of development, gametes divide as all other cells do (a process called *mitosis*), with each set of 23 chromosome pairs duplicating itself. In the final step of gamete division, however, called *meiosis,* each new cell receives only one chromosome from each original pair. Thus, each gamete has only 23 chromosomes instead of 23 *pairs*. When a child is conceived, the 23 chromosomes in the ovum and the 23 in the sperm combine to form the 23 *pairs* that will be part of each cell in the newly developing body.

The chromosomes, in turn, are composed of long strings of molecules of a chemical called **deoxyribonucleic acid** (DNA). In an insight for which they won the Nobel Prize, James Watson and Francis Crick (1953) deduced that DNA is in the shape of a *double helix,* a kind of twisted ladder. The remarkable feature of this ladder is that the rungs are made up in such a way that the whole thing can "unzip" and then each half can guide the duplication of the missing part, thus allowing multiplication of cells so that each new cell contains the full set of genetic information.

The string of DNA that makes up each chromosome can be subdivided further into segments, called **genes,** each of which controls or influences a particular feature or a portion of some developmental pattern. A gene controlling or influencing some specific characteristic, such as your blood type or your hair color, always appears in the same place (the *locus*) on the same chromosome in every individual of the same species. The locus of the gene that determines whether you have type A, B, or O blood is on chromosome 9; the locus of the gene that determines whether you have the Rh factor in your blood is on chromosome 1; and so forth. Geneticists have made remarkable strides in recent years in mapping the genes for a great many features or characteris-

tics—a scientific achievement that has allowed similarly giant strides in our ability to diagnose various genetic defects or inherited diseases before a child is born.

X and Y Chromosomes

A further complexity comes from the fact that there are actually two types of chromosomes. In 22 of the chromosome pairs, called *autosomes,* the members of the pair look
alike and contain exactly matching genetic loci. The twenty-third pair, however, operates differently. The chromosomes of this pair, which determine the child's sex and are
therefore called the *sex chromosomes,* come in two varieties, referred to by convention
as the *X* and the *Y* chromosomes. A normal human female has two X chromosomes on
this twenty-third pair (an XX pattern), while the normal human male has one X and one
Y (an XY pattern). The X chromosome is considerably larger than the Y and contains
many genetic loci not matched on the Y.

Note that the sex of the child is determined by the sex chromosome it receives from
the sperm. Because the mother has *only* X chromosomes, every ovum carries an X. But
because the father has both X and Y chromosomes, when the father's gametes divide,
half the sperm will carry an X, half a Y. If the sperm that fertilizes the ovum carries an X,
then the child inherits an XX pattern and will be a girl. If the fertilizing sperm carries a
Y, then the combination is XY, and the child will be a boy.

Geneticists have pushed this understanding a step further, discovering that only
one very small section of the Y chromosome actually determines maleness—a segment
referred to as *TDF,* or *testis-determining factor* (Page et al., 1987). Fertilized ova that are
genetically XY but that lack the TDF develop physically as female. This finding is one
of many that led geneticists to conclude that the fetus is inherently female, that the female form is the "default option" in prenatal development. According to this argument, femaleness is a kind of passive process, occurring in the absence of any specific
signal, while maleness requires the additional genetic signal of the TDF. However,
very recent work calls this widely accepted description into question. A number of scientists (Arn et al., 1994; Bardoni et al., 1994) have found indications that a "femaleness"
gene may also exist, or perhaps there is a whole collection of genes required to stimulate the appropriate development of female genitalia and internal reproductive organs.
As in so many areas of science, the more we discover, the more complex we see the
process really is.

Incidentally, the mother does have some indirect effect on the likelihood of an XX
or an XY conception because the relative acidity or alkalinity of the mucus in the vagina
affects the survival rate of X-carrying or Y-carrying sperm. This chemical balance
varies both from one woman to the next and during the course of each woman's
monthly cycle. So a woman's typical chemical balance or the timing of intercourse can
sharply alter the probability of conceiving a child of a particular gender, even though it
is still true that the X or Y in the sperm is the final determining factor.

Patterns of Genetic Inheritance

When the 23 chromosomes from the father and the 23 from the mother come together
at conception, they provide a mix of instructions, not always matching. When the two
sets of instructions are the same at any given locus (such as genes for blue eyes from
both parents), geneticists say they are **homozygous.** When the two sets of instructions
differ, the genes are said to be **heterozygous,** such as a gene for blue eyes from one
parent and a gene for brown eyes from the other, or a combination of genes contributing to shyness from one parent and to gregariousness from the other. How are these
differences resolved? Geneticists are still a long way from having a complete answer to
this question, but some patterns are very clear.

Dominant and Recessive Genes

Whenever a given trait is governed by a *single* gene, as is true for some 1000 individual physical characteristics, inheritance patterns follow well-understood rules. In a few cases when heterozygosity occurs, the child may express *both* characteristics. For example, type AB blood results from the inheritance of a type A gene from one parent and a type B gene from the other. More typically, one of the two contrasting genes is *dominant* over the other and only the dominant gene is actually expressed. The nondominant gene, called a *recessive* gene, has no visible effect on the individual's behavior, although it continues to be part of the genotype and can be passed on to offspring through meiosis.

Table 2.1 gives a few examples of physical characteristics that follow these simple rules for recessive and dominant genes. You can see from this abbreviated list that this type of inheritance pattern characterizes both ordinary physical characteristics, such as hair color, and some inherited diseases, such as sickle-cell anemia. Figure 2.2 gives you a schematic look at how the dominant/recessive inheritance pattern works, using sickle-cell disease as the example. Because sickle-cell anemia is controlled by a *recessive* gene, an individual must inherit the disease gene from *both* parents in order for the actual disease to occur. A *carrier* is someone who inherits the disease gene from only one parent. Such a person does not actually have the disease but can pass the disease gene on to his or her children. If two carriers have children together (example *c* in the figure), or if a carrier and someone with the disease have children (example *d* in the figure), their offspring may inherit disease genes from both parents and thus have the disease.

Sex-Linked Genetic Transmission

A variation of the dominant/recessive transmission pattern occurs when the locus for some specific gene is on the X chromosome. Because a boy has only one X chromosome, from his mother, he inherits many genes on his X chromosome that are not

Critical Thinking

Assume for the moment that the inheritance pattern for eye color is that brown is always dominant over blue. Can you figure out what your parents' genotype for eye color would be, based on the eye color of yourself, your siblings, and your grandparents?

Table 2.1

Some Physical Characteristics That Follow a Dominant-Recessive Genetic Pattern

Dominant	Recessive
Curly hair	Straight hair
Dark hair	Blond hair
Dimples in the chin or face	No dimples
Type A blood	Type O blood
Type B blood	Type O blood
Rh-positive blood	Rh-negative blood
Normal blood cells	Sickle-cell anemia

Source: McKusick, 1994.

Note: Eye color does not appear in this list because geneticists now believe that it results from the action of several genes (polygenic). Between blue and brown eye genes, brown is normally dominant; however, it *is* possible for two blue-eyed parents to have a brown-eyed child.

Figure 2.2

Some examples of how a recessive genetic disease, like sickle-cell anemia, is transmitted. In (a), a mother who has the disease passes her sickle-cell gene to all her children, but since her partner is normal, the children are all carriers and do not actually express the disease. In (b), a normal mother and a carrier father have no children with the disease, but each of their children has a 50 percent chance of inheriting the sickle-cell gene from the carrier father. A child can inherit the actual disease in one of three ways: with two carrier parents (c), with one carrier parent and one affected parent (d), or with two affected parents (not shown in the figure).

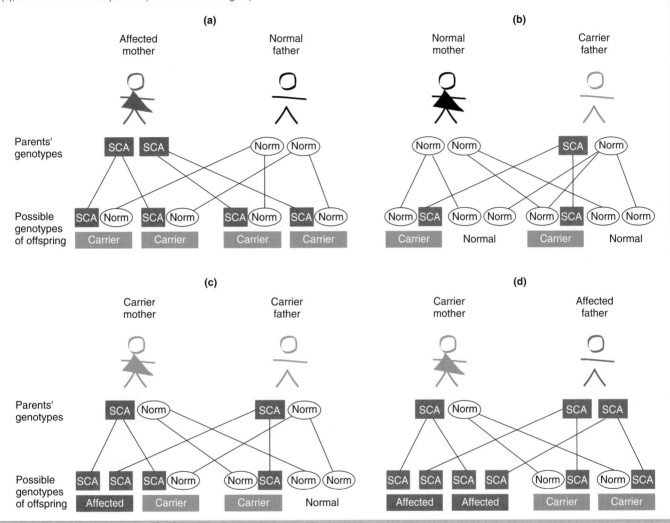

matched by, or counteracted by, equivalent genetic material on the smaller Y chromosome. Among other things, this means that recessive diseases or other characteristics that have their loci on the nonmatched parts of the X chromosome may be inherited by a boy directly from his mother, a pattern called **sex-linked transmission,** illustrated in Figure 2.3 with the disease hemophilia (see p. 44).

You can see from the figure that, as with other recessive-gene characteristics, a girl can inherit a sex-linked disease such as hemophilia only if she inherits the recessive gene from both parents. However, a male can inherit the disease by receiving the recessive gene only from his mother. Since his Y chromosome from his father contains no parallel locus for this characteristic, there are no counteracting instructions, and the mother's recessive gene dominates. Each of the sons of women who carry such recessive disease genes will have a 50 percent chance of having the disease; the daughters

Figure 2.3

Compare the pattern of sex-linked transmission of a recessive disease with the patterns already shown in Figure 2.2 (see p. 43). In the inheritance of a sex-linked disease such as hemophilia, a carrier mother will, on average, pass on the disease to half her sons because there is no offsetting gene on the Y chromosome. But a daughter of a carrier mother will not inherit the disease itself unless her father has the disease.

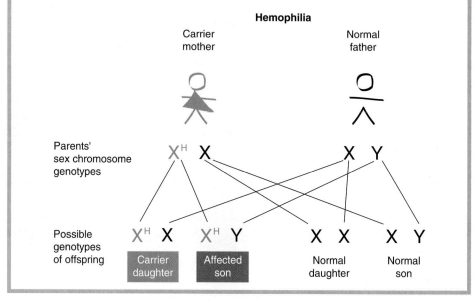

will have a 50 percent chance of being carriers. The sons of those carrier daughters, in turn, will have a 50 percent chance of inheriting the gene for the disease.

Polygenic Inheritance

Characteristics that follow the pattern of dominant and recessive genes are normally either/or characteristics: You either have them or you do not. The majority of human characteristics, however, aren't like that. Height varies along a whole continuum, as do intelligence, personality, and rate of growth, among many others. Geneticists argue that such highly varying traits are much more likely to be caused by multiple genes, a pattern called **polygenic inheritance,** rather than by a single dominant or recessive gene. Researchers have not yet discovered all the rules by which such multiple-gene transmission may occur, which means that for complex, polygenetic traits like intelligence or personality, we have to *infer* the presence of a genetic influence from other information, such as the twin studies and adoption studies I described in Chapter 1.

Twins and Siblings

In most cases, babies are conceived and born one at a time. However, 2 to 3 out of each 100 births in the United States today are multiple births (Centers for Disease Control, 1997a; Guyer et al., 1997), a number that has risen dramatically in recent decades in the United States, in large part because widely prescribed new medications given to infertile women frequently stimulate multiple ovulation. The great majority of multiple births are twins; triplets or higher multiples occur only about once in every 800 births.

Roughly two-thirds of twins are **fraternal twins.** This situation occurs when two ova have been produced and both have been fertilized, each by a separate sperm. Such twins, also called **dizygotic twins,** are no more alike genetically than any other pair of

Critical Thinking

Speculate for a minute: How do you think our society would differ if one in four of us, or half of us, had a twin? How would family life be different? How might schools differ?

siblings and need not even be of the same sex. The remaining one-third are **identical twins** (also called **monozygotic twins**). In such cases, a single fertilized ovum apparently initially divides in the normal way, but then for unknown reasons separates into two parts, usually just before implantation in the uterus, with each part developing into a separate individual. Because identical twins develop from precisely the same original fertilized ovum, they have identical genetic heritages. You'll remember from Chapter 1 that comparisons of the degree of similarity of these two types of twins is one of the major research strategies in the important field of behavior genetics.

Genotypes and Phenotypes

Using data from twin and adoption studies, behavior geneticists have made great strides in identifying those skills, characteristics, or traits that are influenced by heredity. Despite these scientific advances, no geneticist proposes that an inherited combination of genes fully *determines* any outcome for a given individual. Geneticists (and psychologists) make an important distinction between the genotype, which is the specific set of "instructions" contained in a given individual's genes, and the **phenotype,** which is the set of actual observed characteristics of the individual. The phenotype is a product of three things: the genotype, environmental influences from the time of conception onward, and the interaction between the environment and the genotype. A child might have a genotype associated with high IQ, but if his mother drinks too much alcohol during the pregnancy, there may be damage to the nervous system, resulting in mild retardation. Another child might have a genotype including the mix of genes that contribute to a "difficult" temperament, but if his parents are particularly sensitive and thoughtful, he may learn other ways to handle himself.

The distinction between genotype and phenotype is an important one. Genetic codes are not irrevocable signals for this or that pattern of development, or this or that disease. The eventual developmental outcome is also affected by the specific experiences the individual may have from conception onward.

Development from Conception to Birth

If we assume that conception takes place two weeks after a menstrual period, when ovulation normally occurs, then the period of gestation of the human infant is 38 weeks (about 265 days). Most physicians calculate gestation as 40 weeks, counting from the beginning of the last menstrual period. However, all the specifications of weeks of gestation I've given here are based on the 38-week calculation, counting from the presumed time of conception.

These 38 weeks have been subdivided in several different ways. Physicians typically talk in terms of three equal 3-month periods called *trimesters.* In contrast, biologists and embryologists divide the weeks of gestation into three unequal subperiods, linked to specific changes within the developing organism. These stages are the *germinal,* which lasts roughly 2 weeks; the *embryonic,* which continues until about 8 weeks after conception; and the *fetal,* which makes up the remaining 26 to 30 weeks.

The Germinal Stage: From Conception to Implantation

Conception occurs in one of the two fallopian tubes; the fertilized ovum then spends roughly a week floating down the tube to the uterus. Cell division begins 24 to 36 hours after conception; within two to three days, there are several dozen cells and the whole mass is about the size of a pinhead. Approximately four days after conception, the mass of cells, now called a **blastocyst,** begins to subdivide, forming a hollow sphere with two layers of cells around the perimeter. The outermost layer will form the various

Critical Thinking

Can you think of other examples in which the phenotype would be different from the genotype?

Most parents find the nine months of a pregnancy to be a time of delighted anticipation. It is also a time in which the genetic patterning for the child (the genotype) is established and in which complex maturational sequences unfold.

Figure 2.4

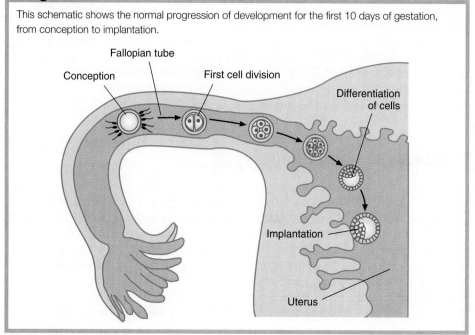

This schematic shows the normal progression of development for the first 10 days of gestation, from conception to implantation.

structures that will support the developing organism, while the inner layer will form the **embryo** itself. When it touches the wall of the uterus, the outer shell of cells breaks down at the point of contact. Small tendrils develop and attach the cell mass to the uterine wall, a process called **implantation.** When implantation is complete, normally ten days to two weeks after conception, the blastocyst has perhaps 150 cells (Tanner, 1990). You can see the sequence schematically in Figure 2.4.

The Embryonic Stage

The embryonic stage begins when implantation is complete and continues until the various support structures are fully formed and all the major organ systems have been laid down in at least rudimentary form. This process normally takes another six weeks.

Development of Support Structures. The outer layer of cells specializes further into two parts, each of which forms critical support structures. An inner membrane, called the **amnion,** creates a sac or bag, filled with liquid (*amniotic fluid*), in which the baby floats. From the outer layer, called the **chorion,** two further organs develop, the **placenta** and the **umbilical cord.** The placenta, which is fully developed by about 4 weeks of gestation, is a plate-like mass of cells that lies against the wall of the uterus. It serves as liver, lungs, and kidneys for the embryo and fetus. Connected to the embryo's circulatory system via the umbilical cord, it also serves as a critical filter between the mother's circulatory system and the embryo's. Nutrients such as oxygen, proteins, sugars, and vitamins from the maternal blood can pass through to the embryo or fetus; digestive wastes and carbon dioxide from the infant's blood pass back through to the mother, whose own body can eliminate them. At the same time, many (but not all) harmful substances, such as viruses or the mother's hormones, are filtered out because they are too large to pass through the various membranes in the placenta. Most drugs and anesthetics, however, do pass through the placenta, as do some disease organisms.

Development of the Embryo. While the support structures are developing, the mass of cells that will form the embryo is itself differentiating further into several types of cells that form the rudiments of skin, sense receptors, nerve cells, muscles, circulatory

Table 2.2

Milestones of Early Gestation

Week	Developmental Events
	Germinal Stage
1	Fertilization; beginning differentiation.
2	Further differentiation; implantation.
	Embryonic Stage
3	First missed menstrual period; pregnancy test is positive; amnion, chorion, and umbilical cord begin to develop; neural tube begins to form.
4	Placenta fully developed; primitive heartbeat begins; neural tube closes (otherwise spina bifida occurs); eyes, blood vessels, and lungs begin to develop; total length roughly $\frac{1}{4}$ inch.
5	Primitive mouth, arm and leg buds, and fingerlike appendages on hands appear; brain divides into three main sections of forebrain, midbrain, and hindbrain; beginning development of peripheral nerves.
6	Primitive nose and ear develop; facial structures fuse (otherwise facial defects are seen).
7	Eyelids begin; gene that determines maleness "turns on" and begins the chain of events resulting in male genitalia.
8	Ovaries and testes distinguishable; gross structure of the nervous system established; abdominal ultrasound can detect the presence of the embryo; total length now over 1 inch.

Sources: Rosenblith, 1992; Needlman, 1996; Allen, 1996.

system, and internal organs. A heartbeat can be detected roughly 4 weeks after conception; the beginnings of lungs and limbs also are apparent at this time. By the end of the embryonic period, rudimentary fingers and toes, eyes, eyelids, nose, mouth and external ears are all present, as are the basic parts of the nervous system—a set of changes summarized in Table 2.2 and shown visually in Figure 2.5 (see p. 48). When this preliminary organ formation is complete, a new stage, that of the **fetus,** begins.

The Fetal Stage

In the seven months of the fetal stage, all these primitive organ systems are refined. You can get some feeling for the rapidity of the changes by looking at Table 2.3 (see p. 48), which lists some of the milestones of fetal development.

Development of the Nervous System. One vital system that develops most fully during the fetal period is the nervous system, which exists in only the most rudimentary form at the end of the embryonic stage. First to form is a hollow cylinder called the **neural tube,** out of which both the brain and the spinal cord develop. You can see the early form of this tube in the schematic of the brain of a 25-day embryo in Figure 2.6 (see p. 49), which also shows the dramatic changes in the brain over the succeeding 33 weeks of gestation.

The nervous system is made up of two basic types of cells, **neurons** and **glial cells.** The glial cells are the "glue" that holds the whole nervous system together, providing firmness and structure to the brain, helping to remove debris after neuronal death or injury, segregating neurons from one another. It is the neurons that do the job

Figure 2.5

A 6-week-old embryo.

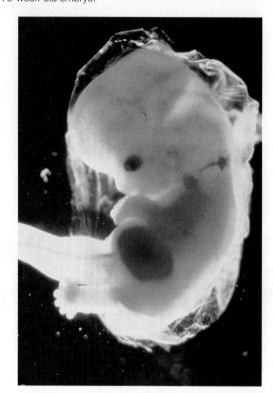

Table 2.3

Milestones of Fetal Development

Weeks	Developmental Events
8–12	Some reflexes visible, such as the startle and sucking reflexes; movement of arms and legs; primitive facial expressions; total length at 12 weeks is about 3 inches, with the head making up roughly half this length.
13–16	Beginning of second trimester: external genitalia fully differentiated and detectable; skin and true hair; bony skeleton develops; breathing and swallowing motions appear.
17–20	Mother first notices movement ("quickening"); heartbeat audible through stethoscope; 20 weeks is the usual lower limit of viability, with a weight of roughly 460 grams, but the great majority of infants born this small do not survive.
21–28	Eyes open by 28 weeks; subcutaneous fat added; myelination of spinal cord begins; eyelids and eyebrows fully form; further development of circulatory system; average weight 1300 grams. Good chance of survival if born this early.
29–37	Further subcutaneous fat added; weight added; fine hair that covered the body earlier begins to disappear; myelination of brain cells begins.
38	Birth

Sources: Rosenblith, 1992; Needlman, 1996; Allen, 1996.

Figure 2.6

Stages in the prenatal development of the brain, beginning with the neural tube in the embryonic period.

(*Source:* From drawings by Tom Prentiss in "The Development of the Brain" by W. Maxwell Cowan in *Scientific American*, September 1979, pp. 112–114+. Adapted by permission of Nelson H. Prentiss.)

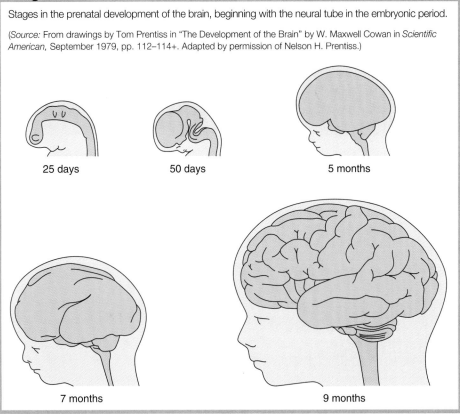

25 days　　　　　50 days　　　　　5 months

7 months　　　　　　　　　　9 months

of receiving and sending messages from one part of the brain or one part of the body to another.

Neurons have four main parts, shown schematically in Figure 2.7 (see p. 50): (1) a cell body, which is most commonly a pyramid-like shape; (2) branch-like extensions of the cell body (called **dendrites**) that are the major receptors of nerve impulses; (3) a tubular extension of the cell body called the **axon,** which can extend as far as a meter (about 3 feet); and (4) branch-like terminal fibers at the end of the axon, which form the primary transmitting apparatus of the nervous system. Because of the branch-like appearance of dendrites, physiologists often use botanical terms to describe them, speaking of the "dendritic arbor" or of "pruning" of the arbor.

The point at which two neurons communicate, where the axon's transmitting fibers come into close contact with another neuron's dendrites, is called a **synapse;** the communication across the synapse is accomplished with chemicals called **neurotransmitters,** such as serotonin, dopamine, or endorphins. The number of such synapses is vast. A single cell in the part of the brain that controls vision, for instance, may have as many as 10,000 to 30,000 synaptic inputs to its dendrites (Greenough et al., 1987).

Glial cells begin to develop about 13 weeks after conception and continue to be added until perhaps two years after birth. The great majority of neurons are formed between 10 and 18 weeks of gestation (Huttenlocher, 1994; Todd et al., 1995), forming initially as cell bodies in one part of the brain and then migrating to other sections of the brain. With rare exceptions, these prenatally created neurons are all the neurons the individual will ever have. Neurons lost later are not replaced.

In these early weeks of the fetal period, neurons are very simple. They consist largely of the cell body with short axons and little dendritic development. It is in the last two months before birth and in the first few years after birth that the lengthening of the

Figure 2.7

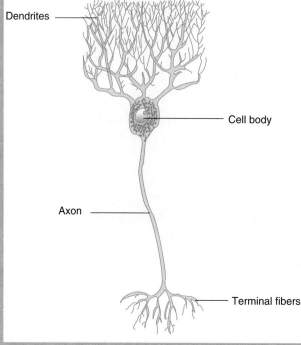

The structure of a single developed neuron. The cell bodies are the first to be developed, primarily between 10 and 20 weeks of gestation. Axons and dendrites begin to develop in the last two months of gestation and continue to increase in size and complexity for several years after birth.

Dendrites

Cell body

Axon

Terminal fibers

axons and the major growth of the "dendritic arbor" occurs. Indeed, as the dendrites first develop in the eighth and ninth months of gestation, they appear to be sent out in a kind of exploratory system; many of these early dendrites are later reabsorbed, with only the useful expansions remaining. In these final fetal months, however, synapse formation is much slower; most synapses are formed after birth. For example, in the part of the brain involved in vision, babies have about 10 times the number of synapses at 6 months as they had at birth (Huttenlocher, 1994).

Development of Length and Weight. Similarly, the major growth in fetal size occurs late in the fetal period. The fetus is about half her birth length by about 20 weeks of gestation, but she does not reach half her birth weight until nearly three months later, at about 32 weeks.

An Overview of Prenatal Development

One of the most important points about the child's prenatal development is how remarkably regular and predictable it is. If the embryo has survived the early, risky period (roughly the first 8 to 10 weeks), development usually proceeds smoothly, with the various changes occurring in what is apparently a fixed order, at fixed time intervals, following a clear maturational ground plan.

This sequence of development is not immune to modification or outside influence, as you'll soon see in detail. Indeed, as psychologists and biologists have looked more carefully at various kinds of teratogens, it has become clear that the sequence is more vulnerable than we had once thought. But before I begin talking about the various things that can go wrong, I want to make sure to state clearly that the maturational system is really quite robust. Normal prenatal development requires an adequate environment, but "adequate" seems to be a fairly broad range. *Most* children are quite normal.

Critical Thinking

Can you think of any practical consequences of the fact that all the neurons one is ever going to have are present by about 28 weeks of gestation?

The list of things that *can* go wrong is long and getting longer as our knowledge expands. However, many of these potential problems are quite rare, many are partially or wholly preventable, and many need not have permanent consequences for the child. Keep this in mind as you read through the next few pages.

The potential problems fall into two large classes: genetic errors, and those damaging environmental events called teratogens. Genetic errors occur at the moment of conception and cannot be altered—although new technology may change that eventually; teratogens, in contrast, may affect development any time from conception onward.

Genetic Errors

In perhaps 3 to 8 percent of all fertilized ova, the genetic material itself contains errors caused by imperfect meiosis in the sperm or ovum, resulting in either too many or too few chromosomes. Current estimates are that 90 to 95 percent of these abnormal conceptuses are aborted spontaneously (Tanner, 1990). Only about 0.5 percent of live newborns have such abnormalities.

Over 50 different chromosomal anomalies have been identified, many of them very rare. The most common is **Down syndrome** (also called *trisomy 21*), in which the child has three copies of chromosome 21 rather than the normal two. Roughly 1 in every 800 to 1000 infants is born with this abnormality (Rogers et al., 1996). These children have distinctive facial features, most notably a flattened face and somewhat slanted eyes with an epicanthic fold on the eyelid (as you can see in the photo), reduced total brain size, and often other physical abnormalities such as heart defects. Typically, they are retarded.

The risk of bearing a child with this deviant pattern is considerably higher for older mothers. For those age 35, the risk is 1 in 385 births; for a woman of 45, it is 1 in 30 (Centers for Disease Control, 1995a). Research by epidemiologists also suggests a link between exposure to environmental toxins of various kinds and the risk of having an offspring with Down syndrome. For example, one large study in Canada shows that men employed as mechanics, farm laborers, or sawmill workers, all of whom are regularly exposed to solvents, oils, lead, and pesticides, are at higher risk for fathering Down syndrome children than are men who work in cleaner environments (Olshan et al., 1989). Findings like these suggest that chromosomal anomalies may not be purely random events but may themselves be a response to various teratogens. Such results also underline the fact that fathers as well as mothers can contribute to teratogenic effects.

Note the distinctive facial characteristics of this Down syndrome child.

Sex-Chromosome Anomalies

A second class of anomalies, associated with an incomplete or incorrect division of either sex chromosome, occurs in roughly 1 out of every 400 births (Berch & Bender, 1987). The most common is an XXY pattern, called Klinefelter's syndrome, which occurs in approximately 1 out of every 1000 males. Affected boys most often look quite normal, although they have characteristic long arms and legs and underdeveloped testes. Most are not mentally retarded, but language and learning disabilities are common. Somewhat rarer is an XYY pattern. These children also develop as boys; typically they are unusually tall, with mild retardation. A single-X pattern (XO), called Turner's syndrome, and a triple-X pattern (XXX) may also occur, and in both cases the child develops as a girl. Girls with Turner's syndrome—perhaps 1 in every 3000 live female births (Tanner, 1990)—show stunted growth and are usually sterile. Without hormone therapy, they do not menstruate or develop breasts at puberty. These girls also show an interesting imbalance in their cognitive skills: They often perform particularly poorly on tests that measure spatial ability but usually perform at or above normal levels on tests of verbal skill (Golombok & Fivush, 1994). Girls with an XXX pattern are of normal size but are slow in physical development. In contrast to Turner's syndrome girls, they have markedly *poor* verbal abilities and overall low IQ, and they do particularly poorly in school compared with other groups with sex-chromosome anomalies (Bender et al., 1995; Rovet & Netley, 1983).

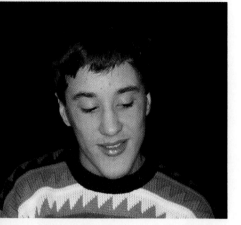

This boy diagnosed with fragile X syndrome has the long narrow face and prominent chin common in those with this abnormality.

Fragile X Syndrome

A quite different type of genetic anomaly is referred to as a "fragile X," which occurs in its full form in about 1 out of every 1300 males (Adesman, 1996; Rose, 1995). The problem arises not from an improper number of chromosomes but rather from a mutation of a specific gene on the X chromosome. The X chromosome is "fragile" in the sense that it has a greater tendency to break at that locus when exposed to various kinds of chemicals or other stresses. This is an *inherited* disorder, following the sex-linked inheritance pattern illustrated earlier in Figure 2.3 (see p. 44).

The majority of affected children have distinctive facial features, including a long, narrow face and a prominent, pointed chin (as in the photograph); large, prominent ears are also common. Almost all those with fragile X have at least some degree of mental retardation; very often they show a drop in IQ scores of perhaps 10 points between toddlerhood and adolescence, a decline that often shifts them from a level of mild retardation to one of moderate retardation. Current estimates are that among males, 5 to 7 percent of all retardation is caused by this syndrome (Zigler & Hodapp, 1991).

Single-Gene Defects

Problems also can occur at conception if the child inherits a gene for a specific disease. The great majority of such diseases are caused by a recessive gene and thus follow the inheritance pattern shown in Figure 2.2 (see p. 43). I've listed a few examples in Table 2.4, but this list cannot really convey the diversity of such disorders. Among known causes of mental retardation are 141 diseases or disorders with known genetic loci and 361 more whose locus has not yet been identified (Wahlström, 1990).

Table 2.4

Some of the Major Inherited Diseases

Phenylketonuria	A metabolic disorder that prevents metabolism of a common amino acid (phenylalanine). Treatment consists of a special phenylalanine-free diet. The child is not allowed many types of food, including milk. If not placed on the special diet shortly after birth, the child usually becomes very retarded. Affects only 1 in 8000 children. Diagnostic tests for this disorder are now routinely given at birth; cannot be diagnosed prenatally.
Tay-Sachs disease	An invariably fatal degenerative disease of the nervous system; virtually all victims die within the first 3 to 4 years. This gene is most common among Jews of Eastern European origin, among whom it occurs in approximately 1 in 3500 births. Can be diagnosed prenatally with amniocentesis or chorionic villus sampling.
Sickle-cell anemia	A sometimes fatal blood disease, with joint pain, increased susceptibility to infection, and other symptoms. The gene for this disease is carried by about 2 million Americans, most often blacks. Can now be diagnosed prenatally through amniocentesis or chorionic villus sampling.
Cystic fibrosis	A fatal disease affecting the lungs and intestinal tract. Many children with CF now live into their twenties. The gene is carried by more than 10 million Americans, most often whites. In families affected by the disease, carriers can be identified before pregnancy, and affected children can be diagnosed prenatally. Two carriers have a 1 in 4 chance of having a child with CF in each pregnancy.
Muscular dystrophy	A fatal muscle-wasting disease, carried on the X chromosome and thus found almost exclusively among boys. The gene for the most common type of MD, Duchenne's, has been located, and prenatal diagnosis is now available.

The Real World
Prenatal Diagnosis of Genetic Errors

Not so many years ago, when a child was conceived, that child was born with whatever deformities, diseases, or anomalies happened to come along. The parents had no choices. That is no longer true. Parents today may have access to genetic testing, genetic counseling, and any one of several prenatal diagnostic tests that can detect fetal abnormalities.

Prepregnancy Genetic Testing. Before conceiving, you and your spouse can have blood tests done that will tell you whether you are carriers of genes for those specific diseases for which the loci are known, such as Tay-Sachs or sickle-cell anemia. Because the locations of genes for all genetic diseases have not yet been determined, carriers of many diseases cannot yet be identified in this way. Still, such a genetic analysis may be an important step if you and your spouse belong to a subgroup known to be likely to carry particular recessive genes.

Prenatal Diagnosis of the Fetus. Four prenatal diagnostic strategies are now available. Two of these, the **alpha-fetoprotein test** (AFP) and **ultrasound,** are primarily used to detect problems in the formation of the neural tube, the structure that becomes the brain and spinal cord. If the tube fails to close at the bottom end at the fourth week of gestation, a disability called spina bifida occurs. Children with this defect (roughly 1500 of whom are born each year in the United States) are often partially paralyzed, and many (but not all) are retarded.

Alpha-fetoprotein is a substance produced by the fetus and is detectable in the mother's blood. If the levels are abnormally high, there may be some problem with the spinal cord or brain. The blood test is normally not done until the second trimester. If the AFP value is high, it does not mean a problem definitely exists; it means there is a higher *risk* of problems, and further tests are usually indicated.

One such further test is ultrasound, which involves the use of sound waves to provide an actual "moving picture" of the fetus. It is frequently possible to detect, or rule out, neural tube defects and some other physical abnormalities with this method. The procedure is not painful and gives parents an often delightful chance to see their unborn child moving; very often it can also show whether the fetus is a boy or a girl. But ultrasound cannot provide information about the presence of chromosomal anomalies or inherited diseases.

If you want the latter information, you have two choices: **amniocentesis** or **chorionic villus sampling** (CVS). In both cases, a needle is used to take small samples of cells. In CVS, normally done at 10 to 12 weeks of gestation, the sample is taken from what will become the placenta; in amniocentesis, normally done at about 15 weeks of gestation, the sample is from the amniotic fluid.

Both CVS and amniocentesis will provide information about any of the chromosomal anomalies and about the presence of genes for many of the major genetic diseases. Each technique has advantages and disadvantages. Amniocentesis was developed earlier and is the more widely used of the two. Its major drawback is that because the amniotic sac must be large enough to allow a sample of fluid to be taken with very little danger to the fetus, the test cannot be done until fairly late in pregnancy, and the results are not typically available until 17 to 18 weeks of pregnancy, well into the second trimester. If the test reveals an abnormality and the parents decide to abort, it is quite late for an abortion to be performed. CVS, in contrast, is done much earlier, so decisions can be made before the pregnancy is so far along. On the other side of the ledger is the fact that CVS is associated with slightly higher rates of miscarriage than is amniocentesis. (When amniocentesis is done as early as 12 weeks, it too is linked to higher miscarriage rates [Canadian Early and Mid-Trimester Amniocentesis Trial Group, 1998].) CVS is also associated with a *slightly* increased risk of missing or abnormal limbs, fingers, or toes (Centers for Disease Control, 1995a). The absolute risk for such abnormalities remains low, even with CVS (about 3.5 cases per 10,000 CVS procedures), but the risk is higher than when no CVS has been done.

Because of the risks associated with either procedure, parents need to think over the options carefully. Most physicians recommend one of the two for women over 35, because of the increased risk of Down syndrome, and for any women with a known or probable family risk of particular inherited diseases, such as Tay-Sachs or cystic fibrosis.

By the time you are facing such a choice, the decision may have been simplified by the development of new lower-risk diagnostic techniques using maternal blood samples. Experimental evidence already indicates that such a technique may be suitable for diagnosing Down syndrome or even the sex of the fetus (Lo et al., 1989; Wald et al., 1988). But no matter what technique you may select, the moral and ethical choices you may be called upon to make are far from easy.

Geneticists estimate that the average adult carries genes for four different recessive diseases or abnormalities (Scarr & Kidd, 1983), but for any one disease the distribution of genes is not random. For example, sickle-cell genes are more common among blacks, and Tay-Sachs is most common among Jews of Eastern European origin.

Teratogens: Diseases and Drugs

Deviant prenatal development can also result from variations in the environment in which the embryo and fetus is nurtured. I pointed out in Chapter 1 that the effect of most teratogens seems to depend heavily on their *timing* (an example of *critical periods*). That is, a particular teratogen, such as a drug or a disease in the mother, will result in a defect in the embryo or fetus *only* if it occurs during a particular period of days or weeks of prenatal life. The general rule is that each organ system is most vulnerable to disruption at the time when it is developing most rapidly (Moore & Persaud, 1993). Because most organ systems develop most rapidly during the first 8 to 10 weeks of gestation, this is the period of greatest risk for most teratogens. Figure 2.8 shows the maximum times of vulnerability for different parts of the body.

Of the many teratogens, the most critical are probably diseases the mother may have and drugs she may take.

Figure 2.8

Critical periods in the prenatal development of various body parts. The purple portion of each line signifies the period during which any teratogen is likely to produce a major structural deformity in that particular body part. The orange part of each line shows the period in which more minor problems may result. The embryonic period is generally the time of greatest vulnerability.

(*Source:* Moore, K. L. and Persaud, T., *The Developing Human: Clinically Oriented Embryology,* 5th ed. © 1993 by W. B. Saunders. By permission.)

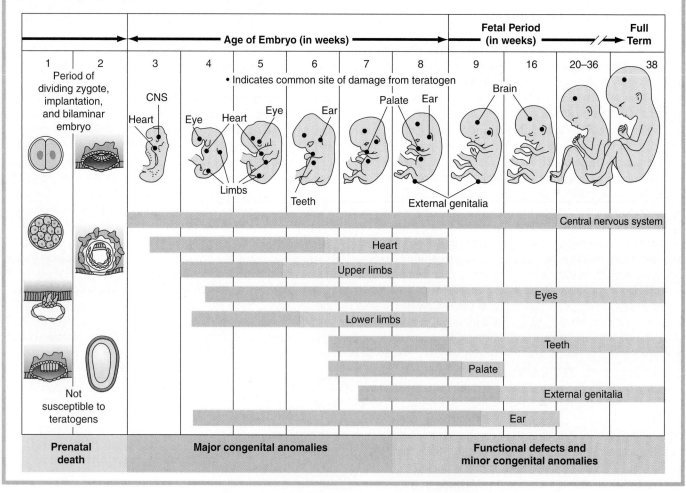

Research Report

Rh Factor: Another Type of Genetic Problem

Another possible problem, Rh factor incompatibility, is neither a genetic defect nor an inherited disease, but rather an incompatibility between the mother's genes and the baby's. One of the many factors in the blood is the presence or absence of a red-cell antigen, called the Rh factor because rhesus monkeys have it. Humans who have this factor are called Rh+ (Rh-positive), while those who lack it are Rh– (Rh-negative). Only about 15 percent of whites and 5 percent of blacks in the United States are Rh–; most Asians and Native Americans are Rh+.

Problems arise if the mother is Rh– and the baby is Rh+. Because Rh+ is dominant, a baby with an Rh+ father could inherit an Rh+ gene from him, even though the mother is Rh–. If the mother's and fetus's blood mix in the uterus, the mother's body considers the baby's Rh+ factor to be a foreign substance, and her immune system tries to fight it off by producing antibodies. These antibodies cross the placenta and attack the baby's blood, breaking down the red blood cells and producing a chemical substance called bilirubin. Babies with high levels of bilirubin look quite yellow; if untreated, they can suffer brain damage.

The risk of damage to the fetus increases with each succeeding pregnancy in which an Rh– mother carries an Rh+ baby. Normally, the placenta keeps the two blood systems separate, but during birth some mixing usually occurs. So after the first baby, the mother produces some antibodies. With a second incompatible baby, these antibodies attack the infant's blood, producing negative effects.

This problem used to be treated with rather heroic measures, such as complete exchange of the infant's blood shortly after birth, to remove all the antibodies. Fortunately, scientists have now discovered a much simpler and safer treatment. At the birth of her first child, an Rh– mother can be injected with antibodies that will remove any Rh+ cells from her system and thus protect subsequent infants, even if they are also Rh+.

Diseases of the Mother

A disease in the mother can affect the embryo or fetus by any one of three mechanisms. Some diseases, particularly viruses, can attack the placenta, reducing the amount of nutrients available to the embryo. Some others have molecules small enough to pass through the placental filters and attack the embryo or fetus directly. Examples of this type include rubella and rubeola (both forms of measles), cytomegalovirus (CMV), syphilis, diphtheria, influenza, typhoid, serum hepatitis, and chicken pox. The third possibility is that disease organisms present in the mucus membranes of the birth canal may infect the infant during birth itself. Herpes simplex, for example, is transmitted this way. As far as researchers now know, AIDS is transmitted both directly through the placenta and during delivery, as well as through breast milk after birth (Van de Perre et al., 1991). Among these many diseases, the riskiest for the child are rubella, AIDS, and CMV.

Rubella. The critical period for a negative effect from **rubella** (also called *German measles*) is the first few weeks of gestation. Most infants exposed in the first four to five weeks show some abnormality, while only about 10 percent of those exposed in the final six months of the pregnancy are negatively affected (Moore & Persaud, 1993). Deafness, cataracts, and heart defects are the most common abnormalities.

Fortunately, rubella is preventable. Vaccination is available and should be given to all children as part of a regular immunization program. Adult women who were not vaccinated as children can be vaccinated later, but vaccination must be done at least three months before a pregnancy to provide complete immunity.

AIDS. Worldwide, an estimated 3 million women are infected with HIV, the virus that causes AIDS, and the number of infected women of childbearing age is rising everywhere. In the United States, an estimated 1.7 out of every 1000 childbearing women are infected (Centers for Disease Control, 1995b). In areas with a high population of drug users, such as inner cities, as many as 3 to 5 percent of all pregnant women are now HIV-infected. Approximately 7000 infants are born to these infected mothers each year (Centers for Disease Control, 1996c).

These grim numbers are counterbalanced by several bits of good news. First, we now know that only about a quarter of infants born to HIV-infected mothers actually become infected (Abrams et al., 1995; Newell & Peckham, 1994). Transmission appears to be much more likely when the mother has developed the symptoms of AIDS than when she is HIV-positive but is not yet experiencing symptoms of the disease (Abrams et al., 1995).

Even more encouraging is the finding that infected women who are treated with the drug AZT (more technically called *zidovudine*) during their pregnancy have a markedly lowered risk of transmitting the disease to their children—as low as 8 percent (Centers for Disease Control, 1994b; Fiscus et al., 1996). Because most HIV-positive women are asymptomatic and are unaware they are infected, the Centers for Disease Control recommend routine HIV counseling and voluntary testing for all pregnant women early in their pregnancies so that they can begin a course of AZT, should that be necessary.

CMV. A much less well known but remarkably widespread and potentially serious disease is cytomegalovirus (CMV), a virus in the herpes group. It is now thought to be the single most important known infectious cause of both congenital mental retardation and deafness. CMV typically has few, if any, symptoms in an adult. In most cases an affected person doesn't even know she carries this virus, although in an active phase it sometimes has mononucleosis-like symptoms, including swollen glands and low fever. In infants who are infected prenatally or during birth, however, the virus can sometimes produce crippling disabilities.

Roughly half of *all* women of childbearing age have antibodies to CMV (Spector, 1996), indicating that they have been infected at some time. Perhaps 2 percent of babies whose mothers have CMV antibodies become infected prenatally, which means that approximately 1 out of every 100 babies is congenitally infected. When the mother becomes newly infected during her pregnancy, the transmission rate is much higher—on the order of 40 percent (Nelson & Demmler, 1997). In the United States, these various rates of infection mean that roughly 40,000 infants are born each year who test positive for this virus. Of these 40,000, 10 to 20 percent exhibit congenital CMV syndrome at birth or during the first year of life, a syndrome that includes a variety of symptoms of neurological damage, including mental retardation, small head size, and calcifications in the brain. Deafness, vision, and dental problems are also common. As many as 30 percent of infants who show this syndrome die in infancy (Hagay et al., 1996).

Transmission appears to follow the same three pathways we see with HIV: prenatally, during delivery, and through breast milk. Unlike the case for HIV infection, however, researchers have not yet found any effective treatment for CMV in pregnancy, and no general screening for this virus is presently recommended for pregnant women.

Taken together, this information about CMV can be quite scary for a woman to read, whether she is now pregnant or planning to become pregnant. Here is a common disease that may have massive negative effects on your child, and there is really nothing you can do about it. (A vaccine is under development but is not yet available [Nelson & Demmler, 1997].) However, keep the statistics correctly in mind: If the mother's disease is not active, fewer than 1 percent of babies become infected. Of those who do become infected, only 10 to 20 percent show symptoms of the disease—which means that at most 4 out of every 1000 infants whose mothers carry an inactive antibody will show any effect. Until someone figures out a treatment or develops a vaccine, that's the most optimism I can offer.

Herpes Simplex. Like CMV, herpes virus can also be transmitted to the fetus during delivery if the mother's disease is in the active phase at that time. Not only will the child then periodically experience the genital sores characteristic of the disease, but other complications are also possible, most notably *meningoencephalitis,* a potentially serious inflammation of the brain and spinal cord. Because of this increased risk, many physi-

Critical Thinking

Should pregnant women be *required* to be tested for HIV infection? Medical ethicists have offered strong arguments on both sides of this question. What do you think?

cians now recommend surgical delivery (cesarean section) of infants of mothers with herpes, although vaginal delivery is possible if the disease is inactive.

Drugs Taken by the Mother

There is now a huge literature on the effects of prenatal drugs, involving everything from aspirin to antibiotics to alcohol and cocaine. Sorting out their effects has proved to be an immensely challenging task, not only because it is clearly not possible to assign women randomly to various drug groups in order to test effects experimentally, but also because in the real world many women take multiple drugs during their pregnancy. For example, women who drink alcohol are also more likely than nondrinkers to smoke; those who use cocaine are also likely to take other illegal drugs or to smoke or drink to excess. What's more, the effects of drugs may be subtle, visible only many years after birth in the form of minor learning disabilities or increased risk of behavior problems. Still, we are creeping toward some fairly clear conclusions in several areas. Let me give you some examples.

Smoking. One consistent result stands out from the large body of research: Infants of mothers who smoke are on average about half a pound lighter at birth than are infants of nonsmoking mothers (Floyd et al., 1993) and are nearly twice as likely to be born with weights below 2500 grams (5 pounds 8 ounces), the common definition of low birth weight. The more the mother smokes, the greater the negative impact on the infant's weight (Nordentoft et al., 1996), and the older the mother, the more likely it is that her smoking will be linked to low birth weight (U.S. Bureau of the Census, 1997). The primary causal mechanism seems to be that nicotine constricts the blood vessels, reducing blood flow and nutrition to the placenta. The resulting lowered birth weight has a variety of potential negative consequences I'll talk about later.

The moral seems clear: The safest plan is to refrain from smoking during pregnancy. If you are a smoker, quit as soon as you learn you are pregnant. Smokers who quit smoking early in their pregnancy have the same rates of low-birth-weight infants as do those who did not smoke at all (Ahlsten et al., 1993). The research also shows a relationship between the "dose" (the amount of nicotine you are taking in) and the severity of consequences for the child. So if you cannot quit entirely, at least cut back.

Drinking. Recent work on the effects of maternal drinking on prenatal and postnatal development also carries a clear message—the very message I tried to convey to my daughter-in-law: To be safe, don't drink during pregnancy.

The effects of alcohol on the developing fetus range from mild to severe. At the extreme end of the continuum are children who exhibit a syndrome called **fetal alcohol syndrome (FAS),** which affects between 0.5 and 3 of every 1,000 infants in the United States (Stratton et al., 1996). Projecting these figures to all children born in the United States, this means that between 2,000 and 12,000 children with FAS are born every year. These children, whose mothers were usually heavy drinkers or alcoholics, are generally smaller than normal, with smaller brains and often with distinct physical anomalies or deformities (Swayze et al., 1997). They frequently have heart defects, and their faces have certain common features (visible in the two photos in Figure 2.9 on p. 58), with a somewhat flattened nose and nose bridge and often an unusually long space between nose and mouth. As children, adolescents, and adults, they continue to be shorter than normal, have smaller heads, and have IQ scores in the range of mild mental retardation. Indeed, FAS is the leading known cause of retardation in the United States, exceeding even Down syndrome (Streissguth et al., 1991). As adults, those with FAS show very high rates of mental illness as well as trouble with the law and alcohol and drug problems, among other difficulties (Streissguth, 1997).

Recent evidence also points to milder effects of moderate or "social" drinking, such as two glasses of wine a day. Children of mothers who drink at this level during pregnancy are more likely to have IQ scores below 85 and to show poorer attention span. I've given details about one of the best studies in the Research Report on page 59,

Figure 2.9

These two children, from different countries and different racial backgrounds, have both been diagnosed as having fetal alcohol syndrome (FAS). Both are mentally retarded and have relatively small heads. Note also the short nose and low nasal bridge typical of FAS children. (Copyright George Steinmetz.)

so you can get some feeling for how investigators have gone about studying this problem.

We do not yet know whether there is any safe level of alcohol consumption during pregnancy, although most researchers who work in this field are convinced that there is a linear relationship between the amount of alcohol ingested (the "dose") and the risk to the infant. This means that even infrequent drinking at low dosage carries *some* increased risk. Occasional bouts of heavy drinking, such as five or more drinks on one occasion (called *binge drinking*), carries even greater risk (Olson et al., 1992; Streissguth et al., 1990). In the face of our remaining ignorance, the *safest* course is not to drink at all.

Cocaine. Significant numbers of pregnant women in the United States (and presumably elsewhere in the world) also take various illegal drugs, most notably cocaine. The best current estimates are that roughly 3 percent of all babies born in the United States have been exposed prenatally to cocaine. In some inner-city hospitals, as many as 50 percent of mothers delivering have used cocaine or crack cocaine during their pregnancies (Shore, 1997).

Cocaine appears to cross the placental barrier quite readily. About a third of all cocaine-exposed babies are born prematurely, and among those born after a normal gestation period, many are lower than normal in birth weight. In addition, cocaine-exposed infants are three times as likely to have a very small head circumference or to show some signs of neurological abnormalities (Needlman et al., 1995; Singer et al., 1993). Some (but not all) also show significant drug withdrawal symptoms after birth, such as irritability, restlessness, shrill crying, and tremors. What is not yet clear is whether any long-term consequences can be ascribed clearly to prenatal cocaine exposure. Some studies show long-term negative effects (e.g., Bender et al., 1995); others do not (Griffith et al., 1994; Richardson & Day, 1994). The most likely possibility is that prenatal cocaine exposure, like prenatal alcohol exposure, does indeed have lasting effects on the child, but that the effects are fairly subtle and thus hard to pin down. As of this moment, we simply don't know what those long-term effects may be (Lester et al., 1995).

Critical Thinking

Another question of medical ethics for you to ponder: There are now several cases of pregnant women being held in custody to prevent them from excessive drinking or drug taking, on the grounds that the court has the responsibility to prevent harm to the fetus. What do you think about this?

Research Report
Streissguth's Study of Prenatal Alcohol Exposure

The best single study of the consequences of prenatal alcohol exposure has been done by Ann Streissguth and her colleagues (Olson et al., 1992; Streissguth et al., 1980; 1981; 1984; 1989; 1990; 1995), who have followed a group of over 500 women and children beginning in early pregnancy. Because the study was begun before there were widespread warnings about the possible impact of alcohol during pregnancy, the sample includes many well-educated middle-class women with good diets who did not use many other recreational drugs but who did drink alcohol in moderate or even fairly heavy amounts while pregnant—a set of conditions that would be impossible to duplicate today, at least in the United States or other countries in which the risks of alcohol in pregnancy are well advertised.

Streissguth tested the children repeatedly, beginning immediately after birth, again later in infancy, at age 4, at school age, and again at ages 11 and 14. She found that the mother's alcohol consumption in pregnancy was associated with sluggishness and weaker sucking in infancy; lower scores on measures of intelligence at 8 months, 4 years, and 7 years; and problems with attention and vigilance at 4, 7, 11, and 14. Teachers also rated the 11-year-olds on overall school performance and on various behavior problems, and on both of these measures, children whose mothers had consumed the most alcohol during pregnancy were rated significantly worse.

Streissguth also was careful to obtain information about other drug use in pregnancy, including smoking, and asked mothers about their diet, their education, and their life habits. She found that the links between alcohol consumption and poor outcomes for the child held up even when all these other variables were controlled statistically.

Setting aside those cases in which the child was diagnosed with the full fetal alcohol syndrome, the effects of moderate levels of alcohol use during pregnancy are not large in absolute terms, but they have significant practical consequences. For example, the difference in IQ scores at age 7 between children of abstainers and children of women who drank 1 ounce or more of alcohol per day during their pregnancy (roughly equivalent to 2 ounces of hard liquor or one 8-ounce glass of wine) was only about 6 points in Streissguth's sample (Streissguth et al., 1990). However, this relatively small absolute difference means that 3 times as many alcohol-exposed children have IQs below 85 than is true among children of abstainers. Alcohol-exposed children are thus greatly overrepresented in special classes in schools and probably also appear in overlarge numbers among high school dropouts and the underemployed in adulthood—although those links remain for longer-term longitudinal studies to confirm.

Other Teratogens

Other known teratogens include excess amounts of vitamin A, the drug diethylstilbestrol, methylmercury, and lead. Many other drugs or chemicals are suspected of being teratogens, but we have too little information to be sure. The latter category includes anticonvulsant medication taken by epileptics, polychlorinated biphenyls (PCBs, compounds widely used in electrical transformers and paint), radiation at high doses, aspirin, some antidepressants and other prescription medications, some artificial hormones, and some pesticides (Vorhees & Mollnow, 1987). I don't have room to go into detail about what we know (or don't know) in each case, but let me say just a word about several items that have clear practical significance.

Diethylstilbestrol (DES). DES is a synthetic estrogen that at one time was commonly given to pregnant women to prevent miscarriages. The daughters of such women have been found to have higher rates of some kinds of cancers; sons have higher rates of congenital malformations of the genitalia. Some—but not all—research suggests that the sons also have higher rates of infertility (Rosenblith, 1992; Wilcox et al., 1995).

Vitamin A. Vitamin A in small doses is essential for the development of the embryo. But when taken in very large doses during the first two months of pregnancy—10,000 International Units (IU) or more per day—it may increase the risk of birth defects, particularly malformations of the head, face, heart, and nervous system (e.g., Rothman et al., 1995). The recommended daily allowance of Vitamin A is 2,700 IU. Most multivitamin pills contain 4,000 to 5,000 units, but some brands contain as much as 10,000, and straight Vitamin A capsules can contain as much as 25,000 units. If you are pregnant or planning a pregnancy, check your intake of this vitamin.

Aspirin. One of the most widely used drugs, aspirin is teratogenic in animals when given in high doses. People rarely take high enough doses to produce such effects directly, but it turns out that aspirin in moderate amounts can have negative effects on the human fetus if it is ingested along with benzoic acid, a chemical widely used as a food preservative, such as in ketchup. This combination, especially in the first trimester, seems to increase the risk of physical malformations in the embryo/fetus.

Lead. In most industrialized countries, adults are exposed to fairly high dosages of lead, although the introduction of unleaded gasoline has helped to lower dosages significantly. So did the outlawing of lead-based paint in 1978 in the United States, although any house built before 1978 is quite likely to have at least some lead-based paint. Children may be exposed to lead prenatally (through the mother's blood lead levels) or postnatally, through contact with lead paint (from breathing paint dust in the air in an older house, or from chewing on a painted windowsill), from car exhaust, or from living near a factory that emits high levels of lead.

Because most children who are exposed to high levels of lead prenatally are *also* exposed to high levels postnatally, it is extremely difficult to sort out the unique impact of prenatal lead. The best information comes from several excellent longitudinal studies following children from birth through early childhood (e.g., Baghurst et al., 1992, 1995; Dietrich et al., 1993). These researchers find a consistent but small relationship between elevated blood lead levels in newborns and lower IQ scores later in childhood. Exposure to high levels of lead during childhood appears to have a further, even larger, negative effect, not only on IQ scores but also on distractibility and (perhaps) aggressiveness (Needleman et al., 1996). Even at quite low levels—levels previously classified as "safe" by U.S. guidelines and found in children who live in houses without lead-based paint—we see negative effects. Until recently, for example, a level of 20 micrograms per deciliter was thought to be acceptable; newer research shows that children with this level of lead have IQ scores that average 2.6 points lower than do those with only 10 micrograms per deciliter of blood lead (Schwartz, 1994). Because of such evidence, the Centers for Disease Control have changed their guidelines, now listing 10 micrograms as the desirable upper limit.

By current estimates, 3 to 6 percent of U.S. infants and young children have blood lead levels that exceed this amount (Centers for Disease Control, 1997b), the greatest percentage of them black or Latino children living in inner-city neighborhoods (Berney, 1996). Lead exposure may thus be one of the many small factors contributing to the lower average IQ scores of children living in poverty.

Eliminating leaded gasoline clearly has not solved all the problems of air pollution, although it has benefited children by reducing their exposure to lead.

As the study of teratogens expands, psychologists are realizing that prenatal development is less insulated, less fully protected than we had first thought. In particular, many chemicals associated with modern industrial societies may have unforeseen effects on the fetus.

Other Influences on Prenatal Development

Diet

Another significant factor for prenatal development is the mother's diet. Both the general adequacy of the diet, measured in terms of calories, and the presence of certain key nutrients are critical.

Malnutrition. At a minimum, a mother needs sufficient overall calories and protein to prevent malnutrition. When a woman experiences severe malnutrition during pregnancy, particularly during the final three months, she has a greatly increased risk of a stillbirth, low infant birth weight, or infant death during the first year of life (Stein et al., 1975). The impact appears to be greatest on the developing nervous system—a pattern found in studies of both humans and other mammals. For example, rats whose caloric intake has been substantially restricted during the fetal and early postnatal periods show a pattern described as *brain stunting,* resulting in lighter brains with less dendritic development and less rich synaptic formation (Pollitt & Gorman, 1994).

In humans, we see similar effects in cases in which prenatal malnutrition has been severe enough to cause the death of the fetus or newborn. Autopsies show that these infants have smaller brains with fewer and smaller brain cells than normal (Georgieff, 1994).

What is far less clear is whether similarly lasting effects on brain development occur in cases of prenatal *sub*nutrition, such as the chronic protein-energy malnutrition common in many populations around the world. For one thing, children who experience such subnutrition prenatally are highly likely to encounter mal- or subnutrition after birth as well, frequently accompanied by lower levels of stimulation in the home. This makes it extremely difficult to sort out the effects of the *pre*natal nutrition from the effects of *post*natal insufficiencies. At the moment, most experts in this area have abandoned the idea that common levels of prenatal subnutrition have some direct, irremediable, negative effect on the developing brain (Pollitt et al., 1996; Ricciuti, 1993). Instead, what seems to happen is some variation of the interaction pattern I described in Chapter 1 (recall Figure 1.3, p. 15): Prenatal subnutrition may make the infant more "vulnerable," perhaps because it makes him less energetic or responsive or less able to learn from his experiences. In a nonstimulating environment, or one in which the child experiences continuing subnutrition, such a vulnerable child is likely to do poorly. But a stimulating environment can overcome the vulnerability.

This pattern is illustrated nicely in the results of a small study by Philip Zeskind and Craig Ramey (1981). They have looked at the outcomes for a small group of 10 infants, all born to poverty-level mothers and all extremely thin at birth—usually a sign of prenatal malnutrition. Half of these babies happened to have been assigned randomly to a special enriched day-care program beginning when they were 3 months old. The other 5 malnourished babies received nutritional supplements but were reared at home in much less stimulating circumstances. Other children in the day-care center had been of normal weight at birth, as were other home-reared children included in the study. Table 2.5 (see p. 62) gives the IQ scores of these four groups of children when they were 3 years old. As you can see, the results match Horowitz's model very well. Malnourished infants did well in the stimulating environment of the day-care center but extremely poorly in a less supportive environment. Well-nourished infants also did better in the day-care environment than at home, but the difference was not nearly so large.

Table 2.5

IQ Scores of 3-Year-Old Children

	Prenatal Nutritional Status	
Experience After Birth	**Malnourished**	**Well Nourished**
Enriched day care	96.4	98.1
Home-reared	70.6	87.7

Source: Zeskind & Ramey, 1981, p. 215.

Thus, malnutrition appeared to create a "vulnerability" that could be overcome only by an enriched environment.

Folic Acid. A vital specific nutrient, whose importance during pregnancy has only recently become clear, is folic acid, a B vitamin found primarily in liver, beans, leafy green vegetables, broccoli, orange juice, fortified breakfast cereals, and grain products, especially wheat germ. Inadequate amounts of this nutrient have been clearly linked to the risk of neural tube defects such as spina bifida, a deformity in which the lower part of the spine does not close (e.g., Butterworth & Bendich, 1996). Many (but not all) such children are retarded; most have some lower-body paralysis. Because the neural tube develops primarily during the very earliest weeks of pregnancy, before a woman may even know she is pregnant, it is important for women who plan a pregnancy to achieve and maintain at least the minimum level of folic acid: 400 micrograms daily. Most women, however, do not receive enough folic acid from ordinary food sources or multivitamin pills to reach this minimum level (Daly et al., 1997). To help raise the normal intake above the desired level, new regulations by the Food and Drug Administration in the United States now require that 140 micrograms of folic acid be added to each 100 grams of enriched flour, thus greatly increasing the likelihood that the majority of women will receive sufficient quantities of folic acid.

Weight Gain. A woman's caloric needs go up 10 to 20 percent during a pregnancy in order to support the needed weight gain. As recently as the late 1960s in the United States, physicians routinely advised pregnant women to limit their weight gain to 15 or 20 pounds; greater gains were thought to increase the risk of labor abnormalities and other problems. Beginning in the 1970s, however, new data accumulated showing that weight gains in that low range were associated with increased risk of bearing a low-birth-weight infant and with neurological impairment in the infant (e.g., Carmichael & Abrams, 1997; Hickey et al., 1996; Zhou & Olsen, 1997). Such information led to significant increases in the recommended weight gain. The most recent guidelines, published in 1990 by the National Institute of Medicine, base the recommended gain on a woman's prepregnancy weight-for-height, as shown in Table 2.6.

Unfortunately, the very women who are otherwise at highest risk for various kinds of problems are also most likely to gain too little weight: those who are lightweight for their height before pregnancy, women older than 35, those with low education, and African-American women, for whom higher levels of weight gain during pregnancy seem optimal (Abrams, 1994; Centers for Disease Control, 1992).

At the same time, there are also risks associated with gaining too much. In particular, women who gain more than the amounts recommended in the table are more likely to have cesarean section delivery (Abrams, 1994; Brost et al., 1997); they are also prone to postpartum obesity, which carries a whole set of other health risks, including heart disease and diabetes (Johnson & Yancey, 1996). Gains within the recommended ranges appear optimal, although there is wide variability from one woman to the next.

Finally, women who are obese before they become pregnant have some additional risks, regardless of the amount of weight they gain. Such women are about twice as

Critical Thinking

What kind of study would you have to do to figure out whether it is okay for pregnant women to maintain high levels of exercise, such as running 30 miles a week?

Table 2.6

Currently Recommended Weight Gains During Pregnancy

Prepregnant Weight Category	Recommended Weight Gain
Below normal (90% or less of recommended weight for height)	28 to 40 lbs
Normal	25 to 35 lbs
Overweight (120% to 135% of recommended weight for height)	15 to 25 lbs
Obese (135% or more of recommended weight for height)	15 lbs or more

Source: Taffel et al., 1993.

likely to have infants with neural tube defects, regardless of their intake of folic acid (Shaw et al., 1996; Werler et al., 1996)—a finding that argues in favor of weight loss *before* pregnancy for women who are classed as obese.

The Mother's Age

One of the particularly intriguing trends in modern family life in the United States and many other industrialized countries is the increasing likelihood that women will postpone their first pregnancy into their late twenties or early thirties. In 1994, 22.1 percent of first births in the United States were to women over 30, more than double the rate in 1970 (U.S. Bureau of the Census, 1996). Of course, women have many reasons for such delayed childbearing, chief among them the increased need for second incomes in families and the desire of many young women to complete job training and early career steps before bearing children. I'm not going to debate all the pros and cons of such a choice. What I do want to do is explore the question that is relevant for the subject of this chapter, namely, the impact of maternal age on the mother's experience of pregnancy and on the developing fetus.

Current research suggests that the optimum time for childbearing is in a woman's early twenties. Mothers over 30 (particularly those over 35) are at increased risk for several kinds of problems, including miscarriage, stillbirth, complications of pregnancy such as high blood pressure or bleeding, cesarean section delivery, and death during pregnancy or delivery (Berkowitz et al., 1990; Hoyert, 1996; McFalls, 1990; Peipert & Bracken, 1993).

The infants born to these older mothers also appear to have higher risk of some kinds of problems. In particular, a number of large studies in several different industrialized countries show that the risk of fetal death—from any of a variety of causes—is higher for mothers of 35 and older, even when the mothers in every age group have received good prenatal care (Cnattingius et al., 1993; Fretts et al., 1995). Other than the well-established risk of Down syndrome, children born to older mothers do not seem to be at higher risk for congenital anomalies, but delayed childbearing clearly does continue to carry some added risk for both mother and child, despite improvements in prenatal and neonatal care.

Risks for mother and child are also higher at the other end of the age continuum, among very young mothers. Because teen mothers are also more likely to be poor and less likely to receive adequate prenatal care, it has been difficult to sort out the causal factors. An unusually well designed new study, however, makes the link quite clear.

Alison Fraser and her colleagues (1995) studied 135,088 white girls and women, aged 13 to 24, who gave birth in the state of Utah between 1970 and 1990. This is an un-

Older mothers, like this one, are becoming much more common in the United States and other industrialized countries. Mothers over age 30 (especially those over 35) and their infants have somewhat higher risks of problems during pregnancy and delivery, a point to bear in mind if you choose to delay childbearing.

usual sample for studies on this subject: Almost two-thirds of the teenage mothers in this group were married, and most had adequate prenatal care; 95 percent remained in school. These special conditions have enabled Fraser to disentangle the effects of ethnicity, poverty, marital status, and the mother's age—all of which are normally confounded in studies of teenage childbearing. Overall, Fraser found higher rates of adverse pregnancy outcomes among mothers age 17 and younger than among the mothers age 20 and up. The rate of preterm births was twice as high; the incidence of low birth weight was almost twice as high. And these differences were found even when Fraser looked only at teenage mothers who were married, in school, and had adequate prenatal care. Outcomes were riskier still among teenage mothers who lacked adequate prenatal care, but good care alone did not eliminate the heightened risk of problems linked to teenage birth.

Just why such a heightened risk should exist for teen mothers is not entirely clear. The most likely possibility is that there is some negative biological consequence of pregnancy in a girl whose own growth is not complete.

Stress and Emotional State

The idea that emotional or physical stresses are linked to poor pregnancy outcomes is firmly established in folklore, but "its foundation in science is much less secure" (Grimes, 1996). Results from studies in animals are clear: Exposure of the pregnant female to stressors such as heat, light, noise, shock, or crowding significantly increases the risk of low-birth-weight offspring as well as later problems in the offspring (Schneider, 1992). Studies in humans are harder to interpret because they necessarily involve quasi-experimental designs rather than random assignment of subjects. Women who experience high levels of stress are quite likely to be different in other ways from those who do not, so it is harder to uncover clear causal connections. Nonetheless, a number of careful recent studies do show that stressful life events, emotional distress, and physical stress are all linked to slight increases in problems of pregnancy, such as low birth weight, heightened maternal blood pressure, and certain physical problems in the infants, such as cleft palate or respiratory problems (e.g., Hedegaard et al., 1996; Henriksen et al., 1995; Sandman et al., 1997). The effect appears to be small, but my own conclusion from reading this literature is that stress does have a deleterious effect.

An Overview of Risks and Long-Term Consequences of Prenatal Problems

Every time I write this chapter, I am aware that the list of things that can go wrong seems to get longer and longer and scarier and scarier. Physicians, biologists, and psychologists keep learning more about both the major and the subtle effects of prenatal environmental variations, so the number of warnings to pregnant women seems to increase yearly, if not monthly. One of the ironies of this is that too much worry about such potential consequences can make a woman more anxious, and anxiety is on the list of warnings! So before you begin worrying too much, let me try to put this information into perspective.

First, let me say again that *most* pregnancies are normal and largely uneventful, and most babies are healthy and normal at birth. Second, any woman can take specific preventive steps to reduce the risks for herself and her unborn child. She can be properly immunized; she can quit smoking and drinking (since FAS and its milder cousins can be entirely prevented by abstaining from alcohol); she can watch her diet and make sure her weight gain is sufficient; and she and the child's father can get genetic counseling. In addition, she can get early and regular prenatal care. Many studies show that mothers who receive adequate prenatal care reduce the risks to themselves and their infants (e.g., Hoyert, 1996). Just one example: Jann Murray and Merton Bernfield (1988), in a study of more than 30,000 births, found that the risk of giving birth to a low-birth-weight infant was more than three times as great among women who had received inadequate prenatal care as among those receiving adequate care, and this pattern held among both blacks and whites. The percentage of women receiving adequate prenatal care has been increasing in the United States in recent years, but there is still some distance to go. In 1996, 18.2 percent of all mothers did not begin their prenatal care until at least the second trimester, and 4.1 percent either had no care at all or saw a health care provider only in the final few months (Guyer et al., 1996). Inadequate care was twice as common among black mothers as among whites, and in both groups inadequate care was more common among mothers living in poverty and among teenage mothers.

Given such statistics, it is perhaps not surprising that the United States continues to have a relatively high rate of **infant mortality**—defined as a death at birth or within the first year of life. The good news is that this rate has been declining steadily and quite dramatically over the past decades, dropping from 20.0 infant deaths per 1000 births in 1970 to 7.2 per 1000 in 1996 (Guyer et al., 1997). The bad news is that infant mortality is more than twice as high for blacks as for whites (14.6 and 6.3, respectively, in 1996) and that even an overall rate of 7.2 places the United States twenty-first in the world. Virtually all European countries, where prenatal care is typically free or low cost and universally available, have lower infant mortality rates, as do Japan (with the lowest rate in the world), Hong Kong, and Singapore.

Incidentally, the United States looks bad in such comparisons in part because we really do have more high-risk infants, especially those with very low birth weight (disproportionately African-American infants). At the same time, the traditional comparative statistics are also weighted against the United States because we count every infant who lives even a few minutes as a live birth, whereas many other countries do not. This means that some of the very small infants who die some hours or days after delivery are counted as *infant* deaths in the United States but are counted as stillbirths or in some other category in other countries (e.g., Sachs et al., 1995). Yet even if the U.S. statistics are adjusted by excluding all deaths in the first hour after birth, the U.S. infant mortality rate would still be higher than the rates in 17 other countries (Wegman, 1996).

The black/white difference in infant mortality in the United States is also troubling and deserves a further word. A somewhat heightened risk also exists for Native American infants, although *not* for Latino babies, a set of findings that raises a whole host of questions (Singh & Yu, 1995). The black/white difference has existed at least since record keeping began (in 1915) and has *not* been declining. It is found even when researchers compare only infants born to college-educated mothers (Schoendorf et al., 1992). Physicians and physiologists do not yet understand all the reasons for this discrepancy, although it is clear that one significant factor is that infants born to African-American mothers are much more likely to be born before the full gestational period is completed, and thus have low birth weight. When only full-term, normal-weight babies are compared, infant mortality is about the same in the two groups. Yet saying that only pushes the explanation back one step. We still need to know why African Americans have more preterm, low-birth-weight babies, and the answer to this question remains unclear.

A third basic point to be made about prenatal problems is that if something does go wrong, chances are good that the negative consequences to the child will be short-term rather than permanent. And many physical defects can be treated successfully after birth.

Of course some negative outcomes *are* permanent and have long-term consequences for the child. Chromosomal anomalies, including Down syndrome and deviations in sex-chromosome patterns, are permanent and are usually associated with lasting mental retardation or school difficulties. Some teratogens also have permanent effects; fetal alcohol syndrome and deafness resulting from rubella, for example, are serious conditions. And as you'll see in Chapter 3, *very* low-birth-weight infants (those under about 1500 grams) have an increased risk of persistent, long-term learning problems or low IQ, regardless of the richness of the environment in which they are reared.

However, many of the effects I have talked about in this chapter may be detectable only for the first few years of the child's life, and then only in certain families. The relationship between prenatal problems and long-term outcomes, in fact, generally follows the same pattern I talked about with regard to malnutrition: We are more likely to see persisting problems if the child is reared in an unstimulating or unsupportive environment than if he grows up in a more optimal family situation. Claire Kopp puts it this way:

> To use an analogy, some perinatal risks (e.g., infections, anoxia, low-birth-weight) appear to act like a jolt to the system in which the system is hurt but is not irreparably damaged. With care and nurturance the system can fully mend in time whereas in the absence of adequate care, the system only partially recovers. (1994, p. 19)

So it is not the prenatal problem by itself that is the cause of the later difficulties; it is the combination of a prenatal problem and a relatively poor early environment that seems to produce long-term negative effects. So don't despair when you read the long list of cautions and potential problems. The story isn't as gloomy as it first seems.

Sex Differences in Prenatal Development

Because nearly all prenatal development is controlled by maturational sequences that are the same for all members of our species—male and female alike—there aren't very many sex differences in prenatal development. Still, there are a few, and they set the stage for some of the physical differences we'll see at later ages.

- Sometime between 4 and 8 weeks after conception, the male embryo begins to secrete the male hormone *testosterone* from the rudimentary testes. If this hormone is not secreted or is secreted in inadequate amounts, the embryo will be "demasculinized," even to the extent of developing female genitalia. Female embryos do not appear to secrete any equivalent hormone prenatally. However, the accidental presence of male hormone at the critical time (such as from some drug the mother may take, or from a genetic disease called *congenital adrenal hyperplasia*) acts to "defeminize" or masculinize the female fetus, sometimes resulting in malelike genitalia and frequently resulting in masculinization of later behavior, such as more rough-and-tumble play (Collaer & Hines, 1995).

- The several hormones that affect the development of genitalia prenatally (particularly testosterone in males) also appear to affect the pattern of brain development, resulting in subtle brain differences between males and females and affecting patterns of growth-hormone secretions in adolescence, levels of physical aggression, and the relative dominance of the right and left hemispheres of the brain (Ruble & Martin, 1998; Todd et al., 1995). The research evidence in this area is still fairly sketchy; it is clear that whatever role such prenatal hormones play in brain architecture and functioning is highly complex, but the early research has raised some very intriguing questions.

- Girls are a bit faster in some aspects of prenatal development, particularly skeletal development. They are 4 to 6 weeks ahead in bone development at birth (Tanner, 1990).

- Despite the more rapid development of girls, boys are slightly heavier and longer at birth, with more muscle tissue and fewer fat cells. U.S. data, for example, show the 50th percentile birth length and weight for boys is 20 inches and $7\frac{1}{4}$ pounds, compared with $19\frac{1}{4}$ inches and 7 pounds for girls (Needlman, 1996).

- Boys are considerably more vulnerable to all kinds of prenatal problems. Many more boys than girls are conceived—on the order of about 120 to 150 male embryos to every 100 female—but more of the males are spontaneously aborted. At birth, there are about 105 boys for every 100 girls. Boys are also more likely to experience injuries at birth (perhaps because they are larger), and they have more congenital malformations (Zaslow & Hayes, 1986).

The striking sex difference in vulnerability is particularly intriguing, especially since it seems to persist throughout the life span. Males have shorter life expectancy, higher rates of behavior problems, more learning disabilities, and usually more negative responses to major stresses such as divorce. One possible explanation for at least some of this sex difference may lie in the basic genetic difference. The XX combination affords the girl more protection against the fragile X syndrome and against any "bad" genes that may be carried on the X chromosome. For instance, geneticists have found that a gene affecting susceptibility to infectious disease is carried on the X chromosome (Brooks-Gunn & Matthews, 1979). Because boys have only one X chromosome, such a gene is much more likely to be expressed phenotypically in a boy.

Social Class Differences

I will be talking much more fully about the impact of poverty and other social class differences on development in Chapter 14, but I cannot leave this chapter without saying a word about the impact of social class on the risks of pregnancy and birth.

The basic sequence of fetal development is clearly no different for children born to poor mothers than for children born to middle-class mothers, but many of the problems that can affect prenatal development negatively are more common among the poor. For example, in the United States, mothers who have not graduated from high school are about twice as likely as mothers with a college education to have a low-birth-weight infant or to have a stillborn infant. Poor women are also likely to have their first pregnancy earlier and to have more pregnancies overall, and they are less likely to be immunized against such diseases as rubella. They are also less likely to seek prenatal care, or they seek it much later in their pregnancies. A significant portion of this difference could be overcome in the United States if we were willing to devote the resources needed to provide good, universal prenatal care. We could significantly reduce not only the rate of infant death but also the rate of physical abnormalities and perhaps even mental retardation. Equal access to care is not the only answer. In the Nordic countries, for example, in which such care is universally available, social class differences in low-birth-weight deliveries and in infant mortality rates remain (Bakketeig et al., 1993). Nonetheless, I am still convinced that access to good-quality prenatal care is a minimum goal. Among other things, it would create cost savings over the long run, because it costs a great deal less to provide prenatal care than it does to care for a low-birth-weight infant or a child with significant learning disabilities. Ultimately, though, the argument is broader than that: Every child, in my view, has a *right* to begin with the best possible start in life.

Summary

1. At conception, the 23 chromosomes from the sperm join with 23 from the ovum to make up the set of 46 that will be reproduced in each cell of the new child's body. Each chromosome consists of a long string of deoxyribonucleic acid (DNA) made up of specific segments called genes.

2. The child's sex is determined by the twenty-third pair of chromosomes, a pattern of XX for a girl and XY for a boy.

3. Geneticists distinguish between the genotype, which is the pattern of inherited characteristics, and the phenotype, which is the result of the interaction of genotype and environment.

4. During the first days after conception, called the germinal stage of development, the initial cell divides, travels down the fallopian tube, and is implanted in the wall of the uterus.

5. The second stage, the period of the embryo, which lasts until 8 weeks after fertilization, includes the development of the various structures that support fetal development, such as the placenta, as well as primitive forms of all organ systems.

6. The final 30 weeks of gestation, called the fetal period, are devoted primarily to enlargement and refinements in all the organ systems.

7. All the neurons an individual will ever have are developed between 10 and 20 weeks of gestation, but the development of the axon and dendrites of each neuron occurs primarily in the final two months of gestation and in the first few years after birth.

8. Normal prenatal development seems heavily determined by maturation—a "road map" contained in the genes. Disruptions in this sequence can occur; the timing of the disruption determines the nature and severity of the effect, illustrating the principle of critical periods.

9. Deviations from the normal pattern can be caused at conception by any of a variety of chromosomal anomalies, such as Down syndrome, or by the transmission of genes for specific diseases.

10. Prior to conception, it is possible to test parents for the presence of genes for many inherited diseases. After conception, several diagnostic techniques exist to identify neural tube defects, chromosomal anomalies, or recessive-gene diseases in the fetus.

11. Some diseases contracted by the mother may affect the child, including rubella, AIDS, and CMV. Any of these may result in disease or physical abnormalities in the child.

12. Drugs such as alcohol and nicotine appear to have significantly harmful effects on the developing fetus; the greater the dose, the larger the potential effect appears to be.

13. The mother's diet is also important. If she is severely malnourished, there are increased risks of stillbirth, low birth weight, and infant death during the first year of life. Long-term consequences of milder subnutrition, however, have been more difficult to establish.

14. Sufficient levels of folic acid in the diet are also necessary to help prevent neural tube defects.

15. Older mothers and very young mothers also run increased risks, as do their infants.

16. High levels of anxiety or stress in the mother may also increase the risk of complications of pregnancy or difficulties in the infant, although the research findings here are mixed.

17. During the embryonic period, the XY embryo secretes the hormone testosterone, which stimulates the growth of male genitalia and shifts the brain into a "male" pattern. Without that hormone, the embryo develops as a girl, as do normal XX embryos.

18. Other sex differences in prenatal development are few in number. Boys are slower to develop, bigger at birth, and more vulnerable to most forms of prenatal stress than are girls.

Key Terms

alpha-fetoprotein test A prenatal diagnostic test frequently used to screen for the risk of neural tube defects. May also be used in combination with other tests to diagnose Down syndrome and other chromosomal anomalies. **p. 53**

amniocentesis A medical test for genetic abnormalities in the embryo/fetus, which may be done at 15 to 18 weeks of gestation. **p. 53**

amnion The sac or bag, filled with liquid, in which the embryo and fetus floats during prenatal life. **p. 46**

axon The long appendage-like part of a neuron; the terminal fibers of the axon serve as transmitters in the synaptic connection with the dendrites of other neurons. **p. 49**

blastocyst Name for the mass of cells from roughly 4 to 10 days after fertilization. **p. 45**

chorion The outer layer of cells during the blastocyst stage of prenatal development, from which both the placenta and the umbilical cord are formed. **p. 46**

chorionic villus sampling A technique for prenatal genetic diagnosis, involving taking a sample of cells from the placenta. Can be performed earlier in the pregnancy than amniocentesis but carries slightly higher risks. **p. 53**

chromosomes The structures, arrayed in 23 pairs, contained in each cell in the body that contains genetic information. Each chromosome is made up of many segments, called genes. **p. 39**

dendrites The branch-like part of a neuron that forms one half of a synaptic connection to other nerves. Dendrites develop rapidly in the final two prenatal months and the first year after birth. **p. 49**

deoxyribonucleic acid Called DNA for short, this is the chemical of which genes are composed. **p. 40**

dizygotic twins See *fraternal twins*. **p. 44**

Down syndrome A genetic anomaly in which every cell contains three copies of

chromosome 21 rather than two. Children born with this genetic pattern are usually mentally retarded and have characteristic physical features. **p. 51**

embryo The name given to the developing organism during the period of prenatal development from about 2 to 8 weeks after conception, beginning with implantation of the blastocyst into the uterine wall. **p. 46**

fallopian tube The tube between the ovary and the uterus down which the ovum travels to the uterus and in which conception usually occurs. **p. 39**

fetal alcohol syndrome (FAS) A pattern of physical and mental abnormalities, including mental retardation and minor physical anomalies, found often in children born to alcoholic mothers. **p. 57**

fetus The name given to the developing organism from about 8 weeks after conception until birth. **p. 47**

fraternal twins Children carried in the same pregnancy but resulting from two separate fertilized ova. No more alike genetically than other pairs of brothers and sisters. Also called dizygotic twins. **p. 44**

gametes Sperm and ova. These cells, unlike all other cells of the body, contain only 23 chromosomes rather than 23 pairs. **p. 40**

gene A uniquely coded segment of DNA in a chromosome that affects one or more specific body processes or developments. **p. 40**

genotype The pattern of characteristics and developmental sequences mapped in the genes of any specific individual. Will be modified by individual experience into the phenotype. **p. 39**

glial cells One of two major classes of cells making up the nervous system, glial cells provide the firmness and structure, the "glue" to hold the system together. **p. 47**

heterozygous Term describing the genetic pattern when the pair of genes at any given genetic locus carry different instructions, such

as a gene for blue eyes from one parent and for brown eyes from the other parent. **p. 41**

homozygous Term describing the genetic pattern when the pair of genes at any given genetic locus carry the same instructions. **p. 41**

identical twins Children carried in the same pregnancy who come from the *same* originally fertilized ovum. They are genetic clones of one another. Also called monozygotic twins. **p. 45**

implantation Process by which the blastocyst attaches itself to the wall of the uterus, generally during the second week after fertilization. **p. 46**

infant mortality Death at birth or at any time during the first year of life. The incidence of such deaths in any given country or subgroup is called the *infant mortality rate*. **p. 65**

monozygotic twins See *identical twins*. **p. 45**

neural tube A hollow cylinder formed in the first weeks after conception, out of which both the brain and spinal cord eventually develop. **p. 47**

neuron The second major class of cells in the nervous system, neurons are responsible for transmission and reception of nerve impulses. **p. 47**

neurotransmitters Chemicals at synapses that accomplish the transmission of signals from one neuron to another. **p. 49**

ovum The gamete produced by a woman, which, if fertilized by a sperm from a man, forms the basis for the developing organism. **p. 39**

phenotype The expression of a particular set of genetic information in a specific environment; the observable result of the joint operation of genetic and environmental influences. **p. 45**

placenta An organ that develops during gestation between the fetus and the wall of the uterus. The placenta filters nutrients from the mother's blood, acting as liver, lungs, and kidneys for the fetus. **p. 46**

polygenic inheritance Any pattern of genetic transmission in which multiple genes contribute to the outcome, such as is presumed to occur for complex behaviors such as intelligence or temperament. **p. 44**

rubella A form of measles that, if contracted during the first few weeks of a pregnancy, may have severe effects on the developing embryo or fetus. **p. 55**

sex-linked transmission Pattern of genetic transmission that occurs when the critical gene is carried on a portion of the X chromosome that is not matched by genetic material on the Y chromosome. Diseases such as hemophilia follow this genetic pattern. **p. 43**

synapse The point of communication between two neurons, where nerve impulses are passed from one neuron to another by means of chemicals called neurotransmitters. **p. 49**

ultrasound A form of prenatal diagnosis in which high-frequency sound waves are used to provide a picture of the moving fetus. Can be used to detect many physical deformities, such as neural tube defects, as well as multiple pregnancies and to determine gestational age. **p. 53**

umbilical cord The cord connecting the embryo/fetus to the placenta, containing two arteries and one vein. **p. 46**

uterus The female organ in which the blastocyst implants itself and within which the embryo/fetus develops. (Popularly referred to as the womb.) **p. 39**

Suggested Readings

Bérubé, M. (1996). *Life as we know it: A father, a family, and an exceptional child.* New York: Pantheon Books. A forthright book by a father of a Down syndrome child, described by the *New York Times Book Review* as "an astonishingly good book, important, literate and ferociously articulated."

The Boston Women's Health Collective (1992). *The new our bodies, ourselves: A book by and for women.* New York: Simon & Schuster. This recent revision of a popular book is really focused on the adult female's body, rather than on prenatal development, but it has an excellent discussion of health during pregnancy. This is a strongly feminist book; some of you may not be entirely in sympathy with all the political views included. But it is nonetheless a very good compact source of information on all facets of pregnancy and childbirth.

Moore, K. L., & Persaud, T. V. N. (1993). *The developing human: Clinically oriented embryology* (5th ed.). Philadelphia: Saunders. A highly technical book aimed at medical students. It may give more detail than you want, but I guarantee it will tell you anything you might want to know about prenatal development.

Nightingale, E. O., & Goodman, M. (1990). *Before birth: Prenatal testing for genetic disease.* Cambridge, MA: Harvard University Press. This is an extremely informative, clearly written, helpful small book.

Nilsson, L. (1990). *A child is born.* New York: Delacorte Press. This is a remarkable book, full of the most stunning photographs of all phases of conception, prenatal development, and birth.

Rosenblith, J. F. (1992). *In the beginning: Development in the first two years of life* (2nd ed.) Newbury Park, CA: Sage. A first-rate text covering prenatal development and infancy. Much less technical than Moore and Persaud's book listed above, it would be an excellent next step in your reading if you are interested in this area.

Wright, L. (1995, August 7). Double mystery. *The New Yorker,* 45–62. A fascinating look at all aspects of the study of twins.

Birth and the Newborn Child

Try to imagine that you are a woman 9 months pregnant with your first child. The long months of prenatal life are over and the baby is about to be born. If you are like many of today's mothers, you and your partner have explored your options for the location and conditions for your delivery; both of you may have taken prenatal classes; you have tried to prepare yourselves for what the baby will be like and how the advent of this new member of the family will change your life. You are a little apprehensive about the process of delivery and a bit uncertain about what to expect from the baby and about your own abilities to cope, but you are eager for the whole adventure to begin.

In this chapter I want to try to answer some of the questions that new parents reasonably ask about birth and about newborn babies. Does it make a difference whether the baby is born in a hospital or at home? Does it matter if the father is present or not? What happens if the birth is too early, or if something else goes wrong? I also want to describe the beginnings of the child's independent life so that you can have a clear picture of the qualities and skills with which the infant begins the long developmental journey. In the past few decades, researchers have discovered that the apparently helpless newborn really has a wide range of quite remarkable abilities. This knowledge has changed not only the information given out to new parents, but also our theories of development.

Birth

The Stages of Labor

In the normal process, labor progresses through three stages of unequal length.

The First Stage of Labor. Stage 1 covers the period during which two important processes occur: dilation and effacement. The cervix (the opening at the bottom of the uterus) must open up like the lens of a camera (**dilation**) and flatten out (**effacement**). At the time of actual delivery of the infant, the cervix must normally be dilated to about 10 centimeters (about 4 inches). This part of labor has been likened to putting on a sweater with a neck that is too tight. You have to pull and stretch the neck of the sweater with your head in order to get it on. Eventually, the neck is stretched wide enough so that the widest part of your head can pass through.

A good deal of the effacement may actually occur in the last weeks of the pregnancy, as may some dilation. It is not uncommon for women to begin labor 80 percent effaced and 1 to 3 centimeters dilated. The contractions of the first stage of labor, which are at first widely spaced and later more frequent and rhythmical, serve to complete both processes.

Customarily, stage 1 is itself divided into phases. In the *early* (or *latent*) phase, contractions are relatively far apart and are typically not too uncomfortable. In the *active* phase, which begins when the cervix is 3 to 4 centimeters dilated and continues until dilation has reached 8 centimeters, contractions are closer together and more intense. The last 2 centimeters of dilation are achieved during a period usually called the *transition* phase. It is this period, when contractions are closely spaced and strong, that women typically find the most painful. Fortunately, transition is relatively brief, especially in second or later pregnancies.

Stage 1 lasts an average of about 12 hours for a first birth and about 7 hours for a woman having a second or later child (Moore & Persaud, 1993). Figure 3.1 shows the duration of the several subphases, although neither the figure nor the average numbers convey the wide individual variability that exists. Among women delivering a first child, stage 1 labor may last as little as 3 hours or as long as 20 (Biswas & Craigo, 1994; Kilpatrick & Laros, 1989). The times are generally longer for women receiving anesthesia than for those delivering with natural childbirth.

Figure 3.1

Typical pattern of timing of the phases of stage 1 of labor for first births and for subsequent births. The relatively long latent phase shown here counts from zero centimeters dilated, which increases the total hours somewhat. The total length of stage 1 ranges from 8 to 12 hours for a first birth and from 6 to about 8 hours for later births.

(*Source:* Based on Biswas & Craigo, 1994, from Figures 10–16, p. 216, and 10–17, p. 217.)

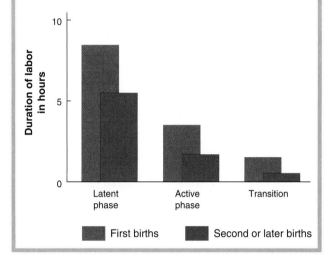

The Second Stage of Labor. At the end of the transition phase, the mother will normally have the urge to help the infant out by "pushing." When the birth attendant (physician or midwife) is sure the cervix is fully dilated, she or he will encourage this pushing, and the second stage of labor—the actual delivery—begins. The baby's head moves past the stretched cervix, into the birth canal, and finally out of the mother's body. Most women find this part of labor markedly less distressing than the transition phase. The average length is about 50 minutes for first infants and 20 minutes for later deliveries (Moore & Persaud, 1993). It rarely takes longer than 2 hours.

Most infants are delivered head first, facing down toward the mother's spine. Three to four percent, however, are oriented differently, either feet first or bottom first (called *breech* presentations) (Brown et al., 1994). Several decades ago most breech deliveries were accomplished with the aid of medical instruments such as forceps; today nearly four-fifths of breech presentations are delivered by cesarean section—a procedure I'll discuss more fully in a moment.

The Third Stage of Labor. Stage 3, typically quite brief, is the delivery of the placenta (also called the *afterbirth*) and other material from the uterus. You can see all these steps schematically in Figure 3.2 (p. 74).

The First Greeting

The brief description I've just given does not begin to convey the emotional impact of the experience of childbirth for the mother or father. Many parents experience intense joy as they greet the infant for the first time, accompanied often by laughter, exclamations of delight at the baby's features, and first tentative and tender touching. Here's an excerpt from one mother's greeting (Macfarlane, 1977, pp. 64–65):

Figure 3.2

The sequence of steps during delivery is shown clearly in these drawings.

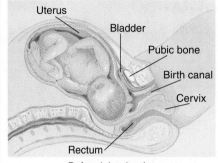

Uterus
Bladder
Pubic bone
Birth canal
Cervix
Rectum

Before labor begins

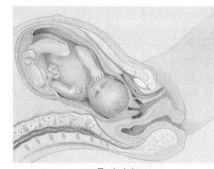

Early labor

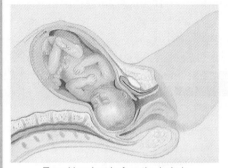

Transition: just before the baby's head enters the birth canal

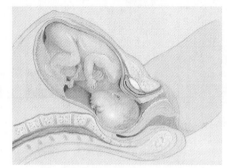

The baby's head before crowning

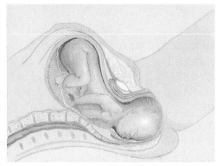

The head crowning

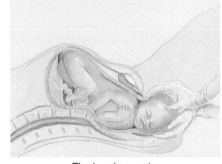

The head emerging

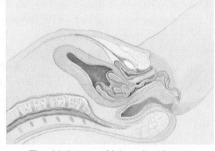

The third stage of labor: the placenta coming loose and about to emerge

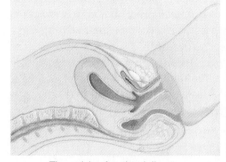

The pelvis after the delivery

She's big, isn't she? What do you reckon? (Doctor makes a comment.) Oh look, she's got hair. It's a girl—you're supposed to be all little. Gosh. Oh, she's lovely. Oh, she's opened her eyes (laughs). Oh lovely (kisses baby).

Most parents are intensely interested in having the baby look at them right away. They are delighted if the baby opens her eyes and will try to stimulate her to do so if she doesn't. The parents' initial tentative touches also seem to have a pattern to them: The parent first touches the infant rather gingerly with the tip of a finger and then proceeds gradually to stroking with the full hand (Klaus & Kennell, 1976; Macfarlane, 1977). The tenderness seen in most of these early encounters is striking.

Critical Thinking

Why do you think parents are so interested in having the baby look at them? Do you think this is a universal pattern?

Birth Choices

What I am going to say here about birth choices is necessarily specific to options and experiences in industrialized countries. In many other cultures there are no decisions to be made about such questions as where the delivery will occur, whether the father should be present, or whether the mother should be given drugs to ease her pain. Custom dictates the answers. In many Western industrialized countries, however, patterns and customs in this area continue to change rapidly, which leaves individual parents with decisions to make—decisions that may affect the child's health or the mother's satisfaction with the delivery. Because many of you will face these choices at some point in the future, I want to give you the best current information I have.

Drugs During Delivery. One key decision concerns the use of drugs during delivery. Three types of drugs are commonly used. (1) *Analgesics* (such as the common drug Demerol) are given during the first stage of labor to reduce pain. All the analgesics in this group are members of the opium family of drugs. (2) *Sedatives* or *tranquilizers* (such as Nembutol, Valium, or Thorazine) are given during stage 1 labor to reduce anxiety. (3) *Anesthesia* is given during transition or the second stage of labor to block pain either totally (general anesthesia) or in portions of the body (local anesthesia). Of the three, anesthesia is least often used in the United States, although the use of one form of local anesthesia, the epidural block, has been increasing, with a current rate of up to 16 percent of all labors (Fields & Wall, 1993).

Studying the causal links between such drug use and the baby's later behavior or development has proved to be monumentally difficult. Controlled experiments are

In the United States, the most common delivery setting is in a hospital, assisted by a physician, as shown in the photo below (with the father in the background); in Europe, home deliveries assisted by a midwife are quite common, as in the French birth shown in the photo at right—again with the father present.

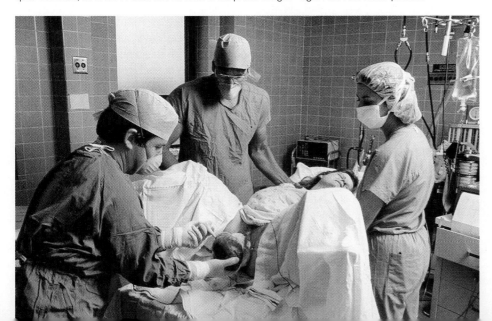

obviously not possible, since women cannot be randomly assigned to specific drug regimens. In the real world, drugs are also given in myriad different combinations. Still, a few reasonably clear conclusions are emerging from the research on this question.

First, nearly all drugs given during labor pass through the placenta and enter the fetal bloodstream. Because the newborn lacks the enzymes necessary to break down such drugs quickly, the effect of any drug lasts longer in the baby than it does in the mother. Not surprisingly, then, drugged infants are slightly more sluggish, gain a little less weight, and spend more time sleeping in the first few weeks than do infants of non-drugged mothers (Maurer & Maurer, 1988). These differences are quite small but have been observed repeatedly.

Second, beyond these first few days there are no consistently observed effects from analgesics and tranquilizers, and there are only hints, from a few studies, of possible longer-term effects of anesthesia (Rosenblith, 1992). Given such findings, only one specific piece of advice seems warranted: If you have received medication, you need to bear in mind that your baby is also drugged and that this will affect her behavior in the first few days. If you allow for this effect and realize that it will wear off, your long-term relationship with your child is unlikely to be affected.

The Location of Birth: Four Alternatives. A second choice parents must make is *where* the baby is to be born. Today in the United States there are typically four alternatives: (1) a traditional hospital maternity unit; (2) a hospital-based birth center or birthing room located within a hospital but providing a more homelike setting, with both labor and delivery completed in the same room and family members often present throughout; (3) a freestanding birth center, like a hospital birth center except located apart from the hospital, with delivery typically attended by a midwife rather than (or in addition to) a physician; and (4) home delivery.

At the turn of the century, only about 5 percent of babies in the United States were born in hospitals; today, the figure is 99 percent (U.S. Bureau of the Census, 1997). The small fraction remaining are born at home or in birthing centers. Limited research in the United States indicates that such nonhospital deliveries, if planned and attended by a midwife or equivalent professional, are no riskier than deliveries in hospitals (e.g., Janssen et al., 1994). More extensive information comes from research in Europe, where home deliveries are encouraged in uncomplicated pregnancies in which the woman has received good prenatal care. For example, in the Netherlands, a third of all deliveries are at home (Eskes, 1992). In this low-risk group, with a trained birth attendant present at delivery, the rate of delivery complications or infant problems is no higher in home or birth center deliveries than in hospital deliveries (Rooks et al., 1989; Tew, 1985). In contrast, infant mortality rates are significantly higher in *unplanned* home deliveries, in those without trained attendants, or when the mother had experienced some complication of pregnancy (Schramm et al., 1987).

The Presence of Fathers at Delivery. A third issue is whether the father should be present at delivery. In the United States today, this is hardly a "decision" any longer. As recently as 1972, only about one-fourth of U.S. hospitals permitted the father to be present in the delivery room; by 1980, four-fifths of them did (Parke & Tinsley, 1984); and today, the father's presence has become the norm—an illustration of how a cultural pattern surrounding an event as important as birth can undergo rapid change.

There have been several compelling arguments offered in favor of this new norm: The father's presence may lessen the mother's anxiety and give her psychological support; by coaching the mother in breathing and other techniques, the father may help her control her pain; and he may become more strongly attached to the infant if he is present at the birth. At least some evidence supports the first two of these arguments, but—perhaps unexpectedly for some of you—the third has little support.

When fathers are present, mothers report lower levels of pain and receive less medication (Henneborn & Cogan, 1975). And when the mother has a coach (the father or someone else), the incidence of problems of labor and delivery goes down, as does the duration of labor (Sosa et al., 1980). Furthermore, at least one study shows that

This couple, like so many today, is taking a prenatal class together. Having the father present at the delivery as coach seems to reduce the mother's pain and even shorten the length of labor.

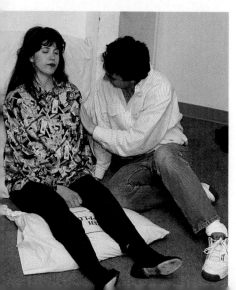

women are more likely to report that the birth was a "peak" experience if the father was present (Entwisle & Doering, 1981).

What is far less clear is whether the father's relationship with his infant is affected positively by being present at delivery or by having an opportunity for early contact with the infant. In the 1970s and 1980s, most parents accepted the statements made by various psychologists and pediatricians that it was essential for the father's bonding with the baby for him to be present at the baby's birth. In fact, it was just such statements that led to the rapid increase in fathers' participation in births in the United States and elsewhere. However, the evidence has failed to support the early arguments. On the plus side is some indication that those fathers whose birth experience has been particularly positive show signs of greater attachment to their infant throughout the first year (Peterson et al., 1979), but this seems to be true whether or not the father is actually present for the birth or not. Presence at delivery seems to have no magical effect. Thus, the father's presence is neither necessary nor sufficient for the father's emerging attachment to his infant (Palkovitz, 1985).

This statement is not in any way intended as an argument against fathers' participation in the delivery process. The fact that the father's presence seems to help the mother control pain, helps reduce medication and labor duration, and may enhance the husband-wife relationship, all seem to me to be compelling reasons for encouraging fathers to be present. In addition, of course, most fathers report powerful feelings of delight at being present at the birth of their children. Reason enough.

Problems at Birth

As with prenatal development, there are some things that can alter the normal pattern I have been describing. One of the most common problems is that the delivery itself may not proceed normally, leading to a surgical delivery through an abdominal incision, called a **cesarean section** (usually abbreviated C-section). A second common problem is that the infant may be born too early.

Cesarean-section Delivery. C-section deliveries occur for a variety of reasons, of which the most common are a previous cesarean delivery, a failure to progress in labor, a breech position of the fetus, or some sign of fetal distress (Cunningham et al., 1993). C-sections are also more common among older mothers in the United States—a group that makes up an increasingly large proportion of all pregnancies (Adashek et al., 1993).

During the 1970s and 1980s, the frequency of C-sections rose rapidly in many industrialized countries, including Australia, Canada, Britain, Norway, and other European countries (e.g., Notzon et al., 1994). In the United States the increase was particularly striking, as you can see in Figure 3.3 (p. 78), rising from a rate of 5.5 percent in 1970 to a peak of nearly 1 out of 4 births in 1988 (U.S. Bureau of the Census, 1994).

By far the largest part of this increase appears to be due to changes in standard medical practice, such as requiring any woman who has had one C-section to have all subsequent deliveries the same way, as well as the widespread use of fetal monitors—equipment that allows the physician to hear the fetal heartbeat and thus to detect signs of fetal distress. Such signs of distress increasingly have been handled with C-sections in order to reduce the apparent risk to the infant.

Recent research calls both these practices into question. The best current conclusion, based on studies in both the United States and Europe, is that the rate of C-sections could be reduced to a range of 10 to 15 percent without any increase in maternal or infant mortality (e.g., Lagrew & Morgan, 1996; Notzon et al., 1994). In light of this information, the Centers for Disease Control (1993) have suggested a goal of lowering the U.S. C-section rate to 12 percent by the year 2000. The first steps toward such a goal are reflected in a modest drop in the rate of C-sections in recent years, reaching 20.6 percent in 1996 (Guyer et al., 1997), as you can see in Figure 3.3.

I do not want to give you the impression that C-sections are never necessary. They clearly are. Breech position births, for example, appear to be safer if done by C-section

Critical Thinking

Have you read or heard that a father wouldn't really "bond" with his baby unless he was present at delivery? Did you believe it? Why? Because it made sense to you, or because the evidence seemed especially good? Will you be more skeptical next time?

Figure 3.3

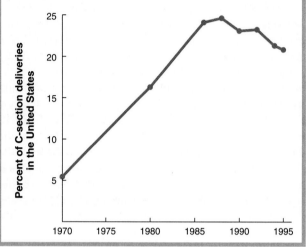

Cesarean section delivery rates rose rapidly and substantially in the United States in the 1970s and 1980s. Increases also occurred in most other industrialized countries in these same decades, although rates rose further and faster in the United States than in any other country.

(*Source:* U.S. Bureau of the Census, *Statistical Abstract of the United States*, 1994.)

than vaginally (Cheng & Hannah, 1993). Nonetheless, obstetricians worldwide agree that the rate has become too high and that it can be considerably reduced without added risk to mothers or infants.

Anoxia (Lack of Oxygen). Another complication that can occur during delivery is an insufficiency of oxygen for the infant, a state called **anoxia.** During the period immediately surrounding birth, anoxia may occur because the umbilical circulation system fails to continue the supply of blood oxygen until the baby breathes, or because the umbilical cord has been squeezed in some way during labor or delivery. Perhaps as many as 20 percent of newborns experience some degree of anoxia.

Long-term effects of anoxia have been hard to pin down. Prolonged anoxia is often (but not invariably) associated with such major consequences as cerebral palsy or mental retardation. Briefer periods of oxygen deprivation appear to have little long-term effect, although that is still a tentative conclusion.

Low Birth Weight. In talking about various teratogens, I have often mentioned low birth weight as one of the clearest negative outcomes. But how low is too low? The optimum weight range for infants—the weight that is associated with the lowest risk of later death or disability—is between about 3000 and 5000 grams (6.6 to 11 pounds) (Rees et al., 1996). Several different labels are used to describe infants whose weight falls below this optimum range. All babies below 2500 grams (5.5 pounds) are described with the most general term of **low birth weight (LBW).** Those below 1500 grams (3.3 pounds) are usually called **very low birth weight,** while those below 1000 grams (2.2 pounds) are called **extremely low birth weight.**

The incidence of low birth weight has declined in the United States in the past decade but is still high: In 1996, 7.4 percent of all newborns were below 2500 grams—a total of about 290,000 infants nationwide (Guyer et al., 1997). About 19 percent of those small babies weighed less than 1500 grams.

Low birth weight is considerably more common among blacks than among either whites or Latinos in the United States. In 1996, the respective rates were 13.0 percent, 6.3 percent, and 6.2 percent (Guyer et al., 1997). (Interestingly, this black/white difference in low birth weight apparently does *not* exist in Cuba [Hogue & Hargraves, 1993].)

Low birth weight occurs for a variety of reasons, of which the most obvious and common is that the infant is born before the full 38 weeks of gestation. Any baby born before 38 weeks of gestation is labeled **preterm.** It is also possible for an infant to have completed the full 38-week gestational period but still weigh less than 2500 grams, or to weigh less than would be expected for the number of weeks of gestation completed, however long that may have been. Such an infant is called **small for date.** Infants in this group appear to have suffered from prenatal malnutrition, such as might occur with constriction of blood flow caused by the mother's smoking, or from other significant problems prenatally. Such infants generally have poorer prognoses than do equivalent-weight infants who weigh an appropriate amount for their gestational age, especially if the small-for-date infant is also preterm (Korkman et al., 1996; Ott, 1995).

All low-birth-weight infants share some characteristics, including markedly lower levels of responsiveness at birth and in the early months of life. Those born more than 6 weeks before term also often suffer from **respiratory distress syndrome.** Their poorly developed lungs lack an important chemical, called *surfactant,* that enables the air sacs to remain inflated; some of the sacs collapse, resulting in serious breathing difficulties. Beginning in 1990, neonatologists began treating this problem by administering a synthetic or animal-derived version of surfactant, a therapy that has reduced the rate of death among very low-birth-weight infants by about 30 percent (Hamvas et al., 1996; Schwartz et al., 1994).

About 80 percent of all low-birth-weight infants now survive long enough to leave the hospital, but the lower the birth weight, the greater the risk of neonatal death. This pattern is especially clear in Figure 3.4 (p. 80), which shows the results from a study of 1765 very low-birth-weight infants born in seven different hospitals around the United States (Hack et al., 1991). The limit of viability is about 500 to 600 grams or about 23 weeks of gestation. Babies born before 23 weeks rarely survive, even with aggressive neonatal care; those born at 24 weeks have better than a 50 percent survival rate (e.g., Allen et al., 1993; La Pine et al., 1995).

Some of these very tiny babies who do survive will have major, continuing developmental problems. Yet some will not. Although we do not yet know all the factors that predict such long-term problems among low-birth-weight infants, a few elements are clear, of which the infant's weight itself is the most significant.

The great majority of those above 1500 grams who are not small for date catch up to their normal peers within the first few years of life. Those below 1500 grams, however, especially those below 1000, have significantly higher rates of long-term problems, including neurological impairment, lower IQ scores, smaller size, and greater problems in school (Breslau et al., 1994; Hack et al., 1994; Koller et al., 1997; O'Shea et al., 1997; Saigal et al., 1991). You can get a better sense of both the type and incidence of such problems from the data in Table 3.1 (p. 80), which lists the results for two studies, one from the United States and the other from Australia.

Two points are worth making about the findings from follow-up studies like those shown in the table. First, some problems do not appear until school age, when the child is challenged by a new level of cognitive tasks. Many surviving LBW children who appear to be developing normally at age 1 or 2 later show significant problems in school. More optimistically, even in the extremely low-birth-weight group, some children seem

Critical Thinking

If you were given the job of designing a program that would drastically reduce the incidence of low-birth-weight infants, what would you do, given what you have read here and in Chapter 2? Where and how would you target your efforts?

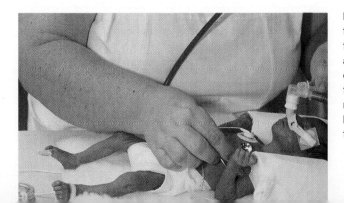

Low-birth-weight infants like this one are not only small; they are also more wrinkled and skinny because the layer of fat under the skin has not fully developed. They are also more likely to have significant breathing difficulties because their lungs lack surfactant.

Figure 3.4

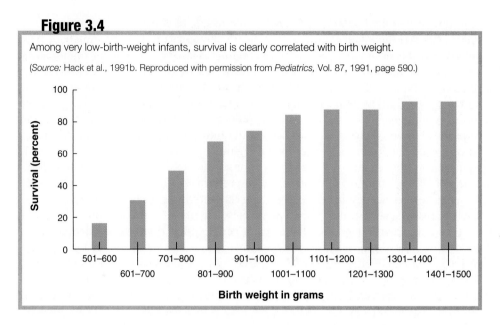

Among very low-birth-weight infants, survival is clearly correlated with birth weight.

(*Source:* Hack et al., 1991b. Reproduced with permission from *Pediatrics,* Vol. 87, 1991, page 590.)

to be fine. So it is not the case that *all* LBW children are *somewhat* affected; rather, *some* LBW children are significantly affected while others develop normally.

Another ingredient in the predictive equation is the quality of care available to the infant (Bendersky & Lewis, 1994). Because medical advances in the care of LBW infants have been enormous in the past few decades, the more recently such a baby was born, the better the long-term prognosis seems to be (Perlman et al., 1995). One piece of good news is that we do now know something about treatments that seem to improve the

Table 3.1

Two Examples of Long-Term Outcomes for Very Low-Birth-Weight Infants

	Australian Study[a]	United States Study[b]	
	500–999 g	< 750 g	750–1500 g
Number of babies followed	89	68	65
Age at testing	8 years	7 years	7 years
Percentage with severe problems of some type (IQ scores below 70, deaf, blind, cerebral-palsied, etc.)	21.3	37.5	17.5
Additional percentage with significant learning problem or IQ scores between 70 and 85	19.1	29.0	20.0

[a]Victorian Infant Collaborative Study Group, 1991. The study included all surviving children of 500–999 grams born in a single state (Victoria) in Australia between 1979 and 1980. A total of 351 infants were born in this weight range, so only a quarter survived. With today's medical techniques, survival rates might be higher.

[b]Hack et al., 1994. The study includes the 68 survivors of a group of 243 children born in an area in Ohio from 1982 to 1986 with birth weights below 750 grams, plus a comparison group born in the same period who weighed between 750 and 1500 grams at birth.

long-term chances of good functioning for LBW infants. Babies provided with special kinds of rhythmic stimulation while still in the hospital, such as water beds, rocking beds, heartbeat sounds, or body massage, are more alert, gain weight faster, and may even have higher IQs later than preterm babies receiving more typical hospital care (Barnard & Bee, 1983; Scafidi et al., 1990). And when special cognitive, emotional, and social supports are provided to such infants and to their families—such as helping the mothers to learn better skills for interaction with their babies or providing stimulating day care for the infants—the infants have a better chance of developing normally (Brooks-Gunn et al., 1993a; Spiker et al., 1993).

Assessing the Newborn

It has become customary in most hospitals to evaluate an infant's status immediately after birth, and then again five minutes later, to detect any problems that may require special care. The most frequently used assessment system is the **Apgar score,** developed by a physician, Virginia Apgar (1953). The newborn is given a score of 0, 1, or 2 on each of the five criteria listed in Table 3.2. A maximum score of 10 is fairly unusual immediately after birth because most infants are still somewhat blue in the fingers and toes at that stage. At the five-minute assessment, however, 85 to 90 percent of infants are scored as 9 or 10, meaning that they are getting off to a good start. Any score of 7 or better indicates that the baby is in no danger. A score of 4, 5, or 6 usually means that the baby needs help establishing normal breathing patterns; a score of 3 or below indicates a baby in critical condition, requiring active intervention, although babies with such low Apgar scores can and often do survive. Given a sufficiently supportive environment, most babies with low Apgar scores at birth will develop normally (Breitmayer & Ramey, 1986).

Another test used to assess newborns, widely used by researchers, is the *Brazelton Neonatal Behavioral Assessment Scale* (Brazelton, 1984). In this test, a skilled examiner checks the neonate's responses to a variety of stimuli; her reflexes, muscle tone, alertness, and cuddliness; and her ability to quiet or soothe herself after being upset. Scores on this test can be helpful in identifying children who may have significant neurological problems. More interestingly, several investigators have found that teaching *parents*

Table 3.2

Evaluation Method for Apgar Score

Aspect of Infant Observed	Score Assigned		
	0	**1**	**2**
Heart rate	Absent	< 100/min.	> 100/min.
Respiratory rate	No breathing	Weak cry and shallow breathing	Good strong cry and regular breathing
Muscle tone	Flaccid	Some flexion of extremities	Well flexed
Response to stimulation of feet	None	Some motion	Cry
Color	Blue; pale	Body pink, extremities blue	Completely pink

Source: Francis et al., 1987, pp. 731–732.

how to administer this test to their own infant turns out to have beneficial effects on the parent-infant interaction, apparently because it heightens the parent's awareness of all the subtle cues the baby provides (e.g., Francis et al., 1987).

Adapting to the Newborn

Learning those subtle cues is one of the several adaptational tasks facing parents of infants. For most adults, the role of parent brings profound satisfaction, a greater sense of purpose and self-worth, and a feeling of being grown up. It may also bring a sense of shared joy between husband and wife (Umberson & Gove, 1989). At the same time, the birth of the first child signals a whole series of changes in parents' lives, not all of which are absorbed without strain. Mark Bornstein offers a particularly clear description of the process:

> By their very coming into existence, infants forever alter the sleeping, eating, and working habits of their parents; they change who parents are and how parents define themselves. Infants keep parents up late into the night or cause them to abandon late nights to accommodate early waking; they require parents to give up a rewarding career to care for them or take a second job to support them; they lead parents to make new circles of friends with others in similar situations and sometimes cause parents to lose or abandon old friends who are not parents. . . . Parenting an infant is a 168-hour-a-week job, whether by the parents themselves or by a surrogate who is on call, because the human infant is totally dependent on parents for survival. (1995, pp. 3–4)

One common consequence of all these changes and new demands is that marital satisfaction typically goes down in the first months and years after the first child is born (Glenn, 1990). Individuals and couples report a sense of strain made up partly of fatigue and partly of a feeling that there is too much to cope with, anxiety about not knowing how best to care for the child, and a strong sense of loss of time and intimacy in the marriage relationship itself (Feldman, 1987). In longitudinal studies in which couples have been observed or interviewed during pregnancy and then again in the months after the first child's birth, spouses typically report fewer expressions of love, fewer positive actions designed to maintain or support the relationship, and more expressions of ambivalence after the child's birth than before (Belsky et al., 1985). Such strains and reduced satisfaction are less noticeable when the child was planned rather than unplanned and among those couples whose marriage was strong and stable before the birth of the child. But virtually all couples experience some strain.

The Newborn: What Can He Do?

Who is this small stranger who brings both joy and strain? What qualities and skills does the newborn bring to this new interactive process? He cries, breathes, looks

The advent of a new baby—especially a first child—is one of those richly ambivalent times for many adults: They are delighted and proud, and yet they also typically feel increased strain.

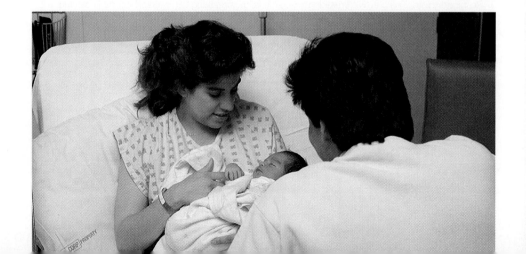

The Real World
Postpartum Depression

An added difficulty for many women after the birth of a child is a period of depressed mood in the first few days or weeks after delivery, often called the "maternity blues" or "postpartum blues." Estimates vary, but Western studies suggest that something between one-half and three-quarters of all women go through such an emotionally low period marked by frequent bouts of crying or feeling unexpectedly "down" in mood (Corter & Fleming, 1995). Most women pass through this depression in a few days and then return to a more positive and stable mood state. For 10 to 15 percent of women, however, this depressed state following delivery is deeper and more lasting (O'Hara, 1997). In these cases, physicians and psychologists label the condition a **postpartum depression** and consider it to be part of the broader category of *clinical depression.*

Clinicians use the phrase *clinical depression* to describe more than just the blues, although sadness or persisting low mood is one of the critical ingredients. To be diagnosed as suffering from a clinical depression, including postpartum depression, a person must also show at least half of the following additional symptoms: poor appetite, sleep disturbances (inability to sleep or excessive sleep), loss of pleasure in everyday activities, feelings of worthlessness, complaints of diminished ability to think or concentrate, or recurrent thoughts of death or suicide.

You can see from this description that such a depressive episode is not a trivial experience, so the fact that as many as 15 percent of women experience such feelings after the birth of a child is striking—although it is worth noting that rates of clinical depression are high among women in general, whether they have just given birth or not, so it is difficult to know what percentage of the depression we see in postpartum women is causally connected with giving birth (O'Hara, 1997). What appears to distinguish a postpartum depression from other types of clinical depression is that it is normally of shorter duration. Six to eight weeks seems to be the typical length, after which the woman gradually recovers her normal mood, although for perhaps 1 or 2 percent of women the depression persists for a year or longer.

The origins of these depressive episodes are not totally clear. Some new research points to the possibility that the radical changes of hormone patterns associated with pregnancy and delivery play a key role, but the findings are quite inconsistent (O'Hara, 1997). More consistently linked to postpartum depression is the presence of particularly stressful life events during pregnancy and after delivery, such as unemployment or a serious illness in a family member. Postnatal depression is also more common in women who did not plan their pregnancy, who were high in anxiety during the pregnancy, or whose partner is not supportive of them or is displeased with the arrival of the child (Campbell et al., 1992; O'Hara, 1997).

Understandably, mothers who are in the midst of a significant postpartum depression interact differently with their infants than do mothers whose mood is more normal. Based on detailed analysis of videotaped interactions between depressed (and nondepressed) mothers and their infants, Edward Tronick and his colleagues (e.g., Tronick & Weinberg, 1997) find that depressed mothers show either a withdrawn/disengaged/emotionally flat pattern of interacting with their infants or an intrusive pattern in which they handle the baby roughly and speak in an angry tone of voice. Infants are understandably disrupted and distressed by both these styles of interaction, with the withdrawn pattern perhaps the more upsetting for the baby. The good news is that these disturbances in the mother's behavior with her child typically do *not* persist after the mother's depression lifts (e.g., Fleming et al., 1988). The not-so-good news is that a persisting maternal depression—whether it is labeled as a postpartum depression or some other variety of clinical depression—seems to have potentially lasting consequences for infants' cognitive and emotional development—at least for some children (Hay, 1997; Murray & Cooper, 1997).

I think it is quite common in our society to pass off a woman's postpartum depression as if it were a minor event, "just the blues." And of course for many women, it is. For a minority, however, the arrival of a child ushers in a much more significant depressive episode, requiring some kind of clinical intervention.

around a bit. But what else can he do in the early hours and days? On what skills does the infant build?

Reflexes

One important part of the infant's repertoire of behaviors is a large collection of **reflexes,** which are physical responses triggered involuntarily by specific stimuli. Some of these persist into adulthood, such as your automatic eyeblink when a puff of air hits

Moro reflex

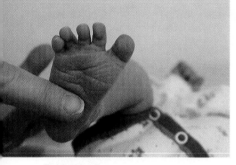

Babinski reflex

your eye or the involuntary narrowing of the pupil of your eye when you're in a bright light. Others, sometimes referred to as *adaptive reflexes,* are essential to the infant's survival but gradually disappear in the first year of life. Sucking and swallowing reflexes are prominent in this category, as is the **rooting reflex**—the automatic turn of the head toward any touch on the cheek, a reflex that helps the baby get the nipple into his mouth during nursing. These reflexes are no longer present in older infants or adults but are clearly highly adaptive for the newborn.

Finally, newborns have a large collection of **primitive reflexes,** so called because they are controlled by the more primitive parts of the brain, the medulla and the midbrain, both of which are close to being fully developed at birth. For example, if you make a loud noise or startle a baby in some other way, you'll see her throw her arms outward and arch her back, a pattern that is part of the **Moro reflex** (also called the *startle reflex*). Stroke the bottom of her foot and she will splay out her toes; this reaction is called the **Babinski reflex.**

These various primitive reflexes disappear over the first year of life (see Table 3.3), apparently superseded by the action of the cortex, which by this age is much more fully developed. Yet, even though these reflexes represent neurologically primitive patterns, they are nonetheless linked to important later behavior patterns. The tonic neck reflex (described in Table 3.3), for example, forms the foundation for the baby's later ability to reach for objects because it focuses the baby's attention on the hand; the grasp reflex, too, is linked to the later ability to hold onto objects.

In a similar way, the walking reflex may be linked to later voluntary walking. In an early study, Zelazo and his colleagues (1972) stimulated the walking reflex repeatedly in some babies every day from the second to the eighth week after birth. By 8 weeks, these stimulated babies showed many more steps per minute when they were held in the walking position than did nonstimulated babies. And at the end of the first year, these stimulated babies learned to walk alone about a month sooner than did comparison babies who had not had their walking reflex stimulated. Esther Thelen, one of the experts on early motor development, points out that to be able to walk, an infant has to have enough muscle strength in his legs to move his legs in a walking movement (1983). Very young infants are light enough to manage such movement, but then they gain weight quickly without an equivalent gain in muscle strength. Only late in the first year do the child's weight and leg muscle strength again come into the appropriate balance. The babies in Zelazo's experiment, however, gained added muscle strength in the early weeks because their legs were exercised—just as you gain muscle strength if you begin a program of regular exercise. According to Thelen, these babies were then able to reach the right balance of weight and strength a bit sooner than normal.

Thus, primitive reflexes are not just curiosities or remnants from our evolutionary past. They can be informative, as when a baby fails to show a reflex that ought to be there or displays a reflex past the point at which it normally disappears. For example, narcotics-exposed infants, or those suffering from anoxia at birth, may show only very weak reflexes; Down syndrome infants have only very weak Moro reflexes and sometimes have poor sucking reflexes. When a primitive reflex persists past the normal point, it may suggest some neurological damage or dysfunction. Reflexes are also the starting point for many important physical skills, including reaching, grasping, and walking.

Perceptual Skills: What the Newborn Sees, Hears, and Feels

Babies also come equipped with a surprisingly mature set of perceptual skills. I'll be describing the development of those skills in Chapter 5; all I want to do here is to give you some sense of the starting point. The newborn can:

Table 3.3

Examples of Primitive and Adaptive Reflexes

Reflex	Stimulation	Response	Developmental Pattern
Tonic neck	While baby is on his back and awake, turn his head to one side.	Baby assumes a "fencing" posture, with arm extended on the side toward which the head is turned.	Fades by 4 months.
Grasping	Stroke the baby's palm with your finger.	Baby will make a strong fist around your finger.	Fades by 3 to 4 months.
Moro	Make a loud sound near the baby, or let the baby "drop" slightly and suddenly.	Baby extends legs, arms, and fingers; arches his back; and draws back his head.	Fades by about 6 months.
Walking	Hold baby under arms with feet just touching a floor or other flat surface.	Baby will make step-like motions, alternating feet as in walking.	Fades by about 8 weeks in most infants.
Babinski	Stroke sole of the baby's foot from toes toward heel.	Baby will fan out his toes.	Fades between 8 and 12 months.
Rooting	Stroke baby's cheek with finger or nipple.	Baby turns head toward the touch, opens mouth, and makes sucking movements.	After 3 weeks, is transformed into a voluntary head-turning response.

- Focus both eyes on the same spot, with 8 to 10 inches being the best focal distance. Within a few weeks the baby can follow a moving object with his eyes—although not yet very efficiently—and he can discriminate his mother's face from other faces almost immediately.

- Easily hear sounds within the pitch and loudness range of the human voice; roughly locate objects by their sounds; discriminate some individual voices, particularly the mother's voice.

- Taste the four basic tastes (sweet, sour, bitter, and salty) and identify familiar body odors, including discriminating the mother's smell from the smell of a strange woman.

Brief as this summary is, several points nonetheless stand out. First of all, newborns' perceptual skills are a great deal better than most parents believe—better than most psychologists or physicians believed until a few years ago. The better our research techniques have become, the more we have understood just how skillful the newborn baby really is—important evidence for the significance of "nature" in the nature-nurture interaction.

Even more striking is how well adapted the baby's perceptual skills are for the interactions he will have with the people in his world. He hears best in the range of the human voice, and he can discriminate his mother (or other regular caregiver) from others on the basis of smell, sight, or sound almost immediately. The distance at which he can focus his eyes best, about 8 to 10 inches, is approximately the distance between the infant's eyes and the mother's face during nursing.

You'll see in Chapter 5 that there is a long way to go in the development of sophisticated perceptual abilities, but the newborn begins life able to make key discriminations and to locate objects through various perceptual cues.

Newborns are quite nearsighted, but they can focus very well at a distance of about 8 to 10 inches—just about the distance between 2-week-old Christian's eyes and his father's face when Dad holds him to give him a bottle.

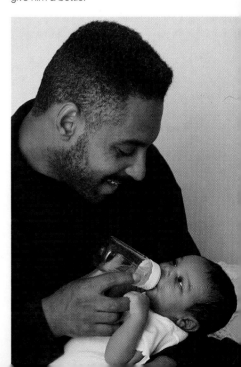

Motor Skills: Moving Around

While the new baby's perceptual skills may be unexpectedly impressive, her motor skills certainly are not. She can't hold up her head; she can't coordinate her looking and her reaching yet; she can't roll over or sit up. These skills emerge only gradually in the early weeks. By 1 month, the baby can hold her chin up off the floor or mattress. By 2 months, she can hold her head steady while she's being held and is beginning to swipe at objects near her with her hands.

These improving motor skills follow two broad patterns: Development proceeds from the head downward, called **cephalocaudal,** and from the trunk outward, called **proximodistal**—patterns originally identified by Gesell. Thus, the baby can hold up his head before he can sit or roll over and can sit before he can crawl.

Another interesting feature of young babies' motor skills is how repetitively they perform their limited range of movements. They kick, rock, wave, bounce, bang, rub, scratch, or sway repeatedly and rhythmically. These repeated patterns become particularly prominent at about 6 or 7 months of age, although you can see some such behavior even in the first weeks, particularly in finger movements and leg kicking. These movements do not seem to be totally voluntary or coordinated, but they also do not appear to be random. For instance, Esther Thelen (1981) has observed that kicking movements peak just before the baby begins to crawl, as if the rhythmic kicking were a part of the preparation for crawling. Thelen's work has helped us see the patterns and order in the apparently random movements of the young infant, but even this understanding does not alter the fact that, by contrast with perceptual abilities, the baby's initial motor abilities are quite limited.

Learning and Habituation

It seems obvious that maturation must play a vital role in these early developmental processes. The body systems and parts of the nervous system required for many perceptual skills are largely complete at birth, while those needed for motor control are not.

But is maturation the only process involved? Can a newborn also learn from her experiences? From a theoretical perspective, this question is obviously crucial for understanding the relative influences of nature and nurture. From a practical point of view, the same question is also important because the answer affects the sort of advice parents may be given about appropriate toys or stimulation for their child. For example, if a child's perceptual abilities develop largely through maturation rather than learning, then it doesn't make much sense to buy expensive mobiles to hang above the baby's crib. On the other hand, if learning is possible from the earliest days of life, then various kinds of enrichment make much more sense.

What does the evidence tell us?

Classical Conditioning. The bulk of the research suggests that the newborn can be classically conditioned, although it is difficult. It is most likely to be successful when the conditioning relates to feeding in some way, perhaps because these responses are so critical for the infant's survival. As one example, Elliott Blass and his colleagues (1984)

Young Lucy was 5 months old when this photo was taken, showing her "airplaning." You can see that by this age, she is able to hold not just her head but part of her chest off the ground—a big advance over the motor skills we see in newborns.

gave 1- to 2-day-old infants sugar water in a bottle (the unconditional stimulus), which prompted sucking (the unconditioned response). Then, just before the sugar water was given, the babies' foreheads were stroked (the conditional stimulus). After several such repetitions, the experimenters stroked the infants' foreheads without giving the sugar water to see if the infants would begin sucking—which they did, thus showing classical conditioning.

By 3 or 4 weeks of age, classical conditioning is no longer difficult to establish; it occurs easily with many different responses. In particular, this means that the conditioned emotional responses I talked about in Chapter 1 may begin to develop as early as the first week of life. Thus, the mere presence of Mom or Dad or another favored person may trigger the sense of "feeling good," a pattern that may contribute to what we see later as the child's attachment to the parent.

Operant Conditioning. Newborns also clearly learn by operant conditioning. Both the sucking response and head turning have been successfully increased by the use of reinforcements, such as sweet-tasting liquids or the sound of the mother's voice or heartbeat (Moon & Fifer, 1990). At the least, the fact that conditioning of this kind can take place means that whatever neurological wiring is needed for learning to occur is present at birth. Results like this also tell us something about the sorts of reinforcements that are effective with very young children. It is surely highly significant for the whole process of mother-infant interaction that the mother's voice is an effective reinforcer for virtually all babies.

Schematic Learning. The fact that babies can recognize voices and heartbeats in the first days of life is also important because it suggests that another kind of learning is going on as well. This third type of learning, sometimes referred to as **schematic learning,** draws both its name and many of its conceptual roots from Piaget's theory. The basic idea is that from the beginning the baby organizes her experiences into expectancies, into "known" combinations. These expectancies, often called *schemas,* are built up over many exposures to particular experiences but thereafter help the baby to distinguish between the familiar and the unfamiliar. Carolyn Rovee-Collier (1986) has suggested that we might think of classical conditioning in infants as being a variety of schematic learning. When a baby begins to move her head as if to search for the nipple as soon as she hears her mother's footsteps coming into the room, this is not just some kind of automatic classical conditioning, but the beginning of the development of expectancies. From the earliest weeks, the baby seems to begin to make connections between events in her world, such as the link between the sound of her mother's footsteps and the feeling of being picked up, or between the touch of the breast and the feeling of a full stomach. Thus, early classical conditioning may be the beginnings of the process of cognitive development.

Habituation. A related concept is that of **habituation.** Habituation is the automatic reduction in the strength or vigor of a response to a repeated stimulus. For example: Suppose you live on a fairly noisy street so that the sound of cars going by is repeated over and over during each day. After a while, you not only don't react to the sound, you quite literally *do not perceive it as being as loud.* The ability to do this—to dampen down the intensity of a physical response to some repeated stimulus—is obviously vital in our everyday lives. If we reacted constantly to every sight and sound and smell that came along, we'd spend all our time responding to these repeated events, and we wouldn't have energy or attention left over for things that are new and deserve attention.

The ability to *dishabituate* is equally important. When a habituated stimulus changes in some way, such as a sudden extra-loud screech of tires on the busy street by your house, you again respond fully. Thus, the reemergence of the original response strength is a sign that the perceiver—infant, child, or adult—notices some significant change.

A rudimentary capacity to habituate and to dishabituate is built in at birth in human babies, just as it is in other species. By 10 weeks of age, this ability is well developed. An infant will stop looking at something you keep putting in front of her face; she

Critical Thinking

Can you think of other examples of classically conditioned emotional responses that might develop in early infancy? What about negative emotions?

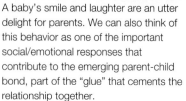

A baby's smile and laughter are an utter delight for parents. We can also think of this behavior as one of the important social/emotional responses that contribute to the emerging parent-child bond, part of the "glue" that cements the relationship together.

will stop showing a startle reaction (Moro reflex) to loud sounds after the first few presentations but will again startle if the sound is changed; she will stop turning her head toward a repeating sound (Swain et al., 1993). Such habituation itself is not a voluntary process; it is entirely automatic. Yet in order for it to work, the newborn must be equipped with the capacity to "recognize" familiar experiences. That is, she must have, or must develop, schemas of some kind.

The existence of these processes in the newborn has an added benefit for researchers: It has enabled them to figure out what an infant responds to as "the same" or "different." If a baby is habituated to some stimulus, such as a sound or a specific picture, the experimenter can then present slight variations on the original stimulus to see the point at which dishabituation occurs. In this way, researchers have begun to get a picture of how the newborn baby or young infant experiences the world around him— a point I'll come back to in Chapter 5.

Social Skills

All the skills of the newborn I have described so far are important for the baby's comfort and survival, but human newborns, unlike those in many other species, are a very long way from being independent. If they are to survive, someone must provide consistent care over an extended period. So the infant's capacity to entice others into the caregiving role is critical. It is here that the "social" skills of infants come into play.

The newborn doesn't have a lot of obvious social abilities. He doesn't talk. He doesn't flirt. He smiles, but not often during the first weeks. Normal newborns nonetheless have a collection of behaviors that are remarkably effective for attracting and keeping the attention of adults, including crying, cuddling, and soothing in response to the parents' caregiving efforts. The converse is also true, as I pointed out in talking about the baby's perceptual abilities: Adult faces and voices are remarkably effective for attracting and keeping the baby's attention too. It would seem from all this that the adult and the baby are programmed from the beginning to join in a crucial social "dance," one that forms the root of the developing relationship between parent and child and that is critical for the formation of the parent's bond to the child.

Because they can't yet talk or move around much, young infants make social connections primarily through their expression of emotion—crying, smiling, or looking surprised, unhappy, or pleased. Parents use these emotional expressions as clues to adapt their own behavior to the baby's, thus creating a mutually responsive social system.

The Emergence of Emotional Expression. There is really no way to know just what emotion a baby actually *feels*. The best we can do is to try to judge what emotion a baby appears to *express* through body and face. Researchers have done this by confronting babies with various kinds of events likely to prompt emotions, photographing or videotaping those encounters, and then asking adult judges to say which emotion the baby's face expresses (Izard & Harris, 1995; Izard & Malatesta, 1987; Izard et al., 1995).

Table 3.4 summarizes the current wisdom about the ages at which various important emotional expressions first appear. As you can see, some rudimentary emotional expressions are visible at birth, including a sort of "half smile" that delights parents even though they cannot figure out how to elicit it consistently. Within a few weeks, though, babies begin to show a full social smile. Happily, one of the earliest triggers for this wonderful baby smile is the kind of high-pitched voice we all seem to use naturally with infants. So adults seem to be preprogrammed to behave in just the ways that babies will respond to positively. Within a few weeks, babies will also smile in response to a smiling face, especially a familiar face.

Within a few months, babies' emotional expressions differentiate even further, so that they express sadness, anger, and surprise. Four-month-olds also begin to laugh— and there are few things in life more delightful than the sound of a giggling or laughing baby! Fear appears as a discrete emotional expression only at about 7 months.

Table 3.4

The Emergence of Emotional Expressions in Infancy and Toddlerhood

Age	Emotion Expressed	Examples of Stimuli That Trigger That Expression
At birth	Interest	Novelty or movement
	Distress	Pain
	Disgust	Offensive substances
	Neonatal smile (a "half smile")	Appears spontaneously for no known reason
3 to 6 weeks	Pleasure/social smile (precursor to joy)	High-pitched human voice; clapping the baby's hands together; hearing a familiar voice; a nodding face
2 to 3 months	Sadness	Painful medical procedure
	Wariness (precursor to fear)	A stranger's face
	Frustration (precursor to anger)	Being restrained; being prevented from performing some established action
	Surprise	Jack-in-the-box
7 months	Fear	Extreme novelty; heights (such as in the visual cliff experiment)
	Anger	Failure or interruption of some attempted action, such as reaching for a ball that has rolled under a couch
	Joy	Immediate delighted response to an experience with positive meaning, such as the caregiver's arrival, or in peekaboo

Sources: Izard & Malatesta, 1987; Mascolo & Fischer, 1995; Sroufe, 1996.

Over these early months, babies' emotional expressions become increasingly responsive to the emotions they see their parents express. The baby's social smile, for example, appears more and more often in response to the parent's own smile or pleasure. Similarly, babies whose parents are depressed show more sad and angry facial expression and fewer expressions of interest, a pattern detectable as early as 3 or 4 months of age (Field, 1995). Indeed, Tiffany Field's research suggests that babies of depressed mothers may actually learn *not* to express interest or delight; instead, they learn to display a kind of depressed look, something they show with strangers as well as with their depressed Moms. Thus, even as early as the first months of life, the expression of emotion is a reciprocal process; infants not only respond to adult emotional expression, they seem to adapt their expressions to match or fit with the adult's typical pattern.

Taking Turns. Yet another social skill the baby brings to the interaction is the ability to take turns. As adults, we take turns all the time, most clearly in conversations and eye contacts. In fact, it's very difficult to have any kind of social encounter with someone who does *not* take turns. Kenneth Kaye (1982) argues that the beginnings of this "turn taking" can be seen in very young infants in their eating patterns. As early as the first days of life, the baby sucks in a "burst-pause" pattern. He sucks for a while, pauses, sucks for a while, pauses, and so on. Mothers enter into this process, such as by jiggling the baby during the pauses, thus creating an alternating pattern: Suck, pause, jiggle, pause, suck, pause, jiggle, pause. The rhythm of the interaction is really very much like a conversation. To be sure, we cannot be certain whether this conversational quality of very early interaction occurs because the adult figures out the baby's natural rhythm and adapts her own responses to the baby's timing, or whether some mutual adaptation is going on. Nonetheless, it is extremely intriguing that we can see this apparent turn taking in an infant 1 day old.

The Daily Life of Infants

Parents are obviously interested in the various skills and capacities of the newborn infant. They are delighted with his smiles and with each new ability as it emerges. For most parents, however, the real questions are more practical: What is it like to live with a newborn? How is the infant's day organized? What sort of natural rhythms occur in the daily cycles?

Researchers who have studied newborns have described five different states of sleep and wakefulness in infants, summarized in Table 3.5. Of these states, the least common in the newborn are the two awake states. At first, babies are awake and not fussing only about two to three hours each day.

The five main states tend to occur in cycles, just as your own states occur in a daily rhythm. Most infants move from deep sleep to lighter sleep to fussing and hunger and then to a brief period of alert wakefulness, after which they become drowsy and drop back into deep sleep. In the newborn, this cycle repeats itself about every 1½ to 2 hours: Sleep, cry, eat, look; sleep, cry, eat, look. Because the first three parts of this repeating pattern—sleeping, crying, and eating—are so crucial for parents, let me say just a word more about each.

Sleeping

Newborns sleep about two-thirds of the time, as you can see in Figure 3.5, which shows the average nighttime and daytime sleep for a sample of U.S. babies at each of various ages. You can see that newborns sleep as much in the day as at night, but within a few weeks, daytime sleep begins to drop and we see signs of day/night sleep rhythms (called *circadian rhythms*)—at least among infants in Western countries, where regular sleep/wake cycles are more highly valued. Babies this age begin to string two or three two-hour cycles together without coming to full wakefulness, at which point we say that the baby can "sleep through the night" (Needlman, 1996; Whitney & Thoman, 1994).

Figure 3.5 gives the average figures, but of course babies vary a lot around these norms. Of the 6-week-old babies in one study, there was one who slept 22 hours a day

Table 3.5

The Basic States of Infant Sleep and Wakefulness

State	Characteristics
Deep sleep	Eyes closed, regular breathing, no movement except occasional startles
Active sleep	Eyes closed, irregular breathing, small twitches, no gross body movement
Quiet awake	Eyes open, no major body movement, regular breathing
Active awake	Eyes open, with movements of the head, limbs, and trunk; irregular breathing
Crying and fussing	Eyes may be partly or entirely closed; vigorous diffuse movement with crying or fussing sounds

Sources: Based on the work of Prechtl & Beintema, 1964; Hutt et al., 1969; Parmelee et al., 1964.

Figure 3.5

The total amount of sleep infants need, and the number of daytime naps they take, typically decline over the first two years of life.

(*Source*: Reprinted with the permission of Simon & Schuster from *How to Solve Your Child's Sleep Problems*, Fig. 1, p. 19, by Richard Ferber and Rick Boyer. Copyright © 1985 by Richard Ferber, M.D.)

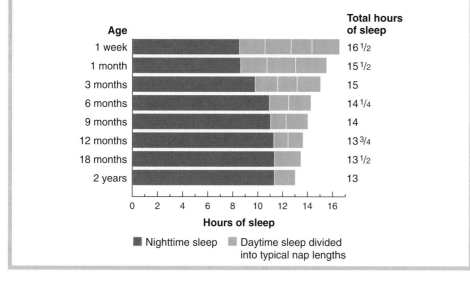

and another who slept only 8.8 hours a day (Bamford et al., 1990). (Now there must be one tired set of parents!) And some babies, even in Western cultures, do not develop a long unbroken nighttime sleep period until late in the first year of life.

All these aspects of the baby's sleep pattern have implications for the emerging parent-infant interaction—as does the place the baby sleeps, a point I've explored in the Cultures and Contexts box on page 92. Psychologists have also been interested in sleep patterns because marked irregularity of sleep patterns may be a symptom of some disorder or problem. For example, some babies born to mothers who used cocaine during pregnancy have difficulty establishing a regular pattern of sleeping and waking. Brain-damaged infants often have the same kind of difficulties, so any time an infant fails to develop clear sleep/waking regularity, it *may* be a sign of trouble.

Crying

Newborns actually cry less than you might think. One researcher studying normal newborns found that they cried from 2 to 11 percent of the time (Korner et al., 1981). This percentage frequently increases over the first few weeks, peaking at 2 to 3 hours of crying a day at 6 weeks and then dropping off to less than 1 hour a day by 3 months (Needlman, 1996). Such a peak in crying at 6 weeks has been observed in infants from a number of different cultures, including cultures in which mothers have almost constant body contact with the infant (St. James-Roberts et al., 1994), suggesting that this crying pattern is not unique to the United States or other Western cultures. Initially, infants cry most in the evening; later, their most intense crying occurs just before feedings.

The basic function of the child's cry, obviously, is to signal need. Because babies can't move *to* someone, they have to *bring* someone to them, and crying is the main way they have to attract attention. In fact, infants have a whole repertoire of cry sounds, with different cries for pain, anger, or hunger. The anger cry, for example, is typically louder and more intense, and the pain cry normally has a very abrupt onset—unlike the more basic kinds of hunger or distress cries, which usually begin with whimpering or moaning. However, not all infants cry in precisely the same way. Some, as you can see

Critical Thinking

The obvious explanation of the mother's greater ability to discriminate among the different cries of her baby is that she spends more time in caregiving than does the father. What kind of study could you design to test this hypothesis?

in the Research Report (opposite) have particularly piercing or grating cries, a pattern that may be diagnostic of an underlying problem of some sort. In the end, each parent learns the sounds of her (or his) own baby. Alen Wiesenfeld and his colleagues (1981) found that mothers (but not fathers) of 5-month-olds could discriminate between taped episodes of anger and pain cries in their own babies, while neither parent could reliably make the same discrimination with the taped cries of another baby.

Colic. Fifteen to 20 percent of infants develop a pattern called **colic,** which involves intense daily bouts of crying totaling more than 3 hours a day. The crying is generally worst in late afternoon or early evening—a particularly inopportune time for parents, of course, because that is just the time when they are tired and needing time with one another. Colic typically appears at about 2 weeks of age and then disappears spontaneously at 3 or 4 months of age. Neither psychologists nor physicians are sure why colic begins, or why it stops without any intervention. Two favorite theories are that colic arises because of (1) a reaction to a specific diet, such as an allergy to cow's milk in formula or to specific foods eaten by a nursing mother, including cow's milk drunk by the mother; or (2) an anxious new parent with a temperamentally difficult or unadaptable infant. Unfortunately, treatments based on these two explanatory hypotheses have not proved to be consistently effective, and the underlying cause remains unclear (e.g., Hill, 1995; Lust et al., 1996; Wolke et al., 1994). There is no doubt that colic is a difficult pattern to live with, but the good news is that it *does* go away, even without any specific intervention.

Responding to Infant Cries. One of the enduring practical questions for parents about a baby's crying is how they should respond to it. If they pick up the baby right away, every time he cries, will that simply reinforce the baby's crying so that he will cry

Cultures and Contexts
Sleeping Arrangements for Infants

When we look at typical infant sleeping arrangements around the world, we find a wonderful example of the contrast between collectivist and individualist cultures, as well as an illustration of how unaware we often are of our own cultural assumptions.

In one edition of his *Baby and Child Care,* Dr. Spock said:

I think it is a sensible rule not to take a child into the parents' bed to sleep for any reason (even as a treat when one parent is away on a trip). . . . Children can sleep in a room by themselves from the time they are born, if convenient, as long as the parents are near enough to hear them when they cry. (Spock & Rothenberg, 1985, pp. 219–220)

Because you are very likely steeped in Euro-American culture, with its strong emphasis on separateness and individuality, you probably agree with Spock. Most of us see separate sleeping as "right" and "natural" and healthiest for children's psychological development (Morelli et al., 1992). Yet in the majority of cultures in the world (and in Western cultures until perhaps 200 years ago), babies sleep in the same bed with their parents, typically until they are weaned, a pattern often called *cosleeping.* Such

an arrangement has many supportive reasons, including lack of alternative space for the infant to sleep in some cases. More often, cosleeping seems to reflect a basic collectivist value, one in which contact and interdependence rather than separateness are emphasized (Harkness & Super, 1995). Morelli and her colleagues (1992) report that the Mayan mothers they interviewed, most of whom practice cosleeping, considered the U.S. practice of separate sleeping as tantamount to child neglect. They are shocked and disbelieving when told that U.S. infants often sleep in a separate room, with no one nearby.

Morelli also reports that bedtime among the Mayan families she studied was rarely a time of discord or difficulty between parent and child, as it so often is in Western families in which infants and toddlers sleep separately from the adults. Mayan children also rarely used stuffed animals or other "transitional objects" to comfort themselves as they fell asleep, while this is common among Western infants and toddlers. Thus, the cultural assumptions affect not only what we consider "normal" and "right" for children; they shape the interaction between parent and child, including the nature of their common disputes or struggles.

Research Report
Variations in Children's Cries

Parents have always known that some babies have cries that are particularly penetrating or grating; other babies seem to have much less noxious crying sounds. Researchers have confirmed this parental observation in a wide range of studies.

Many groups of babies with known medical abnormalities have different-sounding cries, including those with Down syndrome, encephalitis, meningitis, and many types of brain damage. In recent work, Barry Lester has extended this observation to babies who appear physically normal but are at risk for later problems because of some perinatal problem, such as preterm or small-for-date babies (1987; Lester & Dreher, 1989) or those whose mothers were heavy drinkers during pregnancy (Nugent et al., 1996). Such babies typically make crying sounds that are acoustically distinguishable from what you hear in a normal, low-risk baby. In particular, the cry of such higher-risk babies has a more grating, piercing quality. Interestingly, the cries of babies with colic also have some of these same qualities (Lester et al., 1992; Zeskind & Barr, 1997).

On the assumption that the baby's cry may reflect some basic aspect of neurological integrity, Lester also wondered whether one could use the quality of the cry as a *diagnostic* test. Among a group of high-risk babies, for example, could one predict later intellectual functioning from a measure of the gratingness or pitch of the baby's cry? The answer seems to be "yes." Lester found that among preterms, those with higher-pitched cries in the first days of life had lower scores on an IQ test at age 5 years (1987). The same kind of connection has also been found among both normal babies and those exposed to methadone prenatally. In all these groups, the higher the pitch and more grating the cry, the lower the child's later IQ or motor development (Huntington et al., 1990).

Eventually, it may be possible for physicians to use the presence of such a grating or piercing cry as a signal that there may be some underlying physical problem with the infant or as a way of making better guesses about the long-term outcomes for individual babies at high risk of later problems, such as low-birth-weight babies.

more? Or will such an immediate response reassure the child, building the child's expectation that the world is a safe and reliable place?

Ten years ago I was confident that I knew the answer to this question, namely, always to respond immediately. Results from early studies gave no indication that such immediate responding increased the child's crying, and there was a lot of evidence that predictable responding was one ingredient in the development of a secure attachment to the parent. More recent studies, though, make the answer less clear-cut. It now looks as if the parents' response may need to depend on the type of crying the child is doing. Intense crying, such as when the infant is hurt or significantly distressed—very hungry, very wet and uncomfortable, or the like—should be responded to immediately. Whimpering and milder crying, on the other hand, such as what a baby may do when she is put down for a nap, is another matter. When a parent responds immediately to all these milder cries, babies seem to learn to cry more often (Hubbard & van IJzendoorn, 1987). Thus, both reassurance and reinforcement seem to be involved, and it takes real sensitivity on the part of the parent to sort it out. The best rule of thumb seems to be that if you are not sure, pick up the baby when he cries.

Eating

Eating is not among the states listed in Table 3.5 (p. 90), but it is certainly something that newborn babies do frequently! Given that the baby's natural cycle seems to be about two hours long, a newborn may eat as many as 10 times a day. Gradually, the baby takes more and more milk at each feeding and doesn't have to eat so often. By 2 months the average number is down to about $5\frac{1}{2}$ feedings each day, dropping to about 3 feedings by age 8 to 12 months (Barness & Curran, 1996). Both breast-fed and bottle-fed babies eat at about the same frequency, but these two forms of feeding do differ in other important ways.

Breast- Versus Bottle-Feeding. Several decades of extensive research in many countries make it clear that breast-feeding is nutritionally superior to bottle-feeding. Breast milk provides the infant with important antibodies against many kinds of diseases, so breast-fed infants are much less likely to suffer from such problems as diarrhea, gastroenteritis, bronchitis, ear infections, and colic, and they are less likely to die in infancy (Barness & Curran, 1996; Beaudry et al., 1995; Golding et al., 1997a; 1997b; López-Alarcón et al., 1997). Breast milk also appears to promote the growth of nerves and the intestinal tract, to contribute to more rapid weight and size gain (Prentice, 1994), and to stimulate better immune system function (Pickering et al., 1998).

More speculatively, breast-feeding may also be linked to higher IQ at later ages. A number of investigators have found such a correlation (e.g., Lucas et al., 1992; Rogers, 1978), although interpreting the finding has been difficult because, on average, mothers who choose to breast-feed are better educated and have higher IQs than do mothers who choose not to breast-feed. These studies are thus quasi experiments in which it is extremely difficult to match the two groups on an obviously crucial variable. When investigators have attempted to control statistically for social class differences in quasi experiments of this type, they have found no residual link between breast-feeding and IQ (e.g., Gale & Martyn, 1996). However, at least one genuine experiment has now been done in which preterm infants were randomly assigned to groups that received either formula or donor breast milk (Lucas et al., 1994). The researchers report that the breast-fed infants had higher scores on measures of infant intellectual development, although longer-term follow-up tests of intelligence on these children are not yet available. This study strengthens the argument for a causal link between breast-feeding and more optimal intellectual development, but the question is far from settled.

Even if no intellectual benefit is ever confirmed, the health benefits of breast-feeding are clear and well established, leading the World Health Organization to recom-

Figure 3.6

Cultures and Contexts

Cultural and Social Class Differences in Patterns of Breast-Feeding, and Their Consequences

If you look at the incidence of breast-feeding in countries around the world over the past forty or fifty years, you'll find a common pattern. In each country, artificial feeding was first adopted by that society's elite, followed by the urban poor and then by the rural dwellers. Then a reversal, back toward breast-feeding, followed the same path, beginning with the educated middle class (World Health Organization, 1982). The United States and most Western countries began this entire cycle earlier than did most developing countries. Today, countries like Sweden, New Zealand, and the United States are on the rebound toward more breast-feeding, as are countries like Malaysia. For example, in Norway, in 1968 only 30 percent of 12-week-old infants were being breast-fed; in 1991 the rate was 80 percent (Endresen & Helsing, 1995). Similarly, in New Zealand, breast-feeding rates dropped from 80 percent in 1938 to 45 percent in 1968 but then rose to 80 percent in 1992 (Basire et al., 1997). Many developing countries, however, are still in the first phase, with declining rates of exclusive breast-feeding and earlier shifting to some combination of formula, solid food, and breast milk (e.g., Amador et al., 1994; Arnold & Larson, 1993; Mondal et al., 1996; Perez-Escamilla, 1994).

One contributor to the decline of breast-feeding in less industrialized countries appears to have been the marketing of infant formula. Manufacturers of formula often gave free samples or free feeding bottles to new mothers and assured women that formula was as good or better for babies, while frequently failing to provide adequate instruction on how formula should be used. Some women, knowing no better and faced with extreme economic hardship, diluted their infants' formula with water in order to make it stretch further. Sterilization procedures were also not well explained; for many women, proper sterilization was simply not feasible. Worldwide, the concern aroused by this change in normal feeding practices was sufficient to cause the World Health Organization to issue an "International Code of Marketing of Breast-milk Substitutes" in 1981. Marketing practices have since been modified. Yet the decline in breast-feeding has continued in many parts of the world (Stewart et al., 1991).

Such a decline is cause for real concern because bottle-fed babies or those who are weaned early from breast milk in developing or Third World countries are at far higher risk of serious disease or death. In Bangladesh, for example, the risk of death from diarrhea is 3 times higher among bottle-fed than among breast-fed babies; in Brazil, the risk of death from various kinds of infections ranges from $2\frac{1}{2}$ to 14 times higher among the bottle-fed. In all these studies, the risk associated with bottle-feeding is far higher where the sanitary conditions are poorest (Cunningham et al., 1991). Breast-feeding is thus better for two reasons: It provides the baby with needed antibodies against infection, and it is likely to expose the baby to less infection in the first place.

Patterns in the United States

In view of such findings, it is disturbing to note that in the United States the rate of breast-feeding is only about 55 percent, and two-fifths of those are babies who are breast-fed for only one or two months (Abma et al., 1997). Breast-feeding is most common among Latinos and whites and among well-educated and older mothers; it is least common among African-American mothers, among whom only about a quarter breast-feed their infants. The low rates of breast-feeding among poverty-level mothers is of special concern because rates of mortality and illness are already higher among infants born to these women.

A mother's work status also makes some difference in her decision about breast- or bottle-feeding, but it is not the deciding factor in many cases. The majority of women who do *not* work also do not breast-feed, while many working women find creative ways to combine employment (especially part-time work) and breast-feeding (Lindberg, 1996; Ryan et al., 1991).

Overall, it is clear that a large public health task still remains, not only in the United States but around the world, to educate women still further about the importance of breast-feeding and to create the cultural and practical supports needed to make breast-feeding the norm.

mend that infants be exclusively breast-fed for the first 4 to 6 months of life. When and if you have a child, I urge you to follow this advice if at all possible.

Still, I know that for some women, breast-feeding is problematic if not impossible. Some women are physically unable to breast-feed successfully because of inverted or chronically cracked nipples or an insufficient milk supply. Many others, working full-time with only a few weeks of maternity leave, find breast-feeding logistically very complicated. Breast pumps provide some flexibility in such cases, since they make it possible for women to expel breast milk while they are away from their infant and refrigerate it for later feedings. It may also be helpful to know that babies appear to derive some of the protections of breast-feeding with as little as one breast-feeding per day, a regimen that may enable some working women to continue at least partial breast-feeding over more months. For those of you who cannot breast-feed at all, it is also reassuring to know that the *social* interactions between mother and child seem to be unaffected by the type of feeding. Bottle-fed babies are held and cuddled in the same ways as are breast-fed babies, and their mothers appear to be just as sensitive and responsive to their babies, just as bonded to their babies, as are mothers of breast-fed infants (Field, 1977).

The bottom line, though, is that although formula will work as a backup if required, exclusive breast-feeding for at least four months is optimum, and at least partial breast-feeding is healthier for the infant than is exclusive bottle-feeding.

Critical Thinking

What specific changes in policies or practices do you think would increase the rate of breast-feeding in your country?

Individual Differences Among Babies

Most of my emphasis in the past few pages has been on the many ways infants are alike. Barring some kind of physical damage, all babies have similar sensory equipment at birth and can experience the same kinds of happenings around them. They all sleep, eat, and cry. At the same time, babies also differ in important ways—in health, in temperament, even in their patterns of crying.

Health and Death in the First Year

Virtually all babies get sick, most of them repeatedly. Among infants around the world, three types of illnesses are most common: diarrhea, upper respiratory infections, and ear infections.

Diarrhea. Worldwide, one of the most common and deadly illnesses of infancy and early childhood is diarrhea, accounting for an estimated 3.5 million infant and child deaths each year. In developing countries, 1 out of 4 deaths in children under age 5 is due to this illness; in some countries the rate is even higher (Gorter et al., 1995). In the United States, diarrhea rarely leads to death in infants, but virtually every infant or young child has at least one episode of diarrhea each year; about 1 in 10 cases is severe enough for the child to be taken to a doctor (Kilgore et al., 1995).

Virtually all the deaths from diarrhea could be prevented by giving fluids to rehydrate the child. In serious cases, this rehydration should involve a special solution of salts ("oral rehydration salts," or ORS). The World Health Organization has for some years been involved in a program of training health professionals around the world in the use of ORS, with some success (Muhuri et al., 1996). Still, diarrhea remains a very serious illness for infants and children in many parts of the world.

Upper Respiratory Infections. A second common disease of infancy is some kind of upper respiratory infection. In the United States, the average baby has seven colds in the first year of life. (That's a lot of nose-wipes!) Interestingly, research in a number of countries shows that babies in day-care centers have about twice as many such infections as do those reared entirely at home, presumably because babies in group care settings are exposed to a wider range of germs and viruses (e.g., Collet et al., 1994; Hurwitz et al., 1991; Louhiala et al., 1995). In general, the more different people a baby is exposed to, the more colds she is likely to get. This is not the unmitigated negative that it may appear to be. The heightened risk of infection among infants in day care drops after the first few months, while those reared entirely at home have very high rates of illness when they first attend preschool or kindergarten. Attendance at day care thus simply means that the baby is exposed earlier to the various microorganisms typically carried by children.

Ear Infections. One of the most severe forms of upper respiratory infection is an ear infection (more properly called **otitis media**), the early childhood illness that in the United States most often leads to a visit to a doctor (Daly, 1997). Such an infection very often follows a cold or an allergic reaction, either of which may lead to congestion in the eustachian tube—the tube through which middle ear fluid drains. The fluid thus has nowhere to go and accumulates in the middle ear, creating pressure and pain, most often accompanied by fever, headache, and other signs of illness. In the United States as many as 90 percent of children will have at least one serious ear infection before age 2, with the incidence peaking between ages 6 and 18 months (Daly, 1997; Paradise et al., 1997). The earlier a child's first episode, the more likely she is to have repeated infections.

The risk of otitis media is unusually high among many Native American groups as well as Alaskan and Canadian Inuits, and is higher among Caucasian than among black or Latino infants; it is more common in boys than in girls, more common in children in day care than those reared at home, more common among children whose parents smoke, and less common among infants who are breast-fed (e.g., Alho et al., 1996; Golding et al., 1997b; Kemper, 1996; Klein, 1994). It is a serious condition, requiring consistent medical treatment—treatment that is not equally available to all children. When not treated appropriately, repeated episodes can sometimes lead to some permanent hearing loss, which in turn may be linked to language or learning problems at later ages (Gravel & Nozza, 1997; Roberts & Wallace, 1997; Vernon-Feagans et al., 1996).

Infant Mortality. For a small minority of babies, the issue is not a few sniffles but the possibility of death. I mentioned in the last chapter that in 1996, 7.2 babies out of every 1000 in the United States died before age 1 (Guyer et al., 1997). Almost two-thirds of these deaths occurred in the first month of life and were directly linked either to congenital anomalies or to low birth weight. Fewer than 3 deaths per 1000 births occur in the remainder of the first year, and a sizeable fraction of those are cases of **sudden infant death syndrome (SIDS),** in which an apparently healthy infant dies suddenly and unexpectedly. In 1996, 2906 babies in the United States died of SIDS (Guyer et al., 1997).

SIDS occurs worldwide, although for unexplained reasons the rate varies quite a lot from country to country. For example, SIDS rates are particularly high in Australia and New Zealand and particularly low in Japan and Sweden (Hoffman & Hillman, 1992).

Physicians have not yet uncovered the basic cause of these deaths, although they have learned a fair amount about the groups that are at higher risk: babies with low birth weight, males, blacks, those with young mothers, and those whose mothers smoked during pregnancy or after birth. SIDS is also more common in the wintertime and among babies who sleep on their stomachs (Hoffman & Hillman, 1992; Mitchell et al., 1997; Ponsonby et al., 1993; Taylor et al., 1996), especially if the baby is sleeping on a soft or fluffy mattress, pillow, or comforter.

The growing evidence on the role of sleeping position persuaded pediatricians in many countries to change their standard advice to hospitals and families about the best sleeping position for babies. The American Academy of Pediatrics, for example, has been recommending since 1992 that when healthy infants are put down to sleep, they should be positioned on their sides or backs. Physicians in many other countries have made similar recommendations, a change in advice that has been followed by a significant drop in SIDS cases in every country involved (Willinger et al., 1994). In the United States, for example, the number of SIDS cases has dropped by nearly 30 percent since 1992. Still, sleeping position cannot be the full explanation, because of course *most* babies who sleep on their stomachs do not die of SIDS.

Another important contributor is smoking by the mother during pregnancy or by anyone in the home after the child's birth. Babies exposed to such smoke are about four times as likely to die of SIDS as are babies with no smoking exposure (Klonoff-Cohen et al., 1995; Schoendorf & Kiely, 1992; Taylor & Danderson, 1995). One more powerful reason not to smoke.

Temperament

Another way babies differ, other than health, is in their *temperament*. Babies vary in the way they react to new things, in their typical moods, in their rate of activity, in their preference for social interactions or solitude, in the regularity of their daily rhythms, and in many other ways. I'll be talking about temperament at greater length in Chapter 9, but because the concept will come up often as we go along, it is important at this early stage to introduce some of the basic terms and ideas.

Psychologists who have been interested in these differences have proposed several different ways of describing the key dimensions of temperament. Buss and Plomin (1984; 1986) propose three dimensions: emotionality, activity, and sociability. Thomas and Chess (1977) describe nine dimensions, which they organize into three types: the easy child, the difficult child, and the slow-to-warm-up child.

As you'll see in Chapter 9, it is not yet clear whether one of these views, or some other, will eventually carry the theoretical day, but the Thomas and Chess formulation has been the most influential one thus far. Let me describe their three basic types for you.

The Easy Child. Easy children, who comprised approximately 40 percent of Thomas and Chess's original study group, approach new events positively. They try new foods without much fuss, for example. They are also regular in biological functioning, with good sleeping and eating cycles, are usually happy, and adjust easily to change.

The Difficult Child. By contrast, the difficult child is less regular in body functioning and is slow to develop regular sleeping and eating cycles. These children react vigorously and negatively to new things, are more irritable, and cry more. Their cries are also more likely to have the higher-pitched, grating quality I talked about in the Research Report on page 93 (Huffman et al., 1994). Thomas and Chess point out, however, that once the difficult baby has adapted to something new, he is often quite happy about it, even though the adaptation process itself is quite trying. In Thomas and Chess's original sample, about 10 percent of children were clearly classifiable in this group.

The Slow-to-Warm-Up Child. Children in this group are not as negative in responding to new things or new people as is the difficult child. They show instead a kind of passive resistance. Instead of spitting out new food violently and crying, the slow-to-warm-up child may let the food drool out and may resist mildly any attempt to feed her more of the same. These infants show few intense reactions, either positive or negative, although once they have adapted to something new, their reaction is usually fairly positive. Approximately 15 percent of the Thomas and Chess sample followed this pattern.

While these differences in style or pattern of response tend to persist through infancy into later childhood, no psychologist studying temperament suggests that such individual differences are absolutely fixed at birth. Inborn temperamental differences are shaped, strengthened, bent, or counteracted by the child's relationships and experiences. What we do know is that infants enter the world with somewhat different reper-

Of course we can't evaluate a baby's temperament on the basis of one picture, but if we had to guess, we might predict that young Benjamin, smiling delightedly, has an easier temperament than Eleanor, pushing away her food—perhaps an instance of a slow-to-warm-up temperament.

toires or patterns of behavior and that those differences not only affect the experiences the infant may choose, but also help to shape the emerging pattern of interaction that develops between infant and parents. For example, toddlers and preschoolers with difficult temperaments are more often criticized or physically punished by their parents than are easy children, presumably because the child's behavior *is* more troublesome (Bates, 1989). Yet once it is established, such a pattern of criticism and punishment itself is likely to have additional consequences for the child.

Nonetheless, not all parents of difficult children respond in this way. A skilled parent, especially one who correctly perceives that the child's "difficultness" is a temperamental quality and not a result of the child's willfulness or the parent's ineptness, can avoid some of the pitfalls and can handle the difficult child more adeptly.

Sex Differences

Finally, as I did in the last chapter, let me add at least a brief word about sex differences. Most of us, when we hear about a new baby's birth, immediately ask, "Is it a boy or a girl?" A new child's gender is obviously highly salient to all of us. You might assume that such a preoccupation exists because boy and girl babies are really very different from one another. But in fact they are not. There are remarkably few sex differences in physical development in young infants. As was true at birth, girls continue to be ahead in some aspects of physical maturity, such as the development of bone density, although boys have more muscle tissue and are heavier and taller than girls. Boys continue to be more vulnerable, with higher infant mortality rates. More mixed are the findings on activity level. When researchers observe a difference, it is likely to be infant boys who are found to be slightly more active (Campbell & Eaton, 1995), but many investigators report no difference at all (Cossette et al., 1991). Similarly, there appear to be few differences in temperament. Boys are not more often "difficult" in temperament and girls are not more often "easy," even though that is what our stereotypes might lead us to expect. There are actually bigger differences in activity level or temperament between babies from different ethnic groups—which I'll discuss in Chapter 9—than there are between boys and girls. What dominates the system in these early months is not "boyness" or "girlness" but "babyness."

> **Critical Thinking**
>
> Why *do* we all ask immediately whether a new baby is a boy or a girl? Why does this information seem so vital? Think about it.

Summary

1. The normal birth process has three parts: dilation, delivery, and placental delivery.

2. The first "acquaintance" process after delivery may be an especially important one for parents. Most parents show an intense interest in the baby's features, especially the eyes.

3. Most drugs given to the mother during delivery pass through to the infant's bloodstream and have short-term effects on infant responsiveness and on feeding patterns. There may be some longer-term effects, but this possibility remains in dispute.

4. In uncomplicated, low-risk pregnancies, delivery at home or in a birthing center is as safe as hospital delivery.

5. The presence of the father during delivery has a variety of positive consequences, including reduced pain experience for the mother, but does not appear to affect the father's attachment to the infant.

6. Slightly more than one-fifth of all deliveries in the United States today are by cesarean section—a statistic that has been the cause of considerable debate.

7. Several types of problems may occur at birth, including reduced oxygen supply (anoxia) to the infant or low birth weight.

8. Infants born weighing less than 2500 grams are designated as low birth weight; those below 1500 grams are very low birth weight;

those below 1000 grams are extremely low birth weight. The lower the weight, the greater the risk of neonatal death or of significant lasting problems, such as low IQ scores or learning disabilities.

9. Newborns are typically assessed using the Apgar score, which is a rating on five dimensions. The Brazelton Neonatal Behavioral Assessment Scale is another commonly used instrument to evaluate newborn behavior.

10. Most parents experience delight and pleasure at their new role, but there are also strains. The majority of mothers have at least a brief period of "blues"; as many as one-tenth experience a more serious, longer depression. Marital satisfaction also typically declines after a baby is born.

11. The newborn has far more skills than most physicians and psychologists had thought, including excellent reflexes, good perceptual skills, and effective social skills.

12. Infants have a wide range of reflexes. Some, such as the sucking reflex, are essential for life. Other primitive reflexes are present in the newborn but disappear in the first year as cortical development advances.

13. Even primitive reflexes, however, may be linked to later developmental patterns, such as the stepping reflex and later walking.

14. Perceptual skills include focusing both eyes, tracking slowly moving objects, discrimination of the mother by smell and sound, and general responsiveness to smells, tastes, and touch.

15. Motor skills, in contrast, are only rudimentary at birth.

16. Social skills, while rudimentary, are sufficient to bring people close for care and to keep them close for social interactions. A key ingredient is the infant's ability to express a range of emotions, such as pleasure and distress. A true social smile appears at about 1 month.

17. Newborns can learn from the first days of life and can habituate to repeated stimulation.

18. Cycles of sleeping, waking, crying, and eating are present from the beginning. Newborns sleep 16 to 18 hours a day and eat perhaps 10 times.

19. In Western countries, babies most often sleep separate from their parents; in many other cultures, babies sleep in the same bed with their parents.

20. Babies cry several hours per day, on average, with the amount of crying peaking at about 6 weeks. Some infants show more persistent, inconsolable crying (colic), which may last until age 3 to 4 months.

21. Persisting irregularity of sleep patterns, or a particularly high-pitched or grating cry, may be indications of some neurological problem.

22. Breast-feeding has clear benefits to the baby, providing antibodies against diseases and reducing the risk of disease.

23. Common illnesses of childhood include diarrhea (which is linked to many deaths in infants worldwide) and upper respiratory infections. Of the latter, ear infections (otitis media) are often the most serious. All forms of upper respiratory illness are more common among children in day care than in those reared at home.

24. In the United States and other industrialized countries, most infant deaths in the first weeks are due to congenital anomalies or low birth weight; past the first weeks, sudden infant death syndrome is the most common cause of death in the first year. The risk of SIDS is higher in black infants, those with young mothers, and those whose mothers smoked. The cause is not yet understood.

25. Babies differ from one another on several dimensions, including vigor of response, general activity rate, restlessness, irritability, and cuddliness. These temperamental dimensions, which Thomas and Chess have grouped into "easy," "difficult," and "slow-to-warm-up" types, appear to be at least somewhat stable.

26. Male and female babies differ at birth on a few dimensions. Girls are more mature physically. Boys are more active, have more muscle tissue, and are more vulnerable to stress. No sex differences are found, however, on temperamental dimensions such as cuddliness or sootheability.

Key Terms

anoxia A shortage of oxygen. If it is prolonged, it can result in brain damage. This is one of the potential risks at birth. **p. 78**

Apgar score An assessment of the newborn completed by the physician or midwife at 1 minute and again at 5 minutes after birth, assessing five characteristics: heart rate, respiratory rate, muscle tone, response to stimulation, and color. **p. 81**

Babinski reflex A reflex found in very young infants in which they splay out their toes in response to a stroke on the bottom of the foot. **p. 84**

cephalocaudal One of two basic patterns of physical development in infancy (the other is proximodistal), describing development that proceeds from the head downward. **p. 86**

cesarean section Delivery of the child through an incision in the mother's abdomen. **p. 77**

colic A pattern of persistent and often inconsolable crying, totaling more than 3 hours a day, found in some infants in the first 3 to 4 months of life. **p. 92**

dilation A key process in the first stage of childbirth, when the cervix widens sufficiently to allow the infant's head to pass into the birth canal. Full dilation is 10 centimeters. **p. 72**

effacement The flattening of the cervix, which, along with dilation, is a key process of the first stage of childbirth. **p. 72**

extremely low birth weight Any birth weights below 1000 grams (2.2 pounds). **p. 78**

habituation An automatic decrease in the intensity of a response to a repeated stimulus, enabling a child or adult to ignore the familiar and focus attention on the novel. **p. 87**

low birth weight (LBW) Any baby born with a weight below 2500 grams (5.5 pounds) is given this label, including both those born too early (preterm) and those who are "small for date." **p. 78**

Moro reflex When startled (e.g., by a loud sound or a sensation of being dropped), the infant extends his legs, arms, and fingers, arches his back, and draws back his head. **p. 84**

otitis media The technical name for what most parents call an ear infection: the collection of fluid in the middle ear, often accompanied by other symptoms of acute illness. **p. 96**

postpartum depression A severe form of the common experience of postpartum blues. Affecting perhaps 15 percent of women, this form of clinical depression typically lasts six to eight weeks. **p. 83**

preterm infant Descriptive phrase widely used to label infants born before 38 weeks gestational age. **p. 79**

primitive reflexes Collection of reflexes seen in young infants, controlled by the more primitive parts of the brain, that gradually disappear during the first year of life, including the Moro, Babinski, and stepping reflexes. **p. 84**

proximodistal One of two basic patterns of physical development in infancy (the other is cephalocaudal), describing development that proceeds from the center outward, such as from the trunk to the limbs. **p. 86**

reflexes Automatic body reactions to specific stimulation, such as the knee jerk or the Moro reflex. Many reflexes remain among adults, but the newborn also has some "primitive" reflexes that disappear as the cortex develops. **p. 83**

respiratory distress syndrome A problem frequently found in infants born more than 6 weeks before term in which the infant's lungs lack the chemical surfactant needed to keep air sacs inflated. **p. 79**

rooting reflex Stroke an infant on the cheek near the mouth and the baby will reflexively turn toward the touch, open his mouth, and make sucking movements. **p. 84**

schematic learning The development of expectancies of what actions lead to what results, or what events tend to go together. Classical conditioning may be thought of as a subset of schematic learning. **p. 87**

small-for-date infant An infant who weighs less than is normal for the number of weeks of gestation completed. **p. 79**

sudden infant death syndrome (SIDS) Unexpected death of an infant who otherwise appears healthy. Also called crib death. Cause is unknown. **p. 97**

very low birth weight Any birth weight below 1500 grams (3.3 pounds). **p. 78**

Suggested Readings

Field, T. M. (1990). *Infancy*. Cambridge, MA: Harvard University Press. Another of the fine small books published by Harvard University Press. Field reviews what we know about infancy in an engaging and clear style.

Kemper, K. J. (1996). *The wholistic pediatrician*. New York: HarperCollins. A fine new book providing advice for parents concerning the major illnesses of infancy and childhood, including asthma, colds, colic, diarrhea, ear infections, and many others. Kemper reviews what we know about the full range of therapeutic options, from simple things a parent can do at home, through various natural remedies, to traditional medical treatments.

Rosenblith, J. F. (1992). *In the beginning: Development in the first two years of life* (2nd ed.). Newbury Park, CA: Sage. A fine basic text on infant development.

4

Physical Development

When my daughter (who is now 29) was about 8½, a lot of well-rehearsed family routines seemed to unravel. She was crankier than usual, both more assertive and more needful of affection, and alternately compliant and defiant. What on earth was happening? Had I done something dreadfully wrong? Was something going on at school? I mentioned my problems to several colleagues, many of whom told me their own tales about the special difficulties they had had with their daughters between ages 8 and 9. It finally occurred to us all that there might be a physical explanation: Girls of 8 or 9 are beginning to experience the first hormone changes of puberty. Perhaps the inconsistent and uncomfortable behaviors I was seeing were one form of response to the changing hormones in the system.

It may amuse you to think of the clever psychologist missing such an obvious possibility, but in fact developmental psychologists have often placed too little emphasis on physical growth. We describe it briefly and then take it for granted. But I am convinced, both by the research literature on the effects of physiological change and by my observations as a parent, that an understanding of physical development is an absolutely critical first step in understanding children's progress, for at least four reasons.

Four Reasons for Studying Physical Development

The Child's Growth Makes New Behaviors Possible. Specific physical changes are needed before the infant can crawl or walk. Similarly, the development of full reproductive capacity at adolescence is based on a complex sequence of physical changes. Thus, nonobvious physical changes are often the necessary underpinning of behavior change.

The flip side of this is that the *lack* of a particular physical development may set limits on the behaviors a child is capable of performing. An infant of 10 months cannot be toilet trained, no matter how hard parents may try, because the anal sphincter muscle is not yet fully mature. Toddlers cannot easily pick up raisins or Cheerios from their highchair trays until the muscles and nerves required for thumb-forefinger opposition have developed. Six-year-olds cannot reliably hit baseballs or throw basketballs through hoops, no matter how much their parents (or their coaches) may pressure them.

The Child's Growth Determines Experience. A child's range of physical capacities or skills can also have a major indirect effect on cognitive and social development by influencing the variety of experiences she can have. An infant who is able to sit up can now reach more easily for objects around her; an infant who is able to crawl can explore still more widely, an experience that may have both positive and negative consequences. For example, Bennett Bertenthal and his colleagues (1994) have shown that babies develop a fear of heights several weeks after they learn to crawl, but crawling also ushers in new skills in searching for lost objects. At an older age, a child who learns to ride a bike widens her horizons still further, as she explores her neighborhood on her own, perhaps for the first time.

The Child's Growth Affects Others' Responses. The child's new physical skills also change the way others respond to her. For example, parents react quite differently to an infant who can crawl than to one who cannot. They begin to say "no" more often, put things out of reach, or put the baby in a playpen. Such changes in the pattern of interaction between parent and child may have both immediate and long-term consequences for the child's emotional or mental development.

Adults' expectations for children are also affected by the child's size and shape, attractiveness, and physical skills. Children who are pretty, tall, or well coordinated are treated differently from those who are homely, petite, or clumsy (Lerner, 1985). A Little League baseball coach may be more supportive of a child with advanced large-muscle

This 6-year-old is still unsteady on her bike, but once she masters this new physical skill, her life will change as she ranges more independently.

coordination (good for home runs), while a classroom teacher may be especially appreciative of children whose small-muscle coordination is superior (good for writing and drawing).

Adults and children are also biased in favor of some specific body types. In the terminology introduced by Sheldon (1940) many years ago, the most favored type for boys is one that is well muscled and square in build, called *mesomorphic*. *Endomorphic* (rounded) and *ectomorphic* (skinny, tall, bony) body types are less preferred by both children and adults—a pattern of preferences that has been found not only in the United States but also in samples of Japanese and Mexican children and adults (Lerner, 1985; 1987). Thus, individual differences in physical patterns or speed of growth can have profound effects on children's early experiences.

The Child's Growth Affects Self-concept. The final reason for us to pay close attention to physical development is that physical characteristics and physical skills (or lack of them) have a significant influence on a child's self-concept or sense of self-efficacy—that inner belief that one can (or cannot) successfully accomplish some task (Bandura, 1997). I'll be talking about this topic much more fully in Chapters 9 and 10, but let me only point out here that this is another example of the importance of internal models, a concept I introduced in Chapter 1. A child's body image and her sense of self-efficacy are not simply direct reflections of observable reality. Rather, these are internal models, shaped by a variety of things, including direct experience of physical successes, what the child overhears from others, and the child's ideas about the cultural image of an ideal body. Like all internal models, these ideas, once created, become relatively difficult to change. A child's choice of activities, her behavior in social situations, and her sense of self-worth are all likely to be affected throughout childhood and adolescence, perhaps even into adulthood, by the body image and sense of physical self-efficacy formed early in childhood. My own body image, for example, includes a strong element of "gawkiness," since I was always taller than everyone else and saw myself as uncoordinated. Whether that is *objectively* true is less important than the fact that I *believe* it to be true and base my behavior, my choices, and my interpretations of my own behavior on that belief.

For all four of these reasons, I think it is important to begin our exploration of development with a fairly detailed look at physical growth and change.

Basic Sequences and Common Patterns

Size and Shape

The most obvious thing about children's physical development is that they get bigger as they get older. Yet even this simple and obvious statement may conceal some surprises. The biggest surprise for most people is the fact that at birth an infant is already one-third of his final height; by age 2 he is about *half as tall* as he will be as an adult (hard to believe, isn't it?). Another possible surprise is the fact that growth from birth to maturity is neither continuous nor smooth. Figure 4.1 shows the four different phases in the development of height in boys and girls.

During the first phase, which lasts for about the first two years, the baby gains in height very rapidly, adding 10 to 12 inches in length in the first year and tripling his body weight in the same span. At about age 2, the child settles down to a slower but steady addition of 2 to 3 inches and about 6 pounds a year until adolescence.

The third phase is the dramatic adolescent "growth spurt," when the child may add 3 to 6 inches a year for several years, after which the rate of growth again slows until final adult size is reached. The figure makes it clear that this growth spurt is, on average, much larger for boys than for girls, but virtually all children show a period of more rapid growth some time between the ages of about 9 and 15.

The shape and proportions of the child's body also change over the years of development. In an adult, the head is about one-eighth or one-tenth of the total height. In a

Critical Thinking

Think of examples of how the same processes have operated in your own life: How has your self-image been affected by your early growth or by your physical size or shape? How have your beliefs about your own physical capacities affected your choices or your behavior?

These Texas first graders are all the same age, but not all the same size. Because he is so much smaller, the little guy on the left in the front row is likely to be treated quite differently from his classmates.

Figure 4.1

These curves show the gain in height for each year from birth through adolescence, based on recent data from many hundreds of thousands of American children. You can see the several clear phases: very rapid growth in infancy, slower growth in the preschool and elementary school years, a growth spurt at adolescence, and the cessation of growth at adulthood.

(*Sources:* Tanner, 1990, p. 14; Malina, 1990; Lindsay et al., 1994; Baumgartner et al., 1986.)

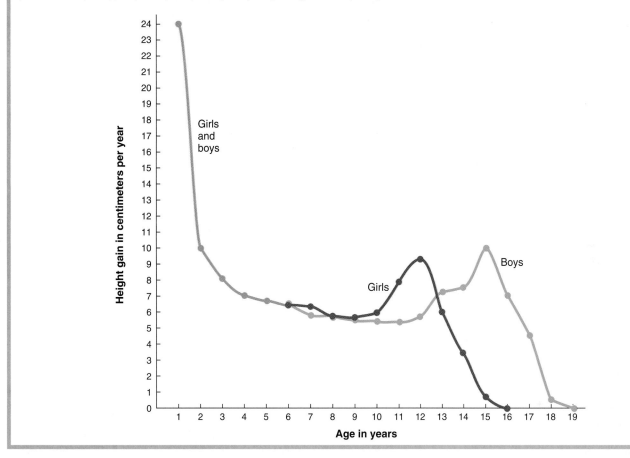

toddler, in contrast, the head is proportionately far larger—about one-fourth of the total body length—in order to accommodate the nearly adult-sized brain of the infant.

Individual body parts do not all grow at the same rate. In a reversal of the typical proximodistal pattern, a child's hands and feet normally reach full adult size some time in late elementary school or early adolescence, followed by the arms and legs, which grow most rapidly in early adolescence, with the trunk usually the last to complete its growth. Because of this asymmetry in the body parts, we often think of adolescents as "awkward" or uncoordinated. Interestingly, research does not bear this out. Robert Malina (1990), who has done extensive research on physical development, has found no point in the adolescent growth process at which teenagers become consistently less coordinated or less skillful in physical tasks.

All these visible changes in size and shape are the result of changes on the inside in bones, muscles, and fat.

Bones

The hand, wrist, ankle, and foot all have fewer bones at birth than they will have at full maturity. For example, an adult has nine separate bones in his wrist while a 1-year-old has only three. The remaining six develop over the period of childhood, with complete growth by adolescence. Like many aspects of physical development, this process occurs earlier in girls than in boys. The wrist bones are normally complete by 51 months in girls but only at 66 months in boys (Needlman, 1996).

In one part of the body, though, the bones fuse rather than differentiating. The skull of a newborn is made up of several bones separated by spaces called **fontanels.** Fontanels allow the head to be compressed without injury during the birth process, and they give the brain room to grow. In most children, the fontanels are filled in by bone by 12 to 18 months, creating a single connected skull bone.

Bones change also in quality as well as number over the course of development. An infant's bones are softer, with a higher water content, than adults' bones. The process of bone hardening, called **ossification,** occurs steadily from birth through puberty, following such a regular and predictable pattern that physicians use **bone age** as the best single measure of a child's physical maturation; X-rays of the hand and wrist show the stage of development of wrist and finger bones. In infancy and toddlerhood, the sequence of development generally follows the two patterns I mentioned in Chapter 3, moving from the head downward (*cephalocaudal*) and from the trunk outward (*proximodistal*). For example, bones of the hand and wrist harden before those in the feet.

Bone hardening may seem to be a fairly minor aspect of development, but the process has some direct practical relevance. Soft bones are clearly needed if the fetus is going to have enough flexibility to fit into the cramped space of the uterus. Yet that very flexibility contributes to a newborn human's relative floppiness and motor immaturity. As the bones stiffen, the baby and toddler is able to manipulate his body more surely, which increases the range of exploration he can enjoy and makes him much more independent.

Muscles

Although virtually all muscle fibers are present at birth (Tanner, 1990), muscles—like bones—change in quality from infancy through adolescence, becoming longer, thicker, and less watery at a fairly steady rate throughout childhood.

At adolescence, muscles go through a growth spurt, just as height does, so that adolescents become quite a lot stronger in just a few years. Both boys and girls show this increase in strength, but the increase is much greater in boys. For example, in a cross-sectional study in Canada involving 2673 children and teenagers, Smoll and Schutz (1990) measured strength by having each child hang as long as possible from a bar, keeping his or her eyes level with the bar. As you can see in Figure 4.2, 9-year-old boys could maintain this flexed arm hang for about 40 percent longer than could girls the same age; by age 17, boys could sustain it almost 3 times as long as girls. This substantial difference in strength is one reflection of the sex difference in muscle tissue: In adult men, about 40 percent of total body mass is muscle compared to only about 24 percent in adult women.

Such a sex difference in muscle mass (and accompanying strength) seems to be largely a result of hormone differences, although sex differences in exercise patterns or fitness may also play some role. For example, the sex difference in *leg* strength is much less than the difference in arm strength, a pattern that makes sense if we assume that all teenagers walk and use their legs a similar amount but that boys use their arm muscles in various sports activities more than girls do, especially in the teenage years, when girls increasingly drop out of sports programs (Kann et al., 1995). Still, there does seem to be a basic hormonal difference as well, because we know that very fit girls and women are still not as strong as very fit boys and men.

Fat

Another major component of the body is fat, most of which is stored immediately under the skin. This *subcutaneous fat* is first laid down beginning at about 34 weeks pre-

Figure 4.2

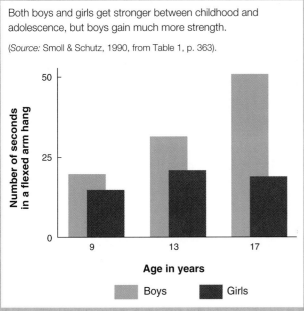

Both boys and girls get stronger between childhood and adolescence, but boys gain much more strength.

(*Source:* Smoll & Schutz, 1990, from Table 1, p. 363).

natally and has an early peak at about 9 months after birth (the so-called baby fat); the thickness of this layer of fat then declines until about age 6 or 7, after which it rises until adolescence.

Once again we see a sex difference in these patterns. From birth, girls have slightly more fat tissue than boys do, and this difference becomes gradually more marked during childhood. At adolescence, the difference grows still further. The size of the change is illustrated nicely in the results of the same Canadian study reflected in Figure 4.2 (Smoll & Schutz, 1990). Between ages 13 and 17, the percentage of body weight made up of fat rose from 21.8 to 24.0 percent among girls in this study but dropped from 16.1 to 14.0 percent among boys. So during and after puberty, proportions of fat rise among girls and decline among boys, while the proportion of weight that is muscle rises in boys and declines in girls.

Heart and Lungs

Puberty also brings important changes in other body organs. In particular, the heart and lungs increase considerably in size and the heart rate drops. Both of these changes are more marked for boys than for girls—another of the factors that increases the capacity for sustained effort for boys relative to girls. Before puberty, boys and girls are fairly similar in physical strength, speed, and endurance, although even at these earlier ages, when a difference exists, it favors the boys. After puberty, boys have a clear advantage in all three (Smoll & Schutz, 1990).

The Nervous System

Growth in height and weight involves changes you can see. Even the changes in muscles, bones, and fat can be detected fairly easily in the child's longer legs, greater strength, or softness or leanness of body. Two other, enormously important, types of developmental changes in the body are not so easy to perceive—those in the nervous system and in hormones.

Composition of the Nervous System. Figure 4.3 (p. 108) shows the main structures of the brain. At birth, as I mentioned briefly in Chapter 3, the **midbrain** and the **medulla**

Critical Thinking

Current U.S. laws require equal treatment of males and females in school sports. But imagine for the moment that that weren't the case, and you were a member of a local school board being asked to decide whether teenage boys and girls should be allowed to play on the same competitive teams in sports such as volleyball, soccer, and baseball. Given what you have read so far, how would you decide the issue, and why?

Figure 4.3

The medulla and the midbrain are largely developed at birth. In the first two years after birth, it is primarily the cortex that develops, although increases in the dendritic arbor and in synapses also occur throughout the nervous system.

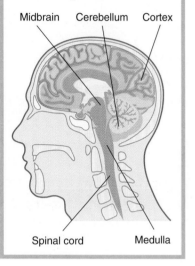

are most fully developed. These two parts, both in the lower part of the skull and connecting to the spinal cord, regulate such basic tasks as attention and habituation, sleeping, waking, elimination, and movement of the head and neck (but not movement of the trunk or limbs)—all tasks a newborn can perform at least moderately well. The least-developed part of the brain at birth is the **cortex,** the convoluted gray matter that wraps around the midbrain and is involved in perception, body movement, and all complex thinking and language.

Recall from Chapter 2 that all these structures are composed of two basic types of cells, *neurons* and *glial cells*. Virtually all these cells are already present at birth. The developmental process after birth is primarily the creation of synapses between neurons, which involves enormous growth of both the dendritic arbor and the axons and their terminal fibers. Most of that dendritic growth occurs in the cortex, primarily during the first three years after birth, resulting in a tripling of the overall weight of the brain during those years. By age 2, a baby has as many synapses as an adult; by age 3, toddlers have more than 1000 trillion synapses—roughly twice as many as the average adult (Shore, 1997). Thus, the child's brain is denser and more complex in organization than is an adult's.

This fact has been one of the great surprises of modern neuroscientific research. The currently accepted explanation is that the developing brain creates many times more neurons and more synapses than it will eventually need, following a built-in pattern. Put another way, we can think of the organism as being programmed to develop certain kinds of neural connections, which it does in abundance, creating redundant pathways (Greenough et al., 1987). This unwieldy mass of synapses is then gradually *pruned,* with unneeded or unused synapses dropping out. The pruning process appears to occur throughout childhood and to be largely complete by late adolescence, at which time about half the synapses have been eliminated (Huttenlocher, 1994). For example, early in development each skeletal muscle cell seems to develop synaptic connections with several motor neurons in the spinal cord. After the pruning process has occurred, however, each muscle fiber is connected to only one neuron.

Although pruning continues throughout childhood and early adolescence, it does not occur at the same time in all parts of the brain. For example, the maximum density of synapses in the portions of the brain that have to do with language comprehension and production occurs at about age 3 years, while the part of the cortex devoted to vision is maximally dense at 4 *months* of age, with rapid pruning thereafter (Huttenlocher, 1994).

The crucial new understanding that has emerged from this research is that the pruning process is heavily dependent on the child's specific experience. Each time some experience stimulates a neural pathway, it leaves behind a kind of chemical signal, which is strengthened with each repeated use of that same pathway. When the signal strength reaches some threshold level, that particular neural connection appears to become immune to the pruning process and becomes a permanent part of brain architecture. Conversely, pathways that are not used at all, or not used often enough, do not reach this threshold strength and are later pruned out.

There are several critical implications of this new information. First, it becomes clear that brain development follows the old dictum *Use it or lose it*. A child growing up in a rich or intellectually challenging environment will thus retain a more complex network of synapses than one growing up with fewer forms of stimulation—a variation of the nature-nurture interaction pattern Aslin calls *attunement*. The evidence to support this proposal comes from several kinds of research, including work with animals. For example, if rat infants are reared in highly stimulating environments, as adults they will have a denser network of neurons, dendrites, and synaptic connections (e.g., Escorihuela et al., 1994). We also know that in both subhuman primates and humans, infants who experience significant sensory deprivation, such as from being blind in one eye, develop (or retain) less dense synaptic networks in the part of the brain linked to that particular function (e.g., Gordon, 1995). Finally, we have a growing body of information showing the importance for human babies of being talked to—not from an inanimate source like television, but by an attentive, conversational adult. Such conversation appears to help stimulate and organize the infant's brain (e.g., Fifer & Moon, 1994; Kuhl, 1993); babies exposed to more such verbal stimulation retain denser and more complex networks of synapses. This denser network, in turn, provides an enduring base for later complex thinking. Thus, these early months look like a sensitive period for the retention of synapses; neural complexity that is not retained in these early years does not redevelop later. Love and affection, while critical to the infant for other reasons, are not enough to optimize brain organization; the baby needs patterned visual and auditory stimulation, particularly language.

A second implication of this same basic idea is that the very flexibility of the early brain means that babies and children can adapt to whatever environmental demands they may face; those adaptations are then built into their brains throughout their lives. A child growing up in a physically dangerous environment may retain and strengthen an acute sensitivity to certain signals of danger; a child who lives in a hunting culture will retain an especially acute ability to notice some categories of environmental detail; a child growing up in a noisy urban environment "learns" how to filter out the unnecessary noise (Shore, 1997).

A third basic point is that the "programmed plasticity" of the brain is at its height in infancy. Perhaps paradoxically, this period of maximum plasticity is also the period in which the child may be most vulnerable to major deficits, making these early years a kind of critical period for brain development. Just as the time of most rapid growth of any body system prenatally is the time when the fetus is most vulnerable to teratogens, so the young infant needs sufficient stimulation and predictability in his environment to maximize the early period of rapid growth and plasticity (de Haan et al., 1994). A really inadequate diet or a serious lack of stimulation—particularly verbal stimulation—in the early months will thus have subtle but long-range effects on the child's later cognitive progress.

Myelination. Another crucial process in neuronal development is the development of sheaths around individual axons, which electrically insulate them from one another and improve the conductivity of the nerve. This sheath is made up of a substance called **myelin;** the process of developing the sheath is called **myelination.**

The sequence with which nerves are myelinated follows both cephalocaudal and proximodistal patterns. Thus, nerves serving muscle cells in the arms and hands are myelinated earlier than are those serving the lower trunk and the legs. Myelination is most rapid during the first two years after birth, then continues at a slower pace throughout childhood and adolescence. For example, the parts of the brain that govern motor movements are not fully myelinated until perhaps age 6 (Todd et al., 1995).

To understand the importance of myelin, it may help you to know that multiple sclerosis is a disease in which the myelin begins to break down. An individual with this disease gradually loses motor control, with the specific symptoms depending on the portion of the nervous system affected by the disease.

Critical Thinking

Programs like Head Start, aimed at providing cognitive enrichment for children growing up in impoverished circumstances, are focused on children aged 3 to 5. The newer work on brain development, however, suggests that this may be too little, too late. Do you think enrichment programs for infants would make more sense? Are such programs likely to be socially acceptable or practically feasible?

Andrea's mother seems to be providing her with just the kind of engaged, attentive verbal stimulation that babies need to shape and optimize their brain development.

Table 4.1

Major Hormones Involved in Physical Growth and Development

Gland	Some of the Key Hormone(s) Secreted	Aspects of Growth Influenced
Thyroid	Thyroxine	Normal brain development and overall rate of growth.
Adrenal	Adrenal androgen (chemically highly similar to testosterone)	Some changes at puberty, particularly the development of skeletal maturity and mature muscles, especially in boys.
Leydig cells in the testes (in boys)	Testosterone	Crucial in the formation of male genitals prenatally; triggers the sequence of primary and secondary sex characteristic changes at puberty in the male; stimulates increased output of growth hormone and affects bones and muscles.
Ovaries (in girls)	Several estrogens, the most critical of which is estradiol	Development of the menstrual cycle, breasts, and pubic hair in girls.
Pituitary	Growth hormone (GH), thyroid-stimulating hormone (TSH), and the gonadotrophic hormones: follicle-stimulating hormone (FSH) and luteinizing hormone (LH)	Growth hormone governs the rate of physical maturation; other pituitary hormones signal the respective sex glands to secrete; follicle-stimulating hormone and luteinizing hormone help control the menstrual cycle.

Source: Tanner, 1990.

Hormones

A second crucial set of changes over the years of childhood and adolescence is in *hormones*—secretions of the various **endocrine glands** in the body. Hormones govern growth and physical changes in several ways, summarized in Table 4.1.

Of all the endocrine glands, the most critical is the pituitary, since it provides the trigger for release of hormones from other glands. For example, the thyroid gland secretes thyroxine only when it has received a signal to do so in the form of a specific thyroid-stimulating hormone secreted by the pituitary. The pituitary hormones are, in turn, controlled by the hypothalamus, a brain structure near the pituitary and linked to it by blood vessels. Nerve cells in the hypothalamus release chemical messengers to the pituitary, with each pituitary hormone having its own unique chemical trigger.

Hormones play a role at every stage of physical development, perhaps most strikingly at adolescence but significantly at earlier stages as well.

Prenatal Hormones. Thyroid hormone (thyroxine) is present from about the fourth month of gestation and appears to be involved in stimulating normal brain development. Growth hormone is also produced by the pituitary, beginning as early as 10 weeks after conception. Presumably, it helps to stimulate the very rapid growth of cells and organs of the body. And as I mentioned in Chapter 2, testosterone is produced prenatally in the testes of the developing male and influences both the development of male genitals and some aspects of brain development.

Hormones Between Birth and Adolescence. Between birth and adolescence, physical growth is largely governed by thyroid hormone and pituitary growth hormone. Thyroid hormone is secreted in greater quantities for the first two years of life and then falls to a lower level and remains steady until adolescence (Tanner, 1990), a secretion pattern that obviously matches the pattern of change in height you saw in Figure 4.1 (p. 105).

Secretions from the testes and ovaries, as well as adrenal androgen, remain at extremely low levels until about age 7 or 8, when adrenal androgen begins to be secreted in increased amounts, a pattern shown in the upper part of Figure 4.4 (McClintock & Herdt, 1996). The role of adrenal androgen, which is chemically very similar to testosterone, remains a bit of a mystery. It used to be thought that it was critical in the development of secondary sex characteristics in girls, particularly the development of pubic and underarm hair. Recent research calls that into question (Tanner, 1990). At the moment, the only established role of this hormone is in prompting and controlling skeletal development, which suggests that it plays some part in the adolescent growth spurt, perhaps particularly for girls (Tanner, 1990). More speculatively, it may play a role in the development of sexual attraction, which begins at about age 10, well before the onset of most pubertal changes but when adrenal androgen has already begun to rise (McClintock & Herdt, 1996).

Figure 4.4

Changes in hormones prior to and at adolescence. The top graph shows changes in adrenal androgen, which are equivalent in boys and girls; the bottom graphs show increases in estradiol for girls in picograms per milliliter, and testosterone for boys in nanograms per milliliter.

(*Sources:* Androgen data from M. K. McClintock and G. Herdt, from "Rethinking Puberty: The Development of Sexual Attraction," *Current Directions in Psychological Science,* Vol. 5, No. 6 (December 1996), p. 181, Fig. 2. © 1996 American Psychological Association. By permission of Cambridge University Press. Estradiol and testosterone data from Elizabeth Susman, Fig. 2 from "Modeling Developmental Complexity in Adolescence: Hormones and Behavior in Context,: p. 291, *Journal of Research on Adolescence,* 7, 1997. © 1997 by Lawrence Erlbaum Associates, Inc. By permission of the publisher and author.)

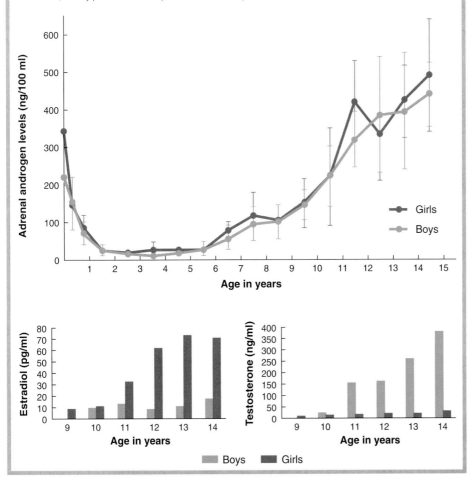

Hormones in Adolescence. The rise in adrenal androgen is followed by a complex sequence of further hormone changes, beginning with a signal from the hypothalamus to the pituitary to begin secreting increased levels of **gonadotrophic hormones** (two in males, three in females). These in turn stimulate the development of the glands in the testes and ovaries that then begin to secrete more hormones, *testosterone* in boys and a form of **estrogen** called *estradiol* in girls. Over the course of puberty, the levels of testosterone increase 18-fold in boys while levels of estradiol increase 8-fold in girls (Biro et al., 1995; Nottelmann et al., 1987), a pattern evident in the lower part of Figure 4.4. Note that the age of onset of these several hormonal changes is essentially the same in boys as in girls, although the peak of testosterone production occurs a year or so later in boys than does the peak of estradiol secretion in girls.

Development of Sexual Maturity

The physical result of the hormonal changes that take place during **puberty** is not only a spurt in height but, more important, a set of physical changes that bring about full sexual maturity. Included are changes in the reproductive systems themselves (called *primary sex characteristics*), such as the testes and penis in the male, and the ovaries, uterus, and vagina in the female, as well as changes in *secondary sex characteristics:* the development of breasts in girls, changing voice pitch and beard growth in boys, and the growth of body hair in both sexes.

Each of these physical developments occurs in a defined sequence. Following the work of J. M. Tanner (1978), each sequence is customarily divided into 5 stages. Stage 1 always describes the preadolescent stage, stage 2 the first signs of pubertal change, stages 3 and 4 the intermediate steps, and stage 5 the final adult characteristic. Table 4.2 gives one example of these sequences for each sex. These stages have proved to be extremely helpful not only for describing the normal progress through puberty, but also for assessing the rate of development of individual youngsters.

Table 4.2

Examples of Tanner's Stages of Pubertal Development

Stage	Breast Development	Male Genital Development
1	No change except for some elevation of the nipple.	Testes, scrotum, and penis are all about the same size and shape as in early childhood.
2	Breast bud stage: elevation of breast and the nipple as a small mound. Areolar diameter is enlarged over stage 1.	Scrotum and testes are slightly enlarged. Skin of the scrotum is reddened and changed in texture, but little or no enlargement of the penis.
3	Breast and areola both enlarged and elevated more than in stage 2, but no separation of their contours.	Penis slightly enlarged, at first mainly in length. Testes and scrotum are further enlarged.
4	Areola and nipple form a secondary mound projecting above the contour of the breast.	Penis further enlarged, with growth in breadth and development of glans. Testes and scrotum further enlarged, and scrotum skin still darker.
5	Mature stage. Only the nipple projects, with the areola recessed to the general contour of the breast.	Genitalia are adult in size and shape.

Source: Petersen & Taylor, 1980, p. 127.

Sexual Development in Girls

Studies of preteens and teens in both Europe and North America (Malina, 1990) reveal that for girls, the various sequential changes are interlocked in a particular pattern, shown schematically in Figure 4.5. The first steps are typically the early changes in breasts and pubic hair, followed by the peak of the growth spurt. Only then does first menstruation occur, an event called **menarche** (pronounced MEN-are-kee). Menarche typically occurs two years after the beginning of other visible changes and is succeeded only by the final stages of breast and pubic hair development. Ninety-five percent of all girls experience this event between the ages of 11 and 15.

The red box on each bar in Figure 4.5 indicates the average age at which girls reach that particular stage, based on a number of older studies. Very recent data in the United States, however, suggest that all these changes may be occurring considerably earlier among children today. In a cross-sectional study of more than 17,000 girls whose sexual maturity was assessed by 225 pediatricians around the country, Herman-Giddens and her colleagues (1997) found that the average age for stage 2 breast development was 9.96 years among white girls and 8.87 years among African-American girls. The equivalent average ages for stage 2 pubic hair development were 10.51 and 8.78 years—all a year or more earlier than the averages shown in Figure 4.5. Despite these much earlier signs of pubertal changes, however, the average age of menarche among the girls in Herman-Giddens's study was essentially the same as what other investigators have found in recent decades both in the United States and in other industrialized countries: age 12.88 for white girls and 12.16 for African-American girls.

There are a number of methodological reasons why we should be cautious about drawing sweeping conclusions about the timing of puberty based on the Herman-Giddens data, including the possibility that the 225 pediatricians may have used the Tanner category system inaccurately or inconsistently. Nonetheless, these results raise

Figure 4.5

The figure shows the normal sequence and timing of pubertal changes for girls. The red box on each black line represents the average age of attainment of that change, while the line indicates the range of normal times. Note the *wide* range of normality for all of these changes. Also note how relatively late in the sequence the growth spurt and menarche occur.

(*Sources:* Chumlea, 1982; Garn, 1980; Malina, 1990; Tanner, 1990.)

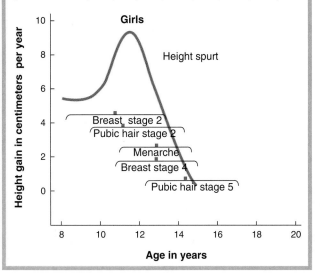

both red flags and a series of important and intriguing questions. For example, if the age of onset of pubertal changes has really declined a year or more recently, what might be causing such a shift? Why would African-American girls experience pubertal onset significantly sooner than European-American girls? What are the implications of such early puberty for the educational system, for sexual behavior, for teenage pregnancy rates?

The age of onset of puberty has changed in other historical eras as well. In particular, the timing of menarche dropped rather dramatically between the mid-nineteenth and mid-twentieth centuries. In 1840, menarche occurred, on average, at age 17 in Western countries; that average then dropped about 4 months a decade to a level of approximately age 13 in 1970, where it has remained since then (Roche, 1979), an example of what psychologists call a **secular trend.** Most observers have attributed this pattern of change to significant alterations in life-style and diet, particularly increases in protein intake. It is not clear, however, whether the same explanation can account for the findings Herman-Giddens reports.

Menarche does not signal full sexual maturity. In as many as three-quarters of the cycles in the first year, and in half the cycles in the second and third years after menarche, no ovum is produced (Vihko & Apter, 1980). Full adult fertility thus develops over a period of years.

This initial menstrual irregularity has some significant practical consequences for sexually active teenagers. For one thing, such irregularity no doubt contributes to the widespread assumption among girls in their early teens that they cannot get pregnant because they are "too young." In fact, pregnancy *can* occur any time after the first menstruation. Menstrual irregularity also makes any form of rhythm contraception unreliable, even among teenagers who have enough basic reproductive knowledge to realize that the time of ovulation is normally the time of greatest fertility—knowledge that is not widespread.

Sexual Development in Boys

In boys, as in girls, the peak of the growth spurt typically comes fairly late in the sequence, as you can see in Figure 4.6. Malina's data suggest that, on average, a boy completes stages 2, 3, and 4 of genital development and stages 2 and 3 of pubic hair development before the growth peak is reached (Malina, 1990), with facial hair and the lowering of the voice coming only quite near the end of the sequence. Precisely when in this sequence the boy begins to produce viable sperm is very difficult to determine, although current evidence places this event some time between ages 12 and 14, usually *before* the boy has reached the peak of the growth spurt (Brooks-Gunn & Reiter, 1990).

Two things are particularly interesting about these sequences. First, if you look again at Figure 4.4 (p. 111) and compare it to Figures 4.5 (p. 113) and 4.6, you will see that while boys experience the onset of major hormone changes and the first steps of changes in primary and secondary sex characteristics at about the same time that girls do, their growth spurt comes about two years later. Most of you remember that period in late elementary school or junior high when all the girls were suddenly taller than the boys.

A second intriguing thing is that while the order of development seems to be highly consistent *within* each sequence (such as breast development or pubic hair development), quite a lot of variability occurs *across* sequences. I've given you the normative or average pattern, but individual teenagers often deviate from the norm. For instance, a girl might move through several stages of pubic hair development before the first clear breast changes, or experience menarche much earlier in the sequence than is usual. It is important to keep this variation in mind if you are trying to make a prediction about an individual teenager.

Figure 4.6

The sequence of pubertal changes begins about two years later for boys than for girls, but as with girls, the height spurt occurs relatively late in the sequence.

(*Sources:* Chumlea, 1982; Malina, 1990; Tanner, 1990.)

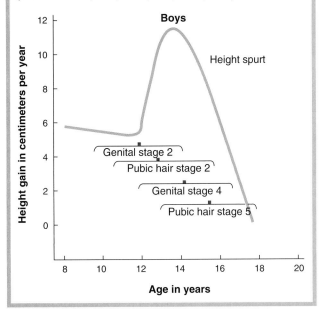

Adolescent Sexual Behavior

The many physical changes of puberty mean that the young person is stronger and faster and better coordinated than before. Those same changes also obviously make mature sexual attraction and behavior possible. Recent studies suggest that, on average, children experience their first feeling of sexual attraction—heterosexual or homosexual—very early in the pubertal process, at about age 10 or 11 (McClintock & Herdt, 1996); they begin to spend significant amounts of time thinking about the opposite sex at about the same age (Richards et al., 1998). Most, however, do not become sexually active as early as that. What do we know about the choices teenagers make about their sexual activity?

As is usually the case, the data I have to draw on are almost entirely specific to the United States or to other industrialized countries. It is good to keep in mind that the whole question of adolescent sexuality is a central issue for those of us in such cultures in large part because we have created such a long delay between physical sexual maturity and social maturity: Young people are physically mature at 13 or 14, but they are not financially independent or fully trained until age 20 or later. In cultures in which 12- or 14-year-olds are considered ready to take on adult tasks and responsibilities, to marry and to bear children, adolescent sexuality is handled very differently.

Adolescent sexual activity has increased fairly dramatically in the United States since the late 1950s (Miller et al., 1993). Surveys in the 1990s consistently show that roughly half of all high school students have had intercourse at least once (e.g., Resnick et al., 1997). Figure 4.7 (p. 116) gives some representative data, drawn from a national survey by the Centers for Disease Control (Kann et al., 1995), showing that this percentage increases steadily over the years of high school. You can also see in the figure that at every age, more boys than girls report sexual activity—although this sex difference is far smaller now than it was a decade ago. Comparable surveys in Canada show that

Figure 4.7

These data, from a nationally representative sample of 16,296 U.S. high school students interviewed in 1993 by the Centers for Disease Control, show that the likelihood of sexual activity increases steadily with age among current U.S. teenagers and is above 50 percent for high school students as a whole.

(*Source: Morbidity and Mortality Weekly Reports*, 44, 1993, Centers for Disease Control.)

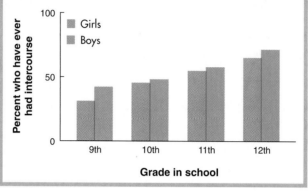

half of 16-year-olds and two-thirds of 18-year-olds have experience of intercourse (Herold & Marshall, 1996).

The number of teens reporting multiple sexual partners has also risen in recent years. In the 1993 survey by the Centers for Disease Control, 18.8 percent of all high school students and 27.0 percent of high school seniors reported having had four or more partners; among black male high school students, the equivalent rate was twice as high (Kann et al., 1995). Indeed, at every age we find similar ethnic differences in sexual activity, with black teens reporting higher rates of sexual activity than Latinos or whites. In the 1993 survey, for example, 79.7 percent of black high school students reported at least one experience of intercourse compared with 56.0 percent of Latinos and 48.4 percent of whites.

Although sexual activity is somewhat correlated with the amount of testosterone in the blood among boys (Halpern et al., 1993; Udry & Campbell, 1994), social factors are much better predictors of teen sexual activity than are hormones. Those who begin sexual activity early are more likely to live in poor neighborhoods in which young people have little monitoring by adults; they come from poorer families or from families in which sexual activity is condoned and dating rules are lax; they are more likely to use alcohol. Among girls, those who are sexually active are also more likely to have had early menarche, to have low interest in school, and to have a history of sexual abuse (Billy et al., 1994; Hovell et al., 1994; Small & Luster, 1994). In general, these same factors predict sexual activity among whites, blacks, and Latinos.

Reproductive Knowledge and Contraceptive Use. Despite their high levels of sexual activity, teenagers know relatively little about physiology and reproduction—a fact that highlights widespread weaknesses in sex education programs in schools (or at home.) For example, only about half of white and a quarter of black teenagers can describe the time of greatest fertility in the menstrual cycle (Freeman & Rickels, 1993; Morrison, 1985). Despite such ignorance, contraceptive use has risen significantly in recent years. Two-thirds of young people now report using some form of contraception (barrier methods, withdrawal, or some form of rhythm method) at their first sexual intercourse (Sells & Blum, 1996). Approximately half report having used a condom during their last experience of intercourse; another 18 percent report that they or their partner used birth control pills (Kann et al., 1995). Contraceptive use is lower among Latinos than among whites and in all groups is least likely among younger girls. Contraceptive use is

Critical Thinking

How many different reasons can you think of why teenagers would *not* use contraceptives? Which of those explanations might account for the lower use of contraception among Latinos?

Research Report
Homosexuality Among Adolescents

For the great majority of teenagers, "sexual activity" is heterosexual activity. A minority, however, are sexually drawn to their own gender. In a recent study of nearly 35,000 youth in Minnesota public schools, Remafedi and colleagues (1992) found that slightly fewer than 1 percent of the adolescent boys and only 0.4 percent of the girls *defined* themselves as homosexual, but about 1 in 10 said they were "unsure" of their sexual orientation, and 2 to 6 percent reported that they were attracted to others of the same sex. Similarly, in a smaller study of nearly 500 students in grades 10 to 12 in Australia, Buzwell and Rosenthal (1996) found that only 2 subjects described themselves as homosexual, but 4.2 percent had had at least one homosexual experience, although they labeled themselves as heterosexual.

These figures are a bit lower than but still generally consistent with the newest and most comprehensive data on sexual orientations among U.S. adults (Laumann et al., 1994): 2 to 3 percent of adults say they think of themselves as homosexual or bisexual; nearly twice that many say they are attracted to those of the same sex.

Recent evidence has greatly strengthened the hypothesis that homosexuality has a biological basis (Gladue, 1994; Pillard & Bailey, 1995). For example, several new twin studies show that when one twin is homosexual, the probability that the other will also be homosexual is 50 to 60 percent. For fraternal twins, this "concordance rate" is only about 20 percent, and among pairs of biologically unrelated boys adopted into the same families, the rate is only about 11 percent (Bailey & Pillard, 1991; Bailey et al., 1993; Whitam et al., 1993). More direct comparisons of gene patterning and brain architecture of homosexual and heterosexual men also point to the possibility (not yet firmly established) that homosexual behavior may be "hard-wired" (e.g., Hamer et al., 1993; LeVay, 1991).

Additional studies suggest that prenatal hormone patterns may also be causally involved in homosexuality. For example,

women whose mothers took the drug diethylstilbestrol (DES, a synthetic estrogen) during pregnancy are more likely to be homosexual as adults than are women who did not have such DES exposure (Meyer-Bahlburg et al., 1995).

Finally, there is accumulating information indicating that boys who show strong cross-sex-typed behavior in infancy and early childhood are highly likely to show homosexual preferences when they reach adolescence (Bailey & Zucker, 1995), findings that are consistent with the hypothesis that homosexuality is built-in by the time of birth.

Such biological evidence does not mean that environment plays no role in homosexuality. No behavior is entirely controlled by either nature or nurture, as I have said many times. At the very least, we know that 40 or 50 percent of identical twins do *not* share the same sexual orientation. Something beyond biology must be at work, although we do not yet know what environmental factors may be involved.

Whatever the cause, homosexual teenagers are a minority who face high levels of prejudice and stereotyping. Many are verbally attacked or ridiculed; as many as a third are physically assaulted by their peers (Remafedi et al., 1991; Savin-Williams, 1994). For these and other reasons, these young people are at high risk for a variety of problems. In Remafedi's Minneapolis study (1987a), for example, four-fifths of homosexual teens showed deteriorating school performance, and more than one-fourth dropped out of high school. They must also cope with the decision about whether to "come out" about their homosexuality. Those who do come out are far more likely to tell peers than parents, although telling peers carries some risk: In his Minneapolis study, Remafedi (1987b) found that 41 percent of homosexual male youths had lost a friend over the issue; a majority have not told either parent (Savin-Williams, 1998).

There is obviously much that we do not know about homosexual adolescents. What is clear is that the years of adolescence are likely to be particularly stressful for this subgroup.

more widespread in several European countries (e.g., Sweden and the Netherlands) in which such use is culturally acceptable and contraceptive information is readily available (Jones et al., 1986).

Teenage Pregnancy

There is no necessary connection between teenage sexual activity and pregnancy; it is possible to have high rates of adolescent sexual activity and low rates of teen pregnancy. In the Netherlands, for example, only 14 girls out of every 1000 between the ages of 15 and 19 get pregnant each year, even though the majority of teens are sexually active; in Canada, the equivalent rate is about 49 pregnancies per 1000 teenage girls per

The Real World

Which Teenagers Get Pregnant?

Whether a young woman becomes pregnant during her teenage years depends on many of the same factors that predict sexual activity in general, including family background, educational aspirations, timing of sexual activity, and subcultural attitudes (Coley & Chase-Lansdale, 1998). The likelihood of pregnancy is *higher*:

- The younger a girl is when she becomes sexually active
- Among girls from poor families, from single-parent families, or from families with relatively uneducated parents
- Among girls whose mothers became sexually active early and who bore their first child early
- Among girls who were rejected by their peers in elementary school, especially if they were high in aggressiveness (Underwood et al., 1996)

The likelihood of pregnancy is *lower*:

- Among girls who do well in school and have strong educational aspirations (such girls are more likely to use contraception if they are sexually active)
- Among girls with more stable and committed relationships with their sexual partners

- Among girls who have good communication with their mothers about contraception and whose mothers support the use of contraception
- Among girls who were popular with their peers in elementary school

Black and Latino teenagers are more likely than are Anglos to become pregnant, but for different reasons. Blacks are more likely to be sexually active, while Latinos, who have lower rates of sexual activity, are less likely to use contraception than are Anglos.

The riskiest time for teen pregnancy is in the first year or so after a girl has become sexually active. It is during these early months that girls are least likely to seek out contraceptive information or to use contraception consistently.

Finally, I should note that young women do not become pregnant all by themselves. The fathers involved are typically late teenagers or even in their twenties rather than 14- or 15-year-olds. They, too, bear responsibility for obtaining and using contraceptives and for supporting their children.

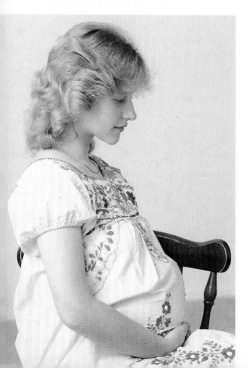

Teenage sexual activity is not more common in the United States than in most Western industrialized countries, but teen pregnancy is. Girls like this 14-year-old who give birth during their teens are more likely to have problems in adulthood, including lower income, less education, and higher risk of divorce, although many teenage mothers manage to surmount these difficulties.

year (Wadhera & Millar, 1997). In the United States, despite the increase in contraceptive use, the rate is markedly higher: about 120 pregnancies per 1000 girls per year, of which four-fifths are unintended (Henshaw, 1994), a rate that is higher than in any other developed Western country (Ambuel, 1995). Within the U.S. population, the pregnancy rate is nearly 3 times higher among African-American and Latino teen girls than among whites (Coley & Chase-Lansdale, 1998). Sandra Hofferth (1987a) estimates that fully 44 percent of all teenage girls in the United States will be pregnant at least once before the age of 20. About half these pregnancies are carried to term.

Let me try to put these fairly astonishing numbers into some kind of context. Birth rates have actually dropped among the entire U.S. population since the 1960s and early 1970s, *including among teenagers*. Indeed, the proportion of all births in the United States that are teenage births has declined steadily since 1975. What has increased since the 1960s is the rate of births to *nonmarried* teens. In 1995, 75 percent of all girls between the ages of 15 and 19 who gave birth in the United States were unmarried, compared with only 53 percent in 1970; among black girls, the current rate is 95 percent (Coley & Chase-Lansdale, 1998). Thus, it is not that more and more teenagers are bearing children, but that more and more teenage girls are choosing to rear their children without marrying.

Whether one sees this as a worrisome trend or not depends not only on one's religious or moral beliefs but also on evidence about the long-term consequences of adolescent childbearing for the adult lives of the girls involved and for the lives of the children they bear. The bulk of that evidence points to negative consequences for the teenage mothers (e.g., Coley & Chase-Lansdale, 1998; Hardy, et al., 1997), although it has been difficult to sort out which effects are due to early childbearing itself and which might be due to self-selection or the impact of poverty. Most studies indicate that teenage childbearing—whether the woman was married or unmarried—is associated with a larger total number of children, more closely spaced; fewer years of total education throughout adult life; lower levels of occupational success; lower income in adulthood; a greater chance of being on welfare; and higher likelihood of divorce in adult life. These relationships are found among African-American, Latino, and Anglo teens, so these negative outcomes are not just ethnic differences in disguise (Astone, 1993; Hofferth, 1987b; Moore et al., 1993).

The picture is certainly not entirely bleak. Pregnant teens who manage to complete their high school education, often through the support of special school programs, have better prospects. Happily, more than half of girls who become pregnant before age 18 do manage to complete high school by the time they are in their early twenties (Upchurch, 1993). Further, many teenage mothers who struggle economically in their early adult years manage to recover in their thirties and forties (e.g., Werner & Smith, 1992). Nonetheless, it is still true that teenage mothers, on average, are disadvantaged. For black inner-city girls in particular, the chances of moving out of poverty in adulthood seem to be far better for those who delay childbearing into their twenties than for those who bear children in adolescence (Freeman & Rickels, 1993).

For the *children* of these teenage mothers, the news is not good. These children are simply far more likely to grow up in poverty, with all the accompanying negative consequences for the child's optimum development (Duncan & Brooks-Gunn, 1997).

Using the Body: Motor Development

This brief picture of physical changes in the first 15 years of life should give you some sense of the alterations in muscles, fat, internal organs, and nervous system. What this description does not convey is the impact of all those changes on the child's ability to use his body to move about in the world, which psychologists call **motor development.** Included are both *movement skills,* often called *gross motor skills,* such as crawling, walking, running, and bike riding; and *manipulative skills,* often called *fine motor skills,* such as grasping or picking up objects, holding a crayon or a pencil, or threading a needle. Both gross and fine motor skills are present in some form at every age, as you can see in Table 4.3 (p. 120), but as a general rule, gross motor skills develop earlier, with fine motor abilities lagging behind. Thus, 6-year-olds can run well, hop, skip, jump and climb; many can ride a two-wheeled bike. But children this age are not yet skilled at using a pencil or crayon or cutting accurately with scissors. When they use such tools, their whole body is still involved—the tongue moving and the whole arm and back involved in the writing or cutting motion—a pattern plain in the photograph of the boy cutting (bottom). In the elementary school years, fine motor skills improve rapidly, making it possible for most children not only to write more clearly and easily, but also to play a musical instrument, draw, and develop sports skills that require fine motor coordination.

All these changes, particularly the baby's early shifts from sitting to crawling to walking, are normally a delight for parents to observe and encourage. Motor skill improvements have clear practical ramifications as well. One obvious example: Until a baby is able to crawl or walk, it is not necessary to put dangerous or fragile objects out of reach. When he begins to move around independently, childproofing the house becomes critical. Similarly, the types of toys you would buy or make for a child are obviously influenced by the child's motor skills. For example, at about age 2 or 3, the child may for the first time enjoy drawing with *large* crayons or pencils but cannot yet grasp smaller ones.

The emergence of motor skills also has an impact on the appropriate timing of children's sports activities—an application I've explored in the Real World box on page 121.

Variations in Rate of Development

Although virtually all children and teenagers go through the various sequences of physical development in the same order, children vary widely in the *rate* at which they

By age 1, young Nellie can not only walk; she can begin to navigate stairs. By age 5 or 6, most children have developed very good large-muscle skills, such as those the young soccer players need to run and kick. Yet the same 5- or 6-year-old who confidently rides a bike or throws a ball will approach a fine motor task like cutting with tense concentration and slow, still imprecise body movements.

Table 4.3

Sequences of Development of Various Motor Skills

Age	Locomotor/Gross Motor Skills	Manipulative/Fine Motor Skills
1–3 mos.	Stepping reflex; lifts head; sits with support.	Holds object if placed in hand; begins to swipe at objects.
4–6 mos.	Rolls over; sits with self-support by 6 months; creeps.	Reaches for and grasps objects, using one hand to grasp.
7–9 mos.	Sits without support.	Transfers objects from one hand to the other. By 9 months, can grasp with thumb and finger ("pincer grasp").
10–12 mos.	Pulls himself to standing; walks grasping furniture, then walks without help; squats and stoops.	Grasps a spoon across palm, but has poor aim of food to mouth.
13–18 mos.	Walks backward and sideways; runs (14–20 months).	Stacks two blocks; puts objects into small containers and dumps them.
2–4 yrs.	Runs easily; walks upstairs using one foot per step; skips on both feet; pedals and steers a tricycle.	Picks up small objects (e.g., Cheerios); holds crayon with fingers (age 2–3), then between thumb and first two fingers (age 3–4); cuts paper with scissors.
4–7 yrs.	Walks up and downstairs using one foot per step; walks on tiptoe; walks a thin line; jumps, throws, and catches fairly well.	Threads beads but not needle (age 4–5); threads needle (age 5–6); grasps pencil maturely but writes or draws with stiffness and concentration.

Sources: Connolly & Dalgleish, 1989; Capute et al., 1984; Den Ouden et al., 1991; Fagard & Jacquet, 1989; Gallahue & Ozmun, 1995; Hagerman, 1996; Mathew & Cook, 1990; Needlman, 1996; Thomas, 1990b.

go through all the body and motor changes I have described. Some children walk at 7 or 8 months, others not until 18 months. Some are skillful soccer players at 7 or 8 years, others not until much later (if at all). Such differences in the rate of development are particularly striking at puberty. Among 12- or 13-year-old girls, for example, some are already at stage 4 or 5 of breast development while others are still clearly prepubescent. Some 14-year-old boys are already fully developed, with lowered voices and full beards, while others still have the narrow, slim bodies of children.

As a general rule, a child tends to be consistently early, average, or late in most aspects of physical development. The child who shows slower bone development is also likely to walk later and to have later puberty (Tanner, 1990). There are exceptions to this generalization, but what Tanner calls the *tempo of growth* is a powerful element in development. These differences are interesting in their own right, but they are also important because of the ways in which they can affect a child's self-image, her relationships with her peers, or her general contacts with the world around her.

Most of the research on the psychological impact of early versus late or fast versus slow development has focused on puberty, where earliness or lateness of development appears to have especially strong psychological meaning. Researchers who have explored these issues have proposed an interesting and complex hypothesis that focuses on the role of internal models in shaping the experience of puberty. The general idea is that each young child or teenager has an internal model about the "normal" or "right" timing for puberty (Faust, 1983; Lerner, 1987; Petersen, 1987). Each girl has an internal model about the right age to develop breasts or begin menstruating; each boy has an internal model or image about when it is right to begin to grow a beard or for his voice to get lower. According to this hypothesis, it is the discrepancy between an adolescent's expectation and what actually happens that determines the psychological effect. Those whose development occurs outside the desired or expected range are likely to think less well of themselves and to be less happy with their bodies and with the process of puberty. They may also have fewer friends and experience other signs of distress.

The Real World

Sports for Children

In the United States, and increasingly in other industrialized countries, children no longer play much in the street or in backyards; they play on organized teams and groups: soccer teams, Little League baseball, swimming clubs, and the like. Many children begin such programs when they are 6 or 7, often with great enthusiasm, but participation peaks by age 10 or 11 and then declines rapidly. Why?

Children drop out of such programs for many reasons, but a key factor is the strong emphasis on competition and winning in many sports programs (Anshel, 1990; Harvard Education Letter, 1992). Children of 6 or 7 get involved in sports mostly because they simply enjoy moving their bodies rather than out of any desire to defeat some opponent. They want to do their best, but they care more about having a chance to play than they do about winning. Yet coaches in many organized sports, even those for young children, emphasize winning rather than fun or fair play or even basic exercise—a process sometimes called the "professionalization of play" (Hodge & Tod, 1993). Mark Anshel tells this story:

> The volunteer coach for the city league was meeting just before the game with his young athletes, boys aged nine and ten years. He was talking about how important it was for everyone to play well and win; this was a "big game." Then he asked whether anyone had any questions. A youngster raised his hand and asked, "Coach, will everyone get a chance to play?" "What's more important," the coach snapped back, "everyone playing, or winning?" (1990, p. 327)

Further, amateur coaches often have a poor understanding of normal motor skills among 6- or 7-year-olds. When they see a child who does not yet throw a ball skillfully or kicks a ball awkwardly, they label this child as clumsy or uncoordinated. From then on, these perfectly normal boys and girls get little playing time or encouragement. Only the stars—children with unusually good or early motor skill development—get maximum attention and exercise. Coaches may also overtly compare children's abilities, criticizing those who don't play as well rather than emphasizing effort and improvement. Children drop out of sports by age 10 or 11 because they have a clear impression that they are "not good enough" (Anshel, 1990) or because they experience their coaches as too critical and not supportive enough (Smith & Smoll, 1997).

In fact, 6 or 7 is really too early for most children to be playing on full-sized playing fields or in competitive games (Kolata, 1992). It would be far better to wait until age 9 or 10—if then—for competitive games. Children should spend the earlier years learning and perfecting basic skills in activities that are fun regardless of skill level and that involve as much movement as possible. Among sports activities, soccer and swimming are particularly likely to meet these conditions, not only because everyone is likely to get at least some aerobic exercise, but also because the basic skills are within the abilities of 6- or 7-year-olds. Baseball, in contrast, is *not* a good sport for most children this age because it requires real eye-hand coordination to hit or catch the ball, coordination that most 7-year-olds do not yet have. By age 10 or so, many children will be ready to play sports such as basketball, but many organized sports, such as tennis, are still difficult for the average child of this age.

If you want to encourage your children to be involved in some organized sport (as opposed to simply encouraging active games or outdoor play), choose carefully. Let the child try several sports—individual sports as well as team sports—to see which one or ones he or she may enjoy. The child's body type or size may suggest which sports are likely to be best. A lean child of average or below-average height may find soccer or gymnastics a good choice; a larger child with broader shoulders may make a good swimmer; taller children may be inclined toward basketball—although small size certainly does not disqualify a child from this sport (Malina, 1994). Whatever program you choose, make sure to select specific instructors or programs that deemphasize competition and offer skills training and encouragement to *all* children. Finally, don't push too fast or too hard. If you do, your child is likely to drop out of any type of organized sport by age 10 or 11, saying—as many do—that they feel inadequate, or that it isn't fun anymore.

In the U.S. culture today, most young people seem to share the expectation that pubertal changes will happen sometime between ages 12 and 14; anything earlier is seen as "too soon," and anything later is thought of as late. If you compare these expectations to the actual average timing of pubertal changes, you'll see that such a norm includes girls who are average in development and boys who are *early*. So we should expect these two groups—normal-developing girls and early-developing boys—to have the best psychological functioning. Early-maturing boys are also more likely to be of the preferred *mesomorphic* body type, with wide shoulders and a large amount of muscle. This body type is consistently preferred for boys at all ages, and because boys with this body type tend to be good at sports, the early-developing boy should be particularly advantaged. In contrast, late-developing boys, and to a lesser extent, late-developing girls, should be at some psychological disadvantage.

Research in the United States generally confirms these predictions. Girls who are early developers (before 11 or 12 for major body changes) show consistently more negative body images, such as thinking themselves too fat. Such girls are also more likely to engage in risky behavior like smoking or drinking; they more often get involved with misbehaving peer groups; they become sexually active at an earlier age; and they are more likely to be depressed later in adolescence (Alsaker, 1995; Brooks-Gunn & Paikoff, 1993; Ge et al., 1996; Silbereisen & Kracke, 1993). Very late development in girls also appears to be somewhat negative, but the effect of lateness is not so striking for girls as it is for boys. Among boys, the relationship is essentially linear: The earlier the boy's development, the more positive his body image, the better he does in school, the less trouble he gets into, and the more friends he has (Duke et al., 1982).

In nearly all these studies, earliness or lateness has been defined in terms of the actual physical changes. The results are even clearer when researchers have instead asked teenagers about their internal model of earliness or lateness. For example, Rierdan and colleagues (1989) have found that the negativeness of a girl's menarcheal experience was predicted by her *subjective* sense of earliness and not by the actual age of her menarche; girls who perceived themselves as early reported a more negative experience.

This link between the internal model and the outcome is especially vivid in a study of ballet dancers by Jeanne Brooks-Gunn (Brooks-Gunn, 1987; Brooks-Gunn & Warren, 1985). She studied 14- to 18-year-old girls, some of whom were serious ballet dancers studying at a national ballet company school. In this group, a very lean, almost prepubescent body is highly desirable. Brooks-Gunn therefore expected that among dancers, those who were very late in pubertal development would actually have a better image of themselves than those who were on time. And that is exactly what she found, as you can see in Figure 4.8. Among nondancers the same age, normal-time menarche was associated with a better body image than late menarche, but exactly the reverse was true for the dancers.

Thus, it seems to be the discrepancy or mismatch between the desired or expected pattern and a youngster's actual pattern that is critical, not the absolute age of pubertal development. Because the majority of young people in any given culture share similar expectations, we can see common effects of early or late development. To predict the effect of early or late development in any individual teenager, however, we would need to know more about her or his internal model or the shared internal models of his cultural subgroup.

Health and Illness

The study of both the common patterns and individual differences in normal physical growth forms the core of psychological research on physical development. For parents, as well as for physicians and for society as a whole, another key aspect of a child's

Figure 4.8

Serious ballet dancers clearly prefer to have a very late puberty. In this study, those dancers whose menarche was "on time" by ordinary standards actually had a poorer body image than did those who were objectively quite late, while the reverse was true for nondancers. Thus, it is perception of timing and not actual timing that is critical.

(*Source:* Brooks-Gunn & Warren, 1985, from Table 1, p. 291.)

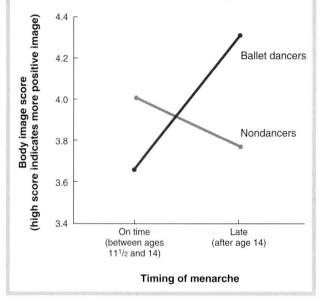

physical status is her health or illness. Let's start at the most negative end of the continuum of health, with mortality.

Mortality

Those of us who live in countries with relatively low rates of infant and childhood mortality are accustomed to thinking of childhood as a basically healthy time. Yet in the world at large, over 10 percent of children die before age 5; in many countries, the rate is higher than 20 percent, as you can see in Figure 4.9 (p. 124). In less developed countries, the most common cause of death is diarrhea, confounded with malnutrition. In contrast, the leading cause of children's deaths in the United States is accidents, particularly motor vehicle accidents (National Center for Health Statistics, 1996).

Happily, the rate of deaths in childhood in the United States has been declining an average of about 2 percent every year for the past five decades (Singh & Yu, 1996), suggesting that, as a society, we have begun to control at least some of the causes of mortality, particularly through the use of car seat belts and bicycle helmets. However, we continue to have wide ethnic variation in mortality rates among children. African-American children—especially African-American boys—have the highest death rates, primarily because of much higher rates of accidents and homicide; Asian-American children have the lowest rates, with Euro-American children falling in between (Singh & Yu, 1996).

Nonfatal Illnesses and Accidents

Nonfatal accidents are also common hazards for children. In any given year, about a quarter of all children under 5 in the United States have at least one accident that requires some kind of medical attention (U.S. Bureau of the Census, 1997; Starfield, 1991).

Figure 4.9

I find this a stunning figure, showing so clearly the different prospects for children in technologically developed countries like the United States compared to children in poorer countries.

(*Source:* "Child Survival: What Are the Issues?" by Mandelbaum, J. K., *Journal of Pediatric Health Care,* 6, 1992, p. 133, Fig. 1. © 1992 The National Association of Pediatric Nurse Associates and Practitioners. By permission of Mosby-Year Book, Inc. Based on data from Galway, Wolff, and Sturgis, *Child Survival: Risks and the Road to Health,* 1987.)

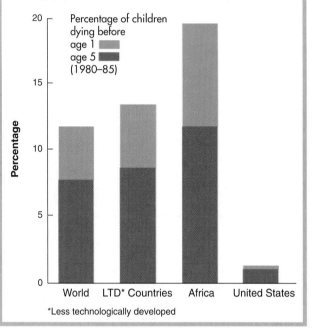

Most kids this age are sick in bed about five days a year, most often with a cold or the flu.

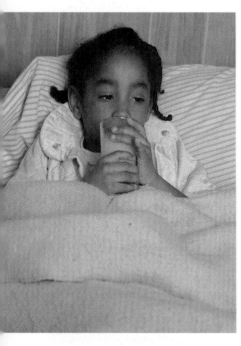

Critical Thinking

Children who are sick a lot early in life have a higher risk of health problems in adolescence and adulthood. How many different explanations can you propose to account for such a finding?

Among older children and adolescents, accident rates are even higher (Bussing et al., 1996). Falls and auto accidents are the two leading causes of accidental injuries.

At every age, accidents are more common among boys than among girls, presumably because of boys' more active and daring styles of play. Elementary school boys in the United States and Canada, for example, have an average of about 0.8 accidents per year, while girls have only about 0.6 (Bussing et al., 1996; Christoffel et al., 1996). Children who are less well supervised, such as (often) those from single-parent families or those in highly stressed families, also have more accidents (Christoffel et al., 1996).

Both *chronic illnesses* (generally, those lasting longer than 6 months) and briefer sicknesses (called *acute illnesses*) are also common in childhood. The most common chronic condition is *asthma,* from which nearly 7 percent of all U.S. children suffer (Centers for Disease Control, 1996a). The incidence of asthma has been rising rapidly in recent years; it is particularly common among children living in inner-city poverty, those who live with someone who smokes, or those living in crowded conditions. In such groups, current childhood asthma rates are often as high as 14 percent (Crain et al., 1994).

Even more common are acute illnesses, particularly upper respiratory problems such as the common cold or flu. I mentioned in Chapter 3 that the average baby has seven or eight respiratory illnesses in the first year. Preschool children have perhaps six such brief sicknesses a year, while in middle childhood the rate drops to perhaps four to six a year (Parmelee, 1986; Starfield, 1991).

Poverty and Health

At every age, children who are experiencing high levels of stress or family upheaval are more likely to become ill. We can see this effect in studies of children growing up in

Research Report
Child Abuse and Neglect

One of the most harrowing of all the dangers of childhood is the possibility of physical, sexual, or psychological abuse. Although figuring out what qualifies as abuse is not always simple, most psychologists today would follow definitions proposed by Douglas Barnett and his colleagues (1993; Rogosch et al., 1995b): *physical abuse* involves the nonaccidental infliction of bodily injury on the child—anything from a black-and-blue mark to injuries so extreme that the child requires hospitalization or dies; *sexual abuse* involves any kind of sexual contact between a child and a responsible adult that is for the purpose of the *adult's* gratification or gain; *physical neglect* includes both the failure to provide adequately for the child's nurturance and basic care and the failure to provide supervision adequate for the child's age.

It is extremely difficult to determine how common abuse may be, although all observers agree that it is disturbingly common in the United States. Most estimates suggest that about 1 child out of every 70 is abused in any given year (National Center on Child Abuse and Neglect, 1988; U.S. Bureau of the Census, 1997), although some researchers conclude that the rate may be as much as double that (Sedlak & Broadhurst, 1996; Straus & Gelles, 1986). Of this number, about half are cases of physical neglect, a fourth are cases of physical abuse, and a tenth involve primarily sexual abuse (Emery & Laumann-Billings, 1998). Children between ages 2 and 9 are most likely to be abused; infants are least often abused, although they are the most likely to die of any abuse they receive (National Center on Child Abuse & Neglect, 1988; U.S. Bureau of the Census, 1997). Of these abused children, perhaps a quarter to a third suffer extreme forms of violence; the remaining children experience milder forms of abuse (Emery & Laumann-Billings, 1998).

Why do parents abuse their children? There is no easy answer. We can identify certain risk factors, but abuse does not normally occur unless several of these risks occur in the same family at the same time (Rogosch et al., 1995a; 1995b; Spieker et al., 1996). Three elements appear to be key.

First is the role of the *parents' stress* in triggering abuse. The risk of abuse is higher in any family experiencing significant stress, whether that stress arises from unemployment, poverty, neighborhood violence, a lack of social support, or an especially difficult or demanding infant. No doubt each of us has some threshold of stress above which we are likely to snap—reacting with a fit of anger, with aggression, or, in some cases, with abuse of a child.

Still, stress alone, even fairly severe stress, is not enough to make abuse a certainty. Another key ingredient is the *parent's skill in dealing with the child* and with the stresses of her or his life. Some parents, who were themselves abused, simply know no other way to deal with frustration and stress or with disobedience in their child, other than striking the child in some way.

Others are depressed or unable to form the kind of emotional bond to the child that would help to prevent abuse. Alcohol and drug dependence, too, play a significant role in a great many cases (Emery & Laumann-Billings, 1998).

A third key element is a *lack of social support* or some sort of social isolation. When several of these key ingredients intersect—a high level of stress, a lack of personal support, a lack of alternative strategies or skills, and the personal inability to deal well with stress—abuse of a child (or a spouse) becomes highly likely.

The long-term prospects for abused children are not terribly hopeful, especially for the subset that have been most frequently or severely maltreated (Emery & Laumann-Billings, 1998). Physically abused children are far more likely than are nonabused children to become aggressive or delinquent at school age or adolescence, and they are more likely to be violent as adults (including such behaviors as date rape or spousal abuse.) They are more likely to be substance abusers in adolescence and adulthood, to attempt suicide, to have emotional problems such as anxiety or depression or more serious forms of emotional illness, and to have lower IQs and poorer school performance (Malinosky-Rummell & Hansen, 1993; National Research Council, 1993; Rogosch et al., 1995b). They have more difficulty forming intimate friendships at school age and adolescence (Parker & Herrera, 1996).

Sexually abused children also show a wide variety of disturbances, including fears, behavior problems, sexual promiscuity or sexual offenses in adolescence and adulthood, poor self-esteem, and *posttraumatic stress disorder*—a pattern of disturbance that includes flashbacks of the traumatic event, nightmares, persistent efforts to avoid thinking about or being reminded of the traumatic event, and signs of heightened arousal such as hypervigilance, exaggerated startle reactions, sleep disturbances, and interference with concentration and attention (Kendall-Tackett et al., 1993; National Research Council, 1993; Pynoos et al., 1995).

Children who suffer either type of abuse do not typically show *all* these symptoms, but they are far more likely than are their nonabused peers to show some form of significant disturbance. The more lasting and severe the abuse, the greater the likelihood of problems of these types.

The picture is not totally bleak. Some abused children are remarkably resilient, showing no measurable symptoms. Others show a decline in symptoms of distress when the abuse is stopped, especially if the child's mother was supportive and protective. Despite these few comforting words, though, let us not lose sight of the fact that long-term problems are common among children who experience this degree of hostility or hurt, nor of the fact that our society has not yet found good ways of reducing the incidence of such abuse.

Table 4.4

Comparison of Health Problems of Poor Versus Nonpoor Children

Problem	Rate for Poor Vs. Rate for Nonpoor
Low birth weight	1.5 to 2 times higher
Delayed immunization	3 times higher
Asthma	Somewhat higher
Lead poisoning	3 times higher
Neonatal mortality	1.5 times higher
Child deaths from accidents	2 to 3 times higher
Child deaths from disease	3 to 4 times higher
Reported to be in fair or poor health (rather than good health)	2 times higher
Percentage with conditions limiting school activity	2 to 3 times higher
Physical stunting (being in the 5th percentile or lower for height)	2 times higher
Days sick in bed or lost school days	40 percent higher
Severely impaired vision	2 to 3 times higher
Severe iron-deficiency anemia	2 times higher

Sources: Starfield, B., "Childhood Morbidity: Comparisons, Clusters, and Trends," *Pediatrics*, 88, 1991, pp. 519–526; Brooks-Gunn, J., and Duncan, G. J., "The Effects of Poverty on Children," *The Future of Children*, 7(2), 1997, pp. 55–71.

single-parent families, who have more accidents, more asthma, more headaches, and a generally higher vulnerability to illnesses of many types than do those living with both biological parents (Christoffel et al., 1996; Dawson, 1991). More generally, we know that children growing up in poverty have significantly more health problems than do those living in more affluent circumstances, as you can see from Table 4.4.

A sobering list, isn't it? This pattern is not unique to the United States. Equivalent risk differentials exist in virtually all countries. Nor are explanations hard to come by. Poor children have more limited access to health care, so they are less likely to receive timely or full immunizations, and they see health care professionals later in an illness. They also live in more dangerous home and neighborhood environments, with higher fire risks, higher exposures to lead, more neighborhood violence, and a higher likelihood of living with someone who smokes (Zill et al., 1995). They are also more likely to be malnourished, or at the least to experience periods of hunger or malnutrition (Community Childhood Hunger Identification Project, 1991; Meyers et al., 1995). Poorer health and nutrition, in turn, affect the child's ability to learn in school. We know, for example, that children who come to school without breakfast think more slowly and show smaller gains in achievement over a school year than do those who have breakfast each day (Meyers et al., 1989; Pollitt, 1995). Thus, poverty has a direct and cumulative effect on children's health and development.

Obesity

The other side of the coin from malnutrition is obesity—a problem that is growing in the United States, Canada, and many European countries. Although there is no standard definition of **obesity** or overweight for children, two definitions are common: (1) a body weight 20 percent or more above the normal weight for height given in standard weight charts, or (2) a body mass index (BMI) at the 85th percentile or above. The BMI is a more precise adjustment of weight for height. The specific BMI formula is

$$\frac{weight\ in\ kilograms}{(height\ in\ centimeters)^2}$$

Using the BMI measure, researchers have found that more than 20 percent of elementary school–age children in the United States are now classed as obese, a rate that has risen steadily since the early 1960s (Freedman et al., 1997; Troiano et al., 1995). Equivalently high rates of obesity are common in other Western countries as well. For example, researchers in Italy found that 23.4 percent of a sample of 10-year-old boys and 12.7 percent of girls were obese (Maffeis et al., 1993), while Canadian researchers report rates of about 20 percent (Lechky, 1994).

U.S. surveys also tell us that obesity (at least in the United States) is more common among Latino and African-American children than among whites, with the highest rates among Mexican Americans (Troiano et al., 1995). In the latter group, 26.7 percent of the boys and 29.0 percent of the girls are classed as obese in the most recent survey. In part, these ethnic differences are really poverty differences in disguise. Among poor children, obesity (as well as hunger) is common for the simple reason that higher-fat or higher-calorie foods are likely to be cheaper than are fruits and vegetables.

Obesity in childhood is a problem for two reasons. First, fat children are more likely to be fat as adults, and we know that obesity in adulthood is linked to higher health risks of various kinds. The reassuring fact is that the connection between childhood fatness and adult overweight is not automatic. The more extreme the child's overweight, the more likely he is to remain fat throughout childhood and into adulthood, but almost 80 percent of fat infants and toddlers, and roughly half of overweight school-age children, are not obese as adults (Serdula et al., 1993). (Conversely, more than half of obese adults were *not* fat as children.) Nonetheless, significantly overweight children are clearly at higher risk for adult obesity, a state linked to shorter life expectancies and higher risk of heart disease, high blood pressure, diabetes, gallbladder disease, and respiratory problems (Pi-Sunyer, 1995).

Obesity in childhood is also a problem because fat children are more likely than their thinner peers to be rejected or ridiculed. In one study, elementary school children described silhouettes of fat children as "lazy, dirty, stupid, ugly, cheats, and liars" and were less likely to choose them as friends (Stunkard & Sobol, 1995).

Causes of Obesity. Why are some children fat in the first place? Obesity in either childhood or adulthood appears to result from an interaction between a genetic predisposition and environmental factors that promote overeating or low levels of activity. Both twin and adoption studies show a clear genetic component. Adult identical twins have extremely similar adult weights even if they are reared apart, while fraternal twins differ much more in weight (Stunkard et al., 1990). Even more persuasive are studies of adopted children, which show that those reared by obese parents are less likely to be obese than are the natural children of obese parents (Stunkard et al., 1986).

Clear as these results are, we still cannot attribute all obesity to genetic heritage. For one thing, if heredity were the only factor involved, there would be no reason to find steady *increases* in rates of childhood obesity, as we have observed in most Western countries. Some environmental factors must be at work to produce such an increase.

One obvious environmental factor is diet. We know that the average child in the United States today eats a diet too high in fat and too low in fruits, vegetables, and grains (Muñoz et al., 1997), a pattern linked to increased risk of obesity. We also know that obesity is inversely related to levels of physical activity and that today's children are getting less physical exercise than was true even a few decades ago. The decline in physical activity is linked to a variety of causes. Among other factors, physical education classes have diminished in frequency and intensity in schools, and children now spend proportionately more time playing video games or watching TV than in active outdoor play (Andersen et al., 1998). One influential researcher, Steven Gortmaker

This overweight child not only has different kinds of encounters with his peers—he is also more likely to be fat as an adult, with accompanying increased health risks.

(Gortmaker et al., 1996) has pushed this a step further, arguing that there is a causal connection between the amount of time a child spends watching TV and the risk of obesity—not only because children who watch TV are more sedentary, but also because they are bombarded with ads for high-fat and high-sugar foods, so they develop less healthy eating habits and less healthy ideas about foods (Centers for Disease Control, 1996b). In a four-year longitudinal study, Gortmaker found that teenagers who watched five or more hours of television a day were four to five times as likely to show increases in overweight than were those who watched less than two hours a day. The prescription for children, and for our society as a whole, seems pretty clear: more exercise, healthier food, and less TV and other sedentary activities.

Special Health Problems in Adolescence

Adolescents have fewer acute illnesses than do infants, toddlers, or school-age children, but teenagers engage in many forms of risky behavior, often described as sensation seeking, that lead to markedly increased rates of accidents, injuries, and illnesses in this age range. Indeed, Jeffrey Arnett proposes, "Adolescence bears a heightened potential for recklessness compared to other developmental periods in every culture and in every time" (1992, p. 339). The form this recklessness takes, and the extent to which it is allowed expression, varies from one culture and one historical time to the next. In the United States, at this time, the cultural mores allow—perhaps even encourage—a wide variety of risky behaviors. Adolescents engage in more unprotected sex, drive faster, tailgate more often, and use seat belts less than do adults (Arnett, 1992; Centers for Disease Control, 1994a; Kann et al., 1995). Rates of driving while intoxicated are also high among adolescents, although arrests for driving while intoxicated are actually at their peak among those in their mid-twenties (U.S. Bureau of the Census, 1994). All these forms of risky behavior are more common among teenage boys than girls, although the rates for girls are rising in many instances. For both sexes, risky behavior is linked to health problems of various kinds.

Sexually Transmitted Diseases. One form of risky behavior is unprotected sex, which may result not only in an unplanned pregnancy but also in a **sexually transmitted disease (STD),** the label for any one of a cluster of diseases spread by sexual contact (also called venereal diseases). The most common of these are *chlamydia* and *genital warts,* which are contracted by somewhere between 10 and 40 percent of sexually active girls (Sells & Blum, 1996). *Gonorrhea* and *syphilis* are less common but potentially more serious, while *HIV* is life-threatening. Most of these infections can be treated successfully with antibiotics; if left untreated, they may cause pelvic inflammatory disease in females (which is linked to later infertility in many cases) or increase the risk of cervical cancer or arthritis. Untreated syphilis can cause paralysis, brain damage, convulsions, and sometimes death.

STDs are more common among teenagers and young adults than in any other age group, accounting for two-thirds of all the cases. Among adolescents in the United States, approximately 4 percent contract an STD each year. This high rate of infection among the young occurs for a variety of reasons, including the higher likelihood of multiple sexual partners, inconsistent use of condoms, a belief in their own invulnerability, and an unwillingness to seek medical treatment if they experience symptoms (Biro & Rosenthal, 1995).

The good news is that the use of condoms among sexually active teens has risen in recent years, as has their knowledge about sexually transmitted diseases, especially through AIDS instruction in schools. Despite these gains in prevention, STDs remain a significant problem among U.S. adolescents.

Smoking. Smoking is another risky behavior that is disturbingly common among teenagers, with well-established long-term health risks. Adolescents, however, are not uniformly convinced of those risks. Nearly half of eighth graders think that smoking a pack or two of cigarettes a day carries no great risk. By senior year, only about 30 percent still believe this, but by then many have a well-established smoking habit. In fact, nearly all first tobacco use occurs before high school graduation; most of those who do not smoke in high school never develop the habit, while most of the 3 million adolescents who smoke regularly become addicted and are unable to quit, even when they try (Centers for Disease Control, 1994a).

Ethnic groups differ widely in tobacco use, with African-American youth smoking the least and white youth smoking the most (Kandel et al., 1997; Wills & Cleary, 1997). In one study, researchers found that fewer than 5 percent of African-American high school seniors smoke daily, compared with about 12 percent of Latinos and more than 20 percent of whites (Hilts, 1995). These differences appear to reflect variations in peer pressure to smoke (among whites) or *not* to smoke (among blacks).

Alcohol and Drug Use. Alcohol and drug use are also disturbingly common among adolescents. National data suggest that many types of teenage drug use declined in the United States in the 1970s and 1980s, reaching a low point in 1992. For example, in 1979, 26.7 percent of adolescents between the ages of 12 and 17 reported that they had used marijuana; by 1992, this had dropped to 9.1 percent (National Household Survey on Drug Abuse, 1997a). Since 1992, however, illegal drug use among teenagers has risen rather rapidly (National Household Survey on Drug Abuse, 1997a; 1997b; Leukefeld et al., 1998). By 1996, marijuana use in this same age group had risen to 16.8 percent, and 22.1 percent said they had used some kind of illegal drug at least once; 9.0 percent said they had used an illegal drug in the past month (National Household Survey on Drug Abuse, 1997b).

Alcohol use among junior high and high school students is also high—although unlike the use of illegal drugs such as marijuana or cocaine, alcohol use has not increased in recent years; current rates of alcohol use among teenagers are markedly lower than what we saw in the late 1970s and early 1980s. Recent estimates, from the National Household Survey on Drug Abuse (1997b), indicate that 38.8 percent of teens aged 12 to 17 have tried alcohol at least once; 18.8 percent have had at least one drink in the past month, while 7.9 percent report a drinking "binge" in that same month—a binge being defined as five or more drinks on a single occasion.

Risky Behavior in Context. These various risky behaviors appear to be unusually common in adolescence because they help many teenagers to meet important psychological and social goals, including gaining peer acceptance or respect, establishing autonomy from parents and from other authority figures, coping with anxiety or fear of failure, and affirming maturity. Richard Jessor (1992) argues that these are absolutely normal, central goals of adolescence. So when some risky behavior, such as smoking, drinking, or early sexual activity, helps individual teenagers to meet those goals, such behaviors will be hard to change *unless* alternative ways of meeting these same goals are available or encouraged.

Jessor's argument also implies that those teenagers who will be most likely to show high-risk behaviors are those who enter adolescence with few social skills and

Many kinds of risky behaviors are at their peak in the adolescent years, with highly negative implications for the adolescent's health. Both alcohol and drug use are on the increase among U.S. teens.

hence few alternative avenues for meeting their social and personal goals. And that is indeed what researchers have found. For one thing, we know that reckless behaviors tend to cluster together: The same teenager who smokes is also more likely to drink in binges, use marijuana, have multiple sexual partners, not use a bike helmet, and get into fights or carry a weapon (Escobedo et al., 1997). Furthermore, those teens who show high rates of such reckless behaviors are likely to have had poor school records, low self-esteem, early rejection by peers, neglect at home, or some combination of these early problems (Leukefeld et al., 1998; Robins & McEvoy, 1990). By default, such children or teens are drawn to peers who share their patterns and their internal models of the world.

Bulimia and Anorexia. Two forms of eating disorder, bulimia and anorexia nervosa, are also significant problems among adolescents, particularly among girls. Many psychologists argue that these disorders are in fact only the extreme end of a continuum of problems relating to dieting and obsession about body shape and size that appear to be epidemic among white teenage (and increasingly preteen) girls in the United States and in Britain and some other European countries (e.g., Smolak et al., 1996).

Bulimia (sometimes called *bulimia nervosa*) involves three elements: (1) a preoccupation with eating and an irresistible craving for food, leading to episodes of binge eating; (2) an intense fear of fatness; and (3) some method of "purging" to counteract the effects of the binge eating so as to avoid weight gain. Typical purging methods are self-induced vomiting, excessive use of laxatives, or excessive exercise (Garfinkel, 1995). Alternating periods of restrained and binge eating are common among individuals in all weight groups. Only when binge eating occurs as often as twice a week and is combined with repeated episodes of some kind of purging is the syndrome properly called bulimia. Bulimics are ordinarily not exceptionally thin, but they are obsessed with their weight, feel intense shame about their abnormal behavior, and often experience significant depression. The physical consequences can include marked tooth decay (from repeated vomiting), stomach irritation, dehydration, lowered body temperature, disturbances of body chemistry, loss of hair, and in extreme cases cardiovascular problems (Mitchell, 1995; Muscari, 1996).

Most experts conclude that the incidence of bulimia has increased in recent decades in many Western countries, although firm figures have been hard to establish. Current estimates are that from 1 to 3 percent of adolescent girls and young adult women show the full syndrome of bulimia; as many as 20 percent of girls in Western industrialized countries show at least some bulimic behaviors, such as occasional purging (Attie & Brooks-Gunn, 1995; Brooks-Gunn & Attie, 1996; Graber et al., 1994). Many more are sufficiently concerned about their weight to diet regularly or constantly. None of these behaviors is found in countries where food is scarce.

Those adolescents most at risk for bulimia are those in cultural settings where slenderness is strongly emphasized, particularly if the girl herself wishes to pursue a career in which thinness is required, such as dance, gymnastics, modeling, or acting (Brownell & Fairburn, 1995). Bulimia also appears to be more common among girls who have been sexually abused, although this connection remains controversial among researchers (Perkins & Luster, 1997).

Anorexia nervosa is less common but potentially more deadly. It is characterized by a refusal to maintain body weight at or above a minimally normal level, with extreme dieting to maintain an abnormally low weight, an intense fear of gaining weight, and obsessive exercise. The weight loss can eventually produce a variety of physical symptoms associated with starvation: sleep disturbance, cessation of menstruation, insensitivity to pain, endocrine disorders, loss of hair on the head, low blood pressure, a variety of cardiovascular problems, and reduced body temperature. An anorexic's body image is so distorted that she can look in the mirror at a skeletally thin body and remain convinced that she is "too fat." As many as 10 percent of anorexics die as a result of their eating disorder. Some literally starve themselves to death; others die because of some type of cardiovascular dysfunction (Litt, 1996).

This 17-year-old has been hospitalized for anorexia. When she looks at herself in the mirror, chances are she sees herself as "too fat," despite her obvious emaciation.

As is true for bulimia, anorexia is far more common among girls and women than among boys or men. Perhaps 1 girl out of every 500 in Western countries (0.2%) is anorexic. Among European and European-American girls, especially those from professional families, the rate may be as high as 1 out of 100 (Brooks-Gunn & Attie, 1996; Litt, 1996). As is true for bulimia, the rate is considerably higher among subgroups who are under pressure to maintain extreme thinness, such as ballet dancers and high-performance athletes in sports in which thinness is highly valued, such as gymnastics (Stoutjesdyk & Jevne, 1993).

Both bulimia and anorexia typically begin with persistent dieting, reinforcing the idea that eating disorders represent the extreme end of a continuum that includes other forms of concern about weight (Cooper, 1995; Polivy & Herman, 1995). Such a link between dieting and eating disorders is further strengthened by recent evidence that in countries like Taiwan, Singapore, and China, where dieting has become a recent fad, eating disorders—almost never seen earlier—are becoming more common (Goleman, 1995a).

Yet a great many young women (and some young men) diet regularly, even obsessively, but never shift into a frank eating disorder. What tips a dieter into bulimia or anorexia?

Linda Smolak and Michael Levine (1996) propose the following scenario. A key factor is a strong "thinness schema"—a firm belief, common in many Western cultures, that thinness is an essential ingredient of beauty. Denise Wilfley and Judith Rodin point out that "a healthy woman of normal weight has 22% to 25% body fat, yet our current aesthetic ideal is based on actresses and models who have only 10% to 15% body fat" (1995, p. 80). A great many teenagers, especially white teens in the United States and Europe, accept this ideal and make valiant efforts to achieve it. Current research, for example, shows that three-quarters of teenage girls have dieted or are dieting. If you look only at chronic dieters (those who have dieted at least 10 times in the past year), the percentages are lower but still striking, as you can see in Figure 4.10. These numbers come from a questionnaire study of all junior and senior high school students in Minnesota in 1987 and 1988—a total of more than 36,000 teenagers (Story

Figure 4.10

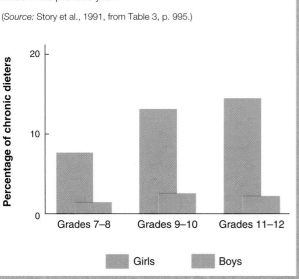

The percentage of junior high and high school students in Minnesota in 1987–88 who reported having dieted at least 10 times in the previous year.

(*Source:* Story et al., 1991, from Table 3, p. 995.)

Critical Thinking

If you had the power to change our culture in such a way that the rate of bulimia and anorexia would go way down, what changes would you want to make? Why, and how?

et al., 1991). You can see that chronic dieting was far less common among boys than among girls. Such dieting was also less common among black than among Latino and white girls.

When an adolescent combines such a thinness schema with perfectionism, body dissatisfaction (such as might be caused by teasing an overweight child), a strong emphasis on weight and shape within the family, and low self-esteem, she (or, less often, he) is more likely to shift from chronic dieting to an eating disorder.

The final ingredient in Smolak and Levine's scenario is some kind of precipitator or trigger. For some, this can be early puberty. One of the effects of puberty in girls is to increase the amount of body fat. This is particularly true of early-developing girls, who characteristically acquire and retain higher fat levels than do later-maturing girls. Indeed, early-developing girls are nearly twice as likely to have an eating disorder as are normal- or late-developing girls (Graber et al., 1994; Killen et al., 1992).

For others, the trigger may be some significant stressful life event, such as breaking up with a boyfriend. When several significant changes occur together (such as a girl who hits puberty just as she switches to junior high school, just as her parents divorce), the risk of an eating disorder seems especially high. Smolak and Levine propose that when a teenager with a strong thinness schema is able to deal with the stresses and tasks of adolescence one at a time, she is likely to develop some kind of disturbed eating pattern or chronic dieting but does not develop bulimia or anorexia. When stresses pile up, though, for a teenager with a strong thinness schema, perfectionism, low self-esteem, and poor familial relationships, the likelihood of an eating disorder is very high.

Of the two problems, bulimia is considerably easier to treat; anorexics frequently have relapses, even after extensive treatment. Newer treatment programs, however, offer some promise. In particular, treatment of both types of eating disorders increasingly involves antidepressant drugs, because depression very frequently precedes or accompanies the eating problem (Riggs, 1997). Among bulimics, antidepressant medication appears to be effective in about a third of cases.

Determinants of Growth: Explanations of Physical Development

In what I have said so far, I have mostly been dealing with description, with answering "what" questions. But "why" questions are equally important. Why does physical development occur as it does, and what can affect it?

Maturation

Maturational sequences certainly seem to be part of the explanation, especially for such central patterns as neuronal changes and changes in muscles, bones, and fat. In all these areas, while the *rate* of development varies from one child to the next, the *sequence* is virtually the same for all children, even those with marked physical or mental handicaps. Whenever we find such robust sequences, maturation of some kind seems an obvious explanation.

At the same time, Esther Thelen, one of the leading experts on motor development, points out that most of us have an overly simplistic view of the whole idea of maturation (Lockman & Thelen, 1993; Thelen, 1995). There is no "crawling gene" or "walking gene" that somehow "unfolds" in a sequence. Instead, she argues, any new movement or motor skill is a "final common pathway," a result of a complex system of forces operating together, including cognition, perception, and motivation, as well as underlying physical changes.

For example, for the toddler to learn to use a spoon to feed herself requires development of muscles in the hand and wrist, bone development in the wrist, eye-hand coordination skills that allow her to readjust the aim of the spoon as she moves it toward her mouth, and coordination of all these with properly timed mouth opening (Connolly & Dalgleish, 1989).

Obviously, Thelen is not denying the fundamental significance of the maturation of nerves and muscles. But she is saying that the concept of maturation alone does not *explain* the development of motor skills. In addition, of course, we should not forget the other elements in the explanatory equation.

Heredity

Our genetic heritage is individual as well as species-specific, so that each of us receives instructions for unique as well as shared growth tendencies. I've already given you some evidence indicating that the tendency toward obesity has a substantial genetic component. Many other aspects of body size and shape are also affected by the genotype. The heights of identical twins reared together, for example, are virtually the same; the correlations are in the range of .95, which is as close to a perfect correlation as one is likely to find in any psychological or physiological research. In contrast, the heights of fraternal twins of the same sex are correlated about .60. That is, fraternal twins are still quite similar in height—considerably more similar than pairs of strangers picked at random—but not as similar as identical twins.

Other body features influenced by heredity include arm and leg length, sitting height, hip width, and the breadth of the head, length of nose, and width between the eyes (Tanner, 1990). (Some ancestor certainly passed on a gene for long arms to me!)

Rate or tempo of growth, as well as final shape or size, seems to be affected by genes as well. Parents who were themselves early developers, as measured by such things as bone age or age of menarche, tend to have children who are faster developers too (Garn, 1980). Studies of identical and fraternal twins confirm this effect. For example, the age of menarche for identical twin girls is, on average, only 2 to 3 months apart, while for fraternal twin girls menarche occurs an average of 10 months apart (Tanner, 1990).

All in all, heredity clearly plays a significant role in the size and shape of the child's body and in the relative earliness or lateness of development.

Environmental Effects

At the same time, there are potent external influences on physical growth as well. One of the clearest pieces of evidence pointing toward such environmental influences is the observation that children in different birth cohorts grow at different rates, such as the steady and substantial decline in the average age of menarche among European (and American) girls between 1840 and 1970 I described earlier. Over the same decades, average final height and weight have increased, not only among European populations but among the Japanese as well.

What could account for such changes over time? The most obvious possibility is that there have been changes in life-style and diet.

Diet. Differences in diet may not only help to explain such secular trends; they also contribute to the individual differences we see in rates of physical development in any one cohort. I mentioned in Chapter 2 that mothers who are malnourished during pregnancy are more likely to have stillborn infants or infants who die in the first year. It seems logical to assume that the baby's diet after birth would also make a difference in many aspects of physical development, perhaps especially neurological development.

This hypothesis has turned out to be very difficult to test clearly, in large part because most babies who are undernourished are also growing up in environments that are low in other types of stimulation as well. What we do know is that poorly nourished children grow more slowly and don't end up as large (Malina, 1982). If their diet later improves, such children may show some catch-up in height or growth rate, but they are typically shorter and slower than their peers. In addition, of course, malnourished or undernourished children have less energy, which in turn can affect the nature of the interactions the child has with both the objects and the people around him. For example, in a study of schoolchildren in Kenya, Michael Espinosa and his colleagues (1992) observed that undernourished youngsters were more solitary and less active on the playground than their well-nourished peers. The children in this study were not severely malnourished. They were taking in about 1500 calories per day, which is enough to sustain a child but not enough to provide the energy needed for play, or perhaps for concentration in school over long periods.

Prenatal Environmental Influences. Prenatal environments can also have long-term effects on a child's physical development. One example is the impact of prenatal exposure to alcohol. Streissguth and her colleagues, whose work I described in Chapter 2, have found that 4-year-olds whose mothers drank while pregnant, compared to those whose mothers did not drink or drank less, had poorer balance and poorer fine motor skills, such as hand steadiness or the ability to tap rapidly with a finger (Barr et al., 1990). Caffeine ingestion and high use of aspirin during the pregnancy were also related to poorer fine motor skills among the 4-year-olds.

Practice. We can also think of environmental influences on physical development in terms of the child's own opportunities to practice various physical activities. Does a baby who spends a lot of time in a toy called an infant walker, which holds up the baby while he moves around, learn independent walking any sooner than a baby who never has that practice? Does a toddler who has many chances to climb stairs learn to climb them sooner, or more skillfully, than a toddler who is rarely exposed to stairs?

The answer, as usual, is fairly complicated. Two conclusions are reasonably clear. First, the development of such universal, basic skills as crawling or walking requires some minimum amount of practice just to keep the system working as it should. Children who are deprived of such normal practice develop motor skills much more slowly, and not in the normal sequence. A classic early study by Wayne Dennis of children raised in Iranian orphanages is a good illustration (1960). The babies in one of the institutions were routinely placed on their backs in cribs with very lumpy mattresses. They had little or no experience of lying or moving on their stomachs as a normal baby would, and they even had difficulty rolling over because of the hollows in the mattresses. These babies almost never went through the normal sequence of learning to walk—presumably because they didn't have enough opportunity to practice all the on-the-stomach parts of the skill. They did learn to walk eventually, but they were about a year late.

We also know that the development of really smooth, coordinated skill in virtually all complex motor tasks requires practice. The strength and coordination required to throw a basketball high enough to reach the basket may develop in predictable ways over the early years, assuming the environment is sufficiently rich to provide needed

To acquire the basic skills needed to run, even to throw an object like a ball, a child probably doesn't need any special practice. But to be able to run and throw well enough to be a good baseball player requires an enormous amount of very specific practice.

maintenance. However, to develop the skill needed to get the ball through the hoop with regularity, from different angles and distances, requires endless practice.

We are still uncertain, however, about the role of practice in the acquisition of many basic component skills, such as sitting, walking up stairs, climbing, or catching objects. Early studies seemed to show that extra practice in such basic skills didn't speed up their development at all, perhaps because virtually all children have enough opportunity for minimal practice in their ordinary lives. However, some recent studies contradict this conclusion, including one I already mentioned (in Chapter 3) showing that very young infants who are given more practice with the stepping reflex later walk at an earlier age. A more recent study by the same researcher (Zelazo et al., 1993) similarly shows that very young babies who are given more practice sitting are able to sit upright longer than those without such practice. So it may be that special practice helps to strengthen the muscles or affects the neural wiring diagram in some way that speeds up certain aspects of development. In Aslin's terms (recall Figure 1.1, p. 8), practice may have a *facilitating* effect, although the evidence is still pretty mixed.

As a final point about physical development, let me remind you of something I said at the very beginning of the chapter: The links between experience and physical development operate in both directions. Experience affects the child's skills, but the rate and pattern of the child's physical development also affect his self-image, his personality, and his interactions with the world around him. So physical development influences experience as much as the reverse.

Summary

1. It is important to know something about physical growth and development because specific new behaviors are triggered by physical changes, because physical skills affect the kinds of experiences the child can have, and because the child's feelings about her own body can affect self-concept and personality.

2. Changes in height and weight are rapid during the first year and then level off to a steady pace until adolescence, when a sharp "growth spurt" occurs.

3. Bones increase in number and harden slowly. Muscle tissue increases primarily in density and length of fibers, with a much larger increase at adolescence for boys than for girls.

4. Fat cells are added in the early years and then again rapidly at adolescence, in this case more for girls than for boys.

5. Changes in the nervous system are extremely rapid in the first two years. In most parts of the brain, dendritic and synaptic development reaches its peak by about age 3, with pruning of synapses occurring throughout childhood and early adolescence. Myelination of nerve fibers also occurs rapidly in the early years.

6. Specific experience plays a significant role in the pruning process; unused or underused synapses or pathways are pruned, while those that have been repeatedly stimulated are retained. Thus, a rich early environment helps the child retain a more complex neural network.

7. The physical changes of adolescence are triggered by a complex set of hormonal changes, beginning at about age 8 or 9. Very large increases in gonadotrophic hormones, which in turn trigger increased production of estrogen and testosterone, are central to the process.

8. Effects are seen in a rapid growth spurt in height and an increase in muscle mass and in fat. Boys add comparatively more muscle and girls more fat. A further pruning of dendrites also occurs, as does an increase in size of both heart and lungs.

9. In girls, mature sexuality is achieved in a set of changes beginning as early as age 8 or 9. Menarche occurs relatively late in the sequence.

10. Sexual maturity is later in boys, with the growth spurt occurring a year or more after the start of genital changes.

11. Sexual activity among teens has increased in recent decades in the United States, where roughly half of all high school students are sexually active and 1 in 10 teenage girls becomes pregnant each year.

12. Long-term consequences for girls who bear children during adolescence are negative on average, although a significant minority of such girls are able to overcome their early disadvantages.

13. Variations in the rate of pubertal development have some psychological effects. In general, children whose physical development is markedly earlier or later than they expect or desire show more negative effects than do those whose development is "on time."

14. The collective changes in bone, muscle, fat, and nervous system make possible the emergence of the various motor skills. Children of 6 or 7 have confident use of most gross motor skills, although there are refinements still to come; fine motor skills needed for many school tasks are not fully developed until into the elementary school years.

15. Childhood mortality is very low in most industrialized countries; in less developed countries as many as one in five children die before age 5.

16. Acute illnesses are a normal part of children's early lives. Young children have brief illnesses six to nine times each year. Chronic illness is less common, although some chronic illnesses, such as asthma, are rising in frequency.

17. Virtually all forms of physical disability, chronic illness, acute illness, and accidents are more frequent among children living in poverty. Explanations focus on lowered access to health care and on more dangerous home and neighborhood situations among the poor, as well as on higher levels of general stress.

18. Adolescents have fewer acute illnesses than younger children but more deaths from accidents, particularly automobile accidents. In general, they show higher rates of various kinds of risky behavior.

19. Alcohol and drug use are both high among teenagers; drug use has risen in the past five years. Those most likely to use or abuse drugs are those who also show other forms of deviant or problem behavior, including poor school achievement.

20. Eating disorders such as bulimia and anorexia, more common in teenage girls than boys, are rising in frequency in most Western countries. A primary cause appears to be societal emphasis on a thin body ideal, leading to dieting, a pattern that shifts to a more serious eating disorder in many girls who face unusual stresses.

21. Maturation is a key process underlying physical growth and development, but maturation alone cannot account for the patterns that we see. Some environmental support is required, and specific heredity, prenatal teratogens, and prenatal and postnatal diet affect both the rate and pattern of development in individual children.

22. The role of practice is complex. A minimum amount of practice is required to sustain development of basic physical skills; for more complex skills, specific practice is required for skill acquisition.

Key Terms

anorexia nervosa A serious eating disorder characterized by extreme dieting, intense fear of gaining weight, and distorted body image. **p. 130**

bone age A measure of physical maturation based on X-ray examination of bones, typically the wrist and hand bones. Two children of the same chronological age may have different bone age because they differ in rate of physical maturation. **p. 106**

bulimia An eating disorder characterized by an intense concern about weight combined with binge eating followed by purging, either through self-induced vomiting, excessive use of laxatives, or excessive exercise. **p. 130**

cortex The convoluted gray portion of the brain, which governs most complex thought, language, and memory. **p. 108**

endocrine glands Glands—including the adrenals, the thyroid, the pituitary, the testes, and the ovaries—that secrete hormones governing overall physical growth and sexual maturing. **p. 110**

estrogen The female sex hormone secreted by the ovaries. **p. 112**

fontanels The "soft spots" in the skull that are present at birth. These disappear when the several bones of the skull grow together. **p. 106**

gonadotropic hormones Two hormones secreted by the pituitary—follicle-stimulating hormone (FSH) and luteinizing hormone (LH)—that, at the beginning of puberty, stimulate the development of the glands in the testes and ovaries that then begin to secrete testosterone or estrogen. **p. 112**

medulla A portion of the brain that lies immediately above the spinal cord; largely developed at birth. **p. 107**

menarche Onset of menstruation in girls. **p. 113**

midbrain A section of the brain lying above the medulla and below the cortex that regulates attention, sleeping, waking, and other "automatic" functions; largely developed at birth. **p. 107**

motor development Growth and change in ability to perform both gross motor skills (such as walking or throwing) and fine motor skills (such as drawing or writing). **p. 119**

myelin Material making up an insulating sheath that develops around the axon in most neurons. This sheath is not completely developed at birth but develops over the first several years of life. **p. 109**

myelination The process by which myelin is added. **p. 109**

obesity Most often defined as a body weight 20 percent or more above the normal weight

for height, or a body mass index at the 85th percentile or above. **p. 126**

ossification The process of hardening by which soft tissue becomes bone. **p. 106**

puberty The collection of hormonal and physical changes at adolescence that brings about sexual maturity. **p. 112**

secular trends Patterns of change in some characteristic over several cohorts, such as systematic changes in the average timing of menarche or average height or weight. **p. 114**

sexually transmitted diseases (STDs) Also called venereal diseases. Category of disease spread by sexual contact, including chlamydia, genital warts, syphilis, gonorrhea, and HIV. **p. 128**

Suggested Readings

Brownell, K. D., & Fairburn, C. G. (Eds.). (1995). *Eating disorders and obesity: A comprehensive handbook.* New York: Guilford Press. Short, comprehensible chapters on every aspect of eating disorders and obesity. The book focuses primarily on adolescents and adults, although the issues raised and most of the findings are applicable to younger children as well.

Gullotta, T. P., Adams, G. R., & Montemayor, R. (Eds.). (1993). *Adolescent sexuality.* Newbury Park, CA: Sage. A first-rate volume of papers on all aspects of this important subject. Of particular interest are a paper by Dyk reviewing information on physical changes at adolescence and one by Miller et al. on sexual behavior in adolescents.

Kemper, K. J. (1996). *The wholistic pediatrician.* New York: HarperCollins. A fine new book providing advice for parents concerning the major illnesses of infancy and childhood, including asthma, colds, colic, diarrhea, ear infections, and many others. Kemper reviews what we know about the full range of therapeutic

options, from simple things a parent can do at home, through various natural remedies, to traditional medical treatments.

Malina, R. M. (1990). Physical growth and performance during the transitional years (9–16). In R. Montemayor, G. R. Adams, & T. P. Gullotta (Eds.), *From childhood to adolescence: A transitional period?* (pp. 41–62). Newbury Park, CA: Sage. Malina is one of the key researchers studying physical growth. This particular paper focuses on puberty, but it contains references to much of Malina's work on other ages as well.

Millstein, S. G., Petersen, A. C., & Nightingale, E. O. (Eds.). (1993). *Promoting the health of adolescents: New directions for the twenty-first century.* New York: Oxford University Press. An excellent volume covering all aspects of the important question of how we can promote better health and health habits in adolescence.

National Research Council. (1993). *Understanding child abuse and neglect.*

Washington, DC: National Academy Press. This excellent book summarizes the work of a panel of experts, brought together to analyze all of what we now know about maltreatment of children.

Shore, R. (1997). *Rethinking the brain: New insights into early development.* New York: Families and Work Institute. You may have some difficulty finding this book (I had to order it specially), but it is worth the effort. It is an excellent, readable, up-to-date summary of current research and theorizing about brain development, including environmental influences on brain development.

Tanner, J. M. (1990). *Foetus into man: Physical growth from conception to maturity.* Cambridge, MA: Harvard University Press. This is a revised and updated version of Tanner's classic 1978 volume of the same title. It provides a detailed but very thorough and remarkably understandable discussion of what we know about physical growth.

5

Perceptual Development

Have you ever seen a baby trying to feed herself something mushy and messy like chocolate pudding? It is a wonderful and fascinating sight—more charming, of course, if someone else has to clean up the child afterward! In the beginning, babies don't have very good aim, so the chocolate pudding goes in the hair, all over the face, and down the front of the shirt. Most babies are not at all bothered by the mess and will look at you with delighted grins in the midst of the goo.

In fact, it is no small task for the toddler to get that spoon reliably into her mouth. It obviously involves motor skills, since she has to be able to grasp the spoon and move her hand and arm toward her mouth. Motor skills alone, however, are not enough. She also has to use a wide range of *perceptual* information. She has to see the spoon and/or feel it in her hand, estimate the distance from the mouth and gauge the appropriate trajectory, meanwhile coordinating the visual and kinesthetic information as she goes along, so that she can change her aim if she needs to.

In Chapter 4 I tried hard to make the case that we cannot understand the development of the child's thinking, or of her emerging social relationships, without having some understanding of physical development. Here I want to make the same case for perceptual development. Perceptual processes form a part of virtually every task a child must perform, of every motor or cognitive skill that is developed. To identify Mom or Dad she has to discriminate among voices, faces, or even smells. To recognize faces, she must pay attention to (and remember) individual features or patterns of features. To learn to talk she must hear differences among sounds, focusing eventually on the repertoire of sounds used in the language spoken around her.

To understand a child's development, then, we have to understand what kinds of sense impressions are possible for her, both at birth and over the years of development. And we have to understand how the child comes to interpret those sense impressions—to discriminate among them, to recognize or understand patterns. In this sense the study of perceptual development forms a kind of bridge between the study of physiological changes, such as the changes in the nervous system I described in the last chapter, and the study of thinking, which I'll be turning to in Chapter 6.

The study of perceptual development has also been significant because it has been a key battleground for the dispute about nature versus nurture. Theorists who study perceptual development have always labeled this as the contrast between **nativism** and **empiricism** rather than nature versus nurture, but the issue is precisely the same: How much of our basic perceptual understanding of the world is built-in? How much is the product of experience? This issue has been so central in studies of perception that researchers have focused almost all their attention on young infants; it is only among infants that we can observe the organism when it is relatively uninfluenced by specific experience. The early months are also the time of most rapid change in perceptual skills, and hence a time of greater interest to psychologists trying to understand the processes of development. For both these reasons, most of the information I'll be giving you in this chapter describes perceptual processes in very young children. But that age limitation makes the issues no less fascinating.

Success! The spoon is in the mouth! At 1 year, Genevieve isn't very skillful yet, but she is already able to coordinate the perceptual and motor skills involved in this complex task at least a bit.

Ways of Studying Early Perceptual Skills

It took a while for psychologists to figure out how to study infants' perceptual skills. Babies can't talk and can't respond to ordinary questions, so how were we to decipher just what they could see, hear, or discriminate? Eventually, clever researchers figured out three basic methods that allow us to "ask" a baby about what he experiences.

In the *preference technique,* devised by Robert Fantz (1956), the baby is simply shown two pictures or two objects, and the researcher keeps track of how long the baby looks at each one. If many infants shown the same pair of pictures consistently look longer at one picture than the other, it not only tells us that babies see some difference between the two but also may reveal something about the kinds of objects or pictures that capture babies' attention.

Another strategy takes advantage of the processes of *habituation* and *dishabituation* I described in Chapter 3. You first present the baby with a particular sight or sound over and over until he habituates—that is, until he stops looking at it or showing interest in it. Then you present another sight or sound or object that is slightly different from the original one and watch to see if the baby shows renewed interest (dishabituation). If the baby does show such renewed interest, you know he perceives the slightly changed sight or sound as "different" in some way from the original.

The third option is to use the principles of *operant conditioning* I described in Chapter 1. For example, an infant might be trained to turn her head when she hears a particular sound, using the sight of an interesting moving toy as a reinforcement. After the learned response is well established, the experimenter can vary the sound in some systematic way to see whether or not the baby still turns her head.

Research using variations on these three techniques has now yielded a rich array of information about young infants' perceptual capacities. To simplify the descriptive task, let me divide the information into two groups we might refer to as "basic" and "more complex" skills. The distinction I am using here is similar to the distinction between sensation and perception given in most psychology texts. When we study *sensation,* we are asking just what information the sensory organs receive. Does the structure of the eye permit infants to see color? Are the structure of the ear and the cortex such that a very young infant can discriminate among different pitches? When we study *perception,* we are asking what the individual does with the sensory information, how it is interpreted or combined.

Basic Sensory Skills

The common theme running through all of what I will say about basic sensory skills is that newborns and young infants have far more sensory capacity than physicians or psychologists thought even as recently as a few decades ago. Perhaps because babies' motor skills are so obviously poor, we assumed that their sensory skills were equally poor. But we were wrong. A newborn does not have all the sensory capacities of a 2-month-old, a 1-year-old, or an adult. Still, most of the basic skills are in place in at least rudimentary form.

🖥 Seeing

For example, until twenty-five or thirty years ago, many medical texts stated that the newborn infant was blind. Now we know that the newborn has poor visual **acuity** but is quite definitely not blind. The usual standard for visual acuity in adults is "20/20" vision. This means that you can see and identify something that is 20 feet away that the average person can also see at 20 feet. A person with 20/100 vision, in contrast, has to be as close as 20 feet to see something that the ordinary person can see at 100 feet. In other words, the higher the second number, the poorer the person's visual acuity. At birth the infant's acuity is in the range of 20/200 to 20/400, but it improves rapidly during the first year as a result of all the swift changes occurring in the brain I described in the last chapter, including myelination, dendritic development, and pruning. Most infants reach the level of 20/20 vision by about 1 year of life (Haith, 1990).

The fact that the newborn sees so poorly is not so negative a thing as it might seem at first. Of course it does mean that a baby doesn't see faraway things very clearly; he probably can't see well enough to distinguish two people standing nearby. But he sees quite well close up, which is all that is necessary for most encounters with the people

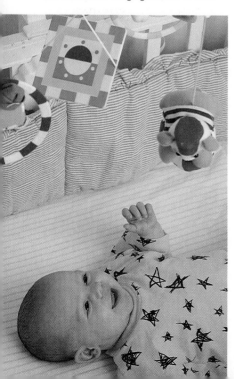

At 2 months, Eleanor's visual acuity is good enough that she can clearly see the colorful mobile hanging above her crib.

who care for him or with objects immediately at hand, such as breast, bottle, or mobiles hanging above his crib.

Tracking Objects in the Visual Field. When our young chocolate pudding eater tries to get the spoon in her mouth, one of the things she needs to do is keep her eyes on her hand or the spoon as she moves it toward herself. This process of following a moving object with your eyes is called **tracking,** and you do it every day in a variety of situations. You track the movement of other cars when you are driving; you track as you watch a friend walk toward you across the room; a baseball outfielder tracks the flight of the ball so that he can catch it. Because a newborn infant can't yet move independently, a lot of her experiences with objects are with things that move toward her or away from her. If she is to have any success in recognizing objects, she has to be able to keep her eyes on them as they move; she must be able to track.

Studies by Richard Aslin (1987a) and others show that tracking is initially fairly inefficient but improves quite rapidly. Infants younger than 2 months show some tracking for brief periods if the target is moving very slowly, but somewhere around 6 to 10 weeks a shift occurs, and babies' tracking becomes skillful rather quickly. You can see the change graphically in Figure 5.1, taken from a study by Aslin.

Color Vision. The tale I can tell about color vision is similar. Researchers in this field have established that the types of cells in the eye (cones) necessary for perceiving red and green are clearly present by 1 month, perhaps at birth; those required for perceiving blue are probably present by then as well (Bornstein et al., 1992). Thus, infants can and do see and discriminate among various colors.

Taken together, these findings certainly do not support the notion that an infant is blind at birth. While it is true that the infant's acuity is initially poor, it improves rapidly, and other visual capacities are remarkably well developed early on. There are also some interesting hints that some kind of "shifting of gears" may take place at approximately 2 months; a number of skills, including the scanning of objects and tracking, improve incrementally at about that age (Bronson, 1994). But we don't yet know whether such a change is the result of such neurological changes as the rapid proliferation of synapses and the growth of dendrites, of changes in the eye itself, or perhaps of the child's experience.

Hearing

Acuity. Although children's hearing improves up to adolescence, newborns' auditory acuity is actually better than their visual acuity. Current research evidence suggests that within the general range of pitch and loudness of the human voice, newborns hear nearly as well as adults do. Only with high-pitched sounds is their auditory skill less than that of an adult; such a sound needs to be louder before the newborn can hear it than is true for older children or adults (Werner & Gillenwater, 1990).

Detecting Locations. Another basic auditory skill that exists at birth but improves with age is the ability to determine the location of a sound. Because your two ears are separated from one another, sounds arrive at one ear slightly before the other, which allows you to judge location. Only if a sound comes from a source equidistant from the two ears (the "midline") does this system fail. In this case, the sound arrives at the same time to the two ears and you know only that the sound is somewhere on your midline. We know that newborns can judge at least the general direction from which a sound has come because they will turn their heads in roughly the right direction toward some sound. Finer-grained location of sounds, however, is not well developed at birth. For example, Barbara Morrongiello has observed babies' reactions to sounds played at the midline and then sounds coming from varying degrees away from the midline. Among infants 2 months old, it takes a shift of about 27 degrees off of midline before the baby shows a changed response; among 6-month-olds, only a 12-degree shift is needed,

Critical Thinking

Can you think of other examples of tracking in your everyday life or examples of activities in which the ability to track well would be especially important? What about playing basketball or target shooting or playing soccer?

Figure 5.1

The red line in each figure shows the trajectory of the moving line that babies tried to follow with their eyes in Aslin's experiment. The black line represents one baby's eye movements at 6 weeks and again at 10 weeks. At 6 weeks, the baby more or less followed the line, but not smoothly. By 10 weeks, the same baby's tracking skill was remarkably smooth and accurate.

(*Source:* Aslin, Richard N., "Motor Aspects of Visual Development in Infancy," *Handbook of Infant Perception: Vol. 1, From Sensation to Perception,* P. Salapatek and L. Cohen, eds. © 1987 by Academic Press. Adapted by permission.)

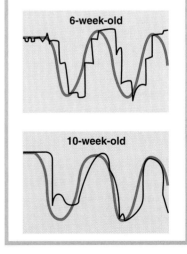

while by 18 months, discrimination of a 4-degree shift is possible—nearly at the skill level seen in adults (Morrongiello, 1988; Morrongiello et al., 1990).

Other Senses

Smelling and Tasting. The senses of smell and taste have been studied much less, but we do have some basic knowledge. As with adults, the two senses are intricately related—that is, if you cannot smell for some reason (like when you have a cold), your taste sensitivity is also significantly reduced. Taste is detected by the taste buds on the tongue, which register four basic tastes: sweet, sour, bitter, and salty. Smell is registered in the mucous membranes of the nose and has nearly unlimited variations.

Newborns appear to respond differentially to all four of the basic flavors (Crook, 1987). Some of the clearest demonstrations of this come from an elegantly simple set of early studies by Jacob Steiner (Ganchrow et al., 1983; Steiner, 1979). Newborn infants who had never been fed were photographed before and after flavored water was put into their mouths. By varying the flavor, Steiner could determine whether the babies reacted differently to different tastes. As you can see in Figure 5.2, babies responded quite differently to sweet, sour, and bitter flavors.

Babies as young as 1 week old can also tell the difference between such complex smells as personal body odors. Specifically, they can discriminate between their mother's and other women's smells, although this seems to be true only for babies who are being breast-fed and who thus spend quite a lot of time with their noses against their mothers' bare skin (Cernoch & Porter, 1985).

Figure 5.2

These are three of the newborns Steiner observed in his experiments on taste response. The left-hand column shows each baby's normal expression; the remaining columns show the change in expression when they were given sweet, sour, and bitter tastes. What is striking is how similar the expressions are for each taste.

(*Source:* Steiner, J. E., "Human Facial Expressions in Response to Taste and Smell Stimulation," in *Advances in Child Development and Behavior*, Vol. 13, H. W. Reese and L. P. Lipsitt, eds. © 1979 by Academic Press. By permission.)

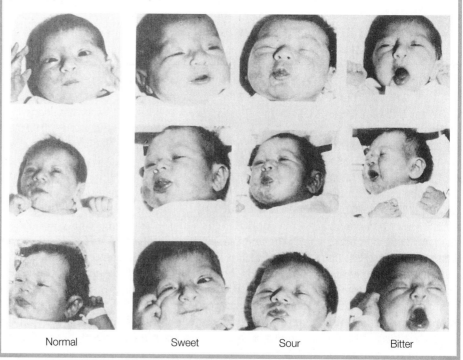

| Normal | Sweet | Sour | Bitter |

Senses of Touch and Motion. The infant's senses of touch and motion may well be the best developed of all. Certainly these senses are sufficiently well developed to get the baby fed. If you think back to the list of reflexes in the newborn I gave you in Chapter 3, you'll realize that the rooting reflex relies on a touch stimulus to the cheek while the sucking reflex relies on touch in the mouth. Babies appear to be especially sensitive to touches on the mouth, the face, the hands, the soles of the feet, and the abdomen, with less sensitivity in other parts of the body (Reisman, 1987).

I am aware that all of what I have said about these sensory abilities is fairly dry and technical. The important point for you to remember is that, as Reisman puts it, "we think of infants as helpless but they are born with some exquisitely tuned sensory abilities" (1987, p. 265).

Complex Perceptual Skills: Preferences, Discriminations, and Patterns

When we turn to studies of more complex perceptual skills, the abilities of very young infants seem even more striking. Very young infants are able to make remarkably fine discriminations among sounds, sights, and feelings, and they pay attention to and respond to *patterns*, not just to individual events. Let's begin again with vision.

Looking

Depth Perception. One of the complex skills that has been most studied is depth perception. You need this ability any time you reach for something or decide whether you have room to make a left turn before an oncoming car gets to you.

Similarly, an infant needs to be able to judge depth in order to perform all kinds of simple tasks, including judging how far away an object is so that he can reach for it, or how far it is to the floor if he has ideas about crawling off the edge of the couch, or how to aim a spoon toward a bowl of chocolate pudding.

It is possible to judge depth using any (or all) of three rather different kinds of information: First, *binocular* cues involve both eyes, each of which receives a slightly different visual image of an object; the closer the object is, the more different these two views are. In addition, of course, information from the muscles of the eyes also tells you something about how far away an object may be. Second, *pictorial* information, sometimes called *monocular* cues, requires input from only one eye. For example, when one object is partially in front of another one, you know that the partially hidden object is further away—a cue called *interposition*. The relative size of two similar objects, such as telephone poles or two people you see in the distance, may also indicate that the smaller-appearing one is further away. Linear perspective (like railroad lines that seem to get closer together as they are further away) is another monocular cue. Third, *kinetic* cues come from either your own motion or the motion of some object: If you move your head, objects near you seem to move more than objects further away (a phenomenon called *motion parallax*). Similarly, if you see some object moving, such as a person walking across a street or a train moving along a track, closer objects appear to move over larger distances in a given space of time.

How early can an infant judge depth, and which of these cues does he use? This is still an active area of research, so the answer I can give you is not final. The best conclusion at the moment seems to be that kinetic information is used first, perhaps by about 3 months of age; binocular cues are used beginning at about 4 months; and pictorial (monocular) cues are used last, perhaps at 5 to 7 months (Bornstein et al., 1992).

I don't have enough room to talk about the research on each of these three types of cues, so let me concentrate on the most extensive and most fascinating line of research, which has involved the use of kinetic cues. In a remarkably clever early study, Eleanor Gibson and Richard Walk (1960) devised an apparatus called a *visual cliff*. You can see

Critical Thinking

Think of three or four other everyday situations in which the ability to judge depth is critical.

One of the many skills 5-month-old Peter has to have to reach for and grasp his toy is the ability to judge depth. How far away is the toy? Is it near enough for him to reach with his hand?

from the picture in Figure 5.3 that it consists of a large glass table with a sort of runway in the middle. On one side of the runway is a checkerboard pattern immediately below the glass; on the other side—the "cliff" side—the checkerboard is several feet below the glass. The baby could judge depth here by several means, but it is primarily kinetic information that is useful, since the baby in motion would see the nearer surface move more than the further surface. If a baby has no depth perception, she should be equally willing to crawl on either side of the runway, but if she can judge depth, she should be reluctant to crawl out on the "cliff" side.

Since an infant had to be able to crawl in order to be tested in the Gibson and Walk procedure, the original subjects were all 6 months old or older. Most of these infants did *not* crawl out on the cliff side but were quite willing to crawl out on the shallow side. In other words, 6-month-old babies have depth perception.

What about younger infants? The traditional visual cliff procedure can't give us the answer, since the baby must be able to crawl in order to "tell us" whether he can judge depth. With younger babies, researchers have studied kinetic cues by watching babies react to apparently looming objects. Most often the baby observes a film of an object moving toward him, apparently on a collision course. If the infant has some depth perception, he should flinch, move to one side, or blink as the object appears to come very close. Such flinching has been consistently observed in 3-month-olds (Yonas & Owsley, 1987). Most experts now agree that this is about the lower age limit of depth perception.

Figure 5.3

In this "visual cliff" apparatus, like the one used by Gibson and Walk, Mom tries to entice her baby out onto the "cliff" side. But because the infant can perceive depth, he thinks he will fall if he comes toward her, so he stays put, looking concerned.

What Babies Look At. Even though a baby cannot judge depth right away, her behavior is governed by visual information from the very first minutes of life. We know that from the beginning, babies look at the world around them in a nonrandom way. In Marshall Haith's phrase (1980), there are "rules babies look by." Furthermore, those rules seem to change with age.

In the first two months, a baby's visual attention is focused on *where* objects are in his world (Bronson, 1991). Babies scan the world around them—not very smoothly or skillfully, to be sure, but nonetheless regularly, even in the dark. This general scanning continues until they come to a sharp light/dark contrast, which typically signals the edge of some object. Once he finds such an edge, a baby stops searching and moves his eyes back and forth across and around the edge. Thus, the initial rule seems to be: Scan till you find an edge and then examine the edge. Motion also captures a baby's attention at this same age, so he will look at things that move as well as things with large light/dark contrast.

These rules seem to change between 2 and 3 months, perhaps because the cortex has then developed more fully. At about this time the baby's attention seems to shift from *where* an object is to *what* an object is. Put another way, the baby seems to move from a strategy designed primarily to *find* things to a strategy designed primarily to *identify* things. Babies this age begin to scan rapidly across an entire figure rather than getting stuck on edges. As a result, they spend more time looking at the internal features of some object or array of objects and are thus better able to identify the objects.

What is amazing about this shift is the degree of detail infants now seem to be able to take in and respond to. They notice whether two pictures are placed horizontally or vertically, they can tell the difference between pictures with two things in them and pictures with three things in them, and they clearly notice patterns, even such apparently abstract patterns as "big thing over small thing."

One early study that illustrates this point particularly well comes from the work of Albert Caron and Rose Caron (1981), who used stimuli like those in Figure 5.4 in a habituation procedure. The babies were first shown a series of pictures, like those labeled *training stimuli* in Figure 5.4, that shared some particular relationship. The example I've shown in the figure is "small over big." After the baby stopped being interested in these training pictures (that is, after he habituated), the Carons showed him another figure (the "test stimulus") that either followed the same pattern or followed some other pattern, such as those you can see at the bottom of Figure 5.4. If the baby had really habituated to the *pattern* of the original pictures (small over big), he should show little interest in stimuli like the A test stimulus ("Ho hum, same old boring small over big thing"), but he should show renewed interest in test stimulus B ("Hey, here's something new!"). Caron and Caron found that 3- and 4-month-old children did precisely that. So even at this early age, babies find and pay attention to patterns, not just to specific stimuli.

Faces: An Example of Responding to a Complex Pattern. From the beginning of this new era of research on infant perception, researchers have been especially interested in babies' perception of faces, not only because of the obvious relevance for parent-infant relationships, but because of the possibility that there might be a built-in preference for faces or facelike arrangements—a variant of the now familiar nativism/empiricism issue. After thirty years of research, we do not yet have all the answers. In fact, research brings new surprises all the time. Here is a sample of what we think we know at this point.

First, there is little indication that faces are uniquely interesting to infants, which fails to support one of the early assumptions of many nativists. That is, babies do not systematically choose to look at faces rather than at other complex pictures.

On the other hand, among faces, babies clearly prefer some to others. They prefer *attractive* faces (an intriguing result that I've discussed in the Research Report on page 146), and it now looks as if they prefer the *mother's* face from the earliest hours of life, a finding that has greatly surprised psychologists, although it may not surprise you.

For years I have been telling my friends and relatives that there was clear research showing that babies can't recognize their mothers' faces until at least 1 or 2 months of

Figure 5.4

In the Carons' study, the researchers first habituated each baby to a set of training stimuli (all "small over large" in this case), then showed each baby two test stimuli: one that had the same pattern as the training stimuli (A), and one that had a different pattern (B). Babies aged 3 and 4 months showed renewed interest in the B stimulus but not the A stimulus, indicating that they pay attention to the pattern and not just to specific stimuli.

(*Source:* Caron, A. J., and Caron, R. F., "Processing of Relational Information as an Index of Infant Risk," *Pre-term Birth and Psychological Development*, S. Friedman and M. Sigman, eds. © 1981 Academic Press. By permission.)

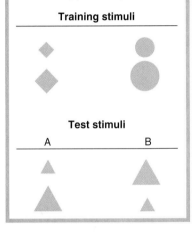

Training stimuli

Test stimuli

A   B

Research Report

Langlois' Studies of Babies' Preferences for Attractive Faces

So many of the current studies on infant perception seem to point toward the conclusion that many more abilities and preferences are built-in than we had supposed. Among all this new work, Judith Langlois' studies of infant preferences for attractive faces rank as some of the most surprising and intriguing. Langlois has found that babies as young as 2 months old will look longer at a face that adults rate as attractive than at one adults judge to be less attractive.

In the first study in this series, Langlois and her colleagues (1987) tested 2- to 3-month-olds and 6- to 8-month-olds. Each baby, while seated on Mom's lap, was shown pairs of color slides of 16 adult Caucasian women, half rated by adult judges as attractive, half rated as unattractive. On each trial, the baby saw two slides simultaneously shown on a screen, with each face approximately life-size, while the experimenter peeked through a hole in the screen to count the number of seconds the baby looked at each picture. Each baby saw some attractive/attractive pairs, some unattractive/unattractive pairs, and some mixed pairs. With mixed pairs, even the 2- and 3-month-old babies consistently looked longer at the attractive faces.

One of the nice features of this study is that the researchers used a variety of attractive and unattractive faces. In a later study, Langlois added even more variability by using pictures of both white men and women as well as African-American women's faces and baby faces (Langlois et al., 1991). Again she found that for all these types of face pairs, babies looked longer at the faces that had been rated by adults as more attractive.

In another exploration of this same issue, Langlois observed 1-year-old babies interacting with an adult wearing either an attractive or an unattractive mask (Langlois et al., 1990). She found that the toddlers showed more positive affective tone, less withdrawal, and more play involvement with the stranger in the attractive mask. These 1-year-olds also played more with an attractive than an unattractive doll.

It is hard to imagine what sort of learning experiences could account for such a preference in a 2-month-old. Instead, these findings raise the possibility that there is some inborn template for the "correct or "most desired" shape and configuration for members of our species, and that we simply prefer those who match this template better. Indeed, in support of this possibility, Langlois has found that the faces babies (and adults) find most attractive and prefer to look at are those that represent the mathematical average of human faces (Langlois & Roggman, 1990; Langlois et al., 1994)—faces that are highly symmetrical and regular. These preferences have real implications for the ways parents interact with their infants and for the way teachers, other adults, and peers later judge and behave toward attractive and unattractive children. For example, Langlois and her colleagues (1995) have found that mothers of infants that judges rate as more attractive show more affection and playfulness toward their newborns than do mothers of infants rated as less attractive. Langlois also finds that, across a variety of studies, attractive children are judged as having greater competence and as being better-adjusted and more socially appealing. They have fewer negative and more positive interactions with peers and adults and receive more attention and caregiving (Langlois et al., 1997). All in all, Langlois' results raise a whole host of fascinating, and highly practical, questions.

Average Looking Time

	2- to 3-month-olds	6- to 8-month-olds	Male and female	Black women	Baby faces
Attractive faces	9.22*	7.24*	7.82*	7.05*	7.16*
Unattractive faces	8.01	6.59	7.57	6.52	6.62

Sources: Langlois et al., 1987, from Table 1, p. 365; Langlois et al., 1991, Table 1, p. 81.
*Contrast between attractive and unattractive faces is statistically significant.

Critical Thinking

Does this mean that researchers ought to believe mothers and fathers more often when they describe their infants and what the babies can do? How should scientists weigh anecdotal evidence against research evidence?

age but that they can recognize the mother by sound or smell immediately. None of my friends or relatives believed me; they all said, "I don't care what the research says; I know my baby could recognize my face right away." Well, it looks like they were right, and the older research (and I) was wrong.

Several studies now show this (e.g., Pascalis et al., 1995). One of the clearest and cleanest is by Gail Walton and her colleagues (1992). Walton videotaped the faces of 12 mothers of newborns and then matched each of these faces with the face of another woman whose hair color, eye color, complexion, and hair style were the same as the mother's. Each baby was then tested with one picture at a time in a modification of the preference technique. The babies could keep the picture turned on by sucking on a pacifier. The experimenters could then count how often the babies sucked in order to keep Mom's picture available, compared to their sucking rate for the non-Mom photo. These babies, who were only a day or two old at the time of the testing, clearly preferred to look at their Moms, as you can see in Figure 5.5. Walton also has some preliminary information that babies do *not* discriminate, or do not prefer, their fathers' faces as early as this, even in cases in which the father had spent more time with the baby than the mother had.

This is a fascinating result. Clearly, the baby has to *learn* the mother's features in those first hours after birth. Yet how is this possible? Is there some kind of imprinting going on here to the first face the baby sees after it is born? If so, then the process should be affected by birth practices or by the amount of contact the baby had had with various individuals. In the particular hospital where Walton's subjects were born, babies spend as much as an hour with their mother immediately after birth—even when the birth is by cesarean section—so the mother's face is usually the first one the baby sees. It would be very interesting to see if Walton's result would be replicated when someone else was the first face or when the mother and infant spent only a moment together after delivery. As is often the case, this one study seems to settle one question but raise many more.

Beyond the issue of preference, we also have to answer the question of just what it is that babies are looking at when they scan a face. Before about 2 months of age, babies seem to look mostly at the edges of the faces (the hairline and the chin), a conclusion buttressed by the finding by Pascalis and his colleagues (1995) that newborns could not discriminate Mom's face from a stranger's if the hairline was covered. After 4 months, however, covering the hairline did not affect the baby's ability to recognize Mom. In general, babies appear to begin to focus on the internal features of a face, particularly the eyes, at about 2 to 3 months—yet another example of the basic shift in rules at 2 months that I already described.

Listening

When we turn from looking to listening, we find similarly intriguing indications that very young infants not only make remarkably fine discriminations among individual sounds but also pay attention to patterns.

Discriminating Speech Sounds. One of the central questions has to do with how early a baby can make discriminations among different speech sounds. This has obvious relevance for language development, since a baby cannot learn language until he can hear the individual sounds as distinct. Researchers interested in perception have also been investigating this question because the answers may tell us about what may be built into the neurological system. Much of this research is quite technical, but I will do my best to try to convey to you why psychologists have found the results so remarkable.

For starters, researchers have established that as early as 1 month, babies can discriminate between speech sounds like *pa* and *ba* (Trehub & Rabinovitch, 1972). Studies using conditioned head-turning responses have shown that by perhaps 6 months of age, babies can discriminate between two-syllable "words" like *bada* and *baga* and can even respond to a syllable that is hidden inside a string of other syllables, like ti*ba*ti or ko*ba*ko (Fernald & Kuhl, 1987; Goodsitt et al., 1984; Morse & Cowan, 1982). Even more remarkable, it doesn't seem to matter what voice quality the sound is said in. By 2 or 3 months of age, babies respond to individual sounds as the same whether they are spoken by male or female voices or by a child's voice (Marean et al., 1992).

That's already pretty impressive evidence that infants listen to quite fine variations in speech sounds, not just at the beginnings of words but in other vocal positions as well. Even more striking is the finding that babies are actually better at discriminating some kinds of speech sounds than adults are. Each language uses only a subset of all possible speech sounds. Japanese, for example, does not use the *l* sound that appears in English; Spanish makes a different distinction between *d* and *t* than occurs in English. It turns out that up to about 6 months of age, babies can accurately discriminate all

Figure 5.5

The babies in this study were 12 to 36 hours old at the time they were tested. They sucked more to see a picture of Mom than a picture of another woman who looked very like her, thus showing that they could discriminate between the two faces.

(*Source:* Walton et al., 1992, p. 267.)

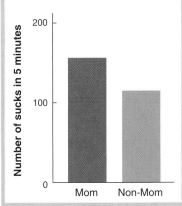

At 2 weeks, Rosa can already discriminate her mother's face from the face of another woman; she can also identify Mom by voice and smell.

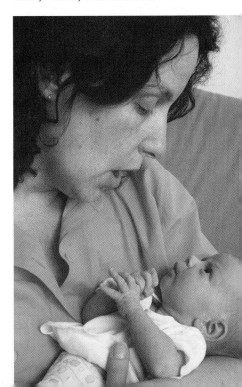

sound contrasts that appear in *any* language, including sounds they do not hear in the language spoken to them. At about 6 months of age, they begin to lose the ability to distinguish pairs of vowels that do not occur in the language they are hearing; by age 1, the ability to discriminate nonheard consonant contrasts begins to fade (Polka & Werker, 1994).

Some of the best evidence on this point comes from the work of Janet Werker and her colleagues (Werker & Desjardins, 1995; Werker & Tees, 1984). They have tested 6- and 10-month-old infants on various consonant pairs, including one pair that is meaningful in English (*ba* versus *da*); a pair that occurs in a North American Indian language, Salish (*ki* versus *qi*); and one from Hindi, a language from the Indian subcontinent (*ta* versus *ta*). Other infants were tested with both English and German vowel contrasts. Figure 5.6 shows the results for babies growing up in English-speaking families on contrasts that do not occur in English. You can see that at 6 months, these babies could still readily hear the differences between pairs of foreign consonants but were already losing the ability to discriminate foreign vowels. Infants aged 10 and 12 months could not readily hear either type of contrast. Similarly, Werker has found that 12-month-old Hindi infants can easily discriminate a Hindi contrast but not an English contrast. So each group of infants loses only the ability to distinguish pairs that do not appear in the language they are hearing.

It seems to me that these findings are entirely consistent with what we now know about the pattern of rapid, apparently preprogrammed, growth of synapses in the early

Figure 5.6

These data from Werker's studies are for babies growing up in English-speaking families, but she has similar results from Hindi-language and Salish-language infants. In every case, 6-month-olds can still "hear" the distinctions between consonant pairs that do not occur in their family's language, but by 12 months that ability has largely disappeared. Discrimination of nonheard vowel pairs disappears even earlier.

(*Source:* "Listening to Speech in the First Year of Life: Experimental Influences on Phoneme Perception" by Werker and Desjardins, *Current Directions in Psychological Science*, Vol. 4, No. 3 (June 1995), p. 80, Fig. 2. By permission of Cambridge University Press.)

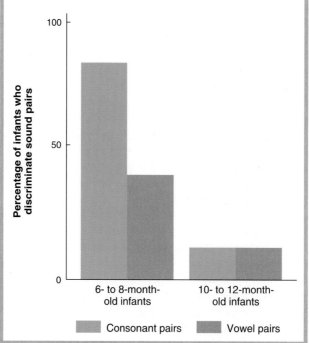

Research Report
Babies Even Learn Sound Patterns *in Utero*

The ability to recognize complex sound patterns is present even before birth. A study by Anthony DeCasper (DeCasper & Spence, 1986) is a particularly striking example. He had pregnant women read a particular children's story (such as Dr. Seuss's *The Cat in the Hat*) out loud each day for the final six weeks of the pregnancy. After the infants were born, he played recordings of the mother reading either this same story or another previously unheard story, to see which the infant preferred. The newborns clearly preferred the sound of the story they had heard *in utero.*

In a more recent study (DeCasper et al., 1994), done in France, DeCasper had pregnant women recite a short chil-

dren's rhyme out loud each day between the thirty-third and thirty-seventh weeks of their pregnancy. In the thirty-eighth week, he played a recording either of the same rhyme the mother had been reading or of another rhyme, and measured the fetal heart rate. He found that fetal heart rates dropped during the recording of the familiar rhyme, but not during the unfamiliar rhyme. These studies obviously tell us that key features of the auditory system are well developed some weeks before birth. They also tell us that even in the last weeks of gestation, the fetus is already paying attention to and discriminating among complex patterns of sounds.

months of life, followed by synaptic pruning. Many connections are initially created, permitting discriminations along all possible sound continua, but only those pathways that are actually used in the language the child hears are strengthened or retained.

Discriminating Individual Voices. Newborns also seem to be able to discriminate between individual voices. DeCasper and Fifer (1980) have found that the newborn can tell the mother's voice from another female voice (but not the father's voice from another male voice) and prefers the mother's. This is easier to account for than is the newborn's preferences for the mother's face, since the baby could learn the sound of the mother's voice while still *in utero.* Nonetheless, the fact that a baby can discriminate the mother's voice from a stranger's voice at birth is striking.

By 6 months, babies even know which voice is supposed to go with which face. If you put an infant of this age in a situation where she can see both her father and mother and can hear a tape-recorded voice of one of them, she will look toward the parent whose voice she hears (Spelke & Owsley, 1979).

Discriminating Other Sound Patterns. As was true with studies of looking, there is also evidence that infants pay attention to *patterns* or sequences of sounds from the very beginning. For example, Sandra Trehub and her colleagues (1984; 1985) have found that as early as 6 months of age, babies listen to melodies and recognize the patterns. Trehub trained 6-month-old babies to turn their heads toward a loudspeaker for a particular six-tone melody and then tested the babies with melodies that varied in a number of ways. Babies continued to turn their heads to new melodies if the melody had the same contour (notes going up and down in the same sequence) and were in approximately the same pitch range. They responded to them as different if the contour changed or if the notes were much higher or much lower. Thus, as is true with patterns of looking, within the first few months of life, babies appear to pay attention to and respond to pattern and not just the specific sounds. Such pattern perception skills appear to be present even before birth, as described in the Research Report above.

Combining Information from Several Senses

I have been talking about each sense separately, as if we experienced the world through only one sense at a time. Yet if you think about the way you receive and use perceptual information, you'll realize that you rarely have information from only one sense at a time. Ordinarily, you have *both* sound and sight, touch and sight, or still

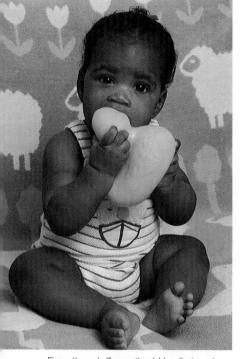

Even though 7-month-old Leslie is not looking at this toy while she chews on it, she is nonetheless learning something about how it *ought* to look, just based on how it feels in her mouth and in her hands—an example of cross-modal transfer.

more complex combinations of smell, sight, touch, and sound. Psychologists have been interested in knowing how early an infant can combine such information. For example, how early can an infant integrate information from several senses, such as knowing which mouth movements go with which sounds? Even more complex, how early can a baby learn something via one sense and transfer that information to another sense (for example, at what age can a child recognize solely by feel a toy he has seen but never felt before)? The first of these two skills is usually called **intersensory integration,** while the latter is called **cross-modal transfer** (or intermodal transfer).

Piaget believed that both these skills were simply not present until quite late in the first year of life, after the infant had accumulated many experiences with specific objects and how they simultaneously looked, sounded, and felt. Other theorists, including James Gibson and Eleanor Gibson, have argued that some intersensory integration or even transfer is built-in from birth. The baby then builds on that inborn set of skills with specific experience with objects. Research favors the Gibsonian view: Empirical findings show that cross-modal transfer is possible as early as 1 month and becomes common by 6 months (Rose & Ruff, 1987).

For example, if you attach a nubby or a smooth sphere to a pacifier and give one or the other to each of several babies to suck, you can test for cross-modal transfer using Fantz's preference technique: You show the babies pictures of the two spheres to see if infants look longer at one than at the other. In one early study following this method, Meltzoff and Borton (1979) found that 1-month-old babies preferred to look at the picture of the object they had sucked on earlier. In a similar recent study, Kaye and Bower (1994) have demonstrated such transfer in infants 12 *hours* old—strong evidence for the nativist side of the ancient argument.

In older children, intersensory integration and transfer can be readily demonstrated, not only between touch and sight but between other modalities such as sound and sight. For instance, in several delightfully clever early experiments, Elizabeth Spelke showed that 4-month-old infants can connect sound rhythms with movement (1979). She showed babies two films simultaneously, one showing a toy kangaroo bouncing up and down, the other a donkey bouncing up and down, with one of the animals bouncing at a faster rate. Out of a loudspeaker located between the two films, the infant heard a tape recording of a rhythmic bouncing sound that matched the bounce pattern of one of the two animals. In this situation, babies showed a preference for looking at the film showing the bounce rate that matched the sound.

An even more striking illustration of the same basic process comes from the work of Jeffery Pickens (1994). He showed 5-month-old babies two films side by side, each displaying a train moving along a track. Then out of a loudspeaker he played engine sounds of various types, such as getting gradually louder (thus appearing to come closer) or getting gradually fainter (thus appearing to be moving away). The babies in this experiment looked longer at a picture of a train whose movement matched the pattern of engine sounds. That is, they appeared to have some understanding of the link between the pattern of sound and the pattern of movement—knowledge that demonstrates not only intersensory integration but also surprisingly sophisticated understanding of the accompaniments of motion.

In the same vein, researchers have shown that 4- to 5-month-old babies will look longer at a face of a person mouthing a vowel that the baby hears spoken over a loudspeaker than at the face of a person mouthing another vowel (Kuhl & Meltzoff, 1984; Walton & Bower, 1993). Similarly, somewhat older infants shown a photo of a male and one of a female will look longer at the face that matches the gender of a voice heard over a loudspeaker—although only when the photo/voice match is female (Poulin-Dubois et al., 1994).

I do not want to leave you with the impression that intersensory integration or transfer is a completely automatic process in young infants. It isn't. In 4- and 5-month-olds, it often doesn't occur at all, or only under special circumstances (Lewkowicz, 1994). What is clear is that young infants have at least some ability to link simultaneous information from several senses, a conclusion that raises several interesting theoretical issues. For one thing it is now perfectly clear that a baby or child does not need language to transfer information from one mode to another. And the fact that at least some transfer is possible within the first few weeks of life certainly points rather strongly to the possibility that *some* connections may be built-in, although experience with specific objects and combinations clearly makes a difference as well. So this body of information enriches but does not settle the nativism/empiricism debate.

Ignoring Perceptual Information: The Perceptual Constancies

All of what I have said so far has been aimed at persuading you that from early in life, babies are remarkably skillful at making perceptual discriminations of various kinds. At the same time, the infant must acquire another, very different, kind of perceptual skill—the ability to *ignore* some kinds of perceptual data. Specifically, the child must acquire a set of rules we call **perceptual constancies.**

When you see someone walking away from you, the image of the person on your retina actually becomes smaller. Yet you don't see the person getting smaller. You see him as the same size but moving farther away. When you do this, you are demonstrating **size constancy;** you are able to see the size as constant even though the retinal image has changed.

Other constancies include the ability to recognize that shapes of objects are the same even though you are looking at them from different angles, called (logically enough) **shape constancy,** and the ability to recognize that colors are constant even though the amount of light or shadow on them changes, called **color constancy.**

Taken together, the several specific constancies add up to the larger concept of **object constancy,** which is the recognition that objects remain the same even when the sensory information you have about them has changed in some way. Babies begin to show signs of these constancies at 3 or 4 months of age and become more skilled over the first several years. Let me use shape constancy as an illustration.

Shape constancy has perhaps the most obvious day-to-day relevance for the baby. She has to realize that her bottle is still her bottle even though it is turned slightly and thus presents a different shape to her eyes; she has to figure out that her toys are the same when they are in different positions. The beginnings of this understanding seem to be present by about 2 or 3 months of age. The classic study was done by Thomas Bower (1966), who first trained 2-month-old babies to turn their heads when they saw a particular rectangle. He then showed them tilted or slightly turned images of the same rectangle to see if the babies would respond to these as "the same," even though the retinal image cast by these tilted rectangles was actually a trapezoid and not a rectangle at all. Two-month-olds did indeed continue to turn their heads to these tilted and turned rectangles, showing that they have some shape constancy.

One of the ironies about perceptual development is that at a later age, when learning to read, a child has to *unlearn* some of these shape constancies. Pairs of letters like *b* and *d, p* and *q,* or *p* and *b* are the same shape except with the direction reversed or one upside down. So to learn to read (at least the Latin alphabet) the child must now learn to pay attention to something she has learned to ignore—namely, the rotation of the letter in space.

Of course learning to read involves a good deal more than simply ignoring shape constancy (and I'll have more to say about it in Chapter 8, when I talk about language development). But we do know that among 5-year-olds, those who have difficulty discriminating between mirror images of shapes also have more difficulty learning to read (Casey, 1986).

The Object Concept

Grasping the various object constancies is only part of a larger task facing the child; he must also figure out the nature of objects themselves. First of all, an infant must somehow learn to treat some combinations of stimuli as "objects" and others not, a process now usually referred to as *object perception*. For example, if a baby sees a heap of blocks on a carpet, does she "know" that each block is a separate object? Does she treat the carpet as an object as well? What makes an object an object?

A still more sophisticated aspect of the infant's emerging concept of objects is the understanding that objects continue to exist even when they are out of view. I know that my computer is still sitting here even when I am not in the room. Does a baby know that Mom continues to exist when she leaves the room or that her bottle still exists when she drops it over the edge of the crib? Such an understanding is usually referred to as **object permanence.**

Object Perception

The most thorough and clever work on object perception in infants has been done by Elizabeth Spelke and her colleagues (Spelke, 1982; 1985; Spelke et al., 1989). Spelke believes that babies are born with certain built-in assumptions about the nature of objects. One of these is the assumption that when two surfaces are connected to each other, they belong to the same object; Spelke calls this the *connected surface principle*. To study this (Spelke, 1982), she first habituated some 3-month-old babies to a series of displays of two objects; other babies were habituated to the sight of one-object displays. Then the babies were shown two objects touching each other, such as two square blocks placed next to each other so that they created a rectangle. Under these conditions, the babies who had been habituated on two-object displays showed renewed interest, clearly indicating that they "saw" this as different, presumably as a single object. Babies who had seen the one-object displays during habituation showed no renewed interest. Spelke has also shown that babies as young as 2 and 3 months old are remarkably aware of what kinds of movements objects are capable of, even when the objects are out of sight. They expect objects to continue to move on their initial trajectory, and they show surprise if the object's movement violates this expectancy. They also seem to have some awareness that solid objects cannot pass through other solid objects.

In one experiment, Spelke (1991) used the procedure shown schematically in the upper part of Figure 5.7. Two-month-old babies were repeatedly shown a series of events like that in the "familiarization" section of the figure: A ball starting on the left-hand side was rolled to the right and disappeared behind a screen. The screen was then taken away and the baby could see that the ball was stopped against the wall on the right. After the baby got bored looking at this sequence (habituated), he or she was tested with two variations, one "consistent" and one "inconsistent." In the consistent variation, a second wall was placed behind the screen and the sequence run as before, except now when the screen was removed, the ball could be seen resting up against the nearer wall. In the inconsistent variation, the ball was surreptitiously placed on the *far* side of the new wall. When the screen was removed, the ball was visible in this presumably impossible place. Babies in this experiment were quite uninterested in the consistent condition but showed sharply renewed interest in the inconsistent condition, as you can see in the lower part of Figure 5.7, which shows the actual results of this experiment.

Spelke is not suggesting that all the child's knowledge of objects is built-in; she is suggesting that *some* rules are built-in and that others are learned through experience. Others, such as Renée Baillargeon (1994), argue that basic knowledge is not built-in, but that strategies for learning are innate. According to this view, infants initially develop basic hypotheses about the way objects function—how they move, how they con-

Critical Thinking

I find it astonishing that a 2-month-old baby can have enough understanding of the physical world to "know" in some fashion that it is unexpected for the ball to be on the other side of the middle wall in this experiment. Are you also astonished by this result?

Figure 5.7

The top part of the figure shows a schematic version of the three conditions Spelke used. The bottom half shows the actual results. You can see that the babies stopped looking at the ball and screen after a number of familiarization trials, but they showed renewed interest in the inconsistent version—a sign that the babies saw this as somehow different or surprising. The very fact that the babies found the inconsistent trial surprising is itself evidence that infants as young as 2 months have far more knowledge about objects and their behavior than most of us had thought.

(*Source:* E. S. Spelke, from Figures 5.3 and 5.4, "Physical Knowledge in Infancy: Reflections on Piaget's Theory" in *The Epigenesis of Mind: Essays on Biology Cognition,* S. Carey and R. Gelman (eds.). © 1991 by Lawrence Erlbaum Associates, Inc. By permission of the publisher and author.)

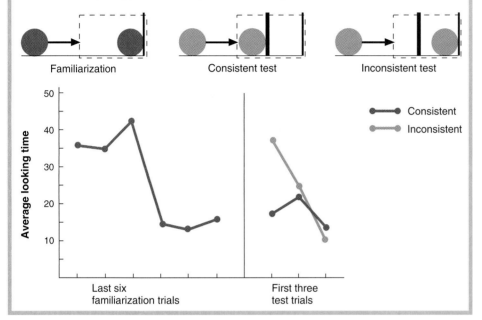

nect to one another. Then these early basic hypotheses are quite rapidly modified, based on the baby's experience with objects. For example, Baillargeon finds 2- to 3-month-old infants are already operating with a basic hypothesis that an object will fall if it isn't supported by something, but they have no notion of how much support is required. By about 5 months of age, this basic hypothesis has been refined, so that they understand that the smiling-face block in the arrangement in the middle of Figure 5.8 (a) will stay supported, but the block in the arrangement on the bottom (b) will not (Baillargeon, 1994). At this point, I can't tell whether Spelke or Baillargeon will ultimately turn out to be correct about the extent to which these forms of knowledge are built-in. In either case, it is striking to see just how early babies know such complex things about the physical world.

Object Permanence

The study of object perception is a rather new area of research. In contrast, object permanence has been extensively explored, in large part because this particular understanding was strongly emphasized in Piaget's theory of infant development. According to his observations, replicated frequently by later researchers, the first sign that the baby is developing object permanence comes at about 2 months of age. Suppose you show a toy to a child of this age and then put a screen in front of the toy and remove the toy. When you then remove the screen, the baby shows some indication of surprise, as if she knew that something should still be there. The child thus seems to have a rudimentary schema or expectation about the permanence of an object. At the same time, infants of this age show no signs of searching for a toy they may have dropped over the

Figure 5.8

Renée Baillargeon's research suggests that 2- and 3-month-old babies think that the smiling-face block will not fall under either of these conditions, but by 5 months, they realize that only the condition shown in (a) is stable. In condition (b), the block will fall.

(*Source:* "How Do Infants Learn About the Physical World" by Baillargeon, R., *Current Directions in Psychological Science,* Vol. 3, No. 5 (October 1994), p. 134, Fig. 1. By permission of Cambridge University Press.)

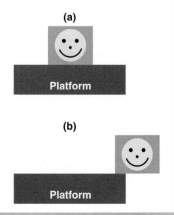

edge of the crib or that has disappeared beneath a blanket or behind a screen—a pattern of reaction that parents take advantage of when an infant is fussing for some toy or object he can't reach, or when the parent wants an infant to stop fooling with some object. With young infants, the parent can simply put the object out of sight. Out of sight, out of mind.

At about 6 or 8 months of age, this begins to change. Babies will now look over the edge of the crib for the dropped toys or for food that was spilled. (In fact, babies of this age may drive their parents nuts playing "dropsy" in the high chair.) Infants this age will also search for partially hidden objects. If you put a favorite toy under a cloth but leave part of it sticking out, the infant will reach for the toy, which suggests that in some sense the infant "recognizes" that the whole object is there even though she can see only part of it. Yet if you cover the toy completely with the cloth or put it behind a screen, the infant will stop looking at it and will not reach for it, even if she has seen you put the cloth over it—a pattern shown in the photos in Figure 5.9.

This changes again somewhere between 8 and 12 months. At this age, the "out of sight, out of mind" parental strategy no longer works at all. Infants this age will reach for or search for a toy that has been covered completely by a cloth or hidden by a screen. Thus, by 12 months, most infants appear to grasp the basic fact that objects continue to exist even when they are no longer visible.

Object constancy has intrigued researchers and theorists in part because it forms one kind of bridge between studies of perception and early cognitive development. Many have also been struck by a possible link between the emergence of object constancy and the infant's earliest attachment. It seems reasonable to assume that some kind of object permanence is required before the baby can become attached to an individual person, such as his mother or father. Since we know that clear single attachments don't appear much before 5 months, right about the time that the baby is showing signs of object permanence, the connection seems very reasonable. Interestingly, and surprisingly to a lot of us, most direct tests of this hypothesis have not shown much sign of such a causal link. Still, the problem may be with our research techniques rather than the hypothesis. As John Flavell says:

Figure 5.9

A typical response of a 7- or 8-month-old baby to the standard object permanence test. The infant stops reaching as soon as the screen is put in front of the toy and shows no sign of knowing that the toy is still there. An older baby would keep searching or push the screen aside to reach for the toy. (Note that the type of hook-on-the-table seat shown in these photos is dangerous and is no longer recommended.)

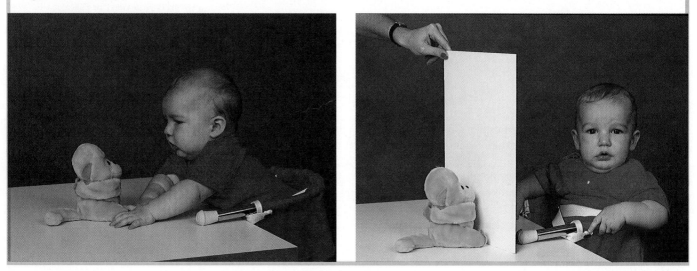

▟ Cultures and Contexts
Object Permanence in Zambian Infants

Piaget believed that the emergence of the child's understanding of object permanence followed a universal sequence. One way to test this assumption, of course, is to observe or test children in non-Western societies, particularly infants or children whose early experiences are different from what we see in the United States or Europe. Susan Goldberg's longitudinal study of 38 Zambian infants (1972) gives us one such cross-cultural look.

Goldberg's two years of observations in Zambia made clear that the typical experience of a Zambian baby was quite different in a number of respects from that of most Western infants. From shortly after birth, Zambian babies are carried about in a sling on their mother's back. They spend very little time on the floor or in any position in which they have much chance of independent movement until they are able to sit up at about 6 months. At that point they are usually placed on a mat in the yard of the house. From this vantage the baby can watch all the activity around the house and in the neighborhood, but he has few objects to play with. Goldberg noted that the Zambian mothers did not see it as their task to provide play objects for their infants or to structure the child's play in any way. Indeed, Goldberg says she rarely saw the babies playing with objects, even those that might have been available in the yards.

Yet despite this very limited experience manipulating objects, tests of object permanence showed that the Zambian babies were *ahead* of the U.S. averages on a measure of the object concept at 6 months of age. At 9 and 12 months of age, the Zambian babies were slightly behind the U.S. norms, but Goldberg believes this difference is due not to any cognitive failure but to the fact that at these ages the Zambian babies were quite unresponsive and passive toward objects and thus were very difficult to test. One possible explanation of this is that in Zambian culture, at least as Goldberg observed it, obedience is a quality highly valued in a child. The babies are trained from very early to be particularly obedient to prohibitions of various kinds. When the baby plays with some object that he is forbidden to touch, the object is taken away. Perhaps, then, the infants learn that when an object is removed, it means "Don't play with that," so a baby makes no further move to reach for a toy during the object permanence test. This does not necessarily mean that the baby has not understood these later stages of object permanence; it could also mean that our traditional ways of measuring this understanding would need to be modified for these children.

Goldberg's observations thus illustrate both the robustness of some basic developmental patterns *and* the impact of culture on the ways those patterns are displayed by children. Babies in Zambia appear to develop the early steps of the understanding of object permanence even though they have little chance to manipulate objects. At the same time, their response to objects is also affected by their training and experience.

> How ever could a child persistently yearn and search for a specific other person if the child were still cognitively incapable of mentally representing that person in the person's absence? (1985, p. 135)

I find Flavell's logic persuasive, but as usual we will have to wait for further research evidence to be sure.

Perception of Social Signals

Thus far I have been talking almost entirely about babies' perception of physical objects and their properties. Even the description of the infant's ability to discriminate faces treats faces as if they were purely physical objects, with fixed properties such as eye characteristics, hairlines, or the like. But of course other people's faces also provide *social* signals in the form of varying emotional expressions. Variations in vocal intonations and body language similarly provide social cues. These are important bits of information for a baby to detect and decipher. Parents, teachers, and other adults convey a great deal of information through their emotional expression. In peer interactions, too, the ability to read another's emotion is essential for any kind of sustained cooperative play or for the subtle adaptations required for the formation of enduring friendships.

Early Discrimination of Emotional Expressions

The evidence suggests that infants begin to pay attention to such social/emotional cues at about 2 or 3 months of age. We know, for example, that at that age infants begin to smile more to human faces than to a doll's face or another inanimate object, suggesting that at this early stage, the baby is already responding to the added social signals available in the human face (Ellsworth et al., 1993; Legerstee et al., 1987). The orientation of the face seems to be one critical ingredient in this early preferential smiling. Albert Caron and his colleagues (1997) find that babies smile more only when the face is turned toward them; if the face is turned aside, the baby does not smile more.

Infants this age are not just reacting differently to face versus nonface; they are also beginning to notice and respond differently to variations in others' emotional expressions. Initially, they discriminate emotions best when they receive information on many channels simultaneously—such as when they see a particular facial expression and hear the same emotion expressed in the adult's voice (Walker-Andrews, 1997). For example, Haviland and Lelwica (1987) found that when mothers expressed happiness in both face and voice, 10-week-old babies looked happy and interested and gazed at the mother; when the mothers expressed sadness, babies showed increased mouth movements or looked away; when the mothers expressed anger, some babies cried vigorously, while others showed a kind of still or "frozen" look.

By 5 to 7 months, babies can begin to "read" one channel at a time, responding to facial expression alone, or vocal expression alone, even when the emotions are displayed by a stranger rather than Mom or Dad (Balaban, 1995). Specifically, they can tell the difference between happy and sad voices (Walker-Andrews & Lennon, 1991) and between happy, surprised, and fearful faces (Nelson, 1987). They also seem to have some preliminary understanding that vocal and facial emotional expressions typically go together. For example, Nelson Soken and Anne Pick (1992) showed 7-month-olds pairs of faces displaying happy and angry expressions while the babies listened to words spoken in either a happy or an angry voice. The infants looked longer at the face that matched the emotion in the speaking voice.

Social Referencing

Late in the first year of life, infants take another important step and link the information about the other's emotional expression with the environmental context. For example, a 12-month-old, faced with some new and potentially fearful event such as a new toy or a strange adult, may first look at Mom's or Dad's face to check for the adult's emotional expression. If Mom looks pleased or happy, the baby is likely to explore the new toy with more ease or to accept the stranger with less fuss. If Mom looks concerned or frightened, the baby responds to those cues and reacts to the novel situation with equivalent fear or concern. Researchers have described this as a process of **social referencing** (Walker-Andrews, 1997).

Understanding Emotions at Later Ages

Through the preschool years, children's emotional vocabulary increases gradually, so that they recognize more and more variations in others' expressions. By age 4, most children can recognize facial expressions and situations that convey the emotions happy, sad, mad, loving, and scared. Preschoolers also increasingly grasp the links between other people's emotions and their circumstances. For example, a child this age understands that another person will feel sad if she fails or happy if she succeeds. The preschool child also begins to figure out that particular emotions occur in situations involving specific relationships between desire and reality. Sadness, for example, normally occurs when someone fails to acquire some desired object or loses something desired (Harris, 1989).

All this may make it sound as if 4- and 5-year-olds have already understood everything they need to know about reading others' emotions. In fact, though, there is a good deal more sophisticated knowledge still to come. For example, 4-year-olds cannot yet accurately detect expressions of pride or shame; these more complex and subtle emotions are correctly discriminated only in middle childhood (Harter & Whitesell, 1989). Similarly, by age 6, children understand that a person can switch rather rapidly from sadness to happiness if circumstances change, but it is only at about age 10 that children begin to understand that a person can feel and express opposite feelings at the same moment (ambivalence) (Harter & Whitesell, 1989).

Cross-Cultural Commonalities and Variations

It is reasonable to ask—as with virtually all the developmental sequences I have given you in this book—whether children in every culture learn about emotions in this same way. In this case, we have a bit of evidence.

The Utka, an Inuit band in northern Canada, have two words for fear, distinguishing between fear of physical disaster and fear of being treated badly. Some African languages have no separate words for fear and sorrow. Samoans use the same word for love, sympathy, and liking, and Tahitians have no word at all that conveys the notion of guilt. These examples, drawn by James Russell (1989) from the anthropological literature, remind us that we need to be very careful when we talk about the "normal" process of a child learning about emotional expression and emotional meaning. From an English-speaking, Western perspective, emotions like fear or anger seem like "basic" emotions that all infants would understand early and easily. But what would be the developmental sequence for a child growing up in a culture in which fear and sorrow are not distinguished?

At the same time, the work of Paul Ekman (1972; 1973; 1989) has given us evidence of a strong cross-cultural similarity in people's facial expressions when conveying certain of these same "basic" emotions, such as fear, happiness, sadness, anger, and disgust. (Figure 5.10 shows two such common expressions.) In all cultures studied so far, adults understand these facial expressions as having the same core meaning. Cultural variations are laid on top of these basic expressive patterns, and cultures have different rules about which emotions may be expressed and which must be masked. One could hypothesize that infants and toddlers are quite good at discriminating and understanding the core, shared patterns; even 2-year-olds can recognize and categorize happy and sad expressions. Beyond that basic understanding, the child must then slowly learn all the cultural overlays—the links between emotion and situation that hold for each culture, the specific meanings of emotional language, the scripts that govern the appropriate expression of emotion in a given culture. No small task. What is remarkable is just how much of this information the preschooler already comprehends and reflects in his own behavior.

Individual Differences in Perception: Speed and Efficiency

I pointed out in the last chapter that the shared patterns of physical development are extremely robust. Highly similar sequences are seen in all children. The same is clearly true for many of the patterns of perceptual development I've been describing here. Nonetheless, as with physical development, there are significant individual variations in the process, of which the most interesting are the indications that babies may differ in the efficiency with which they are able to deal with perceptual information.

The most extensive body of research has dealt with variations in "recognition memory" among infants—the ability to recognize that one has seen or experienced

Critical Thinking

You judge others' emotions quite automatically, using all the subtle cues you have learned. Analyze the process for a moment, though: What are the specific cues you use to decide that someone is expressing pride, or shame, or ambivalence? How are these complex emotions expressed in the face or body movement? Does tone of voice enter in?

Figure 5.10

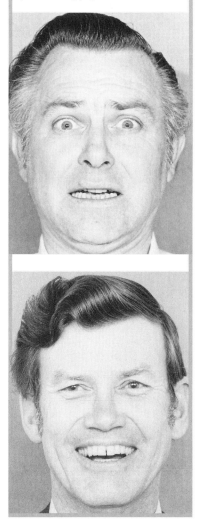

What emotion is being expressed in each of these photos? If you said fear and happiness, you agree with virtually all observers, in many countries, who have looked at these pictures. Copyright Paul Ekman.

some object or person before. One way to measure this is with a standard habituation test. That is, we can count how many repeated exposures it takes before a baby stops responding with interest to some stimulus. The speed with which such habituation takes place may tell us something about the efficiency of the perceptual/cognitive system and its neurological underpinnings. And if such efficiency lies behind some of the characteristics we normally call "intelligence," then it is possible that individual differences in rate of habituation in the early months of life may predict later intelligence test scores.

This is exactly what researchers have found in studies over the past 15 years. The rate of habituation shown by 4- to 5-month-old babies is correlated positively with IQ and language development at 3 or 4 years of age or older. That is, faster habituation is associated with higher IQ and better language, and slower habituation is associated with lower IQ and poorer language. The average correlation in studies in both the United States and England is in the range of .45 to .50 (Rose & Feldman, 1995; Slater, 1995). This correlation is certainly not perfect, but it is remarkably high, given the difficulties involved in measuring habituation rate in babies.

Certainly these correlations do not prove that intelligence, as we measure it on an IQ test, is *only* a reflection of some kind of "speed of basic processing." Results like these nonetheless underline the potential importance of individual differences in perceptual efficiency in early infancy.

Explanations of Perceptual Development

I pointed out at the beginning of this chapter that the study of perception, more than any other topic in developmental psychology except perhaps intelligence, has been dominated by questions of nature versus nurture, nativism versus empiricism. Certainly there are now other theoretical approaches or issues to choose from, but given the importance of the historical argument between the nativists and the empiricists, it's worthwhile to take a look at just where we stand on this question in our current understanding of perceptual development.

Arguments for Nativism

It is not hard to find strong arguments for a nativist position on perceptual development. As researchers have become more and more clever in devising ways to test infants' perceptual skills, they have found more and more skills already present in newborns or very young infants: Newborns have good auditory acuity, poor but adequate visual acuity, excellent tactual and taste perception. They have at least some color vision and at least rudimentary ability to locate the source of sounds around them. More impressive still, they are capable of making quite sophisticated discriminations from the earliest days of life, including being able to identify their mother by sight, smell, or sound.

Newborn or very young babies also do not have to be taught what to look at. There are "rules" for looking, listening, and touching that can be detected at birth. As Kagan puts it: "Nature has apparently equipped the newborn with an initial bias in the processing of experience. He does not, as the nineteenth-century empiricists believed, have to learn what he should examine" (1971, p. 60). Furthermore, studies like Spelke's on babies' object understanding point to the strong possibility that other "assumptions" or biases about the way the world is organized may also be built-in.

The fact that the "rules" seem to change with age can also be explained in nativist terms, since we know that the nervous system is undergoing rapid maturation during the early months of life, much of it apparently in an automatic way, as preprogrammed synapses are formed rapidly. Furthermore, these rule changes seem to occur in bursts. One such set of changes seems to occur at about 2 to 3 months, when infants appear to shift away from fixation on contours or edges and toward more detailed analysis of objects or figures. At about the same age, the baby becomes able to track objects

Critical Thinking

What do you think this finding—that babies who habituate faster later have higher IQs—means in practical terms? Could it mean that babies who have had more stimulation in the early months develop more quickly? Could it mean that what we measure with IQ is really all just wiring? What other possibilities can you think of?

smoothly. Another shift seems to occur at about 4 months, when we see a whole host of discrimination skills for the first time, including depth perception based on kinetic cues and consistent evidence of cross-modal transfer, especially coordination of auditory and visual information.

Of course it is possible that this apparent pileup of changes at 4 months reflects the accidental fact that many researchers have chosen to study babies of this age rather than younger babies, so we simply know a great deal more about 4-month-olds. Perhaps, though, one major reason that researchers choose this age to study is that babies this age are significantly easier to test—because there has now been some underlying maturational shift that makes them more attentive, more able to focus, more stable in state.

Finally, we can find support for a nativist position in comparisons of the perceptual development of babies born *after* the normal gestational period versus those born preterm or at the normal term. In one such study, Yonas (1981) compared the response of two groups of 6-week-old babies: normal-term babies and a group of babies born 3 to 4 weeks late (postterm). Both sets of infants were tested for depth perception using the method of looming objects. Yonas found that the postterm infants showed more consistent reactions to the looming objects, even though both groups had had precisely the same number of weeks of experience with objects since birth. Thus, it looks as if it is maturational age, and not experience, that matters in this case, which strengthens a nativist or biological position.

Arguments for Empiricism

On the other side of the ledger, however, we can find a great deal of evidence from research with other species that some *minimum level* of experience is necessary to support the development of the perceptual systems—the pattern of environmental effect Aslin calls maintenance. For example, animals deprived of light show deterioration of the whole visual system and a consequent decrease in perceptual abilities (Hubel & Weisel, 1963).

It is also possible to find support for the negative version of Aslin's facilitation effect: Infants lacking sufficient perceptual stimulation may develop more slowly. Wayne Dennis's study of orphanage babies in Iran, which I described in Chapter 4, illustrates this possibility. The infants who didn't have a chance to look at things, to explore objects with hands and eyes and tongue, and who were deprived of the opportunity to move around freely were retarded in the development of both perceptual and motor skills.

Attunement may also occur. Evidence from studies of other species suggests that those who are completely deprived of visual experiences in the early months of life never develop the same degree of depth perception as do those with full visual experience (Gottlieb, 1976b).

The relationship between the built-in process and the role of the environment is a little like the difference between computer hardware and software. The perceptual hardware (specific neural pathways, rules for examining the world, a bias toward searching for patterns, and the like) may be preprogrammed, while the software (the specific program that governs the child's response to a particular real environment) depends on specific experience. A child is *able* to make visual discriminations between people or among objects within the first few days or weeks of life. That's built into the hardware. The specific discriminations she learns and the number of separate objects she learns to recognize, however, will depend on her experience. She is initially able to discriminate all the sound contrasts that exist in any spoken language, but the specific sound contrasts she eventually focuses on and the actual language she learns depend on the language she hears. The basic system is thus adapted to the specific environment in which the child finds herself. A perfect example of this, of course, is the newborn's ability to discriminate her mother's face from that of a very similar woman's face. Such a discrimination *must* be the result of experience, yet the capacity to make the distinction must be built-in.

Thus, as is true of virtually all dichotomous theoretical disputes, both sides are correct. Both nature and nurture are involved.

Perceptual Development: A Summing-Up

The research on perceptual development in the early years of life has called into question a whole series of previously cherished beliefs about infants and their abilities. Despite their many limitations, infants seem to approach and respond to the world around them in a much more organized and sophisticated way than most psychologists thought twenty or thirty years ago. And the fact that babies respond to *patterns* of stimulation, to underlying information and not just to the surface sensory input, means that the infant is capable of far more complex cognitive processes than we had given her credit for.

Summary

1. A central issue in the study of perceptual development continues to be the nativism/empiricism controversy: Are sensory and perceptual skills built-in at birth? If not, how early do they develop?

2. Studies of perceptual development have been greatly aided by methodological advances, such as Fantz's preference technique and the use of habituation or operant conditioning paradigms with very young infants.

3. Most basic sensory capacities are present in at least rudimentary form at birth or develop soon thereafter.

4. Color vision is present at birth, but visual acuity and visual tracking skill are relatively poor at birth and then develop rapidly during the first few months.

5. Basic auditory skills are more fully developed at birth; acuity is good for the range of the human voice, and the newborn can locate at least the approximate direction of sounds. The sensory capacities for smelling, tasting, and the senses of touch and motion are also well developed at birth.

6. Depth perception is not present at birth; it is present in at least rudimentary form by 3 months, initially using kinetic cues, then binocular cues, and finally pictorial cues by about 5 to 7 months.

7. Visual attention appears to follow definite rules, even in the first hours of life. Newborns search for objects and focus on the edges, on points of dark/light contrast, or on movement. At about 2 months of life, babies' focus shifts toward examining the middle as well as the edges and attending to more complex relationships and patterns.

8. Babies can discriminate the mother's face from other faces, and the mother's voice from other voices, almost immediately after birth.

9. From the beginning, babies appear to attend to and discriminate among speech contrasts present in all possible languages; by the age of 1 year, the infant makes fine discriminations only among speech sounds salient in the language he is actually hearing.

10. From early in life, certainly by 4 months, babies also attend to and discriminate among different patterns of sounds, such as melodies or speech inflections.

11. Touch/sight and sound/sight cross-modal transfers have been demonstrated as early as 1 month and are found reliably by 4 months.

12. Perceptual constancies such as size constancy, brightness constancy, and shape constancy are all present in at least rudimentary form by 4 months, perhaps earlier.

13. Young babies also have quite complex understanding of objects, their properties, and their possible movements. The understanding of object permanence (the realization that objects exist even when they are out of sight) begins at 2 or 3 months of age and is quite well developed by 10 months.

14. Babies differ in the apparent speed or efficiency of perceptual processes, such as habituation to a repeated stimulus. Such variations in habituation rate are correlated with later measures of IQ and language skill.

15. Both the empiricists and the nativists appear to be partially correct about the origin of perceptual skills. Many basic perceptual abilities, including strategies for examining objects, appear to be built into the system at birth or to develop as the brain develops over the early years. But specific experience is required both to maintain the underlying system and to learn fundamental discriminations and patterns.

Key Terms

acuity Sharpness of perceptual ability—how well or clearly one can see, hear, or use other senses. **p. 140**

color constancy The ability to see the color of an object as remaining the same despite changes in illumination or shadow. One of the basic perceptual constancies that make up object constancy. **p. 151**

cross-modal transfer The ability to transfer information gained through one sense to another sense at a later time; for example, identifying visually something you had previously explored only tactually. **p. 150**

empiricism Opposite of nativism. The theoretical point of view that all perceptual skill arises from experience. **p. 139**

intersensory integration The combining of information from two or more senses to form a unified perceptual whole, such as the sight of mouth movements combined with the sound of particular words. **p. 150**

nativism See *empiricism*. The view that perceptual skills are inborn and do not require experience to develop. **p. 139**

object constancy The general phrase describing the ability to see objects as remaining the same despite changes in retinal image. **p. 151**

object permanence Part of the object concept. The recognition that an object continues to exist even when it is temporarily out of sight. **p. 152**

perceptual constancies A collection of constancies, including shape, size, and color constancy. **p. 151**

shape constancy The ability to see an object's shape as remaining the same despite changes in the shape of the retinal image. A basic perceptual constancy. **p. 151**

size constancy The ability to see an object's size as remaining the same despite changes in size of the retinal image. A key element in this constancy is the ability to judge depth. **p. 151**

social referencing Using another person's emotional reaction to some situation as a basis for deciding one's own reaction. A baby does this when she checks her parent's facial expression or body language before responding positively or negatively to something new. **p. 156**

tracking Also called smooth pursuit. The smooth movements of the eye used to follow the track of some moving object. **p. 141**

Suggested Readings

Aslin, R. N. (1987). Visual and auditory development in infancy. In J. D. Osofsky (Ed.), *Handbook of infant development* (2nd ed., pp. 5–97). New York: Wiley-Interscience. Aslin has written a number of summaries and reviews of the research on early perceptual development, of which this is perhaps the most easily understood by a nonexpert. Even so, the article is quite technical and considerably more detailed than I have been in this chapter.

Baillargeon, R. (1994). How do infants learn about the physical world? *Current Directions in Psychological Science, 3,* 133–140. This is a wonderful brief paper describing some of Baillargeon's fascinating work on young infants' understanding of objects and the physical world. The paper was written for a general audience of fellow psychologists rather than for experts in perception, so with a little effort it should be comprehensible to an undergraduate student.

Bower, T. G. R. (1989). *The rational infant.* New York: Freeman. Bower has been one of the major researchers and theorists in the area of perceptual development. In this book he lays out the evidence and his interpretation of it.

Haith, M. M. (1990). Progress in the understanding of sensory and perceptual processes in early infancy. *Merrill-Palmer Quarterly, 36,* 1–26. In this relatively brief paper, Haith looks back on the last 25 years of research on perceptual development. He comments not only on the knowledge gained but also on the processes by which scientific progress has been made and the tasks still facing the field. Very interesting reading.

6

Cognitive Development I: Structure and Process

Think for a minute about the kinds of things you do in an ordinary day. Since most of you reading this are students, I will assume that you are involved in a whole set of typical "studentish" things: You go to class, listen to lectures and take notes, read assignments, go to the library to look up material for a term paper, and so on. It is tempting to put these academic activities into a special category of "intellectual" pursuits, but that would be a mistake. Virtually every task you undertake in an ordinary nonstudent day also has some intellectual or "cognitive" component. You try to recall a phone number or remember a list of things to buy at the grocery store; you balance your checkbook; you follow directions to a friend's home you've never been to before, or you find it by using a map. Even the simple act of reading your watch and knowing how much time you have before an appointment involves thinking—highly automatic thinking, to be sure, but you had to learn how do it originally.

These activities are all part of what we normally describe as *cognitive functioning* or "intelligence." What I will be exploring in this chapter and the next is how we have all acquired the ability to do these things. One-year-olds cannot use maps, balance a checkbook, or take notes in a lecture. How do children come to be able to do so? And how do we explain the fact that not all children learn these things at the same rate or become equally skilled?

Answering questions like these has been complicated by the fact that there are three distinctly different views of cognition or intelligence, each of which has led to a separate body of research and commentary. Blending the three turns out to be a tricky task—one that I don't want to attempt until I have first presented each view separately.

Three Views of Intelligence

Historically, the first approach to studying cognitive development or intelligence was focused on the basic observation that people clearly differ in their intellectual skill— their ability to remember lists for the grocery store, the speed with which they solve problems or learn new words, their ability, as Robert Sternberg puts it, to "respond flexibly to challenging situations" (1997, p. 1030). When we say someone is "bright" or "very intelligent," it is just such skills we mean, and our label is based on the assumption that we can rank-order people in their degree of "brightness." It was precisely this assumption that led to the development of intelligence tests, which were designed simply to give us a way of measuring such individual differences in intellectual skill or power.

This "power" definition of intelligence, also referred to as a *psychometric* approach, held sway for many years. But it has one great weakness: It does not deal with the equally compelling fact that intelligence develops. As children grow, their thinking becomes more and more abstract and complex. If you give a 5-year-old a mental list of things to remember to buy at the grocery store, she will have trouble remembering more than a few items. She is also very unlikely to use good strategies to aid her memory, such as rehearsing the list or organizing the items into groups. An 8-year-old would remember more things and probably would rehearse the list under his breath or in his head as he was walking to the store.

The fact that intelligence develops in this way forms the foundation of the second great tradition in the study of cognitive development, the *cognitive-developmental* approach of Jean Piaget and his many followers. Piaget's focus was on the development of cognitive *structures* rather than on intellectual power, on patterns of development that are *common* to all children rather than on individual differences.

These two traditions have lived side by side for several decades, rather like not-very-friendly neighbors who smile vaguely at one another when they meet but never get together for coffee. In recent years, though, the two have developed a mutual

Critical Thinking

Is this what you mean when you say someone is "bright" or "intelligent"? What else do you mean by these terms?

Three-year-old Anna is having a fine time figuring out how to lift the spoon with a magnet. How might you describe the "intelligence" of her behavior from each of the three different perspectives?

friend—a third view, called the **information processing approach,** that partially integrates the first two. Proponents of this third view argue: "Intelligence is not a faculty or trait of the mind. Intelligence is not mental content. *Intelligence is processing*" (Fagan, 1992, p. 82). According to this view, if we are to understand intelligence we need to uncover and find ways to measure the basic processes that make up cognitive activity. Once we have identified such basic processes, we can then ask questions about *both* developmental processes and individual differences: Do these basic processes change with age? Do people differ in their speed or skill in using the basic processes? The information on individual differences in infants' speed of habituation or "recognition memory," which I described briefly in Chapter 5, is an example of one body of research that has emerged from this new theoretical model.

Each of these three views tells us something useful and different about intelligence, so we need to look at all three. As I have done in earlier chapters, I want to begin here with the developmental patterns—the observable changes in the child's strategies and understanding with increasing age, both as Piaget described them and as current information processing theorists conceptualize them. In Chapter 7, I'll look at individual differences in IQ.

Piaget's Perspective

Imagine the following scene: Your 5-year-old, John, and your 8-year-old, Anne, come into the kitchen after playing outside, both asking for juice. With both children watching, you take two identical small cans of juice from the refrigerator and pour them into two nonidentical glasses. One glass is narrower than the other, so the juice rises higher in that glass. The 5-year-old, having been given the fatter glass, complains: "Anne got more than I did!" To which Anne replies (with the wonderful grace of the 8-year-old to her sibling): "I did not, you dummy. We both got the same amount. The two cans were just alike." To restore family harmony, you get out another glass identical to Anne's and pour John's juice into this new glass. The level of the liquid is now the same, and John is satisfied.

If this were an item on an IQ test, we'd say that Anne was "right" and John was "wrong." But such an emphasis on rightness or wrongness misses an essential point about this interchange: There seems to be a *developmental* change, a shift in the way the child sees or understands the world and the relationships of objects. John is not being pigheaded or "dumb." He is merely operating with a different kind of reasoning than Anne's. In a year or two, John will sound like Anne does now.

If we are to understand how children think, we need to understand such changes in the *form* or *structure* of their thinking. How do children come to understand the world around them? What kind of logic do they use, and how does it change over time?

These were precisely the kinds of questions that Jean Piaget asked in his many years of research on children's thinking. Despite the fact that many aspects of his theory have been called into question by later research, his theory set the agenda for most research in this area for the past thirty years and still serves as a kind of scaffolding for much of our thinking about thinking. So let me begin by giving you a fairly detailed description of Piaget's original ideas.

Basic Ideas

Piaget set out to answer a fundamental question: How does a child's knowledge of the world develop? In answering this question, Piaget's most central assumption was that the child is an active participant in the development of knowledge, *constructing* his own understanding. This idea, perhaps more than any other, has influenced the thinking of all those who have followed Piaget. The modern metaphor is that of the child as a "little scientist," engaged in active exploration, seeking understanding and knowledge.

Research Report
Piaget's Clever Research

Piaget had an enormous impact on developmental psychologists not only because he proposed a novel and provocative theory, but also because of the cleverness of many of the strategies he devised for testing children's understanding. These strategies often showed children doing or saying very unexpected things—results that other theorists found hard to assimilate into their models.

The most famous of all Piaget's clever techniques is probably his method for studying *conservation.* Piaget would begin with two equal balls of clay, show them to the child, and let the child hold and manipulate the clay until she agreed that they had the same amount. Then in full view of the child, Piaget would squish one of the balls into a pancake or roll it into a sausage. Then he'd ask the child whether there was still the same amount of clay or whether the pancake or sausage or the ball had more. Children of 4 and 5 consistently said that the ball had more; children of 6 and 7 consistently said that the amounts were still the same, indicating that they had grasped the concept of conservation—that the quantity of clay is *conserved* even though it is changed in some other dimension.

In another study, Piaget explored the concept of *class inclusion*—the understanding that a given object can belong simultaneously to more than one category. Fido is *both* a dog and an animal; a high chair is both a chair and furniture. Piaget usually studied this by having children first create their own classes and subclasses, and then asking them questions about them. One 5½-year-old child, for example, had been playing with a set of flowers and had made two heaps, one large group of primroses and a smaller group of other mixed flowers. Piaget then had this conversation with the child:

> Piaget: If I make a bouquet of all the primroses and you make one of all the flowers, which will be bigger?
>
> Child: Yours.
>
> Piaget: If I gather all the primroses in a meadow, will any flowers remain?
>
> Child: Yes. (Piaget & Inhelder, 1959, p. 108)

The child understood that there are other flowers besides primroses but did *not* yet understand that all primroses are flowers—that the smaller, subordinate class is *included in* the larger class.

In these conversations with children, Piaget was always trying to understand how the child thought rather than whether the child could come up with the right answer. So he used a "clinical method" in which he followed the child's lead, asking probing questions or creating special exploratory tests to try to discover the child's logic. In the early days of Piaget's work, many U.S. researchers were critical of this method, since Piaget did not ask precisely the same questions of each child. Still, the results were so striking, and often so surprising, that they couldn't be ignored. And when stricter research techniques were devised, investigators often discovered that Piaget's observations and insights were accurate.

In constructing such an understanding, Piaget thought that the child tries to *adapt* to the world around himself in ever more satisfactory ways. In Piaget's theory, this process of adaptation is in turn made up of several vital subprocesses.

Schemes. A pivotal Piagetian concept—and one of the hardest to grasp—is that of a **scheme** (sometimes written as *schema*). This term is often used as roughly analogous to the word *concept* or the phrases *mental category* or *complex of ideas,* but Piaget used it even more broadly than that. He saw knowledge not as merely passive mental cate-

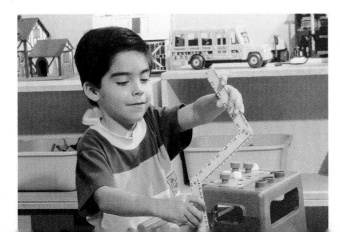

The metaphor of the child as a "little scientist," constructing his understanding of the world, comes directly from Piaget's theory.

gories but as *actions,* either mental or physical, and each of these actions is what he means by a scheme. So a scheme is not really a category, but the *action of categorizing* in some particular fashion. Some purely physical or sensory actions are also schemes. If you pick up and look at a ball, you are using your "looking scheme," your "picking-up scheme," and your "holding scheme." Piaget proposed that each baby begins life with a small repertoire of simple sensory or motor schemes, such as looking, tasting, touching, hearing, reaching. For the baby, an object *is* a thing that tastes a certain way, feels a certain way when touched, or has a particular color. Later, the toddler and child develops mental schemes as well, such as categorizing or comparing one object to another. Over development, the child gradually adds extremely complex mental schemes, such as deductive analysis or systematic reasoning. According to Piaget, the shift from the simple sensorimotor schemes of infancy to the increasingly complex mental schemes of later childhood is achieved through the operation of three basic processes: **assimilation, accommodation,** and **equilibration.**

Assimilation. Assimilation is the process of *taking in,* of absorbing some event or experience to some scheme. Piaget would say that when a baby looks at and then reaches for a mobile above her crib, she has assimilated the mobile to the looking and reaching schemes; when an older child sees a dog and labels it "dog," she is assimilating that animal to her dog category or scheme. When you read this paragraph, you are assimilating the information, hooking the concept onto whatever other concepts (schemes) you have that may be similar.

The key here is that assimilation is an *active* process. For one thing, we assimilate information selectively. We don't absorb everything we experience, like a blotter; instead, we pay attention only to those aspects of any experience for which we already have schemes. For example, when you listen to an instructor give a lecture, you may try to write everything down in your notebook or store it in your brain, but in fact you only assimilate ("take in") the thoughts you can connect to some concept or model you already have. Similarly, when I was living in Germany several years ago and struggling to learn German, I could assimilate only a portion of what my German teacher said—the portion for which I already had schemes. And I could imitate or use only the parts that I had assimilated.

Assimilation also changes the information that is assimilated, because each assimilated event or experience takes on some of the characteristics of the scheme to which it was assimilated. If I label your new sweater as green (that is, if I assimilate it to my "green" scheme) even though it is really chartreuse, I will remember it as more green and less yellow than it really is.

Accommodation. The complementary process is accommodation, which involves *changing the scheme* as a result of the new information you have taken in by assimilation. As I assimilated new German words and grammar, I gradually changed (accommodated) my concepts and categories, so that I had mental categories for several forms of past tense instead of only one, or mental groupings of words with a given prefix. The baby who sees and grasps a square object for the first time will accommodate her grasping scheme, so the next time she reaches for an object of that shape, her hand will be more appropriately bent to grasp it. Thus, in Piaget's theory, the process of accommodation is the key to developmental change. Through accommodation, we reorganize our thoughts, improve our skills, change our strategies.

Critical Thinking

Think of three or four more examples of assimilation and accommodation in your everyday life.

Piaget would say that baby Eleanor is assimilating this ball to her looking and grasping schemes. As she adapts her way of holding, she is also accommodating.

Equilibration. The third aspect of adaptation is equilibration. Piaget assumed that the child is always striving for coherence, to stay "in balance," to have an understanding of the world that makes overall sense. This is not unlike what a scientist does when she develops a theory about some body of information (and hence the metaphor of the child as a "little scientist"). The scientist wants to have a theory that will make sense out of every observation, that has internal coherence. When new research findings come along, she assimilates them to the existing theory; if they don't fit perfectly, she might simply set aside the deviant data, or she may make minor modifications in her theory. However, if enough nonconfirming evidence accumulates, the scientist may have to throw out her theory altogether or change some basic theoretical assumptions; either response would be a form of equilibration.

A road map analogy will also work here. Suppose you have just moved to a new city, and instead of buying a local map you try to learn your way around with only a hand-drawn map given to you by a friend. As you make your way through this new city, you make corrections on your map, redrawing it and writing notes to yourself. This redrawn and revised map is certainly an improvement over the original sketchy version, but eventually you will find that it is both impossible to read and still seriously flawed. So you start over and draw a new map, based on all your information. You carry this around with you, revising it and writing on it until it, too, is so full of annotations that you need to start over. The corrections and annotations you make to your map are analogous to accommodations in Piaget's theory; the process of starting over and drawing a new map is analogous to equilibration.

Piaget thought that a child operated in a similar way, creating coherent, more or less internally consistent models or theories. However, since the infant starts with a very limited repertoire of schemes (a very primitive initial map), the early "theories" or structures the child creates are simply not going to be adequate. Such inadequacies, so Piaget thought, force the child to make periodic major changes in her internal structure.

Piaget saw three particularly significant reorganization or equilibration points, each ushering in a new stage of development. The first is at about 18 months, when the toddler shifts from the dominance of simple sensory and motor schemes to the use of the first symbols. The second is normally between ages 5 and 7, when the child adds a whole new set of powerful schemes Piaget calls **operations.** These are far more abstract and general mental actions, such as mental addition or subtraction. The third major equilibration is at adolescence, when the child figures out how to "operate on" ideas as well as events or objects. These three major equilibrations create four stages:

The **sensorimotor stage** from birth to about 18 months

The **preoperational stage** from 18 months to about age 6

The **concrete operations stage** from 6 to about 12

The **formal operations stage** from age 12 onward

You will see as we go along that cognitive progress is considerably less stagelike than Piaget originally proposed. Still, Piaget's stages have formed an important framework for cognitive-developmental research for many decades. In this discussion, then, I will follow the general structure of Piaget's stages, describing Piaget's view of each period, and then examining some of the newer research on children of that age.

Infancy

Piaget's View of the Sensorimotor Period

Piaget assumes that the baby is engaged in the basic adaptive process of trying to make sense out of the world around her. She assimilates incoming information to the limited array of sensory and motor schemes she is born with—such as looking, listening, sucking, grasping—and accommodates those schemes based on her experiences. According to Piaget, this is the starting point for the entire process of cognitive development. He called this primitive form of thinking *sensorimotor intelligence*.

In the beginning, in Piaget's view, the baby is entirely tied to the immediate present, responding to whatever stimuli are available. She does not remember events or things from one encounter to the next and does not appear to plan or intend. This gradually changes during the first 18 months as the baby comes to understand that objects continue to exist even when they are out of sight and becomes able to remember objects, actions, and individuals over periods of time. Yet Piaget insisted that the sensorimotor infant is not yet able to *manipulate* these early mental images or memories. Nor does she use symbols to stand for objects or events. It is the new ability to manipulate internal symbols, such as words or images, that marks the beginning of the next stage, preoperational thought, at 18 to 24 months of age. John Flavell summarizes all this very nicely:

> [The infant] exhibits a wholly practical, perceiving-and-doing, action-bound kind of intellectual functioning; she does not exhibit the more contemplative, reflective, symbol-manipulating kind we usually think of in connection with cognition. The infant "knows" in the sense of recognizing or anticipating familiar, recurring objects and happenings, and "thinks" in the sense of behaving toward them with mouth, hand, eye, and other sensory-motor instruments in predictable, organized, and often adaptive ways. . . . It is the kind of noncontemplative intelligence that your dog relies on to make its way in the world. (1985, p. 13)

The change from the limited repertoire of schemes available to the newborn to the ability to use symbols at about 18 months is gradual, although Piaget identified six substages, summarized in Table 6.1.

Each substage represents some specific advance. Substage 2 is marked especially by the beginning of those important coordinations between looking and listening, reaching and looking, and reaching and sucking that are such central features of the 2-month-old's means of exploring the world. The term **primary circular reactions** refers to the many simple repetitive actions we see at this stage, each organized around the infant's own body. The baby accidentally sucks his thumb one day, finds it pleasurable, and repeats the action. **Secondary circular reactions,** in substage 3, differ only in that the baby is now repeating some action in order to trigger a reaction outside his own body. The baby coos and Mom smiles, so the baby coos again, apparently in order to get Mom to smile again; the baby accidentally hits the mobile hanging above his crib, it moves, and he then repeats his arm wave, apparently with some intent to make the mobile move again. These initial connections between bodily actions and external consequences are pretty automatic, very like a kind of operant conditioning. Only in substage 4 (according to Piaget) do we see the beginnings of real understanding of causal connections, and at this point the baby really moves into exploratory high gear.

In substage 5 this becomes even more marked with the emergence of what Piaget calls **tertiary circular reactions.** In this pattern the baby is not content merely to repeat the original behavior but tries out variations. The baby in substage 5 might try out many other sounds or facial expressions to see if they will trigger Mom's smile, or try moving his hand in new ways or directions in order to make the mobile move in new ways. At this stage the baby's behavior has a purposeful, experimental quality. Nonetheless, Piaget thought that even in substage 5 the baby does not have internal *symbols* to stand for objects. The development of such symbols is the mark of substage 6.

Piaget's descriptions of this sequence of development, largely based on remarkably detailed observations of his own three children, provoked a very rich array of research, some that confirms the general outlines of his proposals and some that does not. You have already seen some of the relevant information in Chapter 5, all of which points to the conclusion that in a number of important respects, Piaget underestimated

Critical Thinking

Think back to everything I said about perceptual skills in infancy in Chapter 5. Does Flavell's description of the sensorimotor infant match what you already know?

Table 6.1

Substages of the Sensorimotor Period According to Piaget

Substage	Age	Piaget's Label	Characteristics
1	0–1 mos.	Reflexes	Practice of built-in schemes or reflexes such as sucking or looking. No imitation; no ability to integrate information from several senses.
2	1–4 mos.	Primary circular reactions	Accommodation of basic schemes, as baby practices them endlessly—grasping, looking, sucking. Beginning coordination of schemes from different senses, such as looking toward a sound; baby does not yet link his bodily actions to some result outside his body.
3	4–8 mos.	Secondary circular reactions	Baby becomes much more aware of events outside his own body and makes them happen again in a kind of trial-and-error learning. Imitation may occur, but only of schemes already in the baby's repertoire. Beginning understanding of the "object concept."
4	8–12 mos.	Coordination of secondary schemes	Clear intentional means-ends behavior. The baby not only goes after what she wants; she may combine two schemes to do so, such as knocking a pillow away to reach a toy. Imitation of novel behaviors occurs, as does transfer of information from one sense to the other (cross-modal transfer).
5	12–18 mos.	Tertiary circular reactions	"Experimentation" begins, in which the infant tries out new ways of playing with or manipulating objects. Very active, very purposeful trial-and-error exploration.
6	18–24 mos.	Beginning of representational thought	Development of use of symbols to represent object or events. Child understands that the symbol is separate from the object. Deferred imitation occurs first here.

the ability of infants to store, remember, and organize sensory and motor information. Research on infant memory and on imitation generally points to the same conclusion.

Memory

The first hint we have that infants are capable of greater feats of memory than Piaget proposed is that habituation and dishabituation are already present at birth—research I talked about in Chapter 3. Habituation, you'll recall, involves a lessening of response to a repeated stimulus. For it to work, the baby must have at least some ability to store

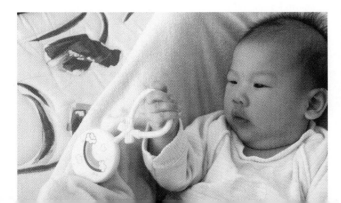

Three-month-old Andrea may be showing a secondary circular reaction here, shaking her hand repeatedly to hear the sound of the rattle. In learning theory language, we could say that the pleasure in the sound is reinforcing her hand-shaking behavior.

(remember) information about the previous occurrences. Similarly, for dishabituation to occur, the baby must recognize that the new event is somehow different, which suggests that the baby's memory contains a fairly detailed image or template of the original event (Schneider & Bjorklund, 1998).

A second source of evidence that quite young babies can remember specific events over periods of time comes from a series of clever studies by Carolyn Rovee-Collier and her colleagues (Bhatt & Rovee-Collier, 1996; Hartshorn & Rovee-Collier, 1997; Hayne & Rovee-Collier, 1995; Rovee-Collier, 1993). In her most widely used procedure, Rovee-Collier uses an ingenious variation of an operant conditioning strategy. She first hangs an attractive mobile over the baby's crib and watches to see how the baby responds. In particular, she is interested in how often the baby normally kicks his legs while looking at the mobile. After three minutes of this "baseline" observation, she attaches a string from the mobile to the baby's leg, as you can see in Figure 6.1, so that each time the baby kicks his leg, the mobile moves. Babies quickly learn to kick repeatedly in order to make this interesting new thing happen (what Piaget would call a secondary circular reaction). Within three to six minutes, 3-month-olds double or triple their kick rates, showing that learning has clearly occurred. Rovee-Collier then tests the baby's memory of this learning by coming back some days later and hanging the same mobile over the crib, but *not* attaching the string to his foot. The crucial issue is whether the baby will kick at the mere sight of the mobile. If the baby remembers the previous occasion, he should kick at a higher rate than he did when he first saw the mobile, which is precisely what 3-month-old babies do, even after a delay of as long as a week.

Figure 6.1

This 3-month-old baby in one of Rovee-Collier's memory experiments will quickly learn to kick her foot in order to make the mobile move. And several days later, she will remember this connection between kicking and the mobile.

(*Source:* Rovee-Collier, 1993, p. 131.)

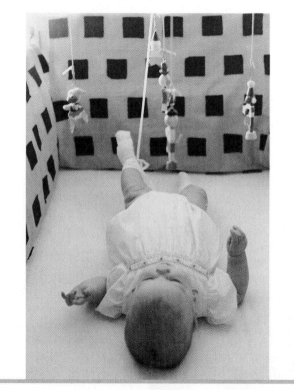

Why is this so interesting? Primarily because it shows us that the young infant is cognitively a whole lot more sophisticated than we (and Piaget) had supposed. At the same time, Rovee-Collier's work also offers some kind of support for Piaget's views, since she observes systematic gains over the months of infancy in the baby's ability to remember. A 2-month-old can remember the kicking action for only one day; a 3-month-old can remember over a week; and by 6 months the baby can remember over two weeks. Rovee-Collier also finds that all these early infant memories are *strongly* tied to the specific context in which the original experience occurred. Even 6-month-olds do not recognize or remember the mobile if the investigator makes even a very small change, such as hanging a different cloth around the crib in which the child was originally tested. Thus, babies do remember—far more than Piaget believed—but their memories are highly specific. With age, their memories become less and less tied to specific cues or contexts.

Imitation

Another active area of study has been the ability of the infant to imitate. If you look again at Table 6.1, you'll see that Piaget thought that the ability to imitate emerged quite gradually over the early months. In broad terms, Piaget's proposed sequence has been supported. For example, imitation of someone else's hand movements or their actions with objects seems to improve steadily during the months of infancy, starting at 1 or 2 months of age; imitation of two-part actions develops only in toddlerhood, perhaps at 15 to 18 months (Poulson et al., 1989). In two areas, however, Piaget appears to have been wrong about infants' imitative abilities.

First, although Piaget thought babies could not imitate other people's facial gestures until about substage 4 (8–12 months), quite a lot of research now shows that newborns are able to imitate at least some facial gestures, particularly tongue protrusion (Anisfeld, 1991; Field et al., 1982b; Meltzoff & Moore, 1977), as in the photos in Figure 6.2. So newborns *do* imitate, a striking and surprising fact—although it is entirely consistent with the research I described in Chapter 5 showing that newborns are capable of tactual/visual cross-modal transfer.

Figure 6.2

Although researchers still disagree on just how much newborns will imitate, everyone agrees that they will imitate the gesture of tongue protrusion, demonstrated here by Andrew Meltzoff from the earliest study of this kind.

(*Source:* Meltzoff & Moore, 1977. Copyright 1997 by the AAAS.)

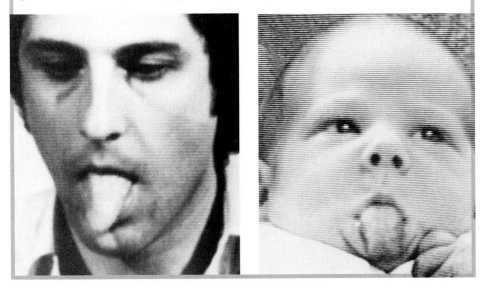

Piaget also argued that *deferred* imitation, in which a child sees some action and then imitates it at a later time when the model is no longer visible, was possible only at substage 6 (about age 18 months), since deferred imitation requires some kind of internal representation. Once again, more recent research points to earlier development of this ability. At least one study (Meltzoff, 1988) shows that babies as young as 9 months can defer their imitation over as long as 24 hours. By 14 months, toddlers can recall and later imitate someone's actions over periods of 2 days (Hanna & Meltzoff, 1993). This finding makes it clear that children of this age can and do learn specific behaviors through modeling, even when they have no chance to imitate the behavior immediately. Even very young toddlers are thus busily learning by watching others, playmates as well as adults.

More broadly, the results of research on both memory and imitation, like many of the studies I talked about in Chapter 5, suggest that in a number of important respects, Piaget underestimated the ability of infants to store, remember, and organize sensory and motor information. Very young babies pay much more attention to patterns, to sequence, to prototypical features than Piaget thought, and babies can apparently remember these things over at least short intervals. Many current theorists have taken this evidence to mean that the baby comes equipped with a wide range of built-in knowledge or inborn constraints on his ways of understanding the world around him.

Arrayed on the other side of the argument, however, is the obvious fact that newborns, despite their unexpectedly good perceptual and cognitive abilities, are *not* as skilled as 6-month-olds or 12-month-olds. Newborns do not use gestures to communicate, they do not talk, and they do not show deferred imitation. At 6 months, babies do not combine several strategies to achieve some goal, and they do not seem to experiment with objects in the same way as we see later. Even at 12 months, toddlers do not seem to use symbols to stand for things in any general way. They use a few words but don't yet show pretend play, for example. So despite all the new and fascinating evidence showing very early skills, it still appears to be correct to describe the infant as *sensorimotor* rather than *symbolic* in her thinking. Over the first 18 to 24 months, the baby seems to be building toward such symbol use, a shift that John Flavell correctly sees as remarkable:

> A cognitive system that uses symbols just seems . . . to be radically, drastically, qualitatively different from one that does not. So great is the difference that the transformation of one system into the other during the first 2 years of life still seems nothing short of miraculous to me, no matter how much we learn about it. (1985, p. 82)

It is precisely this shift that Piaget saw as the beginning point of the next stage.

The Preschool Years

Piaget's View of the Preoperational Stage

During the years from 2 to 6, Piaget saw the evidence of symbol use in many aspects of the child's behavior. Children this age begin to pretend in their play, for example (a development I've talked about in the following Real World box). At age 2 or 3 or 4, a broom may become a horsie or a block may become a train. We can also see such symbol use in the emergence of language (which I'll talk about in Chapter 8) and in the preschooler's primitive ability to understand scale models or simple maps (DeLoache, 1995).

Beyond the accomplishment of symbol use, Piaget's description of the preoperational stage focused mostly on all the things the preschool-age child still *cannot* do, giving an oddly negative tone to his description of this period. Piaget saw the preschooler's thinking as rigid, captured by appearances, insensitive to inconsistencies,

The Real World

Young Children's Play

If you watch young children during their unstructured time, you'll see them building towers out of blocks, talking to or feeding their dolls, making "tea" with the tea set, racing toy trucks across the floor, dressing up in grown-up clothes. They are, in a word, *playing.* This is not trivial or empty activity; it is the stuff of which much of cognitive development seems to be built.

The form of this play changes in very obvious ways during the years from 1 to 6, following a sequence that matches Piaget's stages rather well (Rubin et al., 1983).

First pretend play.

Sensorimotor Play. The child of 12 months or so spends most of her playtime exploring and manipulating objects, using all the sensorimotor schemes in her repertoire. She puts things in her mouth, shakes them, moves them along the floor.

Constructive Play. Such simple exploratory play with objects does continue past 12 months, especially with some totally new object, but by age 2 or so, children also begin to use objects to build or construct things—creating a block tower, putting together a puzzle, making something out of clay or with blocks—a form of play that makes up nearly half the play of children aged 3 to 6.

First Pretend Play. Pretend play also begins at about the same time. The first sign of such pretending is usually something like a child's using a toy spoon to "feed" himself or a toy comb to comb his hair. The toys are still used for their actual or typical purposes (e.g., a spoon for feeding) and the actions are still oriented to the *self,* but pretending is involved. Between 15 and 21 months, a shift occurs: The recipient of the pretend action now becomes another person or a toy, most often a doll. The child is still using objects for their usual purposes (such as drinking from a cup), but now she is using the toy cup with a doll instead of herself. Dolls are especially good toys for this kind of pretending, because it is not a very large leap from doing things

to yourself to doing things with a doll. So children feed dolls imaginary food, comb their hair, soothe them.

Substitute Pretend Play. Between 2 and 3 years of age, children begin to use objects to stand for something altogether different. They may comb the doll's hair with a baby bottle while saying that it is a comb, use a broom to be a horsie, or make "trucks" out of blocks. By age 4 or 5, children spend as much as 20 percent of their playtime in this new, complicated kind of pretending (Field et al., 1982a).

Sociodramatic Play. Somewhere in the preschool years, children also begin to play parts or take roles. This is really still a form of pretending, except that now several children create a mutual pretense. They play "daddy and mommy," "cowboys and Indians," "doctor and patient," and the like. At first, children simply take up these roles; later, they name the roles to one another and may give each other explicit instructions about the right way to pretend a particular role. You can begin to see this form of play in some 2-year-olds; by age 4, virtually all children engage in some play of this type (Howes & Matheson, 1992). Interestingly, at about the same ages a great many children seem to create imaginary companions (M. Taylor et al., 1993). For many years psychologists believed that the existence of an imaginary companion was a sign of disturbance in a child; now it is clear that such a creation is a normal part of the development of pretense in many children.

Children clearly get great delight out of all these often elaborate fantasies. Equally important, by playing roles, pretending to be someone else, they also become more and more aware of how things may look or feel to someone else, and their egocentric approach to the world declines (Rogoff, 1998). In Vygotsky's view, play also "creates its own zone of proximal development of the child. In play a child is always above his average age, above his daily behavior; in play it is as though he were a head taller than himself" (1978, p. 102).

Sociodramatic play.

and tied to his own perspective—a quality Piaget (1954) called **egocentrism.** The child is not being selfish; rather, she simply thinks (assumes) that everyone sees the world as she does.

Figure 6.3 is a photo of a classic experiment illustrating this kind of egocentrism. The child is shown a three-dimensional scene with mountains of different sizes and colors. From a set of drawings, he picks out the one that shows the scene the way he sees it. Most preschoolers can do this without much difficulty. Then the examiner asks the child to pick out the drawing that shows how someone *else* sees the scene, such as the little clay man or the examiner. At this point preschool children have difficulty. Most often they again pick the drawing that shows their *own* view of the mountains (Gzesh & Surber, 1985). In Piaget's view, for the child to be able to succeed at this task, she must "decenter"—she must shift from using herself as the only frame of reference to seeing things from another perspective. He thought that preschool children could not yet do this.

The preschool child's focus on the appearance of objects is an equally important theme in Piaget's description of this period, evident in some of the most famous of his studies, those on **conservation.** It was a problem of conservation that confronted Anne and John and their juice glasses; to understand that both glasses of juice hold the same amount, John would have to ignore the *appearance* of difference and understand that the amount of juice is "conserved"—remains the same—despite variations in the shape of the container. This is an example of conservation of quantity, one of six different conservations Piaget studied (listed in Table 6.2). In every case, his measurement technique (described in the Research Report on p. 165) involved first showing the child two equal sets or objects, getting the child to agree they were equal in some key respect such as weight or quantity or length or number, and then shifting or deforming one of the objects and asking the child if they were still equal. Children rarely show any of these forms of conservation before age 5; Piaget took this fact to be a sign that they were still captured by the appearance of change and did not focus on the underlying unchanging aspect.

Notice that the understanding of conservation is part of a chain of development that begins with the various object constancies and object permanence in infancy. The sensorimotor infant eventually figures out that objects may remain the same even though they appear to change in some respects (such as color or shape), and he under-

Critical Thinking

Can you think of any examples of egocentrism in your own behavior? What about buying someone else a gift you were hoping to receive yourself? Other examples?

Figure 6.3

One of the types of experimental arrangements used to study egocentrism in children.

Table 6.2

Different Types of Conservation Studied by Piaget

Number	Two rows with equal numbers of pennies or buttons are laid out parallel to one another with the items matching. Then one row is stretched out longer or squeezed together or rearranged in some other way, and the child is asked, "Are there the same number?"
Length	Two pencils of identical length are laid one above the other so that they match perfectly. Then one is displaced to the right or left so that one pencil's point sticks out further than the other, and the child is asked if they are now the same length.
Quantity	Two equal beakers are filled with equal amounts of water. One is then poured into a differently shaped glass (tall and thin or short and squat), and the child is asked if there is still the same amount to drink in each.
Substance or mass	Two equal balls of clay are shown to the child. One is then squished into another shape, such as a sausage or a pancake. The child is asked if there is now the same amount of clay in each.
Weight	Two equal balls of clay are weighed on a balance scale so that the child sees that they weigh the same amount. One is then deformed into another shape, and the child is asked if they still weigh the same or "have the same amount of weight."
Volume	Two balls of clay are placed in two equal beakers of water so that the child sees that they each displace the same amount of water. Then one ball is deformed, and the child is asked if they will still "take up the same amount of space."

stands that objects continue to exist even when they are out of sight. Now in the preschool years he must come to understand that other, more abstract aspects of objects, such as their mass or weight, also remain constant despite apparent changes.

Newer Views of the Preschool Child's Thinking

These same two themes—egocentrism/perspective taking and the child's ability to understand the distinction between appearance and reality—continue to dominate much of the research on the thinking of the preschool-age child. A rich and intriguing new body of evidence suggests that preschoolers are a great deal less egocentric than Piaget thought but that they do indeed struggle with the problem of distinguishing between appearance and reality.

Perspective Taking. Research on the child's ability to take others' perspectives shows that children as young as 2 and 3 have at least *some* ability to understand that other people see things or experience things differently than they do. For example, children this age will adapt their speech or their play to the demands of their companion. They play differently with older or younger playmates, and they talk differently to a younger or a disabled child (Brownell, 1990; Guralnick & Paul-Brown, 1984).

Yet such understanding is clearly not perfect at this young age. John Flavell has proposed two levels of perspective-taking ability. At level 1, the child knows *that* some other person experiences something differently. At level 2, the child develops a whole series of complex rules for figuring out precisely *what* the other person sees or experiences (Flavell et al., 1990). Children at ages 2 and 3 have level 1 but not level 2 knowledge. We begin to see some level 2 knowledge in 4- and 5-year-olds.

Appearance and Reality. This shift seems to be part of a much broader change in the child's understanding of appearance and reality. Flavell has studied this change in a variety of ways, such as by showing objects under colored lights to change their apparent color or by putting masks on animals to make them look like other animals. He finds that 2- and 3-year-olds consistently judge things by their appearance; by age 5, the child begins to be able to separate the appearance from the underlying reality and knows that some object isn't "really" red even though it looks red under a red-colored light, or that a cat with a dog mask is still "really" a cat (Flavell et al., 1987; 1989).

In the most famous Flavell procedure, the experimenter shows the child a sponge that has been painted to look like a rock. Three-year-olds, faced with this odd object, will either say that the object looks like a sponge and is a sponge or that it looks like a rock and is a rock. Children aged 4 and 5 can distinguish the two; they realize that the object looks like a rock but *is* a sponge (Flavell, 1986). Thus, the older child now understands that the same object can be represented differently, depending on one's point of view.

Using the same type of materials, investigators have also asked whether a child can grasp the principle of a **false belief.** For example, after the child has felt the sponge/rock and has answered questions about what it looks like and what it "really" is, a researcher can ask something like this: "Your friend John hasn't touched this, he hasn't squeezed it. If John just sees it over here like this, what will he think it is? Will he think it's a rock or will he think that it's a sponge?" (Gopnik & Astington, 1988, p. 35). By and large, 3-year-olds think that John will believe it is a sponge, while 4- and 5-year-olds realize that because John hasn't felt the sponge, he will have a false belief that it is a rock—a finding replicated in research in a number of different cultures, described in the Cultures and Contexts box on appearance and reality (opposite). Thus, the child of 4 or 5 understands that someone else can believe something that isn't true *and will act on that belief.*

Theories of Mind. Evidence like this has led a number of theorists (e.g., Astington & Gopnik, 1991; Gopnik & Wellman, 1994; Harris, 1989) to propose that the 4- or 5-year-old has developed a new and quite sophisticated **theory of mind.** The child this age has begun to understand that she cannot predict what other people will do solely from observing the situation itself; the other person's desires and beliefs also enter into the equation. So the child develops various theories about other people's ideas, beliefs, and desires and about how those ideas or beliefs will affect the other person's behavior.

Such a theory of mind does not spring forth full-blown at age 4. As early as 18 months, toddlers have some beginning understanding of the fact that people (but not inanimate objects) operate with goals and intentions (Meltzoff, 1995). Children this age also understand something about other people's emotions and desires, as I mentioned in Chapter 5. For example, when they see an adult looking happy after eating one food and looking disgusted after eating another, 18-month-olds understand that the adult will choose to eat the pleasing food (Repacholi & Gopnik, 1997). A 2½-year-old will restate a request in clearer language if a listener's behavior shows that she did not understand the first try, thus indicating that the toddler has some awareness of the level of the other person's understanding (Shwe & Markman, 1997). By age 3, children understand that a person who wants something will try to get it and that a person may still want something even if she can't have it (Lillard & Flavell, 1992). What the 3-year-old does not yet understand, however, is the basic principle that each person's actions are based on his own *representation* of reality and that a person's representation may differ from what is "really" there. People act on the basis of what they believe or feel, even if what they believe is incorrect or what they feel is unexpected or apparently inconsistent in a given situation. Thus, a person who feels sad even though she has succeeded at something will act on that sadness, not on the visible success. It is this new aspect of the theory of mind that seems to be absent in the 3-year-old but that clearly emerges at about age 4 or 5.

Despite this major cognitive accomplishment, there is still much that the 4- or 5-year-old doesn't yet grasp about other people's thinking. The child of this age understands that other people think, but he does not yet understand that those same other people think about *him.* In the famous infinite regress, the 4-year-old understands "I know that you know," but he does not yet fully understand that this process is reciprocal, that "You know that I know." Such an understanding of the reciprocal nature of thought seems to develop between ages 5 and 7 for most children (Perner & Wimmer,

Cultures and Contexts
Understanding of Appearance and Reality in Other Cultures

A number of studies from widely differing parts of the globe, and in widely different cultures, suggest that the shift at about age 4 in children's understanding of appearance and reality and of false belief may well be a universal developmental pattern.

Jeremy Avis and Paul Harris (1991) adapted the traditional false belief testing procedure for use with a pygmy tribe, the Baka, who live in Cameroon. The Baka are a hunter-gatherer people who live together in camps. Each child was tested in his or her own hut, using materials with which she was completely familiar. She watched one adult named Mopfana (a member of the tribe) put some mango kernels into a bowl. Mopfana then left the hut, and a second adult (also a tribe member) told the child they were going to play a game with Mopfana: They were going to hide the kernels in a cooking pot. Then he asked the child what Mopfana was going to do when he came back. Would he look for the kernels in the bowl or in the pot? And he asked the child whether Mopfana's heart would feel good or bad before he lifted the lid of the bowl. Younger children—2-, 3-, and early 4-year-olds—were much more likely to say that Mopfana would look for the seeds in the pot or to say that he would be sad before he looked in the bowl, while older 4- and 5-year-olds were nearly always right on all three questions.

Similarly, when Flavell used his sponge/rock task with children in mainland China, he found that Chinese 3-year-olds were just as confused about this task as are U.S. or British 3-year-

olds, whereas 5-year-old Chinese children had no difficulty with the problem (Flavell et al., 1983).

Using a somewhat different kind of problem, but one that still touches on the difference between appearance and reality, Paul Harris and his colleagues have asked children in several cultures how characters in a story *really* feel and what emotion *appears* on their faces. For example:

Diana is playing a game with her friend. At the end of the game Diana wins and her friend loses. Diana tries to hide how she feels because otherwise her friend won't play any more. (Harris, 1989, p. 134)

Four-year-old children in Britain and the United States, faced with such stories, have no trouble saying how the character will really feel, but they have more trouble saying how the character would look. By 5 or 6, however, the child grasps the possible difference. Harris and his colleagues have found that the same age shift occurs in Japan (Gardner et al., 1988), and Joshi and MacLean (1994) found a similar shift in India, despite the fact that both the Japanese and Indian cultures put far more emphasis on the disguising of emotions than is true in British or U.S. culture.

In these very different cultures, then, something similar seems to be occurring between ages 3 and 5. In these years, all children seem to understand something general about the difference between appearance and reality and seem to develop a type of theory of mind.

1985; Sullivan et al., 1994)—a particularly important development because it is probably necessary for the creation of genuinely reciprocal friendships, which we see in the elementary school years.

Metacognition and Metamemory. An increased awareness of the ways in which thinking operates is also apparent in other areas. For example, between ages 3 and 5, children figure out that in order to tell if a rock painted like a sponge is really a sponge or a rock, a person would need to touch or hold it. Just looking at it doesn't give enough information (Flavell, 1993; O'Neill et al., 1992). In a similar vein, 4-year-olds (but not 3-year-olds) understand that to remember or forget something, one must have known it at a previous time (Lyon & Flavell, 1994). These developments are important because they seem to be the first signs of what psychologists now call **metamemory** and **metacognition**— knowing about the process of memory and the process of thinking. By about age 4 or 5, children seem to have some very elementary grasp of these processes.

John Flavell's research suggests that by age 4, a child understands that there is some kind of process called thinking that people do and that is distinct from knowing or talking (Flavell et al., 1995). They also understand in some preliminary way that people can think about imaginary objects or events as well as real ones. Despite these major advances, however, 4- and 5-year-olds do not yet understand that thinking is a process or that it occurs continuously (Wellman & Hickling, 1994). In particular, they don't realize that *other people* are thinking all the time, and when asked, they are bad at guessing what the other person might be thinking about, even when the clues are quite clear—such as when the other person is reading or listening to something. All these skills are much more highly developed in 7- and 8-year-olds, who seem to have figured out that their own and other people's thinking goes on constantly and follows certain rules.

All this new work on the child's theory of mind has not only opened up a fascinating new area of research; it has also clearly demonstrated that the preschool child is vastly less egocentric than Piaget supposed. By age 4, and in more limited ways at earlier ages, the child has the ability to understand other points of view and can predict other people's behavior on the basis of deductions about their beliefs.

These emerging understandings seem to be aided by at least two things: practice at pretend play, especially shared pretense with other children (Dockett & Smith, 1995); and certain aspects of language skill, especially the learning of words for feelings, desires, and thoughts—words like *want, need, think,* or *remember* (Astington & Jenkins, 1995). Indeed, some level of language facility may be a necessary condition for the development of a theory of mind. Jennifer Jenkins and Janet Astington (1996) have found that children simply do not succeed at false belief tasks until they have reached a certain threshold of general language skill. Further support for the same point comes from the finding that children as old as 13 who were born deaf and learned no sign language before school age—who thus had no structured language to work with during the preschool years—typically fail false belief tests and other measures of the theory of mind (Peterson & Siegal, 1995).

Understanding and Regulating Emotions.   Another necessary skill for the emergence of a representational theory of mind is the child's ability to understand or "read" others' emotions—a process I described in Chapter 5. You know that by age 4, children's emotional vocabulary has expanded enough that they can recognize facial expressions and situations that convey the emotions happy, sad, mad, loving, and scared. In keeping with their emerging theory of mind, 4- and 5-year-olds also begin to understand the links between other people's emotions and their circumstances; so, for example, they understand that another person will feel sad if she fails or happy if she succeeds. They also begin to grasp the fact that another person's feelings are based on his *thoughts* as much as or more than on the current situation. As one example, children of this age have some understanding of the fact that a person might feel sad if some cue *reminds* him of a sad experience (Lagattuta et al., 1997).

During these same years, the child also learns to regulate or modulate her *own* expression of emotion (Dunn, 1994). Part of this process is the development of *impulse control,* sometimes called *inhibitory control*—the growing ability to inhibit a response, to wait rather than to weep, to yell rather than to hit, to go slowly rather than fast (e.g., Kochanska et al., 1997). When an infant is upset, it is the parents who help to regulate that emotion by cuddling, soothing, or removing the child from the upsetting situation. Over the preschool years, this regulation process is gradually taken over more and more by the child as the various prohibitions and instructions are internalized. A 2-year-old is only minimally able to modulate feelings or behavior in this way, but by age 5 or 6 most children have made great strides in controlling the intensity of their expression of strong feelings, so that they don't automatically hit someone or something when they are angry, cry inconsolably when they are frustrated, or sulk when they are denied (Sroufe, 1996).

A second aspect to the child's regulation of emotion—one that is clearly linked to the cognitive processes I'm talking about in this chapter—is the need to learn the social rules of specific emotional expressions. When and where is it permissible to express various feelings? What form may that expression take? When should you smile? When should you *not* frown or smile, regardless of the feeling you may be experiencing? For example, as early as age 3, children begin to learn that there are times when they ought to smile—even when they do not feel completely happy. Thus begins the "social smile," a facial expression that is quite distinct from the natural, delighted smile. Similarly, over the years of childhood, children learn to use abbreviated or constricted forms of other emotions, such as anger or disgust (Izard & Malatesta, 1987), and they learn to conceal their feelings in a variety of situations. Such concealment appears to rest on the child's emerging theory of mind. For example, for a child to conceal some emotion in order not to hurt someone else's feelings requires that she have some sense of what will cause the other person's feelings to be hurt. Equally, the preschool child learns to use her own emotional expression to get things she wants, crying or smiling as needed. This control of emotions, in turn, rests at least partially on her grasp of the links between her behavior and others' perception of her behavior, an understanding that develops rapidly between ages 3 and 4 as part of the more sophisticated theory of mind.

Conservation. In contrast to the work on perspective taking, studies of conservation have generally confirmed Piaget's basic observations. Although younger children can demonstrate some understanding of conservation if the task is made very simple (Gelman, 1972; Wellman, 1982), most children do not begin to solve conservation problems until age 5 or 6 or later (e.g., Sophian, 1995).

The relatively late development of the child's understanding of conservation makes sense if we think of conservation tasks as a particularly sophisticated form of the problem of appearance and reality. When I pour juice from a short fat glass into a tall thin glass, the amount of juice appears to increase (rises higher in the glass) even though in reality it remains the same. Thus, conservation cannot be grasped until after the child has made considerable progress in understanding the distinction between appearance and reality, typically by age 5 or so.

Overview of the Preschool Child's Thinking

How can we add up these bits and pieces of information about the preschool child's thinking? At the least, we can say that preschool children are capable of forms of logic that Piaget thought impossible at this stage. In particular, by age 4, and certainly by age 5, not only can they take others' perspectives, but they understand at least in a preliminary way that other people's behavior rests on inner beliefs and feelings.

Of course it might be that Piaget was right about the basic sequences but simply got the ages wrong, that the transition he saw at 6 or 7 really happens at around age 4 or 5. Certainly the various understandings that children seem to come to at about that age—about false belief, about appearance and reality, about other people's physical perspective, and about the meanings of emotional expressions—are remarkably stage-like in that they all tend to appear at about the same time.

Or it might be that the newer research exaggerates the preschooler's abilities to at least some degree. Preschoolers can indeed do some sophisticated-looking things, but their understanding remains specific rather than general. It is still tied heavily to specific situations or can be displayed only with a good deal of support. Studies of both conservation and children's logic show that sophisticated performances can be *elicited* in 2-, 3-, and 4-year-old children, but preschoolers do not typically show such skills spontaneously. In order for the preschool child to demonstrate these relatively advanced forms of thinking, you have to make the task quite simple, eliminate distractions, or give special clues. The fact that children this age can solve these problems at all is striking, but Piaget was clearly correct in pointing out that preschool children think differently from older children. The very fact that they can perform certain tasks *only* when the tasks are made very simple or undistracting is evidence for such a difference.

More broadly, preschoolers do not seem to experience the world or think about it with as general a set of rules or principles as we see in older children, and thus they do not easily generalize something they have learned in one context to a similar but not identical situation. It is precisely such a switch to general rules that Piaget thought characterized the thinking of the school-age child.

Finally, all the newer research has helped to confirm a basic proposition of Vygotsky's theory: Children's cognitive development is fostered to a considerable degree by *social* interactions. Piaget saw the child's development as being dependent mostly on independent play with objects. Such play is surely important, but play with other children and interactions with various adults are probably even more so, for it is here that the child learns about others' feelings and reactions—experiences that are necessary for the

At age 2, young Christian is still at an age when he needs his father's help to handle his sadness or frustration. In the next few years, though, he will develop new abilities to handle his own feelings, including learning the rules about when he can, and when he should not, express certain feelings.

child's emerging theory of mind. For example, Charlie Lewis and his colleagues (1996) have shown that among preschool children in Crete and Cyprus, those with many adult kin and many older siblings are more likely to understand false belief than are those with smaller family circles. Similarly, Ted Ruffman and his colleagues (1998) have found that both English and Japanese preschool-age children who have older siblings (but not those with only younger sibs) show more advanced understanding of false belief. Thus, social encounters both support and foster a child's cognitive development.

The School-Age Child

Piaget's View of Concrete Operations

The new skills we see at age 6 or 7 build on all the small changes we have already seen in the preschooler, but from Piaget's perspective, a great leap forward occurs when the child discovers or develops a set of immensely powerful, abstract, general "rules" or "strategies" for examining and interacting with the world. Piaget called these new skills *concrete operations*. By an operation, Piaget meant any of a set of powerful, abstract, internal schemes such as reversibility, addition, subtraction, multiplication, division, and serial ordering. All these operations are critical building blocks of logical thinking, providing internal rules about objects and their relationships. The child now understands the *rule* that adding something makes it more and subtracting makes it less; she understands that objects can belong to more than one category at once and that categories have logical relationships.

Piaget thought that of all the operations, the most critical was **reversibility**—the understanding that both physical actions and mental operations can be reversed. The clay sausage in a conservation experiment (described in the Research Report on p. 165) can be made back into a ball; the water can be poured back into the shorter, fatter glass. This understanding of the basic reversibility of actions lies behind many of the gains made during this period. For example, if you understand reversibility, then knowing that *A* is larger than *B* also tells you that *B* is smaller than *A*. The ability to understand hierarchies of classes, such as "Fido," "spaniel," "dog," and "animal," also rests on this ability to go backward as well as forward in thinking about relationships.

Piaget also proposed that during this third stage the child develops the ability to use **inductive logic:** He can go from his own experience to a general principle. For example, he can move from the observation that when you add another toy to a set and then count the set, it has one more toy than it did before, to a general principle that adding always makes it more.

Elementary school children are pretty good observational scientists and will enjoy cataloging, counting species of trees or birds, or figuring out the nesting habits of

Because elementary school students are good at observational science and inductive reasoning, field trips like this fossil-hunting expedition are a particularly effective way of teaching.

guinea pigs. What they are not yet good at is **deductive logic,** which requires starting with a general principle and then predicting some outcome or observation, like going from a theory to a hypothesis. For example, suppose I asked you to think of all the ways human relationships and societies would be different if women were physically as strong as men. Answering this question requires deductive, not inductive, logic; the problem is hard because you must imagine things that you have not experienced. The concrete operations child is good at dealing with things he knows or can see and manipulate—that is, he is good with *concrete* things; he does not do well with mentally manipulating ideas or possibilities. Piaget thought that deductive reasoning did not develop until the period of formal operations in junior high or high school.

Piaget did not say, by the way, that all these concrete operations skills popped out all at the same moment, as if a light bulb had gone on in the child's head. He understood that it took the child some years to apply these new cognitive skills to all kinds of problems. At the same time, he argued that the shift to concrete operations involved a profound change in the way the child thinks, the strategies she uses, and the depth of understanding she can achieve.

Critical Thinking

Try thinking about this question and watch yourself as you are thinking about it. Can you see how your deductive logic works? Can you think of everyday situations in which you use inductive or deductive logic?

Direct Tests of Piaget's Ideas

Researchers who have followed up on Piaget's descriptions of the concrete operations period have generally found that Piaget was right about the ages at which children first show various skills or understandings. Studies of conservation, for example, consistently show that children grasp conservation of mass or substance by about age 7. That is, they understand that the amount of clay is the same whether it is in a pancake or a ball or some other shape. They generally understand conservation of weight (that the two balls of clay weigh the same amount no matter their shape) at about age 8, but they understand conservation of volume (that an amount of water or clay takes up the same amount of *space* no matter its shape) only at about age 11.

Studies of classification skills similarly confirm Piaget's observations, showing that at about age 7 or 8 the child first grasps the principle of **class inclusion,** that subordinate classes are *included* in larger, superordinate classes. Bananas are included in the class "fruit," fruits are included in the class "food," and so forth. Preschool children understand that bananas are *also* fruit, but they do not yet fully understand the relationship between the classes—that the class "fruit" is superordinate, including all bananas as well as all other subtypes, such as oranges or apples.

A good illustration of these several cognitive changes comes from an early longitudinal study of concrete operations tasks by Carol Tomlinson-Keasey and her colleagues (1979). They followed a group of 38 children from kindergarten through third grade, testing them with five traditional concrete operations tasks each year: conservation of mass, weight, and volume; class inclusion; and hierarchical classification. You can see from Figure 6.4 (p. 182) that the children got better at all five tasks over the three-year period, with a spurt between the end of kindergarten and the beginning of first grade (about the age Piaget thought that concrete operations really began) and another spurt during second grade.

New Themes: Memory and Strategy Development

Some researchers, rather than simply repeating Piaget's tasks, have tried to devise other ways to test the proposition that school-age children, compared with younger children, approach tasks in ways that are more general, based on broader principles. In particular, the notion that older children intentionally use *strategies* for solving problems or for remembering things has been the basis for a whole new look at cognitive development. Work on memory and memory strategies is a particularly good example (Schneider & Bjorklund, 1998).

Critical Thinking

How would you go about remembering this list of things to do? Would you write down the list? Would you rehearse the list in your mind? What other strategies might you use?

Rehearsal Strategies. Suppose you need to run the following set of errands: Stop at the cleaners; buy some stamps; copy your IRS forms; and buy milk, bread, orange juice, carrots, lettuce, spaghetti, and spaghetti sauce at the grocery store. To remember such a list, you might use any one of several possible strategies, some of which I have listed (with examples) in Table 6.3. In this particular case, one option would be to rehearse the list over and over in your mind.

Do children do this when they try to remember? One classic early study (Keeney et al., 1967) indicated that school-age children did but younger children did not. Keeney showed children a row of seven cards with pictures on them and told the children to try to remember all the pictures in the same order they were laid out. A "space helmet" placed over the child's head then kept the child from seeing the cards but allowed the experimenter to see if the child seemed to be rehearsing the list by muttering under his breath. Children under 5 almost never showed any rehearsal, but 8- to 10-year-old children usually did. Interestingly, when 5-year-olds were *taught* to rehearse, they were able to do so and their memory scores improved. Yet when these same 5-year-olds were then given a new problem without being reminded to rehearse, they stopped rehearsing. That is, they could use the strategy if they were reminded, but they did not produce it spontaneously—a pattern described as a **production deficiency.**

More recent work suggests that preschool-age children show some kinds of strategies in their remembering if the task is quite simple, such as the game of hide-and-seek Judy DeLoache (1989) has used in her studies. In one of DeLoache's studies, the child watches the experimenter hide an attractive toy in some obvious place (e.g., behind a

Figure 6.4

In this longitudinal study, children were tested with the same set of concrete operations tasks five different times, beginning in kindergarten and ending in the third grade.

(*Source:* Tomlinson-Keasey et al., 1979, adapted from Table 2, p. 1158.)

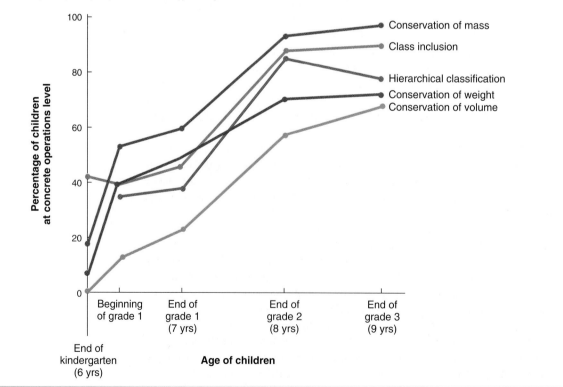

Table 6.3

Some Common Strategies Involved in Remembering

- **Rehearsal.** Perhaps the most common strategy, which involves either mental or vocal repetition or repetition of movement (as in learning to dance). May occur in children as young as 2 years under some conditions.

- **Clustering.** Grouping ideas or objects or words into clusters to help in remembering them, such as "all animals," or "all the ingredients in the lasagna recipe," or "the chess pieces involved in the move called castling." This is one strategy that clearly benefits from experience with a particular subject or activity, since possible categories are learned or are discovered in the process of exploring or manipulating a set of material. Primitive clustering occurs in 2-year-olds.

- **Elaboration.** Finding shared meaning or a common referent for two or more things that need to be remembered. The helpful mnemonic for recalling the names of the lines on the musical staff ("Every Good Boy Does Fine") is a kind of elaboration, as is associating the name of a person you have just met with some object or other word. This form of memory aid is not used spontaneously by all individuals and is not used skillfully until fairly late in development, if then.

- **Systematic searching.** When you try to remember something, you can "scan" the memory for the whole domain in which it might be found. Children aged 3 and 4 can begin to do this to search for actual objects in the real world but are not good at doing this in memory. So search strategies may be first learned in the external world and then applied to inner searches.

Source: Flavell, 1985.

couch) and is then told that when a buzzer goes off she can go and find the toy. While playing with other toys during the four-minute delay interval, 2-year-olds often talked about, pointed to, or looked at the toy's hiding place—all of which seem clearly to be early forms of mnemonic strategies.

These results and others like them tell us that no magic shift from nonstrategic to strategic behavior occurs at age 5 or 6 or 7. Children as young as 2 use primitive strategies, but school-age children seem to have larger repertoires of strategies and to use them more flexibly and efficiently, a quality of thinking that becomes increasingly evident in older schoolchildren (Bjorklund & Coyle, 1995). For example, when learning a list of words, 8-year-olds are likely to practice the words one at a time ("cat, cat, cat") while still older children practice them in groups ("desk, lawn, sky, shirt, cat"). The 8-year-olds, tested again a year later, show signs of a shift toward the more efficient strategy (Guttentag et al., 1987).

Other Memory Strategies. Other strategies that help improve memory involve putting the items to be learned or remembered into some meaningful organization. For example, in trying to remember the list of items you need to buy at the grocery store, you could aid your memory by thinking of the items as ingredients in a recipe (e.g., "what I need to make spaghetti and meatballs"). Another common strategy is to mentally group the items into categories such as "fruits and vegetables" and "canned goods," a strategy called *clustering* or *chunking*.

Studies of clustering often involve having children or adults learn lists of words that have potential categories built into them. For example, I might ask you to remember this list of words: *chair, spaghetti, lettuce, cat, desk, chocolate, duck, lion, table.* I give you two minutes to try to memorize the list, using whatever method(s) you wish, making sure you understand that you don't have to remember them in the order I listed them, but in any order you like. I'm interested only in how many you can recall. Then I ask you to list the words for me. If you have used some kind of clustering technique, you are likely to list the same-category words together (*cat, duck,* and *lion; chair, desk, table;* and *spaghetti, chocolate, lettuce*).

Research Report

Memory and the Child as Witness

In England, a 7-year-old was able to provide the police with details of her experience after a sexual assault and was later able to identify her attacker in a lineup (Davies, 1993). In several famous cases in the United States, children as young as 3 have testified in court about physical or sexual abuse by nursery school teachers, testimony that has sometimes led to convictions—convictions often overturned later on the grounds that the children's testimony had been either coerced or suggested by interviewers.

The controversy surrounding children's testimony has centered on two main issues: (1) Can young children accurately remember faces or events and report on their experiences, even after a period of time has passed? (2) Are children more suggestible than adults about what they might have seen or experienced? (Will they report what they have been told to say, what may have been suggested to them, or what they actually saw or felt?) The answer to both questions seems to be "yes," which leaves us in a real dilemma regarding the overall accuracy of children's testimony (Ceci & Bruck, 1995; 1998). Let's look at some of the evidence that supports this mixed conclusion.

First, recall of specific events or of the faces of people seen at a previous time does improve with age, but even preschoolers can recall action-related events with considerable accuracy. When experimenters have staged various crises or happenings, preschoolers and school-age children can describe what happened and can pick out a photo of the "culprit" almost as well as adults can. They report less detail than adults do, but they rarely report something that didn't actually occur (Baker-Ward, 1995; Baker-Ward et al., 1993; Ceci & Bruck, 1993; Davies, 1993). In several real-life studies, Margaret Steward (1993; Steward & Steward, 1996) has asked preschool children to describe their experiences on a recent visit to a medical clinic—visits that had been videotaped. The children reported only a quarter of the actual occasions when they had been touched on some part of their body by a medical person, but 94 percent of the reports they did give were accurate. When the same children were interviewed again after 6 months, their reports were not always consistent, but the items they did report consistently were nearly always accurate. Even when they were under stress at the time of some event, such as being injured in an accident and treated at a hospital, young children remember the event quite accurately (Peterson & Bell, 1996).

At the same time, younger children, particularly preschoolers, *are* more suggestible than older children or adults (Ceci & Bruck, 1995). One common way to study this is to show a film or tell a story to children and adults. Then, while asking questions about what the subject saw, the investigator injects some misleading question into the set—a question that assumes something that didn't really happen (e.g., "He was carrying a pipe wrench when he came into the room, wasn't he?"). Some days or weeks later, the subjects are again asked to describe what happened in the film or story. In this way the researcher can check to see whether the inaccurate or misleading suggestion has been absorbed into the story. Young children are more affected than are older children or adults by such misleading suggestions (Leichtman & Ceci, 1995). Indeed, it is possible to mislead young children enough so that they will report inaccurately about specific physical events, such as having been kissed while being bathed or having been spanked (Bruck et al., 1995; Ceci & Bruck, 1993).

Most interviewers who deal with prospective child witnesses do not introduce deliberately false information, but research by Maggie Bruck and Stephen Ceci (1997) makes it clear that *interviewer bias* can and does affect a child's recall in both direct and subtle ways. This seems to be particularly true when the child is questioned repeatedly about some event that may or may not have occurred. Even when the event did *not* happen, many preschoolers and some school-age children will say that it did after they have been asked about it many times (Ceci & Bruck, 1998; Muir-Broaddus, 1997). Thus, when the interviewer believes that some misbehavior has occurred, such as sexual abuse, that belief may affect the way she or he conducts the interview and can influence the content of the child's recall, especially with preschool children (Ceci & Bruck, 1995). When misinformation comes from parents, children are even more likely to incorporate the parents' version into their own free recall (Ricci et al., 1995). Furthermore, these incorporated false reports persist over time; when children are reinterviewed later, many of the false reports are repeated. Adult witnesses are *also* susceptible to suggestions of various kinds, a point made in repeated clever studies by Elizabeth Loftus (e.g., 1992). So the difference here is one of degree and not of kind.

From the legal point of view, all this does not mean that children should not testify; it speaks only to the weight one might give their recollections. The research also points to the vital importance of extensive training for interviewers, so that they can use appropriate care in framing questions, beginning with the very first interview with the child (Bruck et al., 1998).

School-age children show this kind of internal organization when they recall things, while preschoolers generally do not. And among school-age children, older children use this strategy more efficiently, using a few large categories rather than many smaller ones (Bjorklund & Muir, 1988). Interestingly, recent research shows that children often spontaneously use such a strategy but derive no apparent memory benefit from it, a pattern called a **utilization deficiency** (Bjorklund et al., 1997; Schneider & Bjorklund, 1998)—in a sense the opposite pattern from what we see with a production deficiency, in which a child will use and benefit from a strategy if reminded to do so, but does not use it spontaneously. Utilization deficiencies are intriguing to theorists because they suggest that the child assumes, at some level, that using some kind of strategy is a good thing to do, but does not fully understand how to go about it. This form of deficiency is more common in children under age 6 or 7, but it occurs among older children and teenagers as well (Bjorklund et al., 1997).

Let me sum up for you: We can see some primitive signs of memory strategies under optimum conditions as early as age 2 or 3; and with increasing age, children use more and more powerful ways of helping themselves remember things. In the use of each strategy, children also appear to shift from a period in which they don't use it at all, to a period in which they will use it if reminded or taught, to one in which they use it spontaneously even when they don't always benefit from it, to a final stage in which they use strategies skillfully and generalize them to more and more situations. These are obviously changes in the *quality* of the child's strategies as well as the quantity.

Expertise

However—and this is a big however—all these apparent developmental changes may well turn out to be as much a function of expertise as they are of age. Piaget obviously thought that children apply broad forms of logic to all their experiences in any given stage. If that's true, then the amount of specific experience a child has had with some set of material shouldn't make a lot of difference. A child who understands hierarchical classification but who has never seen pictures of different types of dinosaurs still ought to be able to create classifications of dinosaurs about as well as a child who has played a lot with dinosaur models. A child who understands the principle of transitivity (that if *A* is greater than *B*, and *B* is greater than *C*, then *A* is greater than *C*) ought to be able to demonstrate this ability with sets of strange figures as well as she could with a set of toys familiar to her. But in fact that seems not to be the case.

We now have a great deal of research showing that specific knowledge makes a huge difference. Children and adults who know a lot about some subject or some set of materials (dinosaurs, baseball cards, mathematics, or whatever) not only categorize information in that topic area in more complex and hierarchical ways; they are also better at remembering new information on that topic and better at applying more advanced forms of logic to material in that area. Furthermore, such expertise seems to generalize very little to other tasks (Ericsson & Crutcher, 1990). A child who is a devout soccer fan will be better than a nonfan at recalling lists of soccer words or the content of a story about soccer, but the two children are likely to be equally good at remembering random lists of words (Schneider & Bjorklund, 1992; Schneider et al., 1995).

The research on expertise also tells us that even the typical age differences in strategy use or memory ability disappear when the younger group has more expertise than the older. For example, Michelene Chi, in her now classic early study (1978), showed that expert chess players can remember the placement of chess pieces on a board much more quickly and accurately than can novice chess players, *even when the expert chess players are children and the novices are adults*—a finding since replicated several times (e.g., Schneider et al., 1993). To paraphrase Flavell (1985), expertise makes any of

Critical Thinking

Think about your own areas of expertise and about the areas in which you have little knowledge. Can you see any differences in the *way* you think about these different areas, in the form of logic you use, or in the way you go about remembering?

us look very smart, very cognitively advanced; lack of expertise makes us look very dumb.

Since young children are novices at almost everything, while older children are more expert at many things, perhaps the apparent age difference in the use of cognitive strategies is just the effect of the accumulation of more specific knowledge and *not* the result of stagelike changes in fundamental cognitive structures.

Variability in Children's Thinking

Yet another strong argument against strict stagelike change comes from recent work of Robert Siegler (1996), who has shown that individual children may use a wide variety of types of reasoning or strategies—from very simple to quite sophisticated—on the same type of problem on different attempts on the same day. For example, if you give first or second graders simple addition problems (3 + 6, 9 + 4, etc.), they may solve each problem in any of a variety of ways. If they have committed a particular sum to memory, they may retrieve the answer directly from memory without calculation—the strategy most adults use with simple addition problems. On other problems, children may simply count, starting at 1, until they reach the sum. So 6 + 3 becomes "One, two, three, four, five, six, seven, eight, nine."

Alternatively, they may use what the researchers call a *min strategy,* a somewhat more sophisticated technique in which the child starts with the larger number and then adds the smaller one by counting. In this method, the 3 + 6 sum is arrived at by saying to yourself, "Six, seven, eight, nine." Finally, a child might use a still more sophisticated *decomposition strategy,* which involves dividing a problem into several simpler ones. So a child might add 9 + 4 by thinking, "10 + 4 = 14, 9 is one less than 10, 14 − 1 = 13, so 9 + 4 = 13" (Siegler, 1996, p. 94). (You may use this method for more complicated problems, such as multiplying 16 × 9. You might think, "9 × 10 = 90; 9 × 6 = 54; 54 + 90 = 144.") With increasing age, elementary school children use counting less and less while increasing their use of retrieval, the min strategy, and decomposition—a finding that is entirely consistent with the notion of a gradual increase in use of more complex strategies. What Siegler has added to this information is the finding that the same child may use *all* these different strategies on different addition problems on the same day. So it isn't that each child systematically shifts from one level of strategy to another, but rather that at any given time the child may have a whole variety of strategies and use all of them on different problems. Over time, the child's repertoire of likely strategies does indeed shift toward more and more complex or sophisticated ones, just as Piaget and others have described. But the process is not step-like; instead, it is more like a series of

These school-age chess players, unless they are rank novices, would remember a series of chess moves or the arrangement of pieces on a chessboard far better than I could, since they have expertise and I do not.

Figure 6.5

Siegler's "overlapping wave" model of cognitive development is probably a better description of the way children move toward more complex forms of thinking than is the step-like stage model Piaget originally proposed.

(*Source:* Siegler, 1996, Figure 4.4, p. 89.) From *Emerging minds: the process of change in children's thinking* by Robert S. Siegler. Copyright © 1996 by Oxford University Press, Inc. Used by permission of Oxford University Press, Inc.)

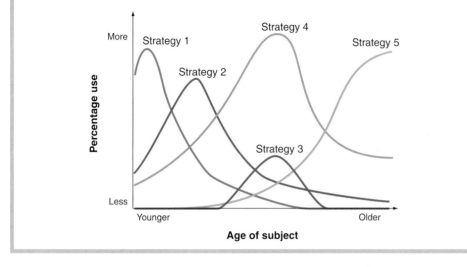

waves, as in Figure 6.5. When children add a new strategy, they do not immediately give up old ones; instead, they continue to use the old and new for some while. Gradually, as the new strategies become more firmly established and better rehearsed, the less efficient or less effective strategies drop out.

Siegler's model fits nicely with what we now know about expertise. When a child has had a lot of experience with some particular problem or subject, he is far more likely to use the most sophisticated strategies in his repertoire when working on that particular kind of problem; when he is dealing with a subject he knows little about, or a type of problem with which he has little experience, he is much more likely to use the most primitive or simplistic strategies in his repertoire.

If we pull together all we know about cognitive development in this period, we thus find both support and nonconfirmation of Piaget's broad ideas. On the one hand, Piaget's core concept of **constructivism**—that children are active thinkers, constantly trying to construct new strategies and advanced understandings—is strongly supported. Siegler points out that children will continue to construct new strategies for solving some given kind of problem, such as addition problems, "even when they already know perfectly adequate ones for solving them" (Siegler & Ellis, 1996, p. 211). Piaget also seems to have been on the mark in arguing for genuine qualitative change in the form of the child's thinking. The 8-year-old, in contrast to a 4-year-old, approaches new tasks differently. He is more likely to attempt a complex strategy; if that strategy fails, he is more likely to try another one.

Yet it looks very much as if these new cognitive skills do not arise from any broad reorganization of schemes at about age 6 or 7, as Piaget proposed. Instead, the developmental process appears to be both gradual and heavily affected by the amount of experience the child has in a particular domain.

Cognitive Development in Adolescence

Many of the same paradoxes emerge in the research on adolescent thinking, an age when Piaget thought the most complex forms of thinking, formal operations, emerged.

Piaget's View of Formal Operations

Formal operations, which Piaget believed emerged fairly rapidly between about ages 12 and 16, has a number of key elements.

From the Actual to the Possible.   One of the first steps in the process is for the child to extend her concrete operational reasoning abilities to objects and situations that she has not seen or experienced firsthand or that she cannot see or manipulate directly. Instead of thinking only about real things and actual occurrences, as the younger child can do, the teenager must start to think about possible occurrences. The preschool child plays "dress up" by putting on real clothes. The teenager *thinks* about options and possibilities, imagining herself in different roles, going to college or not going to college, marrying or not marrying, having children or not. She can imagine future consequences of actions she might take now, so that some kind of long-term planning becomes possible.

Systematic Problem Solving.   Another important feature of formal operations is the ability to search systematically and methodically for the answer to a problem. To study this, Piaget and his colleague Barbel Inhelder (Inhelder & Piaget, 1958) presented adolescents with complex tasks, mostly drawn from the physical sciences. In one of these tasks, subjects were given varying lengths of string and a set of objects of various weight that could be tied to the strings to make a swinging pendulum. They were shown how to start the pendulum by pushing the weight with differing amounts of force and by holding the weight at different heights. The subject's task was to figure out which one or combination of length of string, weight of object, force of push, or height of push determines the "period" of the pendulum, that is, the amount of time for one swing. (In case you have forgotten your high school physics, the answer is that only the length of the string affects the period of the pendulum.)

If you give this task to a concrete operational child, she will usually try out many different combinations of length, weight, force, and height in an inefficient way. She might try a heavy weight on a long string and then a light weight on a short string. Because she has changed both string length and weight in these two trials, there is no way she can draw a clear conclusion about either factor.

In contrast, an adolescent using formal operations is likely to be more organized, attempting to vary just one of the four factors at a time. She may try a heavy object with a short string, then with a medium string, then with a long one. After that, she might try a light object with the three lengths of string. Of course not all adolescents (or all adults, for that matter) are quite this methodical in their approach. Still, there is a very dramatic difference in the overall strategy used by 10-year-olds versus 15-year-olds that marks the shift from concrete to formal operations.

Logic.   Another facet of this shift is the appearance of what Piaget called **hypothetico-deductive reasoning** in the child's repertoire of skills. Piaget suggested that the concrete operational child can use inductive reasoning, which involves arriving at a conclusion or a rule based on a lot of individual experiences. The more difficult kind of reasoning, using *deductive logic,* involves considering hypotheses or hypothetical premises and then deriving logical outcomes. For example, the statement "If all people are equal, then you and I must be equal" involves logic of this type. Although children as young as 4 or 5 can understand some deductive relationships if the premises given are factually true, only at adolescence are young people able to understand and use the basic *logical* relationships (e.g., Ward & Overton, 1990).

A great deal of the logic of science is of this hypothetico-deductive type. We begin with a theory and propose, "If this theory is correct, then I should observe such and such." In doing this, we are going well beyond our observations. We are conceiving things we have never seen that *ought* to be true or observable. We can think of this change as part of a general decentering process that began much earlier in cognitive development. The preoperational child gradually moves away from his egocentrism and comes to be able to take the physical or emotional perspective of others. During

Critical Thinking

Suppose you find yourself having one cold after another or one sinus infection after another. Could the cause be an allergy? Could it be some more basic health problem? How might you go about finding out? Would you need to use some kind of systematic problem solving to find the answer?

One aspect of formal operations is the use of deductive logic, which is normally required first in high school, especially in math and science classes, like this chemistry class.

formal operations, the child takes another step by freeing himself even from his re-liance on specific experiences.

Post-Piagetian Work on Adolescent Thought

A good deal of post-Piagetian research confirms Piaget's basic observation. Edith Neimark summarizes the accumulated information succinctly:

> An enormous amount of evidence from an assortment of tasks shows that adoles-cents and adults are capable of feats of reasoning not attained under normal cir-cumstances by [younger] children, and that these abilities develop fairly rapidly during the ages of about 11 to 15. (1982, p. 493)

Adolescents, much more than school-age children, operate with possibilities in addi-tion to reality, and they are more likely to use deductive logic. As Flavell puts it, the think-ing of the school-age child "hugs the ground of . . . empirical reality" (1985, p. 98), while the teenager is more likely to soar into the realm of speculation and possibility. An 8-year-old thinks that "knowing" something is a simple matter of finding out the facts; a teenager is more likely to see knowledge as relative, as less certain (Bartsch, 1993). Deanna Kuhn and her colleagues (1995) have also found that teenagers and young adults, faced with disconfirming evidence, are more likely than are younger children to change their theory or their initial guesses; they are also more systematic in seeking out new information that will help hone their hypotheses—both hallmarks of formal operations reasoning.

Some research illustrations would probably make the change clearer. In an early cross-sectional study, Susan Martorano (1977) tested 20 girls at each of four grades (sixth, eighth, tenth, and twelfth) on 10 different tasks that require one or more of what Piaget called formal operations skills. Indeed, many of the tasks she used were those Pi-aget himself had devised. Results from two of these tasks are shown in Figure 6.6. The pendulum problem is the same one I described earlier; the "balance" problem requires a youngster to predict whether or not two varying weights, hung at varying distances on either side of a scale, will balance. To solve this problem using formal operations, the teenager must consider both weight and distance simultaneously. You can see in the figure that older students generally did better, with the biggest improvement in scores between eighth and tenth grades (between ages 13 and 15).

Figure 6.6

These are the results from 2 of the 10 different formal operations tasks used in Martorano's cross-sectional study.

(*Source:* Martorano, 1977, p. 670. Copyright by the American Psycholog-ical Association.)

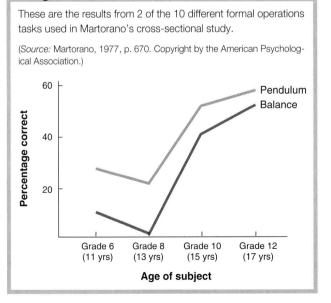

In a more practical vein, Catherine Lewis (1981) has shown that these new cognitive abilities alter the ways teenagers go about making decisions. Older teenagers are more focused on the future, on possibilities, and on options when they consider decisions. Lewis asked eighth-, tenth-, and twelfth-grade students to respond to a set of dilemmas, each of which involved a person facing a difficult decision, such as whether or not to have an operation to remove a facial disfigurement or how to decide which doctor to trust when different doctors give differing advice. Forty-two percent of the twelfth graders, but only eleven percent of the eighth graders, mentioned future possibilities in their answers to these dilemmas.

In answer to the cosmetic surgery dilemma, for example, a twelfth grader said:

> Well, you have to look into the different things . . . that might be more important later on in your life. You should think about, will it have any effect on your future and with, maybe, the people you meet. . . . (p. 541)

An eighth grader, in response to the same dilemma, said:

> The different things I would think about in getting the operation is like if the girls turn you down on a date, or the money, or the kids teasing you at school. . . .
> (p. 542)

The eighth grader, as is characteristic of the preadolescent or early adolescent, is focused on the here and now, on concrete things. The teenager is considering things that *might* happen in the future.

Note, though, that even among the twelfth graders in Lewis's study, nearly three-fifths did not show this type of future orientation. And take another look at Figure 6.6 (p. 189); only about 50 to 60 percent of twelfth graders solved the two formal operations problems. In fact, only 2 of the 20 twelfth graders in Martorano's study used formal operations logic on all 10 problems.

These findings reflect a common pattern in research on adolescent thinking: By no means do all teenagers (or adults) use these more abstract forms of logic and thought. Keating (1980) estimates that only about 50 to 60 percent of 18- to 20-year-olds in industrialized countries use formal operations at all, let alone consistently. In nonindustrialized countries the rates are even lower.

Why Doesn't Every Teenager Use Formal Logic?

There are several possible explanations for such low levels of formal operations thought. One is that expertise is once again the crucial element. That is, most of us have some formal operational ability, but we can only apply it to topics or tasks with which we are highly familiar. For example, I use formal operations reasoning about psychology because it is an area I know well, but I am a lot less skillful at applying the same kind of reasoning to fixing my car—about which I know next to nothing. Willis Overton and his colleagues (1987) have found considerable support for this possibility in their research. They have found that as many as 90 percent of adolescents can solve quite complex logic problems if the problems are stated using familiar content, while only half can solve identical logic problems when they are stated in abstract language.

Another possibility is that most of our everyday experiences and tasks do not require formal operations. Inductive reasoning or other simpler forms of logic are quite sufficient most of the time. So we get into a cognitive rut, applying our most usual mode of thinking to new problems as well. We can kick our thinking up a notch under some circumstances, especially if someone reminds us that it would be useful to do so, but we simply don't rehearse formal operations very much.

Critical Thinking

What was the last major decision you had to make? Think for a minute about how you went about it. What factors did you consider? Did you think about future consequences or only about the here and now?

The fact that formal operations thinking is found more often among young people or adults in Western or other industrialized cultures can be interpreted in the same way. Such cultures include high levels of technology and complex life-styles. They may therefore demand more formal operational thought. By this argument, all nonretarded teenagers and adults are thought to have the *capacity* for formal logic, but only those of us whose lives demand its development will actually acquire it.

Notice that all these explanations undermine the very notion of a universal "stage" of thinking in adolescence. Yes, more abstract forms of thinking may develop in adolescence, but they are neither universal nor broadly used by individual teenagers or adults. Whether one develops or uses these forms of logic depends heavily on experience, expertise, and environmental demand.

Preliminary Conclusions and Questions

I have been raising a variety of questions as I have gone along, so you already know that many puzzles about cognitive development remain to be solved. To set the stage for a discussion of information processing, let me pause for a quick review.

The child comes a long way in only about fifteen years. As Robert Siegler puts it:

> Among the most remarkable characteristics of human beings is how much our thinking changes with age. When we compare the thinking of an infant, a toddler, an elementary school student, and an adolescent, the magnitude of the change is immediately apparent. (1994, p. 1)

In broad outline, Piaget's observations about this sequence have been frequently confirmed. Children do clearly change not only in what they know but in the way they approach problems. Yet it now seems quite unlikely that this developmental progression involves coherent, general stages of the kind Piaget envisioned. Children's performance is much more variable than that. The same child may use quite sophisticated strategies for one kind of problem and very primitive strategies for another (Siegler, 1996). The expert child chess player, who can demonstrate quite extraordinary feats of memory and conceptual sophistication while playing chess, has no better memory for strings of numbers than does another child of the same age. In the current language used by cognitive theorists, children's thinking is quite *domain-specific* (Hirschfeld & Gelman, 1994).

Nor do new cognitive skills emerge full-blown. Rather, they are preceded by more rudimentary or partial versions of the same skills at earlier ages. For example, virtually all the achievements of the concrete operations period are present in at least rudimentary or fragmentary form in the preschool years. This observation undermines the basic notion of a stage as Piaget proposed it.

Yet even if we are now able to reject Piaget's highly "domain-general" theory, we are still left with a wide range of possibilities. Development might be *totally* situation-(domain-) specific, or it might have at least some generality, with some basic skills or understandings changing with age and being applied across several different domains or tasks. We see some sign of just such a semigeneral, almost stagelike shift in children's theory of mind at about age 4. Indeed, the very use of the word *theory* in this label implies that the child has some kind of coherent model that gets applied to a variety of situations (Gopnik & Wellman, 1994). On the other side of the coin, the research on expertise makes thinking look highly domain-specific.

A second major puzzle is just how to explain the broad sweep of changes that we do observe. Are these really qualitative changes involving the emergence of genuinely new skills? If so, then what is pushing those changes? Alternatively, perhaps children simply become more and more efficient at using the same basic set of cognitive processes.

The information processing approach to the study of intellectual development offers new ways to think about and study both of these disputes.

Information Processing in Children

The information processing approach is not really a theory of cognitive development; it is an approach to studying thinking and remembering—a set of questions and some methods of analysis. The basic metaphor underlying this approach has been that of the human mind as computer. We can think of the "hardware" of cognition as the physiology of the brain itself and the "software" of cognition as the set of strategies or "programs" that use the basic hardware. To understand thinking in general, we need to understand the processing capacity of the hardware and just what programs have to be "run" to perform any given task. What inputs (facts or data) are needed? What coding, decoding, remembering, or analyzing are required? To understand cognitive *development,* we need to discover whether the basic processing capacity of the system, or the programs, changes in any systematic way with age. Do children develop new types of processing (new programs)? Or do they simply learn to use basic programs on new material?

Changes in Processing Capacity

One obvious place to look for an explanation of developmental changes in cognitive skills is in the hardware itself. Any computer has physical limits on the number of different operations it can perform at one time or in a given space of time. As the brain and nervous system develop in the early years of life, with synapses formed and then pruned to remove redundancies, perhaps the capacity of the system increases.

This has turned out to be a very difficult hypothesis to test. The most commonly cited evidence in support of an increase in processing capacity is the finding that over the years of childhood, children are able to remember longer and longer lists of numbers, letters, or words, a pattern clear in the data shown in Figure 6.7. The difficulty with these results, however, is that they could also be simply another reflection of age differences in expertise, because older children naturally will have more experience with numbers, letters, or words. Thus, the memory-span data don't give us a clear-cut answer to the question of whether basic processing capacity increases with age. Most developmental psychologists today would agree that, while it is plausible to assume that capacity increases, we haven't yet found an appropriate way to demonstrate it.

Increases in Processing Efficiency

In contrast, we have persuasive evidence that processing *efficiency* increases steadily with age. Indeed, most developmentalists now see such a change in efficiency as the basis on which cognitive development occurs (Case, 1985; Halford et al., 1994; Kuhn, 1992).

The best evidence on this point is that cognitive processing gets steadily faster with age. Robert Kail (1991; Kail & Hall, 1994) has found an exponential increase with age in processing speed on a wide variety of tasks, including such perceptual-motor tasks as tapping, simple response time to a stimulus (like pressing a button when you hear a buzzer), and cognitive tasks such as mental addition. He has found virtually identical patterns of speed increases in studies in Korea and the United States, adding a useful bit of cross-cultural validity to the argument.

The most plausible explanation for this common pattern is that over time, the physical system changes in some fundamental way that allows greater and greater speed of both response and mental processing. The most likely candidates for such a basic

Figure 6.7

Psychologists have tried to measure basic memory capacity by asking subjects to listen to a list of numbers, letters, or words and then repeat back the list in order. This figure shows the number of such items that children of various ages are able to remember and report accurately.

(*Source:* Dempster, 1981, from Figures 1–3, pp. 66–68.)

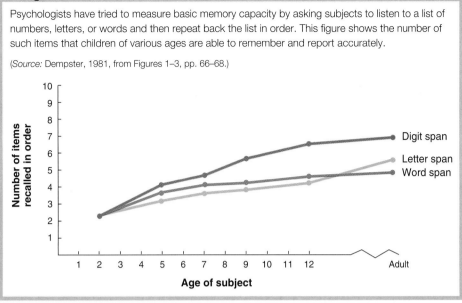

change are the "pruning" of synapses and the myelination of the nerves, both of which I talked about in Chapter 4 (Hale et al., 1993). For example, if pruning begins at about 12 to 18 months and then continues steadily throughout childhood, one effect is to make the "wiring diagram" steadily more efficient and thus faster.

Greater efficiency in processing is also gained because the child acquires new strategies for solving problems or recalling information. Of course the new strategies themselves may appear because of increased underlying capacity or efficiency. Or new strategies may arise because of the child's experimentation and experience with a particular kind of problem or material, as I've already discussed. Once present, however, these more powerful strategies make the whole system more efficient, much as we see in the behavior of experts at some task, who can perform that type of task with remarkable speed and directness.

One form of new strategy or new "software" is the child's increasing awareness of her own mental processes. If I asked you how you had tried to recall the list of nine words (*chair, spaghetti, lettuce . . .*) I listed earlier, I am sure you could describe your mental processes. You may even have consciously considered the various alternative strategies and then selected the best one. You could also tell me other things about the way your mind works, such as good ways to study particular subjects, or which kinds of tasks will be hardest, and why. These are all examples of *metamemory* or *metacognition*—knowing about remembering, or knowing about knowing. Such skills are a part of a larger category that information processing theorists refer to as **executive processes:** planning what to do and considering alternative strategies.

These skills are of particular interest because there is some suggestion that it may be precisely such metacognitive or executive skills that emerge (gradually) with age. Performance on a whole range of tasks will be better if the child can monitor her own performance or can recognize when a particular strategy is called for and when it is not. I pointed out earlier that 4- and 5-year-old children do show some such monitoring, but it is rarely found earlier than that, and it clearly improves fairly rapidly beginning at school age. Schoolchildren begin to understand what they will need to do in order to learn something; they are aware of what they know and do not know. Among other things, some metacognitive ability is critical for learning skillful reading. A child learning to read needs to recognize which words he knows and which he does not, or

Critical Thinking

Write down three good ways to study. In choosing one of these methods, does it matter what subject you are studying? How do you know all this? Do you think about it consciously when you are starting to study?

which sentences he understands and which he does not, and needs to have some idea of how to get the information he needs. He needs to be able to recognize the difference between easy sentences and hard ones so that he can concentrate more and put more effort into the harder ones. A variety of research tells us that younger and poorer readers are less good at all these metacognitive tasks, while better or older readers can do them more readily and skillfully (Flavell et al., 1993).

A Summary of Developmental Changes in Information Processing

If I add up these pieces of evidence about information processing capacity and skills, I arrive at a set of tentative generalizations:

1. There may or may not be any increase in the basic processing capacity of the system (the hardware), but there clearly is an increase in the efficiency with which the hardware is used, resulting in steadily greater processing speed.

2. The sheer amount of specific knowledge the child has about any given task increases as the child experiments, explores, and studies things. This leads to more and more "expert" approaches to remembering and solving problems, which in turn improve the efficiency of the processing system.

3. Genuinely new strategies are acquired, probably in some kind of order. In particular, a school-age child seems to develop some "executive" or "metacognitive" abilities—she knows that she knows, and she can *plan* a strategy for the first time.

4. Existing strategies are applied to more and more different domains, and more and more flexibly. If a child learns to rehearse on one kind of memory problem, an older child is more likely to try it on a new memory task; a younger child (particularly younger than 5 or 6) is not likely to generalize the strategy to the new task.

5. With increasing age, a wider range of different strategies can be applied to the same problem, so that if the first doesn't work, a backup or alternative strategy can be used. If you can't find your misplaced keys by retracing your steps, you try a backup, such as looking in your other purse or your jacket pocket, or searching each room of the house in turn. Young children do not do this; school-age children and adolescents do.

Thus, some of the changes that Piaget observed and chronicled with such detail and richness seem to be the result simply of increased experience with tasks and problems and increased speed and efficiency of processing (all quantitative changes, if you will). At the same time, there also seems to be a real qualitative change in the complexity, generalizability, and flexibility of strategies used by the child.

Having lost one of his shoes, this school-age boy first searches in the most obvious places. If that strategy doesn't work, he is likely to have a number of fallback options, unlike a preschooler, who tends to get stuck in his first strategy.

Summary

1. Studies of cognitive development have been guided by three different theoretical perspectives: the study of individual differences in intellectual "power," such as what we measure on an IQ test; the study of changes with age in the way children go about solving problems, typified by Piaget's approach; and the newest approach, the study of information processing.

2. Piaget assumed that the child was an active agent in his own development, constructing his own understandings and adapting to the environment by changing his basic schemes.

3. Schemes and their interrelationships are changed through the processes of assimilation, accommodation, and equilibration, beginning with primitive schemes at birth and progressing sequentially through several stages.

4. Piaget's first stage is the sensorimotor period, birth to 18 months; the infant begins with a small repertoire of basic schemes, from which she moves toward symbolic representation in a series of six substages.

5. Substage 1 is essentially "automatic pilot"; substage 2 includes coordination of different modalities; in substage 3, the baby focuses more on the outside world; in substage 4, causal connections are understood and the object concept is grasped in a preliminary way; in substage 5, the baby begins to experiment more fully; and in substage 6, we see the first signs of symbol usage.

6. Post-Piagetian studies of infant cognition show infants to be far more cognitively skilled than Piaget thought. They can imitate from the earliest weeks and remember events; both appear to involve some kind of internal representation.

7. In Piaget's preoperational period, from 18 months to 6 years, the child is able to use mental symbols to represent objects to himself internally. Despite this advance, the preschool child still lacks many sophisticated cognitive characteristics. In Piaget's view, such children are still egocentric, rigid in their thinking, and generally captured by appearances.

8. Research on the cognitive functioning of preschoolers makes it clear that they are much less egocentric than Piaget thought. By age 4, they can distinguish between appearance and reality in a variety of tasks, and they develop a surprisingly sophisticated theory of how minds work. They understand that other people's actions are based on thoughts and beliefs, not on "reality."

9. By age 4 or 5, children also understand some of the links between specific situations and other people's likely emotions.

10. In Piaget's third stage—concrete operations, from ages 6 to 12—the child acquires powerful new mental tools called operations, such as reversibility, addition, subtraction, multiplication, and serial ordering.

11. Recent research on this period confirms many of Piaget's descriptions of sequences of development but calls into question Piaget's basic concept of stages.

12. Studies of expertise also indicate that specific task experience is more important in the sophistication of the child's thinking than Piaget believed.

13. Siegler's work shows that cognitive development is less stepwise than Piaget proposed; children may use a variety of different strategies, varying in complexity, on the same kind of problem. Still, the strategy repertoire does become more complex with age.

14. Piaget's fourth stage, formal operations, is said to develop from age 12 onward, characterized by the ability to apply basic operations to ideas and possibilities as well as to actual objects and by the emergence of hypothetico-deductive logic and systematic problem solving.

15. Researchers have found clear evidence of such advanced forms of thinking in at least some adolescents. Yet formal operations thinking is not universal, nor is it consistently used even by those who possess the ability.

16. Collectively, these findings make Piaget's strong stage concept untenable, but there is still disagreement about whether the observed changes nonetheless occur in clusters or groups and whether the changes are qualitative or quantitative.

17. Information processing theorists have searched for the basic building blocks of cognition, both the "hardware" and the "software."

18. Most theorists conclude that there are no age-related changes in the capacity of the mental "hardware,"

but there are clearly improvements in speed and efficiency.

19. One form of increased efficiency is the greater and greater use of various types of processing strategies with age, including strategies for remembering. Preschoolers use some strategies, but school-age children use them more often and more flexibly. Indeed, the inability to use strategies flexibly is one of the hallmarks of mental retardation.

20. At school age, most children also develop some "executive skills," the ability to monitor their own cognitive processes and thus to plan their mental activity.

Key Terms

accommodation That part of the adaptation process proposed by Piaget by which a person modifies existing schemes as a result of new experiences or creates new schemes when old ones no longer handle the data. **p. 166**

assimilation That part of the adaptation process proposed by Piaget that involves the "taking in" of new experiences or information into existing schemes. Experience is not taken in "as is," however, but is modified (or interpreted) somewhat so as to fit the preexisting schemes. **p. 166**

class inclusion The relationship between classes of objects, such that a subordinate class is included in a superordinate class, as bananas are part of the class "fruit" and the class "fruit" is included in the class "food." **p. 181**

concrete operations stage The stage of development between ages 6 and 12, as proposed by Piaget, in which mental operations such as subtraction, reversibility, and multiple classification are acquired. **p. 167**

conservation The concept that objects remain the same in fundamental ways, such as weight or number, even when there are external changes in shape or arrangement. Typically understood by children after age 5. **p. 174**

constructivism A key concept in Piaget's theory, that from birth a child is actively engaged in a process of constructing an understanding both of his own actions and of the external world. **p. 187**

deductive logic Reasoning from the general to the particular, from a rule to an expected instance, or from a theory to a hypothesis. Characteristic of formal operations thinking. **p. 181**

egocentrism A cognitive state in which the individual (typically a child) sees the world only from his own perspective, without awareness that there are other perspectives. **p. 174**

equilibration The third part of the adaptation process, as proposed by Piaget, involving a periodic restructuring of schemes into new structures. **p. 166**

executive processes Proposed subset of information processes involving organizing and planning strategies. Similar in meaning to *metacognition*. **p. 193**

false belief Incorrectly believing something to be true, and acting on that belief. The child's understanding of the principle of false belief is one key sign of the emergence of a representational theory of mind. **p. 176**

formal operations stage Piaget's name for the fourth and final major stage of cognitive development, occurring during adolescence, when the child becomes able to manipulate and organize ideas as well as objects. **p. 167**

hypothetico-deductive reasoning Piaget's term for the form of reasoning that is part of formal operational thought, involving not just deductive logic but more broadly the ability to consider hypotheses and hypothetical possibilities. **p. 188**

inductive logic Reasoning from the particular to the general, from experience to broad rules. Characteristic of concrete operations thinking. **p. 180**

information processing approach Phrase used to refer to a new, third approach to the study of intellectual development that focuses on changes with age, and individual differences, in fundamental intellectual skills. **p. 164**

metacognition General and rather loosely used term describing an individual's knowledge of his own thinking processes: knowing what you know, and how you go about learning or remembering. **p. 177**

metamemory A subcategory of metacognition; knowledge about your own memory processes. **p. 177**

operation Term used by Piaget for complex, internal, abstract, reversible schemes, first seen at about age 6. **p. 167**

preoperational stage Piaget's term for the second major stage of cognitive development, from age 18 months to about age 6, marked at the beginning by the ability to use symbols and by the development of basic classification and logical abilities. **p. 167**

primary circular reactions Piaget's phrase to describe the baby's simple repetitive actions in the second substage of the sensorimotor stage, organized around the baby's own body; the baby repeats some action in order to have some desired outcome occur again, such as putting his thumb in his mouth to repeat the good feeling of sucking. **p. 168**

production deficiency Phrase used to describe a situation in which an individual can use some physical or mental strategy if reminded to do so, but fails to "produce" the strategy spontaneously. **p. 182**

reversibility One of the most critical of the "operations" Piaget identified as part of the concrete operations period. The child understands that actions can be reversed, thus returning to a previous state. **p. 180**

scheme Piaget's word for the basic actions of knowing, including both physical actions (sensorimotor schemes, such as looking or reaching) and mental actions (such as classifying or comparing or reversing). An experience is assimilated to a scheme, and the scheme is modified or created through accommodation. **p. 165**

secondary circular reactions Repetitive actions in the third substage of the sensorimotor period, oriented around external objects; the infant repeats some action in order to have some outside event recur, such as hitting a mobile repeatedly to watch it move. **p. 168**

sensorimotor stage Piaget's term for the first major stage of cognitive development, from birth to about 18 months, when the child moves from reflexive to voluntary action. **p. 167**

tertiary circular reactions The deliberate experimentation with variations of previous actions, characteristic of the fifth substage of sensorimotor intelligence, according to Piaget. **p. 168**

theory of mind A phrase used to describe one aspect of the thinking of 4- and 5-year-olds, when they show signs of understanding not only that other people think differently, but that other people will base their behavior on what they believe or know or feel rather than on the visible situation. **p. 176**

utilization deficiency Term used by researchers to describe the use of some specific strategy without deriving benefit from it. **p. 185**

Suggested Readings

Ceci, S. J., & Bruck, M. (1995). *Jeopardy in the courtroom: A scientific analysis of children's testimony*. Washington, DC: American Psychological Association. A highly readable, sobering discussion of children's testimony in child abuse cases, and the factors that can influence that testimony. An even more current (but more technical) discussion is in Ceci & Bruck (1998).

Flavell, J. H. (1992). Cognitive development: Past, present, and future. *Developmental Psychology, 28,* 998–1005. This brief paper by one of the leading thinkers and researchers in the field of cognitive development gives a quick tour of what Flavell thinks we now know, don't know, and are still arguing about.

Flavell, J. H., Miller, P. H., & Miller, S. A. (1993). *Cognitive development* (3rd ed.). Englewood Cliffs, NJ: Prentice Hall. This is an update of one of the best texts in the field, written by one of the major current figures in cognitive development theory (Flavell). The introductory chapter and the chapter on infancy may be especially helpful if you find Piaget's theory somewhat hard to grasp.

Goldstein, J. H. (Ed.). (1994). *Toys, play, and child development*. Cambridge, England: Cambridge University Press. A collection of current papers on the role of play in children's development. Included is an interesting chapter on war toys and their effect.

Kuhn, D. (1992). Cognitive development. In M. H. Bornstein & M. E. Lamb (Eds.), *Developmental psychology: An advanced textbook* (3rd ed., pp. 211–272). Hillsdale, NJ: Erlbaum. A first-rate discussion of the strengths and limitations of both Piagetian and information processing approaches.

Thomas, R. M. (1990). Basic concepts and applications of Piagetian cognitive development theory. In R. M. Thomas (Ed.), *The encyclopedia of human development and education: Theory, research, and studies* (pp. 53–55). Oxford: Pergamon Press. This is one of the best short descriptions of Piaget's theory I have found. If you need another run at the basic ideas, expressed in someone else's language, this is a good place to look.

7

Cognitive Development II: Individual Differences in Cognitive Abilities

Several years ago (as I mentioned earlier), my husband and I lived in Germany for eight months. Because he was born in Germany and has many relatives there who speak no English, it seemed like a good idea for me to learn enough German to be able to speak to his family. So I took intensive German classes and struggled to learn new vocabulary and complex grammar. The entire process turned out to be far harder than I had expected, but it certainly gave me a chance to observe the ways I go about learning, remembering, and using new information. I had, throughout, an almost physical sense of my brain at work, struggling to create order and sense out of a mass of new information.

In our everyday lives, each of us faces myriad tasks that call for the same kinds of skills I had to use in learning a new language. In Chapter 6 I talked about the *development* of such cognitive skills through the years of childhood and adolescence. Here I want to talk about the incontrovertible fact that children (and adults) do not all perform these various cognitive tasks equally well or equally quickly, or develop them at the same speed. Such individual differences in intellectual skill or power have traditionally been described in terms of variations in **intelligence,** as measured by any one of a variety of intelligence tests. An alternative approach, emerging in recent years, is to describe individual differences in intellectual ability in terms of information processing skill or speed. Let's begin with the more traditional approach, the measurement of intelligence with standardized tests.

Measuring Intellectual Power: IQ Tests and Other Measures

Intelligence tests have a certain mystique about them, and most of us have a greatly inflated notion of the permanence or importance of an IQ score. If you are going to acquire a more realistic view, it's important for you to know something about what such tests were designed to do and something about the beliefs and values of the men and women who devised them.

The First IQ Tests

The first modern intelligence test was published in 1905 by two Frenchmen, Alfred Binet and Theodore Simon (1905). From the beginning, the test had a practical purpose, namely, to identify children who might have difficulty in school. For this reason, the tests Binet and Simon devised were very much like some school tasks, including measures of vocabulary, comprehension of facts and relationships, and mathematical and verbal reasoning. For example, can the child describe the difference between wood and glass? Can the young child touch his nose, his ear, his head? Can he tell which of two weights is heavier?

Lewis Terman and his associates at Stanford University modified and extended many of Binet and Simon's original tests when they translated and revised the test for use in the United States (Terman, 1916; Terman & Merrill, 1937). The several Terman revisions, called the **Stanford-Binet,** consist of sets of six individual tests, one set for children of each consecutive age. A child taking the test is given the set of tests beginning for the age below his actual age, then the set for his age, then those for each successively older age until the child reaches a level at which he fails all six tests.

Terman initially described a child's performance in terms of a score called an **intelligence quotient,** later shortened to IQ. This score was computed by comparing the child's chronological age (in years and months) with his **mental age,** defined as the level of questions he could answer correctly. For example, a child who could solve the problems for a 6-year-old but not those for a 7-year-old would have a mental age of 6. The formula used to calculate the IQ score was as follows:

$$\frac{\text{Mental age}}{\text{Chronological age}} \times 100 = \text{IQ}$$

This formula results in an IQ score above 100 for children whose mental age is higher than their chronological age and an IQ score below 100 for children whose mental age is below their chronological age.

This old system for calculating an IQ score is not used any longer, even in the modern revisions of the Stanford-Binet. IQ score calculations are now based on a direct comparison of a child's performance with the average performance of a large group of other children his own age, with a score of 100 still typically defined as average.

The majority of children achieve scores that are right around the average of 100, with a smaller number scoring very high or very low. Figure 7.1 shows the distribution of IQ scores that we would see if we gave the test to thousands of children. You can see that two-thirds of all children will achieve scores between 85 and 115, while 96 percent will achieve scores between 70 and 130. The groups we refer to as *gifted* or *retarded*, both of which I'll discuss in some detail in Chapter 15, clearly represent only very small fractions of the distribution.

One advantage of this new method of calculating the IQ score is that it allows the test makers to restandardize the test periodically, so that the average remains at 100. Such readjustments are needed because IQ test scores have been rising steadily over the past fifty or sixty years. If we used the same standards today as were used in 1932, when tests like the Stanford-Binet were first devised, the average score would be 115 and not 100—an increase that has been found among children and adults all over the world (Flynn, 1994). That is, the average child today can solve problems that only an above-average child could solve forty or fifty years ago. These overall increases in measured IQ scores have been attributed to a variety of factors, including increased school attendance; increased complexity of children's toys and activities, including some kinds of TV and video games; less emphasis in schools on rote learning and more on analytic or reasoning skills; increased urbanization; smaller families; and improvements in health and nutrition (Williams, 1998). Whatever the causes, it is good to bear in mind that, contrary to some arguments you may see in the press, children are not getting dumber and dumber. On the contrary. As the culture has become more complex, children's (and adults') ability to respond to the complexity has also increased.

Figure 7.1

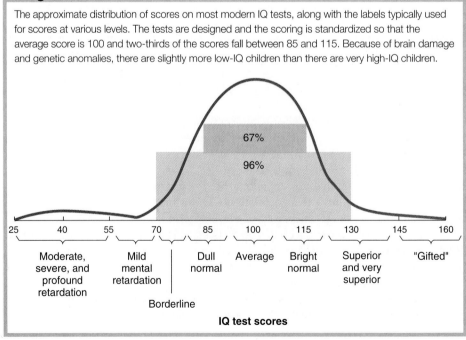

The approximate distribution of scores on most modern IQ tests, along with the labels typically used for scores at various levels. The tests are designed and the scoring is standardized so that the average score is 100 and two-thirds of the scores fall between 85 and 115. Because of brain damage and genetic anomalies, there are slightly more low-IQ children than there are very high-IQ children.

Modern IQ Tests

The two tests used most frequently by psychologists today are the Revised Stanford-Binet and the third revision of the Wechsler Intelligence Scales for Children, called the **WISC-III,** a test originally developed by David Wechsler (1974). (Several other well-known tests are listed in Table 7.1.) The WISC involves 10 different types of problems, each ranging from very easy to very hard. The child begins with the easiest problem of each type and continues with that type of item until he cannot go further, then goes on to the next problem type. Five of the tests, called *verbal tests,* rely strongly on verbal skills (e.g., vocabulary, describing similarities between objects, general information); the other five, collectively called *performance tests,* demand less verbal types of thinking, such as arranging pictures in an order that tells a story or copying a pattern using a set of colored blocks. Many psychologists find this distinction between verbal and performance tests helpful because significant unevenness in a child's test skill may indicate particular kinds of learning problems.

Infant Tests. Neither the Binet nor the WISC-III can be used with children much younger than about age 3. Infants and toddlers don't talk well, if at all, and most child-

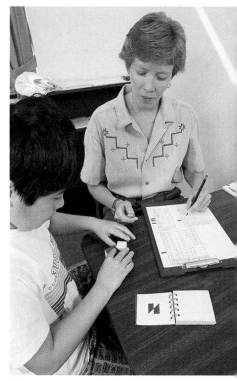

This second grader is working on one of the subtests of the WISC, in which he must use a set of blocks to try to copy the design shown in the book.

Table 7.1

Other Widely Used Tests That May Be Used in Place of the Stanford-Binet and the Wechsler by Researchers or Educators

Peabody Picture Vocabulary Test (PPVT)	Not originally designed as an IQ test, but widely used as a quick measure of intelligence because the scores correlate so highly with Binet or Wechsler scores. Includes 150 pages, each page with four pictures, with the pages arranged in order of increasing difficulty. The examiner names one of the four and asks the child to point to the appropriate picture, as in the example on the right below. Widely used with preschool children. (This is the test used in the study described in Table 8.4 on p. 246.)
Raven's Progressive Matrices	Each of the 36 items shows a pattern on a rectangular space, such as a set of dots covering the space. One section of the rectangle is blanked out, and the subject must choose which of six alternative fill-in options will match the original matrix, like the one on the left below. Designed as a nonverbal measure of intelligence.
Kaufman Assessment Battery for Children (KABC)	Kaufman does not call this an intelligence test, although it is often used in this way. Suitable for children aged 2½ to 12; includes three tests of *sequential processing* (such as number recall) and seven tests of *simultaneous processing* (including face recognition), combined to provide an overall IQ score, based primarily on nonverbal measures. Six achievement subtests can also be given, including vocabulary, riddles, and reading. The test also allows flexible testing procedures, including the use of other languages, alternative wording, and gestures, all of which make the test one of the fairest for ethnic minorities and children from poverty-level families.

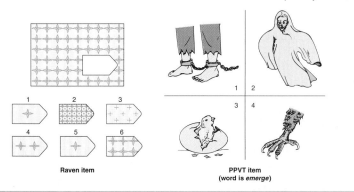

Raven item

PPVT item
(word is *emerge*)

Sources: Reprinted and adapted with the permission of The Free Press, a division of Simon & Schuster, Inc. and Methuen & Co., an imprint of Routledge, from *Bias in mental testing* by Arthur R. Jensen. Copyright © 1980 by Arthur R. Jensen.

Katherine, at 22 months, would clearly pass the 17-month item on the Bayley Scales of Infant Development that calls for the child to build a tower of three blocks.

hood tests rely heavily on language. (Even the Peabody Picture Vocabulary Test, described in Table 7.1 on p. 201, requires the child to understand individual words.) So how do we measure "intelligence" in an infant? This becomes an important question if we want to be able to identify, during infancy, those children who are not developing normally or if we want to predict later intelligence or school performance.

Most "infant IQ tests," such as the widely used **Bayley Scales of Infant Development** (Bayley, 1969, revised 1993), have been constructed rather like IQ tests for older children in that they include sets of items of increasing difficulty. However, instead of testing "school-like" skills—skills an infant does not yet have—the items measure primarily sensory and motor skills, such as reaching for a dangling ring (an item for a typical baby at 3 months), putting cubes in a cup on request (9 months), or building a tower of three cubes (17 months). Some more clearly cognitive items are also included, such as uncovering a toy hidden by a cloth, an item used with 8-month-old infants to measure an aspect of object permanence.

Bayley's test and others like it, such as the Denver Developmental Screening Test, have proved helpful in identifying infants and toddlers with serious developmental delays (Lewis & Sullivan, 1985). As a more general predictive tool to forecast later IQ scores or school performance, however, such tests have not been nearly as useful as many had hoped. On the whole, it looks as if what is being measured on typical infant tests is not the same as what is tapped by the common childhood or adult intelligence tests (Colombo, 1993).

Achievement Tests

Another kind of test of intellectual skill with which you are probably more personally familiar is the **achievement test,** which nearly all of you have taken in elementary and high school. Achievement tests are designed to test *specific* information learned in school, using items like those in Table 7.2. The child taking an achievement test doesn't end up with an IQ score, but his performance is still compared to that of other children in the same grade across the country.

How are these tests different from an IQ test? IQ tests are intended to tell us something about how well a child *can* think and learn, while an achievement test tells us something about what a child *has* learned. Or to put it another way, the designers of IQ tests thought they were measuring the child's basic capacity (her underlying **competence**), while an achievement test is intended to measure what the child has actually learned (her **performance**). This is an important distinction. Each of us presumably has some upper limit of ability—what we could do under ideal conditions, when we are maximally motivated, healthy, and rested. Yet, since everyday conditions are rarely ideal, we typically perform below our hypothetical ability.

The authors of the famous IQ tests believed that by standardizing the procedures for administering and scoring the tests, they could come close to measuring competence. But because we can never be sure that we are assessing any ability under the best of all possible circumstances, we are *always* measuring performance at the time the test

In the United States, virtually all fourth graders—like these in Austin, Texas— are given achievement tests so that schools can compare their students' performance against national norms.

Table 7.2

Some Sample Items from a Fourth-Grade Achievement Test

Vocabulary

jolly old man
1. angry
2. fat
3. merry
4. sorry

Reference Skills

Which of these words would be first in ABC order?
1. pair
2. point
3. paint
4. polish

Language Expression

Who wants _____ books?
1. that
2. these
3. them
4. this

Spelling

Jason took the *cleanest* glass.
right _____ wrong _____

Mathematics

What does the "3" in 13 stand for?
1. 3 ones
2. 13 ones
3. 3 tens
4. 13 tens

Mathematics Computation

79	149	62
+14	– 87	×3

Source: From Comprehensive Tests of Basic Skills, Form S. Reprinted by permission of the publisher, CTB/McGraw-Hill, Del Monte Research Park, Monterey, CA 93940. Copyright © 1973 by McGraw-Hill, Inc. All rights reserved. Printed in the USA.

is taken. What this means in practical terms is that the distinction between IQ tests and achievement tests is one of degree rather than of kind. IQ tests include items that are designed to tap fairly fundamental intellectual processes like comparison or analysis; the achievement tests call for specific information the child has learned in school or elsewhere. College entrance tests, like the Scholastic Aptitude Test (SAT), fall somewhere in between. They are designed to measure basic "developed abilities," such as the ability to reason with words, rather than just specific knowledge. But all three types of tests measure aspects of a child or young person's performance and not competence.

Stability and Predictive Value of IQ Tests

For most psychologists, arguments about whether IQ tests measure capacity or performance are beside the point. The more critical practical questions are whether the scores are stable and whether they predict anything interesting or useful.

Stability of Test Scores

One of the bits of folklore about IQ tests is that a particular IQ score is something you "have," like blue eyes or red hair—that a child who achieves a score of, say, 115 at 3 years of age will continue to score in about the same range at age 6 or 12 or 20.

IQ scores are, in fact, very stable, although there are also some exceptions to this general statement. One such exception is the weak link between scores on infant IQ tests like the Bayley and later IQ scores. The typical correlation between a 12-month

The Real World

Performance Tests: A New Way to Measure School Achievement

Traditional achievement tests, like IQ tests, are designed to show how well a given child, or a classroom of children, performs against some average or norm. Hence, both achievement and IQ tests are sometimes referred to as *norm-referenced*. In both cases the norm is the performance of the average child of a given age. An alternative way to think about testing is to define some criterion, some absolute standard that you think all children should meet, and to compare each child's performance to that criterion. Many educators today are advocating exactly such *criterion-referenced* tests, especially the form of criterion- referenced test called a **performance test.** For example, suppose that one of the goals of an educational system is that each student be able to write clearly and persuasively, using complete sentences and correct grammar. Such a skill can be assessed only with a test that actually asks the students to write something. Then each student's writing can be evaluated as acceptable or not acceptable against some absolute standard.

For example, in one reading/writing test devised as part of the Maryland School Performance Assessment Program, eighth graders are asked to read and write about the intense cold of the winter in the Yukon Territory of Canada. They read a story by Jack London, "To Build a Fire," about a man who dies of the cold. Later they also read a brief excerpt titled "Hypothermia: Causes, Effects, Prevention." Over several days, the students answer questions in test booklets about these readings and discuss some of the material in class. At the end they must write some form of commentary, such as a piece giving advice to a group of friends about what they would need to do to stay safe on a winter hiking trip; a story, play, or poem expressing their feelings about extreme states; or a speech intended to persuade people not to travel in the Yukon (Mitchell, 1992).

Similarly, a performance test in science or mathematics might involve completing and describing an actual science experiment, or it might ask a student to explain some mathematical principle. The following example comes from a mathematics performance test for junior high school students:

Five students have test scores of 62, 75, 80, 86, and 92. Find the average score. How much is the average score increased if each student's score is increased by 1, 5, 8, or X points? Write a statement about how much the average score is increased if each individual score is increased X points, and *write an argument to convince another student that the statement is true.* (Mitchell, 1992, p. 67)

The students' performance on both the writing and mathematics tests are normally scored (by experts, usually on a statewide basis) on a 4- or 6-point scale, with the top 1 or 2 points reserved for those performances that meet the criterion and lower scores for unacceptably poor responses. Thus, the issue is not whether the students in some class or school do better or worse than other children, but whether each one individually meets some absolute standard.

Tests like these are now in use in parts of the United States, as well as in England and Wales, where many of the performance tests of science and mathematics were first devised. They are more complicated (and more expensive) to administer and score than are norm-referenced achievement tests. They are growing in popularity, however, not only because they assess the actual behaviors or skills educators are interested in, but also because the very existence of such tests shapes the way reading, writing, science, and mathematics are taught in the classroom. Just as teachers who know that their students will be tested with standard achievement tests inevitably "teach to the test," so teachers who know that their students will be tested with performance tests of reading, writing, math, or science must change the way they teach these subjects to be sure that their students acquire the needed reasoning and communication skills. Since these are precisely the skills that most educators believe should be taught in schools, performance tests may prove to be a vehicle for educational reform.

Bayley mental test score and a 4-year-old Binet IQ score is only about .20 to .30 (Bee et al., 1982)—significant but not robust. Newer tests of infant intelligence, such as those based on habituation rates or other basic processes, may ultimately prove to be more helpful predictors (Colombo, 1993), but at the moment, there is no widely used method that allows us to predict with any reliability which 1-year-olds will later have high or low IQ scores.

However, beginning at about age 3, consistency in IQ test performance on tests like the Binet or WISC-III increases markedly. If two tests are given a few months or a few years apart, the scores are likely to be very similar. The correlations between adjacent-year IQ scores in middle childhood, for example, are typically in the range of .80 (Honzik, 1986). This high level of predictability, however, masks an interesting fact: Many children show quite wide fluctuations in their scores. When children are given IQ tests repeatedly over a period of years, the common finding is that about half show little or no significant fluctuation in their scores while the remaining half show at least small changes from one test to another, with perhaps 15 percent showing rather substantial change (Caspi et al., 1996; McCall, 1993). One example comes from the big New Zealand longitudinal study I have mentioned before, in which all 1037 children born in the town of Dunedin over a one-year period in the 1970s were followed through childhood and adolescence. Among many other measures, the researchers measured the children's IQs with the WISC every two years starting at age 7. They found that over any two-year period, 10 percent of the children's IQ scores changed as much as 15 points—a very large change (Caspi et al., 1996). Another 13 percent showed major changes over longer periods; 15 of the children showed cumulative shifts of more than 50 points over six years. In most cases, however, these large shifts represent "bounce" or "rebound" rather than permanent shifts upward or downward. That is, some children seemed to respond to specific life experiences—stresses or special advantages—with a decline or a rise in IQ score. A few years later, their IQ score then returned to something closer to the original score.

Such fluctuations, while intriguing, occur against a background of increasing IQ test score stability with age. The general rule of thumb is that the older the child, the more stable the IQ score becomes. Older children may show some fluctuation in scores in response to major stresses such as parental divorce, a change in schools, or the birth of a sibling, but by age 10 or 12, IQ scores are normally highly stable.

What IQ Tests Predict

The information on long-term stability of IQ tests tells us something about the *reliability* of the tests. What about *validity*? Validity, as you'll recall from introductory psychology, has to do with whether a test is measuring what it is intended to measure. One way to assess a test's validity is to see whether scores on that test predict real behavior in a way that makes sense. In the case of IQ tests, the most central question is whether IQ scores predict school performance. That was what Binet originally intended the test to do; that is what all subsequent tests were designed to do. The research findings on this point are quite consistent: The correlation between a child's test score and her grades in school or performance on other school tests typically falls between .45 and .60 (Brody, 1992; 1997; Carver, 1990; Neisser et al., 1996). A correlation in this range suggests a strong but by no means perfect relationship. It tells us that on the whole, children with top IQ scores will also be among the high achievers in school, and those who score low will be among the low achievers. Still, some children with high IQ scores don't shine in school while some lower-IQ children do.

IQ scores predict future grades as well as current grades. Preschool children with high IQ scores tend to do better when they enter school than those with lower scores; elementary school children with higher IQ scores later do better in high school. Further, IQ scores predict the total number of years of education a child is likely to complete. Higher-IQ elementary school children are more likely to complete high school and are more likely to decide to go on to college (Brody, 1997).

It is important to point out that these predictive relationships hold *within* each social class and racial group in the United States. Among the poor, and among African Americans and Latinos, as well as among middle-class Anglos, those children with higher IQ are most likely to get good grades, complete high school, and go on to

Critical Thinking

Given the degree of variability I have described, does it make sense to select children for special classes, such as classes for the gifted, on the basis of a single test score? How else could you go about it?

Among these high school students, those with higher IQ are not only likely to get better grades; they are more likely to go on to college. Intelligence also adds to the child's resilience—his ability to survive stress, including poverty.

Critical Thinking

How or why do you think having a higher IQ score makes a child more resilient? For example, in what specific ways might the life of a brighter child living in a slum be different from the life of a less bright child in the same environment?

college (Brody, 1992). Such findings have led a number of theorists to argue that intelligence adds to the child's *resilience*—a concept I talked about in Chapter 1. Numerous studies now show that poor children, be they white, Latino, African American, or from another minority group, are far more likely to develop the kind of self-confidence and personal competence it takes to move out of poverty if they have higher IQ scores (Luthar & Zigler, 1992; Teachman et al., 1997; Werner & Smith, 1992).

At the other end of the scale, low intelligence is associated with a number of negative long-term outcomes, including adult illiteracy, delinquency in adolescence, and criminal behavior in adulthood (Stattin & Klackenberg-Larsson, 1993). For example, in a 20-year longitudinal study of a group of children born to black teenage mothers in Baltimore, Nazli Baydar has found that the best single predictor of adult literacy or illiteracy was each subject's childhood IQ score (Baydar et al., 1993). This is not to say that all lower-IQ individuals are illiterate or criminals. That is clearly not the case. But low IQ makes a child more vulnerable, just as high IQ increases the child's resilience.

Limitations of Traditional IQ Tests

Judging from the evidence I've just presented, we can argue that IQ tests are valid: They measure what they purport to measure. However, they do not measure everything. Most important, they do not measure underlying competence. An IQ score cannot tell you (or a teacher, or anyone else) that your child has some specific, fixed, underlying intellectual capacity.

Traditional IQ tests also do not measure a whole host of skills that are likely to be highly significant for getting along in the world. IQ tests were originally designed to measure only the specific range of skills that are needed for success in school. They do this reasonably well. But these tests do not tell us how well a particular person may perform other cognitive tasks requiring skills such as creativity, insight, "street smarts," or ability to read social cues.

Finally, it is worth pointing out yet again that IQ scores are not etched on a child's forehead at birth. Although these scores do become quite stable in late childhood, individual children can and do shift in response to especially rich or especially impoverished environments, or in response to any stress in their lives (McCall, 1993; Pianta & Egeland, 1994a).

In the past decade, a number of psychologists have been particularly struck by these limitations in the traditional ways of thinking about intelligence. Howard Gardner (1983), for example, proposes six separate types of intelligence (linguistic, musical, logical-mathematical, spatial, bodily-kinesthetic, and personal), only two of which are actually measured on traditional IQ tests. Another current view, which I find even more intriguing because it has some obvious practical implications, is Robert Sternberg's **triarchic theory of intelligence.**

An Alternative View: Sternberg's Triarchic Theory of Intelligence

Sternberg (1985; Sternberg & Wagner, 1993) argues that there are three aspects or types of intelligence. The first, which he now calls **analytical intelligence** (originally called *componential intelligence*), includes what we normally measure on IQ and achievement tests. Planning, organizing, and remembering facts and applying them to new situations are all part of analytical intelligence.

The second aspect he calls **creative intelligence** (originally labeled *experiential intelligence*). A person with well-developed creative intelligence can see new connections between things, can relate to experiences in insightful ways. A graduate student who can come up with good ideas for experiments, who can see how a theory could be applied to a totally different situation, or who can synthesize a great many facts into a new organization is high in creative intelligence. You might like to try your hand at some of the kinds of tests Sternberg has devised to measure this kind of ability, shown in Table 7.3. The answers are at the bottom in case you are stumped—as many people are.

The third aspect Sternberg calls **practical intelligence** (originally labeled *contextual intelligence*), sometimes also called "street smarts." People who are skilled in this are good at seeing how some bit of information may be applied to the real world, or

Table 7.3

Insight Questions from Sternberg's Tests of Creative Intelligence

1. Aeronautical engineers have made it possible for a supersonic jet fighter to catch up with the bullets fired from its own guns with sufficient speed to shoot itself down. If a plane, flying at 1000 miles an hour, fires a burst, the rounds leave the plane with an initial velocity of about 3000 miles an hour. Why won't a plane that continues to fly straight ahead overtake and fly into its own bullets?

2. If you have black socks and brown socks in your drawer, mixed in a ratio of 4 to 5, how many socks will you have to take out to make sure of having a pair of the same color?

3. In the Thompson family, there are five brothers, and each brother has one sister. If you count Mrs. Thompson, how many females are there in the Thompson family?

In solving the following analogies, assume that the statement given before the analogy is true, whether it actually is true or not, and use that assumption to solve the analogy.

4. LAKES are dry.
   TRAIL is to HIKE as LAKE is to:
   a. swim
   b. dust
   c. water
   d. walk

5. DEER attack tigers.
   LION is to COURAGEOUS as DEER is to:
   a. timid
   b. aggressive
   c. cougar
   d. elk

Answers: 1. Gravity pulls the bullets down. If the plane continues to fly a level course, it cannot shoot itself. 2. Three (the proportion of black and brown socks is irrelevant). 3. Two, the mother and her daughter, who is sister to each brother. 4. d. 5. b.

Source: Excerpts adapted from *Intelligence applied, understanding and increasing your intellectual skills* by Robert J. Sternberg. © 1986 by Harcourt Brace & Company. Reprinted by permission of the publisher.

Critical Thinking

It's fairly easy to come up with a list of occupations for which analytical intelligence is especially useful, but what about practical intelligence? For what jobs might a high level of practical intelligence be especially useful?

finding some practical solution to a real-life problem such as finding shortcuts for repetitive tasks or figuring out which of several different-sized boxes of cereal or laundry soap in the grocery store is the best buy. (Nowadays, of course, the grocery store does this particular calculation for you by providing cost-per-unit information on each item.) Practical intelligence may also involve being skilled at reading social cues or social situations, such as knowing not to give your boss bad news when she is clearly in a bad mood over something else, or knowing how to persuade your superiors to invest a large amount of money on your favorite sales plan (Sternberg et al., 1995).

As an aside, I should note that these social aspects of practical intelligence overlap with what Daniel Goleman, in a recent popular book, labels **emotional intelligence,** a skill requiring the ability to understand others' emotions and to regulate one's own, "such as being able to motivate oneself and persist in the face of frustrations; to control impulses and delay gratification; to regulate one's moods and keep distress from swamping the ability to think; to empathize and to hope" (1995b, p. 34).

Sternberg's most basic point about these several types of intelligence is not just that standard IQ tests do not measure all three, but that in the world beyond the school walls, creative or practical intelligence may be required as much as or more than the type of skill measured on an IQ test (Sternberg & Wagner, 1993). These are important points to keep in mind as we move on to questions about the origins of individual differences in IQ scores. What we know about "intelligence" is almost entirely restricted to information about analytical intelligence—the kind of intelligence most often demanded (and tested) in school. We know almost nothing about the origins or long-term consequences of variations in creative or practical intelligence.

Explaining Differences in IQ Scores

You will not be surprised to discover that the arguments about the origins of differences in IQ test scores nearly always boil down to a dispute about nature versus nurture. When Binet and Simon wrote the first IQ test, they did not assume that intelligence as measured on an IQ test was fixed or inborn. However, many of the U.S. psychologists who revised and promoted the use of the tests *did* believe that intellectual capacity is inherited and largely fixed at birth. Those who share this view, and those who believe that the environment is crucial in shaping a child's intellectual performance, have been arguing—often vehemently—for at least sixty years. Both groups can muster research to support their views.

Evidence for the Importance of Heredity

Both the twin studies and studies of adopted children show strong hereditary influences on IQ scores, as you already know from the Research Report in Chapter 1 (p. 6). Identical twins are more like one another in IQ scores than are fraternal twins, and the IQs of adopted children are better predicted from the IQs of their natural parents than from those of their adoptive parents (Brody, 1992; Loehlin et al., 1994; Scarr et al., 1993). This is precisely the pattern of correlations we would expect if there were a strong genetic element at work.

Evidence for the Importance of Environment

Adoption studies also provide some strong support for an environmental influence on IQ scores, because the actual *level* of IQ scores of adopted children is clearly affected by the environment in which they have grown up. Early studies of adopted children involved mostly children born to poverty-level parents who were adopted into middle-class families. Such children typically have an IQ score 10 to 15 points higher than that of their birth mothers (Scarr et al., 1983), suggesting that the effect of the middle-class adoptive family is to raise the child's IQ score. What this finding doesn't tell us is whether a *less* stimulating adoptive family would *lower* the test score of a child born to average-IQ or above-average-IQ parents. That piece of information is now available from a French study by Christiane Capron and Michel Duyme (1989), who studied a group of 38 French children, all adopted in infancy. Approximately half the children had been born to better-educated parents of higher social class, while the other half had been born to working-class or poverty-level parents. Some of the children in each group had then been adopted by higher-social-class parents, while the others grew up in poorer families. Table 7.4 shows the children's IQ scores in adolescence. If you compare the two columns in the table, you can see the effect of rearing conditions: The children reared in upper-class homes have IQ scores that are 11 or 12 points higher than those reared in lower-class families, regardless of the social class or education of the birth parents. At the same time, you can see a genetic effect if you compare the two rows in the table: The children *born to* upper-class parents have higher IQ scores than do those from lower-class families, no matter what kind of rearing environment they encountered.

Social Class Differences. This relationship between social class and IQ score, so clear in the Capron and Duyme study, is echoed in a great deal of other research. But just what is meant by "social class"?

Every society is divided into social strata of some kind. In Western societies, an individual's social status or **social class** is typically defined or measured in terms of three dimensions: education, income, and occupation. Thus, a person with higher status is one with more education, higher income, and a more prestigious occupation. In other societies, the dimensions of status might be different, but some status differences exist in every society. Distinctions between "blue collar" and "white collar," or "middle class" and "working class," are fundamentally status distinctions.

Dozens of research studies tell us that children from poor or working-class families, or from families in which the parents are relatively uneducated, have lower average IQ scores than do children from middle-class families. You can see this effect particularly vividly in Figure 7.2 (p. 210), which is based on data from a huge national study of more than 50,000 children born in 12 different hospitals around the United States between 1959 and 1966 (Broman et al., 1975). In this figure, in order to make sure that we are not confounding social class and racial differences, I have given only the results for white children who were tested with the Stanford-Binet at age 4, a total sample of more than 11,800 children. As you can see in the figure, the average IQ score of the children rises as the family overall social class rises and as the mother's education rises.

These differences are *not* found on standardized tests of infant intelligence such as the Bayley (Golden & Birns, 1983). After age $2\frac{1}{2}$ or 3, however, social class differences

Table 7.4

IQ Scores at Adolescence for Capron and Duyme's Adopted Children

| | | Social Class of Adoptive Parents | |
		High	Low
Social Class of Biological Parents	**High**	119.60	107.50
	Low	103.60	92.40

Source: From Capron, C., and Duyme, M., "Assessment of Effects of Socio-Economic Status on IQ in a Full Cross-fostering Study," *Nature*, 340, 1989, p. 553. By permission of the publisher, Macmillian Magazines, Ltd. and the authors.

Figure 7.2

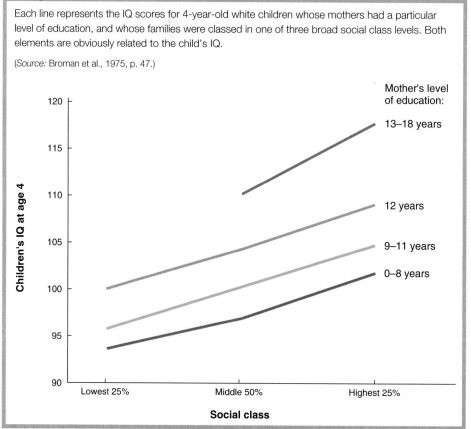

Each line represents the IQ scores for 4-year-old white children whose mothers had a particular level of education, and whose families were classed in one of three broad social class levels. Both elements are obviously related to the child's IQ.

(*Source:* Broman et al., 1975, p. 47.)

appear to widen steadily (Farran et al., 1980), producing what is sometimes called a **cumulative deficit.** That is, the longer the child lives in poverty, the more negative the effect on IQ test scores and other measures of cognitive functioning (Duncan, 1993; Smith et al., 1997). These cumulative effects are especially large on *verbal* tests (Jordan et al., 1992).

Genetic differences are obviously contributing to the pattern in Figure 7.2, since brighter parents typically have more education and better jobs and also pass on their "bright" genes to their children. Clearly, though, environment plays a significant role in accentuating the differences apparent in the figure, particularly for those parents who live in poverty. Poverty exerts a significant negative effect on children's IQ scores, over and above what may be contributed by the parents' own genes or the level of enrichment they may provide to their children. As you'll recall from Chapter 4, children born into or living in poverty are at higher risk for prenatal problems and poorer general health. For example, poor children are likely to be exposed to higher levels of lead, and we know that lead exposure is causally linked to lower test scores (Baghurst et al., 1992; 1995; Dietrich et al., 1993; Tesman & Hills, 1994). Children living in poverty are also more likely to suffer from periodic or chronic subnutrition. We know that this contributes to lower IQ scores because experimental studies in developing countries show that when children living in poverty are given high-quality nutritional supplements in infancy and early childhood, they later have higher IQ scores or vocabularies compared to nonsupplemented children (Pollitt & Gorman, 1994).

In addition to all these physical factors, real differences in the treatment of infants and children in poor versus middle-class families are independently important in cognitive development. It is these differences in early experiences that have been the focus of most of the research on environmental effects on IQ.

Specific Family Characteristics and IQ Scores. When we watch the ways individual families interact with their infants or young children and then follow the children over time to see which ones later have high or low IQ scores, we can begin to get some sense of the kinds of specific family interactions that foster higher scores. At least five dimensions of family interaction or stimulation seem to make a difference. Parents of higher-IQ children, or of children whose IQ scores show a rising pattern over age, tend to do the following:

- They provide an *interesting and complex physical environment* for the child, including play materials that are appropriate for the child's age and developmental level (Bradley et al., 1989; Molfese et al., 1997; Pianta & Egeland, 1994a). New research on brain development in infancy and childhood, discussed in Chapter 4, makes it clear that such a complex environment in the early months and years is a critical factor in stimulating the retention of greater synaptic density.

- They are *emotionally responsive to* and *involved with* their child. They respond warmly and contingently to the child's behavior, smiling when the child smiles, talking when the child speaks, answering the child's questions, and in myriad ways responding to the child's cues (Barnard et al., 1989; Lewis, 1993; Murray & Hornbaker, 1997).

- They *talk to their child* often, using language that is diverse, descriptively rich, and accurate (Hart & Risley, 1995; Sigman et al., 1988).

- When they play with or interact with the child, they operate in what Vygotsky referred to as the *zone of proximal development* (described in Chapter 1), aiming their conversation, their questions, and their assistance at a level that is just above the level the child could manage on her own, thus helping the child to master new skills (e.g., Landry et al., 1996).

- They *avoid excessive restrictiveness,* punitiveness, or control, instead giving the child room to explore, even opportunities to make mistakes (Bradley et al., 1989; Murray & Hornbaker, 1997; S. Olson et al., 1992). In a similar vein, they ask questions rather than giving commands (Hart & Risley, 1995).

- They *expect* their child to do well and to develop rapidly. They emphasize and press for school achievement (Entwisle & Alexander, 1990).

You may have figured out the methodological problem in research of this type—the same problem that exists in comparisons of the IQs of children in families that differ in social class. Because parents provide *both* the genes and the environment, we can't be sure that these environmental characteristics are really causally important. Perhaps these are simply the environmental features provided by brighter parents, and it is the genes and not the environment that cause the higher IQ scores in their children. The way around this problem is to look at the link between environmental features and IQ in adopted children. Fortunately, we have a few studies of this type, and they point to the same critical environmental features. That is, among adoptive families, those that

This kind of rich, complex, stimulating environment is consistently linked to higher IQ in children.

👥 Cultures and Contexts
Maternal "Responsiveness" in Different Cultures

Many studies in the United States and other Western countries have pointed to the central importance of parental *responsiveness* for the child's intellectual and social development. Mothers and fathers who respond to their infant's noises by talking to the baby, who smile when the baby smiles, who notice the baby's other signals have children who later turn out to have higher IQ scores, better language, and more secure attachments.

Since this aspect of the parent-infant interaction appears to be so significant, it seems especially important for us to discover if the same relationship holds in other cultures and contexts. Amy Richman and her colleagues (1992) have taken a first step toward answering this question with two studies in other cultures. They compared responsiveness among U.S. and Kenyan mothers, and they observed the responsiveness of Mexican mothers who varied in level of education.

In the Kenyan/U.S. comparison, Richman observed marked differences in the ways mothers responded to their babies. When the Kenyan babies vocalized, cried, or looked at the mother, their mothers were most likely to pick them up and hold them. Mothers in Boston were far more likely to talk to or look at their babies in response to the same baby signals.

Profound cultural differences are at work here. The Kenyan mothers, all from the Gusii tribe, said that they thought it was ridiculous to talk to a baby before the baby is capable of speech. This culture also has different social conventions about eye contact during speech: Mutual gaze is much less common than in the United States and other Western cultures. Thus, the way the mothers behave with their babies is entirely consistent with cultural beliefs and interaction patterns.

It is also important to note that the two groups did not differ in their absolute amount of responsiveness. Thus, both groups of mothers are "responsive" to their babies. But they respond in very different ways. The Gusii mothers "show a pattern of responsiveness that is strikingly designed to reduce distress and maintain calm in the infant during the 1st year of life" (p. 620). In contrast, the responsiveness of the Boston mothers seems designed to stimulate the baby and encourage further interaction.

The Mexican mothers, as a group, showed yet another pattern. They were most likely to look at the baby when the infant vocalized or looked at them and less likely to pick the baby up than were the Gusii mothers. But they responded to the baby's signals with speech about as often as the Boston mothers did. What is especially interesting here is that Richman found that the amount of formal education the Mexican mothers had received was related to their pattern of responsiveness. The more formal education they had (and the maximum was only about 8 or 9 years), the more their pattern of responsiveness was like the Boston mothers'. Studies in the United States also show that the mother's education is linked in this same way to her manner of interacting with her baby. This does not mean that the Gusii mothers behave as they do because they have little formal education. We don't know if that is the case, and we do know that other cultural values and beliefs among the Gusii contribute to the pattern of responsiveness these mothers show. But the results from the Mexican women show at least that the link between education and patterns of responsiveness is not unique to U.S. samples.

What Richman's study does not tell us is whether these varying styles of responsiveness have differential effects on the child's cognitive development. That piece of the puzzle will have to await further cross-cultural research.

behave in the ways listed earlier have adopted children who score higher on IQ tests (Plomin et al., 1985).

Differences in Environments Within Families. Within families the experiences of individual children also differ in ways that affect IQ test scores. Being the oldest of a large family, for example, is a very different experience from being the youngest or being in the middle; being the only girl in a family of boys is different from being a girl with only sisters. Psychologists are just beginning to study these within-family variables. Thus far, we have been looking mostly at fairly obvious differences, like how many children are in a family or the child's position within the family, both of which seem to be at least slightly related to the child's IQ score. *On average,* the more children in the family, the lower the IQ scores of the children. And on average, firstborn children have the highest IQ scores, with average scores declining steadily as you go down the birth order (Zajonc, 1983; Zajonc & Marcus, 1975; Zajonc & Mullally, 1997). Children who are born very close together also have slightly lower IQ scores on average than do those born further apart (Storfer, 1990). One fairly typical set of data is in Figure 7.3, based on scores of nearly 800,000 students who took the National Merit Scholarship Examination in 1965, with the scores converted to the equivalent of IQ scores.

Two points are important about results like these. First, these differences are found consistently when you average over many children or adults. However, when you look at individual families, the pattern is much weaker or not obvious at all. (In the same way, we know that if you compare large groups of smokers and nonsmokers, the smokers have a much higher probability of developing lung cancer than the nonsmokers, but this doesn't mean that every smoker will develop such a cancer [Zajonc & Mullally, 1997].) So you need to be careful about extrapolating the aggregated data reflected in Figure 7.3 to your own family or other individual families. *Some* significant effect of birth order is detected with large samples, but that particular effect may or may not be present in an individual family.

A second point about the birth-order comparisons is that the absolute differences in IQ scores are not huge, even in the aggregated data. Still, this pattern has been observed repeatedly, in European samples as well as in the United States, leaving us with a puzzle. Why would such a pattern occur? Robert Zajonc's hypothesis is that, on average, the birth of each succeeding child "dilutes" the intellectual climate of the home. The oldest child initially interacts only with his parents and thus has a maximally complex and enriching environment. Second- or later-born children, in contrast, experience a lower average intellectual level in the family simply because they interact with both other children and adults. A later-born child *may* have an advantage if the children are very widely spaced, since then he is interacting entirely with others who are intellectually advanced, including both parents and much older siblings.

This hypothesis has prompted a good deal of debate and criticism (Rogers, 1984); most researchers have concluded that it is probably not the right way to conceptualize what is going on, because the data do not always fit the predictions. But no one has yet offered a better explanation. To solve this puzzle, we will need to know a good deal more about the actual experiences of children in different birth-order positions and in large versus small families.

Figure 7.3

These data from the 1965 National Merit Scholarship Qualifying Test show the commonly found relationship between test scores and family size and birth order. Within each family size, the average score is highest for the firstborn and declines with each position in the birth-order sequence.

(*Sources:* Data from Breland, 1974, recalculated by Storfer, 1990, Table 7, p. 32.)

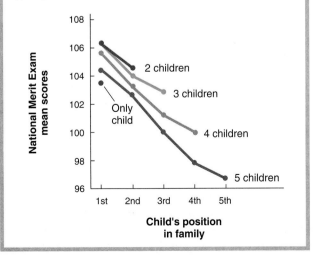

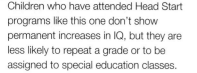

Children who have attended Head Start programs like this one don't show permanent increases in IQ, but they are less likely to repeat a grade or to be assigned to special education classes.

School Experience and Special Interventions. Home environments and family interactions are not the only source of environmental influence. Many young children also spend a very large amount of time in group care settings, including day care, special programs like Head Start, or regular preschools. How much effect do these environments have on the child's intellectual performance?

On a theoretical level, this question is of interest because it may tell us something about early experience in general and about the resilience of children. Are the effects of an initially impoverished environment permanent, or can they be offset by an enriched experience, such as a special preschool? In Aslin's terms (Figure 1.1, p. 8), the question is whether special programs can produce *attunement*—a permanent gain over the level of performance the child would have shown without the added enrichment. At a practical level, programs like Head Start are based squarely on the assumption that it *is* possible to modify the trajectory of a child's intellectual development, especially with early intervention.

Attempts to test this assumption have led to a messy body of research. In particular, children are rarely assigned randomly to Head Start or non–Head Start groups, so interpretation is difficult. Still, researchers agree generally on the effects. Children enrolled in Head Start or other enriched preschool programs, compared to similar children without such preschool, normally show a gain of about 10 IQ points during the year of the Head Start experience. This IQ gain typically fades and then disappears within the first few years of elementary school (Zigler & Styfco, 1993), but on other measures, a clear residual effect can be seen. Children with Head Start or other quality preschool experience are less likely to be placed in special education classes, somewhat less likely to repeat a grade, and somewhat more likely to graduate from high school (Darlington, 1991; Haskins, 1989). They also have better health, better immunization rates, and better school adjustment than their peers (Zigler & Styfco, 1993). So although poor children with preschool experience do not typically *test* much higher than their non-preschool-attending peers on standardized achievement tests (and, in most studies, do *not* differ in IQ score), they *function* better in school. When some kind of supportive intervention continues into the early years of elementary school, or when the school the child moves to is of decent quality, the beneficial effects on school performance are even clearer (Currie & Thomas, 1997; Reynolds, 1994; Zigler & Styfco, 1993).

Furthermore, the one study that has looked at adult outcomes of such preschool attendance suggests lasting effects. Young adults who had attended a particularly good experimental preschool program, the Perry Preschool Project in Milwaukee, had higher rates of high school graduation, lower rates of criminal behavior, lower rates of unemployment, and a lower probability of being on welfare than did their peers who did not have the advantage of the preschool experience (Barnett, 1993). Thus, the potential effects of such early education programs may be broad—even though the programs appear to have no lasting effect on standardized IQ test scores.

At the same time, I should emphasize that the Perry Preschool Project was *not* a Head Start program; we have *no* equivalent information about children who have attended run-of-the-mill Head Start, so we can't be sure that the long-term effects would be as great as in the Perry project, although it is reasonable to expect that well-run, comprehensive Head Start programs would have similar effects (Zigler & Styfco, 1996).

Overall, despite the bits of encouraging information, we should be careful about making too-sweeping assertions about the benefits of Head Start. Edward Zigler—the nation's leading expert on Head Start—says, "Early childhood intervention alone cannot transform lives. Its positive effects can be overpowered by the longer and larger experience of growing up in poverty" (Zigler & Styfco, 1996, p. 152). Programs like Head Start are well worth our support, but we should not expect them to solve all problems.

Interventions in Infancy. More promising still—although far more expensive and complex—are enrichment programs that begin in infancy rather than at age 3 or 4. IQ scores of poverty-level children who have attended such very early programs *do* show an attunement effect: The scores remain elevated even after the intervention has ended—a result we might expect, given what we now know about the importance of early stimulation for the growth of neural connections in the brain. The best-designed and most meticulously reported of the infancy interventions has been carried out by Craig Ramey and his colleagues at the University of North Carolina (Burchinal et al., 1997; Campbell & Ramey, 1994; Ramey, 1993; Ramey & Campbell, 1987). Infants from poverty-level families whose mothers had low IQ scores were randomly assigned either to a special day-care program, eight hours a day, five days a week, or to a control group that received nutritional supplements and medical care but no special enriched day care. The special-care program, which began when the infants were 6 to 12 weeks of age and lasted until they began kindergarten, involved very much the kinds of "optimum" stimulation I described earlier. When they reached kindergarten age, half the children in each group were enrolled in a special supplemental program that focused on family support and increasing educational activities at home. The remaining children had only the normal school experience.

The average IQ scores of the children at various ages are shown in Figure 7.4. You can see that the IQ scores of the children who had been enrolled in the special program were higher at every age, whether they had the school-age supplementary program or not, although the scores for both groups declined in the elementary school years. What is not shown in the figure but is perhaps more practically significant is the fact that fully 44.0 percent of the control group children had IQ scores classified as borderline or retarded (scores below 85), compared to only 12.8 percent of the children who had been in the special program. In addition, the enriched infant care group had significantly higher scores on both reading and mathematics achievement tests at age 12 and were only half as likely to have repeated a grade (Campbell & Ramey, 1994).

Ramey found additional insights in the varying experiences of the control group children. Some of them had been reared primarily at home while others had spent peri-

Figure 7.4

In the Ramey study, children were randomly assigned in infancy to an experimental group with special day care (the "full intervention" group) or to a control group. From kindergarten through third grade, half of each group received supplementary family support, while the other half received none. Thus, the "preschool intervention" group had the intervention for 5 years, but nothing beyond that; the "school-age intervention" group had no intervention before school age but did have assistance in early elementary school. The difference in IQ between the intervention and control groups remained statistically significant even at age 12.

(*Source:* Campbell, F. A., and Ramey, C. T., "Effects of achievement: A follow-up study of children from low-income families," Fig. 1, p. 690, *Child development,* 65, (1994), 684–698. By permission of the Society for Research in Child Development.)

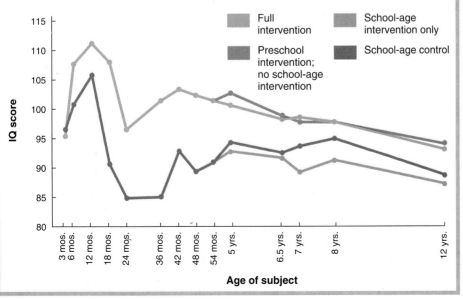

Research Report

Later Schooling and IQ Scores

The results from the Ramey infancy intervention shown in Figure 7.4 (p. 215) suggest that children's measured IQ scores may go down when they enter elementary school. Interestingly, there is now a variety of evidence pointing to a somewhat contrary conclusion: that the more years of school a group of children or young people has completed, the higher their average IQ score. The relationship between the two variables—length of schooling and IQ—appears to be reciprocal. Children who enter school with higher IQ scores tend to stay in school longer, but staying in school longer also seems to have the effect of *raising* the measured IQ score. Stephen Ceci and Wendy Williams (1997) have marshaled a variety of types of evidence in support of the latter point:

1. *Intermittent schooling.* Children who go to school only intermittently have lower IQ scores than children from the same types of families who attend regularly. An example comes from a very early study of children living in remote Appalachian mountain "hollows" in the 1930s (Sherman & Key, 1932). Those who lived in the most remote hollows, who attended school only sporadically, had substantially lower IQ scores than those who lived in nearer or more accessible hollows and attended school regularly. Because both groups came from the same ethnic stock and did not differ in overall poverty, Ceci and Williams argue that these results are not likely to be the result of any kind of self-selection or other factor and must be due to variations in schooling.

2. *Delayed school start-up.* Similarly, children whose entrance into school is delayed by some essentially random event, such as a war or the lack of availability of a teacher, have lower measured IQ scores compared to children whose schooling is not delayed.

3. *The effect of dropping out of school.* Dropping out before completing high school has a negative impact on IQ scores. Ceci and Williams cite particularly research in Sweden, where Harn-

qvist (1968) studied a random sample of 10 percent of all the young men born in 1948, who had been given an IQ test at age 13. When they reached age 18, 4616 were retested as part of their normal military registration. Harnqvist compared boys who were similar in IQ score, social class, and school grades at 13, some of whom had dropped out of school before completing high school and some of whom had remained in school. He found that for each year of high school missed, the young men's average IQ score was 1.8 points lower. For those who missed all of high school, the IQ score difference was nearly 8 points.

4. *Summer vacations.* A number of studies in the United States also show that children drop in IQ (and achievement test) scores over the summer, when they are not in school. The drop is not large but has been found repeatedly, according to Ceci and Williams.

5. *Early-year birthdates.* Children all born in a given year in the United States differ in the amount of schooling they have completed because school entrance rules dictate that those born between October and December of a given year have to wait a year longer than other children born that year before they can begin kindergarten. Thus, for example, among a group of children who were all 10 years old at the end of some year, three-quarters will have had one more year of school than the remaining quarter. Research comparing such groups of children, of various ages, suggests that each additional year of schooling brings an IQ score gain of approximately 3.5 points (Neal & Johnson, as cited in Heckman, 1995, a result paralleled by studies in Germany by Baltes & Reinert, 1969).

Research like this not only emphasizes the practical value of remaining in school; it also underlines the point that IQ tests do not measure only some inherited, basic capacity. The analytical abilities IQ tests measure are affected by specific experience, in-

Critical Thinking

Considering the results of Ramey's study, would you be in favor of providing such enriched day care to all infants from high-risk or poverty-level families? What are the arguments, pro and con?

ods of time in other types of day care or preschool programs. When he compared the IQ scores of these two groups with those in the special intervention program, he found a consistent rank order: Children in the special program had the highest scores, followed by those who had had some kind of day-care experience, with those reared wholly at home the lowest. The IQ scores at age 4 for these three groups were 101.1, 94.0, and 84.2, respectively (Burchinal et al., 1989). So the length and quality of the intervention appeared to be directly related to the size of the effect. Other researchers have confirmed the basic conclusion that the most effective programs are those that begin early and provide consistent, frequent stimulation (Ramey & Ramey, 1998).

These results do *not* mean that all mental retardation could be "cured" by providing children with heavy doses of special education in infancy. What they do show is that the intellectual power (analytical intelligence, at least) of those children who begin life with few advantages can be significantly increased if richer stimulation is provided early in life (Ramey & Ramey, 1998).

Interaction of Heredity and Environment

When we put together all the information about the role of heredity and environment in influencing IQ scores, it is clear that both factors are highly significant. Studies around the world consistently yield estimates that about half the variation in IQ scores within the population is due to heredity (Neisser et al., 1996; Plomin & Rende, 1991; Rogers et al., 1994). The remaining half is clearly due to environment or to interactions between environment and heredity.

One useful way to conceptualize this interaction is with the idea of **reaction range.** The basic idea is that genes establish some range, some upper and lower boundaries, of possible functioning. Where a child's IQ score will fall within those boundaries will be determined by environment. Richard Weinberg (1989) estimates that the reaction range for IQ scores is about 20 to 25 points. That is, given some specific genetic heritage, each child's actual IQ test performance may vary as much as 20 or 25 points, depending on the richness or poverty of the environment in which he grows up. When we change the child's environment for the better, the child moves closer to the upper end of his reaction range. When we change the environment for the worse, the child's effective intellectual performance falls toward the lower end of his reaction range. Thus, even though intelligence as measured on an IQ test is highly heritable, the absolute score within the reaction range is determined by environment.

We could also think about the interaction between heredity and environment in terms rather like Horowitz's model (recall Figure 1.3, p. 15), or we could use Aslin's concept of maintenance. Some theorists (Turkheimer & Gottesman, 1991) have argued that *within the normal range of environments,* IQ scores may be largely a function of heredity, not because environment is unimportant but simply because most environments are sufficiently rich to support or maintain normal intellectual development. It is only when environmental quality falls below some crucial threshold that it has a major effect on the level of measured IQ, such as might be true for children reared in an orphanage or in a severely impoverished environment. This view does not necessarily contradict the concept of reaction range. Rather, the argument is that the lower end of any given child's reaction range is likely to be manifested only if the child is reared in an environment that falls below the critical threshold. If we think about it in this way, then it makes sense that special-education programs like Ramey's would be effective for children from poverty-level environments, since the program brings the child's experience up into the sufficiently supportive range and thus adequately supports normal intellectual development. The same program provided to a child from a more enriched family environment, however, should have little or no effect on IQ scores—which is essentially what researchers have found.

Group Differences in IQ Scores

So far I have sidestepped two difficult issues, namely, racial and sex differences in IQ or cognitive power. Because these issues have powerful personal and political ramifications and can easily be blown out of proportion, I do not want to place too much emphasis on either topic. But you need to see what we know, what we don't know, and how we are trying to explain both kinds of differences.

Racial Differences

Debates about racial differences in IQ scores were re-energized by the publication in 1994 of a highly controversial book, *The Bell Curve,* in which Richard Herrnstein and Charles Murray reviewed and analyzed the evidence. That evidence points to several

Research Report

Stereotype Threat: Another Possible Factor in Poorer Minority Performance

A further factor tending to reduce test scores among African Americans, particularly for those who are most committed to academic achievement, is what Claude Steele (1997) labels *stereotype threat.* This is a subtle but powerful sense of pressure people feel when they are attempting to perform well in an area for which a negative stereotype exists for their group. Girls and women experience such stereotype threat when they are taking tests in math, an area in which the stereotype suggests girls are less able; elderly adults may experience stereotype threat when they are given tests of memory; African-American students experience such threat when they are faced with almost any kind of school exam, achievement test, or IQ test, in light of the general cultural stereotype that blacks are less intellectually able than others. Steele has found that when stereotype threat is strengthened, such as by telling girls before taking a difficult math test that this is a test on which girls generally do less well than boys or by telling African-American students that some test of verbal skills is a measure of their basic intellectual ability, the stereotyped group's performance is lowered. When stereotype threat is reduced, however, such as by telling girls that boys and girls usually do equally well on a given math test or by telling African-American students that the verbal test is simply a laboratory task unrelated to ability, the stereotyped group performs as well as a nonstereotyped comparison group. Thus, on the *same* test, we can see different levels of performance, depending on the potency of the stereotype threat.

The graph at right illustrates the pattern with data from one of Steele's studies of black and white college students who were given a difficult verbal test. Half the subjects were randomly assigned to a condition in which they were told, before taking the test, that the test was diagnostic of their general intellectual ability; the other half were told that the test was just a laboratory exercise and had nothing to do with general ability.

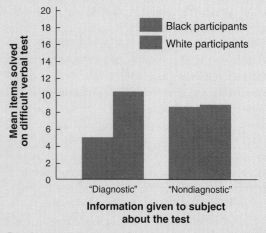

(*Source:* From "A threat in the air: How stereotypes shape intellectual identity and performance" by Claude M. Steele, *American psychologist,* 52 (June 1997), p. 621, Fig. 2. © 1992 American Psychological Association. Reprinted within guidelines of the American Psychological Association and by permission of the author.)

You can see that the black students' scores were significantly lower when stereotype threat was high but were equal to those of whites when the threat was low.

The general psychological principle underlying Steele's hypothesis is the well-established inverted U-shaped relationship between anxiety and performance. That is, performance on any kind of test or activity is best when a person is somewhat anxious; when anxiety rises above that middle level, however, performance declines. Steele is proposing that knowing that you are expected to do poorly on some test or task raises your level of anxiety to the point where your performance suffers. In this way, stereotype threat contributes to the observed lower IQ and achievement test scores among African-American children and adolescents.

racial differences in intellectual performance. First, Asian and Asian-American students typically test 3 to 6 points higher on IQ tests and do consistently better on achievement tests (especially math and science tests) than do Caucasian children (Geary, 1996; Geary et al., 1996; Stevenson et al., 1990; Sue & Okazaki, 1990; Williams & Ceci, 1997). More troubling for researchers and theorists is the finding (discussed at length by Herrnstein and Murray) that in the United States, African-American children consistently score lower than Euro-American children on standard measures of intelligence. This difference, which is on the order of 12 IQ points, is *not* found on infant tests of intelligence or on measures of infant habituation rate (Fagan & Singer, 1983), but it becomes apparent by the time children are 2 or 3 years old (Brody, 1992; Peoples et al., 1995). There is some indication that the size of the IQ difference between black and white children declined during the 1970s and 1980s and may now be less than 10 points (Neisser et al., 1996; Williams & Ceci, 1997). Yet a noticeable difference persists.

Some scientists, including the authors of *The Bell Curve,* while acknowledging that the environments of the two groups are, on average, substantially different, nonetheless argue that the IQ score difference must reflect some genetic differences between the races (Jensen, 1980). Other scientists, even granting that IQ is highly heritable, point out that the 12-point difference falls well within the presumed reaction range of IQ. They emphasize that there are sufficiently large differences in the environments in which black and white children are typically reared to account for the average difference in score (Brody, 1992). Black children in the United States are more likely to be born with low birth weight, more likely to suffer from subnutrition, more likely to have high blood levels of lead, and less likely to be read to or provided with a wide range of intellectual stimulation. Each of these environmental variations is known to be linked to lower IQ scores.

Cultural Variations. Cultural differences also clearly contribute to the observed differences, as black psychologists have long pointed out (e.g., Ogbu, 1994). We can see such differences at work in the way children from different cultures respond to the testing situation itself. For example, in a study of adopted black children, Moore (1986) found that those who had been reared in white families (and thus imbued with the majority culture) not only had higher IQ scores than those adopted into black families (117 versus 103) but also approached the IQ-testing situation quite differently. They stayed more focused on the task and were more likely to try some task even if they didn't think they could do it. Black children adopted into middle-class black families did not show this pattern of persistence and effort. They asked for help more often and gave up more easily when faced with a difficult task. When Moore then observed each adoptive mother teaching her child several tasks, he could see parallel differences. The white mothers were more encouraging and less likely to give the child the answer than were the black mothers.

Findings like these persuade me that the IQ difference we see is primarily a reflection of the fact that the tests, and the schools, are designed by the majority culture to promote a particular form of intellectual activity (Sternberg's analytical intelligence) and that many black or other minority families rear their children in ways that do not promote or emphasize this particular set of skills. In fact, Sternberg has argued that in some black subcultures it is practical intelligence that is particularly emphasized and trained (Sternberg & Suben, 1986).

In a similar vein, Harold Stevenson and others have argued that the differences between Asian and U.S. children in performance on mathematics achievement tests result not from genetic differences in capacity, but from differences in cultural emphasis on the importance of academic achievement, the number of hours spent on homework, and the quality of math instruction in the schools (Chang & Murray, 1995; Geary, 1996; Schneider et al., 1994; Stevenson & Lee, 1990; Stigler et al., 1987)—a possibility I've explored in the Cultures and Contexts box on page 220.

Although we may be able to account for such racial differences in IQ scores or achievement test performance by appealing to the concept of reaction range, to stereotype threat (discussed in the preceding Research Report), or to cultural or subcultural variations, that fact does not make the differences disappear, nor does it make them trivial. But it may put such findings into a less explosive framework.

Sex Differences

In contrast, comparisons of total IQ test scores for boys and girls do *not* reveal consistent differences. It is only when we break down the total score into several separate skills that some patterns of sex differences emerge. On average, elementary school girls are slightly better at verbal tasks and at arithmetic computation. Because computation skills make up a large portion of math achievement tests in these early years, girls typically get higher scores on such tests through elementary school, and they also get better grades in school. Boys, on the other hand, are somewhat better at numerical reasoning, a difference that becomes clearer on tests in high school, when reasoning

Critical Thinking

Some psychologists have argued that IQ tests and achievement tests are biased against blacks and members of other minority groups. What kind of research results would demonstrate such bias? What kind would argue against it?

Cultures and Contexts
How Asian Teachers Teach Math and Science So Effectively

One highly significant contributor to the observed Asian/U.S. differences in science and mathematics achievement may be the different ways school is taught in these several cultures. The clearest information comes from research by James Stigler and Harold Stevenson (Stevenson, 1994; Stigler & Stevenson, 1991). After observing in 120 classrooms in Japan, Taiwan, and the United States, they are convinced that Asian teachers have devised a particularly effective mode of teaching both mathematics and science.

Japanese and Chinese teachers approach mathematics and science by crafting a series of "master lessons," each organized around a single theme or idea. These lessons are like good stories, with a beginning, a middle, and an end. They frequently begin with a problem posed for the students. Here is one example from a fifth-grade class in Japan:

> The teacher walks in carrying a large paper bag full of clinking glass. . . . She begins to pull items out of the bag, placing them, one-by-one, on her desk. She removes a pitcher and a vase. A beer bottle evokes laughter and surprise. She soon has six containers lined up on her desk. . . . The teacher, looking thoughtfully at the containers, poses a question: "I wonder which one would hold the most water?" . . . the teacher calls on different students to give their guesses: "the pitcher," . . . "the teapot." The teacher stands aside and ponders: "Some of you said one thing, others said something different. . . . How can we know who is correct?" (Stigler & Stevenson, 1991, p. 14)

The lesson continues as the students agree on a plan for determining which container will hold the most. In such lessons, students are frequently divided into small groups, each assigned to part of the problem. These small groups then report back to the class as a whole. At the end of the lesson, the teacher reviews the original problem and what the students have learned. In this particular case, the children have learned not only something about measurement but also something about the process of hypothesis testing.

In U.S. classrooms, in contrast, teachers rarely spend 30 or 60 minutes on a single coherent math or science lesson involving the whole class of children and a single topic. Instead, they shift often from one topic to another during a single math or science "lesson." They might do a brief bit on addition, then talk about measurement and then about telling time, and then shift back to addition. Asian teachers shift *activities* in order to provide variety, such as shifting from lecture format to small-group work; U.S. teachers shift *topics* for the same purpose.

Stigler and Stevenson also found striking differences in the amount of time teachers actually spend leading instruction for the whole class. In the U.S. classrooms they observed, group instruction occurred only 49 percent of the time; it occurred 74 percent of the time in Japan and 91 percent of the time in Taiwan.

Stigler and Stevenson point out that the Asian type of teaching is not new to Western teachers. U.S. educators frequently recommend precisely such techniques. "What the Japanese and Chinese examples demonstrate so compellingly is that when widely implemented, such practices can produce extraordinary outcomes" (p. 45).

---

problems make up a larger portion of math exams. For example, on the math portion of the Scholastic Aptitude Test (SAT), the average score for boys is consistently higher than the average score for girls, a difference that has persisted over the past three decades among students in the United States (Brody, 1992; Byrnes & Takahira, 1993; Halpern, 1997; Jacklin, 1989) and that has been found in studies in Europe and Asia as well (Schweingruber, 1997).

Two other differences are also still found regularly. First, among children who test as gifted in mathematics, boys are considerably more common (Benbow, 1988; Lubinski & Benbow, 1992). Second, on tests of spatial visualization, like the ones illustrated in Figure 7.5, boys have somewhat higher average scores. On measures of mental rotation, illustrated by item (c) in the figure, the sex difference is substantial and becomes larger with age (Eagly, 1995; Voyer et al., 1995).

I want to point out that even on tests of mental rotation the two distributions overlap. That is, some girls and women are good at this type of task while some boys and men are not. Still, the average difference is quite large. The fact that girls score lower on such tests does not mean that no women are qualified for occupations that demand

Figure 7.5

Three illustrations of spatial ability tests. (a) *Spatial visualization.* The figure at the top represents a square piece of paper being folded. A hole is punched through all the thicknesses of the folded paper. Which figure shows what the paper looks like when it is unfolded? (b) *Spatial orientation.* Compare the three cubes on the right with the one on the left. No letter appears on more than one face of a given cube. Which of the three cubes on the right could be a different view of the cube on the left? (c) *Mental rotation.* In each pair, can the three-dimensional objects be made congruent by rotation?

(*Source:* D. Halpern, *Sex differences in cognitive abilities,* Figures 3.1 and 3.2, pp. 50 and 52. © 1986 by Lawrence Erlbaum Associates, Inc. By permission of the publisher and author.)

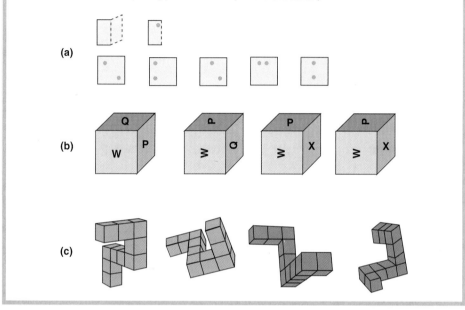

such skill, such as architecture or some kinds of engineering; it does mean that fewer girls or young women will be able to meet the training requirements for such jobs.

Where might such differences come from? The explanatory options should be familiar by now. Biological influences have been most often argued in the case of sex differences in spatial abilities, where there may be both genetic differences and—more speculatively—differences in brain functioning resulting from prenatal variations in hormones (Newcombe & Baenninger, 1989). These initial differences in potential ability may then be shaped further by sex-related differences in play activities in childhood and school experiences in high school. Young boys play more with construction toys,

In elementary school, girls get better grades and higher scores on achievement tests than do boys. What explanations can you think of for such a difference?

for example, and high school boys are more likely to take the kind of math and science classes that will strengthen spatial abilities. Girls who are very good at spatial skills seem to share both these characteristics: They are likely to have inherited some potential for spatial skill, and they have been given (or have chosen) many opportunities to develop that skill (Casey, 1996).

In contrast, more purely environmental explanations have been prominent in discussions of the sex differences in mathematical or verbal reasoning. Especially in the case of mathematics, we have considerable evidence that girls' and boys' skills are systematically shaped by a series of environmental factors characteristic of U.S. culture:

- Boys take more math courses than girls do, not primarily because boys have higher math aptitude but because they have more positive attitudes about mathematics (Eccles & Jacobs, 1986). When the number of math courses girls and boys have taken is held constant, the sex difference in math test scores becomes much smaller.

- Parental attitudes about mathematics are markedly different for boys and girls. Parents are more likely to attribute a daughter's success in mathematics to effort or good teaching; they attribute poor performance by a girl to lack of ability. In contrast, parents attribute a boy's success to ability and his failure to lack of application (Holloway & Hess, 1985; Parsons et al., 1982).

- Girls and boys have different experiences in math classes. In elementary school, teachers pay more attention to boys during math instruction (and more attention to girls during reading instruction). In high school, math teachers direct more of their questions and comments to boys, even when girls are outspoken in class.

Critical Thinking

As you can see, a lot of effort has been spent trying to discover or explain possible sex differences in mathematical ability. What are the practical implications either way?

The cumulative effect of these differences in expectation and treatment show up in high school, when sex differences on standardized math tests usually become evident. In part, then, the sex differences in math achievement test scores appear to be perpetuated by subtle family and school influences on children's attitudes (as well as by stereotype threat). Whether these differences can explain the greater percentage of boys than girls who show real giftedness in mathematics is not so clear. One possibility is that because tests of mathematical ability involve at least some items that require mental rotation ability, very high scores on such tests are less likely for girls. Indeed, one recent study (Casey et al., 1995) shows that when mental rotation ability is subtracted out, the sex difference in SAT math scores among high-ability groups disappears. Still, this question—like a number of the questions I've touched on in this chapter—remains hotly debated.

The Measurement of Intelligence: A Last Look

One of the questions that students often ask at about this point is whether, given all the factors that can affect a test score, it is worth bothering with IQ tests at all. I think that these tests do assess some important aspects of children's intellectual performance and that they can be helpful in identifying children who may have difficulties in school or gifted children who would benefit from special programs. But it is worth emphasizing again that IQ tests do *not* measure a lot of other things we may be interested in, including the other two types of intelligence Sternberg describes. An IQ test is a specialized tool, and like many such tools, it has a fairly narrow range of appropriate use. I don't want to throw out this tool, but we have to keep its limitations firmly in mind when we use it.

Individual Differences in Information Processing

Another way of looking at individual differences in cognitive skill or power is in terms of variations in information processing speed or efficiency. In Chapter 6 I talked about developmental changes in information processing strategies. Could we use some of the same concepts to understand better just what it is we are measuring on an IQ test? Do high- and low-IQ children or adults use different cognitive processes? Do they differ primarily in processing speed? All these are questions we can address within an information processing framework.

Speed of Information Processing

Since it is becoming clear that increases in speed or efficiency of processing underlie age changes in cognitive skills, it makes sense to hypothesize that differences in speed may also underlie individual differences in IQ scores. A number of different investigators have found just such a link: Subjects with faster reaction times or speed of performance on a variety of simple tasks also have higher average IQ scores on standard tests (Fry & Hale, 1996; Vernon, 1987). We even have a few studies in which speed of processing has been directly linked to central nervous system functioning and to IQ. For example, it is now possible to measure the speed of conduction of impulses along individual nerves, such as nerves in the arm. Philip Vernon (1993; Vernon & Mori, 1992) has found that such a measure correlates about .45 with IQ test scores.

Most of this research has been done with adults, but a link between speed of reaction time and IQ scores has also been found in a few studies with children (Keating et al., 1985; Saccuzzo et al., 1994). Furthermore, there are some pretty clear indications that such speed-of-processing differences may be built-in at birth. Indeed, the link between infant habituation or recognition memory and later IQ scores—a finding I talked about in Chapter 5—seems to be primarily a result of basic variations in speed of processing (Rose & Feldman, 1997).

Other IQ/Processing Links

Other researchers have explored the connections between IQ and information processing by comparing the information processing strategies used by normal-IQ and retarded children.

Judy DeLoache has compared the searching strategies of groups of 2-year-olds who either were developing normally or showed delayed development (Deloache & Brown, 1987). When the search task was very simple, such as looking for a toy hidden in a distinctive location in a room, the two groups did not differ in search strategies or skill. But when the experimenter surreptitiously moved the toy before the child was allowed to search, normally developing children were able to search in alternative, plausible places, such as in nearby locations; delayed children simply persisted in looking in the place where they had seen the toy hidden. They either could not change strategies or did not have alternative, more complex strategies in their repertoires.

Other research underlines this difference in the flexibility of strategy use. In several studies, Joseph Campione and Ann Brown (1984; Campione et al., 1985) have found that both retarded and normal-IQ children could learn to solve problems like items (a), (b), and (c) in Figure 7.6 (p. 224), but the retarded children could not transfer this learning to a more complex problem of the same general type, like item (d) in the figure, while normal-IQ children could. Both sets of studies suggest that flexibility of use of any given strategy may be another key dimension of individual differences in intelligence.

Cognitive Development: Putting the Three Approaches Together

The information processing approach offers us some important bridges between the power and structure theories of intelligence in children. It now looks as if some basic, inborn strategies exist (such as noting differences or similarities). It is also clear that these strategies change during the early years of life, with more complex strategies or

Figure 7.6

For panels (a) through (d) the subject must figure out the "system" in each set and then describe what pattern should go in the empty box in the bottom right-hand corner. Panel (a) shows rotation; panel (b) shows addition of two elements; panel (c) shows subtraction. The figure in panel (d) is harder because the subject must apply *two* principles at once, in this case both addition and rotation rules. Retarded children could do problems like (a), (b), and (c) as well as normal-IQ children, but they did much more poorly on problems like (d).

(*Source:* Campione et al., 1985, Figure 1, p. 302, and Figure 4, p. 306.)

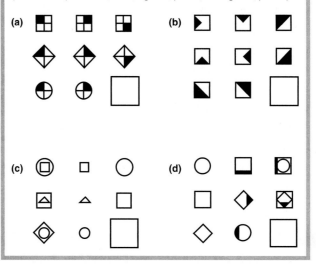

rules emerging and old strategies used more flexibly. Plain old experience is a key part of the process of change. The more a child plays with blocks, the better she will be at organizing and classifying blocks; the more a person plays chess, the better he will be at seeing and remembering relationships among pieces on the board. So some of the changes that Piaget thought of as changes in underlying structure are instead specific task learning. But there seems to be some structural change as well, such as the emergence of new strategies, particularly metacognitive strategies.

Individual differences in what we normally think of as intelligence can then be conceived of as resulting both from inborn differences in the speed or efficiency of the basic processes (differences in the hardware, perhaps) and from differences in expertise or experience. The child with a slower or less efficient processing system is going to move through all the various steps and stages more slowly; he will *use* the experience he has less efficiently or effectively and may never develop as complete a range of strategies as does the initially quicker child. But when this less innately gifted child has sufficient expertise in some area, that specialized knowledge can compensate for the lower IQ.

This point is nicely illustrated in a study of expertise done in Germany (Schneider & Bjorklund, 1992). School-age children who were very knowledgeable about soccer (experts) had better recall of soccer-related lists than did nonexperts. But high-IQ novices did as well as low-IQ experts on these same tasks. So rich knowledge in some area can compensate somewhat for lower IQ, but it does not create equality. High-IQ experts are still going to be better than medium- or low-IQ experts in any given area.

The information processing approach may also have some real practical applications. The studies of recognition memory in infancy, for example, may give us a way to identify retarded children very early in life or to sort out from among low-birth-weight infants those who seem at particular risk for later problems. By identifying the key differences between retarded and nonretarded children (or between brighter and less bright children), we may also be able to identify specific kinds of training that would be useful for a retarded child or for a child with a learning disability.

I do not want to wax too rhapsodic about the information processing approach. It is well to remember that we do not yet have any tests of information processing ability that could realistically replace the careful use of IQ tests in schools and clinics, although a few psychologists believe that a clinically useful biological measure of intelligence will be available within several decades (Matarazzo, 1992). Nor are the sequential theories of information processing development far enough along yet to explain all the differences we see between infants, preschoolers, and older children in performance on various Piagetian tasks. In short, information processing is an important, integrative addition to our understanding of cognitive development, but it does not replace all the other approaches.

Summary

1. When we study the development of "intelligence," we need to distinguish between measures of intellectual power and measures of intellectual structure. IQ tests tap individual differences in intellectual power.

2. The most commonly used individually administered tests for children are the current revisions of the Stanford-Binet and the Wechsler Intelligence Scales for Children (WISC).

3. All current IQ tests compare a child's performance to that of others her or his age. Scores above 100 represent better-than-average performance; scores below 100 represent poorer-than-average performance.

4. Both IQ tests and school achievement tests measure a child's performance, not capacity or underlying competence. Achievement tests, however, test much more specific school-related information than do IQ tests.

5. Criterion-referenced tests, which compare a student's performance against some specific criterion such as the ability to write clearly, have become more common lately as an alternative to norm-referenced achievement tests.

6. IQ scores are quite stable from one testing to the next, and this becomes more and more true the older the child gets. But individual children's scores still may fluctuate or shift 20 or 30 points or more over the course of childhood.

7. IQ test scores are quite good predictors of school performance and years of education, a correlation that gives one piece of evidence for the validity of the tests.

8. IQ tests do not measure many other facets of intellectual functioning in which we might be interested, including what Sternberg calls creative and practical intelligence.

9. Studies of identical twins and of adopted children clearly show a substantial genetic influence on measured IQ scores. Most psychologists agree that approximately half the variation in individual IQ scores can be attributed to heredity.

10. The remaining half is attributed to environmental variation: Poor children consistently test lower than do children from middle-class families; children whose families provide appropriate play materials and encourage the child's intellectual development score higher on IQ tests.

11. Environmental influence is also shown by increases in test performance or school success among children who have been in special enriched preschool or infant day-care programs and by children who attend school longer.

12. One way to understand the interaction of heredity and environment is with the concept of reaction range. Heredity determines some range of potential; environment determines the level of performance within that range.

13. A consistent difference of about 12 points on IQ tests is found between African-American and Caucasian children in the United States. It seems most likely that this difference is due to environmental and cultural differences between the two groups, such as differences in health and prenatal care, and in the type of intellectual skills trained and emphasized at home. Stereotype threat may also play some role in lowering test scores.

14. Males and females do not differ on total IQ test scores, but they do

differ in some subskills. The largest differences are on measures of spatial reasoning, on which males are consistently better.

15. Another way to look at individual differences is through the lens of information processing. Higher-IQ individuals, for example, appear to process information more quickly and to apply strategies or knowledge more broadly.

Key Terms

achievement test Test designed to assess a child's learning of specific material taught in school, such as spelling or arithmetic computation; typically given to all children in designated grades. **p. 202**

analytical intelligence One of three types of intelligence in Sternberg's triarchic theory of intelligence; that type of intelligence typically measured on IQ tests, including analytic thinking, remembering facts, and organizing information. **p. 207**

Bayley Scales of Infant Development The best-known and most widely used test of infant "intelligence," revised most recently in 1993. **p. 202**

competence The level of skill displayed by a person under ideal or perfect circumstances. It is not possible to measure competence directly. **p. 202**

creative intelligence One of three types of intelligence described by Sternberg in his triarchic theory of intelligence; includes insight and the ability to see new relationships among events or experiences. **p. 207**

cumulative deficit Any difference between groups in IQ (or achievement test) scores that becomes larger over time. **p. 210**

emotional intelligence A type of intelligence proposed by Daniel Goleman, including "abilities such as being able to motivate oneself and persist in the face of frustrations; to control impulses and delay gratification; to regulate one's moods and

keep distress from swamping the ability to think; to empathize and to hope" (1995b, p. 34). **p. 208**

intelligence Defined in various ways by different psychologists. Most definitions include the ability to reason abstractly, the ability to profit from experience, and the ability to adapt to varying environmental contexts. **p. 199**

intelligence quotient (IQ) Originally defined in terms of a child's mental age and chronological age, IQ scores are now computed by comparing a child's performance with that of other children of the same chronological age. **p. 199**

mental age Term used by Binet and Simon and Terman in the early calculation of IQ scores; the age level of IQ test items the child can successfully pass. When compared to the child's chronological age, allows calculation of an IQ score. **p. 199**

performance The behavior shown by a person under real-life rather than perfect or ideal circumstances. Even when we are interested in competence, all we can ever measure is performance. **p. 202**

performance test A new category of criterion-referenced test used in some school systems today, in which students are required to demonstrate actual skills, such as writing, performing experiments, or mathematical reasoning, with performance assessed against a specified criterion. **p. 204**

practical intelligence One of three types of intelligence in Sternberg's triarchic theory of intelligence; often also called "street smarts," this type of intelligence includes skill in adapting to an environment and in adapting an environment to one's own needs. **p. 207**

reaction range Term used by some psychologists for the range of possible outcomes (phenotypes) on some variable, given basic genetic patterning (genotype). In the case of IQ scores, the reaction range is estimated at 20 to 25 points. **p. 217**

social class Term widely used to describe broad variations in economic and social positions within any given society. Four broad groups are most often described: upper class, middle class, working class, and lower class (also called poverty level). For an individual family, the designation is based on the income, occupation, and education of the adults in the household. **p. 209**

Stanford-Binet The best-known U.S. intelligence test. It was written by Lewis Terman and his associates on the basis of the first tests by Binet and Simon. **p. 199**

triarchic theory of intelligence A theory advanced by Robert Sternberg, proposing the existence of three types of intelligence: analytical, creative, and practical. **p. 206**

WISC-III The most recent revision of the Wechsler Intelligence Scale for Children, a well-known IQ test developed in the United States that includes both verbal and performance (nonverbal) subtests. **p. 201**

Suggested Readings

Brody, N. (1992). *Intelligence* (2nd ed.). San Diego, CA: Academic Press. Dense and detailed, but the best current source I know for further information about all aspects of this subject.

Elliott, R. (1988). Tests, abilities, race, and conflict. *Intelligence, 12*, 333–350. An especially clear and fascinating discussion of the several lawsuits about the use of IQ tests in the schools.

Neisser, U., Boodoo, G., Bouchard, T. J., Jr., Boykin, A. W., Brody, N., Ceci, S. J., Halpern, D. F., Loehlin, J. C., Perloff, R., Sternberg, R. J., & Urbina, S. (1996). Intelligence: Knowns and unknowns. *American Psychologist, 51*, 77–101. A remarkable paper prepared as a collaborative effort by nearly all the leading experts on intelligence, designed in part as a response to *The Bell Curve*.

These scientists were asked by the American Psychological Association to prepare a summary of the basic, agreed-upon facts about intelligence and its measurement. The paper is dense, but it includes good explanations of most of the key concepts. It is a wonderful source for further study.

The Development of Language

8

A friend of mine listened one morning at breakfast while her 6-year-old and 3-year-old daughters had the following conversation about the relative dangers of forgetting to feed the goldfish versus overfeeding the goldfish:

6-year-old: It's worse to forget to feed them.

3-year-old: No, it's badder to feed them too much.

6-year-old: You don't say badder, you say worser.

3-year-old: But it's baddest to give them too much food.

6-year-old: No it's not. It's worsest to forget to feed them.

Most of us are amused and charmed when we listen to children's language like this. It is so delightfully creative and unexpected, and yet completely clear. Linguists have also learned an enormous amount about children's language by studying "errors" like *baddest* or *worsest*—just as Piaget learned an enormous amount about the child's thinking by studying children's "wrong" answers. Yet one of the really remarkable things about language is that children make so few errors of this kind. Out of the enormously complex set of sounds they hear in the language of those around them, children somehow learn to speak their native tongue with fluency and accuracy within only a few years. At 6 or 8 months, a baby will babble a few sounds; by 18 months, the child will probably be using twenty or thirty separate words; and by 3 years, children construct long and complex sentences, like those of the 3-year-old in the conversation about the goldfish. Parents usually find this whole sequence fun to listen to, but most of us don't spend a lot of time worrying about just how a child manages all this.

For psychologists and linguists, though, the child's rapid and skillful acquisition of language has remained an enduring puzzle. Is some kind of language-learning faculty built into the organism? Is the child "taught" language in some direct way? Does the child "figure it out" on the basis of what he hears?

In attempting to answer such questions, the vast majority of linguists have looked at changes in both grammar (which the linguists call **syntax**) and word meaning (called **semantics**). Lately, some attempts have also been made to explain differences in the rate of language development from one child to the next and differences in individual children's style of language learning. Before I can explore any of these questions, I need to go back a step.

What Is Language Anyway?

What do we mean by *language?* What are we trying to explain? As most linguists use the term, it has several key features:

1. It is an "arbitrary system of *symbols*" (Brown, 1965, p. 246). Words (or gestures) *stand for* things, but because the particular combination of sounds (or gestures) used to stand for some object, event, or relationship varies from one language to another, the symbols are arbitrary.

2. It is *rule-governed*. Every language has certain rules for stringing together individual symbols, such as rules for the order of words in sentences; every language also has rules for creating new words, such as the rules for creating comparatives and superlatives (like *nice, nicer, nicest*), past tenses, or plurals.

3. Within those rules, language is *creative*. Speakers of a language combine symbols in new ways to create new meanings. When you talk, you are not restricted to some repertoire of sentences you have heard and learned; you create sentences according to your need at the moment, following the rules of your language.

Thus, language is not just a collection of sounds. Very young babies make several different sounds, but we do not consider that they are using language since they do not appear to use those sounds to *refer* to things or events (that is, they do not use the sounds as symbols), and they do not combine individual sounds into different orders to create varying meaning. So far as we know, for example, the meaning does not change if a 6-month-old says "kikiki bababa" versus "bababa kikiki."

Some other animals, most notably primates like chimpanzees and possibly other mammals like dolphins, can also learn to use sound or gestural systems in the symbolic way that we define as language. Chimps, for example, can learn to use sign language or point to sequences of symbols, even creating new combinations of such symbols. Like human children, chimps also understand a good deal more than they can express, and they can follow quite complex verbal requests. However, in most cases it takes a good deal of effort to teach them to use expressive language in creative ways (Savage-Rumbaugh et al., 1993). In contrast, as Flavell puts it, "Draconian measures would be needed to *prevent* most children from learning to talk" (1985, p. 248). And as any parent can tell you, once they learn, it is virtually impossible to shut them up!

The developmental process in infants and young children, from prelanguage sounds and gestures to language, follows a common set of steps.

Before the First Word: The Prelinguistic Phase

The process actually begins in the months before the baby speaks his first word, a period called the **prelinguistic phase.**

Early Perception of Language

Let's start with the basic perceptual skills. A baby cannot learn language until he can hear the individual sounds as distinct. Just how early can he do that? Recall from Chapter 5 that babies are born with, or very soon develop, remarkably good ability to discriminate speech sounds. By 1 or 2 months they pay attention to and can tell the difference between many individual letter sounds; within a few more months they clearly can discriminate among syllables or words. They also have figured out that these speech sounds are matched by the speaker's mouth movements.

Researchers have also found that babies in these early months are sensitive to the intonational and stress patterns of the speech they are listening to. You'll remember from Chapter 5, for example, that 8-month fetuses respond differently to familiar than to unfamiliar rhymes (DeCasper et al., 1994). This sensitivity to stress and pattern becomes even more evident in the early months of life. For example, Anne Fernald (1993) has found that 5-month-olds will smile more when they hear tapes of adults saying something in an approving tone than when they speak in a prohibiting tone, whether

Chimps like Nim Chimpsky can fairly easily learn signs for individual objects or actions and can understand and follow quite complex instructions. Here he signs "I see."

the words are in Italian, German, or English. Even more impressive is a study showing that by 9 months of age, babies listening to English prefer to listen to words that have the typical English stress pattern of stressing the first syllable (such as *falter, comet,* or *gentle*) rather than those that stress the second syllable (e.g., *comply* or *assign*) (Jusczyk et al., 1993). Presumably, babies listening to other languages would come to prefer listening to whatever stress pattern was typical of that language. All this research shows that from very early—from birth and perhaps even before birth—the baby is paying attention to crucial features of the language she hears, such as stress and intonation.

Early Sounds

This early perceptual skill is not matched right away by much skill in producing sounds. From birth to about 1 month of age, the most common sound an infant makes is a cry, although infants also make other fussing, gurgling, and satisfied sounds. This sound repertoire expands at about 1 or 2 months with the addition of some laughing and **cooing** vowel sounds, like *uuuuuu*. Sounds like this are usually signals of pleasure in babies and may show quite a lot of variation in tone, running up and down in volume or pitch.

Consonant sounds appear only at about 6 or 7 months, when for the first time the baby has the muscle control needed to combine a consonant sound with a vowel sound. Between 6 and 9 months, we hear a rapid increase in the amount of vowel-consonant combinations. This type of vocalization, called **babbling,** makes up about half of babies' noncrying sounds from about 6 to 12 months of age (Mitchell & Kent, 1990).

Much of the early babbling involves repetitive strings of the same syllables, such as *dadadada* or *nananana* or *yayayaya*. Even in these early months, though, we also hear a form of babbling that is even more like conventional speech, called **jargon** or *variegated babbling,* in which the baby strings together sets of different syllables, often with sentence-like inflections (Bloom, 1993).

Adults find babbling delightful to listen to; Lois Bloom (1998) also points out that these new sound combinations are much easier for adults to imitate than are the earlier baby sounds, because babbling has more of the rhythm and sound of adult speech. The imitative game that may then develop between parent and child is not only a pleasure for both; it may also be helpful to the baby in learning language.

Babbling is an important part of the preparation for spoken language in other ways as well. For one thing, we now know that infants' babbling gradually acquires some of the intonational pattern of the language they are hearing—a process Elizabeth Bates refers to as "learning the tune before the words" (Bates et al., 1987). At the very least, infants do seem to develop at least two such "tunes" in their babbling. Babbling with a rising intonation at the end of a string of sounds seems to signal a desire for a response; a falling intonation requires no response.

A second important thing about babbling is that when babies first start babbling, they typically babble all kinds of sounds, including some that are not part of the language they are hearing. Then, beginning at about 9 or 10 months, their sound repertoire gradually begins to shift toward the set of sounds they are listening to, with the nonheard sounds dropping out (Oller, 1981)—a pattern that clearly parallels the Werker findings you saw in Figure 5.6 (p. 148) and that matches what we now know about early synaptic development and pruning. Findings like these do not tell us that babbling is *necessary* for language development, but they certainly make it look as if babbling is part of a connected developmental process that begins at birth.

Early Gestures

Another part of that connected developmental process appears to be a kind of gestural language that develops at around 9 or 10 months. At this age we first see babies "demanding" or "asking" for things by using gestures or combinations of gestures and sound. A 10-month-old baby who apparently wants you to hand her a favorite toy may

Critical Thinking

Why do you suppose babies babble? Do you think babbling is just the vocal equivalent of rhythmic foot kicking, or can you think of some other purpose it might serve?

Research Report
Early Gestural "Language" in the Children of Deaf Parents

Deaf children of deaf parents are a particularly interesting group to study if we want to understand language development. The children do not hear oral language, but they are nevertheless exposed to *language*—sign language. Do these children show the same early steps in language development as do hearing children, only using gestural language?

The answer seems to be "yes." Deaf children show a kind of "sign babbling" between about 7 and 11 months of age, much as hearing children babble sounds in these same months. Then at 8 or 9 months of age, deaf children begin using simple gestures, such as pointing, which is just about the same age that we see such gestures in hearing babies of hearing parents. At about 12 months of age, deaf babies seem to display their first *referential* signs—that is, signs in which a gesture appears to stand for some object or event, such as signaling that they want a drink by making a motion like a cup being brought to the mouth (Petitto, 1988).

Folven and Bonvillian (1991) have studied an equally interesting group—hearing children of deaf parents. These babies are exposed to sign language from their parents and to hearing language from their contacts with others in their world, including TV, teachers, other relatives, and playmates. In the small sample of nine babies these researchers observed, the first sign appeared at an average age of 8 months, the first referential sign at 12.6 months, and the first spoken word at 12.2 months. What is striking here is that the first referential signs and the first spoken words appeared at such similar times and that the spoken words appeared at such a completely normal time, despite the fact that these children of deaf parents hear comparatively little spoken language.

This marked similarity in the sequence and timing of the steps of early language in the deaf and the hearing child provides strong support for the argument that the baby is somehow primed to learn "language" in some form, be it spoken or gestural.

stretch and reach for it, opening and closing her hand, making whining sounds or other heartrending noises. There is no mistaking the meaning. At about the same age, babies will enter into those gestural games much loved by parents, like "patty-cake," "soooo-big," or "wave bye-bye" (Bates et al., 1987).

Receptive Language

Interestingly, we see the first signs that the infant understands the meaning of individual words spoken to her (which linguists call **receptive language**) also at about 9 or 10 months. Larry Fenson and his colleagues (1994) asked hundreds of mothers about their babies' understanding of various words. The mothers of 10-month-olds identified an average of about 30 words their infants understood; by 13 months, that number was up to nearly 100 words. Since infants of 9 to 13 months typically speak few, if any, individual words, findings like these make it clear that receptive language comes before **expressive language.** Children understand before they can speak. Babies as young as 9 or 10 months are already actively learning the language they are listening to. Not only can they understand some simple instructions, but they can benefit from being exposed to a rich array of language.

Adding up these bits of information, we can see that a whole series of changes seem to come together at 9 or 10 months: the beginning of meaningful gestures, the "drift" of babbling toward the heard language sounds, imitative gestural games, and the first comprehension of individual words. It is as if the child now understands something about the process of communication and is intending to communicate to the adult.

The First Words

Somewhere in the midst of all the babbling, the first words appear, typically at about 12 or 13 months (Fenson et al., 1994). Although the baby's first word is an event that parents eagerly await, it is actually fairly easy to miss. A *word,* as linguists usually define it,

What do you think this young fellow is "saying" with his pointing gesture? Before they speak their first words, babies successfully use gestures and body language in consistent ways to communicate meaning.

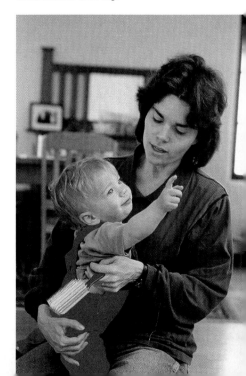

Table 8.1

Brenda's Vocabulary at 14 and 19 Months

14 Months	19 Months*		
aw u (I want, I don't want)	baby	nice	boat
nau (no)	bear	orange	bone
d di (daddy, baby)	bed	pencil	climb
d yu (down, doll)	big	write	checkers
nene (liquid food)	blue	paper	corder
e (yes)	Brenda	pen	cut
ada (another, other)	cookie	see	I do
	daddy	shoe	jump
	eat	sick	met
	at	swim	Pogo
	(hor)sie	tape	Ralph
	mama	walk	you too
	mommy	wowow	

Source: R. Scollon, *Conversations with a one-year-old.* Honolulu: University of Hawaii Press, 1976, pp. 47, 57–58.

*Brenda did not actually pronounce all these words the way an adult would. I have given the adult version since that is easier to read.

is any sound or set of sounds that is used consistently to refer to some thing, action, or quality. But it can be *any* sound; it doesn't have to be a sound that matches words the adults are using. Brenda, a little girl studied by Ronald Scollon (1976), used the sound *nene* as one of her first words. It seemed to mean primarily liquid food, since she used it for "milk," "juice," and "bottle," but she also used it to refer to "mother" and "sleep." (You can see some of Brenda's other early words in the left-hand column of Table 8.1.)

Often, a child's earliest words are used only in one or two specific situations and in the presence of many cues. The child may say "doggie" or "bow-wow" only to such promptings as "How does the doggie go?" or "What's that?" Typically, this early word learning is very slow, requiring many repetitions for each word. In the first six months of word usage (roughly between 12 and 18 months of age), children may learn to say as few as 30 words. Most linguists (e.g., Nelson, 1985) have concluded that in this earliest word-use phase, the child learns each word as something connected to a set of specific contexts. The toddler has apparently not yet grasped that words are *symbolic*—that they refer to objects or events regardless of context.

The Naming Explosion

Somewhere between 16 and 24 months, after the early period of very slow word learning, most children begin to add new words rapidly, as if they have figured out that things have names. According to Fenson's very large cross-sectional study, based on mothers' reports, the average 16-month-old has a speaking vocabulary of about 50 words—a shift you can see illustrated in young Brenda's 19-month vocabulary in Table 8.1; by 24 months this has multiplied more than sixfold to about 320 words (Fenson et

Figure 8.1

Each line in this figure represents the vocabulary growth of one of the children followed by Goldfield and Reznick in their longitudinal study.

(*Source:* B.A. Goldfield and J. S. Reznick, Figure 3, p. 177, "Early lexical acquistion: Rate, content, and the vocabulary spurt," *Journal of child language*, 17 (1990), 171–183. By permission of Cambridge University Press.)

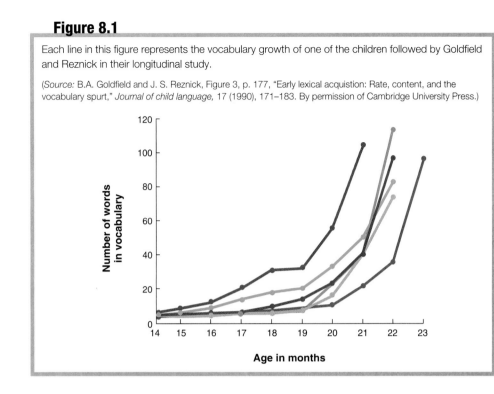

al., 1994). A parallel study in Italy by Elizabeth Bates and her colleagues (Caselli et al., 1997) shows that this rapid rate of vocabulary growth is not unique to children learning English. In this new phase, children seem to learn new words with very few repetitions and generalize these new words to many more situations.

For the majority of children, this naming explosion is not a steady, gradual process; instead, vocabulary "spurts" beginning right about the time that the child has acquired 50 words. You can see this pattern in Figure 8.1, which shows the vocabulary growth curves of six children studied longitudinally by Goldfield and Reznick (1990)—a pattern found by other researchers as well (e.g., Bloom, 1993).

Not all children show precisely this pattern. In Goldfield and Reznick's study, for example, 13 children showed a vocabulary spurt; 11 other children in the study followed varying growth patterns, including several who showed no spurt at all but only gradual acquisition of vocabulary. Still, a rapid increase over a period of a few months is the most common pattern.

During this early period of rapid vocabulary growth, the bulk of new words are names for things or people, like *ball, car, milk, doggie, he,* or *that.* Verblike words tend to develop later, perhaps because they label relationships between objects rather than just a single object (E. Bates et al., 1994; Gleitman & Gleitman, 1992). For example, in Fenson's large cross-sectional study (1994), 63.0 percent of the words mothers said their children knew by age 2 were nouns, while only 8.5 percent were verbs. Studies of children learning other languages show very similar patterns, as you can see in the Cultures and Contexts box on page 234.

Later Word Learning

During the preschool years, children continue to add words at remarkable speed. At age 2½, the average vocabulary is about 600 words, about a quarter of which are verbs (E. Bates et al., 1994); by age 5 or 6, total vocabulary has risen to perhaps 15,000 words—an astonishing increase of 10 words *a day* (Pinker, 1994). Children can accomplish this feat because by age 3 or 4, they seem to pay attention to words in whole

Cultures and Contexts
Early Words by Children in Many Cultures

Cross-cultural studies of children's early language support the generalization that in their earliest word learning, children learn words for people or things before they learn words for actions or other parts of speech. Below are some (translated) samples from the very early vocabularies of one child from each of four cultures, all studied by Dedre Gentner (1982). It is impressive how very similar these early vocabularies are. Of course there are some variations, but all these children had names for Mommy and Daddy, for some other relative, for other live creatures, for food. All but the Chinese child had words for toys or clothes. All four had also learned more naming words than any other type, with very similar proportions. They didn't know the *same* words, but the pattern is remarkably similar.

	German boy	English girl	Turkish girl	Chinese girl
Some of the words for people or things	Mommy	Mommy	Mama	Momma
	Papa	Daddy	Daddy	Papa
	Gaga	babar	Aba	grandmother
	baby	baby	baby	horse
	dog	dog	food	chicken
	bird	dolly	apple	uncooked rice
	cat	kitty	banana	cooked rice
	milk	juice	bread	noodles
	ball	book	ball	flower
	nose	eye	pencil	wall clock
	moon	moon	towel	lamp
Some of the nonnaming words	cry	run	cry	go
	come	all gone	come	come
	eat	more	put on	pick up
	sleep	bye-bye	went pooh	not want
	want	want	want	afraid
	no	no	hello	thank you
Total percentage of naming words	**67%**	**69%**	**57%**	**59%**

groups, such as words that name objects in a single class (e.g., types of dinosaurs or kinds of fruit) or words with similar meanings.

In middle childhood, children continue to add vocabulary at the rate of 5,000 to 10,000 words a year. This figure comes from several recent, careful studies by Jeremy Anglin (1993; 1995), who estimates children's total vocabularies by testing them on a sample of words drawn at random from a large dictionary. Figure 8.2 shows Anglin's estimates for first-, third-, and fifth-grade children. Between third and fifth grades, Anglin finds the largest gain occurs in knowledge of the type of words he calls *derived words:* words that have a basic root to which some prefix or suffix is added, such as happ*ily* or *un*wanted.

Anglin argues that at about age 8 or 9, the child shifts to a new level of understanding of the structure of language, figuring out relationships between whole categories of words, such as between adjectives and adverbs (*happy* and *happily, sad* and *sadly*) or between adjectives and nouns (*happy* and *happiness*). Having understood such relationships, the child can now understand and create a whole class of new words, and his vocabulary thereby increases rapidly.

Critical Thinking

For those of you who have seriously studied another language: Do you think there are similar steps in learning vocabulary in a second language—a first stage in which each word is learned laboriously with many repetitions, followed by a vocabulary spurt? Are the same mechanisms involved?

Figure 8.2

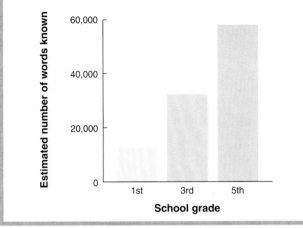

Anglin's estimates of the total vocabulary of first, third, and fifth graders.

(*Source:* From "Word Learning and the Growth of Potentially Knowable Vocabulary" by Jeremy M. Anglin (1995), p. 7, Fig. 6. By permission of Jeremy M. Anglin.)

Speaking in Sentences: The Development of Grammar

After the first word, the next big step is when the child begins to string words into sentences, initially using only two words together, then three, four, and more. The first two-word sentences usually appear between 18 and 24 months. This is not a random or independent event. Recent research, such as Fenson's large cross-sectional study (Fenson et al., 1994), suggests that sentences appear only when a child has reached some threshold level of vocabulary size—somewhere around 100 to 200 words.

Just as the first spoken words are preceded by apparently meaningful gestures, the first two-word sentences have gestural precursors as well. Toddlers often combine a single word with a gesture to create a "two-word meaning" before they actually use two words together in their speech. Elizabeth Bates suggests an example: The infant may point to Daddy's shoe and say "Daddy," as if to convey "Daddy's shoe." Or she may say "Cookie!" while simultaneously reaching out her hand and opening and closing her fingers, as if to say "Give cookie!" (Bates et al., 1987). In both cases, a sentence-like meaning is conveyed by the use of gesture and body language combined with a word. Linguists call these word-and-gesture combinations **holophrases;** they are common between the ages of 12 and 18 months.

Once the actual speaking of two-word sentences begins, the child moves rapidly through a series of steps or stages, so that within a year or two, most children are able to create remarkably complex sentences—as witness the 3-year-old I quoted at the beginning of this chapter.

First Sentences: 18 to 27 Months

The first sentences—which Roger Brown, a famous observer of child language, called stage 1 grammar—have several distinguishing features: They are *short*—generally two or three words—and they are *simple*. Nouns, verbs, and adjectives are usually included, but virtually all the purely grammatical markers (which linguists call **inflections**) are missing. At the beginning, for example, children learning English do not normally use the *s* for plurals or put the *ed* ending on verbs to make the past tense, nor do they use

Table 8.2

Some of the Different Meanings Children Express in Their Earliest Simple Sentences

Meaning	Examples
Agent-action	Sarah eat; Daddy jump
Action-object	Eat cookie; read book
Possessor–possessed object	Mommy sock; Timothy lunch
Action-location	Come here; play outside
Located object–location	Sweater chair; juice table
Attribute-modified object	Big book; red house
Nomination	That cookie; it dog
Recurrence	More juice; other book

Source: Maratsos, 1983.

the 's of the possessive or auxiliary verbs like *am* or *do*. So, for example, they might say "I tired" or "Me tired" rather than "I am tired," or "I not want it" rather than "I don't want it." Because only the really critical words are present in these early sentences, Brown (1973; Brown & Bellugi, 1964) described this as **telegraphic speech.** The child's language sounds rather like what we say when we send a telegram. We keep in all the essential words—usually nouns, verbs, and modifiers—and leave out all the prepositions, auxiliary verbs, and the like.

Interestingly, linguists are no longer sure that precisely this form of telegraphic speech occurs in children learning all languages. Some research seems to show that what determines the words that children use in their early sentences is the amount of *stress* normally placed on such words when that particular language is spoken. In English (and in many other languages), nouns, verbs, and adjectives are stressed in speech while the inflections are not. In languages in which inflections are more stressed, however, such as Turkish, children seem to use inflections much earlier (Gleitman & Wanner, 1988). Findings like these certainly raise some interesting questions about the universality of some of the patterns Brown and others have described.

In contrast, there is no dispute about the assertion that even at this earliest stage, children create sentences following rules. Not adult rules, to be sure, but rules nonetheless. Children focus on certain types of words and put them together in particular orders. They also manage to convey a variety of different meanings with their simple sentences.

For example, young children frequently use a sentence made up of two nouns, such as *Mommy sock* or *sweater chair* (Bloom, 1973). We might conclude from this that a "two-noun" form is a basic grammatical characteristic of early child language, but such a conclusion misses the complexity. For instance, the child in Bloom's classic study who said *Mommy sock* said it on two different occasions. The first time was when she picked up her mother's sock, and the second was when the mother put the child's own sock on the child's foot. In the first case, *Mommy sock* seems to mean "Mommy's sock," which is a possessive relationship. In the second instance, the child seems to convey "Mommy is putting a sock on me," which is an *agent* (Mommy)–*object* (sock) relationship.

Table 8.2 lists some other different meanings that children convey with their earliest sentences. Not all children express all these relationships or meanings in their early word combinations, and there does not seem to be a fixed order in which these meanings or constructions are acquired, but all children appear to express at least a few of these patterns in their earliest, simplest sentences (Maratsos, 1983).

Grammar Explosion: 27 to 36 Months

Just as a vocabulary explosion follows an early, slow beginning, so a grammar explosion follows several months of short, simple sentences. One sign of the change is that children's sentences get longer, as you can see in Figure 8.3, which shows the maximum sentence length reported by parents of toddlers of various ages, drawn from Fenson's very large cross-sectional study. Most 18- to 20-month-olds are still using one- and two-word sentences. By 24 months, the longest sentences include four and five words; by 30 months, the maximum sentence length has almost doubled again.

This grammar explosion is strongly linked to vocabulary development. Fenson finds a correlation of .84 between the complexity of a child's sentences and the size of her speaking vocabulary—an astonishingly high correlation for behavioral research (Fenson et al., 1994). That is, children whose grammar is more complex and advanced also have larger vocabularies. Just what such a link may tell us about how children learn language is still a matter of debate. Is a large vocabulary *necessary* for grammar development? Alternatively, perhaps having begun to understand the ways in which sentences can be constructed, a child also understands new words better and hence learns them more readily. Whatever the eventual explanation, Fenson's research gives us an important new piece of data to work with.

In this same period, children's speech ceases to be telegraphic, as they rather quickly add many of the inflections and function words. Within a few months, they use plurals, past tenses, auxiliary verbs such as *is* or *does*, prepositions, and the like. You can get a feeling for the sound of the change from Table 8.3 (p. 238), which lists some of

Figure 8.3

In this cross-sectional study, Fenson and his colleagues asked 1130 parents of toddlers (aged 16 to 30 months) to describe the longest sentence used by their child.

(*Source:* From "Variability in Early Communicative Development" by Fenson, Dale, Reznick, Bates, Thal, and Pethick, *Monographs of the Society for Research in Child Development*, 59, No. 242 (1994), p. 82, Fig. 27. By permission of the Society for Research in Child Development.)

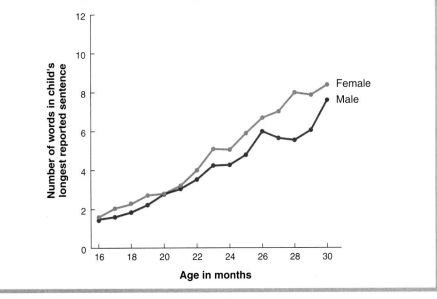

Table 8.3

Examples of Daniel's Stage 1 and Stage 2 Sentences

Stage 1 (Simple) Sentences, Age 21 Months	Stage 2 (More Complex) Sentences, Age 23 Months
A bottle	A little boat
Here bottle	Doggies here
Hi Daddy	Give you the book
Horse doggie	It's a boy
Broke it	It's a robot
Kitty cat	Little box there
Poor Daddy	No book
That monkey	Oh cars
Want bottle	That flowers
	Where going?

Source: Reprinted by permission of the publisher. D. Ingram, Early patterns of grammatical development, in R. E. Stark (Ed.), *Language behavior in infancy and early childhood,* Tables 6 and 7, pp. 344–345. Copyright © 1981 by Elsevier Science Publishing Co., Inc.

the sentences of a little boy named Daniel, recorded by David Ingram (1981). The left-hand column lists some of Daniel's sentences at about 21 months of age, when he was still using the simplest forms; the right-hand column lists some of his sentences only 2½ months later (age 23 months), when he had shifted into a higher gear.

Adding Inflections. Daniel obviously did not add all the inflections at once. In this sample, he uses only a few, such as the *s* for plural, although the beginning of a negative construction is apparent in "No book," and the beginning of a question form shows in "Where going?" even though he has not yet added the auxiliary verb to the question.

Within each language community, children seem to add inflections and more complex word orders in fairly predictable sequences. In a classic early study, Roger Brown (1973) found that the earliest inflection among children learning English is most often the *ing* added onto a verb, as in *I playing* or *doggie running*. Then come (in order) prepositions like *on* and *in*, the plural *s* on nouns, irregular past tenses (such as *broke* or *ran*), possessives, articles (*a* and *the* in English), the *s* that English adds to third-person verbs such as *he wants*, regular past tenses like *played* and *wanted*, and the various forms of the auxiliary verb, as in *I am going*.

Questions and Negatives. We also hear predictable sequences in the child's developing use of questions and negatives. In each case, the child seems to go through periods when he creates types of sentences that he has not heard adults use but that are consistent with the particular set of rules he is using. For example, in the development of questions in English, there is a point at which the child puts a *wh* word (*who, what, when, where, why*) at the front end of a sentence but doesn't yet have the auxiliary verb in the right place, as in *Why it is resting now?* Similarly, in the development of negatives, there is a stage in which the *not* or *n't* or *no* is included but the auxiliary verb is omitted, as in *I not crying, There no squirrels,* or *This not fits* (Bloom, 1991). Then children rather quickly figure out the correct forms and stop making these "mistakes."

Overregularization. Another intriguing phenomenon of this second phase of sentence construction is **overregularization** or overgeneralization. This is what the two little girls were doing in the conversation about the goldfish when they created new regularized forms of superlatives (*badder, baddest, worser,* and *worsest*). We can hear the same thing in children's creation of past tenses like *wented, blowed,* or *sitted,* or in plurals like *teeths* or *blockses* (Fenson et al., 1994; Kuczaj, 1977; 1978). Stan Kuczaj has pointed out that young children initially learn a small number of irregular past tenses and use them correctly for a short time. Then children rather suddenly seem to discover the rule of adding *ed* and overgeneralize this rule to all verbs. Then they relearn the exceptions one at a time. Even among preschoolers this type of "error" is not hugely common, comprising only about 2 to 3 percent of all past tenses in English according to one recent study (Marcus et al., 1992). These overregularizations nonetheless stand out because they are so distinctive and because they illustrate yet again that children create forms that they have not heard but that are logical within their current grammar.

Complex Sentences: 30 to 48 Months

After children have figured out the inflections and basic sentence forms like negation and questions, they soon begin to create remarkably complex sentences, using conjunctions like *and* or *but* to combine two ideas or using embedded clauses. Here are some examples from de Villiers and de Villiers (1992):

I didn't catch it but Teddy did!

I'm gonna sit on the one you're sitting on.

Where did you say you put my doll?

Those are punk rockers, aren't they?

Still more complex and difficult sentence forms are added throughout elementary school, and recurrent overregularization errors are eliminated (Bowerman, 1985). For instance, passive forms, like *The food is eaten by the cat,* are not well understood even by 5- and 6-year-olds and are not used much in spontaneous speech until several years later. But these are refinements. The really giant strides occur between ages 1 and about 4, as the child moves from single words to complex questions, negatives, and commands.

The Development of Word Meaning

To understand language development, it is not enough to know how children learn to string words together to form sentences. We also have to understand how the words in those sentences come to have meaning. Linguists are still searching for good ways to describe (or explain) children's emerging word meaning. So far, several sets of questions have dominated the research.

Which Comes First, the Meaning or the Word?

The most fundamental question is whether the child learns a word to describe a category or class he has *already* created through his manipulations of the world around him or whether the existence of a word forces the child to create new cognitive categories. This may seem like a highly abstract argument, but it touches on the fundamental issue of the relationship between language and thought. Does the child learn to represent objects to himself *because* he now has language, or does language simply come along at about this point and make the representations easier?

Not surprisingly, the answer seems to be "both" (Clark, 1983; Cromer, 1991; Greenberg & Kuczaj, 1982). On the cognitive side of the argument are several pieces of evidence I described in Chapter 6, such as the fact that young babies are able to remember and imitate objects and actions over periods of time, long before they have language to assist them. Further evidence of cognitive primacy comes from the study of the child's use of various prepositions like *in, between,* or *in front of,* each of which seems to be

Critical Thinking

Children learning English also learn the rules for "tag questions" quite late—these are the questions we put on the ends of sentence to make questions, like "isn't it?" or "haven't you?" or "aren't they?" Can you figure out the rule that you use to decide what is the correct tag?

Does this 18-month-old know the word *doll* because she first had a concept of doll and later learned the word, or did she learn the word first and then create a category or concept to go with the word?

What I've said so far about early language development describes what happens when a child learns a *single* language. What about children who are exposed to two or more languages from the beginning? How confusing is this for a child? And how can parents ease the process? At least two important practical questions surround this issue of bilingualism:

- Should parents who speak different native languages try to expose their children to both, or will that only confuse the child and make any kind of language learning harder? What's the best way to handle this situation?
- If a child arrives at school age without speaking the dominant language of schooling, what is the best way for the child to acquire that second language?

Learning Two Languages at the Same Time

Parents should have no fears about exposing their child to two or more languages from the very beginning. Such simultaneous exposure usually slows the child down a bit in word learning and early sentence construction; your child will probably "mix" words or grammar from the two languages in individual sentences at the beginning, too (Genesee, 1993). After this earlier, slower period, however, bilingual children catch up rapidly to their monolingual peers and by age 2 or 3 can switch readily from one language to the other.

The experts agree that the best way to help a child learn two languages fluently is to speak both languages to the child from the beginning, *especially* if the two languages come to the child from different sources. For example, if Mom's native language is English and Dad's is Italian, Mom should speak only English to the infant/toddler and Dad should speak only Italian. If both parents speak both languages to the child or mix them up in their own speech, the situation is much more difficult for the child, and language learning will be delayed (McLaughlin, 1984). The child can also learn two languages if one language is always spoken at home and the other in a day-care center, with playmates, or in some other outside situation.

Bilingual Education

For many children, the need to be bilingual does not begin in the home, but only at school age. In the United States today, there are 2.5 million school-age children for whom English is not the primary language of the home (Hakuta & Garcia, 1989). In California, 19 percent of all the children enrolled in public schools are Spanish-speaking with limited proficiency in English. What is the best way to teach children a second language at the same time as the child is also being taught basic subject matter such as reading and mathematics? Let me describe the alternatives as they exist in U.S. classrooms (Rossell & Baker, 1996).

The most common system in the United States is **bilingual education,** in which the instruction in reading, writing, and basic subject matter (social studies, science, etc.) is in the children's native tongue during the first two or three years of schooling. The children are then gradually shifted into full English instruction over several years. A much smaller number of children are in **English as a second language (ESL)** programs, in which the child spends most of her day in a regular English-speaking classroom, but then has an hour or two of special instruction in English in a separate classroom with other children of limited English proficiency.

A third choice is **structured immersion,** in which all the children in the classroom speak the same non-English native tongue and the teacher speaks both English and the children's native language. In such classrooms, the basic instruction is in English, paced so that the children can comprehend, with the teacher translating only when absolutely necessary.

Finally, there is **submersion,** sometimes called the "sink or swim" approach, in which the non-English-speaking child is simply assigned to a regular English-speaking classroom, without any added support or supplemental instruction.

The only way to find out which of these alternatives is best is with studies in which children are assigned randomly to several of these types of programs and then followed over time. Christine Rossell and Keith Baker (1996), in their recent comprehensive review of all such controlled, comparative studies, report that bilingual education is not consistently better than submersion, ESL, or structured immersion. Indeed, on measures of English reading proficiency, students in structured immersion programs performed consistently better than those in traditional bilingual education or ESL programs. Rossell and Baker conclude that some version of "structured immersion" is best—similar to programs used in Canada. Note, though, that such a system would not be feasible for a school system whose student body includes a few children speaking each of many different native languages. For such children, either submersion or some version of an ESL program are the only alternatives.

As a further caveat, let me hasten to add that the research findings are extremely messy and the whole issue remains fraught with controversy (e.g., Crawford, 1991; Goldenberg, 1996; Rossell & Baker, 1996). Different observers draw varying conclusions from the existing research evidence, and the great majority of bilingual educators remain committed to some version of traditional bilingual education.

Finally, note that even the very best program will not be effective for children who come to school without good spoken language in their native tongue. Learning to read, in any language, requires that the child have a fairly extensive awareness of the structure of language. Any child who lacks such awareness—because she has been exposed to relatively little language or was not read to or talked to much in infancy and preschool years—will have difficulty learning to read, whether the instruction is given in the native language or in English.

used spontaneously in language only after the child has understood the concept (Johnston, 1985).

The naming explosion may also rest on new cognitive understandings. Vygotsky noted many years ago (1962) that somewhere in the second year, the child seems to "discover" that objects have names and begins to ask for the names of objects all around her. This new discovery, in turn, may rest on another new cognitive ability, the ability to categorize things. In several studies, Alison Gopnik and Andrew Meltzoff (1987; 1992) have found that the naming explosion typically occurs just after, or at the same time as, children first show spontaneous categorization of mixed sets of objects, such as putting balls into one group and blocks into another. Having discovered "categories," the child may now rapidly learn the names for already existing categories. However, such a linkage is still uncertain: In one recent set of studies, Lisa Gershkoff-Stowe and her colleagues (1997) repeatedly failed to replicate the Gopnik and Meltzoff result. Gershkoff-Stowe proposes that while some basic understanding of the existence of *kinds* of things or categories may well be required for a child to show the naming explosion, such an understanding is not *sufficient*. Many other factors can influence the precise timing of the naming explosion and of the ability to classify objects into different types.

At the same time, the causality runs the other way as well, from language to thought: Once the child understands in some primitive way that names refer to categories, learning a new name suggests the existence of a new category (Waxman & Hall, 1993); thus, the name affects the child's thinking as much as the reverse.

Extending the Class

Just what kind of categories does the child initially create? Suppose your 2-year-old, on catching sight of the family tabby, says, "See kitty." No doubt you will be pleased that the child has applied the right word to the animal. But this sentence alone doesn't tell you much about the word meaning the child has developed. What does the word *kitty* mean to the child? Does he think it is a name only for that particular fuzzy beast? Or does he think it applies to all furry creatures, all things with four legs, things with pointed ears, or what?

One way to figure out the kind of class or category the child has created is to see what other creatures or things a child also calls a kitty. That is, how is the class *extended* in the child's language? If the child has created a "kitty" category that is based on furriness, then many dogs and perhaps sheep would also be called "kitty." If having a tail is a crucial feature for the child, then some breeds of cat that have no tails might not be labeled "kitty." Or perhaps the child uses the word *kitty* only for the family cat, or only when petting the cat. This would imply a very narrow category indeed. The general question for researchers has been whether young children tend to use words narrowly or broadly, overextending or underextending them.

The research tells us that underextension is most common at the earliest stages, particularly before the naming explosion (Harris, 1992), which suggests that most children initially think of words as belonging to only one thing, not as names for categories. Once the naming explosion starts, however, the child appears to grasp the idea that words go with categories, and overextension becomes more common. At that stage, we're more likely to hear the word *cat* applied to dogs or guinea pigs than we are to hear it used for just one animal or for a very small set of animals or objects (Clark, 1983). All children seem to show overextensions, but the particular classes the child creates are unique to each child. One child Eve Clark observed used the word *ball* to refer not only to toy balls but also to radishes and stone spheres at park entrances. Another child used the word *ball* to refer to apples, grapes, eggs, squash, and a bell clapper (Clark, 1975).

These overextensions *may* tell us something about the way children think, such as that they have broad classes. However, linguists like Eve Clark remind us that part of

Chances are that this toddler has a word for *ball*, and chances are also good that he uses the word *ball* to refer to a variety of other round things, which would be an example of overextension.

the child's problem is that he simply doesn't know very many words. A child who wants to call attention to a horse may not know the word *horse* and so may say "dog" instead. Overextensions may thus arise from the child's desire to communicate and may not tell us that the child fails to make the discriminations involved (Clark, 1987). As the child learns the separate labels that are applied to the different subtypes of fuzzy four-legged creatures the overextension disappears.

Constraints on Word Learning

Another fundamental question about word meanings, the subject of hot debate among linguists in recent years, is just how a child figures out which part of some scene a word may refer to. The classic example: A child sees a brown dog running across the grass with a bone in its mouth. An adult points and says "doggie." From such an encounter the toddler is somehow supposed to figure out that *doggie* refers to the animal and not to "running," "bone," "dog plus bone," "brownness," "ears," "grass," or any other combination of elements in the whole scene.

Many linguists have proposed that a child could cope with this monumentally complex task only if he operated with some built-in biases or **constraints** (e.g., Golinkoff et al., 1994; Waxman & Kosowski, 1990; Woodward & Markman, 1998). For example, the child may have a built-in assumption that words refer to whole objects and not to their parts or attributes—this is referred to as the *whole object constraint.* The *mutual exclusivity constraint* leads children to assume that objects will have only one name.

Another related constraint is the *principle of contrast,* which is the assumption that every word has a different meaning. Thus, if a new word is used, it must refer to some different object or a different aspect of an object (Clark, 1990). For example, in a widely quoted early study, Carey and Bartlett (1978) interrupted a play session with 2- and 3-year-old children by pointing to two trays and saying, "Bring me the chromium tray, not the red one, the chromium one." These children already knew the word *red* but did not know the word *chromium.* Nonetheless, most of the children were able to follow the instruction by bringing the nonred tray. Furthermore, a week later about half of the children remembered that the word *chromium* referred to some color and that the color was "not red." Thus, they learned the meaning by contrast.

If Dad says *goose* while he and his toddler are looking at this scene, how does the boy know that *goose* means the animal and not "white" or "dirt" or "honk honk" or some other feature? In fact, in this case as in most instances, the child first *points* and then the father labels, which greatly simplifies the problem.

Early proponents of constraints argued that such constraints are innate—built into the brain in some fashion. Another alternative is that the child learns the various principles over time (e.g., Merriman, 1991; Merriman & Bowman, 1989). For example, Carolyn Mervis and Jacquelyn Bertrand (1994) have found that not all children between 16 and 20 months use the principle of contrast to learn the name of a new, unknown object. In their sample, those children who did use this principle also had larger vocabularies and were more likely to be good at sorting objects into sets. Results like these tell us that constraints may be a highly useful way for children to learn words quickly but that they may be a *product* of cognitive/linguistic development rather than the basis for it.

A more sweeping argument against the notion of built-in constraints comes from Katherine Nelson (1988), who points out that the child rarely encounters a situation in which the adult points vaguely and gives some word. By far the most common scenario is that the parent follows the child's lead, labeling things the child is already playing with or pointing at (Harris, 1992). In fact, children whose parents do more such responsive, specific labeling seem to learn language somewhat faster (Dunham et al., 1993; Harris, 1992). Other theorists also emphasize that the situations in which children hear new words are rich with cues and clues to help the children figure out what the words may refer to—including the parents' facial expressions, the emphasis in their words, and the entire context in which the new word is given (Akhtar et al., 1996; Samuelson & Smith, 1998). To the extent that this is true, then, the child doesn't *need* a whole collection of constraints in order to figure out new words.

As these few examples illustrate, the study of the development of word meanings has been much more difficult to conceptualize than has the development of grammar. Linguists are obviously searching for the rules that govern this process so that we can understand how and why children use words the way they do. The study of constraints, whether they are ultimately conceived of as built-in or as acquired, has moved us some distance forward, but there is still a long road to travel.

Using Language: Communication and Self-direction

In the past decade or so, linguists have also turned their attention to a third aspect of children's language, namely, the way children learn to *use* speech, either to communicate with others (an aspect of language often called **pragmatics**) or to regulate their own behavior. How early do children know what kind of language to use in specific situations? How early do they learn the "rules" of conversation, such as that you are supposed to take turns?

Language Pragmatics. Children seem to learn the pragmatics of language at a remarkably early age. For example, children as young as 18 months show adultlike gaze patterns when they are talking with a parent: They look at the person who is talking, look away at the beginning of their own speaking turn, and then look at the listener again when they are signaling that they are about to stop talking (Rutter & Durkin, 1987).

Furthermore, a child as young as 2 years adapts the form of his language to the situation he is in or the person he is talking to—a point I made in Chapter 6 as well, when talking about children's egocentrism. He might say "Gimme" to another toddler as he grabs the other child's cup but might say "More milk" to an adult. Among older children, language is even more clearly adapted to the listener: 4-year-olds use simpler language when they talk to 2-year-olds than when they talk to adults (Tomasello & Mannle, 1985); first graders explain things more fully to a stranger than to a friend (Sonnenschein, 1986) and are more polite to adults and strangers than to peers. Both of these trends are still clearer among fourth graders. Thus, from very early, probably from the

Critical Thinking

Do you recognize this pattern? Next time you are in a two-person conversation, monitor yourself and your partner and see if this isn't how it works.

beginning, the child's language is meant to *communicate,* and the child adapts the form of his language in order to achieve better communication.

Language and Self-control. Children also use language to help control or monitor their own behavior. Such "private speech," which may consist of fragmentary sentences, muttering, or instructions to the self, is detectable from the earliest use of words and sentences. For example, when 2- or 3-year-olds play by themselves, they give themselves instructions, or stop themselves with words, or describe what they are doing: "No, not there," "I put that there," or "Put it" (Furrow, 1984).

Piaget thought that this was *egocentric* speech, but Vygotsky thought Piaget was quite wrong about this. Vygotsky insisted instead that in using private speech the child is communicating with herself for the explicit purpose of guiding her own behavior. He believed that such self-directing use of language is central to all cognitive development.

In young children such self-directing speech is audible. In older children it is audible only when the child is facing a challenging task; in other situations it has gone "underground." For example, you may recall from Chapter 6 that Flavell found that young elementary school children muttered to themselves while they were trying to remember lists; among 9- or 10-year-olds this is much less common (Bivens & Berk, 1990). If we connect this set of findings with the work on information processing I talked about in Chapter 6, it begins to sound as if the child uses language audibly to remind himself of some new or complex processing strategy; as the strategy becomes better rehearsed and more flexibly learned, overt language is no longer needed. Such an interpretation is bolstered by the observation that even adults will use audible language in problem solving when they are faced with especially difficult tasks.

Even this brief foray into the research on the child's use of language points out that a full understanding of language development is going to require knowledge both of cognitive development and of the child's social skills and understanding. Lois Bloom, one of the foremost theorists and observers of children's language, argues that indeed "children learn language in the first place because they strive to . . . *share* what they and other persons are feeling and thinking" (1993, p. 245). From birth, the child has been able to communicate feelings and thoughts through facial expressions, somewhat later through gestures. But these are imperfect vehicles for communication; language is much more efficient. Such an argument reminds us once again that the child is not divided into tidy packages labeled "physical development," "social development," and "language development" but is instead a coherent, integrated system.

Explaining Language Development

If merely describing language development is hard—and it is—explaining it is still harder. Indeed, explaining how a child learns language has proved to be one of the most compelling and difficult challenges within developmental psychology. This may surprise you. I suspect that most of you just take for granted that a child learns to talk by listening to the language she hears. What is magical or complicated about that? Yet

Critical Thinking

Do you ever use audible "private speech" this way? Are you more likely to use it when you are working on a hard problem? How does whispering or speaking out loud help you?

Twenty-month-old Clare already knows many of the social rules about how language is used, including rules about who is supposed to look at whom during a conversation.

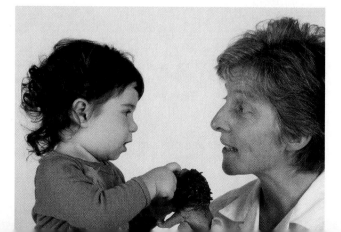

the more you think about it, the more amazing and mysterious it becomes. For one thing, as Steven Pinker (1987) points out, there is a veritable chasm between what the child hears as language input and the language the child must eventually speak. The input consists of some set of sentences spoken to the child, with intonation, stress, and timing. They are spoken in the presence of objects and events, and the words are given in a particular order. All that may be helpful, even essential, but what the child must acquire from such input is nothing less than a set of rules for *creating* sentences. How does the child accomplish this feat? Theories abound. Let me start on the nurture end of the theoretical continuum.

Imitation and Reinforcement

The earliest theories of language were based either on learning theory or on the commonsense idea that language is learned by imitation. Imitation obviously has to play some part, because the child learns the language she hears. Babbling drifts toward the sounds in the heard language; children imitate sentences they hear; they learn to speak with the accent of their parents. Furthermore, those toddlers who most readily imitate an adult when the adult speaks a new word are also the ones who show the most rapid vocabulary growth in the first year or two of the language explosion; this fact tells us that imitation is an important ingredient in the process (Masur, 1995). Still, imitation alone can't explain all language acquisition because it cannot account for the creative quality of the child's language. In particular, children consistently create types of sentences and forms of words that they have never heard—words like *goed* or *footses*.

Reinforcement theories such as Skinner's (1957) fare no better. Skinner argued that, in addition to the role they play in imitation, parents shape language through systematic reinforcements, gradually rewarding better and better approximations of adult speech. Yet when researchers have listened to parents talking to children, they find that parents don't seem to do anything like what Skinner proposed. Instead, parents are remarkably forgiving of all sorts of peculiar constructions and meaning (Brown & Hanlon, 1970; Hirsh-Pasek et al., 1984); they reinforce children's sentences on the basis of whether the sentence is true rather than whether it is grammatically correct. In addition, children learn many forms of language, such as plurals, with relatively few errors. In sum, it is plain that some process other than shaping must be involved.

Newer Environmental Theories: Talking to the Child

Still, it seems obvious that what is said to the child has to play *some* role in the process. At the simplest level, we know that if children have parents who talk to them often, read to them regularly, and use a wide range of words in their speech, they begin to talk sooner, develop larger vocabularies, use more complex sentences, and learn to read more readily when they reach school age (Hart & Risley, 1995; Huttenlocher, 1995; Snow, 1997). Thus, the sheer quantity of language a child hears is a significant factor.

Furthermore, the children who are exposed to less (and less varied) language in their earliest years don't seem to catch up later in vocabulary, a point illustrated with the data in Table 8.4 (p. 246). These numbers come from the National Longitudinal Survey of Labor Market Experience of Youth (NLSY), a 12-year longitudinal study of a large sample of young women in the United States, begun when they were still teenagers. Table 8.4 shows one piece of information about the preschool-age *children* of these young women, namely, the percentage who had vocabulary scores *below* the 30th percentile on the most commonly used measure of vocabulary—the Peabody Picture Vocabulary Test (PPVT) described in Table 7.1 (p. 201). We know that the amount and quality of language spoken to the child varies with the mother's level of poverty: Poor mothers talk less, read to their children less, and use less complex sentences. The data in Table 8.4 tell us that one consequence for the child is a considerably higher risk of poor language.

By age 4, the difference in vocabulary between poor and better-off children is already substantial, and the gap only widens over the school years. Similarly, Catherine Snow (1997) finds that 4-year-old children reared in poverty use shorter and less complex sentences than do their better-off peers. Many factors no doubt contribute to these differences, but the richness and variety of the language a child hears is obviously highly significant. Of all these factors, being read to less often may be one of the most critical, as you can see from the Research Report on reading to children (opposite).

Motherese. Beyond the mere quantity of language directed at the child, the quality of the parents' language may also be important in helping the child learn language. In particular, we know that adults talk to children in a special kind of very simple language, originally called **motherese** by many linguists, now more scientifically described as **infant-directed speech**—a speech pattern you also read about in a Cultures and Contexts box in Chapter 1 (p. 29). This simple language is spoken in a higher-pitched voice and at a slower pace than is talk between adults. The sentences are short and grammatically simple, with concrete vocabulary. When speaking to children, parents also repeat a lot, introducing minor variations ("Where is the ball? Can you see the ball? Where is the ball? There is the ball!"). They may also repeat the child's own sentences but in slightly longer, more grammatically correct forms—a pattern referred to as an *expansion* or a *recasting*. For example, if a child said "Mommy sock," the mother might recast it as, "Yes, this is Mommy's sock," or if a child said "Doggie not eating," the parent might say "The doggie is not eating."

We also know that babies as young as a few days old can discriminate between motherese and adult-directed speech and that *they prefer to listen to motherese,* whether it is spoken by a female or a male voice (Cooper & Aslin, 1994; Pegg et al., 1992). This preference exists even when the motherese is being spoken in a language other than the one normally spoken to the child. Janet Werker and her colleagues (1994), for example, have found that both English and Chinese infants prefer to listen to infant-directed speech, whether it is spoken in English or in Cantonese (one of the major languages of China).

The quality of motherese that seems to be particularly attractive to babies is its higher pitch. Once the child's attention is drawn by this special tone, the very simplicity and repetitiveness of the adult's speech may help the child to pick out repeating grammatical forms.

Children's attention also seems to be drawn to recast sentences. For example, Farrar (1992) found that a 2-year-old was two or three times more likely to imitate a correct grammatical form after he had heard his mother recast his own sentences than he was when the mother used that same correct grammatical form in her normal conversation.

Critical Thinking

Imagine yourself talking to an infant you are holding in your arms. Can your hear yourself using "motherese"?

Table 8.4

Percentage of Children Aged 4 to 7 Who Score Below the 30th Percentile on the Peabody Picture Vocabulary Test, as a Function of Family Poverty

Type of Family	Number of Cases	Observed Percentage	Adjusted Percentage[*]
AFDC (Welfare)	196	60%	52%
Poor but not AFDC	116	47%	42%
Nonpoor	659	27%	30%

Source: From "The life circumstances and development of children in welfare families: A profile based on national survey data" by Zill, Moore, Smith, Stief, and Coiro, *Escape from poverty: What makes a difference for children,* P. L. Chase-Lansdale and J. Brooks-Gunn, eds., p. 45, Table 2.3. © 1995 by Cambridge University Press. By permission of Cambridge University Press.

*These percentages have been adjusted statistically to subtract out the effects of differences in parents' education, family structure, family size, and age, sex, and ethnicity of the child.

Research Report
The Importance of Reading to the Child

A series of studies by G. J. Whitehurst and his colleagues gives us strong evidence for the importance of the child's environment in early language learning. In their first study (Whitehurst et al., 1988), they trained some parents to read picture books to their toddlers and to interact with them in a special way during the reading, using a style Whitehurst calls *dialogic* reading. Specifically, they were trained to use questions that could not be answered just by pointing. So a mother reading Winnie the Pooh might say, "There's Eeyore. What's happening to him?" Or, pointing to some object shown in a book, the parent might ask, "What's the name of that?" Or she might ask a question about some character in a story, such as "Do you think the kitty will get into trouble?" Other parents were encouraged to read to their children but were given no special instructions about how to read. After a month, the children in the experimental group showed a larger gain in vocabulary than did the children in the comparison group.

Whitehurst has now replicated this study in day-care centers for poor children in both Mexico and New York City (Valdez-Menchaca & Whitehurst, 1992; Whitehurst et al., 1994) and in a large number of Head Start classrooms (Whitehurst et al., 1995). In the Mexican study, one teacher in a day-care center was trained in dialogic reading. She then spent ten minutes each day for six to seven weeks reading with each of ten 2-year-olds. A comparison group of children in the same day-care center spent an equivalent amount of time with the same teacher each day, but they were given arts and crafts instruction rather than reading. At the end of the intervention, the children who had been read to had higher vocabulary scores on a variety of standardized tests, and they used more complex grammar when talking with an adult other than their teacher.

In Whitehurst's U.S. day-care and Head Start studies, children were read to in this special way either by their teacher or by both their mother and the teacher, while control group children experienced normal interactions with day-care workers or teachers. In both studies, the children who had participated in dialogic reading gained in vocabulary significantly more than did the control group children, and the effect appears to last.

Similarly, Catherine Crain-Thoreson and Philip Dale (1995) found that they could significantly increase language skills in language-delayed children by teaching either parents or teachers to read to the children in this special way.

The fact that we now have evidence of the same types of effects in two different cultures, with two different languages, with both teachers and parents, with both poor and middle-class children, and with language-delayed children, greatly strengthens the argument that richer interactive language between adult and child is one important ingredient in fostering the child's language growth.

Experimental studies confirm this effect of recastings. Children who are deliberately exposed to higher rates of specific types of recast sentences seem to learn the modeled grammatical forms more quickly than do those who hear no recastings (Nelson, 1977).

Sounds good, doesn't it? The language the child hears seems to be important, perhaps even formative. Still, this theory of language acquisition has some holes in it. For one thing, while children who hear more expansions or recastings may learn grammar sooner, in normal parent-toddler conversations recasts are actually relatively rare, in some cases almost nonexistent. Yet children nevertheless acquire a complex grammar, which suggests that the kind of feedback provided by recastings is unlikely to be a major source of grammatical information for most children (Morgan et al., 1995). And while motherese does seem to occur in the vast majority of cultures and contexts, it does not occur in *all*. For example, Pye (1986) could find no sign of motherese in one Mayan culture, and studies in the United States show it is greatly reduced among depressed mothers (Bettes, 1988). Children of these mothers nonetheless learn language. Thus, while infant-directed speech may be helpful, it is probably not *necessary* for language.

Innateness Theories

On the other side of the theoretical spectrum we have the innateness theorists, who argue that much of what the child needs for learning language is built into the organism. Early innateness theorists like Noam Chomsky (1965; 1975; 1986; 1988) were especially

Cultures and Contexts
Universals and Variations in Early Language

In the early years of research on children's language development, linguists and psychologists were strongly impressed by the apparent similarities across languages in children's early language. You've already seen some of the evidence that supports this impression in an earlier Cultures and Contexts box (p. 234), which illustrated large similarities in early vocabularies. Studies in a wide variety of language communities, including Turkish, Serbo-Croatian, Hungarian, Hebrew, Japanese, a New Guinean language called Kaluli, German, and Italian, have revealed other important similarities in early language:

- The prelinguistic phase seems to be identical in all language communities. All babies coo, then babble; all babies understand language before they can speak it; babies in all cultures begin to use their first words at about 12 months.
- In all language communities studied so far, a one-word phase precedes the two-word phase, with the latter beginning at about 18 months.
- In all languages studied so far, prepositions describing locations are added in essentially the same order. Words for *in, on, under,* and *beside* are learned first. Then the child learns the words *front* and *back* (Slobin, 1985a).
- Children seem to pay more attention to the ends of words than to the beginnings, so they learn suffixes before they learn prefixes.

At the same time, cross-linguistic comparisons show that children's beginning sentences are not nearly so similar as the early innateness theorists had supposed. For example:

- The specific word order that a child uses in early sentences is not the same for all children in all languages. In some languages a noun-verb sequence is fairly common; in others a verb-noun sequence may be heard.
- Particular inflections are learned in highly varying orders from one language to another. Japanese children, for example, begin very early to use a special kind of marker, called a *pragmatic* marker, that tells something about the feeling or the context. For instance, in Japanese the word *yo* is used at the end of a sentence when the speaker is experiencing some resistance from the listener; the word *ne* is used when the speaker expects approval or agreement. Japanese children begin to use these markers very early, much earlier than other inflections appear in most languages.
- Most strikingly, there are languages in which there seems to be no simple two-word-sentence stage in which the sentences contain no inflections. Children learning Turkish, for example, use essentially the full set of noun and verb inflections by age 2 and never go through a stage of using uninflected words. Their language is simple, but it is rarely ungrammatical from the adult's point of view (Aksu-Koc & Slobin, 1985; Maratsos, 1998).

Obviously, any theory of language acquisition must account for both the common ground and the wide variations from one language to the next.

struck by two phenomena: the extreme complexity of the task the child must accomplish, and the apparent similarities in the steps and stages of children's early language development across languages and among all children. Newer cross-language comparisons now make it clear that more variability exists than first appeared—a set of findings I've described in the Cultures and Contexts box above. Nonetheless, innateness theories are alive and well and increasingly accepted.

One particularly influential innateness theorist is Dan Slobin (1985a; 1985b), who assumes a basic language-making capacity in any child, made up of a set of fundamental *operating principles.* Slobin is arguing that just as the newborn infant seems to come programmed with "rules to look by," infants and children are programmed with "rules to listen by."

You've already encountered a good deal of evidence consistent with this proposal in earlier chapters. We know that from earliest infancy babies focus on individual sounds and syllables in the stream of sounds they hear, that they pay attention to sound rhythm, and that they prefer speech of a particular pattern, namely, motherese. Slobin also proposes that babies are preprogrammed to pay attention to the beginnings and endings of strings of sounds and to stressed sounds—a hypothesis supported by research (e.g., Morgan, 1994). Together, these operating principles would help to explain some of the features of children's early grammars. In English, for example, the stressed words in a sentence are normally the verb and the noun—precisely the words that English-speaking children use in their earliest sentences. In Turkish, on the other hand, prefixes and suffixes are stressed, and Turkish-speaking children learn both very early. Both these patterns make sense if we assume that the preprogrammed rule is not "verbness" or "nounness" or "prefixness" but "pay attention to stressed sounds."

The fact that this model is consistent with the growing information about apparently built-in perceptual skills and processing biases is certainly a strong argument in its favor. Even so, this is not the only compelling theoretical option. In particular, some theorists argue persuasively that what is important is not the built-in biases or operating principles but the child's *construction* of language as part of the broader process of cognitive development. In this view, the child is a "little linguist," applying her emerging cognitive understanding to the problem of language, searching for regularities and patterns (e.g., Tomasello & Brooks, in press).

Constructivist Theories

One prominent proponent of this view, Melissa Bowerman, puts the proposition this way: "When language starts to come in, it does not introduce new meanings to the child. Rather, it is used to express only those meanings the child has already formulated independently of language" (1985, p. 372). Even more broadly, Lois Bloom argues that from the beginning of language, the child's intent is to communicate, to share the ideas and concepts in his head. He does this as best he can with the gestures or words he knows, and he learns new words when they help him communicate his thoughts and feelings (1993; 1997).

One type of evidence in support of this argument comes from the observation that it is children and not mothers who initiate the majority of verbal exchanges (Bloom, 1997). Further evidence comes from studies showing links between achievements in language development and the child's broader cognitive development. For example, symbolic play, such as drinking from an empty cup, and imitation of sounds and gestures both appear at about the same time as the child's first words, suggesting some broad "symbolic" understanding that is reflected in a number of behaviors. In children whose language is significantly delayed, both symbolic play and imitation are usually delayed as well (Bates et al., 1987; Ungerer & Sigman, 1984).

A second example occurs later: At about the point at which two-word sentences appear, we can also see children begin to combine several gestures into a sequence in their pretend play, such as pouring imaginary liquid, drinking, and then wiping the mouth. Those children who are the first to show this sequencing in their play are also the first to show two- or three-word sentences in their speech (e.g., McCune, 1995; Shore, 1986).

These apparent linkages between language and cognition are impressive, but an interesting bit of counterevidence comes from recent studies of children with Williams syndrome, a genetic disorder that causes mental retardation. Williams syndrome children and adults, like those with Down syndrome, have general deficiencies in most aspects of cognitive functioning; their IQ scores are in the range of 50 to 60. Unlike Down syndrome children, however, Williams syndrome children develop good language skills—large vocabularies and complex grammar. They acquire vocabulary slowly in the early years, but once their vocabulary reaches the usual "critical mass" of several hundred words, their grammar development proceeds fairly normally. Their eventual language skill—both comprehension and production—does contain some deficits, but it is much nearer to normal than is their nonverbal intelligence (Karmiloff-Smith et al., 1997; Maratsos, 1998; Mervis et al., 1995; Wang & Bellugi, 1993). In these children, then, there seems to be a far weaker linkage between overall cognitive development and language development, a result that obviously poses problems for Bowerman's model.

Table 8.5

A Summary of Theories of Language Development

Theory	Supporting Evidence	Problem Evidence
Imitation	Child clearly learns the language he hears, including regional accent; children who imitate more learn vocabulary more quickly.	Child's sentence construction frequently includes patterns not heard from adults.
Reinforcement	Child gets reinforced when he speaks clearly because he is more likely to get what he wants.	Parents rarely use explicit reinforcement to train language; children learn some grammatical forms with few errors and thus no corrections or reinforcements.
Other environmental theories	Children who are talked to more have larger vocabularies and faster grammar development; children prefer to listen to motherese; children's grammar development is helped by recastings and expansions.	Children who do not hear recastings or motherese nonetheless learn language.
Innateness	From birth, children have biases in what aspects of language they pay attention to; at later ages, children appear to operate with shared word meaning constraints; the early stages of language development are pretty much the same, regardless of the language being learned.	Early grammar varies more from one language community to another than some innateness theories would imply; some word meaning constraints appear to be learned rather than built-in.
Constructivist	Certain aspects of language development appear only when the child has developed a more general cognitive ability to support it, such as a general ability to "combine" as a precursor to two-word sentences.	Cannot ignore the evidence of built-in "operating principles" in early infancy.

Table 8.5 summarizes the several alternative explanations, so you can see the contrast as clearly as possible. My own view is that at this stage we need not choose between Slobin's and Bowerman's approaches. Both may be true. The child may begin with built-in operating principles that aim the child's attention at crucial features of the language input. The child then processes that information according to her initial (perhaps built-in) strategies or schemes. Then she modifies those strategies or rules as she receives new information, such as by arriving at some of the constraints about word meanings. The result is a series of rules for understanding and creating language. The strong similarities we see among children in their early language constructions come about both because all children share the same initial processing rules and because most children are exposed to very similar input from the people around them. But because the input is not identical, because languages differ, language development follows less and less common pathways as the child progresses.

As these brief descriptions of theory make clear, linguists and psychologists who have studied language have made progress. We know a lot more now about how *not* to explain language, but we have not yet cracked the code. The fact that children learn complex and varied use of their native tongue within a few years remains both miraculous and largely mysterious.

Individual Differences in Language Development

The sequences of development of language I have been describing are accurate on the average, but the speed with which children acquire language skill varies widely. There also seem to be important style differences.

Differences in Rate

Some children begin using individual words at 8 months, others not until 18 months; some do not use two-word sentences until 3 years or even later. You can see the range of normal variation in sentence construction very clearly in Figure 8.4, which shows the average sentence length (referred to by linguists as the **mean length of utterance ([MLU])** of 10 children, each studied longitudinally. Eve, Adam, and Sarah were studied by Roger Brown (1973); Jane, Martin, and Ben (all African-American children) by Ira Blake (1994); and Eric, Gia, Kathryn, and Peter by Lois Bloom (1991). I have drawn a line at the MLU level that normally accompanies a switch from simple, uninflected two-word sentences to more complex forms. You can see that Eve was the earliest to make this transition, at about 21 months, while Adam and Sarah passed over this point about a year later. These variations are confirmed in Fenson's much larger cross-sectional study of more than 1000 toddlers whose language was described by their parents. In this group, the earliest age at which parents reported more complex than simple sentences was about 22 months, with an average of about 27 months. However, as many as a quarter of children had not reached this point by 30 months (Fenson et al., 1994).

Figure 8.4

The 10 children whose language is charted here, studied by three different linguists, moved at markedly different times from simple one- and two-word sentences to more complex sentences.

(*Sources:* Adapted from *A First Language: The Early Stages,* p. 55, Fig. 1, by Roger Brown; copyright © 1973 by the President and Fellows of Harvard College, reprinted by permission of Harvard University Press. Lois Bloom, *Language Development from Two to Three,* p. 92, Table 3.1; Cambridge, England: Cambridge University Press, 1991. I. K. Blake, "Language Development and Socialization in Young African-American Children," *Cross-Cultural Roots of Minority Children,* Greenfield and Cocking, eds., p. 169, Table 9.1 and p. 171, Fig. 9.1; Hillsdale, NJ: Lawrence Erlbaum Associates, Inc., 1994.)

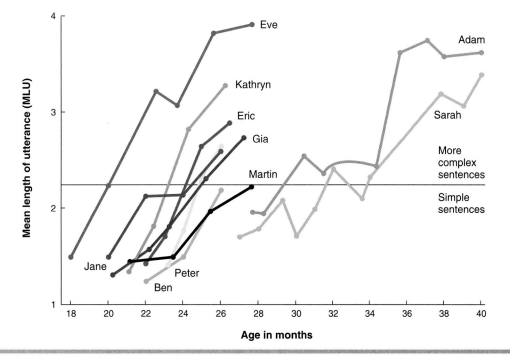

I should point out that more than half of children who talk late eventually catch up. The subset who do not catch up is primarily made up of children who *also* have poor *receptive language* (Bates, 1993; Thal et al., 1991). This group appears to remain behind in language development and perhaps in cognitive development more generally. In practical terms, this means that if your child, or a child you care for, is significantly delayed in *understanding* as well as speaking language, you should seek professional help to try to diagnose the problem and begin appropriate intervention.

How can we explain these variations in speed of early language development? The alternative possibilities should be familiar by now.

Genetic Explanations. One possibility is that the rate of language development may be something you inherit—in the same way that intelligence or the rate of physical development may be affected by heredity. Certainly if we assume that some language-processing patterns are built into the brain, it makes sense to think that some children may inherit a more efficient built-in system than others, just as some babies habituate faster to repeated stimuli.

Twin studies designed to test this possibility show that vocabulary size, but *not* grammatical complexity, is more similar in identical than in fraternal twins (Mather & Black, 1984). Adoption studies show that 2-year-olds' language skill can be predicted about equally well from the IQ scores or language skills of either their natural or their adoptive parents (Plomin & DeFries, 1985).

What this all looks like to me is that some aspects of language development are strongly related to the child's overall information processing abilities, such as speed of learning new words and understanding other people's language. Since cognitive abilities have a significant genetic influence, so do these language abilities. Other aspects of language, however, such as pronunciation and possibly the rate of grammatical development, may be equally influenced by variations in the richness of the child's linguistic environment.

Environmental Explanations. I have already talked about some environmental influences. Parents who talk more, who read to the child more and elicit more language from the child, and who respond contingently to the child's language seem to have children who develop language more rapidly. The problem with such studies, including the one shown in Table 8.4 (p. 246), is that the parents are providing both the genes and the environment, so it is difficult to tease out the environmental effect alone. Adoption studies give us cleaner information; in this case, the research shows that among adoptive families, those who talk the most and provide the most toys have children whose language is more advanced, a finding that confirms the results shown in Table 8.4.

Overall, as with IQ, it seems obvious that both the particular genes the child inherits and the environment in which the child is growing up contribute to the rate of language development she will show. I should emphasize once again, though, that although children do differ widely in the timing of their language development, virtually all children progress through the sequence of steps I have been describing. Nearly all children learn to communicate at least adequately; most do so with considerable skill, regardless of their early rate of progress. One moral for parents is that you should not panic if your child is still using fairly primitive sentences at age 2½ or even 3—providing, of course, that the child appears to understand what is said to her. Instead of worrying, I would urge you to listen with pleasure to your child's emerging language—to the poetry of it, the wonderfully funny mistakes, the amazingly rapid changes. It is a fascinating process.

Differences in Style

A quite different kind of language variation, one that has intrigued linguists far more than variations in rate, is variation in the *style* of children's early language. Katherine Nelson (1973) was the first to point our attention at such style differences. She noted that some toddlers use what she called an **expressive style,** also referred to in current

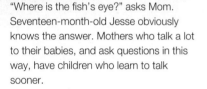

"Where is the fish's eye?" asks Mom. Seventeen-month-old Jesse obviously knows the answer. Mothers who talk a lot to their babies, and ask questions in this way, have children who learn to talk sooner.

writings as a *holistic* style (E. Bates et al., 1994). Such children's early vocabulary is not predominantly made up of nounlike words. Instead, most of their early words are linked to social relationships rather than objects. They often learn pronouns (*you, me*) early and use many more of what Nelson calls "personal-social" words, such as *no, yes, want,* or *please.* Their early vocabulary may also include some multiword strings, like *love you* or *do it* or *go away.* This is in sharp contrast to the children who use what Nelson calls a **referential style,** whose early vocabulary is made up predominantly of names for things or people. Later researchers have found further signs of such a difference in both grammar and articulation, summarized in Table 8.6.

Elizabeth Bates and her colleagues (1988; Thal & Bates, 1990) argue that the difference between these two styles may run fairly deep. Referential-style children are, in some sense, more cognitively oriented. They are drawn to objects, spend more of their time in solitary play with objects, and interact with other people more often around objects. They are much more likely to show a clear spurt in vocabulary development in the early stages, adding a whole lot of object names in a very short space of time, as if they—more than expressive children—had understood the basic principle that things have names. Such children are also advanced in their ability to understand complex adult language.

Expressive-style toddlers, on the other hand, are oriented more toward people, toward social interactions. Their early words and sentences include a lot of "strings" of words that are involved in common interactions with adults. Since many such strings include grammatical inflections, expressive children's early language often sounds more advanced than that of a referential child, but their vocabularies are typically smaller, with no obvious spurt in vocabulary growth.

Just how these differences come about is still not clear. The most obvious possibility is that a child's early language is a reflection of the type of language she is hearing. There is some evidence, for example, that referential-style children, more than expressive-style children, have mothers who spend time naming objects and describing the child's environment (e.g., Furrow & Nelson, 1984; Goldfield, 1993). Yet it is also likely that the quality of the mother's speech is at least partially a *response* to the child's own language quality or style rather than, or in addition to, being a cause of it. Thus, referential children appear to elicit much more noun naming and equivalent referential speech from the mother than do expressive-style children (Pine et al., 1997). Another

If you had to guess, which of the two styles of early language learning would you bet young Shifra shows?

Table 8.6

Some Differences Between Expressive and Referential Children in Early Language

	Expressive	**Referential**
Early words	Low proportion of nouns and adjectives.	High proportion of nouns and adjectives.
Vocabulary growth	Slow, gradual; rarely any spurts.	Rapid, with clear spurt at one-word stage.
Articulation	Less-clear speech.	Clearer speech.
Early sentences	May have inflections at stage 1, because of high use of "rote strings" (formulas) inserted into sentences (e.g., "What do you want?").	Few rote strings at stage 1 grammar; speech is clearly telegraphic at this stage, with no inflections.

Sources: Thal & Bates, 1990; Shore, 1995.

Critical Thinking

There are some indications that girls are more likely to follow a referential pattern, while boys may be more often expressive. Can you think of any possible explanations for such a difference?

explanatory alternative is that the two styles might reflect underlying temperamental variations, although the one study I know of that explores this possibility directly has not found such a link (Bates et al., 1988).

Whatever the source, the existence of such large differences in the form or style of early language raises serious questions about the assumption that the early stages of language development are the same for all children—an assumption crucial to nativist theories of language development. If all children learn language using the same built-in operating principles, then where do the style differences come from? Either there is more variability of process than innateness theories propose, or there must be larger differences in the way parents talk to "referential" and "expressive" children than the existing evidence suggests. All in all, the literature on style differences in language learning, which seemed like an interesting sidelight when Nelson first described the phenomenon, has turned out to lead to a fascinating set of new questions.

An Application of the Basic Knowledge: Learning to Read

In Chapter 5, I talked briefly about some of the *perceptual* aspects of learning to read; but of course reading involves language as well. Researchers have found that a child's knowledge of both the sound and the structure of language plays an important role in early reading. Especially significant are two very specific bits of knowledge: (1) the child's ability to recognize individual letters, and (2) the child's awareness that spoken and written words are made up of individual sounds (Adams et al., 1998).

You know from Chapter 5 that very young babies pay attention to individual sounds, which linguists call *phonemes*. (The word *cat*, for example, has three phonemes; the word *bark* has four). The understanding that words are made up of strings of such sounds—an understanding referred to as *phonemic awareness* or *phonological sensitivity*—seems to be a more advanced understanding, one that is essential to reading.

Suppose you say to a child, "Tell me a word that starts the same as *tap*." To respond correctly to such a request, the child has to be able to identify which sound in the string of sounds comes first in the word *tap*. He must also be able to recognize this same sound in other words. You can assess this same skill in other ways, such as by asking children to recognize or produce rhyming words or by reading them two words that differ in only one sound, such as *sing* and *sink*, and asking if the two words are the same or different. We now have abundant evidence that children who are more skilled at such tasks at age 3, 4, or 5 later learn to read much more easily (Adams et al., 1998; Bryant et al., 1990; Hansen & Bowey, 1994; Wagner et al., 1997; Whitehurst, 1995). Furthermore, if you train preschoolers or kindergartners in phonemic awareness, their reading skills in first grade improve—a result that has been found in studies in Scandinavia and Germany as well as the United States (Schneider et al., 1995).

Where does such early language awareness come from? How does it happen that some 5- and 6-year-olds have extensive understanding of the way words are put together, while others have little? One possible hypothesis might be that measures of phonemic awareness are really just tapping general IQ. In fact, though, IQ test scores are only very weakly correlated with tests of phonemic awareness (Adams et al., 1998), so that can't be the central explanation. Instead, the explanation seems to lie in exposure and expertise. For a child to learn about letters and sounds, he has to have had a great deal of exposure to language, both written and spoken. Such children are talked to a lot as infants, are read to regularly, may have toy letters to play with, are told the sounds that go with each letter, or may be quite specifically taught the alphabet at an early age.

Nursery rhymes are also frequently a significant part of the early experience of good readers. In one study, researchers found that among a sample of children in England, those who knew more nursery rhymes at age 3½ later had greater phonemic awareness and learned to read more readily than did those who knew fewer rhymes (Maclean et al., 1987). Because nursery rhyme knowledge was *not* predictive of the child's later mathematical ability in this study, it looks very much as if we are dealing here with a quite specific body of expertise.

Of all the types of early experience that may contribute to such expertise, the most crucial seems to be the experience of being read to, regularly and in a fashion that invites the child's attention and response—a point I already made in the Research Report on page 247. In families that do not engage in such reading, or do not encourage other prereading experiences, children have far more difficulty learning to read once they begin school.

For those lacking such expertise at the start of school, the only solution is to try to build a parallel base of knowledge through many of the same kinds of experiences that more expert readers have had at home. This means that poor readers need a great deal of exposure to sound/letter combinations. They also need to learn how to recognize patterns of letters in words. One need not—indeed must not—choose between those two hotly contesting educational systems, phonics and "whole word" training. Both are needed, along with instruction in syntax, so that the child will understand better what words *could* appear in certain places in sentences.

Marilyn Adams (1990), who has analyzed all the evidence, also makes a persuasive case that the poor reader must have maximum possible success in oral reading, preferably with texts that are full of the sort of rhyme and repetition that will help to foster phonemic awareness and learning of language regularities. Programs with this emphasis have been highly successful with poor readers, while more drill-like phonics programs have not (Hatcher et al., 1994). In other words, poor readers seem to learn to read most easily through programs that to some degree mimic the naturally occurring home experiences of good readers: a great deal of reading, "play" with words, active questioning, and experimentation.

Children who are read to often have an easier time learning to read later. And it doesn't have to be the parent who does the reading; this 9-year-old is reading to her younger sister.

Summary

1. Language can be defined as an arbitrary system of symbols that permits us to say (in words or gestures), and to understand, an infinite variety of messages. It is rule-governed and creative.

2. Many of the developments during the "prelinguistic" phase (before the first word) are significant precursors to language. The child discriminates language sounds, babbles sounds that more and more closely approximate the sounds he hears, and uses gestures in communicative ways.

3. At about 1 year of age the earliest words appear. Some of these early words are combined with gestures to convey whole sentences of meaning, a pattern called a holophrase.

4. Vocabulary grows slowly at first and then usually spurts in a "naming explosion." By 16 to 20 months, most children have a vocabulary of 50 or more words; by 30 months, the average vocabulary is 600 words. Children continue to add approximately one word every two hours through elementary school.

5. The first two-word sentences normally appear between 18 and 24 months and are short and grammatically simple, lacking the various grammatical inflections. The child can nonetheless convey many different meanings, such as location, possession, or agent-object relationships.

6. During a "grammar explosion" the child quickly adds the many grammatical inflections and learns to create questions and negative sentences.

7. By age 3 or 4, most children can construct remarkably complex sentences. Later skills are mostly just refinements, such as learning to understand and use passive sentences.

8. The development of word meanings (semantic development) follows a less predictable course. Children appear to have many concepts or categories before they have words for them, but learning new words also creates new categories.

9. The earliest words are typically highly specific and context-bound in meaning; later, children typically "overextend" their usage.

10. Many (but not all) linguists have concluded that in determining word meanings, a child has built-in constraints or biases, such as the assumption that words refer to objects or actions but not both, or the principle of contrast. Others think that such constraints exist but are acquired rather than built-in.

11. Children appear to have two uses for language: to communicate and to direct their own activity. Communication is the dominant use. As early as age 2, children adapt their language to the needs of the listener and begin to follow culturally specific customs of language usage.

12. Several theories have been offered to explain language development. Two early environmental explanations, based on imitation or reinforcement, have been largely set aside. More recently, emphasis has been placed both on the helpful quality of the simpler form of parent-to-child language called motherese or infant-directed language and on the role of expansions and recastings of children's sentences.

13. Innateness theories are also prominent. They assume the child is born with a set of "operating principles" that focus him on relevant aspects of language input. Others emphasize the child as a "little linguist" who constructs a language as he constructs all cognitive understandings.

14. Children show differences in the rate of development of both vocabulary and grammar, differences explained by both heredity and environmental influences. Despite these variations in rate of early development, however, most children learn to speak skillfully by about age 5 or 6.

15. In the early years of language development, two styles of language can be distinguished: "referential" (focusing on objects and their description) and "expressive" (focusing on words and forms that describe or further social relationships).

16. Research on language can also help to explain the development of reading skill. Metalinguistic awareness of the grammar, semantics, and segmented sounds of language seems to be critical for reading.

Key Terms

babbling The frequently repetitive vocalizing of consonant-vowel combinations by an infant, typically beginning at about 6 months of age. **p. 230**

bilingual education As practiced in the United States, a system of education for non-English-proficient students in which the instruction in reading, writing, and basic subject matter is in the children's native tongue during the first two or three years of schooling, with a gradual transition to full English instruction over several years. **p. 240**

constraint As used in discussions of language development, this refers to presumed built-in or early-learned assumptions ("default options") by which a child figures out what words refer to. Examples include the principle of contrast and the whole object constraint. **p. 242**

cooing An early phase of the prelinguistic period, from about 1 to 4 months of age, when vowel sounds are repeated, particularly the *uuu* sound. **p. 230**

English as a second language (ESL) An alternative to bilingual education; non-English-proficient students spend most of their school day in a full-English classroom but then spend several hours in a separate class with special instruction in English. **p. 240**

expressive language Term used to describe the child's skill in speaking and communicating orally. **p. 231**

expressive style One of two styles of early language proposed by Nelson, characterized by low rates of nounlike terms and high use of personal-social words and phrases. **p. 252**

holophrase A combination of a gesture with a single word that conveys a sentence-like meaning; often seen and heard in children between 12 and 18 months. **p. 235**

infant-directed speech The formal scientific term for "motherese"; that special form of simplified, higher-pitched speech adults use with infants and young children. **p. 246**

inflections The various grammatical "markers" such as the *s* for plurals or the *ed* for past tenses, auxiliary verbs such as *is*, and the equivalent. **p. 235**

jargon A form of babbling in which the infant strings together a series of different vowel-consonant combinations rather than repeating the same combination over and over. **p. 230**

mean length of utterance (MLU) The average number of meaningful units in a sentence. Each basic word is one meaningful unit, as is each inflection. **p. 251**

motherese See *infant-directed speech*. **p. 246**

overregularization The tendency on the part of children to make the language regular by creating regularized versions of irregular speech forms, such as past tenses or plurals—for example (in English), *beated* or *footses*. **p. 238**

pragmatics The rules for the use of language in communicative interaction, such as the rules for taking turns, the style of speech appropriate for varying listeners, and the equivalent. **p. 243**

prelinguistic phase The period before the child speaks her first words. **p. 229**

receptive language A term used to describe the child's ability to understand (receive) language, as contrasted to his ability to express language. **p. 231**

referential style The second style of early language proposed by Nelson, characterized by emphasis on objects and their naming and description. **p. 253**

semantics The rules for conveying meaning in language. **p. 228**

structured immersion An alternative to traditional bilingual education in which all children in a given classroom speak the same non-English native tongue. All basic instruction is in English, paced so that the children can comprehend, with the teacher translating only when absolutely necessary. **p. 240**

submersion Label used to describe programs for non-English-proficient students in which they are simply assigned to a regular English-speaking classroom without any supplemental language assistance. Also known as "sink or swim" programs. **p. 240**

syntax The rules for forming sentences; also called grammar. **p. 228**

telegraphic speech Term used by Roger Brown to describe the earliest sentences created by most children, because these sentences sound a bit like telegrams, including key nouns and verbs but generally omitting all other words and grammatical inflections. **p. 236**

Suggested Readings

Adams, M. J., Trieman, R., & Pressley, M. (1998). Reading, writing, and literacy. In W. Damon (Ed.), *Handbook of child psychology: Vol. 4. Child psychology in practice* (5th ed., pp. 275–355). New York: Wiley. A remarkably readable detailed discussion of the development of reading skill. Although this paper is aimed at professional psychologists and is thus quite technical in places, the writing style is informal and accessible. For those of you who plan to be teachers, this should be "must" reading.

de Villiers, P. A., & de Villiers, J. G. (1992). Language development. In M. H. Bornstein & M. E. Lamb (Eds.), *Developmental psychology: An advanced textbook* (3rd ed., pp. 337–418). Hillsdale, NJ: Erlbaum. A remarkably thorough and clear review of this subject, much easier to read than many current discussions or descriptions of language development, and touching on many of the issues I have raised here. Strongly recommended as a next source.

Harris, M. (1992). *Language experience and early language development: From input to uptake*. Hove, England: Erlbaum. Margaret Harris is a thoughtful researcher and theorist who argues in this book for the importance of the language input for the child's language development. She lays out the alternative theories nicely and presents a variety of evidence from her own research observations of mothers talking to their infants and toddlers.

Pinker, S. (1994). *The language instinct: How the mind creates language*. New York: Morrow. This splendid book, written by one of the most articulate and easy-to-understand linguists, lays out the argument for a built-in language instinct.

Shore, C. M. (1995). *Individual differences in language development*. Thousand Oaks, CA: Sage. A small book summarizing what we know about individual differences in rate and style of language development and the alternative explanations of those differences.

9

Personality Development: Alternative Views

Imagine yourself sitting in a day-care center, invisible to the eyes of the children but able to watch a group of 2-year-olds. Since you've just read all about cognitive and language development, your attention may be drawn at first to the ways the children play with toys or the way they talk to one another and to the teacher. At the same time, it won't take you long to notice that cognitive and language skills, however fascinating, are only part of the picture. The other part is the child's emerging *social* skills.

You'll see conflict over toys ("Mine!"), often settled with physical aggression or tears, although signs of helpfulness or altruism are also likely to be visible. You'll see children playing and moving about fairly independently, but you will also see that they still turn to the teacher often for attention and reassurance, sometimes physically clinging to her. You'll see boys and girls playing together, but little sign of any real individual friendships.

If you watched the same group of children a few years later, many of these patterns would have changed. By age 5 or 6 we see some friendships formed—although almost entirely between children of the same gender. Clinging and obvious dependence on adults is less in evidence, and disputes are more likely to be dealt with by yelling and name-calling than by grabbing or hitting.

These are all developmental changes, analogous to the changes in cognitive structure I talked about in Chapter 6. At the same time, you cannot watch children for very long without seeing the striking variations in children's approaches to these social tasks. The child who hung about on the edge of the group in nursery school is likely to show something similar in kindergarten; the child who clung more often to the teacher at age 2 or 3 is more likely to be the one who can hardly bear to let go of Mom on the first day of school. The gregarious toddler is probably the one who decides what game everyone will play at recess in first grade.

Psychologists normally use the word **personality** to describe these differences in the way children and adults go about relating to the people and objects in the world around them. Like the concept of intelligence, the concept of personality is designed to describe *enduring individual differences* in behavior. Whether we are gregarious or shy, independent or dependent, confident or uncertain, whether we plunge into new things or hold back—all these (and many more) are usually thought of as elements of personality.

Just as was true for cognition, we need to look at and try to understand both the common developmental patterns in children's social development and the individual differences in personality. Why do 5-year-olds normally show signs of individual friendships while 2-year-olds do not? What change makes that possible? Why are same-sex play groups much more obvious at school age than among preschoolers?

Each of these Texas junior high students has a distinct personality. Where do the differences come from?

And where do the personality differences come from? How does one child come to be shy and another gregarious? How does one child become a bully, another an accepted and popular friend? How does one child become securely attached, another insecurely attached, and what are the consequences of those variations over the long term?

I think the most helpful way to begin to try to answer this set of questions is to look at what we know about individual differences in personality and to consider the major theories that have been offered to explain personality development and its variations. Then in the following two chapters, we can look more directly at the research on developmental changes in social behavior.

Defining Personality in Adults

Like the concept of intelligence, the concept of personality has been hard to define clearly. Most theorists and researchers have thought of personality in terms of variations on a set of basic traits or dimensions, such as shyness versus gregariousness or activity versus passivity. If we could identify the basic dimensions, we could then describe any individual's personality as a profile of those key traits. That sounds straightforward, but coming to agreement on the nature of the key dimensions has been no simple task. Over the years, researchers and theorists have disagreed vehemently about how many such dimensions there might be, how they should be measured, or even whether there were any stable personality traits at all. Yet in the past decade, somewhat to the surprise of many psychologists, researchers in this disputatious field have reached consensus that adult personality can be adequately described as a set of variations along five major dimensions, often referred to as the **Big Five,** described in Table 9.1: **extraversion, agreeableness, conscientiousness, neuroticism,** and **openness/intellect** (Digman, 1990; John et al., 1994; McCrae & John, 1992).

Table 9.1

The Big Five Personality Traits

Trait	Basic Feature(s)	Qualities of Individual High in That Trait
Extraversion	Extent to which a person actively engages the world versus avoiding intense social experiences	Active, assertive, enthusiastic, outgoing, talkative
Agreeableness	Extent to which a person's interpersonal nature is characterized by warmth and compassion versus antagonism	Affectionate, forgiving, generous, kind, sympathetic, trusting
Conscientiousness	Extent and strength of impulse control; ability to delay gratification in the service of more distant goals	Efficient, organized, planful, reliable, responsible, thorough
Neuroticism; also called emotional (in)stability	Extent to which a person experiences the world as distressing or threatening	Anxious, self-pitying, tense, touchy, unstable, worrying
Openness/Intellect	Reflects the depth, complexity, and quality of a person's mental and experiential life	Artistic, curious, imaginative, insightful, original, having wide interests

Sources: McCrae & Costa, 1990; John et al., 1994, Table 1, p. 161; Caspi, 1998, p. 316.

These same five dimensions have been identified in studies of adults in a variety of countries, including some non-Western cultures, which lends some cross-cultural validity to this list. At the very least, we know that this set of dimensions is not unique to U.S. adults (Bond et al., 1975; Borkenau & Ostendorf, 1990). We also have good evidence that these five are stable traits: Among adults, scores on these five dimensions have been shown to be stable over periods as long as a decade or two (Costa & McCrae, 1994). Finally, the usefulness of the Big Five as a description of personality has been validated by a variety of studies linking scores on these dimensions to behavior in a wide variety of real-life situations. For example, adults who are high in extraversion are more likely to be satisfied with their lives than are those low in extraversion. Similarly, those high in neuroticism have poorer health habits (they more often smoke, for example) and complain more about their health than do those low in neuroticism (Costa & McCrae, 1984). Thus, the Big Five, as measured either through self-reports or through reports by observers, appear to be both reliable and valid descriptions of personality.

Defining Personality in Children

When we apply this new model to children's personality, we have to ask two questions. The first is, do these same five dimensions accurately describe children's personality? The second question is much trickier: What connection, if any, do these five dimensions have to infant and early childhood temperament? The great bulk of research on individual differences in infants' and children's style and manner of interaction with the world has been couched in terms of temperament, not personality, so how do we link these two bodies of research? Let's take the easier question first.

The Big Five in Childhood

A small but growing body of research suggests that the Big Five provide a decent description of personality structure in late childhood and adolescence, as well as adulthood (e.g., Caspi, 1998; Hartup & van Lieshout, 1995; Huey & Weisz, 1997). For example, Cornelis van Lieshout and Gerbert Haselager (1994), in a large study of children and adolescents in the Netherlands, found that the five clearest dimensions characterizing their young subjects matched the Big Five very well, and this was true for both boys and girls and for preschoolers as well as adolescents. In this sample, agreeableness and emotional (in)stability (equivalent to the neuroticism dimension) were the clearest dimensions, followed by conscientiousness, extraversion, and openness.

Similar results have come from a longitudinal study in the United States. Oliver John and his colleagues (1994) have studied a random sample of nearly 500 boys initially selected from among all fourth graders in the Pittsburgh public school system and followed up to age 13. Like the Dutch researchers, John has found strong evidence that the five-factor model captures the personality variations among these preteen boys. John's study is also helpful as a test of the validity of the five-factor model because he has information on other aspects of the boys' behavior, such as their school success or their delinquent behavior. By comparing the personality profiles of boys who differ in some other way, he can check to see if the personality patterns differ in ways that make theoretical and conceptual sense. For example, Figure 9.1 (p. 262) contrasts the personality profiles of boys who reported delinquent activity versus boys who reported none. As John predicted, delinquent boys were markedly lower than nondelinquent boys in both conscientiousness and agreeableness. John also found that boys higher in conscientiousness did slightly better in school, just as you would expect.

A nice cross-cultural validation of the five-factor model comes from a study by Geldolph Kohnstamm and his colleagues (Havill et al., 1994; Kohnstamm et al., 1994), who asked parents in the United States, the Netherlands, Belgium, and Suriname to describe their child, using whatever language they chose. He found that 70 to 80 percent

Critical Thinking

Look over the list of qualities for each of the Big Five traits given in Table 9.1. How would you rate yourself on each of these dimensions?

Figure 9.1

Twelve-year-olds who report more delinquent acts have quite different personality profiles than do nondelinquent 12-year-olds—a set of results that helps to validate the usefulness of the Big Five personality traits as a description of children's personality.

(*Source:* O. P. John et al., from "The 'little five': Exploring the nomological network of the five factor model of personality in adolescent boys," *Child development*, 65, 160–178. By permission of the Society for Research in Child Development.)

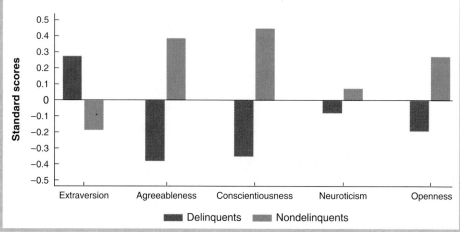

of the qualities mentioned by parents in each of these four cultures could be classified in one of the Big Five personality traits.

These early results are impressive and point to the usefulness of the five-factor model, but it is still too soon to tell whether the Big Five will turn out to be the optimal way of describing children's personality. In particular, we may need more than five dimensions to describe children. For example, both John and his colleagues in their U.S. study and van Lieshout and Haselager in their Dutch study found two additional dimensions describing children's personality: irritability and activity level. Since both these dimensions typically appear in descriptions of temperament, this brings us to the more difficult question: What is the connection between all the Big Five research and studies of infant and child temperament?

Links to Temperament

I talked about temperament in both Chapters 1 and 3, so the concept is not completely new. What is confusing (even to most psychologists) is the question of whether *temperament* is just another word for *personality* or whether the two concepts are really different.

Mary Rothbart and John Bates, two of the leading researchers in this area, define **temperament** as "constitutionally based individual differences in emotional, motor, and attentional reactivity and self-regulation" (1998, p. 109). These authors, and most others who study temperament, conceive of these qualities as the emotional *substrate* of personality—that set of core qualities or response patterns that are visible in infancy and reflected in such things as typical activity level, irritability or emotionality, soothability, fearfulness, and sociability (Hartup & van Lieshout, 1995, p. 658). In this way of thinking, temperament is "the matrix from which later child and adult personality develops" (Ahadi & Rothbart, 1994, p. 190).

This distinction between temperament and personality is a little like the difference between a genotype and a phenotype. The genotype sets the basic pattern, but the eventual outcome depends on the way the basic pattern is affected by specific experience. Thus, temperament may represent the basic pattern; what we measure as personality later in childhood or adulthood reflects the basic pattern affected by myriad life experiences.

If this model is correct, then variations in temperament ought to bear some (perhaps considerable) resemblance to the five basic personality dimensions we see in adulthood, although early temperament will probably not map directly onto the Big Five traits.

Dimensions of Temperament

Discovering whether this conceptualization actually matches the data has been made difficult by the fact that temperament researchers, unlike adult-personality researchers, have not yet agreed on the best way to characterize the variations in early temperament. Instead, we have had several rather different category systems, each influencing a body of research.

One of the most influential temperament category systems has been Chess and Thomas's description of *difficult, easy,* and *slow-to-warm-up* temperaments, reflecting profiles on nine different dimensions—a system I described in Chapter 3. In contrast, Buss and Plomin originally proposed only three key dimensions: *activity level, emotionality* (primarily negative emotionality), and *sociability* (Buss, 1989; Buss & Plomin, 1984; 1986). The questionnaire they devised to measure these three qualities has been widely used by researchers studying infants, children, and adults. Yet a third key figure has been Jerome Kagan, who has focused on only a single dimension, which he calls *behavioral inhibition*—an aspect of what most people mean by "shyness" (Kagan et al., 1990; 1993).

No one of these conceptualizations has quite won the day. Temperament researchers are still struggling to define the key dimensions and have not reached a clear agreement. However, the most recent writings of many of the primary researchers offer some hope of consensus (Ahadi & Rothbart, 1994; Belsky et al., 1996; Kagan, 1997; Martin et al., 1994; Rothbart & Bates, 1998). Many theorists are now emphasizing the following five key dimensions and are actively exploring the possible links between these key dimensions of temperament and the Big Five (e.g., Caspi, 1998).

- *Activity level.* A tendency to move often and vigorously, rather than to remain passive or immobile. High activity is most often hypothesized as a precursor to extraversion (Martin et al., 1994), a link found in one recent longitudinal study in Sweden (Hagekull & Bohlin, 1998).

- *Approach/positive emotionality.* A tendency to move toward rather than away from people, new things, or objects, usually accompanied by positive emotion. This is similar to what Buss and Plomin call sociability and seems to be another obvious precursor to extraversion at later ages. It may also be a precursor to what is later measured as agreeableness (Caspi, 1998; Rothbart & Bates, 1998).

- *Inhibition and anxiety.* The flip side of approach is a tendency to respond with fear or withdrawal to new people, new situations, or new objects. This dimension has been intensely studied by Jerome Kagan and his colleagues (e.g., Kagan, 1994; 1997; Kagan et al., 1990), who see this as the precursor to what is called shyness in everyday language. In the five-factor model, inhibition and anxiety would be reflected in very low scores on extraversion and low scores on openness, and may also contribute to high scores on neuroticism at later ages.

- *Negative emotionality/irritability/anger.* A tendency to respond with anger, fussing, loudness, or irritability; a low threshold of frustration. This appears to be what Thomas and Chess are tapping with their concept of the "difficult" child and what Buss and Plomin call emotionality. It is an obvious precursor to what is later called neuroticism (e.g., Hagekull & Bohlin, 1998).

Cultures and Contexts

Cultural Differences in Infant Temperament

Are infants all over the world alike in their temperaments? Are we just as likely to see a highly active infant in China or among the Navaho as among Caucasian infants? Several investigators have concluded that the answer is "no." There appear to be cultural differences in certain aspects of temperament, beginning as early as the first few months of life.

Daniel Freedman (1979) observed newborn babies from four different cultures: Euro-American, Chinese, Navaho, and Japanese. Of the four, he found that the Euro-American babies were the most active and irritable and the hardest to console (the most "difficult," in Chess and Thomas's terms). Both the Chinese and the Navaho infants were relatively placid, while the Japanese infants responded vigorously but were easier to quiet than the Euro-American infants.

Jerome Kagan and his colleagues (1994) have replicated part of these results in their comparison of Chinese, Irish, and Euro-American 4-month-olds. They found that the Chinese infants were significantly less active, less irritable, and less vocal than were babies in the other two groups. The white American infants showed the strongest reactions to new sights, sounds,

or smells. Similarly, Chisholm (1989) has replicated Freedman's research on Navaho babies, finding them to be significantly less irritable, less excitable, and more able to quiet themselves than Euro-American babies.

Since such differences are visible in newborns, they cannot be the result of systematic shaping by the parents. But the parents, too, bring their temperament and their cultural training to the interaction, which may tend to strengthen or perpetuate such temperamental differences. For instance, Freedman and other researchers have observed that both Japanese and Chinese mothers talk much less to their infants than do Caucasian mothers. These differences in mothers' behavior were present from their first encounters with their infants after delivery, so the pattern is not a response to the babies' quieter behavior. Nonetheless, such similarity of temperamental pattern between mother and child is likely to strengthen the pattern in the child, which would tend to make the cultural differences larger over time.

One of the key points from this research is that our notions of what is "normal" behavior for an infant may be strongly influenced by our own cultural patterns and assumptions.

In this photo, 4-year-old Sayde appears to have a high degree of "effortful control," one of the dimensions of temperament identified by current researchers.

- *Effortful control/task persistence.* An ability to stay focused, to manage attention and effort. Caspi (1998) suggests that this temperamental quality may contribute to several later personality dimensions, including conscientiousness, agreeableness, and openness to experience.

This is obviously not a final list; temperament researchers are still working their way toward common ground. But this set of traits or qualities is probably fairly close to the list they will eventually agree on. At the very least, we know that babies and young children do differ on these dimensions, and we have some reasonable hypotheses about how these early variations may link with later stable personality characteristics. That's saying a lot.

Despite these advances, we are still left with several huge questions to answer. Where do these differences come from, and how are they transformed into adult personality? It is also important not to ignore the common developmental patterns. Are there phases or stages all children appear to go through in forming an adult personality?

Questions like these obviously take us into the realm of theory. So we're going on a fast trip through the theoretical landscape, including *biological, learning,* and *psychoanalytic* explanations of personality. Let me lay out each of these alternative models as a set of propositions.

Genetic and Biological Explanations

The biological argument runs like this:

Proposition 1: Each individual is born with genetically determined characteristic patterns of responding to the environment and to other people. Virtually every researcher who studies temperament shares the assumption that temperamental qualities are *inborn,* carried in the genes. The idea here is not so very different from the notion of "inborn biases" or "constraints" I have talked about in earlier chapters except that here we are talking about *individual* rather than shared behavioral dispositions.

Clear, strong evidence supports such an assertion (Rose, 1995; Saudino, 1998), both in studies of adult personality (discussed in the Research Report on p. 266) and in studies of children's temperament. Studies of twins in many countries show that identical twins are quite a lot more alike in their temperament or personality than are fraternal twins (Rose, 1995). Hill Goldsmith and his colleagues (1997a) have recently combined the results from many studies in which twins have been rated by their parents on some version of the Buss and Plomin temperament categories. Table 9.2 shows that the correlations on each dimension are a great deal higher for pairs of identical twins than for fraternal twins, indicating a strong genetic effect. Table 9.2 also shows one parallel result from a study of behavioral inhibition by Robert Plomin and his collaborators (1993). They studied 100 pairs of identical twins and 100 pairs of fraternal twins at age 20 months, measuring behavioral inhibition by observing how each child reacted to a strange adult and strange toys in a special laboratory playroom. Did the child approach the novel toys quickly and eagerly, or did she hang back or seem fearful? Did she approach the strange adult, or did she remain close to Mom? You can see from Table 9.2 that identical twins were much more similar in their responses to this situation than were fraternal twins.

Proposition 2: These genetic differences operate via variations in fundamental physiological processes. Many (but not all) temperament theorists take the argument a step further and trace the basic differences in behavior to variations in underlying physiological patterns, particularly to variations in the reactivity of underlying neural systems (Derryberry & Rothbart, 1998; Gunnar, 1994; Nelson, 1994; Rothbart & Bates, 1998). Recall, for example, that Rothbart and Bates define temperament as *constitutionally based.* One specific example: Jerome Kagan has suggested that differences in behavioral inhibition are based on differing thresholds for arousal in those parts of the brain—the amygdala and the hypothalamus—that control responses to uncertainty (1994; Kagan et al., 1990; 1993). Arousal of these parts of the brain leads to increases in muscle tension and heart rate. Shy or inhibited children are thought to have a *low* threshold for such a reaction. That is, they more readily become tense and alert in the presence of uncertainty, perhaps even interpreting a wider range of situations as uncertain. What we inherit, then, is not "shyness" or some equivalent but a tendency for the brain to react in particular ways.

Table 9.2

Similarity of Temperament Ratings in Identical and Fraternal Twin Preschoolers

	Correlation	
Temperament Scale	**Identical Twins**	**Fraternal Twins**
Combined Results from Many Studies		
Emotionality	.57	.11
Activity	.64	−.08
Sociability	.59	.10
Plomin Study of Behavioral Inhibition	.45	.17

Source: From "Toddler and childhood temperament: Expanded content, stronger genetic evidence, new evidence for the importance of environment" by H. H. Goldsmith, K. A. Buss, and K. S. Lemery, *Developmental psychology,* 33 (1997), p. 892, Table 1; © 1997 American Psychological Association, reprinted within guidelines of the American Psychological Association and by permission of H. Hill Goldsmith. Plomin et al., "Genetic change and continuity form fourteen to twenty months: The MacArthur longitudinal twin study," *Child development,* 64 (1994), p. 1364, Table 2, Ann Arbor: Society for Research in Child Development, 1994.

Research Report

The Inheritance of Personality Patterns: Evidence from Adults

In the past decade, a number of methodologically careful new studies of adult twins have repeatedly demonstrated that identical twins are more like one another than are fraternal twins both on measures of the Big Five personality traits and on measures of temperament using Buss and Plomin's categories (see Caspi, 1998, for a review).

For example, a group of researchers including Nancy Pedersen and Robert Plomin (Bergeman et al., 1993; Pedersen et al., 1988) has taken advantage of the existence of an amazingly extensive and up-to-date twin registry in Sweden that includes 25,000 pairs of twins born between 1886 and 1958. From this set, they were able to identify 99 pairs of identical twins and 229 pairs of fraternal twins reared apart and could then compare these with similar groups of twins reared together. On each of the Big Five personality dimensions, identical twins were more similar than were fraternal twins. The degree of similarity was less for identical twins reared apart, but these pairs were nonetheless significantly more alike than were fraternal twins reared apart.

A smaller but much more famous study in the United States is the Minnesota Twin Study (Bouchard, 1984; Lykken et al., 1992; Tellegen et al., 1988)—a study that has been the subject of a great many articles in the popular press. These researchers have been particularly interested in identical twins reared apart, frequently arranging for them to meet one another for the first time. On standard personality tests they find the now familiar pattern: Identical twins are simply much more like one another than are fraternal twins, even when the identical twins did not grow up to-

gether. This was true on such measures as positive and negative emotionality, but also on less obvious measures such as a sense of "social potency" or a sense of well-being. Even a measure of "traditionalism"—an affinity for traditional values and a strong allegiance to established authority—shows slightly higher correlations among identical than among fraternal twins.

What have intrigued the popular press much more, though, are the less precise but far more striking descriptions of the similarities in clothing preferences, interests, posture and body language, speed and tempo of talking, favorite jokes, and hobbies in pairs of identical twins reared apart:

> One male pair who had never previously met arrived in England sporting identical beards, haircuts, wire-rimmed glasses and shirts. . . . One pair had practically the same items in their toilet cases, including the same brand of cologne and a Swedish brand of toothpaste. . . . [One pair] had the same fears and phobias. Both were afraid of water and had adopted the same coping strategy: Backing into the ocean up to their knees. (Holden, 1987, p. 18)

It is difficult to imagine what sort of genetic process could account for similar preferences in hairstyles or for a particular brand of toothpaste. Still, we can't dismiss the results merely because they are hard to explain. At the very least, these findings point to strong genetic components in many of the elements of personal style and emotional responsiveness that temperament and personality researchers are trying to identify and track in children.

In support of this argument, Kagan reports correlations in the range of .60 between a measure of behavioral inhibition in children aged 2 to 5 and a series of physiological measures, such as muscle tension, heart rate, dilation of the pupil of the eye, and chemical composition of both urine and saliva, all of which strongly suggests that temperament is based on physiological responses and is not simply a set of learned habits (1994; Kagan et al., 1990).

Proposition 3: Temperamental dispositions persist through childhood and into adulthood. No theorist in this tradition proposes that initial temperamental dispositions remain unchanged by experience—a point I'll come back to in a moment. Still, if temperamental patterns create a bias in the system toward particular behaviors, we ought to see at least some stability of temperament over time. Such stability ought to show itself in the form of at least modest correlations between measures of a given temperamental dimension from one age to another.

Although the research evidence is somewhat mixed, we have growing evidence of consistency in temperamental ratings over rather long periods of infancy and childhood. For example, Australian researchers studying a group of 450 children found that mothers' reports of children's irritability, cooperation/manageability, inflexibility, rhythmicity, persistency, and tendency to approach (rather than avoid) contact were all quite consistent from infancy through age 8 (Pedlow et al., 1993). Similarly, in a U.S. longitudinal study covering the years from age 1 to age 12, Diana Guerin and Allen Gottfried (1994a; 1994b) found strong consistency in parent reports of their children's overall "difficultness" as well as approach versus withdrawal, positive versus negative mood, and activity level.

Kagan has also found considerable consistency over the same age range in his measure of inhibition, which is based on direct observation of the child's behavior rather than on the mother's or father's ratings of the child's temperament. He reports that half of babies in his longitudinal study who had shown high levels of crying and motor activity in response to a novel situation when they were 4 months old were still classified as highly inhibited at age 8, while three-fourths of those rated as uninhibited at 4 months remained in that category eight years later (Kagan et al., 1993). Furthermore, the inhibited toddlers in Kagan's sample were *less* likely than their more uninhibited peers to be rated as highly aggressive or delinquent at age 11 (Schwartz et al., 1996).

Thus, babies who readily and positively approach the world around them continue to be more positive as young teenagers, while cranky, temperamentally difficult babies continue to show many of the same temperamental qualities 10 years later, and strongly behaviorally inhibited babies are quite likely to continue to show such "shyness" at later ages. Such consistency is probably stronger among children whose temperamental patterns are initially fairly extreme, such as highly inhibited youngsters or those with particularly clear patterns of negative emotionality (e.g., Rubin et al., 1997), but even among children with less extreme patterns we find some degree of consistency.

Proposition 4: Temperamental characteristics interact with the child's environment in ways that may either strengthen or modify the basic temperamental patterns. Despite all this clear evidence for genetic/biological influences on temperament, genetics is clearly not destiny here; there is still a good deal of room for environmental influences. For example, the extent to which parents express warmth toward their children seems to be a significant factor in shaping the child's own tendency toward positive affect and approach rather than withdrawal (Rothbart & Bates, 1998).

In most cases, the resultant personality develops through some interaction between the child's temperamental tendencies and the environment the child encounters or creates. One factor that tends to strengthen a child's built-in qualities is the fact that each of us—including young children—*chooses* our experiences. Highly sociable children seek out contact with others; children low on the activity dimension are more likely to choose sedentary activities like puzzles or board games than baseball. Similarly, temperament may affect the way in which a child *interprets* a given experience—a factor that helps to account for the fact that two children in the same family may experience the family pattern of interaction quite differently.

Imagine, for example, a family that moves often, such as a military family. If one child in this family has a strong built-in pattern of behavioral inhibition, the myriad changes and new experiences will trigger fear responses over and over. This child

This 1-year-old may just be having a bad day. But if this is a typical reaction, one sign of a "difficult" temperament, she will be at higher risk for a variety of problems at later ages.

comes to anticipate each new move with dread and is likely to interpret his family life as highly stressful. A second child in the same family, with a more strongly approach-oriented temperament, finds the many moves stimulating and energizing and is likely to think of his childhood in a much more positive light.

A third environmental factor that often reinforces built-in temperamental patterns is the tendency of parents (and others in the child's world) to respond differently to children with varying temperaments. The sociable child, who may smile often, is likely to elicit more smiles, more positive interactions with parents, simply because she has reinforced their behavior by her positive temperament. Buss and Plomin (1984) have proposed the general argument that children in the middle range on temperament dimensions typically adapt *to* their environment, while those whose temperament is extreme—like extremely difficult children—force their environment to adapt to them. Parents of difficult children, for example, adapt to the children's negativity by punishing them more and providing them with less support and stimulation than do parents of more adaptable children (Luster et al., 1993; Rutter, 1978). This pattern may well contribute to the higher rates of significant emotional problems in such children, a set of results I have explored in the Research Report below.

Critical Thinking

The finding that difficult children are punished more often could be interpreted in several ways. How many alternative explanations can you think of?

Research Report
Temperament and Behavior Problems

One of the consistent findings in research on temperament is that children with difficult temperaments are much more likely to show various kinds of emotional disturbance or *behavior problems* than are children with less extreme temperaments. Included in the category of behavior problems (which I'll be talking about in more detail in Chapter 15, when I discuss abnormal development) are such patterns as overaggressiveness, depression, anxiety, and hyperactivity (Rothbart & Bates, 1998).

The typical finding is that children who are rated as having aspects of difficult temperament, or those who are high in negative affectivity or with poor impulse control, are perhaps twice as likely to show one or another of these behavior problems as are children with less difficult temperaments (Bates, 1989; Chess & Thomas, 1984; Hagekull, 1994). So babies with more difficult temperaments are more likely to become preschoolers who show some behavior problem, and preschoolers whose temperament is rated as difficult or who are "lacking in control" are more likely to have behavior problems at age 10 or 15 or even as adults (Caspi et al., 1995).

Such findings may sound like a simple restatement of consistency of temperament. Perhaps hyperactivity, inattentiveness, aggressiveness, or other behavior problems in 5-year-olds or 7-year-olds are simply further manifestations of a basically difficult temperament. But it is not so easy. The majority of children who are rated as showing "difficult" temperament in infancy or in the preschool years do *not* develop behavior problems at later ages. They are more *likely* to exhibit such problems, but the relationship is not at all inevitable.

As usual, a complex interactive process is involved. The key seems to be whether the infant's or child's "difficultness" is acceptable to the parents or can be managed by the family in some effective way. For example, Fish, Stifter, and Belsky (1991) have studied changes and continuities in crying patterns in a small sample of infants. They found that those babies who had cried a great deal as newborns but cried much less at 5 months had mothers who were highly responsive and sensitive to the infant. Babies who cried a lot at both time points had much less responsive mothers. Thus, the responsive mother may have reshaped the baby's inborn temperamental behavior. Difficult temperament also seems to increase the risk of behavior problems when there are other stresses in the family system (such as divorce) or other deficits in the child, such as physical disability or retardation (Chess & Korn, 1980).

Thus, difficult temperament does not *cause* later behavior problems. Rather, it creates a *vulnerability* in the child. Such children seem to be less able to deal with major life stresses. Nevertheless, in a supportive, accepting, low-stress environment, many such children move through childhood without displaying any significant behavior problems.

The lesson for parents is not always an easy one. If you are under severe stress, that is precisely the moment when it is hard to provide a maximally supportive, accepting environment for any child, let alone a temperamentally difficult child. It may still help to keep in mind that a child with a difficult temperament is going to need more attention, more help, more support than will a temperamentally less volatile child under any kind of stress, such as when the family moves, when the child changes schools or baby-sitters, or if the family pet dies.

Buss and Plomin's proposal, while accurate, doesn't convey the additional complexities of the process. First of all, sensitive and responsive parents can moderate the more extreme forms of infant or child temperament. A particularly nice example comes from the work of Megan Gunnar (1994) and her colleagues, who have studied a group of highly inhibited toddlers who differed in the security of their attachment to their mothers. In a series of studies (Colton et al., 1992; Nachmias, 1993), they found that *insecurely* attached inhibited toddlers showed the usual physiological responses to challenging or novel situations. *Securely* attached temperamentally inhibited toddlers, on the other hand, showed no such indications of physiological arousal in the face of novelty or challenge. Thus, the secure attachment appears to have modified a basic physiological/temperamental response. Over time, the child's personality pattern may shift away from extreme inhibition or shyness.

Another example, also with inhibited/fearful children, comes from the work of Kenneth Rubin and his colleagues (1997), who found that highly inhibited children with oversolicitous mothers showed more persistent inhibition across situations than did those whose mothers were more relaxed and less intrusive or intense.

Thus, while many forces within the environment tend to reinforce the child's basic temperament and thus create stability and consistency of temperament/personality over time, environmental forces can also push a child toward new patterns or aid a child in controlling extreme forms of basic physiological reactions.

Critique of Biological Theories

The biological approach to the origins of personality has two great strengths. First, it is strongly supported by a large body of empirical research. There is simply no refuting the fact that built-in genetic and physiological patterns underlie what we think of as both temperament and personality. This approach thus provides a powerful counterweight to the longtime dominance of psychoanalytic and learning theories of personality development, both of which had strongly emphasized environmental influences.

Paradoxically, the second strength I see is that this is not a *purely* biological approach; it is an interactionist approach, very much in keeping with much of the current theorizing about development. The child is born with certain behavioral tendencies, but his eventual personality depends on the transactions between his initial characteristics and the responses of his environment.

On the other side of the ledger, I see a number of problems, not the least of which is the continuing lack of agreement on the basic dimensions of temperament. Researchers have used such varying definitions and varying measures that it is often difficult to add up the results of different investigations.

A second problem has been that many biologically oriented temperament theories have not been fundamentally *developmental* theories. They allow for change through the mechanism of interaction with the environment, but they do not tell us whether we might expect systematic age differences in children's responses to new situations or to people; they do not tell us whether the child's emerging cognitive skills have anything to do with changes in the child's temperamental patterns. They do not, in a word, tell us how the *shared* developmental patterns may interact with the inborn individual differences. A few theorists have begun to talk about such developmental patterns (e.g., Rothbart & Bates, 1998), but this remains a set of questions in need of exploration.

Neither of these concerns constitutes a refutation of any of the basic tenets of this theoretical approach. We can simply no longer ignore the importance of genetic differences and basic biology in shaping individual differences in temperament or personality.

Learning Explanations

The emphasis shifts rather dramatically when we look at social learning approaches. Instead of focusing on what the child brings to the equation, learning theorists have

This child, clinging to her mom's leg, might be rated as relatively high in "behavioral inhibition," but she is also being reinforced for her clinging or shy behavior, thus strengthening it.

Critical Thinking

Can you think of other real-life examples of partial reinforcement in action? What about things you do to please someone important to you, for which you get a smile only some of the time?

looked at the reinforcement patterns in the environment as the primary cause of differences in children's patterns of behavior. Of course, theorists in this tradition do not reject biology. Albert Bandura, arguably the most influential theorist in this group, grants that biological factors such as hormones or inherited propensities (such as temperament, presumably) also affect behavior. But he and others of this persuasion look to the environment as the major source of influence.

These are not new ideas for you. You already read about the basic concepts in Chapter 1 and encountered a version of such a theory in Skinner's explanation of language acquisition. The question here is how to apply this theory specifically to such temperamental characteristics as activity level or gregariousness, or such social behaviors as aggressiveness or dependency—both often thought of as aspects of personality.

The learning camp includes several distinct schools of thought. Some investigators, often called *radical behaviorists,* argue that only the basic principles of classical and operant conditioning are needed to account for variations in behavior, including personality. Others, like Bandura, emphasize not only observational learning but also important cognitive elements. Both groups would agree with the first two propositions I've listed below; the remaining propositions emerge primarily from Bandura's work.

Proposition 1: Behavior is "strengthened" by reinforcement. If this rule applies to all behavior, then it should apply to attachment, shyness, sharing, or competitiveness. Children who are reinforced for clinging to their parents, for example, should show more clinging than do children who are not reinforced for it. Similarly, a nursery school teacher who pays attention to children only when they get rowdy or aggressive should find that the children in her care get steadily more rowdy and aggressive over the course of weeks or months.

Proposition 2: Behavior that is reinforced on a "partial schedule" should be even stronger and more resistant to extinction than behavior that is consistently reinforced. I talked briefly about this phenomenon in Chapter 1, so you have some idea of what is involved. Most parents are inconsistent in their reinforcements of their children, so most children are on partial schedules of some kind, whether the parent intends that or not. That is, they are sometimes reinforced for a particular behavior, but not every time. Because behavior that is rewarded in this way is highly persistent—highly *resistant to extinction,* in the language of learning theory—partial reinforcement patterns are a major factor in the establishment of those distinctive and stable patterns of behavior defined as personality.

An immense collection of studies supports these first two propositions. For example, in several studies, experimenters systematically rewarded some children for hitting an inflated rubber clown on the nose. When the researchers later watched the children in a free play situation with peers, they found that the children who had been rewarded showed more hitting, scratching, and kicking than did children who hadn't been rewarded for punching the clown (Walters & Brown, 1963). Partial reinforcement in the form of inconsistent behavior from parents also has the expected effect. For example, Sears, Maccoby, and Levin (1977) found that parents who permit fairly high levels of aggression in their children, but occasionally react by punishing it quite severely, have children who are more aggressive than are children whose parents neither permit nor punish aggression.

Gerald Patterson's research on families with aggressive or noncompliant children, which I described in Chapter 1, also illustrates the significance of these basic principles. If you go back and look at Figure 1.2 (p. 11), you'll see that the heart of Patterson's model is a link between "poor parental discipline" and resultant conduct problems in the child. He is arguing here that both normal personality patterns and deviant forms of social behavior have their roots in daily social exchanges with family members. For example, imagine a child playing in his very messy room. The mother tells the child to clean up his room. The child whines or yells at her that he doesn't want to do it or won't do it. The mother gives in and leaves the room, and the child stops whining or shouting.

The Real World

Applying Learning Principles at Home

It is a lot harder than you may think to apply basic learning principles consistently and correctly with children at home or in schools. Virtually all parents do try to reinforce some behaviors in their children by praising them or by giving them attention or treats. And most of us try to discourage unpleasant behavior through punishment. But it is easy to misapply the principles or to create unintended consequences because we have not fully understood all the mechanisms involved.

For example, suppose you have a favorite armchair in your living room that is being systematically ruined by the dirt and pressure of little feet climbing up the back of the chair. You want the children to *stop* climbing up the chair. So you scold them. After a while you may even stoop to nagging. If you are really conscientious and knowledgeable, you may carefully try to time your scolding so that it operates as a negative reinforcer, by stopping your scolding when they stop climbing. But nothing works. They keep on leaving those dirty footprints on your favorite chair. Why? It could be because the children *enjoy* climbing up the chair. So the climbing is intrinsically reinforcing to the children, and that effect is clearly stronger than your negative reinforcement or punishment. One way to deal with this might be to provide something *else* for them to climb on.

Another example: Suppose your 3-year-old son repeatedly demands your attention while you are fixing dinner (a common state of affairs, as any parent of a 3-year-old can tell you). Because you don't want to reinforce this behavior, you ignore him the first six or eight times he says "Mommy" or tugs at your clothes. After the ninth or tenth repetition, though, with his voice getting louder and whinier each time, you can't stand it any longer and finally say something like "All *right!* What do you want?" Since you have ignored most of his demands, you might well be convinced that you have not been reinforcing his demanding behavior, but what you have actually done is to create a partial reinforcement schedule; you have rewarded only every tenth demand or whine. And we know that this pattern of reinforcement helps to create behavior that is very hard to extinguish. So your son may continue to be demanding and whining for a very long time, even if you later succeed in ignoring his behavior completely.

If such situations are familiar to you, it may pay to keep careful records for a while, keeping track of each incident and your response, and then see if you can figure out which principles are really at work and how you might change the pattern.

Patterson analyzes this exchange as a pair of negatively reinforced events. When the mother gives in to the child's defiance, her own behavior (giving in) is negatively reinforced by the ending of the child's whining or yelling. This makes it more likely that she will give in the next time. She has *learned* to back down in order to get the child to shut up. At the same time, the child has been negatively reinforced for yelling or whining, since the unpleasant event for him (being told to clean his room) stopped as soon as he whined. So he has learned to whine or yell. Imagine such exchanges occurring over and over, and you begin to understand how a family can create a *system* in which an imperious, demanding, noncompliant child rules the roost (Snyder et al., 1994).

As I pointed out in Chapter 1, Patterson's thinking has moved beyond the simple propositions I have outlined here. Like the current temperament theorists, he emphasizes that what happens in a given family, for a particular child, is a joint product of the child's own temperament or response tendencies, the parents' discipline skills, the parents' personalities, and the social context of the parents' lives. Patterson is nonetheless still assuming that basic learning principles can both describe and explain the ways in which the child's behavior pattern (his "personality") is formed or changed. And he and others have shown that it is possible to *change* the child's typical behavior by helping families learn new and more effective reinforcement and management strategies, and in this way to reduce the likelihood of later delinquency (Tremblay et al., 1995a; Wierson & Forehand, 1994).

Proposition 3: Children learn new behaviors largely through modeling. Bandura has argued that the full range of social behaviors, from competitiveness to nurturance, is

Three-year-old Marvin is not only learning something about how to use a screwdriver from observing and working next to his dad; he's also learning his father's attitudes about work and perhaps the beginnings of self-efficacy.

Critical Thinking

Suppose you were trying to learn a new sport, such as tennis or soccer, by observing an expert. Can you see how these four principles would affect what you could learn from the model?

learned not just by direct reinforcement but also by watching others perform those actions. Thus, the child who sees her parents taking a casserole next door to the woman who has just been widowed will learn generosity and thoughtful behavior. The child who sees her parents hitting each other when they are angry will most likely learn violent ways of solving problems.

Children learn from TV, too, and from their peers, their teachers, and their brothers and sisters. A boy growing up in an environment where he observes playmates and older boys hanging around street corners, shoplifting, or selling drugs is going to learn all those behaviors. His continuous exposure to such antisocial models makes it that much harder for his parents to reinforce more constructive behavior.

These many effects of observational learning have been demonstrated experimentally in literally hundreds of studies (Bandura, 1973; 1977). One interesting—and very practical—sidelight to the process of modeling has been the repeated finding that modeling works better than preaching. So displaying the desired behavior yourself—such as generosity, fairness, or diligent work—is more effective than simply telling children that it is good to be generous, fair, or hardworking.

For example, in one early study, Joan Grusec and her co-workers (1978) had elementary school children play a miniature bowling game, ostensibly to test the game. The children first observed an adult "test" the game and saw the adult win 20 marbles. Next to the bowling game was a poster that said "Help poor children. Marbles buy gifts." Under the poster was a bowl with some marbles in it. Half the subjects saw the adult model donate half his newly won marbles to this bowl; the other half of the children did not see the model donating marbles. In addition, the model either "preached" about donating marbles or said nothing. To some of the children he preached in specific terms, saying that the child should donate half his marbles when he played the game, since it would be good to make poor children happy by doing that. To other children, he preached in more general terms, saying that the child should donate half his marbles because it is a good thing to make other people happy by helping them any way one can. After demonstrating the game, the adult model then left the room, and the child had an opportunity to play the bowling game and to decide whether to donate any marbles. You can see in Figure 9.2 how many children in each group (out of a maximum of 16) donated marbles. Clearly, modeling worked better than preaching. The results also illustrate the point that when a conflict exists between what the model says and what the model does—such as when parents smoke but tell their kids that they should not smoke—children generally follow the behavior and not the verbal message. So the old adage "Do what I say and not what I do" doesn't seem to work.

However, learning from modeling is not an entirely automatic process. Bandura points out that what a child (or adult) learns from watching someone else will depend on four things: what she pays attention to and what she is able to remember (both *cognitive* processes), what she is physically able to copy, and what she is motivated to imitate. Because attentional abilities, memory, and other cognitive processes change with age through infancy and childhood, what a baby or child can or will learn from any given modeled event will also change through development (Grusec, 1992).

Proposition 4: Children learn not only overt behavior but also ideas, expectations, internal standards, and self-concepts from reinforcement and modeling. The child learns standards for his own behavior and expectancies about what he can and cannot do—which Bandura (1997) calls *self-efficacy*—from specific reinforcements and from modeling. In this way, the child *internalizes* what he has learned. Once those standards and those expectancies or beliefs are established, they affect the child's behavior in consistent and enduring ways and form the core of what can be called personality.

Critique of Learning Models

Several implications of this overall theoretical approach are worth emphasizing. First of all, learning theorists can handle either consistency or inconsistency in children's be-

Figure 9.2

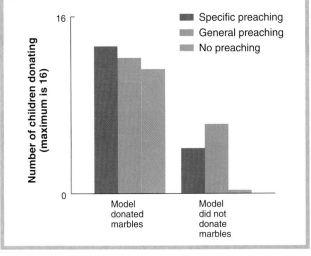

These results from Grusec's modeling study illustrate the general finding that modeling is more powerful than preaching in changing children's behavior.

(*Source:* Grusec et al., 1978, from Table 1, p. 922.)

havior. The behavior of a child who is friendly and smiling both at home and at school, for example, could be explained by saying that the child is being reinforced for that behavior in both settings rather than by assuming that the child has strong "approach tendencies" or a "gregarious temperament." Similarly, if the child is helpful at school but defiant at home, we need only invoke the principle that different reinforcement contingencies are at work in the two settings. To be sure, because individuals tend to choose settings that support or reward their accustomed behavior and because a person's behavior tends to *elicit* similar responses (reinforcements) from others in many settings, there is a bias toward consistency. But learning theorists have less trouble accounting for normal "situational variability" in behavior than do other theorists.

A related implication is that learning theorists are supremely optimistic about the possibility of change. Children's behavior can change if the reinforcement system (or their beliefs about themselves) changes, so "problem behavior" can be modified. In contrast, biologically oriented temperament theorists, while agreeing that environmental variations can alter or shift the child's built-in temperamental tendencies, are more pessimistic about the likelihood of change, particularly for children whose temperamental pattern is extreme. Extremely inhibited children, for example, tend to remain that way, even in supportive environments; extremely irritable, angry, inattentive children ("difficult" in Chess and Thomas's conceptualization), unless they learn extremely good strategies for self-control, are highly likely to become aggressive, interpersonally difficult schoolchildren with a higher-than-normal likelihood of developing antisocial or delinquent patterns later (e.g., Eisenberg et al., 1997; Moffitt & Harrington, 1996).

The great strength of the learning view of personality and social behavior is that it gives an accurate picture of the way in which many specific behaviors are learned. It is perfectly clear that children do learn through modeling; it is equally clear that children (and adults) will continue to perform behaviors that "pay off" for them.

The cognitive elements in Bandura's theory add further strength, offering a beginning integration of learning models and cognitive-developmental approaches. If we were to apply Piaget's language to Bandura's theory, we could talk about the acquisition of a "self-scheme"—a concept of one's own capacities, qualities, standards, and experiences. New experiences are then assimilated to that scheme. You will recall from

This toddler may be happily helping his father wash windows (yet another example of modeling), but there is no guarantee that he will be equally helpful to his mother—a kind of inconsistency that learning theorists can handle more easily than biological temperament theorists can.

Chapter 6 that one of the characteristics of the process of assimilation as Piaget proposed it is that new information or experiences are modified as they are taken in. In the same way, Bandura is saying that once the child's self-concept is established, it affects what behaviors she chooses to perform, how she reacts to new experiences, whether she persists or gives up on some new task, and the like. If a child believes he is unpopular, for example, then he will not be surprised if others do not choose to sit by him in the lunchroom; if someone does sit next to him, he's likely to explain it in such a way that he retains his central belief, such as by saying to himself, "There must have been no place else to sit." In this way the underlying scheme isn't modified (accommodated) very much.

Just as biological temperament theorists argue that inborn temperament serves as a central mediating process, shaping the child's choices and behavior, so in social learning theory the self-concept or self-scheme acts as a central mediator, leading to stable differences in behavior of the kind we typically call personality. It *can* be modified (accommodated) if the child accumulates enough experience or evidence that doesn't fit with the existing scheme (in learning theory language, if the reinforcement contingencies change in some dramatic way). If the "unpopular" child noticed that classmates regularly chose to sit next to him at lunch even when there were other seats available, he might eventually change his self-scheme, coming to think of himself as "somewhat popular." However, since the child (like the adult) will choose activities or situations that fit his self-concept, such as sitting in the corner where no one is likely to see him, he will be partially protected from such "nonconfirming" experiences.

To be sure, Bandura and Piaget would not agree on how this self-concept or self-scheme develops. Piaget emphasizes internal processes while Bandura emphasizes reinforcement and modeling as causal factors. What they agree on is the impact that such a scheme will have once it has developed.

At the same time, these learning theories have significant weaknesses, particularly the more radical versions. First, from the perspective of many psychologists, these theories still place too much emphasis on what happens *to* the child and not enough on what the child is doing with the information he has. Bandura's theory is much less vulnerable to this charge, but most learning theories of personality are highly mechanistic and focused on external events. Second, like biological temperament theories, these are not really *developmental* theories. They can say how a child might acquire a particular behavior pattern or belief, but they do not take into account the underlying developmental changes that are occurring. Do 3-year-olds and 10-year-olds develop a sense of self-efficacy in the same way? Do they learn the same amount or in the same way from modeling? Given Bandura's emphasis on the cognitive aspects of the modeling process, a genuinely developmental social learning theory could be proposed, although no such theory now exists. Still, despite these limitations, all the theories in this group offer useful descriptions of one source of influence on the child's developing pattern of behavior.

Psychoanalytic Explanations

Like many temperament theorists, and like social learning theorists of Bandura's stripe, psychoanalytic theorists believe that the interaction between the child's inborn characteristics and the environment plays a central role in shaping differences in personality. However, unlike most temperament or learning approaches, psychoanalytic theories are clearly *developmental* as well, describing systematic changes in children's sense of self, in their needs or drives, and in their relationships with others.

In Chapter 1 I described a number of the key propositions of this approach. Here let me simply summarize Freud's and Erikson's views:

Proposition 1: Behavior is governed by unconscious as well as conscious motives and processes. Freud emphasized three sets of instinctual drives: the sexual drive (libido);

Critical Thinking

Think for a minute about the ways you choose activities that are consistent with your self-image or self-scheme. What would it take for you to change some of the key portions of your self-scheme?

life-preserving drives, including avoidance of hunger and pain; and aggressive drives. Erikson emphasizes a more cognitive process, the drive for identity.

Proposition 2: Personality structure develops over time, as a result of the interaction between the child's inborn drives/needs and the responses of the key people in the child's world. Because the child is often prevented from achieving instant gratification of his various drives, he is forced to develop new skills—planning, talking, delaying, and other cognitive techniques that allow gratification of the basic needs in more indirect ways. Thus, the ego is created, and it remains the planning, organizing, thinking part of the personality. The superego, in turn, develops because the parents try to restrain certain kinds of gratification; the child eventually incorporates these parental standards into his own personality.

Proposition 3: Development of personality is fundamentally stagelike, with each stage centered on a particular task or a particular form of basic need. I'll describe both Freud's and Erikson's stages in some detail in a moment. For now the key point is only that there *are* stages in these theories.

Proposition 4: The specific personality a child develops depends on the degree of success the child has in traversing these various stages. In each stage, the child requires a particular kind of supportive environment for successfully resolving that particular dilemma or for meeting that need. A child lacking the needed environment will have a very different personality than one whose environment is partially or wholly adequate. However, while each stage is important, all the psychoanalytic theorists strongly emphasize the crucial significance of the very earliest stages and focus especially on the adequacy of the relationship between the baby and the central caregiver, usually the mother. This is not quite like saying that infancy is a sensitive period for personality development; rather, Freud and later psychoanalytic theorists argue that the earliest relationship establishes a pattern and sets the child on a particular pathway through the remainder of the stages.

Some Differences Between Freud and Erikson

All four of these general propositions are contained in both Freud's and Erikson's theories, but both the details and the emphases differ in important respects. In Freud's theory, for example, cognitive skills develop only because the child needs them to obtain gratification; they have no independent life. In Erikson's theory (and in many other variations of psychoanalytic theory), cognitive skills are part of a set of ego functions that are presumed to develop independently, rather than being entirely in the service of basic gratification.

Basic physical maturation is also more central to Freud's theory than to Erikson's. In Freud's theory, the stages shift from one to the next in part because of maturation of the nervous system. In each stage, the child is attempting to gratify basic physical ("sexual") needs through stimulation of a particular part of the body—that part of the body that is most sensitive at that time. As neurological development proceeds, maximum body sensitivity shifts from the mouth to the anus to the genitals, and this maturational change is part of what drives the stage changes. Erikson grants such physical changes but places greater emphasis on shifts in the demands of the social environment. Each stage centers on a specific social conflict, resulting in a psychosocial crisis. For example, stage 4 ("industry versus inferiority") begins at about age 6 because that is when the child goes off to school; in a culture in which schooling is delayed, the timing of the developmental task might be delayed as well.

Because of such theoretical differences, Erikson and Freud have described the stages of development differently. Because both sets of stages have become part of the vocabulary of developmental psychology, you need to be conversant with both, so let me describe each.

Table 9.3

Freud's Stages of Psychosexual Development

Stage	Age (years)	Erogenous Zones	Major Developmental Task (potential source of conflict)	Personality Traits of Adults "Fixated" at This Stage
Oral	0–1	Mouth, lips, tongue	Weaning	Oral behavior, such as smoking and overeating; passivity and gullibility.
Anal	1–3	Anus	Toilet training	Orderliness, parsimoniousness, obstinacy, or the opposite.
Phallic	3–5	Genitals	Oedipus conflict; identification with same-sex parent	Vanity, recklessness, or the opposite.
Latency	5–12	No specific area; sexual energy quiescent	Development of ego defense mechanisms	None; fixation does not normally occur.
Genital	12–18 and adulthood	Genitals	Mature sexual intimacy	Adults who have successfully integrated earlier stages should emerge with a sincere interest in others and mature sexuality.

Freud's Psychosexual Stages

Freud proposed five **psychosexual stages,** which I've summarized in Table 9.3.

The Oral Stage: Birth to 1 Year. The mouth, lips, and tongue are the first center of pleasure for the baby, and his earliest attachment is to the one who provides pleasure in the mouth, usually his mother. For normal development the infant requires some optimum amount of oral stimulation—not too much and not too little. If the optimum amount of stimulation is unavailable, then some libidinal energy may remain attached to (*fixated* on, in Freud's terms) the oral mode of gratification. Such an individual, so Freud thought, will continue to have a strong preference for oral pleasures in later life, as you can see in the right-hand column in Table 9.3.

The Anal Stage: 1 to 3 Years. As the trunk matures, the baby becomes more and more sensitive in the anal region. At about the same time, her parents begin to place great emphasis on toilet training and show pleasure when she manages to perform in the right place at the right time. These two forces together help to shift the major center of physical/sexual energy from the oral to the anal erogenous zone.

The key to the child's successful completion of this stage (according to Freud) is whether the parents allow the child sufficient anal exploration and pleasure. If toilet training becomes a major battleground, then some fixation of energy at this stage may occur—with the possible adult consequences of excessive orderliness, stinginess, or the opposite.

The Phallic Stage: 3 to 5 Years. At about 3 or 4 years of age, the genitals increase in sensitivity, ushering in a new stage. One sign of this new sensitivity is that children of both sexes quite naturally begin to masturbate at about this age.

In Freud's view, the most important event that occurs during the phallic stage is the so-called **Oedipus conflict.** He described the sequence of events more fully (and more believably!) for boys, so let me trace that pattern for you.

Freud thought that babies put things into their mouths because that is where they have the most pleasurable sensations. If babies don't get enough oral stimulation, he argued, they may become fixated at the oral stage.

According to Freud, this stage begins at about age 3 or 4, when the genitals increase in sensitivity. He proposed that during this stage, the boy, having discovered his penis, rather naively wishes to use this newfound source of pleasure to please his oldest source of pleasure, his mother. He becomes envious of his father, who has access to the mother's body in a way that the boy does not. The boy also sees his father as a powerful and threatening figure who has ultimate power—the power to castrate. The boy is caught between desire for his mother and fear of his father's power.

Most of these feelings and the resultant conflict are unconscious. The boy does not have overt sexual feelings or behavior toward his mother. But unconscious or not, the result of this conflict is anxiety. How can the little boy handle this anxiety? In Freud's view, the boy responds with a defensive process called **identification:** The boy "incorporates" his image of his father and attempts to match his own behavior to that image. By trying to make himself as like his father as possible, the boy not only reduces the chance of an attack from the father; he takes on some of the father's power as well. Furthermore, it is the "inner father," with his values and moral judgments, that serves as the core of the child's superego.

A parallel process is supposed to occur in girls. The girl sees her mother as a rival for her father's sexual attentions and has some fear of her mother (though less than the boy has of his father, since the girl may assume she has already been castrated). In this case too, identification with the mother is thought to be the "solution" to the girl's anxiety.

The Latency Stage: 5 to 12 Years. Freud thought that after the phallic stage came a sort of resting period before the next major change in the child's sexual development. The child has presumably arrived at some preliminary resolution of the Oedipus conflict and now goes through a kind of calm after the storm. One of the obvious characteristics of this stage is that the identification with the same-sex parent that defined the end of the phallic stage is now extended to others of the same sex. So it is during these years that children's peer interactions are almost exclusively with members of the same sex and that children often have "crushes" on same-sex teachers or other adults.

The Genital Stage: 12 to 18 and Older. The further changes in hormones and the genital organs that take place during puberty reawaken the sexual energy of the child. During this period a more mature form of sexual attachment occurs. From the beginning of this period, the child's sexual objects are people of the opposite sex. Freud placed some emphasis on the fact that not everyone works through this period to a point of mature heterosexual love. Some people have not had a satisfactory oral period and thus do not have a foundation of basic love relationships. Some have not resolved the Oedipus conflict with a complete or satisfactory identification with the same-sex parent, a failure that may affect their ability to cope with rearoused sexual energies in adolescence.

Optimum development at each stage, according to Freud, requires an environment that will satisfy the unique needs of each period. The baby needs sufficient oral and

Critical Thinking

Can you think of any kind of study that would tell us whether Freud was right or not about the Oedipus conflict?

In elementary school, boys play with boys, girls play with girls. How would Freud explain this?

Critical Thinking

Does the idea that one carries unresolved issues forward into adulthood make sense to you? Can you think of any examples from your own experience?

anal stimulation; the 4-year-old boy needs a father present with whom to identify and a mother who is not too seductive. An inadequate early environment will leave a residue of unresolved problems and unmet needs, which are then carried forward to subsequent stages.

This emphasis on the formative role of early experience, particularly early family experience, is a hallmark of psychoanalytic theories. In this view, the first five or six years of life are critical for the creation of the individual personality.

Erikson's Psychosocial Stages

Erikson shared most of Freud's basic assumptions, but there are some crucial differences between the two theories. First, Erikson de-emphasized the centrality of sexual drive and instead focused on a stepwise emergence of a sense of identity. Second, although he agreed with Freud that the early years are highly important, he argued that

Table 9.4

The Eight Stages of Development Proposed by Erikson

Approximate Age (years)	Ego Quality to Be Developed	Some Tasks and Activities of the Stage
0–1	Basic trust versus basic mistrust	Trust in mother or central caregiver and in one's own ability to make things happen; a key element in an early secure attachment.
2–3	Autonomy versus shame, doubt	Walking, grasping, and other physical skills lead to free choice; toilet training occurs; child learns control but may develop shame if not handled properly.
4–5	Initiative versus guilt	Organize activities around some goal; become more assertive and aggressive. Oedipus-like conflict with parent of same sex may lead to guilt.
6–12	Industry versus inferiority	Absorb all the basic cultural skills and norms, including school skills and tool use.
13–18	Identity versus role confusion	Adapt sense of self to physical changes of puberty, make occupational choice, achieve adultlike sexual identity, and search for new values.
19–25	Intimacy versus isolation	Form one or more intimate relationships that go beyond adolescent love; marry and form family groups.
26–40	Generativity versus stagnation	Bear and rear children, focus on occupational achievement or creativity, and train the next generation.
41+	Ego integrity versus despair	Integrate earlier stages and come to terms with basic identity. Accept self.

identity is not fully formed at the end of adolescence but continues to move through further developmental stages in adult life. You can see in Table 9.4 that he proposes eight stages, three of which are reached only in adulthood.

In Erikson's view, maturation plays a relatively little role in the sequence of stages. Far more important are common cultural demands for children of a particular age, such as the demand that the child become toilet trained at about age 2, that the child learn school skills at age 6 or 7, or that the young adult form an intimate partnership. Each stage, then, centers on a particular dilemma, a particular social task. Thus, he calls his stages **psychosocial stages** rather than psycho*sexual* stages. Let me give you a bit more detail on the five stages in childhood that Erikson described.

Basic Trust Versus Basic Mistrust: Birth to 1 Year. The first task (or "dilemma," as Erikson sometimes said) occurs during the first year of life, when the child must develop a sense of basic trust in the predictability of the world and in his ability to affect the events around him. Erikson believed that the behavior of the major caregiver (usually the mother) is critical to the child's successful or unsuccessful resolution of this crisis. Children who emerge from the first year with a firm sense of trust are those whose parents are loving and respond predictably and reliably to the child. A child who has developed a sense of trust will go on to other relationships, carrying this sense with him. Those infants whose early care has been erratic or harsh may develop *mis*trust, and they too carry this sense with them into later relationships.

Erikson never said, by the way, that the ideal position on any one of the dilemmas is at one extreme pole. In the case of the first stage, for example, there is some risk in being too trusting. The child also needs to develop some healthy mistrust, such as learning to discriminate between dangerous and safe situations.

Autonomy Versus Shame and Doubt: 2 to 3 Years. Erikson saw the child's greater mobility during the toddler years as forming the basis for the sense of independence or autonomy. But if the child's efforts at independence are not carefully guided by the parents and she experiences repeated failures or ridicule, then the results of all the new opportunities for exploration may be shame and doubt instead of a basic sense of self-control and self-worth. Once again the ideal is not for the child to have *no* shame or doubt; some doubt is needed for the child to understand which behaviors are acceptable and which are not, which are safe and which are dangerous. But the ideal does lie toward the autonomy end of the continuum.

Initiative Versus Guilt: 4 to 5 Years. This phase, roughly equivalent to Freud's phallic stage, is again ushered in by new skills or abilities in the child. The 4-year-old is able to plan a bit, to take the initiative in reaching particular goals. The child tries out these new cognitive skills, attempts to conquer the world around him. He may try to go out into the street on his own; he may take a toy apart, then find he can't put it back together and throw it—parts and all—at his mother. It is a time of vigor of action and of behaviors that parents may see as aggressive. The risk is that the child may go too far in his forcefulness or that the parents may restrict and punish too much—either of which

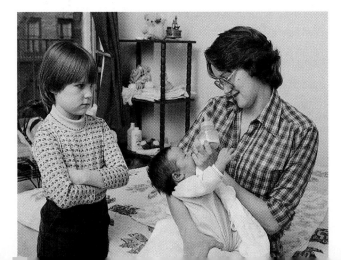

If looks could kill! This child is clearly jealous of the new baby and may well be harboring all sorts of angry and aggressive thoughts. A younger child would probably act out those thoughts and feelings directly. But a child of this age, probably in the period Erikson calls *initiative versus guilt*, feels guilty about her feelings and inhibits the angry actions.

can produce guilt. Some guilt is needed, since without it there would be no conscience, no self-control. The ideal interaction between parent and child is certainly not total indulgence, but too much guilt can inhibit the child's creativity and free interactions with others.

Industry (Competence) Versus Inferiority: 6 to 12 Years. The beginning of schooling is a major force in ushering in this stage. The child is now faced with the need to win approval through specific competence—through learning to read, to do sums, and to succeed at other school skills. The task of this period is thus simply to develop the repertoire of abilities society demands of the child. If the child is unable to develop the expected skills, he will develop instead a basic sense of inferiority. Yet some failure is necessary so that the child can develop some humility; as always, balance is at issue. Ideally, the child must have sufficient success to encourage a sense of competence but should not place so much emphasis on competence that failure is unacceptable or that she becomes a kind of "workaholic."

Identity Versus Role Confusion: 13 to 18 Years. The task occurring during puberty is a major one in which the adolescent reexamines his identity and the roles he must occupy. Erikson suggests that two "identities" are involved—a "sexual identity" and an "occupational identity." What should emerge for the adolescent from this period is a reintegrated sense of self, of what one wants to do and be, and of one's appropriate sexual role. The risk is that of confusion, arising from the profusion of roles opening to the child at this age.

Other Psychoanalytic Views: Bowlby's Model of Attachment

Before looking at some of the evidence supporting (or refuting) the psychoanalytic view, I want to reemphasize that Erikson is not the only influential modern theorist whose thinking has been strongly affected by Freud or psychoanalysis. Among those interested particularly in very early child development, John Bowlby has had a particularly large impact with his theory of the development of attachment (1969; 1973; 1980).

Bowlby offered an interesting blend of psychoanalytic and biological approaches. Like Freud, he assumed that the root of human personality lies in the earliest childhood relationships. Significant failure or trauma in those relationships will permanently shape the child's development. Bowlby focused his attention on the child's first attachment to the mother because it is usually the earliest and is arguably the most central.

To describe how that attachment comes about, Bowlby introduced several concepts from *ethological theory,* which brings evolutionary concepts to bear on the study of behavior. Human evolution, Bowlby suggested, has resulted in the child's being born with a repertoire of built-in, instinctive behaviors that elicit caregiving from others—behaviors like crying, smiling, or making eye contact. Similarly, the mother (or other adult) is equipped with various instinctive behaviors toward the infant, such as responding to a baby's cry or speaking to the baby in a high-pitched voice. Together these instinctive patterns bring mother and infant together in an intricate chain of stimulus and response that causes the child to form a specific attachment to that one adult— a process I'll be talking about in some detail in Chapter 11.

Although Bowlby's theory is not a full-fledged stage theory of development in the manner of Freud or Erikson, it is nonetheless based on many of the underlying psychoanalytic assumptions. It has also stimulated and profoundly influenced the large body of current research on attachment.

Evidence and Applications

Empirical explorations of Freud's or Erikson's theories are relatively rare, largely because both theories are so general that specific tests are very difficult to perform. For example, to test Freud's notion of fixation, we would need much more information about how to determine whether a given child is fixated at some stage. What is a sign that a child is fixated at the oral or the anal stage? Should we expect some automatic connection between how early a child is weaned and such ostensibly oral adult behavior as smoking or overeating? When researchers have searched for such direct linkages, they have not found them.

Despite these difficulties, researchers have managed to devise tests of some of the basic propositions. Let me mention two bodies of work of this type, studies of the Oedipal period and studies of the security of attachment.

The Oedipal Period. One 4-year-old boy, after his mother told him that she loved him, said, "And I love you too, and that's why I can't ever marry someone else" (Watson & Getz, 1990a, p. 29). In their studies of Oedipal behavior, Malcolm Watson and Kenneth Getz (1990a; 1990b) have indeed found that children of about 4 or 5 are likely to make comments like this. More generally, they have found that 4-year-olds, more than any other age group, show more affectionate behavior toward the opposite-sex parent and more aggressive or antagonistic behavior toward the same-sex parent. You can see the second half of this result in Figure 9.3. Whether Freud's explanation of this phenomenon is the correct one remains to be seen, but these results are certainly consistent with his theory.

Security of Attachment. A second research area that has its roots in psychoanalytic theory is the current work on the security or insecurity of children's early attachments. Both Erikson and Freud argued that the quality of the child's first relationship with the central caregiver will shape her relationships with other children and with other adults at later ages. And of course Bowlby's theory is designed specifically to examine that earliest relationship. I'll be talking a great deal more about early attachments in Chapter 11, but let me give you at least a taste of the research in this area, since it provides a good deal of support for the basic psychoanalytic hypothesis that the quality of the child's earliest relationship affects the whole course of her later development. In dozens

Figure 9.3

The data in this figure are based on the detailed reports of parents on the affectionate and aggressive behavior of their child toward them. Scores above 0 mean that the child was more aggressive toward the same-sex parent than toward the opposite-sex parent, while scores below 0 mean the reverse.

(*Source:* Watson & Getz, 1990b, from Table 3, p. 499.)

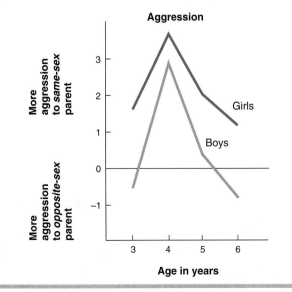

The Real World

The Effects of Divorce: One Test of Psychoanalytic Theory

Some 40 percent of children born in the United States in 1980 had already experienced their parents' divorce by the time they were 16 (Cherlin, 1992a; Hernandez, 1997). What is the effect on the child of such an experience? I'll talk much more broadly about the effects of divorce in Chapter 13; for now, let me focus on just one issue, because it is a kind of test of psychoanalytic theory. If Freud is correct, the negative impact of divorce should be greatest if the divorce occurs before or during the Oedipal period (ages 3 to 5 approximately), since the successful resolution of the Oedipus conflict and the resulting identification process require the presence of both parents. Further, if the children live with their mother after a divorce, then the detrimental effect should be much greater for boys than for girls. A girl still has her mother to identify with, so at least her sex-role identification is appropriate. The boy, in contrast, lacking a father, may never go through the identification process properly and may end up with a very confused sex-role orientation and perhaps a weaker superego.

The results of studies of children in divorced families give partial support to the second, but not the first, of these hypotheses. Virtually all children show some negative effects of divorce, but the most common finding is that boys experience somewhat more problems (Amato, 1993; Hetherington & Stanley-Hagan, 1995). They are more likely than are girls to show behavior problems or have increased difficulty in school after a divorce. I should note, however, that this generalization may not hold for teenagers, among whom girls seem to show more negative responses to their parents' divorce (e.g., Chase-Lansdale & Hetherington, 1990; Lee et al., 1994), although this point is not yet fully clear. What is clear is that preschool-age children do not consistently show more profound or more lasting negative effects of parental divorce than do children of other ages; this fact calls some of Freud's hypotheses about the Oedipus conflict into question.

of longitudinal studies, children whose attachment security has been assessed at age 1 or 2 have then been followed over a period of years—in some cases throughout childhood and adolescence. The consistent finding is that children who had a more secure attachment in infancy later have more positive relationships with others and are more socially skillful (Thompson, 1998). Thus, the relationship formed during the earliest stage of psychosocial development seems to create a prototype for later relationships, as Bowlby and Erikson proposed. Recall, too, the result from Megan Gunnar's study that I described earlier: Temperamentally inhibited toddlers who have formed a secure attachment to their mothers show little or no physiological sign of fearfulness in a novel setting. Thus, the quality of the child's early attachment can at least partially override the basic temperamental tendencies in forming the child's personality.

Critique of Psychoanalytic Theories

Psychoanalytic theories like Freud's or Erikson's have several great attractions. Most centrally, they focus our attention on the importance of the emotional quality of the child's relationship with the caregivers. Furthermore, both these theories suggest that the child's needs or "tasks" change with age, so that the parents must constantly adapt to the changing child. One of the implications of this is that we should not think of "good parenting" as if it were a global quality. Some of us may be very good at meeting the needs of an infant but quite awful at dealing with teenagers' identity struggles; others of us may have the opposite pattern. The child's eventual personality, and her overall emotional "health," thus depends on the interaction or transaction that develops in the particular family. This is an extremely attractive element of these theories because more and more of the research within developmental psychology is moving us toward just such a transactional conception of the process.

Psychoanalytic theory has also given us a number of helpful concepts, such as defense mechanisms and identification, that have been so widely adopted that they have become a part of everyday language as well as theory. These strengths have led to a resurgence of influence of both Erikson's theory and the several second-order or third-order psychoanalytic approaches such as Bowlby's.

The great weakness of all the psychoanalytic approaches is the fuzziness of many of the concepts. Identification may be an intriguing theoretical notion, but how are we to measure it? How do we detect the presence of specific defense mechanisms? Without more precise operational definitions, it is impossible to disconfirm the theory. Those areas in which the general concepts of psychoanalytic theory have been fruitfully applied to our understanding of development have nearly always been areas in which other theorists or researchers have offered more precise definitions or clearer methods for measuring some Freudian or Eriksonian construct, such as Bowlby's concept of security of attachment. Psychoanalytic theory may thus sometimes offer a provocative framework for our thinking, but it is not a precise theory of development.

A Possible Synthesis

I have given you three different views of the origins of those unique, individual patterns of behavior we call personality. Each view can be at least partially supported with research evidence; each has clear strengths. Do we need to choose among them, or can we combine them in any sensible way? Some argue that theories as different as these cannot ever be combined because they make such different assumptions about the child's role in the whole process (Overton & Reese, 1973). I agree in part. I do not think we can simply add up the different sources of influence and say that personality is merely the sum of inborn temperament, reinforcement patterns, interactions with parents, and some kind of self-scheme.

Nonetheless, more complex combinations, like the one shown in Figure 9.4 (p. 284), may still be fruitful. In this model I am suggesting that the child's inborn temperament is a beginning point—an initial, highly significant bias in the system. Arrow 1 suggests a *direct* relationship between that inborn temperament and the eventual personality we see in the child and later in the adult.

Arrow 2 suggests a second direct effect, between the pattern of the child's environment and his eventual personality and social behavior. Whether the parents respond reliably and contingently to the infant will affect his trust or the security of his attachment, which will show up in a range of behaviors later; whether the parents reinforce aggressive or friendly behavior will influence the child's future as well.

These direct effects are straightforward, even obvious, but most of what happens is much more complicated than that. The way the child is treated is influenced by her temperament (arrow 3), and both the basic temperament and the family environment affect the child's self-scheme—her expectations for others and herself, her beliefs about her own abilities (arrows 4 and 5). This self-scheme, or self-concept (including the child's sense of self-efficacy), in turn, helps to shape the behavior we see, the "personality" of the child (arrow 6).

This system does not exist in a vacuum. In keeping with the ecological approach of Bronfenbrenner and others, arrow 7 suggests that the parents' ability to maintain a loving and supportive relationship with their child is influenced by the parents' own outside experiences, such as whether they like their jobs or whether they have enough emotional support to help them weather their own crises.

For example, Mavis Hetherington (1989) reports that children with difficult temperaments show more problem behavior in response to their parents' divorce than do those with easier temperaments, but this difference exists only if the mother is also depressed and has inadequate social support. In this study, those difficult children whose divorcing mothers were *not* depressed did not show heightened levels of problems. Thus, the child's temperament clearly seems to have an impact, but the effect of temperament can be and is modified by the parents' pattern of response.

Critical Thinking

In recent years the concept of "vulnerable" and "resilient" children has become prominent in developmental research. How might vulnerability be conceptualized or explained by theorists of each of the several persuasions described in this chapter?

Figure 9.4

Here is one version of a complex interactive model describing the formation of individual personality. The effects of inborn temperament and environmental influences do not merely add. Each affects the other, helping to create the child's unique self-scheme, which in turn affects the child's experiences. All this occurs within the context of the family, which is itself influenced by the parents' own life experiences. What we think of as personality is a complex product of all these forces.

A model of personality development

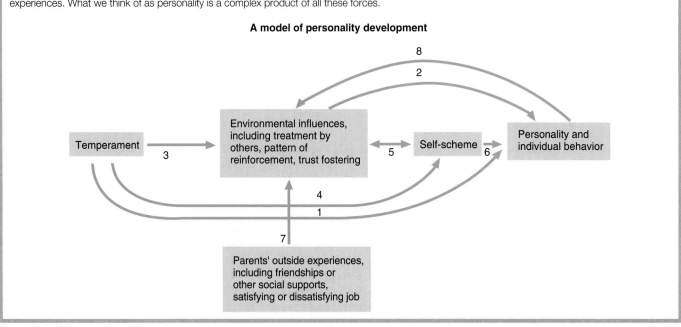

Another illustration of the intricacy of the whole system comes from an early study by Susan Crockenberg (1981), who studied a group of 46 mothers and infants over the first year of life. She measured each child's irritability (an aspect of temperament) when the baby was 5 to 10 days old and assessed the security of the child's attachment to the mother when the child was 12 months old. We might expect that irritable babies would be more likely to be insecurely attached, merely because they are more difficult to care for. In fact, Crockenberg found a small effect of this kind (see Table 9.5). But Crockenberg didn't stop there. She also measured the level of the mother's social support—the degree to which she had family and friends who were sufficiently helpful to assist her in dealing with the strains of having a new child or other life changes she might be experiencing. The results of the study show that insecure attachment in the child was most likely when the mother had *both* an irritable infant *and* low levels of support. If the baby was irritable but the mother had good support, the child's attachment nearly always developed securely. Only when two difficult conditions occurred together did a poor outcome result for the child.

In a later study, Crockenberg (1987) found that a higher level of anger and noncompliant behavior (perhaps reflections of what is called neuroticism in the Big Five formula) was common in toddlers who had been irritable as infants *and* whose mothers were angry and punitive toward them. Furthermore, such angry and punitive behavior in the mother was more likely if the mother had experienced rejection in her own childhood and if she experienced little support from her partner. We are dealing here with a *system* of effects.

Finally, I have included arrow 8 in Figure 9.4 to underline the *transactional* elements of the system. Once the child's unique pattern of behaviors and attitudes (personality) is formed, this affects the environment she will encounter, the experiences she will choose, and the responses of the people around her, which in turn affect her behavior (Bandura, 1997; Scarr & McCartney, 1983; Sroufe et al., 1993).

Table 9.5

Influence of Child's Temperament and Mother's Social Support on the Child's Secure or Insecure Attachment

Child's Irritability	Mother's Support	Securely Attached Children	Insecurely Attached Children
High	Low	2	9
High	High	12	1
Low	Low	7	2
Low	High	13	2

Source: From S. B. Crockenberg, Table 5, 862, "Infant Irritability, Mother Responsiveness, and Social Support Influences on the Security of Infant-Mother Attachment," *Child Development,* 52, 1981, p. 857–865. By permission of the Society for Research in Child Development.

No doubt even this fairly complex system underestimates the intricacy of the process of personality development in the child. Most of our research does not yet encompass all the pieces of the puzzle. But the very fact that developmental psychologists are turning toward such complex models seems to me to be a very good thing. Development *is* this complex, and we will not be able to describe it or explain it until we begin to examine and try to measure all these separate forces.

Summary

1. The word *personality* refers to the unique, individual, relatively enduring pattern of relating to others and responding to the world that is characteristic of each individual.

2. Researchers studying adult personality have agreed on a set of five dimensions (the Big Five) that capture most of the variation among individuals: extraversion, agreeableness, conscientiousness, neuroticism, and openness/intellect.

3. Recent research suggests that the same five dimensions may give us an accurate picture of variations in children's and adolescents' personality as well.

4. Researchers studying infants and young children have studied *temperament* rather than personality. Temperament is now widely seen as the built-in, constitutionally based behavior tendencies that form the emotional substrate of personality.

5. Sizeable differences remain among temperament theorists regarding how best to characterize the basic dimensions of temperament, but reasonable agreement exists on five key dimensions: activity level, approach/positive emotionality, inhibition and anxiety, negative emotionality/irritability/anger, and effortful control/task persistence.

6. Explanations of personality variations center around three distinct theoretical approaches: biological/genetic theories, learning theories, and psychoanalytic theories.

7. Biological explanations of temperament/personality, focusing on genetic differences in patterns or styles of reacting to people and objects, are well supported by research.

8. Evidence is also accumulating that specific differences in neurological and chemical responses underlie many observed variations in behavior.

9. However, temperament is clearly not totally determined by heredity or ongoing physiological processes, although the child's built-in temperament does shape her interactions with the world and affect others' responses to the child.

10. Traditional learning theorists emphasize the role of basic learning processes, such as reinforcement patterns, in shaping individual behaviors, including patterns of interaction with others.

11. Social/cognitive learning theorists like Bandura also emphasize the role of observational learning as well as the role of the child's learned expectancies, standards, and self-efficacy beliefs in creating more enduring patterns of response.

12. Psychoanalytic theorists emphasize the importance of unconscious motives and processes as well as the stagelike emergence of personality. In this approach, the relationship of the child with significant adults, particularly in early infancy, is seen as critical.

13. Freud's psychosexual stages are strongly affected by maturation. Particularly significant is the phallic stage, beginning at about age 3 or 4, when the Oedipus conflict is met and mastered through the process of identification.

14. Erikson's psycho*social* stages are influenced both by social demands and by the child's physical and intellectual skills. Each of the major stages has a central task or "crisis" relating to some aspect of the development of identity.

15. Bowlby's theory of attachment, with roots in psychoanalytic thought, is particularly influential today.

16. Psychoanalytic theory is difficult to test because of its imprecision, but in some areas it has been broadly confirmed, such as in studies of the impact of early attachments on later functioning.

17. Elements of all three views can be combined into an interactionist view of personality development. Temperament may serve as the base from which personality grows, both by affecting behavior directly and by affecting the way others respond to the child. Both the temperament and the specific pattern of response from the people in the child's environment affect the child's self-concept or self-scheme, which then helps to create stability in the child's unique pattern of behavior.

Key Terms

agreeableness One of the "Big Five" personality traits; characterized by trust, generosity, kindness, and sympathy. **p. 260**

Big Five The five primary dimensions of personality variation identified by researchers, including extraversion, agreeableness, conscientiousness, neuroticism, and openness/intellect. **p. 260**

conscientiousness One of the "Big Five" personality traits, characterized by efficiency, organization, planfulness, and reliability. **p. 260**

extraversion One of the "Big Five" personality traits, characterized by assertiveness, energy, enthusiasm, and outgoingness. **p. 260**

identification The process of taking into oneself ("incorporating") the qualities and ideas of another person, which Freud thought was the result of the Oedipus conflict at ages 3 to 5. The child attempts to become like the parent of the same sex. **p. 277**

neuroticism One of the "Big Five" personality traits, characterized by anxiety, self-pity, tenseness, and emotional instability. **p. 260**

Oedipus conflict The pattern of events Freud believed occurred between ages 3 and 5, when the child experiences a "sexual" desire for the parent of the opposite sex; the resulting fear of possible reprisal from the parent of the same sex is resolved when the child "identifies" with the parent of the same sex. **p. 276**

openness/intellect One of the "Big Five" personality traits, characterized by curiosity, imagination, insight, originality, and wide interests. **p. 260**

personality The collection of individual, relatively enduring patterns of reacting to and interacting with others that distinguishes each child or adult. Temperament is thought of as the emotional substrate of personality. **p. 259**

psychosexual stages The stages of personality development suggested by Freud, including the oral, anal, phallic, latency, and genital stages. **p. 276**

psychosocial stages The stages of personality development suggested by Erikson, including trust, autonomy, initiative, industry, identity, intimacy, generativity, and ego integrity. **p. 279**

temperament Term sometimes used interchangeably with *personality*, but best thought of as the emotional substrate of personality, at least partially genetically determined. **p. 262**

Suggested Readings

Erikson, E. H. (1980). *Identity and the life cycle.* New York: Norton. (Originally published 1959.) The middle section of this book, "Growth and Crises of the Healthy Personality," is the best description I have found of Erikson's model of the psychosocial stages of development.

Grusec, J. E. (1992). Social learning theory and developmental psychology: The legacies of Robert Sears and Albert Bandura. *Developmental Psychology, 28,* 776–786. One of a series of papers to mark the centennial of the American Psychological Association, describing and celebrating the work of key theorists.

Kagan, J. (1994). *Galen's prophecy.* New York: Basic Books. A detailed presentation, for the lay reader, of Kagan's ideas about the biological bases of temperament, particularly the aspect of temperament he calls behavioral inhibition.

Rothbart, M. K., & Bates, J. E. (1998). Temperament. In W. Damon (Ed.), *Handbook of child psychology: Vol. 3. Social, emotional, and personality development* (5th ed., pp. 105–176). New York: Wiley. An extremely thorough, technical, up-to-date review of what we know about temperament, including its linkage to the Big Five personality dimensions.

The Concept of Self in Children

10

Try an experiment for me. Before you read any further, write down 20 answers to the question "Who am I?" Now look at your list and think about what you wrote. My own list includes items like these:

I am a logical, analytic person.

I like closure and am uncomfortable with uncertainty.

I am a stubborn, determined person who finishes what she starts.

I am generous with my money and my time.

I am a person with many roles: wife, mother, stepmother, grandmother, daughter, sister, singer, board member.

I have many cherished women friends.

I am lots taller than average and sometimes clumsy.

I am not a traditionally feminine person.

My list, as yours probably does, includes something about what I look like, something about the roles I occupy, and something about my qualities, attitudes, and beliefs about myself. These are all aspects of my **self-concept**—in Piagetian-style language, my *self-scheme*. For each of us, the self-concept serves as a sort of filter for experience, shaping our choices and affecting our responses to others. Our ideas about our own sex role form a powerful part of that self-concept. Because these beliefs and attitudes about ourselves are so central to our personality and hence to our behavior, it is important for us to try to understand how they develop.

The Development of the Concept of Self

Our thinking about the child's emerging sense of self has been strongly influenced by both Freud and Piaget, each of whom assumed that the baby begins life with *no* sense of separateness. Freud emphasized what he called the *symbiotic* relationship between the mother and young infant, in which the two are joined together as if they were one. He believed that the infant does not initially understand himself to be separate from the mother; only gradually does the baby realize he is distinct. This idea was elaborated by Margaret Mahler (1977), a well-known psychoanalytic theorist who proposed that the infant had a "psychological birth" some months after the biological birth.

Even more influential than either Freud or Piaget, however, has been the thinking of the early American psychologist William James (1890; 1892), who made a critical distinction between two aspects of the self, which he called the "I" and the "me." The "I" self is often called the *subjective self*; it is that inner sense that "I am," "I exist." The "me" aspect is sometimes called the *objective self*; it is the set of properties or qualities that are objectively known or knowable about the person, including physical characteristics, temperament, and social skills. It is the "me" self that has come to be called the self-concept—the collection of ideas or beliefs each of us has about our own qualities. However, it is the "I" self that *creates* the self-concept, that *has* the beliefs and ideas about itself. So when you describe yourself to someone else, or when you answer questions like the "Who am I?" task I asked you to do at the beginning of the chapter, it is the "me" you are describing, but it is the "I" who is doing the describing.

James's distinction reappears in most current descriptions of the emergence of the sense of self, although the labels current researchers and theorists use for the two aspects of the self are quite varying. In his current writings, for example, Michael Lewis (1991; 1994) refers to the I-self as *the machinery of the self*, while he labels the me-self *the idea of me*. Robbie Case (1991) echoes the same distinction with his categories of the *implicit self* (the I-self) and the *explicit self* (the me-self). In the following discussion, I'm going to use the labels **subjective self** and **objective self** because I find them to be the clearest of the alternatives.

The Subjective Self

Most modern students of self-development would dispute Freud's claim about the initial symbiotic link between infant and parent in which the infant has no sense of separateness (Harter, 1998). Most would now argue that the baby has some primitive sense of separateness from the beginning. In the early months, the baby's task is to begin to coordinate the various sources of information he has about his own actions and their impact. In particular, over the first year, the infant develops a sense of himself as an *agent* in the world—as able to make things happen. The delight the baby shows when he is able to make a mobile move, or to create a noise by squeezing a squeaky toy, is evidence of the baby's emerging sense of himself as an agent. In a similar vein, Albert Bandura argues that the roots of the sense of *self-efficacy* are found during this first year, when the infant realizes he can control certain events in the world.

This sense of efficacy or control occurs not just with inanimate objects but perhaps even more centrally in interactions with adults, who respond contingently to the child's behavior—smiling back when the baby smiles, making funny faces when the baby does particular things, playing repetitive games while changing diapers or feeding the baby, playing peekaboo. Of course the baby is not "causing" these things to happen in most cases; it is the parents who are often initiating the games or patterns. But within these games and patterns are myriad repetitions of sequences in which the baby does something and the parent replies/responds with some predictable behavior. From the baby's perspective, he has "made it happen," and his sense of self, of efficacy or agency, is established.

Piaget also argued that a critical element in the development of the subjective self is the understanding of object permanence at about 9 to 12 months. Just as the infant is figuring out that Mom and Dad continue to exist when they are out of sight, he is figuring out—at least in some preliminary way—that *he* exists separately and has some permanence.

The Objective Self

The second major step is for the toddler to come to understand that she is also an *object* in the world. Just as a ball has properties—roundness, the ability to roll, a certain feel in the hand—so the "self" also has qualities or properties, such as gender, size, a name, or qualities like shyness or boldness, coordination or clumsiness. It is this *self-awareness* that is the hallmark of the "me-self."

When 12-month-old Deepak plays peekaboo with his grandmother, he is not only delighted; he is engaging in just the kind of repetitive social exchange that theorists think are critical for the formation of the baby's "I-self" and his sense of self-efficacy.

At 4 months, Lucy's pleasure at looking at herself in a mirror comes from the fact that this is an interesting moving object to inspect, not from any understanding that this is *herself* in the mirror.

Studying Self-awareness. When does a child first have such self-awareness? This has been a very hard question to answer, although several different strategies point to 15 to 18 months as the transition point. The most commonly used measurement procedure involves a mirror. First the baby is placed in front of a mirror, just to see how she behaves. Most infants of about 9 to 12 months will look at their own images, make faces, or try to interact with the baby-in-the-mirror in some way. After allowing this free exploration for a time, the experimenter, while pretending to wipe the baby's face with a cloth, puts a spot of rouge on the baby's nose and then again lets the baby look in the mirror. The crucial test of self-recognition, and thus of awareness of the self, is whether the baby reaches for the spot on her *own* nose rather than on the nose on the face in the mirror.

The results from one of Lewis's studies using this procedure are shown in Figure 10.1. As you can see, none of the 9- to 12-month-old children in this study touched their noses, but by 21 months, three-quarters of the children showed that level of self-recognition. The figure also shows the rate at which children refer to themselves by name when they are shown a picture of themselves, which is another commonly used measure of self-awareness. You can see that this development occurs at almost exactly the same time as self-recognition in a mirror. Both are present by about the middle of the second year of life (Bullock & Lütkenhaus, 1990).

Figure 10.1

Mirror recognition and self-naming develop at almost exactly the same time.

(*Source:* Lewis & Brooks, 1978, pp. 214–215.)

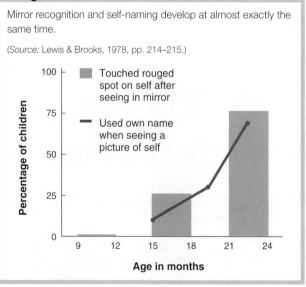

Once the toddler achieves such self-awareness, his behavior is affected in a whole range of ways. Self-aware toddlers now begin to insist on doing things for themselves and show a newly proprietary attitude toward toys or other treasured objects ("Mine!"). Looked at this way, much of the legendary "terrible twos" can be understood as an outgrowth of self-awareness. In a quite literal sense, toddlers are self-willed for the first time.

Another behavioral change ushered in by the toddler's newly emerging self-awareness is the expression of such self-conscious emotions as embarrassment, pride, or shame. These emotions are not normally expressed until late in the second year of life, presumably because they all involve some aspect of self-evaluation, not present until the toddler has achieved at least minimal self-awareness (Lewis et al., 1989; 1992). According to Lewis, emotions like shame or pride also require the child to be aware of some standards of conduct and to compare himself to those standards—a development that also occurs late in the second year of life. It is only at this age, for example, that children begin to use words like *dirty* to describe themselves or some object, suggesting that they are judging themselves or others against some standard. The emotion of shame is then expressed when the child feels he has not met the standard, while pride occurs when the child is able to meet the standard—to build the block tower as high as the teacher wants, to wash his hands well enough to be "clean," or the like. One facet of this whole development is that after age 2, children become increasingly eager for adult approval, using the adult's response as a signal that they have (or have not) met some standard or lived up to some expectation. By school age, children have largely internalized those standards and expectations and thus become more autonomous in their self-judgments (Schaffer, 1996), in the same way that they internalize the parents' rules and regulations, thereby becoming better able to regulate their emotional expression and behavior—a point you'll recall from Chapter 6.

Early Self-definitions. Having achieved an initial self-awareness, the preschool child begins to define "who I am" by learning about her own qualities and her social roles. The 2-year-old not only knows her own name; she can probably also tell you if she is a girl or a boy and whether she is big or little. By about ages 5 to 7, a child can give you quite a full description of himself on a whole range of dimensions. For example, Susan Harter (1987; 1990; Harter & Pike, 1984) has found that children this age have clear notions of their own competence on a whole range of specific tasks, such as solving puzzles, counting, knowing a lot in school, climbing or skipping or jumping rope, or being able to make friends.

Beginning in the second year, children also seem to become aware of themselves as players in the social game. By age 2, the toddler has already learned a variety of social "scripts"—routines of play or interaction with others in her world. Case (1991) points out that the toddler now begins to develop some implicit understanding of her own roles in these scripts. So she begins to think of herself as a "helper" in some situations or as "the boss" when she is telling some other child what to do. You can see this clearly in children's sociodramatic play among preschoolers, who begin to take explicit roles: "I'll be the daddy and you be the mommy" or "I'm the teacher." As part of the same process, the preschool child also gradually understands her place in the network of family roles. She has sisters, brothers, father, mother, and so on.

These are major advances in the child's understanding. Yet this is still a *concrete* self. For one thing, each facet of a preschool child's self-concept seems to be quite separate, rather like a list: "I'm good at running"; "I don't like to play with dolls"; "I live in a big house"; "I have blue eyes" (Harter, 1998). These separate aspects of the "self-scheme" or internal working model of the self have not yet coalesced into a *global* sense of self-worth (Harter, 1987; 1990; Harter & Pike, 1984). Children this age do not say things like "I am a terrible person" or "I really like myself." Their perceptions of themselves are more tied to specific settings and specific tasks.

The self-concept of a preschool child is concrete in another way as well: He tends to focus on his own visible characteristics—whether he's a boy or girl, what

Critical Thinking

Can you think of some social scripts that a 2- or 3-year-old is likely to learn? Bedtime rituals? Others?

he looks like, what or who he plays with, where he lives, what he is good or bad at doing—rather than on more enduring, inner qualities. This pattern obviously parallels what we see in cognitive development at the same ages; it is in these same years that children's attention tends to be focused on the external appearance of objects rather than on their enduring properties, a pattern we see clearly in conservation tasks, such as when the child thinks there are now more pennies in a row because you have spread out the row or there is more water when it is poured into a taller, thinner glass.

Self-concept at School Age

Over the elementary school years, this concrete self-concept gradually shifts toward a more abstract, more comparative, more generalized self-definition. A 6-year-old might describe herself as "smart" or "dumb"; a 10-year-old is more likely to say he is "smarter than most other kids" or "not as good at baseball as my friends" (Rosenberg, 1986; Ruble, 1987). At the same time, the child's self-concept also becomes gradually less focused on external characteristics and more on internal qualities. The school-age child also begins to see her own (and other people's) characteristics as relatively stable, and for the first time she develops a global sense of her own self-worth.

A number of these themes are illustrated nicely in an older study by Montemayor and Eisen (1977) of self-concepts in 9- to 18-year-olds. Using the same "Who am I?" question I asked you to answer at the beginning of this chapter, these researchers found that the younger children in this study were still using mostly surface qualities to describe themselves, as in the description by this 9-year-old:

> My name is Bruce C. I have brown eyes. I have brown hair. I have brown eyebrows. I am nine years old. I LOVE! Sports. I have seven people in my family. I have great! eye site. I have lots! of friends. I live on 1923 Pinecrest Dr. I am going on 10 in September. I'm a boy. I have a uncle that is almost 7 feet tall. My school is Pinecrest. My teacher is Mrs. V. I play Hockey! I'm almost the smartest boy in the class. I LOVE! food. I love fresh air. I LOVE school. (pp. 317–318)

In contrast, look at the self-description of this 11-year-old girl in the sixth grade:

> My name is A. I'm a human being. I'm a girl. I'm a truthful person. I'm not very pretty. I do so-so in my studies. I'm a very good cellist. I'm a very good pianist. I'm a little bit tall for my age. I like several boys. I like several girls. I'm old-fashioned. I play tennis. I am a *very* good swimmer. I try to be helpful. I'm always ready to be friends with anybody. Mostly I'm good, but I lose my temper. I'm not well-liked by some girls and boys. I don't know if I'm liked by boys or not. (pp. 317–318)

This girl, like the other youngsters of this age in the Montemayor and Eisen study, not only describes her external qualities but also emphasizes her beliefs, the quality of her relationships, and general personality traits. Thus, as the child moves through the elementary school years (Piaget's concrete operations period), her self-definition becomes more complex, more comparative, less tied to external features, more focused on feelings, on ideas.

Self-judgments in School. The increasingly comparative self-assessments we see in middle childhood are particularly visible in the school context. Kindergarten and first-grade children pay relatively little attention to how well others do at a particular task; in fact the great majority will confidently tell you that they are the smartest kid in their class—an aspect of a general tendency at this age to identify self-qualities as positive (Harter, 1998). By third grade, however, children begin to notice whether their classmates finish a test sooner than they did or whether someone else got a better grade or more corrections on his spelling paper (Stipek, 1992). Their self-judgments begin to include both positive and negative elements.

Teachers' behavior shows a similar change: In the first few grades, teachers emphasize effort and work habits. Gradually they begin to use more comparative judgments. By junior high, teachers compare children not only to each other but to fixed standards, students at other schools, or national norms (Stipek, 1992). These processes are sometimes subtle, but they can be powerful. Robert Rosenthal (1994), in his famous "Pygmalion in the classroom" studies, has shown that a teacher's belief about a given student's ability and potential has a small but significant effect on her behavior toward that student and on the student's eventual achievement. This set of results has now been replicated many times. Rosenthal's standard procedure is to tell teachers at the beginning of a school year that some of the children in the class are underachievers and just ready to "bloom" intellectually, although in fact the children labeled in this way are chosen randomly. At the end of the year, those students labeled as having more potential have typically shown more academic gains than those who have not been labeled in this way. So the comparative judgments teachers make about individual children can have pervasive effects.

Similarly, parents' judgments and expectations also play a role. For example, you may recall from Chapter 7 that parents in the United States are more likely to attribute a daughter's good performance in math to hard work but a son's good math grades to ability. Children absorb these explanations and adjust their behavior accordingly.

The beliefs about their own abilities that students develop through this process are usually quite accurate. Students who consistently do well in comparison to others come to believe that they are academically competent. Further, and perhaps more important, they come to believe that they are in control of academic outcomes—in Bandura's terms, they have a strong sense of their own academic self-efficacy. Interestingly, this seems to be less true of girls than of boys, at least in U.S. culture. On average, girls get better school grades than boys do, but girls have lower perceptions of their own ability. When they do well, they are more likely to attribute their success to hard work rather than to ability; when they do poorly, they see their failure as their own fault (Stipek & Gralinski, 1991).

Self-concept at Adolescence

The trend toward greater abstraction in the self-definition continues during adolescence. Compare the answers of this 17-year-old to the "Who am I?" question with the ones you read earlier:

> I am a human being. I am a girl, I am an individual. I don't know who I am. I am a Pisces. I am a moody person. I am an indecisive person. I am an ambitious person. I am a very curious person. I am not an individual. I am a loner. I am an American (God help me). I am a Democrat. I am a liberal person. I am a radical. I am a conservative. I am a pseudoliberal. I am an atheist. I am not a classifiable person (i.e., I don't want to be). (Montemayor & Eisen, 1977, p. 318)

Obviously, this girl's self-concept is even less tied to her physical characteristics or even her abilities than is that of the 11-year-old. She is describing abstract traits or ideology. Figure 10.2 (p. 294) shows this shift from concrete to abstract self-definitions, based

Critical Thinking

There is clearly a chicken/egg problem here: Do children come to describe themselves more and more comparatively because that is a natural aspect of increasing cognitive complexity, or are they responding to the higher rate of comparisons made by teachers? How could you find out?

These fourth graders are already developing fairly clear ideas about their academic abilities, comparing their own successes and failures to those of other children in their class. These ideas then become incorporated in the children's self-schemes, affecting their choices and sense of self-efficacy.

Figure 10.2

As they get older, children and adolescents define themselves less and less by what they look like and more and more by what they believe or feel.

(*Source:* Montemayor & Eisen, 1977, from Table 1, p. 316.)

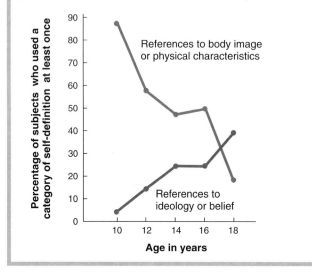

on the answers of all 262 subjects in the Montemayor and Eisen study. Each of the subjects' answers to the "Who am I?" question was placed in one or more specific categories, such as references to physical properties ("I am tall," "I have blue eyes") or references to ideology ("I am a Democrat," "I believe in God"). The figure makes it clear that appearance was still a highly salient dimension in the preteen and early teen years but became less dominant in late adolescence, at a time when ideology and belief became more salient. By late adolescence, most teenagers think of themselves in terms of enduring traits, beliefs, personal philosophy, and moral standards (Damon & Hart, 1988).

Identity in Adolescence

A somewhat different way to look at adolescent self-concept is through the lens of Erikson's theory. In this model, the central task or dilemma of adolescence is that of *identity*

If you asked them to define themselves, these teenagers would surely give much more abstract and comparative answers than you would hear from a 6-year-old.

versus role confusion. Erikson argued that the child's early sense of identity comes partly "unglued" at puberty because of the combination of rapid body growth and the sexual changes of puberty. He referred to this period as one in which the adolescent mind is in a kind of *moratorium* between childhood and adulthood. The old identity will no longer suffice; a new identity must be forged, one that must serve to place the young person among the myriad roles of adult life—occupational roles, sexual roles, religious roles. Confusion about all these role choices is inevitable. Erikson put it this way:

> In general it is primarily the inability to settle on an occupational identity which disturbs young people. To keep themselves together they temporarily overidentify, to the point of apparent complete loss of identity, with the heroes of cliques and crowds. . . . They become remarkably clannish, intolerant, and cruel in their exclusion of others who are "different," in skin color or cultural background . . . and often in entirely petty aspects of dress and gesture arbitrarily selected as *the* signs of an in-grouper or out-grouper. It is important to understand . . . such intolerance as the necessary *defense against a sense of identity confusion,* which is unavoidable at [this] time of life. (1980, pp. 97–98)

The teenage clique or crowd thus forms a base of security from which the young person can move toward a unique solution of the identity process. Ultimately, each teenager must achieve an integrated view of himself, including his own pattern of beliefs, occupational goals, and relationships.

Nearly all the current work on the formation of adolescent identity has been based on James Marcia's descriptions of **identity statuses** (Marcia, 1966; 1980), which are rooted in but go beyond Erikson's general conceptions of the adolescent identity process. Following one of Erikson's ideas, Marcia argues that the formation of an adolescent identity has two key parts: a *crisis* and a *commitment*. By a "crisis" Marcia means a period of decision making when old values and old choices are reexamined. This may occur as a sort of upheaval—the classic notion of a crisis—or it may occur gradually. The outcome of the reevaluation is a commitment to some specific role, some particular ideology.

If you put these two elements together, as in Figure 10.3 (p. 296), you can see that four different "identity statuses" are possible.

- **Identity achievement:** The person has been through a crisis and has reached a commitment to ideological or occupational goals.

- **Moratorium:** A crisis is in progress but no commitment has yet been made.

- **Foreclosure:** A commitment has been made without the person's having gone through a crisis. No reassessment of old positions has been made. Instead, the young person has simply accepted a parentally or culturally defined commitment.

- **Identity diffusion:** The young person is not in the midst of a crisis (although there may have been one in the past) and no commitment has been made. Diffusion may represent either an early stage in the process (before a crisis) or a failure to reach a commitment after a crisis.

Erikson's theory and Marcia's model assume that some kind of identity crisis is both normal and healthy. These assumptions have not always been supported by the evidence. For one thing, the whole process of identity formation may occur later than Erikson thought, when it occurs at all. In one combined analysis of eight separate cross-sectional studies, Alan Waterman (1985) found that the identity achievement status occurred most often in college, not during the high school years. Among these subjects, the moratorium status was also relatively uncommon except in the early years of college. So if most young people are going through an identity crisis, the crisis is occurring fairly late in adolescence and not lasting terribly long. What's more, about a third of the young people at every age were in the foreclosure status, which may indicate

Critical Thinking

The implication in Marcia's formulation is that the foreclosure status is less developmentally mature—that one must go through a crisis in order to achieve a mature identity. Does this idea make sense to you?

that many young people simply do not go through a crisis at all, but follow well-defined grooves.

As a further caveat, I should point out that all the subjects in the studies Waterman analyzed were either in college or in college-preparatory high school programs. This may give a false impression of the process of identity formation for young people who do not go to college, who do not have the luxury of a long period of questioning but must work out some kind of personal identity while still in their teens (e.g., Munro & Adams, 1977).

The whole conception of an adolescent identity crisis has also been strongly influenced by current cultural assumptions in Western societies, in which full adult status is postponed for almost a decade after puberty. In such cultures, young people do not normally or necessarily adopt the same roles or occupations as their parents. Indeed, they are encouraged to choose for themselves. In such a cultural system, adolescents are faced with what may be a bewildering array of options, a pattern that might well foster the sort of identity crisis Erikson described. In less industrialized cultures, especially those with clear initiation rites of the type described in the following Cultures and Contexts box, there may well be a shift in identity from that of child to that of adult, but without a crisis of any kind. Some anthropologists, in fact, refer to such cultures as *foreclosed*, in the sense that adolescent identity alternatives are distinctly limited (Coté, 1996).

For all these reasons, both Marcia and Waterman would now agree that the various identity statuses do not form a clear developmental pathway followed by all or most teenagers and young adults, even in Western cultures. Teens do not routinely move from foreclosure through moratorium to a clear identity status. Instead, the four types may more reasonably be thought of as different approaches young people may take to the task of identity formation, depending on culture as well as on the young person's individual situation (Marcia, 1993; Waterman, 1988). In this view, it is not correct to say that a young person in the foreclosure status has not achieved any identity. She

Figure 10.3

The four identity statuses proposed by Marcia, based on Erikson's theory. A fully achieved identity, according to this model, requires the young person to have examined his or her values or goals and to have reached a firm commitment.

(*Source:* Marcia, 1980.)

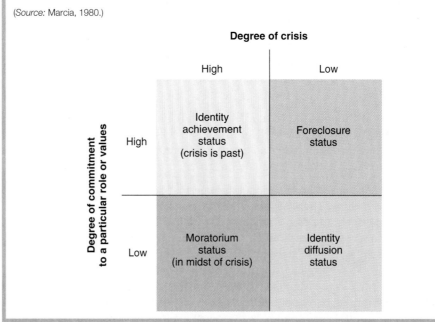

⟨image⟩ Cultures and Contexts
Adolescent Initiation Rituals

So important is the change in status and identity between childhood and adulthood that many societies have marked this passage—and eased the identity shift—with some kind of rite or ritual. Such rituals vary enormously in content, but certain practices are especially common (Cohen, 1964).

One such practice, more common for boys than for girls, is the separation of the child from the family, referred to by anthropologists as *extrusion*. The child may spend the day with his family but sleep elsewhere or may live in a separate dwelling with other boys or with relatives. For example, among the Kurtatchi of Melanesia, boys go through an extrusion ceremony at about age 9 or 10, after which they sleep in a special hut used by boys and unmarried men. Similarly, in traditional Hopi and Navaho cultures, boys typically sleep apart from the family beginning at age 8 or 10. This practice obviously symbolizes the separation of the child from the birth family, marking a coming of age. It also emphasizes that the child "belongs" not just to the family but to the larger group of kin or societal/tribal members.

A related theme is the accentuation of differences between females and males. In many cultures, for example, nudity taboos begin only at adolescence. In other societies, adolescents are forbidden to speak to any opposite-sex siblings, a taboo that may extend until one of the siblings marries. This practice seems to have at least two purposes. First and most obviously, it strengthens the incest taboo that is so important to avoid inbreeding. Second, it signifies the beginning of the time in life when males and females have quite different life patterns. Girls and boys have begun to learn gender-appropriate tasks long before adolescence, but at adolescence they take up their distinct roles far more completely.

These two patterns may form the backdrop for the initiation ritual itself, which is usually brief and fairly intense, often including considerable drama and pageantry. During this time—usually in groups and separately for each sex—youth are indoctrinated by the elders into the customary practices of their tribe or society. They may learn the history and songs of their people as well as special religious rituals or practices, such as the learning of Hebrew as preparation for the bar mitzvah or bat mitzvah in the Jewish tradition.

Physical mutilation or trials of endurance also play a part in the initiation in some cases. Boys may be circumcised or cut so as to create certain patterns of scars, or they may be sent out into the wilderness to undergo spiritual purification or to prove their manhood by achieving some feat. This is less common in girls' initiation rituals, but physical trials or mutilation does occur, such as the removal of the clitoris, whipping, or scarification.

Among the Hopi, for example, both boys and girls go through specific rituals in which they are taught the religious ceremonies of the kachina cult and are whipped. After these ceremonies, they may participate fully in the adult religious practices.

In modern U.S. culture, as in most other Western cultures, we have no universally shared initiation rites, but there are still many changes of status and a few experiences that have some properties in common with traditional adolescent rites of passage. For example, we do not deliberately separate adolescents from family or from adults, but we do send adolescents to a new level of school, thus effectively segregating them from all but their peers. Boot camp, for those who enter the military, is a more obvious parallel because the recruits are sent to a separate location and undergo various physical trials before they are accepted. Until relatively recent times, it was also common for adolescent boys and girls in our culture to attend separate schools. Even within coeducational schools, physical education classes were sex-segregated until very recently, as were such traditional gender-stereotyped classes as home economics and shop. Various other changes in legal standing also mark the passage to adult status in modern Western cultures. In the United States, for example, young people can have a driver's license at 16 and can see R-rated movies at 17. At 18, they can vote, marry or enter the military without parental consent, and be tried in adult rather than juvenile court for any legal offense.

These various remnants of older initiation patterns are considerably less condensed in modern society than are traditional initiation rites. Thus, passage into adult status is much fuzzier for young people in most industrialized countries, perhaps contributing to a greater sense of "identity crisis" among Western teens than is true in cultures in which the path to adulthood is more clearly signposted.

has an identity, but one that is adopted from parental or other societal rules, without significant questioning.

Thus, the *developmental* aspect of the Erikson/Marcia model is very likely not to be correct. In contrast, the second half of the model—the notion that an identity crisis and its resolution is a psychologically healthy process—is confirmed by a whole variety of research. In Western cultures, at least, young people who have made a commitment to some identity (that is, those who are classed in either identity achievement or foreclosure statuses) have higher self-esteem and lower levels of depression and are more goal-directed. Identity achievers, more than those in any of the other statuses, are also more likely to be using formal operations reasoning and to have greater capacity for intimacy in their personal relationships. In this last area, those in a foreclosure status tend to be more stereotyped in their approach to relationships, while those in identity diffusion have the most difficulties with intimacy (Waterman, 1992). All this evidence suggests that while a variety of roads may lead to some kind of personal identity, not all roads are psychologically equivalent. What Marcia calls the identity achievement status, in particular, is linked with more mature and emotionally healthy behavior in a variety of other domains.

Ethnic Identity in Adolescence

Minority teenagers, especially those of color in a predominantly white culture, face another task in creating an identity in adolescence: They must also develop an ethnic or racial identity, including self-identification as a member of some specific group, commitment to that group and its values and attitudes, and some evaluative attitudes (positive or negative) about the group to which they belong. Some of this self-identification occurs in middle childhood (Aboud & Doyle, 1995); 7- and 8-year-old minority children already understand the differences between themselves and majority children and most often prefer their own subgroup.

Further steps in the ethnic identity process occur in adolescence. Jean Phinney (1990; Phinney & Rosenthal, 1992; Phinney et al., 1997) proposes that in adolescence, the development of a complete ethnic identity moves through three rough stages. The first stage is an "unexamined ethnic identity," equivalent to what Marcia calls a foreclosed status. For some subgroups in U.S. society, such as African Americans and Native Americans, this unexamined identity typically includes the negative images and stereotypes common in the wider culture. Indeed, it may be especially at adolescence, with the advent of the cognitive ability to reflect and interpret, that the young person becomes keenly aware of the way in which his own group is perceived by the majority. As Spencer and Dornbusch (1990) put it, "The young African-American may learn as a child that black is beautiful but conclude as an adolescent that white is powerful" (p. 131). The same is doubtless true of other minority groups in the United States. An African-American journalist, Sylvester Monroe, who grew up in an urban housing project, clearly describes this negative feeling:

> If you were black, you didn't quite measure up. . . . For a black kid there was a certain amount of self-doubt. It came at you indirectly. You didn't see any black people on television, you didn't see any black people doing certain things. . . . You don't think it out but you say, "Well, it must mean that white people are better than we are. Smarter, brighter—whatever." (Spencer & Dornbusch, 1990, pp. 131–132)

Not all minority teenagers arrive at such negative views of their own group. Individual teenagers may have very positive ethnic images if that is the content of the identity conveyed by parents or others around the child. Phinney's point is, rather, that this initial ethnic identity is not arrived at independently but comes from outside sources.

The second stage is the "ethnic identity search," parallel to the *crisis* in Marcia's analysis of ego identity. This search is typically triggered by some experience that makes ethnicity salient—perhaps an example of blatant prejudice or merely the widening experience of high school. At this point the young person begins to arrive at her *own* judgments.

This exploration stage is eventually followed by a resolution of the conflicts and contradictions—analogous to Marcia's status of identity achievement. This is often a difficult process. For example, some African-American adolescents who wish to try to compete in and succeed in the dominant white culture may experience ostracism from their black friends, who accuse them of "acting white" and betraying their blackness. Latinos often report similar experiences. Some resolve this by keeping their own ethnic group at arm's length. Some search for a middle ground, adopting aspects of both the majority and minority cultures, a pattern Phinney calls a "blended bicultural" identity (Phinney & Devich-Navarro, 1997). Others deal with it by creating essentially two identities (a pattern Phinney calls an "alternating bicultural" identity), as expressed by one young Chicano interviewed by Phinney:

> Being invited to someone's house, I have to change my ways of how I act at home, because of culture differences. I would have to follow what they do . . . I am used to it now, switching off between the two. It is not difficult. (Phinney & Rosenthal, 1992, p. 160)

Still others resolve the dilemma by wholeheartedly choosing their own ethnic group's patterns and values, even when that choice may limit their access to the larger culture.

In both cross-sectional and longitudinal studies, Phinney has found that African-American teens and young adults do indeed move through these steps or stages toward a clear ethnic identity. Furthermore, there is evidence that among African-American, Asian-American, and Mexican-American teens and college students, those who have reached the second or third step in this process—those who are searching for or who have reached a clear identity—have higher self-esteem and better psychological adjustment than do those who are still in the "unexamined" stage (Phinney, 1990). In contrast, among Caucasian students, ethnic identity has essentially no relationship to self-esteem or adjustment.

This stagelike model may be a decent beginning description of the process of ethnic identity formation, but let us not lose sight of the fact that the details and the content of the ethnic identity will differ markedly from one subgroup to another. Those groups that encounter more overt prejudice will have a different road to follow than will those who may be more easily assimilated; those whose own ethnic culture espouses values that are close to those of the dominant culture will have less difficulty resolving the contradictions than will those whose subculture is at greater variance with the majority. Whatever the specifics, young people of color and those from clearly defined ethnic groups have an important additional identity task in their adolescent years.

Self-esteem

Thus far I have mostly talked about the self-concept as if there were no values attached to the categories by which we define ourselves. Yet clearly the self-concept contains an evaluative aspect. Note, for example, the differences in tone in the answers to the "Who am I?" question that I have already quoted. The 9-year-old makes a lot of positive statements about himself while the two older subjects offer more mixed evaluations.

These evaluative judgments have several interesting features. First of all, over the years of elementary school and high school, children's evaluations of their own abilities become increasingly *differentiated,* with quite separate judgments about skills in academics or athletics, physical appearance, peer social acceptance, friendships, romantic appeal, and relationships with parents (Harter, 1990; 1998).

Paradoxically, however, it is at school age—around age 7—that children first develop a *global* self-evaluation. Children at age 7 or 8 readily answer questions about how well they like themselves as people, how happy they are, or how well they like the way they are leading their lives. It is this global evaluation of one's own worth that is usually referred to as **self-esteem,** and this global evaluation is *not* merely the sum of all the separate assessments the child makes about his skills in different areas.

Instead, as Susan Harter's extremely interesting research on self-esteem tells us, each child's level of self-esteem is a product of two internal assessments or judgments

(Harter, 1987; 1990). First, each child experiences some degree of discrepancy between what he would like to be (or thinks he *ought* to be) and what he thinks he is—between his *ideal self* and what he perceives to be his *real self* (Harter, 1998). When that discrepancy is low, the child's self-esteem is generally high. When the discrepancy is high—when the child sees himself as failing to live up to his own goals or values—self-esteem is much lower.

The standards are not the same for every child. Some value academic skills highly; others value sports skills or having good friends. The key to self-esteem, Harter proposes, is the amount of discrepancy between what the child desires and what the child thinks he has achieved. Thus, a child who values sports prowess but who isn't big enough or coordinated enough to be good at sports will have lower self-esteem than will an equally small or uncoordinated child who does not value sports skill so highly. Similarly, being good at something, like singing, playing chess, or being able to talk to one's mother, won't raise a child's self-esteem unless the child values that particular skill.

Culture obviously plays some role here. Each culture or subculture assigns value to particular qualities or skills, whether intellectual skills, sports prowess, kindness, or whatever. A child's own choice of goals or desired qualities is clearly shaped by such cultural values. At the very broadest level, children growing up in individualist cultures are likely to evaluate themselves against individual achievement standards—getting good grades, winning a blue ribbon at the county fair, or scoring the winning goal in a soccer game. Children growing up in collectivist cultures would be more likely to judge themselves against communal qualities, such as the ability to get along with others.

The second major influence on a child's self-esteem, according to Harter, is the overall sense of support the child feels from the important people around her, particularly parents and peers. Children who feel that other people generally like them the way they are have higher self-esteem scores than do children who report less overall support.

Both these factors are clear in the results of Harter's own research. She asked third, fourth, fifth, and sixth graders how important it was to them to do well in each of five domains and how well they thought they actually did in each. The total discrepancy between these sets of judgments made up the discrepancy score. Remember that a high discrepancy score indicates that the child reported that he was *not* doing well in areas that mattered to him. The social support score was based on children's replies to a set of questions about whether they thought others (parents and peers) liked them as they were, treated them as a person, or felt that they were important. Figure 10.4 shows the results for the third and fourth graders. The findings for the fifth and sixth graders are virtually identical, and both sets of results strongly support Harter's hypothesis, as does other research, including studies of African-American youth (DuBois et al., 1996; Luster & McAdoo, 1995). Note that a low discrepancy score alone does not protect the child completely from low self-esteem if she lacks sufficient social support. And a lov-

According to Harter's model, these children's musical skill or the quality of their performance will have an impact on their global self-esteem only if musical skill is something they value.

Figure 10.4

For the children in Harter's studies, self-esteem was about equally influenced by the amount of support the child saw herself as receiving from parents and peers and by the degree of discrepancy between the value the child placed on various domains and the skill she saw herself having in each of those domains.

(*Source:* From S. Harter, "The Determinants and mediational role of global self-worth in children," *Contemporary topics in developmental psychology*, N. Eisenberg (ed.), p. 227. © 1987 by John Wiley and Sons. By permission of Wiley-Interscience.)

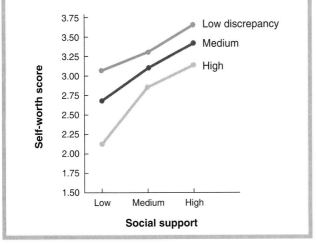

ing and accepting family and peer group do not guarantee high self-esteem if the youngster does not feel she is living up to her own standards.

A particularly deadly combination occurs when the child perceives that the parents' support is *contingent* on good performance in some area—getting good grades, making the first-string football team, winning the audition to play the solo with the school orchestra, being popular with other kids. If the child does not measure up to the standard, he experiences both an increased discrepancy between ideal and achievement and a loss of support from the parents.

Consistency of Self-esteem over Time

How stable are these self-judgments? Is a third grader with low self-esteem doomed to feel less than worthy for the rest of his life? A number of longitudinal studies of elementary school children and teenagers show that global self-esteem is moderately stable in the short term but somewhat less so over periods of several years. The correlation between two self-esteem scores obtained a few months apart is generally about .60. Over several years, this correlation drops to something more like .40 (Alsaker & Olweus, 1992), a level of consistency that has been found over periods as long as a decade, from early adolescence into early adulthood (Block & Robins, 1993). So it is true that a child with high self-esteem at age 8 or 9 is more likely to have high self-esteem at age 10 or 11. It is also true that there is a good deal of variation around that stability.

Self-esteem seems to be particularly unstable—and particularly likely to decline—in the years of early adolescence, especially at the time of the shift from elementary school to junior high school. In one study, Edward Seidman and his colleagues (1994) followed a group of nearly 600 Latino, black, and white youngsters over the two years from sixth grade through junior high—roughly ages 12 to 14. Seidman found a significant drop in average self-esteem between the last year in elementary school and the first year in junior high, a decline that occurred in each of the three ethnic groups. Similarly, David DuBois and his colleagues (1996), in a cross-sectional study of 1800 children in grades 5 through 8, found that eighth graders had significantly lower global self-esteem than did fifth graders.

Critical Thinking

Think about the following somewhat paradoxical proposition: If Harter's model is correct, then our self-esteem is most vulnerable in the area in which we may appear (and feel) the most competent. Does this fit with your experience?

Playing catch with Dad is a classic father-son activity in American culture. One of the side effects is likely to be that the son comes to believe that skill in sports is highly valued by his father.

This decline seems to be linked not so much to age as to stress and major life changes, such as changing schools at the same time as puberty occurs (DuBois et al., 1996; Harter, 1990). Researchers have noted it especially among students—both white and African American—who shift to junior high school at seventh grade (Seidman et al., 1994; Wigfield et al., 1991). When the transition process is more gradual, such as for children in a middle school that includes fifth through eighth grades, we see no parallel drop in self-esteem in early adolescence.

Consequences of Variations in Self-esteem

Harter and others have found that the child's level of self-esteem is *strongly* negatively correlated with depression in both middle childhood and adolescence. That is, the lower the self-esteem score, the more depressed the child describes himself to be. The correlations in several of Harter's studies range from –.67 to –.80—remarkably high for research of this type (Harter, 1987; Renouf & Harter, 1990). Bear in mind, though, that this is still correlational evidence. These findings don't prove that there is a causal connection between low self-esteem and depression. They only tell us that the two tend to go together.

In a similar vein, Bandura (1997) finds that children and adults who have a low sense of self-efficacy (that is, who have little faith in their own ability to achieve goals that they value) are more likely to become depressed. Depression seems especially likely when the individual sets high (perhaps unrealistically high) goals but feels unable to achieve at that high level—such as, perhaps, an uncoordinated child who dreams of being a star quarterback or a child who has incorporated a family expectation that he should get good grades but believes himself unable to achieve that. With goals that are more realistic, so that he feels a stronger sense of his own ability to reach the goal, failure or difficulty does not typically lead to depression, but rather has the effect of motivating the child (or adult) to work harder.

Origins of Differences in Self-esteem

If we accept Harter's model and assume that self-esteem is a product of each person's comparison of her desired or valued qualities with her actual qualities, we still have to ask where each child's values and self-judgments come from. How does a child come to think of herself as good at one thing or bad at something else? Why does she value one quality and not another?

There are at least three sources of information. First, of course, a child's own direct experience with success or failure in various arenas plays an obvious role. Children in elementary school become aware of their relative academic successes; they gain equally direct comparative information when they play sports, take clarinet lessons, or try out for the school play.

Second, the value a child attaches to some skill or quality is obviously affected fairly directly by peers' and parents' attitudes and values. Peer (and general cultural) standards for appearance establish benchmarks for all children and teens. A child who is "too tall" or "too fat" or deviates in some other way from the accepted norms is likely to feel a sense of inadequacy. Similarly, the degree of emphasis parents place on the child's performing well in some domain, whether it is schoolwork, athletics, or playing chess, is an important element in forming the child's aspirations in each area.

Finally, labels and judgments from others play a highly significant role. To a very considerable extent, we come to think of ourselves as others think of us (Cole, 1991a). Children who are repeatedly told that they are "smart," "a good athlete," or "pretty" are likely to have higher self-esteem than are children who are told that they are "dumb," "clumsy," or a "late bloomer." A child who brings home a report card with C's and B's on it and hears "That's fine, honey—we don't expect you to get all A's" draws conclusions both about the parents' expectations and about their judgments of his abilities. From all these sources, the child fashions his ideas (his internal model) about what he should be and what he is.

The Self-concept: A Summing-Up

Many questions remain to be answered, but I want to emphasize once again that a child's self-concept, including her level of self-esteem and her sense of self-efficacy, appears to be a highly significant mediating concept. Once such a "theory" of the self and the self's capacities is well established, once a global judgment of one's self-worth is established, we can see reverberations throughout the child's behavior. Among other things, she systematically chooses experiences and environments that are consistent with her beliefs about herself. The child who believes she can't play baseball behaves differently from the child who believes that she can. She is likely to denigrate the importance of sports or to avoid baseballs, bats, playing fields, and other children who play baseball. If forced to play, she may make self-deprecating remarks like "You know I can't play," or she may play self-defeating games, such as refusing to watch the ball when she swings at it or not running after the ball in right field because she knows she couldn't catch it even if she did get there on time. (If you think all this sounds autobiographical, you're right!)

A child who believes that she can't do long division will behave quite differently in the classroom from the child whose self-concept includes the idea "I am good at math." If she believes she is less competent, she may not try to work long division problems on the theory that if you don't try, you can't fail. At a later age, such a child is much less likely to take further math courses, thus reducing her occupational options. These beliefs are pervasive; many develop early; and although they are somewhat responsive to changing circumstances, they act as self-fulfilling prophecies and thus help to shape the trajectory of the person's life throughout childhood, adolescence, and adulthood.

The Development of Gender and Sex-Role Concepts

A central aspect of the child's self-concept that I have not yet discussed is the gender concept and the accompanying concept of sex roles. How do children come to understand that they are boys or girls, and when and how do they learn to identify behaviors and attitudes considered appropriate for their gender in their particular culture? I have saved this set of questions for a separate discussion partly because this has been an area of hot debate and extensive research in the past several decades, so there is a lot to say (e.g., Eagly, 1995; Jacklin, 1989; Maccoby, 1988; 1995), and partly because this set of questions has such central personal relevance for so many of us. Women's and men's roles are changing rapidly in most industrialized societies, but our stereotypes about men and women, and our own inner sense of what it means to be "male" or "female," have not always kept pace. If we are to understand ourselves—and perhaps rear our children with less confusion—we need to know more about the ways in which children learn about gender and sex roles.

The child has several related tasks. On the cognitive side, she must learn the nature of the sex/gender category itself—that boyness or girlness is permanent, unchanged by such things as modifications in clothing or hair length. This understanding is usually called the **gender concept**. On the social side, she has to learn what behaviors go with being a boy or a girl. That is, she must learn the **sex role** (sometimes called the *gender role*) defined as appropriate for her gender in her particular culture.

All roles involve sets of expected behaviors, attitudes, rights, duties, and obligations. Teachers are supposed to behave in certain ways, as are employees, mothers, or

Critical Thinking

Think back to your own early school years. Can you remember what labels or descriptors your parents and others applied to you? Were you "the smart one" or "the pretty one" or "the one who's good at music"? Think about how those labels—whatever they were—affected your own self-image and self-esteem.

Critical Thinking

Can you think of examples of how your own self-concept affects your choices and your behavior?

This mother is not only teaching her daughter how to cook; she is also transmitting information about sex roles and reinforcing traditional sex-typing.

baseball managers—all roles in our culture. Gender roles are somewhat broader than most other roles, but they are nonetheless roles, so we can think of a gender role as the set of expected behaviors, attitudes, rights, duties, and obligations involved in filling the role of "girl," "woman," "boy," or "man." Put another way, a gender role is a "job description" for being a man or woman in a given culture.

A child's or adult's behavior is said to be **sex-typed** to the degree that it matches the gender-role expectations for his or her own gender. A girl may know quite well that she is a girl and be able to describe the cultural sex roles accurately but still behave in a tomboyish way. In this case we would say that her **sex-role behavior** is less sex-typed than is the behavior of a girl who adopts more traditional behavior patterns.

If we are going to understand the development of the child's concept of gender, we have to understand all these elements. How early does the child know what sex/gender she is? How and when does she develop ideas about gender roles? And how well and how early do children match their behavior to the gender roles or the stereotypes?

Developmental Patterns

The Development of the Gender Concept. How soon does a child figure out that she is a girl or he is a boy? It depends on what we mean by "figure out." There seem to be three steps. First comes **gender identity,** which is simply a child's ability to label his own sex correctly and to identify other people as men or women, boys or girls. By 9 to 12 months, babies already treat male and female faces as if they were different categories, apparently using hair length as the primary differentiating clue (Fagot & Leinbach, 1993; Ruble & Martin, 1998). Within the next year, they begin to learn the verbal labels that go with these different categories. By age 2, if you show them a set of pictures of a same-sex child and several opposite-sex children and ask "Which one is you?" most children can correctly pick out the same-sex picture (Thompson, 1975). Between ages 2 and 3, children learn to identify and label others correctly by sex, such as by pointing out "which one is a girl" or "which one is a boy" in a set of pictures (Ruble & Martin, 1998). Hair length and clothing seem to be especially important cues in these early discriminations.

Accurate labeling, though, does not signify complete understanding. As is true with all the concepts I talked about in Chapter 6, which show increasing subtlety and complexity over the preschool and early school years, the gender concept undergoes further refinements. The second step is **gender stability,** the understanding that people stay the same gender throughout life. Researchers have measured this by asking children such questions as "When you were a little baby, were you a little girl or a little boy?" or "When you grow up, will you be a mommy or a daddy?" Slaby and Frey, in

Even at age 2, these children have the beginning of a gender concept: They can correctly identify their own gender and that of other children.

their classic study (1975), found that most children understand this aspect of gender by about age 4.

The final component, usually referred to as **gender constancy,** is the understanding that someone stays the same biological sex even though he may appear to change by wearing different clothes or changing his hair length. For example, boys don't change into girls by wearing dresses. This is an appearance/reality problem very much like Flavell's sponge/rock test I described in Chapter 6. The child must figure out that although a boy wearing a dress may *look like* a girl, he is *really* still a boy, just as the sponge painted to look like a rock may look like a rock but is really still a sponge. When children are asked the gender constancy question in this way, many 4-year-olds and most 5-year-olds can answer correctly, just as 4- and 5-year-olds understand other appearance/reality distinctions (Martin & Halverson, 1983). Sandra Bem has found that to reach this level of understanding, a child must have at least some grasp of the basic genital differences between boys and girls and some understanding that genital characteristics are what make a child "really" a boy or a girl. In her study, 4-year-olds who did not yet understand genital differences also did not show gender constancy (Bem, 1989).

In sum, children as young as 2 or 2½ know their own sex and that of people around them, but children do not have a fully developed concept of gender until they are 4 or 5.

The Development of Sex-Role Concepts and Stereotypes. Obviously, figuring out your sex/gender and understanding that it stays constant is only part of the story. Learning what goes with, or ought to go with, being a boy or a girl is also a vital part of the child's task.

In every culture, adults have clear sex-role stereotypes. Indeed, the content of those stereotypes is remarkably similar in cultures around the world. John Williams and Deborah Best (1990), who have studied adult gender stereotypes in 28 different countries and children's stereotypes in 24 countries (described in the Cultures and Contexts box on p. 306), find that the most strongly stereotyped traits are weakness, gentleness, appreciativeness, and softheartedness for women and aggression, strength, cruelty, and coarseness for men.

Studies of children show that these stereotyped ideas develop early, even in families that espouse gender equality. The 3-year-old daughter of an egalitarian-minded friend announced one day that "mommies use the stove and daddies use the grill." Another friend told me the story of a 4-year-old who came home from nursery school one day insisting that doctors were always men and nurses were always women—even though his own father was a nurse! Even 2-year-olds already associate certain tasks and possessions with men and women, such as vacuum cleaners and food with women and cars and tools with men. By age 3 or 4, children can assign occupations, toys, and activities to the stereotypic gender (Ruble & Martin, 1998; Signorella et al., 1993). By age 5, children begin to associate certain personality traits with males or females, and such knowledge is well developed by age 8 or 9 (Martin, 1993; Serbin et al., 1993).

Studies of children's ideas about how men and women (or boys and girls) *ought* to behave add an interesting further element. An early study by William Damon (1977) illustrates the point particularly nicely. He told children aged 4 through 9 a story about a little boy named George who likes to play with dolls. George's parents tell him that only little girls play with dolls; little boys shouldn't. The children were then asked a batch of questions about this, such as "Why do people tell George not to play with dolls?" or "Is there a rule that boys shouldn't play with dolls?"

Four-year-olds in this study thought it was okay for George to play with dolls. There was no rule against it and he should do it if he wanted to. Six-year-olds, in contrast, thought it was *wrong* for George to play with dolls. By about age 9, children had differentiated between what boys and girls usually do and what is "wrong." One boy said, for example, that breaking windows was wrong and bad, but that playing with dolls was not bad in the same way: "Breaking windows you're not supposed to do. And if you play with dolls, well you can, but boys usually don't."

Cultures and Contexts
Sex-Role Stereotypes Around the World

A child is shown a silhouette of a man and one of a woman and is told a story: "One of these people is emotional. They cry when something good happens as well as when everything goes wrong. Which person is the emotional person?" Or, "One of these people is always pushing other people around and getting into fights. Which person gets into fights?" (Williams & Best, 1990).

In response to stories like these, third-grade children in the United States identify the male figure as aggressive 90 percent of the time and the female figure as emotional 79 percent of the time. Fourth graders give the stereotyped answer to both stories 100 percent of the time. Are these stereotypes unique to U.S. culture, or does something similar exist in every culture? An amazing cross-cultural study by John Williams and Deborah Best (1990) gives us some answers.

They asked 5- and 8-year-old children in 24 countries these same questions, translated where necessary. Included were countries from every continent, with varying levels of industrialization.

Williams and Best had expected to find some common ground; as they put it, "We were not prepared, however, for the high degree of pancultural generality that we found" (p. 303). In every country, the children had less strong sex stereotypes than did adults in that same country, but in every country, the qualities associated with men were stronger and more active than those associated with women, and this was true of young children as well as adults.

Among the children, the characteristics most consistently ascribed to males were aggression, strength, and cruelty, and those most consistently ascribed to females were weakness, gentleness, and appreciativeness. These patterns became stronger with age in all countries, so 8-year-olds gave more stereotypic responses than 5-year-olds. And in virtually all countries, the male stereotype was clearer or more consistent than the female.

There were a few differences, naturally. Children in some countries seem to learn the sex stereotype very early, in others somewhat later. Children in Pakistan and New Zealand, for example, already had very clear stereotypes at age 5, while those in Brazil and France showed little stereotyping at 5 but clearer stereotyping at 8—a pattern also found among African Americans. Sex stereotypes in particular countries also contain unique content. German children, for instance, choose "adventurous," "confident," "jolly," and "steady" as female items, although these are more normally male items in other cultures. Pakistani children identify "emotional" with men; Japanese children associate independence and severity with neither sex. But these are variations on a common theme. In *all* 24 countries, 8-year-olds choose the male figure for stories about aggression, strength, cruelty, coarseness, and loudness, and they choose the female figure for stories about weakness. In 23 of 24 countries, 8-year-olds also choose the female character for gentleness, appreciativeness, and softheartedness. Thus, not only does every culture appear to have clear sex-role stereotypes, but the content of those stereotypes is remarkably similar across cultures.

What seems to be happening is that the 5- or 6-year-old, having figured out that she is permanently a girl or he is a boy, is searching for a *rule* about how boys and girls behave (Martin & Halverson, 1981). The child picks up information from watching adults, from watching TV, from listening to the labels that are attached to different activities (e.g., "boys don't cry"). Initially they treat these as absolute, moral rules. Later they understand that these are social conventions, at which point sex-role concepts become more flexible (Katz & Ksansnak, 1994).

Four-year-olds and 9-year-olds think it is okay for a boy to play with dolls, but many 6-year-olds think it is simply wrong for boys to do girl things or for girls to do boy things.

In a similar way, many kinds of fixed, biased ideas about other people—such as bias against obese children, against those who speak another language, or against those of other races—are at their peak in the early school years and then decline throughout the remaining years of childhood and into adolescence (Doyle & Aboud, 1995; Powlishta et al., 1994). Another way to put it is that children this age have a strong sense of "us" versus "them," of in-group versus out-group. They classify other children as "like me" or "not like me" on whatever dimension, and they develop strong preferences for those who are like themselves and highly stereotyped (often negative) ideas about those who are "not like them." In the same way, and for the same reason, minority children begin to show strong preferences for those of their own ethnic group only at about age 7 or 8 (Aboud & Doyle, 1995).

This entire stereotyping process seems to be totally normal, part of the child's attempt to create rules and order, to find patterns that can guide his understanding and his behavior. Just as an English-speaking 2- or 3-year-old discovers the rule of adding *ed* to a verb to make the past tense and then overgeneralizes that rule, so the 6- or 7-year-old discovers the "rules" about boys and girls, men and women, "us" and "them," and overgeneralizes. In fact, most 6- and 7-year-olds believe that gender-role differences are determined by nature rather than nurture. By age 9, they understand that at least some differences in behavior between boys and girls are the result of training or experience rather than being built-in (Taylor, 1996).

Another of the interesting sidelights in the research on stereotyping is that the male stereotype and sex-role concept seem to develop a bit earlier and to be stronger than the female stereotype or sex-role concept—and this is true in virtually all countries studied. More children agree on what men are or should be like than on what women are or should be like. This might happen because children have direct experience with women in several significant roles (mother and teacher, for example), while their primary experience with men is in the role of father. Or it could mean that the female role in most societies is more flexible than the male role. At any rate, it is clear that in Western societies, the qualities attributed to the male are more highly *valued* than are the female traits (Broverman et al., 1970). We see it as "good" to be independent, assertive, logical, and strong; it is less good to be warm, quiet, tactful, and gentle. Perhaps girls recognize early that the male role is seen more positively and so aspire to some of the valued male qualities. That would lead to a female role's being perceived more broadly. Whatever the reason, it is an interesting finding—one with considerable relevance for understanding adult male and female sex roles and stereotyping.

The Development of Sex-Role Behavior. The final element in the equation is the actual behavior children show with their own sex and with the opposite sex. The unexpected finding here is that children's *behavior* is sex-typed earlier than are their ideas about sex roles or stereotypes.

By 18 to 24 months, children begin to show some preference for sex-stereotyped toys, such as dolls for girls or trucks or building blocks for boys, which is some months *before* they can normally identify their own gender (O'Brien, 1992). By age 3, children begin to show a preference for same-sex playmates and are much more sociable with playmates of the same sex—at a time when they do not yet have a concept of gender stability (Maccoby, 1988; 1990; Maccoby & Jacklin, 1987). By school age, peer relationships are almost exclusively same-sex. You can see the early development of this preference in Figure 10.5 (p. 308), which shows the results of a study of preschool play groups. The researchers counted how often children played with same-sex or opposite-sex playmates (La Freniere et al., 1984). You can see that by age 3, about 60 percent of play groups were same-sex groupings, and the rate rose from there.

The other intriguing pattern is that in early elementary school, children seem to begin to pay more attention to the behavior of same-sex adults or playmates than to that of people of the opposite sex and to play more with new toys that are labeled as appropriate for their own sex (e.g., Bradbard et al., 1986). Overall, then, we see many signs that children are both aware of and affected by gender from very early, perhaps by

Critical Thinking

How many explanations can you think of for the fact that children begin to prefer to play with same-sex peers as early as age 3?

Figure 10.5

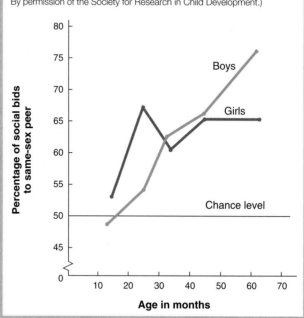

Same-sex playmate preference among preschoolers.

(*Source:* La Freniere et al., from Fig. 1, p. 1961, "The emergence of same-sex affiliative preferences among pre-school peers: A developmental/ethological perspective," *Child development*, 55 (1984), 1958–1965. By permission of the Society for Research in Child Development.)

age 1, certainly by age 2. Gender becomes a still more potent force in guiding behavior and attitudes at around age 5 or 6.

Explaining Sex-Role Development

Theorists from most of the major traditions have tried their hand at explaining these patterns of development. Freud relied on the concept of identification to explain the child's adoption of appropriate sex-role behavior, but his theory founders on the fact that children begin to show clearly sex-typed behavior long before age 4 or 5, when Freud thought identification occurred.

Social Learning Theory. Social learning theorists, such as Bandura (1977) and Walter Mischel (1966; 1970), have naturally emphasized the role of both direct reinforcement and modeling in shaping children's sex-role behavior and attitudes. This model has been far better supported by research than have Freud's ideas. Parents do seem to reinforce sex-typed activities in children as young as 18 months old, not only by buying different kinds of toys for boys and girls, but by responding more positively when their sons play with blocks or trucks or when their daughters play with dolls (Fagot & Hagan, 1991; Lytton & Romney, 1991). Some evidence also suggests that toddlers whose parents are more consistent in rewarding sex-typed toy choice or play behavior, and whose mothers favor traditional family sex roles, learn accurate gender labels earlier than do toddlers whose parents are less focused on the gender-appropriateness of the child's play (Fagot & Leinbach, 1989; Fagot et al., 1992)—findings clearly consistent with the predictions of social learning theory.

Interestingly, researchers have also accumulated a fair amount of evidence that—in U.S. culture at least—differential treatment of sons and daughters is more common among fathers than mothers and that fathers are particularly likely to be concerned with the appropriate sex-role behavior of their sons (Siegal, 1987). Many fathers seem to be especially uncomfortable with "girlish" behavior in their sons and are much more

Social learning theorists argue that little boys prefer to play with trucks because parents buy them more trucks and reinforce them directly for such play.

likely to show disapproval of such behavior in their sons than they are to disapprove of "tomboyish" behavior in their daughters—which may be one reason that the male stereotype develops earlier and is stronger than is the female stereotype.

Cross-cultural evidence also supports a social learning view. Anthropologist Beatrice Whiting, after examining patterns of gender socialization in 11 different cultures, concludes that "we are the company we keep" (Whiting & Edwards, 1988). In most cultures, girls and boys keep different company, beginning quite early, with girls spending more time with women as well as in child-care responsibilities. To the extent that this is true, it would provide each sex with more same-sex than opposite-sex models and more opportunity for reinforcement of sex-appropriate behavior.

Still, helpful as it is, a social learning explanation is probably not sufficient. In particular, parents differentially reinforce "boy" versus "girl" behavior less than you'd expect, and probably not enough to account for the very early and robust discrimination children seem to make on the basis of gender (Fagot, 1995). Even children whose parents seem to treat their young sons and daughters in highly similar ways nonetheless learn gender labels and show same-sex playmate choices.

Cognitive-Developmental Theories. A second alternative, based strongly on Piagetian theory, is Lawrence Kohlberg's suggestion that the crucial aspect of the process is the child's understanding of the gender concept (1966; Kohlberg & Ullian, 1974). Once the child realizes that he is a boy or she is a girl forever, he or she becomes highly motivated to learn to behave in the way that is expected or appropriate for that gender. Specifically, Kohlberg predicted that we should see systematic same-sex imitation only *after* the child has shown full gender constancy. Most studies designed to test this hypothesis have supported Kohlberg: Children do seem to become much more sensitive to same-sex models after they have understood gender constancy (Frey & Ruble, 1992). What Kohlberg's theory cannot easily handle, however, is the obvious fact that children show clearly differentiated sex-role behavior, such as toy preferences, long before they have achieved full understanding of the gender concept.

Gender Schema Theory. The most fruitful current explanation is usually called **gender schema theory** (Bem, 1981; Martin, 1991; Martin & Halverson, 1981), a model that has its roots in information processing theories of cognitive development as well as in Kohlberg's theory. Just as the self-concept can be thought of as a "scheme" or "self-theory," so the child's understanding of gender can be seen in the same way. The gender schema begins to develop as soon as the child notices the differences between male and female, knows his own gender, and can label the two groups with some consistency—all of which happens by age 2 or 3.

Why would children notice gender so early? Why is it such a salient category? One possibility, suggested by Maccoby (1988), is that because gender is clearly an either/or category, children seem to understand very early that this is a key distinction, so the category serves as a kind of magnet for new information. Another alternative is that young children pay a lot of attention to gender differences because our culture is chockablock with gender references. Adults and other children emphasize gender distinctions in innumerable small ways. The first question we ask about a new baby is "Is it a boy or a girl?" We buy blue baby clothes for boys and pink for girls; we ask toddlers whether their playmates are boys or girls. A preschool teacher emphasizes gender if she says "Good morning, boys and girls" or divides her charges into a boys' team and a girls' team (Bigler, 1995). In all these ways, we signal to the child that this is an important category and thus further the very early development of a gender scheme that matches our cultural norms and beliefs. Whatever the origin of this early scheme, once it is established, a great many experiences are assimilated to it, and children may begin to show preference for same-sex playmates or for gender-stereotyped activities (Martin & Little, 1990).

Preschoolers first learn some broad distinctions about what kinds of activities or behavior go with each gender, both by observing other children and through the reinforcements they receive from parents. They also learn a few gender "scripts"—whole sequences of events that normally go with a given gender, such as "fixing dinner" or "building with tools" (Levy & Fivush, 1993)—just as they learn other social scripts at about this age. One study (Bauer, 1993) even suggests that boys (but not girls) may be aware of and more willing to imitate gender-matched scripts as early as age 2—yet another indication that gender socialization occurs earlier and is stronger for boys than for girls, at least in this culture.

Between ages 4 and 6 the child learns a more subtle and complex set of associations for his or her *own* gender—what children of his own gender like and don't like, how they play, how they talk, what kinds of people they associate with. Only at about ages 8 to 10 does the child develop an equivalently complex view of the opposite gender (Martin et al., 1990).

The key difference between this theory and Kohlberg's is that for the initial gender schema to be formed, the child need not understand that gender is permanent. When

The Real World

Sex Stereotyping on TV and in Children's Books

In modern cultures, one obvious source from which children acquire information for their sex-role schemas is the TV programs they watch. From early preschool age, children in the United States spend an average of two to four hours a day in the presence of a TV set that is running (Huston & Wright, 1998). (I put it that way because we don't know how much of the time children actually *watch* the moving image.) Before they begin school, children have already been exposed to thousands of hours of TV; by age 18, the average child has spent more time in front of a TV set than in a classroom (Huston et al., 1990).

How are men and women portrayed in all those TV programs and commercials? Highly stereotypically. The most current estimates suggest that in U.S. television programs, males outnumber females by 2 or 3 to 1 on virtually every kind of programming; in programming aimed specifically at children, the ratio is more like 5 to 1 (Huston & Wright, 1998). The frequency of males and females is more equal in commercials, but the "voice-over" on commercials is nearly always male. In both commercials and regular programming, women are more often shown at home or in romantic situations; men more often appear in work settings, with cars, or playing sports. Men are shown solving problems and being more active, aggressive, powerful, and independent. Women are most often portrayed as submissive, passive, attractive, sensual, nurturing, emotional, and less able to deal with difficult situations (Golombok & Fivush, 1994; Huston & Wright, 1998).

A continuous exposure to these stereotyped males and females does seem to have at least a small effect on a child's vision of men and women and their roles. In two longitudinal studies, Morgan (1982; 1987) has found that among elementary and high school students, those who watched a lot of TV at the beginning of the study increased in their traditional sex-role stereotyping a year later. They were more likely, for example, to think that household chores should be done by women rather than

by men. Even more persuasive is an early experiment by Emily Davidson, who deliberately exposed some 5- and 6-year-olds to highly sex-stereotyped cartoons. Those who had seen such cartoons, compared to control children who had seen neutral cartoons, later gave more stereotyped answers to questions about the qualities of men and women (Davidson et al., 1979).

At a more subtle level, Aletha Huston and her colleagues (1984) have found that toy commercials aimed at boys and those aimed at girls are simply designed differently. Boys' commercials are fast, sharp, and loud—lots of quick cuts, loud music, activity. Girls' commercials are gradual, soft, and fuzzy. They have camera fades and dissolves rather than sharp cuts, and they use softer background music. Children as young as first grade notice these differences. They can watch a commercial of some nonstereotyped toy and tell you whether the *style* of the commercial is suited to a boys' or girls' toy.

Children's books are also quite stereotyped. Fifty years ago, three or four times as many boys as girls appeared as central characters in such books. Today the ratio is more like 2 to 1, but boys are still more common protagonists in picture books and early reading books (Kortenhaus & Demarest, 1993). Even in books that have won the Caldecott Medal, given to the most distinguished children's picture book each year, male characters outnumber females by about 2 to 1 (Golombok & Fivush, 1994). When girls do appear as leading characters in such books, they are often depicted as adventurous, but it is still comparatively rare for girls to be central figures.

TV and books are clearly not the only sources of information children have about sex roles. We know that children growing up without TV nonetheless acquire sex-role stereotypes. Yet TV and books do have an impact on children's ideas about men and women, most often accentuating rather than minimizing gender stereotypes.

gender constancy is understood at about 5 or 6, children develop a more elaborated rule or schema of "what people who are like me do" and treat this "rule" the same way they treat other rules—as absolute. By late childhood and early adolescence, teenagers understand that these are social conventions, and sex-role concepts become more flexible (Katz & Ksansnak, 1994). What is more, teenagers have largely abandoned the automatic assumption that whatever their own gender does is better or preferable (Powlishta et al., 1994). Indeed, a significant minority of teenagers and youths begin to define themselves as having both masculine and feminine traits—a point I'll come back to in a moment.

Many of us, committed to the philosophical goal of equality for women, have taken the rigidity of children's early sex stereotypes as evidence that we have made little progress toward equality ("Mommy, you can't be a psychology doctor, you have to be a psychology nurse"). Gender schema theorists emphasize that such rule learning is absolutely normal, and so is the rigid stereotyping that we see in children's ideas about sex roles between ages 5 and 8 or 9. Children are searching for order, for rules that help to make sense of their experiences. And a rule about "what men do" and "what women do" is a helpful schema for them.

Gender schema theory is surely not the last word. It, too, has limitations. For example, when researchers have measured preschool children's understanding of gender and then looked at how sex-typed their behavior is, they often find only very weak connections (Bussey & Bandura, 1992; Martin, 1993). So 3-year-olds who show the clearest preferences for same-sex playmates are not necessarily the same ones who have the most advanced cognitive understanding of gender. Ultimately, some combination of social learning theory and gender schema theory may be proposed that will handle the data better.

Individual Differences in Sex-Typing and Sex-Role Stereotypes

The developmental patterns I have been describing seem to hold for virtually all children. Nevertheless, as usual, we also see quite a lot of variation from child to child in the rigidity of the gender rules they develop or in the sex-typing of their behavior.

As a group, boys usually have stronger (more rigid and more traditional) sex-role stereotypes. Among both boys and girls, however, children whose mothers work outside the home have *less* stereotypic views—that is, more flexible rules (Powell & Steelman, 1982). Parallel evidence comes from a study of children who were cared for in early life by their fathers instead of their mothers. These children, too, later have less stereotyped views of sex roles (Williams et al., 1992). Such a finding makes perfectly good sense if the child's sex-role schema is formed primarily (or at least originally) by observing the parents' roles.

Cross-Sex Children. Another interesting group are children with cross-sex preferences—girls who would rather be boys and boys who would rather be girls. Having been a tomboy myself, I find such children especially intriguing. How does a child come to wish to be the other sex or to choose cross-sex playmates or toys?

One possibility is that such children are directly trained that way. They may have been specifically reinforced for aspects of the role ascribed to the opposite sex. Some girls are given trucks and carpentry tools and taught football by their fathers (or mothers). They may come to wish to be boys. We know that tomboy behavior is more accepted and reinforced than is "girlish" behavior in a boy, so it makes sense from a social learning perspective that many more girls say they would like to be boys than the reverse.

Social learning theory does not fare so well, though, in explaining the results of research by Carl Roberts and his colleagues (1987). They studied a group of boys who showed strong preference for female toys and playmates from their earliest years of

In our society, "tomboys," as this girl would probably be labeled, are fairly common and largely accepted. But a boy this age who showed "girlish" behavior would experience much more pressure to change, perhaps especially from Dad.

Critical Thinking

Can you think of any other way to explain the fact that there are more tomboys than there are "girlish" boys?

life. When Roberts compared these boys to a group of boys with more typical masculine sex-role behaviors, he found little evidence that the more feminine boys had been specifically reinforced for these behaviors or that their fathers were providing models for such behavior. Rather, Roberts found that the feminine boys were more feminine in appearance from earliest babyhood, that they were more often ill or hospitalized early in life, and that they had relatively less contact with both their mothers and fathers on a daily basis, compared to the more masculine boys. This pattern of findings does not fit nicely with a simple social learning explanation.

Alternatively, there might be some biological differences. The finding by Roberts and his colleagues that the more behaviorally feminine boys already looked more feminine from earliest infancy is at least consistent with some biological difference, as is their finding that in adulthood, three-quarters of the more feminine boys were homosexual or bisexual. Further evidence for some biological influence on cross-sex behavior comes from studies of girls who have experienced heightened levels of androgen prenatally. (Recall from Chapter 4 that androgen is largely a "male" hormone.) These "androgenized" girls, in comparison to their normal sisters, more often prefer to play with boys (Hines & Kaufman, 1994), show less interest in dolls or babies, and have fewer fantasies about being a mother (Meyer-Bahlburg et al., 1986). Some evidence also suggests that these androgenized girls are more interested in rough-and-tumble play, although here the findings are not consistent (Hines & Kaufman, 1994).

Findings like these suggest that actual sex-typing of behavior is at least partially affected by prenatal hormones. At the same time, it is also clear that a child's basic gender identity—the gender she thinks of herself as being—is strongly influenced by the label she is given and the treatment she receives from her parents. Children born with ambiguous genitalia, for example, usually grow up to think of themselves as being whichever gender they were reared as, even if that gender does not match their genotype (Money, 1987).

Clearly, the gender a child *thinks* he is affects the gender *schema* he develops, and the environment is extremely potent in helping to shape that schema. At the same time, I think we must keep an open mind about the possible biological origins of some sex-role behaviors. The evidence is not all in yet.

Androgyny. A different approach to the study of cross-sex sex-typing can be found in research on individual gender schemas or orientations. We can ask, about any given child or adolescent (or adult), not only how closely his behavior matches the sex-role stereotype, but also how he thinks of himself and his own gender-related qualities. In the early years of this research, the issue was usually phrased as *masculinity* versus *femininity*, and these were thought of as being on opposite ends of a single continuum. A person could be masculine or feminine but couldn't be both. Following the lead of Sandra Bem (1974) and of Janet Spence and Robert Helmreich (1978), psychologists today most often conceive of masculinity and femininity as two separate dimensions, with masculinity centered around *agentic/instrumental* qualities and femininity centered around *expressive/communal* qualities. A person can be high or low on either or both. Indeed, if we categorize people as high or low on each of these two dimensions, based on each individual's self-description, we end up with four basic sex-role types, called **masculine, feminine, androgynous,** and **undifferentiated**—as you can see in Figure 10.6. The masculine and feminine types are the traditional combinations in which a person sees himself or herself as high in one quality and low in the other. A "masculine" teenager or adult, by this conceptualization, is thus one who perceives himself (or herself) as having many traditional masculine qualities and few traditional feminine qualities. A feminine teenager or adult shows the reverse pattern. In contrast, androgynous individuals see themselves as having *both* masculine and feminine traits; undifferentiated individuals describe themselves as lacking both—a group that sounds a lot like those with a "diffuse" identity in Marcia's system.

This categorization system says nothing about the accuracy of the child's or the adult's general rule or schema about sex roles. A teenage girl, for example, could have a

Figure 10.6

Four sex-role types are created when we think of masculinity and femininity as separate dimensions rather than as two ends of the same dimension.

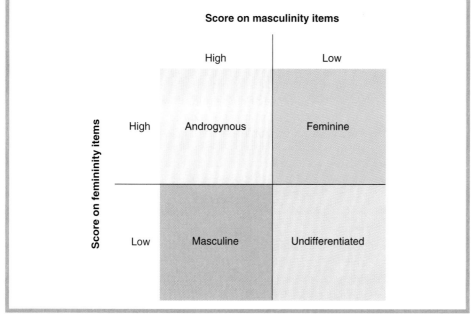

Score on masculinity items

	High	Low
High (Score on femininity items)	Androgynous	Feminine
Low	Masculine	Undifferentiated

clear notion of the norms for male or female behavior and still perceive *herself* as having some stereotypically masculine qualities. In some sense, then, when we study masculinity/femininity/androgyny, we are studying the intersection between the self-scheme and the gender scheme.

Perhaps because young children's ideas about sex roles are still quite rigid, we find little sign of androgyny among children younger than 9 or 10. Among late elementary school students and adolescents, however, variations in androgyny, masculinity, and femininity clearly do exist. In the United States, 25 to 35 percent of high school students define themselves as androgynous (e.g., Lamke, 1982; Rose & Montemayor, 1994). More girls than boys seem to show this pattern, and more girls fall into the masculine category than boys into the feminine group.

More striking is the finding that either an androgynous or a masculine sex-role self-concept is associated with higher self-esteem among *both* boys and girls (Boldizar, 1991; Burnett et al., 1995; Rose & Montemayor, 1994). This finding makes sense if we assume the existence of a kind of "masculine bias" in U.S. and other Western societies, such that traditionally masculine qualities like independence and competitiveness are more valued by both men and women than are many traditionally female qualities. If such a bias exists—and there is good reason to think it does—then the teenage boy's task is simpler than the teenage girl's. He can achieve high self-esteem and success with his peers by adopting a traditional masculine sex-role, while a girl who adopts a traditional gender role is adopting a less valued role, with attendant risks of lower self-esteem and a reduced sense of competence (Massad, 1981; Rose & Montemayor, 1994).

Findings like these suggest the possibility that while the creation of rigid rules or schemas for sex roles is a normal—even essential—process in young children, a blurring of those rules may be an important process in adolescence, particularly for girls, for whom a more masculine or androgynous self-concept is associated with more positive outcomes.

I have been careful in the preceding few paragraphs to say, repeatedly, "in Western cultures." I have done so because it is not entirely obvious to me that androgyny and masculinity are the optimum patterns for adolescent self-esteem in every culture. Would we find this same link in a collectivist culture, in which cooperation and respectfulness are more highly valued than assertiveness and independence? The more general rule may be that higher self-esteem in teenagers (and in adults) is linked to a self-perception that matches the most valued traits in the culture in which one grows up. In the United States, where assertiveness and independence are highly valued, adolescents who perceive themselves as having these qualities not only describe themselves as more masculine or androgynous but also have higher self-esteem. In a collectivist culture, those teens who see themselves as having the more stereotypically feminine qualities of cooperativeness and respectfulness might have higher self-esteem. I know of no data that test this hypothesis, but it is yet another reminder that we have to be cautious about generalizing from U.S. or Western data to all cultures.

Summary

1. The child's emerging self-concept has several elements, including the awareness of a separate self and the understanding of self-permanence (which may be collectively called the subjective self) and awareness of oneself as an object in the world (the objective self).

2. The subjective self develops in the first year of life; we see real self-awareness and the emergence of the objective self in the second year.

3. The sense of self-efficacy may also have its origins in this first year of life, as the infant learns that he can have effects on the world around him.

4. Self-conscious emotions, such as shame or pride, appear only after the toddler has achieved self-awareness.

5. In early childhood, the child begins to place herself in basic categories such as age, size, and gender. These early self-definitions are quite concrete, based primarily on physical attributes and things the child can do.

6. The self-concept becomes steadily more abstract in the elementary and high school years, coming to include not only actions but also likes and dislikes, beliefs, and more general personality characteristics.

7. At adolescence, there may also be a reevaluation of the self, a process Erikson talks of as the "identity crisis." In theory, adolescents move from a diffuse sense of future occupational or ideological identity, through a period of reevaluation (moratorium), to a commitment to a new self-definition. Current data raise doubts about whether the identity process has such a clear developmental aspect.

8. Beginning at about age 7 or 8, the child also develops a global sense of self-worth (self-esteem). Self-esteem is shaped both by the degree of discrepancy between a child's goals and his accomplishments and by the degree of emotional support the child perceives from parents and peers. Children with high self-esteem show lower levels of depression, as do children with greater feelings of self-efficacy.

9. Gender identity is part of the self-concept. Children generally acquire gender identity (labeling themselves and others correctly) by about age 2 or 3. They develop gender stability (knowing that people stay the same gender throughout life) by about 4, and they understand gender constancy (people don't change gender by changing appearance) by about 5 or 6.

10. Children in all cultures studied so far have knowledge of cultural sex-role stereotypes by age 7 or 8; these stereotypes are remarkably similar across cultures.

11. In early elementary school, children create maximally rigid rules about what boys and girls ought to do or are allowed to do. Older children are aware of the social conventions but do not treat them as incontrovertible rules.

12. Sex-typed behavior is visible from about 18 months of age. Children this age begin to show sex-typed toy preferences; by 2½ or 3 they begin to choose same-sex playmates—*before* they have clearly understood gender stability.

13. Theorists of several different traditions have attempted to explain these patterns. The most widely accepted current theory, gender schema theory, proposes that children begin to acquire a rule about what boys do and what

girls do as soon as they figure out the difference, and this schema forms the basis of both stereotyping and sex-typed behavior.

14. More girls than boys show cross-sex preferences in toy choices and

behavior. Both environmental and biological elements may play a part in such cross-sex choices.

15. Young people also differ in the extent to which they see themselves as having feminine and/or masculine qualities or traits. Those

who describe themselves with both sets of qualities are called androgynous. Both girls and boys who describe themselves as androgynous or masculine have somewhat higher self-esteem—at least in U.S. culture.

Key Terms

androgynous One of four sex-role types suggested by the work of Bem and others; label applied to a person whose self-concept includes and whose behavior expresses high levels of both masculine and feminine qualities. **p. 312**

feminine One of four sex-role types suggested by the work of Bem and others; a pattern of high scores on femininity measures and low scores on masculinity measures. **p. 312**

foreclosure One of four identity statuses proposed by Marcia, involving an ideological or occupational commitment without a previous reevaluation. **p. 295**

gender concept Term used to describe the full understanding that gender is permanent and constant, unchanged by appearance. **p. 303**

gender constancy The final step in developing a gender concept, in which the child understands that gender doesn't change even though there are external changes in things like clothing or hair length. **p. 305**

gender identity The first step in gender concept development, in which the child labels herself correctly and categorizes others correctly as male or female. **p. 304**

gender schema theory A theory explaining gender concept and sex-role behavior development; proposes that each child creates a fundamental schema beginning at

age 18 months or younger, by which the child categorizes people, objects, activities, and qualities by gender. **p. 309**

gender stability The second step in gender concept development, in which the child understands that a person's gender continues to be stable throughout the lifetime. **p. 304**

identity achievement One of four identity statuses proposed by Marcia, involving the successful resolution of an identity "crisis," resulting in a new commitment. **p. 295**

identity diffusion One of four identity statuses proposed by Marcia, involving neither a current reevaluation nor a firm personal commitment. **p. 295**

identity statuses Four categories suggested by James Marcia, created by combining high and low identity crisis and high and low identity commitment: identity achievement, moratorium, foreclosure, and identity diffusion. **p. 295**

masculine One of four sex-role types suggested by the work of Bem and others; a pattern of high scores on masculinity measures and low scores on femininity measures. **p. 312**

moratorium One of four identity statuses proposed by Marcia, involving an ongoing reexamination but without a new commitment as yet. **p. 295**

objective self Second major step in the development of the self-concept; awareness of the self as an object with properties. **p. 289**

self-concept The "me" aspect of self; the set of qualities attributed to the self. **p. 288**

self-esteem A global judgement of self-worth; how well you like who you perceive yourself to be; how well you measure up when judged against your own valued qualities or skills. **p. 299**

sex role The set of behaviors, attitudes, rights, duties, and obligations that are part of the "role" of being a boy or a girl, a male or a female in any given culture. **p. 303**

sex-role behavior The performance of behavior that matches the culturally defined sex role, such as choosing "sex-appropriate" toys or playing with same-sex children. **p. 304**

sex-typing See *sex-role behavior*. **p. 304**

subjective self The first major step in the development of the self-concept; the initial awareness that "I exist" separate from others. **p. 289**

undifferentiated One of four sex-role types suggested by the work of Bem and others; a pattern of low scores on both masculinity and femininity measures. **p. 312**

Suggested Readings

Adams, G. R., Gullotta, T. P., & Montemayor, R. (Eds.). (1992). *Adolescent identity formation.* Newbury Park, CA: Sage. One of a series of excellent books on facets of adolescence edited by these three psychologists. It includes a paper by

Waterman on the Erikson/Marcia view of identity, as well as Phinney's paper on ethnic identity.

Golombok, S., & Fivush, R. (1994). *Gender development.* Cambridge, England: Cambridge University Press. A basic,

up-to-date description of all facets of gender development.

Harter, S. (1987). The determinants and mediational role of global self-worth in children. In N. Eisenberg (Ed.), *Contemporary topics in developmental psychology* (pp. 219–242). New York: Wiley-Interscience. I think Harter's work is the best being done today on the subject of self-esteem. This paper is a very good introduction to her ideas.

Harter, S. (1998). The development of self-representations. In W. Damon (Ed.), *Handbook of child psychology: Vol 3. Social, emotional, and personality development* (5th ed., pp. 553–617). New York: Wiley. This recent summary of current theory and research on self-concept and self-esteem by one of the leading psychologists in this area is definitely aimed at fellow professionals, so it is highly detailed and quite technical. Nonetheless, it is well worth your effort.

11

The Development
of Social Relationships

Not long ago, as I had lunch in a restaurant with a friend, we were both happily distracted by the sight of an adorable baby at the next table. The baby, 4 or 5 months old, was sitting on her mom's lap, facing outward, and gazing with delight at an older woman sitting across from her—perhaps her grandmother. As the older woman talked to the baby in a high and lilting voice, smiled, and tickled the baby's tummy, the infant responded with one huge smile after another. My friend and I stopped talking as we watched, and could hardly restrain ourselves from trying to join in the whole process. I had my "talking-with-baby voice" all warmed up and ready to go and found myself smiling as if to try to entice an answering smile from the infant—although the baby didn't look our way at all.

Even as I was personally drawn into this small scene, the psychologist in me was also aware of many aspects of the interaction. The baby's social skills, her ability to entice, were on clear display, as were the skills of the older woman who was eliciting the baby's smiles. My guess was that this older woman was familiar to the baby and had played this interactive game many times before. Chances are good that had I tried to entice a smile or two, I would have had some success, but nothing like what we were watching. Just as dance partners need to learn each other's moves in order to dance smoothly, so babies and the adults who care for them must adapt to one another's style and rhythm.

This brief scene focuses our attention on an aspect of development I have largely neglected so far, namely, the child's relationships with others—surely a central aspect of any child's (or adult's) life.

Willard Hartup (1989), one of the most astute students of social development, suggests that each child needs experience in two rather different kinds of relationships: *vertical* and *horizontal*. A vertical relationship involves an attachment to someone who has greater social power or knowledge, such as a parent, a teacher, or even an older sibling. Such relationships are complementary rather than reciprocal. The bond may be extremely powerful in both directions, but the actual behaviors the two partners show toward one another are not the same. For example, when a child bids for attention, the parents don't respond with some bid for attention of their own but rather provide nurturance. A horizontal relationship, in contrast, is reciprocal and egalitarian. The individuals involved, such as same-age peers, have equal social power, and their behavior toward one another comes from the same repertoire.

Hartup's point is that these two kinds of relationships serve different functions for the child; both are needed for the child to develop effective social skills. Vertical relationships are necessary to provide the child with protection and security. In these relationships the child creates his basic internal working models and learns fundamental social skills. But it is in horizontal relationships—in friendships and in peer groups—that the child practices his social behavior and acquires those social skills that can be learned only in a relationship between equals: cooperation, competition, and intimacy. The psychological significance of these peer relationships is attested to by the many studies showing that having friends is associated with a greater sense of well-being among both children and adults (Hartup & Stevens, 1997).

Let's begin by looking at vertical relationships, in particular at the core relationship between child and parent.

Attachment Theory: Concepts and Terminology

The strongest theoretical influence in modern-day studies of infant-parent relationships is attachment theory, particularly the work of John Bowlby and Mary Ainsworth (Ainsworth, 1972; 1982; 1989; Ainsworth et al., 1978; Bowlby, 1969; 1973; 1980; 1988a; 1988b). You'll recall from Chapter 9 that Bowlby's thinking has roots in psychoanalytic thought, particularly in the emphasis on the significance of the earliest relationship between mother and child. To this theoretical base, he added important evolutionary and ethological concepts. In his view, "The propensity to make strong emotional bonds to particular individuals [is] a basic component of human nature, already present in germinal form in the neonate" (Bowlby, 1988a, p. 3). Such relationships have *survival value* because they bring nurturance to the infant. They are built and maintained by an interlocking repertoire of instinctive behaviors that create and sustain proximity between parent and child or between other bonded pairs.

In Bowlby's and Ainsworth's writings, the key concepts are the affectional bond, attachment, and attachment behaviors. Ainsworth defines an **affectional bond** as "a relatively long-enduring tie in which the partner is important as a unique individual and is interchangeable with none other. In an affectional bond, there is a desire to maintain closeness to the partner" (1989, p. 711). An **attachment** is a subvariety of affectional bond in which a person's sense of security is bound up in the relationship. When you are attached, you feel (or hope to feel) a special sense of security and comfort in the presence of the other, and you can use the other as a *safe base* from which to explore the rest of the world.

In these terms, the child's relationship with the parent is an attachment, but the parent's relationship with the child is usually not, since the parent presumably does not feel a greater sense of security in the presence of the infant or use the infant as a safe base. A relationship with one's adult partner or with a very close friend, however, is likely to be an attachment in the sense Ainsworth and Bowlby mean the term.

Because affectional bonds and attachments are internal states, we cannot see them directly. Instead we deduce their existence by observing **attachment behaviors,** which are all those behaviors that allow a child or adult to achieve and retain proximity to someone else to whom he is attached. These could include smiling, making eye contact, calling out to the other person across a room, touching, clinging, or crying.

It is important to make clear that there is no one-to-one correspondence between the number of different attachment behaviors a child (or adult) shows on any one occasion and the strength of the underlying attachment. Attachment behaviors are elicited primarily when the individual has need of care or support or comfort. An infant is in such a needy state a good deal of the time; an older child would be likely to show attachment behaviors only when he is frightened, tired, or otherwise under stress. It is the *pattern* of these behaviors, not the frequency, that tells us something about the strength or quality of the attachment or the affectional bond.

To understand the early relationship between the parent and the child, we need to look at both sides of the equation—at the development of the parent's bond to the child and the child's attachment to the parent.

Critical Thinking

Think about your own relationships. In Bowlby's, and Ainsworth's terms, which are attachments and which are affectional bonds?

Critical Thinking

Pick one of your attachment relationships and make a list of all the attachment behaviors you show toward that person. Are any of these the same as the kind of attachment behaviors we see in an infant?

In this "vertical" social relationship, the son is attached to his dad, but in Ainsworth's terms, the father's relationship to his son is an affectional bond rather than an attachment.

The Parent's Bond to the Child

The Initial Bond

If you read the popular press at all, I am sure you have come across articles proclaiming that mothers (or fathers) must have immediate contact with their newborn infant if they are to become properly bonded with the baby. This belief has been based primarily on the work of two pediatricians, Marshall Klaus and John Kennell (1976), who proposed the hypothesis that the first few hours after an infant's birth are a critical period for the mother's development of a bond to her infant. Mothers who are denied early contact, Klaus and Kennell thought, are likely to form weaker bonds and thus to be at higher risk for a range of disorders of parenting.

Their proposal was one of many factors leading to significant changes in birth practices, including the now-normal presence of fathers at delivery. I would certainly not want to turn back the clock on such changes, even though it now looks as if Klaus and Kennell's hypothesis is essentially incorrect. Immediate contact does not appear to be either necessary or sufficient for the formation of a stable, long-term affectional bond between parent and child (Myers, 1987).

A few studies show some short-term beneficial effects of very early contact. In the first few days after delivery, mothers with such contact may show more tender fondling or more gazing at the baby than is true of mothers who first held their babies some hours after birth (e.g., de Chateau, 1980). However, there is little indication of a lasting effect. Two or three months after delivery, mothers who had immediate contact with their newborns do not smile at them more or hold them differently than do mothers who had delayed contact. Only among mothers who are otherwise at higher risk for problems with parenting—such as first-time mothers, mothers living in poverty, or very young mothers—do we find a few signs that early contact may make a difference. Among such mothers, extended or early contact with the infant in the first days of life *may* help prevent later problems, such as abuse or neglect (O'Connor et al., 1980). For the majority of mothers, however, neither early nor extended contact appears to be an essential ingredient in forming a strong affectional bond.

The Development of Interactive Skill

What *is* essential in the formation of that bond is the opportunity for the parent and infant to develop a mutual, interlocking pattern of attachment behaviors, a smooth "dance" of interaction. The baby signals his needs by crying or smiling; he responds to being held by quieting or snuggling; he looks at the parents when they look at him. The parents, in their turn, enter into this two-person dance with their own repertoire of caregiving behaviors. They pick the baby up when he cries, wait for and respond to his signals of hunger or other need, smile at him when he smiles, gaze into his eyes when he looks at them. Some researchers and theorists have described this as the development of *synchrony* (Isabella et al., 1989).

One of the most intriguing things about this process is that we all seem to know how to do this particular dance, and we do it in very similar ways. In the presence of a young infant, most adults will automatically display a distinctive pattern of interactive behaviors, including a smile, raised eyebrows, and very wide-open eyes. We also use our voices in special ways with babies, as you'll remember from the discussion of motherese in Chapter 8. Parents all over the world use the characteristic high-pitched and lilting pattern of motherese; they also use similar intonation patterns. For example, in a study of mother-infant interactions, Hanus Papousek and Mechthild Papousek (1991) found that Chinese, German, and U.S. mothers all tended to use a rising voice inflection when they wanted the baby to "take a turn" in the interaction and a falling intonation when they wanted to soothe the baby.

Yet while we can perform all these attachment *behaviors* with many infants, we do not form a bond with every baby we coo at in a restaurant or grocery store. For an

Critical Thinking

Watch yourself next time you interact with a baby. Does your facial expression match the "mock surprise" in the photos at the top of the facing page? Does your intonation pattern follow the pattern in the Papousek study?

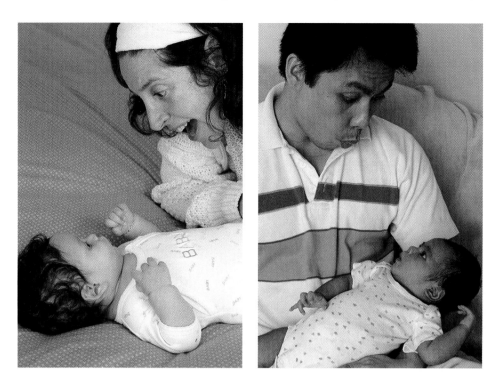

Adults all over the world, both mothers and fathers, show this same "mock surprise" expression when they are talking to or playing with a baby. The eyebrows are raised, the eyes are wide, and the forehead is wrinkled. A wide-open, smiling mouth, like the mother shows here, is often part of the expression too.

adult, the critical ingredient for the formation of a bond seems to be the opportunity to develop real synchrony—to practice the dance until the partners follow one another's lead smoothly and pleasurably. This takes time and many rehearsals, and some parents (and infants) become more skillful at it than others. In general, the smoother and more predictable the process becomes, the more satisfying it seems to be to the parents and the stronger their bond to the infant becomes.

This second step appears to be far more important than the initial contact at birth in establishing a strong parental bond to the child. But this second process, too, can fail. I've explored some of the possible reasons for such a failure in the Real World box on page 322.

Father-Child Bonds

Most of the research I have talked about so far has involved studies of mothers. Still, many of the same principles seem to hold for fathers as well. In particular, fathers seem to direct the same repertoire of attachment behaviors toward their infant as do mothers. In the early weeks of the baby's life, dads touch, talk to, and cuddle their babies in the same ways as mothers do, and they show the same physiological responses when they interact with their new infant, including increased heart rate and blood pressure (Corter & Fleming, 1995).

Past these earliest weeks, however, we see signs of some specialization of parental behaviors with infants and toddlers. Studies in the United States show that fathers spend more time playing with a baby, using more physical roughhousing. Mothers spend more time in routine caregiving and talk to and smile at the baby more (Parke, 1995; Walker et al., 1992). This does not mean that fathers have a weaker affectional bond with the infant; it does mean that the behaviors they show toward the infant are typically somewhat different from those mothers show.

However, we should not leap to the conclusion that this sex difference is somehow built-in; instead, it looks as if it rests on cultural patterns. Researchers in England and in India have found higher levels of physical play by fathers than by mothers, but other researchers in Sweden, Israel, Italy, China, and Malaysia have not (Parke & Buriel, 1998). Findings like this are a nice illustration of the usefulness of cross-cultural research for identifying patterns of behavior that are influenced by varying cultural expectations or training.

Ryan's dad, like most fathers, is far more likely to play with him by tossing him around than is his mom.

The Real World

Failure of Parental Bonding: Causes and Consequences

Not all parents appear to form a strong emotional bond with their infant. What might cause such a failure of bonding, and what are the consequences for the child?

The simplest answer to the "why" question is that such a failure can occur if either the baby or the parents lack the skills to enter into the "dance" of interaction fully. Of the two, the more serious problems seem to arise if it is the parent who lacks skills, but problems can also arise when the baby is physically disabled or otherwise lacks the full repertoire of attachment behaviors (van IJzendoorn et al., 1992).

For example, blind babies smile less and do not show mutual gaze, and preterm infants are typically very unresponsive in the early weeks and months (Fraiberg, 1974; 1975). Most parents of disabled or premature infants form a strong bond to the child despite the baby's problems, but the rate of child abuse is higher among the parents of preterm babies and among families whose babies are sick a lot in the first few months than among those with more robust children (Belsky, 1993). If we take abuse as one sign of a failure of bonding on the parents' part, then these findings suggest that the child's own qualities can, at times, contribute to such a breakdown.

On the other side of the interaction, a parent might lack "attachment skill" because she or he did not form a secure attachment with her or his own parents, perhaps because of abuse (Crittenden et al., 1991). Of those adults who were themselves abused as children, something on the order of 30 percent will abuse their own children, with higher rates for those with a prolonged history of abuse; of those adults who maltreat their children, some three-quarters were themselves abused. Thus while the majority of adults with a history of abuse manage to break the cycle of violence and refrain from abusing their own children, it is still true that there is a substantial risk of intergenerational transmission of this behavior pattern (Belsky, 1993; Kaufman & Zigler, 1989; Rogosch et al., 1995a; Spieker et al., 1996). Those who are unable to break this cycle are typically those who lack other social skills, who have no adequate social supports, or who are living under high levels of stress.

Another serious problem on the parents' side of the equation is a parent's depression, which disrupts both the parent's nurturing behavior and child's response. Babies who interact regularly with a depressed mother express more negative and fewer positive emotions. They smile less, show more sad and angry facial expressions, and are more disorganized and distressed (Dawson et al., 1997; Field et al., 1990; Pickens & Field, 1993). Depressed mothers, for their part, are slower to respond to their infants' signals and are more negative—even hostile—to their infants (Rutter, 1990). These deficiencies in the mother's behavior with the infant persist after the mother is no longer depressed, and they generalize beyond the mother-infant dyad; babies with depressed mothers show similar distressed or nonsynchronous behaviors when they interact with a nondepressed adult (Field et al., 1988). Such children are also at higher risk for later behavior problems, including either heightened aggression or withdrawal (Cummings & Davies, 1994).

All these pieces of evidence tell us that although the parent-child attachment/bonding process is normally powerful and positive, the system can indeed break down, with negative consequences for the child.

The Baby's Attachment to the Parent

Like the parent's bond to the baby, the baby's attachment emerges gradually. Bowlby (1969) suggested three phases in the development of the infant's attachment, sketched schematically in Figure 11.1.

Phase 1: Nonfocused Orienting and Signaling. Bowlby thought the baby begins life with a set of innate behavior patterns that orient him toward others and signal his needs. Mary Ainsworth describes these as "proximity-promoting" behaviors: They bring people closer. In the newborn's repertoire, these include crying, making eye contact, clinging, cuddling, and responding to caregiving efforts by being soothed.

At this stage there is little evidence that the baby is attached to the parents. As Ainsworth says, "These attachment behaviors are simply emitted, rather than being directed toward any specific person" (1989, p. 710). Nonetheless, the roots of attachment are to be found in this phase. The baby is building up expectancies and schemas about interaction patterns with the parents, as well as developing the ability to discriminate Mom and Dad from others in many contexts.

Figure 11.1

This schematic may help you see how the various threads of development of attachment are woven together.

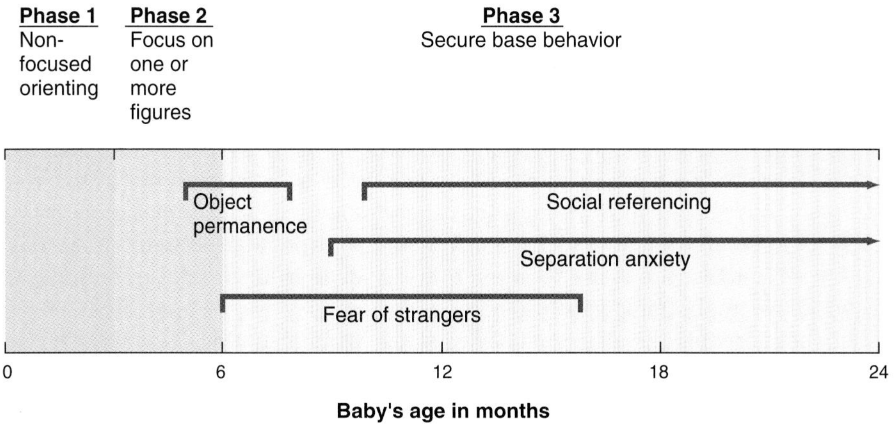

| **Phase 1** | **Phase 2** | **Phase 3** |
| Non-focused orienting | Focus on one or more figures | Secure base behavior |

Object permanence

Social referencing

Separation anxiety

Fear of strangers

0   6   12   18   24

Baby's age in months

Phase 2: Focus on One or More Figure(s). By 3 months of age, the baby begins to aim her attachment behaviors somewhat more narrowly. She may smile more at the people who regularly take care of her and may not smile readily at a stranger. Yet despite the change, Bowlby and Ainsworth have argued that the infant does not yet have a full-blown attachment. The child still favors a number of people with her "proximity-promoting" behaviors, and no one person has yet become the "safe base." Children in

Cultures and Contexts
Attachment in a Very Different Cultural System

Is the sequence of phases Bowlby and Ainsworth describe universal? Do all babies go through this same sequence, no matter what kind of family or culture they live in? Maybe yes, maybe no. Ainsworth herself observed the same basic three phases in forming a clear attachment among children in Uganda, although they showed a more intense fear of strangers than is usually found in U.S. samples (Ainsworth, 1972). But among the Ganda, as in U.S. and other Western families, the mother is the primary caregiver. What would we find in a culture in which the child's early care is much more communal?

Edward Tronick and his colleagues (1992) have studied just such a culture, a pygmy group called the Efe, who forage in the forests of Zaire. They live in small groups of perhaps twenty individuals in camps, each consisting of several extended families, often brothers and their wives.

Infants in these communities are cared for communally in the early months and years of life. They are carried and held by all the adult women, and they interact regularly with many different adults. If they have needs, they are tended by whichever adult or older child is nearby; they may even be nursed by women other than their mothers, although they normally sleep with their mothers.

Tronick and his colleagues report two things of particular interest about early attachment in this group. First, Efe infants seem to use virtually any adult or older child in their world as a safe base, which suggests that they may have no single central attachment. But at the same time, beginning at about 6 months, the Efe infant nonetheless seems to insist on being with his mother more and to prefer her over other women, although other women continue to help care for the child.

Thus, even in an extremely communal rearing arrangement, we can still see some sign of a central attachment, albeit perhaps less dominant. At the same time, it is clear, as Inge Bretherton says, that "attachment behavior is never purely instinctive, but is heavily overlain with cultural prescriptions" (1992b, p. 150).

this phase show no special anxiety at being separated from their parents and no fear of strangers.

Phase 3: Secure Base Behavior. Only at about 6 months of age, according to Bowlby, does the baby form a genuine attachment—about the same time that the baby develops some preliminary understanding that objects and people continue to exist when they are out of sight (object permanence). For the first time, the infant uses the "most important person" as a safe base from which to explore the world around her—one of the key signs that an attachment exists.

At roughly that same age, the dominant mode of the baby's attachment behavior changes. Because the 6- to 7-month-old begins to be able to move about the world more freely by creeping and crawling, she can move *toward* the caregiver as well as entice the caregiver to come to her. Her attachment behaviors therefore shift from mostly "come here" signals (proximity promoting) to what Ainsworth calls "proximity seeking," which we might think of as "go there" behaviors.

I should note that not all infants have a *single* attachment figure, even at this early point. Some show strong attachments to both parents or to a parent and another caregiver. However, under stress, these babies usually show a preference for one of their favored persons over the others.

Once the child has developed a clear attachment, several related behaviors also appear. One of these is social referencing, which I talked about in Chapter 5. The 10-month-old uses his ability to discriminate among various facial expressions to guide his safe-base behavior. He begins to check out Mom's or Dad's expression before deciding whether to venture forth into some novel situation. At about the same age or a little earlier, babies also typically show both fear of strangers and separation anxiety.

Fear of Strangers and Separation Anxiety. Both these forms of distress are rare before 5 or 6 months, then rise in frequency until about 12 to 16 months and then decline. The research findings are not altogether consistent, but it looks as though fear of strangers normally appears first, at about the same time as babies show fearful reactions in other situations as well. Anxiety at separation starts a bit later but continues to be visible for a longer period, a pattern I've marked in Figure 11.1 (p. 323).

Such increases in stranger fear and separation anxiety have been observed in children from a number of different cultures and in both home-reared and day-care-reared children in the United States, all of which makes it look as if some basic age-related developmental timetables underlie this pattern (Kagan et al., 1978). Virtually all children show at least mild forms of these two types of distress, although the intensity of the reaction varies widely. Some babies protest briefly; others are virtually inconsolable. Some of this variation undoubtedly reflects basic temperamental differences in behavioral inhibition (Kagan et al., 1994). Heightened fearfulness may also be a response to some upheaval or stress in the child's life, such as a recent move or a change in the

A few months ago, this baby would probably have let himself be held by just about anyone without a fuss; now all of a sudden he's afraid of strangers. Parents are often puzzled by this behavior, but it is absolutely normal.

daily schedule. Whatever the origin of such variations in fearfulness, the pattern does eventually diminish in most toddlers, typically by the middle of the second year.

Attachments in the Preschool and Elementary School Years

By age 2 or 3, while the child's attachment to the mother and father remains powerful, most attachment behaviors have become less continuously visible. Children this age are cognitively advanced enough to understand Mom if she explains why she is going away and that she will be back, so their anxiety at separation wanes. They can even use a photograph of their mother as a "safe base" for exploration in a strange situation (Passman & Longeway, 1982), which reflects another cognitive advance. By age 3 or 4, a child can also deal with her potential anxiety at separation by creating shared plans with the parents ("I'll be home after your nap time") (Crittenden, 1992). Attachment behaviors have naturally not completely disappeared. Two-year-olds still want to sit on Mom's or Dad's lap; they are still likely to seek some closeness or proximity when Mom returns from some absence. But in nonfearful or nonstressful situations, toddlers and preschoolers are able to wander farther and farther from their safe base without apparent distress.

Bowlby referred to this new form of attachment as a **goal-corrected partnership.** The infant's goal, to put it most simply, is always to have the attachment figure within sight or touch. The preschooler's goal is also to be "in contact" with the parent, but "contact" no longer requires constant physical presence. The preschooler not only understands that his mother will continue to exist when she isn't there; he now also understands that the *relationship* continues to exist even when the partners are apart. This enables the toddler or preschooler to modify ("correct") her goal of contact with her attachment figure by engaging in collaborative planning, agreeing on when and how the two will be together, or what the child will do if he gets scared or anxious, or who the replacement security person will be.

In elementary school, overt attachment behaviors like clinging or crying are even less visible, so it is easy to lose sight of the fact that children this age are still strongly attached to their parents. The child of this age may be the one who now takes primary responsibility for maintaining contact with the parent (Kerns, 1996), but he wants to know that Mom or Dad is there when he needs them. Such a need is most likely to arise when the child faces some stressful situation, such as perhaps the first day of school, illness or upheaval in the family, or the death of a pet. Because fewer experiences are new and potentially stressful to the 7- or 8-year-old than to the preschooler, we see much less obvious safe-base behavior and less open affection from child to parent (Maccoby, 1984). These changes do not, however, signify that the child's attachment to the parent has weakened.

Critical Thinking

Children aged 7 and 8 often seem to actively reject public displays of affection from their parents, squirming away from hugs or refusing kisses—especially in front of peers. Do you have any guesses about how to explain such behavior?

Because school-age children roam farther from home, spending more and more time with peers, we might be tempted to assume that they are less strongly attached to their parents. But this assumption is wrong. Children this age still depend on their parents to be a safe base.

Parent-Child Relationships at Adolescence

In adolescence, the scene shifts somewhat because teenagers have two, apparently contradictory, tasks in their relationships with their parents: to establish autonomy from the parents and to maintain their sense of relatedness (attachment) with their parents. The push for autonomy shows itself in increases in conflict between parent and adolescent; the maintenance of connection is seen in the continued strong attachment of child to parent.

Increases in Conflict. The rise in conflict has now been repeatedly documented (e.g., Flannery et al., 1994; Laursen, 1995; Steinberg, 1988). In the great majority of families, it seems to consist of an increase in mild bickering or conflicts over everyday issues like chores or personal rights—such as whether the adolescent should be allowed to wear a bizarre hair or clothing style or whether and when the teen should be required to do family chores. Teenagers and their parents also interrupt each other more often and become more impatient with one another.

This increase in discord is widely found, but we need to be careful not to assume that it signifies a major disruption of the quality of the parent-child relationship. Laurence Steinberg (1990), one of the key researchers in this area, estimates that only 5 to 10 percent of families in the United States experience a substantial or pervasive deterioration in the quality of parent-child relationship in these years of early adolescence. Those families at highest risk for persistently heightened conflict are those in which the parents have a history of low levels of warmth and supportiveness toward their child in earlier years as well as during adolescence (Rueter & Conger, 1995; Silverberg & Gondoli, 1996). When parents continue to express warmth and supportiveness and are open to hearing the teenager's opinions and disagreements, the period of heightened conflict seems to be relatively brief.

If the rise in conflict doesn't signal that the relationship is falling apart, what does it mean? A variety of theorists have suggested that the temporary discord, far from being a negative event, may instead be a developmentally healthy and necessary part of the adolescent's identity formation process. In order to become his own person, the teenager needs to push away from the parents, disagree with them, try out his own limits—an **individuation** process not unlike what we see in the toddler who begins to say "no" to the parents during that famous period called the terrible twos (Grotevant & Cooper, 1985).

One type of evidence supporting the idea that the rise in conflict is a normal developmental process comes from studies linking the increase with the hormonal changes of puberty rather than age. For example, Steinberg (1988) followed a group of teenagers over a one-year period, assessing their stage of puberty and the quality of their relationship with their parents at the beginning and end of the year. He found that as the early pubertal stages began, family closeness declined, parent-child conflict rose, and the child's autonomy increased. Other researchers (e.g., Inoff-Germain et al., 1988) have taken this a step further by measuring actual hormone levels and showing links between the rise of the various hormones of puberty and the rise in aloofness toward or conflict with parents. Among girls, conflict seems to rise after menarche (Holmbeck & Hill, 1991).

The pattern of causes is obviously complex. Hormonal changes may be causally linked to increases in assertiveness, perhaps especially among boys. Parents' reactions to pubertal changes may also be highly important parts of the mix. Visible pubertal changes, including menarche, alter parents' expectations of the teenager and increase their concern about guiding and controlling the adolescent to help her avoid the shoals of too great a level of independence.

In the midst of the increased conflict, and perhaps partially as a result of it, the overall level of the teenager's autonomy within the family increases steadily throughout the adolescent years. Parents give the youngster more and more room to make independent choices and to participate in family decision making.

Attachment to Parents. Paradoxically, in the midst of this distancing and temporarily heightened family conflict, teenagers' underlying emotional attachment to their parents remains strong. Results from a study by Mary Levitt and her colleagues (1993) illustrate the point.

Levitt interviewed African-American, Latino, and Anglo children aged 7, 10, and 14. Each child was shown a drawing with a set of concentric circles. They were asked to place in the middle circle those "people who are the most close and important to you—people you love the most and who love you the most." In the next circle outward from the middle, children were asked to place the names of "people who are not quite as close but who are still important—people you really love or like, but not quite as much as the people in the first circle." A third circle contained names of somewhat more distant members of this personal "convoy." For each person listed, the interviewer then asked about the kind of support that person provided.

Levitt found that for all three ethnic groups, at all three ages, parents and other close family were by far the most likely to be placed in the inner circle. Even 14-year-olds rarely placed friends in this position. So the parents remain central. At the same time, it is clear from Levitt's results that peers become increasingly important as providers of support, as you can see in Figure 11.2. This figure shows the total amount of support the children and adolescents described from each source. Friends clearly provided more support for the 14-year-olds than for the younger children, a pattern that is clear for all three ethnic groups.

Despite this evidence of greater support from or intimacy with peers, the research evidence tells us that, in general, a teenager's sense of well-being or happiness is more strongly correlated with the quality of his attachment to his parents than to the quality of his attachments to his peers (Greenberg et al., 1983; Raja et al., 1992). Furthermore, the stronger the sense of connectedness (attachment) a teenager has with his parents, the less likely he is to engage in any of the risky or delinquent behaviors I talked about in Chapter 4 (Resnick et al., 1997). Thus, even while the teenager is becoming more autonomous, the parents seem to continue to provide a highly important psychological safe base.

Critical Thinking

You might find it interesting to complete such a "personal convoy" map for your own relationships. Are your parents in the center circle? Friends? Partner?

Figure 11.2

African-American (Af), Anglo-American (An), and Hispanic-American/Latino (Hs) children and teens were asked about the amount and type of support they received from various members of their "social convoy." Note that for teens, friends become more significant sources of support, but parents do not become substantially *less* important.

(*Source:* Levitt, M.; Guacci-Franco, N.; and Levitt, J., 1993. "Convoys of social support in childhood and early adolescence: Structure and function," *Developmental psychology*, 29, p. 815. Copyright © 1993 by the American Psychological Association. Reprinted with permission of the American Psychological Association and M. Levitt.)

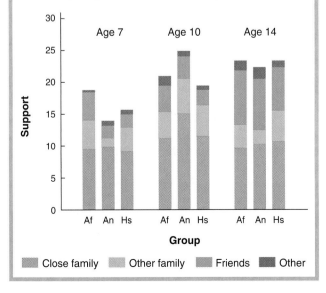

The fact that young Edwin's dad changes his diapers is probably not the crucial causal variable in Edwin's forming a strong attachment to his father, but diaper changing may signify a greater involvement by this father with his infant, and that greater involvement may be linked to the baby's stronger attachment.

Critical Thinking

If internal working models tend to persist and to affect later relationships, is this the same as saying that the first few years of life are a critical period for the creation of patterns of relationships? How else could we conceptualize this model?

Attachments to Mothers and Fathers

I pointed out earlier that both fathers and mothers appear to form strong bonds to their infants, although their behavior with infants varies somewhat. But what about the child's half of this relationship? Are infants and children equally attached to their fathers and mothers?

In general, yes. From the age of 7 to 8 months, when strong attachments are first seen, infants prefer *either* the father or the mother to a stranger. And when both the father and the mother are available, an infant will smile at or approach either or both, *except* when he is frightened or under stress. When that happens, especially between 8 and 24 months, the child typically turns to the mother rather than the father (Lamb, 1981).

As you might expect, the strength of the child's attachment to the father at this early age seems to be related to the amount of time Dad has spent with the child. In one early study, for example, Gail Ross found she could predict a baby's attachment to the father by knowing how many diapers the dad changed in a typical week. The more diapers, the stronger the attachment (Ross et al., 1975). But greatly increased time with the father does not seem to be the only element, since Michael Lamb and his Swedish colleagues (1983) have found that infants whose fathers were their major caregivers for at least a month in the first year of the child's life were nonetheless more strongly attached to their mothers than to their fathers. For the father to be consistently *preferred* over the mother would probably require essentially full-time paternal care. As this option becomes more common in our society, it will be possible to study such father-child pairs to see whether a preference for the father develops.

Variations in the Quality of Infants' Attachments

What I have been describing is the normal developmental sequence for a baby's attachment to parent or caregiver. Equally important is the *quality* of the child's attachment. Go to a day-care center and watch the way the babies or toddlers greet their parents at the end of the day. Some are calmly pleased to see Mom or Dad, running to be hugged, showing a new toy, or smiling when picked up, showing no distress. Others may run to the parent, crying and clinging; still others may show little interest, even turning away when Mom or Dad approaches. These babies may all have formed an attachment to their parents, but the quality of that attachment differs markedly. In Bowlby's terminology, these children have different **internal working models** of their relationship with parents and key others.

This concept introduces a distinctly cognitive flavor to the discussion, very like the concepts of the "self-scheme" or the "gender schema" I talked about in Chapter 10. The internal working model of attachment relationships includes such elements as the child's confidence (or lack of it) that the attachment figure will be available or reliable, the child's expectation of rebuff or affection, and the child's sense of assurance that the other is really a safe base for exploration.

The internal model begins to be formed late in the child's first year of life and becomes increasingly elaborated and firm over the first 4 or 5 years. By age 5, most children have clear internal models of the mother (or other caregiver), a self-model, and a model of relationships. Once formed, such models shape and explain experiences and affect memory and attention. We notice and remember experiences that fit our model and miss or forget experiences that don't match. More importantly, the model affects the child's behavior: The child tends to re-create, in each new relationship, the pattern with which he is familiar. Alan Sroufe gives a nice example that may make this point clearer:

> What is rejection to one child is benign to another. What is warmth to a second child is confusing or ambiguous to another. For example, a child approaches another and asks to play. Turned down, the child goes off and sulks in a corner. A second child receiving the same negative reaction skips on to another partner and successfully engages him in play. Their experiences of rejection are vastly different. Each receives confirmation of quite different inner working models. (1988, p. 23)

In a sense, these internal models are not unlike the social scripts that the preschooler develops in other areas (Bretherton, 1993). They contain expectations for sequences of behavior, rules for behavior with various individuals, and interpretations of others' actions; they help shape what the child pays attention to and what she remembers (Kirsh & Cassidy, 1997).

Secure and Insecure Attachments

All the theorists in this tradition share the assumption that the first attachment relationship is the most influential ingredient in the creation of the child's working model, just as Erikson argued that the child's resolution of his first stage—*trust versus mistrust*—formed the foundation for later relationships. Variations in this first attachment relationship are now almost universally described using Mary Ainsworth's category system (Ainsworth et al., 1978). She distinguishes between **secure attachment** and two types of **insecure attachment,** most often assessed using a procedure called the **Strange Situation.**

The Strange Situation consists of a series of episodes in a laboratory setting, typically used when the child is between 12 and 18 months of age. The child is placed first with the mother, then left with the mother and a stranger, then alone with the stranger, then completely alone for a few minutes, then reunited with the mother, then left alone again, and finally reunited first with the stranger and then with the mother. Ainsworth suggested that children's reactions to this situation could be classified into three types: *securely attached, insecure/avoidant,* and *insecure/ambivalent* (also sometimes called *resistant*). Mary Main has suggested a fourth group, which she calls *insecure/disorganized/disoriented* (Main & Solomon, 1990). I have listed some of the characteristics of the different types in Table 11.1. As you read the descriptions, note that whether the child cries when he is separated from his mother is *not* a helpful indicator of the security of his attachment. Some securely attached infants cry then, while others do not, as is true of insecurely attached infants as well. It is the entire pattern of the child's response to the Strange Situation that is critical, not any one response.

These attachment types have been observed in studies in many different countries, and in every country secure attachment is the most common pattern—as you can see from the information in the Cultures and Contexts box on page 330.

Table 11.1

Categorization of Secure and Insecure Attachment in Ainsworth's Strange Situation

Securely attached	Child readily separates from caregiver and easily becomes absorbed in exploration; when threatened or frightened, child actively seeks contact and is readily consoled; child does not avoid or resist contact if mother initiates it. When reunited with mother after absence, child greets her positively or is easily soothed if upset. Clearly prefers mother to stranger.
Insecurely attached (detached/avoidant)	Child avoids contact with mother, especially at reunion after an absence. Does not resist mother's efforts to make contact, but does not seek much contact. Shows no preference for mother over stranger.
Insecurely attached (resistant/ambivalent)	Child shows little exploration and is wary of stranger. Greatly upset when separated from mother, but not reassured by mother's return or her efforts at comforting. Child both seeks and avoids contact at different times. May show anger toward mother at reunion, and resists both comfort from and contact with stranger.
Insecurely attached (disorganized/ disoriented)	Dazed behavior, confusion, or apprehension. Child may show contradictory behavior patterns simultaneously, such as moving toward mother while keeping gaze averted.

Sources: Ainsworth et al., 1978; Carlson & Sroufe, 1995; Main & Solomon, 1990.

This category system, and the theory that lies behind it, have prompted an enormous amount of research and new theory, much of it fascinating and much of it with practical ramifications. So let me take some time to explore a few of the issues and implications.

Origins of Secure and Insecure Attachments. Where do these differences come from? Studies of parent-child interactions suggest that the crucial ingredients for the development of a secure attachment seem to be both acceptance of the infant by the parents and some aspect of *sensitivity* to the child—a quality that has been measured and labeled in various ways, including *synchrony, mutuality,* and *contingent responsiveness* (De Wolff & van IJzendoorn, 1997; Isabella, 1993; Pederson et al., 1990; Thompson, 1998). This key quality is more than merely love and affection. To be rated as sensitive or high in contingent responsiveness, the parents must be attuned to the child's signals and cues and respond appropriately. They smile when the baby smiles,

Cultures and Contexts
Secure and Insecure Attachments in Different Cultures

Studies in a variety of countries have pointed to the possibility that secure attachments may be more likely in certain cultures than others. The most thorough analyses have come from a Dutch psychologist, Marinus van IJzendoorn, who has examined the results of 32 separate studies in 8 different countries. You can see the percentage of babies classified in each category for each country in the table below.

Cross-Cultural Comparisons of Secure and Insecure Attachments

Country	Number of studies	Percentage		
		Secure	Avoidant	Ambivalent
West Germany	3	56.6	35.3	8.1
Great Britain	1	75.0	22.2	2.8
Netherlands	4	67.3	26.3	6.4
Sweden	1	74.5	21.6	3.9
Israel	2	64.4	6.8	28.8
Japan	2	67.7	5.2	25.0
China	1	50.0	25.0	25.0
United States	18	64.8	21.1	14.1
Overall average		65%	21%	14%

Source: Based on Table 1 of van IJzendoorn & Kroonenberg, 1988, pp. 150–151.

We need to be cautious about overinterpreting the information in this table because in most cases there are only one or two studies from a given country, normally with quite small samples. The single study from China, for example, included only 36 babies. Still, the findings are thought-provoking.

The most striking thing about these data is actually their consistency. In each of the eight countries, a secure attachment is the most common pattern, found in more than half of all babies studied; in five of the eight, an avoidant pattern is the more common of the two forms of insecure attachment. Only in Israel

and Japan is this pattern significantly reversed. How can we explain such differences?

One possibility is that the Strange Situation is simply not an appropriate measure of attachment security in all cultures. For example, because Japanese babies are rarely separated from their mothers in the first year of life, being left totally alone in the midst of the Strange Situation may be far more stressful for them, which might result in more intense, inconsolable crying and hence a classification of ambivalent attachment. The counterargument is that comparisons of toddlers' actual behavior in the Strange Situation suggest few cultural differences in such things as proximity seeking or avoidance of the mother, all of which gives us more confidence that the Strange Situation is tapping similar processes among children in many cultures (Sagi et al., 1991).

It is also possible that the *meaning* of a "secure" or "avoidant" pattern is different in different cultures, even if the percentages of each category are similar. German researchers, for example, have suggested that an insecure-avoidant classification in their culture may reflect not indifference by mothers but rather explicit training toward greater independence in the baby (Grossmann et al., 1985).

On the other hand, research in Israel (Sagi, 1990) shows that the Strange Situation attachment classification predicts the baby's later social skills in much the same way as is found in U.S. samples, which suggests that the classification system is valid in both cultures.

At the moment the most plausible hypothesis is that the same factors in mother-infant interaction contribute to secure and insecure attachments in all cultures and that these patterns reflect similar internal models. But it will take more research like the Israeli work, in which the long-term outcomes of the various categories are studied, before we can be sure if this is correct.

Research Report

Intergenerational Transmission of Secure and Insecure Attachment

Researchers who study attachment have begun to ask a new set of questions about the long-term consequences of early attachment patterns: Do adults' internal models of attachment—presumably a product of their own early history—affect the way they behave with their children, and thus shape the child's emerging attachment patterns? That is, is there some kind of intergenerational transmission of secure or insecure attachment?

Mary Main and her colleagues have devised an interview that allows them to classify the security or insecurity of an adult's attachment to his or her own parents (Main & Hesse, 1990; Main et al., 1985), so we are now able to explore this question. In this interview, adults (or sometimes teenagers) are asked about their childhood experiences and their current relationship with their parents. In one question, interviewees are asked to choose five adjectives to describe their relationship with each parent and to say why they chose each adjective. They are also asked whether they ever felt rejected in childhood and how they feel about their parents currently. On the basis of the interview, the adult's internal working model of attachment is classified as being one of three types:

- *Secure/autonomous/balanced.* These individuals value attachment relations and see their early experiences as influential, but they are objective in describing both good and bad qualities. These subjects speak coherently about their early experiences and have thoughts about what motivated their parents' behavior.
- *Dismissing or detached.* These adults minimize the importance or the effects of early family experience. They may idealize their parents, perhaps even denying the existence of any negative childhood experiences. They emphasize their own personal strengths.
- *Preoccupied or enmeshed.* These adults often talk about inconsistent or role-reversed parenting. They are still engrossed with their relationship with their parents, still actively struggling to please them or very angry at them. They are confused and ambivalent, but still engaged.

When these adult models are linked to the security of attachment displayed by the *children* of those adults, the expected pattern emerges strongly: Adults with secure models of attachment to their own parents are much more likely to have infants or toddlers with secure attachments. Those with dismissing models are more likely to have infants with avoidant attachments, while adults with preoccupied attachments are more likely to have infants with ambivalent attachments. Across 20 studies, the typical finding is that three-quarters of the mother-infant pairs share the same attachment category (van IJzendoorn, 1995; 1997). Diane Benoit has even found marked consistency across *three* generations: grandmothers, young mothers, and infants (Benoit & Parker, 1994).

This is not a genetic transmission—at least not directly. Rather, the link across generations appears to lie in the mother's own behavior toward her child, which varies as a function of her own internal working model of attachment. Mothers who are themselves securely attached are more responsive and sensitive in their behavior toward their infants or young children (van IJzendoorn, 1995). For example, Judith Crowell and Shirley Feldman (1988) observed mothers with their preschoolers in a free-play setting. In the middle of the play period, the mother left the child alone for several minutes and then returned. Mothers who were themselves classed as secure in their attachment model were more likely to prepare the child ahead of time for the impending separation, had less difficulty themselves with the separation, and were most physically responsive to the child during reunion. Preoccupied mothers were themselves more anxious about separating from the child and prepared the child less. Dismissing mothers also prepared the child very little, but they left without difficulty and remained physically distant from their children after returning to the playroom.

Crowell and Feldman also noted that mothers with dismissing or preoccupied internal models interpreted the child's behavior very differently than did the secure moms:

> One [dismissing] mother observed her crying child through the observation window and said, "See, she isn't upset about being left." At reunion, she said to the child, "Why are you crying? I didn't leave." (1991, p. 604).

Thus, not only does the mother's own internal model affect her actual behavior, but it affects the meaning she ascribes to the child's behavior, both of which will affect the child's developing model of attachment.

---

talk to the baby when he vocalizes, pick him up when he cries, and so on (Ainsworth & Marvin, 1995; Sroufe, 1996).

Our certainty that this type of responsiveness is a key ingredient has been strengthened by research in the Netherlands by Dymphna van den Boom (1994), who has demonstrated the link experimentally. She identified 100 lower-class Dutch mothers whose infants had all been rated as high in irritability shortly after birth. Half the mothers were then assigned randomly to participate in a set of three relatively brief training sessions aimed at helping them improve their responsiveness to their infants. The other mothers received no such help. When the babies were 12 months old, van den Boom observed the mothers interacting with their infants at home as well as in the standard Strange Situation. The effects were quite clear: The trained mothers had indeed become more responsive to their babies, and their babies were more likely to be securely attached, as you can see from the results in Table 11.2. In a follow-up study, van den Boom (1995) later found that these same differences persisted to at least age 18 months.

A low level of responsiveness thus appears to be an ingredient in any type of insecure attachment. Beyond this common factor, each of the several subvarieties of insecure attachment has additional distinct antecedents. For example, a disorganized/disoriented pattern seems especially likely when the child has been abused, as well as in families in which the parents had some unresolved trauma in their own childhoods, such as either abuse or their own parents' early death (Cassidy & Berlin, 1994; Main & Hesse, 1990). An ambivalent pattern is more common when the mother is inconsistently or unreliably available to the child. Mothers may show such unavailability or periodic neglect for a variety of reasons, but a common ingredient is depression in the mother (Teti et al., 1995)—a phenomenon I talked about briefly in the Real World box on page 322. When the mother rejects the infant or regularly (rather than intermittently) withdraws from contact with the infant, the infant is more likely to show an avoidant pattern of attachment.

Stability of Attachment Classification. Do these variations in the quality of the child's early attachment persist over time? Does a 1-year-old who is securely or insecurely attached to his mother still show the same quality of attachment when he's 2 or 6 or 16? This question is a particularly important one for those researchers and therapists who are concerned about the possible permanence of effects of early abuse or neglect or other sources of insecure attachment. Can children recover from such unfortunate early treatment? Conversely, is a child who is securely attached at 1 year of age forever buffered from the effects of later difficult life circumstances?

The answer, perhaps not surprisingly, is that both consistency and inconsistency occur, depending on the circumstances (Thompson, 1998; van IJzendoorn, 1997). When the child's family environment or life circumstances are reasonably consistent, the security or insecurity of attachment usually remains constant as well, even over many years. For example, in one small study, Claire Hamilton (1995) found that 16 of 18 adolescents who had been rated as insecurely attached at 12 months of age were still rated as insecurely attached at age 17, while 7 of the 11 teens who had been classed as securely attached as infants were still rated as securely attached at 17. Similar high levels

Table 11.2

The Effect of Mothers' Responsiveness Training on Infants' Attachment Security

	Attachment Classification of Infants at 12 Months	
	Secure	Insecure
Training	31	19
No training	11	39

Source: van den Boom, 1994, from Table 5, p. 1472.

of stability have been observed in a sample of middle-class families studied by Everett Waters and his colleagues (1995a) from infancy to age 18, as well as in a shorter-term study in Germany (Wartner et al., 1994), in which 82 percent of a group of youngsters from stable, middle-class families were rated in the same category of attachment security at age 6 as they had been at age 1.

When the child's circumstances change in some major way, however—such as when she starts going to day care or nursery school, grandma comes to live with the family, or the parents divorce or move—the security of the child's attachment may change as well, either from secure to insecure or the reverse. For example, in Everett Waters's long-term study (Waters et al., 1995b), the subset of subjects whose attachment classification changed between infancy and young adulthood had nearly all experienced some major upheaval, such as the death of a parent, physical or sexual abuse, or a serious illness.

The very fact that a child's security can change from one time to the next does not refute the notion of attachment as an internal working model. Bowlby suggested that for the first two or three years, the particular pattern of attachment a child shows is in some sense a property of each specific *relationship*. For example, studies of toddlers' attachments to mothers and fathers show that about 30 percent of the time, the child is securely attached to one parent and insecurely attached to the other, with both possible combinations equally represented (Fox et al., 1991). It is the quality of each relationship that determines the child's security with that specific adult. If that relationship changes markedly, the security of the baby's attachment to that individual may change, too. However, Bowlby argued that by age 4 or 5, the internal working model becomes more general, more a property of the *child*, more generalized across relationships, and thus more resistant to change. At that point, the child tends to impose it on new relationships, including relationships with teachers or peers.

Thus, a child may "recover" from an initially insecure attachment or lose a secure one, but consistency over time is more typical, both because children's relationships tend to be reasonably stable for the first few years and because once the internal model is clearly formed, it tends to perpetuate itself.

Long-Term Consequences of Secure and Insecure Attachment. Ainsworth's classification system has proved to be extremely helpful in predicting a remarkably wide range of other behaviors in children, both as toddlers and in later childhood, as I mentioned in Chapter 9. Dozens of studies show that children rated as securely attached to their mothers in infancy, compared to those rated as insecurely attached, are later more sociable, more positive in their behavior toward friends and siblings, less clinging and dependent on teachers, less aggressive and disruptive, more empathetic, and more emotionally mature in their approach to school and other nonhome settings (e.g., Carlson & Sroufe, 1995; Leve & Fagot, 1995).

At adolescence, those who were rated as securely attached in infancy or who are classed as secure on the basis of interviews in adolescence (using the Adult Attachment Interview described in the Research Report on p. 331) have more intimate friendships, are more likely to be rated as leaders, and have higher self-esteem (Black & McCartney, 1995; Lieberman et al., 1995; Ostoja et al., 1995). Those with insecure attachments—particularly those with avoidant attachments—not only have less positive and supportive friendships in adolescence but are also more likely to become sexually active early and to practice riskier sex (O'Beirne & Moore, 1995).

One particularly clear demonstration of some of these links comes from a longitudinal study by Alan Sroufe and his co-workers (1993; Urban et al., 1991; Weinfield et al., 1997). These researchers assessed the security of attachment of a group of several hundred infants and then followed the children through childhood and adolescence, testing and observing them at regular intervals. One of their observations in early adolescence involved inviting some of their subjects to participate in a specially designed summer camp. The counselors rated each child on a range of characteristics, and observers noted how often children spent time together or with the counselors. Naturally, neither the counselors nor the observers knew what the children's initial attachment classification had been. The findings are clear: Those with histories of secure attachment in infancy were rated as higher in self-confidence and social competence. They complied more readily with counselor requests, expressed more positive emotions, and had a greater sense of their ability to accomplish things (a quality Sroufe calls *agency,* essentially the same as what Bandura calls *self-efficacy*). Secure subjects created more friendships, especially with other securely attached youngsters, and engaged in more complex activities when playing in groups. In contrast, the majority of those with histories of insecure attachment showed some kind of deviant behavior pattern at age 11, such as isolation from peers, bizarre behavior, passivity, hyperactivity, or aggressiveness. Only a few of the originally securely attached children showed any of these patterns.

Collectively the findings point to potentially long-term consequences of attachment patterns or internal working models of relationships constructed in the first year or two of life. At the same time, fluidity and change also occur, and we need to know much more about the factors that tend to maintain, or alter, the earliest models.

Relationships with Peers: Playmates and Friends

Because most theories of social and personality development have strongly emphasized the centrality of parent-child interactions, until recently most psychologists thought of relationships with peers as much less important. But that view is now changing as it becomes clear that peer relationships play a unique and significant role in a child's development.

Peers in Infancy and the Preschool Years

Children first begin to show some positive interest in other infants as early as 6 months of age. If you place two such babies on the floor facing each other, they will touch each other, pull each other's hair, reach for each other's clothing. By 10 months, these behaviors are even more evident. By 14 to 18 months, we begin to see two or more children playing together with toys—occasionally cooperating together, but more often simply playing side by side with different toys, a pattern Mildred Parten (1932) first described as **parallel play.** Toddlers this age express interest in one another, gazing at or making noises at each other. Only at around 18 months, however, do we begin to see much coordinated play, such as when one toddler chases another or imitates the other's action with some toy. By 3 or 4, children appear to prefer to play with peers rather than alone, and their play with one another is much more cooperative and coordinated, including various forms of group pretend play.

Emerging Friendships. We also see the first signs of emerging playmate preferences or friendships in these toddler and preschool years. A few pairs show signs of specific playmate preferences as early as age 18 months; by age 3 or 4, more than half of children have at least one mutual friendship. Furthermore, the majority of these friendships last for at least 6 months, many of them for far longer (Dunn, 1993; Howes, 1996).

To be sure, these early "friendships" are not nearly as deep or intimate as what we see among school-age or adolescent friend pairs. Toddler friends ignore one another's bids for interaction as often as not. Still, these preschool friend pairs show unmistakable signs that their relationship is more than merely a passing fancy. They display more mutual liking, more reciprocity, more extended interactions, more positive and less negative behavior, more forgiveness, and more supportiveness in a novel situation than is true between nonfriend pairs at this same age. When they quarrel, they are more likely than are nonfriends to try to patch it up (Dunn, 1993; Hartup et al., 1998; Newcomb & Bagwell, 1995).

There is every reason to believe that play with such a friend is a highly important arena for children to practice a whole host of social skills. As John Gottman says, in order to play collaboratively, friends "must coordinate their efforts with all the virtuosity of an accomplished jazz quartet" (1986, p. 3). Often, they must subdue their own desires

By age 3, most children play with one another in coordinated ways rather than merely side by side.

 **The Real World**

Sibling Relationships

Playmates and friends play a highly significant role in children's development, but so too can another important "horizontal" relationship, that with brothers and sisters. What do we know about these relationships?

Preschool-Age Siblings. Stories such as the tale of Cain and Abel might lead us to believe that rivalry or jealousy is the key ingredient of sibling relationships. Certainly the birth of a new brother or sister radically changes the life of the older sibling. The parents have less time for the older child, who may feel neglected and angry, leading both to more confrontations between the older child and the parents and to feelings of rivalry toward the new baby (Furman, 1995). Yet rivalry is not the only quality of these early sibling relationships; observations of preschoolers with their siblings point toward other ingredients as well. Toddlers and preschoolers help their brothers and sisters, imitate them, and share their toys. Judy Dunn, in a detailed longitudinal study of a group of 40 families in England, observed that the older child often imitated a baby brother or sister; by the time the younger child was a year old, he or she began imitating the older sibling, and from then on most of the imitation flowed in that direction, with the younger child copying the older one (Dunn & Kendrick, 1982).

At the same time, brothers and sisters also hit each other, snatch toys, and threaten and insult each other. The older child in a pair of preschoolers is likely to be the leader and is therefore likely to show more of both aggressive and helpful behaviors (Abramovitch et al., 1982). For both members of the pair, however, the dominant feature seems to be ambivalence. Both supportive and negative behaviors are evident in about equal proportions. In Abramovitch's research, such ambivalence occurred whether the pair were close in age or further apart and whether the older child was a boy or a girl. Naturally there are variations on this theme; some pairs show mostly antagonistic or rivalrous behaviors while some show mostly helpful and supportive behaviors. Most sibling pairs show both types of behavior.

School-Age Siblings. How do those themes play out in middle childhood? First of all, as a general rule, sibling relationships seem to be less central in the lives of school-age children than are relationships with either friends or parents (Buhrmester, 1992). Children of elementary school age are less likely to turn to a sibling for affection than to parents, and they are less likely to turn to a brother or sister for companionship or intimacy than they are to a friend.

While this is true in general, sibling relationships also vary enormously. On the basis of direct studies of young children as well as retrospective reports by young adults about their sibling relationships when they were at school age, researchers have identified several patterns or styles of sibling relationships: (1) a *caregiver* relationship, in which one sibling serves as a kind of quasi parent for the other, a pattern that seems to be more common between an older sister and younger brother than in any other combination; (2) a *buddy* relationship, in which both members of the pair try to be like one another and take pleasure in being together; (3) a *critical* or conflictual relationship, which includes attempts by one sibling to dominate the other, teasing, and quarreling; (4) a *rival* relationship, which contains many of the same elements as a critical relationship but is also low in any form of friendliness or support; and (5) a *casual* or *uninvolved* relationship, in which the siblings have relatively little to do with one another (Murphy, 1993; Stewart et al., 1995).

Rivalrous or critical relationships seem to be more common when siblings are close together in age (4 or fewer years apart) and in families in which the parents are less satisfied with their marriage (Buhrmester & Furman, 1990; McGuire et al., 1996). Friendly and intimate relationships appear to be somewhat more common in pairs of sisters (Buhrmester & Furman, 1990), while rivalry seems to be highest in boy-boy pairs (Stewart et al., 1995).

Do you recognize your own middle-childhood sibling relationships in these categories? Has your relationship with your brothers and sisters changed in the years since you were in elementary school?

---

in the interests of joint play, which requires some awareness of the other's feelings and wishes as well as an ability to modulate one's own emotions. You already know that these cognitive and control skills emerge during the preschool years; what the research on friendships tells us is that play with peers, especially play with friends, may be a crucial ingredient in that development.

One of the really intriguing facts about such early friendships is that they are more likely between same-sex pairs, even among children as young as 2 or 3. John Gottman (1986) reports that perhaps 65 percent of friendships between preschool children in the United States are with same-sex peers. Social interactions with children other than the chosen friend(s) are also more likely to be with children of the same sex, beginning as early as age 2½ or 3 (Maccoby, 1988; 1990; Maccoby & Jacklin, 1987)—a pattern you already saw in Figure 10.5 (p. 308).

Figure 11.3

O'Brien and Bierman's results illustrate the change between elementary and high school in children's ideas about what defines a "group" of peers.

(*Source:* O'Brien & Bierman, 1988, Table 1, p. 1363.)

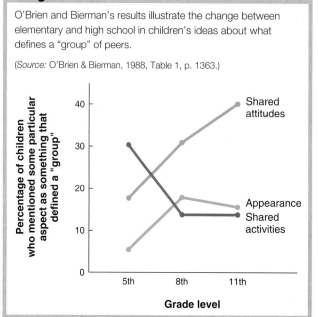

Peers at School Age

Peers become even more important among school-age children. Indeed, among children aged 7 through 10, playing with pals (along with watching TV) takes up virtually all their time when they are not in school, eating, or sleeping (Timmer, 1985).

Shared play interests form the major basis of these school-age peer relationships, just as is true among preschoolers. Furthermore, kids this age *define* play groups in terms of common activities rather than in terms of common attitudes or values. You can see this pattern in Figure 11.3, which shows the results of a study by Susan O'Brien & Karen Bierman (1988). They asked children in fifth, eighth, and eleventh grades to tell them about the different groups of kids that hang around together at their school and then to say how they could tell that a particular bunch was a "group." For the fifth graders, the single best criterion of a "group" was that the children did things together. For eighth graders, shared attitudes and common appearance became much more important.

I'll be talking much more about the child's *understanding* of social relationships and processes in Chapter 12, but let me just point out here that this "concreteness" in the elementary school child's view of peers is entirely consistent with what I've already told you about the character of the self-concepts of children this same age, as well as with Piaget's ideas about the thinking of a concrete operational child.

Gender Segregation. Beyond the centrality of shared activities, the most striking thing about peer group interactions in the elementary school years is how gender-segregated they are, a pattern that appears to exist in every culture in the world (Cairns & Cairns, 1994; Harkness & Super, 1985). Boys play with boys, girls play with girls, each in their own areas and at their own kinds of games. There are some ritualized "boundary violations" between these separate territories, such as chasing games (Thorne, 1986), but on the whole, girls and boys between the ages of 6 and 12 actively avoid interacting with one another and show strong favoritism toward their own gender and negative stereotyping of the opposite gender (Powlishta, 1995). Given a forced choice between playing with a child of the opposite gender or a child of a different race, researchers have found that at elementary school age, children will make the cross-race choice rather than the cross-gender choice (Maccoby & Jacklin, 1987).

Why is this preference for same-gender playmates so very strong at this age? Eleanor Maccoby (1990), one of the leading researchers and theorists in this area, suggests two reasons. First, girls appear to be "put off" by the typical boy's rough-and-tumble play style and by the strong emphasis on competition and dominance that is so much a part of boy-boy interactions. Second, Maccoby argues that girls find it hard to influence boys. Girls make polite suggestions to each other, a style of influence attempt that school-age boys simply don't comply with very often. In response, argues Maccoby, girls withdraw into their own pairs or groups where their own "rules" of behavior are familiar and effective. Why boys avoid girls is more of a mystery, although it is clear that they do at this age. Indeed, boys' preference for same-gender playmates is, if anything, even stronger than is girls'.

Friendships. Gender segregation is even more pronounced when we look at friendships among school-age children. In one recent large study of third and fourth graders, researchers found that only 14 percent had a cross-sex friendship; for only 3 percent of these children was the cross-sex relationship the child's primary or most central friendship (Kovacs et al., 1996).

School-age children spend more time with their friends than do preschoolers, and they gradually develop a larger collection of **reciprocal friendships**—pairs in which each child names the other as a friend or as a "best friend." Thomas Berndt, in several studies (e.g., Berndt & Hoyle, 1985), finds that most first graders have only one such reciprocal friendship. This number gradually rises through elementary school, so that by eighth grade, the average child has two to three reciprocal friendships. If we simply ask children to name their friends—regardless of whether the friendship is reciprocated—the numbers are still higher. Second graders name about four friends each, while seventh graders name about seven (Reisman & Shorr, 1978).

Children in this age range also behave differently with friends than they do with strangers, just as preschoolers do. They are more open and more supportive with chums, smiling and looking at each other, laughing and touching each other more than nonfriends; they talk more with friends and cooperate with and help each other more. Pairs of friends are also more successful than are nonfriends in solving problems or performing some task together (Newcomb & Bagwell, 1996). Yet school-age children are also more critical of friends and have more conflicts with them than they do with strangers (Hartup, 1996). At the same time, when such conflicts with friends occur, children are more concerned about resolving them than is true of disagreements among nonfriends. Thus, friendships are an arena in which children can learn how to manage conflicts (Newcomb & Bagwell, 1995).

Sex Differences in Friendship Quality. The qualities of the friendships girls and boys create also differ in intriguing ways. Waldrop and Halverson (1975) refer to boys' relationships as *extensive* and to girls' relationships as *intensive*. Boys' friendship groups are larger and more accepting of newcomers than are girls'. Boy friends play more outdoors and roam over a larger area in their play. Girl friends are more likely to play in pairs or in smaller groups, and they spend more playtime indoors or near home or school (Gottman, 1986; Benenson, 1994).

In the elementary school years, gender segregation in play groups is almost total: Boys play with boys, girls with girls.

At the level of actual interaction, we also see sex differences—a fact that won't surprise you, given what I've already said about the reasons for gender segregation in this age group. Boys' groups and boys' friendships appear to be focused more on competition and dominance than are girls' friendships (Maccoby, 1995). In fact, among school-age boys, we see *higher* levels of competition between pairs of friends than between strangers, the opposite of what we see among girls. Friendships between girls also include more agreement, more compliance, and more self-disclosure than is true for boys. For example, Campbell Leaper (1991) finds that "controlling" speech—a category that includes rejecting comments, ordering, manipulating or challenging, defiance or refutation, or resisting the other's attempt to control—is twice as common among pairs of 7- and 8-year-old male friends as among pairs of female friends. Among the 4- and 5-year-olds in this study, there were no sex differences in controlling speech.

None of this should obscure the fact that the interactions of male and female friendship pairs have a great many characteristics in common. For example, collaborative and cooperative exchanges are the most common forms of communication in both boys' and girls' friendships in these years. Nor should we necessarily conclude that boys' friendships are less important to them than are girls'. Nevertheless, it seems clear that there are differences in form and style that may well have enduring implications for the patterns of friendship over the full life span.

Peer Relationships at Adolescence

Many of these patterns change at adolescence. Mixed-sex groups begin to appear, conformity to peer group values and behaviors increases, and parents' influence on the child wanes even while the attachment to the parents remains strong. In the United States, teenagers spend more than half their waking hours with other teenagers and less than 5 percent of their time with either parent. Their friendships are also increasingly intimate, in the sense that adolescent friends share more and more of their inner feelings and secrets and are more knowledgeable about each other's feelings. Loyalty and faithfulness become centrally valued characteristics of friendship. These adolescent friendships are also more likely to endure for a year or longer. In one longitudinal study, Robert Cairns and Beverly Cairns (1994) found that only about 20 percent of friendships among fourth graders lasted as long as a year, while about 40 percent of friendships formed by these same youngsters when they were tenth graders were long-lasting.

Beyond these changes in individual relationships, the *function* of the peer group changes in adolescence. In elementary school, peer groups are mostly the setting for mutual play and for all the learning about relationships and the natural world that is part of such play. The teenager uses the peer group in another way. He is struggling to make a slow transition from the protected life of the family to the independent life of adulthood; the peer group becomes the *vehicle* for that transition.

One sign of this shift is that teenagers begin to use their peers, rather than their parents, as their primary confidants. You've seen one illustration of this change in Figure 11.2 (p. 327). An equally striking set of findings comes from research by Duane Buhrmester (1996). Figure 11.4 shows the combined findings from several studies in which children, teenagers, or adults were asked to rate the level of intimate disclosure they experienced with parents, friends, and a romantic partner. You can see three clear stages. Before adolescence, children report higher levels of self-disclosure with their parents. At adolescence, this changes in a major way: Self-disclosure with parents drops abruptly while self-disclosure with friends becomes dominant. Then in adulthood, a second shift occurs as a romantic partner takes the dominant role.

Another facet of this change in the centrality of peer relationships is a strong clannishness and intense conformity to the group. Such conformity, which Erikson saw as an entirely normal aspect of adolescence, seems to peak at about age 13 or 14 (at about

Figure 11.4

Before adolescence, parents are most often a child's closest confidants; in adolescence, it is peers in whom the young person confides.

(*Source:* From "Need Fulfillment, Interpersonal Competence, and the Developmental Context of Early Adolescent Friendship" by D. Buhrmester, *The company they keep: Friendship in childhood and adolescence,* W. M. Bukowski, A. F. Newcomb, and W. W. Hartup (eds.), p. 168, Fig 8.2. © 1996 Cambridge University Press. By permission of Cambridge University Press.)

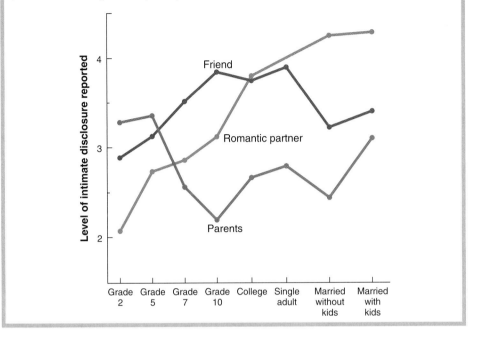

the same time that we see a drop in self-esteem) and then wanes as the teenager begins to arrive at a sense of identity that is more independent of the peer group.

However, while it is very clear that peers do indeed put pressure on each other to conform to peer group behavior standards, it is also true that peer group pressures are less potent and less negative than popular cultural stereotypes might lead you to believe (Berndt, 1992). Adolescents, like all of us, *choose* their friends, and they are likely to choose to associate with a group that shares their values, attitudes, and behaviors. If the discrepancy between their own ideas and those of their friends becomes too great, teens are more likely to move toward a more compatible group of friends than to be persuaded to shift toward the first group's values or behaviors. Furthermore, teenagers report that when explicit peer pressure is exerted, it is most likely to be pressure toward positive activities, such as school involvement, and *away* from misconduct. Thus, while Erikson appears to be quite correct in saying that peers are a major force in shaping a child's identity development in adolescence, peer influence is neither monolithic nor uniformly negative (Berndt & Keefe, 1995a; Brown et al., 1995).

One important exception to this rather rosy view of the impact of peer pressure is what we see among those teens who spend time with peers who lean toward aggressive, delinquent, or disruptive behavior. Such peer subgroups often do provide explicit pressure toward misconduct or lawbreaking, to which some teens are susceptible. Whether an adolescent will be drawn to such a group in the first place, and whether he or she will be pushed toward more deviant behavior once he begins to "hang out" with such a group, appears to depend a good deal on the individual teenager's own qualities—such as whether the teenager has good social skills or is already showing some disruptive behavior before adolescence. For example, Frank Vitaro and his colleagues (1997) have found that among a group of 868 boys they studied from age 11 to 13, those who had been *moderately* disruptive at age 11 were more likely to be delinquent at age 13 if they had had aggressive/disruptive friends at ages 11 and 12 than if their friends

Research Report

Are African-American Adolescents More Susceptible to Peer Influence?

One assumption made by a great many adults, including many social scientists, is that African-American youth, more than any other group, are likely to be strongly peer-oriented and to be vulnerable to peer pressure. One typical argument is that because black teenagers are more often living in single-parent families, they are more likely to depend on peers for affiliation and support. Several recent studies call this assumption into question.

Peggy Giordano and her colleagues (1993) studied a group of 942 teenagers, chosen as a representative sample of all adolescents living in Toledo, Ohio. Half the members of the group were black, the remainder mostly non-Hispanic whites. These teens were asked a wide variety of questions about their friendships and their relationships with peers, such as these:

How important is it to you to do things your friends approve of?
How important is it to you to have a group of friends to hang around with?

They were also asked about family intimacy (e.g., "I'm closer to my parents than a lot of kids my age are") and about parental supervision and control.

In this sample, African-American adolescents reported significantly *more* family intimacy, *more* parental supervision and control, *less* need for peer approval, and *less* peer pressure than did white teens.

Similarly, Vicki Mack, in a study of nearly 1000 teens in Detroit, found that the African-American youth described *lower* levels of compliance to friends and *higher* scores on measures of the importance of their relationship with their parents (Mack et al., 1995). These two studies certainly raise questions about widespread cultural assumptions.

had been less disruptive. Thus, those boys who were leaning toward bad behavior were drawn further toward disruptive activities by their crowd. However, the boys in this study who were already showing *highly* disruptive behavior at age 11 most often continued with delinquent or disruptive behavior at age 13, regardless of the type of friends they hung out with. These teenagers were already set on a course of negative behavior; their participation in "druggie" or "tough" crowds did not exacerbate that pattern, nor did nondeviant friends steer them away from delinquent choices. Findings like these suggest that negative peer group influences occur primarily for a particular group of marginal teens, perhaps especially those whose parents are ineffective in monitoring and discipline, or perhaps those who have insecure attachments to their parents (e.g., Dishion et al., 1995b; Resnick et al., 1997).

Changes in Peer Group Structure in Adolescence. The structure of the peer group also changes over the years of adolescence. The classic, widely quoted early study is Dunphy's observation of the formation, dissolution, and interaction of teenage groups in a high school in Sydney, Australia, between 1958 and 1960 (Dunphy, 1963). Dunphy identified two important subvarieties of groups. The first type, which he called a **clique,** is made up of four to six young people who appear to be strongly attached to one another. Cliques have strong cohesiveness and high levels of intimate sharing. In the early years of adolescence, these cliques are almost entirely same-sex groups—a residual of the preadolescent pattern. Gradually, however, the cliques combine into larger sets Dunphy called **crowds,** which include both males and females. Finally, the crowd breaks down again into heterosexual cliques and then into loose associations of couples. In Dunphy's study, the period of the fully developed crowd was between approximately ages 13 and 15—the very years when we see the greatest conformity to peer pressure.

Bradford Brown and others of the current generation of adolescence researchers have changed Dunphy's labels somewhat (Brown, 1990; B. Brown et al., 1994). Brown uses the word *crowd* to refer to the "reputation-based" group with which a young person is identified, either by choice or by peer designation. In U.S. schools these groups have labels like "jocks," "brains," "nerds," "dweebs," "punks," "druggies," "toughs," "normals," "populars," "preppies," or "loners." Studies in U.S. junior and senior high schools make it clear that teenagers can readily identify and have quite stereotypic—even caricatured—descriptions of each of the major crowds in their school (e.g., "The partiers goof off a lot more than the jocks do, but they don't come to school stoned like the burnouts do"). Each of these descriptions serves as what Brown calls an "identity prototype" (B. Brown et al., 1994, p. 133): Labeling others and labeling oneself as belonging to one or more of these groups helps to create or reinforce the adolescent's own identity. Such labeling also helps the adolescent identify potential friends or foes. Thus, identification as a member in one crowd or another channels each adolescent toward particular activities and particular relationships.

Within any given school, these various crowds are organized into a fairly clear, widely understood pecking order. In U.S. schools, the groups labeled as some variant of "jocks," "populars," or "normals" are typically at the top of the heap, with "brains" somewhere in the middle and "druggies," "loners," and "nerds" at the bottom (B. Brown et al., 1994).

Through the years of junior high and high school, the social system of crowds becomes increasingly differentiated, with more and more distinct groups. For example, in one Midwest school system, Kinney (1993) found that junior high students labeled only two major crowds, one small high-status group (called "trendies" in this school) and the great mass of lower-status students called "dweebs." A few years later, the same students named five distinct crowds, three with comparatively high social status and two with low status ("grits" and "punkers"). By late high school, these same students identified seven or eight crowds, but by this age the crowds seemed to be less significant in the social organization of the peer group; mutual friendships and dating pairs had become more central (Urberg et al., 1995).

Within (and sometimes across) these crowds, adolescents create smaller friendship groups Brown calls *cliques*—a usage that is very similar to Dunphy's meaning for the same term. Brown, like Dunphy, notes that in early adolescence, cliques are almost entirely same-sex; by late adolescence, they have become mixed in gender, often composed of groups of dating couples.

Whatever specific clique or crowd a teenager may identify with, theorists agree that the peer group performs the highly important function of helping the teenager shift from friendships to "partner" social relationships. The 13- or 14-year-old can begin to try out her new relationship skills in the wider group of the crowd or clique; only after some confidence is developed do we see the beginnings of dating and of more committed pair relationships.

Critical Thinking

Think back to your own high school. Can you draw some kind of diagram or map to describe the organization of crowds and cliques? Were those crowds or cliques more or less important in the last years of high school than they had been earlier?

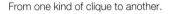
From one kind of clique to another.

Heterosexual Relationships in Adolescence. Of all the changes in social relationships in adolescence, perhaps the most profound is this shift from the total dominance of same-sex friendships to heterosexual relationships (Richards et al., 1998). These new relationships are clearly part of the preparation for assuming a full adult sexual identity. Physical sexuality is part of that role, but so are the skills of personal intimacy with the opposite sex, including flirting, communicating, and reading the form of social cues used by the other gender.

In Western societies, these skills are learned first in larger crowds or cliques and then in dating pairs (Zani, 1993). Studies of adolescents in the United States suggest that dating begins most typically at 15 or 16, as you can see from Table 11.3, which shows results from a representative sample of Detroit teenagers.

You'll recall from Chapter 4 that there are some ethnic differences in such heterosexual behavior within U.S. society. African-American teens begin dating and sexual experimentation earlier than do Anglos or Latinos. Early dating and early sexual activity are also more common among the poor of every ethnic group and among those who experience relatively early puberty. Religious teachings and individual attitudes about the appropriate age for dating and sexual behavior also make a difference, as does family structure. Girls from divorced or remarried families, for example, report earlier dating and higher levels of sexual experience than do girls from intact families, and those with strong religious identity report later dating and lower levels of sexuality (Bingham et al., 1990; Miller & Moore, 1990). In every one of these subgroups, however, these are years of experimentation with presexual and/or sexual relationships.

Behavior with Peers:
Prosocial Behavior and Aggression

This broad sketch of peer relationships from toddlerhood through adolescence makes clear the various roles that peers play in children's development over these years, and how central such relationships are. What it does not convey are all the changes in the actual content or quality of children's peer interactions. To fill in some of the gaps, let me talk briefly about two specific categories of behavior representing the two ends of the positive/negative continuum, namely, prosocial behavior and aggression.

Table 11.3

Age at First Date Among U.S. Adolescents

Age	Percentage	
	Males	**Females**
13 or younger	21.2	8.6
14	17.9	16.2
15	21.2	33.6
16	29.5	29.3
17–18	7.2	10.0

Source: Thornton, 1990, Table 1, pp. 246–247.

Prosocial Behavior

This class of behavior is defined by psychologists as "intentional, voluntary behavior intended to benefit another" (Eisenberg, 1992, p. 3). In everyday language, this is essentially what we mean by **altruism,** and it changes with age, just as other aspects of peer behavior change.

We first see such **prosocial behaviors** in children of about 2 or 3—at about the same time as they begin to show real interest in play with other children. They will offer to help another child who is hurt, offer a toy, or try to comfort another person (Eisenberg & Fabes, 1998; Zahn-Waxler & Radke-Yarrow, 1982; Zahn-Waxler et al., 1992a). As I pointed out in Chapter 6, children this young have only a beginning understanding of the fact that others feel differently from themselves, but they obviously understand enough about the emotions of others to respond in supportive and sympathetic ways when they see other children or adults hurt or sad.

Past these early years, researchers have found a number of trends. Older children are more likely to share objects or money with others (such as donating marbles in the game I described in Chapter 9). School-age children and adolescents are also more likely than are preschoolers to provide physical and verbal assistance to someone in need (Eisenberg, 1992). However, not all prosocial behaviors show this pattern of increase with age. Comforting another child, for example, appears to be more common among preschool and early elementary school children than at older ages (Eisenberg, 1988; 1990).

We also know that children vary a lot in the amount of such altruistic behavior they show, and that young children who show relatively more empathy and altruism are also those who regulate their own emotions well. They show positive emotions readily and negative emotions less often (Eisenberg et al., 1996). These variations among children's level of empathy or altruism seem to be related to specific kinds of child rearing. For those of you interested in knowing more about how helpful or altruistic children come to be that way, I've explored some of the research in the Real World box on page 344.

Aggression

If you have watched children together, you know that all is not sweetness and light in the land of the young. Children do support and share with their friends, and they do show affectionate and helpful behaviors toward one another, but they also tease, fight, yell, criticize, and argue over objects and territory. Researchers who have studied this more negative side of children's interactions have looked mostly at **aggression,** which we can define as behavior with the apparent intent to injure some other person or object.

Every child shows at least some aggression, but the form and frequency of aggression change over the years of childhood. When 2- or 3-year-old children are upset or frustrated, they are more likely to throw things or hit each other. As their verbal skills improve, children shift away from such overt physical aggression toward greater use of verbal aggression, such as taunting or name-calling. In the elementary school and adolescent years, physical aggression becomes still less common, and children learn the cultural rules about when and how much it is acceptable to display anger or aggression. In most cultures, this means that anger is more and more disguised and aggression more and more controlled with increasing age (Underwood et al., 1992).

Sex Differences in Aggression. One interesting exception to this general pattern of declining physical aggression is that in all-boy pairs or groups, at least in U.S. studies, physical aggression seems to remain both relatively high and constant over the years of childhood. Indeed, at every age, boys show more physical aggression and more assertiveness than do girls, both within friendship pairs and in general (Coie & Dodge,

The Real World

Rearing Helpful and Altruistic Children

If you wish to encourage your own children to be more generous or altruistic, here are some specific things you can do, based on the work of Eisenberg and others (Eisenberg, 1992; Eisenberg & Fabes, 1998; Eisenberg & Murphy, 1995; Grusec et al., 1996):

1. *Capitalize on the child's capacity for empathy.* If your child injures someone else, point out the consequences of that injury for the other person: "When you hit Susan it hurts her" or "See, you made Jimmy cry." This strategy seems to be especially effective when parents use it regularly, when they express their feelings strongly, and when they don't combine it with physical punishment.

2. *Create a loving and warm family climate.* When parents express affection and warmth regularly toward their children, those children are more likely to be generous and altruistic. As a corollary, children who are securely attached are also more likely to show prosocial behavior.

3. *Provide rules or guidelines about helpful behavior.* Clear rules about what *to* do as well as what *not* to do are important: "It's always good to be helpful to other people" or "We should share what we have with people who don't have so much." More direct instructions also foster prosocial behavior: "I'd like you to help Keisha with her puzzle" or "Please share your candy with John."

4. *Provide prosocial attributions.* Attribute your child's helpful or altruistic action to the child's own internal character: "You're such a helpful child!" or "You certainly do a lot of nice things for other people." This strategy begins to be effective with children at about age 7 or 8, at about the same time as they are beginning to develop global notions of self-esteem. In this way you may be able to affect the child's self-scheme, which in turn may result in a generalized, internalized pattern of altruistic behavior.

5. *Have children do helpful things.* Assign your children regular household tasks. It doesn't seem to matter just what the tasks are, whether helping to cook or clean,

Having children do helpful things, as these third graders are doing by sorting recyclable material, is one way to increase altruistic behavior in kids.

take care of pets, or watch younger siblings. What matters is that the child have a regular role in everyday household routines, a pattern that seems to encourage the development of concern for others as well as a sense of responsibility. In school, too, children who have a chance to do helpful things such as tutoring younger students seem to develop more empathy and concern. This strategy can backfire, though, if the coercion required to get the child to do the helpful thing is too strong: The child may now attribute his "good" behavior to the coercion ("Mother made me do it") rather than to some inner trait of his own ("I am a helpful/kind person"), and no future altruism is fostered. But as a general rule, it is good for children to practice performing helpful or generous actions.

6. *Model thoughtful and generous behavior.* Stating the rules will do little good if your own behavior does not match what you say! Children (and adults) are simply much more likely to do generous or thoughtful things if they see other people—especially other people in authority, such as parents—performing those same actions.

1998). Table 11.4 gives some highly representative data from a very large, careful survey in Canada (Offord et al., 1991) in which both parents and teachers completed checklists describing each child's behavior—a study you may remember from Figure 1.4 (p. 25). In Table 11.4 I've listed only the information provided by teachers, but parent ratings yielded parallel findings. It is clear that boys are described as far more aggressive on nearly any measure of physical aggressiveness.

Relational Aggression. Results like these have been so clear and so consistent that most psychologists concluded that boys are simply "more aggressive" in every pos-

Table 11.4

Percentage of Boys and Girls Aged 4 to 11 Rated by Their Teachers as Displaying Aggressive Behaviors

Behavior	Boys	Girls
Mean to others	21.8	9.6
Physically attacks people	18.1	4.4
Gets in many fights	30.9	9.8
Destroys own things	10.7	2.1
Destroys others' things	10.6	4.4
Threatens to hurt people	13.1	4.0

Source: Offord et al., 1991, from Table 2.3, p. 39.

sible way. But that may turn out to be wrong or at least misleading. Instead, it begins to look as if girls express aggressiveness in a different way, using what has recently been labeled **relational aggression** instead of either physical aggression or nasty words (Crick & Grotpeter, 1995; Crick et al., 1997; Rys & Bear, 1997; Tomada & Schneider, 1997). Physical aggression hurts others through physical damage or threat of such damage; relational aggression is aimed at damaging the other person's self-esteem or peer relationships, such as by cruel gossiping, by making facial expressions of disdain, or by ostracizing or threatening to ostracize the other child ("I won't invite you to my birthday party if you do that"). Children experience such indirect aggression as genuinely hurtful, and they are likely to shun other kids who regularly use this form of aggression, just as they tend to reject peers who are physically aggressive.

Girls are much more likely to use relational aggression than are boys, especially toward other girls, a difference that begins as early as the preschool years and becomes very marked by the fourth or fifth grade. For example, in one study of nearly 500 children in the third through sixth grades, Nicki Crick found that 17.4 percent of the girls but only 2 percent of the boys were high in relational aggression—almost precisely the reverse of what we see for physical aggression (Crick & Grotpeter, 1995).

What might be the origins of such sex differences in the form of aggression? One obvious possibility is that hormone differences play a part. We know that higher rates of physical aggression in males have been observed in every human society and in all varieties of primates. We also know that girls exposed prenatally to heightened levels of androgen (male hormone), because of a disorder called congenital adrenal hyperplasia, show more physical aggression with playmates than do their normal siblings or cousins (Berenbaum, 1997). Among boys, we also have some evidence of a link between rates of physical aggression and testosterone levels (e.g., Susman et al., 1987), particularly at adolescence and later ages. Thus, differing rates of physical aggression appear to have at least some biological basis. We have no equivalent research regarding relational aggression, so the cultural or possible biological factors shaping this sex difference are still unknown.

Individual Differences in Peer Relationships

Collectively children may move toward greater and greater ability to interact effectively with their peers, toward greater altruism and away from overt expression of aggression, toward greater intimacy in their relationships with peers. Overlaid on these com-

Research Report
Bullies and Victims

Some physically or relationally aggressive children may also fall into the category of bully. Dan Olweus (1995), who has done the most significant work on bullies and victims, defines a bully as one who repeatedly torments some other child with words, gestures, intentional exclusion from a group, or physical aggression. The target of such repeated torment is referred to as the victim. Olweus's studies in Sweden indicate that as many as 9 percent of elementary school children are regularly victims while 7 percent could be called bullies, percentages confirmed in studies in other countries (e.g., Perry et al., 1988).

Victims have certain characteristics in common, including anxiety, passivity, sensitivity, low self-esteem or self-confidence, lack of humor, and comparative lack of friends (Egan & Perry, 1998; Hodges et al., 1997; Olweus, 1995). Among boys, victims are also often physically smaller or weaker than their peers. Whether boys or girls, victims seldom assert themselves with their peers, making neither suggestions for play activities nor prosocial actions. Instead, they submit to whatever suggestions others may make. Other children do not like this behavior and thus do not like the victims (Crick & Grotpeter, 1996; Schwartz et al., 1993). The consequences of such victimization can include loneliness, school avoidance, lower self-esteem, and significant depression at later ages (Kochenderfer & Ladd, 1996; Olweus, 1995).

Not all children faced with a passive and unresponsive playmate turn into bullies. Bullies are distinctive because they are typically aggressive in a variety of situations, not just in relationships with selected victims. Bullies also tend to be more aggressive toward adults than do nonbullies, have little empathy for their victims' pain or unhappiness, and are often impulsive. Olweus's studies do *not* support the common assumption that bullies are basically insecure children who have developed a tough exterior to cover up their insecurity. In fact, the opposite appears to be true. Bullies most often have *low* levels of anxiety and insecurity. Olweus proposes four child-rearing factors that lie behind the development of bullying behavior:

- Indifference and lack of warmth from the parent toward the child in the early years
- Lack of clear or adequate limits on aggressive behavior set by the parents
- The parents' use of physical punishment
- A difficult, impulsive temperament in the child

If you compare this list to the qualities Gerald Patterson has identified in families of delinquent or "out-of-control" children, you'll see a great many similarities. These children tyrannize their families and terrorize their peers.

mon developmental patterns, however, are very large differences in the degree to which children acquire social skills and in their resulting popularity or lack of it.

Popularity and Rejection

Psychologists who study popularity in children have concluded that it is important to distinguish between several subgroups of unpopular children. The most frequently studied are **rejected children.** If you ask children to list peers they would *not* like to play with, or if you observe which children are avoided on the playground, you can get a measure of rejection of this type. **Neglected children** form a second group among the less popular. Children in this category are reasonably well liked but lack individual friends and are rarely chosen as most preferred by their peers. Neglect seems to be much less stable over time than is rejection, but children who are neglected nonetheless seem to share certain qualities. Interestingly, such children often do quite well in school (Wentzel & Asher, 1995), but they are more prone to depression and loneliness than are accepted children, especially if the neglect has persisted over several years (Burks et al., 1995; Cillessen et al., 1992; Rubin et al., 1991). Where might such differences in popularity or peer acceptance come from?

Qualities of Rejected and Popular Children. Some of the characteristics that differentiate popular and unpopular children are factors outside a child's control. In particular, attractive children and physically larger children are more likely to be popular—perhaps merely a continuation of the preference for attractive faces that Langlois detected in young infants and that I described in Chapter 5. The most crucial ingredient, though, is not how the child looks but how the child behaves.

Critical Thinking

One reasonable hypothesis might be that neglected children would be more likely to have had insecure attachments as infants. Can you think of refinements of this hypothesis? And how could you test it?

Popular children behave in positive, supporting, nonpunitive, and nonaggressive ways toward most other children. They explain things, take their playmates' wishes into consideration, take turns in conversation, and are able to regulate the expression of their strong emotions. They are helpful and friendly and have leadership skills (Rubin et al., 1998). Not surprisingly, these more popular children are also more likely than are rejected children to have close reciprocal friendships (Franco & Levitt, 1997), giving them still more opportunity to practice important social skills. Rejected children, in contrast, are aggressive, disruptive, uncooperative, and often unable to control the expression of their strong feelings (Eisenberg et al., 1995b; Pettit et al., 1996; Rubin et al., 1998). They interrupt their play partners more often, fail to take turns in a systematic way, and are less empathetic toward peers (Cohen & Strayer, 1996).

These conclusions emerge from a variety of types of research, including at least a few cross-cultural studies. For example, aggression and disruptive behavior are linked to rejection and unpopularity among Chinese children, just as they are among U.S. children (Chen et al., 1992; 1995). Some of the most informative studies are those in which previously unacquainted children are brought together to spend several sessions playing with one another while researchers observe and note specific behaviors. Later, the children pick their favorite playmates from among the play group (e.g., Coie & Kupersmidt, 1983; Dodge, 1983; Shantz, 1986). In these studies, children who are most consistently positive and supportive during the play sessions are those who end up being chosen as leaders or as friends. Those who consistently participate in conflicts are most often rejected.

Rejected children also seem to have quite different internal working models of relationships and of aggression than do popular children. In a series of studies, Kenneth Dodge has shown that aggressive/rejected children are much more likely to see aggression as a useful way to solve problems (Dodge & Feldman, 1990; Dodge & Frame, 1982; Dodge et al., 1990; Quiggle et al., 1992). They are also much more likely to interpret someone else's behavior as hostile or attacking than is true for less aggressive or more popular children.

Much of this information on rejected children is consistent with Gerald Patterson's work, whose model I described in Chapter 1 (Figure 1.2, p. 11) and in Chapter 9. Patterson is persuaded that a child's excess aggressiveness can be traced originally to ineffective parental control. But once the child's aggressiveness is well established, the child displays this same behavior with peers, is rejected by those peers, and is then driven more and more toward the only set of peers who will accept him, usually other aggressive or delinquent youngsters. These antisocial kids are not friendless, but their friends are almost always other kids with similar antisocial patterns. These friendships tend to be fairly transitory and focused on mutual coercion (Dishion et al., 1995a).

Any pattern of persistent aggression, and the peer rejection that so often accompanies it, are linked to a variety of long-term problems for children.

The seriousness of this set of connected problems is amply demonstrated in a growing body of research showing that rejection by one's peers in elementary school is one of the very few aspects of childhood functioning that consistently predicts behavior problems or emotional disturbances later in childhood, in adolescence, and in adulthood (e.g., Bagwell et al., 1998; Dishion, 1990; Serbin et al., 1991; Stattin & Magnusson, 1996). For example, Melissa DeRosier and her colleagues (1994) followed one group of over 600 children over a four-year period in early elementary school. She found that those children who were most chronically rejected by their peers later showed higher rates of several types of problems, including being absent from school, more depression or sadness, and more behavior problems.

Similarly, John Coie and his colleagues (1995) have followed a group of over 1000 children from the third to the tenth grade. Among the boys, those who were both aggressive and rejected in third grade were far more likely to show delinquency or other behavior problems in high school than were any other group of boys. Among girls, aggressiveness but not peer rejection was linked to later behavior problems.

We might explain such a link between early unpopularity and later behavior problems in any of several ways. Early problems with peers might be merely the most visible reflection of a general maladjustment that later manifests itself as delinquency or emotional disturbance. Alternatively, we might hypothesize that a failure to develop friendships itself causes problems that later become more general. Or the basic difficulty could lie in a seriously warped internal working model of relationships that leads to peer rejection in elementary school and to delinquency, or all of the above.

Happily, not all rejected children remain rejected; not all develop serious behavior problems or delinquency. And not all aggressive children are rejected. Recent research gives us a few hints about what may differentiate among these several subgroups. For example, some aggressive children also show fairly high levels of altruistic or prosocial behavior, and this mixture of qualities carries a much more positive prognosis than does aggression unleavened by helpfulness (Coie & Cillessen, 1993; Newcomb et al., 1993). Distinctions like these may help us not only to refine our predictions but to design better intervention programs for rejected/aggressive children.

Sex Differences

As a final word in this long and complex chapter, let me make a couple of additional brief points about a topic I have only touched on as we have gone along, namely, sex differences in social behavior. The most consistent difference is in the area of aggression/dominance/competitiveness. Boys show more of all of these behaviors, beginning at an early age, just as the widespread gender stereotypes would suggest. But contrary to most expectations, we have only very weak evidence that girls are consistently more nurturant or empathetic or more compliant to adults' wishes. Girls are also not more sociable; they do not, for example, have more friends than boys do. Girls do appear to be somewhat kinder and more considerate, on average, but the difference is not as large as the sex difference in physical aggression.

At a subtler level, however, we are beginning to understand that there are important differences in the *ways* boys and girls go about interacting with one another. I've already mentioned several of the bits of information that point us toward this conclusion, but let me pull them together for you:

- Pairs of boy friends are *more* competitive with each other than are pairs of strangers.
- Aggression between boys does not decline over the years of elementary school, while aggression between girls, and between boys and girls, does drop.
- Friendships between girls are more intimate, with much more self-disclosure.
- Boy friends are more likely to gather in large groups than in paired chumships, and the boys are less likely to exchange confidences and more likely to engage in some mutual activity, such as sports.

We also have a variety of indications that the same differences in style of relationship are evident in adults. Eleanor Maccoby (1990) describes the girls'/women's pattern as an *enabling* style. Enabling includes such behaviors as supporting the partner, expressing agreement, and making suggestions. All these behaviors tend to foster a greater equality and intimacy in the relationship and keep the interaction going. In contrast, boys and men are more likely to show what Maccoby calls a *constricting* or *restrictive* style: "A restrictive style is one that tends to derail the interaction—to inhibit the partner or cause the partner to withdraw, thus shortening the interaction or bringing it to an end" (1990, p. 517). Contradicting, interrupting, boasting, or other forms of self-display are all aspects of this style.

These are subtle but profound differences, and we still know little about how they arise in earliest childhood and whether equivalent differences occur across cultures. But if we are going to be able to make sense out of our own relationships, and out of the rapidly changing gender roles in modern society, we obviously need to know a great deal more about these apparently pervasive gender differences.

Summary

1. Both vertical relationships with adults and horizontal relationships with peers are of central significance in the child's social development. In particular, skills in forming and maintaining reciprocal relationships can be learned only with peers.

2. Bowlby and Ainsworth distinguish between an affectional bond (an enduring tie to a uniquely viewed partner) and an attachment, which involves the element of security and a safe base. An attachment is deduced from the existence of attachment behaviors.

3. For the parents to form a strong bond to the infant, what is most crucial is the learning and repetition of mutually reinforcing and interlocking attachment behaviors, not immediate contact at birth.

4. Fathers as well as mothers form strong bonds with their infants; fathers in most Western cultures show more physically playful behaviors with their children than do mothers.

5. Bowlby proposed that the child's attachment to the caregiver develops through a series of steps, beginning with rather indiscriminate aiming of attachment behaviors toward anyone within reach, through a focus on one or more figures, and finally "secure base behavior," beginning at about 6 months of age, which signals the presence of a clear attachment.

6. Attachment behaviors become less visible during the preschool years except when the child is stressed. By age 4 or 5, the child understands the constancy of the relationship.

7. The basic attachment to the parents remains strong in adolescence, despite an increase in parent-child conflict, the greater independence of the teenager, and the increased role of the peer group.

8. Children differ in the security of their first attachments and thus in the internal working model they develop. The secure infant uses the parent as a safe base for exploration and can be readily consoled by the parent.

9. The security of the initial attachment is reasonably stable and is fostered by sensitivity and contingent responsiveness by the parent.

10. Securely attached children appear to be more socially skillful, more curious and persistent in approaching new tasks, and more mature.

11. Children's relationships with peers become increasingly significant for their social development past the age of about 2. In elementary school, peer interactions are focused mostly on common activities; in adolescence, peer groups also become the vehicle for the transition from dependence to independence.

12. By age 4 or 5, most children have formed individual friendships and show preferential positive behavior toward friends. Friendship becomes more common, and more stable, in the elementary school years, and more intimate in adolescence.

13. Reputation-based groups, called crowds by current researchers, are an important part of adolescent social relationships, particularly in the early high school years. Smaller groups of friends, called cliques, are also present and gradually shift from same-sex to mixed-sex to dating pairs.

14. On average in Western cultures, dating begins at about age 15, but there is wide variability.

15. Prosocial behavior, such as helpfulness or generosity, is apparent as early as age 2 or 3 and generally increases throughout childhood.

16. Physical aggression peaks at age 3 or 4 and is replaced more and more by verbal aggression among older children. Boys show more physical aggressiveness at every age; girls show more relational aggression.

17. Popularity among peers, in elementary school or later, is most consistently based on the amount of positive and supportive social behavior shown by a child toward peers.

18. Socially rejected children are most strongly characterized by high levels of aggression or bullying and low levels of agreement and helpfulness. Aggressive/rejected children are likely to show behavior problems in adolescence and a variety of disturbances in adulthood.

19. Rejected children are more likely to interpret others' behavior as threatening or hostile. Thus, they have different internal models of relationship.

20. Boys and girls appear to have quite different styles of interacting with one another, with girls' pairs or groups showing a more "enabling" style.

Key Terms

affectional bond A "relatively long-enduring tie in which the partner is important as a unique individual and is interchangeable with none other" (Ainsworth, 1989, p. 711). **p. 319**

aggression Behavior that is aimed at harming or injuring another person or object. **p. 343**

altruism Giving away or sharing objects, time, or goods, with no obvious self-gain. **p. 343**

attachment An especially intense and central subtype of affectional bond in which the presence of the partner adds a special sense of security, a "safe base," for the individual. Characteristic of the child's bond with the parent. **p. 319**

attachment behavior The collection of (probably) instinctive behaviors of one person toward another that bring about or maintain proximity and caregiving, such as the smile of the young infant; behaviors that reflect an attachment. **p. 319**

clique Defined by Dunphy as a group of four to six friends with strong affectional bonds and high levels of group solidarity and loyalty; currently used by researchers to describe a self-chosen group of friends, in contrast to reputation-based crowds. **p. 340**

crowd Defined by Dunphy as a larger and looser group of friends than a clique, normally made up of several cliques joined together; defined by current researchers as a reputation-based group, common in adolescent subculture, with widely agreed-upon characteristics (e.g., "brains," "jocks," or "druggies"). **p. 340**

goal-corrected partnership Term used by Bowlby to describe the form of an appropriate child-to-parent attachment in the preschool years in which the two partners, through improved communication, negotiate the form and frequency of contact between them. **p. 325**

individuation Label used by some theorists for the process of psychological, social, and physical separation from parents that begins in adolescence. **p. 326**

insecure attachment An internal working model of relationship in which the child does not as readily use the parent as a safe base and is not readily consoled by the parent if upset. Includes three subtypes of attachment: ambivalent, avoidant, and disorganized/disoriented. **p. 329**

internal working model As applied to social relationships, a cognitive construction, for which the earliest relationships may form the template, of the workings of relationships, such as expectations of support or affection, trustworthiness, and so on. **p. 328**

neglected children Type of unpopular children who are not overtly rejected and are reasonably well liked but are not often chosen as friends. **p. 346**

parallel play Form of play seen in toddlers, in which two children play next to, but not with, one another. **p. 334**

prosocial behavior See *altruism*. **p. 343**

reciprocal friendship Any friendship in which the two partners each name the other as a friend; also a quality of friendship in school-age children, when friendship is for the first time perceived as being based on reciprocal trust. **p. 337**

rejected children Unpopular children who are not just ignored but are explicitly avoided, not chosen as playmates or friends. **p. 346**

relational aggression A form of aggression aimed at damaging the other person's self-esteem or peer relationships, such as by using ostracism or threats of ostracism, cruel gossiping, or facial expressions of disdain. **p. 345**

secure attachment An internal working model of relationship in which the child uses the parent as a safe base and is readily consoled after separation, when fearful, or when otherwise stressed. **p. 329**

Strange Situation A series of episodes used by Mary Ainsworth and others in studies of attachment. The child is observed with the mother, with a stranger, alone, and when reunited with stranger and mother. **p. 329**

Suggested Readings

Bowlby, J. (1988). *A secure base*. New York: Basic Books. This splendid small book, Bowlby's last before his death, includes a number of his most important early papers as well as new chapters that bring his theory up to date. See particularly Chapters 7 and 9.

Bretherton, I. (1992). The origins of attachment theory: John Bowlby and Mary Ainsworth. *Developmental Psychology, 28,* 759–775. A clear, current, thoughtful review of both Bowlby's and Ainsworth's ideas, including new data from anthropology and other cross-cultural analyses.

Dunn, J. (1993). *Young children's close relationships*. Newbury Park, CA: Sage. A wonderful small book, written in a clear and engaging style by one of the experts on children's social relationships.

Eisenberg, N. (1992). *The caring child*. Cambridge, MA: Harvard University Press. A brief, clear, current summary of what we know about the development of prosocial and altruistic behavior.

Karen, R. (1994). *Becoming attached*. New York: Warner Books. In this fine book, Robert Karen, who is both a psychologist and a journalist, tells the story of the early research on attachment, focusing on the central players in the scientific drama, including both Bowlby and Ainsworth. Written for the lay reader, this book will tell you a lot about both attachment and the process of science.

Lickona, T. (1983). *Raising good children*. Toronto: Bantam Books. One of the best "how to" books for parents I have ever seen, with excellent, concrete advice as well as theory. Lickona's emphasis is on many of the issues I raised in the Real World box on rearing altruistic children (p. 344).

Maccoby, E. E. (1990). Gender and relationships: A developmental account. *American Psychologist, 45,* 513–520. In this brief paper, Maccoby reviews the accumulating evidence suggesting that boys and girls show quite different styles of interaction, beginning in the preschool years.

Montemayor, R., Adams, G. R., & Gullotta, T. P. (Eds.). (1994). *Personal relationships during adolescence*. Thousand Oaks, CA: Sage. A first-rate collection of papers, including an especially fascinating discussion of teen crowds by Bradford Brown.

12

Thinking About Relationships:
The Development of Social Cognition

Think for a minute about the conversations you have with your friends. Haven't you said things like "I thought Jack was my friend, but now it turns out I can't really trust him" or "I've been trying to figure Jane out—sometimes she's shy, and sometimes she's the life of the party" or "Lots of people believe that I'm really the confident person I look like on the outside, but my friends know how insecure I really am."

All these statements reflect some aspect of what psychologists have come to call **social cognition**—thinking about people, what they do and should do, how they feel. If you are anything like I am (and I assume you are), then you, too, spend a great deal of time and energy analyzing other people, trying to understand them, trying to predict what your friends, partner, or co-workers will do. Arguably, knowledge about people and relationships is more important in our everyday life than are many of the more abstract kinds of knowledge or thinking I talked about in Chapters 6 and 7. Where does such social knowledge come from? How does children's thinking about people, about relationships, about right and wrong, change over time?

These questions are not new in this book. I have touched on many facets of social cognition as I have gone along. The infant's emerging ability to recognize individuals and to use facial expressions and other body language for social referencing is one kind of social cognition, as is the growing understanding of others' emotions and the development of a theory of others' minds in the preschool years. One could also argue that an "internal working model" of attachment is a kind of social cognition, as is the child's self-scheme. What I need to do now is to pull these various threads together and describe some of the more general ideas about social cognition that have emerged in recent decades. In the process, I hope to build a few bridges between the earlier, separate discussions of thinking and social relationships.

Some General Principles and Issues

One way to think about social cognition is simply to conceive of it as the application of general cognitive processes or skills to a different topic, in this case people or relationships. In Chapter 6 I talked about all the ways in which children's thinking changes from infancy through adolescence. We might assume that at any given age, a child applies these fundamental ways of thinking to his relationships as well as to objects. In this view, the child's understanding of self and others, of social relationships, reflects or is based on her overall level of cognitive development, such as her level of perspective-taking skills (Selman, 1980).

This approach has a powerful intuitive appeal. After all, as John Flavell points out (1985), it is the same head doing the thinking when a child works on a conservation problem and when she tries to understand people. Furthermore, as you will see very clearly as we go through the evidence, many of the same principles that seem to apply to general cognitive development hold here as well, such as the following:

- *Outer to inner characteristics.* Younger children pay attention to the surface of things, to what things look like; older children look for principles, for causes.

- *Observation to inference.* Young children initially base their conclusions only on what they can see or feel; later they make inferences about what ought to be or what might be.

- *Definite to qualified.* Young children's "rules" are very definite and fixed (such as sex-role rules); by adolescence, rules begin to be qualified.

- *Observer's view to general view.* Children also become less egocentric with time—less tied to their own individual views, more able to construct a model of some experience or some process that is true for everyone.

Critical Thinking

Think for a minute about how you can tell when someone else is concealing some feeling. What clues do you use? How sure can you be of your interpretation?

All these dimensions of change describe children's emerging social cognition, just as they describe the development of thinking about objects. But thinking about people or relationships also has some special features that makes it different from thinking about physical objects.

One obvious difference is that people, unlike rocks or glasses of water, behave *intentionally*. In particular, people often attempt to conceal information about themselves, so the ability to "read" other people's cues is one of the key social-cognitive skills. Further, unlike relationships with objects, relationships with people are mutual and reciprocal. Dolls, sets of blocks, or bicycles don't talk back, get angry, or respond in unexpected ways, but people do all these things. In learning about relationships, children must learn enough about other people's motives and feelings to predict such responses.

Children also have to learn special rules about particular forms of social interactions, such as politeness rules, rules about when you can and cannot speak, and rules about power or dominance hierarchies, all forms of social *scripts* (Schank & Abelson, 1977)—a concept I have mentioned several times before. The existence of such scripts allows children to develop strong expectations about how people will behave, in what order, in which settings. Furthermore, these scripts probably change with age not just because children's cognitive skills change, but also simply because the rules (scripts) themselves change as children move from one social setting to another. One obvious example is the set of changes that occurs when children start school. The script associated with the role of "student" is quite different from the one connected with the role of "little kid." Classrooms are more tightly organized, expectations for obedience are higher, and there are more drills and routines to be learned than was probably true at home or even in nursery school. The school script changes when the young adolescent moves into junior high school and then again when she enters high school.

These illustrations make it clear, I hope, that the development of sophisticated social cognitive understanding is more than a simple process of applying basic cognitive processes and strategies to the arena of social interaction. The child must also come to understand the ways in which social relationships are *different* from interactions with the physical world, and she must learn special rules and strategies. Let's begin with the child's growing ability to read others' feelings.

Reading Others' Feelings

Think of sitting in a classroom while your instructor hands back midterm exams. The person on your right, after looking at her exam, raises her head and smiles widely. The person on your left stays hunched over his test and turns down his mouth as he shakes his head a bit. A third person near you breathes a huge sigh and sits in a more relaxed posture, but does not smile. You easily deduce that the first person did well on the test and is happy, that the second person did less well than he expected or hoped and is distressed, perhaps even feeling guilty, and that the third person is relieved. How did you know that? What clues did you use? Presumably you used three types of information: facial expression, other body language, and the context in which the events occurred. Because you knew that tests were being handed back, you were alert for both happy and sad reactions, and you interpreted the body language accordingly. The same body language in another setting might mean something a bit different.

Both cognitive skill and social information are obviously involved in this whole process. You need to be able to identify various body signals, including facial expressions; you need to understand various kinds of emotions and know that it is possible for people to feel several emotions at the same time; you need to understand the social context; and you need to have a theory of mind that helps you link the context with the other person's likely feelings. In this case, you need the basic understanding that another person will be happy or sad depending on how well he does on some task.

Research on children's understanding of others' emotions suggests that they acquire these various forms of knowledge gradually over the years from about age 1 to adolescence. You already know from Chapter 5 that by 10 to 12 months, babies can tell the difference between positive and negative facial and vocal expressions—at that age, they already show social referencing. By age 3 or 4, the child's emotion-recognition repertoire has expanded considerably, and she has some preliminary understanding of the links between other people's emotions and their situations, such as that someone would be sad if she failed. And by age 10, the child understands and can read some emotional blends, even expressions of ambivalence.

Individual Differences in Emotion Knowledge

Not all children (or all adults) are equally skilled in their ability to read other people's emotions or intentions, a variation emphasized in Daniel Goleman's popular book *Emotional Intelligence* (1995b). These individual differences turn out to be quite significant for a child's overall social development and social competence. One illustration comes from research by Kenneth Dodge, which I mentioned briefly in Chapter 11 and which shows that unpopular children are significantly less skilled than are popular children at reading others' intentions.

In one study, Dodge showed videotapes to children in kindergarten, second grade, and fourth grade. Each tape showed an interaction in which one child destroyed the toy of a second child (Dodge et al., 1984). These videos were carefully created so that the destroying child's intent was varied. In some vignettes the intent was clearly hostile; in others it was accidental; in some it was ambiguous; and in others it was prosocial, such as knocking down the playmate's block tower in order to help clean up the room. Dodge found that in each age group, the popular children were better at detecting the actor's intent, with neglected and rejected children least accurate. In particular, neglected and rejected children were more likely to see hostile intent when it was not present, a pattern that has been found in other studies, especially among rejected children (Dodge & Feldman, 1990; Graham & Hudley, 1994).

Carol Izard and her colleagues (1997) have now shown such a linkage longitudinally. In a group of economically disadvantaged children, Izard found that those who had better and more accurate emotion knowledge in preschool later showed greater social competence and fewer behavior problems in first grade. Such a linkage suggests the possibility that an intervention program designed to improve children's basic emotional competence—their ability both to read others and to control their own emotional expressions—might have wide-ranging benefits. One such intervention, the PATHS program, is described in the Research Report on page 356.

The Development of Empathy

To explore the development of the child's ability to read the emotions and cues of others, psychologists have also studied the development of **empathy.** Empathy involves two aspects: apprehending another person's emotional state or condition and then matching that emotional state oneself. An empathizing person experiences the same feeling he imagines the other person to feel, or a highly similar feeling. *Sympathy* involves the same process of apprehending the other's emotional state, but it is accompanied not by a matching emotion but by a general feeling of sorrow or concern for the other (Eisenberg et al., 1989). Generally speaking, empathy seems to be the earlier response developmentally; among older children and adults, sympathy often seems to grow out of an initial empathetic response.

The most thorough analysis of the development of empathy and sympathy has been offered by Martin Hoffman (1982; 1988), who describes four broad steps, summarized in Table 12.1 (p. 357). The first stage, global empathy, which seems to be a kind of automatic empathetic distress response, is visible in quite young infants. Hoffman describes one example:

A preschool child would no doubt label this boy's emotion as "sad." A teenager would understand that the emotions might be much more complicated, such as sadness mixed with anger at himself, or sadness and relief, or other forms of ambivalence.

Critical Thinking

Do you cry at weddings and funerals, even when you do not know the people involved really well? Is that a form of empathy?

Research Report

An Intervention to Increase Children's Emotional Competence

If the abilities to read others' emotions and to regulate one's own emotional expression are both important skills, necessary for a child to form and maintain supportive social relationships, then training children in such emotional competence should reap benefits. This is the premise on which the PATHS (Promoting Alternative THinking Strategies) curriculum is based (Greenberg, 1997; Greenberg et al., 1995).

The PATHS curriculum is a set of 60 lessons specifically designed to teach elementary school children about emotions and how to read them. It also includes lessons teaching children that their own feelings provide helpful information and are okay to have. Children are taught to label their own feelings and learn techniques for controlling the expression of those feelings. For example, with the teachers' help, they are taught to use a "Control Signals Poster," which has a red light to signal "Stop—calm down," a yellow light for "Go slow—think," and a green light to signal "Go—try my plan." At the bottom is the instruction to "Evaluate—how did my plan work?"

Greenberg and his colleagues (1995) have found that children who have participated in this set of lessons do indeed learn more about how to understand, label, and read their own and others' emotions. Further, this group of researchers has taken the argument another step, focusing the PATHS curriculum intervention on a group of early elementary school children who are already showing strong signs of excessive aggression or conduct disorders (McMahon, 1997). In their "Fast Track Project," the researchers have identified nearly 900 such children, in 395 different classrooms in four cities in the United States. For half these children, a special intervention was designed to change the child and his environment at all possible levels, including using the PATHS curriculum in the child's classroom. Early results indicate that after three years, the intervention is having an effect. The children in the experimental group are better at recognizing their own emotions, more competent in their social relationships, and rated as less aggressive by their peers, and they are less likely to be placed in special education programs than are the equivalently aggressive children who have had no intervention (Coie, 1997b; Dodge, 1997).

The Fast Track program also includes an intervention with the parents of these aggressive children. The parents are given special help in learning better child-management skills and are encouraged to create better connections with their child's school. The early results indicate that this parental intervention, too, has had some effect: After two years the parents were using less physical punishment and were more appropriate and effective in their discipline. Because the Fast Track intervention has these several facets, we cannot attribute the reduction in aggression and the improvement in the children's social competence solely to the PATHS training in emotion knowledge; presumably the changes in the parents' behavior had some impact as well. Still, this project provides impressive support for the linkage between the child's emotion knowledge and his social competence. It also gives some reason for optimism about the possibility of altering the developmental trajectory of children with early signs of social incompetence, including excessive aggressiveness.

> An 11-month-old girl, on seeing a child fall and cry, looked as if she was about to cry herself, and then put her thumb in her mouth and buried her head in her mother's lap, which is what she would do if she herself were hurt. (1988, pp. 509–510)

This initial response changes as early as 12 or 18 months, as soon as the child has a clear understanding of the difference between self and other. The toddler still shows a matching emotion but understands that the distress is the other person's and not her own. Nonetheless, her solution to the other's distress is still likely to be egocentric, such as offering the distressed person a teddy bear (Eisenberg & Fabes, 1998).

Children's empathetic and sympathetic responses become more and more subtle over the preschool and elementary school years, as they become better readers of others' emotions. By middle childhood, many children can even empathize with several different emotions at once, as when they see another child make a mistake and fall during a game. The observing child may see and empathize with both the hurt and the sense of shame or embarrassment, and she may be aware that the victim may prefer *not* to be helped. In adolescence a still more abstract level emerges, when the child moves beyond the immediate situation and empathizes (or sympathizes) with another person's general plight.

Table 12.1

Stages in the Development of Empathy Proposed by Hoffman

- **Stage 1: Global empathy.** Observed during the first year. If the infant is around someone expressing a strong emotion, he may match that emotion—for example, by beginning to cry when he hears another infant crying.

- **Stage 2: Egocentric empathy.** Beginning at about 12 to 18 months, when children have a fairly clear sense of their separate selves, they respond to another's distress with some distress of their own, but they may attempt to "cure" the other person's problem by offering what they themselves would find most comforting. They may, for example, show sadness when they see another child hurt, and go to get their *own* mother to help.

- **Stage 3: Empathy for another's feelings.** Beginning as young as age 2 or 3 and continuing through elementary school, children note others' feelings, partially match those feelings, and respond to the other's distress in nonegocentric ways. Over these years, children distinguish a wider and wider (and more subtle) range of emotions.

- **Stage 4: Empathy for another's life condition.** In late childhood or adolescence, some children develop a more generalized notion of others' feelings and respond not just to the immediate situation but to the other individual's general situation or plight. So a young person at this level may become more distressed over another person's sadness if she knows that that sadness is chronic, or if she knows that the person's general situation is particularly tragic, than if she sees it as a more momentary problem.

Sources: Hoffman, 1982; 1988.

Notice that both developmental progressions I've been describing—reading others' emotions and empathizing with them—reflect several of the general principles I outlined earlier and parallel the changes Piaget described. In particular, we see a shift from observation to inference: With increasing age, the child's empathetic response is guided less and less by just the immediate, observed emotions seen in others, such as facial expressions or body language, and much more by the child's inferences or deductions about the other person's feelings. This is not a swift change. For example, research in England by Paul Harris and his associates (1981) shows that not until adolescence do young people become fully aware that other people may hide their emotions or act differently from the way they feel "inside."

As you might expect, not all children show equal amounts of such empathetic responses. Some biological disposition toward empathy appears to be part of the story,

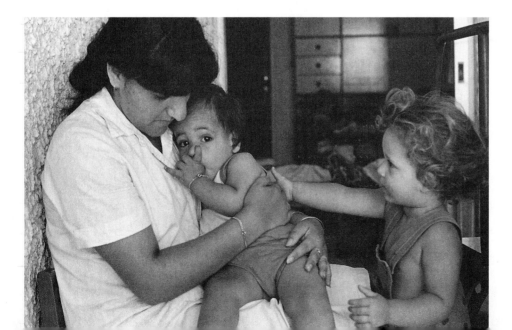

Children as young as age 2 or 3 show this kind of empathetic response to other people's distress or delight.

as evidenced by the greater similarity in levels of empathy among identical than fraternal twins (Zahn-Waxler et al., 1992b). On the environmental side, many of the same factors that contribute to greater altruistic behavior (described in the Real World box on p. 344) also appear to contribute to more empathetic responses in young children. For example, greater maternal warmth is linked to increased empathetic among toddlers (e.g., Strayer & Roberts, 1989). Like altruistic or kind behavior, empathy is also fostered by parental explanations about the consequences of the child's actions for others and by parental discussions of emotions (e.g., Miller et al., 1989). Finally, we have some preliminary evidence that children with histories of secure attachment show more empathy than do others (Kestenbaum et al., 1989).

Describing Other People

Critical Thinking

Before you read the rest of this section, write down a description of a friend or an acquaintance. Then as you read along, compare your description to the ones children give.

We can see the same kind of shift from observation to inference in studies of children's descriptions of others, as well as a clear change in focus from outer to internal characteristics. There seem to be at least three steps. Up to perhaps age 6 or 8, children's descriptions of others are focused almost exclusively on external features—what the person looks like, where he lives, what he does. This description by a 7-year-old boy, taken from a study in England by Livesley and Bromley, is typical:

> He is very tall. He has dark brown hair, he goes to our school. I don't think he has any brothers or sisters. He is in our class. Today he has a dark orange [sweater] and gray trousers and brown shoes. (1973, p. 213)

When young children do use internal or evaluative terms to describe people, they are likely to use quite global terms, such as *nice* or *mean* or *good* or *bad*. Further, young children do not seem to see these qualities as lasting or general traits of the individual, applicable in all situations or over time (Rholes & Ruble, 1984). In other words, the young child has not yet developed a concept we might think of as "conservation of personality."

Then, beginning at about age 7 or 8, at just about the same time as children seem to develop a global sense of self-esteem, a rather dramatic shift occurs in children's descriptions of others. The child begins to focus more on the inner traits or qualities of another person and to assume that those traits will be apparent in many situations (Gnepp & Chilamkurti, 1988). Children this age still describe others' physical features, but now those descriptions are more by way of examples or elaborations of more general points about internal qualities. You can see the change when you compare the 7-year-old's description with this (widely quoted) description by a nearly-10-year-old:

> He smells very much and is very nasty. He has no sense of humour and is very dull. He is always fighting and he is cruel. He does silly things and is very stupid. He has brown hair and cruel eyes. He is sulky and 11 years old and has lots of sisters. I think he is the most horrible boy in the class. He has a croaky voice and always chews his pencil and picks his teeth and I think he is disgusting. (Livesley & Bromley, 1973, p. 217)

This description still includes many external, physical features, but it goes beyond such concrete, surface qualities to the level of personality traits, such as lack of humor or cruelty.

In adolescence, young people's descriptions begin to include more comparisons of one trait with another or one person with another, more recognition of inconsistencies and exceptions, more shadings of gray (Shantz, 1983), as in this description by a 15-year-old:

> Andy is very modest. He is even shyer than I am when near strangers and yet is very talkative with people he knows and likes. He always seems good tempered and I have never seen him in a bad temper. He tends to degrade other people's

achievements, and yet never praises his own. He does not seem to voice his opinions to anyone. He easily gets nervous. (Livesley & Bromley, 1973, p. 221)

I can illustrate these changes less anecdotally with some findings from two early studies by Carl Barenboim (1977; 1981). He asked children ranging in age from 6 to 16 to describe three people. Any descriptions that involved comparing a child's behaviors or physical features with another child, or with a norm, he called *behavioral comparisons* (such as "Billy runs a lot faster than Jason" or "She draws the best in our whole class"). Statements that involved some internal personality construct he called *psychological constructs* (such as "Sarah is so kind" or "He's a real stubborn idiot!"), while any that included qualifiers, explanations, exceptions, or mentions of changes in character he called *organizing relationships* (e.g., "He's only shy around people he doesn't know" or "Usually she's nice to me, but sometimes she can be quite mean"). Figure 12.1 shows the combined findings from the two studies. You can see that behavioral comparisons peaked at around age 8 or 9, psychological constructs peaked at about age 14, and organizing relationships did not appear at all until age 10 and were still increasing at age 16.

I am sure that many of you have noticed the strong resemblance between this series of changes and the development of children's self-descriptions I outlined in Chapter 10 (Figure 10.2, p. 294). This parallel illustrates Flavell's basic point, that it is the same head doing the thinking about self and about others.

Describing Friendships

When we look at children's ideas about relationships, very much the same pattern holds, no matter what type of relationship we study—the relationship with parents,

Figure 12.1

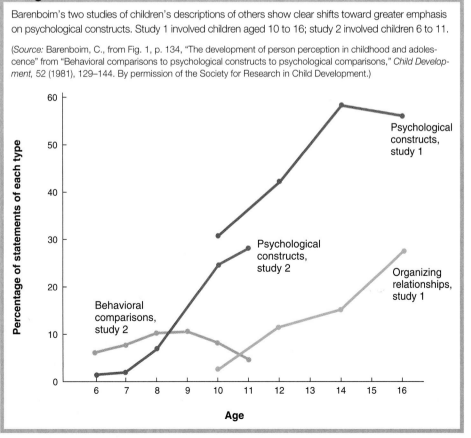

Barenboim's two studies of children's descriptions of others show clear shifts toward greater emphasis on psychological constructs. Study 1 involved children aged 10 to 16; study 2 involved children 6 to 11.

(*Source:* Barenboim, C., from Fig. 1, p. 134, "The development of person perception in childhood and adolescence" from "Behavioral comparisons to psychological constructs to psychological comparisons," *Child Development*, 52 (1981), 129–144. By permission of the Society for Research in Child Development.)

with other authority figures, with groups, or with friends. Let me use descriptions of friendships as an illustration.

In Chapter 11 I described the developmental changes in the actual relationships children have with their friends—what friends do together, how enduring and intimate their relationships are. Here I want to talk about how the child *understands* the nature of friendship itself.

Preschool children seem to understand friendships mostly in terms of common activities. If you ask a young child how people make friends, the answer is usually that they "play together" or spend time physically near each other (Damon, 1977; 1983; Hartup & Stevens, 1997; Selman, 1980). Children this age think of friendship as something that involves sharing toys or giving things to one another.

Robert Selman's research and extensive studies by Thomas Berndt (1983; 1986) show that in elementary school this early view of friendship gives way to one in which the key concept seems to be *reciprocal trust*. Friends are now seen as special people with desired qualities other than mere proximity, as people who are generous with one another, who help and trust one another. Children this age also understand friendship to have a temporal dimension: Friends are people with whom one has a history of connection and interaction, rather than someone one has just met or played with once.

By about age 11 or 12, children begin to talk about *intimacy* as an important ingredient in friendship; by middle adolescence, they expect a friend to be a confidant and to be supportive and trustworthy (Hartup & Stevens, 1997). Understanding of friendship also becomes more qualified, more shaded. Damon's research suggests that in late adolescence, young people understand that even very close friendships cannot fill every need and that friendships are not static: They change, grow, or dissolve as each member of the pair changes. A really good friendship, then, is one that *adapts* to these changes. At this age, young people say things about friendship like "Trust is the ability to let go as well as to hang on" (Selman, 1980, p. 141).

Let me again make these generalizations concrete with some actual research findings, this time from an early cross-sectional study by Brian Bigelow and John La Gaipa (1975). They asked several hundred children in Canada to write an essay about how their expectations of best friends differed from their expectations of other acquaintances. The answers were scored along many dimensions, three of which I have shown in Figure 12.2. You can see that references to *demographic similarity* (e.g., "We live in the same neighborhood") were highest among fourth graders, while mentions of loyalty and commitment were highest among seventh graders. References to intimacy potential (e.g., "I can tell her things about myself I can't tell anyone else") did not appear at all until seventh grade and then increased further in eighth grade.

Taking together all of what I have told you so far, you can see that the patterns of developmental change in children's understanding of themselves, of others, and of relationships are strikingly similar, shifting in all the ways I listed at the beginning of the chapter: from outer to inner characteristics, from observation to inference, from definite to qualified, from an egocentric to a general view.

Making Moral Judgments

A somewhat different facet of the child's emerging social cognition is her understanding of social and moral rules. Beginning some time in the elementary school years, children understand the important distinction between what Elliot Turiel (1983) calls **conventional rules** and **moral rules.** Conventional rules are arbitrary, created by a particular group or culture. School rules about uniforms, not running in the hall, and asking permission before you leave the room are all conventional rules, as are cultural rules about appropriate dress for boys and girls. By age 7 or 8, children begin to grasp the fact that such rules are arbitrary and may vary from one group to another, from one family to another. They should be followed when in the specified group or situation but need not be followed at other times.

Critical Thinking

How would you define a friend or friendship? What do you expect from a friend that you do not expect from an acquaintance? What do you *give* to a friend that you would not give to an acquaintance? Think about these questions for a minute.

Figure 12.2

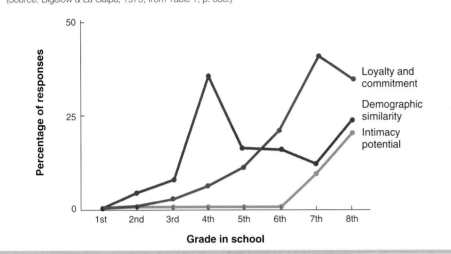

Some of the changes in children's ideas about friendship are clear from these findings from Bigelow and La Gaipa's study.

(*Source:* Bigelow & La Gaipa, 1975, from Table 1, p. 858.)

Moral rules, in contrast, are seen as universal and obligatory, reflecting basic principles that guarantee the rights of others. Not running in the hall is a conventional rule; not hitting other people is a moral rule.

Children judge the breaking of moral rules as far more serious than the breaking of conventional rules (Nucci & Nucci, 1982). The latter kind of wrongdoing is seen as impolite or disruptive but is not typically condemned. Children's judgments of moral transgressions, however, are harsher. Such moral judgments also go through distinct developmental stages as children grapple with the problem of explaining—to themselves and to others—why certain behaviors are morally right or wrong.

Kohlberg's Stages of Moral Development

Piaget (1932) was the first to offer a description of the development of moral reasoning, but Lawrence Kohlberg's work has had the most powerful impact (Colby et al., 1983; Kohlberg, 1964; 1976; 1980; 1981). Building on and revising Piaget's ideas, Kohlberg pioneered the practice of assessing moral reasoning by presenting a subject with a series of hypothetical dilemmas in story form, each of which highlighted a specific moral issue, such as the value of human life. One of the most famous is the dilemma of Heinz:

> In Europe, a woman was near death from a special kind of cancer. There was one drug that the doctors thought might save her. It was a form of radium that a druggist in the same town had recently discovered. The drug was expensive to make, but the druggist was charging ten times what the drug cost him to make. He paid $200 for the radium and charged $2000 for a small dose of the drug. The sick woman's husband, Heinz, went to everyone he knew to borrow the money, but he could only get together about $1000 which is half of what it cost. He told the druggist that his wife was dying, and asked him to sell it cheaper or let him pay later. But the druggist said, "No, I discovered the drug and I'm going to make money from it." So Heinz got desperate and broke into the man's store to steal the drug for his wife. (Kohlberg & Elfenbein, 1975, p. 621)

After hearing this story, the child or young person is asked a series of questions, such as whether Heinz should have stolen the drug. What if Heinz didn't love his wife? Would that change anything? What if the person dying was a stranger? Should Heinz steal the drug anyway?

Table 12.2

Kohlberg's Stages of Moral Development

LEVEL I: Preconventional Morality

- **Stage I: Punishment and obedience orientation.** The child decides what is wrong on the basis of what is punished. Obedience is valued for its own sake, but the child obeys because the adults have superior power.

- **Stage 2: Individualism, instrumental purpose, and exchange.** The child follows rules when it is in his immediate interest. What is good is what brings pleasant results.

LEVEL II: Conventional Morality

- **Stage 3: Mutual interpersonal expectations, relationships, and interpersonal conformity.** Moral actions are those that live up to the expectations of the family or other significant group. "Being good" becomes important for its own sake.

- **Stage 4: Social system and conscience.** Moral actions are those so defined by larger social groups or the society as a whole. One should fulfill duties one has agreed to and uphold laws except in extreme cases.

LEVEL III: Principled or Postconventional Morality

- **Stage 5: Social contract or utility and individual rights.** Acting so as to achieve the "greatest good for the greatest number." The teenager or adult is aware that most values are relative and laws are changeable, although rules should be upheld in order to preserve the social order. Still, there are some basic nonrelative values, such as the importance of each person's life and liberty.

- **Stage 6: Universal ethical principles.** The adult develops and follows self-chosen ethical principles in determining what is right. These ethical principles are part of an articulated, integrated, carefully thought-out, and consistently followed system of values and principles.

Sources: After Kohlberg, 1976, and Lickona, 1978.

On the basis of answers to dilemmas like this one, Kohlberg concluded that there were three main levels of moral reasoning, with two stages within each level, summarized briefly in Table 12.2.

At Level I, **preconventional morality,** the child's judgments of right and wrong are based on sources of authority who are close by and physically superior to himself—usually the parents. Just as his descriptions of others at this same stage are largely external, so the standards the child uses to judge rightness or wrongness are external rather than internal. In particular, it is the outcome or consequences of his actions that determine the rightness or wrongness of those actions.

In stage 1 of this level—the *punishment and obedience* orientation—the child relies on the physical consequences of some action to decide whether it is right or wrong. If he is punished, the behavior was wrong; if he is not punished, it was right. He is obedient to adults because they are bigger and stronger.

In stage 2—*individualism, instrumental purpose, and exchange*—the child begins to do things that are rewarded and to avoid things that are punished. (For this reason, the stage is sometimes called a position of "naive hedonism.") If something feels good or brings pleasant results, it is good. Some beginning of concern for other people is apparent during this phase, but only if that concern can be expressed as something that benefits the child himself as well. So he can enter into agreements like "If you help me, I'll help you."

As illustration, here are some responses to variations of the Heinz dilemma, drawn from studies of children and teenagers in a number of different cultures, all of which would be rated as stage 2:

He should steal the food for his wife because if she dies he'll have to pay for the funeral, and that costs a lot. (Taiwan)

He should steal the drug because "he should protect the life of his wife so he doesn't have to stay alone in life." (Puerto Rico)

Suppose it wasn't his wife who was starving but his best friend. Should he steal the food for his friend?

Yes, because one day when he is hungry his friend would help. (Turkey) (Snarey, 1985, p. 221)

At the next major level, **conventional morality,** the young person shifts from judgments based on external consequences and personal gain to judgments based on rules or norms of a group to which the individual belongs, whether that group is the family, the peer group, a church, or the nation. What the chosen reference group defines as right or good *is* right or good in the child's view, and the child internalizes these norms to a considerable extent.

Stage 3 (the first stage of Level II) is the stage of *mutual interpersonal expectations, relationships, and interpersonal conformity* (sometimes also called the *good boy/nice girl* stage). Children at this stage believe that good behavior is what pleases other people. They value trust, loyalty, respect, gratitude, and maintenance of mutual relationships. Andy, a boy Kohlberg interviewed who was at stage 3, said:

I try to do things for my parents, they've always done things for you. I try to do everything my mother says, I try to please her. Like she wants me to be a doctor and I want to, too, and she's helping me get up there. (Kohlberg, 1964, p. 401)

Another mark of stage 3 is that the child begins to make judgments based on intentions as well as on outward behavior. If someone "means well" or "didn't mean to do it," their wrongdoing is seen as less serious than if they did it "on purpose."

Stage 4, the second stage of the conventional level, shows the child turning to larger social groups for her norms. Kohlberg labeled this the stage of *social system and conscience*. People reasoning at this stage focus on doing their duty, respecting authority, following rules and laws. The emphasis is less on what is pleasing to particular people (as in stage 3) and more on adhering to a complex set of regulations. The regulations themselves are not questioned.

The transition to Level 3, **principled morality** (also called **postconventional morality**), is marked by several changes, the most important of which is a shift in the source of authority. At Level 1, children see authority as totally outside themselves; at Level 2, the judgments or rules of external authority are internalized, but they are not questioned or analyzed; at Level 3, a new kind of personal authority emerges in which individual choices are made, with individual judgments based on self-chosen principles.

By this age, the majority of teenagers—like this group of Venezuelan adolescents—are using stage 3 moral reasoning: What is good is what family or peers define as good and right. Do you think that the level of moral reasoning a teenager shows has any connection to his or her conformity to peers at this same age?

In stage 5 at this level—called the *social contract orientation* by Kohlberg—we see the beginning of such self-chosen principles. Rules, laws, and regulations are still seen as important because they ensure fairness, and they are seen as logically necessary for society to function. However, people operating at this level also see times when the rules, laws, and regulations need to be ignored or changed. Our U.S. system of government is based on moral reasoning of this kind, since we have provisions for changing laws and for allowing personal protests against a given law, such as during the civil rights protests of the 1960s, the Vietnam War protests of the 1960s and 1970s, or the protests against apartheid in the 1980s.

Stage 6, the second stage in Level III reasoning, is simply a further extension of this same pattern, with the individual searching for and then living in a way that is consistent with the deepest set of moral principles possible. Kohlberg referred to this as the *universal ethical principles orientation*. People who reason in this way assume personal responsibility for their own actions on the basis of fundamental and universal principles, such as justice and basic respect for persons (Kohlberg, 1978; Kohlberg et al., 1990). In their case studies of modern adults who reason and act at this level, Ann Colby and William Damon (1992) note that another quality such people share is "open receptivity"—a willingness to examine their ideas and convictions, even while they act firmly and generously in support of their ideals. Such people are not common. Two famous examples are Gandhi and Mother Teresa, both of whom devoted their lives to humanitarian causes.

In all this, it is *very* important to understand that what defines the stage or level of a person's moral judgment is not the specific moral choice but the *form of reasoning* used to justify that choice. For example, either the choice that Heinz should steal the drug or that he should not could be justified with logic at any given stage. I've already given you some examples of a stage 2 justification for Heinz's stealing the drug; here's a stage 5 justification of the same choice, drawn from a study in India:

What if Heinz was stealing to save the life of his pet animal instead of his wife?

If Heinz saves an animal's life his action will be commendable. The right use of the drug is to administer it to the needy. There is some difference, of course—human life is more evolved and hence of greater importance in the scheme of nature—but an animal's life is not altogether bereft of importance. . . . (Snarey, 1985, p. 223, drawn originally from Vasudev, 1983, p. 7)

If you compare this answer to the ones I quoted before, you can clearly see the difference in the form of reasoning used, even though the action being justified is precisely the same.

Kohlberg argued that this sequence of reasoning is both universal and hierarchically organized, just as Piaget thought his proposed stages of cognitive development were universal and hierarchical. That is, each stage follows and grows from the preceding one and has some internal consistency. Individuals should not move "down" the sequence but only "upward" along the stages, if they move at all. Kohlberg did *not* suggest that all individuals eventually progress through all six stages or even that each stage is tied to specific ages, but he insisted that the order is invariant and universal. Let me take a critical look at these claims.

Age and Moral Reasoning. Kohlberg's own findings, confirmed by many other researchers (e.g., Walker et al., 1987), show that preconventional reasoning (stages 1 and 2) is dominant in elementary school, with stage 2 reasoning still evident among many early adolescents. Conventional reasoning (stages 3 and 4) emerges as important in middle adolescence and remains the most common form of moral reasoning in adulthood. Postconventional reasoning (stages 5 and 6) is relatively rare, even in adulthood. For example, in one study of men in their forties and fifties, only 13 percent were rated as using stage 5 moral reasoning (Gibson, 1990).

Let me give you two research examples illustrating these overall age trends. The first, shown in Figure 12.3, comes from Kohlberg's own longitudinal study of 58 boys,

Critical Thinking

Imagine a society in which everyone handled moral issues at Kohlberg's stage 3. Now think about one in which everyone operated at stage 5. How would these two societies be likely to differ?

Kohlberg thought that there were at least a few people, perhaps like Mother Teresa, whose moral reasoning was based on universal ethical principles.

Figure 12.3

These findings are from Colby and Kohlberg's long-term longitudinal study of a group of boys who were asked about Kohlberg's moral dilemmas every few years from age 10 through early adulthood. Note that postconventional or principled reasoning was quite uncommon, even in adulthood.

(*Source:* Colby, et al., from Fig. 1, p. 46, "Longitudinal study of moral judgment," *Monographs of the society for research in child development,* 48 (1–2, Serial No. 200) (1983). By permission of the Society for Research in Child Development.)

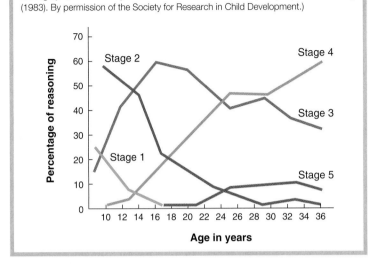

first interviewed when they were 10, and followed for more than twenty years (Colby et al., 1983). Table 12.3 shows cross-sectional data from a study by Lawrence Walker and his colleagues (1987). They studied 10 boys and 10 girls at each of four ages, interviewing the parents of each child as well. Note that Walker scored each response on a 9-point scale rather than just scoring the five main stages. This system, which has become quite common, allows for the fact that many people's reasoning falls between two specific stages.

The results of these two studies, although not identical, point to remarkably similar conclusions about the order of emergence of the various stages and about the approximate ages at which they predominate. In both studies, stage 2 reasoning dominates at age 10, and stage 3 reasoning is most common at about age 16.

Table 12.3

Percentage of Children and Parents Who Show Moral Reasoning at Each of Kohlberg's Stages

Age	Stage								
	1	**1–2**	**2**	**2–3**	**3**	**3–4**	**4**	**4–5**	**5**
6 (grade 1)	10	70	15	5	–	–	–	–	–
9 (grade 4)	–	25	40	35	–	–	–	–	–
12 (grade 7)	–	–	15	60	25	–	–	–	–
15 (grade 10)	–	–	–	40	55	5	–	–	–
Parents	–	–	–	1	15	70	11	3	–

Source: Walker et al., from Table 1, p. 849, "Moral Stages and moral orientations in real-life and hypothetical dilemmas," *Child development,* 60 (1987), 157–160. By permission of the Society for Research in Child Development.

Sequence of Stages. The evidence also seems fairly strong that the stages follow one another in the sequence Kohlberg proposed. For example, in three long-term longitudinal studies of teenagers and young adults, one in the United States (Colby et al., 1983), one in Israel (Snarey et al., 1985), and one in Turkey (Nisan & Kohlberg, 1982), the changes in subjects' reasoning nearly always occurred in the hypothesized order. Subjects did not skip stages, and only about 5 to 7 percent of the time was there any indication of regression (movement down the sequence rather than up). Similarly, when Walker (1989) retested the subjects in his study two years later, he found that only 6 percent had moved down, mostly only half a stage, while 22 percent had moved up and none had skipped a stage. Such a rate of regression is about what you would expect to find, given the fact that the measurements of stage reasoning are not perfect. On the whole, I agree with James Rest (1983) that the evidence is "fairly compelling" that moral judgment changes over time in the sequence Kohlberg describes.

Universality. Might this sequence of stages be only a phenomenon of Western culture, or has Kohlberg uncovered a genuinely universal process? Thus far, variations of Kohlberg's dilemmas have been presented to children or adults in at least 27 different countries or subcultures, both Western and non-Western, industrialized and nonindustrialized (Snarey, 1985).

John Snarey, who has reviewed and analyzed these many studies, notes several things in support of Kohlberg's position: (1) In studies of children, an increase in stage of reasoning with age is found consistently; (2) the few longitudinal studies report "strikingly similar findings" (1985, p. 215), with subjects moving upward in the stage sequence with few reversals; and (3) cultures differ in the highest level of reasoning observed. In complex urban societies (both Western and non-Western), stage 5 is typically the highest stage observed, while in those cultures Snarey calls "folk" societies, stage 4 is typically the highest. Collectively, this evidence seems to provide quite strong support for the universality of Kohlberg's stage sequence.

Moral Development: A Critique. Kohlberg's theory has been one of the most provocative theories in all of developmental psychology. Over 1000 studies have explored or tested aspects of the theory, and several competing theories have been proposed. The remarkable thing is how well Kohlberg's ideas have stood up to this barrage of research and commentary. There does appear to be a clear set of stages in the development of moral reasoning, and these stages seem to be universal.

Still, the theory has not emerged unscathed. Some psychologists are less impressed than Snarey with the data on universality (Shweder et al., 1987). Also troubling is the fact that so few teenagers or adults seem to reason at the postconventional level (stages 5 and 6). Shweder points out that the effective range of variation is really only from stage 2 to stage 4, which is not nearly so interesting or impressive as is the full range of stages.

Even more vocal critics have been those who argue that Kohlberg is really not talking about all aspects of "moral reasoning." Instead, as Kohlberg himself acknowledged in his later writings (Kohlberg et al.,1983), he is talking about the development of reasoning about *justice and fairness*. We might also ask about moral reasoning about doing good or reasoning based on some ethic other than justice, such as an ethic based on concern for others or for relationships. Let me take a quick look at two such alternative views.

Eisenberg's Model of Prosocial Reasoning

Most of the moral dilemmas Kohlberg posed for his subjects deal with wrongdoing—with stealing, punishment, disobeying laws. Few tell us anything about the kind of reasoning children use in justifying *prosocial behavior*. I mentioned in Chapter 11 that altruistic behavior is visible in children as young as 2 and 3; but how do children explain and justify such behavior?

Nancy Eisenberg and her colleagues (Eisenberg, 1986; Eisenberg et al., 1987; 1995a) have explored such questions by proposing dilemmas to children in which self-interest is set against the possibility of helping some other person. One story for younger children, for example, involves a child walking to a friend's birthday party. On the way, he comes upon another child who has fallen and hurt himself. If the party-bound child stops to help, he will probably miss the cake and ice cream. What should he do?

In response to dilemmas like this, preschool children most often use what Eisenberg calls **hedonistic reasoning,** in which the child is concerned with self-oriented consequences rather than moral considerations. Children this age say things like "I'd help because he'd help me the next time" or "I wouldn't help because I'd miss the party." This approach gradually shifts to one Eisenberg calls **needs-oriented reasoning,** in which the child expresses concern rather directly for the other person's need, even if the other's need conflicts with the child's own wishes or desires. Children operating on this basis say things like "He'd feel better if I helped." At this stage, children do not express their choices in terms of general principles or indicate any reflectiveness about generalized values; they simply respond to the other's needs.

Still later, typically in adolescence, children say they will do good things because it is expected of them, a pattern highly similar to Kohlberg's stage 3 reasoning. Finally, in late adolescence, some young people give evidence that they have developed clear, internalized values that guide their prosocial behavior: "I'd feel a responsibility to help because of my values" or "If everyone helped, society would be a lot better."

Some sample data from Eisenberg's longitudinal study of a small group of U.S. children, in Figure 12.4, illustrate the shift from hedonistic to needs-oriented reasoning. By early adolescence, hedonistic reasoning has virtually disappeared, while needs-oriented reasoning has become the dominant form. Eisenberg reports that similar patterns have been found among children in West Germany, Poland, and Italy, but that kibbutz-reared Israeli elementary school children show little needs-oriented reasoning (Eisenberg, 1986). Instead, this particular group of Israeli children is more likely to reason on the basis of internalized values and norms and the humanness of recipients, a pattern consistent with the strong emphasis on egalitarianism and communal values in the kibbutzim. These findings point to perhaps a larger role of culture in children's prosocial reasoning than in reasoning about justice, although that is still a highly tentative conclusion.

Figure 12.4

Every two years Eisenberg asked the same group of children what a person should do when confronted with each of a series of dilemmas about doing good, such as helping someone who is hurt. She then analyzed their form of reasoning, using a measure for which the minimum score is 4 and the maximum is 16.

(*Source:* Eisenberg et al., "Pro-social development in late adolescence," *Child development,* 66, 1995, pp. 1179–1197.)

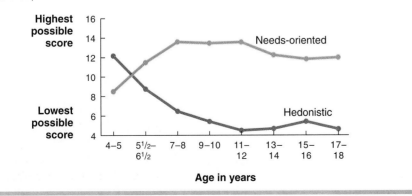

There are obviously strong parallels between the sequences of changes in prosocial reasoning Eisenberg has described and Kohlberg's levels and stages of moral reasoning. Children seem to move from a self-centered orientation ("What feels good to me is right") to a stance in which social approval guides reasoning about both justice and doing good ("What is right is what other people define as right; I should do good things because others will approve of me if I do"). Much later, some young people seem to develop internalized, individualized norms to guide both kinds of reasoning.

Despite these obvious parallels, though, researchers have typically found only moderate correlations between children's reasoning about prosocial dilemmas such as Eisenberg's and their reasoning about Kohlberg's justice or fairness dilemmas. The sequences of steps may be similar, but as was true of so many of the developments I talked about in Chapter 6, children's reasoning in one arena doesn't necessarily generalize to a related area.

Eisenberg's research, as well as the work of others in the same vein, helps to broaden Kohlberg's original conception, without changing the fundamental arguments. In contrast, Carol Gilligan has questioned some of the basic tenets of Kohlberg's model.

Gilligan's Ethic of Caring

Carol Gilligan (1982; Gilligan & Wiggins, 1987) is fundamentally dissatisfied with Kohlberg's focus on justice and fairness as the defining features of moral reasoning. Gilligan argues that there are at least two distinct "moral orientations": justice and care. Each has its own central injunction: not to treat others unfairly (justice), and not to turn away from someone in need (caring). Boys and girls learn both of these injunctions, but Gilligan has hypothesized that girls are more likely to operate from an orientation of caring or connection, while boys are more likely to operate from an orientation of justice or fairness. Because of these differences, she argues, they tend to perceive moral dilemmas quite differently.

Given the emerging evidence on sex differences in styles of interaction and in friendship patterns, which I talked about in Chapter 11, Gilligan's hypothesis makes some sense. Perhaps girls, focused more on intimacy in their relationships, judge moral dilemmas by different criteria. In fact, however, research on moral dilemmas has not shown that boys are more likely to use justice reasoning or that girls more often use care reasoning. Several studies of adults have shown such a pattern (e.g., Lollis et al., 1996; Lyons, 1983), but studies of children, adolescents, or college students generally have not (Jadack et al., 1995; Smetana et al., 1991; Walker, 1991). What matters far more than gender in determining whether a given child or adult will use a care or a justice orientation in addressing a moral dilemma is the nature of the dilemma itself. Dilemmas relating to interpersonal relationships, for example, are more likely to be dealt with using a care orientation, whereas dilemmas directly addressing issues of fairness are more likely to be addressed with a justice orientation. It may be that adult women are more likely to *interpret* moral dilemmas as personal rather than impersonal, but both men and women use both care and justice arguments in resolving moral dilemmas (Turiel, 1998).

Gilligan argues that these young women are much more likely to be using an "ethic of caring" than an "ethic of justice" as a basis for their moral judgments, while the reverse is true among boys and men. Such a difference *may* exist among adults, but research on children and adolescents shows no such pattern.

For example, Lawrence Walker scored children's answers to moral dilemmas using both Kohlberg's fairness scheme and Gilligan's criteria for a care orientation. He found no sex difference either for hypothetical dilemmas like the Heinz dilemma or for real-life dilemmas suggested by the children themselves (Walker et al., 1987). Only among adults did Walker find a difference, in the direction that Gilligan would expect.

Gilligan's arguments have often been quoted in the popular press as if they were already proven, when in fact the empirical base is really quite weak. Gilligan herself has done no systematic studies of children's (or adults') care reasoning. Yet despite these weaknesses, I am not ready to discard all of her underlying points, primarily because the questions she is asking seem to me to fit so well with the newer research on sex differences in styles of relationship. The fact that we typically find no differences between boys and girls in their tendencies to use care versus justice orientations does not mean that there are no differences in the assumptions males and females bring to relationships or to moral judgments. This seems to me to be clearly an area in which we need to learn a great deal more.

Social Cognition and Behavior

In Chapter 11 I talked about children's social behavior; in this chapter I have been talking about children's thinking about relationships. What is the connection between the two? Can we predict a child's behavior, such as his moral choices, his generous behavior, or the quality of his relationships, from knowing the stage or level of his social cognition? Yes and no. Knowing the form or level of a child's reasoning cannot tell us *precisely* what he will do in a real-life social situation, but there are nevertheless some important links between thinking and behavior.

Empathetic Understanding, Prosocial Reasoning, and Behavior. One possible link is the one between empathy and prosocial behavior. The findings are not completely consistent, but Eisenberg's research generally shows that more empathetic or other-oriented children are somewhat more likely to share or help others in real situations and less likely to show socially disruptive or highly aggressive behavior (Eisenberg & Mussen, 1989). For example, George Bear and Gail Rys (1994) gave four of Eisenberg's dilemmas to a group of second- and third-grade students drawn from 17 different classrooms. The teacher in each classroom also rated each child's level of disruptive and aggressive behavior (collectively referred to as "acting out") as well as each child's positive social skills, including being friendly toward peers, having friends, being able to cope with failure, being comfortable as a leader, and so on. Bear and Rys found that children who used predominantly hedonistic reasoning were rated by their teachers as lower in social competence than children who used mostly needs-oriented (empathetic) or higher levels of social reasoning. Teachers also described the hedonistic boys, but not the hedonistic girls, as more likely to act out, a pattern you can see in Figure 12.5 (p. 370). The hedonistic boys also had fewer friends and were more likely to be rejected by their peers. Bear and Rys argue that higher levels of prosocial moral reasoning help to curtail a child's acting-out behavior, keeping it at a socially acceptable level, thus helping to prevent peer rejection.

Similarly, Eisenberg has found that certain types of prosocial reasoning are correlated with a child's altruistic behavior. For instance, in a group of 10-year-olds, she found that hedonistic reasoning was negatively correlated with a measure of the children's willingness to donate to UNICEF the nickels they earned for participating in the study (Eisenberg et al., 1987). In another study, among a group of 4- and 5-year-olds, those who both were high in empathetic responses to others' distress and used some other-oriented prosocial reasoning (needs-oriented reasoning) were especially likely to spend time helping a needy peer (Miller et al., 1996).

Friendship Understanding and Friendship Behavior. Equivalent links appear in studies of reasoning about friendships. As a general rule, children with more mature reasoning

Critical Thinking

Suppose Gilligan is right, and adult women typically reason with an ethic of care while men reason with an ethic of justice. What do you think would be the implications of such a difference—for male-female relationships, for men and women as political leaders, or in other ways?

Figure 12.5

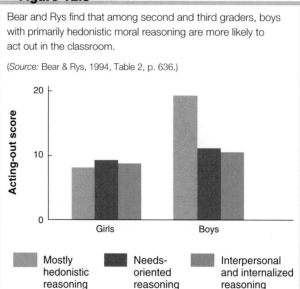

Bear and Rys find that among second and third graders, boys with primarily hedonistic moral reasoning are more likely to act out in the classroom.

(*Source:* Bear & Rys, 1994, Table 2, p. 636.)

about friendships are less likely to be aggressive with their peers and more likely to show sharing or other helpful behavior toward their friends in actual interactions.

In one study, Lawrence Kurdek and Donna Krile (1982) found that among children in third through eighth grade, those with higher scores on a measure of understanding of individuals and friendships were more likely to be involved in mutual friendships than were children with lower scores. Similarly, Selman (1980) compared children's scores on a measure of social reasoning with teachers' ratings of the children's social strengths and weaknesses. He found that children with more mature reasoning were more likely to be described by their teachers as showing higher levels of helpful or other prosocial behaviors.

An intriguing exception to this pattern, however, is the finding I reported in Chapter 11, that in friendships between boys, competition, and not sharing or helpfulness, is often the dominant pattern. Furthermore, Berndt (1983) finds that among boys, the level of competition or cooperation is unrelated to their level of social cognitive reasoning about either friendship or the justification for helpfulness. Thus, while we usually find a correlation between the maturity of a child's social reasoning and his friend-making skills, more mature reasoning does not invariably increase the level of helpfulness or cooperation in actual friendship pairs among males. Once again, then, we have evidence that the "relationship rules" are different for boys than for girls, a pattern that I think is both fascinating and important.

Moral Judgment and Behavior. Kohlberg's theory has sometimes been criticized on the grounds that children's or adults' moral behavior does not always match their reasoning. In fact, Kohlberg never said that there should be a one-to-one correspondence

Why do you think it is that among boys, competition is such a strong feature of friendship interactions, no matter what level of reasoning the boys may otherwise have about relationships or morality?

between the two. Reasoning at stage 4 (conventional reasoning) does not mean that you will never cheat or that you will always be kind to your mother. Still, the form of reasoning a young person typically applies to moral problems should have at least *some* connection with real-life choices or behavior.

One such connection proposed by Kohlberg is that the higher the level of reasoning a young person shows, the stronger the link to behavior ought to become. Thus, young people reasoning at stage 4 or stage 5 should be more likely to follow their own rules or reasoning than should children reasoning at lower levels.

For example, Kohlberg and Candee (1984) studied students involved in the early "free speech" movement at Berkeley in the late 1960s (a precursor to the Vietnam War protests). They interviewed and tested the moral judgment levels of a group that had participated at a sit-in in the university administration building, plus a group randomly chosen from the campus population. Among students who thought it was morally right to sit in, nearly three-quarters of those reasoning at stage 4 or 5 actually did sit in, compared to only about one-quarter of those reasoning at stage 3. Thus, the higher the stage of reasoning, the more consistent the behavior was with the reasoning.

In other research, Kohlberg and others approached the question simply by asking whether a link exists between the stage of moral reasoning and the probability of making some "moral choice," such as not cheating. In one early study, Kohlberg (1975) found that only 15 percent of college students reasoning at the principled level (stage 5) cheated when they were given an opportunity, while 55 percent of conventional-level and 70 percent of preconventional students cheated.

A similar argument lies behind studies in which the moral reasoning of highly aggressive or delinquent youngsters is compared to that of nondelinquent peers. The repeated finding is that delinquents (male or female) have lower levels of moral reasoning than do nondelinquents, even when the two groups are carefully matched for levels of education, social class, and IQ (Smetana, 1990). In one study of this type, Virginia Gregg and her colleagues (1994) found that only 20 percent of a group of incarcerated male and female delinquents were reasoning at stage 3 or higher, while 59 percent of a carefully matched comparison group of nondelinquents were reasoning at this level. Like younger children who act out more in school, delinquents are most likely to use highly hedonistic reasoning, scored at Kohlberg's stage 2 (Richards et al., 1992).

Yet despite this abundance of evidence for a link between moral reasoning and behavior, no one has found the correspondence to be perfect. After all, in Kohlberg's studies, 15 percent of the principled moral reasoners did cheat, and a quarter of stage 4 and stage 5 reasoners who thought it morally right to participate in a sit-in did not do so. As Kohlberg says, "One can reason in terms of principles and not live up to those principles" (1975, p. 672).

What else besides level of reasoning might matter? James Rest suggests three other elements (1983; Rest & Narvaez, 1991). *Moral sensitivity* is the awareness that some moral problem is involved in a given situation. Unless a person sees such a moral problem in some particular setting, there is no reason for moral reasoning to affect the person's behavior. The tendency to perceive such moral dilemmas is affected by both empathy and role-taking skill.

A second element, *moral motivation,* is the process by which the individual weighs competing values and needs. For example, in any given situation, even though you might think it morally right to take some action, you may not see that action as morally necessary or obligatory. Or the cost may be too high. If helping someone else has little cost in time, money, or effort, then most children and adults will help, regardless of their overall level of social cognitive reasoning. It is when there is some cost—such as was the case for the children in Eisenberg's study who were asked if they wanted to donate some of the nickels they earned to help other children—that we find a more consistent correlation between level of reasoning and behavior. This suggests the more general principle that moral reasoning becomes a factor in moral behavior only when

Critical Thinking

Do you think that a person's stage or level of moral reasoning has any impact on political behavior, such as whether or not a person votes or has liberal or conservative party preferences? Can you generate a hypothesis about such a link and figure out how you might test it?

something about the situation heightens the sense of moral conflict, such as when a cost is involved or when the individual feels personally responsible.

Competing motives or ethics are often at work as well, such as the pressure of a peer group or motives for self-protection or self-reward. Gerson and Damon (1978) found this very clearly in a study in which they asked groups of four children to divide up 10 candy bars. The candy was a reward for work the children had done on a project, and some of the group members had worked harder than others. When asked separately about how the candy bars ought to be divided, children usually argued for various kinds of fair arrangements, such as a model in which the child who worked the hardest should get the most. When faced with the actual distribution of the candy bars, however, some children gave themselves the most; others went along with a group consensus and divided the candy equally. We might expect that in early adolescence, when the impact of the peer group is particularly strong, this group effect on moral actions might be especially strong, too.

Rest's final element, *ego strength or moral character,* is the set of processes that allow a person to persist in pursuing a moral course of action despite difficulties or distractions. An individual's moral behavior in any given situation, according to Rest, is the joint result of all three of these factors, in addition to that person's level of moral reasoning.

Kohlberg's own fascination with the links between moral reasoning and moral behavior, and with the question of how one raises a person's level of moral reasoning, led him and his colleagues to a series of bold attempts to apply the theory to schooling. I've explored some of this research in the Real World box on the facing page.

Social Cognition and General Cognitive Development

Before I leave this subject, I need to explore one other set of linkages, namely, the potential connection between the sequences of development of social cognition and the broader sequences of cognitive development I described in Chapter 6. Earlier in this chapter I suggested several key dimensions that seem to characterize both sets of changes, such as a shift in focus from outer to inner characteristics. What evidence do we have that such parallels or connections actually exist?

We know that IQ is weakly linked to a child's level of social reasoning (Shantz, 1983). The correlations, which are in the range of +.20 to +.40, mean that children with higher IQs typically show slightly more advanced forms of social reasoning than do children of the same age with lower IQs.

Surprisingly, we know much less about any possible connections between overall cognitive *structure* and social-cognitive reasoning. The most concrete proposal was offered by Kohlberg, who hypothesized that the child first moves to a new level of logical thought, then applies this new kind of logic to relationships as well as objects, and only then applies this thinking to moral problems. More specifically, Kohlberg argued that at least some formal operations and at least some mutual perspective taking in relation-

Most children and adults will readily show helpful actions like this if there is little personal cost attached. But if the cost of helping goes up—as when you're in a hurry to get somewhere else—then those with higher levels of moral reasoning are more likely to help.

The Real World

Application of Kohlberg's Theory to Education

A lot of what I have said about Kohlberg's theory may seem pretty abstract to you. In Kohlberg's own view, though, there were many potential practical implications for education. The question that interested him was whether children or young people could be taught higher stages of moral reasoning, and if so, whether such a change in moral reasoning would change their behavior in school.

We know from early research by Elliot Turiel (1966) that at least under some conditions, exposing young people to moral arguments one step above their own level of reasoning can lead to an increase in their level of moral judgment. Young people who attend college also continue to show increases in moral stage scores, while those who quit school after high school typically show no further increase (Rest & Narvaez, 1991; Rest & Thoma, 1985). Because arguments about moral and philosophical issues in class and over coffee (or a few beers) in the wee small hours of the night are one of the hallmarks of the college experience for many young people, perhaps it is the discussion—the exposure to other people's ideas, other people's logic—that makes a difference.

If that's true, what would happen if high school students were given systematic opportunities to explore moral dilemmas; would that change them, too? Apparently it can.

One educational application has involved the creation of special discussion classes in which moral dilemmas similar to those Kohlberg devised are presented and argued. In the process, the teacher attempts to model higher levels of reasoning. Other programs are broader-based, involving not just discussion but also cross-age teaching (to encourage nurturance and caring), empathy training, cooperation games, volunteer service work, and the like. The dozens of studies on the effectiveness of programs of this kind show that on average, the programs succeed in shifting young people's moral reasoning upward about half a stage (Schaefli et al., 1985). The largest effects are generally found in programs focusing exclusively on discussions of moral dilemmas, but broader-based programs work, too. Courses lasting longer than three or four weeks seem to work better than very short programs, and the effects are generally larger with older students—college students and even post-college-age adults. Among high school students, we see some impact, but it is not as large. Even larger effects have been found for classes that emphasize the direct teaching of concepts from moral philosophy and ethics (Rest & Narvaez, 1991).

An even broader-based educational application, designed to change students' moral behavior as much as their moral reasoning, has been the development of the so-called "just community." Such an experimental school, typically set up as a "school within a school," operates as a kind of laboratory for moral education (Higgins, 1991; Higgins et al., 1984; Kohlberg & Higgins, 1987; Kuther & Higgins-D'Alessandro, 1997; Power & Reimer, 1978; Power et al., 1989).

Kohlberg insisted that the crucial feature of these just communities must be complete democracy: Each teacher and student has one vote, and community issues and problems have to be discussed in open forum. Rules are typically created and discussed at weekly community-wide meetings. In this way, students become *responsible* for the rules, and for one another.

In experimental schools following this model, Kohlberg and his co-workers found that as students' level of Kohlbergian moral reasoning shifted upward, so did their reasoning about responsibility and caring. The link between moral reasoning and moral behavior was strengthened as well. For example, stealing and other petty crime virtually disappeared in one school after the students had repeatedly discussed the problem and arrived—painfully—at a solution that emphasized the fact that stealing damaged the whole community, and thus the whole community had to be responsible. For example, after one stealing episode, the group agreed that if the stolen money had not been returned (anonymously) by a specified date, each community member would be assessed 15 cents to make up the victim's loss (Higgins, 1991).

This effect of just communities makes sense when you think about the factors that seem to affect moral behavior. In these schools, two elements were added that would tend to support more moral behavior: a sense of personal responsibility and a group norm of higher moral reasoning and caring.

Among teenagers, the emotional impact of the group pressure may be especially significant, in addition to whatever effect there may be from exposure to more mature arguments. If you find yourself in the minority in some argument about a moral issue, the "social disequilibrium" you feel may help to make you more open to other arguments, and thus to change your view. Certainly in experimental schools like those studied by Kohlberg, this added emotional impact is no doubt part of the process (Haan, 1985).

Classes in moral education have not proved to be the "quick fix" that many educators hoped for. The gains in moral reasoning are typically only moderate, and they may not be reflected in increases in moral behavior in the school unless there is an effort to alter the overall moral atmosphere of the entire school. Nonetheless, these programs do show that there are provocative and helpful applications of some of the abstract developmental theories.

Critical Thinking

Why might it be important, either practically or theoretically, if there is any link between children's approach to moral dilemmas and their level of Piagetian cognitive reasoning?

ships are necessary (but not sufficient) for the emergence of conventional moral reasoning. Full formal operations and still more abstract social understanding may be required for postconventional reasoning.

The research examining such a sequential development is scant, but it supports Kohlberg's hypothesis. Lawrence Walker (1980) found that among a group of fourth to seventh graders he had tested on all three dimensions (concrete and formal operations, social understanding, and moral reasoning), half to two-thirds were reasoning at the same level across the different domains, which makes the whole system look unexpectedly stagelike. When a child was ahead in one progression, the sequence was always that the child developed logical thinking first, then more advanced social understanding, and then the parallel moral judgments.

This research seems to tell us that there is *some* coherence in a child's or young person's thinking or reasoning about quite different problems. Children who have not yet understood principles of conservation are not likely to understand that another person's behavior may not match her feelings. However, once conservation is understood, the child begins to extend this principle to people and to relationships. Similarly, a young person still using concrete operations is unlikely to use postconventional moral reasoning. However, such coherence is not automatic. The basic cognitive understanding makes advances in social and moral reasoning *possible* but does not guarantee them. Experience in relationships, and with moral dilemmas, is necessary, too.

The moral of this (if you will excuse the pun) is that a young person or adult who shows signs of formal operations will *not* necessarily show sensitive, empathetic, and forgiving attitudes toward friends or family. You may find it helpful to bear this in mind in your own relationships.

Summary

1. Many of the principles of developmental change that describe overall cognitive development also describe the changes in social cognition, including a shift in focus from outer to inner characteristics, from observation to inference, from definite to qualified judgment, and from a particular to a general view.

2. Social cognition differs from other aspects of cognition, however, in that the child must learn that people behave with intention, mask feelings, and operate by special socially defined scripts or rules.

3. Children learn to interpret many basic emotional expressions fairly early, but more complex emotions and emotional blends can be correctly read only later.

4. The ability to read others' emotions and intentions is an important element in the child's general social competence; those who are less skilled, who have less "emotion knowledge," are more likely to be rejected by their peers.

5. Empathy—being able to match or approximate the emotion of another—is seen in young infants, but it becomes less egocentric and more subtle through the preschool and elementary school years.

6. Children's descriptions of others shift from a focus on external features to a focus on personality traits and to a more qualified, comparative description at adolescence, paralleling the shifts in children's self-descriptions.

7. Children's thinking about their relationships, such as friendships, shows strongly parallel shifts, moving from definitions of friends as people who share physical space or activities, to definitions emphasizing trust, and finally, at adolescence, to definitions emphasizing intimacy.

8. By elementary school, children begin to understand the distinction between conventional rules and moral rules.

9. Kohlberg described six distinct stages in children's (and adults') reasoning about moral rules.

10. These six stages are divided into three levels. The child moves from preconventional morality (dominated by punishment and "what feels good"), to conventional morality (dominated by group norms or laws), to postconventional or principled morality (dominated by social contracts and basic ethical principles).

11. Cross-sectional and longitudinal research shows that the stages occur in subjects from all countries studied, that the stages occur in the order listed, and that the modal

level for young adults is conventional morality.

12. Alternative models of moral reasoning include Eisenberg's stages of prosocial reasoning (reasoning about why to do something good) and Gilligan's proposal about a parallel ethic of caring.

13. Gilligan's hypothesis that girls are more likely than boys to use caring, rather than justice, as a basis for moral judgments has not been supported by research.

14. A child's level of social cognition is at least somewhat predictive of the type of social behavior she will show. Children with more hedonistic reasoning are more likely to act out in class and to have lower general social competence; children with higher levels of reasoning about friendships have more and more intimate friendships.

15. Higher-level moral reasoning is associated with a higher likelihood of "moral" behavior and a lower likelihood of delinquency, although the relationship is not perfect.

16. Rest suggests three other factors that influence specific moral behavior: moral sensitivity (particularly empathy), moral motivation, and ego strength or moral character.

17. Social-cognitive development is somewhat related to broader sequences of cognitive development. In particular, conventional levels of moral reasoning seem to require (as a necessary but not sufficient condition) at least beginning formal operations, as well as fairly advanced reasoning about social relationships.

Key Terms

conventional morality The second level of moral judgment proposed by Kohlberg, in which the person's judgments are dominated by considerations of group values and laws. **p. 363**

conventional rules One of the two types of rules suggested by Turiel: arbitrary, socially defined rules specific to a particular culture, subculture, or group, such as "Don't run in the halls" or "Smoking allowed only in designated areas." **p. 360**

empathy As defined by Hoffman, "a vicarious affective response that does not necessarily match another's affective state but is more appropriate to the other's situation than to one's own" (1984, p. 285). **p. 355**

hedonistic reasoning A form of prosocial moral reasoning described by Eisenberg in which the child is concerned with self-oriented consequences rather than moral considerations. Roughly equivalent to Kohlberg's stage 2. **p. 367**

moral rules One of the two types of rules suggested by Turiel: rules seen as universal and obligatory, reflecting basic principles that guarantee the rights of others. **p. 360**

needs-oriented reasoning A form of prosocial moral reasoning proposed by Eisenberg in which the child expresses concern directly for the other person's need, even if the other's need conflicts with the child's own wishes or desires. **p. 367**

postconventional morality See *principled morality*. **p. 363**

preconventional morality The first level of morality proposed by Kohlberg, in which moral judgments are dominated by consideration of what will be punished and what feels good. **p. 362**

principled morality The third level of morality proposed by Kohlberg, in which considerations of justice, individual rights, and contracts dominate moral judgment. **p. 363**

social cognition Term used to describe an area of research and theory focused on the child's *understanding* of social relationships. **p. 353**

Suggested Readings

Flavell, J. H., Miller, P. H., & Miller, S. A. (1993). *Cognitive development* (3rd ed.). Englewood Cliffs, NJ: Prentice Hall. This third edition of an excellent text has a very helpful chapter on social cognition.

Hoffman, M. L. (1988). Moral development. In M. H. Bornstein & M. E. Lamb (Eds.), *Developmental psychology: An advanced textbook* (2nd ed., pp. 497–548). Hillsdale, NJ: Erlbaum. Not all psychologists are as persuaded as I am of the general validity of Kohlberg's stage theory. Hoffman is one of the articulate skeptics, so this paper will give you a look at an alternative view.

Kurtines, W. M., & Gewirtz, J. L. (Eds.). (1991). *Handbook of moral behavior and development*. Hillsdale, NJ: Erlbaum. This is a massive three-volume work, prepared as a commemoration of the work of Lawrence Kohlberg. Volume 1 deals with theory, volume 2 with research, and volume 3 with application. If this area intrigues you, there is no more complete source.

13

The Ecology of Development: The Child Within the Family System

Six months ago, Sam McKenzie, age 35, lost his job as a machinist when his company laid off several hundred workers. Sam's wife, Edith, still has her job as a clerk in the local grocery store, but Sam's unemployment compensation is running out, and he hasn't been able to find another job. Money is tight. Sam has tried hard to persuade himself that these things happen to people, but mostly he blames himself and his lack of education. He thinks it is a man's job to support his family, so he finds it very difficult to have to rely so much on Edith's income. Over the months, he has become increasingly gloomy and irritable. He drinks more and has trouble sleeping, and he and Edith have been arguing more. The kids have also felt the change—not just in the things they can't buy now, but in the whole atmosphere at home. Sam snaps at them often and has become strict with them—though sometimes he seems to pay no attention to them at all. The kids also notice that he hugs them a lot less. David, who is 13, has started yelling back much more frequently than he used to and has been spending more and more time with his school buddies. Nine-year-old Jennifer has reacted differently; she's become quite withdrawn and depressed and no longer spends much time with her friends. Both the children have had a lot more colds and other illnesses than usual, too.

What the McKenzies have experienced is fairly typical of families when the father loses his job or when a single mother loses her job (Conger et al., 1995; Crouter & McHale, 1993; McLoyd et al., 1994). Their experience also illustrates two important points—points I made in a preliminary way in Chapter 1 but that may have gotten a bit lost in all the intervening chapters.

First, to understand the child's development, we must go beyond the child himself and whatever intrinsic developmental patterns may exist; we must go beyond the parent-child dyads. We need to look at the whole ecology of development—at the pattern of interaction within the entire family and at the influences of the larger culture on that family. David and Jennifer McKenzie have been affected by Sam's job loss both directly and indirectly, and some of those effects may be very long-lasting. Glen Elder's studies of families in the Great Depression of the 1930s, for example, show that some children whose families experienced major financial upheavals in the Depression continued to show the emotional scars well into adult life (Elder, 1974; 1981; 1984).

Second, the McKenzies' story illustrates a *system* of influences at work. The loss of Sam's job was not just an economic event. It affected Sam's attitudes, his self-esteem, and his behavior; it reverberated through the entire family system, affecting every other person and every relationship.

In this chapter and the next, I want to explore this larger psychological and ecological system in which the child's development occurs. I introduced some of the current thinking about such family and cultural influences in Chapter 1, but let me both refresh your memory and set the stage by delving a bit more deeply into the theoretical issues.

Theoretical Approaches

Thirty years ago, most child development texts and books of advice to parents emphasized the role of the parents in "molding" the child, as if the child were a lump of clay. The parents' task was thought to be to *socialize* the child, to shape the child's behavior to fit well into the expectations and rules of society. This clay-molding view has now given way to a far more complex model, most commonly called *systems theory*.

Systems Theory

Systems theorists such as Arnold Sameroff (1995) emphasize that any system—biological, economic, psychological—has several key properties. First and foremost, a system has "wholeness and order," which is another way of saying that the whole is greater than the sum of its parts. The whole consists of the parts and their *relationship* to one another. The usual analogy is to a melody, which is far more than a set of individual notes. It is the relationship of those notes to each other that creates the melody.

A second feature of any system is that it is *adaptive* in precisely the same way that Piaget talks about the child's cognitive system being adaptive. When any part of the system changes or some new element is added, the system will "assimilate" if it can but will "accommodate" if it must. So systems resist change as much as they can by absorbing new data or new parts into the existing structure; then only if that doesn't work—as it often doesn't—will the system change. For example, when a second child is born into a family, the parents may try to keep to their old routines as much as possible, but the presence of this new individual in the family system will inevitably force accommodations as well. That will be particularly true if the new baby is temperamentally very different from the first child.

Combining these two features of systems, you can see that any change in any one part of a system will affect every other part. Furthermore, feedback loops occur. In the McKenzie family's experience, for example, Sam's distress led him to be more negative toward Edith, which made their relationship worse. Such a worsening of the marital relationship, along with Sam's own basic distress, led to changes in both parents' behavior toward the children, to which the kids reacted with changes of their own. Once set in motion, the changes in David's and Jennifer's behavior affected Sam and Edith. David became more defiant, to which Sam responded by becoming even more strict and demanding, which affected David's behavior in still more negative ways.

Although virtually all psychologists would now grant the general validity of such a systems approach, figuring out how to conceptualize the various parts of such systems has been no small task. Urie Bronfenbrenner, who originally coined the phrase *ecology of development,* has offered one approach.

Bronfenbrenner's Ecological Approach

Bronfenbrenner (1979; 1989), whose ideas I talked about briefly in Chapter 1, proposes that we think of the ecological system in which the child develops as having a series of layers or concentric circles. The most central circle, made up of elements he calls *microsystems,* includes all those settings in which the child has direct personal experience, such as the family, school, a day-care center, or a job setting where a teenager works.

The next layer, which Bronfenbrenner calls *exosystems,* includes a whole range of system elements that the child does not experience directly but that influence the child because they affect one of the microsystems, particularly the family. The parents' work and workplace is one such element, as is the parents' network of friends.

Finally, Bronfenbrenner describes a *macrosystem* that includes the larger cultural or subcultural setting in which both the micro- and exosystems are embedded. The poverty or wealth of the family, the neighborhood in which the family lives, the ethnic identity of the family, and the larger culture in which the entire system exists are all parts of this macrosystem.

Figure 13.1 is a schematic drawing of these three layers for two hypothetical 4-year-old U.S. children, one from the majority Euro-American culture in an intact middle-class family with parents both employed, the other a Latino child living with both parents and a grandmother in a working-class, largely Spanish-speaking neighborhood, with the mother at home full-time. If you try to imagine yourself living inside each of these systems, you can get a feeling for all the complex ways in which they differ and how all the pieces of the system interact with one another. Bronfenbrenner's point is that until we really understand the ways in which all the elements in such complex systems interact to affect the child, we will not understand development.

I am sure it is obvious to you that trying to understand development in this way is *immensely* difficult. It is hard to keep all the elements of the system in mind at once, let alone to try to study all the relevant parts simultaneously. Perhaps frustrated by that

Critical Thinking

We can also think of cultures as systems in this same sense. So when you change one aspect of a given culture, everything is affected. As an experiment, imagine that all violent TV, all highly aggressive games, and all handguns were banned. How might such a change reverberate through the entire cultural system?

Critical Thinking

Draw an equivalent set of concentric circles and describe the ecology of your life at about age 5. What were the microsystems that affected you? What exosystems had an impact? What larger cultural influences (macrosystems) do you think were significant?

Figure 13.1

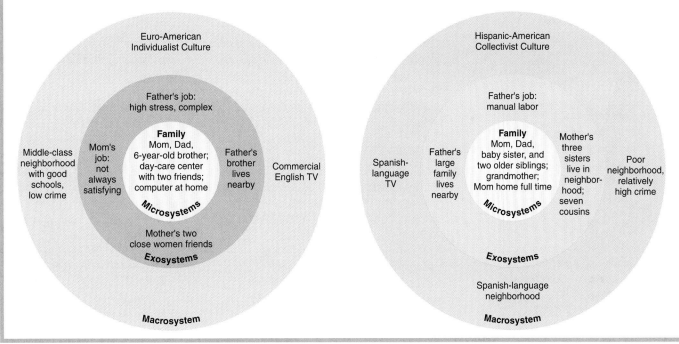

Two hypothetical children, growing up in widely different ecological settings, illustrate the layers in Bronfenbrenner's model. To understand how the environment affects a child, we would need to study every aspect of this complex system simultaneously—a tall order.

difficulty, or perhaps because of the long tradition of examining family and cultural effects in more linear ways, psychologists have continued to design research that explores only small pieces of the total system. Thus, much of what we know about family and cultural influences on children is piecemeal rather than systemic. Nonetheless, let us plunge in, using Bronfrenbrenner's model as a general framework. I want to begin in this chapter by looking more closely at that most studied and most obviously influential microsystem, the family. I'll also explore some of the exosystem influences on the family. Then in Chapter 14 I'll look at other microsystems affecting the child directly, such as child-care settings, as well as at the larger macrosystem/cultural influences.

Naturally I have talked about family influences on the child many times already. You have seen how family interaction patterns affect the child's language, cognitive development, or the security of the child's attachment. What I have not talked about is the family system, with all its complexities. To understand how that system works and how it might affect the child, we need first to have some way of describing the many possible patterns of interaction that can occur in families. Then we have to try to understand the ways in which other factors inside and outside the family will affect those patterns—factors such as the parents' personalities, the family structure, and the parents' job experiences.

Dimensions of Family Interaction

Those researchers who have focused most directly on patterns of parent-child interaction have identified several major dimensions on which families differ that seem to be significant for the child. These include the emotional tone of the family, the responsiveness of the parent to the child, the manner in which control is exercised, and the quality and amount of communication.

I am sure it is obvious to you that loving a child is a critical ingredient in the child's optimum development. But sometimes it helps to restate the obvious.

The Emotional Tone of the Family

The first key element for the child seems to be the relative **warmth versus hostility** of the home. "Warmth" has been difficult to define and measure, but intuitively and theoretically we know that it is highly important for the child. A warm parent cares about the child, expresses affection, frequently or regularly puts the child's needs first, shows enthusiasm for the child's activities, and responds sensitively and empathetically to the child's feelings (Maccoby, 1980). On the other end of the continuum are parents who overtly reject their children—saying in words or behavior that they do not love or want the child.

Such differences have profound effects. Psychologists have found that children in warm and loving families are more securely attached in the first two years of life; have higher self-esteem; are more empathetic, more altruistic, and more responsive to others' hurts or distress; and have higher IQ scores in preschool and elementary school and do better in school (Maccoby, 1980; Pettit et al., 1997a; Simons et al., 1989). They are also less likely to show high levels of aggression or delinquent behavior in later childhood or in adolescence (Maughan et al., 1995). High levels of affection can even buffer the child against the negative effects of otherwise disadvantageous environments. Several studies of children and teens growing up in poor, tough neighborhoods show that the single ingredient that most clearly distinguishes the lives of those who do *not* become delinquent from those who do is a high level of maternal love (Glueck & Glueck, 1972; McCord, 1982). Similarly, in a recent longitudinal study, Gregory Pettit and his colleagues (1997a) find that children growing up in poverty environments whose parents provide more "supportive parenting" (including warmth) are less likely to develop aggressive or delinquent behavior than are equally poor children in less emotionally supportive families.

At the other end of the continuum of warmth, parental hostility is linked to declining school performance and higher risk of delinquency (Melby & Conger, 1996). When hostility is expressed as physical abuse or neglect, the consequences may be even more severe, as I discussed in the Research Report in Chapter 4 (p. 125).

I suspect that the role of warmth in fostering a secure attachment of the child to the parent is one of the key elements in this picture. You already know from Chapter 11 that securely attached children are more skillful with their peers, more exploratory, more sure of themselves. Warmth also makes children generally more responsive to guidance, so the parents' affection and warmth increase the potency of the things that parents say to their children as well as the efficiency of their discipline (MacDonald, 1992).

Responsiveness

A second key element of family interaction patterns is **responsiveness** by the parent to the child, a concept I've mentioned repeatedly in earlier chapters. Responsive parents are those who "pick up on" the child's signals appropriately and then react in sensitive ways to the child's needs (Ainsworth & Marvin, 1995; Sroufe, 1996). Children of parents who do more of this learn language somewhat more rapidly; show higher IQ scores and more speedy cognitive development; and are more likely to be securely attached, more compliant with adult requests, and more socially competent (e.g., Bornstein, 1989; Kochanska, 1997; van den Boom, 1994).

Methods of Control

It is the nature of children that they will often do things their parents do not want, ask for things they cannot have, or refuse to obey their parents' requests or demands. From early days, parents are inevitably faced with the task of controlling the child's behavior and training the child to follow basic rules, a process more popularly called *discipline*. Since I have not yet talked much about this aspect of parent-child interactions, I need to break the subject up into several elements.

One element of control is the *consistency of rules*—making it clear to the child what the rules are, what the consequences are of disobeying (or obeying) them, and then enforcing them consistently. Some parents are very clear and consistent; others waffle or are fuzzy about what they expect or will tolerate. Studies of families show that parents who are clear and consistent have children who are much less likely to be defiant or noncompliant—a pattern you'll remember from Gerald Patterson's research (recall Figure 1.2, p. 11). The same pattern, incidentally, can be observed in day-care centers or preschools: Children who are cared for by teachers who are lax and inconsistent in their response to misbehavior are more likely to misbehave (Arnold et al., 1998). Consistency of rules does not produce little robots. Children from families with consistent rules are more competent and sure of themselves and less likely to become delinquent or show significant behavior problems than are children from less consistent families.

One piece of research that nicely illustrates this pattern is Lawrence Kurdek and Mark Fine's study of 850 junior high school students (Kurdek & Fine, 1994). They measured the level of control in the family by asking the young adolescents to say whether each of the following three statements was true or not true (on a 7-point scale) about their families:

Someone in my family makes sure that my homework is done.

Generally, someone in my family knows where I am and what I'm doing.

Someone in my family keeps a close eye on me.

Kurdek and Fine also had information about each child's self-esteem and sense of self-efficacy, which they combined into a measure of "psychological competence." You can see the relationship between these two pieces of information in Figure 13.2: Greater control was clearly associated with greater psychological competence.

Such a link between good parental control and positive outcomes for the child has been found among African-American as well as Euro-American youth. For example, Craig Mason and his colleagues (1996) found that among working-class black families, those in which the parents maintained the most consistent monitoring and control over their adolescents had teenagers who were least likely to show problem behavior. Interestingly and importantly, the link between parental control and lower rates of problem behavior in Mason's study was especially clear in cases in which the child had many

Figure 13.2

Junior high school students who report higher levels of parental control and supervision also describe themselves as having higher self-esteem and self-efficacy.

(*Source:* Kurdek, L., and Fine, M., from Fig. 1, p. 1143, "Family acceptance and family control as predictors of adjustments in young adolescents," *Child development*, 65 (1994), 1137–1146. By permission of the Society for Research in Child Development.)

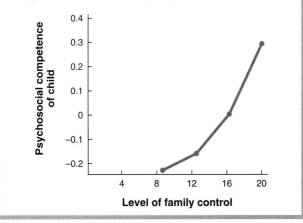

peers who were engaging in problem behavior. Thus, the parents, by applying consistent rules and monitoring the child's activities, could at least partially counteract the negative effects of "hanging out" with misbehaving peers.

A related element of parental control is the *level of expectations* the parents have for the child's behavior. Is the child expected to show relatively more mature behavior, or does the parent feel it is important not to expect too much, too soon? Studies of such variations show that, within limits, higher expectations seem to be associated with better outcomes. Children whose parents make high demands on them—expecting them to help around the house or to show relatively mature behavior for their age—have higher self-esteem, show more generosity and altruism toward others, and have lower levels of aggression. Obviously this can be carried much too far. It is unrealistic and counterproductive to expect a 2-year-old to set the table for dinner every day or to tie his own shoes. But when parents expect the child to be as independent and helpful as possible for his age, they seem to foster a sense of competence in the child that carries over into other situations.

Finally, to understand the process of control, we have to understand the role of *punishment*. Punishment is one form of discipline, one method of training and controlling. It is most often aimed at getting a child to stop doing something prohibited, such as writing on the wall, hitting her brother, or staying out past a curfew, but it may also be used to try to push a child to do something that he is resisting, such as cleaning his room. Punishments almost invariably involve some negative consequence for the child, ranging from withholding privileges or treats, assigning extra chores, sending a child to his room, or "grounding" to more severe forms of verbal scolding or spanking. The most controversial of these is spanking. Because of the importance of the question, I have explored the pros and cons of such physical punishment in the Real World discussion on the facing page. Here I want to make a number of other points about punishment strategies in general.

First, as Gerald Patterson says, "Punishment 'works.' If you use it properly it will produce rapid changes in the behavior of other people" (1975, p. 19). The operative word here, though, is *properly*. The most effective punishments—those that produce long-term changes in the child's behavior without unwanted or negative side effects—are those used early in some sequence of misbehavior, with the lowest level of emotion possible and the mildest level of punishment possible. Taking a desired toy away when the child *first* uses it to hit the furniture (or a sibling), or consistently removing small privileges when a child misbehaves, will "work," especially if the parent is also warm, clear about the rules, and consistent. It is far less effective to wait until the screams have reached a piercing level, or until the fourth time a teenager has gone off without telling you where she's going, and then weigh in with yelling, loud comments, and strong punishments.

Second, to a considerable degree, parents get back what they give out in the way of punishment. As I pointed out in Chapter 9, children learn by observation as well as by doing, so they learn the adults' ways of coping with stress and forms of punishment. Yelling at children to stop doing something, for example, may bring a *brief* change in their behavior (which thus reinforces the parent for yelling, by the way), but it also increases the chances that children will yell back on other occasions.

Communication Patterns

A fourth important dimension of the family system is the quality of the communication between parent and child. Two things about such communication seem to make a difference for the child: the amount and richness of language spoken *to* the child (which I already talked about in Chapter 8) and the amount of conversation and suggestions *from* the child that the parent encourages. Listening is important as well as talking.

When I say *listening*, I have in mind more than merely saying "uh-huh" periodically when the child talks. I also mean conveying to the child the sense that what he has to

Critical Thinking

Think about your own upbringing. What types of control strategies did your parents use? What kinds of punishment? How might you want to change these patterns in bringing up your own children?

The Real World

To Spank or Not to Spank

In Sweden, there is a law against physical punishment of children (Palmérus & Scarr, 1995). In the United States, no such law exists, and 9 out of 10 parents of preschoolers say that they spank their children at least occasionally, most often in response to some aggressive act (Holden et al., 1995). Among middle-class parents, a quarter say they spank their child with their hand at least weekly; 35 percent use an object such as a hairbrush to hit their child at least occasionally; and 12 percent say they hit their child hard enough on occasion to cause considerable pain (Graziano et al., 1996). Spanking teenagers is less common than is spanking preschoolers or elementary school children, but about half of parents of teenagers say they use spanking at least occasionally (Straus, 1991a; Straus & Donnelly, 1993). Parents who spank think of it as an effective way of discipline. I think they are wrong, and so does the American Academy of Pediatrics which recently issued new "Guidance for Effective Discipline" (1998).

Note please: I am not talking here about physical abuse, although certainly some parents do abuse their children by spanking excessively with a switch or a belt or hitting them with fists. I'm talking about the ordinary kind of spanking that most people think of as normal and helpful: two or three hard swats on the rear or a quick slap. Let me give you some of the arguments against using this form of discipline.

In the short term, spanking a child usually *does* get the child to stop the particular behavior you didn't like, and to have a *temporary* effect of reducing the chance that the child will repeat the bad behavior. Since that's what you wanted, it may seem like a good strategy, but even in the short term there are some negative side effects. The child may have stopped misbehaving, but after a spanking he is likely to be crying, which may be almost as distressing as the original misbehavior.

Another short-term side effect is that *you* are being negatively reinforced for spanking whenever the child stops misbehaving after you spank her. Thus, you are being "trained" to use spanking the next time, and a cycle is being built up.

In the longer term, the effects are clearly negative. First, when you spank, the child observes you using physical force as a method of solving problems or getting people to do what you want. You thus serve as a model for a behavior you do *not* want your child to use with others. Second, by repeatedly pairing your presence with the unpleasant or painful event of spanking, you are undermining your own positive value for your child. Over time, this means that you are less able to use any kind of reinforcement effectively. Eventually even your praise or affection will be less powerful in influencing your child's behavior. That is a very high price to pay.

Third, spanking frequently carries a strong underlying emotional message—anger, rejection, irritation, dislike of the child. Even very young children read this emotional message quite clearly (Rohner et

al., 1991). Spanking thus helps to create a family climate of rejection instead of warmth, with all the attendant negative consequences.

Finally, we have research evidence that children who are spanked—just like children who are abused—at later ages show higher levels of aggression and less popularity with their peers, lower self-esteem, more emotional instability, higher rates of depression and distress, and higher levels of delinquency and later criminality (Laub & Sampson, 1995; Rohner et al., 1991; Strassberg et al., 1994; Turner & Finkelhor, 1996). As adults, children who have been spanked are more likely to be depressed than are those who were never or rarely spanked (Straus, 1995), and they also have higher risks of various other types of adult problems, including problems holding a job, divorce or violence within a relationship, and criminality (Maughan et al., 1995). All these negative effects are especially clear if the physical punishment is harsh and erratic, but the risks for these poor outcomes are increased even with fairly mild levels of physical punishment.

I am *not* saying that you should never punish a child. I *am* saying that *physical punishment,* such as spanking, is not a good way to go about it. Yelling at the child is not a good alternative strategy, either. Strong *verbal* aggression by a parent toward a child is also linked to many poor outcomes in the child, including increased risk of delinquency and adult violence (Straus, 1991b).

At the same time, an important caveat is in order. Virtually all the research that shows such a link between physical punishment and poor outcomes has been done with European-American children. We now have a handful of studies suggesting that the same links may not occur in African-American families. For example, Deater-Deckard and his colleagues (1996) found that white children whose parents used higher levels of physical punishment were more likely to be aggressive in school; the same link did not occur for black children in the same study—unless the physical discipline was severe. One possible explanation is that spanking and other forms of physical punishment may have negative effects primarily when they are combined with low levels of emotional warmth (Deater-Deckard & Dodge, 1997). If physical discipline is more likely to be combined with emotional coldness in European-American families than is true for African Americans, then this would help to account for the difference between these ethnic groups. Another possibility is that the urban black poor, in particular, use physical punishment as a means of maintaining tighter monitoring and control in a highly dangerous environment, with the benefits of improved monitoring outweighing the adverse effects of physical punishment. Whatever the reason, results like this remind us once again that we must be very careful about generalizing from one group to another. For now, what I can tell you is that among Euro-Americans, spanking seems to have consistently negative consequences and that *harsh* or erratic physical punishment has negative effects in every group studied.

This dad seems to be willing to listen carefully to his son, even though the boy is angry and accusatory.

say is *worth* listening to, that he has ideas, that his ideas are important and should be considered in family decisions.

We have much less research on the quality of communication within families than on some of the other dimensions I have been describing, so we are a long way from understanding all the ramifications. In general, children from families with open communication are seen as more emotionally or socially mature (Baumrind, 1971; Bell & Bell, 1982).

Open communication may also be important for the functioning of the family as a unit. For example, in a study of a national sample of families with adolescents, Howard Barnes and David Olson (1985) measured communication by asking the parents and teenagers to agree or disagree with statements like "It is easy for me to express all my true feelings to my (mother/father/child)." As you can see in Figure 13.3, the investigators found that parents and children who reported good, open communication, compared to those with poorer communication, also described their families as more adaptable in the face of stress or change and said they were more satisfied with their families.

Figure 13.3

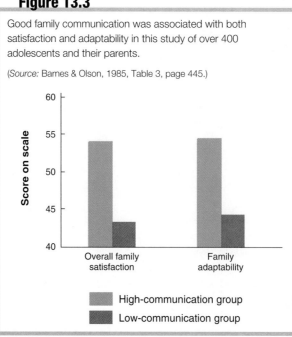

Good family communication was associated with both satisfaction and adaptability in this study of over 400 adolescents and their parents.

(*Source:* Barnes & Olson, 1985, Table 3, page 445.)

Patterns or Styles of Child Rearing

Each of these dimensions of parental behavior has a demonstrable effect on the child, but if we are going to try to use a systems theory approach, it is not enough to look at each dimension independently. We also have to think about how the dimensions interact with one another to create *styles* or *patterns* of child rearing.

Baumrind's Model

The most influential proposal about such styles has come from Diana Baumrind (1973), who has looked at combinations of the dimensions I've just described: (1) warmth or nurturance; (2) level of expectations, which she describes in terms of "maturity demands"; (3) the clarity and consistency of rules; and (4) communication between parent and child. Baumrind saw three specific combinations of these characteristics:

- The **permissive style** is high in nurturance but low in maturity demands, control, and communication.
- The **authoritarian style** is high in control and maturity demands but low in nurturance and communication.
- The **authoritative style** is high in all four.

Maccoby and Martin's Variation

Eleanor Maccoby and John Martin (1983) extended Baumrind's category system, proposing a model that has been widely influential. They emphasized two dimensions, as you can see in Figure 13.4: the degree of demand or control and the amount of acceptance/rejection or responsiveness. The intersection of these two dimensions creates four types, three of which correspond fairly closely to Baumrind's authoritarian, authoritative, and permissive types. Maccoby and Martin's fourth type, the uninvolved **neglecting style,** was not identified by Baumrind in her early work, although recent research shows clearly that this is an important group to study.

Figure 13.4

Maccoby and Martin expanded on Baumrind's categories in this two-dimensional typology.

(*Source:* Maccoby, E. and Martin, J., adapted from Fig. 2, p. 39, "Socialization in the context of the family: Parent-child interaction," *Handbook of child psychology: Socialization, personality, and social development,* Vol. 4, 1983, pp. 1–102. © 1983 by Wiley. By permission.)

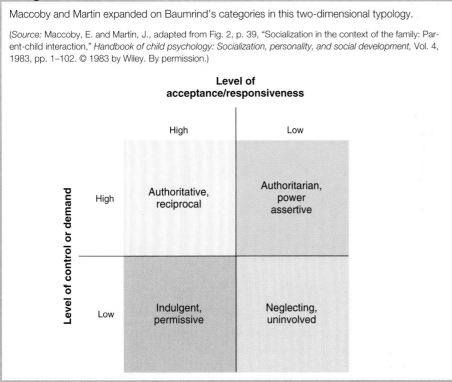

The Authoritarian Type. Authoritarian parents, as Kristan Glasgow and her colleagues describe them, are highly demanding of their children while being quite unresponsive: "These parents attempt to mold and control the behavior and attitudes of their children according to a set of standards. They tend to emphasize obedience, respect for authority, and order. [They] also discourage verbal give-and-take with their children, expecting rules to be followed without further explanation" (1997, p. 508). Children growing up in such families do less well in school, are typically less skilled with peers than are children from other types of families, and have lower self-esteem (Baumrind, 1991; Maccoby & Martin, 1983). Some of these children appear subdued; others may show high aggressiveness or other indications of being out of control. Which of these two outcomes occurs may depend in part on how skillfully the parents use the various disciplinary techniques. Patterson finds that the "out-of-control" child is most likely to come from a family in which the parents are authoritarian by inclination but lack the skills to enforce the limits or rules they set.

The Permissive Type. Children growing up with indulgent or permissive parents, who are tolerant and warm but exercise little authority, also show some negative outcomes. They do slightly less well in school in adolescence, and they are likely to be more aggressive—particularly if the parents are specifically permissive toward aggressiveness—and to be somewhat immature in their behavior with peers and in school. They are less likely to take responsibility and are less independent (Maccoby & Martin, 1983).

The Authoritative Type. The most consistently positive outcomes have been associated with the authoritative pattern, in which the parents are high in both control and warmth, setting clear limits, expecting and reinforcing socially mature behavior, and at the same time responding to the child's individual needs. Note, please, that this style of parenting is *not* one in which the parents let the child rule the roost. Authoritative parents are quite willing to discipline the child appropriately if the child misbehaves. They are less likely to use *physical* punishment than are authoritarian parents, preferring instead to use "time out" or other mild punishments, but it is important to understand that these parents are not wishy-washy. Children reared in such families typically show higher self-esteem. They are more independent but at the same time are more likely to comply with parental requests, and they may show more altruistic behavior as well. They are self-confident and achievement-oriented in school and get better grades in elementary school, high school, or college (e.g., Crockenberg & Litman, 1990; Dornbusch et al., 1987; Steinberg et al., 1989; Weiss & Schwarz, 1996). In late adolescence they are more likely to use postconventional moral reasoning (Boyes & Allen, 1993).

The Neglecting Type. The most consistently negative outcomes are associated with the fourth pattern, the neglecting or uninvolved type. You may remember from the discussion of secure and insecure attachments in Chapter 11 that one of the family characteristics often found in children rated insecurely attached is the "psychological unavailability" of the mother. The mother may be depressed or may be overwhelmed by other problems in her life, or she simply may not have made any deep emotional connection with the child. Whatever the reason, such children continue to show disturbances in their relationships with peers and with adults for many years. At adolescence, for example, youngsters from neglecting families are more impulsive and antisocial and much less achievement-oriented in school (Block, 1971; Lamborn et al., 1991; Pulkkinen, 1982). Lack of parental monitoring appears to be a critical aspect of this pattern: Children and teens whose parents show poor monitoring are far more likely to become delinquent (Patterson et al., 1992).

A Research Example: The Work of Steinberg and Dornbusch

The best single piece of research demonstrating the effects of these several styles is a study of nearly 11,000 high school students in California and Wisconsin, by Laurence Steinberg and Sanford Dornbusch and their colleagues. Of this sample, 6,902 were followed over a two-year period, providing valuable longitudinal information (Dornbusch et al., 1987; Glasgow et al., 1997; Lamborn et al., 1991; Steinberg et al., 1989; 1991; 1992b; 1994; 1995). The researchers measured parenting styles by asking the teenagers themselves to respond to questions about their relationship with their parents and their family life, including questions about both parental acceptance/responsiveness and parental control or demand—the dimensions that define Maccoby and Martin's category system. For example, they were asked to indicate the extent to which each of the following statements was true or not true:

I can count on my parents to help me out if I have some kind of problem.

When [my father] wants me to do something he explains why.

My parents know exactly where I am most afternoons after school.

On the basis of students' answers to such questions, Steinberg and Dornbusch were able to classify most of the subjects' families in the Maccoby/Martin category system and could then look at the relationship between these family styles and a variety of behaviors in the teenagers. They found that teenagers from authoritative families showed the most optimum pattern on every measure they used. These teenagers had higher self-reliance, higher social competence, better grades, fewer indications of psychological distress, and lower levels of school misconduct, drug use, and delinquency. Teenagers from authoritarian families had the lowest scores on the several measures of social competence and self-reliance; those from neglecting families had the least optimal scores on measures of problem behaviors and school achievement (Steinberg et al., 1994). Figure 13.5 gives two of these results, one showing variations in grade point average, the other self-reported delinquent acts, including such things as carrying a weapon, stealing, and getting into trouble with the police.

In a longitudinal analysis of the data for the nearly 7000 students for whom they have two years of information, these same researchers have found that students who described their parents as most authoritative at the beginning of the study showed

Figure 13.5

School grades and delinquency both vary as a function of parental style in Steinberg and Dornbusch's large sample of teenagers. Delinquent behavior in this case reflects the adolescent's own report of the frequency with which he or she carries a weapon, steals, or gets into trouble with the police.

(*Source:* Steinberg et al., 1994, from Table 5, p. 762.)

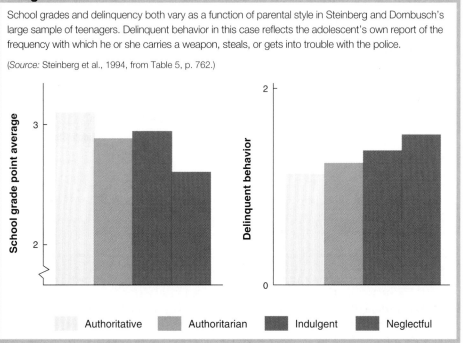

more *improvement* in academic competence and self-reliance and the smallest increases in psychological symptoms and delinquent behavior over the succeeding two years, suggesting that the family style has a causal, continuing effect.

These results are impressive, but in fact the family system is more complex than the simple comparison of the four types may make it sound. For example, authoritative parents not only create a good family climate and thereby support and motivate their child optimally; they also behave differently toward the child's school. They are much more likely to be involved with the school, attending school functions or talking to teachers, and this involvement seems to play a crucial role. When an otherwise authoritative parent is *not* also involved with the school, the outcomes for the student are not so clearly positive. Similarly, a teenager whose parent is highly involved with the school but is *not* authoritative shows less optimal outcomes. It is the combination of authoritativeness and school involvement that is associated with the best results (Steinberg et al., 1992b).

In another indication of the complexity of these relationships, this research group has recently found that the young people in their study whose *friends* had more authoritative parents showed more optimum outcomes, regardless of the style of interaction in their own families. Even authoritatively reared teenagers had better grades and lower delinquency when they hung out with friends whose families were also authoritative than when they chose pals from families with other styles (Fletcher et al., 1995).

Ethnic Group Differences in Styles. An additional complexity appears when we look at these relationships separately within each of several ethnic groups. Steinberg and Dornbusch's sample is large enough to allow them to do this for subgroups of African-American, Latino, and Asian-American youth and their families, as well as for Euro-Americans (Steinberg et al., 1991). The results suggest both common processes and unique cultural variations.

Table 13.1 shows the percentages of families from each of the four ethnic groups involved in this study who could be classed as authoritative, broken down further by social class and the intactness of the family. The authoritative pattern was most common among white families and least common among Asian Americans, but in each ethnic group, authoritative parenting was more common among the middle class and (with one exception) more common among intact families than in single-parent or stepparent families.

The more important question is whether the same predictive relationships between family style and child outcomes obtain in all groups. For some outcomes, the answer is

Table 13.1

Ethnic Differences in Authoritative Parenting

	Percentage of Authoritative Families			
	Working Class		Middle Class	
Ethnic Group	**Intact**[a]	**Not Intact**	**Intact**	**Not Intact**
White	17.2	11.5	25.0	17.6
Black	13.4	12.2	14.0	16.0
Hispanic	10.7	9.8	15.8	12.9
Asian	7.5	6.1	15.6	10.8

Source: Steinberg, L; Mounts, N. S.; Lamborn, S. D.; and Dornbusch, S. D.; from Table 1, p. 25, "Authoritative parenting and adolescent adjustment across varied ecological niches," in *Journal of research on adolescence*, 1, 1991. © 1991 by Lawrence Erlbaum and Associates. By permission of the publisher and L. Steinberg.

[a]*Intact* means the child is still living with both biological parents; *not intact* means either a single-parent family, a stepfamily, or any family configuration other than both natural parents.

"yes." In all four groups, for example, teenagers from authoritative families showed more self-reliance and less delinquency than did those from nonauthoritative families.

On the other hand, school performance was *not* linked to authoritative parenting in the same ways in all four groups. In this study, good grades were linked to such a parenting style for whites and for Latinos, but only very weakly for Asian Americans—a group of students who do extremely well in school even though their parents are among the least authoritative. Among African-American families, too, the linkage between authoritative parenting and good school performance was either weak or nonexistent—a result replicated by other researchers (Lamborn et al., 1996; Norwood, 1997).

How can we explain these differences? One possibility is that the four styles of parenting simply don't capture the most crucial features of family interaction that affect academic performance. Steinberg and Dornbusch have pursued this possibility by examining a wide variety of other aspects of family and cultural systems (Steinberg et al., 1992a). They conclude that an additional key element is the belief students and parents have about the importance of education for later success in life. All four ethnic groups they studied share a belief that doing well in school will lead to better chances later, but the groups disagree on the consequences of doing poorly in school. Asian-American students, more than any other group, believe that a good job is unlikely to follow a bad education, while both Latinos and African Americans are more optimistic (or more cavalier) about the risks associated with poor school performance. Perhaps as a result of their greater fear of failure, Asian-American students spend much more time on homework than do other groups.

Furthermore, Asian-American students (and whites) get very good peer support for academic achievement while African-American teens get little. This factor undermines the beneficial effects of any authoritative parenting in this subgroup. Indeed, interviews with the African-American students in the Steinberg and Dornbusch study suggest that academically oriented African-American youths have difficulty finding a peer group that will support their academic goals. As Steinberg puts it, "The sad truth is that many students, and many Black students in particular, are forced to choose between doing well in school and having friends" (1996, p. 161).

Another possibility is that the four styles suggested by Maccoby and Martin are themselves ethnocentric and simply do not (perhaps cannot) capture the elements that make individual cultural patterns unique (Parke & Buriel, 1998). For example, Ruth Chao (1994) notes that Chinese-American parents, who require obedience, are usually scored high on traditional measures of authoritarian parenting. But in Asian culture, strictness and a demand for obedience are perceived as aspects of concern and caring, not as reflecting any lack of warmth. For the Chinese, says Chao, the key concept is *training,* which means teaching or educating and carries with it not only the element of control but also high involvement and closeness to the child. Chinese parents control their children not in order to dominate—an aspect implicit in the authoritarian style as

Critical Thinking

Can you come up with any possible explanations for the observation that Asian-American families are high in authoritarian style but still have children who do well in school? How many different hypotheses can you generate?

Asian parents very often score high on measures of authoritarian parental style. But their high level of strictness and control is embedded in a different set of cultural values, and it thus has a different meaning for the child and a different effect on the child's behavior—yet another illustration of the fact that psychologists need to be careful in generalizing theories and results across cultures.

Baumrind described it—but rather to ensure that harmonious relations within the family and the culture will be maintained. According to Chao, the traditional measures of the authoritarian style simply fail to capture these values and thus badly misrepresent the quality of the parent-child interaction within the Chinese family.

Adding Up What We Know About Parental Style

I think the accumulating evidence makes it clear that the concept of parental style has been and will continue to be highly useful descriptively and predictively. For one thing, it focuses our attention on the family *system* rather than merely on individual behaviors.

However, we may not yet have zeroed in on the best ways to describe family styles. The four types Baumrind and Maccoby and Martin suggest are probably only a first approximation. Many Euro-American families cannot be tidily described in this system at all, and—as you've already seen—the model may not capture the important qualities of family interaction in other ethnic or cultural groups.

The model also does not tell us *why* authoritative parenting is linked to greater competence in children. Are particular elements of the system especially critical, or is it the full configuration that matters? Addressing this question, Nancy Darling and Laurence Steinberg (1993) propose that we make a major distinction between parental *styles* and parental *behavior*. They suggest that we think of parenting style as a kind of basic climate in the family, as a set of attitudes and values rather than as a set of specific parenting practices or behaviors. Specific parenting behaviors or practices, in contrast, are responses to particular situations or goals, such as getting a child to stop hitting his sister or making sure a child does her homework. Style and parenting behaviors are obviously linked in various ways because some specific parental practices are more common in some styles than in others, but Darling and Steinberg argue that we need to look at them separately. They propose that parenting practices affect the child directly, increasing or decreasing the likelihood of specific behaviors. Parenting style, in contrast, has a more indirect effect. In particular, so Darling and Steinberg argue, parenting style "alters the parents' capacity to socialize their children by changing the effectiveness of their parenting practices" (p. 493). Thus, an authoritative parenting style is effective because it creates a climate in which the child is more open to the parents' influences and makes the specific parenting practices more potent. One result I reported earlier provides support for this idea: Parental involvement with the child's school is more strongly associated with good academic outcomes in authoritative than in authoritarian families. Both groups of parents may attend school functions regularly, talk to their children's teachers, and supervise homework. That is, their parenting *behavior* is the same. But the effects are different. Authoritative parents, by creating a climate that encourages discussion, by using explanations rather than orders, are more effective in their attempts to influence their child's school involvement and success.

The Darling/Steinberg proposal may yet prove to be a heuristic framework, but even this more complex type of analysis of the family system will not be sufficient in the long run. We need to remember that a great many variables beyond parental style are involved in family dynamics. Each child brings her own temperament or other qualities to the mixture; parents bring their own personalities and habits; the relationship between siblings may have a powerful effect, as the structure of the family itself clearly does. Let me look at each of these added elements in the family system.

Other Aspects of Family Dynamics

The Child's Characteristics

One of the first things to understand is that the influences in the parent-child system flow both ways. Children influence their parents as well as the other way around. I have already talked about one important influence of this type, namely, the child's temperament. Children with "difficult" temperaments seem to elicit more punishment (especially if the family is under some kind of stress) and may also affect a parent's mood. More generally, such children may have much more difficulty adapting to any change in the family system, such as a divorce.

Birth Order. Children's relationships with their parents may also be affected by where they stand in the family sequence (referred to as **birth order** or **ordinal position**). Early research on birth order suggested that birth order had, at most, very small effects. Parents generally have higher expectations for maturity in their firstborn and may well be more responsive, more child-centered with the first child. Firstborns are also punished more, in part because parents are simply less skilled in using non-coercive forms of control with their first child. Perhaps responding to the higher expectations, oldest children (firstborns or onlies) are somewhat more likely to be achievement-oriented. Compared to later-borns, they have slightly higher IQ scores, are more likely to go on to college, and are more likely to achieve some degree of eminence as adults (Sutton-Smith, 1982). Various explanations of these slight differences have been offered, but most psychologists concluded from this early research that birth order was not a terribly helpful way of looking at family interaction patterns.

An intriguing new book by historian Frank Sulloway, *Born to Rebel* (1996), however, reopens the debate. After a detailed analysis of the lives of over 7000 historical figures, he finds that firstborns nearly always support the status quo while later-borns are the rebels, likely to support new ideas or new political movements. Sulloway's central proposal is that each child must find some niche within the family configuration, some effective way to "curry parental favor." In this battle for successful niches, firstborns have a decided advantage. They are bigger and stronger and can defend the position of "biggest" or "most responsible." (My older sister used to chant at me, in that wonderful singsong voice children use to taunt one another, "I'm bigger 'n better than you, I'm bigger 'n better than you.") Firstborns, as a group, have more self-confidence and identify with authority and power. This combination allows them to achieve within the existing social system, committing them to the status quo from very early on.

Later-borns, in contrast, are automatically underdogs within the family. Sulloway argues that they are more open to experience because such an openness helps them to find an unoccupied niche. Their openness also makes them more empathetic, imaginative, and independent-minded than firstborns. Most explorers, heretics, and revolutionaries, according to Sulloway's research, were later-borns.

Sulloway's position is flexible enough to explain exceptions to these patterns. The key argument is that all children try to find some niche within the family. If the firstborn, perhaps because of a genetically patterned difficult temperament, becomes the family rebel, then the second child can capture the niche of the family achiever, the traditionalist. Birth order, then, is not destiny. However, if Sulloway is right—and it remains for psychologists to test his theory in various ways—then birth order may give us further important clues about why children in the same family are often so different.

Child Age. The child's age also makes a difference—a point that may seem obvious but is well worth reemphasizing. As the child develops, very different demands are made on the parents. As any parent can tell you, caring for an infant is quite a different task from caring for a 2-year-old or a 12-year-old. The areas in which control will be needed change over time; the degree of push for independence changes; the child's intellectual and language abilities change. Parents quite naturally adapt to these changes, altering their own patterns—perhaps even their style—as the child grows older. At the same time, parents show some consistency in their behavior toward children of the same age. That is, parents behave similarly toward the second child when he is 2 as they had toward the first child when she was 2, even though they are now treating the older child as a 4-year-old (Boer et al., 1992). Such a clearly rational set of changes in the parents' behavior as their children grow older has the effect of changing the family system over time.

Cultures and Contexts
China's One-Child Policy

A particularly fascinating cultural experiment regarding sibling effects and family size has been under way in China since 1979, when the government instituted an intense family-planning effort to reduce the normal family size to one child. This was done for economic and political reasons, since China has about 21 percent of the population of the world but only 7 percent of the arable land. The Chinese were facing the prospect of enormous food shortages with attendant social unrest if something was not done about their population explosion. What they did was adopt a one-child policy. This policy, nowadays somewhat loosely followed in rural areas but still rigorously followed in urban areas, has had a variety of consequences, not the least of which is a sizeable number of girl babies abandoned because the culture has such a strong preference for sons. There is also some indication that girl fetuses are being deliberately aborted for the same reason. These consequences have been, and continue to be, serious problems.

Another potential problem, anticipated by the Chinese at the inception of the one-child policy, is negative psychological effects of a culture full of only children. The Chinese authorities feared that only children would become family tyrants, spoiled by parents and grandparents. Recent studies do not confirm that fear. Toni Falbo, a U.S. researcher who has been involved in a series of large survey studies of Chinese children, reports that she can find few differences between only and nononly children, either in school performance or in personality (1992; Falbo & Poston, 1993). Another recent study indicates, in fact, that children born after the one-child policy went into effect reported *less* fear, anxiety, and depression than did youngsters with siblings, born a few years before the one-child policy began (Yang et al., 1995). Thus, by Chinese standards, the one-child policy has been a success. The policy has not led to a generation of "little emperors" as some had feared, although it is still early to know what effects it will have on the society as a whole in the decades to come, when the only children have become adults. A culture made up of only children (with a preponderance of males) is likely to differ in a whole variety of ways, many of them unanticipated, from one in which larger families prevail. In particular, if Sulloway is right about firstborns (including onlies) being generally supportive of the status quo, then a whole culture of only children should create few pressures for societal change. An interesting thought.

Differential Treatment of Siblings

Such changes over time, as well as ordinal position differences like those Sulloway proposes, may contribute to a phenomenon that has been puzzling developmental psychologists more and more in recent years—namely, the fact that two children from the same family so often turn out quite differently. I think that until recently, most of us assumed that parental style was rather like the weather in a given location: If it's raining, it's raining equally hard on everyone in the same place. In just the same way, we assumed that if one child experienced an authoritative style, then such a style must characterize the *family*; all other children in the same household would experience the same style, and the children would therefore end up with similar skills, similar personalities, similar strengths and weaknesses. But both pieces of this assumption now look wrong. Children growing up in the same family end up quite different, and the family system, perhaps even the family style, can be quite different for each child.

Some of the best evidence comes from several studies by Judy Dunn in both England and the United States (Dunn & McGuire, 1994). She has found that parents may express warmth and pride toward one child and scorn toward another, may be lenient toward one and strict with another. Here's an example from one of Dunn's observations, of 30-month-old Andy and his 14-month-old sister, Susie:

> Andy was a rather timid and sensitive child, cautious, unconfident, and compliant. . . . Susie was a striking contrast—assertive, determined, and a handful for her mother, who was nevertheless delighted by her boisterous daughter. In [one] observation of Andy and his sister, Susie persistently attempted to grab a forbidden object on a high kitchen counter, despite her mother's repeated prohibitions.

Critical Thinking

Are you and your siblings alike in a lot of ways, or do you have quite different traits, skills, attitudes? Can you trace any of those differences to variations in the way you were treated as children?

Finally, she succeeded, and Andy overheard his mother make a warm, affectionate comment on Susie's action: "Susie, you *are* a determined little devil!" Andy, sadly, commented to his mother, "*I'm* not a determined little devil!" His mother replied, laughing, "No! What are you? A poor old boy!" (Dunn, 1992, p. 6)

Not only are such episodes common in family interactions, but children are highly sensitive to such variations in treatment. Notice that Andy monitored his mother's interaction with Susie and then compared himself to his sister. Children this age are already aware of the emotional quality of exchanges between themselves and their parents as well as between their siblings and their parents. Dunn finds that those who receive less affection and warmth from their mothers are likely to be more depressed, worried, or anxious than are their siblings. And the more differently the parents treat siblings, the more rivalry and hostility brothers and sisters are likely to show toward one another (Brody et al., 1992).

Of course parents treat children differently for many reasons, *including* the child's age. Susie and Andy's mother may have been just as accepting of naughty behavior from Andy when he was a toddler. But Andy does not remember that; what he sees is the contrast between how he and Susie are treated now. Thus, even when parents are consistent in the way they respond to each child at a given age, at any moment they are *not* behaving consistently toward all children, and the children notice this and create internal models about the meaning of those differences in treatment.

Parents also respond to temperamental differences in their children, to gender differences, and to variations in the children's skills or talents, creating a unique pattern of interaction for each child. If Sulloway's theory is correct, then the child's effort to find her own niche within the family will also affect the way parents (and siblings) respond to her. It is becoming increasingly clear that such differences in treatment are an important ingredient in the child's emerging internal model of self and contribute greatly to variations in behavior between children growing up in the same families.

The Parents' Characteristics

The parents bring their own life histories, their own personalities, and the quality of their relationship with one another into the family dynamic as well. I could devote a whole chapter to the parents' half of this equation, but lacking such space, let me give only a few brief illustrations.

First, significant depression in either parent has a profound effect on the entire family system. You already know from Chapter 11 that an insecure attachment is more likely when the mother is depressed. Depressed parents also perceive their children as more difficult and problematic and are more critical of them, even when objective observers cannot identify any difference in the behavior of such children and the children of nondepressed mothers (Richters & Pellegrini, 1989; Webster-Stratton & Hammond, 1988). Thus, the parent's depression changes not only her behavior but her perception of the child's behavior, both of which alter the family system.

The parent's own internal working model of attachment also seems to have a very strong effect on the family system and thus on the child. You'll recall from the Research Report in Chapter 11 (p. 331), that those adults who are themselves securely attached are much more likely to have a child who is also securely attached.

Perhaps most broadly, the quality of the parents' own relationship with one another spills over into their relationship with their children. Couples with satisfying marital relationships are more warm and supportive toward their children; those whose marriage is full of discord also have more negative relationships with their children (Erel & Burman, 1995; Parke & Buriel, 1998). Their children show the effects in heightened risk of anxiety, depression, and delinquent behavior (Harold & Conger, 1997). In general, fathers' relationships with their children seem to be more strongly affected by

Critical Thinking

Can you think of other parental qualities, skills, or attributes that might affect the family system?

Critical Thinking

If cultures are systems too, then this large increase in the number of children experiencing a single-parent family structure has to have some impact on the whole system. What might be the long-term effects of this change?

the quality of their marital relationship than is true for mothers, but the spillover occurs for both parents.

Family Structure

Another obvious aspect of the family system is the particular configuration of people who live together in a given family unit—an aspect usually called *family structure*. For those of us who live in cultures with high rates of divorce and single-parent families, this is an issue of profound practical importance.

Only about half of all children in the United States in 1995 lived with both their biological parents (Hernandez, 1997). If we ask what percentage spend their entire childhood living with both natural parents, the numbers are even lower. Donald Hernandez, in his remarkable book *America's Children* (1993), estimated that only about 40 percent of the children born in 1980 have spent all their years up to age 18 living with both natural parents. Among African Americans, Hernandez estimates, this figure is only 20 percent, while among Euro-Americans it is about 55 percent. These figures are nearly double the rate of single-parent family experience over what occurred earlier in this century. In the 1920s, for example, 31 percent of whites and 57 percent of blacks spent at least some part of their childhood living with only one parent. In addition, the *reasons* for the pattern have changed. In 1920, the most common reason for a child to be living with only one parent was that a parent had died; today, the most common reasons are divorce or that the mother has never married.

You can get some feeling for the variety of family structures in which children live today from Figure 13.6, which shows the percentages of five different structures in the families of white, African-American, and Latino 13-year-olds in the United States, based on a nationally representative sample of over 21,000 children studied by Valerie Lee and her colleagues (1994). Even this chart, though, doesn't begin to convey the variety of family structures or the number of changes in family structure a child may experience over time. Divorced mothers, for example, may have had live-in relationships with one or more men before a remarriage, or they may have lived for a while with their own parents. And many children, especially children with never-married mothers, live in extended families with grandparents and other family members as well as a parent. All in all, the evidence makes it inescapably clear that the *majority* of children in the United States today experience at least two different family structures, often many more than that, in the course of their growing up. This is especially true of African Americans, but it is increasingly true of other ethnic groups in our culture as well.

In other industrialized countries, single-parent families are less common, but they are on the rise everywhere. By the mid-1980s, the proportions ranged widely: less than

When we think of "the family," many of us still think of a configuration with a father and mother and several children. But in fact, in the United States it now is the exception rather than the rule for a child to spend his or her entire childhood and adolescence in such a family system.

Figure 13.6

Variations in family structure among today's 13-year-olds.

(*Source:* Lee, V. E.; Burkham, D. T.; Zimiles, H.; and Ladewski, B.; from Table 2, p. 419, "Family structure and its effect on behavioral and emotional problems in young adolescents," in *Journal of research on adolescence*, 4, 1994. © 1994 by Lawrence Erlbaum Associates. By permission of the publisher and V. Lee.)

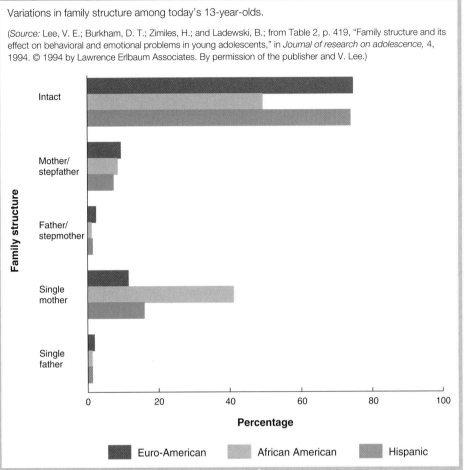

5 percent in Japan; about 15 percent in Australia, the United Kingdom, and Sweden; and nearly 25 percent in the United States (Burns, 1992). Because cultures are complex, knowledge gleaned about the impact of family structure on children's development in one country may not hold elsewhere, but the issue is growing in importance in many parts of the world.

What do we know about the impact on children of being reared in such varied or varying family structures?

Single-Parent Families. One place to begin is to look at what happens to children who are reared with both natural parents versus those with only one natural parent. Sara McLanahan, a sociologist who has studied this question extensively (McLanahan, 1997; McLanahan & Sandefur, 1994), concludes:

> Children who grow up with only one biological parent are less successful, on average, than children who grow up with both parents. These differences extend to a broad range of outcomes, and they persist into adulthood. (McLanahan, 1997, p. 37)

Children of single parents are about twice as likely to drop out of high school, twice as likely to have a child before age 20, and less likely to have a steady job in their late teens or early twenties (McLanahan & Sandefur, 1994).

These negative consequences seem to occur regardless of whether the cause of the parent's absence is that the mother was never married or that the parents divorced. In contrast, children of widowed mothers, on average, do nearly as well as children reared by both natural parents—a finding for which we do not yet have any good explanations.

This does *not* mean that single parenthood is the cause of all evil. Rather, as McLanahan points out, it is but one of many factors that increase the risk that a child

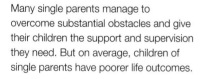

Cultures and Contexts
The Benefits of Extended Families

Because single-parent families have become so common in the United States, researchers here tend to develop a kind of tunnel vision when it comes to studies of "family structure." For us, the question nearly always translates to a comparison of single-parent families with two-parent families. But in many parts of the world, the normative form of family life is not the nuclear or two-parent family but rather an *extended* family, in which several generations live together in the same household. One recent study from the Sudan provides a kind of antidote to our typical cultural myopia.

Ahmed El Hassan Al Awad and Edmund Sonuga-Barke (1992) compared the incidence of childhood problems for children who lived in Western-style nuclear families (mother and father only) versus those who lived in traditional extended families with three generations in the same household. All these families lived in towns near Khartoum (the capital of Sudan), and the two groups were matched for social status and approximate income. The mothers were interviewed about their children's behavior and problems.

The findings are very clear: Children reared in extended households had fewer conduct problems, fewer sleep problems, and better self-care, and they were less likely to be overly dependent. The best single predictor of these good outcomes was the involvement of the child's grandmother in the child's care, and this was true within the group of nuclear families as well as in the comparison of nuclear and extended families.

How many different explanations for this result can you think of? Should we generalize this finding to Western cultures and conclude that extended families would be better for children in our society as well? How could you investigate such a hypothesis?

will do poorly in school or become delinquent. Nor does living in an intact family buffer a child against all problems. Many young people whose parents are still together nonetheless drop out of school or experience other significant personal problems. But living with only one parent substantially increases the risks.

Why are the risks higher for this group? One obvious but nevertheless highly significant reason is that such families are simply much more likely to be poor. For example, data from the United States indicate that after a divorce, a woman's income drops an average of 40 to 50 percent (Smock, 1993). Never-married mothers, too, are far more likely to be poor. Poverty, in turn, reduces the resources available to the child, increases the parent's level of stress, and makes it far less likely that the child will receive the financial or emotional support needed to finish high school or to go on to college—a point I'll come back to in Chapter 14 when I talk more generally about poverty. McLanahan estimates that approximately half the difference in educational achievement between children reared by both parents and those in single-parent families can be attributed to differences in income. The other half of the difference can be attributed to two factors: Children in single-parent families receive less parental supervision, and, be-

Many single parents manage to overcome substantial obstacles and give their children the support and supervision they need. But on average, children of single parents have poorer life outcomes.

Cultures and Contexts
Explaining the High Rate of Single Parenthood Among African Americans

Why is the rate of single parenthood so much higher among African Americans than in other subgroups in U.S. culture? Andrew Cherlin (1992a) suggests that the situation reflects historical trends in childbearing and marriage within the African-American community rather than any increase in sexual activity among young black women. Unmarried black teens or young adults are no more likely to give birth today than they were in the 1960s. The *proportion* of all black births to unmarried young women has risen because the birth rate among older black women declined over those years, particularly among *married* women. At the same time, the rate of marriage declined steadily among blacks, a pattern that Cherlin attributes to two factors.

First, economic conditions for many black males worsened as unemployment rose in the 1980s and early 1990s; even today, with unemployment at much lower levels nationally, job opportunities for unskilled men are severely limited. Furthermore, although black working women earn less than black working men, this gender difference is smaller among African Americans than among Euro-Americans. Taken together, this means that black men, particularly inner-city black men, have become less and less able to take on the role of provider for a family, while black women have become more and more able to support themselves. These conditions, according to Cherlin, made African-American women less likely to marry at all and less tolerant of unsatisfactory relationships.

Cultural traditions stemming from African styles of extended families have also contributed to this lesser emphasis on marriage as the foundation of family life. Instead, networks of relationships across several households, or multiple generations within a single household, are both common and approved.

These various factors help to put the large ethnic differences in the rate of single-parent families into a wider context. Yet explaining such a difference does not eliminate the effects on children. To be sure, extended kin networks can help to buffer children from the generally negative outcomes associated with single parenthood, but the risks are still higher than for children of two-parent families.

cause their families move more often, they have less access to what sociologists call *social capital*—the whole range of other relationships and resources available to the child.

Ethnicity, incidentally, is *not* a causal factor here. Yes, a larger percentage of African-American children grow up in single-parent families. But the same negative outcomes occur in white single-parent families, and the same positive outcomes are found in two-parent minority families. For example, the school dropout rate for white children from disrupted families is higher than the dropout rate for Latino or African-American children reared in two-parent families.

Stepparent Families. For a single parent, marriage or remarriage is not a "quick fix" for all these various problems. Adding a stepparent to the family system does usually reduce the economic hardship, but it doesn't eliminate the increased emotional and intellectual risks for the children. After reviewing all the available research, McLanahan concludes that children in stepparent families do about as well or poorly as those

Five-year-old Keith is a whole lot less sure than his mother that her second marriage is a joyous occasion!

reared by a single parent—and less well than those in intact families. One specific finding, shown in Figure 13.7, illustrates the point. The data are from the same large study of adolescents by Valerie Lee from which I drew the data in Figure 13.6 (p. 395). You can see that she finds that any family structure other than two biological parents is linked to higher levels of problems in the teenagers. Findings from the Steinberg/Dornbusch study I've been describing throughout this chapter offer one possible explanation of such a result; they find that stepparent families show higher levels of authoritarian and lower levels of authoritative child-rearing styles (Dornbusch et al., 1987).

Divorce

All of what I have just been saying about the impact of single parenthood and stepfamilies is obviously relevant to any discussion of the effects of divorce on children. But some special additional strains are associated with divorce.

All observers agree that "divorce is not an event, but a *process* that unfolds over a long period of time" (Goodman et al., 1998, p. 786). The first two to four years after the divorce are a period of special strain. In these years, children typically become more defiant, more negative, more aggressive or depressed or angry. If they are of school age, their school performance often drops for at least a while (Furstenberg & Cherlin, 1991; Hetherington & Stanley-Hagan, 1995; Morrison & Cherlin, 1995).

The same sort of disruption occurs in the parents' behavior as well. The adults may show wide mood swings, experience problems at work, or suffer from poor health. Their parenting style also changes, becoming much less authoritative, almost neglectful (Hetherington, 1989; Hetherington et al., 1998). In particular, single parents do much less well at monitoring their children's behavior and setting clear rules or limits, a pattern that typically persists for several years, even if the mother or father remarries (Hetherington & Clingempeel, 1992).

As a general rule, these immediate negative effects are slightly larger for boys than for girls, although this difference now appears smaller than earlier research had led us to conclude. Among adolescents, in particular, girls show equally or even greater negative consequences (Amato, 1993; Hetherington & Stanley-Hagan, 1995). Age differences in the severity of the child's reaction are also not clear-cut. If there is one age associated with higher rates of problems, it is early adolescence, especially if a remarriage occurs at the time the child is moving into adolescence (Hetherington et al., 1998).

Figure 13.7

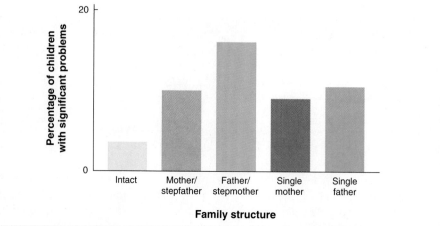

Children in stepparent families, especially father/stepmother, are more likely than are those in intact families to show behavior problems of one type or another.

(*Source:* Lee et al., 1994, from Table 1, p. 417.)

Evidence on long-term problems is more consistent: All researchers agree that *on average,* children and adults from divorced families have more adjustment problems, more school difficulties, and higher rates of divorce themselves (Parke & Buriel, 1998). Where disagreement still exists is over the extensiveness of such problems. Some researchers, notably Judith Wallerstein (1989), have concluded that the majority of children and adults with divorced parents have significant and persisting psychological problems. Others assess the situation more positively. Yes, adults whose parents divorced are two to three times more likely than are those growing up with both parents to show long-term psychological problems (Goodman et al., 1998; Hetherington et al., 1998), but such a rate still means that 70 to 80 percent of children whose parents divorce become "reasonably competent and well-adjusted individuals" (Hetherington & Stanley-Hagan, 1995, p. 234). On most measures of longer-term functioning, the overall difference is fairly modest.

In all this, it is not clear yet just what the causal agent is, because so many changes happen at the same time when a couple divorces: a rise in conflict between the parents, the loss of one member of the family system, increased economic hardship, and other stressful life changes. The short-term disruption in the children's and adults' behavior seems to result from some combination of these factors, although of them all, the degree of open conflict between the parents may well be the most critical for the child's emotional stability (Amato, 1993).

Open parental conflict has negative effects on children whether the parents divorce or not—a point already clear from what I've said about the impact of marital harmony/disharmony (Amato, 1993; Coiro, 1995; Harold et al., 1997; Isabella, 1995). Children whose parents fight often, physically or verbally, show more distress, more anger, more aggression than do children whose parents fight less openly or less often, even when the parents are still together (Davies & Cummings, 1994; Harold & Conger, 1997). Indeed, many children in divorcing families already show heightened rates of negative behavior before the divorce occurs, presumably as a result of pre-divorce exposure to parental discord or hostility (e.g., Cherlin et al., 1991). So we should be careful not to blame all the bad outcomes on the divorce itself, although that process does create further disruption and distress. Such distress is exacerbated if the parents continue to argue or bicker after the divorce, increasing the psychological risks for the child.

Summing Up What We Know About Family Structure

Where does all this leave us in our effort to understand the impact of family structure? My own reading of this growing body of evidence is that any family structure other than two biological parents has less optimal effects for three key reasons.

First, single parenthood or divorce reduces the financial and emotional resources available to support the child. With only one parent, the household typically has only one income and only one adult to respond to the child's emotional needs. Second, *any* family transition involves upheaval. This is true of the birth of a new sibling in an intact family. It is even more true of divorce or of remarriage. Both adults and children adapt slowly and with difficulty to the subtraction or addition of new adults to the family system (Hetherington & Stanley-Hagan, 1995). Parents can take specific actions to reduce this disruption (as discussed in the Real World box on p. 400), but some disruption is unavoidable.

Finally and perhaps most importantly, single parenthood, divorce, and stepparenthood all increase the likelihood that the family climate or style will shift away from authoritative parenting (or other forms of supportive parenting) toward less optimal forms. We see this in the first few years after a divorce when the custodial parent (usually the mother) is distracted or depressed and less able to manage warm control; we see it in stepfamilies as well, where rates of authoritative parenting are lower than in intact families.

The key thing to understand is that authoritative child rearing is linked to low levels of disturbed behaviors and higher levels of psychological adjustment in the child, *no matter what family structure the child grows up in*. And authoritarian or neglecting parenting is linked to poor outcomes whether it is the normal family pattern or was triggered by a

Critical Thinking

Given what you have just read, how would you answer someone who asks you whether it is worse for an unhappy couple to get divorced or to stay together even though they fight all the time? What kind of study might you do to try to answer this question better?

The Real World

Softening the Effects of Divorce

Given the rate of divorce in our culture, a significant percentage of you reading these words will likely go through a divorce when you have children still living at home. You cannot eliminate all the short-term disruptive effects of such an event on your children, but here are some specific things you can do that are likely to soften or shorten the effects:

1. Try to keep the number of separate changes the child has to cope with to a minimum. If at all possible, keep the children in the same school, in the same house or apartment, or in the same day-care setting. This advice holds not just for the period immediately following the divorce but for several subsequent years as well (Buchanan et al., 1996).

2. If the children live with you full-time, help them stay in touch with the noncustodial parent. Buchanan's large study of adolescents in divorced families (Buchanan et al., 1996) suggests that this is especially important for children with a custodial father. If they did not maintain regular contact with their noncustodial mother, then even a warm relationship with the father did not prevent a higher rate of emotional problems. If you are the noncustodial parent, maintain as much contact as possible with your children, calling regularly, seeing them regularly, attending school functions, and so on. If you live at some distance from your children, then phone calls and predictable visits in the summer or over school holidays may be sufficient, especially with older children. Whatever you do, don't forget the child's birthday or other special occasions!

3. Keep the conflict between you and your ex-spouse to a minimum. Most of all, try not to fight in front of the children; it is the conflict the children experience, rather than the conflict the parents feel, that seems to be critical (Buchanan et al., 1996).

The consequences are particularly bad when the conflict is prolonged, is openly angry or violent, and focuses on or involves the child (Goodman et al., 1998).

4. Whatever else you do, do not use the child as a go-between or talk disparagingly about your ex-spouse to your child. Children who feel caught in the middle between the two parents are more likely to show various kinds of negative symptoms, such as depression or behavior problems (Buchanan et al., 1991).

5. Maintain your own network of support, and use that network liberally. Stay in touch with friends; seek out others in the same situation; join a support group. In whatever way you can, nurture yourself and your own needs (Hetherington & Stanley-Hagan, 1995).

6. *Consider* the possibility of a dual-residence arrangement in which the child moves back and forth regularly between the two households—such as weekly or monthly. The evidence is scant and not entirely consistent (Goodman et al., 1998), but a few studies suggest that such arrangements are slightly better. For example, Buchanan's large study of adolescents in divorced families suggested that children in this kind of joint custody had slightly better adjustment than did those in the custody of only one parent. Such an arrangement will not work in every case. Certainly if the level of acrimony between the divorcing couple is very high or they do not live close to one another, dual residence is impossible. Still, when it is feasible, such an arrangement seems to be beneficial because it allows the child to maintain a close relationship with both parents.

In the midst of your own emotional upheaval from a divorce, these are not easy prescriptions to follow. But if you are able to do so, your children will suffer less.

divorce, by a stressful remarriage, by the father's loss of a job, or by any other stress (Goldberg, 1990). Ultimately, it is this *process* within the family that is significant for the child. The likelihood of a nonoptimal family process is greater in single-parent families, but this does not mean that the probability is 100 percent. Many single parents are able to find the strength within themselves to maintain a supportive relationship with their children. After all, we know that three-quarters of children reared in single-parent or step-families manage to finish high school, and roughly half of those high school graduates go on to at least some college (McLanahan & Sandefur, 1994). Similarly, the great majority of children reared by a single parent or in a stepfamily do not become delinquent or show significant behavior problems. Indeed, one recent study of inner-city African-American teenage boys suggests that those in single-parent households are no more likely to be delinquent than are those in two-parent households because in this sample, the single mothers actually had more supportive relationships with their sons than did many of the married or remarried mothers (Zimmerman et al., 1995). It is thus clearly possible for single or divorced parents to surmount the extra problems. Still, we need to face up to the fact that such family systems are less stable and, on average, less supportive for children.

Some Exosystem Effects:
Parents' Work and Social Support

Beyond family structure, the family process is affected by a wide range of experiences in the *parents'* lives—experiences that occur outside the family's interactions but that nonetheless affect those interactions. The two examples I want to talk about are the parents' jobs and their network of social support.

Parents' Jobs

The existing research on the effects of parents' work on children contains an odd quirk: Nearly all the research on mothers' employment compares mothers who work with those who do not, while nearly all the work on the impact of fathers' employment focuses on fathers who have *lost* their jobs. We have little research on mothers who lose their jobs or on stay-at-home fathers compared with employed fathers. Given our cultural history, I suppose this pattern of research makes sense, although it certainly leaves some significant gaps in our knowledge. Fortunately, a new body of work is beginning to emerge that asks a very different kind of question, namely: What is the impact of the *quality* of the parents' work experience on family life?

Mothers' Employment. How is life different for children whose mothers work, compared to those whose mothers stay home? Do these two groups of children differ in any systematic way? These questions are obviously not entirely separable from all the issues about child care I'll be talking about in Chapter 14, since it is precisely because the mother is working that most children are in alternative care. But the question is also relevant when we look at families with school-age children, where the impact of the mother's work is not so totally confounded with the effects of the child's alternative care.

Most of the research on the impact of mothers' employment points to a neutral or slightly positive effect for children, at least in this culture at this time in history (Parke & Buriel, 1998). Girls whose mothers work are more independent and admire their mothers more than do girls whose mothers do not work. And both boys and girls whose mothers work have more egalitarian sex-role concepts. The effects of the mother's employment on the children's academic performance are less clear. Many studies show no differences (e.g., A. E. Gottfried et al., 1994); some studies show that among boys, those whose mothers work full-time are doing slightly less well in school (Hoffman, 1989). One recent large study (Muller, 1995), involving a nationally representative sample of 24,599 eighth graders, shows a very small negative effect of the mother's employment on adolescents' math grades and test scores—a difference that seems to flow from the fact that when mothers work, they are less involved with the child's school and are less likely to supervise the teenager's schoolwork during after-school hours. Working mothers who find ways to provide such supervision and who remain involved with their children's schools have kids who do as well as children of homemaker mothers.

In the United States today, nearly two-thirds of women with children under age 6 and three-quarters of women with school-age or adolescent children work at least part-time (U.S. Bureau of the Census, 1997). In general, the effects seem to be neutral or beneficial for the children.

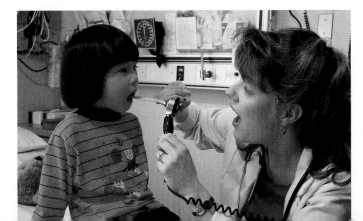

These fired Latino garment workers in San Antonio are protesting the loss of their jobs. Such a loss affects the worker's family not only economically but also psychologically. Adults typically become less authoritative in their child rearing in the face of such stress.

These findings point to the fact that it is not the mother's job per se that produces the various effects that are linked to maternal employment, but rather that her employment alters the family system in various ways. For one thing, having a job may affect the mother's own view of herself by improving her self-esteem or her morale and thereby changing the way she relates to the rest of the family. For example, a woman who begins working generally acquires more power in the spousal relationship, in part because she now has demonstrable earning power, and because she may feel more independent (Spitze, 1988). Such power or self-esteem also spills over into her interactions with her children, perhaps especially with a daughter. For example, Bronfenbrenner finds that working mothers give more positive descriptions of their young daughters than do nonworking mothers (Bronfenbrenner et al., 1984).

The mother's employment also forces changes in daily routines and in interaction patterns simply because she is not at home for as many hours. Fathers in dual-worker families spend somewhat more time in child care and household tasks than do fathers with homemaker wives, although it is still true that working mothers do about twice as much of this labor as do fathers (Blair & Johnson, 1992; Parke & Buriel, 1998). This change in the division of labor may then have an effect on the quality of the parents' interaction with children, as well as altering the role model each parent provides for the child.

Finally, of course, when the mother works, she has less time available for one-on-one interaction with the children, including supervision of their homework. These effects of employment on the woman and on her family are not automatic or uniform. The mother's attitude toward her work is an important intervening variable. Numerous studies show that the most negative outcomes are found among children in two subgroups: those with mothers who would prefer to work but are staying at home and those with working mothers who dislike their jobs or are unwilling workers (DeMeis et al., 1986; Lerner & Galambos, 1986). The most positive outcomes occur when the mother wants to work and works at a job she likes. In such families, the mother's style of child rearing is more likely to be authoritative (Greenberger & Goldberg, 1989).

Fathers' Employment or Unemployment. I have already touched on the effects of a father's job loss when I talked about the McKenzie family at the beginning of this chapter. The research evidence tells us that when a man loses his job, it puts enormous strain on his marriage; marital conflict rises, and both parents show more symptoms of depression. The resulting effects on family dynamics look much like what we see in divorcing families or in families facing other sorts of stresses: Both parents become less consistent in their behavior toward their children, less affectionate, and less good at monitoring (Conger et al., 1995). The children respond to this deterioration in their parents' behavior as they do during a divorce: They show a variety of symptoms, including sometimes depression, aggression, or delinquency. Often their school performance declines (Conger et al., 1992; 1994; Flanagan & Eccles, 1993). The negative pattern can be softened if the unemployed father receives enough emotional support from his wife and is generally cured when the father again finds work, but the whole sequence illustrates nicely how an event outside the family affects the child through the impact on the parents' behavior toward one another and toward the child.

Quality of Parents' Work. Research examining the effects of the *quality* of the parents' work points to a similar conclusion. The now classic studies were done by Melvin Kohn and Carmi Schooler (Kohn, 1980; Kohn & Schooler, 1983), who found that men (or women) whose jobs require higher levels of self-direction and autonomy show increases in intellectual flexibility over time. In contrast, routine, highly supervised jobs lead to decreases in intellectual flexibility. Kohn's work, as well as that of several current researchers (Greenberger et al., 1994; Parcel & Menaghan, 1994), shows that these differences spill over into family life. Men and women who work at routine jobs come to place greater emphasis on obedience from their children than is true for parents in more intellectually flexible jobs, a pattern that has been found among African-American parents as well as Euro-Americans (Mason et al., 1994). Furthermore, when a mother who has been at home with her children begins work at a job that is low in complexity, the child's home environment deteriorates, becoming less stimulating and supportive than it was before; in contrast, the mother's beginning work at an intellectually complex job is linked to improvements in the child's environment (Menaghan & Parcel, 1995). In the terms I have been using in this chapter, complex jobs are linked to increases in authoritative and decreases in authoritarian child rearing. Thus, the character of the job a parent has affects his or her way of thinking, particularly about authority, and parents apply their thinking to their interactions with their children.

Social Support for Parents

A second aspect of parents' lives that affects the family microsystem is the quality of their network of relationships and their satisfaction with the social support they receive from that network. The general point is fairly easy to state: Parents who have access to adequate emotional and physical support—from each other or from friends and family—are able to respond to their children more warmly, more consistently, and with better control (Crnic et al., 1983; Parke & Buriel, 1998; R. Taylor et al., 1993). Their children, in turn, look better on a variety of measures (Melson et al., 1993). For example, children whose parents have access to more assistance from friends complete more years of school than do children whose parents have less support of this type (Hofferth et al., 1995).

The effect of social support on parents is particularly evident when they are experiencing stress of some kind, such as job loss, chronic poverty, teenage childbirth, a temperamentally difficult or handicapped infant, divorce, or even just fatigue. You may recall the discussion in Chapter 9 of a study by Susan Crockenberg (1981) that illustrates the point nicely. She found that temperamentally irritable infants had an increased likelihood of ending up with an insecure attachment to their mothers only when the mother lacked adequate social support. When the mother felt that she had enough support, similarly irritable children were later securely attached. There are many other examples of this "buffering effect" of social support, for example:

- New mothers who lack good social and emotional support are more likely to suffer from postpartum depression than are those with adequate support (Cutrona & Troutman, 1986).

- Divorced parents who have help and emotional support from friends or family members are much more able to maintain a stable and affectionate environment for their children than are those who grapple with the problem in isolation (Hetherington, 1989).

- Among African-American single mothers, those who have enough aid and emotional support from kin show a more authoritative style of parenting than do single mothers lacking such aid (R. Taylor et al., 1993).

As a general rule, social support seems to allow parents to mobilize the best parenting skills they may have in their repertoire. Of course not all "help" from families or friends feels like support. (I'm sure you have all been given unwanted advice from your parents or in-laws or friends!) The key is not the objective amount of contact or advice received but rather the parent's *satisfaction* with the level and quality of the support he or she is experiencing. The moral seems to be that at those times of greatest difficulty or stress—when a new child is born, when a child presents special difficulties, when the family moves or experiences major changes—you most need the emotional and physical support of others. Yet if you wait until that difficult moment to look around and see who is there to help, you may not find what you need. Social networks must be developed and nurtured over time. But they certainly seem to pay dividends for parents, and thus for children.

Summary

1. To understand children's development, we must move beyond examination of the child alone or of the mother-child pair; we must examine the total ecological system.

2. A system is understood as being more than the sum of its parts. It is also adaptive to change, and any change in any one part of the system affects every other part.

3. Bronfenbrenner conceives of the child's ecological system as composed of three elements: microsystems, such as the family or the school, in which the child is directly involved; exosystems, such as the parent's job, which affect the child indirectly by influencing some aspect of a microsystem; and macrosystems, such as the ethnic subculture or the broader society or culture in which the family exists.

4. Within the family microsystem, several dimensions of parental behavior toward children seem to be particularly significant, including the emotional tone of the family, the method of maintaining control, and the patterns of communication.

5. Families that provide high levels of warmth and affection, compared to those that are more cold or rejecting, have children with more secure attachments and better peer relationships.

6. Families that have clear rules and standards and enforce those rules and expectations consistently have children with the greatest self-esteem and the greatest competence across a broad range of situations.

7. Children who are talked to frequently, in complex sentences, and who are listened to in turn not only develop language more rapidly; they also have more positive and less conflicted relationships with their parents.

8. The elements of parental behavior occur in combinations or styles of child rearing. Four such styles, suggested by several theorists, are authoritarian, authoritative, permissive, and neglecting.

9. The authoritative style is high in nurturance, control, communication, and maturity demands; the authoritarian style is high in control and maturity demands but low in warmth and communication; the permissive style is high in warmth and low in communication, control, and maturity demands; the neglecting style is low on all dimensions.

10. The authoritative style appears to be the most generally effective for producing confident, competent, independent, and affectionate children. The most negative outcomes are found in neglecting families.

11. Research by Steinberg and Dornbusch suggests ethnic differences in the ways in which family styles affect children. In particular, Asian-American children do generally very well in school despite low rates of authoritative parenting, which may indicate that the categorization of family styles is culture-specific.

12. The family system is also affected by the child's characteristics, such as temperament, age, gender, and position in the family.

13. The family system is, in essence, different for each child, helping to explain why siblings growing up in the same family often turn out very differently.

14. Parental characteristics that affect the family system include depression, the parent's own internal working model of attachment, and the quality of the parents' marital relationship.

15. The structure of the family also has an impact on family functioning, which in turn affects children's behavior. The majority of children born in the United States today will spend at least a portion of their childhood in a one-parent family structure.

16. Children reared in single-parent families are at higher risk for a variety of negative outcomes, including school dropout, teen parenthood, and delinquency. Stepfamilies, too, are associated with heightened risks of poorer outcomes for children.

17. Any change in family structure, such as after a divorce, is likely to produce short-term disruption (often including an increase in authoritarian or neglecting child-rearing style) before the system adapts to a new form.

18. A mother's employment affects the family system by changing the mother's self-image, increasing her power, and altering the distribution of labor. The effects on the children are generally positive, especially for girls.

19. Loss of job by a father disrupts the family system, increasing authoritarian child rearing and reducing marital satisfaction. Children often show disrupted behavior.

20. The character of a parent's job also has an effect on family interactions. Complex jobs that demand greater independence are linked to increased authoritative parenting, while less complex, routine jobs are linked to increases in authoritarian control.

21. The impact of family change or stress is mitigated by the availability of a sufficient amount of social support from the parents' social network.

Key Terms

authoritarian style One of the three parental styles described by Baumrind, characterized by high levels of control and maturity demands and low levels of nurturance and communication. **p. 385**

authoritative style One of the three parental styles described by Baumrind, characterized by high levels of control, nurturance, maturity demands, and communication. **p. 385**

birth order A child's position in the sequence of children within a family, such as firstborn, later-born, or only. **p. 391**

neglecting style A fourth major parenting style, suggested by Maccoby and Martin, involving low levels of both acceptance and control. **p. 385**

ordinal position See *birth order.* **p. 391**

permissive style One of the three parenting styles described by Baumrind, characterized

by high levels of nurturance and low levels of control, maturity demands, and communication. **p. 385**

responsiveness An aspect of parent-child interaction; a responsive parent is sensitive to the child's cues and reacts appropriately, following the child's lead. **p. 380**

warmth versus hostility The key dimension of emotional tone used to describe family interactions. **p. 380**

Suggested Readings

Boer, F., & Dunn, J. (Eds.). (1992). *Children's sibling relationships: Developmental and clinical issues.* Hillsdale, NJ: Erlbaum. A first-rate collection of papers on a subject that is of growing interest to many psychologists. Each paper is relatively brief and reviews the available literature on one aspect of sibling relationships.

Boynton, R. S. (1996, October 7). The birth of an idea. *The New Yorker,* 72–81. A fascinating review and analysis of Frank Sulloway's somewhat revolutionary ideas on the importance of birth order in shaping individual personality and behavior.

Furstenberg, F. F., Jr., & Cherlin, A. J. (1991). *Divided families: What happens to children when parents part.* Cambridge, MA: Harvard University Press. A relatively brief, reasonably current review of this important subject, aimed at lay readers and decision makers rather than at psychologists. The focus is on the impact of divorce on children.

Hernandez, D. J. (1993). *America's children: Resources from family, government, and the economy.* New York: Russell Sage Foundation. A dense, difficult, but remarkable book based on U.S. Census data, exploring everything that we know about the status of children in the United States. Hernandez focuses particularly on

the changing demographics of mother's employment, single parenthood, and family incomes as they affect children. Not easy reading, but fascinating.

McLanahan, S. S., & Sandefur, G. (1994). *Growing up with a single parent: What hurts, what helps.* Cambridge, MA: Harvard University Press. A sobering book based on a careful reading of five major national studies, several of them longitudinal in design. I think you will find its not-too-technical style comprehensible. A briefer review of the evidence on single parenthood is in McLanahan's 1997 paper, listed in the references.

14

Beyond The Family:
The Impact of the Broader Culture

The ecological approach to studying the family's influence on the child's development has brought us many new insights, among them the realization that we cannot stop at the edges of the family. To understand a child's development, we also have to understand the impact of other institutions that affect the child directly. As a final step, we need to try to understand the ways in which all of these institutions are embedded in still broader subcultural and cultural contexts. In the best of all possible worlds, we would look at these beyond-the-family effects in many different cultural systems: in collectivist as well as individualist cultures, in nonindustrialized as well as highly industrialized systems, in stable cultures and those undergoing change, in cultures in which schooling is rare or brief as well as those in which schooling is a normal part of childhood, and so on and on. Ultimately, we will need such an analysis to understand the ways in which nonfamily influences shape the child's development. But not only is such an analysis beyond the scope of this book; it is beyond the scope of our knowledge. So what I want to try to do here is to take our own complex culture as a kind of case study, looking at what we know about the ways in which nonfamily institutions affect the child, beginning with several institutions with which the child is likely to have direct experience: child care, schools, part-time jobs, and television.

Child Care

In virtually every industrialized country in the world, women have gone into the work force in great numbers in the past two decades. In the United States the change has been particularly rapid and massive: In 1970, only 18 percent of married women with children under age 6 were in the labor force; by 1996, this number had risen to 62.5 percent (U.S. Bureau of the Census, 1997). More than half of women with children under age 1—including more than half of women with husbands present—are now working outside the home at least part-time, a rate that appears to be higher than in any other country in the world (Cherlin, 1992b; U.S. Bureau of the Census, 1996). It is now typical for infants as well as school-age children to spend a significant amount of time being cared for by someone other than a parent. One recent study, based on a carefully selected sample of over 1300 families from throughout the United States, indicated that by age 1, 80 percent of infants had experienced some regular nonmaternal child care; the majority entered such care before 6 months of age (NICHD Early Child Care Research Network, 1997b). Although similar changes have occurred in other countries to a lesser degree, raising the same kinds of fundamental questions, in the discussion to follow, I'm going to be talking almost exclusively about child care as it exists in the United States.

The key question for psychologists—as well as for teachers and other child-care professionals—is what effect such nonparental care may have on infants and young children. As you can easily imagine, this is *not* a simple question to answer, for a whole host of reasons:

- An enormous variety of different care arrangements are all lumped under the general title "day care" or "child care."

- Children enter these care arrangements at different ages and remain in them for varying lengths of time.

- Some children have the same alternative caregiver over many years; others shift often from one care setting to another.

- Child care varies hugely in quality.

- Families who place their children in day care are undoubtedly different in a whole host of ways from those who care for their children primarily at home.

How can we be sure that effects attributed to child care are not the result of these other family differences instead?

Much of the research we have to draw on does not really take these complexities into account. Early studies typically compared children "in day care" with those "reared at home" and ascribed any differences between the two groups to the day-care experience. Recent studies are much better, so we are moving toward clearer answers, although many uncertainties remain. Nonetheless, because the question is so critical, you need to be aware of what we know, as well as what we do not yet know.

Who Is Taking Care of the Children?

Let me begin at the descriptive level. Just who is taking care of all those children while their parents work? In some countries, such as France or Belgium, child care is organized and subsidized by the government and is free to all parents, though of course paid for by higher taxes (Bergmann, 1996). In the United States, we have no such governmental system, so each family must make its own arrangements as best it can.

Figure 14.1 summarizes the solutions working parents have found, based on 1993 Census Bureau data for all children under age 6 (Hofferth, 1996). These numbers may contain some surprises for you. When most people think of "child care" or "day care," they think of a day-care center or perhaps someone caring for a group of other people's children in her own home (an arrangement called **family day care**). The use of center care has increased considerably in recent years, rising from 6 percent in 1965 to 31 percent by 1995 (Scarr, 1998). Figure 14.1 shows that despite this increase, half of preschool children with employed parents are still cared for by a family member rather than in a center or in family day care. Most such children are cared for in their own homes rather than in someone else's home.

These numbers do vary somewhat depending on the age of the child and the family's economic status. Infants are much more likely to be cared for at home by a father, grandparent, or other relative and much less likely to be placed in a day-care center

Figure 14.1

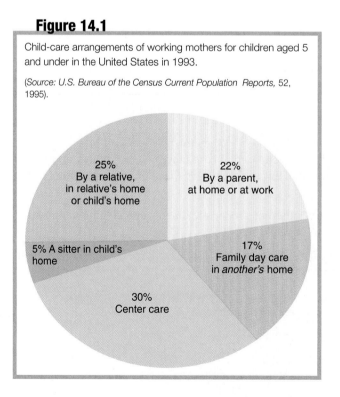

Child-care arrangements of working mothers for children aged 5 and under in the United States in 1993.

(*Source: U.S. Bureau of the Census Current Population Reports*, 52, 1995).

25%
By a relative, in relative's home or child's home

22%
By a parent, at home or at work

5% A sitter in child's home

17%
Family day care in *another's* home

30%
Center care

(NICHD Early Child Care Research Network, 1997b). Poverty-level families, lacking the funds for many kinds of paid care, rely more often on grandparents or other family members to provide care; middle-class families are more likely to choose family day care or center care (Lamb, 1998; NICHD Early Child Care Research Network, 1997c).

The data in Figure 14.1 can only begin to convey the enormous variety of solutions parents arrive at in seeking alternative care for their children. For example, in one national survey, almost a third of employed mothers reported that their children were in some type of *combined* care, such as family day care some of the time and care by a relative part of the time—arrangements that are often dictated by the fact that the parent works an evening or night shift or at variable times (Folk & Yi, 1994). Furthermore, a great many families are unable to find consistent care arrangements, so their children experience multiple arrangements over the years of infancy and preschool. In the large national sample studied by the National Institutes of Child Health and Development (NICHD Early Child Care Research Network, 1997b), a third of 1-year-olds had experienced at least three different nonparental care arrangements; more than half had been placed in two different situations.

Comparisons of Alternative Care Settings. High-quality care is possible in any of the care settings represented in Figure 14.1, although they do differ from one another in systematic ways. For example, center care typically provides the most cognitive enrichment, including a variety of toys to play with, a high rate of verbal exchange with caregivers, and reading aloud. Family day-care homes typically provide the lowest levels of such enrichment. In contrast, both center care and family day care give the child an opportunity to play with same-age peers, while at-home care normally does not.

Such variations make it very difficult to talk about global effects of child care. Furthermore, many researchers have studied only those children in center care, and we cannot be sure that these findings will generalize to children in family day care or with at-home care by someone other than a parent (let alone to some other culture altogether!). Still, let me tell you what the current evidence suggests.

Effects on Cognitive Development

We have a good deal of evidence that good-quality, cognitively enriched child care has beneficial effects on many children's overall cognitive development. In the most recent large study, by the NICHD Early Child Care Research Network (1997a), the researchers found a small but significant positive effect of high-quality care on children's overall cognitive skills and on their language. Other research tells us that this positive effect is even larger among infants and children from poor families, who show significant and lasting gains in IQ scores and later school performance after attending highly enriched child care throughout infancy and early childhood—research you'll recall from Chapter 7 (Campbell & Ramey, 1994; Ramey, 1993; Ramey & Campbell, 1987).

Even middle-class children sometimes show cognitive benefits when they are in good care (e.g., Peisner-Feinberg, 1995). For example, Alison Clarke-Stewart found that

The majority of children in the United States have at least some experience with nonparental care, although center care of the kind shown in both these photos is not the most common arrangement.

regardless of the economic situation of the child's parents, the more cognitively enriched the child's daytime experience, the higher the child's later cognitive performance (Clarke-Stewart et al., 1994). Children who were read to, talked to, and explicitly taught showed greater cognitive gains than did children who spent their days in less stimulating environments—and this was true whether they were cared for entirely at home or in some other care setting. Several longitudinal studies in Sweden confirm such a positive effect of high-quality child care: Those children who had spent the most time in Sweden's very good quality day-care centers had better school performance or better intellectual test scores throughout elementary school than did children who had been totally home-reared or those who had been in family day care (Andersson, 1992; Broberg et al., 1997).

A few studies suggest a less rosy picture, perhaps particularly for middle-class children. For example, in one large study of over a thousand 3- and 4-year-olds, Baydar and Brooks-Gunn (1991) found that white children—but *not* black children—who began some kind of alternative care in the first year of life had the lowest vocabulary scores later in preschool, whether they were from advantaged or poverty-level families. No negative effects were found for those who entered day care after age 1. In a similar large study of 5- and 6-year-olds (Caughy et al., 1994), researchers found that children from poor families who began day care before age 1 had *higher* reading or math scores at the start of school, while those from middle-class families who entered day care in infancy had *poorer* scores.

How can we reconcile these conflicting findings? One fairly straightforward possibility is that the critical factor is the discrepancy between the level of stimulation the child would receive at home and the quality of the child care. When the particular day-care setting for a given child provides *more* enrichment than the child would have received at home, then we see some beneficial cognitive effects of child-care attendance; when the child care is less stimulating than full-time home care would have been for that child, then child care may have negative cognitive effects. Most (but not all) of the results I've described are consistent with this hypothesis, but we don't yet have enough good large studies to be confident that this is the right way to conceptualize the process.

Effects on Personality

When we look at the impact of nonhome child care on children's personality, we find yet another somewhat confusing story. A number of investigators have found that children in day care are more sociable and more popular and have better peer-play skills than do those reared primarily at home. Andersson found this in his longitudinal study in Sweden (1989; 1992), as have researchers in the United States (Scarr & Eisenberg, 1993). However, this is by no means the universal finding. Many other researchers find child-care attendance linked to heightened aggression with peers and lower compliance with teachers and parents at later ages.

For example, in one very well designed large study, John Bates and his colleagues (1994) found that kindergarten children who had spent the most time in child care—in infancy, toddlerhood, or preschool years—were more aggressive and less popular with their peers at school age than were children who had been reared entirely at home or who had spent fewer years in child care. Bates did not find that those who had entered day care early in infancy were worse off; the critical variable was the total length of time in nonhome care, not the timing of that care. These negative effects are fairly small. A child's level of aggressiveness in elementary school is influenced by a whole variety of things, including temperament and the effectiveness of the parents' disciplinary techniques. Yet the fact that child care is implicated in this equation certainly raises a cautionary flag.

Confusing, isn't it? By some measures, day-care children seem to be *more* socially competent than home-reared children; by other measures, they seem less so. One possible way to resolve this discrepancy is again to look at the relative quality of care at

Critical Thinking

Do you accept this argument? What other explanation(s) can you come up with?

home or in day care. Consistent with this argument is a finding by Tiffany Field (1991) that the beneficial effects of day-care experience on the child's social competence holds only for *good-quality* care. Similarly, Alison Clarke-Stewart, in a study comparing various types of nonhome child care with home care, finds that what is critical for the child's level of aggression is whether the child spends the daytime hours in an organized, well-structured situation versus a messy, unstimulating one—no matter if the unstructured and messy setting is at home or in day care (Clarke-Stewart et al., 1994). If this argument holds, then it is not child care per se that is at issue, but the child's actual experiences on a day-to-day basis. Yet even if this turns out to be the best explanation of the observed negative effects, it is hardly cause for cheering. The children in Bates's study, for example, were in ordinary, everyday types of child-care situations. If such run-of-the-mill care is of sufficiently poor quality that it has even small negative effects on children's later behavior, we need to be concerned.

Effects on Attachments

Another vital question is whether an infant or toddler can develop a secure attachment to her mother and father if she is repeatedly separated from them. We know that the majority of infants develop secure attachments to their fathers, even though fathers typically go away every day to work, so it is clear that regular separations do not *preclude* secure attachment. Still, the early research created enough concern that psychologist Jay Belsky, in a series of papers and in testimony before a congressional committee, sounded an alarm (Belsky, 1985; 1992; Belsky & Rovine, 1988). Combining data from several studies, he concluded that there was a slightly heightened risk of an insecure attachment among infants who entered day care before their first birthday, compared with those cared for at home throughout the first year. Subsequent analyses supported Belsky's conclusion. For example, summing across the findings from 13 different studies involving 897 infants, Michael Lamb noted that 35 percent of infants who had experienced at least five hours per week of nonmaternal care were insecurely attached, compared with 29 percent of the infants with exclusively maternal care (Lamb et al., 1992).

What did such results mean? Psychologists disagreed strongly and vocally, in person and in print (e.g., Clarke-Stewart, 1990; Roggman et al., 1994; Sroufe, 1990). Some concluded that these findings meant that day care itself increased the chances of an insecure attachment. Others pointed out that most of the existing research included so many confounding variables that it was impossible to draw any clear conclusion. For example, perhaps the problem was not day care itself, but rather poor-quality care. The self-selection problem was also troubling. Mothers who work are different in other ways from mothers who do not. More are single mothers, and more prefer to work or find child care onerous. So how could we be sure that any heightened probability of insecure attachment is due to the day-care experience and not to other factors?

In a wonderful example of the way dispute and disagreement can often lead to very good science, 25 researchers at 14 different universities—including all the main protagonists in the dispute—got together in 1991 to design and carry out a very large study that would address all these questions (NICHD Early Child Care Research Network, 1996a; 1997d). They enrolled over 1300 infants and their families in the study, including black and Latino families, mothers with little education as well as those with college or more, and both single mothers and two-parent families.

The basic design of the study is summarized in Table 14.1 (p. 412). As you can see, the researchers first visited each home when the baby was 1 month old. During that visit they obtained information about the family's organization and income and about the mother's temperament, her level of depression, and her attitude toward working. They also asked her to rate the baby's temperament, using a standard questionnaire.

When the babies were 6 months old, the researchers returned to each home, asking the mother again about her level of depression and her view of her child's temperament. During this visit, they also observed the mother's interactions with her infant during a play session and evaluated the quality of the overall caregiving environment in

Table 14.1

Design of the National Institutes of Child Health and Development (NICHD) Study of Early Child Care

Age of infant at each contact	Measures used at that age
1 month	• Mother's personality
	• Mother's level of depression
	• Mother's attitude toward employment
	• Mother's rating of the infant's temperament
	• Household composition and family income
6 months	• Mother's rating of the infant's temperament
	• Mother's level of depression
	• Observation of quality of home caregiving environment
	• Observation of mother and infant during play
	• Rating of quality of any nonhome care setting
15 months	• Mother's level of depression
	• Observation of mother and child during play
	• Observation of quality of home caregiving environment
	• Rating of quality of any nonhome care setting
	• Child's security of attachment in the Strange Situation

Source: NICHD Early Child Care Research Network, 1996a, from Table 3.

the home using another standard instrument. In these observations, the researchers were looking particularly at the level of the mother's sensitivity/responsiveness toward the infant—a quality we know is linked to security of attachment.

At 15 months, they made one more home visit, repeating their evaluation of the home environment and their direct observation of the mother and child during play. Each pair was also brought to a laboratory where mother and child were put through the series of episodes of the Strange Situation. For those children who were in child care at 6 months and 15 months, the researchers also visited the care setting and rated its quality.

Given the complexity of the study, the results are surprisingly clear: Child care, of itself, was unrelated to the security of the child's attachment. Only among those infants whose mothers were relatively insensitive to the infant's needs at home did day care or other child care have some negative effects. For these children, low-quality care was linked to less secure attachment. Only the infants who experienced the combination of two poor conditions—an insensitive mother and poor care—had a higher risk of being insecurely attached. Infants with insensitive mothers whose alternative child care was of good quality were just as likely as any other child to be securely attached.

Here too, though, there are a few small cautionary flags. The NICHD study researchers also found that the mothers of children in child care showed a very slight (but statistically significant) increased tendency to behave less sensitively toward their children, compared to mothers who reared their children entirely at home. Note that this effect was not sufficient to affect the likelihood that the child would be securely attached to the mother. Children in day care were just as likely as those reared entirely at

The Real World

Latchkey Children

Questions associated with child care do not end when the child reaches school age. Working parents also face the problem of arranging before- or after-school care for their school-age children. When they are unable to make such arrangements, many parents are forced to leave their child or children to care for themselves in the hours between the end of school and the parent(s)' return from work. Such an arrangement is labeled *self-care* by psychologists, although this term is at least somewhat misleading, since many such children are in the care of an older sibling at least part of the time (e.g., Marshall et al., 1997). The more popular label for children who spend their after-school hours without adult supervision is *latchkey children.*

It has been very difficult to discover just how many latchkey children there are, in part because the practice of leaving children alone has had a lot of bad press, so parents may be reluctant to acknowledge that their children care for themselves part of the time. Most current estimates are that between 5 and 10 percent of all children between ages 6 and 13 in the United States spend at least some part of their days in self-care (Zigler & Gilman, 1996). In families in which all the adults are working, the rate is about twice that (Cain & Hofferth, 1989).

Self-care is most likely for children age 10 and over, and for only a short time each day, most often after school. Contrary to what you may assume, such care arrangements are *not* found primarily among families in poverty environments; roughly the same percentage of families from every social class level use such arrangements.

There is relatively little decent research to tell us what effect self-care may have on children. The better recent studies, however, suggest mild to moderate negative effects, with latchkey children showing greater vulnerability to peer pressure and substance abuse, poorer social skills, lower school grades, or higher rates of aggression/delinquency (Pettit et al., 1997b; Zigler & Gilman, 1996). Some of these negative effects, especially in levels of aggression or delinquency, are stronger among low-income urban latchkey children; latchkey children from middle-class, suburban, or rural areas do appear to have somewhat lower school grades, but they show little or no increased risk of other problem behavior (e.g., Galambos & Maggs, 1991; Marshall et al., 1997; Pettit et al., 1997b). Other studies point to the possibility that latchkey children may not differ from other kids in their school performance, self-concept, or susceptibility to peer pressure *if* they have a clear routine, are in daily contact with the parent(s) by phone during the self-care hours, and have neighbors or others to turn to in case of need (Cole & Rodman, 1987). When these conditions cannot be met, self-care may simply exacerbate existing problems.

Among adolescents who lack supervision for parts of each day, those who stay in their own homes for the unsupervised hours seem to do better than those who spend the time "hanging out" or at a friend's house. The latter groups seem to be especially susceptible to peer pressure during the peer-sensitive years of early adolescence (Steinberg, 1986).

Overall, the relatively scant research literature suggests that self-care by children is not a uniformly negative arrangement, as many reports in the popular press might lead us to believe. It is possible for parents to organize such care without apparent detrimental consequences. At the same time, it is also increasingly clear that self-care carries risks, especially for children from poor families, in which it is likely to be only one part of a constellation of problems, including a lack of alternative supervisory adults, dangerous neighborhoods, and high levels of family distress and upheaval.

home to be securely attached to their mothers. Still, we can see a small potential negative effect.

Combining these findings with what I've already said about the impact of child care on intellectual development and other aspects of personality, you can see that the quality of the alternative care is a critical factor. Good-quality care is generally linked with positive or neutral outcomes while inconsistent or poor-quality custodial care can be actively detrimental to the child (e.g., Lamb, 1998; Peisner-Feinberg & Burchinal, 1997; Scarr, 1998).

Unfortunately, child care in the United States is not always—not even typically—high-quality care. Most researchers who have evaluated child care conclude that the average quality is at best fair or mediocre; some is quite dreadful (Scarr, 1998). If you are facing a decision about your own child's care, how do you judge what is good quality and what is not? Table 14.2 gives you a starting point, listing the characteristics of good-quality programs.

Table 14.2

Ideal Characteristics of a Day-Care Setting

- **Low adult-to-child ratio.** For children younger than age 1, the ratio recommended by professional associations is 1 to 3; for children aged 1 to 2, the recommended ratio is 1 to 5; for children aged 2 to 3, a ratio of 1 to 6 is recommended, with the optimum ratio rising to 1 to 10 for children aged 5 to 6. To protect against the possibility of child abuse, many good centers require at least two adults in each room or with each group of infants or children.

- **Small group size.** The smaller the number of children cared for together—whether in one room in a day-care center or in a home—the better for the child. This factor appears to be *in addition* to the effect of the adult-to-child ratio. So large groups with many adults are less optimal than smaller groups with the same adult-to-child ratios. For infants, a maximum of 6 to 8 per group appears best; for 1- to 2-year-olds, between 6 and 12 per group. For older children, groups as large as 15 or 20 appear to be okay.

- **Low staff turnover.** This is important for all children, but especially for infants. Turnover tends to be highest when caregivers' wages are low.

- **A clean, safe, colorful space, adapted to child play.** Lots of expensive toys are not critical, but there must be a variety of activities that children will find engaging, organized in a way that encourages play.

- **A daily plan with at least some structure,** some specific teaching, some supervised activities. Too much regimentation is not ideal, but children are better off with some structure.

- **A caregiver who is warm, positive, involved, and responsive** to the child, not merely custodial.

- **A caregiver with some knowledge of child development.** Caregivers who have the most advanced education generally are most effective, but even a few courses in child development are better than none.

Sources: Clarke-Stewart, 1992; Howes, 1997; Howes et al., 1992; NICHD Early Child Care Research Network, 1996b; Scarr, 1998; Scarr & Eisenberg, 1993.

The Impact of Schools

School is another vitally important "microsystem" experienced by virtually all children in the great majority of cultures. School normally begins between ages 5 and 7, and in industrialized countries it typically continues through age 16 or older. During these 10 or more years, the child learns an enormous number of facts and develops new and much more complex forms of thinking, many of which I talked about in Chapter 6. What role does schooling itself play in this set of cognitive changes? Is schooling the *cause* of the cognitive shifts Piaget referred to as concrete and formal operations?

Schooling and Cognitive Development

Researchers have attempted to answer this question in several ways. One strategy has been to study children in societies or cultures in which schooling is not compulsory or is not universally available. By comparing similar groups of children, some of them in school and some not, researchers may be able to discover the role that schooling plays in cognitive development.

A second strategy, developed recently, is to compare children whose birthdays fall just before versus just after the arbitrary school district cutoffs for entrance into kindergarten or first grade. If a particular school district sets September 15 as the cutoff, for example, then a child born on September 10 would be eligible for first grade 5 days after he turned 6, while a child born on September 20 would not be eligible for another year, even though he is only 10 days younger. A year later these two children are still essentially the same age, but one has had a year of school and the other has not, so investigators can look at the effect of schooling with age held constant (e.g., Morrison et al., 1995; Stelzl et al., 1995).

Cross-cultural studies—in Mexico, Peru, Colombia, Liberia, Zambia, Nigeria, Uganda, Hong Kong, and many other countries—support the conclusion that school experiences are indeed *causally* linked to the emergence of some advanced cognitive skills. Children who do not attend school not only do not learn some complex concepts and strategies, but they are also not as good at generalizing a learned concept or principle to some new setting. So attending school helps children learn to think—precisely what it is intended to do.

A good example comes from Harold Stevenson's study of the Quechua Indian children of Peru (Stevenson & Chen, 1989; Stevenson et al., 1991). Stevenson and his associates tested 6- to 8-year-old children, some of whom had been in school for about six months and some who had not yet started school or who were living in an area where no school was available. Stevenson found that in both rural and urban areas, schooled children performed better on virtually all tasks, including a measure of seriation (putting things in serial order, such as by size or length) and a measure of concept formation. These differences remained even if the parents' level of education, the nutritional status of the child, and the amount of educational enrichment offered at home were taken into account.

Similarly, studies comparing early versus late school starters in the United States show that schooling itself, rather than merely age, has a direct effect on some kinds of cognitive skills, such as the ability to use good memory strategies. In one such study, Fred Morrison and his colleagues (1995) found that a big improvement in the use of memory strategies occurred in first grade; same-age children who spent the year in kindergarten because they just missed the cutoff did not show the same gain in memory skill—although these children would of course acquire such skill in the following year, when they were in first grade.

This does not mean that schooling is the only way for children to develop complex forms of thinking. Specific experience in some area can also promote expertise, even without any school experience. As just one example, Brazilian street children who sell in the markets are able to make change unerringly, despite their lack of formal schooling (Carraher et al., 1985). Nonetheless, schooling exposes children to many specific skills and types of knowledge and appears to stimulate the development of more flexible, generalized strategies for remembering and solving problems.

Fitting In and Adapting to School

School is not just a neutral setting for acquiring cognitive skills. It is a complex social environment with its own rules and values, intricate new peer relationships, and many new demands. Among children in the United States, a key factor in the child's successful adaptation to this new environment is her readiness to learn to read—a process I discussed in Chapter 8. However, reading readiness is not the only factor. Parent involvement in the school also matters, as do some aspects of the child's temperament.

Parent Involvement. When parents come to parent-teacher conferences, attend school events, and get involved in supervising homework, children are more strongly motivated, feel more competent, and adapt better to school. They learn to read more readily, get better grades through elementary school, and stay in school for more years (Brody et al., 1995; Grolnick & Slowiaczek, 1994; Reynolds & Bezruczko, 1993). As Laurence Steinberg puts it, "All other things being equal, children whose parents are involved in school do better than their peers" (1996, pp. 124–125). This effect of parent involvement has been found within groups of poor children as well as among the middle

Critical Thinking

Suppose your child's birthday is right after your local school district's cutoff for starting kindergarten or first grade. In light of the evidence about the effects of schooling, would you try to get your child in early? Or would it not make any difference in the long run?

class, which tells us that the effect is not just a social class difference in disguise (e.g., Luster & McAdoo, 1996; Reynolds & Bezruczko, 1993). That is, among poverty-level children, those whose parents are most involved with their school and schooling have a better chance of doing well in school than do equivalently poor children whose parents have little or no connection to the school. High levels of parental involvement are less common among poverty-level families, sometimes because they are so overstressed with other aspects of their lives that they simply do not find time, and sometimes because they are simply unaware that such involvement will help their child. But when a parent becomes involved, the child's school performance improves.

Parent involvement is important not just for the child, but for the parent and for the school. Schools that invite and encourage parent participation help to create a stronger sense of community, linking parents with one another and with the teachers. Stronger communities, in turn—be they in poverty-stricken inner cities or middle-class suburbs—provide better supervision and monitoring of the children in their midst, which befits the children. Parents who get involved with their child's school also learn ways to help their children; they may even be motivated to continue their own education (Haynes et al., 1996).

Temperament and Personality.   A child's early success in school is also affected by whether her own personality or temperament matches the qualities valued and rewarded within the school setting. For example, Karl Alexander and his colleagues (1993) have found that children who are enthusiastic, interested in new things, cheerful, and easygoing do better in the early years of school than those who are more withdrawn, moody, or high-strung.

What all this research indicates is that how a child starts out in the first few years of school has a highly significant effect on the rest of her school experience and success. Children who come to school with good skills quickly acquire new academic skills and knowledge and thereby adapt to later school demands more easily. Children who enter school with poor skills, or with less optimal temperamental qualities, learn less in the early years and are likely to move along a slower achievement trajectory throughout their school years. Such a slow trajectory is not immutable. Parent involvement can improve the chances of a less advantaged child, as can a particularly skillful kindergarten or first-grade teacher (Pianta et al., 1995). The key point is that the child does not enter school with a blank slate; she brings her history and her personal qualities with her.

Engagement and Disengagement in School

Over time, these different trajectories diverge more and more, so that by junior high or high school, students fall into two distinct clusters. Some students are highly "engaged"

A range of research tells us that children's school performance improves when their parents participate in school activities like parent-teacher conferences.

Table 14.3

Evidence for Widespread Disengagement from Schooling Among U.S. Teenagers in Steinberg's Study

- Over one-third of students said they get through the school day mostly by "goofing off with their friends."

- Two-thirds of students said they had cheated on a school test in the past year; nine out of ten said they had copied homework from someone else.

- The average U.S. high school student spends only about four hours a week on homework, compared with four hours a *day* among students in other industrialized countries.

- Half the students in Steinberg's sample said they did not do the homework they were assigned.

- Two-thirds of U.S. high school students hold down paying jobs; half work 15 or more hours a week.

- Only about 20 percent of students in Steinberg's study said their friends think it is important to get good grades in school.

- Nearly 20 percent of students in the sample said they do not try as hard as they can in school because they are afraid of what their friends might think.

Source: Steinberg, L., *Beyond the Classroom*, New York: Simon & Schuster, 1996.

in the schooling process—to use Laurence Steinberg's term. They not only enjoy school but are involved in all aspects of it, participating in activities, doing their homework, learning the skills they need. Others, including many middle-class teenagers in suburban schools, are "disengaged" from schooling, particularly the academic part of the process. Steinberg argues—persuasively I think—that this quality of engagement or disengagement is a critical one for the child and her future.

Disengaged Students. Steinberg (1996) paints quite a gloomy picture of the typical level of engagement of U.S. high school students today, based on interviews with and observations of over 20,000 teenagers and their families. A high proportion don't take school or their studies seriously; outside class, they don't often participate in activities that reinforce what they are learning in school (such as doing their homework); the peer culture denigrates academic success and scorns students who try to do well in school. Some of the specifics that support these conclusions are summarized in Table 14.3.

This Texas high school girl, studying in her biology class, has quite firmly developed beliefs about her abilities and potentials, based on her past school successes and failures. These beliefs contribute significantly to her level of engagement in schooling through junior high and high school and will affect important life choices, such as whether to go to college or whether to drop out of school altogether.

Furthermore, a great many U.S. parents today are just as disengaged from their children's schooling as their teenagers are. In Steinberg's large study, more than half the high school students said they could bring home grades of C or worse without their parents getting upset; a third said their parents didn't know what they are studying at school; only about a fifth of the parents in this study consistently attended school programs. In the category system I described in Chapter 13, parents of disengaged students are most likely to be classed as permissive or authoritarian; parents of engaged students are most likely to be rated as authoritative (Steinberg, 1996).

Parents are not the whole story. Peer group norms and values play an equally important role. Asian students, for example, are far more likely than are African-American or Latino students to have friends who value good grades and effort in school; African-American and Latino peer groups are much more likely to devalue academic effort or achievement. In these two groups, parental involvement in school or emphasis on the importance of school is undermined by peer norms. To work hard, to try to achieve, is thought of as "acting white" and is thus denigrated.

This problem is not unique to black or Latino students. The dominant white teen culture in the United States today also takes as one of its central values that high school students should not seem to be working hard—they should get by, but not show off in the process. To put it another way, the widespread peer norm or goal is the *appearance* of uninvolvement. Not surprisingly, many teenagers take this a step too far and become genuinely uninvolved with their schooling, with long-term negative consequences for adult life.

Those Who Drop Out. At the extreme end of the continuum of uninvolvement are the teenagers who actually drop out before completing high school. The good news is that dropping out is a rarer occurrence than you might guess. Approximately three-quarters of young adults in the United States have received a high school diploma, and another 12 percent receive a general equivalency diploma (GED) at some later age. So only about 15 percent of current young adults failed to graduate from high school (McLanahan & Sandefur, 1994). Among students in the most recent high school classes, the rate is even lower. For example, among those students who entered high school in 1988, only 11 percent had failed to graduate by 1993. Latinos have the highest dropout rates (roughly 30 percent). Until quite recently, African Americans had higher dropout rates than Euro-Americans, but this difference has disappeared in the latest comparisons. In both groups today, 86 to 87 percent of young adults have a high school diploma (Holmes, 1996). Overall, social class is a better predictor of school completion than is ethnicity. Kids growing up in poor families—especially poor families with a single parent—are considerably more likely to drop out of high school than are those from more economically advantaged or intact families.

Teenagers who drop out of school list many reasons for such a decision, including not liking school, getting poor grades, being suspended, or needing to find work to support a family. For girls, additional factors are involved. They most often say that they dropped out because they planned to marry, were pregnant, or felt that school was simply not for them (National Center for Educational Statistics, 1987). Some of these same factors appear when we try to *predict* which students will drop out. For example, in their longitudinal study of more than 500 children, Robert Cairns and Beverly Cairns (1994) found two strong predictors of subsequent dropout: whether the teenager had a history of low academic success, often including repeating a grade, and whether the child or teenager had shown a pattern of aggressive behavior. More than 80 percent of boys and about 50 percent of girls who had shown *both* characteristics in seventh grade later dropped out before completing high school. For girls in this study, giving birth or getting married were also strongly linked to dropping out—although it was also true that early pregnancy was more likely among girls who had a history of poor school performance or high levels of aggression. So it is unclear what is cause and what is effect here.

Cairns and his colleagues have also found that among students who were less academically skilled, those who had participated in one or more extracurricular activities

Critical Thinking

Think about your own high school years. Does any of this ring true? Did you risk disapproval from some of your peers if you were diligent in your studies? How did you deal with this?

On average, we'd expect at least one of these ninth graders to drop out of school before completing high school.

in their early years of high school were less than half as likely to drop out as were those who were not involved in school activities (Mahoney & Cairns, 1997). This finding provides further support for Steinberg's basic point about engagement and disengagement: Some kind of connection with the school, even among students who are academically less successful, can act as a counterweight to poor academic performance and help keep many young people in school long enough to graduate.

On the other side of the ledger for some adolescents is their perception that a high school diploma won't buy them much extra in the job world. Some of the young people in the Cairns study (Cairns & Cairns, 1994), for example, were already working part-time at jobs that paid above the minimum wage, and they saw no rationale for staying in school when they could earn more by working full-time. Here are two voices:

> [School] was boring, I felt like I knew all I had to know. . . . I was going to go back . . . , but I figure I was making $6 an hour and nothing in school, so . . . ." (Chuck)
>
> I just hate it. I said well if I could go to school 8 hours a day, I could get me a job 8 hours a day, 5 days a week. I said I'm going to school 40 hours a week and I said I'm not getting paid for it and I said well I'm gonna go get me a job and get paid." (Amy) (Cairns & Cairns, 1994, pp. 180, 181)

Yet in the long term, teens who use such a rationale for dropping out of high school (or for cruising through high school with poor grades) are wrong. Unemployment is higher among high school dropouts than in any other education group, and dropouts who manage to find jobs earn lower wages than do those with a high school diploma. In 1995, for example, the average annual income for adults aged 35–44 who had not completed high school was $20,466, compared with $32,689 for those with a high school education and $57,196 for those with a college degree (Hacker, 1997). Clearly, those who drop out enter a very different—and far less optimal—economic trajectory.

Engaged Students: Those Who Achieve. The other side of the coin are those engaged students who do well in school. Engaged students spend more time on homework, cut class less often, pay more attention in class, and don't cheat. They also tend to spend their time with other students who are engaged or who at least do not ridicule those who make some effort in school, and they are likely to have authoritative parents who expect them to get good grades and who are involved with the child and the school (Brooks-Gunn et al., 1993a; Steinberg, 1996).

You might argue that all the relationships I've just described exist simply because brighter kids have an easier time with schoolwork. There is some truth to that. In fact, the best single predictor of a student's academic performance in high school is his or her IQ score. Bright students also have the advantage of many years of successful

While engaged students, like these three, are likely to have the advantage of higher IQ, they are also interested in school and expend effort to do well.

schooling. Such academic success fosters a greater sense of self-efficacy in these intellectually more able students, in turn increasing their sense of involvement with schooling. Yet Steinberg is also right that the sense of involvement has many other ingredients, which jointly have a strong impact on a teenager's effort and success in school.

Effort and success, in turn, predict more years of subsequent education, a link that exists among children reared in poverty as well as among the middle class (Barrett & Depinet, 1991). Those extra years of education then have a powerful effect on the career path a young person enters in early adulthood, influencing lifetime income and job success (Featherman, 1980; Rosenbaum, 1984). These are not trivial effects, which is why Steinberg's conclusions about the typical level of school engagement among U.S. high school students today are so disturbing.

Joining the Work World: The Impact of Jobs on Teenagers

One possible contributor to the pervasive school disengagement among U.S. high school students is an increasing pattern of part-time jobs for teenagers. Certainly, teenage employment is not a new phenomenon. As in many cultures around the world today, in earlier historical eras in the United States, teenagers already fulfilled normal adult work responsibilities. They worked in the mines, factories, and fields; they herded animals and fished. Child labor laws have changed this picture drastically since the nineteenth century in most industrialized countries. Today, adolescents are in school for many hours each day and are not generally available for full-time adult work. Yet increasingly adolescents have jobs. In the United States, teenage employment rates have risen steadily since the 1950s. Today, roughly three-fifths of all high school juniors have some kind of formal part-time job during at least part of the school year, and the great majority of high school students have had at least some work experience before they graduate (Bachman & Schulenberg, 1993).

For some, work is an economic necessity. Others work to earn money for college or to support their favorite hobbies or habits. Parents are frequently very supportive of such work on the grounds that it "builds character" and teaches young people about "real life." Here's one parental voice:

> Let's face it . . . some time in life, someone is going to tell you what to do. . . . I think work is the only place to learn to deal with it. . . . Parents can give you a little discipline, but it isn't accepted. . . . You can't learn that in school, because there is another so-called tyrant, the teacher. But then they get . . . a boss, and [they] get out there and learn it. (Greenberger & Steinberg, 1986, p. 39)

Most part-time teen jobs are low-skill and low-paying, like selling clothing or working in a fast-food restaurant. Such jobs do not appear to build character but rather to have negative effects.

Figure 14.2

The data on the left come from Steinberg and Dornbusch's study; the data on the right come from Bachman and Schulenberg.

(*Sources:* (left) Steinberg, L., and Dornbusch, S., "Negative correlates of part-time employment during adolescence," *Developmental psychology*, 27, p. 308. © 1991 by the American Psychological Association. By permission of L. Steinberg. (right) Bachman, J., and Schulenberg, J., "How part-time work intensity relates to drug use, problem behavior, time use, and satisfaction among high school seniors," *Developmental psychology*, 29, p. 226. © 1993 by the American Psychological Association. By permission of J. G. Bachman.

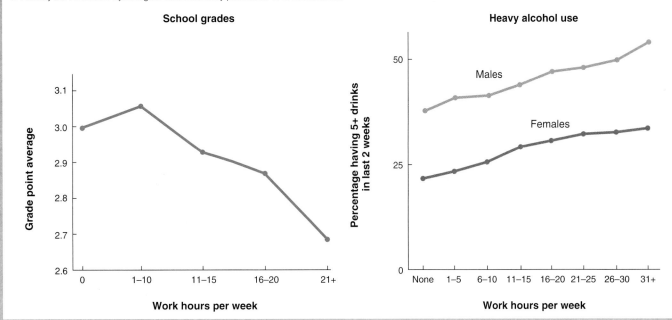

Are parents right about such beneficial effects of work? Does it really teach responsibility and reliability? Maybe, but maybe not. If you look again at Table 14.3 (p. 417), you'll see that Steinberg lists teenage employment as one of the symptoms (or causes) of widespread school disengagement. From his view, the high rate of teenage employment is one aspect of our current culture that needs changing. Other investigators have come to somewhat more optimistic conclusions about the possible beneficial effects of teenage work experience. What does the evidence tell us?

The Pessimistic View

On the pessimistic side we find several major studies suggesting that the more hours adolescents work, the more *negative* the consequences. In the largest single study, Jerald Bachman and John Schulenberg (1993) accumulated information from more than 70,000 high school students, seniors in the graduating classes of 1985 through 1989. Subjects were drawn each year from both private and public schools in every state in the country. Approximately four-fifths of the students worked at least a few hours per week, most of them for pay. He found that 46.5 percent of the boys and 38.4 percent of the girls worked more than 20 hours a week.

Bachman and Schulenberg found that the more hours students worked, the more they used drugs (alcohol, cigarettes, marijuana, cocaine), the more aggression they showed toward peers, the more arguments they had with parents, the less sleep they got, the less often they ate breakfast, the less exercise they got, and the less satisfied they were with life. An impressive list of negatives.

The second major piece of pessimistic evidence comes from the Steinberg/Dornbusch study I have described repeatedly (Steinberg & Dornbusch, 1991; Steinberg et al., 1993). Steinberg and his colleagues have employment information from 5300 of their sample of ninth to twelfth graders, data collected in 1987 and 1988. Like Bachman and Schulenberg, they find that work has a variety of negative effects on teenagers, including lower school grades and weaker commitment to school.

Figure 14.2 (p. 421) gives one finding from each of these studies, so you can see the size of the effects. I should note, by the way, that Steinberg and Dornbusch found essentially the same pattern of results for all the ethnic groups in their study and for students from every economic level, so this is a widespread and significant effect.

At this point, some of you are undoubtedly thinking that results like those in Figure 14.2 may not mean that working during the high school years *causes* bad effects. Instead, the findings might reflect self-selection: Those students who are least engaged in school, who already hang out with others who smoke or drink more, may be the same ones who choose to work more. Bachman and Schulenberg's data are consistent with such an interpretation. They find that those high school seniors who are getting the best grades, who are planning to go on to college, are least likely to work. Note, though, that this is still correlational evidence and doesn't solve the basic problem of interpretation. Steinberg and his colleagues are able to help unravel these two factors because they have longitudinal data. They found that those who *later* worked 20 hours a week had indeed been less involved with or committed to school in earlier years, which illustrates the effect of self-selection. At the same time, they found that these same students became even *more* withdrawn from school and showed not only increases in drug use and delinquency but a *decline* in self-reliance after they began working, illustrating a negative effect of working.

The Optimistic View

A quite different answer to the question of the impact of teenage employment comes from a recent study by Jeylan Mortimer and her colleagues (Mortimer & Finch, 1996; Mortimer et al., 1995), who have followed a group of more than 1000 Minnesota students from ninth through twelfth grades. She found that over these years, teenagers worked more and more hours and their work became somewhat more complex. She also found no correlation between the number of hours students worked and their school grades or risk for problem behavior—with the exception of alcohol use, which was higher among those students who worked more. What mattered more than work per se, in this group of young people, was the quality of work they were doing. Students who had positive work experiences developed increased feelings of competence and efficacy; those students who saw themselves gaining useful skills through their work also seemed to develop that constellation of work-related values and attitudes that most adults mean when they say that work "builds character."

It is not clear how we should add up the results of these several studies. One possible resolution is suggested by Kristelle Miller, who finds that only work on weekdays, and *not* weekend work, has a detrimental effect on high school students' grades (Miller & Pedersen-Randall, 1995). This suggests the hypothesis that work is academically detrimental to the extent that it distracts young people from school tasks. Even Mortimer's findings are consistent with this. In her study, the employed eleventh and twelfth graders often said that spending time on the job made it hard to get homework done and meant they often came to school tired. On the other hand, Mortimer is probably right that the quality of work is a critical ingredient in the equation. Low-skilled work that affords little opportunity for independence and little chance to learn long-term job skills is much more likely to be associated with poor outcomes than is complex, skilled work.

Collectively, these findings are a good illustration of why it is so very difficult to arrive at clear social policy recommendations. At the very least, however, this mixture of results should make parents think twice before they (we) encourage teenagers to work 15 or 20 hours a week.

Critical Thinking

What was your own work experience as a teenager? What lessons do you think you learned from that work, if any? In light of your own experience and the data from this study, would you want your own children to work when they are teenagers?

The Impact of the Mass Media

Another direct influence on children coming from outside the family is the mass media, particularly television. Ninety-eight percent of U.S. homes have a television set. Children between the ages of 2 and 11 spend an average of about 22 hours a week watching TV, adolescents a bit less (American Psychological Association, 1993; Fabrikant, 1996). This number has declined in the past decade, dropping from more than 26 hours a week in 1984, but it is still the case that "by the time American children are 18 years old, they have spent more time watching television than in any other activity except sleep" (Huston et al., 1990). In the United States, high levels of TV viewing are more common among African-American and Latino children and adults than among Euro-Americans and are more common in families in which the parents are less well educated (Anderson et al., 1986).

Viewing rates are not as high in most other countries, but TV ownership is above 50 percent of households in Latin America and in most of Eastern and Western Europe, so this is not an exclusively U.S. phenomenon (Comstock, 1991).

I can give you only a few tidbits from the vast amount of research designed to detect any effects TV viewing may have on children and adults. Still, a taste is better than no meal at all.

Specific Educational Effects

Programs specifically designed to be educational or to teach children positive values do indeed have demonstrable positive effects. This is particularly clear among preschoolers, for whom most such programming is designed. For example, children who regularly watch *Sesame Street* develop larger vocabularies and other school readiness skills than children who do not watch it or who watch it less often, an effect found for children in homes in which Spanish is the dominant language as well as for those who hear English at home (Huston & Wright, 1998; Rice et al., 1990). One recent, carefully designed study by Patricia Collins and her associates (1997) provides particularly clear evidence. They followed more than 500 children from age 5 to late high school and found that those who had been heavier *Sesame Street* viewers as preschoolers had better grades through elementary and high school, read more books, and had more confidence in their academic abilities. The most likely causal chain is that watching *Sesame Street* and other educational programs helps children develop more positive attitudes toward learning and provides them with specific knowledge that will increase their success in first grade, thus getting them off to a good start. Such children are more likely to remain engaged in the entire process of schooling—no small benefit.

Programs that emphasize prosocial behaviors like sharing, kindness, and helpfulness, such as *Mister Rogers' Neighborhood, Sesame Street,* or even *Lassie,* also have some positive impact. Children who regularly view such programs show more kind and helpful behavior than do children who don't view them (Huston & Wright, 1998).

Overall School Achievement

However, when we look at the impact of the *total* amount of TV viewing rather than at only educational programming, we find a small negative correlation between heavy TV viewing and school grades or achievement test scores. That is, children who are heavy viewers, particularly those who spend more than 30 hours a week watching TV, do slightly *less* well in school (Huston & Wright, 1998). This is naturally a correlational statement. We can't be sure how the causality runs. It is quite possible that children who are already doing poorly in school choose to watch more TV, rather than the TV watching interfering with school performance. Longitudinal studies like the Collins study I just described give us some help in untangling the causality. These researchers find that girls who were heavy viewers in preschool got slightly lower school grades overall, especially in science and English, even when they control statistically for each

In the United States, children the age of these two watch an average of three to four hours of TV every day. Amazing.

Research Report
Family Viewing Patterns

The mythical "average child" in the United States watches three to four hours of TV a day. But this average obviously disguises very large variations among families in both viewing patterns and attitudes about television. To a considerable extent, parents control their children's TV viewing through explicit rules and through attitudes—an example of the way in which broad cultural forces interact with individual family styles. Nearly half of families have consistent rules about what type or which specific programs a child may view; about 40 percent restrict the number of hours a child can watch, while another 40 percent encourage the child's viewing at least some of the time (Comstock, 1991).

Michelle St. Peters found that she could classify families into one of four types on the basis of the degree of regulation or encouragement of TV viewing parents imposed (St. Peters et al., 1991). *Laissez-faire* parents had few regulations but did not specifically encourage viewing. *Restrictive* parents had many regulations and little encouragement, while *promotive* parents had few regulations and high levels of encouragement for TV viewing. *Selective* parents had high regulations but encouraged some specific types of viewing.

In a two-year longitudinal study of 5-year-olds and their parents, St. Peters found that children in restrictive families watched the least TV (11.9 hours a week). When they watched, they were most likely to view entertainment or educational programs aimed specifically at children (such as *Sesame Street, Mister Rogers' Neighborhood,* or Disney shows). The heaviest viewers were children with parents classed as promotive, who watched an average of 21.1 hours a week. They watched not only children's programs but also adult comedy, drama, game shows, and action-adventure. Both laissez-faire families (16.7 hours) and selective families (19.2 hours) watched an intermediate number of hours each week.

The key point here is that families create the conditions for children's viewing and thus for what children learn from TV. Not only do parents establish a degree of regulation, but they may also watch with the child and interpret what the child sees. A family that wishes to do so can take advantage of the beneficial things TV has to offer and can minimize exposure to programs with aggressive, violent, or sexist content. The difficulty for many families, however, is that such a planned approach to TV may mean that the parents will have to give up their own favorite programs.

child's early skill in those areas. For boys, early heavy viewing had no such persisting effects in this sample (Collins et al., 1997). Other research, however, suggests that heavy viewing may have (causal) negative effects on the development of reading skills for both boys and girls (Ritchie et al., 1987).

Television and Aggression

By far the largest body of research has focused on the potential impact of TV on children's aggressiveness. On U.S. television, the level of violence is remarkably high and has remained high over the past two decades, despite many congressional investigations and cries of alarm. In prime-time programs, a violent act occurs an average of 5 times per hour; on Saturday morning cartoons, the rate is 20 to 25 times per hour (Gerbner et al., 1994; Murray, 1997). The highest rates of violence are generally found in programs broadcast between 6:00 and 9:00 in the morning or between 2:00 and 5:00 in the afternoon—both times when young children are likely to be watching. Cable TV, now available in 60 percent of homes in the United States, adds to this diet of violence, as do violent video games that are increasingly popular as replacements of TV viewing time. The violence portrayed on these various programs and media is typically shown as socially acceptable or as a successful way of solving problems; it is frequently rewarded in that people who are violent often get what they want (Sege, 1998). In many video games, symbolic violence is the approved means to achieve the game's goal.

Does the viewing of such a barrage of violence *cause* higher rates of aggression or violence in children? Demonstrating such a causal link is a bit like demonstrating a causal connection between smoking and lung cancer. Unequivocal findings would require an experimental design—a strategy ruled out for obvious ethical reasons. One can

neither randomly assign some people to smoke for 30 years nor assign some children to watch years of violent TV while others watch none. However, we have several other types of research evidence that all point strongly toward the existence of a causal link.

The most common type of study, purely correlational in design, involves comparing levels of aggression among children who vary in the amount of TV they watch in their everyday lives. The almost universal finding is that those who watch more TV are more aggressive than their low-TV-watching peers (Huston & Wright, 1998). As is true with all correlational studies like this, such a result leaves us with a problem of interpretation. In particular, children who already behave aggressively appear to *choose* to watch more TV and more violent TV. And families in which TV is watched a great deal may also be more likely to use patterns of discipline that will foster aggressiveness in the child.

One partial solution to this dilemma is to study children longitudinally. In this way we can see whether the amount of violent TV a child watches at one age can predict later aggressiveness, taking into account the level of aggression the child already showed at the beginning of the study. We have several good studies of this type, which show a small but significant effect of TV violence on subsequent aggression. The most famous study in this category is Leonard Eron's 22-year study of aggressiveness from age 8 to age 30 (Eron, 1987). Eron found that the best predictor of a young man's aggressiveness at age 19 was the violence of television programs he watched when he was 8. When Eron interviewed the men again when they were 30, he found that those who had had higher rates of TV viewing at age 8 were much more likely to have a record of serious criminal behavior in adulthood, a set of results shown in Figure 14.3. The pattern is the same for women, by the way, but the level of criminal offenses is far lower, just as the level of aggression is lower among girls in childhood.

Figure 14.3

These data from Leonard Eron's 22-year longitudinal study show the relationships between the amount of TV a group of boys watched when they were 8 and the average severity of criminal offenses they had committed by age 30.

(*Source:* From Eron, L. D., "The development of aggressive behavior from the perspective of a developing behaviorism," *American psychologist,* 42 (1987), p. 40. © 1987 by the American Psychological Association. By permission of the author.)

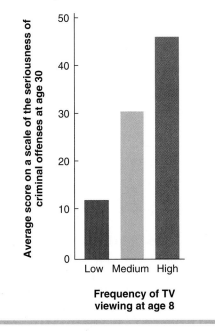

The results shown in the figure, of course, are still a form of correlation. They don't prove that the TV viewing contributed in any causal way to the later criminality, because those children who chose to watch a lot of violent TV at age 8 may already have been the most violent children. Indeed, Eron found just such a pattern: Eight-year-old boys who watched a lot of violent television were already more aggressive with their peers, indicating that aggressive boys select more violent TV programs. However, the longitudinal design allows Eron to tease out some additional patterns. In particular, he finds that among the *already* aggressive 8-year-olds, those who watched the most TV were more delinquent or aggressive as teenagers and as adults than were those who watched TV for fewer hours (Eron, 1987; Hucsmann et al., 1984). Shorter-term longitudinal studies in Poland, Finland, Israel, and Australia show similar links between TV viewing and later increased aggression among children (Eron et al., 1991).

A recent longitudinal study by Frazier, covering the years from age 5 to age 12, adds a further note: The impact of higher levels of violent TV viewing at age 5 was substantially stronger among those children whose families also used harsh physical discipline (Frazier et al., 1997). The combination of physical discipline (spanking) and high levels of violent TV was linked to higher levels of later aggression than was either factor by itself.

These findings, along with Eron's, suggest that children are differentially susceptible to the impact of violent television. Not only do aggressive children prefer violent television, but children who are living in families in which aggressive forms of discipline are used are also more susceptible. What seems clear from this research, however, is that the violent television they see causes these children to be more aggressive.

The best evidence of such a causal connection comes from several dozen genuinely experimental studies in which one group of children has been exposed to a *few* episodes of moderately aggressive TV while others watched neutral programs. Collectively, these studies show a significant short-term increase in observable physical aggression among those who watched the aggressive programs (Huston & Wright, 1998; Paik & Comstock, 1994; Wood et al., 1991). In one study of this type, Chris Boyatzis (1995) found that children of elementary school age who were randomly assigned to watch episodes of a then popular (and highly violent) children's program, *The Mighty Morphin Power Rangers,* showed seven times as many aggressive acts during subsequent free play with peers as did comparable children who had not just viewed the violent program. Virtually all psychologists, after reviewing the combined evidence, would agree with Eron's testimony before a Senate committee:

> There can no longer be any doubt that heavy exposure to televised violence is one of the causes of aggressive behavior, crime and violence in society. The evidence comes from both the laboratory and real-life studies. Television violence affects youngsters of all ages, of both genders, at all socioeconomic levels and all levels of intelligence. The effect is not limited to children who are already disposed to being aggressive and is not restricted to this country. (Eron, 1992, p. S8539)

Other evidence suggests that repeated viewing of TV violence leads to emotional desensitization toward violence, to a belief that aggression is a good way to solve problems, and to a reduction in prosocial behavior (Donnerstein et al., 1994). Violent television is clearly not the only, or even the major, cause of aggressiveness among children or adults. It is nonetheless a significant influence, both individually and at a broader cultural level.

For parents, the clear message from all the research on TV is that television is an educational medium. Children learn from what they watch—vocabulary words, helpful behaviors, attitudes, gender roles, and aggressive behaviors. Huston and Wright point out that "television can be an ally, not an enemy, for parents. Parents can use television programs for their children's benefit just as they use books and toys" (1994, p. 80). However, using television in this way requires considerable vigilance and planning.

Critical Thinking

Given all that you have now read about television and children's development, how could you as a parent maximize the benefits and limit the negative effects of TV viewing? Would you be willing to give up having a television altogether if you thought that was necessary for your child's optimum development?

Macrosystem Effects: The Impact of the Larger Culture

Finally, we come explicitly to the question of contexts and cultures. Each family, and thus each child, is embedded in a series of overlapping contexts, each of which affects the way the family itself interacts, and each of which affects all other parts of the system. These contexts include the overall economic position of the family, the ethnic group to which the family belongs, and the larger culture in which all of this exists. These days we should probably also think about the global culture, because the global marketplace affects job opportunities and standards of living in individual countries. But that is a level of complexity I cannot yet begin to grasp.

Economic Variations: Social Class and Poverty

Every society is made up of social layers, usually called **social classes,** with each layer having a different degree of access to power, goods, or status. In Western societies, the social class of a given family is most often defined in terms of the income and education of the adults in that family. In the United States, four social classes are usually identified: upper-class, middle-class, working-class, and poverty-level families. Members of each social layer tend to share certain values or styles of interaction, with the largest differences found between families living in poverty and those in higher-social-class groups. For children, it is clear that the disadvantages of poverty are enormous—and these disadvantages are not equally distributed across ethnic groups in the United States.

Figure 14.4 shows the percentage of children in the United States who live below the poverty line—defined in 1995 as an income of $15,569 or less per year for a family of four. Happily, these percentages have dropped somewhat in the past few years. In 1993, for example, 45.9 percent of African-American children lived in poverty, compared with the 41.5 percent reflected in the figure for 1995. Still, *proportionately more children live in poverty in the United States than in any other industrialized country in the world.* By way of specific contrast, the poverty rate for children is about 9 percent in Canada and 2 percent in Sweden (McLoyd, 1998).

Figure 14.4 also makes clear that poverty is not equally distributed across ethnic groups in the United States. Nor is it equally distributed across family structures: Children reared by single mothers are far more likely to be living in poverty than children

Figure 14.4

The percentage of children under age 18 living in poverty in the United States in 1995.

(*Source:* U.S. Bureau of the Census, data from Table 737, p. 475, *Statistical abstract of the United States*, 117th Edition, 1997.)

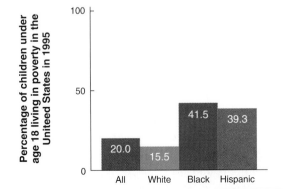

in two-parent families. Approximately 60 percent of black and Latino children and 40 percent of white children reared by single mothers in the United States live in poverty (Zill & Nord, 1994). Many of these mothers have jobs, but the jobs pay too little to raise the family out of poverty (Lichter & Eggebeen, 1994).

Data like those in Figure 14.4 can give us only a slice in time. Perhaps more important for the child is the overall family history of poverty. Such an analysis points to even greater disadvantages for minority children. Greg Duncan notes that two-fifths of black children, but only 6 percent of white children, grow up in families that are poor for all of the child's first five or six years (Duncan et al., 1994). Half of white children grow up in families that are never poor and never live in a poor neighborhood, while this is true for only 5 percent of blacks. Thus, even those black families that do not fall below the poverty line at any one moment are likely to have fallen below it at some time or to spend some time living in a poor neighborhood.

The Effects of Poverty on Families. Among many other things, poverty reduces options for parents. They may not be able to afford prenatal care, so their children are more likely to be born with some sort of disability. When the mother works, she is likely to have fewer choices of affordable child care. Such children spend more time in poor-quality care and shift more from one care arrangement to another. Poor families also live in smaller and less adequate housing, often in decaying neighborhoods with high rates of violence, and many of them move frequently, so their children change schools often. The parents are less likely to feel they have adequate social support, and the children often lack a stable group of playmates (Dodge et al., 1994). Overall, poverty environments are more chaotic, more highly stressed, with fewer psychological and social resources (Brooks-Gunn, 1995; McLoyd & Wilson, 1991).

Mothers and fathers living in poverty also interact with their children in different ways than do parents in working-class or middle-class families in the United States. Poverty-level parents talk and read to their children less, provide fewer age-appropriate toys, spend less time with them in intellectually stimulating activities, explain things less often and less fully, are less warm, and are stricter and more physical in their discipline (Dodge et al., 1994; Sampson & Laub, 1994). In the terms I introduced in Chapter 13, in poor families the parents are more likely to be either neglecting or authoritarian and are less likely to be authoritative.

Some of this pattern of parental behavior seems clearly to be a response to the extraordinary stresses and special demands of the poverty environment—a point buttressed by the repeated observation that those parents living in poverty who nonetheless feel they have enough social support are much less likely to be harshly punitive or unsupportive toward their children (Hashima & Amato, 1994; Taylor & Roberts, 1995). To some extent, the stricter discipline and emphasis on obedience we see among poor parents may be thought of as a logical response to the realities of life in a very poor neighborhood.

Some of the differences in child-rearing patterns between poor and nonpoor parents may also result from straightforward modeling of the way these same parents were reared; some may be a product of ignorance of children's needs. Poor parents with relatively more education, for example, typically talk to their children more, are more responsive, and provide more intellectual stimulation than do equally poor parents with lower levels of education (Kelley et al., 1993). Whatever the cause, children reared in poverty experience both different physical conditions and quite different interactions with their parents.

The Effects of Poverty on Children. Not surprisingly, such children turn out differently. Children from poverty environments have higher rates of illness and disabilities, as you've already seen in Chapter 4. Typically, they also have lower IQ scores and move through the sequences of cognitive development more slowly—effects that have been found in studies in which the researchers controlled for many possible confounding factors, such as the mother's IQ and the family structure (McLoyd, 1998). These children come to school less ready to learn to read, and thereafter they consistently do less

well in school. They are twice as likely as nonpoor children to repeat a grade and are less likely to go on to college (Brooks-Gunn, 1995; Huston, 1994; Zill et al., 1995). As adults, they are more likely to be poor, thus continuing the cycle through another generation. All these effects are greater for those children who live in poverty in infancy and early childhood and for those who have lived continuously in poverty compared to children who have experienced some mixture of poverty and greater affluence (Bolger, 1997; Duncan et al., 1994; Shanahan et al., 1997; Smith et al., 1997).

Figure 14.5 shows one of these effects, drawn from research by Greg Duncan and his colleagues (1994). Duncan has information on family income for a large sample of families over the years from the child's birth to age 5. He looked at the child's IQ score at age 5 as a function of whether the family had been poor in every one of those five years or in only some of those years. The figure compares the IQ scores of each of these groups to the benchmark IQ of children who never lived in poverty. It's clear that constant poverty has a greater negative effect than sometime poverty, and both are worse than nonpoverty. In this analysis, Duncan has controlled for the mother's education and the structure of the household (single mother versus two parents, for example), so these differences seem to be real effects of poverty.

The Special Case of Inner-City Poverty. All these effects are probably much worse for children growing up in poverty-ravaged urban areas—the majority of whom are African American, Latino, or other minorities (Brooks-Gunn et al., 1997). They are exposed to street gangs and street violence, to drug pushers, to overcrowded homes and higher risks of abuse. Whole communities have become like war zones.

In the United States, almost 13 million children live in urban poverty (Garbarino et al., 1991). More than 1.5 million children live in public housing developments, including some with the highest crime rates in the country. Surveys in a number of large cities indicate that nearly half of inner-city elementary and high school students have witnessed at least one violent crime in the past year (Osofsky, 1995); nearly all have

Figure 14.5

In this analysis, the zero line represents the average IQ score of a group of 5-year-old children in Duncan's study who have never lived in poverty. Average IQ scores of children who have lived in poverty some of the time or all of the time are then compared to that benchmark. You can see that children who have spent all of their first five years living in poverty have considerably lower average IQs than those who have lived in poverty only part of the time, and both groups are significantly lower than the benchmark group.

(*Source:* Duncan et al., 1994, from Table 3, p. 306.)

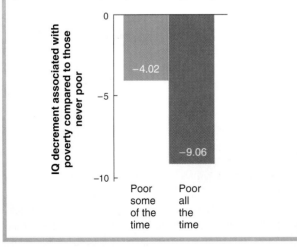

heard guns being shot, seen someone being beaten up, or observed a drug deal (White et al., 1997); as many as 30 percent have seen a homicide by the time they are 15 (Garbarino & Kostelny, 1997). Guns are common in schools as well as on the streets. In a 1993 national survey by the Centers for Disease Control, 22.1 percent of high school students reported that they had carried a weapon (gun, knife, or club) some time in the previous 30 days; 7.9 percent had carried a gun (Kann et al., 1995). Psychologist James Garbarino, who has written extensively about urban poverty, points out that "these figures are much more like the experience of children in the war zones we have visited in other countries . . . than they are of what we should expect for our own children, living in 'peace'" (Garbarino & Kostelny, 1997, p. 33).

A growing body of evidence shows that the effect of living in a concentrated pocket of poverty is to intensify all the ill effects of family poverty (Klebanov et al., 1995; Kupersmidt et al., 1995). Individual family characteristics are still the most important determinants of the child's development, but when the whole neighborhood is poor, especially when residence in the neighborhood is in constant flux, we see intensified negative effects for children (Brooks-Gunn et al., 1997). In such situations, parents have fewer nonfamily resources to rely on, and children have more violent and fewer supportive adult models; rates of child abuse rise, as do rates of aggression and delinquency in the children (Coulton et al., 1995; McLoyd, 1997). When the whole neighborhood also lacks what sociologist William Wilson calls *connectedness* and *stability*—when the adults do not collaborate to monitor the children and do not provide practical or emotional support to one another—the effects are still worse (Sampson, 1997; Wilson, 1995).

Many children living in such neighborhoods show all the symptoms of posttraumatic stress disorder (Garbarino et al., 1992; Jenkins & Bell, 1997), including sleep disturbances, irritability, inability to concentrate, angry outbursts, and hypervigilance. Many experience flashbacks or intrusive memories of traumatic events. And because they are likely to have missed out on many of the forms of intellectual stimulation and consistent family support that would allow them to succeed in school, they have high rates of behavior problems and academic failure. Fewer than half of urban poor children graduate from high school (Garbarino et al., 1991). The reasons for such school failure are complex, as I have already pointed out, but there is little doubt that the chronic stress experienced by poor children is one highly significant component.

The Roles of Stress and Protective Factors. Arnold Sameroff and his colleagues (1987) have argued that the effects of various different kinds of stresses accumulate. A child may be able to handle one or two, but as the stresses and risks pile up, the probability that the child will thrive intellectually, emotionally, or socially declines steadily. For a child growing up in poverty, perhaps especially urban poverty, the chances of experiencing multiple separate types of stress are very high indeed.

Critical Thinking

Are you shocked by such statistics? What do you think we ought to do about the problem of inner-city poverty?

When you look at scenes of urban poverty like this, you can see why some refer to them as "war zones."

The Real World

Children in Danger

I cannot leave the subject of urban poverty—so common now in America—without quoting some of James Garbarino's eloquent words:

> Our efforts to understand the impact of chronic community violence on children and youth around the world and in our own cities highlight several concerns . . . but from our perspective, *the most important of these is that the experience of trauma distorts the values of children.* Unless we reach them with healing experiences and offer them a moral and political framework within which to process their experiences, *traumatized children are likely to be drawn to groups and ideologies that legitimatize and reward their rage, their fear, and their*

hateful cynicism. This is an environment in which gangs flourish and community institutions deteriorate, a "socially toxic" environment. (Garbarino & Kostelny, 1997, p. 40)

> What is truly needed in America's urban war zones is restoration of a safe environment where children can have a childhood, and where parents can exert less energy on protecting children from random gunfire and more on helping children to grow. No one can eliminate all risk from the lives of families. But America does have the resources to make a real childhood a real possibility even for the children of the urban poor. But sometimes the war close to home is the most difficult to see. (Garbarino et al., 1991, p. 148)

At the same time, studies of resilient and vulnerable children suggest that certain characteristics or circumstances may help to protect some children from the detrimental effects of repeated stresses and upheavals (Easterbrooks et al., 1993; Furstenberg & Hughes, 1995; Garmezy & Masten, 1991; Masten & Coatsworth, 1998; Masten et al., 1990; Runyan et al., 1998; Winfield, 1995). Ann Masten and Douglas Coatsworth, in their recent review (1998), provide a list of the key qualities of such resilient children, shown in Table 14.4.

Table 14.4

Characteristics of Resilient Children and Adolescents

Source	Characteristic
Individual	Good intellectual functioning
	Appealing, sociable, easygoing disposition
	Self-efficacy, self-confidence, high self-esteem
	Talents
	Faith
Family	Close relationship to caring parent figure
	Authoritative parenting: warmth, structure, high expectations
	Socioeconomic advantages
	Connections to extended supportive family networks
Extrafamilial context	Bonds to prosocial adults outside the family
	Connections to prosocial organizations
	Attending effective schools

Source: From "The development of competence in favorable and unfavorable environments" by Ann S. Masten, *American psychologist*, 53, p. 212. (1998). Copyright © 1998 by the American Psychological Association. Reprinted within the guidelines of the American Psychological Association and by permission of the author.

Note that these are the same qualities that are linked to competence in children who are *not* growing up in poverty or in other risky environments. As Masten and Coatsworth put it:

> Resilient children do not appear to possess mysterious or unique qualities; rather, they have retained or secured important resources representing basic protective systems in human development. . . . Competence develops in the midst of adversity when, despite the situation at hand, fundamental systems that generally foster competence in development are operating to protect the child or counteract the threats to development. (1998, p. 212)

If you go back and look at the Research Report in Chapter 1 (p. 14) describing the results of Emmy Werner's long-term longitudinal study on the Hawaiian island of Kauai, you can see how these factors operate in real lives (Werner & Smith, 1992). The families of the resilient children/adults in her sample were clearly more authoritative, more cohesive, and more loving than were the equivalently poor families whose children had worse outcomes. Similarly, studies of boys reared in high-crime inner-city neighborhoods show that high intelligence and at least a minimum level of family cohesion are key ingredients affecting a boy's chance of creating a successful adult life pattern (Long & Vaillant, 1984; McCord, 1982; Sampson & Laub, 1994). Boys reared in poverty-level families in which there was alcoholism, or who had parents with strong antisocial tendencies or low IQ, were simply much less likely to develop the competence needed to bootstrap themselves out of their difficult circumstances.

Thus, the outcome depends on some joint effect of the number of stresses the child must cope with and the range of competencies or advantages the child brings to the situation. Poverty does not guarantee bad outcomes, but it stacks the deck against most children. As Judith Musick puts it, these environments are "densely layered with risk" (1994, p. 1).

Ethnicity

In the United States, because poverty status is so much more common among some ethnic groups than others, social class and ethnic group membership are strongly linked to one another. Because of this overlap, it is sometimes tempting to focus our attention solely on poverty or social class as the most powerful factor, ignoring the additional impact of ethnicity. However, if we are to gain an understanding of children's development, we need to understand the separate effects of ethnic group membership. For example, what difference does it make to a child to grow up in a family whose cultural roots emphasize collectivism rather than individualism? I have touched on these questions throughout the book, but let me take one final look at what we know at this point about ethnic effects, using the several major ethnic groups in the United States as illustration.

First, though, we need a better definition of ethnicity and an **ethnic group** than I have given so far. Parke and Buriel define it this way: "Ethnicity refers to an individual's membership in a group sharing a common ancestral heritage based on nationality, language, and culture" (1998, p. 496). Ethnicity *may* include a biological or racial component, but that is not an essential part of the definition. Thus, race and ethnicity are not the same. *Ethnicity* refers primarily to social and cultural characteristics, while *race* normally designates a group with specific physical characteristics. Thus, Latinos, African Americans, and Asian Americans may be viewed as both ethnic and racial categories, while Polish Americans or Italian Americans would be regarded only as ethnic groups.

African Americans. African Americans, the largest ethnic minority group in the United States at about 12 percent of the total population (U.S. Bureau of the Census, 1997), have a culture that has been shaped by their African heritage, their experience of slavery, and a continuing experience of discrimination and segregation. The central values of this ethnic culture include the following (Hill et al., 1994):

- Collectivism or communalism as opposed to individualism; identity is collective as well as personal.

- Person-centered rather than object-centered values; relationships with people are more important than material possessions.

- Mutuality and reciprocity; a belief that "what goes around, comes around," that each person's actions will eventually have repercussions for that individual.

- A strong religious or spiritual orientation, involving acknowledgement of a higher power.

- An emphasis on the importance of children for family continuity.

- Harmony and a sense of connection with nature, including a belief in the "oneness of being" of all humanity.

- Role flexibility.

These values, especially the emphasis on collectivism or communalism and the importance of children, have contributed to a pattern of family structures that is quite different from what exists within the majority Euro-American culture. Euro-Americans think of "the family" as (normatively) a father, a mother, and several children. Within the African-American culture, "family" has a much broader definition, including many variations of extended family structures—a pattern that likely has its roots in West African culture (Sudarkasa, 1993). Martin and Martin, in their book *The Black Extended Family*, defined the African-American family as

> a multigenerational, interdependent kinship system which is welded together by a sense of obligation to relatives; is organized around a dominant figure; extends across geographic boundaries to connect family units to an extended family network; and has a built in mutual aid system for the welfare of its members and the maintenance of the family as a whole. (1978, p. 1)

Thus, the key is not just that three or more generations often live in the same household but that contact with nonresident kin is frequent and integral to the functioning of the family unit. When asked, African Americans overwhelmingly report a strong sense of family solidarity (Hatchett & Jackson, 1993; Wilson, 1986; 1989).

Within this subculture, marriage does not play the dominant role in family formation that it does among Euro-Americans: Far fewer black adults marry, they are less likely to be satisfied with their marriages, and divorce is more common (Broman, 1993). One result is that a much larger percentage of black children are born to or reared by unmarried mothers. However, because of the cultural emphasis on the importance of

These Irish Americans marching in a St. Patrick's Day parade would fit the definition of an ethnic group, but they are not a race.

Cultures and Contexts
Child Rearing and Family Values in West Africa

The emphasis on collectivism that we see in the African-American subculture naturally enough has its roots in African cultural traditions. In many West African cultures, for example (Ivory Coast, Cameroon, and other countries), adults clearly distinguish between social intelligence and "book learning." They say that a person can read and write but be quite dumb, or that a person can be wise without having book learning (Dasen, 1984; Nsamenang & Lamb, 1994). In rearing their children, adults in these cultures pay more attention to the children's social knowledge or skill than to biological age. Children are given new responsibilities or tasks when they seem ready, not at some arbitrary age.

In one study of these cultures, Bame Nsamenang and Michael Lamb (1994) interviewed 389 adults of the Nso tribe in Cameroon. These adults defined a "good child" as one who showed obedience and respect, filial service, hard work, helpfulness, honesty, and intelligence. Although many children in this setting attend school (a training system that is an artifact of colonial rule), adult Nsos see the primary training of children as occurring both through apprenticeships, in which adults act as role models, and through training of younger children by their older sibs or by peers. This is a very different model of child rearing and child development than what we see in the United States and most Western cultures.

children and on communalism, these single mothers occupy a different niche within the African-American culture than is true for single Euro-American mothers. The latter group are more likely to receive financial help from their parents but to live independently; an African-American single mother is more likely to live in an extended family with her own mother or grandmother (Wilson, 1986).

These extended family structures allow individuals to pool their economic resources; they also provide important social and emotional support to the members of the household. The presence of the children's grandmother seems to provide especially helpful support for the young single mother; black children in such three-generation families do better in school and show fewer behavior problems than do black children reared in single-mother households without a grandmother. There is also some evidence that the presence of the grandmother increases the chance that an infant will develop a secure rather than an insecure attachment (Egeland & Sroufe, 1981). Thus, the extended family not only has a cultural history but also seems to be a successful adaptive strategy for many black families.

Religion also appears to play a special, positive role within the African-American community. The church is a place for participation and belonging, a structure in which prestige and status can be conferred on those who take on specific roles. For black children, participation in church activities seems to be a plus as well; a few studies suggest that those who are more active in a church are more likely to be successful in other arenas, such as in school or on the job (Lee, 1985).

The culture of African-American families is also profoundly shaped by the persistence of prejudice and discriminatory housing practices, difficulty in finding good jobs, and an (often accurate) perception that hard work will not necessarily yield good results for them. African-American adolescents who are most aware of such prejudice are most likely to see school achievement as irrelevant (Taylor et al., 1994). In many inner cities, the combined effect of these forces has been to create a subculture in which illegal activity or idleness becomes the norm for African-American teenagers, especially teenage boys (Spencer & Dornbusch, 1990). Among adult black men, such "economic marginality" appears to be a significant precursor to divorce or family strain—a pattern that is not unique to the black subculture but that is particularly relevant for this group precisely because job opportunities are more limited.

Because so many black families and children live in or near poverty, it is very difficult to sort out which patterns are due to economic conditions and which are due to distinctive African-American cultural processes. These factors obviously interact and are further embedded within the larger culture, in which prejudice and discrimination against blacks is still a part of everyday life.

Latinos. Some of the same statements can be made about Latinos, for whom poverty is also endemic. The term *Hispanic* was coined by the Department of Commerce to denote any person with family roots in Spanish-speaking countries or from Central or South America. The term *Latino,* which many in this community prefer, is the Spanish word for the same group. Whichever term is used, it is clear that a wide range of separate groups are included, differing somewhat in values and cultural traditions. Of the present-day 26.3 million U.S. Latinos (now nearly 10 percent of the population), 64 percent are Mexican Americans (also often called Chicanos), 11 percent are Puerto Rican, about 5 percent are Cuban, and the rest are from other Central and South American countries. Within this diverse group, Puerto Ricans have the highest poverty rates; their divorce rates are comparable to what we see among African Americans. Both Chicanos and Cubans have divorce rates closer to the rate in the dominant Euro-American culture.

These subgroups, however, share a number of cultural values, all of which are aspects of a basic collectivist world view (Hill et al., 1994; Parke & Buriel, 1998):

- Preference for group participation or group work rather than individual effort (allocentrism).

- Strong commitment to and adherence to family; placing the family before the individual; self-identity is embedded in the family (*familia*).

- Avoidance of personal conflict; keeping the peace at all costs (*simpatia*).

- Respect for and deference to authority, such as parents, elders, teachers, or government officials (*respeto*).

- Maximal value on personal relationships, seen as more important than reputation or material gain; feelings and needs of others are paramount; competition is discouraged (*personalismo*).

In addition, of course, there is also the common thread of the Spanish language. The great majority of Latinos in the United States today are either monolingual in Spanish or bilingual. Because of rapid recent immigration, more than half of Latino school-age children have only limited English proficiency; a shift toward English as the dominant language generally occurs among second- or third-generation Latinos, but many if not most continue to speak Spanish in the home (Chapa & Valencia, 1993; Grenier, 1985). Many Latino communities also have Spanish-language newspapers and radio and TV stations; in many neighborhoods, Spanish is the dominant tongue.

This Latino family has obviously assimilated some of the larger American culture: They are celebrating Thanksgiving. At the same time, they have doubtless retained many features of Latino culture, including the centrality of family loyalty.

Critical Thinking

Are there any "fictive kin" in your own family network? What is their role within the family?

The significance of family life within Latino culture is hard to exaggerate. The nuclear family is the core of this kin system, although contact with extended family members and with "fictive kin" is frequent. Fictive kin, also common in extended African-American family systems, might include a child's godparents or other friends who take on a long-term connection with the family and with each child (Keefe & Padilla, 1987).

In general, Latinos see frequent contacts with kin not only as enjoyable but as vital signs of the closeness of kin relationships. It is not enough to write or talk on the phone; to maintain close ties, you need to see and touch your relatives and friends. Among Latinos, an individual's self-esteem may also be strongly related to the valuation given by the kin group. William Madsen described it this way:

> When an Anglo fails, he thinks first of how this failure will affect him and his status in society. When a Chicano fails, his first evaluation of the failure is in terms of what it will do to his family and how it will affect his relationship to other family members. (1969, p. 224)

This pattern seems to be stronger in first-generation immigrants, who rely almost exclusively on family members for emotional support and problem solving. Second-generation immigrants seem to have more extensive nonkin networks, and many have shifted somewhat toward an individualist set of values—with accompanying increases in intrafamily stress (Delgado-Gaitan, 1994; Parke & Buriel, 1998). In both newly immigrant and second-generation families, however, the extended family clearly plays a more central role in the daily life of Latinos than it does in the Anglo culture.

This emphasis on the central role of the family is reflected in the values taught to children. Literally translated, *bien educado* means "well educated"; the phrase does not primarily connote many years of formal education, however, but rather the ability to function well in any social setting without disrespect or rudeness. Thus, *bien educado* includes politeness, respect, loyalty, and attachment to the extended family and cooperation with others. Latino mothers emphasize the importance of a child's showing proper demeanor in public; an Anglo mother, in contrast, is likely to be pleased or even proud when her child behaves in some independent but slightly naughty way (Harwood, 1992).

These values are taught in the home through all the mechanisms I have described throughout the book: modeling, direct reinforcement, and style of family interaction. A number of studies suggest that the more fully the parents identify with their Latino ethnic heritage, the more likely it is that the child will show these valued qualities, such as concern for others (Knight et al., 1993).

The collectivist Latino values often conflict with the strong individualism and competitiveness of the dominant Anglo culture. Where the values of the minority and majority cultures overlap is in the value placed on education. Latino parents, like both African-American and Anglo parents, place a strong value on doing well in school. Yet Latino youths are even more likely to drop out of school or to get poor grades in school than are African-American teens. This pattern has been difficult to explain. It is certainly linked partially to poverty, doubtless also to persisting language difficulties. It may also arise in part from the emphasis on deference and respect that are part of *bien educado,* because Latino parents are quite likely to show an authoritarian rearing style. We know that this rearing style is associated with poorer school performance, so it may be that the very aspect of Latino culture that is one of its greatest strengths may also contribute to less optimal school outcomes for children—at least within the larger Anglo cultural system.

Asian Americans. Asian-American culture, too, places great stress on obedience to family, on respect for elders, and on family honor. Asian-American family systems also resemble Latino families in some respects: They often include three generations in the same household; they are generally hierarchically organized, with the father as the clear head; and there is a strong emphasis on the interdependence of family members.

Despite these surface similarities, the mixture of values in Asian-American families is distinctive (American Psychological Association, 1993; Parke & Buriel, 1998):

- Pacifism, self-discipline, and self-control—all values linked to Confucianism, and thus common for those Asian groups with a strong Confucian heritage (Chinese, Korean, and Vietnamese particularly, with lesser influence among Japanese).

- An emphasis on hierarchy and respect in social systems and personal relationships (parents are superior to children, men to women), also based on Confucianism.

- Strong family links; young people are expected to obey elders; family solidarity and harmonious relationships are highly valued; family needs come before individual needs.

- A strong belief that each person controls his or her own destiny.

- A powerful work ethic and belief in the importance of achievement.

The Asian family model includes a striking combination of indulgence, physical contact, comfort, and care on the one hand, high expectations for both obedience and achievement on the other. Children are taught that empathy with others is highly important and yet that respecting the privacy of others is also critical (Lebra, 1994). Overall, children are highly valued, although the family's collective needs normally take precedence over the child's individual needs (Rothbaum et al., 1995).

Asian-American families also believe in individual *effort* as one of the primary roads to success (Harrison et al., 1990; Stevenson, 1988), an element missing from both Latino and Euro-American cultural values. In Euro-American culture, *ability* rather than hard work is seen as the key to success. This difference is not trivial. If you believe in ability as the key ingredient, then there is not much point in pressing for greater effort, and you will accept mediocre performance from your child. An Asian parent, in contrast, believing in the centrality of effort, takes a very different attitude toward both success and failure by a child: The parent takes success more or less for granted but responds to failure by insisting on more effort. Because of these different belief systems, Asian-American parents spend more time tutoring their children and have higher standards for their children's achievement. They are also less likely to be satisfied with their children's schools, believing that schools, too, can always do better. Yet despite what (to Euro-American eyes) seems like strong pressure to achieve, Asian and Asian-American students do not report high feelings of stress or anxiety, while high-achieving Euro-American adolescents *do* report frequent feelings of stress (Crystal et al., 1994).

Given all these differences, we shouldn't be surprised that Asian-American children as a group achieve at higher levels in schools than any other U.S. ethnic group, just as Asian children from Japan, China, Taiwan, and Korea regularly outperform U.S. children and teenagers on standardized tests of math and science. Asian Americans complete high school and college at the highest rate of any group in the United States, including Anglos.

Asian-American families are also more stable and more upwardly mobile than other groups and are quite unlikely to involve single parents. Collectively, all these factors mean that Asian Americans are least likely to live in poverty of any of the minority groups I have described here.

Ethnicity in Perspective. What conclusions can we draw about the role of ethnicity (or culture more broadly) in children's development from these three brief (and necessarily simplistic) sketches? Sadly, not many. First and foremost, of course, I have been talking almost entirely about subgroups within U.S. culture, which tells us little about other cultural systems. And even within these limits, we are working mostly with research that involves comparisons of each ethnic group with children or families in the Anglo culture. Until recently, most of this research assumed that the Anglo culture was

Nine-year-old Brian gets help with his homework from his dad—a common activity in Asian-American households, in which parents typically place great emphasis on the importance of hard work to reach academic goals.

Critical Thinking

Think about your own beliefs for a moment. Do you think of effort or ability as the most significant element in an individual's success? Has your belief about this affected your own choices or behavior at any point in your life?

Research Report

Asian and U.S. Teenagers and Their Parents Define a "Bad Kid"

If I asked you to think about and describe some specific teenager you consider to be a "bad kid," what qualities would define "badness" for you? It turns out that this is a useful question to ask in different cultures as a way to uncover differences in values and expectations for children.

David Crystal and Harold Stevenson (1995) asked this question of nearly 600 eleventh graders in the United States, in Taiwan, and in Japan. The U.S. teens, more than either Asian group, described a "bad kid" as someone who lacked self-control—someone who was "childish" or "immature." Taiwanese teens, more than the other groups, emphasized society-related conduct, such as "makes trouble for society" or "rebels against society," while Japanese students most often referred to lack of interpersonal

harmony, such as "hurting other people's feelings," "being argumentative and starting fights," or "not caring about others." Both U.S. and Taiwanese children also mentioned disruptions of interpersonal harmony as being part of "badness," but this was almost the only category the Japanese students mentioned.

Crystal and Stevenson also interviewed the mothers of these students, asking them the same question, with similar results. In simple terms, these results suggest that for the U.S. teens, failure to achieve an appropriate individuality defines badness, while in both Asian cultures, badness occurs when the child fails to have a proper respect for the collective. It would be interesting to hear the responses of Latino students and their parents to this same question.

right or "normal" and all other variations were inferior or "deviations" from the standard. That assumption has faded, but we rarely have information about all these groups at the same time, and even less often have data about whether the same *processes* operate in each subgroup. What we are left with is a kind of snapshot of each group without being able to tell which characteristics are the most crucial, which attitudes or values the most significant.

For example, if we look for reasons for good or poor school performance in different subcultures, what conclusions can we draw? Bilingualism cannot be the sole answer because both Asian Americans and Latinos are typically bilingual; child-rearing style cannot be the sole answer because Asian-American parents are most likely to be authoritarian (by current research definitions), yet their children do well in school. Doubtless it is the *pattern* of values and parental behavior that is crucial, and not any one variable operating at once. Cultures and subcultures are incredibly complex systems; their effects come from the combination and not merely from the adding up of a set of separate variables. In addition, of course, because we are talking about subcultures here, we have to try to understand how each culture, each set of values, combines or conflicts with the values of the majority culture. For a child growing up with a foot in each culture, these are highly important issues.

Critical Thinking

Imagine a largish group of Euro-Americans set down in the midst of some quite different culture, such as perhaps China or Japan. What cultural conflicts would the children of this subgroup be likely to experience?

The Culture as a Whole

The culture as a whole is also a system, made up of values, assumptions, and beliefs, a political and an economic system, a pattern of personal relationships, and so forth. Each piece of that system affects all the other parts; changing one part changes the whole. The wide cultural consequences of the rapid increase in the number of women in the labor force in the United States and other industrialized countries is a very good example. It has led, among many other things, to a huge new demand for child care (with consequent changes in children's lives), to changes in male-female relationships, to new political alignments, and to shifts in patterns of interactions within families, which in turn affect children in still other ways.

Throughout the book, I have pointed to a variety of patterns or sequences of children's development that seem to occur regardless of cultural context. The stages of moral judgment, the early stages of language development, the creation of internal models of attachment, physical maturation, the development of a theory of mind—all these and many other patterns appear to be universal aspects of development.

At the same time, examples of cultural differences are also easy to come by. At the most visible and measurable level are variations in children's specific beliefs, the social scripts they learn, and the pattern of family and kin relationships they experience.

An interesting example comes from the work of Giyoo Hatano and his colleagues (1993), who compared beliefs about the nature of plants and animals among Japanese, Israeli, and U.S. kindergarten, second-grade, and fourth-grade children. Piaget noted, and others have confirmed, that children typically begin with the idea of *animism,* in which they attribute not only life but also feelings and self-awareness to inanimate objects, to plants, and to animals. Later they differentiate among these several facets of life and understand that plants are alive but have no self-awareness. Hatano's study confirms the broad features of this shift: Younger children in all three cultures had much stronger beliefs in animism. But Hatano also found differences in the developmental pattern, depending on the specific cultural beliefs about life.

Japanese culture includes the belief that plants are much like humans; in the Buddhist system, even a blade of grass is thought to have a mind. In contrast, in Israeli language and culture, plants are put into a quite different category from animals and humans. When children in Japan and Israel, along with U.S. children, were asked whether a tree or a tulip were alive, 91 percent of the Japanese but only 60 percent of the Israeli fourth graders said that it was. One-fifth of Japanese fourth graders attributed sensory properties to plants, saying that a tree or a tulip could feel chilly or could feel pain if it were hit with a stick. Overall, because of their stronger distinction between plants and animals, Israeli children were much slower than either Japanese or U.S. children to come to the understanding that people, animals, and plants are all alive. This study thus illustrates both an underlying developmental pattern that seems to be shared across cultures and the cultural variations laid over that basic pattern.

It is not hard to generate similar examples. For instance, cultures may vary in the proportion of securely and insecurely attached children because of variations in their typical child-rearing styles or beliefs, even while the *process* by which a child becomes securely or insecurely attached is much the same from one culture to another. In a similar way, adolescents in all cultures need to change their identity to at least some extent in order to move into the adult world, but cultures that provide initiation rituals at puberty may make the process much simpler and less confusing.

Certainly we need to know a great deal more about how such cultural variations affect development. But as I pointed out in Chapter 1, we also have to ask a more subtle set of questions. In particular, we need to know whether the *relationship* between environmental events or child characteristics and some outcome for the child is the same in every culture. Is authoritative child rearing optimal in all cultures, or is some other style better to prepare children for adult life in some settings? Are aggressive children unpopular in every culture, or are there some settings in which aggression is highly valued? Indeed, is unpopularity in childhood a major risk factor for adult dysfunction in every culture?

As yet we do not have answers, although researchers are beginning to ask the questions. Steinberg and Dornbusch, for example, asked whether authoritative parental style had the same effects in each of several ethnic groups in the United States. They found that it did not; this finding forces us to reexamine our assumptions about the way parental style affects children's development.

It is extremely difficult to conceptualize the developmental process as part of such a complex system, and even harder to design research that allows us to look at all the pieces of the puzzle at the same time. But it is precisely that kind of research we need if we are to be able to understand the full impact of the ecology of the child's development, including cultural and subcultural influences.

Summary

1. Children's development is directly affected by institutions beyond the family, including child care, school, jobs, and television. It is also affected by the subculture and culture in which children grow up.

2. The majority of children in the United States now spend a part of their infancy or preschool years in some form of nonparental care. The most common forms of such care in the United States are family day care and care in the child's own home by someone other than the mother.

3. Day care often has positive effects on the cognitive development of less advantaged children, but it may have negative effects on advantaged children if the discrepancy between the home environment and the level of stimulation in day care is large.

4. The impact of day care on children's personality is unclear. Some studies show children with a history of day care to be more aggressive; others show them to be more socially skillful.

5. A major new study shows no overall negative effect of day care on the security of children's attachment to their parents.

6. The quality of day care appears to be a highly significant element in determining its effects. Good-quality care involves low adult-to-child ratios, small groups of children, clean spaces designed for children's play, and responsive caregivers trained in child development.

7. Experience with school appears to be causally linked to some aspects of cognitive development, such as the ability to generalize strategies from one situation to another.

8. Children's adaptation to school is affected by their readiness to learn to read as well as by their parents' involvement in the schools and in the children's educational attainment.

9. School experience also shapes a child's sense of self-efficacy. By adolescence, children have a clearly developed idea of their comparative skills and abilities. These beliefs are a significant element in decisions about high school completion or dropping out.

10. The majority of teenagers in the United States work at part-time jobs. Most (but not all) research points to negative effects from such part-time work: The more hours a student works, the lower his school grades, the more drugs or alcohol he uses, and the more aggression he shows.

11. The average U.S. child watches 3 to 4 hours of television per day. Children who watch specifically educational programming can gain specific skills or attitudes.

12. Heavy TV viewing may also contribute to somewhat lower grades and poorer reading skills, although this effect is small and is not found consistently.

13. Experts agree that watching violence on TV also increases the level of personal aggression or violence shown by a child. This effect appears to be especially strong among children who are already aggressive and among those whose parents use harsh physical punishment.

14. Children growing up in poverty, perhaps especially urban poverty, are markedly disadvantaged in many ways, including having lower access to medical care and greater exposure to multiple stresses. They do more poorly in school and drop out of school at far higher rates.

15. Some protective factors, including a secure attachment, higher IQ, authoritative parenting, and effective schools, can help to counterbalance poverty effects for some children.

16. The African-American subculture includes a strong emphasis on extended family households and contact and on religion, but it places a weaker emphasis on marriage as the vehicle for household formation. Because a large fraction of African Americans live in poverty, it is difficult to sort out the separate effects of ethnic culture and poverty.

17. Latinos, too, place great emphasis on family ties. Their emphasis on family honor and solidarity is heightened by the use of a shared language. In this collectivist cultural system, kin contact is frequent and central to daily life. Values taught to children include politeness, respect, and loyalty, an emphasis somewhat at odds with the individualism of the larger society.

18. Asian Americans, too, emphasize respect and loyalty to family, but they also stress the central importance of effort (rather than inherent ability) as the path to achievement. Asian-American families are more stable than others, with lower divorce rates and fewer single-parent families; their children achieve in school at a higher rate than any other group in the United States.

19. As yet we know far too little about the ways in which these varying mixtures of values and family patterns interact to affect children's development.

20. When we compare whole cultures, too, our ignorance exceeds our knowledge. Some patterns of development and some basic developmental processes appear to be independent of culture, such as perhaps moral reasoning and attachment. Other processes and patterns are affected by cultural variation.

Key Terms

ethnic group "A subgroup whose members are perceived by themselves and others to have a common origin and culture, and shared activities in which the common origin or culture is an essential ingredient" (Porter & Washington, 1993, p. 140). **p. 432**

family day care Nonparental care in which the child is cared for in someone else's home, usually with a small group of other children. **p. 408**

social class Term widely used to describe broad variations in economic and social positions within any given society. Four broad groups are most often described: upper class, middle class, working class, and lower class (also called poverty level). For an individual family, the designation is based on the income, occupation, and education of the adults in the household. **p. 427**

Suggested Readings

Duncan, G. J. & Brooks-Gunn, J. (Eds.). (1997). *Consequences of growing up poor.* New York: Russell Sage Foundation. A fine, up-to-date collection of papers on poverty and its effects, focusing primarily—but not exclusively— on poverty in the United States.

Garbarino, J., Dubrow, N., Kostelny, K., & Pardo, C. (1992). *Children in danger: Coping with the consequences of community violence.* San Francisco: Jossey-Bass. A striking, frightening book about children growing up in "war zones," including urban poverty in the United States as well as literal war zones in other countries.

Huston, A. C. (Ed.). (1991). *Children in poverty: Child development and public policy.* Cambridge, England: Cambridge University Press. Another excellent collection of papers on all aspects of poverty.

McAdoo, H. P. (Ed.). (1993). *Family ethnicity: Strength in diversity.* Newbury Park, CA: Sage. A very helpful collection of papers describing the family life and experiences of African Americans, Latinos, Native Americans, Asian Americans, and Muslim families.

Osofsky, J. D. (Ed.). (1997). *Children in a violent society.* New York: Guilford Press. Another excellent collection of papers, focusing on all aspects of violence in society, including family violence and neighborhood and media violence; prevention and intervention strategies are also discussed.

Steinberg, L. (1996). *Beyond the classroom: Why school reform has failed and what parents need to do.* New York: Simon & Schuster. Steinberg is one of my favorite researchers and authors—as I'm sure you have gathered after reading this far. This excellent book is basically an account of the Steinberg/Dornbusch study, written for a lay audience. It is highly readable, and Steinberg does not hesitate to talk about the practical educational and societal applications of his findings. Highly recommended for teachers and would-be teachers, parents and would-be parents.

15

Atypical Development

W hen Jeffrey was 4, he couldn't walk or talk and spent most of his time in a crib. His parents fed him pureed baby food through a bottle. After six years with a loving foster family, at age 10 Jeffrey is now in a special class in a regular elementary school and is learning to print and read.

Nine-year-old Archie seemed "different from other children even when he started school." Often he was "disoriented" or "distractible." Although he scored in the normal range on an IQ test, he had great difficulty learning to read. Even after several years of special tutoring, he could read only by sounding out the words each time; he didn't recognize even familiar words by sight (Cole & Traupmann, 1981).

Janice's parents are worried about her. Right about the time she turned 13, she seemed to change in quite disturbing ways. She's lost weight, even though she's growing fast; she doesn't seem to call up her friends anymore and is listless and gloomy. This has been going on for about six months now, and her parents think this is just not normal; they're going to talk to the school counselor about her and will consider family therapy if it will help.

Each of these children is "atypical" in some way. In each, the developmental processes I have been describing in the past 13 chapters haven't quite worked in the normal way. Jeffrey is a Down syndrome child and is mentally retarded. Archie has some kind of learning disability, while Janice shows many signs of clinical depression.

Frequency of Problems

How common are such problems? Given the critical practical relevance of this question, you'd think that psychologists and epidemiologists would long ago have come to some agreement. But we haven't, in large part because the line between typical and atypical is very much a matter of degree rather than of kind. *Most* children show at least some kinds of "problem behavior" at one time or another. For example, parents in the United States report that 10 to 20 percent of 7-year-olds still wet their beds at least occasionally; 30 percent have nightmares, 20 percent bite their fingernails, 10 percent suck their thumbs, and 10 percent swear enough for it to be considered a problem. Another 30 percent or so have temper tantrums (Achenbach & Edelbrock, 1981). Problems like these, especially if they last only a few months, should more properly be considered part of "normal" development. Usually we label a child's development atypical or deviant only if a problem persists for six months or longer or if the problem is at the extreme end of the continuum for that behavior.

When we count only such extreme or persisting problems, the incidence is much lower—although nonetheless higher than most of you will have guessed. Table 15.1 (p. 444) gives some current estimates for each of a series of deviant patterns. Some of these numbers are based on extensive data and are widely accepted, such as the 3.5 percent rate of mental retardation. Others are still in some dispute, such as the rate of depression in adolescence. Where the findings are not in agreement, I have given the range of current estimates.

We might also want to combine all these individual rates in some way, to give us some idea of the total percentage of children with one kind or problem or another. Unfortunately this is not a simple matter of addition, since the categories overlap a good deal. For example, many children with serious learning disabilities also show an attention deficit disorder or conduct disorders. Still, even if we allow for some overlap, the totals are astonishing: Between 14 and 20 percent of children and teenagers show at least *some* form of significant psychopathology (Costello & Angold, 1995; Simonoff et al., 1997). If we add in cognitive disorders, the total is at least 20 percent. That is, at least one in five, and maybe as many as one in four, children will show at least one form of significantly deviant or abnormal behavior *at some time in their early years*. The majority of these children will require some type of special help in school, in a child guidance clinic,

Table 15.1

Estimated Incidence of Various Types of Atypical Development in the United States and Other Developed Countries

Type of Problem	Percentage of Children Aged 0–18 with That Problem
Psychopathologies	
Externalizing problems	
1. Conduct disorders	5 to 7
2. Arrested by police (delinquency)	3
Internalizing problems	
1. Significant anxiety and fear	2.5
2. Serious or severe depression	
Elementary school–age children	1 to 2
Adolescents	5 to 7
Attention problems/hyperactivity	3 to 7
Intellectual disabilities	
IQ below 70 (mentally retarded)	3.5
Speech and language problems, including delayed language, articulation problems, and stuttering	3.5
Serious learning disability	4
All other problems	
Including blindness, cerebral palsy, hearing impairment, autism	0.5

Sources: Barkley, 1997; Brandenburg et al., 1990; Broman et al., 1987; Buitelaar & van Engeland, 1996; Cantwell, 1990; Chalfant, 1989; Costello & Angold, 1995; Kopp & Kaler, 1989; Marschark, 1993; Merikangas & Angst, 1995; Nolen-Hoeksema, 1994; Rutter, 1989; Rutter & Garmezy, 1983; Simonoff et al., 1997; Tuna, 1989.

Critical Thinking

Do you think that such high rates of problems would be found in every culture? Why or why not?

or in an equivalent setting. When you think of these figures in terms of the demands on the school system and on other social agencies, the prospect is staggering.

If we are going to meet those needs, we must obviously understand the origins of such atypical patterns. In this chapter I can give you only a glimpse of our current knowledge, but I can at least alert you to the issues and remaining questions about the most common forms of deviance.

Developmental Psychopathology: A New Approach

Our knowledge about the dynamics of deviant development in general, and psychopathology in particular, has been enormously enhanced in the past few years by the emergence of a new theoretical and empirical approach called **developmental psychopathology,** pioneered by such researchers as Norman Garmezy, Michael Rutter, Dante Cicchetti, Alan Sroufe, and others (e.g., Cicchetti & Cohen, 1995b; Rutter & Garmezy, 1983; Sroufe, 1997). These theorists have emphasized several key points.

First, normal and abnormal development both emerge from the same basic processes. To understand either, we must understand both and how they interact with one another. The task of a developmental psychopathologist is to uncover those basic processes—to see both how they work "correctly" in the case of normal development and to identify *developmental deviations* and their causes (Sroufe, 1989). Alan Sroufe's studies of the consequences of secure or insecure attachment, which I talked about in Chapter 11, are good examples of research based on such assumptions.

Second, the approach is *developmental*. Theorists in this new subfield are interested in the *pathways* leading to both deviant and normal development, from earliest infancy through childhood and into adult life. Sroufe uses the metaphor of a branching tree, as shown in Figure 15.1 (p. 446). A child may follow a continuously maladaptive or adaptive pathway; alternatively, we might see initially positive adaptations that later turn maladaptive, or the reverse. Our job as psychologists, according to this view, is to try to trace these various pathways: What are the sequences of experiences that lead to increased risk of depression in adolescence? What pathways lead to delinquency or other antisocial behavior or to peer rejection? What factors may inhibit or exacerbate an early deviation or turn an initially normal developmental trajectory into a deviant pattern?

Note that one of the important implications of this model is that the *same* maladaptive behavior may be reached by many different pathways. We should not assume that all depressed teenagers, or all delinquent teens, have the same history, the same roots of their behavior. And it follows that the same treatments will not be effective for all children with similar diagnoses.

Another implication of the model is that change is possible at virtually any point; the tree can branch off in a new direction. At the same time, it is also true that later branchings are at least somewhat constrained by earlier adaptations. As Sroufe puts it, "the longer a maladaptive pathway has been followed . . . the less likely it is that the person will reclaim positive adaptation" (1997, p. 254).

The model in Figure 15.1 also makes it clear that developmental pathologists are especially interested in the concepts of *resilience* and *vulnerability*. One of the unexpected results of many recent studies of children thought to be "at risk" for particular kinds of problems, such as children reared by depressed parents, children in divorcing families, or abused children, has been that some children seem to be unexpectedly resilient in the face of what appear to be disturbing circumstances. The obverse has also been found repeatedly: Some children seem to be unexpectedly vulnerable despite what appear to be supportive life circumstances. Developmental psychopathologists such as Rutter and Garmezy not only have taken the lead in studying resilient children; they have insisted that these "exceptions" to the general rules offer us crucial information about the basic processes of both normal and abnormal development.

Cultures and Contexts
Problem Behaviors Among Children in Kenya and Thailand

A growing body of information links particular cultural values and the type of emotional or behavioral problems children may show. In one recent study, John Weisz and his colleagues (1993) compared the incidence of externalizing and internalizing problems among teenagers in a rural Kenyan group (the Embu) and a rural Thailand group with the rates among rural black and white youth in the United States. Both the Thai and Embu cultures place great emphasis on obedience and politeness, a pattern of cultural values that is thought to be linked to higher rates of "overcontrolled" or internalizing problems, such as shyness, fearfulness, or depression. In contrast, U.S. culture, with its greater emphasis on individual freedom, appears to foster higher rates of "undercontrolled" or externalizing problems, such as fighting, showing off, or hyperactivity.

In each of the three cultures, parents were asked a series of questions about specific behaviors or symptoms their child showed. Weisz found that the Embu teens had the highest rates of internalizing and the lowest rates of externalizing problems, while U.S. white teens had the highest rates of undercontrol, followed by African-American teens. Interestingly, the Thai group showed low rates of both types of problems, although other studies in Thailand have shown high levels of overcontrol problems in this culture.

The fact that the Embu and Thai patterns are not the same certainly reminds us yet again that cultural effects are not going to be so simple as a difference between an emphasis on obedience versus personal freedom. The results also remind us that the pattern of frequencies of various types of problems that we note in U.S. populations is at least in part a product of our culture.

Figure 15.1

A schematic representation of the developmental pathways concept: A, continuity of maladaptation, culminating in disorder; B, continuous positive adaptation; C, initial maladaptation followed by positive change (resilience); D, initial positive adaptation followed by negative change.

(*Source:* Psychopathology as an outcome of development" by L. A. Stroufe, *Development and psychopathology,* 9 (1997), p. 253, Fig. 1. By permission of Cambridge University Press.)

A growing body of research, cast in this framework, can help us examine the origins and manifestations of the array of psychopathologies.

The Psychopathologies of Childhood

Experts in childhood psychopathologies (e.g., Achenbach, 1995) now agree that there are three main categories of such disorders: **externalizing problems** (also described as *disturbances of conduct*), including both delinquency and excessive aggressiveness or defiance, in which the deviant behavior is directed outward; **internalizing problems** (also called *emotional disturbances*), such as depression, anxiety, or eating disorders, in which the deviance is largely internal to the individual; and **attention problems,** most particularly attention deficit hyperactivity disorder (ADHD).

Externalizing Problems

The broadest category of externalizing problems is what in lay terms we might call *antisocial behavior.* In the 1994 revision of the American Psychiatric Association's *Diagnostic and Statistical Manual of Mental Disorders,* called DSM-IV, this type of problem is called a **conduct disorder.** It includes high levels of aggression, argumentativeness, bullying, disobedience, irritability, and threatening and loud behavior.

It has been clear for a long while that there are a number of subvarieties of conduct disorders (e.g., Achenbach, 1993). In Sroufe's terms, there are several distinct pathways, differentiated primarily by the age at which the deviant behavior first begins. One group includes those whose aggression and other antisocial behavior begins in early childhood and persists through adolescence and into adulthood. Children and adolescents who fall in this group also tend to show more serious or severe aggression or delinquent acts than is true of those whose deviant behavior begins later. Stephen Hinshaw and his colleagues (1993) label this group **childhood-onset conduct disorders;** Terrie Moffitt (1993) refers to this same group as *life-course-persistent offenders*.

The second group, labeled **adolescent-onset conduct disorders** by Hinshaw, and *adolescence-limited delinquents* by Moffitt, includes those who begin aggressive or delinquent behavior only in adolescence. Their deviance is typically milder, more transitory, more a function of hanging out with bad companions than a deeply ingrained behavior problem.

The developmental pathway for early-onset conduct disorders is one you are familiar with by now from all I have said about Patterson's research on aggressive children. These are very often children who begin life with a range of vulnerabilities, including difficult temperament, lower intelligence, or both (e.g., Lyons-Ruth et al., 1997; Newman et al., 1997; Prior et al., 1997). In infancy, they are likely to have formed insecure/disorganized or insecure/avoidant attachments (Lynam, 1996; Lyons-Ruth et al., 1997; D. Shaw et al., 1996; van IJzendoorn, 1997). In the preschool years, these children very often throw tantrums and defy parents. They are, in a word, simply very difficult children to handle. If the parents are not up to the task of controlling the child, the child's behavior worsens to overt aggression toward others, who then reject the child. Such peer rejection aggravates the problem, pushing the seriously aggressive child in the direction of other children with similar problems, who become the child's only supportive peer group (Shaw et al., 1994). By adolescence, these youngsters are firmly established in delinquent or antisocial behavior with friends drawn almost exclusively from among other delinquent teens (Tremblay et al., 1995b). They are also highly likely to display a whole cluster of other problem behaviors, including drug and alcohol use, truancy or dropping out of school, and early and risky sexual behavior, including multiple sexual partners (Dishion et al., 1995b).

The degree of continuity of this form of deviant behavior is quite striking. The correlation between aggression in childhood and aggression in adulthood averages .60 to .70—very high for data of this kind, and replicated in studies in both England and the United States (Farrington, 1991). One example, which you may remember from Chapter 14, is Leonard Eron's longitudinal study of aggressive boys. Those who were most aggressive at age 8 were much more likely to show antisocial or damaging aggressive behavior as adults (Eron et al., 1987).

There is also some indication that the early-onset syndrome has a much stronger genetic component than the later-onset pattern (Achenbach, 1993; Deater-Deckard & Plomin, 1997). Thus, the preschooler who already shows defiant and oppositional behavior as well as aggressiveness may have strong inborn propensities for such behavior. But if Patterson is correct—and I think he is—then whether that propensity will develop into a full-fledged, persisting conduct disorder will depend on the unfolding sequence of events, including the parents' ability to handle the child's early defiance as well as the general environment in which the child lives, such as inner-city versus small-town settings (Gottesman & Goldsmith, 1994; Loeber et al., 1989).

One confirmation of Patterson's basic model comes from the Fast Track Project, which I described briefly in a Research Report in Chapter 12 (p. 356). You'll recall that this intervention program, which includes nearly 900 children in 395 classrooms, has been aimed quite directly at altering the behavior of children who already show strong signs of excessive aggression or conduct disorders in early elementary school (McMahon, 1997). Half the children have participated in a special intervention that includes lessons in expressing and labeling emotions as well as training in strategies for interacting with peers and solving social problems. Parents of children in the intervention group have been given special help in learning better child-management skills and

Critical Thinking

What kind of implications for social policy (if any) do you see in the fact that early-onset conduct disorders are most likely to persist to involve adult criminality or violence?

have been encouraged to create better connections with their children's schools. After two years, the children in this intervention program are rated as more competent in their social relationships and as less aggressive than are equivalent children who have had no intervention (Coie, 1997a; Dodge, 1997). This is not an inexpensive program, but if the early results hold up, it not only confirms Patterson's overall model; it demonstrates Sroufe's point that early trajectories *can* be redirected.

Delinquency. Let me also say just a word about **delinquency,** which is a narrower category than conduct disorders, referring only to intentional lawbreaking. Clearly, many children who break laws also show other forms of conduct disorder, so the two categories overlap a great deal. Still, the overlap is not 100 percent, so it is useful to look at delinquency separately.

Some willful misbehavior, such as lying or stealing, is fairly common in children as young as 4 or 5, but it is in adolescence that we see a significant increase in the number of youngsters who display such behaviors as well as a rise in the seriousness and consistency of delinquent behaviors.

It is extremely difficult to estimate how many teenagers engage in delinquent behavior. One window on the problem is to look at the number of arrests—although arrest rates are arguably only the tip of the iceberg. More than 2 million juvenile arrests were recorded in the United States in 1995, suggesting that as many as 5 to 7 percent of all children under age 18 were arrested (U.S. Bureau of the Census, 1997). From age 15 to 17, the arrest rate is more like 10 percent—a higher rate than we see for any other age group across the entire life span. Many of these arrests are for relatively minor infractions, but about a third are for serious crimes, including murder, burglary, rape, and arson.

When adolescents themselves describe their own lawbreaking, they report even higher rates. Four-fifths of U.S. youngsters between ages 11 and 17 say that they have been delinquent at some time or another. One-third admit truancy and disorderly conduct, and one-fifth say they have committed criminal acts, most often physical assaults or thefts (Dryfoos, 1990). Terrie Moffitt (1993) reports similar figures from his New Zealand sample—a sample made up of all the children born in a single New Zealand town over a one-year period in 1972–1973, followed for over twenty years. In this group, 93 percent of the males acknowledged some form of delinquent activity by age 18.

Just as conduct disorders are much more common among boys than girls at preschool and elementary school ages, delinquent acts and arrests are far more common among teenage males than females. Among those actually arrested, the ratio is more than 4 to 1; in self-reports, the ratios vary, but the more physically violent the act, the more common it is among boys rather than girls.

Serious or persistent delinquency is also more common among teens with lower IQ scores (Lynam et al., 1993). This link between IQ score and delinquency cannot be explained away by arguing that the less bright delinquents are more likely to be caught; nor is it simply an artifact of social class or ethnic differences in both delinquency and IQ, because among white middle-class teens it is also the case that delinquents have lower IQs than their nondelinquent peers. Instead, low IQ scores appear to be a genuine risk factor for delinquency, particularly for early-onset patterns of conduct disor-

These boys at the Cook County (Illinois) Juvenile Temporary Detention Center are among the 2 million juveniles arrested each year in the United States.

Research Report

Delinquency Among Girls

When we use the term *delinquent*, most of us think immediately of teenage boys. But although the incidence of delinquency or criminality in girls is much lower, it is not zero. Girls are much less likely to be involved in forms of delinquency that involve violence, just as girls are consistently less aggressive at every age, but girls do get involved in delinquent behaviors, such as shoplifting or the use of illegal drugs (Zoccolillo, 1993).

A study in New Zealand by Avshalom Caspi and his colleagues (1993) provides some interesting insights into the possible origins of such delinquent behavior. The sample of students involved in this study—a study I have referred to several times before—included all the children born in one town in one year (1972–1973), a group of more than 1000. The children were tested and assessed repeatedly, at ages 3, 5, 7, 9, 11, 13, and 15. In one analysis, Caspi looked at rates of delinquency among the girls as a function of the earliness or lateness of their menarche and whether they went to an all-girl or a mixed-sex high school. Caspi's hypothesis was that girls who attended a mixed-sex secondary school would be more likely to be involved in delinquent activities because they would have more rule-breaking models (delinquent boys) among their peers. He also expected to find that girls with early puberty would be more likely to become delinquent, especially in mixed-sex schools.

These hypotheses were generally confirmed, although there are some interesting wrinkles. At age 13, the girls were asked to report on "norm violations," which included a variety of mildly delinquent acts like breaking windows, stealing from schoolmates, getting drunk, swearing loudly in public, or making prank telephone calls. As you can see in the figure, such norm violations were most common among early-maturing girls attending coed schools. Further analysis shows that this difference is almost entirely contributed by a small group of girls who had had a history of high levels of aggression earlier in childhood *and* who had early puberty. Early-ma-

turing girls in coed schools who had no such history of early problems showed no heightened rate of delinquency.

To make it still more complicated, Caspi found that at age 15, early-developing girls in coed schools continued to have high rates of delinquency, but at this age the highest rate of delinquency was found among *on-time-puberty* girls attending coed schools. Puberty, whether early or on time, thus seems to increase the likelihood that vulnerable girls will get involved with antisocial peers. But this is only true of girls in coed schools.

I find this study fascinating not only because it points to the complex relationships between physical maturation and social relationships, but also because it offers an interesting argument in favor of all-girl schools.

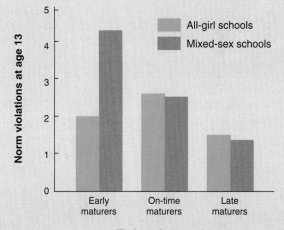

(*Source:* Caspi, A., et al., from Fig 2, p. 24, "Unraveling girls' delinquency: Biological, dispositional, and contextual contributions to adolescent behavior," *Developmental psychology, 29* (1993), 19–30. © 1993 by the American Psychological Association. By permission of Dr. Avshalom Caspi.)

der, for those who show more serious or violent forms of offenses, and for those children who experience some school failure (Hämäläinen & Pulkkinen, 1996). The argument offered by Donald Lynam and others is that school failure reduces a young person's engagement with school and the values it represents. School failure also increases the child's or adolescent's frustration, which raises the likelihood of aggression of some kind. Thus, for many less intelligent young people, traditional social constraints on delinquent behavior are simply weaker.

It is important to emphasize, however, that unlike the broader category of conduct disorders, which are quite stable from childhood to adulthood, the milder forms of delinquency do not invariably or even commonly persist into adulthood. Many teens commit only occasional delinquent acts and show no further problem in adulthood. For them, mild delinquent behavior is merely a phase. It is those who show a syndrome of delinquent acts plus high-risk behavior, and who come from families with low warmth and ineffective control, who are quite likely to show criminality in their adult lives.

Both depressed mood and significant clinical depressions rise in frequency in adolescence.

Internalizing Problems: The Example of Depression

A different set of antecedents, and a different pathway, is found among children who show internalizing forms of psychopathology. The particular form of deviance that has been most often addressed within the framework of developmental psychopathology is **depression,** so let me use that as an example.

For many years, psychiatrists took the position that significant depression could not occur in children or adolescents. This turns out to be quite wrong. We now have abundant evidence that depression is actually quite common in adolescence and occurs at least occasionally among younger children. Perhaps 10 percent of preadolescent children and 30 to 40 percent of adolescents experience significant short-term depressed mood or misery (Compas et al., 1995; Harrington et al., 1996; Petersen et al, 1993). When a depressed mood lasts six months or longer and is accompanied by other symptoms, such as disturbances of sleeping and eating and difficulty concentrating, it is usually referred to as **clinical depression** or a *depressive disorder*—a definition you'll recall from the discussion of postpartum depression in Chapter 3 (p. 83). Estimates of the frequency of clinical depression among children and adolescents vary somewhat; the best epidemiological studies tell us that at any given time, about 1.0 percent of preadolescents and between 1.6 and 8.0 percent of adolescents are in the midst of such an enduring depression (Cicchetti & Toth, 1998). Perhaps twice that many will experience a serious depression at some time in their adolescent years (Compas et al., 1993; Merikangas & Angst, 1995). These are not trivial states of unhappiness. Not only do they last, on average, for seven to nine months, but they are also highly likely to recur: As many as 90 percent of all major depressive episodes are followed by a recurrence within two years (Cicchetti & Toth, 1998). A significant portion of depressed teens also say they think about suicide. In one longitudinal study of youths growing up in a working-class neighborhood in the United States, one-fifth of those who had had a serious depression by age 18 had also attempted suicide (Reinherz et al., 1993).

Interestingly, during the preadolescent years, boys and girls are about equally likely to be unhappy or depressed; beginning somewhere between ages 13 and 15, however, girls are twice as likely to report high or chronic levels of depression. This sex difference persists throughout adulthood and has been found in a number of industrialized countries and among African Americans, Latinos, and Anglo-Americans (Culbertson, 1997; Hankin et al., 1998; Nolen-Hoeksema & Girgus, 1994; Roberts & Sobhan, 1992).

Where do such depressions come from, and why do girls have more of them? The search for the developmental pathways leading to later depression begins with the clear finding that children growing up with depressed parents are much more likely than are those growing up with nondepressed parents to develop depression themselves (Merikangas & Angst, 1995). Of course this could indicate a genetic factor, a possibility supported by at least a few studies of twins and adopted children (Petersen et al., 1993). Or we could understand this link between parental and child depression in terms of the changes in the parent-child interaction that are caused by the parent's depression.

I mentioned in Chapter 11 that depressed mothers are much more likely than nondepressed mothers to have children who are insecurely attached. In particular, the depressed mother's behavior with her child is often so nonresponsive that it seems to foster in the child a kind of helpless resignation. Such a sense of helplessness has been found to be strongly related to depression in both adults and adolescents (Dodge, 1990).

Of course not all children of depressed parents are themselves depressed. About 60 percent show no abnormality at all. Whether or not a child moves along a pathway toward depression seems to be largely a function of the number of other stresses that are present in the family life, such as an illness, family arguments, work stress, loss of income, job loss, or marital separation.

The significant role of stress in the emergence of depression is just as clear among children whose parent or parents are not depressed. Any combination of stresses, such

Research Report

Adolescent Suicide and Its Prevention

Suicide is the third leading cause of death among U.S. adolescents and young adults; among whites in this age group, it is the second leading cause. The rate has also been rising in the past several decades (Sells & Blum, 1996). One recent national survey suggests that as many as a quarter of all teens in the United States have had thoughts about suicide; 19.0 percent say they have made a suicide plan, and 8.6 percent say they have made an attempt (Kann et al., 1995). A second large survey points to somewhat lower numbers, with 10.2 percent of girls and 7.5 percent of boys reporting suicidal thoughts and a total of 3.6 percent reporting a suicide attempt (Resnick et al., 1997). Still, even these lower figures are quite disturbing.

Teenage boys are far more likely than girls to die by suicide. The highest rate is among Native American males, with a rate of 26.3 deaths per 100,000 per year, followed by white males at 22.7, black males at 18.0, and Latinos at 16.3. The rates for girls are far lower, averaging 3.7 deaths per 100,000 per year (Centers for Disease Control, 1994b; National Center for Health Statistics, 1996). In contrast, suicide *attempts* are estimated to be as much as four times more common in girls than in boys (Group for the Advancement of Psychiatry, 1996). The major reason for the difference appears to be that girls, more often than boys, use less "successful" methods such as self-poisoning, whereas boys are more likely to use firearms.

It is obviously very difficult to uncover the contributing factors in successful or completed suicides because the crucial individual is no longer available to be interviewed. Researchers and clinicians are forced to rely on secondhand reports by parents or others about the mental state of the suicide before the act—reports that are bound to be at least partially invalid, because in many cases the parents or friends had no suspicion that a suicide attempt was imminent. Nonetheless, we do have some information about risk factors. First and foremost, some kind of significant emotional disturbance in the suicide or potential suicide, including but not restricted to depression, is virtually a universal ingredient. Behavior problems such as aggression are also common in the histories of completed suicides, as are a history of physical or sexual abuse, the loss of a caregiver because of separation or death, and a family history of psychiatric disorder or suicide (Garland & Zigler, 1993; Wagner, 1997).

These factors, however, are not enough to explain suicidal behavior. After all, many teenagers (and adults) have one or more of these risk factors, and very few actually commit suicide. David Shaffer (Shaffer et al., 1988) suggests at least three other important elements:

1. Some triggering stressful event. Studies of suicides suggest that among adolescents, this triggering event is often a disciplinary crisis with the parents or some rejection or humiliation, such as breaking up with a girlfriend or boyfriend or failure in a valued activity.

2. An altered mental state, which might be an attitude of hopelessness, reduced inhibitions because of alcohol consumption, or rage (Swedo et al., 1991). Among girls, in particular, the sense of hopelessness seems to be common: a feeling that the world is against them *and that they can't do anything about it.*

3. There must be an opportunity—a loaded gun available in the house, a bottle of sleeping pills in the parents' medicine cabinet, or the like (Resnick et al., 1997). Indeed, one likely contributor to the rising teenage suicide rates, especially among boys, is the increased availability of firearms to adolescents.

A fourth element, suggested by the results of the National Longitudinal Study on Adolescent Health (Resnick et al., 1997), is the absence of sufficient emotional "connectedness" with parents. Young people who have warm relationships with their parents, who feel they can go to them with problems and who spend time with their parents, are less likely to commit suicide.

Attempts to prevent teen suicide have not been notably successful. Despite the fact that most suicides and suicide attempters have displayed significantly deviant behavior for some time before the event, most do not find their way to mental health clinics or other professionals, and increasing the availability of such clinics or of hot lines or crisis phones has not proved effective in reducing suicide rates.

Other prevention efforts have focused on education, such as providing training to teachers or to teenagers on how to identify students who are at risk for suicide, in the hope that vulnerable individuals might be reached before they attempt suicide. Risk factors include withdrawal from friends, recent social stresses such as an emotional loss of some kind, self-destructive behavior such as extreme risk taking, and any talk of suicide (Group for the Advancement of Psychiatry, 1996). The problem is that a great many adolescents show several of these risk factors at one time or another and most do not attempt suicide, so it is hard for peers or teachers to single out those at especially high risk.

Another prevention strategy has been to offer special training in coping skills to students, so that teenagers might be able to find a nonlethal solution to their problems. Unfortunately, most such programs appear to be ineffective in changing student attitudes or knowledge (Shaffer et al., 1991).

These discouraging results are not likely to change until we know a great deal more about the developmental pathways that lead to this particular form of psychopathology. What makes one teenager particularly vulnerable to suicide and another able to resist the temptation? What combination of stressful circumstances is most likely to trigger a suicide attempt, and how do those stressful circumstances interact with the teenager's personal resources? Only when we can answer questions of this kind will we be on the road to understanding teenage suicide.

as the parents' divorce, the death of a parent or another loved person, the father's loss of job, a move, or a change of schools, increases the likelihood of depression in the child (Compas et al., 1993). Indeed, the role of such individual life stresses may help to explain the sex differences in depression among adolescents. Anne Petersen has proposed that girls are more likely to experience simultaneous stressful experiences in adolescence, such as pubertal changes combined with a shift in schools (Petersen et al., 1991). In her own longitudinal study, Petersen found that depression was *not* more common among girls than among boys when both groups had encountered equal levels of life stress or simultaneous stressful experiences.

Susan Nolen-Hoeksema (1994; Nolen-Hoeksema & Girgus, 1994) agrees with Petersen that one of the keys is that teenage girls face more stresses than do teenage boys. She also argues that girls respond to their "down" moods quite differently than do boys. Girls (and women) are more likely to *ruminate* about their sadness or distress ("What does it mean that I feel this way?" "I just don't feel like doing anything"). This coping strategy actually accentuates the depression, producing longer-lasting depressive episodes. Boys (and men), on the other hand, are more likely to use distraction—exercising, playing a game, or working—to deal with their blue moods, a coping strategy that tends to reduce depression.

You'll remember from Chapter 10 that low self-esteem is also part of the equation. Susan Harter's studies tell us that young people who feel that they do not measure up to their own standards are much more likely to show symptoms of clinical depression (e.g., Harter & Whitesell, 1996). The fact that depression increases markedly in adolescence makes good sense from this point of view. We know that in adolescence, children are much more likely to define themselves and others in *comparative* terms—to judge themselves against some standard or to see themselves as "less than" or "more than" some other person. We also know that at adolescence, appearance becomes highly salient, and a great many teenagers are convinced that they do not live up to the culturally defined appearance standards. Self-esteem thus drops in early adolescence, and depression rises. Girls in current Western cultures seem especially vulnerable to this process because the increase in body fat that is typical for girls in adolescence runs counter to the desired slim body type—a point I made in Chapter 4 in the discussion of eating disorders.

All this research has taken us a fair distance in our efforts to understand both the rise in depression in adolescence and the marked gender difference in rates of depression. Yet teenagers still vary widely in their responses to what appear to be the same levels of stress. Not every teenager who faces multiple stresses, fails to live up to some standard, is inclined to ruminate rather than use distraction, or is temperamentally shy ends up being clinically depressed. These are all risk factors, but even with these risk factors, some adolescents are more vulnerable than others.

Attention Problems

A third major category of psychopathology includes various problems of attention and inhibitory control. In DSM-IV, the major disorder in this category is called **attention deficit hyperactivity disorder (ADHD).** A glance at the diagnostic criteria, which I've listed in Table 15.2, will tell you quickly that the hallmarks of this disorder are physical restlessness and problems with attention—precisely as the label implies. Russell Barkley (1997), one of the major researchers and theorists in this area, suggests that the underlying problem is a deficit in the child's ability to inhibit behavior—to keep himself from starting some prohibited or unhelpful behavior or reacting to some compelling stimulus, or to stop behaving in some fashion once he has started. In busy, complex environments with many stimuli (such as a classroom), ADHD children are unable to inhibit their reactions to all the sounds and sights around them, so they appear restless and cannot sustain attention on a single activity.

Whether we ought to treat this constellation of problems as a single syndrome or as several distinct subvarieties is still a matter of active debate. You'll note in Table 15.2

Table 15.2

Diagnostic Criteria for Attention Deficit Hyperactivity Disorder

- The child must show either significant *inattention* or significant *hyperactivity-impulsivity* (or both).

- Inattention is indicated by any six or more of the following:

  1. Often fails to give close attention to details or makes careless mistakes in schoolwork or other activities.
  2. Often has difficulty sustaining attention in tasks or play.
  3. Often does not seem to listen when spoken to directly.
  4. Often does not follow through on instructions and fails to finish chores, homework, or duties.
  5. Often has difficulty organizing tasks and activities.
  6. Often avoids, dislikes, or is reluctant to engage in tasks that require sustained mental effort.
  7. Often loses things necessary for tasks or activities (e.g., toys, pencils, books, tools).
  8. Is often easily distracted by extraneous stimuli.
  9. Is often forgetful in daily activities.

- Hyperactivity-impulsivity is indicated by the presence of six of the following, persisting over a period of at least six months:

  1. Often fidgets with hands or feet or squirms in seat.
  2. Often leaves seat in classroom or in other situations in which remaining seated is expected.
  3. Often runs about or climbs excessively or reports feelings of restlessness.
  4. Often has difficulty playing quietly.
  5. Is often "on the go" or often acts as if "driven by a motor."
  6. Often talks excessively.
  7. Often blurts out answers before questions are completed.
  8. Often has difficulty waiting for a turn.
  9. Often interrupts or intrudes on others.

- The onset of the problem must be before age 7.

- At least some of the symptoms must be present in two or more settings, such as home and school or school and play with peers.

- The behavior must interfere with developmentally appropriate social, academic, or occupational functioning.

Source: Reprinted with permission from the *Diagnostic and statistical manual of mental disorders,* Fourth Edition, pp. 83–85. Copyright © 1994 American Psychiatric Association.

that the DSM-IV criteria are divided into two sets, those dealing with attention problems and those dealing with hyperactivity, suggesting the existence of two subtypes. European psychologists recognize only the hyperactivity subtype, which they label **hyperkinetic syndrome** (Taylor, 1995). U.S. psychologists agree that two subtypes exist, but they argue that the most common pattern is for both attention deficit and hyperactivity to occur together. When the child shows an attention problem but not hyperactivity, U.S. practitioners normally use a different name, **attention deficit disorder (ADD).** Because of these wide variations in definition, it is hard to get a good estimate of just how frequent such problems may be. The best current guess, based on studies from around the world, is that something between 3.0 and 7.0 percent of children can be diagnosed with some form of ADHD. Of this number, perhaps 1.5 percent show hyperactivity alone, while ADD alone occurs in perhaps 1.0 percent of children (Barkley, 1997; Buitelaar & van Engeland, 1996). The remainder show both hyperactivity and attention difficulties. All these patterns are three to five times more common in boys than in girls (Heptinstall & Taylor, 1996)—yet another example of the greater vulnerability of boys.

A further diagnostic problem arises from the fact that a great many children are inattentive or overactive at least some of the time. It is tempting—for both teachers and parents—to label a boisterous or obstreperous child as ADD or ADHD. There is no doubt that a good deal of mislabeling of this kind does occur, especially in the United States, where ADD or ADHD are far more common diagnoses than is the equivalent diagnosis in Europe. In fact, though, the full syndrome is quite distinctive. ADHD children's interactions with their peers are so strikingly different that novice observers need to watch videotapes for only a few minutes before they can reliably distinguish between a child diagnosed as ADHD and a normally behaving child—even when the hyperactive child displays no aggression and the sound is turned off (Henker & Whalen, 1989). The body language is distinctive, the level of activity is different, and the child's social behavior is often inappropriate. About half of such children *also* show problems with excessive aggressiveness, and most do poorly in school.

One mother, who had been getting calls from her child's kindergarten teacher about his behavior, gave this description of her son, later diagnosed with ADHD:

> Chris was lying out in the hall, doing somersaults, standing on his head making weird noises. They couldn't get him in line with the rest of the class. He was bouncing off walls in Never-Never Land. (Martell, 1996, p. 1G)

By definition, this is an early-developing disorder. The majority of hyperactive children already show some problems with attention and inhibition of activity by preschool age; many have problems making friends or playing effectively with peers because they are not well tuned to their playmates' cues, even at this early age. They are intrusive and insensitive toward peers, showing a variety of annoying behaviors (Hinshaw & Melnick, 1995; Sandberg et al., 1996). ADHD persists into adolescence in half to three-quarters of cases and into adulthood in one-third to half of cases (Barkley, 1997).

The severity of the long-term problem seems to be strongly influenced by whether or not the child also develops a conduct disorder. It is the combination of hyperactivity and aggressiveness that is especially likely to lead to significant problems with peer rejection in childhood and to persisting problems in adulthood (Barkley et al., 1990). You can see one facet of this effect in the results of Terrie Moffitt's New Zealand longitudinal study (1990), which included 434 boys. When the boys were 13, they were classed in one of four groups based on the presence or absence of two factors: hyperactivity and delinquency. Moffitt then traced backward for each group, looking at scores at earlier ages on measures of antisocial behavior, intelligence, and family adversity. You can see the results for antisocial behavior in Figure 15.2.

It is clear that the boys who showed *both* hyperactivity and delinquency as adolescents had been the most antisocial at every earlier age. Hyperactivity that was not accompanied by antisocial behavior at early ages was also not linked to delinquency at 13.

Origins of the Problem. Where might ADD or ADHD come from? Because the pattern begins so early and has such a strong physical component, most clinicians have assumed that these problems have some kind of biological origin. Early research failed to confirm a biological hypothesis, but more recent evidence makes clear that this is a *neuro*psychiatric disorder (Goldman et al., 1998). Three converging lines of evidence support that conclusion.

First, physicians and psychologists have known for some time that a biological *treatment* is very often effective in reducing or eliminating the deviant behavior. As many as 80 percent of children diagnosed with ADHD in the United States (but many fewer in Europe) are treated with a stimulant medication called methylphenidate (most commonly the brand-name drug Ritalin). The drug works by stimulating the part of the brain that maintains attention. Some 70 to 90 percent of children treated with this drug show improvement, including decreases in demanding, disruptive, and noncompliant behaviors; lessened aggressiveness and noncompliance; more attentiveness in the classroom; and improved performance on many academic tasks (Gillberg et al., 1997; Goldman et al., 1998; Schachar et al., 1996). This evidence is consistent with a biological explanation for

Figure 15.2

The boys in Moffitt's study had been studied every two years from the time they were 5. When they were 13, they were assigned to one of four hyperactivity/delinquency categories, and then Moffitt backtracked from that age. You can see that those who were *both* delinquent and hyperactive at 13 had shown markedly higher rates of antisocial behavior from the time they were 5, while those who were only hyperactive at 13 had been much less socially deviant at earlier ages.

(*Source:* Moffitt, T. E., adapted from Fig. 1, p. 899, "Juvenile delinquency and attention deficit disorder: Boys' developmental trajectories from Age 3 to Age 15," *Child Development,* 61 (1990) pp. 893–910. By permission of the Society for Research in Child Development.)

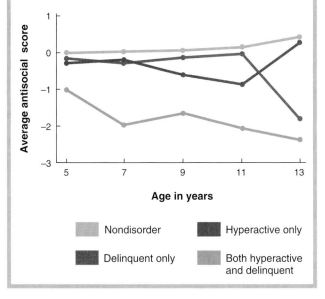

ADHD. More specifically, it suggests that the problem may lie in one of the neurotransmitters, because stimulant medications of the type used with ADHD children act by altering the action of monoamine, one of the key neurotransmitters (Kado & Takagi, 1996).

Additional evidence for an underlying biological cause comes from research in behavior genetics, which suggests that a pattern of hyperactivity is inherited, at least in certain families. About one-quarter of the parents of hyperactive children themselves have a history of hyperactivity. Studies of twins also suggest there is a genetic contribution. Among identical twins, if one is diagnosed as hyperactive, the other is highly likely to have the same diagnosis; among fraternal twins, this "concordance rate" is much lower (Kado & Takagi, 1996).

Finally, newer diagnostic methods have begun to reveal subtle differences in brain structure and brain function between hyperactive and nonhyperactive individuals. For example, studies using magnetic resonance imaging (MRI) suggest that the majority of ADHD children have larger right than left brain hemispheres, while the majority of non-ADHD children show the reverse (Hynd et al., 1993). Other researchers using positron emission tomography (PET) have found slight differences in brain metabolism (e.g., Zametkin et al., 1990).

Researchers have not yet zeroed in on the precise biological mechanism involved, but new research of this type strongly supports the hypothesis that ADHD has a biological basis. Still, being more confident about the origins of ADHD does not settle all the important questions. From the point of view of developmental psychopathology, we also need to understand how this deviant biological pattern affects the child's interactions with parents and peers to produce the common combination of hyperactivity and antisocial behavior. For many hyperactive children, the pathway is very like the one Patterson has described for defiant or aggressive children. These kids are just plain hard to raise. Those parents whose child-management skills are not up to the task of dealing with the hyperactive toddler's typically higher rates of noncompliance, or who face major family stresses that prevent them from maintaining good child-care routines, may find that their child's behavior becomes more and more disruptive, which in turn adversely affects the child's emerging social skills. By school age, parent-child conflict is high, as is child-peer conflict. Poor school performance makes the problem worse by lowering the child's self-esteem. Such children are then on a pathway that is highly likely to lead to continued problems in adolescence and adulthood (Campbell, 1990). In Moffitt's New Zealand study, for example, those boys who eventually showed the combination of hyperactivity and delinquency came from families with much higher than average levels of stress and fewer resources. The hyperactive boys who did not develop the accompanying antisocial behavior came from families with lower than average levels of stress and more resources. Thus, once again we find that the key to either long-term problems or recovery from difficulties lies in the interaction between the child's inborn or early-developed qualities and the capacity of the family and the environment more generally to support the child's optimum behavior. When parents of ADHD children manage to maintain an authoritative style, their children become less aggressive and more socially competent (Hinshaw et al., 1997). In the terminology I have been using throughout the book, children of such parents are more resilient.

Vulnerability and Resilience

This question of vulnerability or resilience has been a persistent theme among developmental psychopathologists. Research findings suggest that the same kinds of protective factors that help poor children rise above their negative circumstances (listed in Chapter 14) also mitigate the effect of other kinds of stresses. Children who are securely attached (whether to a parent or to someone else), who have good cognitive skills, and who have sufficient social skills to make connections with peers are better able to weather the stresses they encounter.

For example, in her studies of resilience among school-age children, Ann Masten (1989) has found that when children have experienced a year with high levels of life stresses, those with higher IQ are much less likely to respond to that stress by becoming disruptive. Masten speculates that such children, who have a history of successful problem solving, have a stronger sense of self-efficacy, which may help to make them more resistant to frustration.

On the other side of the coin are the vulnerable children, who are far more likely to show some kind of significant psychopathology in the face of stress. Some kinds of vulnerabilities are inborn, such as physical abnormalities, prenatal trauma or preterm birth, prenatal malnutrition, or exposure to disease *in utero*. A tendency toward "difficult" temperament, which also seems to be inborn, is another significant vulnerability, not only because by definition such children have greater difficulty adapting to new experiences but also because such children are harder to raise; their parents may be less able to establish regular discipline patterns.

Other vulnerabilities emerge during infancy or early childhood. An insecure early attachment and the internal working model that accompanies it seem to make a child more vulnerable to stress at later ages, particularly to stresses that involve losses or severe strains on key relationships. And any combination of circumstances that results in a high rate of aggressive or disruptive behavior with peers makes a child more vulnerable to a whole variety of stresses in the elementary and high school years (Masten, 1989).

Kenneth Rubin and his colleagues (1991) have proposed a model of the origins of internalizing disorders that combines many of these elements. They argue that one important pathway begins with an infant who shows high levels of behavioral inhibition (a temperamental pattern you'll recall from Chapter 9). Among infants with such a ten-

Whether a child or a teenager will show a behavior problem at a stressful time like moving will depend in part on whether he faces several other stresses or life changes at the same time—such as perhaps his parents' divorce.

dency, those who become securely attached to their parents appear to be okay. In contrast, those who become insecurely attached tend to move down a path that includes anxiety and fearfulness in the preschool years, then anxiety and perhaps victimization by bullies in the early school years; victimization results in more anxiety and withdrawal from peers, eventually leading to a failure to develop helpful social skills. By adolescence, these children are at high risk for depression.

Overall, it seems very helpful to think of each child as possessing some inborn *vulnerabilities,* some *protective factors* such as a secure attachment or an authoritative family, and some *resources,* such as higher IQ, an array of friends, or good peer interaction skills. The child's resilience in the face of stress, or at normal developmental passages like school entry or adolescence, will depend on the relative weight of these three elements at that time—*and* on how many separate stresses the child must face simultaneously. No matter how basically resilient he may be, any child is more likely to show at least a short-term behavior problem when multiple stresses pile up at the same moment.

Critical Thinking

How would you describe your own vulnerabilities, protective factors, and resources?

Developmental Psychopathology: A Reprise

I think that even this brief foray into research on psychopathology makes clear that a developmental framework is the only one that is going to yield real understanding of the emergence of deviant behavior. Even for a disorder such as hyperactivity, which appears to be rooted in an inborn biological dysfunction, its severity and persistence can be best understood in terms of the child's cumulative patterns of interaction and the child's own internal models of relationships. Ultimately, studies within this framework may tell us as much about normal development as about the emergence of pathology.

Intellectually Atypical Development

If you go back and look at Table 15.1 (p. 444), you'll see that the various forms of intellectually atypical development rank right up there with psychopathologies in frequency of occurrence among children. Roughly 1 in 10 children shows at least some form of intellectual abnormality, including learning disabilities, speech problems, and mental retardation.

Mental Retardation

Mental retardation (also referred to as *intellectual disability* by many educators today) is normally diagnosed when a child has "consistently subaverage intellectual functioning," usually operationalized as an IQ score below 70 or 75, *and* has significant problems in *adaptive behavior*—such as an inability to dress or eat alone or a problem getting along with others or adjusting to the demands of a regular school classroom (MacMillan & Reschly, 1997). Thus, a low IQ score is a necessary but not sufficient condition for an individual to be classed as retarded. As Thomas Achenbach says, "Children doing well in school are unlikely to be considered retarded no matter what their IQ scores" (1982, p. 214).

Low IQ scores are customarily divided up into several ranges, with different labels attached to each, as you can see in Table 15.3 (p. 458). The farther down the IQ scale you go, the fewer children there are. More than 80 percent of all children with IQs below 70 are in the mildly retarded range; only about 2 percent of low-IQ youngsters (perhaps 3500 children in the United States) are profoundly retarded (Broman et al., 1987).

Cognitive Functioning in Retarded Children. Some researchers interested in information processing have tried to understand normal intellectual processing by looking at the ways in which retarded children think or approach problems differently than do normal-IQ children (Bray et al., 1997; Campione et al., 1982; DeLoache & Brown, 1987). This research leads to several major conclusions about retarded children:

Table 15.3

IQ Scores and Labels for Children Classified as Retarded

Approximate IQ Score Range	Common Label
68–83	Borderline retarded
52–67	Mildly retarded
36–51	Moderately retarded
19–35	Severely retarded
Below 19	Profoundly retarded

1. They think and react more slowly than normal-IQ children.

2. They think concretely amd have difficulty with abstract reasoning.

3. They require much more complete and repeated instruction in order to learn new information or a new strategy. (Normal-IQ children may discover a strategy for themselves or profit from incomplete instruction.)

4. They do not generalize or transfer something they have learned in one situation to a new problem or task. They thus appear to lack those "executive" functions that enable older higher-IQ children (or adults) to compare a new problem to familiar ones or to scan through a repertoire of strategies until they find one that will work.

On simple, concrete tasks, retarded children learn in ways and at rates that are similar to younger normal-IQ children. The more significant deficit lies in higher-order processing. These children *can* learn, but they do so more slowly and require far more exhaustive and task-specific instruction.

Causes of Retardation. Retarded children can be divided into two distinct subgroups, depending on the cause of the retardation. The smaller subset, making up about 15 to 25 percent of the total, includes children whose retardation is caused by some evident physical damage. Included here are those with a genetic anomaly such as Down syndrome or fragile X syndrome. Damage resulting in retardation can also be caused by a disease, a teratogen such as prenatal alcohol, or severe prenatal malnutrition; it can occur during the birth itself, such as from prolonged anoxia. A small subset of these physically damaged retarded children suffer their injury after birth, often in an auto accident or a fall. Certainly, not all children who are injured in accidents or affected by teratogens are necessarily retarded. Instead, what I'm saying is that some children we know to be retarded have been disabled by some purely physical injury, disease, or anomaly.

The majority of retarded children show no obvious signs of brain damage or other physical disorder. In these cases the cause of the retardation is some combination of genetic and environmental conditions. Typically, these children come from families in which the parents have low IQ or mental illness, family life is highly disorganized, or the home life is emotionally or cognitively deprived. To be sure, in these cases, too, the child's intellectual disability might have been exacerbated by the effects of teratogens or other hazards, such as moderate amounts of prenatal alcohol or elevated levels of prenatal or postnatal lead, but in children in this subset, the retardation is not thought to be attributable solely to such physical causes.

Large-scale studies have now shown quite conclusively that these several causes of retardation are not distributed evenly across the range of low IQ scores. The lower

Fifteen to 25 percent of mentally retarded children have clear physical abnormalities, such as Down syndrome.

the IQ, the more likely it is that the cause is physical rather than environmental (Broman et al., 1987). One implication of this conclusion is that interventions like the enriched day care and preschool Ramey devised (recall Figure 7.4, p. 215) are more likely to be effective in preventing or ameliorating milder retardation that has familial-cultural causes. This is not to say that we should ignore environmental enrichment or specific early training for children with physically caused retardation. Greater breadth of experience will enrich their lives and may help to bring their level of functioning closer to the top end of their "reaction range." But even massive early interventions are not going to make most brain-damaged or genetically anomalous children intellectually normal, although they can help retarded children to function much more independently (Spiker, 1990).

Learning Disabilities

Some children with normal IQs and essentially good adaptive functioning nonetheless have difficulty learning to read, write, or do arithmetic. The typical label for this problem is **learning disability (LD),** although you will also hear terms like *dyslexia* (literally, "nonreading") or *minimal brain damage.* The official definition of this problem includes the presumption that the difficulty arises from some kind of central nervous system dysfunction or damage, in much the same way that many definitions of ADHD assume some kind of biological underpinning. In fact, some children with attention deficit disorder are *also* diagnosed as learning disabled, so these two sets of problem children overlap. Still, the overlap is far from complete; most children diagnosed as learning disabled do not suffer from ADHD.

Diagnosing a learning disability is extremely tricky because it is basically a *residual* diagnosis. It is the label normally applied to a child of average or above average intelligence, with normal vision and hearing, who has significant difficulty absorbing, processing, remembering, or expressing some type of information, such as written words or numbers. Children diagnosed as learning disabled do not show persistent or obvious emotional disturbance, and their difficulties cannot be attributed to any clear cultural or educational deprivation. Thus, we can say what learning disability is not; we cannot say what it *is.* Furthermore, the specific form of a child's learning disability may vary widely, with some displaying difficulties in reading only, some having trouble with reading and spelling (such as the boy whose writing sample is shown in Figure 15.3), and others having more difficulty with arithmetic.

Figure 15.3

This is part of a story written by 13-year-old Luke, who has a significant and persistent learning disability. The little numbers next to some of the words are Luke's word counts. They show that despite his severe writing handicap, his counting abilities are intact.

(*Source:* From *Learning disabilities: a psychological perspective* by Sylvia Farnham-Diggory, p. 61. Copyright © 1978 by Sylvia Farnham-Diggory. By permission of the author.)

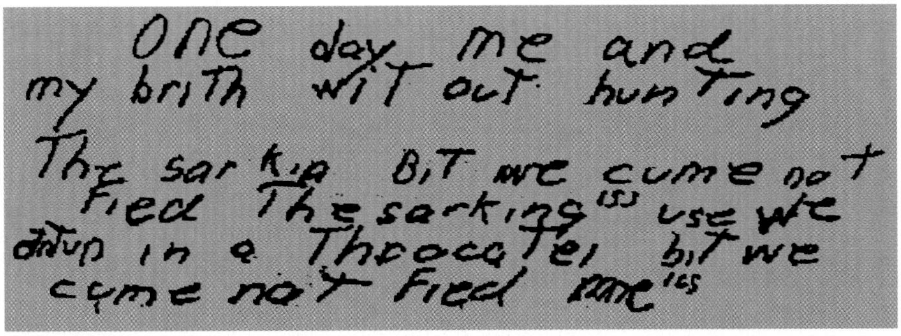

School can surely be a discouraging and frustrating place for a child with a learning disability.

Because of such fuzziness in the definition of the disability, there is a good deal of dispute about just how many LD children there really are. Sylvia Farnham-Diggory (1992), one of the leading experts in the field, argues that up to 80 percent of all children classified by school systems as learning disabled are misclassified. She claims that only about 5 out of every 1000 children are genuinely learning disabled. The remainder of those labeled as LD are more appropriately called slow learners, or they may suffer from another problem, perhaps temporary emotional distress or poor teaching.

Practically speaking, however, the LD label is used very broadly within school systems (at least within the United States) to describe a grab bag of children who have unexpected or otherwise unexplainable difficulty with schoolwork, particularly reading. Nearly 5 percent of all children in the United States are currently labeled in this way (Farnham-Diggory, 1992).

Causes. Given such problems with definition, we shouldn't be surprised that the search for causes has been fraught with difficulties. As Farnham-Diggory says, "We are trying to find out what's wrong with children whom we won't be able to accurately identify until after we know what's wrong with them" (1986, p. 153).

The most central problem has been with the fundamental assumption that learning disability has a neurological basis. The difficulty is that children so labeled (like hyperactive children) rarely show signs of major brain damage on standard neurological tests—perhaps because many children are mislabeled or perhaps because the brain dysfunction is too subtle to detect with standard tests.

Happily, new technologies may make it possible to uncover subtle—but very real and significant—neurological differences between children labeled dyslexic or learning disabled and those who are facile readers. A recent study by Sally Shaywitz and her colleagues (1998) used functional Magnetic Resonance Imaging (MRI) to identify the parts of the brain that become active when an individual is performing various reading-related tasks. When skillful adult readers in the study were working on these tasks, Shaywitz found that a series of brain regions were activated in turn, beginning with sections of the frontal lobe and then moving backward in the brain. Among the dyslexic adults who participated in this study, however, only the frontal lobe was fully activated, suggesting that their brains functioned quite differently on these same tasks.

This difference in brain activation patterns was especially vivid when the subjects were working on tasks that required them to identify individual sounds, such as in a rhyming task—a finding that makes very good sense in light of all the research I talked about in Chapter 8 that links good reading to *phonemic awareness*. The Shaywitz study suggests the possibility that the brains of genuinely dyslexic children and adults may simply not be wired in a way that facilitates the analysis of sounds into their phonologic components, a skill that is necessary for phonemic awareness. To be sure, some children may have difficulty with phonemic tasks simply because they have had too little exposure to language, not because their brains function differently. For others, however—those in the subset that Farnham-Diggory sees as legitimately dyslexic or learning disabled—the problem has a neurological/biological basis. The Shaywitz study will certainly stimulate a whole new body of research. Among other things, we need to discover whether the same differences in the pattern of brain activation that Shaywitz observed in adults also occurs in children. Then, of course, we will need to explore the effects of alternative forms of remediation or training on the brain organization of children who read poorly. Until this new body of research yields clearer answers, parents of poor readers will have to continue to cope with confusion and uncertainty about both diagnosis and available treatment for their learning-disabled children.

Giftedness

For parents whose children lie at the other end of the intellectual continuum, the gifted, the problem is almost as tough. Finding good programs for such children is a continuing dilemma. Let me give you an extreme example, a child named Michael described by Halbert Robinson:

> When Michael was 2 years and 3 months old, the family visited our laboratory. At that time, they described a youngster who had begun speaking at age 5 months and by 6 months had exhibited a vocabulary of more than 50 words. He started to read English when he was 13 months old. In our laboratory he spoke five languages and could read in three of them. He understood addition, subtraction, multiplication, division, and square root, and he was fascinated by a broad range of scientific constructs. He loved to make puns, frequently bilingual ones. (1981, p. 63)

Michael's IQ score on the Stanford-Binet was in excess of 180 at age 2; two years later, when Michael was 4½, he performed on the test like a 12-year-old and was listed as having an IQ score beyond 220.

Definitions and Labels. We can certainly all agree that Michael should be labeled as **gifted,** but defining the term precisely is difficult (Sternberg & Davidson, 1986). A number of authors (e.g., Gardner, 1983) have argued that people with exceptional specific talents, such as musical, artistic, mathematical, or spatial abilities, should be classed as gifted, along with those with very high IQ scores. This broadening of the definition of giftedness has been widely accepted among theorists, who agree that there are many kinds of exceptional ability, each of which may reflect unusual speed or efficiency with one or another type of cognitive function.

Within school systems, however, giftedness is still typically defined entirely by IQ test scores, such as all scores above 130 or 140. Robinson suggested that it may be useful to divide the group of high-IQ children into two sets, the "garden variety gifted" with high IQ scores (perhaps 130 to 150) but without extraordinary ability in any one area, and the "highly gifted" (like Michael) with extremely high IQ scores and/or remarkable skill in one or more areas—a group Ellen Winner (1997) calls *profoundly gifted.* These two groups may have quite different experiences at home and in school.

Cognitive and Social Functioning in Gifted Children. Just as retarded children show slower and less efficient information processing, the gifted show speedy and efficient processing on simple tasks and flexible use of strategies on more complex tasks. They learn quickly and transfer that learning broadly, and they have remarkably good problem-solving skills, often leaping directly to a solution that requires less gifted individuals many intermediate steps to figure out (Sternberg & Davidson, 1985; Winner, 1997). Further, they seem to have unusually good *metacognitive* skills: They know what they know and what they don't know, and they spend *more* time than do average-IQ children in planning how to go about solving some problem (Dark & Benbow, 1993). Winner also notes that profoundly gifted children also have a "rage to master," a powerful drive to immerse themselves in learning in some area.

Whether such advanced intellectual abilities transfer to *social* situations is not so well established. Many parents are concerned about placing their gifted child in a higher grade in school because of fears that the child will not be able to cope socially; others have assumed that rapid development in one area should be linked to rapid development in all areas.

One famous and remarkable early study of gifted children, by Lewis Terman, pointed to the latter conclusion. Terman selected about 1500 children with high IQ scores from the California school system in the 1920s. These children—now adults in their eighties—have been followed regularly throughout their lives (e.g., Holahan, 1988; Terman, 1925; Terman & Oden, 1959). Terman found that the gifted children he studied were better off than their less gifted classmates in many ways other than school performance. They were healthier, they had wider-ranging interests, and they were more successful in later life. Both the boys and the girls in this study went on to complete many more years of education than was typical in their era and had successful careers as adults.

Elizabeth Lovance of Hartland, Wisconsin, on the right, skipped several grades and graduated from high school at age 14. She said of her experience of being accelerated through school: "I would have had a mental breakdown if I had remained where I was."

Most recent research suggests that gifted children have about the same risk of social or emotional problems as normal-IQ children, which means that most are well adjusted and socially adept (A. W. Gottfried et al., 1994). Furthermore, good social development seems to be just as likely for gifted children who have been accelerated through school as for those who have been kept with their age-mates but provided with "enrichment" programs (Robinson & Janos, 1986).

Such optimism about the social robustness of gifted children may have to be tempered somewhat, however, in the case of the profoundly gifted subgroup, such as those with IQs above 180. These children are *so* different from their peers that they are likely to be seen as strange or disturbing. They are often socially solitary and introverted as well as fiercely independent and nonconforming; they have difficulties finding peers who can play at their level and are often quite unpopular with classmates (Kennedy, 1995). These profoundly gifted children are about twice as likely as their less gifted peers to show some kind of significant social or emotional problem (Winner, 1997). Also on the negative side of the ledger is the fact that many gifted children are so bored by school that they become disengaged, even dropping out, often because their school district does not allow acceleration in grade or has no special programs for the gifted. Given the fact that grade skipping does *not* seem to be linked to social maladjustment (and *is* linked to better achievement among the gifted), it seems to make very good sense to encourage accelerated schooling, if only to help ward off terminal boredom for the gifted child.

Critical Thinking

Are you persuaded by my arguments in favor of encouraging grade skipping by gifted children? If you were a parent of a gifted child, what kind of data would you want to have to help make a decision on this question?

Schooling for Atypical Children

Gifted children are naturally not the only group of atypical children who require special adaptations by teachers and schools. Indeed, the majority of public attention has been focused on children with one or another type of learning problem, not on the gifted. Largely as a result of pressure from parents of atypical or disabled children, in 1975 Congress passed Public Law (PL) 94-142, called the *Education for All Handicapped Children Act*. It specifies that every child in the United States must be given access to an *appropriate* education in the *least restrictive environment possible*. PL 94-142 does not say that every child, no matter the nature or degree of her disability, must be educated full-time in a regular classroom. The law allows schools to offer a continuum of services, including separate schools or special classrooms, although the law also indicates that a child should be placed in a regular classroom as a first choice and removed from that setting only if his disability is such that he cannot be satisfactorily educated there.

PL 94-142 and the supplementary laws that followed it (including the Education of the Handicapped Act of 1986 and the Individuals with Disabilities Education Act of 1990) rest most centrally on a philosophical position: that children with disabilities have a right to participate in normal school environments (e.g., Stainback & Stainback, 1985). Proponents have further argued that such **inclusive education** aids the disabled child by integrating him into the nondisabled world, thus facilitating the development of important social skills as well as providing more appropriate academic challenges than are often found in separate classrooms or programs designated for the disabled (Siegel, 1996). Advocates of inclusion are convinced that mildly retarded children and those with learning disabilities will show greater academic achievement if they are in regular classrooms.

Schools and school districts differ widely in the specific model of inclusion they use, although virtually all models involve a team of educators, including combinations of the classroom teacher, one or more special education teachers, classroom aides, and sometimes volunteers. Some schools follow a plan in which the disabled student is placed in a regular classroom only part of each day, with the remainder of the time spent working with a special education teacher in a special class or resource room, a system often called a *pull-out program*. More common today are *full-inclusion* systems in which the child spends his entire schoolday in a regular class but receives help from volunteers, aides, or special education teachers who come to the classroom to work with the child there. In some districts, a group of disabled children are clustered in a single regular classroom; in others, no more than one such child is normally assigned to any one class (Baker & Zigmond, 1995).

There is little argument about the desirability of the overall goal: to provide every child with the best education possible, one that challenges optimally and gives the child the best possible chance to learn the basic intellectual and social skills needed to function in our increasingly complex society. (No small task!) What the experts (and parents) do argue about is whether current inclusion programs are meeting this goal (Gerber, 1995; Martin, 1995; McLeskey & Pugach, 1995; Roberts & Mather, 1995). Are learning-disabled, retarded, or physically disabled children better off intellectually and socially in inclusion programs than in special classes? In which setting do they make more progress in reading or math? In which do they learn better social skills—skills that will enable them to function later in a job situation or with peers? Do they make friends?

For those of you who plan to be teachers, I should note that these theoretical questions are moot. Inclusion programs are legally mandated and here to stay (Putnam et al., 1995). For teachers, the crucial question is more practical: What works best? Among the many varieties of inclusion programs, can we identify features that are consistently associated with better results or poorer results?

All these questions are extremely hard to answer. For all kinds of perfectly understandable reasons, we have little of the kind of research we need to answer them. Inclusion programs vary widely in design and serve children with diverse problems. The teachers who implement them range from highly skilled and inventive to overwhelmed and unskilled. If a particular program pattern appears to work in one school, it is often difficult to tell whether it is successful because of the particular teachers involved, because of the specific characteristics of the children being served, or because of the program itself is especially well designed.

Given all this, it is not surprising that we lack clear answers to the many relevant questions. Still, educators and psychologists have struggled to summarize the information we do have. Most would agree with the following conclusions:

- Children with physical disabilities but no learning problem—such as blind children or some with spina bifida—make better academic gains in full-inclusion programs (Buysse & Bailey, 1993; MacMillan et al., 1986; Odom & Kaiser, 1997).

- For children with learning disabilities, however, full-inclusion programs may be less academically supportive than are pull-out programs or "resource rooms." As Vaughn and Schumm say, "The evidence that does exist for students with learning disabilities suggests that they do not fare well academically in the general education classroom, where undifferentiated, large-group

Both Gina, a child with spina bifida in the photo on the left, and David, the Down syndrome boy in the photo on the right, are in inclusive elementary school classrooms, participating as fully as possible in all activities and assignments.

instruction is the norm" (1995, p. 264). Success for LD children in a regular classroom depends heavily on the ability of the teacher to implement an individualized program.

- Although there may be some social benefits from inclusion, there are also social risks. Some research shows gains in self-esteem and social skills for disabled children in inclusion programs (e.g., Banerji & Dailey, 1995; Cole, 1991b). Yet virtually all groups of disabled children, including the learning disabled, mildly retarded, and physically disabled, are more likely to experience rejection from their peers in regular classes than are nondisabled children (e.g., Sale & Carey, 1995). Learning-disabled students, in particular, are often notably unpopular with their peers in regular classes (Roberts & Mather, 1995).

- Effective inclusion programs require, at a minimum, that teachers be given extensive additional training and substantial support from specialists, aides, or volunteers (Roberts & Mather, 1995)—conditions that very often are not met because of budgetary or other reasons. The majority of teachers feel they are

The Real World

The Impact of an Atypical Child on the Family

How does a family deal with an atypical child? In some instances of course, deficiencies or inadequacies in the family are part of the *cause* of the child's atypical development. But whether the original cause lies in the family or not, once a child does show some form of deviant development, the family is inevitably affected, often adversely.

One of the first reactions is often a form of grief, almost as if the child had died. Indeed, the parent is grieving about the loss of the *fantasy* "perfect child." The parents grieve for the child-that-never-will-be, expressed poignantly by one parent:

> I wept for the perfect baby I had lost, for the sunsets he would never see, for the 4-year-old who would never be able to play outside unsupervised. (Featherstone, 1980, p. 26)

As with other forms of grief, denial, depression, and anger are all natural elements. Many parents also feel some guilt (e.g., "If only I hadn't had those drinks at that party while I was pregnant").

In some cases this process may result in an emotional rejection of the infant, aggravated by the difficulty many atypical infants have in entering fully into the mutually adaptive parent-child process. Such rejection seems to be particularly common when the marital relationship is conflicted or the family lacks adequate social support (Hodapp, 1995).

Once the initial shock and grief is dealt with as well as it can be, the family must work toward an ongoing adaptive system with the disabled child. There are often massive financial burdens; there are problems of finding appropriate schooling; there are endless daily adjustments to the child's special needs.

I look at the people down the street. Their kids are 15 and 18 and now they can just get in the car and take off when they want to . . . and then I think, "When will that happen for us? We'll always have to be thinking of Christopher. . . . We'll never have that freedom." (Featherstone, 1980, p. 17)

The system that evolves most often leaves the mother primarily in charge of the atypical child; fathers of physically disabled children quite often seem to withdraw from interaction with or care of the child (Bristol et al., 1988). This is not a general withdrawal of the father from the family system, since such fathers continue to be involved with their other children. But the father's selective withdrawal leaves the mother with added burdens. One predictable response, among both mothers and fathers, is depression. Parents of atypical children are also more likely to have low self-esteem and to have lower feelings of personal competence (Hodapp, 1995). Where the marital relationship was poor before the birth of the atypical child, the presence of the disabled child in the family system seems to increase the likelihood of further discord. However, there is no consistent indication that having an atypical child results in an average increase in marital disharmony or risk of divorce (Longo & Bond, 1984).

The fact that many (even most) parents manage to adapt effectively to the presence of an atypical child is testimony to the devotion and immense effort expended. But we cannot evade the fact that rearing such a child is very hard work and that it strains the family system in ways that rearing a "typical" child does not.

not prepared to teach students with disabilities; many who have such children in their classrooms feel that they do not receive adequate support (Schumm & Vaughn, 1995).

Reading through this set of statements will convince you that there is no magic bullet here, no single solution for educators, for parents, or for disabled children. If you are planning to become a teacher, you will need to learn as much as possible about the needs of children with various kinds of disabilities as well as about successful strategies for teaching them; if you are a parent of a disabled child, you will need to inform yourself about all the educational alternatives so that you can become your child's consistent advocate within the school system.

Sex Differences in Atypical Development

One of the most fascinating facts about atypical development is that virtually all forms of disorder are more common in boys than in girls. The major exception to this statement is depression, which as I've already mentioned is about twice as common among adolescent girls and among adult women. I've put some of the comparisons in Table 15.4, but even this list does not convey the extent of the difference. With very few exceptions, studies of the impact of environmental stresses show that boys are more adversely affected. This is true in studies of divorce, parental discord, parental mental illness, parental job loss, and many others. In these situations, boys are more likely to show disturbed behavior, a decline in school performance, or some other indication of a problem (Zaslow & Hayes, 1986).

How are we to explain differences like this? One possibility is that having an extra X chromosome gives the girl protection from some types of inherited disorder or anomaly. Girls are obviously less likely to inherit any recessive disease that is carried on the X chromosome. We also have some hints that there may be a gene on the X chromosome that affects the individual's ability to respond effectively to stress. Since girls have two X chromosomes, they are less likely to suffer from any disorder in that gene. If this explanation is valid, then the appropriate conclusion is not that *all* boys are more vulnerable, but that *more* boys than girls have some minor neurological dysfunction or high vulnerability to stressors of various kinds.

Two other physiological factors may also be important, each potentially explaining one or two of the differences listed in Table 15.4. First, hormonal differences may be important contributors. Since it is possible to construct a persuasive argument for the role of male hormones in aggressive behavior (as I attempted to do in Chapter 11), it is not a very great leap to the hypothesis that the higher incidence of conduct disorders among boys may also be related in some way to hormone variations.

A second possible physiological contributor is the comparative level of physical maturity of boys and girls. Because girls of any age are more physically mature than are boys of the same age, girls may have more resources with which to meet various problems. For example, researchers have frequently observed that infant boys are more irritable and less able to achieve physical or emotional equilibrium after being upset than are infant girls (Haviland & Malatesta, 1981). Since such fussiness is also common in *younger* babies, the problem may not be maleness but immaturity.

Experiences after birth may also contribute to the differing rates of deviance. One hypothesis is that adults are simply more tolerant of disruptive or difficult behavior in boys than in girls. By this argument, boys and girls initially respond similarly to stressful situations, but boys learn early that various forms of acting out, tantrums, or defiance are tolerated or not punished severely. Girls learn to inhibit these responses—perhaps even to internalize them—because adults respond quite

Table 15.4

Sex Differences in the Incidence of Atypical Development

Type of Problem	Approximate Ratio of Males to Females
Psychopathologies	
Conduct disorders, including delinquency	5:1
Anxiety and depression in preadolescence	1:1
Anxiety and depression in adolescence	1:2
Attention deficit hyperactivity disorder	3:1–5:1
Estimated number of all children with all diagnoses seen in psychiatric clinics	2:1
Intellectual disabilities	
Mental retardation	3:2
Learning disabilities	3:1
Physical problems	
Blindness or significant visual problems	1:1
Hearing impairment	5:4

Sources: Achenbach, 1982; Nolen-Hoeksema & Girgus, 1994; Rutter, 1989; Rutter & Garmezy, 1983; Todd et al., 1995; Zoccolillo, 1993.

differently to girls. We have only fragments of support for such a hypothesis (e.g., Eme, 1979). Studies of cultures in which *both* boys and girls are discouraged from behaving aggressively or assertively would provide very useful data to test such an explanation.

Whatever the explanation—and none of the existing explanations seems very satisfactory to me—it is nonetheless extremely interesting that girls do seem to be less vulnerable, less likely to show virtually any type of atypical development. Equally fascinating is the exception to this statement: depression among girls in adolescence. If girls are generally more robust, more able to handle stress, why should the stresses of puberty and adolescence be linked to such a significant rise in depression for girls? Is this a purely cultural phenomenon? Again, cross-cultural research would be very helpful in sorting out the various possible causes.

Critical Thinking

Can you think of any other explanations for the sex differences in the rate of atypical development?

A Final Point

As a final point, I think it is crucial for me to state clearly what has been only implicit throughout this chapter: Children whose development is atypical in some respect are much more *like* normally developing children in other respects than they are unlike them. Blind and deaf and retarded children all form attachments in much the same way that physically and mentally normal children do (Lederberg & Mobley, 1990); children with conduct disorders go through the same sequences of cognitive development that more adjusted children show. It is very easy, when dealing with an atypical child, to be overwhelmed by the sense of differentness. But as Sroufe and Rutter and all the other developmental psychopathologists are beginning to say so persuasively, the same basic processes are involved.

Summary

1. Approximately 20 percent of all children in the United States will need some form of special assistance for a significant emotional, cognitive, or physical problem some time in childhood or adolescence.

2. Studies of psychopathology are more and more being cast in a *developmental* framework, with emphasis on the complex pathways that lead to deviance or normality. Such a framework also emphasizes the importance of the child's own resilience or vulnerability to stresses.

3. Psychopathologies are most often divided into three broad groups: externalizing problems, including conduct disorders; internalizing problems, including anxiety and depression; and disorders of attention, including attention deficit hyperactivity disorder (ADHD).

4. Conduct disorders include both patterns of excess aggressiveness and delinquency. Conduct disorders can also be divided into early- and late-onset problems. The former are more serious and persistent.

5. Early-onset conduct disorders appear to have a genetic component and to be exacerbated by poor family interactions and subsequent poor peer relations.

6. Delinquent (lawbreaking) acts increase in adolescence and are found not only among children with early-onset conduct disorders but also among some teens who show a brief period of delinquency without long-term negative consequences.

7. Depression is one form of internalizing problem, relatively uncommon in childhood but common in adolescence.

Depressed youngsters are more likely to have a family history of parental depression, to have developed low self-esteem, or to have a history of being ignored by peers.

8. Depression in adolescence is about twice as common among girls as among boys. No consensus has yet been reached on the explanation for this sex difference.

9. Attention deficit hyperactivity disorder (ADHD), the most common type of disorder of attention, includes problems with both attention and excessive restlessness and activity. Long-term problems are greatest when ADHD is combined with a conduct disorder.

10. ADHD appears to have an initial biological cause, but deviant patterns are aggravated or ameliorated by subsequent experience.

11. Family stress or stress experienced directly by the child, especially multiple simultaneous stresses, exacerbate any existing or underlying tendency toward pathology.

12. Children with inborn vulnerabilities (such as difficult temperament or physical problems), few protective factors, and few resources are more likely to respond to stressful circumstances with pathology.

13. Children with mental retardation, normally defined as IQ below 70 combined with significant problems of adaptation, show slower development and more immature or less efficient forms of information processing strategies.

14. Two groups of retarded children can be identified: those with clear

physical abnormalities, who are overrepresented among the severely retarded; and those without physical abnormalities but with low-IQ parents and/or deprived environments, who are overrepresented among the mildly retarded.

15. Roughly 4 percent of the schoolchildren in the United States are labeled as learning disabled (LD). There is still considerable dispute about how to identify genuine learning disability, and many children may be misclassified as LD.

16. New research supports the hypothesis that learning disabilities have their roots in atypical brain function, although this conclusion remains tentative.

17. *Gifted* is a term applied to children with very high IQ or to those with unusual creativity or special skill. Their information processing is unusually flexible and generalized. Socially they appear to be well adjusted, except for the small group of unusually highly gifted students, who have a higher risk of psychopathology.

18. Inclusive education—in which children with disabilities are primarily educated in regular classrooms alongside nondisabled children—is mandated by law in the United States, although many questions and problems remain. Programs vary widely; some are effective, others are not.

19. Except for adolescent depression, boys show almost all forms of emotional, mental, and physical disability more often than do girls. This may reflect genetic differences, hormone differences, or differences in cultural expectations.

Key Terms

adolescent-onset conduct disorder
A conduct disorder that begins only in adolescence. Typically less severe and persistent than childhood-onset conduct disorders. **p. 447**

attention deficit disorder (ADD) Term sometimes used interchangeably with ADHD, but more properly used to describe the subset of children who show attention problems without hyperactivity. **p. 453**

attention deficit hyperactivity disorder (ADHD) A disorder in which the child shows *both* significant problems with attention and physical hyperactivity. **p. 452**

attention problems One of several major categories of psychopathologies, including attention deficit hyperactivity disorder, attention deficit disorder, and hyperkinetic disorder. **p. 446**

childhood-onset conduct disorder
Conduct disorder beginning in childhood; linked to rejection by peers and to persistent conduct problems into adolescence and adulthood. **p. 447**

clinical depression A combination of sad mood, sleep and eating disturbances, and

difficulty concentrating, lasting six months or longer. **p. 450**

conduct disorder Diagnostic term for a pattern of deviant behavior including high levels of aggressive, antisocial, or delinquent acts. **p. 446**

delinquency A subcategory of conduct disorders involving explicit lawbreaking. **p. 448**

depression A combination of sad mood, sleep and eating disturbances, and difficulty concentrating. When all these symptoms are present, the condition is usually called *clinical depression*. **p. 450**

developmental psychopathology A relatively new approach to the study of deviance that emphasizes that normal and abnormal development have common roots and that pathology can arise from many different pathways or systems. **p. 444**

externalizing problems One of several major categories of psychopathology, including any deviant behavior primarily directed away from the individual, such as conduct disorders. **p. 446**

gifted Normally defined in terms of very high IQ (above 130 or 140), but may also be

defined in terms of remarkable skill in one or more specific areas, such as mathematics, music, or memory. **p. 461**

hyperkinetic syndrome Label used in Europe in place of attention deficit hyperactivity disorder. **p. 453**

inclusive education Term used broadly to describe the education of physically, mentally, or emotionally disabled children in regular classrooms, with any special services required by the child provided in that classroom. **p. 462**

internalizing problems One of several major categories of psychopathology, in which the deviant behavior is directed inward, including anxiety and depression. **p. 446**

learning disability (LD) A term broadly used to describe a child's unexpected or unexplained problem in learning to read, spell, or calculate. More precisely used to refer to a subgroup of such children who have some neurological dysfunction. **p. 459**

mental retardation Defined most often as an IQ below 70 combined with poor adaptive behavior. **p. 457**

Suggested Readings

Alper, S., Schloss, P. J., Etscheidt, S. K., & Macfarlane, C. A. (1995). *Inclusion. Are we abandoning or helping students?* Thousand Oaks, CA: Corwin Press. A small book aimed at teachers, full of highly practical suggestions about strategies for including disabled children in a classroom.

Cicchetti, D., & Cohen, D. J. (Eds.). (1995a). *Developmental psychopathology: Vol 1. Theory and methods. Vol. 2. Risk, disorder, and adaptation.* New York: Wiley. This massive two-volume collection is a highly technical but nonetheless extremely useful

next source on virtually any type of atypical development.

Farnham-Diggory, S. (1992). *The learning-disabled child.* Cambridge, MA: Harvard University Press. This revision of an excellent book is a reasonably up-to-date source, pitched at the level of the lay reader.

Petersen, A. C., Compas, B. C., Brooks-Gunn, J., Stemmler, M., Ey, S., & Grant, K. E. (1993). Depression in adolescence. *American Psychologist, 48,* 155–168. A brief, fairly dense review of the most current information on this important subject.

Rutter, M. (Ed.). (1995). *Psychosocial disturbances in young people: Challenges for prevention.* Cambridge, England: Cambridge University Press. An excellent recent collection of papers on many of the emotional and social problems of adolescence.

Sandberg, S. (Ed.). (1996). *Hyperactivity disorders of childhood.* Cambridge, England: Cambridge University Press. Dense, detailed chapters on every aspect of this problem, written by European experts.

Putting It All Together: The Developing Child

16

I remember the sense of unfairness I had in a world history class in high school when, after I had carefully learned all the kings of England in order and all the kings of France in order, I was asked on a test to say who had been king of France at the same time when Henry VIII had ruled England. I hadn't the foggiest idea; we had never studied it that way.

You may have something of the same feeling about the developing child. For example, you know a good deal about the sequence of development of language and about the sequential changes in cognitive functioning and in attachments, but you probably have not hooked these different developmental sequences to one another very well. If I asked you now what was happening at the same time as the child first used two-word sentences, you would probably have a difficult time answering. So what I want to do in this brief chapter is to put the child back together a bit by looking at the things that are happening at the same time.

I also want to take another look at some of the key questions I raised in Chapter 1: What are the major influences on development? Does the timing of experience matter? What is the nature of developmental change? Are there stages or sequences? And how best can we understand individual differences in development?

Critical Thinking

Think about it. What else is going on when the child first uses two-word sentences?

Transitions, Consolidations, and Systems

I see the process of development as being made up of a series of alternating periods of rapid growth (accompanied by disruption or disequilibrium) and periods of comparative calm or consolidation. Change is obviously going on all the time, from conception to death, but I am persuaded that there are particular times when the changes pile up or when one highly significant change occurs. This might be a major physiological development like puberty, a highly significant cognitive change like the beginning of symbol usage at about 18 months, or some other major shift.

When such a significant change occurs, it has two related effects. First, in systems theory terms, any one change inevitably affects the entire system. So a rapid increase in skill in one area, like language, demands adaptation in all parts of the developing system. Because the child can now talk, her social interactions change, her thinking changes, and no doubt even her nervous system changes as new synapses are created and redundant or underused ones are pruned. Similarly, the child's early attachment may affect her cognitive development by altering the way she approaches new situations; the hormonal changes of puberty affect parent-child relations.

Second, when the system changes in such a major way, the child sometimes seems to come "unglued" for a while. The old patterns of relationships, of thinking, of talking, don't work very well anymore, and it takes a while to work out new patterns. Erikson frequently uses the word *dilemma* to label such periods of semiupheaval. Klaus Riegel (1975) once suggested the phrase *developmental leaps,* which conveys nicely the sense of excitement and blooming opportunity that often accompany these pivotal periods. I'm going to use the more pedestrian term *transition* to describe the times of change or upheaval, and I'll use the term *consolidation* to describe the in-between times when change is more gradual. Collectively, these concepts may help us examine what is happening during each of the major age periods.

From Birth to 18 Months

Figure 16.1 shows the various changes during the first 18 months of life. The rows of the figure roughly correspond to the chapters of this book; what we need to do now is read up and down the figure rather than just across the rows.

Figure 16.1

This brief summary chart shows some of the simultaneous developments during infancy. I have outlined the several developmental changes that seem to me to be pivotal—creating transitional changes.

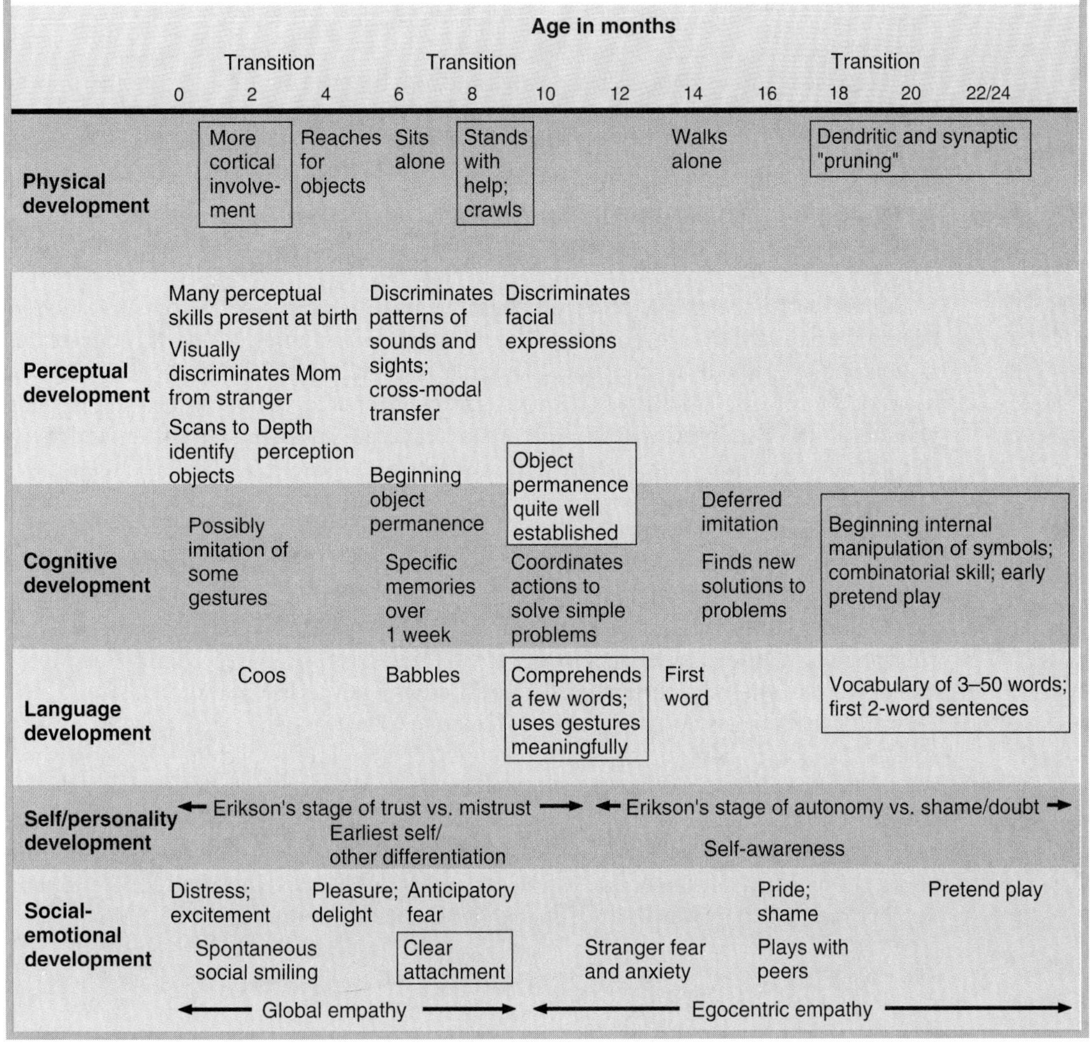

Age in months

	Transition		Transition						Transition		
	0　2	4	6	8	10	12	14	16	18	20	22/24
Physical development	More cortical involvement	Reaches for objects	Sits alone	Stands with help; crawls			Walks alone		Dendritic and synaptic "pruning"		
Perceptual development	Many perceptual skills present at birth — Visually discriminates Mom from stranger — Scans to identify objects	Depth perception	Discriminates patterns of sounds and sights; cross-modal transfer	Discriminates facial expressions							
Cognitive development	Possibly imitation of some gestures		Beginning object permanence — Specific memories over 1 week	Object permanence quite well established — Coordinates actions to solve simple problems			Deferred imitation — Finds new solutions to problems		Beginning internal manipulation of symbols; combinatorial skill; early pretend play		
Language development	Coos		Babbles	Comprehends a few words; uses gestures meaningfully			First word		Vocabulary of 3–50 words; first 2-word sentences		
Self/personality development	← Erikson's stage of trust vs. mistrust →		Earliest self/other differentiation				← Erikson's stage of autonomy vs. shame/doubt → — Self-awareness				
Social-emotional development	Distress; excitement — Spontaneous social smiling	Pleasure; delight	Anticipatory fear — Clear attachment				Stranger fear and anxiety	Pride; shame — Plays with peers			Pretend play
	← Global empathy →			← Egocentric empathy →							

The overriding impression one gets of the newborn infant—despite her remarkable skills and capacities—is that she is very much on automatic pilot. There seem to be built-in rules or schemas that govern the way the infant looks, listens, explores the world, and relates to others.

One of the really remarkable things about these rules, as I pointed out in Chapters 3 and 5, is how well designed they are to lead both the child and the caregivers into the "dance" of interaction and attachment. Think of an infant being breast-fed. The baby has the needed rooting, sucking, and swallowing reflexes to take in the milk; in this position, the mother's face is at just about the optimum distance from the baby's eyes for the infant's best focusing; the mother's facial features, particularly her eyes and mouth, are just the sort of visual stimuli that the baby is most likely to look at; the baby is particularly sensitive to the range of sounds of the human voice, especially the upper register, so the higher-pitched, lilting voice virtually all mothers use is easily heard by the infant; and during breast-feeding the release of a hormone called cortisol in the mother has the effect of relaxing her and making her more alert to the baby's signals. Both the adult and the infant are thus "primed" to interact with one another.

Eight-month-old Laura has a whole set of new skills and understandings: she can crawl, she has a firm attachment to both parents, she can perhaps understand a few words, and she has a beginning understanding of object permanence. All these more or less simultaneous changes alter the system profoundly.

Sometime around 6 to 8 weeks, there seems to be a change, with these automatic, reflexive responses giving way to behavior that looks more volitional. The child now looks at objects differently, apparently trying to identify what an object is rather than merely where it is; at this age, she also begins to reliably discriminate one face from another, she smiles more, she sleeps through the night, and she generally becomes a more responsive creature.

Because of these changes in the baby, and also because it takes most mothers six to eight weeks to recover physically from the delivery (and for the mother and father jointly to begin to adjust to the immense change in their routine), we also see big changes in mother-infant interaction patterns at this time. The need for routine caretaking continues, of course (ah, the joys of diapers!), but as the child stays awake for longer periods and smiles and makes eye contact more, exchanges between parent and child become more playful and smoother-paced.

Once this transition has occurred, there seems to be a brief period of consolidation lasting perhaps five or six months. Of course change continues during this consolidation period. Neurological change, in particular, is rapid, with the motor and perceptual areas of the cortex continuing to develop. The child's perceptual skills also show major changes in these months, with depth perception, clear cross-modal transfer, and identification of patterns of sounds and sights all emerging. Despite all these changes, however, a kind of equilibrium nonetheless exists in this period—an equilibrium that is altered by a series of changes that occur between about 7 and 9 months: (1) The baby forms a strong central attachment, followed a few months later by separation anxiety and fear of strangers; (2) the infant begins to move around independently (albeit very slowly and haltingly at first); (3) communication between infant and parents changes substantially, as the baby begins to use meaningful gestures and to comprehend individual words; (4) object permanence is grasped at a new level, and the baby now understands that objects and people can continue to exist even when they are out of sight. At the very least, these changes profoundly alter the parent-child interactive system, requiring the establishment of a new equilibrium, a new consolidation, a new system.

The baby continues to build gradually on this set of new skills—learning a few spoken words, learning to walk, consolidating the basic attachment—until 18 or 20 months of age, at which point the child's language and cognitive development appear to take another major leap forward—a set of changes I'll describe shortly.

Central Processes

What is causing all these changes? Any short list of such causes is inevitably going to be a gross oversimplification. Still, undaunted, let me suggest four key processes that seem to me to be shaping the patterns shown in Figure 16.1 (p. 471).

Physical Maturation. First and most obviously, the biological clock is ticking very loudly indeed during these early few months. Only at adolescence, and again in old age, do we see such an obvious maturational pattern at work. In infancy, it is the prepatterned growth of neural dendrites and synapses that appears to be the key. The shift in behavior we see at 2 months, for example, seems to be governed by just such built-in changes, as synapses in the cortex develop sufficiently to control behavior more fully.

Important as this built-in program is, it nonetheless *depends on* the presence of a minimum "expectable" environment (Greenough et al., 1987). The brain may be "wired" to create certain synapses, but the process has to be triggered by exposure to particular kinds of experience. Because such a minimum environment exists for virtually all infants, the perceptual, motor, and cognitive developments we see are virtually identical from one baby to the next. But that does not mean that the environment is unimportant.

The Child's Explorations. A second key process is the child's own exploration of the world around her. She is born *ready* to explore, to learn from her experience, but she still has to learn the specific connections between seeing and hearing, to tell the differences between Mom's face and someone else's, to pay attention to the sounds empha-sized in the language she is hearing, to discover that her actions have consequences, and so on.

Clearly, physiological maturation and the child's own exploration are intimately linked in a kind of perpetual feedback loop. The rapid changes in the nervous system, bones, and muscles permit more and more exploration, which in turn affects the child's perceptual and cognitive skills, and these in turn affect the architecture of the brain. For example, we now have a good deal of evidence that the ability to crawl—a skill that rests on a whole host of maturationally based physical changes—profoundly affects the baby's understanding of the world. Before the baby can move indepen-dently, he seems to locate objects only in relation to his own body; after he can crawl, he begins to locate objects with reference to fixed landmarks (Bertenthal et al., 1994). This shift, in turn, probably contributes to the infant's growing understanding of him-self as an object in space.

Attachment. A third key process seems obviously to be the relationship between the infant and the caregiver(s). I am convinced that Bowlby is right about the built-in *readiness* of all infants to create an attachment, but in this domain, the quality of the specific experience the child encounters seems to have a more formative effect than is true for other aspects of development. A wide range of environments are "good enough" to support physical, perceptual, and cognitive growth in these early months. For the establishment of a secure central attachment, however, the acceptable range seems to be narrower.

Still, attachment does not develop along an independent track. Its emergence is linked both to maturational change and to the child's own exploration. For example, the child's understanding of object permanence may be a necessary precondition for the development of a basic attachment. As John Flavell puts it, "How ever could a child persistently yearn and search for a specific other person if the child were still cogni-tively incapable of mentally representing that person in the person's absence?" (1985, p. 135).

We might also turn this hypothesis on its head and argue that the process of estab-lishing a clear attachment may cause, or at least affect, the child's cognitive develop-ment. For example, securely attached youngsters appear to persist longer in their play and to develop the object concept more rapidly (Bates et al., 1982). Such a connection might exist because the securely attached child is simply more comfortable exploring the world around him from the safe base of his secure person. He thus has a richer and more varied set of experiences, which may stimulate more rapid cognitive (and neuro-logical) development.

Internal Working Models. We could also think of attachment as a subcategory of a broader process, namely, the creation of internal working models. Seymour Epstein (1991) proposes that what the baby is doing is nothing less than beginning to create a "theory of reality." In Epstein's view, such a theory includes at least four elements:

- A belief about the degree to which the world is a place of pleasure or pain

- A belief about the extent to which the world is meaningful—predictable, con-trollable, and just versus chaotic, uncontrollable, and capricious

- A belief about whether people are desirable or threatening to relate to

- A belief about the worthiness or unworthiness of the self

The roots of this theory of reality, so Epstein and others argue (Bretherton, 1991), lie in the experiences of infancy, particularly the experiences with caregivers and other hu-mans. Indeed, Epstein suggests that beliefs created in infancy are likely to be the most basic and therefore the most durable and resistant to change at later ages. Not all psy-chologists would agree with Epstein about the broadness of the infant's "theory" of re-ality. However, virtually all would now agree that the baby begins to create at least two significant internal models, one of the self and one of relationships with others (attachment). Of the two, the attachment model seems to be the most fully developed at 18 or 24 months; the model of the self undergoes many elaborations in the years that follow. You'll recall from Chapter 10 that it is only at about age 6 or 7 that the child seems to have a sense of his *global* worth (Harter, 1987; 1990).

Influences on the Basic Processes

These four basic processes are quite robust (Masten et al., 1990). Nonetheless, infants can be deflected from the common trajectory by several kinds of influences.

Organic Damage. The most obvious potential deflector is some kind of damage to the physical organism, either from genetic anomalies, inherited disease, or teratogenic effects *in utero*. Yet even here, nature and nurture interact: Recall from Chapter 2 that the long-term consequences of such damage may be more or less severe, depending on the richness and supportiveness of the environment the baby grows up in.

Family Environment. The specific family environment in which the child is reared also affects the trajectory. On one end of the continuum we can see beneficial effects from an optimal environment that includes a variety of objects for the baby to explore, at least some free opportunity to explore, and loving, responsive, and sensitive adults who talk to the infant often and respond to her cues (Bradley et al., 1989). Among other things, such enriched environments may contribute to the development and retention of a more elaborate and complex network of neural connections. On the other end of the continuum, some environments can be so poor that they fall outside the "good enough" range and thus fail to support the child's most basic development. Severe neglect or abuse would fall into this category, as might deep or lasting depression in a parent or persisting upheaval or stress in family life. In between these extremes are many variations in enrichment, in responsiveness, in loving support, all of which seem to have at least some impact on the child's pattern of attachment, his motivation, the content of his self-concept, his willingness to explore, as well as his specific knowledge. We see the consequences of such differences further down the developmental road, when the child is facing the challenging tasks of school and the demands of relating to other children.

Influences on the Family. I've made the point before, but let me make it again: The baby is embedded in the family, but the family is part of a larger economic, social, and cultural system, all of which can have both direct and indirect effects on the infant.

The most obvious example is the impact of poverty or wealth; the parents' overall economic circumstances may have a very wide-ranging impact on the baby's life experience. Poor families are less able to provide a safe and secure environment. Their infants are more likely to be exposed to environmental toxins such as lead; less likely to have regular health care, including immunizations; and more likely to have nutritionally inadequate diets. If they place their infant in day care, poor parents may be unable to afford good quality care, and they are more likely to have to shift their baby from one care arrangement to another. Collectively, these are large differences. We do not see the effects immediately; babies being reared in poverty-level families do not look much different from babies being reared in more affluent circumstances. By age 2, 3, or 4, though, the differences begin to be obvious.

Overall Impressions of Infancy

One of the strongest impressions one gets from so much of the current research on babies is that they are far more capable than we had thought. They appear to be born with many more skills, many more templates for handling their experiences. At the same time, they are not 6-year-olds, and we need to be careful not to get too carried away with our statements about how much the baby can do.

The Preschool Years

The sense one gets of this period, summarized in Figure 16.2, is that the child is making a slow but immensely important shift from dependent baby to independent child. The toddler and preschooler can now move around easily, can communicate more and more clearly, has a sense of himself as a separate person with specific qualities, and has the beginning cognitive and social skills that allow him to interact more fully and successfully with playmates. In these same years, the child's thinking is *decentering*—to use Piaget's term: She shifts away from using herself as the only frame of reference and becomes less tied to the outside appearances of things.

In the beginning, these newfound skills and this new independence are not accompanied by much impulse control. Two-year-olds are pretty good at doing; they are lousy at *not* doing. If frustrated, they hit things, wail, scream, or shout (isn't language wonderful?). A large part of the conflict parents experience with children at this age comes about because the parent *must* limit the child, not only for the child's own survival but also to help teach the child impulse control (Escalona, 1981).

The preschool years also stand out as the period in which the seeds are sown for the child's—and perhaps the adult's—social skills and personality. The attachment process in infancy continues to be formative because it helps to shape the internal working model of social relationships the child creates. However, in the years from 2 to

Figure 16.2

A brief summary of parallel developments during the preschool years.

	Age in years				
	2	3	4	5	6
Physical development	Runs easily; climbs stairs one step at a time	Rides trike; uses scissors; draws	Climbs stairs one foot per step; kicks and throws large ball	Hops and skips; some ball games with more skill	Jumps rope; skips
Cognitive development	Symbol use; 2- and 3-step play sequences	Flavell's Level 1 perspective taking	Level 2 perspective taking; understands false belief	Representational theory of mind clearly present; conservation of number and quantity	Some meta-cognition and meta-memory; no spontaneous use of rehearsal in memory tasks
Language development	2-word sentences	3- and 4-word sentences with grammatical markers	Continued improvement of inflections, past tense, plurals, passive sentences, and tag questions		
Self/personality development	Self-definition based on comparisons of size, age, gender — Gender identity	Gender stability		Categorical self based on physical properties or skills — Gender consistency	
	Erikson's stage of autonomy ►◄ Erikson's stage of initiative vs. guilt ——————————————► vs. shame/doubt				
Social development	Attachments to parents shown less frequently, mostly under stress				
	Cooperative play; multistep turn-taking sequences in play with peers	Empathy for another's feelings — Some altruism; same-sex peer choice	Beginning signs of individual friendships	Sociodramatic play	Roles in play

6 this early model is revised, consolidated, and established more firmly. The resultant interactive patterns tend to persist into elementary school and beyond. The 3-, 4-, or 5-year-old who develops the ability to share, to read others' cues well, to respond positively to others, and to control aggression and impulsiveness is likely to be a socially successful, popular 8-year-old. In contrast, the noncompliant, hostile preschooler is far more likely to become an unpopular, aggressive schoolchild (Campbell et al., 1991; Eisenberg et al., 1995b; Patterson et al., 1991).

Central Processes

Many forces are at play in creating these changes, beginning with two immense cognitive advances in this period: the 18- or 24-month-old child's new ability to use symbols, and the rapid development, between ages 3 and 5, of a more sophisticated theory of mind.

Symbol Use. The development of symbol use is reflected in many different aspects of the child's life. We see it in the rapid surge of language development, in the child's approach to cognitive tasks, and in play, where the child now pretends, having an object *stand for* something else. The ability to use language more skillfully, in turn, affects social behavior in highly significant ways. For example, the child increasingly uses verbal rather than physical aggression and uses negotiation with parents in place of tantrums or defiant behavior.

Theory of Mind. The emergence of the child's more sophisticated theory of mind has equally broad effects, especially in the social arena, where his newfound abilities to read and understand others' behaviors form the foundation for new levels of interactions with peers and parents. It is probably not accidental that individual friendships between children are first visible at about the time that they also show the sharp drop in egocentrism that occurs with the emergence of the theory of mind.

We also see the seminal role of cognitive changes in the growing importance of several basic schemes. Not only does the 2- or 3-year-old have a more and more generalized internal model of attachment; she also develops a self-scheme and a gender-scheme, each of which forms part of the foundation of both social behavior and personality.

Social Contacts. Important as these cognitive changes are, they are clearly not the only causal factors. Equally important are the child's contacts with adults and peers. When children play together, they expand each other's experience with objects and suggest new ways of pretending to one another, thus fostering still further cognitive growth. When two children disagree about how to explain something or insist on their own different views, each child gains awareness that there *are* other ways of thinking or playing, thus creating opportunities to learn about others' mental processes. Just as Vygotsky suggested, social interactions are the arena in which much cognitive growth occurs. For example, in one recent study, Charles Lewis finds that children who have many siblings or who interact regularly with a variety of adult relatives show more rapid understanding of other people's thinking and acting than do children with fewer social partners (Lewis et al., 1995). Similarly, Jenkins and Astington (1996) find that chil-

Pride and independence!

dren from larger families show more rapid development of a representational theory of mind. Some new research also shows that children with secure attachments show a more rapid shift to understanding false belief and other aspects of a representational theory of mind than do children with insecure attachments (Charman et al., 1995; Steele et al., 1995)—a result that points to the importance of the *quality* as well as the quantity of social interactions for the child's cognitive development.

Play with other children also forms the foundation of the child's emerging gender schema. Noticing whether other people are boys or girls, and what toys boys and girls play with, is itself the first step in the long chain of sex-role learning.

Naturally enough, it is also in social interactions, especially those with parents, that the child's pattern of social behaviors is modified or reinforced. The parents' style of discipline becomes critical here. Gerald Patterson's work shows clearly that parents who lack the skills to control the toddler's impulsivity and demands for independence are likely to end up strengthening noncompliant and disruptive behavior, even if the parents' intention is the reverse (Patterson et al., 1991).

Influences on the Basic Processes

Family Dynamics. The family's ability to support the child's development in these years is affected not only by the skills and knowledge the parents bring to the process but also by the amount of stress they are experiencing from outside forces and the quality of support they have in their personal lives (Crockenberg & Litman, 1990). In particular, mothers who are experiencing high levels of stress are more likely to be punitive and negative toward their children, with resulting increases in the children's defiant and noncompliant behavior (Webster-Stratton, 1988). Maternal negativity, in turn, is implicated in the persistence of noncompliant behavior into elementary school. This link is clear, for example, in Susan Campbell's longitudinal study of a group of such noncompliant children (Campbell & Ewing, 1990; Campbell et al., 1991). Campbell finds that among a group of 3-year-olds who were labeled "hard to manage," those who improved by age 6 had mothers who had been less negative.

The mother's stress is obviously not the only factor in her level of negativity toward the child. Depressed mothers are also more likely to show such behavior (Conrad & Hammen, 1989), as are mothers from working-class or poverty-level families, who may well have experienced such negativity and harsh discipline in their own childhoods. Even so, stress and lack of personal social support are both part of the equation. Thus, the preschooler, like children of every age, is affected by broader social forces outside the family as well as by the family interaction itself.

The Elementary School Years

Figure 16.3 (p. 478) summarizes the changes and continuities of middle childhood. There are obviously many gradual changes: greater and greater physical skill, less and less reliance on appearance, more and more attention to underlying qualities and attributes, and a greater role of peers. The one interval during these years when there seems to be a more rapid change is right at the beginning of middle childhood, at the point of transition from the preschooler to the schoolchild.

The Transition Between 5 and 7

Some kind of transition into middle childhood has been noted in a great many cultures. There seems to be widespread recognition that a 6-year-old is somehow qualitatively different from a 5-year-old: more responsible, more able to understand complex ideas. Among the Kipsigis of Kenya, for example, the age of 6 is said to be the first point at which the child has *ng'omnotet,* translated as "intelligence" (Harkness & Super, 1985).

Critical Thinking

If a parent of a 2-year-old complained to you about the "terrible twoness" of his child, what comments might you make, in light of what you have just read? How could you explain the child's behavior to the parent in a way that might make it easier to deal with?

Figure 16.3

A summary of parallel changes during the elementary school years.

	Age in years						
	6	7	8	9	10	11	12
Physical development	Jumps rope; draws figures like squares	Begins to ride two-wheeled bike	Rides bike well	Beginning puberty for some girls; first stage of breast development	Early menarche	Early genital development in boys	Growth spurt in girls
Cognitive development	Gender constancy; class inclusion; conservation of mass and number; rehearsal and other memory strategies; beginning metacognition		Inductive logic; conservation of weight Better and better use of concrete operations skills				Conservation of space/volume
Social cognition	Kohlberg's stage 1	Kohlberg's stage 2 (naive hedonism) Friendship thought to be based on reciprocal trust		Kohlberg's stage 3 (good boy/nice girl) Descriptions of others begin to emphasize inner traits or qualities			
Self/personality development	Strong sex-role stereotyping; imitation of same-sex models		Global sense of self-worth	Self-definition begins to include more inner qualities, more complex qualities			
	Erikson's stage of industry vs. inferiority ⟶						
Social development	⟵ Same-sex play groups ⟶						
	⟵ Enduring friendships appear regularly ⟶						

The fact that schooling begins at this age seems to reflect an implicit or explicit recognition of this fundamental shift.

Psychologists who have studied development across this transition have pointed to a whole series of changes:

- Cognitively, there is a shift to what Piaget calls concrete operational thinking. The child now understands conservation problems, seriation, and class inclusion. More generally, the child seems to pay less attention to surface properties of objects and more to underlying continuities and patterns, to be captured less by appearance and to focus on the underlying reality. We see this not only in children's understanding of physical objects but also in their understanding of others, of relationships, and of themselves. In studies of information processing, we see a parallel rapid increase in the child's use of executive strategies.

- In the self-concept, we first see a global judgment of self-worth at about age 7 or 8.

- In peer relationships, gender segregation becomes virtually complete by age 6 or 7, especially in individual friendships.

The apparent confluence of these changes is impressive and seems to provide some support for the existence of a Piaget-like stage. On the surface, at least, there seems to be some kind of change in the basic structure of the child's thinking that is reflected in all aspects of the child's functioning. Still, impressive as these changes are, it is not so clear that what is going on here is a rapid, pervasive, structural change to a whole new way of thinking and relating. Children don't make this shift all at once in every area of their thinking or relationships. For example, while the shift from a concrete to a more abstract self-concept may become noticeable at age 6 or 7, it occurs quite gradually and is still going on at ages 11 and 12. Similarly, a child may grasp conservation of quantity at age 5 or 6 but typically does not understand conservation of weight until several years later.

Furthermore, expertise, or the lack of it, strongly affects the pattern of the child's cognitive progress. Thus, while I think most psychologists would agree that a set of important changes normally emerge together at about this age, most would also agree that no rapid or abrupt reorganization of the child's whole mode of operating is occurring.

Central Processes

Cognitive Influences. In trying to account for the developmental shifts we see during middle childhood, my bias has been to see the cognitive changes as most central, the necessary but not sufficient condition for the alterations in relationships and in the self-scheme during this period. A good illustration is the emergence of a global sense of self-worth, which seems to require not only a tendency to look beyond or behind surface characteristics but also the use of inductive logic. The child appears to arrive at a global sense of self-worth by some summative, inductive process.

Similarly, the quality of the child's relationships with peers and parents seems to rest, in part, on a basic cognitive understanding of reciprocity and perspective taking. The child now understands that others read him as much as he reads them. Children of 7 or 8 will now say of their friends that they "trust each other," something you would be very unlikely to hear from a 5-year-old.

Peer Group Influences. Such a cognitive bias dominated theories and research on middle childhood for many decades, largely as a result of the powerful influence of Piaget's theory. This imbalance has begun to be redressed in recent years as the central importance of the peer group and the child's social experience has become better understood. There are two aspects to this revision of thinking. First, we have reawakened to the (obvious) fact that a great deal of the experience on which the child's cognitive progress is based occurs in social interactions. Second, we have realized that social relationships make a unique set of demands, both cognitive and interactive, and have unique consequences for the child's social and emotional functioning. It is in these elementary school years, for example, that patterns of peer rejection or acceptance are consolidated, with reverberations through adolescence and into adult life.

Physical Influences. Just what role physical change plays in this collection of developments I do not know. Clearly there are physical changes going on. Girls, in particular, begin the early steps of puberty during elementary school. What we don't yet know is whether the rate of physical development in these years is connected in any way to the rate of the child's progress through the sequence of cognitive or social understandings. The one thing we know is that bigger, more coordinated, early-developing children are likely to have slightly faster cognitive development and to be somewhat more popular with peers. Obviously this is an area in which we need far more knowledge.

Critical Thinking

As a way to grasp the importance of social contacts, try to imagine a child who grew up without ever playing with another child. How would such a child be different from other children? What kind of adult would he or she become?

Influences on the Basic Processes: The Role of Culture

Most of what I have said about middle childhood—and about other ages as well—is based on research on children growing up in Western cultures. I've tried to balance the scales a bit as I've gone along, but we must still ask, again and again, whether the patterns we see are specific to particular cultures or whether they reflect underlying developmental processes common to all children everywhere.

In the case of middle childhood, there are some obvious differences in the experiences of children in Western cultures versus those growing up in villages in Africa, in Polynesia, or in other parts of the world where families live by subsistence agriculture

Going to school may not always be as filled with joy as this, but there is no doubt that it is a hugely formative experience for children in these ages.

and schooling is not a dominant force in children's lives (Weisner, 1984). In many such cultures, children of 6 or 7 are thought of as "intelligent" and responsible and are given almost adultlike roles. They are highly likely to be given the task of caring for younger siblings, and begin their apprenticeships in the skills they will need as adults, such as agricultural skills or animal husbandry, learning alongside the working adults. In some West African and Polynesian cultures, it is also common for children this age to be sent out to foster care, either with relatives or to apprentice with a skilled worker.

Such children obviously have a very different set of social tasks to learn in the middle childhood years than do children growing up in industrialized countries. They do not need to learn how to relate to or make friends with strangers in a new school environment. Instead, from an early age they need to learn their place in an existing network of roles and relationships. For the Western child, the roles are less prescribed; the choices for adult life are far more varied.

Yet the differences in the lives of children in industrialized and nonindustrialized cultures should not obscure the very real similarities. In all cultures, children this age develop individual friendships, segregate their play groups by gender, develop the cognitive underpinnings of reciprocity, learn the beginnings of what Piaget calls concrete operations, and acquire some of the basic skills that will be required for adult life. These are not trivial similarities. They speak to the power of the common process of development, even in the midst of obvious variation in experience.

Adolescence

Figure 16.4 summarizes the various threads of development during adolescence. A number of experts on this age period argue that it makes sense to divide the years between 12 and 20 into two subperiods, one beginning at 11 or 12, the other perhaps at 16 or 17. Some label these periods as *adolescence* and *youth* (Keniston, 1970), others as *early* and *late* adolescence (Brooks-Gunn, 1988). However we label them, there are distinct differences.

Early adolescence, almost by definition, is a time of transition, a time of significant change in virtually every aspect of the child's functioning. Late adolescence is more a time of consolidation, when the young person establishes a cohesive new identity, with clearer goals and role commitments. Norma Haan (1981), borrowing Piaget's concepts, suggests that early adolescence is a time dominated by assimilation while late adolescence is primarily a time of accommodation.

The 12- or 13-year-old is assimilating an enormous number of new physical, social, and intellectual experiences. While all this absorption is going on, but before it is digested, the young person is in a more or less perpetual state of disequilibrium. Old patterns, old

Figure 16.4

A brief summary of parallel developments during adolescence.

Age in years

	12	13	14	15	16	17	18	19

Physical development

Major pubertal change begins for boys

Girls' height spurt | Average age of menarche | | Boys' maximum height spurt | Puberty completed for girls | | Puberty completed for boys

Cognitive development

Beginning formal operations: systematic analysis

"Early basic" formal operations: deductive logic

Consolidated formal operations (for a few)

Social cognition

Kohlberg's stage 3 continues

Kohlberg's stage 4 ("law and order") for a minority

Descriptions of others and of self begin to include exceptions, comparisons, special conditions; deeper personality traits; empathy with another's general plight

Self/personality development

Incidence of depression rises; self-esteem declines briefly

Self-esteem rises for remainder of adolescence

Clear identity developed for perhaps half

Erikson's stage of identity vs. role diffusion ⟶

Social relationships

Cliques — Crowds — Pairs

Stable and intimate friendships continue and become more intimate

Parent-child conflict peaks at beginning of puberty

Maximum impact of peer group

---

schemes no longer work very well, but new ones have not been established. It is during this early period that the peer group is so centrally important. Ultimately, the 16- or 17- or 18-year-old begins to make the needed accommodations, pulls the threads together, and establishes a new identity, new patterns of social relationships, new goals and roles.

Early Adolescence

In some ways, the early years of adolescence have a lot in common with the early years of toddlerhood. Two-year-olds are famous for their negativism and for their constant push for more independence. At the same time, they are struggling to learn a vast array of new skills. Teenagers show many of these same qualities, albeit at much more abstract levels. Many of them go through a period of negativism, particularly with parents, right at the beginning of the pubertal changes. And many of the conflicts with parents center on issues of independence—adolescents want to come and go when they please; listen to the music they prefer, at maximum volume; and wear the clothing and hair styles that are currently "in."

As is true of the negativism of the 2-year-old, it is easy to overstate the depth or breadth of the conflict between young teenagers and their parents. For the great majority of teenagers, there is no major turmoil but only a temporary increase in the frequency of disagreements or disputes. The depiction of adolescence as full of storm and stress is as much an exaggeration as is the phrase *terrible twos.* What is true is that both ages are characterized by a new push for independence, which is inevitably accompanied by more confrontations with parents over limits.

While this push for independence is going on, young adolescents are also facing a whole new set of demands and skills to be learned—new social skills, new and more complex school tasks, a need to form an adult identity. The sharp increase in the rate of depression (especially among girls) and the drop in self-esteem we see at the beginning of adolescence seem to be linked to this surplus of new demands and changes. A number of investigators have found that those adolescents who have the greatest number of simultaneous changes at the beginning of puberty—changing to junior high school, moving to a new town or new house, perhaps a parental separation or divorce—also show the greatest loss in self-esteem, the largest rise in problem behavior, and the biggest drop in grade point average (e.g., Simmons et al., 1988). Young adolescents who can cope with these changes one at a time, as when the youngster remains in the same school through eighth or ninth grade before shifting to high school, show fewer symptoms of stress.

Facing major stressful demands, the 2-year-old uses Mom (or some other central attachment figure) as a safe base for exploring the world, returning for reassurance when fearful. Young adolescents seem to do the same with the family, using it as a safe base from which to explore the rest of the world, including the world of peer relationships. Parents of young adolescents must try to find a difficult balance between providing the needed security, often in the form of clear rules and limits, and still allowing independence—just as parents of 2-year-olds must walk the fine line between allowing exploration and ensuring safety. Among teenagers, as among toddlers, the most confident and successful are those whose families manage this balancing act well.

Still a third way in which theorists have likened the young teenager to the 2-year-old is in egocentrism. David Elkind (1967) suggested some years ago that egocentrism rises in adolescence. This new egocentrism, according to Elkind, has two facets: (1) the belief that "others in our immediate vicinity are as concerned with our thoughts and behavior as we ourselves are" (Elkind & Bowen, 1979, p. 38), which Elkind describes as having an *imaginary audience;* and (2) the possession of a *personal fable,* a tendency for adolescents to consider their own ideas and feelings unique and singularly important. Egocentrism is typically accompanied by a sense of invulnerability—a feeling that may lie behind many adolescents' apparent attraction to high-risk behavior such as unprotected sex, drugs, drinking, and high-speed driving.

Elkind's research shows that the preoccupation with others' views of the self (imaginary audience behavior) peaks at about ages 13 to 14 (Elkind & Bowen, 1979). Teenagers this age are most likely to say that if they went to a party where they did not know many people, they would wonder a *lot* about what the other kids were thinking of them. They also report that they worry a lot when someone is watching them work, and they feel desperately embarrassed if they discover a grease spot on their clothes or have newly erupted pimples. Of course younger children and adults may also worry about these things, but they seem to be much less disturbed or immobilized by these worries than are 13- and 14-year-olds, who are at an age when the dominance of the peer crowd or clique is at its peak.

Independence of a new and different kind.

Drawing a parallel between the early adolescent and the toddler also makes sense in that both age groups face the task of establishing a separate identity. The toddler must separate herself from the symbiotic relationship with Mom or another central caregiver. The child must figure out not only that she is separate but that she has abilities and qualities. Physical maturation also allows her new levels of independent exploration. The young adolescent must separate himself from his family and from his identity as a child and begin to form a new identity as an adult.

Late Adolescence

To carry the basic analogy further, late adolescence is more like the preschool years. Major changes have been weathered, and a new balance has been achieved. The physical upheavals of puberty are mostly complete, the family system has changed to allow the teenager more independence and freedom, and the beginnings of a new identity have been created. This period is not without its strains. For most young people, a clear identity is not achieved until college age, if then, so the identity process continues. And the task of forming emotionally intimate sexual or presexual partnerships is a key task of late adolescence. Nonetheless, I think Haan is correct that this later period is more one of accommodation than assimilation. At the very least, we know that it is accompanied by rising levels of self-esteem and declining levels of family confrontation or conflict.

Central Processes and Their Connections

In talking about other age periods, I have suggested that changes in one or another of the facets of development may be central to the constellation of transformations we see at a given age. In infancy, underlying physiological change and the creation of a first central attachment appear to have such key causal roles; in the preschool years, cognitive changes seem especially dominant, while among school-age children, both cognitive and social changes appear to be formative. In adolescence, *every* domain shows significant change. At this point, we simply do not have the research data to clarify the basic causal connections among the transformations in these various areas. Still, we have some information about linkages.

The Role of Puberty. The obvious place to begin is with the role of puberty itself. Puberty not only defines the beginning of early adolescence; it clearly affects all other facets of the young person's development, either directly or indirectly.

Direct effects might be seen in several ways. Most clearly, the surges of pubertal hormones stimulate sexual interest while they also trigger body changes that make adult sexuality and fertility possible. These changes seem inescapably causally linked to the gradual shift (for the great majority of teens) from same-sex peer groupings to heterosexual crowds and finally to heterosexual pair relationships.

Hormone changes may also be directly implicated in the rise both in confrontation or conflict between parents and children and in various kinds of aggressive or delinquent behavior. Steinberg's research suggests such a direct link because he finds pubertal stage and not age to be the critical variable in predicting the level of adolescents' conflict with their parents. Other investigators have found that in girls, the rise in estradiol at the beginning of puberty is associated with increases in verbal aggression and a loss of impulse control, while in boys, increases in testosterone are correlated with increases in irritability and impatience (Paikoff & Brooks-Gunn, 1990). However, many studies find no such connection (e.g., Coe et al., 1988), so most theorists conclude that the links between pubertal hormones and changes in adolescent social behavior are considerably more complicated than we had first imagined.

One of the complications is that the physical changes of puberty have highly significant *indirect* effects as well as direct consequences. When the child's body grows and becomes more like that of an adult, the parents begin to treat the child differently, and

Critical Thinking

Does the comparison of early adolescence and toddlerhood make sense to you? If it is a valid comparison, then does that suggest that development is somehow like a spiral, returning to the same issues repeatedly, but at ever higher levels of complexity?

By late adolescence, the form of peer interaction has shifted from mixed-sex cliques to loose associations of pairs.

the child begins to see himself as a soon-to-be-adult. Both of these changes may be linked to the brief rise in parent-adolescent confrontation and may help to trigger some of the searching self-examinations that are part of this period of life.

Physiological changes might conceivably also play some role in the shift to formal operations. We have some indication, for example, that synaptic and dendritic pruning continues through early adolescence, so a final reorganization of the brain may be occurring in these years. At the same time, any link between formal operational thinking and pubertal change cannot be inevitable, because we know that all adolescents experience puberty but not all make the transition to formal operations. The best guess at the moment is that neurological or hormonal changes at adolescence may be *necessary* for further cognitive gains, but they cannot be *sufficient* conditions for such developments.

The Role of Cognitive Changes. An equally attractive possibility to many theorists has been the proposition that it is the cognitive changes that are pivotal in adolescence. The cognitive shift from concrete to formal operations obviously does not cause pubertal changes, but cognitive development may be central to many of the other changes we see at adolescence, including changes in the self-concept, the process of identity formation, increases in level of moral reasoning, and changes in peer relationships.

There is ample evidence, for example, that the greater abstractness in the child's self-concept and in his descriptions of others are intimately connected to the broader changes in cognitive functioning (Harter, 1990). You will also remember from Chapter 12 that the shift in the child's thinking from concrete operations to at least beginning formal operations seems to be a necessary precondition for the emergence of more advanced forms of social cognition and moral judgment. Finally, some ability to use formal operations may also be necessary but not sufficient for the formation of a clear identity. One of the characteristics of formal operational thinking is the ability to imagine possibilities that you have never experienced and to manipulate ideas in your head. These new skills may help to foster the broad questioning of old ways, old values, old patterns that is a central part of the identity formation process. For example, several studies show that among high school and college students, those in Marcia's identity achievement or moratorium statuses are much more likely also to be using formal operations reasoning than are those in the diffusion or foreclosure statuses. In Rowe and Marcia's study (1980), the *only* individuals who showed full identity achievement were those who were also using full formal operations. But the converse was not true. That is, there were a number of subjects who used formal operations but had not yet established a clear identity. Thus, formal operational thinking may *enable* the young person to rethink many aspects of his life, but it does not guarantee that he will do so.

Overall, we are left with the impression that both the physical changes of puberty and the potential cognitive changes of formal operations are central to the phenomena of adolescence, but the connections between them, and their impact on social behavior, remain unclear.

Influences on the Basic Processes

I do not have space enough to detail all the many factors that will influence the teenager's experience of adolescence. Many I have already mentioned, including such cultural variations as the presence or absence of initiation rites, the timing of the child's pubertal development, and the degree of personal or familial stress. But one more general point is worth repeating: Adolescence, like every other developmental period, does not begin with a clean slate. The individual youngster's own temperamental qualities, behavioral habits, and internal models of interaction, established in earlier years of childhood, obviously have a profound effect on the experience of adolescence. Examples are easy to find:

- Alan Sroufe's longitudinal study (1989), which I described in Chapter 11, shows that those who had been rated as having a secure attachment in infancy were more self-confident and more socially competent with peers at the beginning of adolescence.

- Delinquency and heightened aggressiveness in adolescence are most often presaged by earlier behavior problems and by inadequate family control as early as the years of toddlerhood (Dishion et al., 1995b). Even those delinquents who show such antisocial behavior for the first time as teenagers enter adolescence with different qualities, including poorer-quality friendships (Berndt & Keefe, 1995a).

- Depression in the teenage years is more likely among those who enter adolescence with lower self-esteem (Harter, 1987).

Avshalom Caspi and Terrie Moffitt (1991) make the more general point that *any* major life crisis or transition, including adolescence, has the effect of *accentuating* earlier personality or behavioral patterns rather than creating new ones. This is not unlike the observation that the child's attachment to the parent is revealed only when the child is under stress. As one example of the more general process, Caspi and Moffitt point out that girls with very early puberty have higher rates of psychological problems, on average, than do those with normal-time puberty. However, closer analysis reveals that it is only the early-puberty girls who already had social problems before puberty began whose pubertal experience and adolescence is more negative. Very early puberty does not induce psychological problems in girls who were psychologically healthier to begin with.

I think this is an important point for understanding all the various transitions of adult life as well as adolescence. Not only do we carry ourselves with us as we move through the roles and demands of adult life, but existing patterns may be most highly visible when we are under stress. This does not mean that we never change or learn new and more effective ways of responding. Many of us do. Still, we must never lose sight of the fact that by adolescence, and certainly by adulthood, our internal working models and our repertoire of coping behaviors are already established, creating a bias in the system. Another way of putting it is that while change is possible, continuity is the default option.

Returning to Some Basic Questions

With this brief overview in mind, let me now go back to some of the questions I raised in Chapter 1 and see if the answers can be made any clearer.

What Are the Major Influences on Development?

In Chapter 1 and throughout the book, I have contrasted nature and nurture, nativism and empiricism, as basic explanations of developmental patterns. In every instance I have also said that the real answer lies in the interaction between the two. I certainly hope that it is this interactive message that you will take away with you. I can perhaps make the point clearest by going back to Aslin's five models of environmental and internal influences on development I showed in Figure 1.1 (p. 8). You'll recall that he is proposing one purely physical model (which he calls maturation) in which some particular development would occur regardless of environmental input, and one purely environmental pattern (which he calls induction) in which some development is entirely a function of experience. These two "pure" alternatives make logical sense, but in actuality, probably neither of them actually occurs at all. *All* of development is a product of various forms of interaction between internal and external influences.

Even in those areas of development that appear to be the most clearly biologically determined or influenced, such as physical development or early perceptual development, normal development can occur *only* if the child is growing in an environment that falls within the range of adequate or sufficient environments. The fact that the vast majority of environments fall within that range in no way reduces the crucial importance of the environment. John Flavell puts it this way: "Environmental elements do not become any less essential to a particular form of development just because they are virtually certain to be available for its use" (1985, p. 284).

Similarly, even those aspects of development that seem most obviously to be a product of environment, such as the quality of the child's first attachment, rest on a physiological substrate and on instinctive patterns of attachment behaviors. The fact that all intact children possess that substrate and those instincts makes them no less essential for development.

Rutter's Five Principles of the Interaction of Nature and Nurture. At the same time, it is not enough merely to say that all development is a product of interaction between nature and nurture. We need to be able to specify much more clearly just how that interaction operates. Michael Rutter and his colleagues (1997) have recently proposed a set of five general principles governing the interplay between nature and nurture that go beyond Aslin's models and provide a helpful summary analysis:

1. **"Individuals differ in their reactivity to the environment"** (p. 338). Some babies/children/adults are highly reactive, highly sensitive to stress or strangeness; others react with much less volatility. Variations in such reactivity may rest on basic inborn temperamental differences, or they may be the product of cumulative experience. A child exposed to high levels of stress over many months or years, for example, may become more reactive—just as we know that adults who have experienced higher levels of stress are more likely to catch a cold when exposed to a virus (Cohen et al., 1991).

2. **"There is a two-way interplay between individuals and their environments"** (p. 338). It is important not to think of this process as a one-way street. Influences go back and forth. One example from Rutter's analysis: Mothers who experience higher levels of stress are more likely to become depressed, but once they become depressed, the women are later likely to experience still higher rates of stressful life events. Thus, both directions of influence occur: Stress leads to more depression, and depression leads to more stress (Pianta & Egeland, 1994b). Another example: Children whose inborn skills or disabilities make it difficult for them to learn to read will naturally read less. Reading less, in turn, means that they will have fewer of the experiences that help build reading skill. These back-and-forth influences tend to move the child—or the adult—farther and farther along the original trajectory.

3. **"The interplay between persons and their environments needs to be considered within an ecological framework"** (p. 339). Although our research nearly always treats environmental events—such as divorce—as if they were constant, they are not. The event itself will surely vary as a function of culture, poverty, family structure, and a whole host of other variables.

4. **"People *process* their experiences rather than just serve as passive recipients of environmental forces"** (p. 339). I've made this point throughout the book, but it is good to repeat it. Children are actively trying to understand their experience. They create theories or models to explain that experience. We can think of the internal models of attachment, of the self, of gender, of relationships, as examples of this principle, but the principle is even more general. As I said in Chapter 1, it is the *meaning* each child attaches to an experience that governs the effect, not the experience itself. Thus,

The fact that virtually all babies have some chance to reach for and examine objects does not mean that such experience is unimportant in the child's emerging perceptual or motor skills. Most (if not all) so-called maturational sequences require particular kinds of environmental inputs if they are to occur at all.

the "same" experience can have widely differing effects, depending on how the child (or adult) processes or interprets it.

5. **"People *act on their environment* so as to shape and select their experiences"** (p. 339). Experiences are not randomly distributed, independent of how the child or adult behaves. We each choose behaviors and choose niches within the family or within other social groups.

A Continuum of Environmental Influences. A sixth point, not included in Rutter's list, is that the form and extent of the interaction between nature and nurture may well vary as a function of the aspect of development we are talking about. It may help to think of different facets of development along a continuum, with those most fully internally programmed on one end and those most externally influenced on the other.

Physical development defines one end of this continuum, since it is very strongly shaped by internal forces. *Given the minimum necessary environment,* maturational timetables are extremely powerful and robust, particularly during infancy and adolescence. Next along the continuum is probably language (although some experts will argue with this conclusion, given the possible dependency of language development on prior cognitive developments). Language seems to emerge with only minimal environmental support—though here, too, the environment must fall within some acceptable range. At the very least, the child must hear language spoken (or see it signed). Still, specific features of the environment seem to matter a bit more here than is true for physical development. For example, parents who respond contingently to their children's vocalizations seem to be able to speed up the process, an example of what Aslin calls facilitation.

Cognitive development falls somewhere in the middle of the continuum. Clearly, powerful internal forces are at work. Let me quote John Flavell once again:

> There is an impetus to childhood cognitive growth that is not ultimately explainable by this environmental push or that experiential shove. (1985, p. 283)

We don't yet know whether the impressive regularity of the sequences of cognitive development arises from built-in processes like assimilation and accommodation, or whether physiological changes like synapse formation and pruning are the critical factors, or whether some combination of causes might be involved, but it is clear that this engine is moving along a shared track. At the same time, we know that the specific qualities of the environment affect both cognitive power and structure. Children with varied and age-appropriate toys, with encouragement for exploration and achievement, with parents who are responsive to the child's overtures, show faster cognitive development and higher eventual IQ scores—not just facilitation in Aslin's models, but actual attunement.

Social and emotional development lie at the other end of the continuum, where the impact of the environment seems to be the greatest, although even here genetic factors are obviously at work. Some aspects of temperament seem clearly to be built in genetically, and attachment behaviors may be instinctive; both of these inborn factors certainly shape the child's earliest encounters with others. In this area, however, the balance of nature/nurture seems to lean more toward nurture. In particular, the security of the child's attachment, and the quality of the child's relationships with others outside of the family, seem to be powerfully affected by the specific quality of the interactions within the family.

Does Timing Matter?

Finally, we need to remember that the impact of any experience may vary depending on *when* it occurs during development. This issue has been explored in a variety of ways.

Early Experience as Critical. The most pervasive version of the timing question has been to ask whether the early years of life are a critical or sensitive period, establishing many of the trajectories of the child's later development. To borrow Clarke's analogy (Clarke & Clarke, 1976): When we construct a house, does the shape of the foundation determine the final structure partially or completely, or can many final structures be built on the original foundation? Are any flaws or weaknesses in the original foundation permanent, or can they be corrected later, after the house is completed?

Critical Thinking

Try making a list of all the ways you choose your own environment(s). Think about your friendships, your activities, and your choice of major or occupation. What factors influence your choices? How different might your life be if you deliberately made other choices?

There are arguments on both sides. Some psychologists, such as Sandra Scarr, point to the fact that virtually all children successfully complete the sensorimotor period and even mild and moderately retarded children achieve some form of what Piaget called concrete operations. The term that has been widely used to describe such developmental patterns is **canalization,** a notion borrowed from an embryologist named Waddington (1957). He suggested that we think of development metaphorically as a marble rolling down a gully on a hillside, as in Figure 16.5. Where the gully is narrow and deep, development is said to be highly canalized. The marble will roll down that gully with little deviation. Other aspects of development, in contrast, might be better depicted with much flatter or wider gullies, with many side branches. Thus, Scarr and others argue that in the early years of life, development is highly canalized, with strong "self-righting" tendencies. If deflected, the baby's pattern of development rapidly returns to the bottom of the gully and proceeds along the normal track. Such self-righting is illustrated, for example, by the large percentage of low-birth-weight or other initially vulnerable babies who nonetheless catch up to their normal-birth peers in physical and cognitive development by age 2 or 3.

Michael Lewis, in his recent book *Altering Fate* (1997), makes an even more sweeping argument against the primacy of early experience:

> I wish to argue against the idea that development is a sequence of small progressions that are gradual but accumulative, that it has clear directionality, that it is causal—earlier events are connected to later ones—and that prediction therefore is possible. Instead, I would like to argue for the idea that development is based on the pragmatic needs of the present, that the contextual flow of our lives determines our development through adaptation to the current. (pp. 15–16)

He makes the point that chance encounters, upheavals, joys, and stresses change each of us; in a sense, he is saying that we remake ourselves moment to moment and that it is simply a mistake to think of development as if it were a cumulative process, with the earliest steps determining the trajectory of all that follows. My own feeling is that Lewis has taken this argument too far, but he has certainly raised some important and provocative issues.

On the other side of the argument are a whole group of psychologists—many of them with some roots in psychoanalytic thinking—who see infancy and early childhood as especially formative (e.g., Sroufe, 1983). They note that some prenatal influences are permanent; some effects of early cognitive impoverishment, malnutrition, or abuse may also be long-lasting. We also have a good deal of evidence that early psychological adaptations, such as the quality of the earliest attachment or the child's tendency toward aggressive behavior, tend to persist and shape the child's later experiences in a cumulative way.

My own sense is that both these perspectives are valid: The early years of life are *both* a sensitive period for some kinds of development and at the same time highly canalized. How can we resolve such an apparent paradox? Two possible resolutions occur to

If infancy is a critical period for some aspects of personality development, then these preschoolers' characters are already well formed. Whether this is true or not remains one of the most crucial theoretical and practical issues in developmental psychology.

Figure 16.5

Waddington's visual depiction of the concept of canalization. A narrow and deep gully depicts strong canalization. If infancy is highly canalized, it means that almost any environment will support or sustain that development.

(*Source:* "A Catastrophic theory of evolution" by C. H. Waddington in the *Annals of the New York Academy of Science*, 231, pp. 32–42 (1974). By permission.)

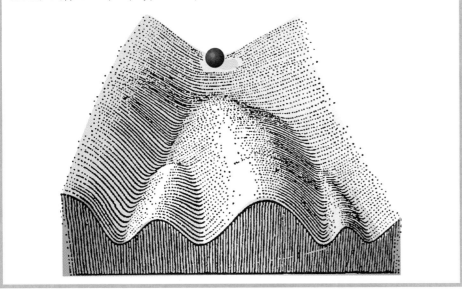

me. First, we might think of such canalization not just as a product of powerful built-in programming but as the result of such programming *occurring in a sufficiently supportive environment*. When we do that, a good deal of the apparent dispute disappears (Turkheimer & Gottesman, 1991). It is only when a child's particular environment falls *outside* the range of sufficiently supportive environments that we see a so-called environmental effect, such as a child reared in an extremely impoverished orphanage setting or a child who is regularly physically abused. In these conditions, environmental effects can be strongly negative and long-lasting. The earlier such a deviation occurs, the more pervasive the effects seem to be. In this way of looking at critical periods versus canalization, infancy may be less *frequently* pivotal in the pattern of the child's development than are more minor deviations in toddlerhood or the preschool years. But *if* the deviations in infancy are extreme enough to deflect the infant from the normal developmental path—as in the case of severe abuse or malnutrition—the effect is larger than at any other age.

Robert Cairns (1991) offers a second resolution to the paradox when he points out that in any given period, some facets of development may be highly canalized while other facets may be strongly responsive to environmental variation. In infancy, for example, physical, perceptual, and perhaps linguistic development may be strongly canalized, but the development of internal working models of attachment is clearly affected by the child's specific family experiences. Indeed, I would argue that all internal working models—of attachment, of gender identity and self-concept, of peer relations—are likely to be more powerfully affected by early than by later experiences, simply because the model, once formed, affects and filters all later experience.

A particularly nice example of this kind of early effect comes from one of Alan Sroufe's studies of the long-term consequences of attachment security. Sroufe and his colleagues (1990) compared two groups of elementary school children. One group had formed a secure attachment in infancy but for various reasons had not functioned well in the preschool years. The second group had shown poor adaptation at both ages. When these two groups of children were assessed at elementary school age, Sroufe found that those who had had a good early start "rebounded" better. They had better emotional health and peer competence at school age than did those who had had poor adaptation

Critical Thinking

Does either of these resolutions of the paradox persuade you? If not, why not?

in infancy, even though both groups had functioned poorly as preschoolers. The infancy experience is not totally formative; the child's current circumstances also have a major impact. But at least in this domain, early experience leaves a lingering trace.

Psychological Tasks at Different Ages. Another way to think about timing is to identify different specific psychological tasks to be dealt with at different ages. Erikson's theory, for example, emphasizes a series of psychological dilemmas. Any experience that affects the way a child resolves a particular task will be formative at that time; at an earlier or later time the same experience might have much less effect. Alan Sroufe and Michael Rutter (1984) have offered a broader list of age-graded tasks, given in Table 16.1. In this way of looking at things, the child is seen as *focusing* on different aspects of the environment at different times. Thus, during the period from 1 to 2½, when the child is focused on mastery of the object world, the quality and range of inanimate experiences the child has access to may be of special importance.

Overall, I do not think that any specific age is "critical" for all aspects of development; I do think that for any aspect of development, some ages are more central than others, and that during those times, patterns are set that affect later experience. As Alan Sroufe says, "Development is hierarchical; it is not a blackboard to be erased and written upon again. Even when children change rather markedly, the shadows of the earlier adaptation remain" (1983, pp. 73–74).

What Is the Nature of Developmental Change?

My bias has no doubt been apparent throughout the book, so you can predict my conclusion that developmental change is more qualitative than quantitative. Certainly, over the years of development, the child acquires more vocabulary words, more information processing strategies. But these are used in different ways by older children than by younger ones. Further, it seems clear that these qualitative changes occur in sequences. Such sequences are apparent in physical development, in cognitive development, in social and moral development.

Stages. Whether it is meaningful to speak of stages, however, is still an open question. Some hierarchically organized stages have certainly been identified, the most obvious example being Kohlberg's stages of moral reasoning. And we can certainly find examples of apparently stagelike changes across domains, such as what happens at about 18 to 24 months when the child seems to discover the ability to combine symbols, an

Table 16.1

Tasks or Issues in Each of Several Age Periods

Age in Years	Issues or Tasks
0–1	Biological regulation; harmonious dyadic interaction; formation of an effective attachment relationship
1–2½	Exploration, experimentation, and mastery of the object world (caregiver as secure base); individuation and autonomy; responding to external control of impulses
3–5	Flexible self-control; self-reliance; initiative; identification and gender concept; establishing effective peer contacts (empathy)
6–12	Social understanding (equity, fairness); gender constancy; same-sex friendships; sense of "industry" (competence); school adjustment
13+	Formal operations (flexible perspective taking, "as-if" thinking); loyal friendships (same-sex); beginning heterosexual relationships; emancipation; identity

Source: Table 1, p. 22, "The domain of developmental psychopathology" by L. A. Sroufe and M. Rutter, *Child development*, 55 (1984), 17–29. By permission of the Society for Research in Child Development.

understanding that is evident in two-word sentences, in thinking, and in multistep play with other children. There also appears to be a quite stagelike shift between ages 3 and 4, of which the new theory of mind is the centerpiece. The majority of the evidence, however, has not supported the notion of pervasive changes in structure. More commonly, each new skill, each new understanding, seems to be acquired in a fairly narrow area first and is only later generalized more fully. In fact, one of the things that differentiates the gifted or higher-IQ child from the lower-IQ or retarded child is how quickly and broadly the child generalizes some new concept or strategy to new instances.

Despite this nonstagelike quality of most developmental change, it is still true that if you compare the patterns of relationship, of thinking, of problem solving of two children of widely differing ages—say, a 5-year-old and an 11-year-old—they will differ in almost every respect. So there is certainly orderliness in the sequences, and there are some linkages between them, but there are probably not major stages quite like those Piaget proposed.

Continuities. In the midst of all this change, all these sequences, all the new forms of relating and thinking, we also see continuity. Each child carries forward some core of individuality. The notion of temperament certainly implies such a core, as does the concept of an internal working model. Alan Sroufe once again offers an elegant way of thinking about this central core. Continuity in development, he says, "takes the form of coherence across transformations" (1983, p. 51). Thus, the specific behavior that we see in the child may change; the clinging toddler may not be a clinging 9-year-old, but the underlying attachment model or the temperament that led to the clinging will still be at least partially present, manifesting itself in new ways. In particular, it has become increasingly clear that *mal*adaptations often persist over time, as seen in the consistency of high levels of aggression or tantrum behavior and in the persistence of some of the maladaptive social interactions that flow from insecure attachments. Our task as psychologists is to understand both coherence or consistency and the underlying patterns of development or transformation.

Individual Differences

The whole issue of individual continuities emphasizes the fact that development is individual as well as collective. I have talked about individual differences in virtually every chapter, so you know that both inborn differences and emergent or environmentally produced variations are present among children in every aspect of development. All this is familiar stuff by now and bears little repeating, but I want to try to tie together many of the threads I have been weaving in this chapter by returning to a dimension of individual differences I have talked about several times, namely, vulnerability and resilience. I think it is useful to define these concepts somewhat differently than usual, in terms of the *range of environments that will be sufficiently supportive for optimal development.* By this definition, a vulnerable infant is one with a narrow range of potentially supportive environments. For such a child, only the most stimulating, the most responsive, the most adaptive environment will do. When the child's environment falls outside that range, the probability of a poor outcome is greatly increased. A resilient child, in contrast, is one for whom any of a very wide range of environments will support optimum development. A resilient child may thus be more strongly canalized, a vulnerable child less so.

Some kinds of vulnerabilities are inborn, such as genetic abnormalities, or prenatal trauma or stress, or preterm birth, or malnutrition. Any child suffering from these problems will thrive only in a highly supportive environment. You've encountered this pattern again and again through the chapters of this book:

- Low-birth-weight infants typically have normal IQs if they are reared in middle-class homes, but they have a high risk of retardation if they are reared in nonstimulating poverty-level homes (Bradley et al., 1994).

- Prenatally malnourished infants, or those with other complications during pregnancy or delivery, develop more or less normally if they attend highly stimulating special preschools, but they have significantly lower IQs if reared at home by low-education mothers (Breitmayer & Ramey, 1986; Zeskind & Ramey, 1981).

- Children born with cytomegalovirus are much more likely to have learning problems in school if they are reared in poverty-level environments than if they are reared in middle-class families (Hanshaw et al., 1976).

So far that's fairly straightforward. But let me propose a further, more speculative theoretical step: I think that "vulnerability" in this sense does not remain constant throughout life. A more general proposition, which I suggest as a working hypothesis, is that each time the child's environment falls outside the range of acceptably supporting environments *for that child* (that is, each time a mismatch occurs between the child's needs and what is available), the child becomes *more vulnerable,* while each period during which the child's needs are met makes the child more resilient. For example, I would predict that a temperamentally difficult child whose family environment was nonetheless sufficient to foster a secure attachment will become more resilient, more able to handle the next set of tasks, while a temperamentally easy child who nonetheless developed an insecure attachment would become more vulnerable to later stress or environmental insufficiency.

Furthermore, the qualities of the environment that are critical for a child's optimum development no doubt change as the child passes from one age to another. Responsive and warm interactions with parents seem particularly central in the period from perhaps 6 months to 18 months; richness of cognitive stimulation seems particularly central between perhaps 1 year and 4 years; opportunity for practicing social skills with peers may be especially central at a later age. Thus, as the tasks change with age, the optimum environment will change also. Among other things, this means that the same family may be very good with a child of one age and not so good with a child of another age.

Most generally, this model leads to the conclusion that even the most "vulnerable" child can show improvement if her environment improves markedly. Because some congenitally vulnerable children do not encounter sufficiently supportive environments, their vulnerability will continue to increase. For this reason, early problems will often persist. At the same time, improvement is possible, even likely. *Most* children manage to survive and thrive, despite stresses and vulnerabilities. As Emmy Werner puts it, "We could not help being deeply impressed by the resilience of most children and youth and their capacity for positive change and personal growth" (1986, p. 5).

A Final Point: The Joy of Development

On a similarly optimistic note, I want to end both this chapter and the book by pointing out that in the midst of all the "crises" and "transitions" and "vulnerabilities," development has a special *joyous* quality. When a child masters a new skill, she is not just pleased—she is delighted and will repeat that new skill at length, quite obviously getting vast satisfaction from it. A 5-year-old I once knew learned to draw stars and drew them on everything in sight, including paper, walls, clothes, and napkins. It was so much *fun* to draw stars. A 10-year-old who learns to do cartwheels will delightedly display this new talent to anyone who will watch and will practice endlessly.

The same joyous quality can be part of the family's development as well. Confronting and moving successfully through one of the periodic (and inevitable) upheavals in family life can be immensely pleasing. Watching your child progress, liking your child, enjoying walking or talking together are all deeply satisfying parts of rearing children. When parents cry at their son's or daughter's high school graduation or wedding, it is not merely sentiment. It is an expression of that sense of love, pride, and wonderment that you have gotten this far.

Critical Thinking

What I am suggesting is that resilience or vulnerability is a little like a bank account. Vulnerable children start out with little in the account, while resilient children have a lot. Experience then adds to or subtracts from the account. Does this make sense to you? Can you think of any implications of this concept other than those I have suggested here?

I have used this photo at the end of every edition of this book because it speaks to me so eloquently of the quality of joy, of discovery, that is so much a part of development.

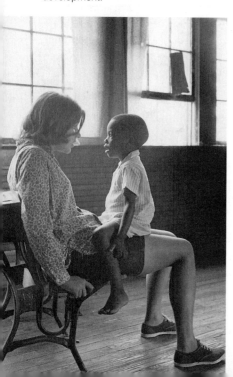

Summary

1. The child's development may be thought of as a series of alternating periods of transition and consolidation. The transitions occur when there are individual major changes or pileups of smaller changes.

2. To understand development we must understand the system, not just the individual parts. A change in any part of the system affects all the other facets.

3. Within infancy, there appear to be at least two transition periods, one at about 2 months, and the other at approximately 8 months.

4. Four key processes appear to underlie the changes we see in infancy: physical maturation, including changes in the nervous system; the child's own explorations of the environment; the process of attachment; and perhaps most broadly, the emergence of the early forms of internal working models.

5. The transition at 18 months is marked by the remarkable emergence of symbolic activity, evidenced in language, in thinking, in play. A general ability to combine words and actions also appears at about this time, with a more sophisticated theory of mind several years later.

6. These cognitive accomplishments combine with major new motor skills to allow the child significantly greater independence, which in turn fosters further cognitive growth.

7. The preschool child basically shifts from dependent to independent behavior and from poor to better impulse control.

8. The transition at ages 5 to 7 is marked by the beginning emergence of still more powerful cognitive skills, by the beginning of school, and by the emergence of a global sense of self-worth.

9. Peer relationships become central for the child's emerging social skills and for the development of skillful social cognition. These relationships are largely gender-segregated.

10. The transition at adolescence is triggered primarily by the physical changes of puberty, but it is accompanied by still further cognitive changes, major alterations in patterns of peer interaction, increases in family disruption, and increases in depression.

11. A shift toward formal operations at adolescence may be one contributor to a rise in self-questioning; pubertal changes may have both direct and indirect effects on the other developments of this period.

12. All facets of development are the product of some combination or interaction of internal and external influences.

13. Five principles can describe the complexity of that interaction: (a) individuals differ in their reactivity to the environment; (b) there is a two-way interplay between individuals and their environments; (c) this interplay occurs within varying ecological frameworks; (d) people *process* their experiences rather than just being passive recipients of them; and (e) people act on their environment, shaping and selecting their experiences.

14. The various facets of development can be arrayed along a continuum from those most affected by internal influences to those most affected by external influences, in the following order: physical development, language, cognition, and social/personality development.

15. Paradoxically, development in the early years of life appears to be both highly canalized and (at extremes of environment) highly sensitive to environmental variation.

16. The early years of life may also be especially important for all children because internal working models are established in that period.

17. Each age period can also be thought of as having a set of central tasks; experiences that are especially important for the successful completion of those tasks will thus be "critical" for that age.

18. Development seems clearly to be made up of a large number of widely shared (if not universal) sequences, but whether broad, structurally different stages occur is less clear.

19. The dimension of vulnerability/ resilience is one way to think about individual differences. The dimension may be defined in terms of the range of environments that will support optimal development for a particular child. A large range implies resilience; a narrow range defines vulnerability.

20. Vulnerability may be increased or decreased over time, depending on the adequacy or inadequacy of environments at each of a series of points in development. Children may thus recover from, or surmount, even very poor starts.

21. For both the child and the parent, development is full of joy as well as travail.

Key Term

canalization Term used to describe the degree to which development during any given period follows some clear, shared "canal" or "channel," difficult to disrupt except by extreme environmental variation.
p. 488

Suggested Readings

Many of the books I have suggested in earlier chapters are relevant here as well, including the Rosenblith (1992), Field (1990), and Osofsky (1987) books on infancy and Montemayor, Adams, and Gulotta's collection of papers on personal relationships in adolescence (Montemayor, Adams, & Gullotta, 1994). Flavell's book on cognitive development (Flavell et al., 1993) also includes an elegant discussion of many of the basic issues I have been talking about in this chapter. In addition, several other books that give the flavor of particular ages:

Collins, W. A. (Ed.). (1984). *Development during middle childhood: The years from six to twelve*. Washington, DC: National Academy Press. This collection of papers is no longer altogether current, but it touches on all facets of school-age children: biology, cognition, self-understanding, family and peer relationships, school, and atypical development. An excellent source of information about this often neglected age period.

Crockett, L. J., & Crouter, A. C. (Eds.). (1995). *Pathways through adolescence*. Mahwah, NJ: Erlbaum. An excellent collection of papers on adolescence, written by many of the current leading researchers.

Feldman, S. S., & Elliott, G. R. (Eds.). (1990). *At the threshold: The developing adolescent*. Cambridge, MA: Harvard University Press. Another good collection of papers on adolescence—an age period that has been "discovered" by psychologists in the past decade.

Shatz, M. (1994). *A toddler's life: Becoming a person*. New York: Oxford University Press. Marilyn Shatz uses her grandson Ricky as an example throughout this engaging book, bringing in research as she goes along.

Glossary

accommodation That part of the adaptation process proposed by Piaget by which a person modifies existing schemes as a result of new experiences or creates new schemes when old ones no longer handle the data. **p. 166**

achievement test Test designed to assess a child's learning of specific material taught in school, such as spelling or arithmetic computation; typically given to all children in designated grades. **p. 202**

acuity Sharpness of perceptual ability-how well or clearly one can see, hear, or use other senses. **p. 140**

adolescent-onset conduct disorder A conduct disorder that begins only in adolescence. Typically less severe and persistent than childhood-onset conduct disorders. **p. 447**

affectional bond A "relatively long-enduring tie in which the partner is important as a unique individual and is interchangeable with none other" (Ainsworth, 1989, p. 711). **p. 319**

aggression Behavior that is aimed at harming or injuring another person or object. **p. 343**

agreeableness One of the "Big Five" personality traits; characterized by trust, generosity, kindness, and sympathy. **p. 260**

alpha-fetoprotein test A prenatal diagnostic test frequently used to screen for the risk of neural tube defects. May also be used in combination with other tests to diagnose Down syndrome and other chromosomal anomalies. **p. 53**

altruism Giving away or sharing objects, time, or goods, with no obvious self-gain. **p. 343**

amniocentesis A medical test for genetic abnormalities in the embryo/fetus, which may be done at 15 to 18 weeks of gestation. **p. 53**

amnion The sac or bag, filled with liquid, in which the embryo and fetus floats during prenatal life. **p. 46**

analytical intelligence One of three types of intelligence in Sternberg's triarchic theory of intelligence; that type of intelligence typi-

cally measured on IQ tests, including analytic thinking, remembering facts, and organizing information. **p. 207**

androgynous One of four sex-role types suggested by the work of Bem and others; label applied to a person whose self-concept includes and whose behavior expresses high levels of both masculine and feminine qualities. **p. 312**

anorexia nervosa A serious eating disorder characterized by extreme dieting, intense fear of gaining weight, and distorted body image. **p. 130**

anoxia A shortage of oxygen. If it is prolonged, it can result in brain damage. This is one of the potential risks at birth. **p. 78**

Apgar score An assessment of the newborn completed by the physician or midwife at 1 minute and again at 5 minutes after birth, assessing five characteristics: heart rate, respiratory rate, muscle tone, response to stimulation, and color. **p. 81**

assimilation That part of the adaptation process proposed by Piaget that involves the "taking in" of new experiences or information into existing schemes. Experience is not taken in "as is," however, but is modified (or interpreted) somewhat so as to fit the preexisting schemes. **p. 166**

attachment An especially intense and central subtype of affectional bond in which the presence of the partner adds a special sense of security, a "safe base," for the individual. Characteristic of the child's bond with the parent. **p. 319**

attachment behavior The collection of (probably) instinctive behaviors of one person toward another that bring about or maintain proximity and caregiving, such as the smile of the young infant; behaviors that reflect an attachment. **p. 319**

attention deficit disorder (ADD) Term sometimes used interchangeably with ADHD, but more properly used to describe

the subset of children who show attention problems without hyperactivity. **p. 453**

attention deficit hyperactivity disorder (ADHD) A disorder in which the child shows both significant problems with attention and physical hyperactivity. **p. 452**

attention problems One of several major categories of psychopathologies, including attention deficit hyperactivity disorder, attention deficit disorder, and hyperkinetic disorder. **p. 446**

authoritarian style One of the three parental styles described by Baumrind, characterized by high levels of control and maturity demands and low levels of nurturance and communication. **p. 385**

authoritative style One of the three parental styles described by Baumrind, characterized by high levels of control, nurturance, maturity demands, and communication. **p. 385**

axon The long appendage-like part of a neuron; the terminal fibers of the axon serve as transmitters in the synaptic connection with the dendrites of other neurons. **p. 49**

babbling The frequently repetitive vocalizing of consonant-vowel combinations by an infant, typically beginning at about 6 months of age. **p. 230**

Babinski reflex A reflex found in very young infants in which they splay out their toes in response to a stroke on the bottom of the foot. **p. 84**

Bayley Scales of Infant Development The best-known and most widely used test of infant "intelligence," revised most recently in 1993. **p. 202**

behavior genetics The study of the genetic basis of behavior, such as intelligence or personality. **p. 5**

Big Five The five primary dimensions of personality variation identified by researchers, including extraversion, agreeableness, con-

495

scientiousness, neuroticism, and openness/intellect. **p. 260**

bilingual education As practiced in the United States, a system of education for non-English-proficient students in which the instruction in reading, writing, and basic subject matter is in the children's native tongue during the first two or three years of schooling, with a gradual transition to full English instruction over several years. **p. 240**

birth order A child's position in the sequence of children within a family, such as firstborn, later-born, or only. **p. 391**

blastocyst Name for the mass of cells from roughly 4 to 10 days after fertilization. **p. 45**

bone age A measure of physical maturation based on X-ray examination of bones, typically the wrist and hand bones. Two children of the same chronological age may have different bone age because they differ in rate of physical maturation. **p. 106**

bulimia An eating disorder characterized by an intense concern about weight combined with binge eating followed by purging, either through self-induced vomiting, excessive use of laxatives, or excessive exercise. **p. 130**

canalization Term used to describe the degree to which development during any given period follows some clear, shared "canal" or "channel," difficult to disrupt except by extreme environmental variation. **p. 488**

cephalocaudal One of two basic patterns of physical development in infancy (the other is proximodistal), describing development that proceeds from the head downward. **p. 86**

cesarean section Delivery of the child through an incision in the mother's abdomen. **p. 77**

childhood-onset conduct disorder Conduct disorder beginning in childhood; linked to rejection by peers and to persistent conduct problems into adolescence and adulthood. **p. 447**

chorion The outer layer of cells during the blastocyst stage of prenatal development, from which both the placenta and the umbilical cord are formed. **p. 46**

chorionic villus sampling A technique for prenatal genetic diagnosis, involving taking a sample of cells from the placenta. Can be performed earlier in the pregnancy than amniocentesis but carries slightly higher risks. **p. 53**

chromosomes The structures carrying genetic information, arrayed in 23 pairs in each cell in the body. Each chromosome is made up of many segments, called genes. **p. 39**

class inclusion The relationship between classes of objects, such that a subordinate class is included in a superordinate class, as bananas are part of the class "fruit" and the class "fruit" is included in the class "food." **p. 181**

classical conditioning One of three major types of learning. An automatic unconditioned response such as an emotion or a reflex comes to be triggered by a new cue, called the conditional stimulus (CS), after the CS has been paired several times with the original unconditional stimulus. **p. 21**

clinical depression A combination of sad mood, sleep and eating disturbances, and difficulty concentrating, lasting six months or longer. **p. 450**

clique Defined by Dunphy as a group of four to six friends with strong affectional bonds and high levels of group solidarity and loyalty; currently used by researchers to describe a self-chosen group of friends, in contrast to reputation-based crowds. **p. 340**

cohort A group of persons of approximately the same age who have shared similar major life experiences, such as cultural training, historical events, or general economic conditions. **p. 25**

colic A pattern of persistent and often inconsolable crying, totaling more than 3 hours a day, found in some infants in the first 3 to 4 months of life. **p. 92**

collectivism A cultural perspective or belief system, contrasted with individualism, in which the emphasis is on collective rather than individual identity, and on group solidarity, decision making, duties and obligations. Characteristic of most Asian, Latino, and African cultures. **p. 12**

color constancy The ability to see the color of an object as remaining the same despite changes in illumination or shadow. One of the basic perceptual constancies that make up object constancy. **p. 151**

competence The level of skill displayed by a person under ideal or perfect circumstances. It is not possible to measure competence directly. **p. 202**

concrete operations stage The stage of development between ages 6 and 12, as proposed by Piaget, in which mental operations such as subtraction, reversibility, and multiple classification are acquired. **p. 167**

conditional stimulus In classical conditioning, the stimulus that, after being paired a number of times with an unconditional stimulus, comes to trigger the unconditioned response. (E.g., the sound of the mother's footsteps may become a conditional stimulus for the baby's turning his head as if to suck.) **p. 21**

conduct disorder Diagnostic term for a pattern of deviant behavior including high levels of aggressive, antisocial, or delinquent acts. **p. 446**

conscientiousness One of the "Big Five" personality traits, characterized by efficiency, organization, planfulness, and reliability. **p. 260**

conservation The concept that objects remain the same in fundamental ways, such as weight or number, even when there are external changes in shape or arrangement. Typically understood by children after age 5. **p. 174**

constraint As used in discussions of language development, this refers to presumed built-in or early-learned assumptions ("default options") by which a child figures out what words refer to. Examples include the principle of contrast and the whole object constraint. **p. 242**

constructivism A key concept in Piaget's theory, that from birth a child is actively engaged in a process of constructing an understanding both of his own actions and of the external world. **p. 187**

control group The group of subjects in an experiment that receives either no special treatment or some neutral treatment. **p. 29**

conventional morality The second level of moral judgment proposed by Kohlberg, in which the person's judgments are dominated by considerations of group values and laws. **p. 363**

conventional rules One of the two types of rules suggested by Turiel: arbitrary, socially defined rules specific to a particular culture, subculture, or group, such as "Don't run in the halls" or "Smoking allowed only in designated areas." **p. 360**

cooing An early phase of the prelinguistic period, from about 1 to 4 months of age, when vowel sounds are repeated, particularly the uuu sound. **p. 230**

correlation A statistic used to describe the degree or strength of a relationship between two variables. It can range from +1.00 to -1.00. The closer it is to 1.00, the stronger the relationship being described. **p. 32**

cortex The convoluted gray portion of the brain, which governs most complex thought, language, and memory. **p. 108**

creative intelligence One of three types of intelligence described by Sternberg in his triarchic theory of intelligence; includes insight and the ability to see new relationships among events or experiences. **p. 207**

critical period Any time period during development when the organism is especially responsive to and learns from a specific type of stimulation. The same stimulation at other points in development has little or no effect. **p. 9**

cross-cultural research Research involving in-depth study of another culture, or research involving comparisons of several cultures or subcultures. **p. 24**

cross-modal transfer The ability to transfer information gained through one sense to another sense at a later time; for example, identifying visually something you had previously explored only tactually. **p. 150**

cross-sectional design A form of research in which samples of subjects from several different age groups are studied at the same time. **p. 24**

cross-sequential design A complex combination of cross-sectional and longitudinal research designs in which groups of subjects of several different ages are initially selected and compared, and then all groups are followed longitudinally. **p. 27**

crowd Defined by Dunphy as a larger and looser group of friends than a clique, normally made up of several cliques joined together; defined by current researchers as a reputation-based group, common in adolescent subculture, with widely agreed-upon characteristics (e.g., "brains," "jocks," or "druggies"). **p. 340**

culture A system of meanings and customs shared by some identifiable group or subgroup, and transmitted from one generation of that group to the next. **p. 12**

cumulative deficit Any difference between groups in IQ (or achievement test) scores that becomes larger over time. **p. 210**

deductive logic Reasoning from the general to the particular, from a rule to an expected instance, or from a theory to a hypothesis. Characteristic of formal operations thinking. **p. 181**

delinquency A subcategory of conduct disorders involving explicit lawbreaking. **p. 448**

dendrites The branch-like part of a neuron that forms one half of a synaptic connection to other nerves. Dendrites develop rapidly in the final two prenatal months and the first year after birth. **p. 49**

deoxyribonucleic acid Called DNA for short, this is the chemical of which genes are composed. **p. 40**

dependent variable The variable in an experiment that is expected to show the impact of manipulations of the independent variable; also called the outcome variable. **p. 29**

depression A combination of sad mood, sleep and eating disturbances, and difficulty concentrating. When all these symptoms are present, the condition is usually called clinical depression. **p. 450**

developmental psychopathology A relatively new approach to the study of deviance that emphasizes that normal and abnormal development have common roots and that pathology can arise from many different pathways or systems. **p. 444**

dilation A key process in the first stage of childbirth, when the cervix widens sufficiently to allow the infant's head to pass into the birth canal. Full dilation is 10 centimeters. **p. 72**

dizygotic twins See fraternal twins. **p. 44**

Down syndrome A genetic anomaly in which every cell contains three copies of chromosome 21 rather than two. Children born with this genetic pattern are usually mentally retarded and have characteristic physical features. **p. 51**

effacement The flattening of the cervix, which, along with dilation, is a key process of the first stage of childbirth. **p. 72**

ego In Freudian theory, that portion of the personality that organizes, plans, and keeps the person in touch with reality. Language and thought are both ego functions. **p. 19**

egocentrism A cognitive state in which the individual (typically a child) sees the world only from his own perspective, without awareness that there are other perspectives. **p. 174**

embryo The name given to the developing organism during the period of prenatal development from about 2 to 8 weeks after conception, beginning with implantation of the blastocyst into the uterine wall. **p. 46**

emotional intelligence A type of intelligence proposed by Daniel Goleman, including "abilities such as being able to motivate oneself and persist in the face of frustrations; to control impulses and delay gratification; to regulate one's moods and keep distress from swamping the ability to think; to empathize and to hope" (1995b, p. 34). **p. 208**

empathy As defined by Hoffman, "a vicarious affective response that does not necessarily match another's affective state but is more appropriate to the other's situation than to one's own" (1984, p. 285). **p. 355**

empiricism Opposite of nativism. The theoretical point of view that all perceptual skill arises from experience. **p. 139**

endocrine glands Glands—including the adrenals, the thyroid, the pituitary, the testes, and the ovaries—that secrete hormones governing overall physical growth and sexual maturing. **p. 110**

English as a second language (ESL) An alternative to bilingual education; non-English-proficient students spend most of their school day in a full-English classroom but then spend several hours in a separate class with special instruction in English. **p. 240**

equilibration The third part of the adaptation process, as proposed by Piaget, involving a periodic restructuring of schemes into new structures. **p. 166**

estrogen The female sex hormone secreted by the ovaries. **p. 112**

ethnic group "A subgroup whose members are perceived by themselves and others to have a common origin and culture, and shared activities in which the common origin or culture is an essential ingredient" (Porter & Washington, 1993, p. 140). **p. 432**

ethnography A detailed description of a single culture or context, based on extensive observation by a resident observer. **p. 27**

executive processes Proposed subset of information processes involving organizing and planning strategies. Similar in meaning to metacognition. **p. 193**

experiment A research strategy in which subjects are assigned randomly to experimental and control groups. The experimental group is then provided with some designated experience that is expected to alter behavior in some fashion. **p. 28**

experimental group The group (or groups) of subjects in an experiment that is given a special treatment intended to produce some specific consequence. **p. 29**

expressive language Term used to describe the child's skill in speaking and communicating orally. **p. 231**

expressive style One of two styles of early language proposed by Nelson, characterized by low rates of nounlike terms and high use of personal-social words and phrases. **p. 252**

externalizing problems One of several major categories of psychopathology, including any deviant behavior primarily directed away from the individual, such as conduct disorders. **p. 446**

extraversion One of the "Big Five" personality traits, characterized by assertiveness, energy, enthusiasm, and outgoingness. **p. 260**

extremely low birth weight Any birth weight below 1000 grams (2.2 pounds). **p. 78**

fallopian tube The tube between the ovary and the uterus down which the ovum travels to the uterus and in which conception usually occurs. **p. 39**

false belief Incorrectly believing something to be true, and acting on that belief. The child's understanding of the principle of false belief is one key sign of the emergence of a representational theory of mind. **p. 176**

family day care Nonparental care in which the child is cared for in someone else's home, usually with a small group of other children. **p. 408**

feminine One of four sex-role types suggested by the work of Bem and others; a pattern of high scores on femininity measures and low scores on masculinity measures. **p. 312**

fetal alcohol syndrome (FAS) A pattern of physical and mental abnormalities, including mental retardation and minor physical anomalies, found often in children born to alcoholic mothers. **p. 57**

fetus The name given to the developing organism from about 8 weeks after conception until birth. **p. 47**

fontanels The "soft spots" in the skull that are present at birth. These disappear when the several bones of the skull grow together. **p. 106**

foreclosure One of four identity statuses proposed by Marcia, involving an ideological or occupational commitment without a previous reevaluation. **p. 295**

formal operations stage Piaget's name for the fourth and final major stage of cognitive development, occurring during adolescence, when the child becomes able to manipulate and organize ideas as well as objects. **p. 167**

fraternal twins Children carried in the same pregnancy but resulting from two separate fertilized ova. No more alike genetically than other pairs of brothers and sisters. Also called dizygotic twins. **p. 44**

gametes Sperm and ova. These cells, unlike all other cells of the body, contain only 23 chromosomes rather than 23 pairs. **p. 40**

gender concept Term used to describe the full understanding that gender is permanent and constant, unchanged by appearance. **p. 303**

gender constancy The final step in developing a gender concept, in which the child understands that gender doesn't change even though there are external changes in things like clothing or hair length. **p. 305**

gender identity The first step in gender concept development, in which the child labels herself correctly and categorizes others correctly as male or female. **p. 304**

gender schema theory A theory explaining gender concept and sex-role behavior development; proposes that each child creates a fundamental schema beginning at age 18 months or younger, by which the child categorizes people, objects, activities, and qualities by gender. **p. 309**

gender stability The second step in gender concept development, in which the child understands that a person's gender continues to be stable throughout the lifetime. **p. 304**

gene A uniquely coded segment of DNA in a chromosome that affects one or more specific body processes or developments. **p. 40**

genotype The pattern of characteristics and developmental sequences mapped in the genes of any specific individual. Will be modified by individual experience into the phenotype. **p. 39**

gifted Normally defined in terms of very high IQ (above 130 or 140), but may also be defined in terms of remarkable skill in one or more specific areas, such as mathematics, music, or memory. **p. 461**

glial cells One of two major classes of cells making up the nervous system, glial cells provide the firmness and structure, the "glue" to hold the system together. **p. 47**

goal-corrected partnership Term used by Bowlby to describe the form of an appropriate child-to-parent attachment in the preschool years in which the two partners, through improved communication, negotiate the form and frequency of contact between them. **p. 325**

gonadotropic hormones Two hormones secreted by the pituitary—follicle-stimulating hormone (FSH) and luteinizing hormone (LH)—that, at the beginning of puberty, stimulate the development of the glands in the testes and ovaries that then begin to secrete testosterone or estrogen. **p. 112**

grand schemes Phrase used in this book to describe the three most comprehensive theories of development: psychoanalytic, cognitive-developmental, and learning theories. **p. 17**

habituation An automatic decrease in the intensity of a response to a repeated stimulus, enabling a child or adult to ignore the familiar and focus attention on the novel. **p. 87**

hedonistic reasoning A form of prosocial moral reasoning described by Eisenberg in which the child is concerned with self-oriented consequences rather than moral considerations. Roughly equivalent to Kohlberg's stage 2. **p. 367**

heterozygous Term describing the genetic pattern when the pair of genes at any given genetic locus carry different instructions, such as a gene for blue eyes from one parent and for brown eyes from the other parent. **p. 41**

holophrase A combination of a gesture with a single word that conveys a sentence-like meaning; often seen and heard in children between 12 and 18 months. **p. 235**

homozygous Term describing the genetic pattern when the pair of genes at any given genetic locus carry the same instructions. **p. 41**

hyperkinetic syndrome Label used in Europe in place of attention deficit hyperactivity disorder. **p. 453**

hypothetico-deductive reasoning Piaget's term for the form of reasoning that is part of formal operational thought, involving not just deductive logic but more broadly the ability to consider hypotheses and hypothetical possibilities. **p. 188**

id In Freudian theory, the first, primitive portion of the personality; the storehouse of basic energy, continually pushing for immediate gratification. **p. 19**

identical twins Children carried in the same pregnancy who come from the same originally fertilized ovum. They are genetic clones of one another. Also called monozygotic twins. **p. 45**

identification The process of taking into oneself ("incorporating") the qualities and ideas of another person, which Freud thought was the result of the Oedipus conflict at ages 3 to 5. The child attempts to become like the parent of the same sex. **p. 277**

identity achievement One of four identity statuses proposed by Marcia, involving the successful resolution of an identity "crisis," resulting in a new commitment. **p. 295**

identity diffusion One of four identity statuses proposed by Marcia, involving neither a current reevaluation nor a firm personal commitment. **p. 295**

identity statuses Four categories suggested by James Marcia, created by combining high and low identity crisis and high and low identity commitment: identity achievement, moratorium, foreclosure, and identity diffusion. **p. 295**

implantation Process by which the blastocyst attaches itself to the wall of the uterus, generally during the second week after fertilization. **p. 46**

inclusive education Term used broadly to describe the education of physically, mentally, or emotionally disabled children in regular classrooms, with any special services required by the child provided in that classroom. **p. 462**

independent variable A condition or event an experimenter varies in some systematic way in order to observe the impact of that variation on the subjects' behavior. **p. 29**

individualism A cultural perspective or belief system, contrasted with collectivism, in which the emphasis is placed on the separateness and independence of individual development and behavior. Characteristic of most Western cultures. **p. 12**

individuation Label used by some theorists for the process of psychological, social, and physical separation from parents that begins in adolescence. **p. 326**

inductive logic Reasoning from the particular to the general, from experience to broad rules. Characteristic of concrete operations thinking. **p. 180**

infant mortality Death at birth or at any time during the first year of life. The incidence of such deaths in any given country or subgroup is called the infant mortality rate. **p. 65**

infant-directed speech The formal scientific term for "motherese"; that special form of simplified, higher-pitched speech adults use with infants and young children. **p. 246**

inflections The various grammatical "markers" such as the *s* for plurals or the *ed* for past tenses, auxiliary verbs such as *is*, and the equivalent. **p. 235**

information processing approach Phrase used to refer to a new, third approach to the study of intellectual development that focuses on changes with age and individual differences in fundamental intellectual skills. **p. 164**

insecure attachment An internal working model of relationship in which the child does not as readily use the parent as a safe base and is not readily consoled by the parent if upset. Includes three subtypes of attachment: ambivalent, avoidant, and disorganized/disoriented. **p. 329**

intelligence Defined in various ways by different psychologists. Most definitions include the ability to reason abstractly, the ability to profit from experience, and the ability to adapt to varying environmental contexts. **p. 199**

intelligence quotient (IQ) Originally defined in terms of a child's mental age and chronological age, IQ scores are now computed by comparing a child's performance with that of other children of the same chronological age. **p. 199**

internal model of experience Currently popular theoretical concept emphasizing that each child creates a set of core ideas or beliefs about the nature of relationships, the self, and the world. The most commonly discussed example is the child's "inner working model" of attachment. **p. 9**

internal working model As applied to social relationships, a cognitive construction, for which the earliest relationships may form the template, of the workings of relationships, such as expectations of support or affection, trustworthiness, and so on. **p. 328**

internalizing problems One of several major categories of psychopathology, in which the deviant behavior is directed inward, including anxiety and depression. **p. 446**

intersensory integration The combining of information from two or more senses to form a unified perceptual whole, such as the sight of mouth movements combined with the sound of particular words. **p. 150**

intrinsic reinforcements Those inner sources of pleasure, pride, or satisfaction that serve to increase the likelihood that an individual will repeat the behavior that led to the feeling. **p. 22**

jargon A form of babbling in which the infant strings together a series of different vowel-consonant combinations rather than repeating the same combination over and over. **p. 230**

learning disability (LD) A term broadly used to describe a child's unexpected or unexplained problem in learning to read, spell, or calculate. More precisely used to refer to a subgroup of such children who have some neurological dysfunction. **p. 459**

libido The term used by Freud to describe the pool of sexual energy in each individual. **p. 18**

longitudinal design A research design in which the same subjects are observed or assessed repeatedly over a period of months or years. **p. 24**

low birth weight (LBW) Any baby born with a weight below 2500 grams (5.5 pounds) is given this label, including both those born too early (preterm) and those who are "small for date." **p. 78**

masculine One of four sex-role types suggested by the work of Bem and others; a pattern of high scores on masculinity measures and low scores on femininity measures. **p. 312**

maturation The sequential unfolding of physical characteristics, governed by instructions contained in the genetic code and shared by all members of a species. **p. 4**

mean length of utterance (MLU) The average number of meaningful units in a sentence. Each basic word is one meaningful unit, as is each inflection. **p. 251**

medulla A portion of the brain that lies immediately above the spinal cord; largely developed at birth. **p. 107**

menarche Onset of menstruation in girls. **p. 113**

mental age Term used by Binet and Simon and Terman in the early calculation of IQ scores; the age level of IQ test items the child can successfully pass. When compared to the child's chronological age, allows calculation of an IQ score. **p. 199**

mental retardation Defined most often as an IQ below 70 combined with poor adaptive behavior. **p. 457**

metacognition General and rather loosely used term describing an individual's knowledge of his own thinking processes: knowing what you know, and how you go about learning or remembering. **p. 177**

metamemory A subcategory of metacognition; knowledge about your own memory processes. **p. 177**

midbrain A section of the brain lying above the medulla and below the cortex that regulates attention, sleeping, waking, and other "automatic" functions; largely developed at birth. **p. 107**

minitheories Term used in this text to describe the narrower, more limited types of theories designed to explain only a particular, somewhat specific phenomenon. **p. 17**

modeling A term used by Bandura and others to describe observational learning. **p. 22**

models Term used in this book to describe the middle level of theories, less comprehensive than a grand scheme, but broader than a minitheory; examples are biological and ecological models. **p. 17**

monozygotic twins See identical twins. **p. 45**

moral rules One of the two types of rules suggested by Turiel: rules seen as universal and obligatory, reflecting basic principles that guarantee the rights of others. **p. 360**

moratorium One of four identity statuses proposed by Marcia, involving an ongoing reexamination but without a new commitment as yet. **p. 295**

Moro reflex When startled (e.g., by a loud sound or a sensation of being dropped), the infant extends his legs, arms, and fingers, arches his back, and draws back his head. **p. 84**

motherese See infant-directed speech. **p. 246**

motor development Growth and change in ability to perform both gross motor skills (such as walking or throwing) and fine motor skills (such as drawing or writing). **p. 119**

myelin Material making up an insulating sheath that develops around the axon in most neurons. This sheath is not completely developed at birth but develops over the first several years of life. **p. 109**

myelination The process by which myelin is added. **p. 109**

nativism See empiricism. The view that perceptual skills are inborn and do not require experience to develop. **p. 139**

needs-oriented reasoning A form of prosocial moral reasoning proposed by Eisenberg in which the child expresses concern directly for the other person's need, even if the other's need conflicts with the child's own wishes or desires. **p. 367**

negative reinforcement The strengthening of a behavior because of the removal or cessation of an unpleasant stimulus. **p. 21**

neglected children Type of unpopular children who are not overtly rejected and are reasonably well liked but are not often chosen as friends. **p. 346**

neglecting style A fourth major parenting style, suggested by Maccoby and Martin, involving low levels of both acceptance and control. **p. 385**

neural tube A hollow cylinder formed in the first weeks after conception, out of which both the brain and spinal cord eventually develop. **p. 47**

neuron The second major class of cells in the nervous system, neurons are responsible for transmission and reception of nerve impulses. **p. 47**

neuroticism One of the "Big Five" personality traits, characterized by anxiety, self-pity, tenseness, and emotional instability. **p. 260**

neurotransmitters Chemicals at synapses that accomplish the transmission of signals from one neuron to another. **p. 49**

obesity Most often defined as a body weight 20 percent or more above the normal weight for height, or a body mass index at the 85th percentile or above. **p. 126**

object constancy The general phrase describing the ability to see objects as remaining the same despite changes in retinal image. **p. 151**

object permanence Part of the object concept. The recognition that an object continues to exist even when it is temporarily out of sight. **p. 152**

objective self Second major step in the development of the self-concept; awareness of the self as an object with properties. **p. 289**

observational learning Learning of motor skills, attitudes, or other behaviors through watching someone else perform them. **p. 22**

Oedipus conflict The pattern of events Freud believed occurred between ages 3 and 5, when the child experiences a "sexual" desire for the parent of the opposite sex; the resulting fear of possible reprisal from the parent of the same sex is resolved when the child "identifies" with the parent of the same sex. **p. 276**

openness/intellect One of the "Big Five" personality traits, characterized by curiosity, imagination, insight, originality, and wide interests. **p. 260**

operant conditioning That type of learning in which the probability of a person performing some behavior is strengthened by positive or negative reinforcements. **p. 21**

operation Term used by Piaget for complex, internal, abstract, reversible schemes, first seen at about age 6. **p. 167**

ordinal position See birth order. **p. 391**

ossification The process of hardening by which soft tissue becomes bone. **p. 106**

otitis media The technical name for what most parents call an ear infection: the collection of fluid in the middle ear, often accompanied by other symptoms of acute illness. **p. 96**

overregularization The tendency on the part of children to make the language regular by creating regularized versions of irregular speech forms, such as past tenses or plurals—for example (in English), beated or footses. **p. 238**

ovum The gamete produced by a woman, which, if fertilized by a sperm from a man, forms the basis for the developing organism. **p. 39**

parallel play Form of play seen in toddlers, in which two children play next to, but not with, one another. **p. 334**

partial reinforcement Reinforcement of behavior on some schedule less frequent than every occasion. **p. 22**

perceptual constancies A collection of constancies, including shape, size, and color constancy. **p. 151**

performance test A new category of criterion-referenced test used in some school systems today, in which students are required to demonstrate actual skills, such as writing, performing experiments, or mathematical reasoning, with performance assessed against a specified criterion. **p. 204**

performance The behavior shown by a person under real-life rather than perfect or ideal circumstances. Even when we are interested in competence, all we can ever measure is performance. **p. 202**

permissive style One of the three parenting styles described by Baumrind, characterized by high levels of nurturance and low levels of control, maturity demands, and communication. **p. 385**

personality The collection of individual, relatively enduring patterns of reacting to and interacting with others that distinguishes each child or adult. Temperament is thought of as the emotional substrate of personality. **p. 259**

phenotype The expression of a particular set of genetic information in a specific environment; the observable result of the joint operation of genetic and environmental influences. **p. 45**

placenta An organ that develops during gestation between the fetus and the wall of the uterus. The placenta filters nutrients from the mother's blood, acting as liver, lungs, and kidneys for the fetus. **p. 46**

polygenic inheritance Any pattern of genetic transmission in which multiple genes contribute to the outcome, such as is presumed to occur for complex behaviors such as intelligence or temperament. **p. 44**

positive reinforcement Strengthening of a behavior by the presentation of some pleasurable or positive stimulus. **p. 21**

postconventional morality See principled morality. **p. 363**

postpartum depression A severe form of the common experience of postpartum blues. Affecting perhaps 15 percent of women, this form of clinical depression typically lasts six to eight weeks. **p. 83**

practical intelligence One of three types of intelligence in Sternberg's triarchic theory of intelligence; often also called "street smarts," this type of intelligence includes skill in adapting to an environment and in adapting an environment to one's own needs. **p. 207**

pragmatics The rules for the use of language in communicative interaction, such as the rules for taking turns, the style of speech appropriate for varying listeners, and the equivalent. **p. 243**

preconventional morality The first level of morality proposed by Kohlberg, in which moral judgments are dominated by consideration of what will be punished and what feels good. **p. 362**

prelinguistic phase The period before the child speaks her first words. **p. 229**

preoperational stage Piaget's term for the second major stage of cognitive development, from age 18 months to about age 6, marked at the beginning by the ability to use symbols and by the development of basic classification and logical abilities. **p. 167**

preterm infant Descriptive phrase widely used to label infants born before 38 weeks gestational age. **p. 79**

primary circular reactions Piaget's phrase to describe the baby's simple repetitive actions in the second substage of the sensorimotor stage, organized around the baby's own body; the baby repeats some action in order to have some desired outcome occur again, such as putting his thumb in his mouth to repeat the good feeling of sucking. **p. 168**

primitive reflexes Collection of reflexes seen in young infants, controlled by the more primitive parts of the brain, that gradually disappear during the first year of life, including the Moro, Babinski, and stepping reflexes. **p. 84**

principled morality The third level of morality proposed by Kohlberg, in which considerations of justice, individual rights, and contracts dominate moral judgment. **p. 363**

production deficiency Phrase used to describe a situation in which an individual can use some physical or mental strategy if reminded to do so, but fails to "produce" the strategy spontaneously. **p. 182**

prosocial behavior See altruism. **p. 343**

proximodistal One of two basic patterns of physical development in infancy (the other is cephalocaudal), describing development that proceeds from the center outward, such as from the trunk to the limbs. **p. 86**

psychosexual stages The stages of personality development suggested by Freud, in-

cluding the oral, anal, phallic, latency, and genital stages. **p. 19, 276**

psychosocial stages The stages of personality development suggested by Erikson, including trust, autonomy, initiative, industry, identity, intimacy, generativity, and ego integrity. **p. 19, 279**

puberty The collection of hormonal and physical changes at adolescence that brings about sexual maturity. **p. 112**

punishment Unpleasant consequences, administered after some undesired behavior by a child or adult, with the intent of extinguishing the behavior. **p. 22**

reaction range Term used by some psychologists for the range of possible outcomes (phenotypes) on some variable, given basic genetic patterning (genotype). In the case of IQ scores, the reaction range is estimated at 20 to 25 points. **p. 217**

receptive language A term used to describe the child's ability to understand (receive) language, as contrasted to his ability to express language. **p. 231**

reciprocal friendship Any friendship in which the two partners each name the other as a friend; also a quality of friendship in school-age children, when friendship is for the first time perceived as being based on reciprocal trust. **p. 337**

referential style The second style of early language proposed by Nelson, characterized by emphasis on objects and their naming and description. **p. 253**

reflexes Automatic body reactions to specific stimulation, such as the knee jerk or the Moro reflex. Many reflexes remain among adults, but the newborn also has some "primitive" reflexes that disappear as the cortex develops. **p. 83**

rejected children Unpopular children who are not just ignored but are explicitly avoided, not chosen as playmates or friends. **p. 346**

relational aggression A form of aggression aimed at damaging the other person's self-esteem or peer relationships, such as by using ostracism or threats of ostracism, cruel gossiping, or facial expressions of disdain. **p. 345**

respiratory distress syndrome A problem frequently found in infants born more than 6 weeks before term in which the infant's lungs lack the chemical surfactant needed to keep air sacs inflated. **p. 79**

responsiveness An aspect of parent-child interaction; a responsive parent is sensitive to the child's cues and reacts appropriately, following the child's lead. **p. 380**

reversibility One of the most critical of the "operations" Piaget identified as part of the concrete operations period. The child understands that actions can be reversed, thus returning to a previous state. **p. 180**

rooting reflex Stroke an infant on the cheek near the mouth and the baby will reflexively turn toward the touch, open his mouth, and make sucking movements. **p. 84**

rubella A form of measles that, if contracted during the first few weeks of a pregnancy, may have severe effects on the developing embryo or fetus. **p. 55**

scaffolding Term used by Bruner to describe the process by which a teacher (parent, older child, or person in the official role of teacher) structures a learning encounter with a child, so as to lead the child from step to step—a process consistent with Vygotsky's theory of cognitive development. **p. 20**

schematic learning The development of expectancies of what actions lead to what results, or what events tend to go together. Classical conditioning may be thought of as a subset of schematic learning. **p. 87**

scheme Piaget's word for the basic actions of knowing, including both physical actions (sensorimotor schemes, such as looking or reaching) and mental actions (such as classifying or comparing or reversing). An experience is assimilated to a scheme, and the scheme is modified or created through accommodation. **p. 165**

secondary circular reactions Repetitive actions in the third substage of the sensorimotor period, oriented around external objects; the infant repeats some action in order to have some outside event recur, such as hitting a mobile repeatedly to watch it move. **p. 168**

secular trends Patterns of change in some characteristic over several cohorts, such as systematic changes in the average timing of menarche or average height or weight. **p. 114**

secure attachment An internal working model of relationship in which the child uses the parent as a safe base and is readily consoled after separation, when fearful, or when otherwise stressed. **p. 329**

self-concept The "me" aspect of self; the set of qualities attributed to the self. **p. 288**

self-esteem A global judgement of self-worth; how well you like who you perceive yourself to be; how well you measure up when judged against your own valued qualities or skills. **p. 299**

semantics The rules for conveying meaning in language. **p. 228**

sensitive period Similar to a critical period except broader and less specific. A time in development when a particular type of stimulation is particularly important or effective. **p. 9**

sensorimotor stage Piaget's term for the first major stage of cognitive development, from birth to about 18 months, when the child moves from reflexive to voluntary action. **p. 167**

sequential design A family of research designs involving multiple cross-sectional, or multiple longitudinal, studies, or a combination of the two. **p. 24**

sex role The set of behaviors, attitudes, rights, duties, and obligations that are part of the "role" of being a boy or a girl, a male or a female in any given culture. **p. 303**

sex-linked transmission Pattern of genetic transmission that occurs when the critical gene is carried on a portion of the X chromosome that is not matched by genetic material on the Y chromosome. Diseases such as hemophilia follow this genetic pattern. **p. 43**

sex-role behavior The performance of behavior that matches the culturally defined sex role, such as choosing "sex-appropriate" toys or playing with same-sex children. **p. 304**

sex-typing See sex-role behavior. **p. 304**

sexually transmitted diseases (STDs) Also called venereal diseases. Category of disease spread by sexual contact, including chlamydia, genital warts, syphilis, gonorrhea, and HIV. **p. 128**

shape constancy The ability to see an object's shape as remaining the same despite changes in the shape of the retinal image. A basic perceptual constancy. **p. 151**

size constancy The ability to see an object's size as remaining the same despite changes in size of the retinal image. A key element in this constancy is the ability to judge depth. **p. 151**

small-for-date infant An infant who weighs less than is normal for the number of weeks of gestation completed. **p. 79**

social class Term widely used to describe broad variations in economic and social positions within any given society. Four broad groups are most often described: upper class, middle class, working class, and lower class (also called poverty level). For an individual family, the designation is based on the income, occupation, and education of the adults in the household. **p. 209, 427**

social cognition Term used to describe an area of research and theory focused on the child's understanding of social relationships. **p. 353**

social referencing Using another person's emotional reaction to some situation as a basis for deciding one's own reaction. A baby does this when she checks her parent's facial expression or body language before responding positively or negatively to something new. **p. 156**

Stanford-Binet The best-known U.S. intelligence test. It was written by Lewis Terman and his associates on the basis of the first tests by Binet and Simon. **p. 199**

Strange Situation A series of episodes used by Mary Ainsworth and others in studies of attachment. The child is observed with the mother, with a stranger, alone, and when reunited with stranger and mother. **p. 329**

structured immersion An alternative to traditional bilingual education in which all children in a given classroom speak the same non-English native tongue. All basic instruction is in English, paced so that the

children can comprehend, with the teacher translating only when absolutely necessary. **p. 240**

subjective self The first major step in the development of the self-concept; the initial awareness that "I exist" separate from others. **p. 289**

submersion Label used to describe programs for non-English-proficient students in which they are simply assigned to a regular English-speaking classroom without any supplemental language assistance. Also known as "sink or swim" programs. **p. 240**

sudden infant death syndrome (SIDS) Unexpected death of an infant who otherwise appears healthy. Also called crib death. Cause is unknown. **p. 97**

superego In Freudian theory, the "conscience" part of personality that develops as a result of the identification process. The superego contains the parental and societal values and attitudes incorporated by the child. **p. 19**

synapse The point of communication between two neurons, where nerve impulses are passed from one neuron to another by means of chemicals called neurotransmitters. **p. 49**

syntax The rules for forming sentences; also called grammar. **p. 228**

telegraphic speech Term used by Roger Brown to describe the earliest sentences created by most children, because these sentences sound a bit like telegrams, including key nouns and verbs but generally omitting all other words and grammatical inflections. **p. 236**

temperament Term sometimes used interchangeably with personality, but best thought of as the emotional substrate of personality, at least partially genetically determined. **p. 262**

teratogen Any outside agent, such as a disease or a chemical, that causes a birth defect. **p. 9**

tertiary circular reactions The deliberate experimentation with variations of previous actions, characteristic of the fifth substage of sensorimotor intelligence, according to Piaget. **p. 168**

theory A relatively broad explanatory system, with specific assumptions and propositions, designed to explain some set of observations. **p. 17**

theory of mind A phrase used to describe one aspect of the thinking of 4- and 5-year-olds, when they show signs of understanding not only that other people think differently, but that other people will base their behavior on what they believe or know or feel rather than on the visible situation. **p. 176**

time-lag design A comparison of groups of subjects of the same age in different cohorts, such as studying drug use in a separate sample of 15-year-olds each year for 20 years; allows a direct examination of cohort changes in some behavior. **p. 27**

tracking Also called smooth pursuit. The smooth movements of the eye used to follow the track of some moving object. **p. 141**

triarchic theory of intelligence A theory advanced by Robert Sternberg, proposing the existence of three types of intelligence: analytical, creative, and practical. **p. 206**

ultrasound A form of prenatal diagnosis in which high-frequency sound waves are used to provide a picture of the moving fetus. Can be used to detect many physical deformities, such as neural tube defects, as well as multiple pregnancies and to determine gestational age. **p. 53**

umbilical cord The cord connecting the embryo/fetus to the placenta, containing two arteries and one vein. **p. 46**

unconditional stimulus In classical conditioning, the cue or signal that automatically triggers the unconditioned response. A touch on a baby's cheek, triggering head turning, is an unconditional stimulus. **p. 21**

unconditioned response In classical conditioning, the basic unlearned response that is triggered by the unconditional stimulus. A baby's turning of his head when touched on the cheek is an unconditioned response. **p. 21**

undifferentiated One of four sex-role types suggested by the work of Bem and others; a pattern of low scores on both masculinity and femininity measures. **p. 312**

uterus The female organ in which the blastocyst implants itself and within which the embryo/fetus develops. (Popularly referred to as the womb.) **p. 39**

utilization deficiency Term used by researchers to describe the use of some specific strategy without deriving benefit from it. **p. 185**

very low birth weight Any birth weight below 1500 grams (3.3 pounds). **p. 78**

warmth versus hostility The key dimension of emotional tone used to describe family interactions. **p. 380**

WISC-III The most recent revision of the Wechsler Intelligence Scale for Children, a well-known IQ test developed in the United States that includes both verbal and performance (nonverbal) subtests. **p. 201**

zone of proximal development In Vygotsky's theory, the zone is that range of tasks or skills that is slightly too difficult for a child to do alone but that she can do successfully with guidance or "scaffolding" by an adult or more experienced child. **p. 20**

References

Abma, J. C., Chandra, A., Mosher, W. D., Peterson, L. S., & Piccinino, L. J. (1997). Fertility, family planning, and women's health: New data from the 1995 National Survey of Family Growth. *Vital and Health Statistics, 23*(9) 1–67.

Aboud, F. E., & Doyle, A. B. (1995). The development of in-group pride in black Canadians. *Journal of Cross-Cultural Psychology, 26,* 243–254.

Abramovitch, R., Pepler, D., & Corter, C. (1982). Patterns of sibling interaction among preschool-age children. In M. E. Lamb & B. Sutton-Smith (Eds.), *Sibling relationships: Their nature and significance across the lifespan* (pp. 61–86). Hillsdale, NJ: Erlbaum.

Abrams, B. (1994). Weight gain and energy intake during pregnancy. *Clinical Obstetrics and Gynecology, 37,* 515–527.

Abrams, E. J., Matheson, P. B., Thomas, P. A., Thea, D. M., Krasinski, K., Lambert, G., Shaffer, N., Bamji, M., Hutson, D., Grimm, K., Kaul, A., Bateman, D., Rogers, M., & New York City Perinatal HIV Transmission Collaborative Study Group. (1995). Neonatal predictors of infection status and early death among 332 infants at risk of HIV-1 infection monitored prospectively from birth. *Pediatrics, 96,* 451–458.

Achenbach, T. M. (1982). *Developmental psychopathology* (2nd ed.). New York: Wiley.

Achenbach, T. M. (1991). *Manual for the Child Behavior Checklist/4–18 and 1991 profile.* Burlington: University of Vermont Department of Psychiatry.

Achenbach, T. M. (1993). Taxonomy and comorbidity of conduct problems: Evidence from empirically based approaches. *Development and Psychopathology, 5,* 51–64.

Achenbach, T. M. (1995). Developmental issues in assessment, taxonomy, and diagnosis of child and adolescent psychopathology. In D. Cicchetti & D. J. Cohen (Eds.), *Developmental psychopathology: Vol. 1. Theory and methods* (pp. 57–80). New York: Wiley.

Achenbach, T. M., & Edelbrock, C. S. (1981). Behavioral problems and competencies reported by parents of normal and disturbed children aged 4 through 16. *Monographs of the Society for Research in Child Development, 46*(1, Serial No. 188).

Adams, G. R., Gullotta, T. P., & Montemayor, R. (Eds.). (1992). *Adolescent identity formation.* Newbury Park, CA: Sage.

Adams, M. J. (1990). *Beginning to read: Thinking and learning about print.* Cambridge, MA: MIT Press.

Adams, M. J., Trieman, R., & Pressley, M. (1998). Reading, writing, and literacy. In W. Damon (Ed.), *Handbook of child psychology: Vol 4. Child psychology in practice* (5th ed., pp. 275–355). New York: Wiley.

Adashek, J. A., Peaceman, A. M., Lopez-Zeno, J. A., Minogue, J. P., & Socol, M. L. (1993). Factors contributing to the increased cesarean birth rate in older parturient women. *American Journal of Obstetrics and Gynecology, 169,* 936–940.

Adesman, A. R. (1996). Fragile X syndrome. In A. J. Capute & P. J. Accardo (Eds.), *Developmental disabilities in infancy and childhood: Vol. 2. The spectrum of developmental disabilities* (2nd ed., pp. 255–269). Baltimore: Brookes.

Ahadi, S. A., & Rothbart, M. K. (1994). Temperament, development, and the Big Five. In C. F. Halverson, Jr., G. A. Kohnstamm, & R. P. Martin (Eds.), *The developing structure of temperament and personality from infancy to adulthood* (pp. 189–207). Hillsdale, NJ: Erlbaum.

Ahlsten, G., Cnattingius, S., & Lindmark, G. (1993). Cessation of smoking during pregnancy improves foetal growth and reduces infant morbidity in the neonatal period: A population-based prospective study. *Acta Paediatrica, 82,* 177–182.

Ainsworth, M. D. S. (1972). Attachment and dependency: A comparison. In J. L. Gewirtz (Ed.), *Attachment and dependency* (pp. 97–138). Washington, DC: Winston.

Ainsworth, M. D. S. (1982). Attachment: Retrospect and prospect. In C. M. Parkes & J. Stevenson-Hinde (Eds.), *The place of attachment in human behavior* (pp. 3–30). New York: Basic Books.

Ainsworth, M. D. S. (1989). Attachments beyond infancy. *American Psychologist, 44,* 709–716.

Ainsworth, M. D. S., Blehar, M., Waters, E., & Wall, S. (1978). *Patterns of attachment.* Hillsdale, NJ: Erlbaum.

Ainsworth, M. D. S., & Marvin, R. S. (1995). On the shaping of attachment theory and research: An interview with Mary D. S. Ainsworth (Fall 1994). *Monographs of the Society for Research in Child Development, 60*(244, Nos. 2–3), 3–21.

Akhtar, N., Carpenter, M., & Tomasello, M. (1996). The role of discourse novelty in early word learning. *Child Development, 67,* 635–645.

Aksu-Koc, A. A., & Slobin, D. I. (1985). The acquisition of Turkish. In D. I. Slobin (Ed.), *The crosslinguistic study of language acquisition: Vol. 1. The data* (pp. 839–878). Hillsdale, NJ: Erlbaum.

Alexander, K. L., Entwisle, D. R., & Dauber, S. L. (1993). First-grade classroom behavior: Its short- and long-term consequences for school performance. *Child Development, 64,* 801–814.

Alho, O., Läärä, E., & Oja, H. (1996). How should relative risk estimates for acute otitis media in children aged less than 2 years be perceived? *Journal of Clinical Epidemiology, 49,* 9–14.

Allen, M. C. (1996). Preterm development. In A. J. Capute & P. J. Accardo (Eds.), *Developmental disabilities in infancy and childhood: Vol. 2. The spectrum of developmental disabilities* (2nd ed., pp. 31–47). Baltimore: Brookes.

Allen, M. C., Donohue, P. K., & Dusman, A. E. (1993). The limit of viability—neonatal outcome of infants born at 22 to 25 weeks' gestation. *The New England Journal of Medicine, 329,* 1597–1601.

503

Alper, S., Schloss, P. J., Etscheidt, S. K., & Macfarlane, C. A. (1995). *Inclusion: Are we abandoning or helping students?* Thousand Oaks, CA: Corwin Press.

Alsaker, F. D. (1995). Timing of puberty and reactions to pubertal change. In M. Rutter (Ed.), *Psychosocial disturbances in young people: Challenges for prevention* (pp. 37–82). Cambridge, England: Cambridge University Press.

Alsaker, F. D., & Olweus, D. (1992). Stability of global self-evaluations in early adolescence: A cohort longitudinal study. *Journal of Research on Adolescence, 2,* 123–145.

Amador, M., Silva, L. C., & Valdes-Lazo, F. (1994). Breast-feeding trends in Cuba and the Americas. *Bulletin of the Pan American Health Organization, 28,* 220–227.

Amato, P. R. (1993). Children's adjustment to divorce: Theories, hypotheses, and empirical support. *Journal of Marriage and the Family, 55,* 23–38.

Ambert, A. (1994). An international perspective on parenting: Social change and social constructs. *Journal of Marriage and the Family, 56,* 529–543.

Ambuel, B. (1995). Adolescents, unintended pregnancy, and abortion: The struggle for a compassionate social policy. *Current Directions in Psychological Science, 4,* 1–5.

American Academy of Pediatrics Committee on Psychosocial Aspects of Child and Family Health. (1998). Guidance for effective discipline. *Pediatrics, 101,* 723–728.

American Psychiatric Association. (1994). *Diagnostic and statistical manual of mental disorders* (4th ed.). Washington, DC: American Psychiatric Association.

American Psychological Association. (1993). *Violence and youth: Psychology's response: Vol. 1. Summary report of the American Psychological Association Commission on Violence and Youth.* Washington, DC: American Psychological Association.

Andersen, R. E., Crespo, C. J., Bartlett, S. J., Cheskin, L. J., & Pratt, M. (1998). Relationship of physical activity and television watching with body weight and level of fatness among children. *Journal of the American Medical Association, 279,* 938–942.

Anderson, D. R., Lorch, E. P., Field, D. E., Collins, P. A., & Nathan, J. G. (1986). Television viewing at home: Age trends in visual attention and time with TV. *Child Development, 57,* 1024–1033.

Andersson, B. (1989). Effects of public day-care: A longitudinal study. *Child Development, 60,* 857–886.

Andersson, B. (1992). Effects of day-care on cognitive and socioemotional competence of thirteen-year-old Swedish schoolchildren. *Child Development, 63,* 20–36.

Anglin, J. M. (1993). Vocabulary development: A morphological analysis. *Monographs of the Society for Research in Child Development, 58*(Serial No. 238).

Anglin, J. M. (1995, April). *Word learning and the growth of potentially knowable vocabulary.* Paper presented at the biennial meetings of the Society for Research in Child Development, Indianapolis.

Anisfeld, M. (1991). Neonatal imitation. *Developmental Review, 11,* 60–97.

Anshel, M. H. (1990). *Sport psychology: From theory to practice.* Scottsdale, AZ: Gorsuch Scarisbrick.

Apgar, V. A. (1953). A proposal for a new method of evaluation of the newborn infant. *Current Research in Anesthesia and Analgesia, 32,* 260–267.

Arn, P., Chen, H., Tuck-Muller, C. M., Mankinen, C., Wachtel, G., Li, S., Shen, C.-C., & Wachtel, S. S. (1994). SRVX, a sex reversing locus in Xp21.2 → p22.11. *Human Genetics, 93,* 389–393.

Arnett, J. (1992). Reckless behavior in adolescence: A developmental perspective. *Developmental Review, 12,* 339–373.

Arnold, D. H., McWilliams, L., & Arnold, E. H. (1998). Teacher discipline and child misbehavior in day care: Untangling causality with correlational data. *Developmental Psychology, 34,* 276–287.

Arnold, L. D. W., & Larson, E. (1993). Immunologic benefits of breast milk in relation to human milk banking. *American Journal of Infection Control, 21,* 235–242.

Aslin, R. N. (1981a). Experiential influences and sensitive periods in perceptual development: A unified model. In R. N. Aslin, J. R. Alberts, & M. R. Petersen (Eds.), *Development of perception. Psychobiological perspectives: Vol. 2. The visual system* (pp. 45–93). New York: Academic Press.

Aslin, R. N. (1981b). Development of smooth pursuit in human infants. In D. F. Fisher, R. A. Monty, & J. W. Senders (Eds.), *Eye movements: Cognition and visual perception* (pp. 31–51). Hillsdale, NJ: Erlbaum.

Aslin, R. N. (1987a). Motor aspects of visual development in infancy. In P. Salapatek & L. Cohen (Eds.), *Handbook of infant perception: Vol. 1. From sensation to perception* (pp. 43–113). Orlando, FL: Academic Press.

Aslin, R. N. (1987b). Visual and auditory development in infancy. In J. D. Osofsky (Ed.), *Handbook of infant development* (2nd ed., pp. 5–97). New York: Wiley-Interscience.

Astington, J. W., & Gopnik, A. (1991). Theoretical explanations of children's understanding of the mind. In G. E. Butterworth, P. L. Harris, A. M. Leslie, & H. M. Wellman (Eds.), *Perspectives on the child's theory of mind* (pp. 7–31). New York: Oxford University Press.

Astington, J. W., & Jenkins, J. M. (1995, April). *Language and theory of mind: A theoretical review and a longitudinal study.* Paper presented at the biennial meetings of the Society for Research in Child Development, Indianapolis.

Astone, N. M. (1993). Are adolescent mothers just single mothers? *Journal of Research on Adolescence, 3,* 353–371.

Attie, I., & Brooks-Gunn, J. (1995). The development of eating regulation across the life span. In D. Cicchetti & D. J. Cohen (Eds.), *Developmental psychopathology: Vol. 2. Risk, disorder, and adaptation* (pp. 332–368). New York: Wiley.

Avis, J., & Harris, P. L. (1991). Belief-desire reasoning among Baka children: Evidence for a universal conception of mind. *Child Development, 62,* 460–467.

Bachman, J. G., & Schulenberg, J. (1993). How part-time work intensity relates to drug use, problem behavior, time use, and satisfaction among high school seniors: Are these consequences or merely correlates? *Developmental Psychology, 29,* 220–235.

Baghurst, P. A., McMichael, A. J., Tong, S., Wigg, N. R., Vimpani, G. V., & Robertson, E. F. (1995). Exposure to environmental lead and visual-motor integration at age 7 years: The Port Pirie cohort study. *Epidemiology, 6,* 104–109.

Baghurst, P. A., McMichael, A. J., Wigg, N. R., Vimpani, G. V., Robertson, E. F., Roberts, R. J., & Tong, S. (1992). Environmental exposure to lead and children's intelligence at the age of seven years. *The New England Journal of Medicine, 327,* 1279–1284.

Bagwell, C. L., Newcomb, A. F., & Bukowski, W. M. (1998). Preadolescent friendship and peer rejection as predictors of adult adjustment. *Child Development, 69,* 140–153.

Bailey, J. M., & Pillard, R. C. (1991). A genetic study of male sexual orientation. *Archives of General Psychiatry, 48,* 1089–1096.

Bailey, J. M., Pillard, R. C., Neale, M. C., & Agyei, Y. (1993). Heritable factors influence sexual orientation in women. *Archives of General Psychiatry, 50,* 217–223.

Bailey, J. M., & Zucker, K. J. (1995). Childhood sex-typed behavior and sexual orientation: A conceptual analysis and quantitative review. *Developmental Psychology, 31,* 43–55.

Baillargeon, R. (1994). How do infants learn about the physical world? *Current Directions in Psychological Science, 3,* 133–140.

Baker, J. M., & Zigmond, N. (1995). The meaning and practice of inclusion for students with learning disabilities: Themes and implications from the five cases. *The Journal of Special Education, 29,* 163–180.

Baker-Ward, L. (1995, April). *Children's reports of a minor medical emergency procedure.* Paper presented at the biennial meetings of the Society for Research in Child Development, Indianapolis.

Baker-Ward, L., Gordon, B. N., Ornstein, P. A., Larus, D. M., & Clubb, P. A. (1993). Young children's long-term retention of a pediatric examination. *Child Development, 64,* 1519–1533.

Bakketeig, L. S., Cnattingius, S., & Knudsen, L. B. (1993). Socioeconomic differences in fetal and infant mortality in Scandinavia. *Journal of Public Health Policy, 14*(Spring), 82–90.

Balaban, M. T. (1995). Affective influences on startle in five-month-old infants: Reactions to facial expressions of emotion. *Child Development, 66,* 28–36.

Baltes, P. B., & Reinert, G. (1969). Cohort effects in cognitive development as revealed by cross-sectional sequences. *Developmental Psychology, 1,* 169–177.

Bamford, F. N., Bannister, R. P., Benjamin, C. M., Hillier, V. F., Ward, B. S., & Moore, W. M. O. (1990). Sleep in the first year of life. *Developmental Medicine and Child Neurology, 32,* 718–724.

Bandura, A. (1973). *Aggression: A social learning analysis.* Englewood Cliffs, NJ: Prentice Hall.

Bandura, A. (1977). *Social learning theory.* Englewood Cliffs, NJ: Prentice Hall.

Bandura, A. (1982). Self-efficacy mechanism in human agency. *American Psychologist, 37,* 122–147.

Bandura, A. (1986). *Social foundations of thought and action: A social cognitive theory.* Englewood Cliffs, NJ: Prentice Hall.

Bandura, A. (1989). Social cognitive theory. *Annals of Child Development, 6,* 1–60.

Bandura, A. (1997). *Self-efficacy. The exercise of control.* New York: Freeman.

Banerji, M., & Dailey, R. A. (1995). A study of the effects of an inclusion model on students with specific learning disabilities. *Journal of Learning Disabilities, 28,* 511–522.

Bardoni, B., Zanaria, E., Guioli, S., Floridia, G., Worley, K. C., Tonini, G., Ferrante, E., Chiumello, G., McCabe, E. R. B., Fraccaro, M., Zuffardi, O., & Camerino, G. (1994). A dosage sensitive locus at chromosome Xp21 is involved in male to female sex reversal. *Nature Genetics, 7,* 497–501.

Barenboim, C. (1977). Developmental changes in the interpersonal cognitive system from middle childhood to adolescence. *Child Development, 48,* 1467–1474.

Barenboim, C. (1981). The development of person perception in childhood and adolescence: From behavioral comparisons to psychological constructs to psychological comparisons. *Child Development, 52,* 129–144.

Barkley, R. A. (1997). Behavioral inhibition, sustained attention, and executive functions: Constructing a unifying theory of ADHD. *Psychological Bulletin, 121,* 65–94.

Barkley, R. A., Fischer, M., Edelbrock, C. S., & Smallish, L. (1990). The adolescent outcome of hyperactive children diagnosed by research criteria: I. An 8-year prospective follow-up study. *Journal of the American Academy of Child and Adolescent Psychiatry, 29,* 546–557.

Barnard, K. E., & Bee, H. L. (1983). The impact of temporally patterned stimulation on the development of preterm infants. *Child Development, 54,* 1156–1167.

Barnard, K. E., Hammond, M. A., Booth, C. L., Bee, H. L., Mitchell, S. K., & Spieker, S. J. (1989). Measurement and meaning of parent-child interaction. In J. J. Morrison, C.

Lord, & D. P. Keating (Eds.), *Applied developmental psychology* (Vol. 3, pp. 40–81). San Diego, CA: Academic Press.

Barnes, H. L., & Olson, D. H. (1985). Parent-adolescent communication and the circumplex model. *Child Development, 56,* 438–447.

Barness, L. A., & Curran, J. S. (1996). Nutrition. In R. E. Behrman, R. M. Kliegman, & A. M. Arvin (Eds.), *Nelson textbook of pediatrics* (15th ed., pp. 141–184). Philadelphia: Saunders.

Barnett, D., Manly, J. T., & Cicchetti, D. (1993). Defining child maltreatment: The interface between policy and research. In D. Cicchetti & S. L. Toth (Eds.), *Child abuse, child development, and social policy* (pp. 7–73). Norwood, NJ: Ablex.

Barnett, W. S. (1993). Benefit-cost analysis of preschool education: Findings from a 25-year follow-up. *American Journal of Orthopsychiatry, 63,* 500–508.

Barr, H. M., Streissguth, A. P., Darby, B. L., & Sampson, P. D. (1990). Prenatal exposure to alcohol, caffeine, tobacco, and aspirin: Effects on fine and gross motor performance in 4-year-old children. *Developmental Psychology, 26,* 339–348.

Barrett, G. V., & Depinet, R. L. (1991). A reconsideration of testing for competence rather than for intelligence. *American Psychologist, 46,* 1012–1024.

Bartsch, K. (1993). Adolescents' theoretical thinking. In R. M. Lerner (Ed.), *Early adolescence. Perspectives on research, policy, and intervention* (pp. 143–157). Hillsdale, NJ: Erlbaum.

Basire, K., Pullon, S., & McLeod, D. (1997). Baby feeding: The thoughts behind the statistics. *New Zealand Medical Journal, 110,* 184–187.

Bates, E. (1993). Commentary: Comprehension and production in early language development. *Monographs of the Society for Research in Child Development, 58*(3–4, Serial No. 233), 222–242.

Bates, E., Bretherton, I., Beeghly-Smith, M., & McNew, S. (1982). Social bases of language development: A reassessment. In H. W. Reese & L. P. Lipsitt (Eds.), *Advances in child development and behavior* (Vol. 16, pp. 8–68). New York: Academic Press.

Bates, E., Bretherton, I., & Snyder, L. (1988). *From first words to grammar: Individual differences and dissociable mechanisms.* Cambridge, England: Cambridge University Press.

Bates, E., Marchman, V., Thal, D., Fenson, L., Dale, P., Reznick, J. S., Reilly, J., & Hartung, J. (1994). Developmental and stylistic variation in the composition of early vocabulary. *Journal of Child Language, 21,* 85–123.

Bates, E., O'Connell, B., & Shore, C. (1987). Language and communication in infancy. In J. D. Osofsky (Ed.), *Handbook of infant development* (2nd ed., pp. 149–203). New York: Wiley.

Bates, J. E. (1989). Applications of temperament concepts. In G. A. Kohnstamm, J. E. Bates, &

M. K. Rothbart (Eds.), *Temperament in childhood* (pp. 321–356). Chichester, England: Wiley.

Bates, J. E., Marvinney, D., Kelly, T., Dodge, K. A., Bennett, D. S., & Pettit, G. S. (1994). Child-care history and kindergarten adjustment. *Developmental Psychology, 30,* 690–700.

Bauer, P. J. (1993). Memory for gender-consistent and gender-inconsistent event sequences by twenty-five-month-old children. *Child Development, 64,* 285–297.

Baumgartner, R. N., Roche, A. F., & Himes, J. H. (1986). Incremental growth tables: Supplementary to previously published charts. *American Journal of Clinical Nutrition, 43,* 711–722.

Baumrind, D. (1971). Current patterns of parental authority. *Developmental Psychology Monograph, 4*(1, Part 2).

Baumrind, D. (1973). The development of instrumental competence through socialization. In A. D. Pick (Ed.), *Minnesota symposium on child psychology* (Vol. 7, pp. 3–46). Minneapolis: University of Minnesota Press.

Baumrind, D. (1991). The influence of parenting style on adolescent competence and substance use. *Journal of Early Adolescence, 11,* 56–95.

Baydar, N., & Brooks-Gunn, J. (1991). Effects of maternal employment and child-care arrangements on preschoolers' cognitive and behavioral outcomes: Evidence from the children of the National Longitudinal Survey of Youth. *Developmental Psychology, 27,* 932–945.

Baydar, N., Brooks-Gunn, J., & Furstenberg, F. F. (1993). Early warning signs of functional illiteracy: Predictors in childhood and adolescence. *Child Development, 64,* 815–829.

Bayley, N. (1969). *Bayley Scales of Infant Development.* New York: Psychological Corporation.

Bear, G. G., & Rys, G. S. (1994). Moral reasoning, classroom behavior, and sociometric status among elementary school children. *Developmental Psychology, 30,* 633–638.

Beaudry, M., Dufour, R., & Marcoux, S. (1995). Relation between infant feeding and infections during the first six months of life. *Journal of Pediatrics, 126,* 191–197.

Bee, H. L., Barnard, K. E., Eyres, S. J., Gray, C. A., Hammond, M. A., Spietz, A. L., Snyder, C., & Clark, B. (1982). Prediction of IQ and language skill from perinatal status, child performance, family characteristics, and mother-infant interaction. *Child Development, 53,* 1135–1156.

Bell, L. G., & Bell, D. C. (1982). Family climate and the role of the female adolescent: Determinants of adolescent functioning. *Family Relations, 31,* 519–527.

Belsky, J. (1985). Prepared statement on the effects of day care. In *Improving child care services: What can be done?* Select Committee on Children, Youth, and Families, House of Representatives, 98th Cong., 2d Sess., Washington, DC: U.S. Government Printing Office.

Belsky, J. (1992). Consequences of child care for children's development: A deconstructionist view. In A. Booth (Ed.), *Child care in the 1990s. Trends and consequences* (pp. 83–94). Hillsdale, NJ: Erlbaum.

Belsky, J. (1993). Etiology of child maltreatment: A developmental-ecological analysis. *Psychological Bulletin, 114,* 413–434.

Belsky, J., Hsieh, K., & Crnic, K. (1996). Infant positive and negative emotionality: One dimension or two? *Developmental Psychology, 32,* 289–298.

Belsky, J., Lang, M. E., & Rovine, M. (1985). Stability and change in marriage across the transition to parenthood: A second study. *Journal of Marriage and the Family, 47,* 855–865.

Belsky, J., & Rovine, M. (1988). Nonmaternal care in the first year of life and the security of infant-parent attachment. *Child Development, 59,* 157–167.

Bem, S. L. (1974). The measurement of psychological androgyny. *Journal of Consulting and Clinical Psychology, 42,* 155–162.

Bem, S. L. (1981). Gender schema theory: A cognitive account of sex-typing. *Psychological Review, 88,* 354–364.

Bem, S. L. (1989). Genital knowledge and gender constancy in preschool children. *Child Development, 60,* 649–662.

Benbow, C. P. (1988). Sex differences in mathematical reasoning ability in intellectually talented preadolescents: Their nature, effects, and possible causes. *Behavioral and Brain Sciences, 11,* 169–232.

Bender, S. L., Word, C. O., DiClemente, R. J., Crittenden, M. R., Persaud, N. A., & Ponton, L. E. (1995). The developmental implications of prenatal and/or postnatal crack cocaine exposure in preschool children: A preliminary report. *Developmental and Behavioral Pediatrics, 16,* 418–424.

Bendersky, M., & Lewis, M. (1994). Environmental risk, biological risk, and developmental outcome. *Developmental Psychology, 30,* 484–494.

Benenson, J. F. (1994). Ages four to six years: Changes in the structures of play networks of girls and boys. *Merrill-Palmer Quarterly, 40,* 478–487.

Benoit, D., & Parker, K. C. H. (1994). Stability and transmission of attachment across three generations. *Child Development, 65,* 1444–1456.

Berch, D. B., & Bender, B. G. (1987, December). Margins of sexuality. *Psychology Today, 21,* 54–57.

Berenbaum, S. A. (1997, April). *How and why do early hormones affect sex-typed behavior?* Paper presented at the biennial meetings of the Society for Research in Child Development, Washington, DC.

Bergeman, C. S., Chipuer, H. M., Plomin, R., Pedersen, N. L., McClearn, G. E., Nessel-

roade, J. R., Costa, P. T., & McCrae, R. R. (1993). Genetic and environmental effects on openness to experience, agreeableness, and conscientiousness: An adoption/twin study. *Journal of Personality, 61,* 159–179.

Bergmann, B. R. (1996). *Saving our children from poverty: What the United States can learn from France.* New York: Russell Sage Foundation.

Berkowitz, G. S., Skovron, M. L., Lapinski, R. H., & Berkowitz, R. L. (1990). Delayed childbearing and the outcome of pregnancy. *The New England Journal of Medicine, 322,* 659–664.

Berndt, T. J. (1983). Social cognition, social behavior, and children's friendships. In E. T. Higgins, D. N. Ruble, & W. W. Hartup (Eds.), *Social cognition and social development: A sociocultural perspective* (pp. 158–192). Cambridge, England: Cambridge University Press.

Berndt, T. J. (1986). Children's comments about their friendships. In M. Perlmutter (Ed.), *Minnesota symposia on child psychology* (Vol. 18, pp. 189–212). Hillsdale, NJ: Erlbaum.

Berndt, T. J. (1992). Friendship and friends' influence in adolescence. *Current Directions in Psychological Science, 1,* 156–159.

Berndt, T. J., & Hoyle, S. G. (1985). Stability and change in childhood and adolescent friendships. *Developmental Psychology, 21,* 1007–1015.

Berndt, T. J., & Keefe, K. (1995a). Friends' influence on adolescents' adjustment to school. *Child Development, 66,* 1312–1329.

Berndt, T. J., & Keefe, K. (1995b, April). *Friends' influence on school adjustment: A motivational analysis.* Paper presented at the biennial meetings of the Society for Research in Child Development, Indianapolis.

Berney, B. (1996). Epidemiology of childhood lead poisoning. In S. M. Pueschel, J. G. Linakis, & A. C. Anderson (Eds.), *Lead poisoning in childhood* (pp. 15–35). Baltimore: Brookes.

Bertenthal, B. I., Campos, J. J., & Kermoian, R. (1994). An epigenetic perspective on the development of self-produced locomotion and its consequences. *Current Directions in Psychological Science, 3,* 140–145.

Bérubé, M. (1996). *Life as we know it: A father, a family, and an exceptional child.* New York: Pantheon Books.

Betancourt, H., & Lopez, S. R. (1993). The study of culture, ethnicity, and race in American psychology. *American Psychologist, 48,* 629–637.

Bettes, B. A. (1988). Maternal depression and motherese: Temporal and intonational features. *Child Development, 59,* 1089–1096.

Bhatt, R. S., & Rovee-Collier, C. (1996). Infants' forgetting of correlated attributes and object recognition. *Child Development, 67,* 172–187.

Bigelow, B. J., & La Gaipa, J. J. (1975). Children's written descriptions of friendships: A

multidimensional analysis. *Developmental Psychology, 11,* 857–858.

Bigler, R. S. (1995). The role of classification skill in moderating environmental influences on children's gender stereotyping: A study of the functional use of gender in the classroom. *Child Development, 66,* 1072–1087.

Billy, J. O. G., Brewster, K. L., & Grady, W. R. (1994). Contextual effects on the sexual behavior of adolescent women. *Journal of Marriage and the Family, 56,* 387–404.

Binet, A., & Simon, T. (1905). Méthodes nouvelles pour le diagnostic du niveau intellectual des anormaux [New methods for diagnosing intellectual level in the abnormal]. *Année Psychologie, 11,* 191–244.

Bingham, C. R., Miller, B. C., & Adams, G. R. (1990). Correlates of age at first sexual intercourse in a national sample of young women. *Journal of Adolescent Research, 5,* 18–33.

Biro, F. M., Lucky, A. W., Huster, G. A., & Morrison, J. A. (1995). Pubertal staging in boys. *Journal of Pediatrics, 127,* 100–102.

Biro, F. M., & Rosenthal, S. L. (1995). Adolescents and sexually transmitted diseases: Diagnosis, developmental issues, and prevention. *Journal of Pediatric Health Care, 9,* 256–262.

Biswas, M. K., & Craigo, S. D. (1994). The course and conduct of normal labor and delivery. In A. H. DeCherney & M. L. Pernoll (Eds.), *Current obstetric and gynecologic diagnosis & treatment* (pp. 202–227). Norwalk, CT: Appleton & Lange.

Bivens, J. A., & Berk, L. E. (1990). A longitudinal study of the development of elementary school children's private speech. *Merrill-Palmer Quarterly, 36,* 443–463.

Bjorklund, D. F., & Coyle, T. R. (1995, April). *Utilization deficiencies, multiple strategy use, and memory development.* Paper presented at the biennial meetings of the Society for Research in Child Development, Indianapolis.

Bjorklund, D. F., Miller, P. H., Coyle, T. R., & Slawinski, J. L. (1997). Instructing children to use memory strategies: Evidence of utilization deficiencies in memory training studies. *Developmental Review, 17,* 411–441.

Bjorklund, D. F., & Muir, J. E. (1988). Remembering on their own: Children's development of free recall memory. In R. Vasta (Ed.), *Annals of child development* (Vol. 5, pp. 79–124). Greenwich, CT: JAI Press.

Black, K. A., & McCartney, K. (1995, April). *Associations between adolescent attachment to parents and peer interactions.* Paper presented at the biennial meetings of the Society for Research in Child Development, Indianapolis.

Blair, S. L., & Johnson, M. P. (1992). Wives' perceptions of the fairness of the division of household labor: The intersection of housework and ideology. *Journal of Marriage and the Family, 54,* 570–581.

Blake, I. K. (1994). Language development and socialization in young African-American children. In P. M. Greenfield & R. R. Cocking (Eds.), *Cross-cultural roots of minority child development* (pp. 167–195). Hillsdale, NJ: Erlbaum.

Blass, E. M., Ganchrow, J. R., & Steiner, J. E. (1984). Classical conditioning in newborn humans 2–48 hours of age. *Infant Behavior and Development, 7,* 223–235.

Block, J. (1971). *Lives through time.* Berkeley, CA: Bancroft.

Block, J., & Robins, R. W. (1993). A longitudinal study of consistency and change in self-esteem from early adolescence to early adulthood. *Child Development, 64,* 909–923.

Bloom, L. (1973). *One word at a time.* The Hague: Mouton.

Bloom, L. (1991). *Language development from two to three.* Cambridge, England: Cambridge University Press.

Bloom, L. (1993). *The transition from infancy to language: Acquiring the power of expression.* Cambridge, England: Cambridge University Press.

Bloom, L. (1997, April). *The child's action drives the interaction.* Paper presented at the biennial meetings of the Society for Research in Child Development, Washington, DC.

Bloom, L. (1998). Language acquisition in its developmental context. In W. Damon (Ed.), *Handbook of child psychology: Vol. 2. Cognition, perception, and language* (5th ed., pp. 309–370). New York: Wiley.

Boer, F., & Dunn, J. (Eds.). (1992). *Children's sibling relationships: Developmental and clinical issues.* Hillsdale, NJ: Erlbaum.

Boer, F., Godhart, A. W., & Treffers, P. D. A. (1992). Siblings and their parents. In F. Boer & J. Dunn (Eds.), *Children's sibling relationships: Developmental and clinical issues* (pp. 41–54). Hillsdale, NJ: Erlbaum.

Boldizar, J. P. (1991). Assessing sex typing and androgyny in children: The Children's Sex Role Inventory. *Developmental Psychology, 27,* 505–515.

Bolger, K. (1997, April). *Children's adjustment as a function of timing of family economic hardship.* Paper presented at the biennial meetings of the Society for Research in Child Development, Washington, DC.

Bond, M. H., Nakazato, H., & Shiraishi, D. (1975). Universality and distinctiveness in dimensions of Japanese person perception. *Journal of Cross-Cultural Psychology, 6,* 346–357.

Borkenau, P., & Ostendorf, F. (1990). Comparing exploratory and confirmatory factor analysis: A study on the five-factor model of personality. *Personality and Individual Differences, 11,* 515–524.

Bornstein, M. H. (1987). Sensitive periods in development: Definition, existence, utility, and meaning. In M. H. Bornstein (Ed.), *Sensitive periods in development: Interdisciplinary perspectives* (pp. 3–18). Hillsdale, NJ: Erlbaum.

Bornstein, M. H. (Ed.). (1989). Maternal responsiveness: Characteristics and consequences. *New Directions for Child Development, 43.*

Bornstein, M. H. (1995). Parenting infants. In M. H. Bornstein (Ed.), *Handbook of parenting: Vol 1. Children and parenting* (pp. 3–39). Mahwah, NJ: Erlbaum.

Bornstein, M. H., Tamis-LeMonda, C. S., Tal, J., Ludemann, P., Toda, S., Rahn, C. W., Pecheux, M., Azuma, H., & Vardi, D. (1992). Maternal responsiveness to infants in three societies: The United States, France, and Japan. *Child Development, 63,* 808–821.

The Boston Women's Health Collective. (1992). *The new our bodies, ourselves: A book by and for women.* New York: Simon & Schuster.

Bouchard, T. J., Jr. (1984). Twins reared apart and together: What they tell us about human diversity. In S. Fox (Ed.), *The chemical and biological bases of individuality.* New York: Plenum Press.

Bouchard, T. J., Jr., & McGue, M. (1981). Familial studies of intelligence: A review. *Science, 212,* 1055–1059.

Bower, T. G. R. (1966). The visual world of infants. *Scientific American, 215,* 80–92.

Bower, T. G. R. (1989). *The rational infant.* New York: Freeman.

Bowerman, M. (1985). Beyond communicative adequacy: From piecemeal knowledge to an integrated system in the child's acquisition of language. In K. E. Nelson (Ed.), *Children's language* (Vol. 5, pp. 369–398). Hillsdale, NJ: Erlbaum.

Bowlby, J. (1969). *Attachment and loss: Vol. 1. Attachment.* New York: Basic Books.

Bowlby, J. (1973). *Attachment and loss: Vol. 2. Separation, anxiety, and anger.* New York: Basic Books.

Bowlby, J. (1980). *Attachment and loss: Vol. 3. Loss, sadness, and depression.* New York: Basic Books.

Bowlby, J. (1988a). Developmental psychiatry comes of age. *American Journal of Psychiatry, 145,* 1–10.

Bowlby, J. (1988b). *A secure base.* New York: Basic Books.

Boyatzis, C. J., Matillo, G., Nesbitt, K., & Cathey, G. (1995, April). *Effects of "The Mighty Morphin Power Rangers" on children's aggression and prosocial behavior.* Paper presented at the biennial meetings of the Society for Research in Child Development, Indianapolis.

Boyes, M. C., & Allen, S. G. (1993). Styles of parent-child interactions and moral reasoning in adolescence. *Merrill-Palmer Quarterly, 39,* 551–570.

Boynton, R. S. (1996, October 7). The birth of an idea. *The New Yorker,* 72–81.

Bradbard, M. R., Martin, C. L., Endsley, R. C., & Halverson, C. F. (1986). Influence of sex stereotypes on children's exploration and memory: A competence versus performance distinction. *Developmental Psychology, 22,* 481–486.

Bradley, R. H., Caldwell, B. M., Rock, S. L., Barnard, K. E., Gray, C., Hammond, M. A., Mitchell, S., Siegel, L., Ramey, C. D., Gottfried, A. W., & Johnson, D. L. (1989). Home environment and cognitive development in the first 3 years of life: A collaborative study involving six sites and three ethnic groups in North America. *Developmental Psychology, 25,* 217–235.

Bradley, R. H., Whiteside, L., Mundfrom, D. J., Casey, P. H., Kelleher, K. J., & Pope, S. K. (1994). Early indications of resilience and their relation to experiences in the home environments of low birthweight, premature children living in poverty. *Child Development, 65,* 346–360.

Brandenburg, N. A., Friedman, R. M., & Silver, S. E. (1990). The epidemiology of childhood psychiatric disorders: Prevalence findings from recent studies. *Journal of the American Academy of Child and Adolescent Psychiatry, 29,* 76–83.

Bray, N. W., Fletcher, K. L., & Turner, L. A. (1997). Cognitive competencies and strategy use in individuals with mental retardation. In W. E. MacLean Jr. (Ed.), *Ellis' handbook of mental deficiency: Psychological theory and research* (3rd ed., pp. 197–217). Mahwah, NJ: Erlbaum.

Brazelton, T. B. (1984). *Neonatal Behavioral Assessment Scale.* Philadelphia: Lippincott.

Breitmayer, B. J., & Ramey, C. T. (1986). Biological nonoptimality and quality of postnatal environment as codeterminants of intellectual development. *Child Development, 57,* 1151–1165.

Breland, H. M. (1974). Birth order, family configuration, and verbal achievement. *Child Development, 45,* 1011–1019.

Breslau, N., DelDotto, J. E., Brown, G. G., Kumar, S., Ezhuthachan, S., Hufnagle, K. G., & Peterson, E. L. (1994). A gradient relationship between low birth weight and IQ at age 6 years. *Archives of Pediatric and Adolescent Medicine, 148,* 377–383.

Bretherton, I. (1991). Pouring new wine into old bottles: The social self as internal working model. In M. R. Gunnar & L. A. Sroufe (Eds.), *Minnesota symposia on child development* (Vol. 23, pp. 1–42). Hillsdale, NJ: Erlbaum.

Bretherton, I. (1992a). The origins of attachment theory: John Bowlby and Mary Ainsworth. *Developmental Psychology, 28,* 759–775.

Bretherton, I. (1992b). Attachment and bonding. In V. B. Van Hasselt & M. Hersen (Eds.), *Handbook of social development: A lifespan perspective* (pp. 133–155). New York: Plenum Press.

Bretherton, I. (1993). From dialogue to internal working models: The co-construction of self in relationships. In C. A. Nelson (Ed.), *The Minnesota symposia on child psychology* (Vol. 26, pp. 237–264). Hillsdale, NJ: Erlbaum.

Bristol, M. M., Gallagher, J. J., & Schopler, E. (1988). Mothers and fathers of young developmentally disabled and nondisabled boys: Adaptation and spousal support. *Developmental Psychology, 24,* 441–451.

Broberg, A. G., Wessels, H., Lamb, M. E., & Hwang, C. P. (1997). Effects of day care on the development of cognitive abilities in 8-year-olds: A longitudinal study. *Developmental Psychology, 33,* 62–69.

Brody, G. H., Stoneman, Z., & Flor, D. (1995). Linking family processes and academic competence among rural African American youths. *Journal of Marriage and the Family, 47,* 567–579.

Brody, G. H., Stoneman, Z., McCoy, J. K., & Forehand, R. (1992). Contemporaneous and longitudinal associations of sibling conflict with family relationship assessments and family discussions about sibling problems. *Child Development, 63,* 391–400.

Brody, N. (1992). *Intelligence* (2nd ed.). San Diego, CA: Academic Press.

Brody, N. (1997). Intelligence, schooling, and society. *American Psychologist, 52,* 1046–1050.

Broman, C. L. (1993). Race differences in marital well-being. *Journal of Marriage and the Family, 55,* 724–732.

Broman, S. H., Nichols, P. L., & Kennedy, W. A. (1975). *Preschool IQ: Prenatal and early developmental correlates.* Hillsdale, NJ: Erlbaum.

Broman, S. H., Nichols, P. L., Shaughnessy, P., & Kennedy, W. (1987). *Retardation in young children.* Hillsdale, NJ: Erlbaum.

Bronfenbrenner, U. (1979). *The ecology of human development.* Cambridge, MA: Harvard University Press.

Bronfenbrenner, U. (1989). Ecological systems theory. *Annals of Child Development, 6,* 187–249.

Bronfenbrenner, U., Alvarez, W. F., & Henderson, C. R., Jr. (1984). Working and watching: Maternal employment status and parents' perceptions of their three-year-old children. *Child Development, 55,* 1362–1378.

Bronson, G. W. (1991). Infant differences in rate of visual encoding. *Child Development, 62,* 44–45.

Bronson, G. W. (1994). Infants' transitions toward adult-like scanning. *Child Development, 65,* 1253–1261.

Brooks-Gunn, J. (1987). Pubertal processes and girls' psychological adaptation. In R. M. Lerner & T. T. Foch (Eds.), *Biological-psychosocial interactions in early adolescence* (pp. 123–154). Hillsdale, NJ: Erlbaum.

Brooks-Gunn, J. (1988). Commentary: Developmental issues in the transition to early adolescence. In M. R. Gunnar & W. A. Collins (Eds.), *Minnesota symposia on child psychology* (Vol. 21, pp. 189–208). Hillsdale, NJ: Erlbaum.

Brooks-Gunn, J. (1995). Children in families in communities: Risk and intervention in the Bronfenbrenner tradition. In P. Moen, G. H. Elder Jr., & K. Lüscher (Eds.), *Examining lives in context: Perspectives on the ecology of human development* (pp. 467–519). Washington, DC: American Psychological Association.

Brooks-Gunn, J., & Attie, I. (1996). Developmental psychopathology in the context of adolescence. In M. F. Lenzenweger & J. J. Haugaard (Eds.), *Frontiers of developmental psychopathology* (pp. 148–189). New York: Oxford University Press.

Brooks-Gunn, J., & Duncan, G. J. (1997). The effects of poverty on children. *The Future of Children, 7*(2), 55–71.

Brooks-Gunn, J., Duncan, G. J., & Aber, J. L. (Eds.). (1997). *Neighborhood poverty: Vol 1. Context and consequences for children.* New York: Russell Sage Foundation.

Brooks-Gunn, J., Guo, G., & Furstenberg, F. F., Jr. (1993a). Who drops out of and who continues beyond high school? A 20-year follow-up of black urban youth. *Journal of Research on Adolescence, 3,* 271–294.

Brooks-Gunn, J., Klebanov, P. K., Liaw, F., & Spiker, D. (1993b). Enhancing the development of low-birthweight, premature infants: Changes in cognition and behavior over the first three years. *Child Development, 64,* 736–753.

Brooks-Gunn, J., & Matthews, W. S. (1979). *He and she: How children develop their sex-role identity.* Englewood Cliffs, NJ: Prentice Hall.

Brooks-Gunn, J., & Paikoff, R. L. (1993). "Sex is a gamble, kissing is a game": Adolescent sexuality and health promotion. In S. G. Millstein, A. C. Petersen, & E. O. Nightingale (Eds.), *Promoting the health of adolescents* (pp. 180–208). New York: Oxford University Press.

Brooks-Gunn, J., & Reiter, E. O. (1990). The role of pubertal processes. In S. S. Feldman & G. R. Elliott (Eds.), *At the threshold: The developing adolescent* (pp. 16–53). Cambridge, MA: Harvard University Press.

Brooks-Gunn, J., & Warren, M. P. (1985). The effects of delayed menarche in different contexts: Dance and nondance students. *Journal of Youth and Adolescence, 13,* 285–300.

Brost, B. C., Goldenberg, R. L., Mercer, B. M., Iams, J. D., Meis, P. J., Moawad, A. H., Newman, R. B., Miodovnik, M., Caritis, S. N., Thurnau, G. R., Bottoms, S. F., Das, A., & McNellis, D. (1997). The preterm prediction study: Association of cesarean delivery with increases in maternal weight and body mass index. *American Journal of Obstetrics and Gynecology, 177,* 333–341.

Broverman, I. K., Broverman, D., Clarkson, F. E., Rosenkrantz, P. S., & Vogel, S. R. (1970). Sex-role stereotypes and clinical judgments of mental health. *Journal of Consulting and Clinical Psychology, 34,* 1–7.

Brown, B. B. (1990). Peer groups and peer cultures. In S. S. Feldman & G. R. Elliott (Eds.), *At the threshold. The developing adolescent* (pp. 171–196). Cambridge, MA: Harvard University Press.

Brown, B. B., Dolcini, M. M., & Leventhal, A. (1995, April). *The emergence of peer crowds: Friend or foe to adolescent health?* Paper presented at the biennial meetings of the Society for Research in Child Development, Indianapolis.

Brown, B. B., Mory, M. S., & Kinney, D. (1994). Casting adolescent crowds in a relational perspective: Caricature, channel, and context. In R. Montemayor, G. R. Adams, & T. P. Gullotta (Eds.), *Personal relationships during adolescence* (pp. 123–167). Thousand Oaks, CA: Sage.

Brown, L., Karrison, T., & Cibils, L. A. (1994). Mode of delivery and perinatal results in breech presentation. *American Journal of Obstetrics and Gynecology, 171,* 28–34.

Brown, R. (1965). *Social psychology.* New York: Free Press.

Brown, R. (1973). *A first language: The early stages.* Cambridge, MA: Harvard University Press.

Brown, R., & Bellugi, U. (1964). Three processes in the acquisition of syntax. *Harvard Educational Review, 334,* 133–151.

Brown, R., & Hanlon, C. (1970). Derivational complexity and order of acquisition. In J. R. Hayes (Ed.), *Cognition and the development of language* (pp. 155–207). New York: Wiley.

Brownell, C. A. (1990). Peer social skills in toddlers: Competencies and constraints illustrated by same-age and mixed-age interaction. *Child Development, 61,* 836–848.

Brownell, K. D., & Fairburn, C. G. (Eds.). (1995). *Eating disorders and obesity: A comprehensive handbook.* New York: Guilford Press.

Bruck, M., & Ceci, S. J. (1997). The suggestibility of young children. *Current Directions in Psychological Science, 6,* 75–79.

Bruck, M., Ceci, S. J., Francoeur, E., & Barr, R. (1995). "I hardly cried when I got my shot!" Influencing children's reports about a visit to their pediatrician. *Child Development, 66,* 193–208.

Bruck, M., Ceci, S. J., & Hembrooke, H. (1998). Reliability and credibility of young children's reports: From research to policy and practice. *American Psychologist, 53,* 136–151.

Bryant, P. E., MacLean, M., Bradley, L. L., & Crossland, J. (1990). Rhyme and alliteration, phoneme detection, and learning to read. *Developmental Psychology, 26,* 429–438.

Buchanan, C. M., Maccoby, E. E., & Dornbusch, S. M. (1991). Caught between parents: Adolescents' experience in divorced homes. *Child Development, 62,* 1008–1029.

Buchanan, C. M., Maccoby, E. E., & Dornbusch, S. M. (1996). *Adolescents after divorce.* Cambridge, MA: Harvard University Press.

Buhrmester, D. (1992). The developmental courses of sibling and peer relationships. In F. Boer & J. Dunn (Eds.), *Children's sibling relationships: Developmental and clinical issues.* Hillsdale, NJ: Erlbaum.

Buhrmester, D. (1996). Need fulfillment, interpersonal competence, and the developmental contexts of early adolescent friendship. In W. M. Bukowski, A. F. Newcomb, & W. W. Hartup (Eds.), *The company they keep: Friendship in childhood and adolescence* (pp. 158–185). Cambridge, England: Cambridge University Press.

Buhrmester, D., & Furman, W. (1990). Perceptions of sibling relationships during middle childhood and adolescence. *Child Development, 61,* 1387–1398.

Buitelaar, J. K., & van Engeland, H. (1996). Epidemiological approaches. In S. Sandberg (Ed.), *Hyperactivity disorders of childhood* (pp. 26–68). Cambridge, England: Cambridge University Press.

Bullock, M., & Lütkenhaus, P. (1990). Who am I? Self-understanding in toddlers. *Merrill-Palmer Quarterly, 36,* 217–238.

Burchinal, M., Lee, M., & Ramey, C. (1989). Type of day-care and preschool intellectual development in disadvantaged children. *Child Development, 60,* 128–137.

Burchinal, M. R., Campbell, F. A., Bryant, D. M., Wasik, B. H., & Ramey, C. T. (1997). Early intervention and mediating processes in cognitive performance of children of low-income African American families. *Child Development, 68,* 935–954.

Burks, V. S., Dodge, K. A., & Price, J. M. (1995). Models of internalizing outcomes of early rejection. *Development and Psychopathology, 7,* 683–695.

Burnett, J. W., Anderson, W. P., & Heppner, P. P. (1995). Gender roles and self-esteem: A consideration of environmental factors. *Journal of Counseling and Development, 73,* 323–326.

Burns, A. (1992). Mother-headed families: An international perspective and the case of Australia. *Social Policy Report, Society for Research in Child Development, 6*(1), 1–22.

Buss, A. H. (1989). Temperaments as personality traits. In G. A. Kohnstamm, J. E. Bates, & M. K. Rothbart (Eds.), *Temperament in childhood* (pp. 49–58). Chichester, England: Wiley.

Buss, A. H., & Plomin, R. (1984). *Temperament: Early developing personality traits.* Hillsdale, NJ: Erlbaum.

Buss, A. H., & Plomin, R. (1986). The EAS approach to temperament. In R. Plomin & J. Dunn (Eds.), *The study of temperament: Changes, continuities and challenges* (pp. 67–80). Hillsdale, NJ: Erlbaum.

Bussey, K., & Bandura, A. (1992). Self-regulatory mechanisms governing gender development. *Child Development, 63,* 1236–1250.

Bussing, R., Menvielle, E., & Zima, B. (1996). Relationship between behavioral problems and unintentional injuries in US children. *Archives of Pediatric and Adolescent Medicine, 150,* 50–56.

Butterworth, C. E., Jr., & Bendich, A. (1996). Folic acid and the prevention of birth defects. *Annual Review of Nutrition, 16,* 73–97.

Buysse, V., & Bailey, D. B., Jr. (1993). Behavioral and developmental outcomes in young chil-

dren with disabilities in integrated and segregated settings: A review of comparative studies. *The Journal of Special Education, 26,* 434–461.

Buzwell, S., & Rosenthal, D. (1996). Constructing a sexual self: Adolescents' sexual self-perceptions and sexual risk-taking. *Journal of Research on Adolescence, 6,* 489–513.

Byrnes, J. P., & Takahira, S. (1993). Explaining gender differences on SAT-Math items. *Developmental Psychology, 29,* 805–810.

Cain, V. S., & Hofferth, S. L. (1989). Parental choice of self-care for school-age children. *Journal of Marriage and the Family, 51,* 65–77.

Cairns, R. B. (1991). Multiple metaphors for a singular idea. *Developmental Psychology, 27,* 23–26.

Cairns, R. B., & Cairns, B. D. (1994). *Lifelines and risks: Pathways of youth in our time.* Cambridge, England: Cambridge University Press.

Campbell, D. W., & Eaton, W. O. (1995, April). *Sex differences in the activity level in the first year of life: A meta-analysis.* Paper presented at the biennial meetings of the Society for Research in Child Development, Indianapolis.

Campbell, F. A., & Ramey, C. T. (1994). Effects of early intervention on intellectual and academic achievement: A follow-up study of children from low-income families. *Child Development, 65,* 684–698.

Campbell, R. L., & Bickhard, M. H. (1992). Types of constraints on development: An interactivist approach. *Developmental Review, 12,* 311–338.

Campbell, S. B. (1990). The socialization and social development of hyperactive children. In M. Lewis & S. M. Miller (Eds.), *Handbook of developmental psychopathology* (pp. 77–92). New York: Plenum Press.

Campbell, S. B., Cohn, J. F., Flanagan, C., Popper, S., & Meyers, T. (1992). Course and correlates of postpartum depression during the transition to parenthood. *Development and Psychopathology, 4,* 29–47.

Campbell, S. B., & Ewing, L. J. (1990). Follow-up of hard-to-manage preschoolers: Adjustment at age 9 and predictors of continuing symptoms. *Journal of Child Psychology and Psychiatry, 31,* 871–889.

Campbell, S. B., Pierce, E. W., March, C. L., & Ewing, L. J. (1991). Noncompliant behavior, overactivity, and family stress as predictors of negative maternal control with preschool children. *Development and Psychopathology, 3,* 175–190.

Campione, J. C., & Brown, A. L. (1984). Learning ability and transfer propensity as sources of individual differences in intelligence. In P. H. Brooks, C. McCauley, & R. Sperber (Eds.), *Learning and cognition in the mentally retarded.* Hillsdale, NJ: Erlbaum.

Campione, J. C., Brown, A. L., & Ferrara, R. A. (1982). Mental retardation and intelligence.

In J. R. Sternberg (Ed.), *Handbook of human intelligence* (pp. 392–492). Cambridge, England: Cambridge University Press.

Campione, J. C., Brown, A. L., Ferrara, R. A., Jones, R. S., & Steinberg, E. (1985). Breakdowns in flexible use of information: Intelligence-related differences in transfer following equivalent learning performance. *Intelligence, 9,* 297–315.

The Canadian Early and Mid-Trimester Amniocentesis Trial (CEMAT) Group. (1998). Randomized trial to assess safety and fetal outcome of early and midtrimester amniocentesis. *The Lancet, 351,* 242–247.

Cantwell, D. P. (1990). Depression across the early life span. In M. Lewis & S. M. Miller (Eds.), *Handbook of developmental psychopathology* (pp. 293–310). New York: Plenum Press.

Capron, C., & Duyme, M. (1989). Assessment of effects of socio-economic status on IQ in a full cross-fostering study. *Nature, 340,* 552–554.

Capute, A. J., Palmer, F. B., Shapiro, B. K., Wachtel, R. C., Ross, A., & Accardo, P. J. (1984). Primitive reflex profile: A quantification of primitive reflexes in infancy. *Developmental Medicine and Child Neurology, 26,* 375–383.

Carey, S., & Bartlett, E. (1978). Acquiring a single new word. *Papers and Reports on Child Language Development, 15,* 17–29.

Carlson, E. A., & Sroufe, L. A. (1995). Contribution of attachment theory to developmental psychopathology. In D. Cicchetti & D. J. Cohen (Eds.), *Developmental psychopathology: Vol. 1. Theory and methods* (pp. 581–617). New York: Wiley.

Carmichael, S. L., & Abrams, B. (1997). A critical review of the relationship between gestational weight gain and preterm delivery. *Obstetrics and Gynecology, 89,* 865–873.

Caron, A. J., & Caron, R. F. (1981). Processing of relational information as an index of infant risk. In S. Friedman & M. Sigman (Eds.), *Preterm birth and psychological development* (pp. 219–240). New York: Academic Press.

Caron, A. J., Caron, R. F., Roberts, J., & Brooks, R. (1997). Infant sensitivity to deviations in dynamic facial-vocal displays: The role of eye regard. *Developmental Psychology, 33,* 802–813.

Carraher, T. N., Carraher, D. W., & Schliemann, A. D. (1985). Mathematics in the streets and in the schools. *British Journal of Developmental Psychology, 3,* 21–29.

Carver, R. P. (1990). Intelligence and reading ability in grades 2-12. *Intelligence, 14,* 449–455.

Case, R. (1985). *Intellectual development: Birth to adulthood.* New York: Academic Press.

Case, R. (1991). Stages in the development of the young child's first sense of self. *Developmental Review, 11,* 210–230.

Caselli, C., Casadio, P., & Bates, E. (1997). *A cross-linguistic study of the transition from first words to grammar* (Technical Report No. CND-9701). Center for Research in Language, University of California, San Diego.

Casey, M. B. (1986). Individual differences in selective attention among prereaders: A key to mirror-image confusions. *Developmental Psychology, 22,* 58–66.

Casey, M. B. (1996). Understanding individual differences in spatial ability within females: A nature/nurture interactionist framework. *Developmental Review, 16,* 241–260.

Casey, M. B., Nuttall, R., Pezaris, E., & Benbow, C. P. (1995). Influence of spatial ability on gender differences in mathematics college entrance test scores across diverse samples. *Developmental Psychology, 31,* 697–705.

Caspi, A. (1998). Personality development across the life course. In W. Damon (Ed.), *Handbook of child psychology: Vol. 3. Social, emotional, and personality development* (5th ed., pp. 311–388). New York: Wiley.

Caspi, A., Harkness, A. R., Moffitt, T. E., & Silva, P. A. (1996). Intellectual performance: Continuity and change. In P. A. Silva & W. R. Stanton (Eds.), *From child to adult: The Dunedin Multidisciplinary Health and Development Study* (pp. 59–74). Aukland: Oxford University Press.

Caspi, A., Henry, B., McGee, R. O., Moffitt, T. E., & Silva, P. A. (1995). Temperamental origins of child and adolescent behavior problems: From age three to age fifteen. *Child Development, 66,* 55–68.

Caspi, A., Lynam, D., Moffitt, T. E., & Silva, P. A. (1993). Unraveling girls' delinquency: Biological, dispositional, and contextual contributions to adolescent misbehavior. *Developmental Psychology, 29,* 19–30.

Caspi, A., & Moffitt, T. E. (1991). Individual differences are accentuated during periods of social change: The sample case of girls at puberty. *Journal of Personality and Social Psychology, 61,* 157–168.

Cassidy, J., & Berlin, L. J. (1994). The insecure/ambivalent pattern of attachment: Theory and research. *Child Development, 65,* 971–991.

Caughy, M. O., DiPietro, J. A., & Strobino, D. M. (1994). Day-care participation as a protective factor in the cognitive development of low-income children. *Child Development, 65,* 457–471.

Ceci, S. J., & Bruck, M. (1993). Suggestibility of the child witness: A historical review and synthesis. *Psychological Bulletin, 113,* 403–439.

Ceci, S. J., & Bruck, M. (1995). *Jeopardy in the courtroom: A scientific analysis of children's testimony.* Washington, DC: American Psychological Association.

Ceci, S. J., & Bruck, M. (1998). Children's testimony: Applied and basic issues. In W. Damon (Ed.), *Handbook of child psychology: Vol. 4. Child psychology in practice* (5th ed., pp. 713–774). New York: Wiley.

Ceci, S. J., & Williams, W. M. (1997). Schooling, intelligence, and income. *American Psychologist, 52,* 1051–1058.

Centers for Disease Control. (1992). Pregnancy risks determined from birth certificate data—United States, 1989. *Morbidity and Mortality Weekly Report, 41*(30), 556–563.

Centers for Disease Control. (1993). Rates of cesarean delivery—United States, 1991. *Journal of the American Medical Association, 269*(18), 2360.

Centers for Disease Control. (1994a). Preventing tobacco use among young people: A report of the Surgeon General. Executive summary. *Morbidity and Mortality Weekly Report, 43*(RR-4), 2–10.

Centers for Disease Control. (1994b). Programs for the prevention of suicide among adolescents and young adults. *Morbidity and Mortality Weekly Report, 43*(RR-6, April 22), 3–7.

Centers for Disease Control. (1994c). Recommendations of the U.S. Public Health Service task force on the use of zidovudine to reduce perinatal transmission of human immunodeficiency virus. *Morbidity and Mortality Weekly Report, 43*(August 5), 1–20.

Centers for Disease Control. (1995a). Chorionic villus sampling and amniocentesis: Recommendations for prenatal counseling. *Morbidity and Mortality Weekly Report, 44*(RR-9), 1–12.

Centers for Disease Control. (1995b). U.S. Public Health Service recommendations for human immunodeficiency virus counseling and voluntary testing for pregnant women. *Mortality and Morbidity Weekly Report, 44*(RR-7), 1–15.

Centers for Disease Control. (1996a). Asthma mortality and hospitalization among children and young adults—United States, 1980–1993. *Morbidity and Mortality Weekly Report, 45*(17), 350–353.

Centers for Disease Control. (1996b). Guidelines for school health programs to promote lifelong healthy eating. *Morbidity and Mortality Weekly Report, 45*(RR-9), 1–41.

Centers for Disease Control. (1996c). HIV testing among women aged 18–44 years—United States, 1991 and 1993. *Morbidity and Mortality Weekly Report, 45*(34), 733–737.

Centers for Disease Control. (1997a). State-specific variation in rates of twin births—United States, 1992–1994. *Morbidity and Mortality Weekly Report, 46*(2), 121–125.

Centers for Disease Control. (1997b). Update: Blood lead levels—United States, 1991–1994. *Morbidity and Mortality Weekly Report, 46*(7), 141–145.

Cernoch, J. M., & Porter, R. H. (1985). Recognition of maternal axillary odors by infants. *Child Development, 56,* 1593–1598.

Chalfant, J. C. (1989). Learning disabilities: Policy issues and promising approaches. *American Psychologist, 44,* 392–398.

Chang, L., & Murray, A. (1995, April). *Math performance of 5- and 6-year-olds in Taiwan and the U.S.: Maternal beliefs, expectations, and tutorial assistance.* Paper presented at the biennial meetings of the Society for Research in Child Development, Indianapolis.

Chao, R. K. (1994). Beyond parental control and authoritarian parenting style: Understanding Chinese parenting through the cultural notion of training. *Child Development, 65,* 1111–1119.

Chapa, J., & Valencia, R. R. (1993). Latino population growth, demographic characteristics, and educational stagnation: An examination of recent trends. *Hispanic Journal of Behavioral Sciences, 15,* 165–187.

Charman, T., Redfern, S., & Fonagy, P. (1995, April). *Individual differences in theory of mind acquisition: The role of attachment security.* Paper presented at the biennial meetings of the Society for Research in Child Development, Indianapolis.

Chase-Lansdale, P. L., & Hetherington, E. M. (1990). The impact of divorce on life-span development: Short and long term effects. In P. B. Baltes, D. L., Featherman, & R. M. Lerner (Eds.), *Life-span development and behavior* (Vol. 10, pp. 107–151). Hillsdale, NJ: Erlbaum.

Chen, X., Rubin, K. H., & Li, Z. (1995). Social functioning and adjustment in Chinese children: A longitudinal study. *Developmental Psychology, 31,* 531–539.

Chen, X., Rubin, K. H., & Sun, Y. (1992). Social reputation and peer relationships in Chinese and Canadian children: A cross-cultural study. *Child Development, 63,* 1336–1343.

Cheng, M., & Hannah, M. (1993). Breech delivery at term: A critical review of the literature. *Obstetrics and Gynecology, 82,* 605–618.

Cherlin, A. J. (1992a). *Marriage, divorce, remarriage.* Cambridge, MA: Harvard University Press.

Cherlin, A. J. (1992b). Infant care and full-time employment. In A. Booth (Ed.), *Child care in the 1990s: Trends and consequences* (pp. 209–214). Hillsdale, NJ: Erlbaum.

Cherlin, A. J., Furstenberg, F. F., Chase-Lansdale, P. L., Kiernan, K. E., Robins, P. K., Morrison, E. R., & Teitler, J. O. (1991). Longitudinal studies of effects of divorce on children in Great Britain and the United States. *Science, 252,* 1386–1389.

Chess, S., & Korn, S. J. (1980). Temperament and behavior disorder in mentally retarded children. *The Journal of Special Education, 23,* 122–130.

Chess, S., & Thomas, A. (1984). *Origins and evolution of behavior disorders: Infancy to early adult life.* New York: Brunner/Mazel.

Chi, M. T. (1978). Knowledge structure and memory development. In R. S. Siegler (Ed.), *Children's thinking: What develops?* (pp. 73–96). Hillsdale, NJ: Erlbaum.

Chisholm, J. S. (1989). Biology, culture, and the development of temperament: A Navaho example. In J. K. Nugent, B. M. Lester, & T. B.

Brazelton (Eds.), *The cultural context of infancy: Vol. 1. Biology, culture, and infant development*. Norwood, NJ: Ablex.

Chomsky, N. (1965). *Aspects of a theory of syntax*. Cambridge, MA: MIT Press.

Chomsky, N. (1975). *Reflections on language*. New York: Pantheon Books.

Chomsky, N. (1986). *Knowledge of language: Its nature, origin, and use*. New York: Praeger.

Chomsky, N. (1988). *Language and problems of knowledge*. Cambridge, MA: MIT Press.

Christoffel, K. K., Donovan, M., Schofer, J., Wills, K., & Lavigne, J. V. (1996). Psychosocial factors in childhood pedestrian injury: A matched case-control study. *Pediatrics, 97,* 33–42.

Chumlea, W. C. (1982). Physical growth in adolescence. In B. B. Wolman (Ed.), *Handbook of developmental psychology* (pp. 471–485). Englewood Cliffs, NJ: Prentice Hall.

Cicchetti, D., & Cohen, D. J. (Eds.). (1995a). *Developmental psychopathology: Vol. 1. Theory and methods. Vol. 2. Risk, disorder, and adaptation*. New York: Wiley.

Cicchetti, D., & Cohen, D. J. (1995b). Perspectives on developmental psychopathology. In D. Cicchetti & D. J. Cohen (Eds.), *Developmental psychopathology. Vol 1: Theory and methods* (pp. 3–20). New York: Wiley.

Cicchetti, D., & Toth, S. L. (1998). The development of depression in children and adolescents. *American Psychologist, 53,* 221–241.

Cillessen, A. H. N., van IJzendoorn, H. W., van Lieshout, C. F. M., & Hartup, W. W. (1992). Heterogeneity among peer-rejected boys: Subtypes and stabilities. *Child Development, 63,* 893–905.

Clark, E. V. (1975). Knowledge, context, and strategy in the acquisition of meaning. In D. P. Date (Ed.), *Georgetown University round table on language and linguistics*. Washington, DC: Georgetown University Press.

Clark, E. V. (1983). Meanings and concepts. In J. H. Flavell & E. M. Markman (Eds.), *Handbook of child psychology: Cognitive development* (Vol. 3, pp. 787–840). New York: Wiley.

Clark, E. V. (1987). The principle of contrast: A constraint on language acquisition. In B. MacWhinney (Ed.), *Mechanisms of language acquisition* (pp. 1–34). Hillsdale, NJ: Erlbaum.

Clark, E. V. (1990). On the pragmatics of contrast. *Journal of Child Language, 41,* 417–431.

Clarke, A. M., & Clarke, A. D. B. (1976). *Early experience: Myth and evidence*. New York: Free Press.

Clarke-Stewart, A. (1990). "The 'effects' of infant day care reconsidered" reconsidered: Risks for parents, children, and researchers. In N. Fox & G. G. Fein (Eds.), *Infant day care: The current debate* (pp. 61–86). Norwood, NJ: Ablex.

Clarke-Stewart, A. (1992). Consequences of child care for children's development. In A. Booth (Ed.), *Child care in the 1990s: Trends and consequences* (pp. 63–82). Hillsdale, NJ: Erlbaum.

Clarke-Stewart, K. A., Gruber, C. P., & Fitzgerald, L. M. (1994). *Children at home and in day care*. Hillsdale, NJ: Erlbaum.

Cnattingius, S., Berendes, H. W., & Forman, M. R. (1993). Do delayed childbearers face increased risks of adverse pregnancy outcomes after the first birth? *Obstetrics and Gynecology, 81,* 512–516.

Coe, C., Hayashi, K. T., & Levine, S. (1988). Hormones and behavior at puberty: Activation or concatenation? In M. R. Gunnar & W. A. Collins (Eds.), *Development during the transition to adolescence: Minnesota symposia on child psychology* (Vol. 21, pp. 17–42). Hillsdale, NJ: Erlbaum.

Cohen, D., & Strayer, J. (1996). Empathy in conduct-disordered and comparison youth. *Developmental Psychology, 32,* 988–998.

Cohen, S., Tyrrell, D. A. J., & Smith, A. P. (1991). Psychological stress and susceptibility to the common cold. *The New England Journal of Medicine, 325,* 606–612.

Cohen, Y. A. (1964). *The transition from childhood to adolescence*. Chicago: Aldine.

Coie, J. D. (1997a, April). *Initial outcome evaluation of the prevention trial*. Paper presented at the biennial meetings of the Society for Research in Child Development, Washington, DC.

Coie, J. D. (1997b, August). *Testing developmental theory of antisocial behavior with outcomes from the Fast Track Prevention Project*. Paper presented at the annual meeting of the American Psychological Association, Chicago.

Coie, J. D., & Cillessen, A. H. N. (1993). Peer rejection: Origins and effects on children's development. *Current Directions in Psychological Science, 2,* 89–92.

Coie, J. D., & Dodge, K. A. (1998). Aggression and antisocial behavior. In W. Damon (Ed.), *Handbook of child psychology: Vol. 3. Social, emotional, and personality development* (5th ed., pp. 779–862). New York: Wiley.

Coie, J. D., & Kupersmidt, J. B. (1983). A behavioral analysis of emerging social status in boys' groups. *Child Development, 54,* 1400–1416.

Coie, J. D., Terry, R., Lenox, K., Lochman, J., & Hyman, C. (1995). Childhood peer rejection and aggression as predictors of stable patterns of adolescent disorder. *Development and Psychopathology, 7,* 697–713.

Coiro, M. J. (1995, April). *Child behavior problems as a function of marital conflict and parenting*. Paper presented at the biennial meetings of the Society for Research in Child Development, Indianapolis.

Colby, A., & Damon, W. (1992). *Some do care: Contemporary lives of moral commitment*. New York: Free Press.

Colby, A., Kohlberg, L., Gibbs, J., & Lieberman, M. (1983). A longitudinal study of moral judgment. *Monographs of the Society for Research in Child Development, 48*(1–2, Serial No. 200).

Cole, D. A. (1991a). Change in self-perceived competence as a function of peer and teacher evaluation. *Developmental Psychology, 27,* 682–688.

Cole, D. A. (1991b). Social integration and severe disabilities: A longitudinal analysis of child outcomes. *The Journal of Special Education, 25,* 340–351.

Cole, D. A., & Rodman, H. (1987). When school-age children care for themselves: Issues for family life educators and parents. *Family Relations, 36,* 92–96.

Cole, M. (1992). Culture in development. In M. H. Bornstein & M. E. Lamb (Eds.), *Developmental psychology: An advanced textbook* (3rd ed., pp. 731–789). Hillsdale, NJ: Erlbaum.

Cole, M., & Traupmann, K. (1981). Comparative cognitive research: Learning from a learning disabled child. In W. A. Collins (Ed.), *Minnesota symposia on child psychology* (Vol. 14, pp. 125–154). Hillsdale, NJ: Erlbaum.

Coley, R. L., & Chase-Lansdale, P. L. (1998). Adolescent pregnancy and parenthood: Recent evidence and future directions. *American Psychologist, 53,* 152–166.

Collaer, M. L., & Hines, M. (1995). Human behavioral sex differences: A role for gonadal hormones during early development? *Psychological Bulletin, 118,* 55–107.

Collet, J. P., Burtin, P., Gillet, J., Bossard, N., Ducruet, T., & Durr, F. (1994). Risk of infectious diseases in children attending different types of day-care setting. Epicreche Research Group. *Respiration, 61,* 16–19.

Collins, P. A., Wright, J. C., Anderson, D. R., Huston, A. C., Schmitt, K. L., McElroy, E. S., & Linebarger, D. L. (1997, April). *Effects of early childhood media use on academic achievement*. Paper presented at the biennial meetings of the Society for Research in Child Development, Washington, DC.

Collins, W. A. (Ed.). (1984). *Development during middle childhood: The years from six to twelve*. Washington, DC: National Academy Press.

Colombo, J. (1993). *Infant cognition: Predicting later intellectual functioning*. Newbury Park, CA: Sage.

Colton, M., Buss, K., Mangelsdorf, S., Brooks, C., Sorenson, D., Stansbury, K., Harris, M., & Gunnar, M. (1992). Relations between toddler coping strategies, temperament, attachment and adrenocortical stress responses. Poster presented at the Eighth International Conference on Infant Studies, Miami, FL.

Community Childhood Hunger Identification Project. (1991). *A survey of childhood hunger in the United States*. Washington, DC: Food Research and Action Center.

Compas, B. E., Ey, S., & Grant, K. E. (1993). Taxonomy, assessment, and diagnosis of depression during adolescence. *Psychological Bulletin, 114,* 323–344.

Compas, B. E., Hinden, B. R., & Gerhardt, C. A. (1995). Adolescent development: Pathways and processes of risk and resilience. *Annual Review of Psychology, 46,* 265–293.

Comstock, G. (1991). *Television and the American child.* San Diego, CA: Academic Press.

Conger, R. D., Conger, K. J., Elder, G. H., Jr., Lorenz, F. O., Simons, R. L., & Whitbeck, L. B. (1992). A family process model of economic hardship and adjustment of early adolescent boys. *Child Development, 63,* 526–541.

Conger, R. D., Ge, X., Elder, G. H., Jr., Lorenz, F. O., & Simons, R. L. (1994). Economic stress, coercive family process, and developmental problems of adolescence. *Child Development, 65,* 541–561.

Conger, R. D., Patterson, G. R., & Ge, X. (1995). It takes two to replicate: A mediational model for the impact of parents' stress on adolescent adjustment. *Child Development, 66,* 80–97.

Connolly, K., & Dalgleish, M. (1989). The emergence of a tool-using skill in infancy. *Developmental Psychology, 25,* 894–912.

Conrad, M., & Hammen, C. (1989). Role of maternal depression in perceptions of child maladjustment. *Journal of Consulting and Clinical Psychology, 57,* 663–667.

Cooper, P. J. (1995). Eating disorders and their relationship to mood and anxiety disorders. In K. D. Brownell & C. G. Fairburn (Eds.), *Eating disorders and obesity: A comprehensive handbook* (pp. 159–164). New York: Guilford Press.

Cooper, R. P., & Aslin, R. N. (1994). Developmental differences in infant attention to the spectral properties of infant-directed speech. *Child Development, 65,* 1663–1677.

Corter, C. M., & Fleming, A. S. (1995). Psychobiology of maternal behavior in human beings. In M. H. Bornstein (Ed.), *Handbook of parenting: Vol. 2. Biology and ecology of parenting* (pp. 87–116). Mahwah, NJ: Erlbaum.

Cossette, L., Malcuit, G., & Pomerleau, A. (1991). Sex differences in motor activity during early infancy. *Infant Behavior and Development, 14,* 175–186.

Costa, P. T., Jr., & McCrae, R. R. (1984). Personality as a lifelong determinant of wellbeing. In C. Z. Malatesta & C. E. Izard (Eds.), *Emotion in adult development* (pp. 141–158). Beverly Hills, CA: Sage.

Costa, P. T., Jr., & McCrae, R. R. (1994). Set like plaster? Evidence for the stability of adult personality. In T. F. Hetherton & J. L. Weinberger (Eds.), *Can personality change?* (pp. 21–40). Washington, DC: American Psychological Association.

Costello, E. J., & Angold, A. (1995). Developmental epidemiology. In D. Cicchetti & D. J. Cohen (Eds.), *Developmental psychopathology: Vol. 1. Theory and methods* (pp. 23–56). New York: Wiley.

Coté, J. E. (1996). Identity: A multidimensional analysis. In J. G. Adams, R. Montemayor, & T. P. Gullotta (Eds.), *Psychosocial development during adolescence: Progress in developmental contextualism* (pp. 131–180). Thousand Oaks, CA: Sage.

Coulton, C. J., Korbin, J. E., Su, M., & Chow, J. (1995). Community level factors and child maltreatment rates. *Child Development, 66,* 1262–1276.

Crain, E. F., Weiss, K. B., Bijur, P. E., Hersh, M., Westbrook, L., & Stein, R. E. K. (1994). An estimate of the prevalence of asthma and wheezing among inner city children. *Pediatrics, 94,* 356–362.

Crain-Thoreson, C., & Dale, P. S. (1995, April). *Parent vs. staff storybook reading as an intervention for language delay.* Paper presented at the biennial meetings of the Society for Research in Child Development, Indianapolis.

Crawford, J. (1991). *Bilingual education: History, politics, theory, and practice* (2nd ed.). Los Angeles: Bilingual Education Services.

Crick, N. R., Casas, J. F., & Mosher, M. (1997). Relational and overt aggression in preschool. *Developmental Psychology, 33,* 579–588.

Crick, N. R., & Grotpeter, J. K. (1995). Relational aggression, gender, and social-psychological adjustment. *Child Development, 66,* 710–722.

Crick, N. R., & Grotpeter, J. K. (1996). Children's treatment by peers: Victims of relational and overt aggression. *Development and Psychopathology, 8,* 367–380.

Crittenden, P. M. (1992). Quality of attachment in the preschool years. *Development and Psychopathology, 4,* 209–241.

Crittenden, P. M., Partridge, M. F., & Claussen, A. H. (1991). Family patterns of relationship in normative and dysfunctional families. *Development and Psychopathology, 3,* 491–512.

Crnic, K. A., Greenberg, M. T., Ragozin, A. S., Robinson, N. M., & Basham, R. B. (1983). Effects of stress and social support on mothers and premature and full-term infants. *Child Development, 54,* 209–217.

Crockenberg, S. B. (1981). Infant irritability, mother responsiveness, and social support influences on the security of infant-mother attachment. *Child Development, 52,* 857–865.

Crockenberg, S. B. (1987). Predictors and correlates of anger toward and punitive control of toddlers by adolescent mothers. *Child Development, 58,* 964–975.

Crockenberg, S. B., & Litman, C. (1990). Autonomy as competence in 2-year-olds: Maternal correlates of child defiance, compliance, and self-assertion. *Developmental Psychology, 26,* 961–971.

Crockett, L. J., & Crouter, A. C. (Eds.). (1995). *Pathways through adolescence.* Mahwah, NJ: Erlbaum.

Cromer, R. F. (1991). *Language and thought in normal and handicapped children.* Oxford, England: Basil Blackwell.

Crook, C. (1987). Taste and olfaction. In P. Salapatek & L. Cohen (Eds.), *Handbook of infant perception: Vol. 1. From sensation to perception* (pp. 237–264). Orlando, FL: Academic Press.

Crouter, A. C., & McHale, S. M. (1993). Familial economic circumstances: Implications for adjustment and development in early adolescence. In R. M. Lerner (Ed.), *Early adolescence: Perspectives on research, policy, and intervention* (pp. 71–91). Hillsdale, NJ: Erlbaum.

Crowell, J. A., & Feldman, S. S. (1988). Mothers' internal models of relationships and children's behavioral and developmental status: A study of mother-child interaction. *Child Development, 50,* 1273–1285.

Crowell, J. A., & Feldman, S. S. (1991). Mothers' working models of attachment relationships and mother and child behavior during separation and reunion. *Developmental Psychology, 27,* 597–605.

Crystal, D. S., Chen, C., Fuligni, A. J., Stevenson, H. W., Hsu, C., Ko, H., Kitamura, S., & Kimura, S. (1994). Psychological maladjustment and academic achievement: A cross-cultural study of Japanese, Chinese, and American high school students. *Child Development, 65,* 738–753.

Crystal, D. S., & Stevenson, H. W. (1995). What is a bad kid? Answers of adolescents and their mothers in three cultures. *Journal of Research on Adolescence, 5,* 71–91.

Culbertson, F. M. (1997). Depression and gender: An international review. *American Psychologist, 52,* 25–31.

Cummings, E. M., & Davies, P. T. (1994). Maternal depression and child development. *Journal of Child Psychology and Psychiatry, 35,* 73–112.

Cunningham, A. S., Jelliffe, D. B., & Jelliffe, E. F. P. (1991). Breast-feeding and health in the 1980s: A global epidemiologic review. *Journal of Pediatrics, 118,* 659–666.

Cunningham, F. G., MacDonald, P. C., Leveno, K. J., Gant, N. F., & Gilstrap, L. C. (1993). *Williams obstetrics* (19th ed.). Norwalk, CT: Appleton & Lange.

Currie, J., & Thomas, D. (1997). Can Head Start lead to long term gains in cognition after all? *SRCD Newsletter, 40*(2), 3–5.

Cutrona, C. E., & Troutman, B. R. (1986). Social support, infant temperament, and parenting self-efficacy: A mediational model of postpartum depression. *Child Development, 57,* 1507–1518.

Daly, K. A. (1997). Definition and epidemiology of otitis media. In J. E. Roberts, I. F. Wallace, & F. W. Henderson (Eds.), *Otitis media in young children: Medical, developmental, and educational considerations* (pp. 3–42). Baltimore: Brookes.

Daly, S., Mills, J. L., Molloy, A. M., Conley, M., Lee, Y. J., Kirke, P. N., Weir, D. G., & Scott, J. M. (1997). Minimum effective dose of folic acid for food fortification to prevent neural-tube defects. *The Lancet, 350,* 1666–1669.

Damon, W. (1977). *The social world of the child.* San Francisco: Jossey-Bass.

Damon, W. (1983). The nature of social-cognitive change in the developing child. In W. F. Overton (Ed.), *The relationship between social and cognitive development* (pp. 103–142). Hillsdale, NJ: Erlbaum.

Damon, W., & Hart, D. (1988). *Self understanding in childhood and adolescence.* New York: Cambridge University Press.

Dark, V. J., & Benbow, C. P. (1993). Cognitive differences among the gifted: A review and new data. In D. K. Detterman (Ed.), *Current topics in human intelligence: Vol. 3. Individual differences and cognition* (pp. 85–120). Norwood, NJ: Ablex.

Darling, N., & Steinberg, L. (1993). Parenting style as context: An integrative model. *Psychological Bulletin, 113,* 487–496.

Darlington, R. B. (1991). The long-term effects of model preschool programs. In L. Okagaki & R. J. Sternberg (Eds.), *Directors of development* (pp. 203–215). Hillsdale, NJ: Erlbaum.

Dasen, P. R. (1984). The cross-cultural study of intelligence: Piaget and the Baoule. *International Journal of Psychology, 19,* 407–434.

Davidson, E. S., Yasuna, A., & Tower, A. (1979). The effect of television cartoons on sex-role stereotyping in young girls. *Child Development, 50,* 597–600.

Davies, G. M. (1993). Children's memory for other people: An integrative review. In C. A. Nelson (Ed.), *The Minnesota symposia on child psychology* (Vol. 26, pp. 123–157). Hillsdale, NJ: Erlbaum.

Davies, P. T., & Cummings, E. M. (1994). Marital conflict and child adjustment: An emotional security hypothesis. *Psychological Bulletin, 116,* 387–411.

Dawson, D. A. (1991). Family structure and children's health and well-being: Data from the 1988 National Health Interview Survey on Child Health. *Journal of Marriage and the Family, 53,* 573–584.

Dawson, G., Panagiotides, H., Klinger, L. G., & Spieker, S. (1997). Infants of depressed and nondepressed mothers exhibit differences in frontal brain electrical activity during the expression of negative emotions. *Developmental Psychology, 33,* 650–656.

de Chateau, P. (1980). Effects of hospital practices on synchrony in the development of the infant-parent relationship. In P. M. Taylor (Ed.), *Parent-infant relationships* (pp. 137–168). New York: Grune & Stratton.

de Haan, M., Luciana, M., Maslone, S. M., Matheny, L. S., & Richards, M. L. M. (1994). Development, plasticity, and risk: Commentary on Huttenlocher, Pollit and Gorman, and Gottesman and Goldsmith. In C. A. Nelson (Ed.), *The Minnesota symposia on child psychology* (Vol. 27, pp. 161–178). Hillsdale, NJ: Erlbaum.

De Peretti, E., & Forest, M. G. (1976). Unconjugated dehydroeplandrosterone plasma levels in normal subjects from birth to adolescence in humans: The use of a sensitive radioimmunoassay. *Journal of Clinical Endocrinology and Metabolism, 43,* 982–991.

de Villiers, P. A., & de Villiers, J. G. (1992). Language development. In M. H. Bornstein & M. E. Lamb (Eds.), *Developmental psychology: An advanced textbook* (3rd ed., pp. 337–418). Hillsdale, NJ: Erlbaum.

De Wolff, M. S., & van IJzendoorn, M. H. (1997). Sensitivity and attachment: A meta-analysis on parental antecedents of infant attachment. *Child Development, 68,* 571–591.

Deater-Deckard, K., & Dodge, K. A. (1997). Externalizing behavior problems and discipline revisited: Nonlinear effects and variation by culture, context, and gender. *Psychological Inquiry, 8,* 161–175.

Deater-Deckard, K., Dodge, K. A., Bates, J. E., & Pettit, G. S. (1996). Physical discipline among African American and European American mothers: Links to children's externalizing behaviors. *Developmental Psychology, 32,* 1065–1072.

Deater-Deckard, K., & Plomin, R. (1997, April). *An adoption study of the etiology of teacher reports of externalizing problems in middle childhood.* Paper presented at the biennial meetings of the Society for Research in Child Development, Washington, DC.

DeCasper, A. J., & Fifer, W. P. (1980). Of human bonding: Newborns prefer their mothers' voices. *Science, 208,* 1174–1176.

DeCasper, A. J., Lecaneut, J., Busnel, M., Granier-Deferre, C., & Maugeais, R. (1994). Fetal reactions to recurrent maternal speech. *Infant Behavior and Development, 17,* 159–164.

DeCasper, A. J., & Spence, M. J. (1986). Prenatal maternal speech influences newborns' perception of speech sounds. *Infant Behavior and Development, 9,* 133–150.

Delgado-Gaitan, C. (1994). Socializing young children in Mexican-American families: An intergenerational perspective. In P. M. Greenfield & R. R. Cocking (Eds.), *Cross-cultural roots of minority child development* (pp. 55–86). Hillsdale, NJ: Erlbaum.

DeLoache, J. S. (1989). The development of representation in young children. In H. W. Reese (Ed.), *Advances in child development and behavior* (Vol. 22, pp. 2–37). San Diego, CA: Academic Press.

DeLoache, J. S. (1995). Early understanding and use of symbols: The model model. *Current Directions in Psychological Science, 4,* 109–113.

DeLoache, J. S., & Brown, A. L. (1987). Differences in the memory-based searching of delayed and normally developing young children. *Intelligence, 11,* 277–289.

DeMeis, D. K., Hock, E., & McBride, S. L. (1986). The balance of employment and motherhood: Longitudinal study of mothers' feelings about separation from their first-born infants. *Developmental Psychology, 22,* 627–632.

Dempster, F. N. (1981). Memory span: Sources of individual and developmental differences. *Psychological Bulletin, 89,* 63–100.

Den Ouden, L., Rijken, M., Brand, R., Verloove-Vanhorick, S. P., & Ruys, J. H. (1991). Is it correct to correct? Developmental milestones in 555 "normal" preterm infants compared with term infants. *Journal of Pediatrics, 118,* 399–404.

Dennis, W. (1960). Causes of retardation among institutional children: Iran. *Journal of Genetic Psychology, 96,* 47–59.

DeRosier, M. E., Kupersmidt, J. B., & Patterson, C. J. (1994). Children's academic and behavioral adjustment as a function of the chronicity and proximity of peer rejection. *Child Development, 65,* 1799–1831.

Derryberry, D., & Rothbart, M. K. (1998). Reactive and effortful processes in the organization of temperament. *Development and Psychopathology, 9,* 633–652.

Dietrich, K. N., Berger, O. G., Succop, P. A., Hammond, P. B., & Bornschein, R. L. (1993). The developmental consequences of low to moderate prenatal and postnatal lead exposure: Intellectual attainment in the Cincinnati Lead Study cohort following school entry. *Neurotoxicology and Teratology, 15,* 37–44.

Digman, J. M. (1990). Personality structure: Emergence of the five-factor model. *Annual Review of Psychology, 41,* 417–440.

Dishion, T. J. (1990). The family ecology of boys' peer relations in middle childhood. *Child Development, 61,* 874–892.

Dishion, T. J., Andrews, D. W., & Crosby, L. (1995a). Antisocial boys and their friends in early adolescence: Relationship characteristics, quality, and interactional process. *Child Development, 66,* 139–151.

Dishion, T. J., French, D. C., & Patterson, G. R. (1995b). The development and ecology of antisocial behavior. In D. Cicchetti & D. J. Cohen (Eds.), *Developmental psychopathology: Vol. 2. Risk, disorder, and adaptation* (pp. 421–471). New York: Wiley.

Dishion, T. J., Patterson, G. R., Stoolmiller, M., & Skinner, M. L. (1991). Family, school, and behavioral antecedents to early adolescent involvement with antisocial peers. *Developmental Psychology, 27,* 172–180.

Dockett, S., & Smith, I. (1995, April). *Children's theories of mind and their involvement in complex shared pretense.* Paper presented at the biennial meetings of the Society for Research in Child Development, Indianapolis.

Dodge, K. A. (1983). Behavioral antecedents of peer social status. *Child Development, 54,* 1386–1399.

Dodge, K. A. (1990). Developmental psychopathology in children of depressed mothers. *Developmental Psychology, 26,* 3–6.

Dodge, K. A. (1997, April). *Testing developmental theory through prevention trials.* Paper presented at the biennial meetings of the Society for Research in Child Development, Washington, DC.

Dodge, K. A., Coie, J. D., Pettit, G. S., & Price, J. M. (1990). Peer status and aggression in boys' groups: Developmental and contextual analysis. *Child Development, 61,* 1289–1309.

Dodge, K. A., & Feldman, E. (1990). Issues in social cognition and sociometric status. In S. R. Asher & J. D. Coie (Eds.), *Peer rejection in childhood* (pp. 119–155). Cambridge, England: Cambridge University Press.

Dodge, K. A., & Frame, C. L. (1982). Social cognitive biases and deficits in aggressive boys. *Child Development, 53,* 620–635.

Dodge, K. A., Murphy, R. R., & Buchsbaum, K. (1984). The assessment of intention-cue detection skills in children: Implications for developmental psychopathology. *Child Development, 55,* 163–173.

Dodge, K. A., Pettit, G. S., & Bates, J. E. (1994). Socialization mediators of the relation between socioeconomic status and child conduct problems. *Child Development, 65,* 649–665.

Donnerstein, E., Slaby, R. G., & Eron, L. D. (1994). The mass media and youth aggression. In L. D. Eron, J. H. Gentry, & P. Schlegel (Eds.), *Reason to hope: A psychosocial perspective on violence and youth* (pp. 219–250). Washington, DC: American Psychological Association.

Dornbusch, S. M., Ritter, P. L., Liederman, P. H., Roberts, D. F., & Fraleigh, M. J. (1987). The relation of parenting style to adolescent school performance. *Child Development, 58,* 1244–1257.

Doyle, A. B., & Aboud, F. E. (1995). A longitudinal study of white children's racial prejudice as a social-cognitive development. *Merrill-Palmer Quarterly, 41,* 209–228.

Dryfoos, J. (1990). *Adolescents at risk: Prevalence and prevention.* New York: Oxford University Press.

DuBois, D. L., Felner, R. D., Brand, S., Phillips, R. S. C., & Lease, A. M. (1996). Early adolescent self-esteem: A developmental-ecological framework and assessment strategy. *Journal of Research on Adolescence, 6,* 543–579.

Duke, P. M., Carlsmith, J. M., Jennings, D., Martin, J. A., Dornbusch, S. M., Gross, R. T., & Siegel-Gorelick, B. (1982). Educational correlates of early and late sexual maturation in adolescence. *Journal of Pediatrics, 100,* 633–637.

Duncan, G. (1993, April). *Economic deprivation and childhood development.* Paper presented at the biennial meetings of the Society for Research in Child Development, New Orleans.

Duncan, G. J., & Brooks-Gunn, J. (Eds.). (1997). *Consequences of growing up poor.* New York: Russell Sage Foundation.

Duncan, G. J., Brooks-Gunn, J., & Klebanov, P. K. (1994). Economic deprivation and early childhood development. *Child Development, 65,* 296–318.

Duncan, R. M. (1995). Piaget and Vygotsky revisited: Dialogue or assimilation? *Developmental Review, 15,* 458–472.

Dunham, P. J., Dunham, F., & Curwin, A. (1993). Joint-attentional states and lexical acquisition at 18 months. *Developmental Psychology, 29,* 827–831.

Dunn, J. (1992). Siblings and development. *Current Directions in Psychological Science, 1,* 6–9.

Dunn, J. (1993). *Young children's close relationships.* Newbury Park, CA: Sage.

Dunn, J. (1994). Experience and understanding of emotions, relationships, and membership in a particular culture. In P. Ekman & R. J. Davidson (Eds.), *The nature of emotion: Fundamental questions* (pp. 352–355). New York: Oxford University Press.

Dunn, J., & Kendrick, C. (1982). Siblings and their mothers: Developing relationships within the family. In M. E. Lamb & B. Sutton-Smith (Eds.), *Sibling relationships: Their nature and significance across the lifespan* (pp. 39–60). Hillsdale, NJ: Erlbaum.

Dunn, J., & McGuire, S. (1994). Young children's nonshared experiences: A summary of studies in Cambridge and Colorado. In E. M. Hetherington, D. Reiss, & R. Plomin (Eds.), *Separate social worlds of siblings: The impact of nonshared environment on development* (pp. 111–128). Hillsdale, NJ: Erlbaum.

Dunphy, D. C. (1963). The social structure of urban adolescent peer groups. *Sociometry, 26,* 230–246.

Eagly, A. H. (1995). The science and politics of comparing women and men. *American Psychologist, 50,* 145–158.

Easterbrooks, M. A., Davidson, C. E., & Chazan, R. (1993). Psychosocial risk, attachment, and behavior problems among school-aged children. *Development and Psychopathology, 5,* 389–402.

Eccles, J. S., & Jacobs, J. E. (1986). Social forces shape math attitudes and performance. *Signs: Journal of Women in Culture and Society, 11,* 367–389.

Egan, S. K., & Perry, D. G. (1998). Does low self-regard invite victimization? *Developmental Psychology, 34,* 299–309.

Egeland, B., & Sroufe, L. A. (1981). Attachment and early maltreatment. *Child Development, 52,* 44–52.

Eisenberg, N. (1986). *Altruistic emotion, cognition, and behavior.* Hillsdale, NJ: Erlbaum.

Eisenberg, N. (1988). The development of prosocial and aggressive behavior. In M. H. Bornstein & M. E. Lamb (Eds.), *Developmental psychology: An advanced textbook* (2nd ed., pp. 461–496). Hillsdale, NJ: Erlbaum.

Eisenberg, N. (1990). Prosocial development in early and mid-adolescence. In R. Montemayor, G. R. Adams, & T. P. Gullotta (Eds.), *From childhood to adolescence: A transitional period?* (pp. 240–268). Newbury Park, CA: Sage.

Eisenberg, N. (1992). *The caring child.* Cambridge, MA: Harvard University Press.

Eisenberg, N., Carlo, G., Murphy, B., & Van Court, P. (1995a). Prosocial development in late adolescence. *Child Development, 66,* 1179–1197.

Eisenberg, N., & Fabes, R. A. (1998). Prosocial behavior. In W. Damon (Ed.), *Handbook of child psychology: Vol 3. Social, emotional, and personality development* (5th ed., pp. 701–778). New York: Wiley.

Eisenberg, N., Fabes, R. A., Murphy, B., Karbon, M., Smith, M., & Maszk, P. (1996). The relations of children's dispositional empathy-related responding to their emotionality, regulation, and social functioning. *Developmental Psychology, 32,* 195–209.

Eisenberg, N., Fabes, R. A., Murphy, B., Maszk, P., Smith, M., & Karbon, M. (1995b). The role of emotionality and regulation in children's social functioning: A longitudinal study. *Child Development, 66,* 1360–1384.

Eisenberg, N., Fabes, R. A., Schaller, M., & Miller, P. A. (1989). Sympathy and personal distress: Development, gender differences, and interrelations of indexes. *New Directions for Child Development, 44,* 107–126.

Eisenberg, N., Fabes, R. A., Shepard, S. A., Murphy, B. C., Guthrie, I. K., Jones, S., Friedman, J., Poulin, R., & Maszk, P. (1997). Contemporaneous and longitudinal prediction of children's social functioning from regulation and emotionality. *Child Development, 68,* 642–664.

Eisenberg, N., & Murphy, B. (1995). Parenting and children's moral development. In M. H. Bornstein (Ed.), *Handbook of parenting: Vol. 4. Applied and practical parenting* (pp. 227–257). Mahwah, NJ: Erlbaum.

Eisenberg, N., & Mussen, P. H. (1989). *The roots of prosocial behavior in children.* Cambridge, England: Cambridge University Press.

Eisenberg, N., Shell, R., Pasternack, J., Lennon, R., Beller, R., & Mathy, R. M. (1987). Prosocial development in middle childhood: A longitudinal study. *Developmental Psychology, 23,* 712–718.

Ekman, P. (1972). Universals and cultural differences in facial expressions of emotion. In J. Cole (Ed.), *Nebraska symposium on motivation, 1971* (pp. 207–282). Lincoln: University of Nebraska Press.

Ekman, P. (1973). Cross-cultural studies of facial expression. In P. Ekman (Ed.), *Darwin and facial expression* (pp. 169–222). New York: Academic Press.

Ekman, P. (1989). The argument and evidence about universals in facial expressions of emotion. In H. Wagner & A. Manstead (Eds.), *Handbook of social psychophysiology* (pp. 143–164). Chichester, England: Wiley.

El Hassan Al Awad, A. M., & Sonuga-Barke, E. J. S. (1992). Childhood problems in a Sudanese city: A comparison of extended and nuclear families. *Child Development, 63,* 906–914.

Elder, G. H., Jr. (1974). *Children of the great depression.* Chicago: University of Chicago Press.

Elder, G. H., Jr. (1981). Scarcity and prosperity in postwar childbearing: Explorations from a life course perspective. *Journal of Family History, 5,* 410–431.

Elder, G. H., Jr. (1984). Families, kin, and the life course: A sociological perspective. In R. D. Parke (Ed.), *Review of child development research: Vol. 7. The family* (pp. 80–136). Chicago: University of Chicago Press.

Elkind, D. (1967). Egocentrism in adolescence. *Child Development, 38,* 1025–1034.

Elkind, D., & Bowen, R. (1979). Imaginary audience behavior in children and adolescents. *Developmental Psychology, 15,* 38–44.

Elliott, R. (1988). Tests, abilities, race, and conflict. *Intelligence, 12,* 333–350.

Ellsworth, C. P., Muir, D. W., & Hains, S. M. J. (1993). Social competence and person-object differentiation: An analysis of the still-face effect. *Developmental Psychology, 29,* 63–73.

Eme, R. F. (1979). Sex differences in childhood psychopathology: A review. *Psychological Bulletin, 86,* 374–395.

Emery, R. E., & Laumann-Billings, L. (1998). An overview of the nature, causes, and consequences of abusive family relationships: Toward differentiating maltreatment and violence. *American Psychologist, 53,* 121–135.

Endresen, E., & Helsing, E. (1995). Changes in breastfeeding practices in Norwegian maternity wards: National surveys, 1973, 1982, and 1991. *Acta Paediatrica, 84,* 719–724.

Entwisle, D. R., & Alexander, K. L. (1990). Beginning school math competence: Minority and majority comparisons. *Child Development, 61,* 454–471.

Entwisle, D. R., & Doering, S. G. (1981). *The first birth.* Baltimore: Johns Hopkins University Press.

Epstein, S. (1991). Cognitive-experiential self theory: Implications for developmental psychology. In M. R. Gunnar & L. A. Sroufe (Eds.), *The Minnesota symposia on child development* (Vol. 23, pp. 79–123). Hillsdale, NJ: Erlbaum.

Erel, O., & Burman, B. (1995). Interrelatedness of marital relations and parent-child relations: A meta-analytic review. *Psychological Bulletin, 118,* 108–132.

Ericsson, K. A., & Crutcher, R. J. (1990). The nature of exceptional performance. In P. B. Baltes, D. L., Featherman, & R. M. Lerner (Eds.), *Life-span development and behavior* (Vol. 10, pp. 188–218). Hillsdale, NJ: Erlbaum.

Erikson, E. H. (1980). *Identity and the life cycle.* New York: Norton. (Originally published 1959)

Eron, L. D. (1987). The development of aggressive behavior from the perspective of a developing behaviorism. *American Psychologist, 42,* 435–442.

Eron, L. D. (1992). Testimony before the Senate Committee on Governmental Affairs. *Congressional Record, 88*(June 18), S8538-S8539.

Eron, L. D., Huesmann, L. R., Dubow, E., Romanoff, R., & Yarmel, P. (1987). Aggression and its correlates over 22 years. In D. Crowell, I. Evans, & C. O'Donnell (Eds.), *Childhood aggression and violence: Sources of influence, prevention and control* (pp. 249–262). New York: Plenum Press.

Eron, L. D., Huesmann, L. R., & Zelli, A. (1991). The role of parental variables in the learning of aggression. In D. J. Pepler & K. H. Rubin (Eds.), *The development and treatment of childhood aggression* (pp. 169–188). Hillsdale, NJ: Erlbaum.

Escalona, K. S. (1981). The reciprocal role of social and emotional developmental advances and cognitive development during the second and third years of life. In E. K. Shapiro & E. Weber (Eds.), *Cognitive and affective growth: Developmental interaction* (pp. 87–108). Hillsdale, NJ: Erlbaum.

Escobedo, L. G., Reddy, M., & DuRant, R. H. (1997). Relationship between cigarette smoking and health risk and problem behaviors among US adolescents. *Archives of Pediatric and Adolescent Medicine, 151,* 66–71.

Escorihuela, R. M., Tobena, A., & Fernández-Teruel, A. (1994). Environmental enrichment reverses the detrimental action of early inconsistent stimulation and increases the beneficial effects of postnatal handling on shuttlebox learning in adult rats. *Behavioural Brain Research, 61,* 169–173.

Eskes, T. K. A. B. (1992). Home deliveries in the Netherlands—perinatal mortality and morbidity. *International Journal of Gynecology and Obstetrics, 38,* 161–169.

Espinosa, M. P., Sigman, M. D., Neumann, C. G., Bwibo, N. O., & McDonald, M. A. (1992). Playground behaviors of school-age children in relation to nutrition, schooling, and family characteristics. *Developmental Psychology, 28,* 1188–1195.

Fabrikant, G. (1996, April 8). The young and restless audience: Computers and videos cut into children's time for watching TV and ads. *The New York Times,* p. C1.

Fagan, J. F., III (1992). Intelligence: A theoretical viewpoint. *Current Directions in Psychological Science, 1,* 82–86.

Fagan, J. F., III, & Singer, L. T. (1983). Infant recognition memory as a measure of intelligence. In L. P. Lipsitt (Ed.), *Advances in infancy research* (Vol. 2, pp. 31–78). Norwood, NJ: Ablex.

Fagard, J., & Jacquet, A. (1989). Onset of bimanual coordination and symmetry versus asymmetry of movement. *Infant Behavior and Development, 12,* 229–235.

Fagot, B. I. (1995). Parenting boys and girls. In M. H. Bornstein (Ed.), *Handbook of parenting: Vol. 1. Children and parenting* (pp. 163–183). Mahwah, NJ: Erlbaum.

Fagot, B. I., & Hagan, R. (1991). Observations of parent reactions to sex-stereotyped behaviors: Age and sex effects. *Child Development, 62,* 617–628.

Fagot, B. I., & Leinbach, M. D. (1989). The young child's gender schema: Environmental input, internal organization. *Child Development, 60,* 663–672.

Fagot, B. I., & Leinbach, M. D. (1993). Gender-role development in young children: From discrimination to labeling. *Developmental Review, 13,* 205–224.

Fagot, B. I., Leinbach, M. D., & O'Boyle, C. (1992). Gender labeling, gender stereotyping, and parenting behaviors. *Developmental Psychology, 28,* 225–230.

Falbo, T. (1992). Social norms and the one-child family: Clinical and policy implications. In F. Boer & J. Dunn (Eds.), *Children's sibling relationships: Developmental and clinical issues* (pp. 71–82). Hillsdale, NJ: Erlbaum.

Falbo, T., & Poston, D. L., Jr. (1993). The academic, personality, and physical outcomes of only children in China. *Child Development, 64,* 18–35.

Fantz, R. L. (1956). A method for studying early visual development. *Perceptual and Motor Skills, 6,* 13–15.

Farnham-Diggory, S. (1986). Time, now, for a little serious complexity. In S. J. Ceci (Ed.), *Handbook of cognitive, social, and neuropsychological aspects of learning disability* (Vol. 1). Hillsdale, NJ: Erlbaum.

Farnham-Diggory, S. (1992). *The learning-disabled child.* Cambridge, MA: Harvard University Press.

Farran, D. C., Haskins, R., & Gallagher, J. J. (1980). Poverty and mental retardation: A search for explanations. *New Directions for Exceptional Children, 1,* 47–66.

Farrar, M. J. (1992). Negative evidence and grammatical morpheme acquisition. *Developmental Psychology, 28,* 90–98.

Farrington, D. P. (1991). Childhood aggression and adult violence: Early precursors and later life outcomes. In D. J. Pepler & K. H. Rubin (Eds.), *The development and treatment of childhood aggression* (pp. 5–30). Hillsdale, NJ: Erlbaum.

Faust, M. S. (1983). Alternative constructions of adolescent growth. In J. Brooks-Gunn & A. C. Petersen (Eds.), *Girls at puberty: Biological and psychosocial perspectives* (pp. 105–126). New York: Plenum Press.

Featherman, D. L. (1980). Schooling and occupational careers: Constancy and change in worldly success. In O. G. Brim Jr. & J. Kagan (Eds.), *Constancy and change in human development* (pp. 675–738). Cambridge, MA: Harvard University Press.

Featherstone, H. (1980). *A difference in the family.* New York: Basic Books.

Feldman, S. S. (1987). Predicting strain in mothers and fathers of 6-month-old infants: A short-term longitudinal study. In P. W. Berman & F. A. Pedersen (Eds.), *Men's transitions to parenthood* (pp. 13–36). Hillsdale, NJ: Erlbaum.

Feldman, S. S., & Elliott, G. R. (Eds.). (1990). *At the threshold: The developing adolescent.* Cambridge, MA: Harvard University Press.

Fenson, L., Dale, P. S., Reznick, J. S., Bates, E., Thal, D. J., & Pethick, S. J. (1994). Variability in early communicative development. *Monographs of the Society for Research in Child Development, 59*(5, Serial No. 242).

Fernald, A. (1993). Approval and disapproval: Infant responsiveness to vocal affect in familiar and unfamiliar languages. *Child Development, 64,* 657–674.

Fernald, A., & Kuhl, P. (1987). Acoustic determinants of infant preference for motherese speech. *Infant Behavior and Development, 10,* 279–293.

Fernald, A., & Morikawa, H. (1993). Common themes and cultural variations in Japanese and American mothers' speech to infants. *Child Development, 64,* 637–656.

Fernald, A., Taeschner, T., Dunn, J., Papousek, M., Boysson-Bardies, B., & Fukui, I. (1989). A cross-language study of prosodic modifications in mothers' and fathers' speech to preverbal infants. *Journal of Child Language, 16,* 477–501.

Field, T. M. (1977). Effects of early separation, interactive deficits, and experimental manipulations on infant-mother face-to-face interaction. *Child Development, 48,* 763–771.

Field, T. M. (1990). *Infancy.* Cambridge, MA: Harvard University Press.

Field, T. M. (1991). Quality infant day-care and grade school behavior and performance. *Child Development, 62,* 863–870.

Field, T. M. (1995). Psychologically depressed parents. In M. H. Bornstein (Ed.), *Handbook of parenting: Vol. 4. Applied and practical parenting* (pp. 85–99). Mahwah, NJ: Erlbaum.

Field, T. M., De Stefano, L., & Koewler, J. H. I. (1982a). Fantasy play of toddlers and preschoolers. *Developmental Psychology, 18,* 503–508.

Field, T. M., Healy, B., Goldstein, S., & Guthertz, M. (1990). Behavior-state matching and synchrony in mother-infant interactions of nondepressed versus depressed dyads. *Developmental Psychology, 26,* 7–14.

Field, T. M., Healy, B., Goldstein, S., Perry, S., Bendell, D., Schanberg, S., Zimmerman, E. A., & Duhn, C. (1988). Infants of depressed mothers show "depressed" behavior even with nondepressed adults. *Child Development, 59,* 1569–1579.

Field, T. M., Woodson, R., Greenberg, R., & Cohen, D. (1982b). Discrimination and imitation of facial expressions by neonates. *Science, 218,* 179–181.

Fields, S. A., & Wall, E. M. (1993). Obstetric analgesia and anesthesia. *Primary Care, 20,* 705–712.

Fifer, W. P., & Moon, C. M. (1994). The role of mother's voice in the organization of brain function in the newborn. *Acta Paediatrica, 397*(Suppl.), 86–93.

Fiscus, S. A., Adimora, A. A., Schoenbach, V. J., Lim, W., McKinney, R., Rupar, D., Kenny, J., Woods, C., & Wilfert, C. (1996). Perinatal HIV infection and the effect of zidovudine therapy on transmission in rural and urban

counties. *Journal of the American Medical Association, 275,* 1483–1488.

Fish, M., Stifter, C. A., & Belsky, J. (1991). Conditions of continuity and discontinuity in infant negative emotionality: Newborn to five months. *Child Development, 62,* 1525–1537.

Flanagan, C. A., & Eccles, J. S. (1993). Changes in parents' work status and adolescents' adjustments at school. *Child Development, 64,* 246–257.

Flannery, D. J., Montemayor, R., & Eberly, M. B. (1994). The influence of parent negative emotional expression on adolescents' perceptions of their relationships with their parents. *Personal Relationships, 1,* 259–274.

Flavell, J. H. (1985). *Cognitive development* (2nd ed.). Englewood Cliffs, NJ: Prentice Hall.

Flavell, J. H. (1986). The development of children's knowledge about the appearance-reality distinction. *American Psychologist, 41,* 418–425.

Flavell, J. H. (1992). Cognitive development: Past, present, and future. *Developmental Psychology, 28,* 998–1005.

Flavell, J. H. (1993). Young children's understanding of thinking and consciousness. *Current Directions in Psychological Science, 2,* 40–43.

Flavell, J. H., Green, F. L., & Flavell, E. R. (1989). Young children's ability to differentiate appearance-reality and level 2 perspectives in the tactile modality. *Child Development, 60,* 201–213.

Flavell, J. H., Green, F. L., & Flavell, E. R. (1990). Developmental changes in young children's knowledge about the mind. *Cognitive Development, 5,* 1–27.

Flavell, J. H., Green, F. L., & Flavell, E. R. (1995). Young children's knowledge about thinking. *Monographs of the Society for Research in Child Development, 60*(1, Serial No. 243).

Flavell, J. H., Green, F. L., Wahl, K. E., & Flavell, E. R. (1987). The effects of question clarification and memory aids on young children's performance on appearance-reality tasks. *Cognitive Development, 2,* 127–144.

Flavell, J. H., Miller, P. H., & Miller, S. A. (1993). *Cognitive development* (3rd ed.). Englewood Cliffs, NJ: Prentice Hall.

Flavell, J. H., Zhang, X., Zou, H., Dong, Q., & Qi, S. (1983). A comparison of the appearance-reality distinction in the People's Republic of China and the United States. *Cognitive Psychology, 15,* 459–466.

Fleming, A. S., Ruble, D. L., Flett, G. L., & Schaul, D. L. (1988). Postpartum adjustment in first-time mothers: Relations between mood, maternal attitudes, and mother-infant interactions. *Developmental Psychology, 24,* 71–81.

Fletcher, A. C., Darling, N. E., Steinberg, L., & Dornbusch, S. M. (1995). The company they keep: Relation of adolescents' adjustment and behavior to their friends' perceptions of authoritative parenting in the social network. *Developmental Psychology, 31,* 300–310.

Floyd, R. L., Rimer, B. K., Giovino, G. A., Mullen, P. D., & Sullivan, S. E. (1993). A review of smoking in pregnancy: Effects on pregnancy outcomes and cessation efforts. *Annual Review of Public Health, 14,* 379–411.

Flynn, J. R. (1994). IQ gains over time. In *The Encyclopedia of Human Intelligence* (pp. 617–623). New York: Macmillan.

Folk, K. F., & Yi, Y. (1994). Piecing together child care with multiple arrangements: Crazy quilt or preferred pattern for employed parents of preschool children? *Journal of Marriage and the Family, 56,* 669–680.

Folven, R. J., & Bonvillian, J. D. (1991). The transition from nonreferential to referential language in children acquiring American Sign Language. *Developmental Psychology, 27,* 806–816.

Fox, N. A., Kimmerly, N. L., & Schafer, W. D. (1991). Attachment to mother/attachment to father: A meta-analysis. *Child Development, 62,* 210–225.

Fraiberg, S. (1974). Blind infants and their mothers: An examination of the sign system. In M. Lewis & L. A. Rosenblum (Eds.), *The effect of the infant on its caregiver* (pp. 215–232). New York: Wiley.

Fraiberg, S. (1975). The development of human attachments in infants blind from birth. *Merrill-Palmer Quarterly, 21,* 315–334.

Francis, P. L., Self, P. A., & Horowitz, F. D. (1987). The behavioral assessment of the neonate: An overview. In J. D. Osofsky (Ed.), *Handbook of infant development* (2nd ed., pp. 723–779). New York: Wiley-Interscience.

Franco, N., & Levitt, M. J. (1997, April). *Friendship, friendship quality, and friendship networks in middle childhood: The role of peer acceptance in a multicultural sample.* Paper presented at the biennial meetings of the Society for Research in Child Development, Washington, DC.

Fraser, A. M., Brockert, J. E., & Ward, R. H. (1995). Association of young maternal age with adverse reproductive outcomes. *The New England Journal of Medicine, 332,* 1113–1117.

Frazier, S., Bates, J. E., Dodge, K. A., & Pettit, G. S. (1997, April). *The effects of television violence and early harsh discipline on children's social cognitions and peer-directed aggression.* Paper presented at the biennial meetings of the Society for Research in Child Development, Washington, DC.

Freedman, D. G. (1979). Ethnic differences in babies. *Human Nature, 2,* 36–43.

Freedman, D. S., Srinivasan, S. R., Valdez, R. A., Williamson, D. F., & Berenson, G. S. (1997). Secular increases in relative weight and adiposity among children over two decades: The Bogalusa Heart Study. *Pediatrics, 99,* 420–426.

Freeman, E. W., & Rickels, K. (1993). *Early childbearing: Perspectives of black adolescents on pregnancy, abortion, and contraception.* Newbury Park, CA: Sage.

Fretts, R. C., Schmittdiel, J., McLean, F. H., Usher, R. H., & Goldman, M. B. (1995). Increased maternal age and the risk of fetal death. *The New England Journal of Medicine, 333,* 953–957.

Freud, S. (1905). *The basic writings of Sigmund Freud* (A. A. Brill, Trans.). New York: Random House.

Freud, S. (1920). *A general introduction to psychoanalysis* (J. Riviere, Trans.). New York: Washington Square Press.

Frey, K. S., & Ruble, D. N. (1992). Gender constancy and the "cost" of sex-typed behavior: A test of the conflict hypothesis. *Developmental Psychology, 28,* 714–721.

Fry, A. F., & Hale, S. (1996). Processing speed, working memory, and fluid intelligence. *Psychological Science, 7,* 237–241.

Furman, W. (1995). Parenting siblings. In M. H. Bornstein (Ed.), *Handbook of parenting: Vol. 1. Children and parenting* (pp. 143–162). Mahwah, NJ: Erlbaum.

Furrow, D. (1984). Social and private speech at two years. *Child Development, 55,* 355–362.

Furrow, D., & Nelson, K. (1984). Environmental correlates of individual differences in language acquisition. *Journal of Child Language, 11,* 523–534.

Furstenberg, F. F., Jr., & Cherlin, A. J. (1991). *Divided families: What happens to children when parents part.* Cambridge, MA: Harvard University Press.

Furstenberg, F. F., Jr., & Hughes, M. E. (1995). Social capital and successful development among at-risk youth. *Journal of Marriage and the Family, 57,* 580–592.

Galambos, D. L., & Maggs, J. (1991). Out-of-school care of young adolescents and self-reported behavior. *Developmental Psychology, 27,* 644–655.

Gale, C. R., & Martyn, C. N. (1996). Breastfeeding, dummy use, and adult intelligence. *The Lancet, 347,* 1072–1075.

Gallahue, D. L., & Ozmun, J. C. (1995). *Understanding motor development* (3rd ed.). Madison, WI: Brown & Benchmark.

Ganchrow, J. R., Steiner, J. E., & Daher, M. (1983). Neonatal facial expressions in response to different qualities and intensities of gustatory stimuli. *Infant Behavior and Development, 6,* 189–200.

Garbarino, J., Dubrow, N., Kostelny, K., & Pardo, C. (1992). *Children in danger: Coping with the consequences of community violence.* San Francisco: Jossey-Bass.

Garbarino, J., & Kostelny, K. (1997). What children can tell us about living in a war zone. In J. D. Osofsky (Ed.), *Children in a violent society* (pp. 32–41). New York: Guilford Press.

Garbarino, J., Kostelny, K., & Dubrow, N. (1991). *No place to be a child: Growing up in a war zone.* Lexington, MA: Lexington Books.

Gardner, D., Harris, P. L., Ohmoto, M., & Hamasaki, T. (1988). Japanese children's understanding of the distinction between real and apparent emotion. *International Journal of Behavioral Development, 11,* 203–218.

Gardner, H. (1983). *Frames of mind: The theory of multiple intelligence.* New York: Basic Books.

Garfinkel, P. E. (1995). Classification and diagnosis of eating disorders. In K. D. Brownell & C. G. Fairburn (Eds.), *Eating disorders and obesity: A comprehensive handbook* (pp. 125–134). New York: Guilford Press.

Garland, A. F., & Zigler, E. (1993). Adolescent suicide prevention: Current research and social policy implications. *American Psychologist, 48,* 169–182.

Garmezy, N. (1993). Vulnerability and resilience. In D. C. Funder, R. D. Parke, C. Tomlinson-Keasey, & K. Widaman (Eds.), *Studying lives through time: Personality and development* (pp. 377–398). Washington, DC: American Psychological Association.

Garmezy, N., & Masten, A. S. (1991). The protective role of competence indicators in children at risk. In E. M. Cummings, A. L. Green, & K. H. Karraker (Eds.), *Life-span developmental psychology: Perspectives on stress and coping* (pp. 151–174). Hillsdale, NJ: Erlbaum.

Garmezy, N., & Rutter, M. (Eds.). (1983). *Stress, coping, and development in children.* New York: McGraw-Hill.

Garn, S. M. (1980). Continuities and change in maturational timing. In O. G. Brim Jr. & J. Kagan (Eds.), *Constancy and change in human development* (pp. 113–162). Cambridge, MA: Harvard University Press.

Ge, X., Conger, R. D., & Elder, G. H., Jr. (1996). Coming of age too early: Pubertal influences on girls' vulnerability to psychological distress. *Child Development, 67,* 3386–3400.

Geary, D. C. (1996). International differences in mathematical achievement: Their nature, causes, and consequences. *Current Directions in Psychological Science, 5,* 133–137.

Geary, D. C., Bow-Thomas, C. C., Liu, F., & Siegler, R. S. (1996). Development of arithmetical competencies in Chinese and American children: Influences of age, language, and schooling. *Child Development, 67,* 2022–2044.

Gelman, R. (1972). Logical capacity of very young children: Number invariance rules. *Child Development, 43,* 75–90.

Genesee, F. (1993). Bilingual language development in preschool children. In D. Bishop & K. Mogford (Eds.), *Language development in exceptional circumstances* (pp. 62–79). Hove, England: Erlbaum.

Gentner, D. (1982). Why nouns are learned before verbs: Linguistic relativity versus natural partitioning. In S. A. Kuczaj II (Ed.), *Language development: Vol. 2. Language, thought, and culture* (pp. 301–334). Hillsdale, NJ: Erlbaum.

Georgieff, M. K. (1994). Nutritional deficiencies as developmental risk factors: Commentary on Pollitt and Gorman. In C. A. Nelson (Ed.), *The Minnesota symposia on child development* (Vol. 27, pp. 145–159). Hillsdale, NJ: Erlbaum.

Gerber, M. M. (1995). Inclusion at the high-water mark? Some thoughts on Zigmond and Baker's case studies of inclusive educational programs. *The Journal of Special Education, 29,* 181–191.

Gerbner, G., Morgan, M., & Signorielli, N. (1994). *Television violence profile no. 16: The turning point—from research to action.* Unpublished manuscript, Annenberg School of Communications, University of Pennsylvania.

Gershkoff-Stowe, L., Thal, D. J., Smith, L. B., & Namy, L. L. (1997). Categorization and its developmental relation to early language. *Child Development, 68,* 843–859.

Gerson, R. P., & Damon, W. (1978). Moral understanding and children's conduct. *New Directions for Child Development, 2,* 41–60.

Gesell, A. (1925). *The mental growth of the preschool child.* New York: Macmillan.

Gibson, D. R. (1990). Relation of socioeconomic status to logical and sociomoral judgment of middle-aged men. *Psychology and Aging, 5,* 510–513.

Gibson, E. J., & Walk, R. D. (1960). The "visual cliff." *Scientific American, 202,* 80–92.

Gillberg, C., Melander, H., von Knorring, A., Janols, L., Thernlund, G., Hägglöf, B., Eidevall-Wallin, L., Gustafsson, P., & Kopp, S. (1997). Long-term stimulant treatment of children with attention-deficit hyperactivity disorder symptoms: A randomized, double-blind, placebo-controlled trial. *Archives of General Psychiatry, 54,* 857–864.

Gilligan, C. (1982). *In a different voice: Psychological theory and women's development.* Cambridge, MA: Harvard University Press.

Gilligan, C., & Wiggins, G. (1987). The origins of morality in early childhood relationships. In J. Kagan & S. Lamb (Eds.), *The emergence of morality in young children* (pp. 277–307). Chicago: University of Chicago Press.

Giordano, P. C., Cernkovich, S. A., & DeMaris, A. (1993). The family and peer relations of black adolescents. *Journal of Marriage and the Family, 55,* 277–287.

Gladue, B. A. (1994). The biopsychology of sexual orientation. *Current Directions in Psychological Science, 3,* 150–154.

Glasgow, K. L., Dornbusch, S. M., Troyer, L., Steinberg, L., & Ritter, P. L. (1997). Parenting styles, adolescents' attributions, and educational outcomes in nine heterogeneous high schools. *Child Development, 68,* 507–529.

Gleitman, L. R., & Gleitman, H. (1992). A picture is worth a thousand words, but that's the problem: The role of syntax in vocabulary acquisition. *Current Directions in Psychological Science, 1,* 31–35.

Gleitman, L. R., & Wanner, E. (1988). Current issues in language learning. In M. H. Bornstein & M. E. Lamb (Eds.), *Developmental psychology: An advanced textbook* (2nd ed., pp. 297–358). Hillsdale, NJ: Erlbaum.

Glenn, N. D. (1990). Quantitative research on marital quality in the 1980s: A critical review. *Journal of Marriage and the Family, 52,* 818–831.

Glueck, S., & Glueck, E. (1972). *Identification of pre-delinquents: Validation studies and some suggested uses of Glueck table.* New York: Intercontinental Medical Book Corp.

Gnepp, J., & Chilamkurti, C. (1988). Children's use of personality attributions to predict other people's emotional and behavioral reactions. *Child Development, 50,* 743–754.

Goldberg, S. (1972). Infant care and growth in urban Zambia. *Human Development, 15,* 77–89.

Goldberg, W. A. (1990). Marital quality, parental personality, and spousal agreement about perceptions and expectations for children. *Merrill-Palmer Quarterly, 36,* 531–556.

Golden, M., & Birns, B. (1983). Social class and infant intelligence. In M. Lewis (Ed.), *Origins of intelligence: Infancy and early childhood* (2nd ed., pp. 347–398). New York: Plenum Press.

Goldenberg, C. (1996). Latin American immigration and U.S. schools. *Social Policy Report, Society for Research in Child Development, 10*(1), 1–29.

Goldfield, B. A. (1993). Noun bias in maternal speech to one-year-olds. *Journal of Child Language, 20,* 85–99.

Goldfield, B. A., & Reznick, J. S. (1990). Early lexical acquisition: Rate, content, and the vocabulary spurt. *Journal of Child Language, 17,* 171–183.

Golding, J., Emmett, P. M., & Rogers, I. S. (1997a). Gastroenteritis, diarrhoea and breast feeding. *Early Human Development, 49*(Suppl.), S83–S103.

Golding, J., Emmett, P. M., & Rogers, I. S. (1997b). Does breast feeding protect against non-gastric infections? *Early Human Development, 49*(Suppl.), S105–S120.

Goldman, L. S., Genel, M., Bezman, R. J., & Slanetz, P. J. (1998). Diagnosis and treatment of attention-deficit/hyperactivity disorder in children and adolescents. *Journal of the American Medical Association, 279,* 1100–1107.

Goldsmith, H. H., Buss, K. A., & Lemery, K. S. (1997a). Toddler and childhood temperament: Expanded content, stronger genetic evidence, new evidence for the importance of environment. *Developmental Psychology, 33,* 891–905.

Goldsmith, H. H., Gottesman, I. I., & Lemery, K. S. (1997b). Epigenetic approaches to developmental psychopathology. *Development and Psychopathology, 9,* 365–387.

Goldstein, J. H. (Ed.). (1994). *Toys, play, and child development.* Cambridge, England: Cambridge University Press.

Goleman, D. (1995a, October 4). Eating disorder rates surprise the experts. *The New York Times,* p. B7.

Goleman, D. (1995b). *Emotional intelligence.* New York: Bantam Books.

Golinkoff, R. M., Mervis, C. B., & Hirsh-Pasek, K. (1994). Early object labels: The case for lexical principles. *Journal of Child Language, 21,* 125–155.

Golombok, S., & Fivush, R. (1994). *Gender development.* Cambridge, England: Cambridge University Press.

Goodman, G. S., Emery, R. E., & Haugaard, J. J. (1998). Developmental psychology and law: Divorce, child maltreatment, foster care, and adoption. In W. Damon (Ed.), *Handbook of child psychology: Vol. 4. Child psychology in practice* (5th ed., pp. 775–874). New York: Wiley.

Goodsitt, J. V., Morse, P. A., Ver Hoeve, J. N., & Cowan, N. (1984). Infant speech recognition in multisyllabic contexts. *Child Development, 55,* 903–910.

Gopnik, A., & Astington, J. W. (1988). Children's understanding of representational change and its relation to the understanding of false belief and the appearance-reality distinction. *Child Development, 59,* 26–37.

Gopnik, A., & Meltzoff, A. (1987). The development of categorization in the second year and its relation to other cognitive and linguistic developments. *Child Development, 58,* 1523–1531.

Gopnik, A., & Meltzoff, A. N. (1992). Categorization and naming: Basic-level sorting in eighteen-month-olds and its relation to language. *Child Development, 63,* 1091–1103.

Gopnik, A., & Wellman, H. M. (1994). The theory theory. In L. A. Hirschfeld & S. A. Gelman (Eds.), *Mapping the mind* (pp. 257–293). Cambridge, England: Cambridge University Press.

Gordon, N. (1995). Apoptosis (programmed cell death) and other reasons for elimination of neurons and axons. *Brain & Development, 17,* 73–77.

Gorter, A. C., Sanchez, G., Pauw, J., Perez, R. M., Sandiford, P., & Smith, G. O. (1995). Childhood diarrhea in rural Nicaragua: Beliefs and traditional health practices. *Boletin de la Oficina Sanitaria Panamericana, 119,* 337–390.

Gortmaker, S. L., Must, A., Sobel, A. M., Peterson, K., Colditz, G. A., & Dietz, W. H. (1996). Television viewing as a cause of increasing obesity among children in the United States, 1986–1990. *Archives of Pediatric and Adolescent Medicine, 150,* 356–362.

Gottesman, I. I., & Goldsmith, H. H. (1994). Developmental psychopathology of antisocial behavior: Inserting genes into its ontogenesis and epigenesis. In C. A. Nelson (Ed.), *The Minnesota symposia on child psychology* (Vol. 27, pp. 69–104). Hillsdale, NJ: Erlbaum.

Gottfried, A. E., Bathurst, K., & Gottfried, A. W. (1994). Role of maternal and dual-earner employment status in children's development: A longitudinal study from infancy through early adolescence. In A. E. Gottfried & A. W. Gottfried (Eds.), *Redefining families: Implications for children's development* (pp. 55–97). New York: Plenum Press.

Gottfried, A. W., Gottfried, A. E., Bathurst, K., & Guerin, D. W. (1994). *Gifted IQ: Early developmental aspects.* New York: Plenum Press.

Gottlieb, G. (1976a). Conceptions of prenatal development: Behavioral embryology. *Psychological Review, 83,* 215–234.

Gottlieb, G. (1976b). The roles of experience in the development of behavior and the nervous system. In G. Gottlieb (Ed.), *Neural and behavioral specificity.* New York: Academic Press.

Gottman, J. M. (1986). The world of coordinated play: Same- and cross-sex friendship in young children. In J. M. Gottman & J. G. Parker (Eds.), *Conversations of friends: Speculations on affective development* (pp. 139–191). Cambridge, England: Cambridge University Press.

Graber, J. A., Brooks-Gunn, J., Paikoff, R. L., & Warren, M. P. (1994). Prediction of eating problems: An 8-year study of adolescent girls. *Developmental Psychology, 30,* 823–834.

Graham, S., & Hudley, C. (1994). Attributions of aggressive and nonaggressive African-American male early adolescents: A study of construct accessibility. *Developmental Psychology, 30,* 365–373.

Gravel, J. S., & Nozza, R. J. (1997). Hearing loss among children with otitis media with effusion. In J. E. Roberts, I. F. Wallace, & F. W. Henderson (Eds.), *Otitis media in young children: Medical, developmental, and educational considerations* (pp. 63–92). Baltimore: Brookes.

Graziano, A. M., Hamblen, J. L., & Plante, W. A. (1996). Subabusive violence in child rearing in middle-class American families. *Pediatrics, 98,* 845–848.

Greenberg, J., & Kuczaj, S. A., II (1982). Towards a theory of substantive word-meaning acquisition. In S. A. Kuczaj II (Ed.), *Language development: Vol. l. Syntax and semantics* (pp. 275–312). Hillsdale, NJ: Erlbaum.

Greenberg, M. T. (1997, April). *Improving peer relations and reducing aggressive behavior: The classroom level effects of the PATHS curriculum.* Paper presented at the biennial meetings of the Society for Research in Child Development, Washington, DC.

Greenberg, M. T., Kusche, C. A., Cook, E. T., & Quamma, J. P. (1995). Promoting emotional competence in school-aged children: The effects of the PATHS curriculum. *Development and Psychopathology, 7,* 117–136.

Greenberg, M. T., Siegel, J. M., & Leitch, C. J. (1983). The nature and importance of attachment relationships to parents and peers during adolescence. *Journal of Youth and Adolescence, 12,* 373–386.

Greenberger, E., & Goldberg, W. A. (1989). Work, parenting, and the socialization of children. *Developmental Psychology, 25,* 22–35.

Greenberger, E., O'Neil, R., & Nagel, S. K. (1994). Linking workplace and homeplace:

Relations between the nature of adults' work and their parenting behaviors. *Developmental Psychology, 30,* 990–1002.

Greenberger, E., & Steinberg, L. (1986). *When teenagers work: The psychological and social costs of adolescent employment.* New York: Basic Books.

Greenfield, P. (1995). Profile: On teaching. Culture, ethnicity, race, and development: Implications for teaching theory and research. *SRCD Newsletter* (Winter), 3–4, 12.

Greenfield, P. M. (1994). Independence and interdependence as developmental scripts: Implications for theory, research, and practice. In P. M. Greenfield & R. R. Cocking (Eds.), *Cross-cultural roots of minority child development* (pp. 1–37). Hillsdale, NJ: Erlbaum.

Greenfield, P. M., & Cocking, R. R. (Eds.). (1994). *Cross-cultural roots of minority child development.* Hillsdale, NJ: Erlbaum.

Greenough, W. T. (1991). Experience as a component of normal development: Evolutionary considerations. *Developmental Psychology, 27,* 11–27.

Greenough, W. T., Black, J. E., & Wallace, C. S. (1987). Experience and brain development. *Child Development, 58,* 539–559.

Gregg, V., Gibbs, J. C., & Basinger, K. S. (1994). Patterns of developmental delay in moral judgment by male and female delinquents. *Merrill-Palmer Quarterly, 40,* 538–553.

Grenier, G. (1985). Shifts to English as usual language by Americans of Spanish mother tongue. In R. O. De La Garza, F. D. Bean, C. M. Bonjean, R. Romo, & R. Alvarez (Eds.), *The Mexican American experience: An interdisciplinary anthology* (pp. 347–358). Austin: University of Texas Press.

Griffith, D. R., Azuma, S. D., & Chasnoff, I. J. (1994). Three-year outcome of children exposed prenatally to drugs. *Journal of the American Academy of Child and Adolescent Psychiatry, 33,* 20–27.

Grimes, D. A. (1996). Stress, work, and pregnancy complications. *Epidemiology, 7,* 337–338.

Grolnick, W. S., & Slowiaczek, M. L. (1994). Parents' involvement in children's schooling: A multidimensional conceptualization and motivational model. *Child Development, 65,* 237–252.

Grossmann, K., Grossmann, K. E., Spangler, G., Suess, G., & Unzner, L. (1985). Maternal sensitivity and newborns' orientation responses as related to quality of attachment in northern Germany. *Monographs of the Society of Research in Child Development, 50*(1–2, Serial No. 209), 233–256.

Grotevant, H. D., & Cooper, C. R. (1985). Patterns of interaction in family relationships and the development of identity exploration in adolescence. *Child Development, 56,* 415–428.

Group for the Advancement of Psychiatry. (1996). *Adolescent suicide.* Washington, DC: American Psychiatric Press.

Grusec, J. E. (1992). Social learning theory and developmental psychology: The legacies of Robert Sears and Albert Bandura. *Developmental Psychology, 28,* 776–786.

Grusec, J. E., Goodnow, J. J., & Cohen, L. (1996). Household work and the development of concern for others. *Developmental Psychology, 32,* 999–1007.

Grusec, J. E., Saas-Kortsaak, P., & Simutis, Z. M. (1978). The role of example and moral exhortation in the training of altruism. *Child Development, 49,* 920–923.

Guerin, D. W., & Gottfried, A. W. (1994a). Temperamental consequences of infant difficultness. *Infant Behavior and Development, 17,* 413–421.

Guerin, D. W., & Gottfried, A. W. (1994b). Developmental stability and change in parent reports of temperament: A ten-year longitudinal investigation from infancy through preadolescence. *Merrill-Palmer Quarterly, 40,* 334–355.

Gullotta, T. P., Adams, G. R., & Montemayor, R. (Eds.). (1993). *Adolescent sexuality.* Newbury Park, CA: Sage.

Gunnar, M. R. (1994). Psychoendocrine studies of temperament and stress in early childhood: Expanding current models. In J. E. Bates & T. D. Wachs (Eds.), *Temperament: Individual differences at the interface of biology and behavior* (pp. 175–198). Washington, DC: American Psychological Association.

Guralnick, M. J., & Paul-Brown, D. (1984). Communicative adjustments during behavior-request episodes among children at different developmental levels. *Child Development, 55,* 911–919.

Guttentag, R. E., Ornstein, P. A., & Siemens, L. (1987). Children's spontaneous rehearsal: Transitions in strategy acquisition. *Cognitive Development, 2,* 307–326.

Guyer, B., MacDorman, M. F., Anderson, R. N., & Strobino, D. M. (1997). Annual summary of vital statistics—1996. *Pediatrics, 100,* 905–918.

Guyer, B., Strobino, D. M., Ventura, S. J., MacDorman, M., & Martin, J. A. (1996). Annual summary of vital statistics—1995. *Pediatrics, 98,* 1007–1019.

Gzesh, S. M., & Surber, C. F. (1985). Visual perspective-taking skills in children. *Child Development, 56,* 1204–1213.

Haan, N. (1981). Adolescents and young adults as producers of their own development. In R. M. Lerner & N. A. Busch-Rossnagel (Eds.), *Individuals as producers of their own development* (pp. 155–182). New York: Academic Press.

Haan, N. (1985). Processes of moral development: Cognitive or social disequilibrium? *Developmental Psychology, 21,* 996–1006.

Hack, M., Horbar, J. D., Mallow, M. H., Tyson, J. E., Wright, E., & Wright, L. (1991). Very low birth weight outcomes of the National Institute of Child Health and Human Devel-

opment Neonatal Network. *Pediatrics, 87,* 587–597.

Hack, M., Taylor, C. B. H., Klein, N., Eiben, R., Schatschneider, C., & Mercuri-Minich, N. (1994). School-age outcomes in children with birth weights under 750 g. *The New England Journal of Medicine, 331,* 753–759.

Hacker, A. (1997). *Money: Who has how much and why.* New York: Scribner.

Hagay, Z. J., Biran, G., Ornoy, A., & Reece, E. A. (1996). Congenital cytomegalovirus infection: A long-standing problem still seeking a solution. *American Journal of Obstetrics and Gynecology, 174,* 241–245.

Hagekull, B. (1994). Infant temperament and early childhood functioning: Possible relations to the five-factor model. In C. J. Halverson Jr., G. A. Kohnstamm, & R. P. Martin (Eds.), *The developing structure of temperament and personality* (pp. 227–240). Hillsdale, NJ: Erlbaum.

Hagekull, B., & Bohlin, G. (1998). Preschool temperament and environmental factors related to the five-factor model of personality in middle childhood. *Merrill-Palmer Quarterly, 44,* 194–215.

Hagerman, R. J. (1996). Growth and development. In W. W. Hay Jr., J. R. Groothuis, A. R. Hayward, & M. J. Levin (Eds.), *Current pediatric diagnosis and treatment* (12th ed., pp. 65–84). Norwalk, CT: Appleton & Lange.

Haith, M. M. (1980). *Rules that babies look by.* Hillsdale, NJ: Erlbaum.

Haith, M. M. (1990). Progress in the understanding of sensory and perceptual processes in early infancy. *Merrill-Palmer Quarterly, 36,* 1–26.

Hakuta, K., & Garcia, E. E. (1989). Bilingualism and education. *American Psychologist, 44,* 374–379.

Hale, S., Fry, A. F., & Jessie, K. A. (1993). Effects of practice on speed of information processing in children and adults: Age sensitivity and age invariance. *Developmental Psychology, 29,* 880–892.

Halford, G. S., Maybery, M. T., O'Hare, A. W., & Grant, P. (1994). The development of memory and processing capacity. *Child Development, 65,* 1338–1356.

Halpern, C. T., Udry, J. R., Campbell, B., & Suchindran, C. (1993). Testosterone and pubertal development as predictors of sexual activity: A panel analysis of adolescent males. *Psychosomatic Medicine, 55,* 436–447.

Halpern, D. F. (1992). *Sex differences in cognitive abilities.* Hillsdale, NJ: Erlbaum.

Halpern, D. F. (1997). Sex differences in intelligence: Implications for education. *American Psychologist, 52,* 1091–1102.

Hämäläinen, M., & Pulkkinen, L. (1996). Problem behavior as a precursor of male criminality. *Development and Psychopathology, 8,* 443–455.

Hamer, D. H., Hu, S., Magnuson, V. L., Hu, N., & Pattatucci, A. M. (1993). A linkage between DNA markers on the X chromosome and male sexual orientation. *Science, 261,* 321–327.

Hamilton, C. E. (1995, April). *Continuity and discontinuity of attachment from infancy through adolescence.* Paper presented at the biennial meetings of the Society for Research in Child Development, Indianapolis.

Hamvas, A., Wise, P. H., Yang, R. K., Wampler, N. S., Noguchi, A., Maurer, M. M., Walentik, C. A., Schramm, W. F., & Cole, F. S. (1996). The influence of the wider use of surfactant therapy on neonatal mortality among blacks and whites. *The New England Journal of Medicine, 334,* 1635–1640.

Hankin, B. L., Abramson, L. Y., Moffitt, T. E., Silva, P. A., McGee, R., & Angell, K. E. (1998). Development of depression from preadolescence to young adulthood: Emerging gender differences in a 10-year longitudinal study. *Journal of Abnormal Psychology, 107,* 128–140.

Hanna, E., & Meltzoff, A. N. (1993). Peer imitation by toddlers in laboratory, home, and day-care contexts: Implications for social learning and memory. *Developmental Psychology, 29,* 701–710.

Hansen, J., & Bowey, J. A. (1994). Phonological analysis skills, verbal working memory, and reading ability in second-grade children. *Child Development, 65,* 938–950.

Hanshaw, J. B., Scheiner, A. P., Moxley, A. W., Gaeav, L., Abel, V., & Scheiner, B. (1976). School failure and deafness after "silent" congenital cytomegalovirus infection. *The New England Journal of Medicine, 295,* 468–470.

Hardy, J. B., Shapiro, S., Astone, N. M., Miller, T. L., Brooks-Gunn, J., & Hilton, S. C. (1997). Adolescent childbearing revisited: The age of inner-city mothers at delivery is a determinant of their children's self-sufficiency at age 27 to 33. *Pediatrics, 100,* 802–809.

Harkness, S., & Super, C. M. (1985). The cultural context of gender segregation in children's peer groups. *Child Development, 56,* 219–224.

Harkness, S., & Super, C. M. (1995). Culture and parenting. In M. H. Bornstein (Ed.), *Handbook of parenting: Vol. 2. Biology and ecology of parenting* (pp. 211–234). Mahwah, NJ: Erlbaum.

Harnqvist, K. (1968). Changes in intelligence from 13 to 18. *Scandinavian Journal of Psychology, 9,* 50–82.

Harold, G. T., & Conger, R. D. (1997). Marital conflict and adolescent distress: The role of adolescent awareness. *Child Development, 68,* 333–350.

Harold, G. T., Fincham, F. D., Osborne, L. N., & Conger, R. D. (1997). Mom and Dad are at it again: Adolescent perceptions of marital conflict and adolescent psychological distress. *Developmental Psychology, 33,* 333–350.

Harrington, R., Rutter, M., & Fombonne, E. (1996). Developmental pathways in depression: Multiple meanings, antecedents, and endpoints. *Development and Psychopathology, 8,* 601–616.

Harris, M. (1992). *Language experience and early language development: From input to uptake.* Hove, England: Erlbaum.

Harris, P. L. (1989). *Children and emotion: The development of psychological understanding.* Oxford: Basil Blackwell.

Harris, P. L., Olthof, T., & Terwogt, M. M. (1981). Children's knowledge of emotion. *Journal of Child Psychology and Psychiatry, 22,* 247–261.

Harrison, A. O., Wilson, M. N., Pine, C. J., Chan, S. Q., & Buriel, R. (1990). Family ecologies of ethnic minority children. *Child Development, 61,* 347–362.

Hart, B., & Risley, T. R. (1995). *Meaningful differences in the everyday experience of young American children.* Baltimore, MD: Brookes.

Harter, S. (1987). The determinants and mediational role of global self-worth in children. In N. Eisenberg (Ed.), *Contemporary topics in developmental psychology* (pp. 219–242). New York: Wiley-Interscience.

Harter, S. (1990). Processes underlying adolescent self-concept formation. In R. Montemayor, G. R. Adams, & T. P. Gullotta (Eds.), *From childhood to adolescence: A transitional period?* (pp. 205–239). Newbury Park, CA: Sage.

Harter, S. (1998). The development of self-representations. In W. Damon (Ed.), *Handbook of child psychology: Vol. 3. Social, emotional, and personality development* (5th ed., pp. 553–617). New York: Wiley.

Harter, S., & Pike, R. (1984). The Pictorial Perceived Competence Scale for Young Children. *Child Development, 55,* 1969–1982.

Harter, S., & Whitesell, N. R. (1989). Developmental changes in children's understanding of single, multiple, and blended emotion concepts. In C. Saarni & P. L. Harris (Eds.), *Children's understanding of emotion* (pp. 81–116). Cambridge, England: Cambridge University Press.

Harter, S., & Whitesell, N. R. (1996). Multiple pathways to self-reported depression and psychological adjustment among adolescents. *Development and Psychopathology, 8,* 761–777.

Hartshorn, K., & Rovee-Collier, C. (1997). Infant learning and long-term memory at 6 months: A confirming analysis. *Developmental Psychobiology, 30,* 71–85.

Hartup, W. W. (1989). Social relationships and their developmental significance. *American Psychologist, 44,* 120–126.

Hartup, W. W. (1996). The company they keep: Friendships and their developmental significance. *Child Development, 67,* 1–13.

Hartup, W. W., Laursen, B., Stewart, M. I., & Eastenson, A. (1988). Conflict and the friendship relations of young children. *Child Development, 59,* 1590–1600.

Hartup, W. W., & Stevens, N. (1997). Friendships and adaptation in the life course. *Psychological Bulletin, 121,* 355–370.

Hartup, W. W., & van Lieshout, C. F. M. (1995). Personality development in social context. *Annual Review of Psychology, 46,* 655–687.

Harwood, R. L. (1992). The influence of culturally derived values on Anglo and Puerto Rican mothers' perceptions of attachment behavior. *Child Development, 63,* 822–839.

Hashima, P. Y., & Amato, P. R. (1994). Poverty, social support, and parental behavior. *Child Development, 65,* 394–403.

Haskins, R. (1989). Beyond metaphor: The efficacy of early childhood education. *American Psychologist, 44,* 274–282.

Hatano, G., Siegler, R. S., Richards, D. D., Inagaki, K., Stavy, R., & Wax, N. (1993). The development of biological knowledge: A multi-national study. *Cognitive Development, 8,* 47–62.

Hatcher, P. J., Hulme, C., & Ellis, A. W. (1994). Ameliorating early reading failure by integrating the teaching of reading and phonological skills: The phonological linkage hypothesis. *Child Development, 65,* 41–57.

Hatchett, S. J., & Jackson, J. S. (1993). African American extended kin systems: An assessment. In H. P. McAdoo (Ed.), *Family ethnicity: Strength in diversity* (pp. 90–108). Newbury Park, CA: Sage.

Haviland, J. M., & Lelwica, M. (1987). The induced affect response: 10-week-old infants' responses to three emotional expressions. *Developmental Psychology, 23,* 97–104.

Haviland, J. M., & Malatesta, C. Z. (1981). The development of sex differences in nonverbal signals: Fallacies, facts, and fantasies. In C. Mayo & N. M. Henley (Eds.), *Gender and nonverbal behavior* (pp. 183–208). New York: Springer-Verlag.

Havill, V. L., Allen, K., Halverson, C. F., Jr., & Kohnstamm, G. A. (1994). Parents' use of Big Five categories in their natural language descriptions of children. In C. F. Halverson Jr., G. A. Kohnstamm, & R. P. Martin (Eds.), *The developing structure of temperament and personality from infancy to adulthood* (pp. 371–386). Hillsdale, NJ: Erlbaum.

Hay, D. F. (1997). Postpartum depression and cognitive development. In L. Murray & P. J. Cooper (Eds.), *Postpartum depression and child development* (pp. 85–110). New York: Guilford Press.

Hayne, H., & Rovee-Collier, C. (1995). The organization of reactivated memory in infancy. *Child Development, 66,* 893–906.

Haynes, N. M., Ben-Avie, M., Squires, D. A., Howley, J. P., Negron, E. N., & Corbin, J. N. (1996). It takes a whole village: The SDP school. In J. P. Comer, N. M. Haynes, E. T. Joyner, & M. Ben-Avie (Eds.), *Rallying the whole village: The Comer process for reforming education* (pp. 42–71). New York: Teachers College Press.

Hazan, C., & Shaver, P. (1990). Love and work: An attachment-theoretical perspective.

Journal of Personality and Social Psychology, 59, 270–280.

Heckman, J. J. (1995). Lessons from *The bell curve: Intelligence and class structure in American life. Journal of Political Economy, 103,* 1091–1120.

Hedegaard, M., Henriksen, T. B., Secher, N. J., Hatch, M. C., & Sabroe, S. (1996). Do stressful life events affect duration of gestation and risk of preterm delivery? *Epidemiology, 7,* 339–345.

Henker, B., & Whalen, C. K. (1989). Hyperactivity and attention deficits. *American Psychologist, 44,* 216–223.

Henneborn, W. J., & Cogan, R. (1975). The effect of husband participation on reported pain and the probability of medication during labour and birth. *Journal of Psychosomatic Research, 19,* 215–222.

Henriksen, T. B., Hedegaard, M., Secher, N. J., & Wilcox, A. J. (1995). Standing at work and preterm delivery. *British Journal of Obstetrics and Gynecology, 102,* 198–206.

Henshaw, S. K. (1994). *U.S. teenage pregnancy statistics.* New York: Alan Guttmacher Institute.

Heptinstall, E., & Taylor, E. (1996). Sex differences and their significance. In S. Sandberg (Ed.), *Hyperactivity disorders of childhood* (pp. 329–349). Cambridge, England: Cambridge University Press.

Herman-Giddens, M. E., Slora, E. J., Wasserman, R. C., Bourdony, C. J., Bhapkar, M. V., Koch, T. G., & Hasemeier, C. M. (1997). Secondary sexual characteristics and menses in young girls seen in office practice: A study from the Pediatric Research in Office Settings Network. *Pediatrics, 99,* 505–512.

Hernandez, D. J. (1993). *America's children: Resources from family, government, and the economy.* New York: Russell Sage Foundation.

Hernandez, D. J. (1994). Children's changing access to resources: A historical perspective. *Social Policy Report, Society for Research in Child Development, 8*(1), 1–23.

Hernandez, D. J. (1997). Child development and the social demography of childhood. *Child Development, 68,* 149–169.

Herold, E. S., & Marshall, S. K. (1996). Adolescent sexual development. In G. R. Adams, R. Montemayor, & T. P. Gullotta (Eds.), *Psychosocial development during adolescence: Progress in developmental contextualism* (pp. 63–94). Thousand Oaks, CA: Sage.

Herrnstein, R. J., & Murray, C. (1994). *The bell curve: Intelligence and class structure in American life.* New York: Free Press.

Hess, E. H. (1972). "Imprinting" in a natural laboratory. *Scientific American, 227,* 24–31.

Hetherington, E. M. (1989). Coping with family transitions: Winners, losers, and survivors. *Child Development, 60,* 1–14.

Hetherington, E. M., Bridges, M., & Insabella, G. M. (1998). What matters? What does not? Five perspectives on the association between marital transitions and children's adjustment. *American Psychologist, 53,* 167–184.

Hetherington, E. M., & Clingempeel, W. G. (1992). Coping with marital transitions: A family systems perspective. *Monographs of the Society for Research in Child Development, 57*(2–3, Serial No. 227).

Hetherington, E. M., & Stanley-Hagan, M. M. (1995). Parenting in divorced and remarried families. In M. H. Bornstein (Ed.), *Handbook of parenting: Vol. 3. Status and social conditions of parenting* (pp. 233–254). Mahwah, NJ: Erlbaum.

Hickey, C. A., Cliver, S. P., McNeal, S. F., Hoffman, H. J., & Goldenberg, R. L. (1996). Prenatal weight gain patterns and birth weight among nonobese black and white women. *Obstetrics and Gynecology, 88,* 490–496.

Higgins, A. (1991). The just community approach to moral education: Evolution of the idea and recent findings. In W. M. Kurtines & J. L. Gewirtz (Eds.), *Handbook of moral behavior and development: Vol. 3. Application* (pp. 111–141). Hillsdale, NJ: Erlbaum.

Higgins, A., Power, C., & Kohlberg, L. (1984). The relationship of moral atmosphere to judgments of responsibility. In W. M. Kurtines & J. L. Gewirtz (Eds.), *Morality, moral behavior, and moral development* (pp. 74–108). New York: Wiley-Interscience.

Hill, D. J. (1995). The colic debate. *Pediatrics, 96,* 165.

Hill, H. M., Soriano, F. I., Chen, S. A., & LaFromboise, T. D. (1994). Sociocultural factors in the etiology and prevention of violence among ethnic minority youth. In L. D. Eron, J. H. Gentry, & P. Schlegel (Eds.), *Reason to hope: A psychosocial perspective on violence and youth* (pp. 59–97). Washington, DC: American Psychological Association.

Hilts, P. J. (1995, April 19). Black teen-agers are turning away from smoking, but whites puff on. *The New York Times,* p. B7.

Hines, M., & Kaufman, F. R. (1994). Androgen and the development of human sex-typical behavior: Rough-and-tumble play and sex of preferred playmates in children with congenital adrenal hyperplasia (CAH). *Child Development, 65,* 1042–1053.

Hinshaw, S. P., Lahey, B. B., & Hart, E. L. (1993). Issues of taxonomy and comorbidity in the development of conduct disorder. *Development and Psychopathology, 5,* 31–49.

Hinshaw, S. P., & Melnick, S. M. (1995). Peer relationships in boys with attention-deficit hyperactivity disorder with and wit out comorbid aggression. *Development and Psychopathology, 7,* 627–647.

Hinshaw, S. P., Zupan, B. A., Simmel, C., Nigg, J. T., & Melnick, S. (1997). Peer status in boys with and without attention-deficit hyperactivity disorder: Predictions from overt and covert antisocial behavior, social isolation, and authoritative parenting beliefs. *Child Development, 68,* 880–896.

Hirsch, H. V. B., & Tieman, S. B. (1987). Perceptual development and experience-dependent changes in cat visual cortex. In M. H. Bornstein (Ed.), *Sensitive periods in development: Interdisciplinary perspectives* (pp. 39–80). Hillsdale, NJ: Erlbaum.

Hirschfeld, L. A., & Gelman, S. A. (1994). Toward a topography of mind: An introduction to domain specificity. In L. A. Hirschfeld & S. A. Gelman (Eds.), *Mapping the mind* (pp. 3–35). Cambridge, England: Cambridge University Press.

Hirsh-Pasek, K., Trieman, R., & Schneiderman, M. (1984). Brown and Hanlon revisited: Mothers' sensitivity to ungrammatical forms. *Journal of Child Language, 11,* 81–88.

Hodapp, R. M. (1995). Parenting children with Down syndrome and other types of mental retardation. In M. H. Bornstein (Ed.), *Handbook of parenting: Vol. 1. Children and parenting* (pp. 233–253). Mahwah, NJ: Erlbaum.

Hodge, K. P., & Tod, D. A. (1993). Ethics of childhood sport. *Sports Medicine, 15,* 291–298.

Hodges, E. V. E., Malone, M. J., & Perry, D. G. (1997). Individual risk and social risk as interacting determinants of victimization in the peer group. *Developmental Psychology, 33,* 1032–1039.

Hofferth, S. L. (1987a). Teenage pregnancy and its resolution. In S. L. Hofferth & C. D. Hayes (Eds.), *Risking the future: Adolescent sexuality, pregnancy, and childbearing. Working papers* (pp. 78–92). Washington, DC: National Academy Press.

Hofferth, S. L. (1987b). Social and economic consequences of teenage childbearing. In S. L. Hofferth & C. D. Hayes (Eds.), *Risking the future: Adolescent sexuality, pregnancy, and childbearing. Working papers* (pp. 123–144). Washington, DC: National Academy Press.

Hofferth, S. L. (1996). Child care in the United States today. *The Future of Children, 6*(2), 41–61.

Hofferth, S. L., Boisjoly, J., & Duncan, G. (1995, April). *Does children's school attainment benefit from parental access to social capital?* Paper presented at the biennial meetings of the Society for Research in Child Development, Indianapolis.

Hoffman, H. J., & Hillman, L. S. (1992). Epidemiology of the sudden infant death syndrome: Maternal, neonatal, and postneonatal risk factors. *Clinics in Perinatology, 19*(4), 717–737.

Hoffman, L. W. (1989). Effects of maternal employment in the two-parent family. *American Psychologist, 44,* 283–292.

Hoffman, M. L. (1982). Development of prosocial motivation: Empathy and guilt. In N. Eisenberg (Ed.), *The development of prosocial behavior* (pp. 281–314). New York: Academic Press.

Hoffman, M. L. (1984). Empathy, its limitations, and its role in a comprehensive moral theory. In W. M. Kurtines & J. L. Gewirtz (Eds.),

Morality, moral behavior, and moral development (pp. 283–302). New York: Wiley.

Hoffman, M. L. (1988). Moral development. In M. H. Bornstein & M. E. Lamb (Eds.), *Developmental psychology: An advanced textbook* (2nd ed., pp. 497–548). Hillsdale, NJ: Erlbaum.

Hogue, C. J. R., & Hargraves, M. A. (1993). Class, race, and infant mortality in the United States. *American Journal of Public Health, 83,* 9–12.

Holahan, C. K. (1988). Relation of life goals at age 70 to activity participation and health and psychological well-being among Terman's gifted men and women. *Psychology and Aging, 3,* 286–291.

Holden, C. (1987). Genes and behavior: A twin legacy. *Psychology Today, 21*(9), 18–19.

Holden, G. W., Coleman, S. M., & Schmidt, K. L. (1995). Why 3-year-old children get spanked: Parent and child determinants as reported by college-educated mothers. *Merrill-Palmer Quarterly, 41,* 431–452.

Holloway, S. D., & Hess, R. D. (1985). Mothers' and teachers' attributions about children's mathematics performance. In I. E. Sigel (Ed.), *Parental belief systems: The psychological consequences for children* (pp. 177–200). Hillsdale, NJ: Erlbaum.

Holmbeck, G. N., & Hill, J. P. (1991). Conflictive engagement, positive affect, and menarche in families with seventh-grade girls. *Child Development, 62,* 1030–1048.

Holmes, S. A. (1996, September 6). Education gap between races closes. *The New York Times,* p. A8.

Honzik, M. P. (1986). The role of the family in the development of mental abilities: A 50-year study. In N. Datan, A. L. Greene, & H. W. Reese (Eds.), *Life-span developmental psychology: Intergenerational relations* (pp. 185–210). Hillsdale, NJ: Erlbaum.

Horowitz, F. D. (1987). *Exploring developmental theories: Toward a structural/behavioral model of development.* Hillsdale, NJ: Erlbaum.

Horowitz, F. D. (1990). Developmental models of individual differences. In J. Colombo & J. Fagen (Eds.), *Individual differences in infancy: Reliability, stability, prediction* (pp. 3–18). Hillsdale, NJ: Erlbaum.

Hovell, M., Sipan, C., Blumberg, E., Atkins, C., Hofstetter, C. R., & Kreitner, S. (1994). Family influences on Latino and Anglo adolescents' sexual behavior. *Journal of Marriage and the Family, 56,* 973–986.

Howes, C. (1996). The earliest friendships. In W. M. Bukowski, A. F. Newcomb, & W. W. Hartup (Eds.), *The company they keep: Friendship in childhood and adolescence* (pp. 66–86). Cambridge, England: Cambridge University Press.

Howes, C. (1997). Children's experiences in center-based child care as a function of teacher background and adult:child ratio. *Merrill-Palmer Quarterly, 43,* 404–425.

Howes, C., & Matheson, C. C. (1992). Sequences in the development of competent play with peers: Social and pretend play. *Developmental Psychology, 28,* 961–974.

Howes, C., Phillips, D. A., & Whitebook, M. (1992). Thresholds of quality: Implications for the social development of children in center-based child care. *Child Development, 63,* 449–460.

Hoyert, D. L. (1996). Fetal mortality by maternal education and prenatal care, 1990. *Vital and Health Statistics, Series 20*(No. 30), 1–7.

Hubbard, F. O. A., & van IJzendoorn, M. H. (1987). Maternal unresponsiveness and infant crying: A critical replication of the Bell & Ainsworth study. In L. W. C. Tavecchio & M. H. v. IJzendoorn (Eds.), *Attachment in social networks* (pp. 339–378). Amsterdam: Elsevier/North-Holland.

Hubel, D. H., & Weisel, T. N. (1963). Receptive fields of cells in striate cortex of very young, visually inexperienced kittens. *Journal of Neurophysiology, 26,* 994–1002.

Huesmann, L. R., Lagerspetz, K., & Eron, L. D. (1984). Intervening variables in the television violence–aggression relation: Evidence from two countries. *Developmental Psychology, 20,* 746–775.

Huey, S. J., Jr., & Weisz, J. R. (1997). Ego control, ego resiliency, and the five-factor model as predictors of behavioral and emotional problems in clinic-referred children and adolescents. *Journal of Abnormal Psychology, 106,* 404–415.

Huffman, L. C., Bryan, Y. E., Pedersen, F. A., Lester, B. M., Newman, J. D., & del Carmen, R. (1994). Infant cry acoustics and maternal ratings of temperament. *Infant Behavior and Development, 17,* 45–53.

Huntington, L., Hans, S. L., & Zeskind, P. S. (1990). The relations among cry characteristics, demographic variables, and developmental test scores in infants prenatally exposed to methadone. *Infant Behavior and Development, 13,* 533–538.

Hurwitz, E., Gunn, W. J., Pinsky, P. F., & Schonberger, L. B. (1991). Risk of respiratory illness associated with day-care attendance: A nationwide study. *Pediatrics, 87,* 62–69.

Huston, A. C. (Ed.). (1991). *Children in poverty: Child development and public policy.* Cambridge, England: Cambridge University Press.

Huston, A. C. (1994). Children in poverty: Designing research to affect policy. *Social Policy Report, Society for Research in Child Development, 8*(2), 1–12.

Huston, A. C., Greer, D., Wright, J. C., Welch, R., & Ross, R. (1984). Children's comprehension of televised formal features with masculine and feminine connotations. *Developmental Psychology, 20,* 707–716.

Huston, A. C., & Wright, J. C. (1994). Educating children with television: The forms of the medium. In D. Zillmann, J. Bryant, & A. C. Huston (Eds.), *Media, children, and the family: Social scientific, psychodynamic, and clinical perspectives* (pp. 73–84). Hillsdale, NJ: Erlbaum.

Huston, A. C., & Wright, J. C. (1998). Mass media and children's development. In W. Damon (Ed.), *Handbook of child psychology: Vol. 4. Child psychology in practice* (5th ed., pp. 999–1058). New York: Wiley.

Huston, A. C., Wright, J. C., Rice, M. L., Kerkman, D., & St. Peters, M. (1990). Development of television viewing patterns in early childhood: A longitudinal investigation. *Developmental Psychology, 26,* 409–420.

Hutt, S. J., Lenard, H. G., & Prechtl, H. E. R. (1969). Psychophysiological studies in newborn infants. In L. P. Lipsitt & H. W. Reese (Eds.), *Advances in child development and behavior* (Vol. 4, pp. 128–173). New York: Academic Press.

Huttenlocher, J. (1995, April). *Children's language in relation to input.* Paper presented at the biennial meetings of the Society for Research in Child Development, Indianapolis.

Huttenlocher, P. R. (1994). Synaptogenesis, synapse elimination, and neural plasticity in human cerebral cortex. In C. A. Nelson (Ed.), *The Minnesota symposia on child psychology* (Vol. 27, pp. 35–54). Hillsdale, NJ: Erlbaum.

Hynd, G. W., Hern, K. L., Novey, E. S., Eliopolus, D., Marshall, R., Gonzalez, J. J., & Voeller, K. K. (1993). Attention deficit–hyperactivity disorder and asymmetry of the caudate nucleus. *Journal of Child Neurology, 8,* 339–347.

Ingram, D. (1981). Early patterns of grammatical development. In R. E. Stark (Ed.), *Language behavior in infancy and early childhood* (pp. 327–358). New York: Elsevier/North-Holland.

Inhelder, B., & Piaget, J. (1958). *The growth of logical thinking from childhood to adolescence.* New York: Basic Books.

Inoff-Germain, G., Arnold, G. S., Nottelmann, E. D., Susman, E. J., Cutler, G. B., Jr., & Chrousos, G. P. (1988). Relations between hormone levels and observational measures of aggressive behavior of young adolescents in family interactions. *Developmental Psychology, 24,* 129–139.

Isabella, G. M. (1995, April). *Varying levels of exposure to marital conflict: Prediction of adolescent adjustment across intact families and stepfamilies.* Paper presented at the biennial meetings of the Society for Research in Child Development, Indianapolis.

Isabella, R. A. (1993). Origins of attachment: Maternal interactive behavior across the first year. *Child Development, 64,* 605–621.

Isabella, R. A., Belsky, J., & von Eye, A. (1989). Origins of infant-mother attachment: An examination of interactional synchrony during the infant's first year. *Developmental Psychology, 25,* 12–21.

Izard, C. E., Fantauzzo, C. A., Castle, J. M., Haynes, O. M., Rayias, M. F., & Putnam, P. H. (1995). The ontogeny and significance of infants' facial expressions in the first 9 months of life. *Developmental Psychology, 31*, 997–1013.

Izard, C. E., & Harris, P. (1995). Emotional development and developmental psychopathology. In D. Cicchetti & D. J. Cohen (Eds.), *Developmental psychopathology: Vol. 1. Theory and methods* (pp. 467–503). New York: Wiley.

Izard, C. E., & Malatesta, C. Z. (1987). Perspectives on emotional development I: Differential emotions theory of early emotional development. In J. D. Osofsky (Ed.), *Handbook of infant development* (2nd ed., pp. 494–554). New York: Wiley-Interscience.

Izard, C. E., Schultz, D., & Ackerman, B. P. (1997, April). *Emotion knowledge, social competence, and behavior problems in disadvantaged children.* Paper presented at the biennial meetings of the Society for Research in Child Development, Washington, DC.

Jacklin, C. N. (1989). Female and male: Issues of gender. *American Psychologist, 44*, 127–133.

Jadack, R. A., Hyde, J. S., Moore, C. F., & Keller, M. L. (1995). Moral reasoning about sexually transmitted diseases. *Child Development, 66*, 167–177.

James, W. (1890). *Principles of psychology.* Chicago: Encyclopaedia Britannica.

James, W. (1892). *Psychology: The briefer course.* New York: Holt.

Janssen, P. A., Holt, V. L., & Myers, S. J. (1994). Licensed midwife–attended, out-of-hospital births in Washington State: Are they safe? *Birth, 21*, 141–148.

Jenkins, E. J., & Bell, C. C. (1997). Exposure and response to community violence among children and adolescents. In J. D. Osofsky (Ed.), *Children in a violent society* (pp. 9–31). New York: Guilford Press.

Jenkins, J. M., & Astington, J. W. (1996). Cognitive factors and family structure associated with theory of mind development in young children. *Developmental Psychology, 32*, 70–78.

Jensen, A. R. (1980). *Bias in mental testing.* New York: Free Press.

Jessor, R. (1992). Risk behavior in adolescence: A psychosocial framework for understanding and action. *Developmental Review, 12*, 374–390.

John, O. P., Caspi, A., Robins, R. W., Moffitt, T. E., & Stouthamer-Loeber, M. (1994). The "little five": Exploring the nomological network of the five-factor model of personality in adolescent boys. *Child Development, 65*, 160–178.

Johnson, J. W. C., & Yancey, M. K. (1996). A critique of the new recommendations for weight gain in pregnancy. *American Journal of Obstetrics and Gynecology, 174*, 254–258.

Johnson, M. H. (1997). *Developmental cognitive neuroscience.* Cambridge, MA: Blackwell.

Johnston, J. R. (1985). Cognitive prerequisites: The evidence from children learning English. In D. I. Slobin (Ed.), *The crosslinguistic study of language acquisition: Vol. 2. Theoretical issues* (pp. 961–1004). Hillsdale, NJ: Erlbaum.

Jones, E. F., Forrest, J. D., Goldman, N., Henshaw, S. K., Lincoln, R., Rosoff, J. L., Westoff, C. F., & Wulf, D. (1986). *Teenage pregnancy in industrialized countries.* New Haven, CT: Yale University Press.

Jordan, N. C., Huttenlocher, J., & Levine, S. C. (1992). Differential calculation abilities in young children from middle- and low-income families. *Developmental Psychology, 28*, 644–653.

Joshi, M. S., & MacLean, M. (1994). Indian and English children's understanding of the distinction between real and apparent emotion. *Child Development, 65*, 1372–1384.

Jusczyk, P. W., Cutler, A., & Redanz, N. J. (1993). Infants' preference for the predominant stress patterns of English words. *Child Development, 64*, 675–687.

Kado, S., & Takagi, R. (1996). Biological aspects. In S. Sandberg (Ed.), *Hyperactivity disorders of childhood* (pp. 246–279). Cambridge, England: Cambridge University Press.

Kagan, J. (1971). *Change and continuity in infancy.* New York: Wiley.

Kagan, J. (1994). *Galen's prophecy.* New York: Basic Books.

Kagan, J. (1997). Temperament and the reactions to unfamiliarity. *Child Development, 68*, 139–143.

Kagan, J., Arcus, D., Snidman, N., Feng, W. Y., Hendler, J., & Greene, S. (1994). Reactivity in infants: A cross-national comparison. *Developmental Psychology, 30*, 342–345.

Kagan, J., Kearsley, R., & Zelazo, P. (1978). *Infancy: Its place in human development.* Cambridge, MA: Harvard University Press.

Kagan, J., Reznick, J. S., & Snidman, N. (1990). The temperamental qualities of inhibition and lack of inhibition. In M. Lewis & S. M. Miller (Eds.), *Handbook of developmental psychopathology* (pp. 219–226). New York: Plenum Press.

Kagan, J., Snidman, N., & Arcus, D. (1993). On the temperamental categories of inhibited and uninhibited children. In K. H. Rubin & J. B. Asendorpf (Eds.), *Social withdrawal, inhibition, and shyness in childhood* (pp. 19–28). Hillsdale, NJ: Erlbaum.

Kail, R. (1991). Processing time declines exponentially during childhood and adolescence. *Developmental Psychology, 27*, 259–266.

Kail, R., & Hall, L. K. (1994). Processing speed, naming speed, and reading. *Developmental Psychology, 30*, 949–954.

Kandel, D., Chen, K., Warner, L. A., Kessler, R. C., & Grant, B. (1997). Prevalence and demographic correlates of symptoms of last year dependence on alcohol, nicotine, marijuana and cocaine in the U.S. population. *Drug and Alcohol Dependence, 44*, 11–29.

Kann, L., Warren, C. W., Harris, W. A., Collins, J. L., Douglas, K. A., Collins, M. E., Williams, B. I., Ross, J. G., & Kolbe, L. J. (1995). Youth risk behavior surveillance—United States, 1993. *Morbidity and Mortality Weekly Reports, 44*(SS 1), 1–55.

Karen, R. (1994). *Becoming attached.* New York: Warner Books.

Karmiloff-Smith, A., Grant, J., Berthoud, I., Davies, M., Howlin, P., & Udwin, O. (1997). Language and Williams syndrome: How intact is "intact"? *Child Development, 68*, 246–262.

Katz, P. A., & Ksansnak, K. R. (1994). Developmental aspects of gender role flexibility and traditionality in middle childhood and adolescence. *Developmental Psychology, 30*, 272–282.

Kaufman, A. S., & Kaufman, N. L. (1983a). *Kaufman Assessment Battery for Children: Interpretive manual.* Circle Pines, MN: American Guidance Service.

Kaufman, A. S., & Kaufman, N. L. (1983b). *Kaufman Assessment Battery for Children: Administration and scoring manual.* Circle Pines, MN: American Guidance Service.

Kaufman, J., & Zigler, E. (1989). The intergenerational transmission of child abuse. In D. Cicchetti & V. Carlson (Eds.), *Child maltreatment: Theory and research on the causes and consequences of child abuse and neglect* (pp. 129–150). New York: Cambridge University Press.

Kaye, K. (1982). *The mental and social life of babies: How parents create persons.* Chicago: University of Chicago Press.

Kaye, K. L., & Bower, T. G. R. (1994). Learning and intermodal transfer of information in newborns. *Psychological Science, 5*, 286–288.

Keating, D. P. (1980). Thinking processes in adolescence. In J. Adelson (Ed.), *Handbook of adolescent psychology* (pp. 211–246). New York: Wiley.

Keating, D. P., List, J. A., & Merriman, W. E. (1985). Cognitive processing and cognitive ability: Multivariate validity investigation. *Intelligence, 9*, 149–170.

Keefe, S. E., & Padilla, A. M. (1987). *Chicano ethnicity.* Albuquerque: University of New Mexico Press.

Keeney, T. J., Cannizzo, S. R., & Flavell, J. H. (1967). Spontaneous and induced verbal rehearsal in a recall task. *Child Development, 38*, 935–966.

Kelley, M. L., Sanches-Hucles, J., & Walker, R. R. (1993). Correlates of disciplinary practices in working- to middle-class African-American mothers. *Merrill-Palmer Quarterly, 39*, 252–264.

Kemper, K. J. (1996). *The wholistic pediatrician.* New York: HarperCollins.

Kendall-Tackett, K. A., Williams, L. M., & Finkelhor, D. (1993). Impact of sexual abuse on children: A review and synthesis of recent empirical studies. *Psychological Bulletin, 113*, 164–180.

Keniston, K. (1970). Youth: A "new" stage in life. *American Scholar, 8*(Autumn), 631–654.

Kennedy, D. M. (1995). Glimpses of a highly gifted child in a heterogeneous classroom. *Roeper Review, 17,* 164–168.

Kerns, K. A. (1996). Individual differences in friendship quality: Links to child-mother attachment. In W. M. Bukowski, A. F. Newcomb, & W. W. Hartup (Eds.), *The company they keep: Friendship in childhood and adolescence* (pp. 137–157). Cambridge: Cambridge University Press.

Kestenbaum, R., Farber, E. A., & Sroufe, L. A. (1989). Individual differences in empathy among preschoolers: Relation to attachment history. *New Directions for Child Development, 44,* 51–64.

Kilgore, P. E., Holman, R. C., Clarke, M. J., & Glass, R. I. (1995). Trends of diarrheal disease–associated mortality in US children, 1968 through 1991. *Journal of the American Medical Association, 274,* 1143–1148.

Killen, J. D., Hayward, C., Litt, I., Hammer, L. D., Wilson, D. M., Miner, B., Taylor, B., Varady, A., & Shisslak, C. (1992). Is puberty a risk factor for eating disorders? *American Journal of Diseases of Childhood, 146,* 323–325.

Kilpatrick, S. J., & Laros, R. K. (1989). Characteristics of normal labor. *Obstetrics and Gynecology, 74,* 85–87.

Kim, U., Triandis, H. C., Kâgitçibasi, Ç., Choi, S., & Yoon, G. (Eds.). (1994). *Individualism and collectivism: Theory, method, and applications.* Thousand Oaks, CA: Sage.

Kinney, D. A. (1993). From "nerds" to "normals": Adolescent identity recovery within a changing social system. *Sociology of Education, 66,* 21–40.

Kirsh, S. J., & Cassidy, J. (1997). Preschoolers' attention to and memory for attachment-relevant information. *Child Development, 68,* 1143–1153.

Klaus, H. M., & Kennell, J. H. (1976). *Maternal-infant bonding.* St. Louis, MO: Mosby.

Klebanov, P. K., Brooks-Gunn, J., Hofferth, S., & Duncan, G. J. (1995, April). *Neighborhood resources, social support and maternal competence.* Paper presented at the biennial meetings of the Society for Research in Child Development, Indianapolis.

Klein, J. O. (1994). Otitis media. *Clinical Infectious Diseases, 19,* 823–833.

Kline, M., Tschann, J. M., Johnston, J. R., & Wallerstein, J. S. (1989). Children's adjustment in joint and sole physical custody families. *Developmental Psychology, 25,* 430–438.

Klonoff-Cohen, H. D., Edelstein, S. L., Lefkowitz, E. S., Srinivasan, I. P., Kaegi, D., Chang, J. C., & Wiley, K. J. (1995). The effect of passive smoking and tobacco exposure through breast milk on sudden infant death syndrome. *Journal of the American Medical Association, 273,* 795–798.

Knight, G. P., Cota, M. K., & Bernal, M. E. (1993). The socialization of cooperative, competitive, and individualistic preferences among Mexican American children: The mediating role of ethnic identity. *Hispanic Journal of Behavioral Sciences, 15,* 291–309.

Kochanska, G. (1997). Mutually responsive orientation between mothers and their young children: Implications for early socialization. *Child Development, 68,* 94–112.

Kochanska, G., Murray, K., & Coy, K. C. (1997). Inhibitory control as a contributor to conscience in childhood: From toddler to early school age. *Child Development, 68,* 263–277.

Kochenderfer, B. J., & Ladd, G. W. (1996). Peer victimization: Cause or consequence of school maladjustment. *Child Development, 67,* 1305–1317.

Kohlberg, L. (1964). Development of moral character and moral ideology. In M. L. Hoffman & L. W. Hoffman (Eds.), *Review of child development research* (Vol. 1, pp. 283–332). New York: Russell Sage Foundation.

Kohlberg, L. (1966). A cognitive-developmental analysis of children's sex-role concepts and attitudes. In E. E. Maccoby (Ed.), *The development of sex differences* (pp. 82–172). Stanford, CA: Stanford University Press.

Kohlberg, L. (1975). The cognitive-developmental approach to moral education. *Phi Delta Kappan,* 670–677.

Kohlberg, L. (1976). Moral stages and moralization: The cognitive-developmental approach. In T. Lickona (Ed.), *Moral development and behavior: Theory, research, and social issues* (pp. 31–53). New York: Holt.

Kohlberg, L. (1978). Revisions in the theory and practice of moral development. *New Directions for Child Development, 2,* 83–88.

Kohlberg, L. (1980). *The meaning and measurement of moral development.* Worcester, MA: Clark University Press.

Kohlberg, L. (1981). *Essays on moral development: Vol. 1. The philosophy of moral development.* New York: Harper & Row.

Kohlberg, L., Boyd, D. R., & Levine, C. (1990). The return of stage 6: Its principle and moral point of view. In T. E. Wren (Ed.), *The moral domain: Essays in the ongoing discussion between philosophy and the social sciences.* Cambridge: MIT Press.

Kohlberg, L., & Candee, D. (1984). The relationship of moral judgment to moral action. In W. M. Kurtines & J. L. Gewirtz (Eds.), *Morality, moral behavior, and moral development* (pp. 52–73). New York: Wiley.

Kohlberg, L., & Elfenbein, D. (1975). The development of moral judgments concerning capital punishment. *American Journal of Orthopsychiatry, 54,* 614–640.

Kohlberg, L., & Higgins, A. (1987). School democracy and social interaction. In W. M. Kurtines & J. L. Gewirtz (Eds.), *Moral development through social interaction* (pp. 102–130). New York: Wiley-Interscience.

Kohlberg, L., Levine, C., & Hewer, A. (1983). *Moral stages: A current formulation and a response to critics.* Basel, Switzerland: Karger.

Kohlberg, L., & Ullian, D. Z. (1974). Stages in the development of psychosexual concepts and attitudes. In R. C. Friedman, R. M. Richart, & R. L. Vande Wiele (Eds.), *Sex differences in behavior* (pp. 209–222). New York: Wiley.

Kohn, M. L. (1980). Job complexity and adult personality. In N. J. Smelser & E. H. Erikson (Eds.), *Themes of work and love in adulthood* (pp. 193–212). Cambridge, MA: Harvard University Press.

Kohn, M. L., & Schooler, C. (1983). *Work and personality: An inquiry into the impact of social stratification.* Norwood, NJ: Ablex.

Kohnstamm, G. A., Halverson, C. F., Jr., Havill, V. L., & Mervielde, I. (1994). Parents' free descriptions of child characteristics: A cross-cultural search for the roots of the Big Five. In S. Harkness & C. M. Super (Eds.), *Parents' cultural belief systems: Cultural origins and developmental consequences.* New York: Guilford Press.

Kolata, G. (1992, April 26). A parents' guide to kids' sports. *The New York Times Magazine,* pp. 12–15, 40, 44, 46.

Koller, H., Lawson, K., Rose, S. A., Wallace, I., & McCarton, C. (1997). Patterns of cognitive development in very low birth weight children during the first six years of life. *Pediatrics, 99,* 383–389.

Kopp, C. B. (1994). Trends and directions in studies of developmental risk. In C. A. Nelson (Ed.), *The Minnesota symposia on child psychology* (Vol. 27, pp. 1–33). Hillsdale, NJ: Erlbaum.

Kopp, C. B., & Kaler, S. R. (1989). Risk in infancy: Origins and implications. *American Psychologist, 44,* 244–230.

Korkman, M., Liikanen, A., & Fellman, V. (1996). Neuropsychological consequences of very low birth weight and asphyxia at term: Follow-up until school-age. *Journal of Clinical and Experimental Neuropsychology, 18,* 220–233.

Korner, A. F., Hutchinson, C. A., Koperski, J. A., Kraemer, H. C., & Schneider, P. A. (1981). Stability of individual differences of neonatal motor and crying patterns. *Child Development, 52,* 83–90.

Kortenhaus, C. M., & Demarest, J. (1993). Gender role stereotyping in children's literature: An update. *Sex Roles, 28,* 219–232.

Kovacs, D. M., Parker, J. G., & Hoffman, L. W. (1996). Behavioral, affective, and social correlates of involvement in cross-sex friendship in elementary school. *Child Development, 67,* 2269–2286.

Kuczaj, S. A., II (1977). The acquisition of regular and irregular past tense forms. *Journal of Verbal Learning and Verbal Behavior, 49,* 319–326.

Kuczaj, S. A., II (1978). Children's judgments of grammatical and ungrammatical irregular past tense verbs. *Child Development, 49,* 319–326.

Kuhl, P. K. (1993). Developmental speech perception: Implications for models of language impairment. *Annals of the New York Academy of Sciences, 682*(July 14), 248–263.

Kuhl, P. K., & Meltzoff, A. N. (1984). The intermodal representation of speech in infants. *Infant Behavior and Development, 7,* 361–381.

Kuhn, D. (1992). Cognitive development. In M. H. Bornstein & M. E. Lamb (Eds.), *Developmental psychology: An advanced textbook* (3rd ed., pp. 211–272). Hillsdale, NJ: Erlbaum.

Kuhn, D., Garcia-Mila, M., Zohar, A., & Andersen, C. (1995). Strategies of knowledge acquisition. *Monographs of the Society for Research in Child Development, 60*(Serial No. 245).

Kupersmidt, J. B., Griesler, P. C., DeRosier, M. E., Patterson, C. J., & Davis, P. W. (1995). Childhood aggression and peer relations in the context of family and neighborhood factors. *Child Development, 66,* 360–375.

Kurdek, L. A., & Fine, M. A. (1994). Family acceptance and family control as predictors of adjustment in young adolescents: Linear, curvilinear, or interactive effects? *Child Development, 65,* 1137–1146.

Kurdek, L. A., & Krile, D. (1982). A developmental analysis of the relation between peer acceptance and both interpersonal understanding and perceived social self-competence. *Child Development, 53,* 1485–1491.

Kurtines, W. M., & Gewirtz, J. L. (Eds.). (1991). *Handbook of moral behavior and development: Vol. 1. Theory. Vol. 2. Research. Vol. 3. Application.* Hillsdale, NJ: Erlbaum.

Kuther, T. L., & Higgins-D'Alessandro, A. (1997, April). *The role of moral reasoning and domain judgment in adolescent risk engagement.* Paper presented at the biennial meetings of the Society for Research in Child Development, Washington, DC.

La Freniere, P., Strayer, F. F., & Gauthier, R. (1984). The emergence of same-sex affiliative preferences among preschool peers: A developmental/ethological perspective. *Child Development, 55,* 1958–1965.

La Pine, T. R., Jackson, J. C., & Bennett, F. C. (1995). Outcome of infants weighing less than 800 grams at birth: 15 years' experience. *Pediatrics, 96,* 479–483.

Lagattuta, K. H., Wellman, H. M., & Flavell, J. H. (1997). Preschoolers' understanding of the link between thinking and feeling: Cognitive cuing and emotional change. *Child Development, 68,* 1081–1104.

Lagrew, D. C., Jr., & Morgan, M. A. (1996). Decreasing the cesarean section rate in a private hospital: Success without mandated clinical changes. *American Journal of Obstetrics and Gynecology, 174,* 184–191.

Lamb, M. E. (1981). The development of father-infant relationships. In M. E. Lamb (Ed.), *The role of the father in child development* (2nd ed., pp. 459–488). New York: Wiley.

Lamb, M. E. (1998). Nonparental child care: Context, quality, correlates, and consequences. In W. Damon (Ed.), *Handbook of child psychology: Vol. 4. Child psychology in practice* (5th ed., pp. 73–133). New York: Wiley.

Lamb, M. E., Frodi, M., Hwang, C., & Frodi, A. M. (1983). Effects of paternal involvement on infant preferences for mothers and fathers. *Child Development, 54,* 450–458.

Lamb, M. E., Sternberg, K. J., & Prodromidis, M. (1992). Nonmaternal care and the security of infant-mother attachment: A reanalysis of the data. *Infant Behavior and Development, 15,* 71–83.

Lamborn, S. D., Dornbusch, S. M., & Steinberg, L. (1996). Ethnicity and community context as moderators of the relations between family decision making and adolescent adjustment. *Child Development, 67,* 283–301.

Lamborn, S. D., Mounts, N. S., Steinberg, L., & Dornbusch, S. M. (1991). Patterns of competence and adjustment among adolescents from authoritative, authoritarian, indulgent, and neglectful families. *Child Development, 62,* 1049–1065.

Lamke, L. K. (1982). Adjustment and sex-role orientation. *Journal of Youth and Adolescence, 11,* 247–259.

Landry, S. H., Garner, P. W. Swank, P. R., & Baldwin, C. D. (1996). Effects of maternal scaffolding during joint toy play with preterm and full-term infants. *Merrill-Palmer Quarterly, 42,* 177–199.

Langlois, J. H., Kalakanis, L. E., Rubenstein, A. J., Larson, A. D., & Hallam, M. J. (1997, April). *Developmental effects of physical attractiveness: A meta-analytic review.* Paper presented at the biennial meetings of the Society for Research in Child Development, Washington, DC.

Langlois, J. H., Ritter, J. M., Casey, R. J., & Sawin, D. B. (1995). Infant attractiveness predicts maternal behaviors and attitudes. *Developmental Psychology, 31,* 464–472.

Langlois, J. H., Ritter, J. M., Roggman, L. A., & Vaughn, L. S. (1991). Facial diversity and infant preferences for attractive faces. *Developmental Psychology, 27,* 79–84.

Langlois, J. H., & Roggman, L. A. (1990). Attractive faces are only average. *Psychological Science, 1,* 115–121.

Langlois, J. H., Roggman, L. A., Casey, R. J., Ritter, J. M., Rieser-Danner, L. A., & Jenkins, V. Y. (1987). Infant preferences for attractive faces: Rudiments of a stereotype? *Developmental Psychology, 23,* 363–369.

Langlois, J. H., Roggman, L. A., & Musselman, L. (1994). What is average and what is not average about attractive faces? *Psychological Science, 5,* 214–220.

Langlois, J. H., Roggman, L. A., & Rieser-Danner, L. A. (1990). Infants' differential social responses to attractive and unattractive faces. *Developmental Psychology, 26,* 153–159.

Laub, J. H., & Sampson, R. J. (1995). The long-term effect of punitive discipline. In J. McCord (Ed.), *Coercion and punishment in long-term perspectives* (pp. 247–258). Cambridge, England: Cambridge University Press.

Laumann, E. O., Gagnon, J. H., Michael, R. T., & Michaels, S. (1994). *The social organization of sexuality: Sexual practices in the United States.* Chicago: University of Chicago Press.

Laursen, B. (1995). Conflict and social interaction in adolescent relationships. *Journal of Research on Adolescence, 5,* 55–70.

Leaper, C. (1991). Influence and involvement in children's discourse: Age, gender, and partner effects. *Child Development, 62,* 797–811.

Lebra, T. S. (1994). Mother and child in Japanese socialization: A Japan-U.S. comparison. In P. M. Greenfield & R. R. Cocking (Eds.), *Cross-cultural roots of minority child development* (pp. 259–274). Hillsdale, NJ: Erlbaum.

Lechky, O. (1994). Epidemic of childhood obesity may cause major public health problems, doctor warns. *Canadian Medical Association Journal, 150,* 78–81.

Lederberg, A. R., & Mobley, C. E. (1990). The effect of hearing impairment on the quality of attachment and mother-toddler interaction. *Child Development, 61,* 1596–1604.

Lee, C. C. (1985). Successful rural black adolescents: A psychological profile. *Adolescence, 20,* 129–142.

Lee, V. E., Burkham, D. T., Zimiles, H., & Ladewski, B. (1994). Family structure and its effect on behavioral and emotional problems in young adolescents. *Journal of Research on Adolescence, 4,* 405–437.

Legerstee, M., Pomerleau, A., Malcuit, G., & Feider, H. (1987). The development of infants' responses to people and a doll: Implications for research in communication. *Infant Behavior and Development, 10,* 81–95.

Leichtman, M. D., & Ceci, S. J. (1995). The effects of stereotypes and suggestions on preschoolers' reports. *Developmental Psychology, 31,* 568–578.

Lerner, J. V., & Galambos, N. L. (1986). Child development and family change: The influences of maternal employment in infants and toddlers. In L. P. Lipsitt & C. Rovee-Collier (Eds.), *Advances in infancy research* (Vol. 4, pp. 40–86). Norwood, NJ: Ablex.

Lerner, R. M. (1985). Adolescent maturational changes and psychosocial development: A dynamic interactional perspective. *Journal of Youth and Adolescence, 14,* 355–372.

Lerner, R. M. (1987). A life-span perspective for early adolescence. In R. M. Lerner & T. T. Foch (Eds.), *Biological-psychosocial interactions in early adolescence* (pp. 9–34). Hillsdale, NJ: Erlbaum.

Lester, B. M. (1987). Prediction of developmental outcome from acoustic cry analysis in term and preterm infants. *Pediatrics, 80,* 529–534.

Lester, B. M., Boukydis, C. F. Z., Garcia-Coll, C. T., Hole, W., & Peucker, M. (1992). Infantile colic: Acoustic cry characteristics, maternal perception of cry, and temperament. *Infant Behavior and Development, 15,* 15–26.

Lester, B. M., & Dreher, M. (1989). Effects of marijuana use during pregnancy on newborn cry. *Child Development, 60,* 765–771.

Lester, B. M., Freier, K., & LaGasse, L. (1995). Prenatal cocaine exposure and child outcome: What do we really know? In M. Lewis & M. Bendersky (Eds.), *Mothers, babies, and cocaine: The role of toxins in development* (pp. 19–39). Hillsdale, NJ: Erlbaum.

Leukefeld, C. G., Logan, T. K., Clayton, R. R., Martin, C., Zimmerman, R., Cattarello, A., Milich, R., & Lynam, D. (1998). Adolescent drug use, delinquency, and other behaviors. In T. P. Gullotta, G. R. Adams, & R. Montemayor (Eds.), *Delinquent violent youth: Theory and interventions* (pp. 98–128). Thousand Oaks, CA: Sage.

LeVay, S. (1991). A difference in hypothalamus structure between heterosexual and homosexual men. *Science, 253,* 1034–1037.

Leve, L. D., & Fagot, B. I. (1995, April). *The influence of attachment style and parenting behavior on children's prosocial behavior with peers.* Paper presented at the biennial meetings of the Society for Research in Child Development, Indianapolis.

Levitt, M. J., Guacci-Franco, N., & Levitt, J. L. (1993). Convoys of social support in childhood and early adolescence: Structure and function. *Developmental Psychology, 29,* 811–818.

Levy, G. D., & Fivush, R. (1993). Scripts and gender: A new approach for examining gender-role development. *Developmental Review, 13,* 126–146.

Lewis, C., Freeman, N. H., Kyriakidou, C., Maridaki-Kassotaki, K., & Berridge, D. M. (1996). Social influences on false belief access: Specific sibling influences or general apprenticeship? *Child Development, 67,* 2930–2947.

Lewis, C. C. (1981). How adolescents approach decisions: Changes over grades seven to twelve and policy implications. *Child Development, 52,* 538–544.

Lewis, C. N., Freeman, N. H., & Maridaki-Kassotaki, K. (1995, April). *The social basis of theory of mind: Influences of siblings and, more importantly, interactions with adult kin.* Paper presented at the biennial meetings of the Society for Research in Child Development, Indianapolis.

Lewis, M. (1991). Ways of knowing: Objective self-awareness of consciousness. *Developmental Review, 11,* 231–243.

Lewis, M. (1994). Myself and me. In S. T. Parker, R. W. Mitchell, & M. L. Boccia (Eds.), *Self-awareness in animals and humans: Developmental perspectives* (pp. 20–34). New York: Cambridge University Press.

Lewis, M. (1997). *Altering fate.* New York: Guilford Press.

Lewis, M., Allesandri, S. M., & Sullivan, M. W. (1992). Differences in shame and pride as a function of children's gender and task difficulty. *Child Development, 63,* 630–638.

Lewis, M., & Brooks, J. (1978). Self-knowledge and emotional development. In M. Lewis & L. A. Rosenblum (Eds.), *The development of affect* (pp. 205–226). New York: Plenum Press.

Lewis, M., & Sullivan, M. W. (1985). Infant intelligence and its assessment. In B. B. Wolman (Ed.), *Handbook of intelligence* (pp. 505–599). New York: Wiley-Interscience.

Lewis, M., Sullivan, M. W., Stanger, C., & Weiss, M. (1989). Self development and self-conscious emotions. *Child Development, 60,* 146–156.

Lewis, M. D. (1993). Early socioemotional predictors of cognitive competence at 4 years. *Developmental Psychology, 29,* 1036–1045.

Lewkowicz, D. J. (1994). Limitations on infants' response to rate-based auditory-visual relations. *Developmental Psychology, 30,* 880–892.

Lichter, D. T., & Eggebeen, D. J. (1994). The effect of parental employment on child poverty. *Journal of Marriage and the Family, 56,* 633–645.

Lickona, T. (1978). Moral development and moral education. In J. M. Gallagher & J. J. A. Easley (Eds.), *Knowledge and development* (Vol. 2, pp. 21–74). New York: Plenum Press.

Lickona, T. (1983). *Raising good children.* Toronto: Bantam Books.

Lieberman, M., Doyle, A., & Markiewicz, D. (1995, April). *Attachment to mother and father: Links to peer relations in children.* Paper presented at the biennial meetings of the Society for Research in Child Development, Indianapolis.

Lillard, A. S., & Flavell, J. H. (1992). Young children's understanding of different mental states. *Developmental Psychology, 28,* 626–634.

Lindberg, L. D. (1996). Women's decisions about breastfeeding and maternal employment. *Journal of Marriage and the Family, 58,* 239–251.

Lindsay, R., Feldkamp, M., Harris, D., Robertson, J., & Rallison, M. (1994). Utah Growth Study: Growth standards and the prevalence of growth hormone deficiency. *Journal of Pediatrics, 125,* 29–35.

Litt, I. F. (1996). Special health problems during adolescence. In R. E. Behrman, R. M. Kliegman, & A. M. Arvin (Eds.), *Nelson textbook of pediatrics* (15th ed., pp. 541–565). Philadelphia: Saunders.

Livesley, W. J., & Bromley, D. B. (1973). *Person perception in childhood and adolescence.* London: Wiley.

Lo, Y. D., Patel, P., Wainscoat, J. S., Sampietro, M., Gillmer, M. D. G., & Fleming, K. A. (1989). Prenatal sex determination by DNA amplification from maternal peripheral blood. *The Lancet,* 1363–1365.

Lockman, J. J., & Thelen, E. (1993). Developmental biodynamics: Brain, body, behavior connections. *Child Development, 64,* 953–959.

Loeber, R., Stouthamer-Loeber, M., Van Kammen, W. B., & Farrington, D. P. (1991). Initiation, escalation and desistance in juvenile offending and their correlates. *Journal of Criminal Law and Criminology, 82,* 36–82.

Loeber, R., Tremblay, R. E., Gagnon, C., & Charlebois, P. (1989). Continuity and desistance in disruptive boys' early fighting at school. *Development and Psychopathology, 1,* 39–50.

Loehlin, J. C., Horn, J. M., & Willerman, L. (1994). Differential inheritance of mental abilities in the Texas Adoption Project. *Intelligence, 19,* 325–336.

Loftus, E. F. (1992). When a lie becomes memory's truth: Memory distortion after exposure to misinformation. *Current Directions in Psychological Science, 4,* 121–123.

Lollis, S., Ross, H., & Leroux, L. (1996). An observational study of parents' socialization of moral orientation during sibling conflicts. *Merrill-Palmer Quarterly, 42,* 475–494.

Long, J. V. F., & Vaillant, G. E. (1984). Natural history of male psychological health: Escape from the underclass. *American Journal of Psychiatry, 141,* 341–346.

Longo, D. C., & Bond, L. (1984). Families of the handicapped child: Research and practice. *Family Relations, 33,* 57–65.

López-Alarcón, M., Villapando, S., & Fajardo, A. (1997). Breast-feeding lowers the frequency and duration of acute respiratory infection and diarrhea in infants under six months of age. *Journal of Nutrition, 127,* 436–443.

Lore, R. K., & Schultz, L. A. (1993). Control of human aggression: A comparative perspective. *American Psychologist, 48,* 16–25.

Louhiala, P. J., Jaakkola, N., Ruotsalainen, R., & Jaakkola, J. J. K. (1995). Form of day care and respiratory infections among Finnish children. *American Journal of Public Health, 85,* 1109–1112.

Lubinski, D., & Benbow, C. P. (1992). Gender differences in abilities and preferences among the gifted: Implications for the math-science pipeline. *Current Directions in Psychological Science, 1,* 61–66.

Lucas, A., Morley, R., Cole, T. J., & Gore, S. M. (1994). A randomized multicentre study of human milk versus formula and later development in preterm infants. *Archives of Disease in Childhood, 70,* 141–146.

Lucas, A., Morley, R., Cole, T. J., Lister, G., & Leeson-Payne, C. (1992). Breast milk and subsequent intelligence quotient in children born preterm. *The Lancet, 339,* 261–264.

Lust, K. D., Brown, J. E., & Thomas, W. (1996). Maternal intake of cruciferous vegetables and other foods and colic symptoms in exclusively breast-fed infants. *Journal of the American Dietetic Association, 96,* 46–48.

Luster, T., Boger, R., & Hannan, K. (1993). Infant affect and home environment. *Journal of Marriage and the Family, 55,* 651–661.

Luster, T., & McAdoo, H. P. (1995). Factors related to self-esteem among African American youths: A secondary analysis of the High/Scope Perry Preschool data. *Journal of Research on Adolescence, 5,* 451–467.

Luster, T., & McAdoo, H. (1996). Family and child influences on educational attainment: A secondary analysis of the High/Scope Perry Preschool data. *Developmental Psychology, 32,* 26–39.

Luthar, S. S., & Zigler, E. (1992). Intelligence and social competence among high-risk adolescents. *Development and Psychopathology, 4,* 287–299.

Lykken, D. T., McGue, M., Tellegen, A., & Bouchard, T. J., Jr. (1992). Emergenesis: Genetic traits that may not run in families. *American Psychologist, 47,* 1565–1577.

Lynam, D. R. (1996). Early identification of chronic offenders: Who is the fledgling psychopath? *Psychological Bulletin, 120,* 209–234.

Lynam, D. R., Moffitt, T. E., & Stouthamer-Loeber, M. (1993). Explaining the relation between IQ and delinquency: Class, race, test motivation, school failure, or self-control? *Journal of Abnormal Psychology, 102,* 187–196.

Lyon, T. D., & Flavell, J. H. (1994). Young children's understanding of "remember" and "forget." *Child Development, 65,* 1357–1371.

Lyons, N. P. (1983). Two perspectives: On self, relationships, and morality. *Harvard Educational Review, 53,* 125–145.

Lyons-Ruth, K., Easterbrooks, M. A., & Cibelli, C. D. (1997). Infant attachment strategies, infant mental lag, and maternal depressive symptoms: Predictors of internalizing and externalizing problems at age 7. *Developmental Psychology, 33,* 681–692.

Lytton, H., & Romney, D. M. (1991). Parents' differential socialization of boys and girls: A meta-analysis. *Psychological Bulletin, 109,* 267–296.

Maccoby, E. E. (1980). *Social development: Psychological growth and the parent-child relationship.* New York: Harcourt Brace Jovanovich.

Maccoby, E. E. (1984). Middle childhood in the context of the family. In W. A. Collins (Ed.), *Development during middle childhood: The years from six to twelve* (pp. 184–239). Washington, DC: National Academy Press.

Maccoby, E. E. (1988). Gender as a social category. *Developmental Psychology, 24,* 755–765.

Maccoby, E. E. (1990). Gender and relationships: A developmental account. *American Psychologist, 45,* 513–520.

Maccoby, E. E. (1995). The two sexes and their social systems. In P. Moen, G. H. Elder Jr., & K. Lüscher (Eds.), *Examining lives in context: Perspectives on the ecology of human development* (pp. 347–364). Washington, DC: American Psychological Association.

Maccoby, E. E., & Jacklin, C. N. (1987). Gender segregation in childhood. In H. W. Reese (Ed.), *Advances in child development and behavior* (Vol. 20, pp. 239–288). Orlando, FL: Academic Press.

Maccoby, E. E., & Martin, J. A. (1983). Socialization in the context of the family: Parent-child interaction. In E. M. Hetherington (Ed.), *Handbook of child psychology: Socialization, personality, and social development* (Vol. 4, pp. 1–102). New York: Wiley.

MacDonald, K. (1992). Warmth as a developmental construct: An evolutionary analysis. *Child Development, 63,* 753–773.

Macfarlane, A. (1977). *The psychology of child birth.* Cambridge, MA: Harvard University Press.

Mack, V., Urberg, K., Lou, Q., & Tolson, J. (1995, April). *Ethnic, gender and age differences in parent and peer orientation during adolescence.* Paper presented at the biennial meetings of the Society for Research in Child Development, Indianapolis.

Maclean, M., Bryant, P., & Bradley, L. (1987). Rhymes, nursery rhymes, and reading in early childhood. *Merrill-Palmer Quarterly, 33,* 255–281.

MacMillan, D. L., Keogh, B. K., & Jones, R. L. (1986). Special educational research on mildly handicapped learners. In M. C. Wittrock (Ed.), *Handbook of research on teaching* (3rd ed., pp. 686–724). New York: Macmillan.

MacMillan, D. L., & Reschly, D. J. (1997). Issues of definition and classification. In W. E. MacLean Jr. (Ed.), *Ellis' handbook of mental deficiency: Psychological theory and research* (pp. 47–74). Mahwah, NJ: Erlbaum.

Madsen, W. (1969). Mexican Americans and Anglo Americans: A comparative study of mental health in Texas. In S. C. Plog & R. B. Edgerton (Eds.), *Changing perspectives in mental illness* (pp. 217–247). New York: Holt, Rinehart and Winston.

Maffeis, C., Schutz, Y., Piccoli, R., Gonfiantini, E., & Pinelli, L. (1993). Prevalence of obesity in children in north-east Italy. *International Journal of Obesity, 14,* 287–294.

Maguin, E., Loeber, R., & LeMahieu, G. (1993). Does the relationship between poor reading and delinquency hold for males of different ages and ethnic groups? *Journal of Emotional and Behavioral Disorders, 1,* 88–100.

Mahler, M. (1977). *The psychological birth of the infant.* New York: Basic Books.

Mahoney, J. L., & Cairns, R. B. (1997). Do extracurricular activities protect against early school dropout? *Developmental Psychology, 33,* 241–253.

Main, M., & Hesse, E. (1990). Parents' unresolved traumatic experiences are related to infant disorganized attachment status: Is frightened and/or frightening parental behavior the linking mechanism? In M. T. Greenberg, D. Cicchetti, & E. M. Cummings (Eds.), *Attachment in the preschool years: Theory, research, and intervention* (pp. 161–182). Chicago: University of Chicago Press.

Main, M., Kaplan, N., & Cassidy, J. (1985). Security in infancy, childhood, and adulthood: A move to the level of representation. *Monographs of the Society for Research in Child Development, 50*(Serial No. 209), 66–104.

Main, M., & Solomon, J. (1990). Procedures for identifying infants as disorganized/disoriented during the Ainsworth Strange Situation. In M. T. Greenberg, D. Cicchetti, & E. M. Cummings (Eds.), *Attachment in the preschool years: Theory, research, and intervention* (pp. 121–160). Chicago: University of Chicago Press.

Malina, R. M. (1982). Motor development in the early years. In S. G. Moore & C. R. Cooper (Eds.), *The young child: Reviews of research* (Vol. 3, pp. 211–232). Washington, DC: National Association for the Education of Young Children.

Malina, R. M. (1990). Physical growth and performance during the transitional years (9–16). In R. Montemayor, G. R. Adams, & T. P. Gullotta (Eds.), *From childhood to adolescence: A transitional period?* (pp. 41–62). Newbury Park, CA: Sage.

Malina, R. M. (1994). Physical growth and biological maturation of young athletes. In J. O. Holloszy (Ed.), *Exercise and sports sciences reviews* (Vol. 22, pp. 389–433). Baltimore: Williams & Wilkins.

Malinosky-Rummell, R., & Hansen, D. J. (1993). Long-term consequences of childhood physical abuse. *Psychological Bulletin, 114,* 68–79.

Mandelbaum, J. K. (1992). Child survival: What are the issues? *Journal of Pediatric Health Care, 6,* 132–137.

Maratsos, M. (1983). Some current issues in the study of the acquisition of grammar. In J. H. Flavell & E. M. Markman (Eds.), *Handbook of child psychology: Cognitive development* (pp. 707–786). New York: Wiley.

Maratsos, M. (1998). The acquisition of grammar. In W. Damon (Ed.), *Handbook of child psychology: Vol. 2. Cognition, perception, and language* (5th ed., pp. 421–466). New York: Wiley.

Marcia, J. E. (1966). Development and validation of ego identity status. *Journal of Personality and Social Psychology, 3,* 551–558.

Marcia, J. E. (1980). Identity in adolescence. In J. Adelson (Ed.), *Handbook of adolescent psychology* (pp. 159–187). New York: Wiley.

Marcia, J. E. (1993). The status of the statuses: Research review. In J. E. Marcia, A. S. Waterman, D. R. Matteson, S. L. Archer, & J. L. Orlofsky (Eds.), *Ego identity: A handbook for psychosocial research* (pp. 22–41). New York: Springer-Verlag.

Marcus, G. F., Pinker, S., Ullman, M., Hollander, M., Rosen, T. J., & Fei, X. (1992). Overregularization in language acquisition. *Monographs of the Society for Research in Child Development, 57*(4, Serial No. 228).

Marean, G. C., Werner, L. A., & Kuhl, P. K. (1992). Vowel categorization by very young infants. *Developmental Psychology, 28,* 396–405.

Marschark, M. (1993). *Psychological development of deaf children.* New York: Oxford University Press.

Marshall, N. L., Coll, C. G., Marx, F., McCartney, K., Keefe, N., & Ruh, J. (1997). After-school time and children's behavioral adjustment. *Merrill-Palmer Quarterly, 43,* 497–514.

Martell, C. (1996, September 22). Disordered lives. *Wisconsin State Journal,* pp. 1G, 4G.

Martin, B., & Hoffman, J. A. (1990). Conduct disorders. In M. Lewis & S. M. Miller (Eds.), *Handbook of developmental psychopathology* (pp. 109–118). New York: Plenum Press.

Martin, C. L. (1991). The role of cognition in understanding gender effects. In H. W. Reese (Ed.), *Advances in child development and behavior* (Vol. 23, pp. 113–150). San Diego, CA: Academic Press.

Martin, C. L. (1993). New directions for investigating children's gender knowledge. *Developmental Review, 13,* 184–204.

Martin, C. L., & Halverson, C. F., Jr. (1981). A schematic processing model of sex typing and stereotyping in children. *Child Development, 52,* 1119–1134.

Martin, C. L., & Halverson, C. F. (1983). Gender constancy: A methodological and theoretical analysis. *Sex Roles, 9,* 775–790.

Martin, C. L., & Little, J. K. (1990). The relation of gender understanding to children's sex-typed preferences and gender stereotypes. *Child Development, 61,* 1427–1439.

Martin, C. L., Wood, C. H., & Little, J. K. (1990). The development of gender stereotype components. *Child Development, 61,* 1891–1904.

Martin, E. P., & Martin, J. M. (1978). *The black extended family.* Chicago: University of Chicago Press.

Martin, E. W. (1995). Case studies on inclusion: Worst fears realized. *The Journal of Special Education, 29,* 192–199.

Martin, R. P., Wisenbaker, J., & Huttunen, M. (1994). Review of factor analytic studies of temperament measures based on the Thomas-Chess structural model: Implications for the Big Five. In C. F. Halverson Jr., G. A. Kohnstamm, & R. P. Martin (Eds.), *The developing structure of temperament and personality from infancy to adulthood* (pp. 157–172). Hillsdale, NJ: Erlbaum.

Martorano, S. C. (1977). A developmental analysis of performance on Piaget's formal operations tasks. *Developmental Psychology, 13,* 666–672.

Mascolo, M. F., & Fischer, K. W. (1995). Developmental transformations in appraisals for pride, shame, and guilt. In J. P. Tangney & K. W. Fischer (Eds.), *Self-conscious emotions: The psychology of shame, guilt, embarrassment, and pride* (pp. 64–113). New York: Guilford Press.

Mason, C. A., Cauce, A. M., Gonzales, N., Hiraga, Y., & Grove, K. (1994). An ecological model of externalizing behaviors in African-American adolescents: No family is an island. *Journal of Research on Adolescence, 4,* 639–655.

Mason, C. A., Cauce, A. M., Gonzales, N., & Hiraga, Y. (1996). Neither too sweet nor too sour: Problem peers, maternal control, and problem behavior in African American adolescents. *Child Development, 67,* 2115–2130.

Massad, C. M. (1981). Sex role identity and adjustment during adolescence. *Child Development, 52,* 1290–1298.

Masten, A. S. (1989). Resilience in development: Implications of the study of successful adaptation for developmental psychopathology. In D. Cicchetti (Ed.), *The emergence of a discipline: Rochester symposium on developmental psychopathology* (Vol. 1, pp. 261–294). Hillsdale, NJ: Erlbaum.

Masten, A. S., Best, K. M., & Garmezy, N. (1990). Resilience and development: Contributions from the study of children who overcome adversity. *Development and Psychopathology, 2,* 425–444.

Masten, A. S., & Coatsworth, J. D. (1995). Competence, resilience, and psychopathology. In D. Cicchetti & D. J. Cohen (Eds.), *Developmental psychopathology: Vol. 2. Risk, disorder, and adaptation* (pp. 715–752). New York: Wiley-Interscience.

Masten, A. S., & Coatsworth, J. D. (1998). The development of competence in favorable and unfavorable environments: Lessons from research on successful children. *American Psychologist, 53,* 205–220.

Masur, E. F. (1995). Infants' early verbal imitation and their later lexical development. *Merrill-Palmer Quarterly, 41,* 286–306.

Matarazzo, J. D. (1992). Biological and physiological correlates of intelligence. *Intelligence, 16,* 257–258.

Mather, P. L., & Black, K. N. (1984). Heredity and environmental influences on preschool twins' language skills. *Developmental Psychology, 20,* 303–308.

Mathew, A., & Cook, M. (1990). The control of reaching movements by young infants. *Child Development, 61,* 1238–1257.

Maughan, B., Pickles, A., & Quinton, D. (1995). Parental hostility, childhood behavior, and adult social functioning. In J. McCord (Ed.), *Coercion and punishment in long-term perspectives* (pp. 34–58). Cambridge, England: Cambridge University Press.

Maurer, D., & Maurer, C. (1988). *The world of the newborn.* New York: Basic Books.

McAdoo, H. P. (Ed.). (1993). *Family ethnicity: Strength in diversity.* Newbury Park, CA: Sage.

McCall, R. B. (1993). Developmental functions for general mental performance. In D. K. Detterman (Ed.), *Current topics in human intelligence: Vol. 3. Individual differences and cognition* (pp. 3–30). Norwood, NJ: Ablex.

McClintock, M. K., & Herdt, G. (1996). Rethinking puberty: The development of sexual attraction. *Current Directions in Psychological Science, 5,* 178–183.

McCord, J. (1982). A longitudinal view of the relationship between parental absence and crime. In J. Gunn & D. P. Farrington (Eds.), *Abnormal offenders, delinquency, and the criminal justice system* (pp. 113–128). London: Wiley.

McCrae, R. R., & Costa, P. T., Jr. (1990). *Personality in adulthood.* New York: Guilford Press.

McCrae, R. R., & John, O. P. (1992). An introduction to the five-factor model and its applications. *Journal of Personality, 60,* 175–215.

McCune, L. (1995). A normative study of representational play at the transition to language. *Developmental Psychology, 31,* 198–206.

McFalls, J. A., Jr. (1990). The risks of reproductive impairment in the later years of childbearing. *Annual Review of Sociology, 16,* 491–519.

McGue, M. (1994). Why developmental psychology should find room for behavior genetics. In C. A. Nelson (Ed.), *The Minnesota symposia on child development* (Vol. 27, pp. 105–119). Hillsdale, NJ: Erlbaum.

McGue, M., & Lykken, D. T. (1992). Genetic influence on risk of divorce. *Psychological Science, 3,* 368–373.

McGuire, S., McHale, S. M., & Updegraff, K. (1996). Children's perceptions of the sibling relationship in middle childhood: Connections within and between family relationships. *Personal Relationships, 3,* 229–239.

McHale, S. M., & Lerner, R. M. (1990). Stages of human development. In R. M. Thomas (Ed.), *The encyclopedia of human development and education* (pp. 163–166). Oxford: Pergamon Press.

McKusick, V. A. (1994). *Mendelian inheritance in man* (11th ed.). Baltimore: Johns Hopkins University Press.

McLanahan, S. S. (1997). Parent absence or poverty: Which matters more? In G. Duncan & J. Brooks-Gunn (Eds.), *Consequences of growing up poor* (pp. 35–48). New York: Russell Sage Foundation.

McLanahan, S. S., & Sandefur, G. (1994). *Growing up with a single parent: What hurts, what helps.* Cambridge, MA: Harvard University Press.

McLaughlin, B. (1984). *Second-language acquisition in childhood: Preschool children* (2nd ed.). Hillsdale, NJ: Erlbaum.

McLeskey, J., & Pugach, M. C. (1995). The real sellout: Failing to give inclusion a chance. A response to Roberts and Mather. *Learning Disabilities Research & Practice, 10,* 233–238.

McLoyd, V. (1997, April). *Reducing stressors, increasing supports in the lives of ethnic minority children in America: Research and policy issues.* Paper presented at the biennial meetings of the Society for Research in Child Development, Washington, DC.

McLoyd, V., & Wilson, L. (1991). The strain of living poor: Parenting, social support, and child mental health. In A. C. Huston (Ed.), *Children in poverty: Child development and public policy* (pp. 105–135). Cambridge, England: Cambridge University Press.

McLoyd, V. C. (1998). Socioeconomic disadvantage and child development. *American Psychologist, 53,* 185–204.

McLoyd, V. C., Jayaratne, T. E., Ceballo, R., & Borquez, J. (1994). Unemployment and work interruption among African American single mothers: Effects on parenting and adolescent socioemotional functioning. *Child Development, 65,* 562–589.

McMahon, R. J. (1997, April). *Prevention of antisocial behavior: Initial findings from the Fast Track Project.* Symposium presented at the biennial meetings of the Society for Research in Child Development, Washington, DC.

Melby, J. N., & Conger, R. D. (1996). Parental behaviors and adolescent academic performance: A longitudinal analysis. *Journal of Research on Adolescence, 6,* 113–137.

Melson, G. F., Ladd, G. W., & Hsu, H. (1993). Maternal support networks, maternal cognitions, and young children's social and cognitive development. *Child Development, 64,* 1401–1417.

Meltzoff, A. N. (1988). Infant imitation and memory: Nine-month-olds in immediate and deferred tasks. *Child Development, 59,* 217–225.

Meltzoff, A. N. (1995). Understanding the intentions of others: Re-enactment of intended acts by 18-month-old children. *Developmental Psychology, 31,* 838–850.

Meltzoff, A. N., & Borton, R. W. (1979). Intermodal matching by human neonates. *Nature, 282,* 403–404.

Meltzoff, A. N., & Moore, M. K. (1977). Imitation of facial and manual gestures by human neonates. *Science, 198,* 75–78.

Menaghan, E. G., & Parcel, T. L. (1995). Social sources of change in children's home environments: The effects of parental occupational experiences and family conditions. *Journal of Marriage and the Family, 57,* 69–84.

Merikangas, K. R., & Angst, J. (1995). The challenge of depressive disorders in adolescence. In M. Rutter (Ed.), *Psychosocial disturbances in young people: Challenges for prevention* (pp. 131–165). Cambridge, England: Cambridge University Press.

Merriman, W. E. (1991). The mutual exclusivity bias in children's word learning: A reply to Woodward and Markman. *Developmental Review, 11,* 164–191.

Merriman, W. E., & Bowman, L. L. (1989). The mutual exclusivity bias in children's word learning. *Monographs of the Society for Research in Child Development, 54*(Serial No. 220).

Mervis, C. B., & Bertrand, J. (1994). Acquisition of the novel name-nameless category (N3C) principle. *Child Development, 65,* 1646–1662.

Mervis, C. B., Bertrand, J., Robinson, B. F., Armstrong, S. C., Klein, B. P., Turner, N. D., Baker, D. E., & Reinberg, J. (1995, April). *Early language development of children with Williams syndrome.* Paper presented at the biennial meetings of the Society for Research in Child Development, Indianapolis.

Meyer-Bahlburg, H. F. L., Ehrhardt, A. A., & Feldman, J. F. (1986). Long-term implications of the prenatal endocrine milieu for sex-dimorphic behavior. In L. Erlenmeyer-Kimling & N. E. Miller (Eds.), *Life-span research on the prediction of psychopathology* (pp. 17–30). Hillsdale, NJ: Erlbaum.

Meyer-Bahlburg, H. F. L., Ehrhardt, A. A., Rosen, L. R., Gruen, R. S., Veridiano, N. P., Vann, F. H., & Neuwalder, H. F. (1995). Prenatal estrogens and the development of homosexual orientation. *Developmental Psychology, 31,* 12–21.

Meyers, A., Frank, D. A., Roos, N., Peterson, K. E., Casey, V. A., Cupples, A., & Levenson, S. M. (1995). Housing subsidies and pediatric undernutrition. *Archives of Pediatric and Adolescent Medicine, 149,* 1079–1084.

Meyers, A. F., Sampson, A. E., Weitzman, M., Rogers, B. L., & Kayne, H. (1989). School breakfast program and school performance. *American Journal of Diseases of Children, 143,* 1234–1239.

Miller, B. C., Christopherson, C. R., & King, P. K. (1993). Sexual behavior in adolescence. In T. P. Gullotta, G. R. Adams, & R. Montemayor (Eds.), *Adolescent sexuality* (pp. 57–76). Newbury Park, CA: Sage.

Miller, B. C., & Moore, K. A. (1990). Adolescent sexual behavior, pregnancy, and parenting: Research through the 1980s. *Journal of Marriage and the Family, 52,* 1025–1044.

Miller, K. E., & Pedersen-Randall, P. (1995, April). *Work, farm work, academic achievement and friendship: A comparison of rural and urban 10th, 11th and 12th graders.* Paper presented at the biennial meetings of the Society for Research in Child Development, Indianapolis.

Miller, P., Eisenberg, N., Fabes, R., Shell, R., & Gular, S. (1989). Mothers' emotional arousal as a moderator in the socialization of children's empathy. *New Directions for Child Development, 44,* 65–83.

Miller, P. A., Eisenberg, N., Fabes, R. A., & Shell, R. (1996). Relations of moral reasoning and vicarious emotion to young children's prosocial behavior toward peers and adults. *Developmental Psychology, 32,* 210–219.

Millstein, S. G., Petersen, A. C., & Nightingale, E. O. (Eds.). (1993). *Promoting the health of adolescents: New directions for the twenty-first century.* New York: Oxford University Press.

Mischel, W. (1966). A social learning view of sex differences in behavior. In E. E. Maccoby (Ed.), *The development of sex differences* (pp. 56–81). Stanford, CA: Stanford University Press.

Mischel, W. (1970). Sex typing and socialization. In P. H. Mussen (Ed.), *Carmichael's manual of child psychology* (Vol. 2, pp. 3–72). New York: Wiley.

Mitchell, E. A., Tuohy, P. G., Brunt, J. M., Thompson, J. M. D., Clements, M. S., Stewart, A. W., Ford, R. P. K., & Taylor, B. J. (1997). Risk factors for sudden infant death syndrome following the prevention campaign in New Zealand: A prospective study. *Pediatrics, 100,* 835–840.

Mitchell, J. E. (1995). Medical complications of bulimia nervosa. In K. D. Brownell & C. G. Fairburn (Eds.), *Eating disorders and obesity: A comprehensive handbook* (pp. 271–275). New York: Guilford Press.

Mitchell, P. R., & Kent, R. D. (1990). Phonetic variation in multisyllable babbling. *Journal of Child Language, 17,* 247–265.

Mitchell, R. (1992). *Testing for learning: How new approaches to evaluation can improve American schools.* New York: Free Press.

Moffitt, T. E. (1990). Juvenile delinquency and attention deficit disorder: Boys' developmental trajectories from age 3 to age 15. *Child Development, 61,* 893–910.

Moffitt, T. E. (1993). Adolescence-limited and life-course-persistent antisocial behavior: A developmental taxonomy. *Psychology Review, 100,* 674–701.

Moffitt, T. E., & Harrington, H. L. (1996). Delinquency: The natural history of antisocial behavior. In P. A. Silva & W. R. Stanton (Eds.), *From child to adult: The Dunedin multidisciplinary health and development study* (pp. 163–185). Aukland: Oxford University Press.

Molfese, V. J., DiLalla, L. F., & Bunce, D. (1997). Prediction of the intelligence test scores of 3- to 8-year-old children by home environment, socioeconomic status, and biomedical risks. *Merrill-Palmer Quarterly, 43,* 219–234.

Mondal, S. K., Sen Gupta, P. G., Gupta, D. N., Ghosh, S., Sikder, S. N., Rajendran, K., Saha, M. R., Sircasr, B. K., & Bhattacharya, S. K. (1996). Occurrence of diarrhoeal diseases in relation to infant feeding practices in a rural community in West Bengal, India. *Acta Paediatrica, 85,* 1159–1162.

Money, J. (1987). Sin, sickness, or status? Homosexual gender identity and psychoneuroendocrinology. *American Psychologist, 42,* 384–399.

Montemayor, R., Adams, G. R., & Gullotta, T. P. (Eds.). (1994). *Personal relationships during adolescence.* Thousand Oaks, CA: Sage.

Montemayor, R., & Eisen, M. (1977). The development of self-conceptions from childhood to adolescence. *Developmental Psychology, 13,* 314–319.

Moon, C., & Fifer, W. P. (1990). Syllables as signals for 2-day-old infants. *Infant Behavior and Development, 13,* 377–390.

Moore, E. G. J. (1986). Family socialization and the IQ test performance of traditionally and transracially adopted black children. *Developmental Psychology, 22,* 317–326.

Moore, K. A., Myers, D. E., Morrison, D. R., Nord, C. W., Brown, B., & Edmonston, B. (1993). Age at first childbirth and later poverty. *Journal of Research on Adolescence, 3,* 393–422.

Moore, K. L., & Persaud, T. V. N. (1993). *The developing human: Clinically oriented embryology* (5th ed.). Philadelphia: Saunders.

Morelli, G. A., Rogoff, B., Oppenheim, D., & Goldsmith, D. (1992). Cultural variation in infants' sleeping arrangements: Questions of independence. *Developmental Psychology, 28,* 604–613.

Morgan, J. L. (1994). Converging measures of speech segmentation in preverbal infants. *Infant Behavior and Development, 17,* 389–403.

Morgan, J. L., Bonamo, K. M., & Travis, L. L. (1995). Negative evidence on negative evidence. *Developmental Psychology, 31,* 180–197.

Morgan, M. (1982). Television and adolescents' sex role stereotypes: A longitudinal study. *Journal of Personality and Social Psychology, 43,* 947–955.

Morgan, M. (1987). Television, sex-role attitudes, and sex-role behavior. *Journal of Early Adolescence, 7,* 269–282.

Morrison, D. M. (1985). Adolescent contraceptive behavior: A review. *Psychological Bulletin, 98,* 538–568.

Morrison, D. R., & Cherlin, A. J. (1995). The divorce process and young children's well-being: A prospective analysis. *Journal of Marriage and the Family, 57,* 800–812.

Morrison, F. J., Smith, L., & Dow-Ehrensberger, M. (1995). Education and cognitive development: A natural experiment. *Developmental Psychology, 31,* 789–799.

Morrongiello, B. A. (1988). Infants' localization of sounds along the horizontal axis: Estimates of minimum audible angle. *Developmental Psychology, 24,* 8–13.

Morrongiello, B. A., Fenwick, K. D., & Chance, G. (1990). Sound localization acuity in very young infants: An observer-based testing procedure. *Developmental Psychology, 26,* 75–84.

Morse, P. A., & Cowan, N. (1982). Infant auditory and speech perception. In T. M. Field, A. Houston, H. C. Quay, L. Troll, & G. E. Finley (Eds.), *Review of human development* (pp. 32–61). New York: Wiley.

Mortimer, J. T., & Finch, M. D. (1996). Work, family, and adolescent development. In J. T. Mortimer & M. D. Finch (Eds.), *Adolescents, work, and family: An intergenerational developmental analysis* (pp. 1–24). Thousand Oaks, CA: Sage.

Mortimer, J. T., Finch, M. D., Dennehy, K., Lee, C., & Beebe, T. (1995, April). *Work experience in adolescence.* Paper presented at the biennial meetings of the Society for Research in Child Development, Indianapolis.

Muhuri, P. K., Anker, M., & Bryce, J. (1996). Treatment patterns for childhood diarrhoea: Evidence from demographic and health surveys. *Bulletin of the World Health Organization, 74,* 135–146.

Muir-Broaddus, J. E. (1997, April). *The effects of social influence and psychological reactance on children's responses to repeated questions.* Paper presented at the biennial meetings of the Society for Research in Child Development, Washington, DC.

Muller, C. (1995). Maternal employment, parent involvement, and mathematics achievement among adolescents. *Journal of Marriage and the Family, 57,* 85–100.

Muñoz, K. A., Krebs-Smith, S. M., Ballard-Barbash, R., & Cleveland, L. E. (1997). Food intakes of US children and adolescents compared with recommendations. *Pediatrics, 100,* 323–329.

Munro, G., & Adams, G. R. (1977). Ego-identity formation in college students and working youth. *Developmental Psychology, 13,* 523–524.

Murphy, S. O. (1993, April). *The family context and the transition to siblinghood: Strategies parents use to influence sibling-infant relationships.* Paper presented at the biennial meetings of the Society for Research in Child Development, New Orleans.

Murray, A. D., & Hornbaker, A. V. (1997). Maternal directive and facilitative interaction styles: Associations with language and cognitive development of low risk and high risk toddlers. *Development and Psychopathology, 9,* 507–516.

Murray, J. L., & Bernfield, M. (1988). The differential effect of prenatal care on the incidence of low birth weight among blacks and whites in a prepaid health care plan. *The New England Journal of Medicine, 319,* 1385–1391.

Murray, J. P. (1997). Media violence and youth. In J. D. Osofsky (Ed.), *Children in a violent society* (pp. 72–96). New York: Guilford Press.

Murray, L., & Cooper, P. J. (1997). The role of infant and maternal factors in postpartum depression, mother-infant interactions, and infant outcome. In L. Murray & P. J. Cooper (Eds.), *Postpartum depression and child development* (pp. 111–135). New York: Guilford Press.

Muscari, M. E. (1996). Primary care of adolescents with bulimia nervosa. *Journal of Pediatric Health Care, 10,* 17–25.

Musick, J. S. (1994, Fall). Capturing the child-rearing context. *Society for Research in Child Development Newsletter, 1,* 6–7.

Myers, B. J. (1987). Mother-infant bonding as a critical period. In M. H. Bornstein (Ed.), *Sensitive periods in development: Interdisciplinary perspectives* (pp. 223–246). Hillsdale, NJ: Erlbaum.

Nachmias, M. (1993, April). *Maternal personality relations with toddler's attachment classification, use of coping strategies, and adrenocortical stress response.* Paper presented at the biennial meetings of the Society for Research in Child Development, New Orleans.

National Center for Educational Statistics. (1987). *Who drops out of high school? From high school and beyond.* Washington, DC: Office of Educational Research and Improvement, U.S. Department of Education.

National Center for Health Statistics. (1996). Leading causes of death by age, sex, race, and Hispanic origin: United States, 1992. *Vital and Health Statistics, Series 20*(29, June).

National Center on Child Abuse and Neglect. (1988). *Study findings: Study of national incidence and prevalence of child abuse and neglect: 1988.*

National Household Survey on Drug Abuse. (1997a). *Main Findings 1995.* Washington, DC: U.S. Department of Health and Human Services.

National Household Survey on Drug Abuse. (1997b). *Population estimates 1996.* Washington, DC: U.S. Department of Health and Human Services.

National Research Council. (1993). *Understanding child abuse and neglect.* Washington, DC: National Academy Press.

Needleman, H. L., Riess, J. A., Tobin, M. J., Biesecker, G. E., & Greenhouse, J. B. (1996). Bone lead levels and delinquent behavior. *Journal of the American Medical Association, 275,* 363–369.

Needlman, R., Frank, D. A., Augustyn, M., & Zuckerman, B. S. (1995). Neurophysiological effects of prenatal cocaine exposure: Comparison of human and animal investigations. In M. Lewis & M. Bendersky (Eds.), *Mothers, babies, and cocaine: The role of toxins in development* (pp. 229–250). Hillsdale, NJ: Erlbaum.

Needlman, R. D. (1996). Growth and development. In R. E. Behrman, R. M. Kliegman, & A. M. Arvin (Eds.), *Nelson textbook of pediatrics* (15th ed., pp. 30–72). Philadelphia: Saunders.

Neimark, E. D. (1982). Adolescent thought: Transition to formal operations. In B. B. Wolman (Ed.), *Handbook of developmental psychology* (pp. 486–502). Englewood Cliffs, NJ: Prentice Hall.

Neisser, U., Boodoo, G., Bouchard, T. J., Jr., Boykin, A. W., Brody, N., Ceci, S. J., Halpern, D. F., Loehlin, J. C., Perloff, R., Sternberg, R. J., & Urbina, S. (1996). Intelligence: Knowns and unknowns. *American Psychologist, 51,* 77–101.

Nelson, C. A. (1987). The recognition of facial expression in the first two years of life: Mechanisms of development. *Child Development, 58,* 889–909.

Nelson, C. A. (1994). Neural bases of infant temperament. In J. E. Bates & T. D. Wachs (Eds.), *Temperament: Individual differences at the interface of biology and behavior* (pp. 47–82). Washington, DC: American Psychological Association.

Nelson, C. T., & Demmler, G. J. (1997). Cytomegalovirus infection in the pregnant mother, fetus, and newborn infant. *Clinics in Perinatology, 24,* 151–160.

Nelson, K. (1973). Structure and strategy in learning to talk. *Monographs of the Society for Research in Child Development, 38*(Serial No. 149).

Nelson, K. (1977). Facilitating children's syntax acquisition. *Developmental Psychology, 13,* 101–107.

Nelson, K. (1985). *Making sense: The acquisition of shared meaning.* New York: Academic Press.

Nelson, K. (1988). Constraints on word learning. *Cognitive Development, 3,* 221–246.

Newcomb, A. F., & Bagwell, C. L. (1995). Children's friendship relations: A meta-analytic review. *Psychological Bulletin, 117,* 306–347.

Newcomb, A. F., & Bagwell, C. L. (1996). The developmental significance of children's friendship relations. In W. M. Bukowski, A. F. Newcomb, & W. W. Hartup (Eds.), *The company they keep: Friendship in childhood and adolescence* (pp. 289–321). Cambridge: Cambridge University Press.

Newcomb, A. F., Bukowski, W. M., & Pattee, L. (1993). Children's peer relations: A meta-analytic review of popular, rejected, neglected, controversial, and average sociometric status. *Psychological Bulletin, 113,* 99–128.

Newcombe, N. S., & Baenninger, M. (1989). Biological change and cognitive ability in adolescence. In G. R. Adams, R. Montemayor, & T. P. Gullotta (Eds.), *Biology of adolescent behavior and development* (pp. 168–194). Newbury Park, CA: Sage.

Newell, M., & Peckham, C. (1994). Vertical transmission of HIV infection. *Acta Paediatrica Supplement, 400,* 43–45.

Newman, D. L., Caspi, A., Moffitt, T. E., & Silva, P. A. (1997). Antecedents of adult interpersonal functioning: Effects of individual differences in age 3 temperament. *Developmental Psychology, 33,* 206–217.

NICHD Early Child Care Research Network. (1996a, April). *Infant child care and attachment security: Results of the NICHD study of early child care.* Paper presented at the International Conference on Infant Studies, Providence, RI.

NICHD Early Child Care Research Network. (1996b). Characteristics of infant child care: Factors contributing to positive caregiving. *Early Childhood Research Quarterly, 11,* 269–306.

NICHD Early Child Care Research Network. (1997a, April). *Mother-child interaction and cognitive outcomes associated with early child care: Results of the NICHD study.* Paper presented at the biennial meetings of the Society for Research in Child Development, Washington, DC.

NICHD Early Child Care Research Network. (1997b). Child care in the first year of life. *Merrill-Palmer Quarterly, 43,* 340–360.

NICHD Early Child Care Research Network. (1997c). Poverty and patterns of child care. In G. J. Duncan & J. Brooks-Gunn (Eds.), *Consequences of growing up poor* (pp. 100–131). New York: Russell Sage Foundation.

NICHD Early Child Care Research Network. (1997d). The effects of infant child care on infant-mother attachment security: Results of the NICHD study of early child care. *Child Development, 68,* 860–879.

Nightingale, E. O., & Goodman, M. (1990). *Before birth: Prenatal testing for genetic disease.* Cambridge, MA: Harvard University Press.

Nilsson, L. (1990). *A child is born.* New York: Delacorte Press.

Nisan, M., & Kohlberg, L. (1982). Universality and variation in moral judgment: A longitudinal and cross-sectional study in Turkey. *Child Development, 53,* 865–876.

Nolen-Hoeksema, S. (1994). An interactive model for the emergence of gender differences in depression in adolescence. *Journal of Research on Adolescence, 4,* 519–534.

Nolen-Hoeksema, S., & Girgus, J. S. (1994). The emergence of gender differences in depression during adolescence. *Psychological Bulletin, 115,* 424–443.

Nordentoft, M., Lou, H. C., Hansen, D., Nim, J., Pryds, O., Rubin, P., & Hemmingsen, R. (1996). Intrauterine growth retardation and premature delivery: The influence of maternal smoking and psychosocial factors. *American Journal of Public Health, 86,* 347–354.

Norwood, M. K. (1997, April). *Academic achievement in African-American adolescents as a function of family structure and child-rearing practices.* Paper presented at the biennial meetings of the Society for Research in Child Development, Washington, DC.

Nottelmann, E. D., Susman, E. J., Blue, J. H., Inoff-Germain, G., Dorn, L. D., Loriaux, D. L., Cutler, G. B., Jr., & Chrousos, G. P. (1987). Gonadal and adrenal hormone correlates of adjustment in early adolescence. In R. M. Lerner & T. T. Foch (Eds.), *Biological-psychosocial interactions in early adolescence* (pp. 303–324). Hillsdale, NJ: Erlbaum.

Notzon, F. C., Cnattingius, S., Pergsjø, P., Cole, S., Taffel, S., Irgens, L., & Dalveit, A. K. (1994). Cesarean section delivery in the 1980s: International comparison by indication. *American Journal of Obstetrics and Gynecology, 170,* 495–504.

Nsamenang, A. B., & Lamb, M. E. (1994). Socialization of Nso children in the Bamenda grassfields of northwest Cameroon. In P. M. Greenfield & R. R. Cocking (Eds.), *Cross-cultural roots of minority child development* (pp. 133–146). Hillsdale, NJ: Erlbaum.

Nucci, L. P., & Nucci, M. S. (1982). Children's social interactions in the context of moral and conventional transgressions. *Child Development, 53,* 403–412.

Nugent, J. K., Lester, B. M., Greene, S. M., Wieczorek-Deering, D., & O'Mahony, P. (1996). The effects of maternal alcohol consumption and cigarette smoking during pregnancy on acoustic cry analysis. *Child Development, 67,* 1806–1815.

O'Beirne, H., & Moore, C. (1995, April). *Attachment and sexual behavior in adolescence.* Paper presented at the biennial meetings of the Society for Research in Child Development, Indianapolis.

O'Brien, M. (1992). Gender identity and sex roles. In V. B. Van Hasselt & M. Hersen (Eds.), *Handbook of social development: A lifespan perspective* (pp. 325–345). New York: Plenum Press.

O'Brien, S. F., & Bierman, K. L. (1988). Conceptions and perceived influence of peer groups: Interviews with preadolescents and adolescents. *Child Development, 59,* 1360–1365.

O'Connor, S., Vietze, P. M., Sandler, H. M., Sherrod, K. B., & Altemeier, W. A. (1980). Quality of parenting and the mother-infant relationships following rooming-in. In P. M. Taylor (Ed.), *Parent-infant relationships* (pp. 349–368). New York: Grune & Stratton.

O'Hara, M. W. (1997). The nature of postpartum depressive disorders. In L. Murray & P. J. Cooper (Ed.), *Postpartum depression and child development* (pp. 3–31). New York: Guilford Press.

O'Neill, D. K., Astington, J. W., & Flavell, J. H. (1992). Young children's understanding of the role that sensory experiences play in knowledge acquisition. *Child Development, 63,* 474–490.

O'Shea, T. M., Klinepeter, K. L., Goldstein, D. J., Jackson, B. W., & Dillard, R. G. (1997). Survival and developmental disability in infants with birth weights of 501 to 800 grams, born between 1979 and 1994. *Pediatrics, 100,* 982–986.

Odom, S. L., & Kaiser, A. P. (1997). Prevention and early intervention during early childhood: Theoretical and empirical bases for practice. In W. E. MacLean Jr. (Ed.), *Ellis' handbook of mental deficiency: Psychological theory and research* (pp. 137–172). Mahwah, NJ: Erlbaum.

Offord, D. R., Boyle, M. H., & Racine, Y. A. (1991). The epidemiology of antisocial behavior in childhood and adolescence. In D. J. Pepler & K. H. Rubin (Eds.), *The development and treatment of childhood aggression* (pp. 31–54). Hillsdale, NJ: Erlbaum.

Ogbu, J. U. (1994). From cultural differences to differences in cultural frame of reference. In P. M. Greenfield & R. R. Cocking (Eds.), *Cross-cultural roots of minority child development* (pp. 365–391). Hillsdale, NJ: Erlbaum.

Oller, D. K. (1981). Infant vocalizations: Exploration and reflectivity. In R. E. Stark (Ed.), *Language behavior in infancy and early childhood* (pp. 85–104). New York: Elsevier/North-Holland.

Olshan, A. F., Baird, P. A., & Teschke, K. (1989). Paternal occupational exposures and the risk of Down syndrome. *American Journal of Human Genetics, 44,* 646–651.

Olson, H. C., Sampson, P. D., Barr, H., Streissguth, A. P., & Bookstein, F. L. (1992). Prenatal exposure to alcohol and school problems in late childhood: A longitudinal prospective study. *Development and Psychopathology, 4,* 341–359.

Olson, S. L., Bates, J. E., & Kaskie, B. (1992). Caregiver-infant interaction antecedents of children's school-age cognitive ability. *Merrill-Palmer Quarterly, 38,* 309–330.

Olweus, D. (1995). Bullying or peer abuse at school: Facts and intervention. *Current Directions in Psychological Science, 4,* 196–200.

Osofsky, J. D. (Ed.). (1987). *Handbook of infant development.* New York: Wiley-Interscience.

Osofsky, J. D. (1995). The effects of exposure to violence on young children. *American Psychologist, 50,* 782–788.

Osofsky, J. D. (Ed.). (1997). *Children in a violent society.* New York: Guilford Press.

Ostoja, E., McCrone, E., Lehn, L., Reed, T., & Sroufe, L. A. (1995, April). *Representations of close relationships in adolescence: Longitudinal antecedents from infancy through childhood.* Paper presented at the biennial meetings of the Society for Research in Child Development, Indianapolis.

Ott, W. J. (1995). Small for gestational age fetus and neonatal outcome: Reevaluation of the relationship. *American Journal of Perinatology, 12,* 396–400.

Overton, W. F., & Reese, H. W. (1973). Models of development: Methodological implications. In J. R. Nesselroade & H. W. Reese (Eds.), *Life-span developmental psychology: Methodological issues* (pp. 65–86). New York: Academic Press.

Overton, W. F., Ward, S. L., Noveck, I. A., Black, J., & O'Brien, D. P. (1987). Form and content in the development of deductive reasoning. *Developmental Psychology, 23,* 22–30.

Page, D. C., Mosher, R., Simpson, E. M., Fisher, E. M. C., Mardon, G., Pollack, J., McGillivray, B., de la Chapelle, A., & Brown, L. G. (1987). The sex-determining region of the human Y chromosome encodes a finger protein. *Cell, 51,* 1091–1104.

Paik, H., & Comstock, G. (1994). The effects of television violence on antisocial behavior: A meta-analysis. *Communication Research, 21,* 516–546.

Paikoff, R. L., & Brooks-Gunn, J. (1990). Physiological processes: What role do they play during the transition to adolescence? In R. Montemayor, G. R. Adams, & T. P. Gullotta (Eds.), *From childhood to adolescence: A transitional period?* (pp. 63–81). Newbury Park, CA: Sage.

Palkovitz, R. (1985). Fathers' birth attendance, early contact, and extended contact with their newborns: A critical review. *Child Development, 56,* 392–406.

Palmérus, K., & Scarr, S. (1995, April). *How parents discipline young children: Cultural comparisons and individual differences.* Paper presented at the biennial meetings of the Society for Research in Child Development, Indianapolis.

Papousek, H., & Papousek, M. (1991). Innate and cultural guidance of infants' integrative competencies: China, the United States, and Germany. In M. H. Bornstein (Ed.), *Cultural approaches to parenting* (pp. 23–44). Hillsdale, NJ: Erlbaum.

Paradise, J. L., Rockette, H. E., Colborn, D. K., Bernard, B. S., Smith, C. G., Kurs-Lasky, M., & Janosky, J. E. (1997). Otitis media in 2253 Pittsburgh-area infants: Prevalence and risk factors during the first two years of life. *Pediatrics, 99,* 318–333.

Parcel, T. L., & Menaghan, E. G. (1994). *Parents' jobs and children's lives.* New York: Aldine de Gruyter.

Parke, R. D. (1995). Fathers and families. In M. H. Bornstein (Ed.), *Handbook of parenting: Vol. 3. Status and social conditions of parenting* (pp. 27–63). Mahwah, NJ: Erlbaum.

Parke, R. D., & Buriel, R. (1998). Socialization in the family: Ethnic and ecological perspectives. In W. Damon (Ed.), *Handbook of child psychology: Vol 3. Social, emotional, and personality development* (5th ed., pp. 463–552). New York: Wiley.

Parke, R. D., & Tinsley, B. R. (1984). Fatherhood: Historical and contemporary perspectives. In K. A. McCluskey & H. W. Reese (Eds.), *Life-span developmental psychology: Historical and generational effects* (pp. 203–248). Orlando, FL: Academic Press.

Parker, J. G., & Herrera, C. (1996). Interpersonal processes in friendship: A comparison of abused and nonabused children's experiences. *Developmental Psychology, 32,* 1025–1038.

Parmelee, A. H., Jr. (1986). Children's illnesses: Their beneficial effects on behavioral development. *Child Development, 57,* 1–10.

Parmelee, A. H., Jr., Wenner, W. H., & Schulz, H. R. (1964). Infant sleep patterns from birth to 16 weeks of age. *Journal of Pediatrics, 65,* 576–582.

Parsons, J. E., Adler, T. F., & Kaczala, C. M. (1982). Socialization of achievement attitudes and beliefs: Parental influences. *Child Development, 53,* 310–321.

Parten, M. B. (1932). Social participation among preschool children. *Journal of Abnormal and Social Psychology, 27,* 243–269.

Pascalis, O., de Schonen, S., Morton, J., Derulle, C., & Fabre-Grenet, M. (1995). Mother's face recognition by neonates: A replication and extension. *Infant Behavior and Development, 18,* 79–85.

Passman, R. H., & Longeway, K. P. (1982). The role of vision in maternal attachment: Giving 2-year-olds a photograph of their mother during separation. *Developmental Psychology, 18,* 530–533.

Patterson, G. R. (1975). *Families: Applications of social learning to family life.* Champaign, IL: Research Press.

Patterson, G. R. (1996). Some characteristics of a developmental theory for early-onset delinquency. In M. F. Lenzenweger & J. J. Haugaard (Eds.), *Frontiers of developmental psychopathology* (pp. 81–124). New York: Oxford University Press.

Patterson, G. R., Capaldi, D., & Bank, L. (1991). An early starter model for predicting delinquency. In D. J. Pepler & K. H. Rubin (Eds.), *The development and treatment of childhood aggression* (pp. 139–168). Hillsdale, NJ: Erlbaum.

Patterson, G. R., DeBarsyshe, B. D., & Ramsey, E. (1989). A developmental perspective on antisocial behavior. *American Psychologist, 44,* 329–335.

Patterson, G. R., Reid, J. B., & Dishion, T. J. (1992). *Antisocial boys.* Eugene, OR: Castalia Press.

Pedersen, N. L., Plomin, R., McClearn, G. E., & Friberg, L. (1988). Neuroticism, extraversion and related traits in adult twins reared apart and reared together. *Journal of Personality and Social Psychology, 55,* 950–957.

Pederson, D. R., Moran, G., Sitko, C., Campbell, K., Ghesquire, K., & Acton, H. (1990). Maternal sensitivity and the security of infant-mother attachment: A Q-sort study. *Child Development, 61,* 1974–1983.

Pedlow, R., Sanson, A., Prior, M., & Oberklaid, F. (1993). Stability of maternally reported temperament from infancy to 8 years. *Developmental Psychology, 29,* 998–1007.

Pegg, J. E., Werker, J. F., & McLeod, P. J. (1992). Preference for infant-directed over adult-directed speech: Evidence from 7-week-old infants. *Infant Behavior and Development, 15,* 325–345.

Peipert, J. F., & Bracken, M. B. (1993). Maternal age: An independent risk factor for cesarean delivery. *Obstetrics and Gynecology, 81,* 200–205.

Peisner-Feinberg, E. S. (1995, April). *Developmental outcomes and the relationship to quality of child care experiences.* Paper presented at the biennial meetings of the Society for Research in Child Development, Indianapolis.

Peisner-Feinberg, E. S., & Burchinal, M. R. (1997). Relations between preschool children's child-care experiences and concurrent development: The Cost, Quality, and Outcomes Study. *Merrill-Palmer Quarterly, 43,* 451–477.

Peoples, C. E., Fagan, J. F., III, & Drotar, D. (1995). The influence of race on 3-year-old children's performance on the Stanford-Binet: Fourth edition. *Intelligence, 21,* 69–82.

Perez-Escamilla, R. (1994). Breastfeeding in Africa and the Latin American and Caribbean region. The potential role of urbanization. *Journal of Tropical Pediatrics, 40,* 137–143.

Perkins, D. F., & Luster, T. (1997, April). *The relationship between sexual abuse and a bulimic behavior: Findings from community-*

wide surveys of female adolescents. Paper presented at the biennial meetings of the Society for Research in Child Development, Washington, DC.

Perlman, M., Claris, O., Hao, Y., Pandid, P., Whyte, H., Chipman, M., & Liu, P. (1995). Secular changes in the outcomes to eighteen to twenty-four months of age of extremely low birth weight infants, with adjustment for changes in risk factors and severity of illness. *Journal of Pediatrics, 126,* 75–87.

Perner, J., & Wimmer, H. (1985). "John thinks that Mary thinks that...": Attribution of second-order beliefs by 5- to 10-year-old children. *Journal of Experimental Child Psychology, 39,* 437–471.

Perry, D., Kusel, S. K., & Perry, L. C. (1988). Victims of peer aggression. *Developmental Psychology, 24,* 807–814.

Petersen, A. C. (1987). The nature of biological-psychosocial interactions: The sample case of early adolescence. In R. M. Lerner & T. T. Foch (Eds.), *Biological-psychosocial interactions in early adolescence* (pp. 35–62). Hillsdale, NJ: Erlbaum.

Petersen, A. C., Compas, B. E., Brooks-Gunn, J., Stemmler, M., Ey, S., & Grant, K. E. (1993). Depression in adolescence. *American Psychologist, 48,* 155–168.

Petersen, A. C., Sarigiani, P. A., & Kennedy, R. E. (1991). Adolescent depression: Why more girls? *Journal of Youth and Adolescence, 20,* 247–272.

Petersen, A. C., & Taylor, B. (1980). The biological approach to adolescence. In J. Adelson (Ed.), *Handbook of adolescent psychology* (pp. 117–158). New York: Wiley.

Peterson, C., & Bell, M. (1996). Children's memory for traumatic injury. *Child Development, 67,* 3045–3070.

Peterson, C. C., & Siegal, M. (1995). Deafness, conversation and theory of mind. *Journal of Child Psychology and Psychiatry, 36,* 459–474.

Peterson, G. H., Mehl, L. E., & Leiderman, P. H. (1979). The role of some birth-related variables in father attachment. *American Journal of Orthopsychiatry, 49,* 330–338.

Petitto, L. A. (1988). "Language" in the prelinguistic child. In F. S. Kessell (Ed.), *The development of language and language researchers: Essays in honor of Roger Brown* (pp. 187–222). Hillsdale, NJ: Erlbaum.

Pettit, G. S., Bates, J. E., & Dodge, K. A. (1997a). Supportive parenting, ecological context, and children's adjustment: A seven-year longitudinal study. *Child Development, 68,* 908–923.

Pettit, G. S., Clawson, M. A., Dodge, K. A., & Bates, J. E. (1996). Stability and change in peer-rejected status: The role of child behavior, parenting, and family ecology. *Merrill-Palmer Quarterly, 42,* 295–318.

Pettit, G. S., Laird, R. D., Bates, J. E., & Dodge, K. A. (1997b). Patterns of after-school care in middle childhood: Risk factors and developmental outcomes. *Merrill-Palmer Quarterly, 43,* 515–538.

Phinney, J. S. (1990). Ethnic identity in adolescents and adults: Review of research. *Psychological Bulletin, 108,* 499–514.

Phinney, J. S., & Devich-Navarro, M. (1997). Variations in bicultural identification among African American and Mexican American adolescents. *Journal of Research on Adolescence, 7,* 3–32.

Phinney, J. S., Ferguson, D. L., & Tate, J. D. (1997). Intergroup attitudes among ethnic minority adolescents: A causal model. *Child Development, 68,* 955–969.

Phinney, J. S., & Rosenthal, D. A. (1992). Ethnic identity in adolescence: Process, context, and outcome. In G. R. Adams, T. P. Gullotta, & R. Montemayor (Eds.), *Adolescent identity formation* (pp. 145–172). Newbury Park, CA: Sage.

Piaget, J. (1932). *The moral judgment of the child.* New York: Macmillan.

Piaget, J. (1952). *The origins of intelligence in children.* New York: International Universities Press.

Piaget, J. (1954). *The construction of reality in the child.* New York: Basic Books. (Originally published 1937)

Piaget, J. (1970). Piaget's theory. In P. H. Mussen (Ed.), *Carmichael's manual of child psychology* (3rd ed., Vol. 1, pp. 703–732). New York: Wiley.

Piaget, J. (1977). *The development of thought: Equilibration of cognitive structures.* New York: Viking Press.

Piaget, J., & Inhelder, B. (1959). *La gènese des structures logiques élémentaires: Classifications et seriations [The origin of elementary logical structures: Classification and seriation].* Neuchâtel: Delachaux et Niestlé.

Piaget, J., & Inhelder, B. (1969). *The psychology of the child.* New York: Basic Books.

Pianta, R. C., & Egeland, B. (1994a). Predictors of instability in children's mental test performance at 24, 48, and 96 months. *Intelligence, 18,* 145–163.

Pianta, R. C., & Egeland, B. (1994b). Relation between depressive symptoms and stressful life events in a sample of disadvantaged mothers. *Journal of Consulting and Clinical Psychology, 62,* 1229–1234.

Pianta, R. C., Steinberg, M. S., & Rollins, K. B. (1995). Teacher-child relationships and deflections in children's classroom adjustment. *Development and Psychopathology, 7,* 295–312.

Pickens, J. (1994). Perception of auditory-visual distance relations by 5-month-old infants. *Developmental Psychology, 30,* 537–544.

Pickens, J., & Field, T. (1993). Facial expressivity in infants of depressed mothers. *Developmental Psychology, 29,* 986–988.

Pickering, L. K., Granoff, D. M., Erickson, J. R., Masor, M. L., Cordle, C. T., Schaller, J. P., Winship, T. R., Paule, C. L., & Hilty, M. D. (1998). Modulation of the immune system by human milk and infant formula containing nucleotides. *Pediatrics, 101,* 242–249.

Pillard, R. C., & Bailey, J. M. (1995). A biologic perspective on sexual orientation. *The Psychiatric Clinics of North America, 18*(1), 71–84.

Pine, J. M., Lieven, E. V. M., & Rowland, C. F. (1997). Stylistic variation at the "single-word" stage: Relations between maternal speech characteristics and children's vocabulary composition and usage. *Child Development, 68,* 807–819.

Pinker, S. (1987). The bootstrapping problem in language acquisition. In B. MacWhinney (Ed.), *Mechanisms of language acquisition* (pp. 399–442). Hillsdale, NJ: Erlbaum.

Pinker, S. (1994). *The language instinct: How the mind creates language.* New York: Morrow.

Pi-Sunyer, F. X. (1995). Medical complications of obesity. In K. D. Brownell & C. G. Fairburn (Eds.), *Eating disorders and obesity: A comprehensive handbook* (pp. 401–405). New York: Guilford Press.

Plomin, R. (1995). Genetics and children's experiences in the family. *Journal of Child Psychology and Psychiatry, 36,* 33–68.

Plomin, R., & DeFries, J. C. (1985). *Origins of individual differences in infancy: The Colorado Adoption Project.* Orlando, FL: Academic Press.

Plomin, R., Emde, R. N., Braungart, J. M., Campos, J., Corley, R., Fulker, D. W., Kagan, J., Reznick, J. S., Robinson, J., Zahn-Waxler, C., & DeFries, J. C. (1993). Genetic change and continuity from fourteen to twenty months: The MacArthur longitudinal twin study. *Child Development, 64,* 1354–1376.

Plomin, R., Loehlin, J. C., & DeFries, J. C. (1985). Genetic and environmental components of "environmental" influences. *Developmental Psychology, 21,* 391–402.

Plomin, R., & McClearn, G. E. (Eds.). (1993). *Nature, nurture, & psychology.* Washington, DC: American Psychological Association.

Plomin, R., Reiss, D., Hetherington, E. M., & Howe, G. W. (1994). Nature and nurture: Genetic contributions to measures of the family environment. *Developmental Psychology, 30,* 32–43.

Plomin, R., & Rende, R. (1991). Human behavioral genetics. *Annual Review of Psychology, 42,* 161–190.

Polivy, J., & Herman, C. P. (1995). Dieting and its relation to eating disorders. In K. D. Brownell & C. G. Fairburn (Eds.), *Eating disorders and obesity: A comprehensive handbook* (pp. 83–86). New York: Guilford Press.

Polka, L., & Werker, J. F. (1994). Developmental changes in perception of nonnative vowel contrasts. *Journal of Experimental Psychology: Human Perception and Performance, 20,* 421–435.

Pollitt, E. (1995). Does breakfast make a difference in school? *Journal of the American Dietetic Association, 95,* 1134–1139.

Pollitt, E., Golub, M., Gorman, K., Grantham-McGregor, S., Levitsky, D., Schürch, B.,

Strupp, B., & Wachs, T. (1996). A reconceptualization of the effects of undernutrition on children's biological, psychosocial, and behavioral development. *Social Policy Report, Society for Research in Child Development, 10*(5), 1–21.

Pollitt, E., & Gorman, K. S. (1994). Nutritional deficiencies as developmental risk factors. In C. A. Nelson (Ed.), *The Minnesota symposia on child development* (Vol. 27, pp. 121–144). Hillsdale, NJ: Erlbaum.

Ponsonby, A., Dwyer, T., Gibbons, L. E., Cochrane, J. A., & Wang, Y. (1993). Factors potentiating the risk of sudden infant death syndrome associated with the prone position. *The New England Journal of Medicine, 329,* 377–382.

Poulin-Dubois, D., Serbin, L. A., Kenyon, B., & Derbyshire, A. (1994). Infants' intermodal knowledge about gender. *Developmental Psychology, 30,* 436–442.

Poulson, C. L., Nunes, L. R. D., & Warren, S. F. (1989). Imitation in infancy: A critical review. In H. W. Reese (Ed.), *Advances in child development and behavior* (Vol. 22, pp. 272–298). San Diego, CA: Academic Press.

Powell, B., & Steelman, L. C. (1982). Testing and undertested comparison: Maternal effects on sons' and daughters' attitudes toward women in the labor force. *Journal of Marriage and the Family, 44,* 349–355.

Power, C., & Reimer, J. (1978). Moral atmosphere: An educational bridge between moral judgment and action. *New Directions for Child Development, 2,* 105–116.

Power, F. C., Higgins, A., & Kohlberg, L. (1989). *Lawrence Kohlberg's approach to moral education: A study of three democratic high schools.* New York: Columbia University Press.

Powlishta, K. K. (1995). Intergroup processes in childhood: Social categorization and sex role development. *Developmental Psychology, 31,* 781–788.

Powlishta, K. K., Serbin, L. A., Doyle, A., & White, D. R. (1994). Gender, ethnic, and body type biases: The generality of prejudice in childhood. *Developmental Psychology, 30,* 526–536.

Prechtl, H. F. R., & Beintema, D. J. (1964). *The neurological examination of the full-term newborn infant: Clinics in developmental medicine, 12.* London: Heinemann.

Prentice, A. (1994). Extended breast-feeding and growth in rural China. *Nutrition Reviews, 52,* 144–146.

Prior, M., Smart, D., Sanson, A., & Oberklaid, F. (1997, April). *Longitudinal trajectories in aggressive behaviour: Infancy to adolescence.* Paper presented at the biennial meetings of the Society for Research in Child Development, Washington, DC.

Pulkkinen, L. (1982). Self-control and continuity from childhood to late adolescence. In P. Baltes & O. G. Brim Jr. (Eds.), *Life span development and behavior* (Vol. 4, pp. 64–107). New York: Academic Press.

Putnam, J. W., Spiegel, A. N., & Bruininks, R. H. (1995). Future directions in education and inclusion of students with disabilities: A Delphi investigation. *Exceptional Children, 61,* 553–576.

Pye, C. (1986). Quiche Mayan speech to children. *Journal of Child Language, 13,* 85–100.

Pynoos, R. S., Steinbert, A. M., & Wraith, R. (1995). A developmental model of childhood traumatic stress. In D. Cicchetti & D. J. Cohen (Eds.), *Developmental psychopathology: Vol. 2. Risk, disorder, and adaptation.* New York: Wiley.

Quiggle, N. L., Garber, J., Panak, W. F., & Dodge, K. A. (1992). Social information processing in aggressive and depressed children. *Child Development, 63,* 1305–1320.

Raja, S. N., McGee, R., & Stanton, W. R. (1992). Perceived attachments to parents and peers and psychological well-being in adolescence. *Journal of Youth and Adolescence, 21,* 471–485.

Ramey, C. T. (1993). A rejoinder to Spitz's critique of the Abecedarian experiment. *Intelligence, 17,* 25–30.

Ramey, C. T., & Campbell, F. A. (1987). The Carolina Abecedarian Project. An educational experiment concerning human malleability. In J. J. Gallagher & C. T. Ramey (Eds.), *The malleability of children* (pp. 127–140). Baltimore: Brookes.

Ramey, C. T., & Ramey, S. L. (1998). Early intervention and early experience. *American Psychologist, 53,* 109–120.

Rees, J. M., Lederman, S. A., & Kiely, J. L. (1996). Birth weight associated with lowest neonatal mortality: Infants of adolescent and adult mothers. *Pediatrics, 98,* 1161–1166.

Reinherz, H. Z., Giaconia, R. M., Pakiz, B., Silverman, A. B., Frost, A. K., & Lefkowitz, E. S. (1993). Psychosocial risks for major depression in late adolescence: A longitudinal community study. *Journal of the American Academy of Child and Adolescent Psychiatry, 32,* 1155–1163.

Reisman, J. E. (1987). Touch, motion, and proprioception. In P. Salapatek & L. Cohen (Eds.), *Handbook of infant perception: Vol 1. From sensation to perception* (pp. 265–304). Orlando, FL: Academic Press.

Reisman, J. M., & Shorr, S. I. (1978). Friendship claims and expectations among children and adults. *Child Development, 49,* 913–916.

Reiss, D. (1998). Mechanisms linking genetic and social influences in adolescent development: Beginning a collaborative search. *Current Directions in Psychological Science, 6,* 100–105.

Remafedi, G. (1987a). Adolescent homosexuality: Psychosocial and medical implications. *Pediatrics, 79,* 331–337.

Remafedi, G. (1987b). Male homosexuality: The adolescent's perspective. *Pediatrics, 79,* 326–330.

Remafedi, G., Farrow, J. A., & Deisher, R. W. (1991). Risk factors for attempted suicide in gay and bisexual youth. *Pediatrics, 87,* 869–875.

Remafedi, G., Resnick, M., Blum, R., & Harris, L. (1992). Demography of sexual orientation in adolescents. *Pediatrics, 89,* 714–721.

Renouf, A. G., & Harter, S. (1990). Low self-worth and anger as components of the depressive experience in young adolescents. *Development and Psychopathology, 2,* 293–310.

Repacholi, B. M., & Gopnik, A. (1997). Early reasoning about desires: Evidence from 14- and 18-month-olds. *Developmental Psychology, 33,* 12–21.

Resnick, M. D., Bearman, P. S., Blum, R. W., Bauman, K. E., Harris, K. M., Jones, J., Tabor, J., Beuhring, T., Sieving, R. E., Shew, M., Ireland, M., Bearinger, L. H., & Udry, J. R. (1997). Protecting adolescents from harm: Findings from the National Longitudinal Study on Adolescent Health. *Journal of the American Medical Association, 278,* 823–832.

Rest, J., & Narvaez, D. (1991). The college experience and moral development. In W. M. Kurtines & J. L. Gewirtz (Eds.), *Handbook of moral behavior and development: Vol 2. Research* (pp. 229–245). Hillsdale, NJ: Erlbaum.

Rest, J. R. (1983). Morality. In J. H. Flavell & E. M. Markman (Eds.), *Handbook of child psychology: Cognitive development* (Vol. 3, pp. 556–629). New York: Wiley.

Rest, J. R., & Thoma, S. J. (1985). Relation of moral judgment development to formal education. *Developmental Psychology, 21,* 709–714.

Reynolds, A. J. (1994). Effects of a preschool plus follow-on intervention for children at risk. *Developmental Psychology, 30,* 787–804.

Reynolds, A. J., & Bezruczko, N. (1993). School adjustment of children at risk through fourth grade. *Merrill-Palmer Quarterly, 39,* 457–480.

Rholes, W. S., & Ruble, D. N. (1984). Children's understanding of dispositional characteristics of others. *Child Development, 55,* 550–560

Ricci, C. M., Beal, C. R., & Dekle, D. J. (1995, April). *The effect of parent versus unfamiliar interviewers on young witnesses' memory and identification accuracy.* Paper presented at the biennial meetings of the Society for Research in Child Development, Indianapolis.

Ricciuti, H. N. (1993). Nutrition and mental development. *Current Directions in Psychological Science, 2,* 43–46.

Rice, M. L., Huston, A. C., Truglio, R., & Wright, J. (1990). Words from "Sesame Street": Learning vocabulary while viewing. *Developmental Psychology, 26,* 421–428.

Richards, H. C., Bear, G. G., Stewart, A. L., & Norman, A. D. (1992). Moral reasoning and classroom conduct: Evidence of a curvilinear relationship. *Merrill-Palmer Quarterly, 38,* 176–190.

Richards, M. H., Crowe, P. A., Larson, R., & Swarr, A. (1998). Developmental patterns and gender differences in the experience of peer companionship during adolescence. *Child Development, 69,* 154–163.

Richardson, G. A., & Day, N. L. (1994). Detrimental effects of prenatal cocaine exposure: Illusion or reality? *Journal of the American Academy of Child and Adolescent Psychiatry, 33,* 28–34.

Richman, A. L., Miller, P. M., & LeVine, R. A. (1992). Cultural and educational variations in maternal responsiveness. *Developmental Psychology, 28,* 614–621.

Richters, J., & Pellegrini, D. (1989). Depressed mothers' judgments about their children: An examination of the depression-distortion hypothesis. *Child Development, 60,* 1068–1075.

Riegel, K. F. (1975). Adult life crises: A dialectic interpretation of development. In N. Datan & L. H. Ginsberg (Eds.), *Lifespan developmental psychology: Normative life crises* (pp. 99–128). New York: Academic Press.

Rierdan, J., Koff, E., & Stubbs, M. L. (1989). Timing of menarche, preparation, and initial menstrual experience: Replication and further analysis in a prospective study. *Journal of Youth and Adolescence, 18,* 413–426.

Riggs, L. L. (1997, April). *Depressive affect and eating problems in adolescent females: An assessment of direction and influence using longitudinal data.* Paper presented at the biennial meetings of the Society for Research in Child Development, Washington, D.C.

Ritchie, D., Price, V., & Roberts, D. F. (1987). Television, reading, and reading achievement: A reappraisal. *Communication Research, 14,* 292–315.

Roberts, C. W., Green, R., Williams, K., & Goodman, M. (1987). Boyhood gender identity development: A statistical contrast of two family groups. *Developmental Psychology, 23,* 544–557.

Roberts, J. E., & Wallace, I. F. (1997). Language and otitis media. In J. E. Roberts, I. F. Wallace, & F. W. Henderson (Eds.), *Otitis media in young children: Medical, developmental, and educational considerations* (pp. 133–162). Baltimore: Brookes.

Roberts, R., & Mather, N. (1995). The return of students with learning disabilities to regular classrooms: A sellout? *Learning Disabilities Research & Practice, 10,* 46–58.

Roberts, R. E., & Sobhan, M. (1992). Symptoms of depression in adolescence: A comparison of Anglo, African, and Hispanic Americans. *Journal of Youth and Adolescence, 21,* 639–651.

Robins, L. N., & McEvoy, L. (1990). Conduct problems as predictors of substance abuse. In L. N. Robins & M. Rutter (Eds.), *Straight and devious pathways from childhood to adulthood* (pp. 182–204). Cambridge, England: Cambridge University Press.

Robinson, H. B. (1981). The uncommonly bright child. In M. Lewis & L. A. Rosenblum (Eds.), *The uncommon child* (pp. 57–82). New York: Plenum Press.

Robinson, N. M., & Janos, P. M. (1986). Psychological adjustment in a college-level program of marked academic acceleration. *Journal of Youth and Adolescence, 15,* 51–60.

Roche, A. F. (1979). Secular trends in human growth, maturation, and development. *Monographs of the Society for Research in Child Development, 44*(3–4, Serial No. 179).

Rogers, B. (1978). Feeding in infancy and later ability and attainment: A longitudinal study. *Developmental Medicine and Child Neurology, 20,* 421–426.

Rogers, J. L. (1984). Confluence effects: Not here, not now! *Developmental Psychology, 20,* 321–331.

Rogers, J. L., Rowe, D. C., & May, K. (1994). DF analysis of NLSY IQ/achievement data: Nonshared environmental influences. *Intelligence, 19,* 157–177.

Rogers, P. T., Roizen, N. J., & Capone, G. T. (1996). Down syndrome. In A. J. Capute & P. J. Accardo (Eds.), *Developmental disabilities in infancy and childhood: Vol 2. The spectrum of developmental disabilities* (2nd ed., pp. 221–243). Baltimore: Brookes.

Roggman, L. A., Langlois, J. H., Hubbs-Tait, L., & Rieser-Danner, L. A. (1994). Infant daycare, attachment, and the "file drawer problem." *Child Development, 65,* 1429–1443.

Rogoff, B. (1998). Cognition as a collaborative process. In W. Damon (Ed.), *Handbook of child psychology: Vol. 2. Cognition, perception, and language* (5th ed., pp. 679–744). New York: Wiley.

Rogosch, F. A., Cicchetti, D., & Aber, J. L. (1995a). The role of child maltreatment in early deviations in cognitive and affective processing abilities and later peer relationship problems. *Development and Psychopathology, 7,* 591–609.

Rogosch, F. A., Cicchetti, D., Shields, A., & Toth, S. L. (1995b). Parenting dysfunction in child maltreatment. In M. H. Bornstein (Ed.), *Handbook of parenting: Vol. 4. Applied and practical parenting* (pp. 127–159). Mahwah, NJ: Erlbaum.

Rohner, R. P., Kean, K. J., & Cournoyer, D. E. (1991). Effects of corporal punishment, perceived caretaker warmth, and cultural beliefs on the psychological adjustment of children in St. Kitts, West Indies. *Journal of Marriage and the Family, 53,* 681–693.

Rooks, J. P., Weatherby, N. L., Ernst, E. K. M., Stapleton, S., Rosen, D., & Rosenfield, A. (1989). Outcomes of care in birth centers: The National Birth Center Study. *The New England Journal of Medicine, 321,* 1804–1811.

Rose, A. J., & Montemayor, R. (1994). The relationship between gender role orientation and perceived self-competence in male and female adolescents. *Sex Roles, 31,* 579–595.

Rose, R. J. (1995). Genes and human behavior. *Annual Review of Psychology, 56,* 625–654.

Rose, S. A., & Feldman, J. F. (1995). Prediction of IQ and specific cognitive abilities at 11 years from infancy measures. *Developmental Psychology, 31,* 685–696.

Rose, S. A., & Feldman, J. F. (1997). Memory and speed: Their role in the relation of infant information processing to later IQ. *Child Development, 68,* 630–641.

Rose, S. A., & Ruff, H. A. (1987). Cross-modal abilities in human infants. In J. D. Osofsky (Ed.), *Handbook of infant development* (2nd ed., pp. 318–362). New York: Wiley-Interscience.

Rosenbaum, J. E. (1984). *Career mobility in a corporate hierarchy.* New York: Academic Press.

Rosenberg, M. (1986). Self-concept from middle childhood through adolescence. In J. Suls & A. G. Greenwald (Eds.), *Psychological perspectives on the self* (Vol 3, pp. 107–136). Hillsdale, NJ: Erlbaum.

Rosenblith, J. F. (1992). *In the beginning: Development in the first two years of life* (2nd ed.). Newbury Park, CA: Sage.

Rosenthal, R. (1994). Interpersonal expectancy effects: A 30-year perspective. *Current Directions in Psychological Science, 3,* 176–179.

Ross, G., Kagan, J., Zelazo, P., & Kotelchuk, M. (1975). Separation protest in infants in home and laboratory. *Developmental Psychology, 11,* 256–257.

Rossell, C., & Baker, K. (1996). The educational effectiveness of bilingual education. *Research in the Teaching of English, 30,* 1–68.

Rothbart, M. K., & Bates, J. E. (1998). Temperament. In W. Damon (Ed.), *Handbook of child psychology: Vol 3. Social, emotional, and personality development* (5th ed., pp. 105–176). New York: Wiley.

Rothbaum, F., Pott, M., & Morelli, G. (1995, April). *Ties that bind: Cultural differences in the development of family closeness.* Paper presented at the biennial meetings of the Society for Research in Child Development, Indianapolis.

Rothman, K. J., Moore, L. L., Singer, M. R., Nguyen, U. D. T., Mannino, S., & Milunsky, A. (1995). Teratogenicity of high Vitamin A intake. *The New England Journal of Medicine, 333,* 1369–1373.

Rovee-Collier, C. (1986). The rise and fall of infant classical conditioning research: Its promise for the study of early development. In L. P. Lipsitt & C. Rovee-Collier (Eds.), *Advances in infancy research* (Vol. 4, pp. 139–162). Norwood, NJ: Ablex.

Rovee-Collier, C. (1993). The capacity for long-term memory in infancy. *Current Directions in Psychological Science, 2,* 130–135.

Rovet, J., & Netley, C. (1983). The triple X chromosome syndrome in childhood: Recent empirical findings. *Child Development, 54,* 831–845.

Rowe, D. C. (1994). *The limits of family influence: Genes, experience, and behavior.* New York: Guilford Press.

Rowe, I., & Marcia, J. E. (1980). Ego identity status, formal operations, and moral development. *Journal of Youth and Adolescence, 9,* 87–99.

Rubin, K. H., Bukowski, W., & Parker, J. G. (1998). Peer interactions, relationships, and groups. In W. Damon (Ed.), *Handbook of child development: Vol. 3. Social, emotional, and personality development* (5th ed., pp. 619–700). New York: Wiley.

Rubin, K. H., Fein, G. G., & Vandenbert, B. (1983). Play. In E. M. Hetherington (Ed.), *Handbook of child psychology: Socialization, personality, and social development* (Vol. 4, pp. 693–774). New York: Wiley.

Rubin, K. H., Hastings, P. D., Stewart, S. L., Henderson, H. A., & Chen, X. (1997). The consistency and concomitants of inhibition: Some of the children, all of the time. *Child Development, 68,* 467–483.

Rubin, K. H., Hymel, S., Mills, R. S. L., & Rose-Krasnor, L. (1991). Conceptualizing different developmental pathways to and from social isolation in childhood. In D. Cicchetti & S. L. Toth (Eds.), *Internalizing and externalizing expressions of dysfunction: Rochester symposium on developmental psychopathology* (Vol. 2, pp. 91–122). Hillsdale, NJ: Erlbaum.

Ruble, D. N. (1987). The acquisition of self-knowledge: A self-socialization perspective. In N. Eisenberg (Ed.), *Contemporary topics in developmental psychology* (pp. 243–270). New York: Wiley-Interscience.

Ruble, D. N., & Martin, C. L. (1998). Gender development. In W. Damon (Ed.), *Handbook of child psychology: Vol 3. Social, emotional, and personality development* (5th ed., pp. 933–1016). New York: Wiley.

Rueter, M. A., & Conger, R. D. (1995). Antecedents of parent-adolescent disagreements. *Journal of Marriage and the Family, 57,* 435–448.

Ruffman, T., Perner, J., Naito, M., Parkin, L., & Clements, W. A. (1998). Older (but not younger) siblings facilitate false belief understanding. *Developmental Psychology, 34,* 161–174.

Runyan, D. K., Hunter, W. M., Socolar, R. R. S., Amaya-Jackson, L., English, D., Landsverk, J., Dubowitz, H., Browne, D. H., Bandiwala, S. I., & Mathew, R. M. (1998). Children who prosper in unfavorable environments: The relationship to social capital. *Pediatrics, 101,* 12–18.

Russell, J. A. (1989). Culture, scripts, and children's understanding of emotion. In C. Saarni & P. L. Harris (Eds.), *Children's understanding of emotion* (pp. 293–318). Cambridge, England: Cambridge University Press.

Rutter, D. R., & Durkin, K. (1987). Turn-taking in mother-infant interaction: An examination of vocalizations and gaze. *Developmental Psychology, 23,* 54–61.

Rutter, M. (1978). Early sources of security and competence. In J. S. Bruner & A. Garton (Eds.), *Human growth and development* (pp. 33–61). London: Oxford University Press.

Rutter, M. (1983). School effects on pupil progress: Research findings and policy implications. *Child Development, 54,* 1–29.

Rutter, M. (1987). Continuities and discontinuities from infancy. In J. D. Osofsky (Ed.), *Handbook of infant development* (2nd ed., pp. 1256–1296). New York: Wiley-Interscience.

Rutter, M. (1989). Isle of Wight revisited: Twenty-five years of child psychiatric epidemiology. *Journal of the American Academy of Child and Adolescent Psychiatry, 28,* 633–653.

Rutter, M. (1990). Commentary: Some focus and process considerations regarding effects of parental depression on children. *Developmental Psychology, 26,* 60–67.

Rutter, M. (Ed.). (1995). *Psychosocial disturbances in young people: Challenges for prevention.* Cambridge, England: Cambridge University Press.

Rutter, M., Dunn, J., Plomin, R., Simonoff, E., Pickles, A., Maughan, B., Ormel, J., Meyer, J., & Eaves, L. (1997). Integrating nature and nurture: Implications of person-environment correlations and interactions for developmental psychopathology. *Development and Psychopathology, 9,* 335–364.

Rutter, M., & Garmezy, N. (1983). Developmental psychopathology. In E. M. Hetherington (Ed.), *Handbook of child psychology: Vol 4. Socialization, personality, and social development* (pp. 775–912). New York: Wiley.

Ryan, A. S., Rush, D., Krieger, F. W., & Lewandoski, G. E. (1991). Recent declines in breast-feeding in the United States, 1984 through 1989. *Pediatrics, 88,* 719–727.

Rys, G. S., & Bear, G. G. (1997). Relational aggression and peer relations: Gender and developmental issues. *Merrill-Palmer Quarterly, 43,* 87–106.

Saccuzzo, D. P., Johnson, N. E., & Guertin, T. L. (1994). Information processing in gifted versus nongifted African American, Latino, Filipino, and white children: Speeded versus nonspeeded paradigms. *Intelligence, 19,* 219–243.

Sachs, B. P., Fretts, R. C., Gardner, R., Hellerstein, S., Wampler, N. S., & Wise, P. H. (1995). The impact of extreme prematurity and congenital anomalies on the interpretation of international comparisons of infant mortality. *Obstetrics and Gynecology, 85,* 941–946.

Sagi, A. (1990). Attachment theory and research from a cross-cultural perspective. *Human Development, 33,* 10–22.

Sagi, A., van IJzendoorn, M. H., & Koren-Karie, N. (1991). Primary appraisal of the Strange Situation: A cross-cultural analysis of pre-separation episodes. *Developmental Psychology, 27,* 587–596.

Saigal, S., Szatmari, P., Rosenbaum, P., Campbell, D., & King, S. (1991). Cognitive abilities and school performance of extremely low birth weight children and matched term control children at age 8 years: A regional study. *Journal of Pediatrics, 118,* 751–760.

Sale, P., & Carey, D. M. (1995). The sociometric status of students with disabilities in a full-inclusion school. *Exceptional Children, 62,* 6–19.

Sameroff, A. J. (1995). General systems theories and developmental psychopathology. In D. Cicchetti & D. J. Cohen (Eds.), *Developmental psychopathology: Vol. 1. Theory and methods* (pp. 659–695). New York: Wiley.

Sameroff, A. J., Seifer, R., Barocas, R., Zax, M., & Greenspan, S. (1987). Intelligence quotient scores of 4-year-old children: Social-environmental risk factors. *Pediatrics, 79,* 343–350.

Sampson, R. J. (1997, April). *Child and adolescent development in community context: New findings from a multilevel study of 80 Chicago neighborhoods.* Paper presented at the biennial meetings of the Society for Research in Child Development, Washington, DC.

Sampson, R. J., & Laub, J. H. (1994). Urban poverty and the family context of delinquency: A new look at structure and process in a classic study. *Child Development, 65,* 523–540.

Samuelson, L. K., & Smith, L. B. (1998). Memory and attention make smart word learning: An alternative account of Akhtar, Carpenter, and Tomasello. *Child Development, 69,* 94–104.

Sandberg, S. (Ed.). (1996). *Hyperactivity disorders of childhood.* Cambridge, England: Cambridge University Press.

Sandberg, S., Day, R., & Gotz, E. T. (1996). Clinical aspects. In S. Sandberg (Ed.), *Hyperactivity disorders of childhood* (pp. 69–106). Cambridge, England: Cambridge University Press.

Sandman, C. A., Wadhwa, P. D., Chicz-DeMet, A., Dunkel-Schetter, C., & Porto, M. (1997). Maternal stress, HPA activity, and fetal/infant outcome. *Annals of the New York Academy of Sciences, 814,* 266–275.

Sapir, E. (1929). The status of linguistics as a science. *Language, 5,* 207–214.

Saudino, K. J. (1998). Moving beyond the heritability question: New directions in behavioral genetic studies of personality. *Current Directions in Psychological Science, 6,* 86–90.

Saudino, K. J., & Plomin, R. (1997). Cognitive and temperamental mediators of genetic contributions to the home environment during infancy. *Merrill-Palmer Quarterly, 43,* 1–23.

Savage-Rumbaugh, E. S., Murphy, J., Sevcik, R. A., Brakke, K. E., Williams, S. L., & Rumbaugh, D. M. (1993). Language comprehension in ape and child. *Monographs of the Society for Research in Child Development, 58*(3–4, Serial No. 223).

Savin-Williams, R. C. (1994). Verbal and physical abuse as stressors in the lives of lesbian, gay male, and bisexual youths: Associations with school problems, running away, substance abuse, prostitution, and suicide. *Journal of Consulting and Clinical Psychology, 62,* 261–269.

Savin-Williams, R. C. (1998). The disclosure to families of same-sex attractions by lesbian, gay, and bisexual youths. *Journal of Research on Adolescence, 8,* 49–68.

Scafidi, F. A., Field, T. M., Schanberg, S. M., Bauer, C. R., Tucci, K., Roberts, J., Morrow, C., & Kuhn, C. M. (1990). Massage stimulates growth in preterm infants: A replication. *Infant Behavior and Development, 13,* 167–188.

Scarr, S. (1998). American child care today. *American Psychologist, 53,* 95–108.

Scarr, S., & Eisenberg, M. (1993). Child care research: Issues, perspectives, and results. *Annual Review of Psychology, 44,* 613–644.

Scarr, S., & Kidd, K. K. (1983). Developmental behavior genetics. In M. M. Haith & J. J. Campos (Eds.), *Handbook of child psychology: Vol. 2. Infancy and developmental psychobiology* (pp. 345–434). New York: Wiley.

Scarr, S., & McCartney, K. (1983). How people make their own environments: A theory of genotype→environment effects. *Child Development, 54,* 424–435.

Scarr, S., Weinberg, R. A., & Waldman, I. D. (1993). IQ correlations in transracial adoptive families. *Intelligence, 17,* 541–555.

Schachar, R., Tannock, R., & Cunningham, C. (1996). Treatment. In S. Sandberg (Ed.), *Hyperactivity disorders of childhood* (pp. 433–476). Cambridge, England: Cambridge University Press.

Schaefli, A., Rest, J. R., & Thoma, S. J. (1985). Does moral education improve moral judgment? A meta-analysis of intervention studies using the Defining Issues Test. *Review of Educational Research, 55,* 319–352.

Schaffer, H. R. (1996). *Social development.* Oxford, England: Blackwell.

Schaie, K. W. (1983). What can we learn from the longitudinal study of adult psychological development? In K. W. Schaie (Ed.), *Longitudinal studies of adult psychological development* (pp. 1–19). New York: Guilford Press.

Schaie, K. W. (1994). Developmental designs revisited. In S. H. Cohen & H. W. Reese (Eds.), *Life-span developmental psychology. Methodological contributions* (pp. 45–64). Hillsdale, NJ: Erlbaum.

Schank, R. C., & Abelson, R. (1977). *Scripts, plans, goals, and understanding.* Hillsdale, NJ: Erlbaum.

Schneider, B., Hieshima, J. A., Lee, S., & Plank, S. (1994). East-Asian academic success in the United States: Family, school, and community explanations. In P. M. Greenfield & R. R. Cocking (Eds.), *Cross-cultural roots of minority child development* (pp. 323–350). Hillsdale, NJ: Erlbaum.

Schneider, M. L. (1992). The effect of mild stress during pregnancy on birthweight and neuromotor maturation in rhesus monkey infants (*Macaca mulatta*). *Infant Behavior and Development, 15,* 389–403.

Schneider, W., & Bjorklund, D. F. (1992). Expertise, aptitude, and strategic remembering. *Child Development, 63,* 461–473.

Schneider, W., & Bjorklund, D. F. (1998). Memory. In W. Damon (Ed.), *Handbook of child psychology: Vol. 2. Cognition, perception, and language* (5th ed., pp. 467–521). New York: Wiley.

Schneider, W., Gruber, H., Gold, A., & Opwis, K. (1993). Chess expertise and memory for chess positions in children and adults. *Journal of Experimental Child Psychology, 56,* 328–349.

Schneider, W., Reimers, P., Roth, E., & Visé, M. (1995, April). *Short- and long-term effects of training phonological awareness in kindergarten: Evidence from two German studies.* Paper presented at the biennial meetings of the Society for Research in Child Development, Indianapolis.

Schoendorf, K. C., Hogue, C. J. R., Kleinman, J. C., & Rowley, D. (1992). Mortality among infants of black as compared with white college-educated parents. *The New England Journal of Medicine, 326,* 1522–1526.

Schoendorf, K. C., & Kiely, J. L. (1992). Relationship of sudden infant death syndrome to maternal smoking during and after pregnancy. *Pediatrics, 90,* 905–908.

Schramm, W. F., Barnes, D. E., & Bakewell, J. M. (1987). Neonatal mortality in Missouri home births, 1978–84. *American Journal of Public Health, 77,* 930–935.

Schumm, J. S., & Vaughn, S. (1995). Getting ready for inclusion: Is the stage set? *Learning Disabilities Research and Practice, 10,* 169–179.

Schwartz, C. E., Snidman, N., & Kagan, J. (1996). Early childhood temperament as a determinant of externalizing behavior in adolescence. *Development and Psychopathology, 8,* 527–537.

Schwartz, D., Dodge, K. A., & Coie, J. D. (1993). The emergence of chronic peer victimization in boys' play groups. *Child Development, 64,* 1755–1772.

Schwartz, J. (1994). Low-level lead exposure and children's IQ: A meta-analysis and search for a threshold. *Environmental Research, 65,* 42–55.

Schwartz, R. M., Anastasia, M. L., Scanlon, J. W., & Kellogg, R. J. (1994). Effect of surfactant on morbidity, mortality, and resource use in newborn infants weighing 500 to 1500 g. *The New England Journal of Medicine, 330,* 1476–1480.

Schweingruber, H. (1997, April). *The effects of gender and exposure to advanced mathematics on achievement and attitudes in four countries.* Paper presented at the biennial meetings of the Society for Research in Child Development, Washington, DC.

Scollon, R. (1976). *Conversations with a one-year-old.* Honolulu: University of Hawaii Press.

Sears, R. R., Maccoby, E. E., & Levin, H. (1977). *Patterns of child rearing.* Stanford, CA: Stanford University Press. (Originally published 1957 by Row, Peterson)

Sedlak, A. J., & Broadhurst, D. D. (1996). *Third national incidence study on child abuse and neglect.* Washington, DC: U.S. Department of Health and Human Services.

Sege, R. D. (1998). Life imitating art: Adolescents and television violence. In T. P. Gullotta, G. R. Adams, & R. Montemayor (Eds.), *Delinquent violent youth: Theory and interventions.* Thousand Oaks, CA: Sage.

Seidman, E., Allen, L., Aber, J. L., Mitchell, C., & Feinman, J. (1994). The impact of school transitions in early adolescence on the self-system and perceived social context of poor urban youth. *Child Development, 65,* 507–522.

Seitz, V. (1988). Methodology. In M. H. Bornstein & M. E. Lamb (Eds.), *Developmental psychology: An advanced textbook* (2nd ed., pp. 51–84). Hillsdale, NJ: Erlbaum.

Sells, C. W., & Blum, R. W. (1996). Morbidity and mortality among US adolescents: An overview of data and trends. *American Journal of Public Health, 86,* 513–519.

Selman, R. L. (1980). *The growth of interpersonal understanding.* New York: Academic Press.

Senchak, M., & Leonard, K. E. (1992). Attachment styles and marital adjustment among newlywed couples. *Journal of Social and Personal Relationships, 9,* 51–64.

Serbin, L., Moskowitz, D. S., Schwartzman, A. E., & Ledingham, J. E. (1991). Aggressive, withdrawn, and aggressive/withdrawn children in adolescence: Into the next generation. In D. J. Pepler & K. H. Rubin (Eds.), *The development and treatment of childhood aggression* (pp. 55–70). Hillsdale, NJ: Erlbaum.

Serbin, L. A., Powlishta, K. K., & Gulko, J. (1993). The development of sex typing in middle childhood. *Monographs of the Society for Research in Child Development, 58*(2, Serial No. 232).

Serdula, M. K., Ivery, D., Coates, R. J., Freedman, D. S., Williamson, D. F., & Byers, T. (1993). Do obese children become obese adults? A review of the literature. *Preventive Medicine, 22,* 167–177.

Shaffer, D., Garland, A., Gould, M., Fisher, P., & Trautman, P. (1988). Preventing teenage suicide: A critical review. *Journal of the American Academy of Child and Adolescent Psychiatry, 27,* 675–687.

Shaffer, D., Garland, A., Vieland, V., Underwood, M., & Busner, C. (1991). The impact of curriculum-based suicide prevention programs for teenagers. *Journal of the American Academy of Child and Adolescent Psychiatry, 30,* 588–596.

Shanahan, M., Sayer, A., Davey, A., & Brooks, J. (1997, April). *Pathways of poverty and children's trajectories of psychosocial adjustment.* Paper presented at the biennial meetings of the Society for Research in Child Development, Washington, DC.

Shantz, C. U. (1983). Social cognition. In J. H. Flavell & E. M. Markman (Eds.), *Handbook of child psychology: Vol. 3. Cognitive development* (pp. 495–555). New York: Wiley.

Shantz, D. W. (1986). Conflict, aggression, and peer status: An observational study. *Child Development, 57,* 1322–1332.

Shatz, M. (1994). *A toddler's life. Becoming a person.* New York: Oxford University Press.

Shaw, D. S., Kennan, K., & Vondra, J. I. (1994). Developmental precursors of externalizing behavior: Ages 1 to 3. *Developmental Psychology, 30,* 355–364.

Shaw, D. S., Owens, E. B., Vondra, J. I., Keenan, K., & Winslow, E. B. (1996). Early risk factors and pathways in the development of early disruptive behavior problems. *Development and Psychopathology, 8,* 679–700.

Shaw, G. M., Velie, E. M., & Schaffer, D. (1996). Risk of neural tube defect–affected pregnancies among obese women. *Journal of the American Medical Association, 275,* 1093–1096.

Shaywitz, S. E., Shaywitz, B. A., Pugh, K. R., Fulbright, R. K., Constable, R. T., Mencl, W. E., Shankweiler, D. P., Liberman, A. M., Skudlarski, P., Fletcher, J. M., Katz, L., Marachione, K. E., Lacadie, C., Gatenby, C., & Gore, J. C. (1998). Functional disruption in the organization of the brain for reading in dyslexia. *Proceedings of the National Academy of Sciences, USA, 95,* 2636–2641.

Sheldon, W. H. (1940). *The varieties of human physique.* New York: Harper.

Sherman, M., & Key, C. (1932). The intelligence of isolated mountain children. *Child Development, 3,* 279–290.

Shore, C. (1986). Combinatorial play, conceptual development, and early multiword speech. *Developmental Psychology, 22,* 184–190.

Shore, C. M. (1995). *Individual differences in language development.* Thousand Oaks, CA: Sage.

Shore, R. (1997). *Rethinking the brain: New insights into early development.* New York: Families and Work Institute.

Shwe, H. I., & Markman, E. M. (1997). Young children's appreciation of the mental impact of their communicative signals. *Developmental Psychology, 33,* 630–636.

Shweder, R. A., Mahapatra, M., & Miller, J. G. (1987). Culture and moral development. In J. Kagan & S. Lamb (Eds.), *The emergence of morality in young children* (pp. 1–82). Chicago: University of Chicago Press.

Siegal, M. (1987). Are sons and daughters treated more differently by fathers than by mothers? *Developmental Review, 7,* 183–209.

Siegel, B. (1996). Is the emperor wearing clothes? Social policy and the empirical support for full inclusion of children with disabilities in the preschool and early elementary grades. *Social Policy Report, Society for Research in Child Development, 10*(2–3), 2–17.

Siegler, R. (1996). *Emerging minds: The process of change in children's thinking.* New York: Oxford University Press.

Siegler, R. S. (1994). Cognitive variability: A key to understanding cognitive development. *Current Directions in Psychological Science, 3,* 1–5.

Siegler, R. S., & Ellis, S. (1996). Piaget on childhood. *Psychological Science, 7,* 211–215.

Sigman, M., Neumann, C., Carter, E., Cattle, D. J., D'Souza, S., & Bwibo, N. (1988). Home interactions and the development of Embu toddlers in Kenya. *Child Development, 59,* 1251–1261.

Signorella, M. L., Bigler, R. L., & Liben, L. S. (1993). Developmental differences in children's gender schemata about others: A meta-analytic review. *Developmental Review, 13,* 147–183.

Silbereisen, R. K., & Kracke, B. (1993). Variations in maturational timing and adjustment in adolescence. In S. Jackson & H. Rodrigues-Tomé (Eds.), *Adolescence and its social worlds* (pp. 67–94). Hove, England: Erlbaum.

Silverberg, S. B., & Gondoli, D. M. (1996). Autonomy in adolescence: A contextualized perspective. In G. R. Adams, R. Montemayor, & T. P. Gullotta (Eds.), *Psychosocial development during adolescence: Progress in developmental contextualism* (pp. 12–61). Thousand Oaks, CA: Sage.

Simmons, R. G., Burgeson, R., & Reef, M. J. (1988). Cumulative change at entry to adolescence. In M. R. Gunnar & W. A. Collins (Eds.), *The Minnesota symposia on child psychology* (Vol. 21, pp. 123–150). Hillsdale, NJ: Erlbaum.

Simonoff, E., Pickles, A., Meyer, J. M., Silberg, J. L., Maes, H. H., Loeber, R., Rutter, M., Hewitt, J. K., & Eaves, L. J. (1997). The Virginia twin study of adolescent behavioral development. *Archives of General Psychiatry, 54,* 801–808.

Simons, R. L., Robertson, J. F., & Downs, W. R. (1989). The nature of the association between parental rejection and delinquent behavior. *Journal of Youth and Adolescence, 18,* 297–309.

Simpson, J. A. (1990). Influence of attachment styles on romantic relationships. *Journal of Personality and Social Psychology, 59,* 971–980.

Singer, L., Arendt, R., & Minnes, S. (1993). Neurodevelopmental effects of cocaine. *Clinics in Perinatology, 20,* 245–262.

Singh, G. K., & Yu, S. M. (1995). Infant mortality in the United States: Trends, differentials, and projections, 1950 through 2010. *American Journal of Public Health, 85,* 957–964.

Singh, G. K., & Yu, S. M. (1996). US childhood mortality, 1950 through 1993: Trends and socioeconomic differentials. *American Journal of Public Health, 86,* 505–512.

Skinner, B. F. (1957). *Verbal behavior.* New York: Prentice Hall.

Slaby, R. G., & Frey, K. S. (1975). Development of gender constancy and selective attention to same-sex models. *Child Development, 46,* 849–856.

Slater, A. (1995). Individual differences in infancy and later IQ. *Journal of Child Psychology and Psychiatry, 36,* 69–112.

Slobin, D. I. (1985a). Introduction: Why study acquisition crosslinguistically? In D. I. Slobin (Ed.), *The crosslinguistic study of language acquisition: Vol. 1. The data* (pp. 3–24). Hillsdale, NJ: Erlbaum.

Slobin, D. I. (1985b). Crosslinguistic evidence for the language-making capacity. In D. I. Slobin (Ed.), *The crosslinguistic study of language acquisition: Vol. 2. Theoretical issues* (pp. 1157–1256). Hillsdale, NJ: Erlbaum.

Small, S. A., & Luster, T. (1994). Adolescent sexual activity: An ecological, risk-factor approach. *Journal of Marriage and the Family, 56,* 181–192.

Smetana, J. G. (1990). Morality and conduct disorders. In M. Lewis & S. M. Miller (Eds.), *Handbook of developmental psychopathology* (pp. 157–180). New York: Plenum Press.

Smetana, J. G., Killen, M., & Turiel, E. (1991). Children's reasoning about interpersonal and moral conflicts. *Child Development, 62,* 629–644.

Smith, J. R., Brooks-Gunn, J., & Klebanov, P. K. (1997). Consequences of living in poverty for young children's cognitive and verbal ability and early school achievement. In G. J. Duncan & J. Brooks-Gunn (Eds.), *Consequences of growing up poor* (pp. 132–179). New York: Russell Sage Foundation.

Smith, R. E., & Smoll, F. L. (1997). Coaching the coaches: Youth sports as a scientific and applied behavioral setting. *Current Directions in Psychological Science, 6,* 16–21.

Smock, P. J. (1993). The economic costs of marital disruption for young women over the past two decades. *Demography, 30,* 353–371.

Smolak, L., & Levine, M. P. (1996). Adolescent transitions and the development of eating problems. In L. Smolak, M. P. Levine, & R. Streigel-Moore (Eds.), *The developmental psychopathology of eating disorders* (pp. 207–233). Mahwah, NJ: Erlbaum.

Smolak, L., Levine, M. P., & Streigel-Moore, R. (Eds.). (1996). *The developmental psychopathology of eating disorders.* Mahwah, NJ: Erlbaum.

Smoll, F. L., & Schutz, R. W. (1990). Quantifying gender differences in physical performance: A developmental perspective. *Developmental Psychology, 26,* 360–369.

Snarey, J. R. (1985). Cross-cultural universality of social-moral development: A critical review of Kohlbergian research. *Psychological Bulletin, 97,* 202–232.

Snarey, J. R., Reimer, J., & Kohlberg, L. (1985). Development of social-moral reasoning among kibbutz adolescents: A longitudinal cross-sectional study. *Developmental Psychology, 21,* 3–17.

Snow, C. E. (1997, April). *Cross-domain connections and social class differences: Two challenges to nonenvironmentalist views of language development.* Paper presented at the biennial meetings of the Society for Research in Child Development, Washington, DC.

Snyder, J., Edwards, P., McGraw, K., Kilgore, K., & Holton, A. (1994). Escalation and reinforcement in mother-child conflict: Social processes associated with the development of physical aggression. *Development and Psychopathology, 6,* 305–321.

Soken, N. H., & Pick, A. D. (1992). Intermodal perception of happy and angry expressive behaviors by seven-month-old infants. *Child Development, 63,* 787–795.

Sonnenschein, S. (1986). Development of referential communication skills: How familiarity with a listener affects a speaker's production of redundant messages. *Developmental Psychology, 22,* 549–552.

Sophian, C. (1995). Representation and reasoning in early numerical development: Counting, conservation, and comparisons between sets. *Child Development, 66,* 559–577.

Sosa, R., Kennell, J. H., Klaus, M. H., Robertson, S., & Urrutia, J. (1980). The effect of a supportive companion on perinatal problems, length of labor and mother-infant interaction. *The New England Journal of Medicine, 303,* 597–600.

Spector, S. A. (1996). Cytomegalovirus infections. In A. M. Rudolph, J. I. E. Hoffman, & C. D. Rudolph (Eds.), *Rudolph's pediatrics* (pp. 629–633). Stanford, CT: Appleton & Lange.

Spelke, E. S. (1979). Exploring audible and visible events in infancy. In A. D. Pick (Ed.), *Perception and its development: A tribute to Eleanor J. Gibson* (pp. 221–236). Hillsdale, NJ: Erlbaum.

Spelke, E. S. (1982). Perceptual knowledge of objects in infancy. In J. Mehler, E. C. T. Walker, & M. Garrett (Eds.), *Perspectives on mental representation* (pp. 409–430). Hillsdale, NJ: Erlbaum.

Spelke, E. S. (1985). Perception of unity, persistence, and identity: Thoughts on infants' conceptions of objects. In J. Mehler & R. Fox (Eds.), *Neonate cognition* (pp. 89–113). Hillsdale, NJ: Erlbaum.

Spelke, E. S. (1991). Physical knowledge in infancy: Reflections on Piaget's theory. In S. Carey & R. Gelman (Eds.), *The epigenesis of mind: Essays on biology and cognition* (pp. 133–169). Hillsdale, NJ: Erlbaum.

Spelke, E. S., & Owsley, C. J. (1979). Intermodal exploration and knowledge in infancy. *Infant Behavior and Development, 2,* 13–27.

Spelke, E. S., von Hofsten, C., & Kestenbaum, R. (1989). Object perception in infancy: Interaction of spatial and kinetic information for object boundaries. *Developmental Psychology, 25,* 185–196.

Spence, J. T., & Helmreich, R. L. (1978). *Masculinity and femininity.* Austin: University of Texas Press.

Spencer, M. B., & Dornbusch, S. M. (1990). Challenges in studying minority youth. In S. S. Feldman & G. R. Elliott (Eds.), *At the threshold: The developing adolescent* (pp. 123–146). Cambridge, MA: Harvard University Press.

Spieker, S. J., Bensley, L., McMahon, R. J., Fung, H., & Ossiander, E. (1996). Sexual abuse as a factor in child maltreatment by adolescent mothers of preschool aged children. *Development and Psychopathology, 8,* 497–509.

Spiker, D. (1990). Early intervention from a developmental perspective. In D. Cicchetti & M. Beeghly (Eds.), *Children with Down syndrome: A developmental perspective* (pp. 424–448). Cambridge, England: Cambridge University Press.

Spiker, D., Ferguson, J., & Brooks-Gunn, J. (1993). Enhancing maternal interactive behavior and child social competence in low birth weight, premature infants. *Child Development, 64,* 754–768.

Spitze, G. (1988). Women's employment and family relations: A review. *Journal of Marriage and the Family, 50,* 595–618.

Spock, B., & Rothenberg, M. (1985). *Dr. Spock's baby and child care.* New York: Pocket Books.

Sroufe, L. A. (1979). The coherence of individual development: Early care, attachment, and subsequent developmental issues. *American Psychologist, 34,* 834–841.

Sroufe, L. A. (1983). Infant-caregiver attachment and patterns of adaptation in preschool: The roots of maladaption and competence. In M. Perlmutter (Ed.), *The Minnesota symposia on child psychology* (Vol. 16, pp. 41–84). Hillsdale, NJ: Erlbaum.

Sroufe, L. A. (1988). The role of infant-caregiver attachment in development. In J. Belsky & T. Nezworski (Eds.), *Clinical implications of attachment* (pp. 18–40). Hillsdale, NJ: Erlbaum.

Sroufe, L. A. (1989). Pathways to adaptation and maladaptation: Psychopathology as developmental deviation. In D. Cicchetti (Ed.), *The emergence of a discipline: Rochester symposium on developmental psychopathology* (pp. 13–40). Hillsdale, NJ: Erlbaum.

Sroufe, L. A. (1990). A developmental perspective on day care. In N. Fox & G. G. Fein (Eds.), *Infant day care: The current debate* (pp. 51–60). Norwood, NJ: Ablex.

Sroufe, L. A. (1996). *Emotional development: The organization of emotional life in the early years.* Cambridge, England: Cambridge University Press.

Sroufe, L. A. (1997). Psychopathology as an outcome of development. *Development and Psychopathology, 9,* 251–268.

Sroufe, L. A., Carlson, E., & Schulman, S. (1993). Individuals in relationships: Development from infancy through adolescence. In D. C.

Funder, R. D. Parke, C. Tomlinson-Keasey, & K. Widaman (Eds.), *Studying lives through time: Personality and development* (pp. 315–342). Washington, DC: American Psychological Association.

Sroufe, L. A., Egeland, B., & Kreutzer, T. (1990). The fate of early experience following developmental change: Longitudinal approaches to individual adaptation in childhood. *Child Development, 61,* 1363–1373.

Sroufe, L. A., & Rutter, M. (1984). The domain of developmental psychopathology. *Child Development, 55,* 17–29.

St. James-Roberts, I., Bowyer, J., Varghese, S., & Sawdon, J. (1994). Infant crying patterns in Manila and London. *Child: Care, Health and Development, 20,* 323–337.

St. Peters, M., Fitch, M., Huston, A. C., Wright, J. C., & Eakins, D. J. (1991). Television and families: What do young children watch with their parents? *Child Development, 62,* 1409–1423.

Stainback, S., & Stainback, W. (1985). The merger of special and regular education: Can it be done? A response to Lieberman and Mesinger. *Exceptional Children, 51,* 517–521.

Starfield, B. (1991). Childhood morbidity: Comparisons, clusters, and trends. *Pediatrics, 88,* 519–526.

Stattin, H., & Klackenberg-Larsson, I. (1993). Early language and intelligence development and their relationship to future criminal behavior. *Journal of Abnormal Psychology, 102,* 369–378.

Stattin, H., & Magnusson, D. (1996). Antisocial development: A holistic approach. *Development and Psychopathology, 8,* 617–646.

Steele, C. M. (1997). A threat in the air: How stereotypes shape intellectual identity and performance. *American Psychologist, 52,* 613–629.

Steele, H., Holder, J., & Fonagy, P. (1995, April). *Quality of attachment to mother at one year predicts belief-desire reasoning at five years.* Paper presented at the biennial meetings of the Society for Research in Child Development, Indianapolis.

Stein, Z., Susser, M., Saenger, G., & Morolla, F. (1975). *Famine and human development: The Dutch hunger winter of 1944–1945.* New York: Oxford University Press.

Steinberg, L. (1986). Latchkey children and susceptibility to peer pressure: An ecological analysis. *Developmental Psychology, 22,* 433–439.

Steinberg, L. (1988). Reciprocal relation between parent-child distance and pubertal maturation. *Developmental Psychology, 24,* 122–128.

Steinberg, L. (1990). Autonomy, conflict and harmony in the parent-adolescent relationship. In S. S. Feldman & G. R. Elliott (Eds.), *At the threshold: The developing adolescent* (pp. 255–276). Cambridge, MA: Harvard University Press.

Steinberg, L. (1996). *Beyond the classroom: Why school reform has failed and what parents need to do.* New York: Simon & Schuster.

Steinberg, L., Darling, N. E., Fletcher, A. C., Brown, B. B., & Dornbusch, S. M. (1995). Authoritative parenting and adolescent adjustment: An ecological journey. In P. Moen, G. H. Elder Jr., & K. Lüscher (Eds.), *Examining lives in context: Perspectives on the ecology of human development* (pp. 423–466). Washington, DC: American Psychological Association.

Steinberg, L., & Dornbusch, S. M. (1991). Negative correlates of part-time employment during adolescence: Replication and elaboration. *Developmental Psychology, 27,* 304–313.

Steinberg, L., Dornbusch, S. M., & Brown, B. B. (1992a). Ethnic differences in adolescent achievement: An ecological perspective. *American Psychologist, 47,* 723–729.

Steinberg, L., Elmen, J. D., & Mounts, N. S. (1989). Authoritative parenting, psychosocial maturity, and academic success among adolescents. *Child Development, 60,* 1424–1436.

Steinberg, L., Fegley, S., & Dornbusch, S. M. (1993). Negative impact of part-time work on adolescent adjustment: Evidence from a longitudinal study. *Developmental Psychology, 29,* 171–180.

Steinberg, L., Lamborn, S. D., Dornbusch, S. M., & Darling, N. (1992b). Impact of parenting practices on adolescent achievement: Authoritative parenting, school involvement, and encouragement to succeed. *Child Development, 63,* 1266–1281.

Steinberg, L., Lamborn, S. D., Darling, N., Mounts, N. S., & Dornbusch, S. M. (1994). Over-time changes in adjustment and competence among adolescents from authoritative, authoritarian, indulgent, and neglectful families. *Child Development, 65,* 754–770.

Steinberg, L., Mounts, N. S., Lamborn, S. D., & Dornbusch, S. D. (1991). Authoritative parenting and adolescent adjustment across varied ecological niches. *Journal of Research on Adolescence, 1,* 19–36.

Steiner, J. E. (1979). Human facial expressions in response to taste and smell stimulation. In H. W. Reese & L. P. Lipsitt (Eds.), *Advances in child development and behavior* (Vol. 13, pp. 257–296). New York: Academic Press.

Stelzl, I., Merz, F., Ehlers, T., & Remer, H. (1995). The effect of schooling on the development of fluid and crystallized intelligence: A quasi-experimental study. *Intelligence, 21,* 279–296.

Sternberg, R. J. (1985). *Beyond IQ: A triarchic theory of human intelligence.* New York: Cambridge University Press.

Sternberg, R. J. (1986). *Intelligence applied.* New York: Harcourt Brace Jovanovich.

Sternberg, R. J. (1997). The concept of intelligence and its role in lifelong learning and success. *American Psychologist, 52,* 1030–1037.

Sternberg, R. J., & Davidson, J. E. (1985). Cognitive development in the gifted and talented. In F. D. Horowitz & M. O'Brien (Eds.), *The gifted and talented: Developmental perspectives* (pp. 37–74). Washington, DC: American Psychological Association.

Sternberg, R. J., & Davidson, J. E. (Eds.). (1986). *Conceptions of giftedness.* Cambridge, England: Cambridge University Press.

Sternberg, R. J., & Suben, J. G. (1986). The socialization of intelligence. In M. Perlmutter (Ed.), *Perspectives on intellectual development: The Minnesota symposia on child psychology* (Vol. 19, pp. 201–236). Hillsdale, NJ: Erlbaum.

Sternberg, R. J., & Wagner, R. K. (1993). The g-ocentric view of intelligence and job performance is wrong. *Current Directions in Psychological Science, 2,* 1–5.

Sternberg, R. J., Wagner, R. K., Williams, W. M., & Horvath, J. A. (1995). Testing common sense. *American Psychologist, 50,* 912–927.

Stevenson, H. W. (1988). Culture and schooling: Influences on cognitive development. In E. M. Hetherington, R. M. Lerner, & M. Perlmutter (Eds.), *Child development in life span perspective* (pp. 241–258). Hillsdale, NJ: Erlbaum.

Stevenson, H. W. (1994). Moving away from stereotypes and preconceptions: Students and their education in East Asia and the United States. In P. M. Greenfield & R. R. Cocking (Eds.), *Cross-cultural roots of minority child development* (pp. 315–322). Hillsdale, NJ: Erlbaum.

Stevenson, H. W., & Chen, C. (1989). Schooling and achievement: A study of Peruvian children. *International Journal of Educational Research, 13,* 883–894.

Stevenson, H. W., Chen, C., Lee, S., & Fuligni, A. J. (1991). Schooling, culture, and cognitive development. In L. Okagaki & R. J. Sternberg (Eds.), *Directors of development* (pp. 243–268). Hillsdale, NJ: Erlbaum.

Stevenson, H. W., & Lee, S. (1990). Contexts of achievement: A study of American, Chinese, and Japanese children. *Monographs of the Society for Research in Child Development, 55*(1–2, Serial No. 221).

Stevenson, H. W., Lee, S., Chen, C., Lummis, M., Stigler, J., Fan, L., & Ge, F. (1990). Mathematics achievement of children in China and the United States. *Child Development, 61,* 1053–1066.

Steward, M. S. (1993). Understanding children's memories of medical procedures: "He didn't touch me and it didn't hurt!" In C. A. Nelson (Ed.), *The Minnesota symposia on child psychology* (Vol. 26, pp. 171–225). Hillsdale, NJ: Erlbaum.

Steward, M. S., & Steward, D. S. (1996). Interviewing young children about body touch and handling. *Monographs of the Society for Research in Child Development, 61*(4, Serial No. 248).

Stewart, J. F., Popkin, B. M., Guilkey, D. K., Akin, J. S., Adair, L., & Flieger, W. (1991). Influences on the extent of breast-feeding: A prospective study in the Philippines. *Demography, 28,* 181–199.

Stewart, R. B., Beilfuss, M. L., & Verbrugge, K. M. (1995, April). *That was then, this is now: An empirical typology of adult sibling relationships.* Paper presented at the biennial meetings of the Society for Research in Child Development, Indianapolis.

Stigler, J. W., Lee, S., & Stevenson, H. W. (1987). Mathematics classrooms in Japan, Taiwan, and the United States. *Child Development, 58,* 1272–1285.

Stigler, J. W., & Stevenson, H. W. (1991, Spring). How Asian teachers polish each lesson to perfection. *American Educator* 12–20, 43–47.

Stipek, D. (1992). The child at school. In M. H. Bornstein & M. E. Lamb (Eds.), *Developmental psychology: An advanced textbook* (3rd ed., pp. 579–625). Hillsdale, NJ: Erlbaum.

Stipek, D., & Gralinski, H. (1991). Gender differences in children's achievement-related beliefs and emotional responses to success and failure in math. *Journal of Educational Psychology, 83,* 361–371.

Storfer, M. D. (1990). *Intelligence and giftedness.* San Francisco: Jossey-Bass.

Story, M., Rosenwinkel, K., Himes, J. H., Resnick, M., Harris, L. J., & Blum, R. W. (1991). Demographic and risk factors associated with chronic dieting in adolescents. *American Journal of Diseases of Childhood, 145,* 994–998.

Stoutjesdyk, D., & Jevne, R. (1993). Eating disorders among high performance athletes. *Journal of Youth and Adolescence, 22,* 271–282.

Strassberg, Z., Dodge, K. A., Pettit, G. S., & Bates, J. E. (1994). Spanking in the home and children's subsequent aggression toward kindergarten peers. *Development and Psychopathology, 6,* 445–461.

Stratton, K. R., Howe, C. J., & Battaglia, F. C. (Eds.). (1996). *Fetal alcohol syndrome: Diagnosis, epidemiology, prevention and treatment.* Washington, DC: National Academy Press.

Straus, M. A. (1991a). Discipline and deviance: Physical punishment of children and violence and other crime in adulthood. *Social Problems, 38,* 133–152.

Straus, M. A. (1991b). New theory and old canards about family violence research. *Social Problems, 38,* 180–194.

Straus, M. A. (1995). Corporal punishment of children and adult depression and suicidal ideation. In J. McCord (Ed.), *Coercion and punishment in long-term perspectives* (pp. 59–77). Cambridge, England: Cambridge University Press.

Straus, M. A., & Donnelly, D. A. (1993). Corporal punishment of adolescents by American parents. *Youth and Society, 24,* 419–442.

Straus, M. A., & Gelles, R. J. (1986). Societal change and change in family violence from 1975 to 1985 as revealed by two national surveys. *Journal of Marriage and the Family, 48,* 465–479.

Strayer, J., & Roberts, W. (1989). Children's empathy and role-taking: Child and parental factors and relations to prosocial behavior. *Journal of Applied Developmental Psychology, 10,* 227–239.

Streissguth, A. (1997). *Fetal alcohol syndrome: A guide for families and communities.* Baltimore: Brookes.

Streissguth, A. P., Aase, J. M., Clarren, S. K., Randels, S. P., LaDue, R. A., & Smith, D. F. (1991). Fetal alcohol syndrome in adolescents and adults. *Journal of the American Medical Association, 265,* 1961–1967.

Streissguth, A. P., Barr, H. M., & Sampson, P. D. (1990). Moderate prenatal alcohol exposure: Effects on child IQ and learning problems at age 7½ years. *Alcoholism: Clinical and Experimental Research, 14,* 662–669.

Streissguth, A. P., Barr, H. M., Sampson, P. D., Darby, B. L., & Martin, D. C. (1989). IQ at age 4 in relation to maternal alcohol use and smoking during pregnancy. *Developmental Psychology, 25,* 3–11.

Streissguth, A. P., Bookstein, F. L., Sampson, P. D., & Barr, H. M. (1995). Attention: Prenatal alcohol and continuities of vigilance and attentional problems from 4 through 14 years. *Development and Psychopathology, 7,* 419–446.

Streissguth, A. P., Landesman-Dwyer, S., Martin, J. C., & Smith, D. W. (1980). Teratogenic effects of alcohol in humans and laboratory animals. *Science, 209,* 353–361.

Streissguth, A. P., Martin, D. C., Barr, H. M., Sandman, B. M., Kirchner, G. L., & Darby, B. L. (1984). Intrauterine alcohol and nicotine exposure: Attention and reaction time in 4-year-old children. *Developmental Psychology, 20,* 533–541.

Streissguth, A. P., Martin, D. C., Martin, J. C., & Barr, H. M. (1981). The Seattle longitudinal prospective study on alcohol and pregnancy. *Neurobehavioral Toxicology and Teratology, 3,* 223–233.

Stunkard, A. J., Harris, J. R., Pedersen, N. L., & McClearn, G. E. (1990). The body-mass index of twins who have been reared apart. *The New England Journal of Medicine, 322,* 1483–1487.

Stunkard, A. J., & Sobol, J. (1995). Psychosocial consequences of obesity. In K. D. Brownell & C. G. Fairburn (Eds.), *Eating disorders and obesity: A comprehensive handbook* (pp. 417–421). New York: Guilford Press.

Stunkard, A. J., Sorensen, T. I. A., Hanis, C., Teasdale, T. W., Chakraborty, R., Schull, W. J., & Schulsinger, F. (1986). An adoption study of human obesity. *The New England Journal of Medicine, 314,* 193–198.

Sudarkasa, N. (1993). Female-headed African American households: Some neglected dimensions. In H. P. McAdoo (Ed.), *Family ethnicity* (pp. 81–89). Newbury Park, CA: Sage.

Sue, S., & Okazaki, S. (1990). Asian-American educational achievements: A phenomenon in search of an explanation. *American Psychologist, 45,* 913–920.

Sullivan, K., Zaitchik, D., & Tager-Flusberg, H. (1994). Preschoolers can attribute second-order beliefs. *Developmental Psychology, 30,* 395–402.

Sulloway, F. (1996). *Born to rebel.* New York: Pantheon Books.

Super, C. M., & Harkness, S. (1982). The infant's niche in rural Kenya and metropolitan America. In L. Adler (Ed.), *Issues in cross-cultural research* (pp. 47–56). New York: Academic Press.

Susman, E. J. (1997). Modeling developmental complexity in adolescence: Hormones and behavior in context. *Journal of Research on Adolescence, 7,* 283–306.

Susman, E. J., Inoff-Germain, G., Nottelmann, E. D., Loriaux, D. L., Cutler, G. B., Jr., & Chrousos, G. P. (1987). Hormones, emotional dispositions, and aggressive attributes in young adolescents. *Child Development, 58,* 1114–1134.

Sutton-Smith, B. (1982). Birth order and sibling status effects. In M. E. Lamb & B. Sutton-Smith (Eds.), *Sibling relationships: Their nature and significance across the lifespan* (pp. 153–165). Hillsdale, NJ: Erlbaum.

Swain, I. U., Zelazo, P. R., & Clifton, R. K. (1993). Newborn infants' memory for speech sounds retained over 24 hours. *Developmental Psychology, 29,* 312–323.

Swayze, V. W., Johnson, V. P., Hanson, J. W., Piven, J., Sato, Y., Geidd, J. N., Mosnik, D., & Andreasen, N. C. (1997). Magnetic resonance imaging of brain anomalies in fetal alcohol syndrome. *Pediatrics, 99,* 232–240.

Swedo, S. E., Rettew, D. C., Kuppenheimer, M., Lum, D., Dolan, S., & Goldberger, E. (1991). Can adolescent suicide attempters be distinguished from at-risk adolescents? *Pediatrics, 88,* 620–629.

Taffel, S. M., Keppel, K. G., & Jones, G. K. (1993). Medical advice on maternal weight gain and actual weight gain. Results from the 1988 National Maternal and Infant Health Survey. *Annals of the New York Academy of Sciences, 678,* 293–305.

Tamis-LeMonda, C., & Bornstein, M. H. (1987). Is there a "sensitive period" in human mental development? In M. H. Bornstein (Ed.), *Sensitive periods in development: Interdisciplinary perspectives* (pp. 163–182). Hillsdale, NJ: Erlbaum.

Tanner, J. M. (1978). *Fetus into man: Physical growth from conception to maturity.* Cambridge, MA: Harvard University Press.

Tanner, J. M. (1990). *Foetus into man* (revised and enlarged ed.). Cambridge, MA: Harvard University Press.

Taylor, E. (1995). Dysfunctions of attention. In D. Cicchetti & D. J. Cohen (Eds.), *Developmental psychopathology: Vol. 2. Risk, disorder, and adaptation* (pp. 243–273). New York: Wiley.

Taylor, J. A., & Danderson, M. (1995). A reexamination of the risk factors for the sudden infant death syndrome. *Journal of Pediatrics, 126,* 887–891.

Taylor, J. A., Krieger, J. W., Reay, D. T., Davis, R. L., Harruff, R., & Cheney, L. K. (1996). Prone sleep position and the sudden infant death syndrome in King County, Washington: A case-control study. *Journal of Pediatrics, 128,* 626–630.

Taylor, M., Cartwright, B. S., & Carlson, S. M. (1993). A developmental investigation of children's imaginary companions. *Developmental Psychology, 29,* 276–285.

Taylor, M. G. (1996). The development of children's beliefs about social and biological aspects of gender differences. *Child Development, 67,* 1555–1571.

Taylor, R. D., Casten, R., & Flickinger, S. M. (1993). Influence of kinship social support on the parenting experiences and psychosocial adjustment of African-American adolescents. *Developmental Psychology, 29,* 382–388.

Taylor, R. D., Casten, R., Flickinger, S. M., Roberts, D., & Fulmore, C. D. (1994). Explaining the school performance of African-American adolescents. *Journal of Research on Adolescence, 4,* 21–44.

Taylor, R. D., & Roberts, D. (1995). Kinship support and maternal and adolescent well-being in economically disadvantaged African-American families. *Child Development, 66,* 1585–1597.

Teachman, J. D., Paasch, K. M., Day, R. D., & Carver, K. P. (1997). Poverty during adolescence and subsequent educational attainment. In G. J. Duncan & J. Brooks-Gunn (Eds.), *Consequences of growing up poor* (pp. 382–418). New York: Russell Sage Foundation.

Tellegen, A., Lykken, D. T., Bouchard, T. J., Wilcox, K. J., Segal, N. L., & Rich, S. (1988). Personality similarity in twins reared apart and together. *Journal of Personality and Social Psychology, 54,* 1031–1039.

Terman, L. (1916). *The measurement of intelligence.* Boston: Houghton Mifflin.

Terman, L. (1925). *Mental and physical traits of a thousand gifted children: Vol. 1. Genetic studies of genius.* Stanford, CA: Stanford University Press.

Terman, L., & Merrill, M. A. (1937). *Measuring intelligence: A guide to the administration of the new revised Stanford-Binet tests.* Boston: Houghton Mifflin.

Terman, L., & Oden, M. (1959). *Genetic studies of genius: Vol. 5. The gifted group at mid-life.* Stanford, CA: Stanford University Press.

Tesman, J. R., & Hills, A. (1994). Developmental effects of lead exposure in children. *Social Policy Report, Society for Research in Child Development, 8*(3), 1–16.

Teti, D. M., Gelfand, D. M., Messinger, D. S., & Isabella, R. (1995). Maternal depression and the quality of early attachment: An examination of infants, preschoolers, and their mothers. *Developmental Psychology, 31,* 364–376.

Tew, M. (1985). Place of birth and perinatal mortality. *Journal of the Royal College of General Practitioners, 35,* 390–394.

Thal, D., & Bates, E. (1990). Continuity and variation in early language development. In J. Colombo & J. Fagen (Eds.), *Individual differences in infancy: Reliability, stability, prediction* (pp. 359–385). Hillsdale, NJ: Erlbaum.

Thal, D., Tobias, S., & Morrison, D. (1991). Language and gesture in late talkers: A 1-year follow-up. *Journal of Speech and Hearing Research, 34,* 604–612.

Thelen, E. (1981). Rhythmical behavior in infancy: An ethological perspective. *Developmental Psychology, 17,* 237–257.

Thelen, E. (1983). Learning to walk is still an "old" problem: A reply to Zelazo. *Journal of Motor Behavior, 15,* 139–161.

Thelen, E. (1995). Motor development: A new synthesis. *American Psychologist, 50,* 79–95.

Thelen, E., & Adolph, K. E. (1992). Arnold L. Gesell: The paradox of nature and nurture. *Developmental Psychology, 28,* 368–380.

Thomas, A., & Chess, S. (1977). *Temperament and development.* New York: Brunner/Mazel.

Thomas, R. M. (Ed.). (1990a). *The encyclopedia of human development and education: Theory, research, and studies.* Oxford: Pergamon Press.

Thomas, R. M. (1990b). Motor development. In R. M. Thomas (Ed.), *The encyclopedia of human development and education: Theory, research, and studies* (pp. 326–330). Oxford: Pergamon Press.

Thomas, R. M. (1990c). Basic concepts and applications of Piagetian cognitive development theory. In R. M. Thomas (Ed.), *The encyclopedia of human development and education: Theory, research, and studies* (pp. 53–55). Oxford: Pergamon Press.

Thompson, R. A. (1998). Early sociopersonality development. In W. Damon (Ed.), *Handbook of child psychology: Vol 3. Social, emotional, and personality development* (5th ed., pp. 25–104). New York: Wiley.

Thompson, S. K. (1975). Gender labels and early sex role development. *Child Development, 46,* 339–347.

Thorne, B. (1986). Girls and boys together . . . but mostly apart: Gender arrangements in elementary schools. In W. W. Hartup & Z. Rubin (Eds.), *Relationships and development* (pp. 167–184). Hillsdale, NJ: Erlbaum.

Thornton, A. (1990). The courtship process and adolescent sexuality. *Journal of Family Issues, 11,* 239–273.

Timmer, S. G., Eccles, J., & O'Brien, K. (1985). How children use time. In F. T. Juster & F. P. Stafford (Eds.), *Time, goods, and well-being* (pp. 353–369). Ann Arbor: Institute for Social Research, University of Michigan.

Todd, R. D., Swarzenski, B., Rossi, P. G., & Visconti, P. (1995). Structural and functional development of the human brain. In D. Cicchetti & D. J. Cohen (Eds.), *Developmental psychopathology: Vol. 1. Theory and methods* (pp. 161–194). New York: Wiley.

Tomada, G., & Schneider, B. H. (1997). Relational aggression, gender, and peer acceptance: Invariance across culture, stability over time, and concordance among informants. *Developmental Psychology, 33,* 601–609.

Tomasello, M., & Brooks, P. J. (in press). Early syntactic development: A construction grammar approach. In M. Barrett (Ed.), *The development of language.* London: UCL Press.

Tomasello, M., & Mannle, S. (1985). Pragmatics of sibling speech to one-year-olds. *Child Development, 56,* 911–917.

Tomlinson-Keasey, C., Eisert, D. C., Kahle, L. R., Hardy-Brown, K., & Keasey, B. (1979). The structure of concrete operational thought. *Child Development, 50,* 1153–1163.

Trehub, S. E., Bull, D., & Thorpe, L. A. (1984). Infants' perception of melodies: The role of melodic contour. *Child Development, 55,* 821–830.

Trehub, S. E., & Rabinovitch, M. S. (1972). Auditory-linguistic sensitivity in early infancy. *Developmental Psychology, 6,* 74–77.

Trehub, S. E., Thorpe, L. A., & Morrongiello, B. A. (1985). Infants' perception of melodies: Changes in a single tone. *Infant Behavior and Development, 8,* 213–223.

Tremblay, R. E., Kurtz, L., Mâsse, L. C., Vitaro, F., & Pihl, R. O. (1995a). A bimodal preventive intervention for disruptive kindergarten boys: Its impact through mid-adolescence. *Journal of Consulting and Clinical Psychology, 63,* 560–568.

Tremblay, R. E., Mâsse, L. C., Vitaro, F., & Dobkin, P. L. (1995b). The impact of friends' deviant behavior on early onset of delinquency: Longitudinal data from 6 to 13 years of age. *Development and Psychopathology, 7,* 649–667.

Troiano, R. P., Flegal, K. M., Kuczmarski, R. J., Campbell, S. M., & Johnson, C. L. (1995). Overweight prevalence and trends for children and adolescents: The National Health and Nutrition Examination Surveys, 1963 to 1991. *Archives of Pediatric and Adolescent Medicine, 149,* 1085–1091.

Tronick, E. Z., Morelli, G. A., & Ivey, P. K. (1992). The Efe forager infant and toddler's pattern of social relationships: Multiple and simultaneous. *Developmental Psychology, 28,* 568–577.

Tronick, E. Z., & Weinberg, M. K. (1997). Depressed mothers and infants: Failure to form dyadic states of consciousness. In L. Murray & P. J. Cooper (Eds.), *Postpartum depression and child development* (pp. 54–81). New York: Guilford Press.

Tuna, J. M. (1989). Mental health services for children: The state of the art. *American Psychologist, 44,* 188–199.

Turiel, E. (1966). An experimental test of the sequentiality of developmental stages in the child's moral judgment. *Journal of Personality and Social Psychology, 3,* 611–618.

Turiel, E. (1983). *The development of social knowledge: Morality and convention.* Cambridge, England: Cambridge University Press.

Turiel, E. (1998). The development of morality. In W. Damon (Ed.), *Handbook of child psychology: Vol 3. Social, emotional, and personality development* (5th ed., pp. 863–932). New York: Wiley.

Turkheimer, E., & Gottesman, I. I. (1991). Individual differences and the canalization of human behavior. *Developmental Psychology, 27,* 18–22.

Turner, H. A., & Finkelhor, D. (1996). Corporal punishment as a stressor among youth. *Journal of Marriage and the Family, 58,* 155–166.

Udry, J. R., & Campbell, B. C. (1994). Getting started on sexual behavior. In A. S. Rossi (Ed.), *Sexuality across the life course* (pp. 187–208). Chicago: University of Chicago Press.

Umberson, D., & Gove, W. R. (1989). Parenthood and psychological well-being. Theory, measurement, and stage in the family life course. *Journal of Family Issues, 10,* 440–462.

Underwood, M. K., Coie, J. D., & Herbsman, C. R. (1992). Display rules for anger and aggression in school-age children. *Child Development, 63,* 366–380.

Underwood, M. K., Kupersmidt, J. B., & Coie, J. D. (1996). Childhood peer sociometric status and aggression as predictors of adolescent childbearing. *Journal of Research on Adolescence, 6,* 201–224.

Ungerer, J. A., & Sigman, M. (1984). The relation of play and sensorimotor behavior to language in the second year. *Child Development, 55,* 1448–1455.

Upchurch, D. M. (1993). Early schooling and childbearing experiences: Implications for post-secondary school attendance. *Journal of Research on Adolescence, 3,* 423–443.

Urban, J., Carlson, E., Egeland, B., & Sroufe, L. A. (1991). Patterns of individual adaptation across childhood. *Development and Psychopathology, 3,* 445–460.

Urberg, K. A., Degirmencioglu, S. M., Tolson, J. M., & Halliday-Scher, K. (1995). The structure of adolescent peer networks. *Developmental Psychology, 31,* 540–547.

U.S. Bureau of the Census. (1994). *Statistical abstract of the United States: 1994* (114th ed.). Washington, DC: U.S. Government Printing Office.

U.S. Bureau of the Census. (1996). *Statistical abstract of the United States: 1996* (116th ed.). Washington, DC: U.S. Government Printing Office.

U.S. Bureau of the Census. (1997). *Statistical abstract of the United States: 1997* (117th ed.). Washington, DC: U.S. Government Printing Office.

Valdez-Menchaca, M. C., & Whitehurst, G. J. (1992). Accelerating language development through picture book reading: A systematic extension to Mexican day care. *Developmental Psychology, 28,* 1106–1114.

Van de Perre, P., Simonen, A., Msellati, P., Hitimana, D., Vaira, D., Bazebagira, A., Van Goethem, C., Stevens, A., Karita, E., Sondag-Thull, D., Dabis, F., & Lepage, P. (1991). Postnatal transmission of human immunodeficiency virus type 1 from mother to infant. *The New England Journal of Medicine, 325,* 593–598.

van den Boom, D. C. (1994). The influence of temperament and mothering on attachment and exploration: An experimental manipulation of sensitive responsiveness among lower-class mothers with irritable infants. *Child Development, 65,* 1457–1477.

van den Boom, D. C. (1995). Do first-year intervention effects endure? Follow-up during toddlerhood of a sample of Dutch irritable infants. *Child Development, 66,* 1798–1816.

van IJzendoorn, M. H. (1995). Adult attachment representations, parental responsiveness, and infant attachment: A meta-analysis on the predictive validity of the Adult Attachment Interview. *Psychological Bulletin, 117,* 387–403.

van IJzendoorn, M. H. (1997, April). *Attachment, morality, and aggression: Toward a developmental socioemotional model of antisocial behavior.* Paper presented at the biennial meetings of the Society for Research in Child Development, Washington, DC.

van IJzendoorn, M. H., & Bakermans-Kranenburg, M. J. (1997). Intergenerational transmission of attachment: A move to the contextual level. In L. Atkinson & K. J. Zucker (Eds.), *Attachment and psychopathology* (pp. 135–170). New York: Guilford Press.

van IJzendoorn, M. H., Goldberg, S., Kroonenberg, P. M., & Frenkel, O. J. (1992). The relative effects of maternal and child problems on the quality of attachment: A meta-analysis of attachment in clinical samples. *Child Development, 63,* 840–858.

van IJzendoorn, M. H., & Kroonenberg, P. M. (1988). Cross-cultural patterns of attachment: A meta-analysis of the Strange Situation. *Child Development, 59,* 147–156.

van Lieshout, C. F. M., & Haselager, G. J. T. (1994). The Big Five personality factors in Q-sort descriptions of children and adolescents. In C. F. Halverson Jr., G. A. Kohnstamm, & R. P. Martin (Eds.), *The developing structure of temperament and personality from infancy to adulthood* (pp. 293–318). Hillsdale, NJ: Erlbaum.

Vaughn, S., & Schumm, J. S. (1995). Responsible inclusion for students with learning disabilities. *Journal of Learning Disabilities, 28,* 264–270.

Vernon, P. A. (Ed.). (1987). *Speed of information-processing and intelligence.* Norwood, NJ: Ablex.

Vernon, P. A. (1993). Intelligence and neural efficiency. In D. K. Detterman (Ed.), *Current topics in human intelligence: Vol. 3. Individual differences and cognition* (pp. 171–187). Norwood, NJ: Ablex.

Vernon, P. A., & Mori, M. (1992). Intelligence, reaction times, and peripheral nerve conduction velocity. *Intelligence, 16,* 273–288.

Vernon-Feagans, L., Manlove, E. E., & Volling, B. L. (1996). Otitis media and the social behavior of day-care-attending children. *Child Development, 67,* 1528–1539.

Victorian Infant Collaborative Study Group. (1991). Eight-year outcome in infants with birth weight of 500-999 grams: Continuing regional study of 1979 and 1980 births. *Journal of Pediatrics, 118,* 761–767.

Vihko, R., & Apter, D. (1980). The role of androgens in adolescent cycles. *Journal of Steroid Biochemistry, 12,* 369–373.

Vitaro, F., Tremblay, R. E., Kerr, M., Pagani, L., & Bukowski, W. M. (1997). Disruptiveness, friends' characteristics, and delinquency in early adolescence: A test of two competing models of development. *Child Development, 68,* 676–689.

Vorhees, C. F., & Mollnow, E. (1987). Behavioral teratogenesis: Long-term influences on behavior from early exposure to environmental agents. In J. D. Osofsky (Ed.), *Handbook of infant development* (2nd ed., pp. 913–971). New York: Wiley-Interscience.

Voyer, D., Voyer, S., & Bryden, M. P. (1995). Magnitude of sex differences in spatial abilities: A meta-analysis and consideration of critical variables. *Psychological Bulletin, 117,* 250–270.

Vuchinich, S., Bank, L., & Patterson, G. R. (1992). Parenting, peers, and the stability of antisocial behavior in preadolescent boys. *Developmental Psychology, 28,* 510–521.

Vygotsky, L. S. (1962). *Thought and language.* New York: Wiley.

Vygotsky, L. S. (1967). Play and its role in the mental development of the child. *Soviet Psychology, 5,* 6–18.

Vygotsky, L. S. (1978). *Mind and society: The development of higher mental processes.* Cambridge, MA: Harvard University Press. (Original works published 1930, 1933, and 1935)

Waddington, C. H. (1957). *The strategy of the genes.* London: Allen.

Waddington, C. H. (1974). A catastrophe theory of evolution. *Annals of the New York Academy of Sciences, 231,* 32–41.

Wadhera, S., & Millar, W. J. (1997). Teenage pregnancies, 1974 to 1994. *Health Reports, 9*(3), 10–16.

Wagner, B. M. (1997). Family risk factors for child and adolescent suicidal behavior. *Psychological Bulletin, 121,* 246–298.

Wagner, R. K., Torgesen, J. K., Rashotte, C. A., Hecht, S. A., Barker, T. A., Burgess, S. R., Donahue, J., & Garon, T. (1997). Changing relations between phonological processing abilities and word-level reading as children develop from beginning to skilled readers: A 5-year longitudinal study. *Developmental Psychology, 33,* 468–479.

Wahlström, J. (1990). Gene map of mental retardation. *Journal of Mental Deficiency Research, 34,* 11–27.

Wald, N. J., Cuckle, H. S., Densem, J. W., Nanchahal, K., Royston, P., Chard, T., Haddow, J. E., Knight, G. J., Palomaki, G. E., & Canick, J. A. (1988). Maternal serum screening for Down's syndrome in early pregnancy. *British Medical Journal, 297,* 883–887.

Waldrop, M. F., & Halverson, C. F. (1975). Intensive and extensive peer behavior: Longitudinal and cross-sectional analysis. *Child Development, 46,* 19–26.

Walker, H., Messinger, D., Fogel, A., & Karns, J. (1992). Social and communicative development in infancy. In V. B. Van Hasselt & M. Hersen (Eds.), *Handbook of social development: A lifespan perspective* (pp. 157–181). New York: Plenum Press.

Walker, L. J. (1980). Cognitive and perspective-taking prerequisites for moral development. *Child Development, 51,* 131–139.

Walker, L. J. (1989). A longitudinal study of moral reasoning. *Child Development, 60,* 157–160.

Walker, L. J. (1991). Sex differences in moral reasoning. In W. M. Kurtines & J. L. Gewirtz (Eds.), *Handbook of moral behavior and development: Vol. 2. Research* (pp. 333–364). Hillsdale, NJ: Erlbaum.

Walker, L. J., de Vries, B., & Trevethan, S. D. (1987). Moral stages and moral orientations in real-life and hypothetical dilemmas. *Child Development, 58,* 842–858.

Walker-Andrews, A. S. (1997). Infants' perception of expressive behaviors: Differentiation of multimodal information. *Psychological Bulletin, 121,* 437–456.

Walker-Andrews, A. S., & Lennon, E. (1991). Infants' discrimination of vocal expressions: Contributions of auditory and visual information. *Infant Behavior and Development, 14,* 131–142.

Wallerstein, J. (1989, January 22). Children after divorce: Wounds that don't heal. *The New York Times Magazine* 19–21, 41–44.

Walters, R. H., & Brown, M. (1963). Studies of reinforcement of aggression: III. Transfer of responses to an interpersonal situation. *Child Development, 34,* 563–571.

Walton, G. E., Bower, N. J. A., & Bower, T. G. R. (1992). Recognition of familiar faces by newborns. *Infant Behavior and Development, 15,* 265–269.

Walton, G. E., & Bower, T. G. R. (1993). Amodal representation of speech in infants. *Infant Behavior and Development, 16,* 233–253.

Wang, P. P., & Bellugi, U. (1993). Williams syndrome, Down syndrome, and cognitive neuroscience. *American Journal of Diseases of Children, 147,* 1246–1251.

Ward, S. L., & Overton, W. F. (1990). Semantic familiarity, relevance, and the development of deductive reasoning. *Developmental Psychology, 26,* 488–493.

Wartner, U. B., Grossman, K., Fremmer-Bombik, E., & Suess, G. (1994). Attachment patterns at age six in south Germany: Predictability from infancy and implications for preschool behavior. *Child Development, 65,* 1014–1027.

Waterman, A. S. (1985). Identity in the context of adolescent psychology. *New Directions for Child Development, 30,* 5–24.

Waterman, A. S. (1988). Identity status theory and Erikson's theory: Communalities and differences. *Developmental Review, 8,* 185–208.

Waterman, A. S. (1992). Identity as an aspect of optimal psychological functioning. In G. R. Adams, T. P. Gullotta, & R. Montemayor (Eds.), *Adolescent identity formation* (pp. 50–72). Newbury Park, CA: Sage.

Waters, E., Merrick, S. K., Albersheim, L. J., & Treboux, D. (1995a, April). *Attachment security from infancy to early adulthood: A 20-year longitudinal study.* Paper presented at the biennial meetings of the Society for Research in Child Development, Indianapolis.

Waters, E., Treboux, D., Crowell, J., Merrick, S., & Albersheim, L. (1995b, April). *From the Strange Situation to the Adult Attachment Interview: A 20-year longitudinal study of attachment security in infancy and early adulthood.* Paper presented at the biennial meetings of the Society for Research in Child Development, Indianapolis.

Watson, J. D., & Crick, F. H. C. (1953). Molecular structure of nucleic acid: A structure for deoxyribose nucleic acid. *Nature, 171,* 737–738.

Watson, M. W., & Getz, K. (1990a). Developmental shifts in Oedipal behaviors related to family role understanding. *New Directions for Child Development, 48,* 29–48.

Watson, M. W., & Getz, K. (1990b). The relationship between Oedipal behaviors and children's family role concepts. *Merrill-Palmer Quarterly, 36,* 487–506.

Waxman, S. R., & Hall, D. G. (1993). The development of a linkage between count nouns and object categories: Evidence from fifteen- to twenty-one-month-old infants. *Child Development, 64,* 1224–1241.

Waxman, S. R., & Kosowski, T. D. (1990). Nouns mark category relations: Toddlers' and preschoolers' word-learning biases. *Child Development, 61,* 1461–1473.

Webster-Stratton, C. (1988). Mothers' and fathers' perceptions of child deviance: Roles of parent and child adjustment and child deviance. *Journal of Consulting and Clinical Psychology, 56,* 909–915.

Webster-Stratton, C., & Hammond, M. (1988). Maternal depression and its relationship to life stress, perceptions of child behavior problems, parenting behaviors and child conduct problems. *Journal of Abnormal Child Psychology, 16,* 299–315.

Wechsler, D. (1974). *Manual for the Wechsler Intelligence Scale for Children–Revised.* New York: Psychological Corp.

Wegman, M. E. (1996). Infant mortality: Some international comparisons. *Pediatrics, 98,* 1020–1027.

Weinberg, R. A. (1989). Intelligence and IQ: Landmark issues and great debates. *American Psychologist, 44,* 98–104.

Weinfield, N. M., Ogawa, J. R. & Sroufe, L. A. (1997). Early attachment as a pathway to adolescent peer competence. *Journal of Research on Adolescence, 7,* 241–265.

Weisner, T. S. (1984). Ecocultural niches of middle childhood: A cross-cultural perspective. In W. A. Collins (Ed.), *Development during middle childhood: The years from six to twelve* (pp. 335–369). Washington, DC: National Academy Press.

Weiss, L. H., & Schwarz, J. C. (1996). The relationship between parenting types and older adolescents' personality, academic achievement, adjustment, and substance use. *Child Development, 67,* 2101–2114.

Weisz, J. R., Sigman, M., Weiss, B., & Mosk, J. (1993). Parent reports of behavioral and emotional problems among children in Kenya, Thailand, and the United States. *Child Development, 64,* 98–109.

Wellman, H. M. (1982). The foundations of knowledge: Concept development in the young child. In S. G. Moore & C. C. Cooper (Eds.), *The young child: Reviews of research* (Vol. 3, pp. 115–134). Washington, DC: National Association for the Education of Young Children.

Wellman, H. M., & Hickling, A. K. (1994). The mind's "I": Children's conception of the mind as an active agent. *Child Development, 65,* 1564–1580.

Wentzel, K. R., & Asher, S. R. (1995). The academic lives of neglected, rejected, popular, and controversial children. *Child Development, 66,* 754–763.

Werker, J. F., & Desjardins, R. N. (1995). Listening to speech in the first year of life: Experiential influences on phoneme perception. *Current Directions in Psychological Science, 4,* 76–81.

Werker, J. F., Pegg, J. E., & McLeod, P. J. (1994). A cross-language investigation of infant preference for infant-directed communication. *Infant Behavior and Development, 17,* 323–333.

Werker, J. F., & Tees, R. C. (1984). Cross-language speech perception: Evidence for perceptual reorganization during the first year of life. *Infant Behavior and Development, 7,* 49–63.

Werler, M. M., Louik, C., Shapiro, S., & Mitchell, A. A. (1996). Prepregnant weight in relation to risk of neural tube defects. *Journal of the American Medical Association, 275,* 1089–1092.

Werner, E. E. (1986). A longitudinal study of perinatal risk. In D. C. Farran & J. D. McKin-

ney (Eds.), *Risk in intellectual and psychosocial development* (pp. 3–28). Orlando, FL: Academic Press.

Werner, E. E. (1993). Risk, resilience, and recovery: Perspectives from the Kauai Longitudinal Study. *Development and Psychopathology, 5,* 503–515.

Werner, E. E. (1995). Resilience in development. *Current Directions in Psychological Science, 4,* 81–85.

Werner, E. E., & Smith, R. S. (1992). *Overcoming the odds: High risk children from birth to adulthood.* Ithaca, NY: Cornell University Press.

Werner, H. (1948). *Comparative psychology of mental development.* Chicago: Follett.

Werner, L. A., & Gillenwater, J. M. (1990). Pure-tone sensitivity of 2- to 5-week-old infants. *Infant Behavior and Development, 13,* 355–375.

Whitam, F. L., Diamond, M., & Martin, J. (1993). Homosexual orientation in twins: A report on 61 pairs and three triplet sets. *Archives of Sexual Behavior, 22,* 187–206.

White, K. S., Bruce, S. E., Farrell, A. D., & Kliewer, W. L. (1997, April). *Impact of exposure to community violence on anxiety among urban adolescents: Family social support as a protective factor.* Paper presented at the biennial meetings of the Society for Research in Child Development, Washington, DC.

Whitehurst, G. J. (1995, April). *Levels of reading readiness and predictors of reading success among children from low-income families.* Paper presented at the biennial meetings of the Society for Research in Child Development, Indianapolis.

Whitehurst, G. J., Arnold, D. S., Epstein, J. N., Angell, A. L., Smith, M., & Fischel, J. E. (1994). A picture book reading intervention in day care and home for children from low-income families. *Developmental Psychology, 30,* 679–689.

Whitehurst, G. J., Falco, F. L., Lonigan, C. J., Fischel, J. E., DeBaryshe, B. D., Valdez-Menchaca, M. C., & Caulfield, M. (1988). Accelerating language development through picture book reading. *Developmental Psychology, 24,* 552–559.

Whitehurst, G. J., Fischel, J. E., Crone, D. A., & Nania, O. (1995, April). *First year outcomes of a clinical trial of an emergent literacy intervention in Head Start homes and classrooms.* Paper presented at the biennial meetings of the Society for Research in Child Development, Indianapolis.

Whiting, B. B., & Edwards, C. P. (1988). *Children of different worlds: The formation of social behavior.* Cambridge, MA: Harvard University Press.

Whitney, M. P., & Thoman, E. B. (1994). Sleep in premature and fullterm infants from 24-hour home recordings. *Infant Behavior and Development, 17,* 223–234.

Wierson, M., & Forehand, R. (1994). Parent behavioral training for child noncompliance:

Rationale, concepts, and effectiveness. *Current Directions in Psychological Science, 3,* 146–150.

Wiesenfeld, A. R., Malatesta, C. Z., & DeLoach, L. L. (1981). Differential parental response to familiar and unfamiliar infant distress signals. *Infant Behavior and Development, 4,* 281–296.

Wigfield, A., Eccles, J. S., MacIver, D., Reuman, D. A., & Midgley, C. (1991). Transitions during early adolescence: Changes in children's domain-specific self-perceptions and general self-esteem across the transition to junior high school. *Developmental Psychology, 27,* 552–565.

Wilcox, A. J., Baird, D. D., Weinberg, C. R., Hornsby, P. P., & Herbst, A. L. (1995). Fertility in men exposed prenatally to diethylstilbestrol. *The New England Journal of Medicine, 332,* 1411–1416.

Wilcox, A. J., Weinberg, C. R., O'Connor, J. F., Baird, D. D., Schlatterer, J. P., Canfield, R. E., Armstrong, E. G., & Nisula, B. C. (1988). Incidence of early loss of pregnancy. *The New England Journal of Medicine, 319,* 189–194.

Wilfley, D. E., & Rodin, J. (1995). Cultural influences on eating disorders. In K. D. Brownell & C. G. Fairburn (Eds.), *Eating disorders and obesity: A comprehensive handbook* (pp. 78–82). New York: Guilford Press.

Williams, E., Radin, N., & Allegro, T. (1992). Sex role attitudes of adolescents reared primarily by their fathers: An 11-year follow-up. *Merrill-Palmer Quarterly, 38,* 457–476.

Williams, J. E., & Best, D. L. (1990). *Measuring sex stereotypes: A multination study* (rev. ed.). Newbury Park, CA: Sage.

Williams, W. M. (1998). Are we raising smarter children today? School- and home-related influences on IQ. In U. Neisser (Ed.), *The rising curve: Long-term changes in IQ and related measures.* Washington, DC: American Psychological Association.

Williams, W. M., & Ceci, S. J. (1997). Are Americans becoming more or less alike? Trends in race, class, and ability differences in intelligence. *American Psychologist, 52,* 1226–1235.

Willinger, M., Hoffman, H. J., & Hartford, R. B. (1994). Infant sleep position and risk for sudden infant death syndrome: Report of meeting held January 13 and 14, 1994, National Institutes of Health, Bethesda, MD. *Pediatrics, 93,* 814–819.

Wills, T. A., & Cleary, S. D. (1997). The validity of self-reports of smoking: Analyses by race/ethnicity in a school sample of urban adolescents. *American Journal of Public Health, 87,* 56–61.

Wilson, M. N. (1986). The black extended family: An analytical consideration. *Developmental Psychology, 22,* 246–258.

Wilson, M. N. (1989). Child development in the context of the black extended family. *American Psychologist, 44,* 380–385.

Wilson, W. J. (1995). Jobless ghettos and the social outcome of youngsters. In P. Moen, G. H. Elder Jr., & K. Lüscher (Eds.), *Examining lives in context: Perspectives on the ecology of human development* (pp. 527–543). Washington, DC: American Psychological Association.

Winfield, L. F. (1995). The knowledge base on resilience in African-American adolescents. In L. J. Crockett & A. C. Crouter (Eds.), *Pathways through adolescence* (pp. 87–118). Mahwah, NJ: Erlbaum.

Winner, E. (1997). Exceptionally high intelligence and schooling. *American Psychologist, 52,* 1070–1081.

Wolke, D., Gray, P., & Meyer, R. (1994). Excessive infant crying: A controlled study of mothers helping mothers. *Pediatrics, 94,* 322–332.

Wood, D. J., Bruner, J. S., & Ross, G. (1976). The role of tutoring in problem solving. *Journal of Child Psychology and Psychiatry, 17,* 89–100.

Wood, W., Wong, F. Y., & Chachere, J. G. (1991). Effects of media violence on viewers' aggression in unconstrained social interaction. *Psychological Bulletin, 109,* 371–383.

Woodward, A. L., & Markman, E. M. (1998). Early word learning. In W. Damon (Ed.), *Handbook of child psychology: Vol. 2. Cognition, perception, and language* (5th ed., pp. 371–420). New York: Wiley.

World Health Organization. (1982). The prevalence and duration of breastfeeding: A critical review of available information. *World Health Statistics Quarterly, 35,* 92–112.

Wright, L. (1995, August 7). Double mystery. *The New Yorker,* 45–62.

Yang, B., Ollendick, T. H., Dong, Q., Xia, Y., & Lin, L. (1995). Only children and children with siblings in the People's Republic of China: Levels of fear, anxiety, and depression. *Child Development, 66,* 1301–1311.

Yonas, A. (1981). Infants' responses to optical information for collision. In R. Aslin N., J. R. Alberts, & M. R. Peterson (Eds.), *Development of perception: Vol. 2. From perception to cognition* (pp. 80–122). Orlando, FL: Academic Press.

Yonas, A., & Owsley, C. (1987). Development of visual space perception. In P. Salapatek & L. Cohen (Eds.), *Handbook of infant perception: Vol. 2. From perception to cognition* (pp. 80–122). Orlando, FL: Academic Press.

Youth sports: Kids are the losers. *The Harvard Education Letter* (1992, July/August) VIII, 1–3.

Zahn-Waxler, C., & Radke-Yarrow, M. (1982). The development of altruism: Alternative research strategies. In N. Eisenberg (Ed.), *The development of prosocial behavior* (pp. 109–138). New York: Academic Press.

Zahn-Waxler, C., Radke-Yarrow, M., Wagner, E., & Chapman, M. (1992a). Development of concern for others. *Developmental Psychology, 28,* 126–136.

Zahn-Waxler, C., Robinson, J., & Emde, R. N. (1992b). The development of empathy in twins. *Developmental Psychology, 28,* 1038–1047.

Zajonc, R. B. (1983). Validating the confluence model. *Psychological Bulletin, 93,* 457–480.

Zajonc, R. B., & Marcus, G. B. (1975). Birth order and intellectual development. *Psychological Review, 82,* 74–88.

Zajonc, R. B., & Mullally, P. R. (1997). Birth order: Reconciling conflicting effects. *American Psychologist, 52,* 685–699.

Zametkin, A. J., Nordahl, T. E., Gross, M., King, A. C., Semple, W. E., Rumsey, J., Hamburger, S., & Cohen, R. M. (1990). Cerebral glucose metabolism in adults with hyperactivity of childhood onset. *The New England Journal of Medicine, 323,* 1361–1366.

Zani, B. (1993). Dating and interpersonal relationships in adolescence. In S. Jackson & H. Rodrigues-Tomé (Eds.), *Adolescence and its social worlds* (pp. 95–119). Hove, England: Erlbaum.

Zaslow, M. J., & Hayes, C. D. (1986). Sex differences in children's responses to psychosocial stress: Toward a cross-context analysis. In M. E. Lamb, A. L. Brown, & B. Rogoff (Eds.), *Advances in developmental psychology* (Vol. 4, pp. 285–338). Hillsdale, NJ: Erlbaum.

Zelazo, N. A., Zelazo, P. R., Cohen, K. M., & Zelazo, P. D. (1993). Specificity of practice effects on elementary neuromotor patterns. *Developmental Psychology, 29,* 686–691.

Zelazo, P. R., Zelazo, N. A., & Kolb, S. (1972). "Walking" in the newborn. *Science, 176,* 314–315.

Zeskind, P. S., & Barr, R. G. (1997). Acoustic characteristics of naturally occurring cries of infants with "colic." *Child Development, 68,* 394–403.

Zeskind, P. S., & Ramey, C. T. (1981). Preventing intellectual and interactional sequelae of fetal malnutrition: A longitudinal, transactional, and synergistic approach to development. *Child Development, 52,* 213–218.

Zhou, W., & Olsen, J. (1997). Gestational weight gain as a predictor of birth and placenta weight according to pre-pregnancy body mass index. *Acta Obstetrica Scandinavica, 76,* 300–307.

Zigler, E. F., & Gilman, E. (1996). Not just any care: Shaping a coherent child care policy. In E. F. Zigler, S. L. Kagan, & N. W. Hall (Eds.), *Children, families, and government: Preparing for the twenty-first century* (pp. 95–116). Cambridge, England: Cambridge University Press.

Zigler, E., & Hodapp, R. M. (1991). Behavioral functioning in individuals with mental retardation. *Annual Review of Psychology, 42,* 29–50.

Zigler, E., & Styfco, S. J. (1993). Using research and theory to justify and inform Head Start expansion. *Social Policy Report, Society for Research in Child Development, 7*(2), 1–21.

Zigler, E. F., & Styfco, S. (1996). Head Start and early childhood intervention: The changing course of social science and social policy. In E. F. Zigler, S. L. Kagan, & N. W. Hall (Eds.), *Children, families, and government* (pp. 132–154). Cambridge, England: Cambridge University Press.

Zill, N., Moore, K. A., Smith, E. W., Stief, T., & Coiro, M. J. (1995). The life circumstances and development of children in welfare families: A profile based on national survey data. In P. L. Chase-Lansdale & J. Brooks-Gunn (Eds.), *Escape from poverty: What makes a difference for children?* (pp. 39–59). Cambridge, England: Cambridge University Press.

Zill, N., & Nord, C. W. (1994). *Running in place: How American families are faring in a changing economy and an individualistic society.* Washington, DC: Child Trends.

Zimmerman, M. A., Salem, D. A., & Maton, K. I. (1995). Family structure and psychosocial correlates among urban African-American adolescent males. *Child Development, 66,* 1598–1613.

Zoccolillo, M. (1993). Gender and the development of conduct disorder. *Development and Psychopathology, 5,* 65–78.

Photo Credits

1: Nancy Sheehan/PhotoEdit
2: Paul Conklin
4 (left): Michael Krasowitz/FPG International LLC, (right): Telegraph Colour Library/FPG International LLC
5: Tony Freeman/PhotoEdit
9: Bob Daemmrich Photography
13 (top): Bob Daemmrich/The Image Works, Inc., (bottom): Laura Dwight Photography
16: Erika Stone
18: Frank Siteman/Index Stock Imagery
21: Laura Dwight Photography
22: Don Smetzer/Tony Stone Images/New York Inc.
26 (left, middle, and right): Jim Whitmer
31: Dan McCoy/Rainbow/PNI
38: Laura Dwight Photography
40: SPL/Photo Researchers, Inc.
45: Mug Shots/The Stock Market, Inc.
48: Science Library/Photo Researchers, Inc
51: Laura Dwight Photography
52: Andrew R. Adesman, M.D.
58 (left and right): George Steinmetz
60: Mark Richards/PhotoEdit/PNI
63: Laura Dwight Photography
71: Judi Bule/Bruce Coleman, Inc.
75 (left): S.I.U./Peter Arnold, Inc., (right): S. Van Rees/Petit Format/Photo Researchers, Inc.
76: David Young-Wolff/PhotoEdit
79: J. Sulley/Image Works
82: Tony Freeman/PhotoEdit
84 (top): Elizabeth Crews/The Image Works, Inc., (bottom): Laura Dwight Photography
85, 86: Laura Dwight Photography
88: Ursula Markus/Photo Researchers, Inc.
94: L. Johnson/ Meadowbrook Press
98 (left and right): Laura Dwight Photography
102: ©1991 John Eastcott/Yva Momatiuk/The Image Works, Inc.
103: Mark Antman/The Image Works, Inc.
104: Bob Daemmrich/The Image Works, Inc.
109: Laura Dwight Photography
118: Bob Daemmrich/Stock Boston, Inc.

119 (top): Laura Dwight Photography, (middle): Tom & DeeAnn McCarthy/The Stock Market, Inc., (bottom): Miro Vintoni/Stock Boston/PNI
124: Brent Jones Photograhy
127: Okoniewski/The Image Works, Inc.
129 (left): Robert Brenner/PhotoEdit, (right): Richard Hutchings
130: William Thompson/Index Stock Imagery
134: Tom & Dee Ann McCarthy/PhotoEdit
138–140: Laura Dwight Photography
142: J. E. Steiner, Human Facial Expressions in response to taste and smell stimulation, in H. W. Reese & L. P. Lipsett (Eds.), Advances in Child Development & Behavior, Vol. 13, Figure 1, p. 269. New York: Academic Press, 1979.
143: Laura Dwight Photography
144: Enrico Ferorelli, Inc.
147, 150: Laura Dwight Photography
154 (left and right): Goodman/Monkmeyer
157: From: "Unmasking The Face" by Paul Ekman and Wallace V. Friesen, Prentice Hall 1975
162, 164: Laura Dwight Photography
165: Tony Freeman/PhotoEdit
167, 169: Laura Dwight Photography
170: Carolyn Rovee-Collier, Current Directions in Science, 2(4), 130-135, 1993
171 (left and right): A. N. Meltzoff and M. F. Moore, "Imitation of Facial and Manual Gestures by Human Neonates," Science, 198, pp. 75-78. Copyright 1977 the American Association for the Advancement of Science.
173: (top and bottom): Laura Dwight Photography
179: Laura Dwight Photography
180: Bob Daemmrich/The Image Works, Inc.
186: R. Sidney/The Image Works, Inc.
188: John Eastcott/YVA Momatiuk/The Image Works, Inc.
194: Michael Newman/PhotoEdit
198: Laura Dwight
201: Bob Daemmrich Photography

202 (top): Laura Dwight Photography, (bottom) Bob Daemmrich/Stock Boston, Inc.
206: Alan Oddie/PhotoEdit
211: David Young-Wolff/PhotoEdit
214: Elizabeth Crews/The Image Works, Inc.
221: Lawrence Migdale, Editorial
227: Laura Dwight Photography
229: H. S. Terrace/Anthro-Photo File
231: Elizabeth Crews/The Image Works, Inc.
239: Laura Dwight Photography
241: Roy Kirby/Stock Boston, Inc.
242: Miro Vintoniv/Stock Boston, Inc.
244, 252, 253, 255: Laura Dwight Photography
258: David Young-Wolff/PhotoEdit
259: Bob Daemmrich Photography
264: Laura Dwight Photography
267: Paula Lerner/Index Stock Imagery
270: Jerry Howard/Positive Images
272: Laura Dwight Photography
273: David Young-Wolff/PhotoEdit
276: Laura Dwight
277: Tony Freeman/PhotoEdit
279: H.Heron/Monkmeyer
289: Ariel Skelley/The Stock Market, Inc.
289, 290: Laura Dwight Photography
293: Kolvoord/Image Works
294: David Young-Wolff/PhotoEdit
300: Bob Daemmrich/Stock Boston, Inc.
302: Michael Newman/PhotoEdit
304 (top): Lawrence Migdale/Photo Researchers, Inc., (bottom) Laura Dwight Photography
306: Laura Dwight Photography
308: Robert W. Ginn/Index Stock Imagery
311: David Young-Wolff/PhotoEdit
317: Elizabeth Crews
319: Frank Siteman/Index Stock Imagery
321 (bottom): Steve Starr/Stock Boston, Inc.; (top left and top right): Laura Dwight Photography
324 (left and right): Michael Newman/PhotoEdit

Name Index

Subject Index